55th Annual Edition

Gun Digest®

2001

Edited by
Ken Ramage

—GUN DIGEST STAFF—

EDITOR
Ken Ramage

ASSOCIATE EDITOR
Ross Bielema

CONTRIBUTING EDITORS

Bob Bell

Holt Bodinson

Raymond Caranta

Doc Carlson

Bill Hanus

John Malloy

Layne Simpson

Larry S. Sterett

Hal Swiggett

Editorial Comments and Suggestions

We're always looking for feedback on our books. Please let us know what you like about this edition. If you have suggestions for articles you'd like to see in future editions, please contact.

Ken Ramage/Gun Digest
700 East State St.
Iola, WI 54990
email: ramagek@krause.com

Manuscripts, contributions and inquiries, including first class return postage, should be sent to the GUN DIGEST Editorial Offices, Krause Publications, 700 E. State Street, Iola, WI 54990-0001. All materials received will receive reasonable care, but we will not be responsible for their safe return. Material accepted is subject to our requirements for editing and revisions. Author payment covers all rights and title to the accepted material, including photos, drawings and other illustrations. Payment is at our current rates.

CAUTION: Technical data presented here, particularly technical data on the handloading and on firearms adjustment and alteration, inevitably reflects individual experience with particular equipment and components under specific circumstances the reader cannot duplicate exactly. Such data presentations therefore should be used for guidance only and with caution. Krause Publications, Inc., accepts no responsibility for results obtained using this data.

Published by

krause
publications

700 E. State Street • Iola, WI 54990-0001
Telephone: 715/445-2214
Web: www.krause.com

Please call or write for our free catalog.

Our toll-free number to place an order or obtain a free catalog is 800-258-0929 or please use our regular business telephone 715-445-2214 for editorial comment and further information.

Library of Congress Catalog Number: 44-32588
ISBN: 0-87341-924-3

NINETEENTH ANNUAL

JOHN T. AMBER LITERARY AWARD

Bob Bell

Bob Bell has won the prestigious John T. Amber Award for his insightful study of John Buhmiller–big-game hunter, wildcat cartridge designer and barrel-maker. "Buhmiller's Big Boomers," published in GUN DIGEST 2000, makes Bell the 19th winner of this prestigious award, placing him in the company of some of the most renowned writers in the firearms field.

Bell is the former editor of *Pennsylvania Game News*, editor of *Handloader's Digest*, and served for a time as associate editor of GUN DIGEST. He has written about guns, hunting and outdoor activities for a number of regional and national magazines including *American Rifleman, Guns,* and *Guns & Ammo,* among others. He is also author of *The Gun Digest Book of Scopes & Mounts.*

After graduating from high school in 1943, Bell enlisted in the Army and served in northern Europe. For several years after his discharge and before attending college, he "knocked around the country" working in logging-camps and owning a handloading shop, among other things.

His first article for GUN DIGEST was accepted in 1959. "It was never published," said Bell. "Probably because it wasn't very good."

The only juried literary award in the firearms field, the John T. Amber Award replaced the Townsend Whelen Award. Now, a $1,000 prize goes to the winner of this annual award–previously the Townsend Whelen Award, originated by the late John T. Amber and re-named in his honor.

Nominations for the competition are made by the GUN DIGEST editor and are judged by a distinguished panel of editors experienced in the firearms field. Entries are evaluated for felicity of expression and illustration, originality and scholarship, and subject importance to the firearms field.

This year's Amber Award nominees, in addition to Bell, were:

* **Geoffrey Boothroyd**: "The British Sporting Gun"
* **Gary M. Brown**: "Pitfalls for Collectors"
* **Colin Greenwood**: "The Three-Sixty Express"
* **Roderick T. Halvorsen**: "It's a Fine Medium Bore"
* **John Malloy**: "Shooting Sideways"
* **Janni Pohojoispaa**: "Children of the 7.62 x 54R"
* **Glen Ruh**: "The 10mm That Won The West"
* **Konrad F. Schreier, Jr.**: "Winchester 69"

Serving as judges for this year's competition were John D. Acquilino, editor of *Inside Gun News*; James W. Bequette, executive editor of *Shooting Times*; David Brennan, editor of *Precision Shooting*, Sharon Cunningham, director of Pioneer Press; Pete Dickey, former technical editor of *American Rifleman*; Robert Elman, former editor-in-chief of Winchester Press, now free-lance editor of Abenake and other publications; Jack Lewis, former editor and publisher of *Gun World*; Bill Parkerson, former editor of *American Rifleman*, now director of research and information for the National Rifle Association and Dave Petzal, executive editor of *Field & Stream.*

About Our Covers...

ON THE OCCASION of this 55th Edition of GUN DIGEST, we illustrate our covers with striking examples selected from some of the finest firearms work by engravers and custom arms makers. The beauty, grace and craftsmanship evident in these arms is a joy to behold and an uplifting experience for all shooting sportsmen and collectors.

Of course, even the most beautifully-executed custom arm cannot be properly appreciated by the reading public unless its image has been captured by a highly talented artisan in the craft of arms photography. Within this 55th Edition, and filling the pages of three books you will shortly read more about, you will see the work of today's most skilled arms photographers.

We extend a special thanks to well-known author Tom Turpin for his part in the preparation of the front and back covers of this edition. He is a long-time contributor to GUN DIGEST, very knowledgeable in all aspects of custom firearms and is, in fact, the author of two richly-illustrated hardcover books on engraving and custom firearms published recently by Krause Publications. Further, he is the author of the well-illustrated section entitled "The Art of the Engraver & Custom Guns," which begins on page 65 of this 55th Edition.

In coming editions, GUN DIGEST will continue to present selected works of custom arms makers, engravers and arms photographers. Readers seeking even more information on this fascinating class of firearms will be interested in the following commentary regarding three Krause hardcover titles which authoritatively – and beautifully – cover the subjects of custom arms-making and engraving. Two are by Tom Turpin; the third by Steven Dodd Hughes, an author whose talent as a custom gunmaker is matched by his talent as an arms photographer.

As always, feel free to contact me via letter or email (ramagek@krause.com). We hope you enjoy this edition. *KR*

Modern Custom Guns, by Tom Turpin

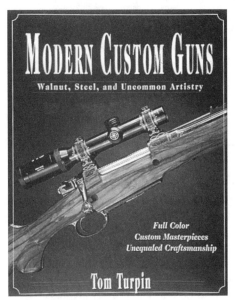

THE REMBRANDTS OF modern guns – the pinnacle of the gunmaker's art – are enjoyed by custom firearms enthusiasts throughout the world as works of art; utilitarian in function, yet exquisite in design. Now a full-color, hardcover book celebrates these creations, paying long-overdue tribute to the best custom-made guns of today and yesterday.

Modern Custom Guns offers details not found elsewhere, along with more than 200 beautiful full-color photographs that capture perfectly the unique elements of each featured gun.

The book covers the top-of-the-line custom work of today's premier gunmakers, engravers, specialists and artisans – reporting on the detailed workmanship and embellishment of stocks, actions and barrels from expert firearms designers. Included are individual profiles of master craftspeople with detailed, close-up representations of their finest works; details on the custom work of some of the major manufacturers and an in-depth look back at custom firearms and custom arms makers of yesteryear.

Modern Custom Guns includes chapters covering ownership of custom guns; custom stocks; custom metalsmithing; actions; barrels; *bells and whistles*; sights and sight mounts; engraving, carving and inlays; custom gun guilds; factory custom guns; semi-custom guns and the state-of-the-art today. Featured are many of today's top custom engravers, including Winston Churchill, Mike Dubber, Ralph Ingle, Lynton McKenzie, Ron Smith, Lisa Tomlin and Claus Willig; such specialists as Ted Blackburn, Kathy Forster, Jim Hasson, Marvin Huey, Dave Talley, Doug Turnbull, and Jim Wisner; and top custom arms makers including Dietrich Apel, Mark Cromwell, Steve Heilmann, Jay McCament, the David Miller Co., Bruce Russell and Ed Webber. The book also includes a source directory of engravers, specialists, and custom makers.

"Both (*a custom rifle and a factory product*) will satisfactorily do the job for which they were designed," Turpin says in the book. "Factory rifles vary in sophistication from the mass-produced Remington 700 and its competitors to the more refined Dakota 76 and similar rifles. They are excellent rifles. Each can be relied upon to deliver a bullet on the target, with groups measuring two minutes-of-angle or less. For the hunter who uses a rifle merely as a tool, an assembly line model – identical to thousands of others – is usually plenty good enough.

"On the other hand, for those who want only the best, or who appreciate beauty and admire technical virtuosity above all else, a full custom job is the only way to go ... They can have precisely what they want and can rest assured that the finished rifle will be the best in the world."

Modern Custom Guns (208 full-color pages; 8 1/2x11; hardcover with full-color dust jacket): $49.95.

From Chapter 8, 'Engraving, Carving, and Inlays' (pages 74&75); *Modern Custom Guns.*

Guns On The Covers

The Front Cover: With no frame of reference, this Farquharson looks to be a standard-size rifle. However, it is an original miniature that is less than half the size of a full-size model. This one has been totally rebuilt with Steve Heilmann doing the metalwork, Darwin Hensley crafting the exquisite stock and Terry Wallace adorning it with his superb engraving. *Photo by Turk's Head Productions, Inc.*

The Back Cover: One of the finest lever-action rifles that I have ever seen. This 1886 Winchester was stocked by Jerry Fisher and engraved by Robert Swartley. Both these artisans have been in the business for many years and each just keeps getting better and better. *Photo by David Wesbrook.*

Tom Turpin

Custom Firearms Engraving, by Tom Turpin

WITH CUSTOM ENGRAVING, the firearm went from a functional tool of survival to a valued showpiece. Now all firearms enthusiasts can enjoy the beauty and craftsmanship of custom engraving through the pages of *Custom Firearms Engraving*, by Tom Turpin. The 208 pages contain over 200 high-quality, full-color photographs of work by some of the world's finest engravers. Sharp close-up photos show the finely detailed work on everything from revolvers to shotguns.

"The earliest examples of firearms found in museums today almost always exhibit some form of embellishment," Turpin said. "Some are exceptionally ornate. Early examples of American-made firearms were by no means ornate, but they were usually decorated in some manner. Most often, this decoration took the form of rather coarse engraving of the brass trim. That, and adding stripes on the stocks, were the most common forms of adornment."

The Austrians and Germans once dominated the firearms engraving field, but recently Americans have come on strong. "Whatever motivated the Yanks to excellence must have kicked into high gear," Turpin said. "As a group, their overall improvement has far exceeded that of their competition from any other country."

The book showcases the work of 74 engravers, most of them American. Each section contains a brief biography of the engraver and large-format, full-color photos of their work.

Opening of 'Inlaying' chapter (pages 26&27); *Custom Firearms Engraving.*

Part I of the book describes engraving techniques – graver and hammer, *Bulino* or banknote, inlaying, chasing or modeling, stippling and filigree. It also describes four engraving styles -- English, American, Germanic and *Bulino* (Italian).

"The book is not a primer on engraving," Turpin said. "It is intended to provide a brief introduction to engraving and give photographic examples of the work of many of the extremely talented people pursuing this career."

Custom Firearms Engraving (208 full-color pages; 8 1/2x11; hardcover with full-color dust jacket): $49.95.

Fine Gunmaking: Double Shotguns, by Stephen Dodd Hughes

MOST FIREARMS ENTHUSIASTS will tell you that nothing compares to the look and feel of a fine double shotgun. Noted gunmaker and author Steven Dodd Hughes takes his readers for a behind-the-scenes look at the design, evolution and creation of quality double guns.

In the 'Foreword', noted author John Barsness says, "Hughes doesn't simply tell us how all those wonderful facets of a fine double come together. Instead, he brings us into his own shop, in both words and photos, and almost puts the gun into our hands as he describes how and why each part of a double gun should work, from buttstock and triggers to forends and chokes."

Fine Gunmaking: Double Shotguns is divided into sections on stock wood and shotgun stocks, gun metal, and engraving and metal finishes. The first section contains chapters detailing the nuances of gunstocks, from the walnut tree to the final coat of hand-rubbed oil finish. The 'gun metal' section takes the mystery out of pertinent gun measurements, shotgun barrels and bores, proper repair, single and double triggers, and more. The third section has perhaps the most complete and detailed explanation of firearms engraving–including the design, process and evaluations of engraving–ever to appear in print.

From 'Full Circle Fox' (pages 152&153); *Fine Gunmaking: Double Shotguns.*

A final section features the history of one custom shotgun–the author's own Hughes/Fox–captured in detailed photographs. Each major step of the fine gun's metamorphosis, from the first file stroke to imaginative engraving, is revealed. A complete glossary of gun-making terms (more than 100 entries) and a selected reading list round out the book.

Hughes has been a professional custom gunmaker since 1978 and is recognized as one of the top custom gunmakers in the United States. *Fine Gunmaking: Double Shotguns* is his first book.

Fine Gunmaking: Double Shotguns (168 pages, including 16 full-color pages; 8-1/2x11; hardcover with full-color dust jacket): $34.95.

Gun Digest 2001

The World's Greatest Gun Book

CONTENTS

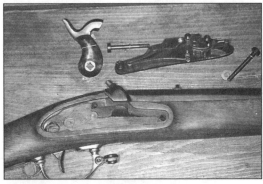

Page 14

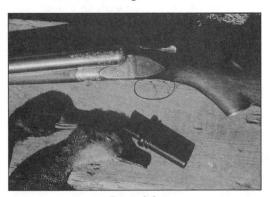

Page 36

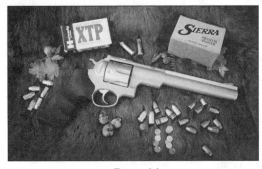

Page 44

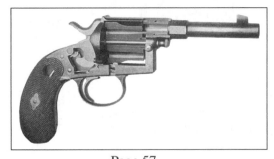

Page 57

Page 77   Page 89

Page 97

CATALOG OF ARMS AND ACCESSORIES

Old lithograph of the Robbins and Lawrence Armory in 1849.

Birth of the Modern Firearm

The transition from colonial gun-making to modern arms manufacturing was the result of many brilliant minds, but it undoubtedly occurred in Windsor, Vermont and principally centered around one man, Richard S. Lawrence.

by Ken Aiken

THE LETTER ADDRESSED to Vermont Governor Erastus Fairbanks at the outbreak of the Civil War, is about a repeating rifle invented during the War of 1812 by Dr. William Church of Chelsea, and who subsequently spent several years bringing it to perfection. The author, Reverend P. Bailey, writes about a fowling piece containing "a magazine of 42 balls [and] sufficient powder to carry them." Being familiar with the weapon he states "you can abstract one bull from [the] magazine [and] powder to carry it [and] discharge it in two seconds of time, or 30 bulls in

a minute." The Reverend Bailey goes on to say: "Church exhibited his gun to our Congress [and] told me that [the] Government offered him 40000 Dollars for [the] invention." I found this letter, with its fading ink, among the archival papers of Vermont's Civil War governor, and it leaves no doubt in my mind that such a gun once existed.

Reuben Ellis had developed a four-shot sliding-block flintlock rifle in 1808 and Lewis Jennings later improved on Ellis's design and patented a three-shot sliding-block repeating flintlock in 1821.[1] Artemus Wheeler

of Boston[2] was making hand-revolving flintlocks around 1818, but those of Elisha Collier, although based on Wheeler's musket design, were more refined and popular.[3] Ormsby's pill-lock revolving rifle, the breech-loading magazine repeating rifle of John Cookson, and Dr. William Church's 42-shot repeating shotgun are examples of some of the technologically advanced designs which are virtually unknown. How many others found inventive solutions to the problems of building multiple-shot firearms, and who then faded into local obscurity, will never be known, but many local

Lawrence became internationally acclaimed as the first successfully mass-produced product machined with interchangeable parts.

After the completion of the first contract in December of 1847, Kendall sold his interest to the other principals and the firm was renamed Robbins & Lawrence. During the following two years the firm completed a second, larger contract for "Mississippi" (Model 1841) rifles, expanded into the manufacturing of railroad cars and had built the most advanced machine shop in the world. In an article in the February 16, 1849 issue of *The Vermont Journal*, this shop is described: "Up to this date nine edifices in all, have been erected and put in use, among which is a rifle-factory and machine-shop, a brick structure 100 feet by 40 and 3 stories; the car-shop, a wooden building of about the same length and breadth, but of less height; 3 blacksmith shops of brick, of smaller size, containing 20 forges and 5 trip-hammers; and 4 other buildings of various dimensions; all of which with the apparatus required for the several species and branches of work cost the sum of $115,000 . . ."

The work being done at Robbins & Lawrence was cutting-edge technology and attracted the best minds of the time—Henry D. Stone,[15] Lemuel Hedge[16] and Frederick Howe[17] among them. The extensive armory described in *The Vermont Journal* was just the beginning, and the year of 1850 brought further expansion and additional contracts. The era of modern firearms was about to begin.

The breech-loading and multiple-shot firearms which had been invented during the first half of the 19th century generally suffered from three major problems: 1) the breech-loading guns leaked gases when the charge was ignited, resulting in less propellant force to the bullet, 2) the relationships between the primer, charge and bullet seal were extremely complicated, and 3) the build-up of corrosive powder fouling in the barrels caused problems after a limited number of repetitive firings. Muzzle-loading firearms had none of these problems. The replacement of primer powder with fulminates and the subsequent development of the copper percussion cap, were major advances that promoted the development of

multiple-shot firearms from 1835 to 1850. Still, problems with the ammunition were recognized as being one of the major obstacles to a repeating weapon; the mechanical precision required in the firearm's construction was the other.

New York inventor Walter Hunt addressed the problem of the ammunition first; he received his patent for "Loaded Balls" in August of 1848.[18] These conical lead bullets were deeply hollowed at the rear; the hollow was packed with black

Fancy patchbox of nickel silver on an under-hammer by N. Kendall & Co.

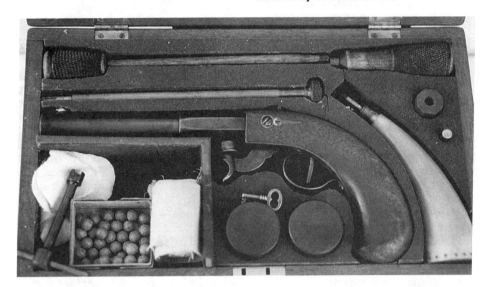

When N. Kendall & Co. ceased operations in 1841, William Smith and David Hall Hilliard began producing under-hammer firearms in their Cornish, NH shop.

◀▼ Fancy-grade under-hammer rifle made by D. H. Hilliard.

powder and capped with a cork disk that had a small hole in the center to allow the flash from a percussion cap to ignite the powder. The lead expanded upon detonation, forming a gas-tight seal and expanding into the rifling grooves and imparting a stabilizing spin to the lead bullet (*This concept was later adopted for the Minie Ball and the Pritchard bullet*). On August 21st of the following year, Hunt was granted a patent for his "Combined Piston Breech and Firing Cock Repeating Gun" or "Volitional Repeater." This repeater was a hammerless rifle that utilized a firing pin and the "Loaded Balls" were held in a tubular magazine; the primer caps were held in a separate magazine. Only one of these guns was produced and it was placed with George A. Arrowsmith (of Gold Street in New York) for improvement and promotion. The project was given to Louis Jennings, a gunsmith working for Arrowsmith who had patented a repeating rifle in 1821. Jennings modified the "Volitional Repeater," replacing the bolt-action mechanism for a standard side-hammer lock and redesigning the way in which the "Loaded Balls" were chambered; by Christmas the new rifle was patented as the "Jennings Repeating Rifle." Within a few months Arrowsmith sold the Hunt and Jennings patents[19] to Mr. Courtlandt C. Palmer, a successful businessman and venture capitalist in New York City, who brought the rifle to Robbins & Lawrence and contracted for improvements and production of 5,000 of these repeating firearms. In September of 1849[20] George Leonard, Jr. of Shrewsbury, Massachusetts patented a "pepperbox pistol" with a revolving hammer – one of many styles invented to avoid Colt's patent on the revolving chamber – and formed the Leonard Pistol Manufacturing Company. He hired Daniel Baird Wesson (younger brother of noted gunsmith and pistol inventor Edwin Wesson)[21] to work on his invention, but the following year Daniel Wesson brought the Leonard pistol and pistol machinery to Robbins & Lawrence in Windsor because the pistol was too complex for Leonard to produce.

On September 12, 1848 Christian Sharps, a Cincinnati machinist, patented the "Sliding Breech Rifle."[22] His first model had a complicated circular cap loader, while his second utilized a Maynard tape primer.

Having difficulty in Pennsylvania with both the production and financing of his rifle, he brought his design to Windsor and contracted Robbins & Lawrence to make improvements and manufacture 5,000 rifles.

All of these complicated firearms were limited by the production methods which were available to gunsmiths (except those in Windsor) in 1850. The fame of the production methods employed at the Robbins & Lawrence armory and the success of the U.S. Army Rifle contract was quick to spread.

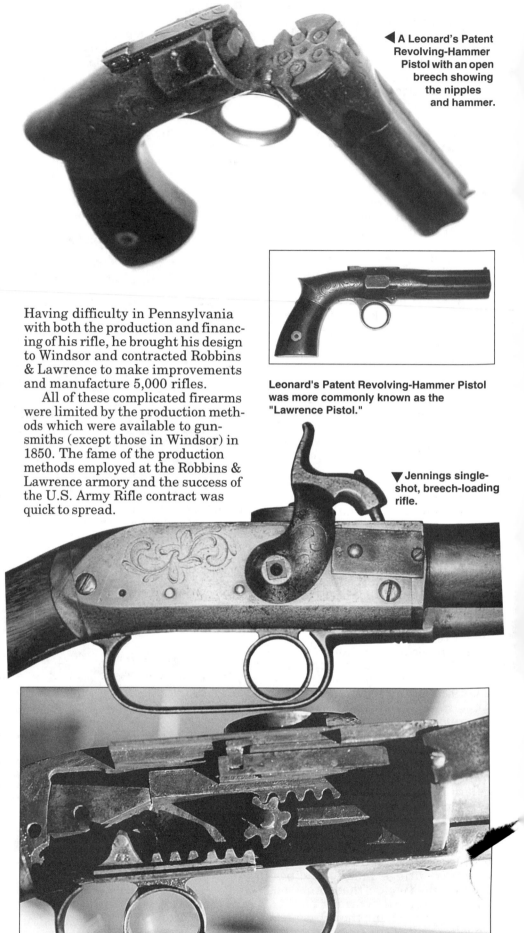

◀ A Leonard's Patent Revolving-Hammer Pistol with an open breech showing the nipples and hammer.

Leonard's Patent Revolving-Hammer Pistol was more commonly known as the "Lawrence Pistol."

▼ Jennings single-shot, breech-loading rifle.

The Jennings single-shot breech-loading rifle utilized a rack and pinion mechanism very different from the lever system used in the 20-shot repeater.

The pill-primer magazine on the Jennings rifle with the brass reservoir in place.

tioning of the repeating rifle. With a contract for the manufacture of 5,000 rifles,[26] Sharps and Lawrence redesigned the Model 2 rifle into the Model 1851 ("box lock") carbine, gun machinery was built and production commenced in 1851. However, Christian Sharps seems to have little involvement with subsequent development of his gun. During 1851, Richard Lawrence corrected the problematic gas leak in the breech, replaced the Maynard tape-primer with an ingenious

When the failure of the railroad car manufacturing end of the business required the company to search for other contracts,[23] Courtlandt Palmer, George Leonard Jr. and Christian Sharps took advantage of the opportunity to have their guns developed and manufactured by the leading "mechanics" of the time.

During 1850 Daniel Wesson and Richard Lawrence simplified the design of the pistol and redesigned the critical hammer spring while the Windsor machinists retooled the machinery brought up from Charles-

◀ A Sharps carbine, Model 1851, in nickel-plated steel with a Maynard tape primer. This photo shows the feed mechanism in the tape primer magazine.

town, Massachusetts. Robbins & Lawrence manufactured and sold the firearm as the Leonard's Patent Revolving-Hammer Pistol, but it became known as the Lawrence Pistol. At this time, Benjamin Tyler Henry and Richard Lawrence were engaged in improving the Jennings rifle; the receiving and chambering methods for the repeater were completely redesigned by them. Two versions were produced — a single-shot breechloader and the twenty-round repeater — using the same patterns for the primary parts.[24] But, it was Lawrence who, in the winter of 1850, solved a major problem with the rifle by inventing the lubricating bullet,[25] thereby eliminating the problem of the barrel clogging with powder fouling after multiple firings, a limitation that had kept earlier breech-loading rifles from gaining popularity and that was essential to the proper func-

A Kendall Harmonica Rifle, circa 1838, showing the steel breechblock and the receiver. Nearby, the indentations on the top of the sliding breech block and the block retaining spring on top of the rifle are clearly visible.

spring-loaded magazine that fed brass primer disks across the nipple when the trigger was pulled,[27] added the knife-edge breech block (that sheared off the end of the paper cartridge) and self-cocking device invented by employee Rollin White, and used his new lubricated bullet to create the Model 1852 ("slanting breech") Sharps carbine. New buildings had been erected in 1850 for the manufacturing of the Jennings rifle; the special machinery required had been designed, built and installed; and production commenced for both the single-shot and repeater models later that same year. At the same time, the machinery for producing the Leonard pistol had been redesigned, installed in one of the many buildings that now comprised the Robbins & Lawrence complex, and production begun on that firearm. The machine tools being designed and built at this time were not only for Robbins & Lawrence's own use, but also for sale to other armories and machine shops. Meanwhile, the California Gold Rush was in full swing and the company was busy filling orders for percussion rifles, shotguns and pistols; "guns were in such demand that we sold all our second-quality work, with good mixed in — anything to make up a working gun — for the full good price,"[28] states Richard Lawrence in his memoirs. The specialized machines and space needed to produce the 5,000 Sharps carbines crowded the existing complex to capacity.

The beginning of the end for the company took place alongside its rapid expansion and came in the guise of international acclaim. The "Crystal Palace" Exhibition (the first world's fair) opened on May 1, 1851 in London; only three American firearms companies sponsored exhibits – Colt's revolvers, Robbins & Lawrence's "Mississippi" rifle and Edwin Maynard's tape primers. Six rifles and a representative had been sent from Windsor to the exhibition where the rifles were frequently disassembled, their parts mingled together and then flawlessly reassembled into six working guns. The demonstration amazed the Europeans, and they coined the term, "the American system," to describe the manufacturing process that produced these military rifles. Ironically, Robbins & Lawrence won a medal of excellence and international acclaim for the least technologically advanced product being manufactured in their factory.

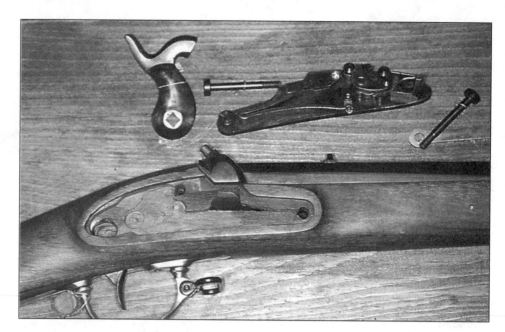

Model 1841 U.S. Army Rifle made by Robbins, Kendall & Lawrence. The bedding in the stock is plainly visible.

A horizontal milling machine designed by Richard Lawrence and Frederick Howe and set up to produce the lock plate of the Model 1841 rifle. These milling machines were one of the primary products manufactured by Robbins & Lawrence Company for sale to other armories.

The exhibiting of these rifles was noticed by certain British ordnance officers; when tension began to build in the Crimea, the Royal Small Arms Commission was formed and representatives were sent to the United States in 1854 to obtain this technology.[29] Orders for gun machinery were placed with several companies, including Robbins & Lawrence, but it was the fatal contract for the manufacture of Enfield rifles[30] that forced Robbins & Lawrence into bankruptcy.

The historical significance of the Robbins & Lawrence Company and what it accomplished in its decade of existence can only be obliquely measured by noting the individuals who worked together and examining their future work. The development of modern firearms was inextricably linked with the precision machine tools invented to manufacture them. The guns designed during this era are as much the inventive genius of the machinist as they were of the gunsmith. The names we remember — Sharps, Smith & Wesson, Colt and Winchester — are associated with guns whose designs were made functional by names we aren't as familiar

An index milling machine designed by Richard Lawrence and Frederick Howe. This was one of the most important machines made by Robbins & Lawrence. Five of these were made for the Enfield contract of 1854.

The brass plate affixed to the index milling machine shown.

▲ A Sharps carbine, Model 1859. Richard Lawrence continued to improve and manufacture the firearm as the chief of armorer (and a principal in) the Sharps Rifle Manufacturing Company of Hartford, CT.

with — R.S. Lawrence, Rollin White, Charles Billings and B. Tyler Henry. The names credited with the founding of the machine-tool industry — Henry D. Stone,[31] Frederick Howe,[32] Charles Billings[33] and George Fairfield[34] — had greater influence on the development of modern firearms than most of the names associated with the guns themselves. There are other names of note which were part of the Windsor school, but even the most basic machine operator, by dint of the cutting-edge technology being developed and used in the armory, was a specialist in his field

Sharps Rifle Manufacturing Company

When the second contract for 15,000 Sharps rifles was made in 1851, more space was needed and none was available in Windsor. Suitable land was found in Hartford, Connecticut and a holding company for the Sharps patents was organized with $100,000 in capital; the holding company — The Sharps Rifle Manufacturing Company — advanced $40,000 to the Robbins & Lawrence Company to purchase the twenty-five acres of land and erect a two-story brick factory measuring 160 feet long by 60 feet wide with an "L" for a forge shop.

Christian Sharps' involvement with the development of his famous rifle after bringing it to Windsor appears to have been minimal. Under the first contract with Robbins & Lawrence, Christian Sharps was paid as a consultant and received a royalty of $1.00 per rifle, but was sim- ply listed as an "engineer" of the Sharps Rifle Manufacturing Company. Both Richard Lawrence and Christian Sharps moved to Hartford in 1852, but all Sharps models were made in Windsor until October of 1856. Lawrence was a principal of the holding company, and when it purchased the Robbins & Lawrence factory in 1856, he continued as a principal and "master armorer" of the Sharps Rifle Manufacturing Company until 1872. Christian Sharps had difficulty with the company and returned to Philadelphia in 1853. He established another company, C. Sharps & Company, then, at the beginning of the Civil War, founded the Carbine and Pistol Manufactory of Sharps & Hankins; the rifles and pistols produced in these other endeavors were different from those of the Sharps Rifle Manufacturing Company, which held his original patents.

A rifling machine designed by Robbins & Lawrence. This one is dated 1851, but the company produced these for sale probably as early as 1849.

Smith & Wesson

The redesigned Jennings single-shot rifle was patented on August 26, 1851 in Courtlandt Palmer's name, while on the same day Horace Smith received a patent for the improvements to the Jennings Repeating Rifle. It's interesting to note that at this time Daniel Wesson was working with B. Tyler Henry in Windsor on improvements to the Jennings repeater and Jennings single-shot rifles; it's also known that R. Tyler Henry was in contact with Horace Smith in Connecticut; that Courtlandt Palmer had also hired Horace Smith to make improvements in the Jennings rifle; that many of the improvements in the repeater had been made by B. Tyler Henry and Richard S. Lawrence in Windsor; and that a Palmer contract was still held by Robbins & Lawrence. Both the repeater and the single-shot rifle were manufactured in Windsor in 1851 and 1852; production ceased sometime during the later part of 1852 and how many were actually made is unknown, but excess parts were used to create muzzle-loading muskets until at least 1854. It's not known whether production stopped because of lack of consumer interest,[36] because Robbins & Lawrence had focused their attention on the Sharps rifle contracts or whether because the rifle needed more work and Smith and Wesson were the ones interested in continuing its development.[37]

Daniel Wesson left Robbins & Lawrence with B. Tyler Henry in 1852. With the financial backing of Courtlandt Palmer and the patents held by him, they continued to develop the Jennings repeater in Horace Smith's gunshop for the following two years. Daniel Wesson made improvements in the "Load Ball" using what appears to be a modified version of the disk primer Lawrence created for the Sharps carbine. This new cartridge allowed the Jennings rifle to be redesigned (eliminating the primer magazine and feed) and the Smith & Wesson company was formed in 1854 with Henry as the superintendent of the new company.

In June of 1855, Horace Smith, Daniel B. Wesson and Courtlandt Palmer incorporated the Volcanic Repeating Arms Company and assigned all their patents to it.[38] This company continued to produce the 36-caliber pistols, rifles and ammunition manufactured by Smith & Wesson; two Navy pistols and three carbines used the tubular magazine and the lever-action feed mechanism that had been patented in 1854. Besides the original Hunt, Jennings, Palmer, Smith and Smith & Wesson patents, the Volcanic Repeating Arms Company also acquired Daniel Wesson's 1854 patent for a center-fire metallic cartridge and the 1856 patent for the Volcanic cartridge.[39,40]

Rollin White, a Vermonter who had worked for Robbins & Lawrence, had formed the Rollin White Arms Company in Lowell, Massachusetts in 1854 and was granted a patent on April 3, 1855[41] that included the boring of a revolver cylinder completely through to enable a cartridge to be loaded from the breech-end of the cylinder. Initially offered to Samuel Colt, who turned it down, Daniel Wesson quickly obtained a license for its exclusive use by Smith & Wesson.[42] One is immediately struck by the similarity between the barrel construction of the Lawrence Pistol and the portion of White's patent application that addresses the drilling of a cylinder; Wesson, who was intimately familiar with this pistol, refused to purchase the patent, but contracted to pay a royalty to White, who was then legally obligated to defend it (as he was forced to do for years).

The Volcanic repeaters, the Smith & Wesson revolver and the Henry rifle all contain elements seen in the guns manufactured in Windsor. The similarity of many components, manufacturing methods and mechanical design are not coincidence, but the continued development and improvement of what was learned while these men worked at Robbins & Lawrence.

and highly sought after by other gun and machine shops.

The machines developed and invented at Robbins & Lawrence – the bandsaw (1847); the plain (1848), profiling (1848), universal (1850) and screw (1852-53) milling machines; the "Combination Threading Machine" (1851); spindle drill presses and the four-spindle "Barrel Driller" (1852); the chain-driven lathe; the perpendicular chuck lathe; and others — were to become the foundation of the machine tool industry, but their creation and initial application was for the manufacture of firearms. The designing of machines to make precision parts — rather than machines to assist hand craftsmanship — was a new approach to gun manufacturing and was immediately recognized as being the key to producing all types of complex mechanisms from pocket watches to steam locomotives.

By the time of the outbreak of the Civil War, the method of mass-manufacturing using interchangeable parts developed at Robbins & Lawrence had been adopted by other machine shops and armories throughout the Northeast,

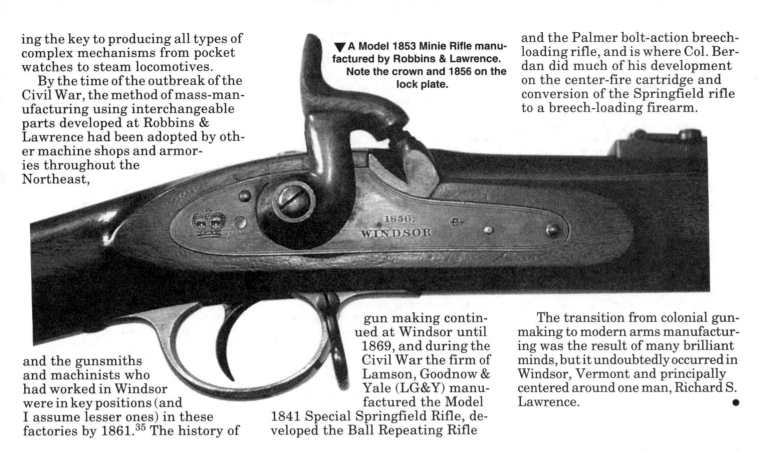

▼A Model 1853 Minie Rifle manufactured by Robbins & Lawrence. Note the crown and 1856 on the lock plate.

and the Palmer bolt-action breech-loading rifle, and is where Col. Berdan did much of his development on the center-fire cartridge and conversion of the Springfield rifle to a breech-loading firearm.

and the gunsmiths and machinists who had worked in Windsor were in key positions (and I assume lesser ones) in these factories by 1861.[35] The history of gun making continued at Windsor until 1869, and during the Civil War the firm of Lamson, Goodnow & Yale (LG&Y) manufactured the Model 1841 Special Springfield Rifle, developed the Ball Repeating Rifle

The transition from colonial gunmaking to modern arms manufacturing was the result of many brilliant minds, but it undoubtedly occurred in Windsor, Vermont and principally centered around one man, Richard S. Lawrence. ●

FOOTNOTES

1. The Ellis-Jennings muzzle-loading repeater was a 54-caliber flintlock with a sliding sidelock, which slid to four different positions, each having its own touch hole, with a swivel primer for the self-priming flashpan. The four separate charges were loaded in the barrel one atop another. An unknown number were made under contract for the NY militia; the barrels marked "US" and "P." Lewis Jennings was granted a patent for this firearm on Sept. 22, 1821.

2. Artemus Wheeler of Boston patented a revolving-cylinder flintlock on June 10, 1818. It is believed they were made by William Bishop of Boston. Two versions were made: a seven-shot, manually-revolved cylinder with a single 32-inch barrel; and a pepperbox carbine with seven 12 1/2-inch barrels. Four (two of each) were purchased by the U.S. Navy in 1821 and tested. The importance of the Wheeler musket is that it was the first patent for a revolving-cylinder firearm in the U.S.; the first revolver purchased by the U.S. Government and is considered to be the first practical revolving firearm.

3. Elisha H. Collier was associated with Artemus Wheeler in either the manufacture or the development of the revolving flintlock in Boston. Collier then went to London where he patented his revolving flintlock, based on Wheeler's principles. Collier's rifles, carbines and pistols were popular in the United States as well as

Europe from 1818 to the early 20s. Elisha H. Collier made about 150 flintlock revolver rifles which vary in size, but the five-shot cylinder (with or without fluting) is the most common. They had an automatically primed flashpan with the powder reservoir located in the heavy frizzen. The design was very advanced with the problem of the gas seal addressed by a protruding lip at the barrel breech; a manually-operated piston wedge was used to seat the cylinder for each chamber (it had to be withdrawn to revolve the cylinder). The original patent allegedly described a spring mechanism for automatic rotation of the cylinder when the hammer was cocked, but all known examples have manually-revolving cylinders.

4. I've seen a photo of a French four-barrel flintlock pepperbox pistol made by Jean Renkin, circa 1790-1810. It has four miniature sidelocks (two on each side) and four triggers; is 41-caliber with 6-inch barrels. A similar rifle is known to exist.

A British seven-barrel flintlock pepperbox revolver, made by Hollis/Chelt circa 1780, is another example of early multiple-firing flintlocks. Each barrel screws off, and there are six clustered around the center one; they measure 2 inches long and are 34-caliber. There is a sliding safety behind the hammer, another sliding safety bar on the left frame to lock the barrels and a fancy wing-nut

on each side of the frame to control the tightness of barrel rotation and lock them to the frame.

A Dutch four-shot flintlock carbine, made around 1720, is of particular interest because it bears a remarkable resemblance to an early Colt. This 67-caliber sidehammer measures 45 inches overall with a round, 24-inch barrel and a 5-inch long, four-chamber cylinder that revolves manually; the cylinder has four separate pans and four separate frizzens and the trigger guard acts as a latch release for the cylinder. It even has an original saddle ring!

5. Joshua Shaw (the artist, not the captain) received an English patent on June 12, 1822 for his copper percussion cap, but he didn't come to America until 1827. Whether copper percussion caps were being manufactured in the United States prior to 1827 is conjecture.

6. Jedediah Caswell of Manlius, NY was granted one of the earliest U.S. patents for an under-hammer lock; he was producing these firearms in the late 1820s and a pistol dated 1828 is known. Another under-hammer pistol, made around 1830 and engraved "Leland" is believed to have been made by one of the Lelan family of Sherborn, MA.; Kendall probably developed his version between 1830 and 1832, but it became the most popular.

7. U.S. Patent #630 was issued to E.A. Bennet and P.F. Haviland on February 15, 1838. A surviving example is a 38-caliber with a 24 1/2-inch octagon rifled barrel, a cherry stock, silver-plated trim and is inscribed "BENNETT'S PATENT" on the barrel strap; the barrel is stamped "N. KENDALL WINDSOR, VT."

8. The Kendall Harmonica Rifle was a 44-caliber with a 20-inch octagonal barrel and measured 39 inches overall. The sliding-breech block had five chambers and was moved side to side for discharge by bringing the underhammer to half cock, depressing the spring catch on top of the frame and manually advancing the block. They are stamped "N. KENDALL WINDSOR, VT PATENTED" on the barrel.

9. The five-shot harmonica rifle made by Jonathan Browning (father of John Moses Browning) looks remarkably like a Kendall harmonica rifle except that it is a side-hammer lock. Like the Kendall, the flat magazine bar has five chambers and five percussion nipples; manually slides and uses a manually-operated thumb lever to lock each chamber in position. Browning called it a "slide gun."

Browning was a Mormon. His first shop was in Nauvoo, Illinois but, in 1842, he emigrated to Council Bluffs, Iowa after anti-Mormon violence. He first advertised his "slide gun" in Council Bluffs, but he emigrated in 1852 to Utah and settled in Ogden, where the four surviving examples of this gun were made. Many of the Mormon, including Brigham Young, moved from Vermont to Illinois and it's probable that Browning had the opportunity to examine one of N. Kendall's harmonica rifles.

10. U.S. Patent #832 was issued to Elijah Jaquith of Brattleboro, VT for a revolving-cylinder firearm. The cylinder revolved above the barrel (i.e. the lower cylinder chamber aligned with the barrel) when the underhammer was cocked and sighting was accomplished through the center of the cylinder. The Jaquith rifle was available in a range of calibers, including as a fowling piece. The Springfield Arms Company made percussion revolvers marked "JAQUITH'S PATENT 1838" but these weren't underhammers, nor did they have the elevated cylinder.

O.W. Whittier of Enfield, NH (about 15 miles from Windsor, VT) produced a revolving cylinder percussion rifle (patent #216 of May 30, 1837). Reported in six, nine and ten-shot variations, it was also produced as a shotgun. Actuating the rear trigger cocked the hammer and rotated the cylinder simultaneously. They were made with octagonal barrels of 31-32 inches length; the deep zigzags on the outside of the cylinder look similar to those on the face of the Jaquith cylin-

der. Samuel Colt owned one of these rifles and it was later modified and improved upon by a Colt engineer, E.K. Root, and patented.

11. John W. Cochran of New York City designed a rifle known as the Cochran Underhammer Revolving Turret Rifle which was made by C.B. Allen in Springfield, MA in the mid-to-late 1830s. Just over 200 were produced. They were made as 36- and 40-caliber nine-shot (seven for the 3rd type), single-action underhammers with a horizontal turret that was revolved manually; they had octagonal barrels with a length of 31-32 inches and the trigger guard was also the hammer. Patent #183 was an improvement (replacing the circular top strap, that retained the turret, with a long rectangular strap that was hinged in the front; with the rear retaining latch functioning as a rear sight -- this made the turret easier to remove and load) but Patent #188 was the original patent – both granted on April 29, 1837. The third model was also produced as a carbine with a round 27-inch barrel.

Henry and Charles Daniels of Chester, CT were producing an under-hammer turret rifle in the late 1830s: Patent #610, granted February 15, 1838 and Patent #677, April 3, 1838. Various calibers and dimensions were produced, but generally the rifle had an 8-shot, manually-revolved turret and an octagonal barrel. The top strap was hinged, with the latch functioning as the rear sight (as in the 2nd and 3rd-type Cochran). A protruding lip on each chamber was locked into the barrel breech by a lever mounted on the left frame below the turret and thus formed a tight gas seal. These were manufactured by C. B. Allen in Springfield, MA. and the influence of the third model Cochran is obvious.

Rufus Nichols and Edward Childs of Conway, MA invented a six-shot percussion revolving rifle (patent #707, granted April 24, 1838). The cylinder is automatically rotated by an outside ratchet when the hammer is cocked – a later version had this mechanism inside the frame. A lever attached to the outside left of the frame secured the cylinder and had to be released prior to cocking. These are sidehammers, but without a forestock (as with underhammers). Produced in five, seven and nine-shot versions with various calibers (36-caliber and 40-caliber probably were the most common); barrel lengths on surviving examples range from 26 to 30 inches. Several features on these rifles, including he Gothic patchbox, are identical to those used on the Jaquith Revolving Rifle, suggesting that an unknown maker produced both the Nichols & Childs and the Jacquith rifles.

James and John Miller were granted a patent in June 1829 (prior to the issuance of patent numbers) for a cylinder magazine; the system of revolving the cylinder and the cylinder stop-lock were

part of this patent. These guns were manufactured by a number of gunsmiths and there is considerable variety; however, they are generally known as Billinghurst rifles after the most prolific maker, William Billinghurst of Rochester, NY, and which were made between 1835 and 1850. They were pill-lock ignition, but later converted to percussion; cylinders chambered for four to nine shots (seven is common) depending on the caliber; and barrels - round, octagon, and a combination - are of various lengths.

12. Samuel Colt's English patent is dated October 22, 1835 and the U.S. one was granted on February 25, 1836. It's important to remember that he wasn't producing firearms at this time, but was trying to raise money for the enterprise; the only known surviving stock certificate for the Paterson, NJ venture was issued on April 18, 1837, more than a year after the patent was granted.

13. Many types of revolver percussion rifles and carbines were already on the market by the time Colt began manufacturing. The Ring Lever rifles were the first to be produced, but his success (with rifles) wasn't assured until the Model 1839 Carbine. One of the company's first orders for this carbine was the Republic of Texas (300 in 1839); the U.S. Dragoons purchased 60 in 1841 and the U.S. Navy purchased 300 of them between 1841 and 1845.

14. Richard Lawrence incorrectly states the bid price per stand in his memoirs: The contract, for 10,000 Model 1841 percussion rifles, for $11.90 per stand, was signed on February 18, 1845 and was extended (a second contract) on January 5, 1848. A letter from Colonel George Talcott to Robbins & Lawrence, National Archives, Record Group 156, Records of the Office of the Chief of Ordnance.

15. Henry D. Stone came to Robbins, Kendall & Lawrence in 1846 and remained in Windsor for the rest of his life. He was the superintendent of Robbins & Lawrence's rifle shop, one of the founders of Vermont Arms Company, and continued with the Lamson companies as a designer and superintendent.

16. Lemuel Hedge of Windsor invented the first machine for ruling paper (1817); a machine for manufacturing precision measuring rules (1827); and the bandsaw (1847) during his notable career.

17. Frederick Howe has often been referred to as one of the founders of the machine tool industry. With Richard Lawrence he designed and invented drill presses, sensitive drills, tapping and threading machines, barrel boring machines, rifling machines, the plain milling machine, the

profiling machine, the universal milling machine and the modem turret lathe.

18. August 10, 1848 - U.S. Patent #5,701

19. Both Hunt patents and the Jennings patent had been assigned to Arrowsmith.

20. September 18, 1849 - U.S. Patent #6,723

21. Edwin Wesson was co-inventor of the Wesson Leavitt revolver manufactured by the Massachusetts Arms Company – a 28-caliber, six-shot, single-action pistol with a Maynard tape primer. Edwin died in 1850 and the successful lawsuit by Colt Arms for patent infringement stopped production around that period – I assume that D. Wesson was hired after his brother's death and took on this job because of the lawsuit.

22. Christian Sharp's first model (1849) were produced with a cap magazine made of brass in which the activation of a lever rotated the wheel in the magazine and from which the nipple picked up a cap. The second model Sharps (Model 1850) used the Maynard tape primer and it was this model that Christian Sharps brought to Windsor. The Sharps Model 1849 and Model 1850 were made in limited numbers by A.S. Nipples in Mill Creek, PA. – a combined total of less than 250 rifles was manufactured during that two-year period. They were distributed by Butterfield & Nippes of Philadelphia.

23. In 1848 Robbins and Lawrence reorganized as the "Windsor Car & Rifle Company" and commenced to manufacture railroad coach cars. Their silent partner was the noted railway builder Sewel Belknap, but his untimely death on June 19, 1849 left the company without any firm contracts; the cars which had been built were sold at a loss and, coupled with an estate settlement against the Windsor Car & Rifle Company, this resulted in a loss of $239,000. The name Robbins and Lawrence was reinstated in 1850 and the principals sought contracts for gun manufacturing either late in 1849 or early in 1850.

24. The single-shot Jennings rifle still used the primer magazine, but the "loaded balls" were fed into the chamber through a small rectangular opening on the side of the receiver (it reminds one of the Winchester rifles of later years). This method is very awkward and it would be difficult to gain access to any jammed or misfired bullet. Having examined several of these, I can't see their advantage over muzzle-loading rifles.

25. Richard Lawrence stated that he invented the lubricating bullet in the winter of 1850 while in New York (Astoria, L.I.) demonstrating the Jennings rifle to a potential buyer from Europe. One of the problems with the rifle was that the inside of the barrel became clogged with powder fouling, (since there was no greased patch used with this ammunition) after repetitive firings. Lawrence used a lathe to cut a groove around the lead bullet and filled it with tallow which, in combination with the expansion of the lead bullet when fired, functioned like the greased patches used in muzzle-loading rifles and cleaned the barrel of the powder fouling from the previous load.

26. Christian Sharps and Richard Lawrence apparently worked together to design the Model 1851 rifle with the nickel-plated receiver and the Maynard tape primer. Only 1,680 of these were produced – all in Windsor, VT.

27. The disk primer system was patented on October 5, 1852 in Christian Sharps' name since the work was under contract, although examination of this device shows it to be a classic example of Richard Lawrence's designs. The degree of Sharps involvement, if any, in the development of the Model 1852 rifle, is pure conjecture.

28. In his memoirs, Richard Lawrence claimed thirty-eight percent of the parts manufactured for the U.S. Army Rifle (mostly barrels) didn't pass inspection. These parts were both sold to local gunsmiths (D.H. Hilliard was a primary buyer) or used by Robbins & Lawrence to build "custom" guns. I've examined muzzle-loading rifles and fowling pieces that utilize Model 1841 barrels and the receivers and stocks of a Jennings. Another example, dated 1853, is an under-hammer pistol that uses the handgrip and breech of a revolving-hammer pistol.

29. Sir John Anderson and Lt. Thomas Picton Warlow were sent to the United States in 1854 by the Royal Small Arms Commission to obtain machinery for the Enfield armory which was then under construction. The committee has visited the Robbins & Lawrence factory in Hartford, CT, but the gun machinery at that location was not yet complete; in August they visited the armory in Windsor, VT. A contract for 150 machines (mostly milling machines) – plus gigs, fixtures and gauges – was awarded to Robbins & Lawrence and this contract was fulfilled.

30. Fox, Henderson & Company, acting as agents for the British war office, contracted with Robbins & Lawrence for 25,000 "Interchangeable Enfield Minie Rifles" at $15.50 each (complete with bayonet) on March 8, 1855. The contract held a penalty clause of $5.00 for any undelivered rifle, but the clause failed to specify the required time for completion of the contract; apparently it was understood by the parties that deliveries of the rifles would begin in June of 1855 and be completed in a year. Delays in obtaining models of the 1853 Enfields placed the tooling behind schedule and the first guns weren't delivered until December 1855. For the next five months production was limited to an average of 650 rifles; production was delayed even further when a drought in Pennsylvania during the summer of 1856 prevented the sawmills from cutting the black walnut needed for the rifle stocks. The unexpected ending of the Crimean War (Feb. 1, 1856) and the signing of the Treaty of Paris (March 30, 1856) coupled with the delays in delivery of the rifles and the completion of the Enfield armory, caused the British agents to rescind the contract in September of 1856 and evoke the penalty clause on 14,600 undelivered rifles. Robbins & Lawrence owed $73,000 against the advance payments and another $73,000 in penalties; the tooling for the Enfield contract coupled with the expenditures of building the factory in Hartford, left the company in a position where it was unable to raise the capital to made the $146,000 payment. On May 22, 1856 the British agents had assigned the held Robbins & Lawrence mortgage to Col. Henry Sebastian Rowan of Her Britannic Majesty's Artillery and the decree of foreclosure took place on June 1, 1857. The Vermont Arms Company which had leased the facility from Col. Rowan and completed the Enfield rifle contract. Upon its completion the armory was put up for auction and was purchased by E.G. Lamson

31. Henry David Stone came to Robbins & Lawrence in 1846, was one of the founders of the Vermont Arms Company (1857) and continued to work with the Lamson Companies (1858-85).

32. Frederick Webster Howe was at Robbins & Lawrence from 1847-56; during 1858-61 he was building guns and gun machinery for North & Savage; from 1861 to 65 he was the superintendent of the armory of the Providence Tool Company manufacturing Springfield rifles; 1865 to 68 he was the president of the Howe Manufacturing (Elias Howe's sewing machine); and in 1868 co-founded Brown & Sharpe as partner and president.

33. Charles Billings worked for Robbins & Lawrence from 1852 to 56; from 1856 to 62 he was a die sinker at Colt Arms; 1862 to 65 he contracted with E. Remington & Sons to forge frames for their revolvers; 1865-68 was working with George Fairchild at Weed Sewing Co.; in 1866 was co-inventor of the Spencer-Roper repeater and in 1869 was a co-founder of the Roper Sporting Arms Company; and 1872 co-founded the drop-forging concern of Billing & Spencer.

34. George Albert Fairfield came to Robbins & Lawrence in 1853 to assist Howe and Stone in building the machinery for the Enfield contract; in 1856 he was the designer of gun machinery for the American Machine Works of Springfield; during 1857 to 65 he was a contractor on machinery to Colt Arms; 1865 to 1876 at the Weed Sewing Machine Company (in the Sharps plant in Hartford); 1876 co-founded (with Spencer) the Hartford Machine Screw Co.; and in 1880 helped establish the Pope Manufacturing Company in Hartford (in the old Sharps plant).

35. Richard Lawrence was producing the Sharps rifle in Hartford during the Civil War; Frederick Howe had developed the gun machinery for North & Savage (1858) and was the superintendent of the armory of the Providence Tool Company and the manufacturing of the Springfield rifle (1861-65); Henry Stone was with Lamson, Goodnow & Yale in Windsor who were manufacturing the Springfield rifle and developing the Ball repeater and Palmer breech-loading carbine during the war; George Fairfield had developed the gun machinery for the American Machine Works of Springfield and during the war was the machinery contractor for Colt Arms; Charles Billings had worked on gun development for Colt Arms and in 1862 began producing the revolver frames for E. Remington & Sons; and George Hubbard of Cresson & Hubbard Co. manufactured special gun machinery, de-mountable guns and invented the bomb fuse during the Civil War. Besides these notables, many of the machine operators who had received their apprenticeship training or had worked at Robbins & Lawrence were employed by armories during this era.

36. During the winter of 1850, Courtlandt's brother, William, was in Paris trying to place orders for the Jennings rifle. The problem with the Jennings rifles was that the powder charge in the "Loaded Ball" was unable to propel the bullet with a force equal to that of the muzzleloaders of the day. This remained the technical limitation of the repeater until the development of rimfire cartridges.

37. The confusion over Daniel Wesson, Horace Smith and B. Tyler Henry's involvement with the Jennings rifle become clear only with Courtlandt Palmer's involvement as a patent holder and financier. When production of the Jennings ceased at Robbins & Lawrence – in 1852 it was Palmer who owned the patents – the terms of Horace Smith's patent and contract with Palmer is unclear. It was Palmer who supplied the funding for continued development of the Jennings repeater in the gunshop of Horace Smith in Norwich, CT. Whether it was Daniel Wesson or C. Palmer who convinced Henry to leave the employ of Robbins & Lawrence is unknown, and how Wesson originally met Smith is mere conjecture, but probably was through Palmer or Henry.

38. The Volcanic Repeating Arms Company was incorporated with capital stock in the amount of $150,000 and 6,000 shares at $25 par; Oliver Winchester purchased 80 shares. In July the three incorporators sold, transferred or assigned their various assets (including patents) to the new corporation for $65,000 in cash (paid in three installments) plus 2,800 shares of stock; they also received an undisclosed sum for the machinery at the Norwich, CT. shop. The three founders never held a corporate office, although H. Smith was plant manager for a short period of time late in 1855. The company was moved to New Haven early in 1856. – *Winchester: The Gun That Won The West*, Harold F. Williamson, Combat Forces Press, Washington D.C. 1952.

39. In August 1854 Daniel Wesson received U.S. Patent #11,496 for an inside-primed, centerfire metallic cartridge; U.S. Patent # 14,147 was granted on Jan. 22, 1856 for the Volcanic cartridge.

40. The "Patent Right Deed and Covenant between Courtlandt Palmer and Horace Smith and Daniel B. Wesson" of June 20, 1854 created confusion over ownership of future patents acquired. Furthermore, part of the agreement made in July 1855 with the Volcanic company stated that "...it shall have the exclusive use and control of all patents and patent rights which the said Smith and the said Wesson or either of them can or may hereafter obtain or acquire for inventions or improvements in firearms or ammunition or upon the matters already patented as aforesaid, including all power of granting licenses, conveying shares and rights, receiving rents and royalties, and recovering and collecting damages for infringements."

41. Rollin White was granted two patents, #12,648 and #12,649 on April 3,1855; it was U.S. Patent #12,648 that contained the relevant clause and the one used by Smith & Wesson. He also invented the knife-edge breechblock and self-cocking mechanism for the Model 1851 Sharps while working for Robbins & Lawrence.

42. Colt Arms then had to wait until Rollin White's patent expired in 1869 before they could use the new type of ammunition and develop the highly successful Colt Peacemaker of 1872.

THE 6MM BENCH REST
— A DOGGER'S DREAM

by Dave Ward

PROJECTS BEGET PROJECTS. A few years back I got interested in a relatively obscure and yet quite useful wildcat cartridge originally developed by Frank Barnes, called the 308 x 1 1/2-inch. The modern version, nearly identical, is the 30 Bench Rest — based on a series of Remington Bench Rest cartridge cases. This delightful little performer was a perfect match for a Remington Model Seven in 308 Winchester languishing in the safe, so I had the Seven re-chambered for the 30 BR. The result was a handy, lightweight rifle chambered for a 200 yard deer, antelope, sheep or goat cartridge. I wrote about the project in *Handloader's Digest #17* should anyone wish a more detailed account. I killed several deer and antelope with the 30 BR over several years with only one real problem: it rapidly became my favorite hunting rifle, but other than trips to the range, I only got to pull the trigger a couple of times a year. It was spending more time in the safe than it should have. But all that was soon to change.

I discovered prairie dogs. Really, I re-discovered prairie dog shooting. Let's be candid here — I became *addicted* to prairie dog shooting.

I had shot prairie dogs before. At that time I owned some property on the southern edge of Denver which held a small population of the little critters. To some, they're cute and cuddly. If you own property, they get un-cute real fast. Why? Because they dig big holes.

My mission became to eliminate the whole batch of 'em. And I did, over a period of several weeks.

Then, last summer, I sold some merchandise to an older gentleman who lives north of Denver. He indicated he was not particularly excited about the thought of taking his life into his own hands and driving into town. I couldn't blame him. Denver's traffic is busy to say the least. On the other hand I didn't want to drive the forty miles or so to his house, either. As I stammered about time and distance, he asked if I liked to shoot prairie dogs. Well, sure, I guess. Why? It seemed that he had 600 or so acres of alfalfa and a prairie dog problem. Hmmm? I had a new Ruger stainless Model 77 in 223 Remington that I'd recently finished load work on — with a lack-of-target prob-

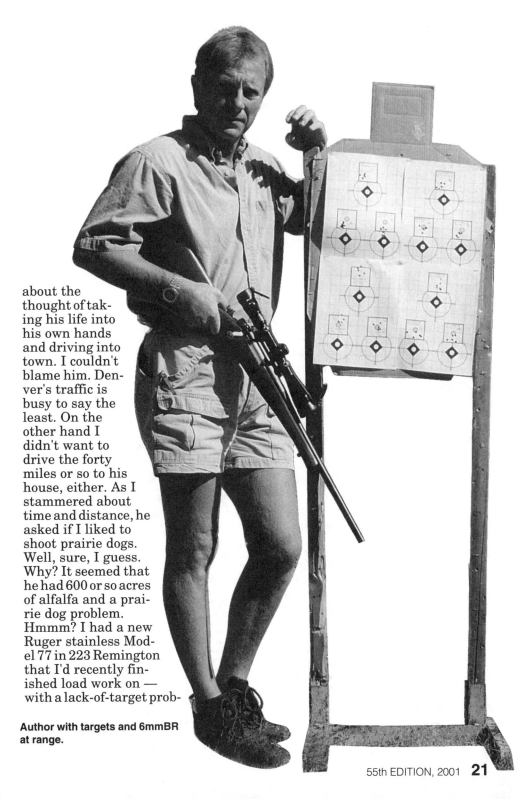

Author with targets and 6mmBR at range.

The finished compact 6mmBR Remington Model Seven measures under 37 inches; the stiff 18-inch medium-weight Douglas barrel adds little weight, gives up nothing in the accuracy department.

lem. Suddenly time and distance were less important. I could deliver, I suppose. Twist my trigger finger.

The next Saturday, I found myself beneath a large cottonwood tree on the edge of an recently mown alfalfa field near the town of Erie. A few miles to the west, the snow-covered Front Range of the Rockies totally dominated the countryside. Toss in a bluer-than-blue sky and just enough breeze to make it interesting, and what else could a person ask for? A couple of things, but what I was interested in at the moment started about 75 yards distant and stretched for another 200 or so. A target-rich environment. Prairie dogs everywhere. Barking. Eating. Digging those *big* holes.

Three shots. Three dogs. Those mountains. The blue sky. Fresh mown alfalfa. I was in heaven, and I was hooked.

Later in the day the breeze picked up and hits, especially at the longer distances, became more challenging (read fewer). I thought, between shots, about bringing the 250 Ackley Improved along with the 223 next time. Those 75-grain hollow-points should do the trick at the longer ranges, especially in the wind. I left shortly thereafter and, after thanking my host profusely and gaining another invite, I thought all the way home about the perfect prairie dog rifle.

Next trip, the 250 Ackley Improved did come along (read about the 250 Ackley Improved in *Handloader's Digest #12)* and performed beautifully at the longer distances. But, since this was primarily a me-

dium- to long-range medium-game cartridge, recoil was up and so were loading costs. It was an excellent long-range prairie dog rig, but not the perfect pack-the-lunch, grab-the-rifle and shoot-all-day doggin' gun. The 223 Ruger stainless with the 19-inch sporter barrel was close. Its 22-inch factory barrel was trimmed to 19 inches for portability - the extra inches ballistically unnecessary - and given a target crown. Happily, it shoots consistently below the one- inch mark with select loads at 100 yards — with minimal recoil. It's cheap to reload. It's only failing appears around 200 yards, in a breeze.

Maybe there was a cartridge out there that would split the differences

between power and recoil, wind drift and expense (the expense now being both in reloading and in the cost of a new rifle). Some version of a 6mm was the obvious choice, but I had additional criteria for the project.

First, the ideal cartridge had to have the same size case head as the 308 Winchester or 30 BR, since I wanted to start with the Model Seven. That eliminated all of the 6mm wildcats based on the smaller 22 centerfire cases, and the 6mm PPC. Second, I wanted modest recoil for those all-day marathons I was already beginning to envision. This eliminated all the big 6mm wildcats, the 243 Winchester and the 6mm Remington. They're all medium-game rifles that double as varminters. I wanted

223 Remington, 6mm BR, 243 Winchester. All work on prairie dogs. Author thinks 6mm BR is about perfect since it handles wind better than the 223 Rem and is much easier on the shoulder than the 243 Winchester.

to go the other way: develop a nearly perfect prairie dog rifle that could also take medium game. I also wanted this rifle to shoot a factory cartridge, or at least a factory case. That didn't leave much to choose from, but then you really only need one choice — if it's the right one. The 6mm Bench Rest was the only one left after the culling. That bothered me not in the least, because I was already so impressed with the 30 Bench Rest.

The one aspect I had not yet dealt with was the barrel. Because the rifle would serve as both a hunting and a varminting rig, I added another requirement: that it remain lightweight and portable. Still, I wanted accuracy: groups no larger than one inch at worst and less than three-quarters of an inch preferred. I liked the length of the Model Seven's factory barrel, but the diameter was just too thin. Frankly, I think the factories make a mistake by offering their compact or carbine models with only a thin, whippy barrel. Something with a bit more beef would improve accuracy without adding significant weight — my opinion.

A couple of telephone conversations later, and Tim Gardner of Douglas Barrels had me convinced I needed a #2 Sporter barrel. Later in the conversation, I convinced him I really did want a varmint rifle with an 18-inch barrel. At that length, the muzzle diameter would be about .650-inch. Stiff enough, not too heavy and still very compact and portable. The finished barrel measures .648-inch at the muzzle. Tim said that a 1-in-12 twist would give best accuracy with the light varmint bullets and still stabilize the 85-grain Nosler Partition I planned to use for

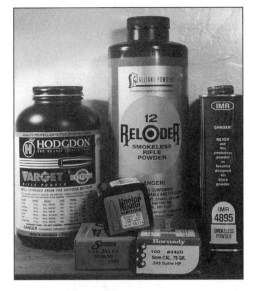

Some of the powders and bullets that shot well in the 6mm BR. Varget, RL-12, and IMR 4895. The 60 gr. Sierra HP, 75 gr Hornady HP and 85 gr. Nosler Partition.

deer, etc. It all sounded good to me so, since Douglas offers complete chambering, turning and other niceties, I let them do most of the work. All I would have to have done was the headspacing and bluing.

While I waited for the barrel, I gathered goodies. A set of full-length dies arrived quickly from RCBS. Brass and bullets, no problem. Rather than finding 40 perfect loads for 10 different bullet weights, I decided to go the other way. One or two great loads for the three or four bullet weights I planned to use. If it didn't work out that way then I'd be stuck

testing a *bazillion* combinations, trying to find one load that shoots well.

Initial bullet selection included, for prairie dogs, the 60-grain Sierra HP, the 70-grain Speer TNT HP, the 70-grain Hornady SP and the 75-grain Hornady HP. For larger varmints, I looked at the 87-grain Hornady, and for big game the 85-grain Nosler Partition, figuring if I could get the Partition to group into 1 1/2 inches I would go with it because of its solid construction and reputation.

For powders, well, there is a surprising amount of data out there. Hornady and Accurate Arms have loads for the 6mm BR in their manuals, but the most complete reference I found was provided by Phil Hodgdon. Allowing for my short barrel, the data was right on, too. I decided to use Hodgdon's Varget, Alliance Reloader 12, Olin 748, and IMR 4320 and 4895. BLC-2 looked intriguing as did H-335 and H-322, but I was out of those and I wanted to see if the rifle/cartridge would shoot well without acquiring additional powders.

The 6mm BR is a solid performer, especially with the lighter bullets. At 75 grains and below, velocities are well above 3100 fps in a 24-inch barrel. I figured that even with the 18-inch barrel, I could comfortably trade some velocity for accuracy. I mean — the biggest, baddest prairie dog out there weighs just over three pounds. Of course, I didn't want to be shooting the equivalent of a super-accurate 25/20, either....

The barrel arrived sooner than I expected (thank you very much, Tim!), but it seemed to take forever to get it headspaced and blued

Hard at work, author Ward looks for smaller groups from his new 6mmBR.

LOAD DATA FOR THE 6mm BENCH REST

Bullet	Powder	Charge(grains)	Velocity (fps)
60 gr. Sierra HP	Varget	33.2	3118
	IMR4895	31.4	3015
	748	34.6	3129
70 gr. Hornady SP	Varget	33.2	3097
	RL-12	33.4	3088
	IMR4895	30.8	2985
70 gr. Speer TNT HP	RL-12	33.2	3095
	748	33.4	3137
75 gr. Hornady HP	Varget	32.2	3028
	RL-12	32.2	3070
	IMR4895	30.4	2927
85 gr. Nosler Partition	Varget	30.9	2951
87 gr. Hornady SP	RL-12	29.7	2805

Velocities measured at 76 F, five-shot strings, CCI 400 primers

Best powders, Varget and RL-12, and bullets, 60 gr. Sierra HP and 75 gr. Hornady HP for author's 6 mm BR.

(thanks a lot, Murphy!). A light bead-blast made for a wonderfully functional matte finish, which I matched with a matte Redfield 5-Star 3x9. Finally assembled, the rifle measured just under 37 inches overall, still quite compact. And, at just over seven pounds, including the scope, it is still quite portable. But would it shoot? Time to find out.

I started with the 85- and 87-grainers. I chose Olin 748, Hodgdon Varget, and Alliance RL-12. Hodgdon's data showed all delivered velocities over 2900 fps, with Varget managing just over 3000 fps. The first fifty rounds were less than exciting. The Nosler 85-grain Partition did its usual thing and grouped around 1.5 to 2.0 inches at 100 yards. Unfortunately, the 87-grain Hornady wasn't all that much better with any of the three powders. I had expected more, especially of the Hornady. And recoil was greater than I anticipated. In order to stay out of the dumps regarding the project, I did the normal thing: I began to rationalize.

It's a new barrel. You can't expect it to be a tack-driver on the first few shots. It needs to be broken in, like a racing engine. That helped a little. *Then, of course, I wasn't expecting much from the Nosler, it's not designed as a varmint/target bullet. As for the Hornady, I wasn't really plan-*

ning to use it on prairie dogs anyway. Too much bullet for the job. And the recoil? *What was it that I expected with nearly twice the bullet weight at almost the same velocity as a 55-grain 223?* Duhhh!

To the next batch of loads, I added the 75-grain Hornady HP. Maybe it would do a bit better. With 748 it was just okay, hovering around the one-inch mark. IMR4895 wasn't much better. Frankly, I was beginning to worry. Just before the Ruger 223 load work I mentioned earlier, I spent many hours and too many rounds on an accuracy project that never did work out. I was beginning to get a feeling of *deja vu*, and I did not like it.

Still, I was far from testing all the load combinations even with the small selection of bullets and powders chosen. There were a lot more fish in the 6mm sea (so to speak), so I went back to work. How about the 75 Hornady and some Varget and RL-12? Maybe that would do better

So, back to the range, early in the morning so the wind wouldn't bother things. Still rationalizing. My first load was the 75 HP and 32.2 grains of Varget (32.5 listed as max by Hodgdon). Five shots went into 9/16-inch from a clean barrel. *I perked up.* The same bullet and 32.4 grains of Varget ballooned to 1 1/4-inch. *I unperked.* The first group must have

been a fluke. I proceeded with the shooting. RL-12 was next with the 75 Hornady HP. Load one at 31.9 grains was so-so. Load two at 32.2 grains slipped into 11/16-inch. I perked again. Load three at 32.4 grains (max of 32.5 grains) did 13/16-inch. Now I was making progress!

Back at the loading bench, I re-did the Varget and RL-12 loads with the 75 HP, and tossed in a few of the Sierra 60 HPs with Varget and RL-12. At the range the next day, I was still a bit concerned the good groups of the previous day were flukes. Not so. The 75 HP repeated with both the Varget and the RL-12. At least I had one bullet and two powders that would shoot to my satisfaction.

Now for the Sierra 60-grain HP, which appeared to be the near-perfect prairie dog bullet, offering good velocity, reasonable recoil and that good 6mm wind-resistance. I crossed my fingers. The first load of 33.0 grains of Varget went into 5/8-inch. Number two load of 33.2 grains of Varget also went into 5/8-inch. Number three load consisted of 33.4 grains of Varget and shot into 1.5 inches. I knew where I didn't want to go. (I should say here the max load from Hodgdon is 34.0 grains of Varget for a velocity of 3442 fps from a 24-inch barrel.) My cases filled to the top of the neck with 33.4 grains and the powder was heavily compressed with the 60-grain HP, a possible reason for the decline in accuracy. My velocities are 3118 fps average for the 33.2-grain load — I doubt the prairie dogs will notice the difference.

I continued testing with the remaining powders and bullets, the results of which are shown in the ac-

A well-engineered shooting system is clearly in evidence as author Ward draws a bead on one of the 'ranch rats'.

and easy to carry. In short, I'm out there walking, so I'll trade that possible quarter-inch for compactness and portability. And, fourth, I don't want to kill them all, that's not the point. I want to keep them relatively under control, and have some shooting in the future. As the old gentleman in Colorado said, "Just shoot the ones in the pasture. Leave 'em along the fence line for brood stock." Makes sense to me.

Perhaps the perfect pair of prairie dog rifles: Remington Model Seven in 6mm BR and Ruger 77 Stainless (shortened) in 223 Remington.

At last, I had the rig and the loads to shoot through it. All I was missing were the prairie dogs. I headed northeast to Springerville, a nice little town on the north side of the White Mountains in east-central Arizona. Rumor had it there were 'dogs on the plains north of there. Well, there were, but after four hunts in three days (mornings and late afternoons only; after all, I had to spend some time with the family) there were thirty or so fewer. It was a perfect test for the 6mm BR because, except for the last morning, the wind was a crisp twenty-plus knots off the port bow. The poor 223 would have been sorely tested, and most of the dogs would have been merely annoyed by the dust it kicked up. But not so with the 6mm BR. Two shots. Two dogs. Distance: about 130 yards with the Sierra 60-

companying chart. Each of the powders did quite well with at least one of the bullets; most did well with several. I could have taken this project to a higher level by using match components, loading tools and techniques and possibly shaved another quarter-inch or so off the groups, but I didn't feel it was necessary. Here's why:

First, I'll take 5/8- to 3/4-inch, five-shot groups from a light hunting rifle — any day. Second, I wanted the results to be attainable by anybody using everyday loading tools and common components at reasonable prices. Third, I don't shoot prairie dogs from a benchrest using a heavy rifle. I sit on the ground and lean against a rock or fence post. To steady the rifle, I use a pair of shooting sticks of lightweight bamboo, tied together with parachute cord. Steady as a rock grain HP. Not a bad start. The longest successful shot on the trip was about 230 yards, in the breeze with a 70-grain Hornady. I was pleased when I heard the *thunk*.

So, I'm back in the prairie dog business with another impressive cartridge from Remington's Bench Rest family. The whole project was easy on the checkbook and would have been easier if I could have re-chambered a 243 Winchester or 6 mm Remington, although the tighter twists typically encountered in rifles chambered for them might reduce the accuracy of the lighter bullets.

Interestingly enough, the 6mm BR clocks 2951 fps with the 85 Nosler. That converts to 1652 ft/lbs of energy at the muzzle, essentially the same as the 30-30 Winchester or the 44 Magnum. At 200 yards, the combination still has 1000 ft/lbs of energy, better that either of those and nearly identical to the 30 BR with the 130-grain Hornady. Since I know from experience that the 30 BR is an excellent medium game cartridge at 200 yards, I'm not the least worried about the 6mm BR performing in that category and, hopefully, the whitetail permit I drew for Arizona will prove that point. So I now have what I consider to be the perfect all-day prairie dog rifle that can easily serve when hunting for deer, javelina, sheep — or any medium game — and it doesn't weigh 15 pounds or measure 44 cumbersome inches long. Interested? Give the 6mm Bench Rest a try. Want some help from me? Good luck, I'll be gone doggin'. •

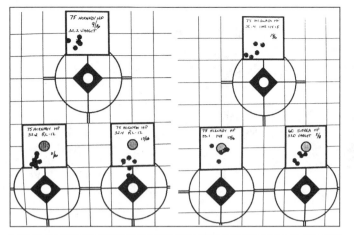

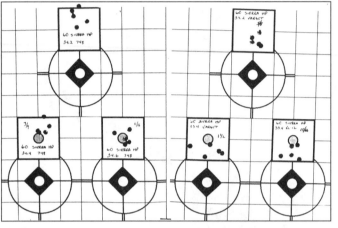

Some groups at 100 yards: (left target, top, counterclockwise) 75 Hornady HP/32.2 gr. Varget; 75 Hornady HP/32.2 gr. RL-12; 75 Hornady HP/32.4 gr. RL-12. (right target, same); 75 Hornady 30.4 gr./IMR 4895; 75 Hornady HP 33.1 gr. 748 and 60 Sierra HP/33.0 gr. Varget.

More groups at 100 yards: (left target, top, counterclockwise) 60 Sierra HP/34.2 gr. 748; 60 Sierra HP/34.4 gr. 748; 60 Sierra HP/34.6 gr. 748. (right target, same); 60 Sierra HP 33.2 gr. Varget; 60 Sierra HP/33.4 gr. Varget; 60 Sierra HP/ 33.4 gr. RL-12. Notice how groups can open or tighten with only 0.2 gr. increase in powder charge.

The Arizona prairie dogs are there for the shooting, although not as plentiful as in the High Plains. A light, accurate rifle and a set of bamboo shooting sticks lets you enjoy the walk, then shoot effectively.

Built on a short-action Interarms Mauser receiver, this early Ball bolt-action muzzleloader turns in exceptional accuracy with Pyrodex Pellets (with either two or three 50-grain pellet loads) and saboted bullets.

Modern Maturity ...

Muzzleloading Enters a New Generation

by Toby Bridges

MUZZLELOADING CONTINUES TO evolve as a true hunting sport and is now more performance-driven than at any other time in history. Today's muzzleloader fancier is a big-game hunter who has turned to the special muzzleloading–or "primitive weapons"–seasons to extend the time he can pursue the whitetail deer and other big game each fall. Nostalgia now plays a minor role in why hunters pick up a muzzleloader–the hi-tech, in-line ignition front-loaders favored by today's hunter can hardly be called primitive weapons.

During the mid-1980s, very modern-looking in-line percussion hunting rifles, like the Knight MK-85, shook up the muzzleloading world by daring to introduce modern firearms features to a centuries-old shooting sport. The guns were built with safeties, faster rates of rifling twist for improved accuracy with ultramodern saboted bullets, receivers drilled and tapped for scope installation and incorporated sleek, modern center-fire rifle lines and handling characteristics.

Black powder shooters who considered front-loaders a historical link to the past hated the new guns, claiming such abominations would jeopardize the special muzzleloading big-game seasons. But they didn't. In fact, the guns have had a completely different effect. The modern features, improved ignition, better accuracy and familiar feel of the new in-line rifles appealed

The removable breech plug of the Henry Ball bolt-action muzzleloader features a chamber, utilizes reusable stainless steel ignition modules and No. 209 shotshell primers.

to cartridge gun hunters, who suddenly joined the ranks of traditionally-minded muzzleloading hunters to take advantage of the special seasons. States responded with increased muzzleloading hunting opportunities.

In 1996, Remington Arms Company introduced their revered Model 700 bolt-action centerfire rifle in an all-new muzzleloading configuration. The Model 700ML retains many of the popular features of the cartridge model, including a modified bolt for faster lock-time than is possible with a plunger-style in-line rifle. The rifle also incorporates features which made the in-line rifles popular in the first place, like a removable breech plug for easy cleaning and a fast 1-in-28-inch rifling twist for outstanding accuracy with hard-hitting saboted bullets. Ruger, Connecticut Valley, Traditions and a new arms-making venture—Austin & Halleck—followed with similar bolt-action in-line percussion rifles.

Knight Rifles and Thompson/Center Arms have since hit the market with still more advanced in-line ignition rifles which tend to push muzzleloader performance beyond its present limits. Both the bolt-action Knight D.I.S.C. Rifle and the break-open T/C Encore have been engineered to rely on exceptionally hot No. 209 shotshell primers for ignition. Not only does the hotter flame guarantee ignition of the powder charge, it does a better job of fully consuming heavy hunting charges, thus delivering better velocity. In fact, when loaded with three of the 50-grain compressed Pyrodex Pellets (150-grain charge), either of these rifles will push a saboted 250- or 260-grain bullet from the muzzle at slightly more than 2,000 fps, compared to approximately 1,700 fps with two of the 50-grain pellets (100-grain charge).

Well, as hi-tech as these modern systems may seem, on the horizon looms further development sure to change this old sport one more time. The rifle and ignition system concept are the brainchild of custom riflesmith Henry Ball, owner and operator of Bill's Custom Guns, in Greensboro, North Carolina.

What makes this front-loading system so different is that here—at last—is a muzzleloader specifically designed and built to be shot *with smokeless powder*!

That's right, a muzzleloader which can be safely loaded and fired with cleaner-burning, more economical-and better-performing—smokeless powder loads. The designer of this

system felt that, since the muzzleloading hunter has been striving to get his front-loader to perform more like a modern centerfire hunting rifle—why not build one that will? The result is a very user-friendly front-loader capable of delivering amazing accuracy and knockdown power.

The heart of a Henry Ball smokeless powder muzzleloader is a modern center-fire rifle action. He has built rifles using everything from surplus Remington rolling-block actions to commercially available Sako bolt-actions. He tends to favor the Howa bolt-actions from Japan. These are readily available to custom riflemakers, reasonably priced and of high quality. Also, the actions have been built to withstand pressures far greater than those created by the smokeless powder loads prescribed by the custom riflesmith for his 21st century front-loader.

Ball's standard rifle is a 50-caliber built with a custom-cut McGowen 4140 match-grade barrel, rifled with a 1-in-24-inch rate of twist for use

Reusable stainless steel ignition modules are easily primed and de-primed. Author Bridges has used some modules more than 150 times.

with saboted bullets. He also offers a 45-caliber rifle, designed to be fired "sabotless", loading a jacketed .452-inch bullet directly atop the powder charge. Either barrel comes with a removable breech plug. The design of the breech plug is covered by one of four patents the designer has to protect this unique muzzleloader.

Instead of relying on a nipple and percussion cap for ignition, this modernistic front-loader actually chambers what Henry Ball refers to as an "ignition module". These are heavy-duty stainless steel cases which precisely fit into a chamber in the breech plug. The reusable modules are easily primed with a No. 209 shotshell primer and, when the bolt of a Howa action locks down behind one of these, this ignition system is fully protected

The rifles built by Henry Ball handle the pressures of certain smokeless powder loads. Here a 34-grain charge of Alliant 2400 is shown with a saboted 300-grain Homady 45 XTP and stainless steel ignition module.

Muzzleloading's new "guru", Henry Ball, prepares to touch off a shot from one of his smokeless powder muzzleloaders, this one built on a Savage Model 110 action.

Henry Ball transformed this Savage Model 11 OFP Tactical Rifle (originally in 308 Winchester) into one of his 21st century smokeless front-loaders. The rifle still retains the look and feel of its center-fire origin.

Ball's conversion of this Savage center-fire into one of his hot front-loaders uses the factory bolt without any modifications.

When the bolt is closed behind the Ball ignition module, the rifle design prevents any escape of fouling or propellant gas, and the ignition system is the most weather-proof system available today.

from the weather. The precise fit of the module in the chamber, plus a tiny .030-inch orifice leading from the chamber into the barrel, prevents blowback. And it is this precise fit which allows this muzzleloader to be loaded and fired with hot smokeless powder loads.

Many of the high performance Pyrodex loads fired out of other in-line ignition muzzleloaders generate a chamber pressure of 14,000 to 18,000 psi. This is especially true with the hefty three 50-grain Pyrodex Pellet loads now advocated by Knight Rifles and Thompson/Center Arms in some of their more recent models. The loads prescribed for the Ball smokeless propellant muzzleloader produce significantly higher pressures, in the 40,000 to 44,000 psi range, just a little shy of the pressure produced by factory 308 Winchester loads, a popular chambering for which the medium-length Howa action is often used. (**Note: These pressures will completely destroy any other muzzleloader**)

One of the ignition modules can be reused hundreds of times, and is easily de-primed with a simple punch pin tapped with a hammer. When the same module is primed, fired, then re-primed and used over and over again for 20 or 30 successive shots, the outside surfaces remain free of fouling residue. All the pressure generated by the smokeless powder loads is contained in the barrel and, to a much smaller degree, inside the heavy-walled ignition module.

One of the powders favored by the rifle's designer has been Alliant 2400. With carefully weighed charges of 30 to 35 grains, I've found the powder produces excellent accuracy with several different saboted bullets out of three different 50-caliber rifles built by Bill's Custom Guns. One sabot and bullet combination which shot extremely well out of all three guns was the 260-grain .451-inch Speer JHP, loaded with a black plastic sabot from Muzzleloading Magnum Products (of Harrison, Arkansas).

Sighting in a beautiful laminate-stocked 50-caliber Ball rifle just prior to the 1998 deer seasons, I settled on 34 grains of Alliant 2400 and the Speer 260-grain jacketed bullet as my most accurate load. At a hundred yards, the rifle would repeatedly print the hollow-point bullet inside of 1 1/2 inches, and one ten-shot group measured just 7/8-inch across at the widest point. The load is good for 2,350 fps at the muzzle and nearly 3,200 ft/lbs of muzzle energy, about the same as a 7mm Remington Magnum.

What really impresses me is the downrange performance. With the scope sighted to print bullet impact 2 inches high at 100 yards, the 260-grain Speer hits just an inch low at 150 and only about five inches below point of aim at 200 yards. In comparison, the same bullet and sabot combination fired out of the same rifle with three 50-grain Pyrodex pellets impacts close to 3 inches below point of aim at 150 yards and nearly a foot below at 200 yards.

I managed to take two good eight-point whitetail bucks with the rifle and load during the course of the season. One of the deer was shot at 210 yards, holding just a few inches above where I wanted the bullet to strike. The other buck was taken at just over 150 yards, using a dead-on hold. Each of these deer was a big-bodied buck which field-dressed over 200 pounds. Still, both these deer were hammered to the ground where they stood. The load is still good for more than 1,700 ft/lbs of energy at 200 yards—or about twice the energy a 100-grain charge of Pyrodex would produce with the same bullet at that distance. Now, that's muzzleloader performance!

During my initial shooting with one of Ball's 50-caliber front-loaders, I tested a variety of saboted .451-inch and .452-inch jacketed bullets—plus several all-copper designs. For a

The Homady .452-inch diameter XTP jacketed hollow point proved to be a great performer from a Ball rifle, using smokeless powder loads delivering velocities up to 2,400 fps, while developing more muzzle energy than a 7mm Remington Magnum.

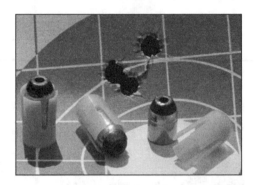

The author found saboted 260-grain Speer 45 JHP bullets, shown here with Knight "Hi-Pressure" sabots, to be exceptionally accurate and devastating on deer. The group was fired with a 50-caliber Howa-actioned Ball rifle and 34 grains of Alliant 2400.

writer who has always preached against shooting smokeless powder in a muzzleloader, the idea went against the grain. I approached the loads Henry Ball recommended with caution; started with a 30-grain charge of Alliant 2400, then moved up in 1-grain increments. When pushing saboted handgun bullets out of a muzzleloader at velocities approaching 2,400 fps, the plastic sabot becomes the weak link in the equation. With loads of 30 to 35 grains of the smokeless propellant, accuracy remained about the same, with many bullets consistently printing inside of 1 1/2 inches at a hundred yards. When I jumped up to 36 grains of 2400, accuracy—with every bullet—went to hell. Recovered sabots looked like a wad of chewed-up chewing gum, indicating the pressures created by the load were too high for the plastic sabot. When I backed off to 35 grains, accuracy returned. My best groups were always shot when the temperatures ranged from 30F to 70F. When the summer sun pushed temperatures into the 80s and 90s, the plastic sabots apparently became too pliable to withstand the sudden pressures produced by heavier 34- and 35-grain charges of 2400. When

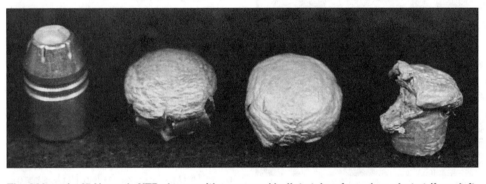

The 300-grain 45 Homady XTP shown with recovered bullets taken from deer shot at (from left to right): 175 yards, 120 yards and 60 yards. All three recovered bullets left the muzzle of a Ball smokeless muzzleloader at about 2,300 fps.

Up 'til now, the Knight D.I.S.C. muzzleloading rifle has reigned as the most advanced muzzleloader available. Now muzzleloading moves into a new era with a new level of performance.

One of the author's concerns has been shooting handgun bullets which were not designed for 2,400 fps-plus velocities. However, more recent designs like the all-copper Barnes Expander-MZ bullets hold up very well at the higher velocities.

Downrange accuracy such as this typical 1-inch three shot group at 100 yards make the Henry Ball smokeless muzzleloader an outstanding big-game rifle.

First time whitetail hunter Debra Bennett cleanly dropped this big-bodied eight-pointer on opening morning at 50 yards, shooting a reduced load of Winchester 571 Ball Powder behind a saboted 45-caliber Speer 225-grain JHP bullet. The load delivered nearly 2,100 fps and 2,200 ft/lbs of knockdown power at the muzzle.

I dropped to 33 grains, groups tightened once again, but only when I allowed the barrel to cool sufficiently between shots. Later in the winter, when temperatures dropped well below freezing, groups fired with the hotter charges also tended to open up to as much as four inches across. Fired sabots recovered five or six yards from the muzzle regularly had one, two, three - or all four - petals missing from the base. This could indicate that at colder temperatures the plastic becomes too brittle and is adversely affected by the higher smokeless powder pressures.

One of the first Ball rifles I played with was built on a Mark-X short action and featured interchangeable 45- and 50-caliber barrels. In just minutes I could switch from one bore size to the other. The 45 barrel was one of Ball's 1-turn-in-14-inches twist "sabotless" barrels, to be loaded and shot specifically with the 300-grain Hornady .452-inch XTP jacketed hollow-point bullet. Accuracy, with charges of up to 39 grains of Alliant 2400, was phenomenal. One three-shot hundred yard group could be completely covered with one thin U.S. dime. The load pushes the big 300-grain hollow-point bullet out of the muzzle at about 2,450 fps, which translates to right at 4,000 ft/lbs. of energy. That's more than the

IMPORTANT:

DO NOT ATTEMPT TO LOAD AND SHOOT ANY SMOKELESS PROPELLANT (OTHER THAN PYRODEX) OUT OF ANY OTHER MUZZLELOADER.

energy produced by a 338 Winchester Magnum with a 250-grain bullet.

When working with hotter smokeless powder loads, Alliant 2400 performed best in the rifles I fired. Slightly reduced loads of Winchester 571 also produced exceptional accuracy, while maintaining some impressive velocities. The hottest load of Winchester 571 the 50-caliber rifles would handle accurately was 32 grains. This load would push one of the saboted 260-grain 45 Speer bullets from the muzzle at just over 2,250 fps, and recoil was considerably less than that produced by factory 308 Winchester loads fired from most bolt-action rifles.

One of the mildest loads worked up for my Howa-actioned 50-caliber rifle consisted of 31 grains of Winchester 571 behind a saboted Speer 225-grain jacketed hollow point. I worked up the load for a young lady going on her first whitetail hunt during the 1998 season. Less than two hours into her first hunt, she cleanly dropped a hefty 200 pound-plus eight-point buck at just 50 yards. That deer was dead before its knees buckled. Muzzle velocity of the load is close to 2,300 fps, with about 2,600 ft/lbs of energy.

Readers should note that loading this system through the muzzle isn't much different than handloading any center-fire rifle or handgun cartridge, only there is no case involved. This system cannot be loaded with just any smokeless powder, as you cannot safely load "just any" smokeless powder into a 300 Winchester Magnum cartridge case. However, with the loads prescribed by the custom maker of this system, the innovative ultramodern

Reusable ignition modules are easily primed with No. 209 shotshell primers, and can be easily de-primed with a punch pin or plain ol' six-penny nail.

This hunter doesn't have to worry about the frosty conditions when packing one of the unique smokeless muzzleloaders. The exceptionally hot No. 209 shotshell primer and fully enclosed ignition system guarantee sure-fire ignition in any weather.

The smokeless loads worked up by author Bridges proved to shoot extremely flat, for a muzzleloader. He dropped this open-country Iowa buck—on the spot—at 210 yards by holding just a few inches above his hundred-yard zero.

Primed stainless steel ignition module ready to be pushed into the chamber with the bolt. This ultra-modern muzzleloader was built on an Interarms short-action Mauser receiver.

muzzleloading rifle can be shot safely with smokeless powder.

No other muzzleloader currently available has been built to withstand the higher pressures. In the past, names like Turner Kirkland, Val Forgett, Warren Center and Tony Knight brought to muzzleloading innovations which have had a profound impact on the sport. Today we have a new front-loading genius who is sure to help shape the sport as we head into the next millennium. One thing is certain, the smokeless powder front-loaders being built one at a time by Henry Ball move muzzleloader performance closer to the performance of today's hottest, hardest-hitting center-fire rifles. Surely some of you reading this are asking yourselves, "Why?" The answer is simple: Today's muzzleloading hunter is no different than today's bow hunter or modern gun hunter. Archers continually turn to higher technology for faster and flatter arrow flight, while center-fire rifle hunters tend to quickly embrace new rifles and ammunition which promise improved accuracy and knockdown power. The muzzleloading hunter is now looking for the same thing, a front-loader which will ensure the buck of a lifetime is laying on the ground when the smoke clears. Whether or not there is actually smoke hanging in the air doesn't seem to matter any more.

Cleaning any of the older muzzleloader designs has always been a major apprehension among shooters looking at muzzleloading for the first time. The thought of cleaning corrosive fouling from the bore and other parts after each and every shooting session has kept many from ever getting into muzzleloading. Now, here is a system which doesn't have to be scrubbed from muzzle to breech after it's been shot. The rifles require basically the same care as any standard center-fire rifle. After a day at the range, I normally wipe the bore with a patch or two saturated with a good bore cleaner. such as that available from Break-Free, then wipe down the outside of the rifle with a lightly oiled cloth. About once a month I'll unthread the breech plug and wipe the threads clean, lubricate them with an anti-seize compound and reinstall the plug—to ensure it will continue to be "removable."

This system is destined for commercial production. It's definitely a better mouse trap! However, the gun is currently available only in custom form from Bill's Custom Guns, 1419 Dorsey Street, Greensboro, North Carolina. At $2,750 a rifle, the deer woods aren't likely to be suddenly overrun with these hi-tech muzzleloaders. And even if one of the major gun companies does arrange production at a much *friendlier* price, some states may attempt to outlaw the system. Recall certain states' reaction to the regular in-line percussion rifles when they hit the market during the mid-80s. Now, a new generation of high performance muzzleloaders will carry the sport into the 21st century with tremendous momentum ... and controversy. (*As this article was being sent off, one of the major gun makers had Henry Ball build a prototype of this system on one of their bolt-action receivers. It is possible that this remarkable front-loader may be one step closer to commercial production.*) ●

AHEAD OF ITS TIME:

The J.C. Higgins Model 20

The J.C. Higgins Model 20 pump action shotgun had many features not usually found on the over-the-counter shotguns, such as the inlaid nameplate and the POWer-PAC choke device.

by **LARRY S. STERETT**

AT ONE TIME Sears, Roebuck and Company was one of the world's largest mail order firms, and their catalog was a real wish book. The old catalogs contained something for everyone, including shooters, and rifles, shotguns, handguns, air rifles and related hunting and shooting equipment were sold by mail for over three-quarters of a century. Back around the turn-of-the century Sears manufactured its own arms. Later, it was apparently more economical to contract for such sporting arms. A slightly modified model of an arm already being produced by a major manufacturer could then be marketed under the Sears, Roebuck label, along with known brand models.

The parent arms of most such Sears sporting arms were easily recognized, but the decade following World War II, brought a change. Sears acquired a controlling interest in High-Standard Manufacturing Co. of Hamden, Connecticut, and again began to manufacture a line of shotguns to be marketed under the Sears label. High-Standard was known for their excellent line of autoloading pistols, but had produced long arms during World War II, including submachine guns. There were three models: the Model 10 (a bolt action), Model 20 (pump action) and Model 60 (gas-operated autoloader). The new shotguns were all repeaters, and all were excellent values for the money.

The pump action Model 20, the subject of this article, was introduced in 1952. According to Sears, based on several decades of selling shotguns, they intended to provide their customers with a shotgun having the "most wanted" features, but at a reasonable

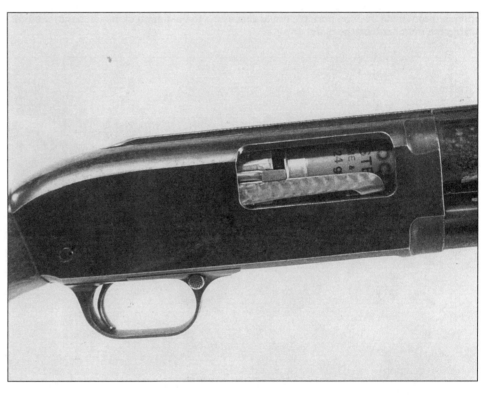

Model 20 lifter aligns the shotshell directly with the chamber, rather than tilting it. Breech bolt and lifter here have been engine-turned; not all Model 20 shotguns are. The solid rib on the receiver is another "custom" feature.

price. They picked the most popular gauge-12-and went from there, providing extras that were usually available only at an added cost.

The result was a shotgun worthy of the Sears label. Although the Sears name is on the shotgun, they wore the same J.C. Higgins label that appeared on all Sears sporting products of that era from golf clubs to fishing tackle. The J.C. portion of the label, according to Colonel Charles Askins, stands for Josephine Clementine, strange as it might seem.

The Model 20 was produced in two grades - Standard and Deluxe. They had the same basic features, with the Standard grade having a plain fixed choke barrel, while the Deluxe grade had a ventilated rib barrel with Power-Pac choke device.

The Model 20 receiver resembles that of the Winchester Model 25, when first viewed, as it is also a solid-frame design, with the barrel permanently interlocked to the steel receiver.

Locking is accomplished by the upper rear of the steel breech bolt

The Model 20's magazine cut-off permits the magazine to be kept full, while loading single rounds through the ejection port. It's easily accessible to the thumb of the left hand, without taking the right hand off the pistol grip.

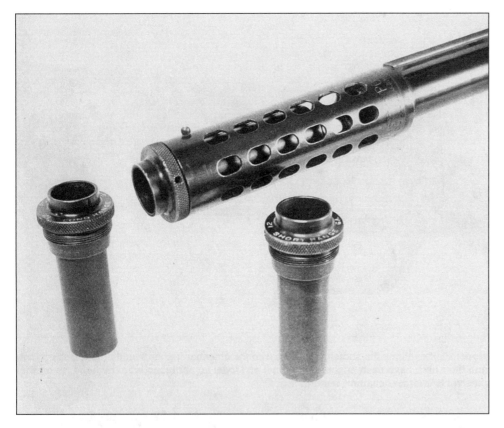

The Deluxe Model 20 features a ventilated Pachmayr POWer-PAC choke device with screwing choke tube. The small hole in the knurled rim is for a lug on the choke wrench. It's easy to figure which is which—Long Range and Short Range are clearly marked.

tilting upward into a notch in the top of the receiver, much the same as on the Winchester Model 25. It also utilizes a sturdy single action bar on the left side, with the action bar release located on the lower left rear of the trigger guard assembly. Sears, Roebuck called it a free-falling action and stated the Model 20 could fire six shots in 3-1/2 seconds. Regardless, the action is smooth in operation and feeding from the magazine flawless on the shotgun tested.

The trigger guard on the Model 20 was an anodized aluminum alloy, with a cross-bolt safety located on the forward portion of the bow. The safety was "on" when pushed to the right.

The carrier on the Model 20 is designed to position the shotshell directly in line with the chamber. This in-line loading feature later appeared on the Mossberg Model 500 a decade later.

The Model 20 had a magazine cutoff on the left side of the receiver. When this lever was moved to the lower or "on" position it prevented any shells in the magazine from being picked up by the carrier. Moving the lever to the upper or "off" position permitted the normal feeding from the magazine onto the carrier. Magazine capacity of the Model 20 was five standard length (2-3/4 inch) 12 gauge shells. This cut-off may not be present on all Model 20 shotguns, as it is not mentioned or illustrated in a 1955 Sears Parts List, nor does the World Parts Corporation list it.

On the Deluxe grade the barrel carried a one-piece steel ventilated rib, with an aligned solid rib positioned on the receiver top. The top surface was roll-marked in a wavy pattern to reduce glare, plus an ivory center bead about mid-way on the rib and a larger metal bead near the muzzle.

Another feature of the Deluxe grade was what Sears called the Choke Control, but which was actually marked POWer-PAC. The POWerPAC, manufactured by the Pachmayr firm in California for many years, had a ventilated cage into which could be screwed one of three interchangeable choke tubes furnished with the Model 20 Deluxe. The compensator on the Model 20 had, we should note, different ventilation slots than those marketed by Pachmayr for after-market installation.

The tubes were marked on the muzzle portion, Short Range, Medium Range, and Long Range, and corresponded to improved cylinder, modified, and full choke. They were knurled on the rim near the muzzle so they could be loosened and tightened by hand, but a special C-wrench was also provided. Thus, the Model 20 was set for hunting everything from quail and rabbits to ducks and deer, simply by changing loads and choke tubes.

Barrel length on the Deluxe Model 20 measured only 22-3/4 inches. The POWer-PAC compensator and choke tube added another four inches, making the total barrel length 26-3/4 inches. Changing choke tubes did

Hunt all this game and more with only 1 gun

Short Range   Medium Range   Long Range   Rifled Slugs

Choke Control has 3 easily changed tubes. Full choke (long range), over 40 yds. and trap. Modified choke (medium range), 25 to 40 yds. Improved cylinder (short range), 15 to 25 yds. and skeet. Remove tubes and you have the ideal gun for firing rifled slugs for deer.

At this low price you get built-in extras USUALLY COSTING $59.50 or more

J.C. Higgins
MODEL "20"
12 GAUGE PUMP SHOTGUN
WITH CHOKE CONTROL-VENTILATED RIB

VENTILATED RIB
usually costing **$25.00** to **$35.00**
Ventilated rib (Deluxe only) for faster and more accurate sighting. Barrel and receiver permanently interlocked.

Deluxe Model "20" **$75.00**

Standard Model "20" without choke control and ventilated rib $64.95

CHOKE CONTROL
usually costing **$18.00** to **$25.50**
Reduces recoil up to 60%—three interchangeable tubes for various ranges.

You can enjoy every hunting thrill with J. C. Higgins Deluxe Model "20." Hunt pheasant in the Dakotas, ducks in Arkansas or deer in Florida with one gun. J. C. Higgins Choke Control compensator changes to give correct pattern and range. And just check these great factory installed "custom-like" features.

Exclusive "free-falling" action makes possible the fastest pump action we know of, and we've tested them all. Fires 6 shots in just 3½ seconds. Extra short pump action travels only 3½ inches to open and close gun. Highest quality steel barrel, proof tested at the factory with loads 50% stronger than regular ammunition. Barrel and receiver permanently interlocked—can't get loose or out of alignment.

3 great safety features: breech lock, hang fire lock and forward safety. Non-glare flat side receiver. Ventilated rib designed to give you faster sighting. Richly grained walnut stock, full pistol grip with grip cap. Rubber recoil pad. Inlaid silver-color name plate (not engraved). Palm filling semi-beavertail fore-end means better grip, better gun control.

FREE-FALLING ACTION
usually costing **$9.50** to **$12.50**
Free-falling action makes possible the fastest, smoothest pump action we know of, 6 shots in 3½ seconds.

RECOIL PAD AND NAME PLATE
usually costing **$9.00** to **$19.00**
Beautifully grained walnut stock, full pistol grip. Silver-color metal name plate. Factory installed rubber recoil pad.

Write to:
Dept. 157
Sears, Roebuck and Co.
in the city nearest you
Chicago, Ill.
Philadelphia, Pa.
Boston, Mass.
Minneapolis, Minn.
Kansas City, Mo.
Memphis, Tenn.
Atlanta, Ga.
Greensboro, N. C.
Dallas, Texas
Los Angeles, Calif.
Seattle, Wash.

Here's how Sears can offer a gun with so many extras at such a low price.
Years of selling guns all over America taught us what gun buyers want in a shotgun. We took the most popular gauge, the most wanted features and concentrated on one model. This permitted efficient assembly line production that greatly reduced costs. Then we built all the wanted "extras" right into the gun at the factory at big cost savings. That's why we can offer what we know is the finest gun value in its field.
See J. C. Higgins Model "20" at your Sears, Roebuck Store or in Sears catalog. If you haven't a catalog and aren't near a Sears store, write the Sears Mail Order House nearest you (list at left). We'll send you more information about the gun and how to order it.

SEARS, ROEBUCK AND CO. America's Sporting Goods Dealer

16

not change the barrel length. The barrel length on the Standard Model 20 was 28 inches, with a fixed choke choice of full or modified.

The Model 20 forearm and buttstock were American walnut. The forearm was a beavertail design with 15 grooves; there was a full pistol grip with plastic cap. The comb was fluted, and there was a ventilated red rubber recoil pad with black base. Forward of the toe was a silver-colored metal plate suitable for engraving initials or name. Strange as it may seem, there was no checkering at all.

The Deluxe Model 20 was introduced at $75, which is about the same price Mossberg put on the Model 500 pump gun when they introduced it a decade later. Sears, Roebuck estimated such "custom" features, ventilated rib, choke device, magazine cutoff, recoil pad, name plate, and center bead, on the Deluxe Model 20 could cost up to $90, if purchased separately, and possibly more depending on installation. If correct, this made the Model 20 a real bargain.

Manufactured only in 12 gauge, chambered for standard length (2-3/4 inch) shells, the Model 20 weighed 7-1/4 to 7-3/4 pounds, depending on whether it was Standard or Deluxe. It felt good in the hands and handled better than some more expensive shotguns of that era. The ventilated POWer-PAC was said to reduce recoil up to 60 percent; changing choke tubes required a bit more effort than using the Poly-Choke, another popular choke device of that era, but no more so than changing modern screw-in choke tubes.

Exactly how many variations of the Model 20 were produced isn't known. The two grades as mentioned were Standard and Deluxe, but when ordering parts forty years ago, Sears wanted you to be sure and mention whether it was for a shotgun stamped 583.59, 583.60, or 583.61 on the barrel. Yet the Model 20 illustrated in this article is marked 583.56. If there were 583.57 and 583.58-marked shotguns, that would amount to at least six variations of a shotgun that was definitely ahead of its time. •

This Sears, Roebuck advertisement for the Model 20 shotgun appeared in some sporting magazines in 1952, makes the whole pitch.

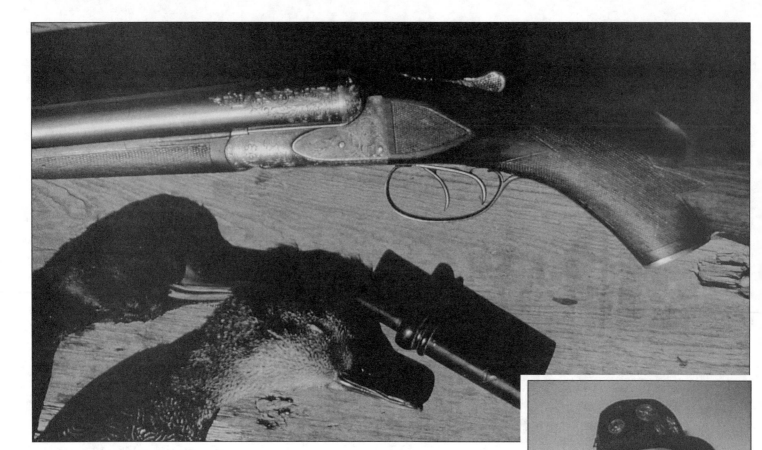

Becker #2, with a pair of mallards and one of Nash's duck calls.

The Saga of Bo Whoop

by H. Lea Lawrence

IT OCCURRED SOME 70 years ago on a slough in the Mississippi River bottoms where two hunters, Col. H. P. Sheldon and Nash Buckingham, were hunting ducks. In Nash's hands was his custom-built 12-gauge 3-inch magnum Becker double shotgun which he referred to as "The Big 'Un."

What happened next became a part of waterfowling history. Here's how Col. H.P. Sheldon described it in his introduction to *Hallowed Years*:

"Nash had 'blinded-up' in a dense thicket of willows at the edge of a clear channel some 150 yards from my own stand. A pair of mallards traveling high and in a hurry went over Nash. Both collapsed and after a moment of complete silence the double boom of the big gun came rolling roundly over the marshes. It sounded exactly like two

solo notes from the bass horn in a symphony orchestra, and I mentioned it to Nash when we got back to the lodge, '*Bo Whoop, Bo Whoop*'." And it was known as *Bo Whoop* from that time on.

Perhaps, as with "a rose by any other name," the gun would have achieved fame without the nickname by being the centerpiece of many of Nash's great waterfowl hunting stories. Still, there's no doubt that being called *Bo Whoop* added a colorful touch to those tales.

Most important to the gun's fame was that Nash was probably the finest wing shot of his time, and possibly, all time. As such, the pairing of this instrument with a highly skilled shooter produced exceptional results.

What isn't commonly known is that there were actually two *Bo Whoops*, the facts about which will emerge as

Nash Buckingham, possibly the best wing shot of all time.

the story continues. But for now, let's go to the beginning.

In 1921, John Olin, president of Western Cartridge Company, and a friend and admirer of Nash's, sent him his personal shotgun and several boxes of a new type of 12 gauge, 3-inch magnum shell to test. The gun was built by Burt Becker, a Philadelphia gunmaker with whom Nash was already familiar. However this was the first magnum he'd encountered and, after shooting with the Olin gun, he was determined to own one. Previous to this experience Nash had been shooting a 12-gauge, 32-inch Super Fox double, and a 12-gauge, 34-inch Parker double.

Nash obtained Becker #1 in 1926. It was built on a heavy Fox frame, with a somewhat thick straight grip and a

The receiver of Becker #2 was richly engraved, and the barrels were engraved for about 2 inches forward.

The bottom of the receiver.

recoil pad. The barrels were 32 inches long, bored full choke and the gun weighed 10 pounds. Also, instead of the streamlined Fox breech lever faired on top of the action, Becker #1 had a different look, with the axis extending almost a quarter-inch above the stock. Nash requested the gun not have a safety, since he believed one should never load a gun until he was ready to shoot. He felt this was safer than becoming dependent on a safety.

Shortly after Nash shot the original loads with Olin's gun, the company came out with the 3-inch Super X shells with copper-coated lead shot. His favorite was 1 3/8 ounces of shot above 4 drams of powder, which was considered to be a real hell-bender.

Becker #1 patterned at around 90% at 40 yards and John Bailey, a close friend of Nash's, said "Not one gunner in 10 million can shoot such a close gun capably. Nash could." And Henry P. Davis, another of his close pals, said he once watched Nash down 17 mallards with 18 shots, none of which were closer than 50 yards.

For the next 22 years, Becker #1 continued to gain fame among waterfowlers, but on December 1, 1948, tragedy struck when Nash, Barry Brooks and Bob Anderson were hunting near Clarendon, Arkansas at the Section 16 club. Nash was the first to bag a limit and, when he came out, two wardens checked his ducks and license. One asked to take a look at *Bo Whoop*, but afterward, instead of giving it back to Nash, he laid it on the car's fender. Barry and Bob were still hunting, and because Nash was cold and wet, he wanted to get back to the hotel. He didn't drive, so he had a friend, Cliff Green, take him to Clarendon. Along the way the gun dropped off the fender. Once this was discovered, a thorough search was initiated, including roadblocks to check cars which had driven the same route. No luck, and even though a reward of $1000 was soon offered for its return, the gun never reappeared.

Nash was devastated by the loss, and he felt the saga of *Bo Whoop* had ended. However, fate had another winning hand in store for him.

George Warner of Lawton, Oklahoma, an admirer of Nash's writings, came to Barry Brooks and said he wanted to see if it was possible to replace the gun. Burt Becker was in retirement, but Brooks told Warner how to contact the gunmaker. Becker had high regard for Nash, and he agreed to

build another custom magnum to replace Becker #1. Becker #2, the last gun Becker was ever to build, was completed in August 1950 at a cost of $500, and Warner and Brooks presented it to Nash in September.

In some ways, Becker #2 was much like its predecessor. Nash gave the following measurements: 32-inch tubes bored full and full, no safety, 1 9/16-inch drop at the comb, 2 1/4-inch drop at heel, 14 1/4-inch pull, and 1/4-inch cast-off. The differences were that due to a misunderstanding, the stock had a pistol grip instead of the straight stock Nash preferred. The second gun was richly ornamented on the action, and the barrels had deeply carved engravings for about 2 inches, forward. The inside diameter of the barrels was .750-inch, with chokes tapering in the last six inches to .700-inch. Using the English system for proofing, a bore just over .740-inch is proved as an 11-gauge, so Nash was actually shooting an 11-gauge gun. Becker #2 delivered 91 percent to 93 percent of its load into a 30-inch circle at 40 yards.

As Col. Sheldon wrote in 1953, "Experienced shotgun shooters will know

I had the privilege of shooting *Bo Whoop* for two days in 1986.

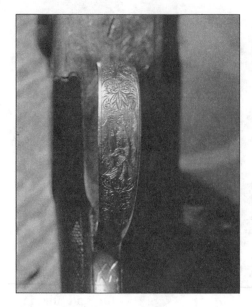

The trigger guard.

The breech lever is different from the usual Fox design.

Engraving on the forearm iron.

by the description that *Bo Whoop* was no gun for that 'puny Peruvian prince' referred to in the defiant speech supposed to have been delivered long ago by an exasperated U.S. senator from Arkansas, nor was it the proper weapon for the average duck hunter regardless of what his opinion might be of his marksmanship. In fact, there are not many among us in these decadent days who are sufficiently skillful to do justice to the extraordinary power of a

true magnum, and that includes the very best of the trap and skeet shooters, too."

I had the privilege of becoming acquainted with *Bo Whoop* in 1986 when I was hosted to a hunt in Mississippi with Dr. William (Chub) Andrews of Memphis, one of Nash's closest friends and hunting companions who, at that time, owned the

Becker #2. Chub wanted me to shoot *Bo Whoop*, and I was happy to be given the opportunity. On the first day, we shot at Nash's favorite blind at the famous Beaverdam Club near Tunica, and the second day from a pit in a flooded soybean field in the same vicinity. The experience was very meaningful, because I had known Nash since 1948, and we had corresponded for more than two decades. He wanted us to hunt together, but every time we made plans, something got in the way. To finally be connected with what I considered to be a part of his heritage was special.

The crowning moment of the second day came when I dropped a greenhead that swung over the pit at about 50 yards. As the duck was falling, Chub leaned over and whispered, "Good shot, Lea. Nash would have been proud of you."

Becker #2 is now owned by Bill Dunavant of Memphis, and is on permanent loan to Ducks Unlimited. Presently it is on display at their headquarters in Germantown, a suburb of Memphis. ●

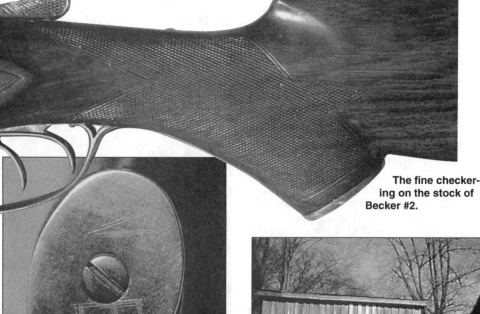

The fine checkering on the stock of Becker #2.

Nash scratched his initial on the metal pistol grip plate.

The keeper's cabin the Beaverdam Club.

LEMON MERINGUE STOCK...

A linseed oil finish   for amateurs

by Nikitas Kypridemos

THERE IS A bit of an alchemist in most hobbyists. We love the lure of the secret formula, not to turn lead into gold but as the means to achieve that something-for-nothing satisfaction. And wood, being a soft part of the gun and consequently more amenable to amateur interventions, receives much of this latent alchemy, mostly in the guise of miracle formulas that will yield, with one simple application, results equaling weeks of toil in the hands of mere crafts-

A 20-gauge shotgun built on a Martini-Henry action. The stock was finished using the lemon meringue method, it took six days from bare wood to this and the stock is still this good in its third season.

men. After all, they do not possess the secret!

There actually are trade secrets, especially in stock work. Only they do not reside in old crusted bottles stopped with rags. Secrets are usu-

ally displayed right out in the open, but the amateur's single-minded search for the genie in the bottle blinds him to what is going on in plain view, maybe because it looks like tedious and hard work.

Your writer once engaged a London coach painter in hours of probing questioning about finish formulas. The craftsman was rubbing a panel with ascending grades of emery paper while talking. I had my eye on the various bottles on the shelf what old half-forgotten secret recipes did they

The materials for the *lemon meringue* stock finish: wet or dry papers in grades 400, 600, 800, 1000; one lemon, one egg, clear alcohol, a small bottle of artistic-grade linseed oil and a large rubber eraser to use as backing.

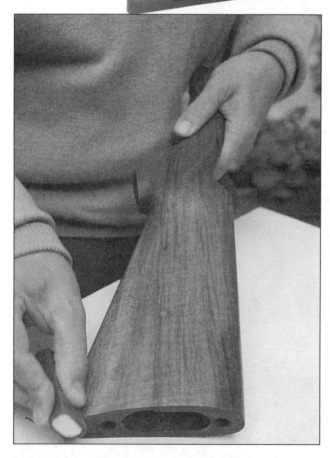

Rubbing with 400 paper used dry and with the backing.

contain within their stained and encrusted hollows? Why, some of the bottles themselves were antiques in their own right, saved by the coach painter's forebears decades before and bearing legends of Victorian patent medicines and digestives.

After a long time of rubbing, the wood of the panel shone like glass. Our faces reflected in it.

"What will you put on it now?" The question casually dropped, not to rouse suspicions of industrial espionage.

The coach painter roared with laughter. It was an outburst so out of place in the subdued atmosphere of the old workshop. "There is no secret, lad. After you make it shine like this any old finish will look good on it," he said and continued to laugh.

Once he calmed down, he patiently explained the first requirement for a good finish on wood, whether it will be painted, varnished or oil finished: The wood must be polished. It took years for the secret to sink in and displace the magic formula theory.

Polishing wood is work, not terribly hard work, but tedious enough to make magic formulas seem like a tempting alternative. After sanding to the finest grade of garnet paper, you start polishing with wet-or-dry, always with a rubber backing block so as not to leave finger grooves on the stock. Finger grooves will not show until the finish is dry. The sanding and polishing strokes follow the grain of the wood, never across the grain because it leaves scars. As in metal, the polishing goes on until all marks of the previous grit have been erased. Care is taken around the edges and where stock meets pad. A good polisher will save his dull paper and go over the wood again, using it with pressure, in a final pass before moving to the next finer grit size. This really puts a shine on wood.

Once the stock is polished to 400 grit it will shine so you can see your reflection in it. This is where polishing stops, for a while. It is time to fill the pores.

Whiskering is based on a seemingly simple principle. Fibers and dust settle in the pores of the wood. Wetting the wood and applying intense heat turns the water to vapor which expels the debris and fiber ends. These are then shaved with steel wool worked against the grain.

But wood is made of fibers. Whiskering the top layer of fibers does not make the rest disappear. The more you whisker the more you need to whisker a stock. If you look at a stock with a powerful magnifying glass you will verify this. A layer of fibers curls up after wetting and heating, always. In some open-grained stocks there is no end to whiskering.

Whiskering had its use in the days when the pores were filled with pumice. It opened the pores enough to

Taking care not to round the stock edges, one more reason to use the backing block.

Leave the checkering alone; rub carefully up to the borders of the checkering. The checkering itself can be cleaned up after the finishing process with a toothbrush or a riffler file.

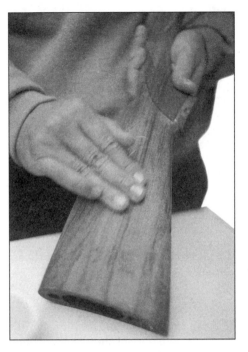

After the 400 paper comes the lemon squeezing directly on the stock.

After the lemon dries, alcohol is generously rubbed into the wood and allowed to dry.

The eggwhite is rubbed into the stock by hand.

enable the absorption of the comparatively large particles of the filler.

For the amateur there is an easier and better way to fill and seal the wood: After the 400-grit polishing, the stock is liberally coated with lemon juice. The exact nature of the reaction between the weak citric acid solution and the wood is probably a complicated chemical process. A chemical engineer said that it probably lowers the pH of the wood and facilitates the oxidization of the linseed oil applied later. Probably he is right. All it takes is the juice of one lemon brushed into the stock until it is absorbed.

After the lemon comes the alcohol—clear surgical alcohol, not the colored wood alcohol, is applied to the stock with a wad of cotton wool. Five passes are enough. The action of alcohol on the wood is hardening. Wood contains albumin and alcohol solidifies albumin. Try it: Pour alcohol onto raw eggwhite and soon it will congeal and turn white, just as if it were cooked. Egg white is pure albumin.

After the lemon and alcohol treatment the stock will look dull. It will have lost its sheen, but there's no need to worry. It will look much worse after the following treatment.

Filling the pores of wood is a requirement to any finishing process. The pores are all those tiny breaks in the surface of the wood. They are not really tiny holes as the name implies. They are the gaps between bunches of fibers. They can be filled with some form of fine powder which

will enter the gaps and then be fixed in place with some type of glue—that is the old pumice powder method. More modern methods consist of liquid synthetic sealers or varnishes applied to the wood, allowed to dry and then sanded off with sealer paper. The idea is that only the sealer that has penetrated into the pores is allowed to remain and the sealer on the surface is removed.

The problem with filling tiny holes, such as the pores of walnut, is the surface tension which prevents liquids from really entering the pores. It is exasperating to apply sealer, sand the surface, repeat the process several times—only to find that the pores are still there.

It is possible to achieve this perfect sealing with a vacuum chamber. The sealer compound is applied to the wood and, while the sealer is still in a runny state, the wood is put in the vacuum chamber and the air removed. The vacuum breaks the surface tension, forcing the sealing compound to be sucked into the pores. Effective, but not for the amateur.

Eggwhite is both more effective and safer than any liquid sealer. It only needs enough skill to break the egg and separate the white from the yolk. The eggwhite is then rubbed into the stock by hand, making sure it is worked into the wood. When the eggwhite dries it is rubbed down to the bare wood with 400 wet-or-dry

It can be done more delicately than this, but separating the eggwhite from the yolk is what really matters, only the white is useful for stock-filling.

paper. Lots of fine white powder is generated during this rubbing down. Good! Leave it in the pores, it helps fill them.

Now apply alcohol to the stock. Let it dry and put on some more eggwhite; let it dry and rub it down with 400 grit wet-or-dry. Remember that alcohol hardens albumin, and albumin is what eggwhite is made of. In effect, the eggwhite and alcohol process is adding to the wood more natural material which is very much like the wood itself. Repeat this routine until most of the pores are filled in.

In case you are wondering, this is a process known and used by the old-time coach painters. It is one of those long-forgotten processes and it works. It takes the eggwhite from one egg to seal and fill the average walnut stock of a shotgun or rifle.

It is impossible to completely fill every single pore of the stock. If some pores remain, do not fret. Some will be filled in by the linseed oil, some by the wax. Now is the time to concentrate on polishing the stock.

Start again with 400 grit wet-or-dry until all traces of eggwhite are removed from the surface of the wood. Go on to 600 grit and polish always with the grain and always using a backing. When all traces of the marks left by the 400 are gone, move on to 800 grit and polish. When you are done, the stock shines like polished bone. Now move on to 1000 grit and polish again. When you are done, take some of the *used* 1000 grit and polish again, using firm pressure and a rubber backing to your paper. At the end of this polishing phase the stock shines so much you can literally see your reflection in it. To a bystander, wood polished to this standard looks like it has been spray-varnished. Now you are ready for the oil.

Linseed oil is made from the flax plant. It's a drying oil and therefore useful as a base for paints and varnishes. It also comes in various grades for various applications.

Linseed oil is refined to remove impurities. The process is called *boiling*, but it is not. So forget boiling and kettles and drums and buy a small bottle of artistic grade linseed oil from an art supply store. It will be described as raw, purified linseed oil or bleached, pure linseed oil. It is a clear liquid with a slight yellow tint. This is the best oil for stocks—forget the heavy, syrupy hardware store stuff.

Linseed oil dries in contact with the air by itself with no need for drying agents. It dries from the outside in. The secret to a good finish is to

After each egg application, more alcohol is used to harden the eggwhite.

And then starts the polishing with 600, 800 and 1000 paper used dry, and with the backing, until the stock shines.

Now comes the oil, one drop on the finger is enough.

The drop of oil applied by hand to the stock, perhaps this gave rise to the term "hand-rubbed oil finish." This is the forend of a Martini-Henry turned into a 20 gauge shotgun. After each coat of oil dries, the process is repeated.

When the oil is dry it is gently polished using fine automotive compound - *gently*!

recognize and use this property of the oil, which means applying it in the thinnest coats, which are allowed to dry. Try an experiment to convince yourself that you do not need to slap on masses of oil. On a sheet of glass apply a very thin smear of linseed oil with your finger and next to it a thick brushload. Check it the next day and see which is dry all the way through.

There are driers which can be added to linseed oil. Most of them are some type of heavy metal derivative such as lead or cadmium. Forget them; they are not needed on stocks.

Applying thin coats of oil is best done by hand. Perhaps that gave rise to the term "hand-rubbed" oil finish. This not a force-intensive procedure as the "hand-rubbed" term implies. You just dip your finger in the oil and you spread it on the stock until it is absorbed. Then you dip your finger again and continue until you have covered the stock with the thinnest of coats. If there is any oil on the surface, remove it by wiping the stock with a clean cotton rag or (old) kitchen towel. Only the oil absorbed into the wood is useful. Let it dry overnight in a place that is warm and airy.

An average density walnut stock will take about six coats, at the rate of one coat per day. You will know that the stock has had enough oil

when the oil stops seeping into the wood and dries on the surface. After the final coat, allow the stock two or three days to dry completely.

At this stage the stock will be smooth but not as shiny as the wood was after the polishing with the 1000 grit. Do not get anxious; the shine is there to be brought back.

Get some automotive rubbing compound, the finest grit paint and body shops use to finish cars. Some compounds are combined with waxes, but they are not suitable for use. Plain fine polishing compound is what is needed.

The compound smooths and polishes the outermost layer of the oil finish. Apply it thinly over the stock, let it dry and then polish it gently with a chamois leather. The shine you get gives the lie to the notion that a linseed oil finish yields a matted dull surface.

After this, the stock is ready for a final waxing with beeswax. Beeswax is a natural material, about as natural as you can get. It is impervious to water and to acids, which means that rain and your own sweat will not get to the linseed oil finish. If there is a secret to this process, it is to treat this final waxing as an essential part and not skip it.

If you cannot locate a commercial beeswax polish, you can make your own very easily. Obtain a block of real beeswax (Orvis used to sell blocks of beeswax) about the size of a shotgun shell. Shred it on a cheese grater and drop it into a jar with four spoonfuls of

real turpentine, the stuff that comes from pine resin, not the synthetic. Shake well and leave for a few hours. The wax will melt in the turpentine, to the consistency of paste. Spread a little of this paste over the stock with a clean cloth and leave to dry for an hour or so. Once dry, rub well with a chamois leather.

Your stock is now finished.

I have used this process on all my shotguns and air rifles and on some old pieces of furniture at home. It stands up to weather and lasts a very long time. It is not as scratch-resistant as polyurethane. On the plus side, it enhances color and the feel of the finish.

Linseed oil continues to oxidize and mature for about six months after a stock is finished. Use no coloring agents of any kind since the oil itself will bring out the best color and grain, but the full effect will not be apparent immediately after a stock is finished. Old-time finishers apply color agents, notably alkanet root which gives the stock a reddish tint. It is not really necessary.

The feel of a stock finished in this way is unique. The polishing to 1000 grit and the soaked-in-oil finish combine to give walnut a feel that has been described as "smooth as ivory." Try getting that from synthetics.

A word to professionals: This is not for you. Every single professional finisher who has seen stocks bearing the finish described here has bet, and lost, that it was not oil but some kind of high polish finish. This formula is strictly for amateurs who either retain—or can attain—the spirit of the alchemist. •

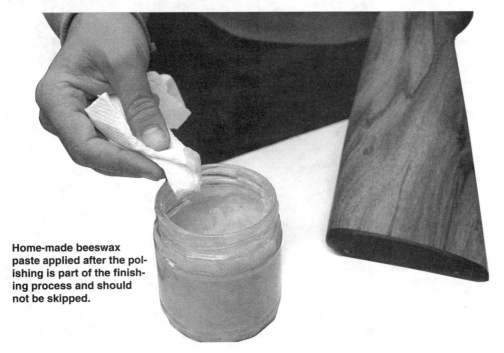

Home-made beeswax paste applied after the polishing is part of the finishing process and should not be skipped.

PUTTING YOUR BEST SHOT

...*FIRST!*

by Michael J. Bilski

photos by Rochelle Bilski

I RECENTLY HAD the factory barrel removed and an eight-inch Shilen barrel mounted on my Ruger Super Redhawk and shortly noticed that some of my old pet loads didn't print the same. With a little experimenting, I discovered the new barrel shot much better with heavier loads.

During my experimentation with these new loads, I asked my father to be my spotter. While I was shooting, he noticed that with each cylinder-full one round would always pull out of the rest of the group. I made sure I was shooting in the same chamber sequence, so we could narrow it down to see if a single chamber was responsible. Sure enough, the same chamber (#1) was responsible for the flyer each time.

Examining my target's shot pattern closely, I found that the groups had a common shape to them. I concluded that if chamber #1 was "doing its own thing" this common shape of my groups may be due to the other five chambers also shooting

independently of one another. Subsequent tests proved me correct—every chamber shot slightly different. I measured the chambers and found their diameters differed by as much as .002-inch in the most extreme case. Those differences, coupled with minute cylinder misalignments common in revolvers, were responsible, I figure, for this chamber grouping.

From nearly two decades of handgun hunting experience, I can honestly say that one shot is all I ever got at a game animal. This does not include the occasional woodchuck or ground squirrel that allows the hunt-

er to shoot at it until he either hits it or runs out of ammo. I decided that sighting in my revolver using the tightest shooting chamber and allowing the others to follow its lead was my best course of action. Armed with this in mind and the 44 in hand, I and my Super Redhawk's favorite diet (300-grain XTP's over 22 grains of H-110) headed off to the local range.

With any test shooting, a solid rest is of great importance. If you have access to a Ransom Rest, then by all means use it. I use old shot bags full of sifted sand to support the revolver and only enough grip to safely control the piece during recoil. An advantage to allowing the rest to support the entire weight of the revolver is the ability to assure positive sight alignment while eliminating as much human error as possible.

A good test for proper sight alignment is to place your *empty* revolver on the bags as though you were going to shoot and align the sights on the bullseye. If you have proper

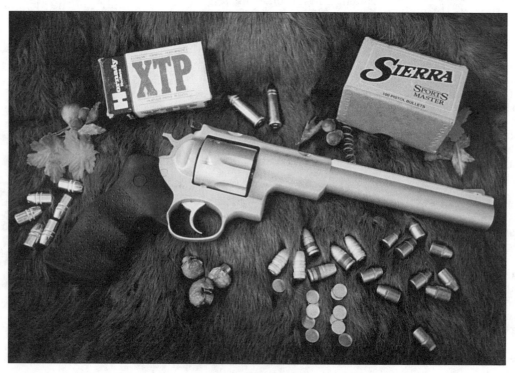

I know people who swear that revolvers do not produce sufficient velocities to expand a bullet. This 300-grain Hornady XTP was recovered after traveling 100 yards and penetrating nine inches into a water-soaked bundle of newspaper. Case closed!

sight alignment, and are not applying undue pressure to the grips of the revolver, you should be able to close your eyes, take a breath, and still be on (or very close to) the bullseye when you open your eyes.

Another important factor in accurate test shooting is to shoot at a distance you are comfortable with; not one that will most impress the boys at the range. I am always amazed at how many shooters do this. If you have an iron-sighted revolver or a low-powered scope, do not plan to do this test at 100 yards. Be true to yourself and the test by staying in relatively close. For this test, 50 yards seemed to work nicely for my Super Redhawk topped with a 2.5-8x Leupold. Because this is my standard distance for testing all my handloads, and because I feel comfortable shooting at that range, it was the obvious choice for me. With less gun, I'd move closer.

Clearly mark each chamber with a number that corresponds to the ones marked on the target.

Once you have established the distance that best suits you, place six (or five, if applicable) bullseyes on a sheet of paper. Make sure the bullseyes are far enough apart to allow you to easily distinguish which chamber shot each group. Mark each bullseye as chamber #1, #2, etc. And at this point, you should already have established which ammunition (factory or handload) shoots best in your revolver and have enough of it on hand to complete the test.

You have to number the chambers to correspond with the bullseyes. There is often a letter or mark of some kind on the face of the cylinder that can serve as a reference point. The test gun has a small letter "S" between two of the chambers, so I chose to make the chamber to the right of the "S" Chamber #1. If your cylinder is devoid of any marks made by the factory, you can arbitrarily assign each chamber

as #1, #2, and mark it with an indelible marker. Once you number your chambers, a rule of thumb to assure that chamber #1 *always* fires first is to place chamber #6 under the hammer when you lock the cylinder. This will work regardless of which direction the cylinder rotates.

Load *all* the chambers and place chamber #6 under the hammer when the cylinder is locked into the frame. Align the sights on the bullseye marked #1, cock the hammer to bring chamber #1 into firing position, and discharge the revolver. Repeat this procedure for each corresponding bullseye and chamber combination. The number of rounds fired at each bullseye is a matter of personal preference. I always shoot five at each for a total of thirty rounds. I feel three rounds is the minimum, and more than five is both overkill and expensive.

With all the chambers tested, you should have found that one or two are better shooters than the others. The performance produced by

A solid rest, sturdy enough to completely support the revolver, is very important.

one brand of ammunition or hand-load may not be the same with another load, so you should write in your logbook that load *XX* shoots tightest out of chamber *X* (logs are not just for reloaders!). In this way, you can keep your heavy hunting loads separate from your plinking or small game loads and still maintain that critical first shot accuracy. If you intend to use only one load for all your shooting, and discover that chamber #4 is your best shooter, make it easy on yourself and change chamber #4 to #1 so it is easier to remember.

Those who are convinced they will get more than one *well-placed* shot at a game animal can use the *two in a row* variation of the test. This variation of the same test involves picking two chambers from your test groups that are side by side in the cylinder that grouped in the same spot on your test paper, (i.e. 2 & 3 both shot a little to the right). Your best chamber may or may not have a chamber next to it that groups in the same spot. In my case, chambers 5 and 6 shot almost identical, with chamber 5 also producing the tightest group. I then sighted in the test gun accordingly. It has been my experience that this is often the case, so you're rarely restricted to that one shot anyway.

Some companies sell out-of-the-box revolvers with much closer tolerances than those I just mentioned. Freedom Arm's 454 Casull is a good example of a revolver with very tight tolerances. Yet after testing one using this method, I found it had three chambers that grouped tightly together, with the two others slightly out of the rest of the group.

Chambers #5 and #6 both shot very well, so I sighted the test gun to hit dead on at 100 yards using both chambers.

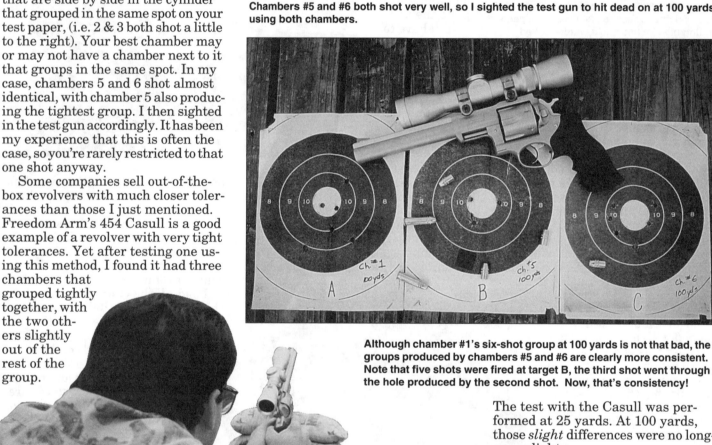

Although chamber #1's six-shot group at 100 yards is not that bad, the groups produced by chambers #5 and #6 are clearly more consistent. Note that five shots were fired at target B, the third shot went through the hole produced by the second shot. Now, that's consistency!

The test with the Casull was performed at 25 yards. At 100 yards, those *slight* differences were no longer so slight.

In the months that have passed since I first told other shooters about this test, I have yet to find anyone who hasn't benefitted from it. By following the method described, you can be assured that when that trophy of a lifetime steps into your crosshairs that at least the revolver will be up to the job. ●

Although recoil was stiff, it was not at all unmanageable.

Cutaway Collection of the Century

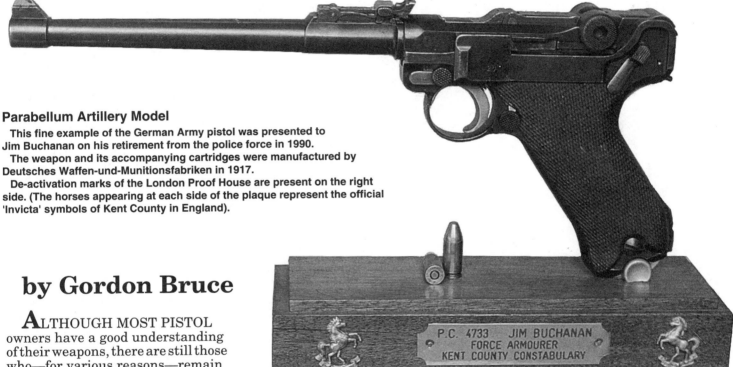

Parabellum Artillery Model

This fine example of the German Army pistol was presented to Jim Buchanan on his retirement from the police force in 1990.

The weapon and its accompanying cartridges were manufactured by Deutsches Waffen-und-Munitionsfabriken in 1917.

De-activation marks of the London Proof House are present on the right side. (The horses appearing at each side of the plaque represent the official 'Invicta' symbols of Kent County in England).

by Gordon Bruce

ALTHOUGH MOST PISTOL owners have a good understanding of their weapons, there are still those who—for various reasons—remain unacquainted with either the construction or general assembly of firearms. Provided the gun works properly and shoots well, owners are generally satisfied and have little concern for what occurs beneath the blued steel exterior.

It is, of course, unfair to condemn this attitude, as it is not easy to appreciate the engineering qualities which have gone into the development of a particular firearm. Without resorting to elaborate X-ray equipment, the user can only speculate about the operating sequence. Only by careful observation of the working components can variation between weapons become apparent.

Ideally, the best means for attaining this knowledge would be by removing portions of the weapon itself—a highly specialized task rarely undertaken by the majority of gun owners because of the costs involved. Moreover, few would have the mechanical ability to undertake the work themselves with satisfactory result. Despite these obvious drawbacks, one enthusiastic firearms collector in England has devoted his time and energy to resolving the matter.

Over the years, Jim Buchanan has accumulated more than 30 examples in a unique assortment of cutaway models. His collection now forms a comprehensive A-to-Z of handguns, ranging from a modern Astra Falcon Model 4000 to the 'Zig-Zag' Mauser revolver of 1878, each one carefully prepared and finished to factory standards.

Jim comes from an engineering background and, for as long as he can remember, has nurtured a passion for technical subjects. On leaving school, he worked for a short period as an apprentice with a gunmaking firm on the outskirts of London, where he was able to focus his interest more on the subject of firearms. He then continued to develop his engineering skills with another company that was engaged on sub-contract work involving the production of machinegun parts for various ordnance factories throughout Britain. It was there that Jim first became fascinated with the design of handguns, plus

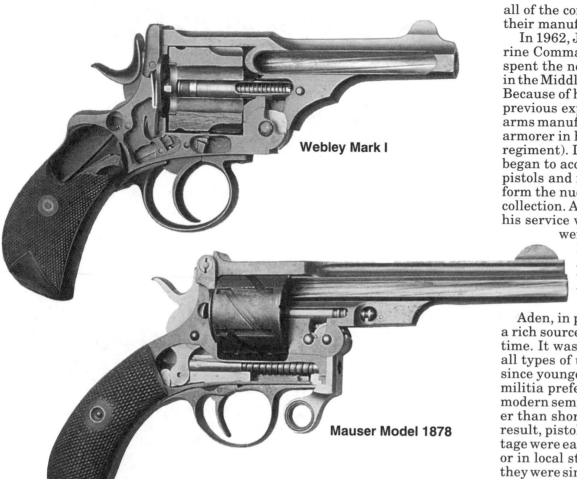

Webley Mark I

Mauser Model 1878

all of the complexities involved in their manufacture.

In 1962, Jim joined the Royal Marine Commandos, with whom he spent the next nine years, serving in the Middle East and the Far East. Because of his special aptitude and previous experience with small arms manufacture, he worked as an armorer in his Commando (Marine regiment). It was then that he first began to acquire the assortment of pistols and revolvers that was to form the nucleus of his own special collection. All were obtained during his service with the Marines and were purchased mainly in Kuwait, Bahrain or in Aden, where he was stationed during the disturbances of the early 1960s.

Aden, in particular, proved to be a rich source for old firearms at the time. It was virtually awash with all types of unwanted handguns, since younger elements of the local militia preferred to be armed with modern semi-automatic rifles, rather than short-range weapons. As a result, pistols of every type and vintage were easy to acquire at bazaars or in local street markets, where they were simply heaped onto tables

Today, most of the Buchanan cutaway models are mounted on individual bases of English oak, each carrying an engraved plate which identifies the weapon concerned. Usually, the pistols and revolvers are displayed by being supported upon the butt of the handle. Some of the guns can be removed easily-particularly certain auto-loading pistols attached to the oak base through the bottom of the magazine. However, not all the pistols can ba dismounted easily by pressing the magazine release and some, especially revolvers, are more permanently attached to their display bases.

Astra Model 4000 Falcon

Chambering: 7.65mm

Developed from the Model 400 and earlier Campo Giro models of 1913 produced by the same factory, this version represents the better class of handguns to emerge from Spain. It differs mainly from previous models in having an external hammer and is manufactured at the factory of Unceta & Company at Guernica, Spain.

A rectangular opening in the frame and slide shows details of the barrel connection. Ribs formed on the lower surface of the barrel allow it to engage and remain in position with grooves on the pistol frame. At the muzzle end, a locking cap secures the barrel collar, which can be seen locked to the slide. A portion has also been removed from the collar to show a large diameter return spring surrounding the barrel. The magazine safety feature is revealed by a smaller cutout in the frame behind the trigger exposing part of an L-shaped lever, which pivots rearwards to block the trigger linkage when the magazine is withdrawn. Engagement of the hammer and sear can be observed through a circular hole above the right-hand grip panel. On the opposite side of the pistol, a section removed from the grip panel reveals action of the trigger bar on the sear.

Browning FN 1900

Chambering: 7.65mm

Designed and patented by John Browning in 1899, this model became the first recoil-operated automatic pistol with an unlocked breech and introduced a new 32-caliber cartridge. It was successfully manufactured for many years in Belgium at the National Arms Factory in Liege.

Sections removed from the right side show the slide return spring and its guide rod positioned above the barrel. A lever pivoted at the rear end of the guide rod operates to bring the striker to a full cocked position. At that setting, an upper end of the lever becomes visible to indicate the pistol is ready to fire.

Other portions removed from the rear side of the pistol frame expose the trigger bar and its connection with the sear. It can then be demonstrated to show the trigger bar only engages under certain conditions. The other side of the weapon remains intact.

and could be purchased for very little cost. Often, a simple barter of items was arranged and weapons obtained by trading quantities of cigarettes or obsolete and discarded military equipment. Given that particular set of circumstances, Jim was able to obtain many pistols and, within a very short period, he gathered quite a selection of early models.

His initial task was to disable the guns in some manner to ensure they would all satisfy the British customs requirements upon an eventual return home. That matter was resolved while Jim was still overseas by the simple process of cutting away strategic areas from each pistol so the weapon could not be fired. The first models on which he experimented were cheap, small-caliber automatic pistols with no special merit in their design and which served merely as practice objects upon which to develop his cutting techniques. They were eventually discarded.

A procedure was planned for every pistol to be sectioned and only after a careful study of available references did he commence work. Once having a proper understanding of the mechanism, he was able to note the salient features in its assembly and could then decide on the cutaways required to show its operation.

On the majority of automatic pistols, the first cut was usually taken from the frame or from the slide. It

(continued on page 57)

Browning M1922

Chambering: 9mm

Designed by John Browning, this weapon is a development of his earlier pistol, first patented in 1910, incorporating many new features. During the Second World War, the Browning model was adopted by the Germans under the special code 626(b). By a simple expedient of interchanging barrels, it is possible to fire either 7.65x17SR Browning (32 ACP) or 9x17mm Browning Short (380 ACP)cartridges in the same pistol. (This particular example is stamped with a Royal Crown and letter W (Queen Wilhelmenia).

Generous portions have been removed from the slide to reveal various aspects of the construction. Two sections at the front reveal the bayonet fitting of a muzzle collar, while a central cutaway shows the four lugs attaching the barrel to the pistol frame. Other cuts at the rear permit the firing mechanism, magazine safety and grip safety operations to be observed.

There are no cutaway sections on the reverse side.

Colt Model 1911

Chambering: 45 ACP

This model is the most familiar of all pistols designed by John Browning. Developed from his original patent of 1897, it has remained an official weapon of the U.S. military forces since 1911 and was also produced commercially in a variety of forms. The typical example shown here features a grip safety and displays the identification 'GOVERNMENT MODEL' stamped onto the right side of the frame.

All sectioning work has been performed on the right side, leaving the left side intact. The distinctive system for locking the barrel and breech can be seen through openings made in the slide, while portions removed from the forward end show the rifling and recoil spring attachment. Other sections at the rear expose actions of the grip safety, disconnector and sear engagement.

Colt Pocket Hammerless Model

Chambering: 32 ACP

Based upon the John Browning patent of 1903 for an unlocked breech design with internal hammer, this model introduced a grip safety feature. Although most were manufactured for the commercial market, the particular example shown here is stamped 'U.S. PROPERTY', suggesting it was once an official military weapon (possibly used by aircrew). These pistols were also produced in 380 ACP.

The barrel bushing and typical Colt left-hand rifling can be seen through openings made at the forward area of the slide.

At the rear, operation of the grip safety mechanism may be observed acting upon the sear. Also visible on the internal hammer is a small roller which bears directly onto the mainspring.

Czech Model 24

Chambering: 9mm Browning Short (380 ACP)

Originally designed in 1922 by Josef Nickl as a locked-breech pistol specifically to fire the powerful 9mm Parabellum cartridge, this weapon was subsequently adopted by the Czech Ministry of National Defense in 1924 to shoot a 9mm short round. The example shown here is one of the initial order for 100,000 pistols delivered during the course of the next seven years. It is marked with a German military acceptance stamp of WaA76 and also carries a Czech 1926 date stamp.

A section cut through the slide shows the method by which the barrel is rotated to disengage from the breech. There are three control lugs on the barrel; one at each side to lock within grooves on the breech slide and the other to engage with a separate guide block beneath it. When the pistol is fired, a helical groove on the guide block causes the barrel to rotate and allows the breech to open.

Nickl also devised a new trigger mechanism to incorporate a disconnection feature and this, together with a safety arrangement, is clearly visible at the left side of the pistol.

The locked-breech system used for the Model 24 was not really necessary for the lower-powered Czech military round of the same caliber. As a consequence, the design was later revised to accommodate a 7.65mm cartridge and so became the Model 27.

Czech Model 27

Chambering: 7.65x17SR Browning (32 ACP)

Adapted from the original Nickl design by Frantisek Myska in 1926 to produce a 7.65mm pistol for use by the Czechoslovakian Police. While this pistol appears to be almost identical to the Model 24, it differs internally by having an unlocked breech system. Externally, the most noticeable difference is in the pattern of serrations at either side of the breech.

A section removed from the slide shows how the barrel is held to a modified guide beneath it.

Czech Model 38

Chambering: 9mm Browning Short(380 ACP)

Designed in 1937 by Frantisek Myska as a 9mm pistol with unlocked breech and double-action firing system, this weapon was manufactured for a brief period at the Czechoslovakian Arms Factory in Strakonice until that region was occupied by the German armed forces in 1939. In the example shown here, the magazine catch has been removed to allow the weapon to be mounted.

The Model 38 is capable of holding nine rounds but can be fired double-action-only (DAO), and so there is no manually-operated safety feature. The barrel is held at its muzzle to a pivoting block on the front of the pistol. Pressing forward on a catch at the left side of the frame allows the slide and barrel to swing up from the rear.

A section removed from the coverplate at the left side of the body, reveals the entire lockwork and also shows a vertical disconnector bar which prevents the weapon from being fired until the breech has been properly closed. Just visible behind the trigger bar is an automatic safety block engaging a notch on the hammer. Unless the trigger is deliberately pulled, the hammer will not strike the firing pin. Smaller cut at the front exposes the recoil spring and its short guide. The other side of the weapon remains intact and carries a 1939 date stamp.

FN Model 1935 High-Power

Chambering: 9mm Parabellum

Based upon a design originally patented by John Browning in 1923, this pistol was eventually produced by the National Military Arms factory at Liege, Belgium. When the factory was captured by the German army during the Second World War, production of the model 1935 was continued for the Waffenamt as Pistole P640(b).

The locking system has been exposed by the removal of sections from the slide and frame units. It involves two ribs at the top of the barrel and a single camming lug beneath to operate the breech disengagement. Also visible is the vertical trigger lever contacting the sear.

Cutaways at the rear of the weapon expose the sear engagement with the hammer and operation of the long hammer strut with its spring in the handle. A magazine safety feature can be observed through an opening made above the magazine release button.

The left side of the model remains intact and displays the usual Belgian proof marks.

Hungarian M37

Chambering: 7.65x17SR Browning (32 ACP)

Produced at the Small Arms Factory in Budapest, this weapon is a variation of the ubiquitous Browning design. Those manufactured under German occupation of the factory during the Second World War were fitted with a manually operated safety device. This particular example is marked with the code stamp jhv with 1943 date, plus a German military acceptance stamp WaA173.

The cut-out section from the slide shows how the barrel is held to the frame by a series of lugs underneath the chamber. The large trigger bar is shown extending over one side of the magazine to make contact with the sear. A shaped cutaway at the rear of the frame reveals the automatic safety arrangement, in which a curved arm on the sear is engaged by the grip safety lever to prevent its movement until the pistol is grasped for firing. Also visible in that area is the action of the disconnector.

The opposite side of this example remains intact and carries the German marking P.Mod.37, Kal.7.65.

Mauser C96

Chambering: 9mm Parabellum

Developed by Friedrich Feederle in collaboration with his brothers Fidel and Josef, this weapon was eventually patented by Paul Mauser in 1895. While it was primarily chambered to fire its own 7.65mm cartridge, a large quantity was produced in 9mm Parabellum for military use during the First World War. Examples in that category were identified by a large number '9' cut into the wooden grip panels and filled with red paint. The example shown here carries a 1920 date stamp on the barrel, plus an Imperial German Eagle proof mark on the magazine. It is complete with wooden shoulder-stock holster and leather fittings.

The mechanism is composed entirely of interlocking components (the screw used for securing the grip panels being the only one in the entire pistol assembly) and these have been exposed by the removal of large sections from the left side of the pistol. Action of the locking block can be observed beneath the breech bolt. The breech bolt itself is also cut away at two places to expose the exceptionally long firing pin and its spring, plus the larger breech return spring.

Secondary cutaways taken from the internal lock mechanism frame also show the unusual position of the hammer spring. The magazine in front of the trigger guard is fed by a nine-round stripper clip.

No sections have been removed from the right side of the weapon.

Nambu 94

Chambering: 8mm Nambu

Designed as a commercial weapon by Kijiro Nambu with features patented in 1935, this model was later manufactured in various military arsenals for issue to officers of the Imperial Japanese Army and also to air force crews during the Second World War. It uses a locked breech system to fire the Japanese 8mm Nambu cartridge. The example shown here was manufactured at the Nambu Works of Nagoya Arsenal in 1943.

Visible at the forward part of the slide is the large diameter recoil spring surrounding the barrel. Another cutaway at the center reveals a separate locking block for connecting the barrel with the breech slide. When the slide is pulled back, the locking block is cammed out of engagement. That same action also actuates a disconnector, which is visible at the top of the trigger. Portions removed from the handle region show the magazine and operation of a magazine safety device.

Revealed by a cutaway at the rear of the pistol body is the internal hammer with its cocking roller at the top. The reverse side of this example is intact.

Parabellum P08 (Luger)

Chambering: 9mm Parabellum

Developed by George Luger in 1900 from an earlier design by Hugo Borchardt, this is a pistol famous throughout the world.

The example shown here is one of the first to be produced in 1941 by the Mauser factory at Oberndorf with the BYF41 code. It also has a German military acceptance mark of Wa655. While the grip panels fitted to the majority of these Mauser wartime models were molded from a black plastic material, those on the cutaway specimen are wooden.

Portions have been removed from both sides of this weapon to show its relevant features. On the left side, a series of cuts into the grip panel reveals the mainspring and operation of the safety catch linkage. Other sections expose the sear, barrel rifling and extractor. At the right side, it is possible to study action of the hold-open device operated by the magazine.

Sauer Model 38

Chambering: 38-caliber

Developed at the factory of J. P. Sauer & Sohn in Suhl during the 1930s, this weapon was one of the more refined pistols to emerge from Germany at that period. It exhibited several interesting new features and was manufactured in large quantities, becoming a popular sidearm with German military officers during the Second World War. Two distinct versions were produced, one with a hammer safety and the other without. The example shown here carries a German nitro proof mark of 1940.

Sections removed from the right grip panel, pistol frame and slide allow operation of the firing mechanism to be observed. The cranked trigger bar is shown extending across the magazine to engage a vertical sear lever, while the long hammer strut and spring can be seen in the handle. In front of the trigger bar is a pivoted lever designed to block the mechanism when the magazine has been withdrawn. The slide has also been cut away to reveal its large diameter return spring encircling the barrel, plus a separate breech block assembly retained by a transverse pin.

At the left side, an opening made in the grip panel permits the most unusual feature of this pistol to be studied in detail. A downward motion of the large milled thumbpiece rotates a lever and causes the hammer to be brought to a cocked position for single-action firing. If the hammer is already cocked, the same motion can also be used to ease it down safely to rest.

Steyr M12

Chambering: 9mm

Developed at the Austrian Arms Factory at Steyr during the period 1910 to 1911 to replace the former Roth-Steyr model of 1907, this weapon also employs a rotary barrel locking system but fires a more powerful 9mm cartridge. Ammunition is stripped from an 8-round clip into the magazine in the handle. The example shown here was manufactured and proof-marked in 1915.

One portion of the slide has been removed to show the twin helical locking ribs on the barrel connecting it to the breech slide. Opening the breech causes the barrel to revolve and disengage from the slide. Other cutaways in the slide expose the bar which connects the trigger to a long sear spring holding the hammer.

The long hammer spring can be viewed through an opening made at the opposite side of the pistol. Two circular holes at that side show a vertical disconnector which blocks the trigger bar until the breech is properly closed. Also visible, the recoil spring serving as a trigger spring.

Swedish Army Pistol M40 (Lahti)

Chambering: 9mm Parabellum

Designed by Aimo Lahti in 1932 and produced initially for the Finnish army as the L35, this modified version was later manufactured under contract in Sweden by the Husqvarna Arms Factory. Many of these models were slotted at the rear of the handle to receive a shoulder stock attachment.

Most of the breech area has been removed to show the angled firing pin, recoil spring and barrel attachment.

A principal feature is the special locking block, in the form of an inverted yoke, housed at the rear of the barrel extension unit. It can be observed moving upwards to release the barrel as the breech travels back. Another special feature is an accelerator lever, located beneath the cartridge chamber, to hasten the opening of the breech.

Due to the hammer being positioned beneath the recoil spring, it is necessary for the firing pin to be set at an angle. Action of the trigger bar can be studied through an opening in the grip panel. The other side of this weapon is unaltered.

Walther P38

Chambering: 9mm Parabellum

Developed from the patents of Fritz Walther and Fritz Barthelmes and first produced at the Walther factory in 1936, this model subsequently became an official military weapon of the German armed forces. The design incorporates many interesting and original features, all of which were patented.

Visible through an opening made at the forward right side of the slide is the special locking block, which operates on a fulcrum under the barrel to release the breech after the pistol has been fired. This weapon also employs a unique recoil system with one small diameter spring positioned at each side of the body to close the breech.

An upper portion of the grip panel has been removed to show the sear in its engagement with the hammer. Another cutout from the lower rear end of the handle reveals the hammer spring serving to actuate the magazine release catch.

At the end of the slide, a small opening reveals an automatic firing pin lock to prevent the pistol from being fired until the breech is safely closed. Operation of the double-action firing system can be studied through another opening at the upper portion of the grip panel.

There is an additional cutout in the firing pin cover to expose the long pin, indicating a cartridge in the chamber.

Webley & Scott Model 1912 Mark I

Chambering: 455 Webley & Scott Auto

Designed originally in 1906 by William Whiting to fire an American 45-caliber cartridge, this pistol was subsequently improved and adopted by the British Royal Navy. It has the distinction of being the only British self-loading pistol to be accepted by the government. The specimen shown here was delivered to the Royal Navy in 1914.

In this example, it was important to show the unique system of interlocking ribs on the barrel which disengage it from the breech. This has been achieved by cutting a rectangular section at one side of the breech unit, permitting the action to be studied while pulling back the slide. Similarly, the unusual breech return mechanism, involving a large V-spring and pivoting lever at one side of the handle, can be observed by the removal of a large portion from the right grip panel.

Smaller cutaways at the rear also reveal the phosphor-bronze firing pin and aspects of the safety operation. Cutaway sections taken from the other side of the pistol show the trigger bar and sear linkage, plus the breech hold-open mechanism.

Roth M7

Chambering: 8x18.5mm Roth M7

Designed from a series of patents registered in the name of George Roth, this weapon was adopted in 1907 as an official sidearm of Austro-Hungarian cavalry regiments. It was manufactured at the Austrian Arms Factory in Steyr and later by the Hungarian Arms Factory in Budapest.

The pistol is striker-fired and the mechanism a double-action system. Cartridges are fed into the magazine from a special 10-round loading device with special plunger. The example shown here was manufactured at Steyr in 1910 and carries the military mark 1FH 152 stamped onto a brass disc at the center of the right grip panel(representing pistol No 152 of the First Howitzer Regiment).

Unlike some earlier models, this specimen incorporates a disconnector in its firing mechanism to prevent double shots. Small rectangular sections taken from the right side expose actions of the disconnector tail against the trigger, plus the sear upon the cocking piece.

Small circular sections allow a study of the cocking piece as it releases the striker and the manner by which the recoil spring also serves as a trigger spring. (As a safety feature, striker must be deliberately cocked by hand—or recoil action—before the trigger can act). A larger portion taken from the forward tubular section shows one of the barrel lugs locking with the breech slide.

The integral lanyard loop was removed from the butt to permit a satisfactory mounting of the pistol. (NOTE: More appropriate cutaways for demonstrating the rotary barrel action could not be made due to the extent of de-activation work carried out at the London Proof house).

Webley & Scott Model 1909

Chambering: 9mm Browning Long

One in a series of automatic pistols designed by William Whiting, this 9mm version was intended as an unlocked breech military pistol. Although the design incorporated several interesting features, all of which were patented, it was never seriously considered for use by the British Army.

The manner by which the barrel is secured by a portion of the trigger guard may be studied through an opening made in the slide. A circular drilling reveals the breech hold-open mechanism and operation of the release button from above. Cut-outs taken from the grip panel show the breech return mechanism involving a large V-spring and lever.

At the opposite side of this weapon, a large section removed from the upper part of the grip panel exposes the connection between trigger and sear. Also at that region is a small disconnector piece which prevents the mechanism from operating when the breech is still open.

Melior Model

Chambering: 7.65mm

While outwardly similar to the Browning model of 1900, this weapon incorporated a modified breech unit and other features patented in 1907 by H. Rosier. It was manufactured in various calibers at the Robar factory in Liege, Belgium. (A pistol with the same features was also produced under the name 'Jieffeco' by the Janssen company).

Generous cutaways at the front expose the recoil spring and its flanged guide rod lying above, and parallel with, the barrel. The breech unit can be pulled back to demonstrate how the spring is compressed against the fixed front casing. At the rear side are openings to reveal the extractor, plus the sear being operated by a rigid bar on the trigger. Action of the manual safety in blocking the firing mechanism can also be studied.

One half of the left grip panel is cut vertically to show engagement of the magazine retaining catch.

French Model 1873

Chambering: 11mm

Developed from the original Colt solid-frame revolver of 1873, this model was typical of several military center-fire revolvers produced in Europe at that same period. Its main difference from the American model existed in the lock work, derived from a design by Chamelot and Delvigne of Paris. In addition to those produced by the French, weapons of this type were also adopted by the armies of Belgium, Italy and Switzerland. The example shown here was manufactured at St Etienne.

An area cut from the cover plate exposes the entire lockwork and allows the mechanism to be seen in operation. The cylinder has been cut in half, while an adjoining slot in the frame shows the method by which the cylinder axis is retained at one side by a spring clip.

At the right side is a hinged loading gate, plus an extractor rod housed within a tube alongside the barrel. The front of the extractor rod is held onto the cylinder axis by spring pressure. That side of the weapon remains intact.

The lanyard swivel has been removed to allow the revolver to be mounted.

Rast-Gasser Model 1898

Chambering: 8mm

Incorporating the improvements patented by August Rast in 1897, this revolver was manufactured at the Rast & Gasser factory in Vienna. It was subsequently adopted by the Austrian War Ministry as a regulation army pistol and remained in service use until the First World War. (A swing-out cylinder version was also produced).

This eight-shot revolver features a separate firing pin, which can be observed through an opening cut from the breech.

A large area has been removed from the hinged cover plate at the left side to show the entire lockwork and its operation by a single mainspring. Part of the tubular housing at the right side is also cut away to show the return spring for the ejector rod.

Dutch Cavalry Revolver Model 1873

Chambering: 11mm

This weapon is typical of many similar handguns adopted by armies of the Netherlands, although the majority were of a smaller (9.4mm) caliber.

All components of the lock mechanism can be studied in operation through openings cut from the left side.

German Reichsrevolver 1883

Italian Service Model 1889

(continued from page 49)

was preceded by a complete disman-tling of the weapon to drill a small pilot hole. The gun was then re-assembled to establish how that hole should beextended and precisely what form the opening should take. Before each subsequent cut, that process was repeated with the gun being constantly taken apart and re-assembled as each stage of work was completed. Since only one part of the weapon could be dealt with on each occasion, it was a very slow and deliberate procedure, requiring much patience to achieve results.

Not having access to a proper mill-ing machine, Jim had to perform most of the shaping work by hand, using just a drill, files and hacksaw. Great care had to be taken on the size and positioning of the cutaway, in order to show a satisfactory inter-pretation of any particular aspect without removing too much material or causing undue weakening of the main structure. During that process, a deliberate effort was made to keep one side of the weapon intact so that it would still appear to be in its orig-inal state when viewed from that side. However, because of the com-plicated arrangement in some as-semblies, that goal was not always been possible to achieve.

In addition, there was the more practical difficulty of actually re-moving the metal from certain

pistols. Those manufactured at the Czechoslovakian arms factory in Strakonice came within that category and two of the CZ models used a steel of a particularly high carbon content. Working on the Model 24 and Model 27, the initial use of hand tools became almost im-possible, as they simply slipped from the hard work surface. To over-come that difficulty, Jim resorted to an annealing process to soften the steel by bringing the metal to a 'red heat' and then allowing it to cool slowly. Only then was he able to con-tinue with his work. However, an-nealing created additional problems by severely discoloring the metal surface so that it was then necessary for the part to be re-pol-ished and blued.

Contrary to his experience with the Czech pistols, Jim found the

British Webley revolver frame and its cylinder to be of a fairly soft material which he could cut and file with relative ease, al-though the cutaways involved were rather more intricate.

After the sectioning work had been completed on a particular pis-tol, the edges of each cut were pol-ished to a smooth finish with a fine file or an emery cloth. Then, in keep-ing with similar cutaways under-taken on military arms for instruction purposes, the sectioned portions were emphasized in red paint, using a standard Humbrol enamel as used by model makers. Gradually, throughout the period of his military service, Jim began to as-semble a sizable and quite varied collection of guns.

After returning to England in 1970, Jim Buchanan left the Royal

Marines and joined the local police force. In due course, the technical knowledge gained through his work with military weapons led to a special appointment as force armorer at the headquarters of Kent Constabulary, where he assumed responsibility for all firearms within that county.

He continued his interest in sectioned handguns, although the pistols then in his possession had not yet been prepared for display but were simply stored away in a cupboard. They were eventually all certified as 'de-activated' weapons by the authorities.

Today, most of the Buchanan cutaway models are mounted on separate wooden bases, each carrying a brass plate identifying the weapon concerned. The brass name plates attached to each base are prepared by a local professional engraver. Prior to engraving, the brass surface is blackened by a chemical treatment in order for the lettering to be defined as the base color.

Jim Buchanan is also an avid collector of small arms ammunition and has a comprehensive assortment. As a result, he was able to mount an inert example of the appropriate ammunition alongside each of the mounted pistols. All cartridges are contemporary with the weapons and each round bears a correct headstamp and date.

Jim Buchanan's private collection has continued to grow slowly, the more recent additions having been acquired as de-activated weapons. His knowledge of firearms generally has also expanded considerably after attending a number of specific firearms courses, including those related to the more modern pistols produced by Heckler & Koch, SIG and Glock. Moreover, he has been able to section a number of other handguns as an aid to his work in the police armory and for the training of firearms officers.

When asked to choose a favorite of all the cutaway pistols of his collection, Jim responds by stating his most exciting specimen is usually the one on which he is working at the moment. "I do not favor any particular one of my cutaways but like certain versions for different reasons, mainly because I like the weapon itself. I have always been fascinated by guns. Rather than shoot them, I prefer to take them apart and see how they are constructed."

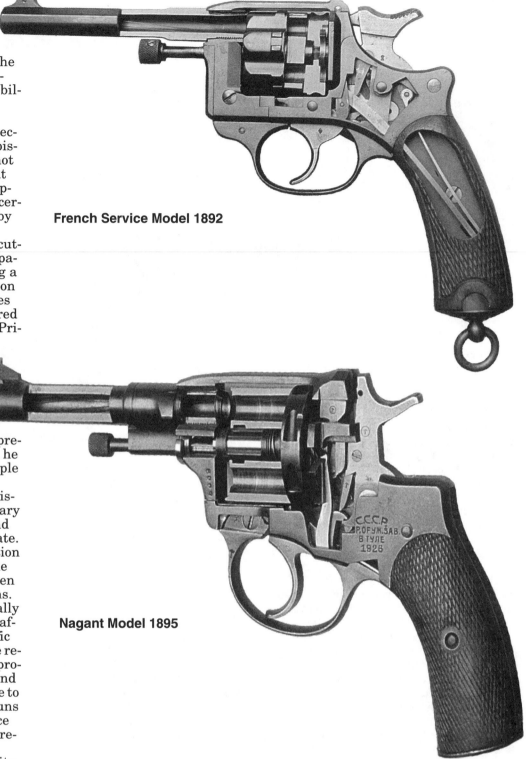

French Service Model 1892

Nagant Model 1895

It has taken a lot of resolve for this collector to drill holes and cut away portions from some of the more valuable models in his gun collection. As it transpires, however, these very weapons have now been better preserved, while so many others have fallen victim to recent British Government legislation. Now that a complete ban on the ownership of handguns in the United Kingdom has been imposed, many pistols of historical importance have been removed from private collections and are lost forever. Fortunately, the examples which remain in the unique Buchanan Cutaway Collection represent an important century of handgun development. ●

The Sedgley Colt Single-Action Rimfire Revolver

by David W. Ploeger

BEFORE WORLD II if you had a desire to shoot a single-action revolver in 22 Long Rifle you didn't have many options. The only solution was to have a custom gunsmith convert an older single-action Colt.

R.F. Sedgley, Inc. is best known for Springfield rifle conversions. This pre-World War II firm converted Springfields, Krags and other rifles to popular sporting patterns. They also made speed-locks, signal pistols, line-throwing pistols and converted Colt Single Action Army and New Service revolvers to 22 Long Rifle or 22 WCF (Hornet).

Through various trades I found myself in possession of a Sedgley-converted Colt Single Action Army chambered for the 22 Long Rifle. This is a very unusual revolver, which has been extensively modi-

fied. *Catalog No. 48*, from R.F. Sedgley, Inc. (established 1897), was printed in 1939 and lists this item: " Colt Single Action Army, Bisley and New Service Revolvers changed to 22 LR or 22 WCF Hornet, including S&W target sights and refinishing, $45.00". It is hard to believe such extensive modifications could be done for $45.00, even in the cheap labor pre-WWII era.

The only thing that appears "original Colt" about this gun is the frame – and even this has been expertly milled and lightened at the top strap and rear recoil shield. The firing pin on the hammer and the frame have been modified to fire rimfire ammo and to hit the rim of those cases on the bottom edge, not the top edge as is typical with 22 LR revolvers. A pre-WWII adjustable S&W rear

sight has been expertly milled into the top strap in much the same manner used to install S & W adjustable sights in the 1960s and 1970s on custom Colt 45 autos. The replacement 6-inch 22-caliber barrel, without ejector tube or rod, is fitted with a blade front sight.

The six-shot, recessed-chamber cylinder is newly-manufactured, of good quality, with flutes. The base pin functions not only as the cylinder pin; it is also the means of taking the cylinder out of the gun and ejecting cases.

The base pin is a new, custom pin which functions in a most unusual manner. It is built into the cylinder and, with the hammer placed at half-cock and the loading gate open, the whole cylinder can be removed from the gun by pulling the base pin

◀ Cylinder removed, the empties are ready for ejection. Note the firing pin strike on the low edge of the rims.

▼ The base pin ejection stroke shows the sturdy star-pattern case ejector and base pin. The cylinder removes from the right side, with the loading gate open and the hammer at half-cock.

outward, away from the frame. The dismounted cylinder is then held in the hand and the base pin pushed back into the cylinder, whereupon a star extractor – just like the one in a double-action, swing-out cylinder revolver – pushes all six shells out of the cylinder. This is a remarkable base pin, very well-engineered, which pulls forward to release the cylinder from the gun and then, when pushed rearward, ejects the empty shells.

Overall, this is a very trim and well-made Colt Single Action. The grips are checkered walnut, slim and attractive. The gun shoots very well; 2-inch groups at 25 yards are usual. The trigger has a very good 3- to 4-pound pull and the action is tight with little play. The cylinder has a very deep drag line, indicating improper timing, but it cycles well.

In this period prior to WWII, when a 22 LR single-action revolver was not available, this could have been a popular conversion. First Generation Colt single-action guns were widely available in pawn shops during this period, so the gun for conversion was generally at hand. The $45.00 fee was a large sum at that time but it could have easily paid for itself in the cost savings of cartridges for center-fire versus rim-fire.

I have only seen one of these conversions; I have heard of three or four more. Based upon samples I am aware of, there do not appear to have been many made – a shame considering the good quality and good design.

Interesting detail of the conversion includes neatly installed S&W adjustable rear sight, relieved recoil shields and a noticeable "droop" to the firing pin tip. Cylinder is well-done, looks original.

The Lone Eagle

Where else would a lone eagle perch, but upon a fence post?

by M. T. Lumly

IV'E NEVER LACKED for reasons to acquire another gun and often the reasons are even plausible. The big single shot from Magnum Research is the most recent example. I chose the 30-30 Winchester chambering because I do a lot of cast bullet shooting and the 30-30's long neck, medium case capacity and strong rim make it a good cast bullet case – plus I also had a bucket full of once-fired brass I wanted to use.

However, I was initially drawn to the Lone Eagle because of its unique rotating locking mechanism. The design borrows somewhat from artillery pieces. It features a rather massive cylindrical breech block, which screws onto an inner cylinder receiver ring, into which the barrel screws. The total shear area of this locking breech mechanism is far greater than any other design I'm aware of. So it's

bank vault strong. An ejector kicks out fired cases when the breechblock is fully opened.

One thing I have learned is that both chamber and cartridge cases should be kept clean to ensure positive ejection. For resizing, I use Lee's case lube, mixed one part to ten parts or so of rubbing alcohol and I don't bother to wipe off what little residue remains. If a lot of shots are fired, less than full ejection may result due to lube residue, but I've not had a partially-ejected case I couldn't coax out.

Cocking the piece is accomplished by pulling back the lever running along the left side of the pistol's synthetic frame, made of Hyloy 610, some new form of tactical Tupperware that's in vogue now. The grip does have a very good feel and it helps tame the felt recoil. The compact design allows a 14-

Lone Eagle fodder, from left: 155-grain cast, 150-grain Speer spitzer and 55-grain Remington Accelerator.

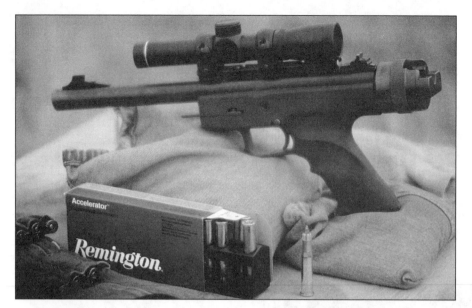

It's in there, scope and all, with extra rounds securely stowed.

Given the pistol's weight, the reclining position works really well when conditions allow.

◀ With the holster completed, enough material remained to make these handy bench bags.

inch barrel with an overall length of only 15 1/8-inches! Even though the beast weighs 4 lbs. 3 oz., without sights and scope, it behaves a lot like a 44 Magnum insofar as muzzle rise goes. Given its weight, shooting offhand is a difficult challenge, which has led me to do most of my shooting from a reclining position or from the bench.

I soon found this pistol thinks it's a rifle! So I installed a 2x Tasco to see how it would do at 100 yards. While more magnification is available, 2x is inexpensive – and all I can manage, anyway. I cut off a bit of the rear of the one-piece base so as to leave the rear sight on as well. While see-through rings might have been used, I prefer the lower, closer to the boreline style.

I now have two 2x scopes, each zeroed for different loads, which can be switched in a couple of minutes – and iron sights for still another loading. The first cast bullet fired was a C.E. Harris design, Lee number C312-155-2R, weighing 155 grains, gas-checked and ALOX-lubed, with AA2520 propellant. The alloy was from a batch of zinc-contaminated wheelweights I just couldn't throw away. Dropped directly from the mould into cold water, they're about linotype hardness. I thought their groups were respectable considering their composition. The 150-grain Speer spitzers really stuck together at 100 yards. I even tried a few Remington Accelerators. They didn't group well by 22 centerfire standards but, given the fact the 1 in 10-inch twist of the 30-30 is far too fast for the little .224-inch bullets, they did the best they could. But if you like speed, these little bullets are going 3,400 fps at the muzzle of a full-length rifle. My shooting is informal and largely at reactive targets, particularly at steel objects. Hitting them is always satisfying and it's great fun to have friends fire on a distant object and, to their happy surprise, find they can hit it more often than not. The good accuracy is due to both the heavy untapered barrel, which is extremely stiff with a good target-crowned muzzle, and a surprisingly good (considering the linkage required) trigger pull.

I realized I now had a good truck gun but, if I were to go afield on foot, I would need to devise a holster of some sort. I made one from a pair of old blue jeans and a 1-inch nylon sling. Even added some cartridge loops which, unlike those of leather, may be left loaded indefinitely. It offers good protection for the gun and is a fairly comfortable way to carry it. I've had a lot of fun loading for, and shooting, this pistol that thinks it's a rifle.

The recoil isn't painful but the muzzle blast is. In fact, I use both plugs and muffs in hopes of preserving what hearing I have left. So I hope you will as well, even if you're only a bystander while others are shooting. The Magnum Research people now offer a wider selection of calibers, including the ubiquitous 7.62x39 Russian. So even reloaders can enjoy the guiltless pleasure of ejecting steel-cased empties off into the weeds.

Now that I think about it, I believe I can feel another reason for acquiring a new gun coming on. As I mentioned earlier, it's a gift I have for that sort of thing. ●

BROWN Model 702 Rifle

by Holt Bodinson

ED BROWN, WELL-KNOWN maker of Model 1911 frames, barrels, a host of prized customizing parts–as well as complete pistols–has turned his sights on the upscale, semi-custom rifle market. Added this year to his extensive Model 1911 lines are six different rifle models that cover the field from big game hunting to tactical.

With a modern manufacturing facility at his command, Brown is capable of doing exactly what he wants–how he wants. His primary objective in building his own action is to offer a platform that is totally straight and concentric. To achieve this, he machines the action and bolt from bar stock that has already been heat-treated to finished specifications; thus, he is able to avoid the almost inevitable warpage that occurs when parts are heat-treated after machining.

The heart of his new Model 702 rifle, a precision action, is made completely in-house. As Brown, a former tool-and-die maker, remarks, "My shop is positioned between a custom gunsmith shop and a full manufacturing facility." And indeed it is, with 13 employees, six CNC machines and full CAD/CAM design and engineering capabilities.

The action is cylindrical in profile, fitted with a separate but massive .300-inch thick recoil lug secured between the receiver ring and the barrel shoulder that can take the stress generated by the largest magnums without flexing. Special attention has been given to the alignment of the front receiver ring with the rear bridge, which accept Talley scope bases secured by extra-stout 8-40 screws. To accomplish this, the rear bridge is actually surface-ground with reference to the front ring to bring both mounting surfaces into perfect alignment.

The push-feed bolt, which features a nicely contoured handle and a three-position safety carried in an elegant bolt sleeve, is hand-lapped into the receiver. The fit is very smooth with no play or binding evident. The extractor resembles an enlarged version of that found on an M-16, while the ejector is a typical spring-loaded pin projecting from the bolt face. The bolt stop and release is pinned and pivots in the left side of the receiver. The trigger is fully adjustable for weight-of-pull and

Ed Brown's Model 702 in 300 Remington Ultra is a refined, tough and accurate sporting rifle.

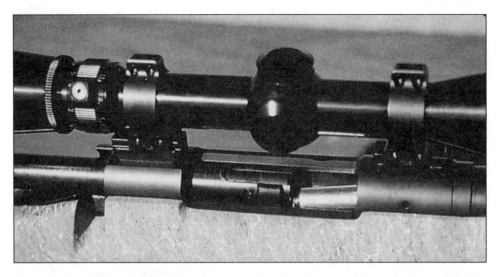

The action is precision-machined from heat-treated steel to insure straightness and concentricity.

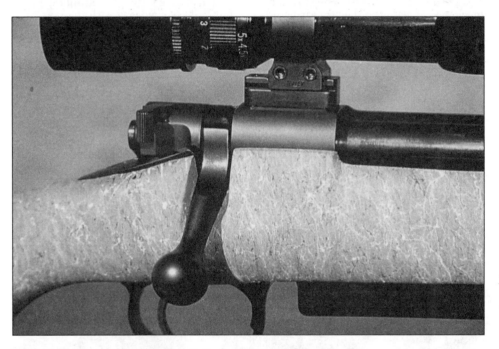

The bolt handle and three-position bolt sleeve are elegantly styled.

Ed Brown's semi-custom rifles are a valuable addition to the upscale firearms market.

over-travel. The lock time of our sample was very fast and snappy.

Brown does not make his own match-grade rifle barrels or synthetic stocks and prefers to buy them from the best of vendors. For example, his stocks are typically from either HS Precision or McMillan.

Our test gun was the Model 702 Savanna chambered in 300 Remington Ultra, featuring an HS Precision stock fitted with their detachable, three-shot magazine and bottom-metal. Typical of the HS Precision line, this synthetic sporter stock featured an aluminum bedding-block that conformed exactly to the action profile. The 24-inch medium-weight barrel was nicely crowned and free-floated for its entire length. Our sample rifle carried Leupold's popular Vari-X III 4-14x power AO scope that is ideal for a long-range big game rifle.

Overall, the new Brown rifle was a good-looking, well-balanced rig that tipped the scales one ounce under 9 pounds–a good weight for a 300 Remington Ultra without a muzzle brake.

Testing was done with the rifle mounted in a Hart pedestal rest, firing Remington's 180-grain Nosler Partition factory load over a PACT Professional chronograph, at 100 yards. Temperature was in the mid-70s and sunny. Simply a delightful day for shooting.

Loading and cycling all the test ammunition through the in-line, three-shot detachable magazine revealed the rifle fed, fired, extracted and ejected without a hitch. The first two shots went into 1/2-inch and the third shot opened the group to 1 1/4-inch.

Looking at the chronograph tape, I found the first two shots averaged 3045 fps while the third shot dropped to 2982 fps. I experienced several other wide swings in extreme spreads as the shooting progressed. The rifle was certainly capable of minute-of-angle at 100 yards with the Remington load as it proved with several three-shot groups at an inch or slightly under.

What was interesting was how slow a 24-inch barrel can be with the large-capacity Ultra case. All the large capacity hunting cases–the Ultra, the Lazzeroni Warbird and Firebird, the 30-378 Weatherby–need at least a 26-inch barrel and, preferably, a 27-inch to obtain all the benefit of the enormous amount of powder being consumed.

Brown's Model 702s are available with a long action or a short action, in a variety of styles suitable for hunting and law enforcement applications. All are built to the reasonable specifications of the customer. There is even a Model 76 "Bushveld" dangerous game rifle in the line that features the Dakota controlled-feed action as the platform.

Priced from $2495-$3000, Ed Brown's semi-custom, precision-made rifles are a valuable addition to the upscale firearms market for those who want something a little bit better. ●

For Additional Information:
Ed Brown Custom, Inc.
P.O. Box 492
Perry, MO 63462
Tel: (573) 565-3261
www.edbrown.com

The Art of the Engraver and Custom Guns

by Tom Turpin

BACK WHEN I was a youngster, or at least a heck of a lot younger than I am now, one of the things I religiously looked forward to each year was the arrival of the new GUN DIGEST. The Editor, John T. Amber, was one of my heroes. He joined the likes of Jack O'Connor, Pete Brown, Warren Page, Col. Charles Askins, Elmer Keith and a few others, as my idols. Amber even published the works of many of my other role models.

While I enjoyed the entire book, particularly if O'Connor or one of the others had a story in the issue, my favorite parts of each and every issue were the *Art of the Engraver* and *Custom Guns* sections. These two sections of the book profiled some of the finest examples of the gunmakers' art. Here, I saw samples of the work of the finest artisans of the day, guys like Goens, Brownell, Biesen, Kennedy, Hartley, Fisher and many other gunmakers. Some of the engravers artistry represented carried names like Griebel, Prudhomme, Kornbrath, Bruhl, Hiptmayer, the Warrens - John and Floyd, and a few others. I spent hours drooling over the pages illustrating such unbelievable talent.

As the years passed, I continued to anxiously await the coming of the next issue of the DIGEST. New names appeared almost every issue and, alas, some of the old-timers dropped out of view. As I gained in experience and traveled a great deal, thanks to a career in the US Army, I was fortunate to meet many of the world's finest artisans. Several became close friends. As I was getting into the writing business, I was fortunate to place one of my very early stories with none other than John T. Amber. We frequently exchanged letters and an occasional phone call or two. In 1978, I attended the Christian DeMoffart International Firearms Expo, held that year in London, England.

The old saw dealing with the kid in the candy store really applied to me at that show. It was there that I finally met Mr. Amber. We spent considerable time together and in time, formed what became practically a father/son-type relationship. He became my mentor in the writing game. Why he took a liking to me, I cannot say. Perhaps he saw in me the talent to become an accomplished outdoor writer, or, perhaps he just wanted to help move me along. Whatever his motivation, he published much of my early material. He knew exactly when to give me a pat on the back and even more important, when to plant a size 10 shoe on my backside. While he had the reputation of being irascible, crotchety and downright obstinate at times, I never saw that side of him. In all the time I spent with him, he was always the perfect gentleman. While he didn't replace my dad in idol worship, he came close at times.

I was saddened when John was replaced at the helm of the DIGEST after more than 30 years as editor. It was only a few years later that he passed away. He was, I believe, in his early eighties. He had suffered numerous afflictions in his elderly years, ranging from heart problems to a detached retina and about everything in-between. Even so, he never stopped living and breathing guns, particularly custom guns, until the very end. I miss him still, even today, a lot of years after his passing.

Ken Warner succeeded John as Editor of GUN DIGEST. While Ken is an admirer of fine custom guns and engraving, his passion was not so great as Amber's. Consequently, the custom and engraving features that I so greatly looked forward to each year were less evident and sometimes not there at all. I missed them greatly.

A new era in the history of GUN DIGEST begins with this issue. Editor Warner decided to move on to other things and has left the helm. I was overwhelmed when Ken Ramage of Krause Publications, the new GUN DIGEST Editor, asked me if I would put together a contemporary version of the old Amber features for the Digest. I took only milliseconds to tell him that I would be delighted.

The Art of the Engraver and Custom Guns, as it appears in this issue, are the beginnings of that endeavor. I sincerely hope the reader enjoys looking at these works of art as much as I did in assembling them for publication. Hopefully we can continue the features for many years to come. Old JTA would be happy. ●

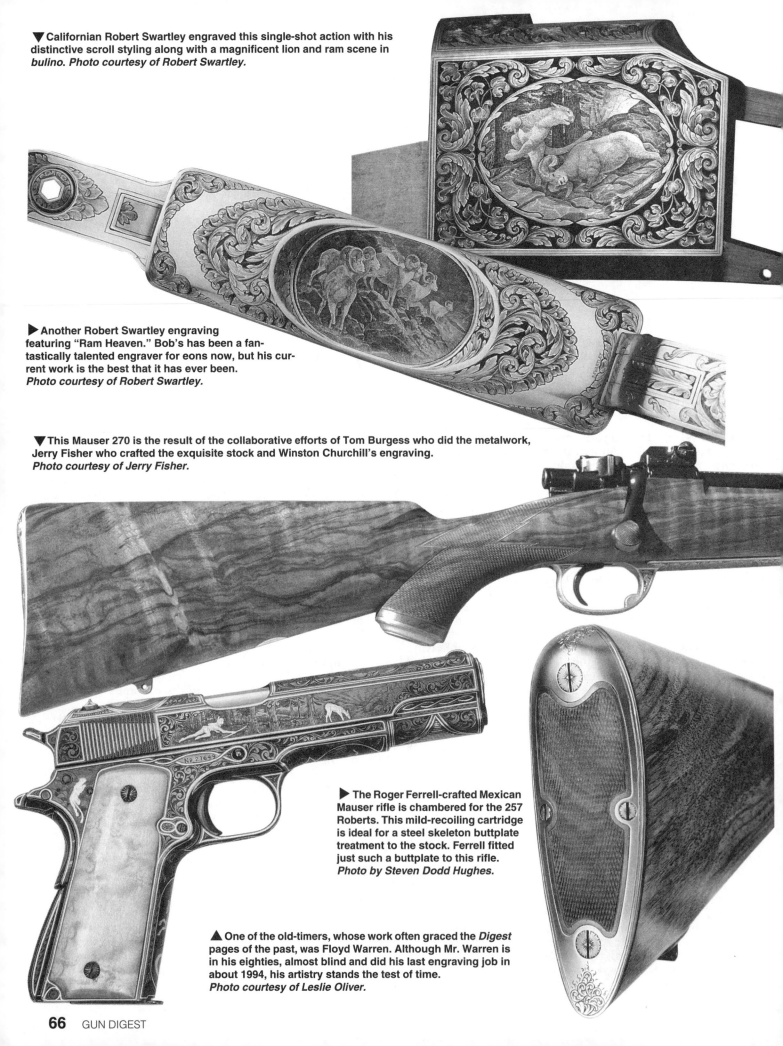

▼ Californian Robert Swartley engraved this single-shot action with his distinctive scroll styling along with a magnificent lion and ram scene in *bulino*. *Photo courtesy of Robert Swartley.*

▶ Another Robert Swartley engraving featuring "Ram Heaven." Bob's has been a fantastically talented engraver for eons now, but his current work is the best that it has ever been. *Photo courtesy of Robert Swartley.*

▼ This Mauser 270 is the result of the collaborative efforts of Tom Burgess who did the metalwork, Jerry Fisher who crafted the exquisite stock and Winston Churchill's engraving. *Photo courtesy of Jerry Fisher.*

▶ The Roger Ferrell-crafted Mexican Mauser rifle is chambered for the 257 Roberts. This mild-recoiling cartridge is ideal for a steel skeleton buttplate treatment to the stock. Ferrell fitted just such a buttplate to this rifle. *Photo by Steven Dodd Hughes.*

▲ One of the old-timers, whose work often graced the *Digest* pages of the past, was Floyd Warren. Although Mr. Warren is in his eighties, almost blind and did his last engraving job in about 1994, his artistry stands the test of time. *Photo courtesy of Leslie Oliver.*

▶ The floorplate of this Mauser 270 rifle provided the canvas for Winston Churchill's artistry in steel and gold. Churchill is one of the world's premiere engravers. *Photo courtesy of Jerry Fisher.*

▼ A close-up of the clean, crisp craftsmanship of Gene Simillion on a Mauser 98 action and a fleur-de-lis checkering pattern. His work is outstanding. *Photo courtesy of Gene Simillion.*

▲ Clean classic lines and superb execution of the details are the hallmarks of the work of Gene Simillion. This Mauser 98 chambered for the 7x57 cartridge is an excellent example of his artistry in wood and metal. *Photo courtesy of Gene Simillion.*

▲ When old-timer Keith Stegall decided to retire, he turned his clientele over to Gene Simillion. He is a worthy successor to Mr. Stegall. This Mauser 98 in 280 Remington is a good example of the work coming from his Gunnison, Colorado shop. *Photo courtesy of Gene Simillion.*

▶ For years, Gary Goudy worked as a machinist for United Airlines during "normal" working hours and crafted fine custom rifles on weekends and after work. He recently retired from United, moved to Dayton, Washington and is now building fine guns on a full-time basis (when he isn't off hunting). This Model 70 is a great example of his outstanding work. *Photo courtesy of Gary Goudy.*

▶ Gary Goudy is one fine craftsman and his stockwork is exquisite. This Mauser-actioned sporter is a fine example of his work. It is clean, crisp and flawless. *Photo courtesy of Gary Goudy.*

▼ This custom Marlin has been totally rebuilt from an old action in the shop of Steven Dodd Hughes. The wonderful case coloring on the frame is an example of the exquisite work of Doug Turnbull. *Photo by Steven Dodd Hughes.*

▶ Starting with a Mexican Mauser action and a 257 barrel, Roger Ferrell turned the components into this wonderfully slim and trim sporting rifle. *Photo by Steven Dodd Hughes.*

▶ This English style magazine rifle is the product of the superb metalwork of Steve Heilmann, including an integral quarter rib and front sight; the stock artistry of James Tucker and the checkering of Bernadette Duckett. The Tucker stock was crafted from an exceptionally dark and dense stick of English walnut. Duckett checkered the stick in a traditional point pattern at 32 lpi. *Photo by Steven Dodd Hughes.*

▶Engraver William Gamradt executed the wonderful scroll engraving on this Steven Dodd Hughes custom Winchester 1873 rifle. The engraving is kept very sparse in keeping with the original rifle, but often more is not necessarily better. This is a great example of the truth of that statement. *Photo by Steven Dodd Hughes.*

▼▶Steven Dodd Hughes is a rather odd duck in the custom gun world. First of all, he is an exceptionally talented gunmaker. In addition, he is a well-published writer and excellent photographer. That combination is curious enough, but the real peculiarity is that he does no work on bolt-action rifles. Instead, he concentrates on fine double shotguns, single-shot rifles and lever-action period pieces. Shown here are two examples of his work. The 1873 Winchester (right) is a completely custom job done in the style of the 1 of 1000 Models. The "modern" single-shot rifle (below) is Hughes' rendition of a Dakota Model 10. Mike Dubber engraved the Hughes/Dakota and William Gamradt engraved the '73. *Photos by Steven Dodd Hughes.*

▼This L.C. Smith 20-bore double is better than anything that ever came out of the original Smith plant. It represents the artistry of metalsmith Pete Mazur, stockmaker Steve Billeb and engraver Robert Evans. It was built as a fund-raising project for the American Custom Gunmaker's Guild. *Photo by Mustafa Bilal*

▲ Although it doesn't look like it, the action on this 416 Rigby was originally a 1917 Enfield. It was extensively modified by metalsmith Ted Blackburn. The late Bob Emmons crafted the wonderful stock and Sam Welch adorned the rifle with his impeccable engraving. *Photo by Mustafa Bilal.*

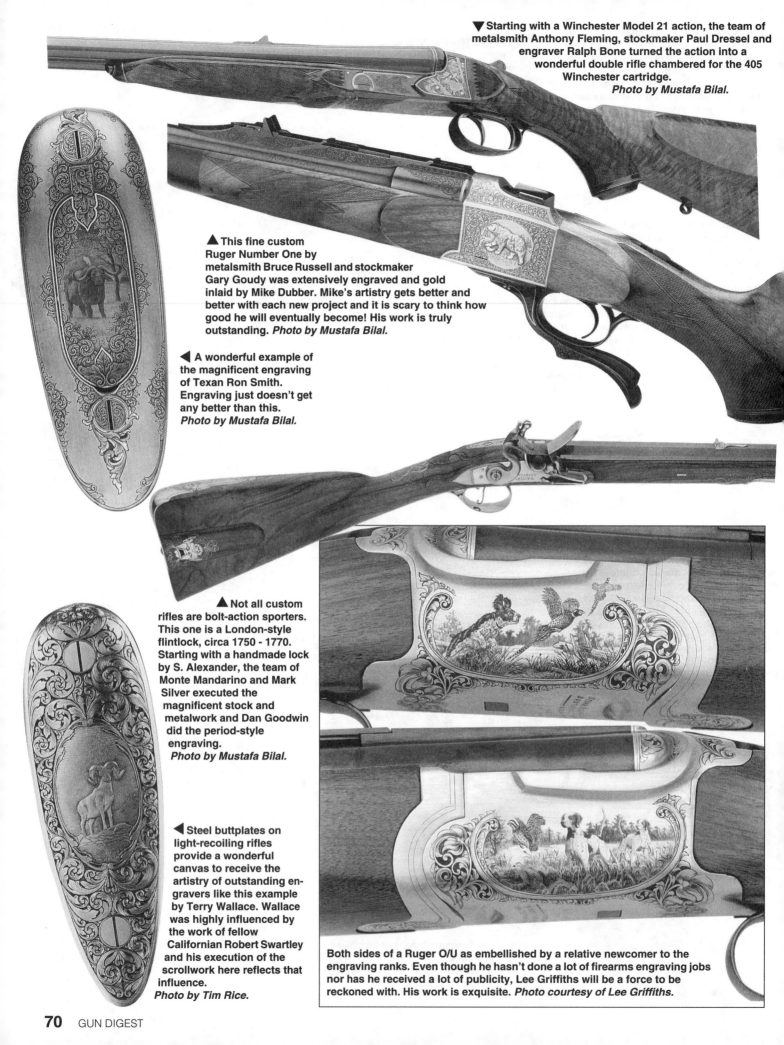

▼ Starting with a Winchester Model 21 action, the team of metalsmith Anthony Fleming, stockmaker Paul Dressel and engraver Ralph Bone turned the action into a wonderful double rifle chambered for the 405 Winchester cartridge. *Photo by Mustafa Bilal.*

▲ This fine custom Ruger Number One by metalsmith Bruce Russell and stockmaker Gary Goudy was extensively engraved and gold inlaid by Mike Dubber. Mike's artistry gets better and better with each new project and it is scary to think how good he will eventually become! His work is truly outstanding. *Photo by Mustafa Bilal.*

◄ A wonderful example of the magnificent engraving of Texan Ron Smith. Engraving just doesn't get any better than this. *Photo by Mustafa Bilal.*

▲ Not all custom rifles are bolt-action sporters. This one is a London-style flintlock, circa 1750 - 1770. Starting with a handmade lock by S. Alexander, the team of Monte Mandarino and Mark Silver executed the magnificent stock and metalwork and Dan Goodwin did the period-style engraving. *Photo by Mustafa Bilal.*

◄ Steel buttplates on light-recoiling rifles provide a wonderful canvas to receive the artistry of outstanding engravers like this example by Terry Wallace. Wallace was highly influenced by the work of fellow Californian Robert Swartley and his execution of the scrollwork here reflects that influence. *Photo by Tim Rice.*

Both sides of a Ruger O/U as embellished by a relative newcomer to the engraving ranks. Even though he hasn't done a lot of firearms engraving jobs nor has he received a lot of publicity, Lee Griffiths will be a force to be reckoned with. His work is exquisite. *Photo courtesy of Lee Griffiths.*

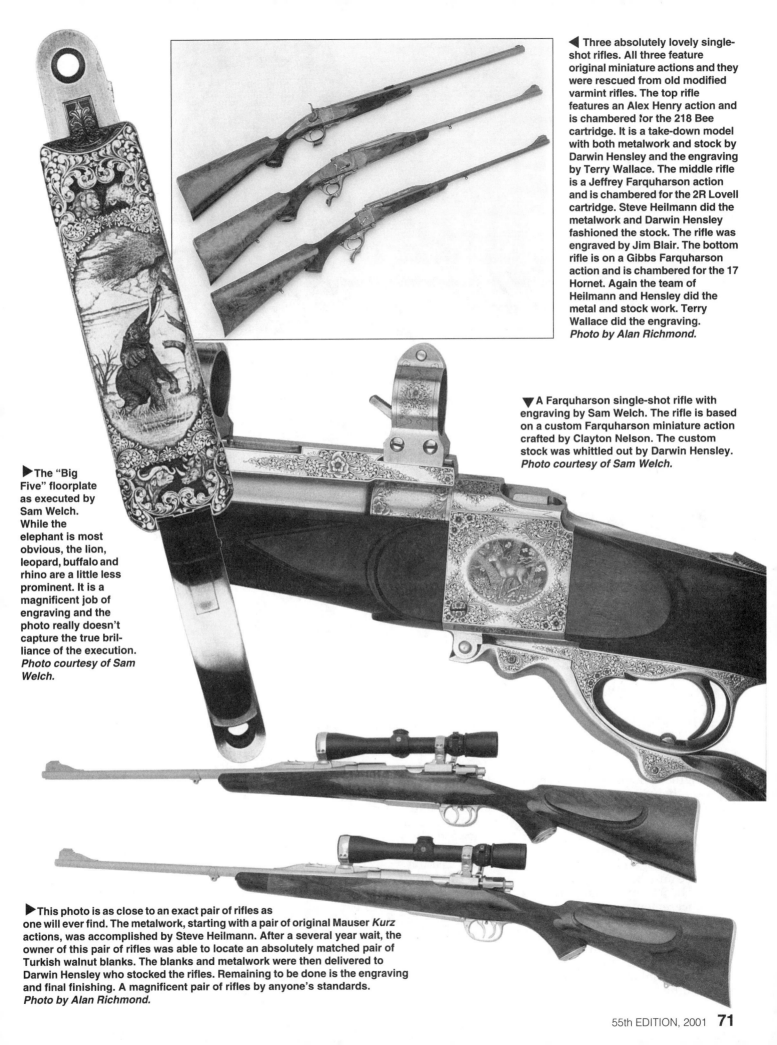

◀ Three absolutely lovely single-shot rifles. All three feature original miniature actions and they were rescued from old modified varmint rifles. The top rifle features an Alex Henry action and is chambered for the 218 Bee cartridge. It is a take-down model with both metalwork and stock by Darwin Hensley and the engraving by Terry Wallace. The middle rifle is a Jeffrey Farquharson action and is chambered for the 2R Lovell cartridge. Steve Heilmann did the metalwork and Darwin Hensley fashioned the stock. The rifle was engraved by Jim Blair. The bottom rifle is on a Gibbs Farquharson action and is chambered for the 17 Hornet. Again the team of Heilmann and Hensley did the metal and stock work. Terry Wallace did the engraving. *Photo by Alan Richmond.*

▶ The "Big Five" floorplate as executed by Sam Welch. While the elephant is most obvious, the lion, leopard, buffalo and rhino are a little less prominent. It is a magnificent job of engraving and the photo really doesn't capture the true brilliance of the execution. *Photo courtesy of Sam Welch.*

▼ A Farquharson single-shot rifle with engraving by Sam Welch. The rifle is based on a custom Farquharson miniature action crafted by Clayton Nelson. The custom stock was whittled out by Darwin Hensley. *Photo courtesy of Sam Welch.*

▶ This photo is as close to an exact pair of rifles as one will ever find. The metalwork, starting with a pair of original Mauser *Kurz* actions, was accomplished by Steve Heilmann. After a several year wait, the owner of this pair of rifles was able to locate an absolutely matched pair of Turkish walnut blanks. The blanks and metalwork were then delivered to Darwin Hensley who stocked the rifles. Remaining to be done is the engraving and final finishing. A magnificent pair of rifles by anyone's standards. *Photo by Alan Richmond.*

John Barlow

The Ideal Man; John H. Barlow in the early 1880s.

The Ideal Man

by Jim Foral

THE AMERICAN-BOUND IMMIGRANT had ample time and occasion to stare out a porthole at the western horizon and give free rein to his imagination. For some, the most aspiring thoughts turned to nothing loftier than the prospects of an evening meal. For most of the others, there were pleasant and expectant images of the American ideal of happiness, success and wealth.

Stirred into the melting pot at Ellis Island, the foreign-born newcomers were unceremoniously poured into the harsh American mainstream and left to their own devices. This new citizen would discover that capturing the American dream would require the precise combination of hard work and good luck. Perseverance, resil-iency and nimbleness also factored into the equation.

1848 was the year the Barlow family, after a wearisome sea voyage from Duckenfield, England, stepped off the boat. Carried over the gangplank and much too young to fantasize about a future, was little John Harwood, the year-old Barlow baby.

Young Barlow's father was by trade a cotton weaver, and drifted into this same work in America. In the 1850s, textile plants worked the help extremely long hours and employed obscenely young children. The wheels started to turn at 5:00 AM and the grind wasn't finished until 12-14 hours later. It was under these conditions that eight year old John Barlow entered the work force. His entire childhood and youth were invested in the mill. The Barlow father and son team considered a way to escape the factory drudgery, and the Civil War provided the opportunity. The senior Barlow put on a blue coat with the 30th U.S. Infantry. Teenager John signed on with the 14th U.S. as an infantryman, and saw action on the battlefield at Richmond. After the war, young Barlow was shipped off to Arizona, where he did his part in subduing the Indian. From there, First Sergeant Barlow was honorably discharged.

Out of military service in 1868, and without a trade or marketable skill with which he could demand a living wage, the young Barlow settled in Meriden, Connecticut and apprenticed himself as a machinist to the Parker Bros. shop. After two years training, he moved to New Haven and accepted a position in the regular machine shop with Winchester Repeating Arms. Barlow was contented with this arrangement. Factory foremen took notice of his abilities and enthusiasm, and he was rewarded with the opportunity to join the firm's contingent of contract labor.

In those days, Winchester's contractors performed the specialty work, produced parts and accessory products. Barlow was assigned to fabricate Winchester loading tools, and he was at the task for the next ten years. Here he was afforded the opportunity to analyze and evaluate the Winchester system. Increasingly more familiar with the design philosophy of the Big Red W, Barlow was aware of the company's prototype tools and what happened to be on

their drawing boards. In addition, he was privy to industry scuttlebutt concerning the plans of the competition. This was a very advantageous position, particularly for an individual with an inventive flair, fresh ideas – and deliberating a career move. In the early 1880s, John Barlow's thoughts and energies centered on devising a practical and patentable cartridge-loading implement.

Before this son of an immigrant stood the whole world. His future was wide open and the sky was the limit. John Barlow took the plunge. In 1884, Barlow severed his connection with Winchester and went to work for himself, selling a limited line of loading tools he'd designed, patented and manufactured. It was trendy in those days to distinguish one's product or company by naming it after a superlative. Very much in step with business fashion was John Barlow and his

newly-christened Ideal Manufacturing Company.

In the world of commerce, Mr. Barlow was the rankest of greenhorns. The man had absolutely no business background or training. Moreover, he lacked the experience to recognize his handicap. Barlow's bread-and-butter items, a tong-type tool he'd patented in March of 1884 and a complete, compact shotshell loader, took a lot of selling. It was difficult to get the hardware and sporting goods trade to even look at his goods. And they steadfastly refused to handle them until it could be proven there was a market.

What Barlow lacked in understanding of his new profession, he made up for in persistence and resourcefulness. Sifting through the magazines, journals and papers devoted to the outdoor sportsman, Barlow wrote a letter to each contributor, correspondent or reader whose name and address could be found. In the mostly rural America of the 1800s, a name and hometown was usually sufficient to assure delivery. Outlining what he had to sell to individuals very likely to be in the market, Barlow slyly promoted his own tools and politely requested the correspondent's consideration.

Barlow's uniquely personal and direct approach was as welcome as a beacon in a tempest and was extraordinarily effective. Letter by letter, Barlow methodically established a core of customers and secured their confidence and acceptance. In the meantime, he advertised when he could afford to. In the March, 1886 sporting bi-weeklies, the first ads for his tong tool appeared. And in the same month, A. D. Clarke of New York City agreed to act as agent for Ideal. Shortly thereafter, other hardware and sporting goods jobbers followed suit and carried the Ideals. A stock of the firm's products was also distributed through firearms companies such as Marlin, Colt, Stevens, Maynard and Winchester.

By the Fall of 1886, Ideal Manufacturing had gotten a bit of opportune ink, the shooting fraternity was increasingly aware of the firm's presence and user reaction was overwhelmingly positive. A *Forest And Stream* correspondent bought a set and declared it to be the "best thing of the kind it has been my good fortune to see." John Barlow had taken his first small step along the uncertain pathway to success.

The Ideal tool's release was advantageously timed. Increasingly, fault

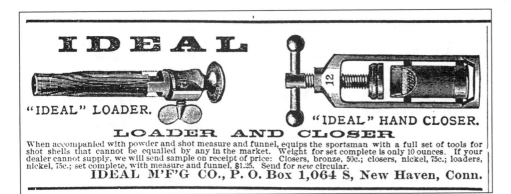

The first Ideal advertisement for shotshell loaders - *Forest And Stream***, May 5th, 1887.**

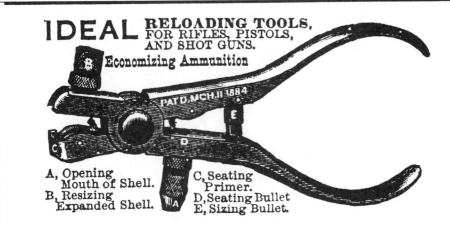

About the earliest Ideal tong tool advertisement you will find, from *Rifle* **- November, 1886.**

Barlow's answer to the need to full-length resize cases, the Ideal Shell Resizing Tool. This particular one is for the 256 Newton and carries the Marlin Firearms Company address.

was found with the reloading tools then on the market. Tools advertised and put out by Winchester, Marlin, Whitney Arms, Providence Tool Co. and the rest, all fell seriously short of satisfying the mainstream 1880s rifle crank. The necessary parts – mould, seater, re- and de-capper – were not combined into a single unit. None of them could sufficiently resize a fired case. But the upstart Ideal product possessed an important point of utility. All of its components were conveniently connected to the polished and nickeled frame of the implement.

Barlow put out a simple set of improved shotshell loading tools consisting of a compact loader and shell closer. Unlike the tools it was supposed to compete with, the ten-ounce Ideal Loader could be tucked into a coat pocket. Just as importantly, it required no table to clamp onto or work upon. This item was instantly popular, and there was a steady demand for it following its release in late 1886.

1887 was not a good year for the New Haven entrepreneur. In early February, a fire at the plant – sabotage by hirelings of a cross-town rival, according to the local gossip – threatened the fledgling enterprise. The buildings escaped serious damage, however, and a week later they were again in complete running order. Later that month, John Barlow lost Ida, his bride for almost thirteen years. Not only was he faced with the day-to-day struggle of maintaining a business, he now had the needs of three very young daughters to attend to.

The basic 1884 hand tool was in a perpetual state of improvement and revision. In November of 1887, John Barlow marched into the New York City publishing offices of *Forest And Stream* magazine and put on an unscheduled demonstration of his newly-patented #2 tool for the staff. The Ideal #2 for pistol cartridges was based upon the familiar 1884 frame, but featured a repositioned recapper and other subtle improvements.

The Ideal tools were wonderful devices for preparing reloads, but as bullet moulds alone, they had two major shortcomings. When the integral mould end was hot enough to do good work, managing the whole assembly required gloved hands. Plus, not everyone who used the Ideal combination tool was contented with the standard cavity attached.

In early 1890, Barlow offered individual moulds formed integral with the frame of the tool. Cool wooden handles allowed for bare-handed casting. Bullet styles numbered in the dozens, and more were added as quickly as Barlow and others could work them up and form the cherries. The immediate acceptance of the Ideal mould was largely attributable to the staggering variety of available designs. In addition, the Ideal moulds featured the same proven and durable hinge system found on the combination tools. John Barlow was able to devise better hinges than his rivals, and it didn't take long for handloaders to recognize this point of superiority.

Casting usable bullets in the late 1880s demanded a good technique and knowledge most folks didn't possess. Typically, casters melted their lead in a pot or kettle, over an open fire or kitchen stove, and spilled the alloy into the mould with a too-hot iron teaspoon. Inescapably, the mould's necessary heat retention was difficult to control and bullet quality suffered according to the proficiency – or pickiness – of the mould's operator. In 1890, Barlow provided the cure – the Ideal dipper for "running bullets". In practice, the nozzle of a full dipper was connected with the mould and both turned vertically as a unit. Plenty of hot metal was forced into the mould. A proper rhythm could be developed, keeping mould and sprue plate

The Ideal Hand Book, **first published June, 1891, is the father of today's many reloading handbooks and manuals. Later the title changed a bit and, today, Lyman offers the** *Reloading Handbook, 47th Edition.* **Courtesy Lyman Products.**

Early Ideal bullet mould with integral wooden handles.

at elaboration was attempted. The mechanics of handload assembly, an explanation of powder suitability and the elemental principles of bullet casting were all condensed into the few paragraphs *Forest And Stream* allowed Barlow in the journal's March 27, 1890 issue.

In June of 1891, Ideal issued a 56-page pamphlet formatted as a manual-cum-catalog. "*The Ideal Handbook of Useful Information for Shooters*" was more than a means of exposing the goods Ideal manufactured. It was a goldmine of information to rifle and revolver enthusiasts.

John Barlow composed the text and presented it in a friendly, chatty manner. All the bases were covered.

He explained basic loading principles, detailed proper casting and lubrication technique, and told how to break in and manage an Ideal bullet mould. Also offered were tips on understanding, preserving and cleaning cartridge cases. For the man who wanted to know if it paid to reload his shells, there were tables showing the cost of factory cartridges compared with the cost of reloaded cartridges.

In addition, tables of bullet diameters and weights, lists of rifling

up to consistent temperature. A perfectly filled-out bullet was the practical result. A ten-pound capacity melting pot and holder rounded out this much needed outfit. Barlow's well-conceived dipper was the first meaningful advancement in the art of moulding lead bullets. It was, and I daresay still is, the caster's most valuable accessory.

The major drawback of the Ideal tong tool was it's inability to re-size a rifle case for it's entire length. This was seldom necessary if the shells were reused in the gun that fired them but, used repeatedly, shells tended to stick in the chamber and benefited from being re-sized full length. For this process, Barlow recommended the Ideal Shell Resizing Tool, an ultra-simple chamber-type die into which the case was driven with a wooded mallet and backed out with a plunger. In 1891, John Barlow was the first to give reloaders a tool of this sort, the forerunner of the modern press-mounted resizing die.

The casual shooter's exposure to any sort of reloading guidance, apart from what little he picked up in the riflemen's press, was the overly concise instruction sheet packed with each Ideal tool. A fair percentage of cranks hungered for particulars, and Barlow obliged as best he could. An effort

twists, and various other peripheral nuggets worth knowing were interspersed with Barlow's humor and homespun philosophy. A number of selected endorsements were impossible to ignore and fostered the trust and confidence of the reader. In the catalog section, each tool and accessory in the line was fully described and artfully illustrated. Between the covers were a few commercial pages of ads, including one from William Lyman, who was then busy setting himself up in the gunsight business. Neither Barlow nor Lyman could have imagined that their companies would eventually come together.

Customers who'd bought a full compliment of tools were not abandoned or left to their own devices. Barlow's objective was to be of service, and he intended to act as the industry's general advisor and instructor to every segment of the reloading public. Right from the start, he encouraged his patrons in need of help or guidance to contact him personally. He invited them to send a sample of their failed work: "A shell and a bullet. State plainly the trouble. A letter from us may overcome all your troubles. We guarantee satisfaction." In this way, Barlow established himself as the friend and mainstay of the gun crank, and this was a strong factor in making Ideal a success.

As products and the handloading scene inevitably evolved, the *Ideal Handbook* was continually updated. Before Barlow was through, this booklet went through nineteen editions. *The Ideal Handbook*, or "Shooter's Koran" as it came to be well-known, wasn't the sort of material halfheartedly browsed through and discarded. Generally, these handy references were shelved with the rest of the books and kept for years.

In shooting circles, John Barlow and Ideal were household words. So identified and inseparably linked was Ideal's principal to his company that he became familiarly known as "The Ideal Man". The new title signified respect and comradeship, and Mr. Barlow was both flattered and pleased to be so regarded.

"Why didn't our people think of that?" must have been the competition's reaction when they noticed the announcement of the Barlow patented bullet sizer in December, 1891. This simple tong tool would size any cast bullet, with the appropriate

The Ideal Loading Flask, from the Ideal Handbook No. 4.

patching. In 1892 Barlow made some minor changes in the original design, placed the improvement on the market, and sold it in a box with an Ideal label. A year previously, Barlow had acquired the rights to Mr. Rabbeth's nifty little loading flask and successfully marketed it as Ideal.

1892 was a banner year for Barlow and Ideal Manufacturing. At the annual New York City Sportsman's Exposition, the Ideal booth displayed the company's complete offering of thirty-six tools in an average of twenty-five different sizes or calibers. The aggregate was startling. And

selected Ideal goods in their massive yearly wish book. Already considered indispensable, a more informative third edition of the *Ideal Handbook* was released in July.

The early 1890s success of the 25-20 Single Shot as a target and small-game cartridge stirred public interest in the quarter-inch bore, and Ideal was kept busy ministering to the wants and needs of the 25-caliber-smitten. Barlow's most valuable contribution was Ideal #25720, a flat-pointed projectile with square grease grooves. In 1892, it stood on the cutting edge of lead bullet design. The basic bullet could be had in a variety of weights ranging from 46-96 grains. Immediately, the 77-grain length became popular. The three dollar Ideal Perfection mould would cast each variation within a single mould and enabled its' operator to put an end to the 25-caliber keyholing problems encountered by many in those days.

In 1893, Capt. W.L. Carpenter of Sackett's Harbor, New York, conceptualized a long, parallel-sided 25-caliber target cartridge. Hopeful of attracting a gunmaker's attention, he drew a rough pencil sketch of what he had in mind and managed to get it printed in *Forest And Stream* that May. After a year of enduring the empty assurances of the people at Winchester, Carpenter turned to the rifleman's friend. At the Ideal plant, John Barlow fashioned a model shell from brass rod and sent the Captain over to the J. Stevens Arms and Tool Co.. With the sample case, and Barlow's recommendation, he took up the matter with company officials. The availability of Stevens rifles chambered for Carpenter's 25-25-100 Stevens Straight was announced in mid-August, 1894.

During this 25-caliber craze, Marlin officials wanted a short 25-caliber for a repeating rifle they had in the drawing board stages. At their request, Barlow designed a compacted 25-20 S.S. on the 32-20 WCF case. Marlin adopted the idea and became the first manufacturer to bring out a 25-20 repeater cartridge.

interchangeable die, to a specified diameter. The Ideal bullet sizer answered a steady demand for such a specialty item.

For reloading the customary single cartridge case at the 200 yard Schuetzen range, Ideal brought out a thoroughly practical five-ounce re/de-capper that fit in the vest pocket. There was also a companion bullet seater for breech-seating the soft lead bullet in front of the charged case. Priced at a dollar each, both tools were new in 1892.

F.J. Rabbeth, the well-known Walnut Hill champion, was the inventor of an adjustable mould for casting cylindrical bullets for paper-

in April Montgomery Ward, the self-professed "Mammoth Mail Order House", decided to include

The #6 Ideal Tool offered changeable, adjustable dies, with integral mould. This specimen reloads the 303 Savage round; the mould cavity casts #308241.

" in Clips....	"	58.00	Bullets, Full Copper Jacketed	
Primed Shells........	"	20.00	or Soft Point..........112 grains.	
Bullets	"	15.00	Cartridges packed 1,000 in a case.	

Adapted to Winchester Repeating Rifles, Model 1892.

Cartridges ....per 1,000, $16.00		Powder ....17 grains.	
Primed Shells........ " 9.00		Bullets, 1 part tin and 60 parts lead.	
Bullets (86 grains).... " 4.00		Cartridges packed 2,000 in a case.	

SMOKELESS CARTRIDGES, .25-20, Model 1892, per 1,000, $19.00.

Adapted to Marlin Repeating Rifles.

Cartridges ....per 1,000, $16.00		Powder .... 17 grains.	
Primed Shells........ " 9.00		Bullets, 1 part tin and 60 parts lead.	
Bullets (86 grains)..... " 4.00		Cartridges packed 2,000 in a case.	

SMOKELESS CARTRIDGES, .25-20 Marlin, per 1,000, $19.00.

See list of SMOKELESS CARTRIDGES, pages 134–137.

Directly compared, the 25-20 Winchester and the 25-20 Marlin appeared thus in the 1899 Winchester catalog.

Presently, Winchester unleashed a nearly identical version for their new Model 1892 rifle. Dimensionally similar to the Marlin 25-20, the 25-20 Winchester Center Fire varied enough to preclude interchangeability. The ballistic advantage using smokeless and an 86-grain bullet – 130 fps – belonged to the Marlin edition, but the W.C.F. number became much more accepted. Winchester standardized cartridge and chamber specifications and the 25-20 Marlin faded into obscurity. The proper, popular choice of lead bullets for either case was Ideal's #25720 in the 86 grain weight.

These were fast-paced, prosperous and happy years at Ideal. More and more, people took up reloading their fired cases as an economical and enjoyable pastime.

Mr. Barlow piloted his company the way his instincts guided him. His business methods were of the "old school", or as he preferred to say, "no school". Unable to forget his cotton mill days, he treated employees fairly, giving them the sort of respect he felt they deserved. By all accounts, he was a fair and decent man to work for.

That most of the Ideal grooved bullets were drawn up by Barlow personally can be readily seen in the similarity, caliber to caliber, of a few basic variations. A sizable percentage, however, were either adopted from client's custom moulds or submitted as simple sketches by outsiders. And there was no shortage of

bullet designers with cranky ideas. In the heyday of the Schuetzen game, there was a rash of 32-40 and 38-55 target bullets designed, mostly by notables in the 200-yard offhand crowd. The reverse-tapered #37586 was reasoned out by Charley and Barney Zettler, the principals behind New York City's Zettler Rifle Club. A popular 32-40 design became known as the French bullet, after New Yorker W.H. French had Barlow shape the cherry for his spitzer-nosed 32-caliber bullet. Doc Carver contributed the odd-looking #315158 and #370163 styles, and Rabbeth the record-breaking #37588. For the 44 Sharps cartridges, Major McFarland dreamed up the unconventional #446188. Dr. Walter Hudson added to Barlow's array numbers #319273 and #375272, both of which required special throating. Hudson was also responsible for the Ideal #1 bullet seater for breech-seating these hardened projectiles. A sea captain came up with an unexpectedly accurate #37580, and used it to shoot big fish. Others found lead bullets just the ticket for small game and it was the Ideal lineup, too.

When long-range 30-caliber shooting developed in the late 1890s, military marksmen looked to Ideal for a mid-range practice bullet. More instrumental in the goal's achievement

were the independent riflemen/experimenters of the day. These men provided the inspiration. Barlow provided the moulds and unlimited cooperation. W.H. Beardsly, with the competing Bridgeport Gun Implement Co., dreamed up an odd-looking short-range projectile – #3086. W.M. Cooper came up with an early full-length bullet – #3081. Horace Kephart, the St. Louis librarian, took the Cooper bullet into the smokeless powder era with his 170-grain #308206. A progressive series of post-1900 30-caliber designs, culminating in the benchmark #308284, were designed by Dr. Walter Hudson. Along the way, the copper gascheck cup evolved from the combined experiments of Hudson and Barlow.

Replace the cast iron powder reservoir on this old #5 Powder Measure with a clear plastic reservoir - and the parentage of today's Lyman #55 Powder Measure becomes clear. Note the Middlefield, Connecticut address cast into the reservoir.

Ideal powder measures evolved with the rest of the company's line.
The Ideal #6 is shown in this small advertisement in *Field And Stream*, November 1904.

To compete with the firmly entrenched 32-40, Barlow also designed a new 32-caliber target cartridge incorporating features he considered important. The straight-walled shell held twenty-five grains of black powder and featured a solid head of brass surrounding a durable primer pocket. The .323-inch 150-grain was equally well thought out and was cataloged as #32360. Appropriately, the U.M.C.-drawn cartridge was named the 32 Ideal. Both Stevens and Winchester chambered their single-shot rifles for it.

The 1890s transition from blackpowder to the early smokeless types was not an especially smooth one. There was a concerted effort to frighten people and convince them the new powders might be dangerous. Widely published excerpts from the *1896 Report to the Chief of Ordnance*, which seemed to caution against the use of these nitro powders, alarmed the masses and generally soured them towards the smokeless propellant. Winchester Repeating Arms issued similar warnings about reloading with the new powders and went on record as wishing "to do its utmost to discourage this practice". Boxes of loaded Winchester ammunition were labeled with this disclaimer.

The real trouble related to failures encountered with government 30-40 Krag shells. Because of brittleness in fired cases, and the likelihood of a rupture at their first reloading, shooters were repeatedly warned to steer clear of reloading the arsenal cases. An incompatibility between the cartridge case and the mercuric primer was at the root of the problem and was, more or less, easily corrected. But the damage had been done. In the minds of many, the new powders were not safe. This uneasiness was not confined to reloading 30-40 shells, but to any smokeless load.

It was in this unhealthy, apprehensive atmosphere that John Barlow struggled to comfort the frightened. He sought to dispel the rifleman's ignorance and fear with enlightenment, and preached that there was safety in knowledge. The nitro was here to stay, and people needed to learn to deal with it. Smokeless powder was a complex material, Barlow explained in a turn-of-the-century Ideal handbook. It couldn't be loaded with blackpowder techniques or charge cups. Owing to the increasing variety of smokeless powders and the diversity of their application, Barlow advised his customers to consult the powder companies for their recommended charges, and stressed the instructions be followed to the letter. It is believed that the powder manufacturers pressed Barlow to take this stance.

Ideal introduced their #10 Tool in 1898 for reloading the trendy rimless cases, and provided the much-needed guidance in the construction of mid-range loads using selected smokeless powders. So, through the medium of the *Ideal Handbooks* and the press, Barlow assured the mainstream rifleman that hand-loading with nitro powders was indeed a safe and practical exercise. In *Recreation* for December, 1904, Barlow's broad-casting that America's leading military marksmen entrusted their performance to nitro reloads was persuasive and bolstered confidence. Cpts. Corwin and Hudson, Lt. Casey and Dr. Cook shot their own assembled cartridges not only in practice, but in important national contests such as the Wimbledon and Leech Cup competitions and the President's Match. An Ideal circular released that winter, listing honors won by Sea Girt contestants employing Ideal tools and smokeless powder handloads, reinforced what the public wanted to hear.

Ideal Manufacturing produced and distributed tools in all calibers chambered by Winchester, Marlin, Colt, *et al*. In the late 1890s, Savage Repeating Arms insisted on control of sales for their trendy 303 Savage caliber. Arthur Savage had taken the step of protecting the 303 Savage designation by trademark. Ideal made the loading tools which were, until 1903, distributed only through Savage.

Ideal did not ignore the shotgun enthusiast, and the #10 Ideal Handbook (July, 1898) describes a number of shotshell loading implements. Besides his original packet tools, there was an assortment of hand closers, shot measures, a shell trimmer and star crimpers. The eighteen pound bench-mounted Ideal Loading Machine for shotshells could be set up for any gauge and load 300 shells per hour. Barlow brought out this foot-operated apparatus for the avid trap

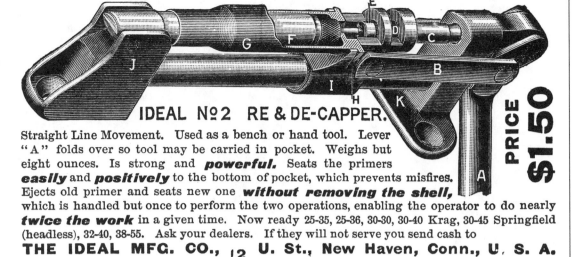
This Ideal No. 2 Re & De-Capper streamlined the priming process and could be operated hand-held or bench-mounted. This advertisement appeared in the December, 1905, issue of *Recreation*.

shooters with high production demands. "They are not the cheapest, but they are the best", Barlow boasted. Regardless, the up-to-the-minute gun club of size couldn't afford to be without one. By September of '98, Ideal was ready to receive orders for this new loader. Rounding out the 1898 Ideal line-up were four types of powder measures and all manner of ancillary items.

Other period Handbooks list an essential Barlow-patented broken shell extractor, an ever-increasing number of bullet styles, prepared bullet lubricant in stick form and a machine to conveniently and effectively size and grease cast bullets. Both the basic operating principle and components of the Barlow-designed Ideal Lubricator and Sizer, a milestone in handloading hardware, haven't changed appreciably in the past hundred years.

By 1900, jobbers courted him for the privilege of distributing the Ideal line. In 1901, Ideal issued a press release informing the trade that Phil. B. Bekeart, the giant San Francisco merchandiser, would be the only authorized Ideal agent for the Pacific Coast after September 1, 1901.

The Spanish-American War had revived the dormant interest in military rifle shooting in the U.S. and, for several years afterwards, eastern National Guard units applied themselves to rifle practice and competition with renewed zeal. Government practice ammunition was substandard even for the purpose, and it was grudgingly dispensed by a crew of miserly War Department bureaucrats.

To get all the shooting they wanted, the troopers turned to reloading their own fired 30-40 Krag cases. Just as he'd supported the 45-70 Springfield rifleman with six-cavity gang moulds and nutcracker tools, Barlow provided for the 30-caliber Krag rifleman of 1900-1907.

The Ideal Man designed and marketed a hefty twenty-five pound loading press capable of full-length resizing the Krag shell. The multi-cavity Armory Mould was cut for a variety of 30-caliber bullets, and it was best filled from Ideal's massive gas smelting furnace, which could liquefy 75 pounds of lead alloy. An Ideal bullet sizer-lubricator and #5 powder measure was likewise essential. Together, these items comprised the Ideal Armory Outfit, indispensable to the National Guard unit armorer who spent his drill time putting up accurate gallery and midrange Krag handloads.

A bench-mounted accessory was available in 1907. The ingenious cast iron, japan-finished Ideal Lightning Decapper was a device designed for expelling spent primers very quickly. New recruits, it was said, were assigned the tedious job and could de-prime 20,000 Krag or Springfield cases during a ten hour Guard drill.

For these Krag riflemen, John Barlow put out an extraordinarily useful sight micrometer – a sight elevating tool – for use with the 1901 Model sight. Each competitor hopeful of finding his name on the winner's list had one in his shooting kit.

Military rifle shooting was among John Barlow's passions. He was,

himself, a former competitor and maintained an intense interest in the activity throughout his life. At the bigger Eastern Regimental shoots or the National Matches, Barlow was a fixture on the sidelines, representing Ideal. At the September, 1906 Sea Girt Matches, Barlow happened to be tented with the famed crackshot Dr. Walter G. Hudson. On any evening, a fly on the tent flap would have witnessed a gathering of America's finest marksmen in their quarters, drawn by the pair's presence.

For the purpose of learning something from the exercise, Barlow and Hudson were once up past midnight, slugging the bores of over three hundred of the troopers' Krag barrels and finding a wider than expected variance. Without hesitation, Barlow delivered his sermon, reminding all within earshot the Hudson-designed Ideal cast bullets for the Krag could be made to fit the tightest – or loosest – of these 30-caliber barrels.

Townsend Whelen regularly bumped into Mr. Barlow at the national competitions. Once, about 1907, they had a little chat about cartridge popularity. Barlow knew the 32-20 WCF was the most popular since Ideal sold twice as many tools to reload this little shell as any other.

It was a tradition, a hundred years ago, for gunmakers, cartridge companies and powder manufacturers to contribute the award for an individual shooting contest. Barlow sponsored the Ideal Match during the glory days of the competition Krag. This event was a rapid-fire

On the occasion of John H. Barlow's retirement from Ideal, *Outdoor Life* ran this photograph in their July, 1910 issue.

worthy successors. Marlin had been an Ideal supporter as long as Barlow had been in New Haven. They used and sold his tools, endorsed his methods and helped in his experiments. Barlow agreed to sell his beloved company. Though negotiations had been ongoing for nearly a year, the announcement of Barlow's retirement and Ideal's transfer of ownership took the sporting goods industry by surprise. On May 16, 1910, Marlin Firearms took over the tools, machinery, stock and immeasurable goodwill of Ideal. Marlin officials retained the entire skilled work force and they placed in charge of it a fifteen-year veteran assistant manager named Joseph A. Derby, Barlow's son-in-law and father to his two grandchildren.

Robert Kane, the editor of *OUTERS BOOK*, once wrote "it is safe to say that he (Barlow) has written more personal letters to the individual shooters of the world, aiding and advising them in various ways, than any other man". Barlow's last communications on the Ideal letterhead were open letters directed to the readers of each of the outdoor magazines, informing them of the takeover and thanking them for their past patronage. Further, he assured his loyal customers that the tools they were familiar with, though Marlin-made, would continue to be "Ideal".

John Barlow spent much of his retirement traveling abroad with his unmarried daughter, Alpha. He had always wanted to visit the place of his birth, and England was his destination when, on the Ides of March, 1912, he suffered a heart attack and died suddenly in Venice, Italy, and was buried there. The sad news was cabled to all quarters of the globe and the world's military and shooting fraternity received the loss of 'Papa' Barlow with a sense of great personal loss. Bob Kane eulogized him in the June, 1912 edition of *OUTERS BOOK* as a "public spirited, large hearted, generous man, beloved by all who knew him".

Some things are over, some things go on. The Ideal Man's legacy is in the iron tools he left behind. The #310 tong tool and a remnant of his timeless original bullet designs are still in demand and are with us yet. More enduring is this gentleman's shining example that class and integrity can complement the inventive and entrepreneurial spirit. And the success of John Barlow is valid reason to question the hardness and fastness of the too-often held misconception "nice guys finish last". ●

regimental team competition, shot with the military rifle and open to all comers. The winner was presented with a trophy known as the Barlow Prize. Even the competitor's ammunition was furnished by the Ideal Man. When a segment of the 1906 Sea Girt program, including the Ideal Match, was cancelled on short notice, Barlow distributed the cartridges along the firing line – a case to this state and a case to that – with the expectation that the shooters would remember where it came from. At lesser events, such as the major Zettler gallery matches, Barlow made a practice of donating

merchandise awards; Ideal sizer-lubricators and loading tools.

During Barlow's tenure at Ideal, two generations of secondhand gun buyers looked to the classified section of the outdoor magazines for bargains. Not unexpectedly, a good indicator of a well-kept piece was the ad closing with the deal-sweetening notice: "Ideal tools included".

After heading the Ideal Manufacturing Co. for twenty-six years, sixty-four year old John H. Barlow elected to retire. During this time, the Ideal Man had enjoyed a long and cordial association with the Marlin Firearms Company and felt they would make

BRUSH-BUCKING BULLETS

.....THAT DIDN'T

by Rob Lucas

I PARKED THE 35 Remington in the coldroom, kicked snow off my boots, and stepped into the warm cabin. It was late. I'd stopped at our other deer camp to see if anybody'd gotten a buck, and no one had. My hunting partner sat cleaning his 6mm and glumly announced he'd missed a six-pointer from 20 yards.

This was two years ago, a year the Michigan Department of Natural Resources called for a poor whitetail harvest, the 44 magnum pistol surpassed the 30-30 rifle as a deer cartridge, and the timber wolf population between Lake Michigan and Lake Superior to reach exactly 112. This last item was no surprise, since a black-and-silver male wolf used our 120 acres as part of his summer range and he was still hanging around at the start of deer season.

Twenty yards? Ken explained he was still-hunting through jackpines when he discovered the buck paralleling him. His scope showed an intervening latticework of brush and pine needles, but when a standing high-lung shot was there for an instant, he took the shot and the buck took off. He tracked it for half a mile to the Federal Highway, where he lost it, without seeing a drop of blood.

All the same I talked him into getting out the flashlights for another look and it turned out there were four deer. Criss-crossing and backtrailing in new and old snow we found the right trail and it led to a six-point buck lying in corn stubble. In the white-on-white halogen glare was an unforgettable mess: between shoulder and belly a square foot of bright red ribcage was exposed. Chunks of shoulder and

flank meat were gone, and a yard-long rope of glistening, un-eaten viscera lay in the snow. Huge canine tracks led away to the near treeline.

The autopsy, kneeling in the dark as Ken's light searched for eyes, was brief. There was no sign in the snow of a chase or fight, Ken's bullet felled the deer and the wolf found it first. The 100-grain Nosler Partition had hit behind the paunch where it broke the right hambone and exited, six inches low and two feet back from where it was aimed. Tight-lipped, Ken tagged his buck and left it for Mr. Canis Lupus.

"That bullet hit something," he said walking out.

Next morning we ducked our hats under snowy limbs to search among the long shadows for bullet-spattered pinebark or a fresh-cut limb dangling. No such luck. But something started that Nosler on a wild tangent, a branch close to the muzzle likely, rather than close to the animal. These things happen; it was nobody's fault.

Then my hunting partner of almost 20 years began talking to himself about more caliber, heavier bullets, even rebarreling his custom Mauser to 308 or even 358. Would something like a 30-caliber RN at 2700 fps have deflected the equivalent of 10 feet at 100 yards? Would a 250-grain 35-caliber flatpoint, or a 300-grain 444 for that matter, have anchored the buck before it left the jackpines? He was talking about brush bullets.

A few doe tags got filled, but Ken's was the only buck we shot that year. At the end of the season some of the clan piled into the cabin for butterfly venison chops and a conversation about wolves and brush bullets. Nothing like a lost deer, under any circumstance, to sharpen the focus. The

Lucas posted on a stump, thumb ready on the Marlin's hammer; sometimes it's that simple.

All the cartridges fired in my tests: 22 RF, 222 Remington, 250 Savage, 250 Savage Improved, 257 Roberts, 257 Roberts Improved, 264 Weatherby Magnum, 7x57mm, 280 Remington, 30-30 Winchester, 300 Savage, 308 Winchester, 348 Winchester, 35 Remington, 35 Whelen Improved, 375 H&H, 404 Jeffrey, 44 Magnum, 45-70 Government and 12 gauge.

"brush bullet" we defined like Jack O'Connor had in the 50s, one that can fly through leafy obstructions in a straight line. There were a dozen of us, age 16 to 77 years, all primarily Upper Penninsula hunters with a collective bag of a quarter-thousand whitetails.

Upper Michigan, like the big-timber country in Maine and Minnesota, is an appropriate place to debate the so-called brush bullet. We find whitetails in cedar swamps, tag alder thickets, hardwood and pine stands and, every-so-often, in a clearcut. Until the '98-99 season, treestands were banned in the UP during the firearms season; we dig holes, build blinds, tuck into up-rooted hemlocks, or sit on a stump and trailwatch. Lots of shots every season are fired through green branches and live brush.

Like everybody else who's argued about brush-shooting, we couldn't come to a consensus. For all its empirical content, this discussion could have taken place at the Lake Geneva Sporting Clays Club. Instead of debunking the whole idea we separated into factions and lined up behind *three* different theoretical brush bullets.

Most of our graybeards, when they can't pick a hole in brush to sneak one through, trust the "new math" brush bullet to get through pine needles. This is a spirepoint at 3000 feet per second or better - the 50-grain 223, the 100-grain 243 and 257 Weatherby, and the 130-grain 270 Winchester. Modern gunwriters, present company excepted, recommend "brush cutters" ahead of yesteryear's "brush busters", the 30-30 and 303 and 35 Remington. Bullets are built for speed and distance, the old-timers argued, and what's good about a bullet that starts slow and flies like a rock, except maybe that it "bucks the brush?" Horse manure.

As for Ken's errant 6mm 100 Nosler, the old guys thought it did everything right; it sliced through 10

inches of deer underside, broke bone and killed the deer—all after losing its speed and shape. Not bad performance from an antelope caliber.

The "new math" brush bullet, like the incomprehensible geometry your kids learn, is a fascinating alternative to a traditional heavyweight brush bullet. It is a complete turnaround, like a dietician saying butter and beer are good for you. Until the 1940s a spitzer bullet was a military bullet. It was prone to "tipping", it caused horrible woulds on impact whether it keyholed or not, and it was not a sportsman's bullet. Forty years later, the attributes which condemned the spitzer—high-velocity, high RPM, high ballistic co-efficient—now make it the *cognoscenti's* choice for brush shooting.

A bullet, the theory goes, is actually a high-speed gyroscope. In flight it spins around its axis at thousands of RPMs, giving it irresistible accuracy and stability. Far from "blowing up on any twig" as often recounted in the day of Jack O'Connor and Elmer Keith, a fast-spinning spitzer that hits brush merely deflects for a nano-second before rotation brings it back on course. The more RPM's the better the brush-bucking probability.

Further, a spitzer with a full length "controlled expansion" jacket is better in brush-shooting than a softpoint with exposed lead, like the 2100 fps roundnose from my 35 Remington pumpkin slinger. Bullets that show lots of soft lead tear on contact with brush and, at their low velocity, virtually plummet to the ground. But bullets with polished copper noses resist nose deformation and redirect themselves. Therefore, light fast premium bullets with heavy jackets—the A-Frames, Bearclaws, and Fail Safes—are the bullets most likely to penetrate a clump of birch in a straight line.

Speaking of famous gunwriters and their experiences, brush bullet believers are quick to quote their heroes. The library in my camp has copies of *Deer Hunting With Dalrymple*, by Byron W. Dalrymple, and the *Book of the Rifle*, by *Outdoor Life* Shooting Editor Jim Carmichel. Dalrymple liked the 243 for whitetails and dismissed the 35 Remington. Other than *GUNDIGEST*, *The Book of the Rifle* has settled the most rifle disputes for us over the years and Carmichel offers a first-rate explanation of what happens to a traditional brush bullet in real brush. In 563 pages on his single subject, rifles, Jim gave the brush bullet the brush-off—just half a page—citing the example of the 444

Bark soup for dinner! Entrance (top) and exit (bottom) of 6mm Nosler 100-grain Partition in a jackpine.

Marlin with its squat 240-grain slug at 2350 fps:

"....The thumb-sized slug with its blunt ice-cream cone nose looks like a brush hunter's dream, but let's take a critical look at the real situation. Since the velocity is low, it is necessary to use a thin jacket in order to insure reliable mushrooming. This is all well and good, and the bullet maker's burden is eased somewhat by the knowledge that hunting shots with the 444 Marlin will seldom exceed 100 yards. The lizard in the stew, however, is that the 444 will most often be used in dense cover where there is some likelihood that the bullet will run into twigs and limbs on its way to the target. But damn it, thin bullet jackets and brush don't go together, especially when the bullet features a full moon nose with lots of exposed lead core. When the bullet hits a finger-thick twig, the exposed leads nags, grabs for an instant. The jacket tears and the bullet becomes misshapen. This is followed by loss of direction and a rapid decay of stability.

....Therefore the best brush buckers are the fast-stepping cartridges loaded with pointed bullets."

Good stuff as far as it goes, but Carmichel knew there was more:

"As a practical matter we're only kidding ourselves with the notion that we can shoot through brush with impunity, if we're equipped with anything less formidable than a 450 No 2 Nitro Express loaded with 480-grain solids."

Byron Dalrymple was one 243 admirer who threw out the baby with the bath water. That is, in knocking the old traditional heavyweight brush-busting bullet, he also trashed the short-range rifles that fired them. He never claimed the 100-grain 243 bullet was a sizzling brush cutter; he thought all bullets deflect to some degree in brush. But he didn't think it made much sense to hunt deer with any gun good for 100 yards:

"The old 35 Remington was a good rifle for short range. It, and the 44 Magnum and a few others have been dubbed 'brush rifle' and touted as such. In my opinion they aren't much as deer rifles. Not when so many better choices are available."

"This whole 'brush bullet' hokum should have been given a quick and unmourned burial years ago. It has almost died out, but it's still kept breathing by a few hunters left who stubbornly cling to the old malarkey about the proper rifle for the East and the proper rifle for the West. I always chuckle to hear this."

"....there's no such thing as eastern and western deer rifles. What I'm getting at is .... the last matter a hunter needs to consider in selecting a deer rifle is the character of the terrain where he'll do most of his hunting."

At this point I'll toss in an opinion. Dalrymple goes one bridge too far. In the brush-bucker debate, it's all-important to separate "brush bullet" from 'brush rifle'. A true timber rifle, woods rifle, saddlegun, or whatever the trade calls them this year, is a joy to handle and deadly quick for the important shot. If the bullets they fire are slow and blunt...so what... it's not about bullets.

Besides, there's always the "tube-feed two-shooter." Credit Layne Simpson for lately making the point that if one wants or needs a softpoint or spitzer boattail in his Model 94 or Marlin 336 to add 50 yards of useful range, the answer is to load just two rounds, one in the chamber and another in the magazine. That way there are no sharp bullet noses resting against the primer of the round in front. And there aren't many aimed third, fourth, or fifth shots in the deep woods.

Brush Bullet No 2 was of course that traditional barrel-shaped heavyweight and it survives in Upper Michigan. I say "survives" because nobody actually buys a new rifle that shoots 170-grain flatpoints at 2200 fps or 190-grain softpoints at 2000 fps, but those who own a 32 Special or a 303 Savage know for sure it'll kill whitetails in the brush. For these hunters, as Dalrymple lamented, it

For the book, Jack did some brush-shooting wherein a 35 Remington (left) beat a 375 H&H. Same result in my Plexiglas shooting.

Carmichael thinks there are no brush bullets until you get to the 450/400 Jeffrey. The two 404s weren't bad — but who cares?

takes a blunt profile, medium velocity, and good "*mementum*" to push through frozen pine boughs. They just wouldn't use anything else.

One 80-year old duffer I know hunts a swamp edge from an old wooden two-holer. Every year I ask him what kind of deer rifle he uses and every year it's the same answer: "I can't think of the name right now but she's a dandy, shoots right through that crud." It's a Remington 141 in 30 Remington.

A hunting uncle uses a 60-year old Model 99A 303 Savage he inherited from his father. A few years ago he shot a deer in his backyard as it rounded the corner of his pole barn. The 190-grain softpoint punched four holes, two in the barn and two in the deer. "Mister", he says, "they put a brush-bucking bullet in that 303 Savage."

Elmer Keith and Jack O'Connor were gunwriters who disagreed a lot in print but did agree about brush bullets. First as young men, then as old men after they changed their minds. Early on, both men recommended heavy roundnose or flatpoint bullets for brush shooting, and this is the stuff O'Connor and Keith fans always remember. O'Connor, more or less summarizing the wisdom of the first four decades of the century, had something to say about brush bullets in the very first GUN DIGEST. From a piece called *"Selecting the Big Game Rifle"*, Jack put this practical spin on it:

"Mr. Average Hunter needs either a heavier bullet of larger diameter or a bullet of higher velocity which, in either case, gives greater shock power to kill or disable whitetails with the typical poorly placed shots in the hams, in the guts, and so on. (Mr. Average)..... is better served with big, round-nosed bullets that will plow through a lot of brush and give a severe wound..."

In *The Big Game Rifle*, published in 1952, Jack described his own brush-bullet experiment, firing hunting bullets through live brush at a full-sized deer sillouette on a sheet of drywall, which helped him form this conclusion:

"..... Shots at whitetails are very often taken when the game is partially obscured by brush and the bullet has to drive through brush on a relatively straight line in order to kill the game. Under those conditions an ultra high velocity bullet is actually a handicap because it is much more apt to be deflected than a heavier, slower moving bullet."

Jack didn't say what type of brush or how thick, but whatever it was, the 35 Remington's 200-grain roundnose at 2200 fps (probably more like 2000 fps like today's factory stuff) hit the drywall deer more often than the 375 H&H Magnum's 300 roundnose at 2500 fps. He surmised that latter's additional velocity was the only explanation.

The bigger tree has two little ones growing under it — which are usually the ones that deflect bullets, or so it seems.

But as the Dean of Gunwriters Jack changed his mind. If I read it once in *Outdoor Life*, I read it a dozen times, he *never* pulled the trigger unless his target, and the path to his target, was clear. He came to feel strongly that the idea in brush shooting is not to hit the damn brush!

Elmer Keith's opinions on brush bullets are some of the most powerful in all gun literature. His "big bullet" advocacy sometimes seemed repetetive but it was never confusing. In books, in his decades of writing for the *American Rifleman* and *Guns and Ammo*, Keith's sermon-like certainty was that in brush shooting a big bullet was good and small one was bad. Chief complaint about light, fast bullets? they "blow up." Chapter One, "Brush and Timber Rifles," *Big Game Rifles and Cartridges*, circa 1936:

"..rifles should be selected that handle cartridges capable of wading through a lot of brush and limbs with a minimum of deflection. The very high velocity rifle has little or no place in dense timber due to the fact it tends to blow up on any small twigs or limbs that may be in line with the game..."

In his expanded 1946 book *Keith's Rifles for Large Game* he amplified as follows, page 163:

"High velocity cartridges are out, as they tend to blow up on intervening brush and also because they seldom give adequate penetration for

Ron Gallman (left) likes his Winchester Model 100 in 308 Winchester. His father, Wellington, prefers a stainless 257 Weatherby, while young Christopher isn't yet sure.

raking shots... I would prefer a good solid frame Model 86 Winchester caliber 45-70/405 with a lightweight 22-inch nickel steel barrel and good sights to any and all 30-caliber bolt action rifles for close range timber shooting on all American species. At times it is absolutely necessary to shoot through some small brush and limbs, and only heavy round or flat-point bullets will do so with any certainty. I have seen high velocity bullets from the 250 Savage, 257 Roberts, and even the 300 Magnum 180-grain open point completely disintegrate on small brush and none of the bullet got through to the game."

But Keith also quit giving this counsel. In 21 years of *"Gun Notes"* columns for *Guns and Ammo*, 1961 through 1982, he hardly mentioned brush shooting. For the October 1973 magazine, an elder statesman now, he reported:

"I have heard many hunters speak of brush guns that will shoot through brush and kill game. In my own experience, and that of many of my friends, the opposite is true. Almost any small limb or brush will deflect or turn even heavy bullets, and high velocity expanding bullets simply blow up in fragments. To be certain, it is best to pick a hole through any brush or limbs that you can get a slug through, or else don't shoot until an opening can be found."

And finally, Brush Bullet No 3 which I call the "Express" Brush Bullet. It is the sneakiest, the most popular, and the one our younger guys voted for.

Generation X likes power and reach for whitetails - seven mags and 30-06s with the biggest, heaviest slugs available. And not just in the county where I hunt. According to the DNR, by far the most popular whitetail combination throughout Upper Michigan is a bolt-action 30-06 and the 180-grain bullet.

Most Upper Michigan deer hunters find out pretty quick that a 44 Magnum 240-grain flatpoint will punch completely through an 8-inch poplar tree and knock down brush on the far side. The same tree will stop a 150-grain seven magnum or 180-grain in 30-06—cold. But the 44 lacks range while the seven has close-in anchoring power plus the trajectory for 250-yard clearcut shooting. The heaviest bullets offered in these calibers shoot "flat enough" on the one hand and offer "brush insurance" on the other. Had my partner used an '06 or even a 308 with 180-roundnose instead of his 6mm he'd have dragged out that six-point... we believe.

Early test results from a 257 Roberts Improved indicated poor brush performance. The sighter made the round hole, the next two Barnes 100-grain X-bullets keyholed.

A Marlin 45-70, aimed where I'm pointing, put three of six rounds in this area below the deer.

This Express idea is more pervasive than you'd imagine. It's for hunters who wouldn't be caught dead carrying a "brush gun" but who still think heavy bullets are the way to go. Two Michigan hunting partners, one with a Browning A-Bolt 7mm-08, the other in a Remington 700 BDL in 7mm Magnum, typify the Express logic. They both handload the old parallel-sided 7x57 Mauser 175-grain softpoint. This drill-rod-shaped slug is only doing 2350 fps in the 7mm-08 but that's the plan, heavy and slow so it won't slide off-line if it hits a maple sapling.

A few years back I hunted with a guy who owned a ten-pound heavy-barrel Ruger 77 25-06, his "all-around rifle" for everything from antelope to black bear. For 120-lb goats at 400 yards he loaded 100-grain Ballistic Tips, but for whitetails in the hardwoods he chose the 117-grain RN Hornady, the only bullet still offered for the 25-35 Winchester Model

Fresh target and Plexiglas are ready for author's 250 Savage, as tested by Tim Bellefleur.

94. He was sure the roundnose busted brush. My experience with this bullet at 2500 fps in a 250 Savage, compared to the 25-35's original 2200, is that it's easy-opening deer dynamite under 200 yards. It is the last brush bullet I'd choose, having the same weakness as a 444 Marlin—a thin jacket and lead dot on top.

So there they were, three different brush bullets in the hopeful hearts of hunters.

Where all this stood me was that nobody had ever *proved* light, fast spitzer bullets deflect in brush and heavy, slow, blunt-nosed bullets plow straight ahead. Or the converse, that today's high-coefficient, high-RPM lightweights cut clean holes through brush and lumbering heavyweights glance or plummet. I hadn't thought much about brush-bucking bullets since I learned to use good binoculars and scopes for close-in shooting, the same as in big country.

Sure, over the years guys have fired bullets through Christmas trees, hedges, buckbrush, wooden dowel rods and "brush" to find out what works, but their results seemed contradictory and sometimes challenged common sense. Like one that had a 243 Winchester whipping a 300 Winchester Magnum. And what *about* Jack O'Connor's 35 Remington outshooting a 375 H&H? How on earth can a bullet with both more mass and velocity lose against one that's lighter and slower in any reasonable comparison?

Of course, the problem's not with the shooter, its the stuff he's shooting

Here's a good look at my "brushpile", clearly showing the path of a 348 bullet through 10 panels of Plexiglas.

into. It's the nature of brush as a test medium.

Brush is random, varies in density, and has holes in it. That's why it's called brush, or scrub, or undergrowth, and not called trees. One bullet hits a limb dead center while the next catches a twig at an angle. There's live green brush, which is limber and stringy, and there's dead stuff which is hard but brittle. A "standard" real-world bullet comparison in brush isn't possible.

I grew up with the brush bullet, and with Eastern/Western Rifle Syndrome. My short-barrel carbine for

the National Forests around Manassas, Virginia, was a buckhorn-sighted Model 94 30-30 and my long-range stalking rifle for cornfields was a 7.65mm Argentine Mauser. Though the bullets were the same caliber and weighed about the same, they were as different as the rifles. It was an accepted fact that the 30-30 170-grain Silvertip flatpoint smashed through spruce limbs while the 7.65 (30-cal) 180-grain spitzer ricocheted.

As a serviceman in the US Army in the 60s, I heard my flatnose brush bullet take a philosophical pounding. Rifle instructors explained that the Army tested bullets in brush prior to introducing the 223 caliber and the 55-grain FMJ bullet for use in jungle warfare. Jungle is brush on steroids. The Army was not advocating the small sharp bullet as a brush penetrator, but it knew the 7.62 NATO/308, and everything else short of the 50 BMG, was no damn good in bamboo either.

Now 30 years later I'm still doing the "East/West" routine but it has nothing to do with brush shooting. At home in the Upper Penninsula I switch back and forth between a 257 Roberts/250 Savage and my 35 Remington Marlin. When I travel west for elk or mule deer, the long range rifle is either a 280 Remington or 35 Whelen and the timber rifle is a 348 with 200-grain flatpoints or a 45-70. Byron Dalrymple's opinions aside, a slab-sided hammer rifle has handling advantages in thick cover, and over the short course the big bullet works best because it doesn't rely on expansion to make a serious hole. Whether or not it bucks brush is of no consequence.

Erect posture helps Lucas roll with the recoil from the 45-70 Marlin.

Table 1:

CARTRIDGE	BULLET	VELOCITY (H-Handload)	Center Hits Out Of 6 Rounds Fired
22 RF	40 gr JSP	1070	0
222 Remington	50 gr SPCL	3090 H	0
243 Remington	100 gr NP	2980 H	1
6mm Remington	100 gr PSP	3100	1
250 Savage	100 gr ST	2820	1
257 Robert Improved	100 gr X	3230 H	0
264 Winchester Magnum	140 gr PSP	3130	1
270 Winchester	130 gr X	3030 H	1
280 Remington	140 gr TB	3000	3
	150 gr NPT	2890	2
	162 gr BST	2825	1
	150 gr NH-M	2850	2
	160 gr FS	2840	3
7x57mm Mauser	175 gr RN Speer	2395 H	2
7mm Remington Magnum	150 gr BT Sierra	3100 H	2
	175 gr RN Speer	2740 H	3
30-06 Springfield	150 gr SP Sierra	2880 H	2
	180 gr SPCL	2700	3
308 Winchester	180 gr ST	2590 H	1
300 Savage	180 gr SPCL	2350	3
30-30 Winchester	170 gr ST	2200	2
348 Winchester	200 gr FP Speer	2480 H	3
35 Remington	200 gr SPCL	2050 H	3
35 Whelen (Imp)	225 gr SA-F	2700 H	4
375 H&H Magnum	270 gr SP Horn	2685 H	1
404 Jeffrey	400 gr SP RWS	2280	5
44 Magnum	420 gr JSP Speer	1760 H	1
45-70 Government	400 gr SPCL	1330	3

NP - Nosler Partition **SPCL** - Soft Point Corelokt
PSP - Power Soft Point **ST** - Silver Tip
X - Barnes X **TB** - Trophy Bonded Bearclaw
BST - Ballistic Silver Tip **NH-M** - Norma H-Mantle
FS - Failsafe **BT** - Soft Point Boat Tail
RN - Round Nose **FP** - Flat Point **SA-F** - Swift A-Frame

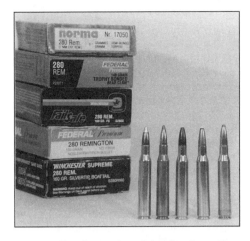

The 280 Remington brush load test candidates, which did not fare well.

There are a half-dozen reasons why the brush bullet won't go away. We can lay some of it off on Generation X rediscovering bullets the Baby Boomers discarded. And there's always a strong current of nostalgia running through the gun business - Cowboy Rifles, and Colt SA clones, and "shooting a deer with grandaddy's gun." Lately there are nifty new rifles from Ruger and Marlin that fire old bullets, the 77/44 bolt-action and the 45-70 Guide Rifle. But that's not why we're still chewing this same old piece of shoe leather.

Despite laser range-finders, infrared heat scanners and beanfield rifles, most of us shoot our annual whitetailed buck at about the same distance as our great grandfathers, well under 100 yards. We like to sneak, skulk, sit or stand to get eyeballing-close to our quarry, where most any good bullet will work now as it did then. In a brushy world it is perfectly natural to wish for a bullet that will fly through a little ground clutter and hold course. But is it wishful thinking, right up there with "cowboys don't lie and heroes don't die?"

Unable to forget my partner's 6mm 100-grain Nosler and wolf-eaten buck, I borrowed a 243 and tried to create a bullet blow-up on a 4-inch jackpine. As a comparison I brought along my 250 Savage and, on a whim, a 12 gauge shotgun and one lead slug. The 100-grain 243 and 250 bullets, both Noslers, zipped right through that tree and kicked up snow on the far side; the 12 gauge slug stayed in the tree! Where the bullets exited the tree there were golfball-sized baldspots in the bark which, as they say in the UP, "jumped out like a crow in a pan of milk."

So I thought I'd better test some bullets in brush myself, with two differences: 1) Every bullet should somehow encounter the same resistance, with nothing random about it; 2) I wanted to see my aimpoint, not just fire blindly. My brush should have a bullseye or a dot so I could see the hits and measure the misses. I had an idea to try 0.10 gauge clear plexiglass, window safety replacement glass, as "brush". Brittle yet somewhat limber, clear plexiglass had some of the properties of real brush.

The "brushpile" was made from plywood strips and 2x2s and ended up looking like a bullet box. I sawed grooves in the frame to hold spaced 12x12 panels tight, as many as 12 at a time if needed, some at 30 degree right and left angles and some dead on. Placing the 5-foot deep box on blocks, I paced back 40 yards and turned to see if I could see through the plexiglass, and sure enough, I could.

Since I was comparing bullets "post-impact", the target size and distance had to be realistic. Like Jack O'Connor, I drew full-sized deer silhouettes on cardboard and put a two-inch aiming point behind the shoulder. The cardboard deer was braced into a frame exactly 15 feet from the brushpile. A bullet that could smash through layers of brush and hit a target five yards back was indeed a brush bullet. With this set up, all Summer and Fall, catch as catch can, my friends and I shot large and small bullets, spitzers and blunts, premiums and blue collars.

To give you an idea of the resistance of plexiglass, a standard velocity 40-grain 22 JSP fired from a 24-inch rifle barrel slipped through a single panel without deflection, and it went through two panels with less than an inch deflection 15 feet beyond. Through three of our fiberglass "twigs," the 22 bullet dropped 4-6

inches low and left spider-shaped holes in the paper deer. Four panels pulled 22s clean off the silhouette.

We fired centerfire cartridges through four panels, but that proved too easy. Everything from a 100-grain 257 Roberts to a 405-grain 45-70 went through on course, and we had our first problem: I could keep adding panels, jam 'em in there until an elephant gun couldn't crash through, but then what conclusions could be drawn? There had to be a stopping point, which introduced subjectivity. I settled on my personal infamous brush buster, a 200-grain roundnose from a 35 Remington, as a baseline.

Going against 10 panels a 35 Remington became a 50% killer. The fiberglass could only take two shots before all panels had to be replaced. Of six 200-grain Corelokts blasted through the box only three made "center hits" in an 8-inch vital zone around the aimpoint. One Corelokt sprayed wide left, one dipped low and one missed everything. There were no keyholes but all five hits were dime-sized, so the bullets had taken a lot of punishment.

Therefore, in a good timber rifle, a 35 Remington is a hard-hitting caliber, but its' bullets aren't much in brush.

Good intentions to simply chart cartridges side-by side with the 35 Remington almost got out of hand. Questions popped up that were worthwhile—but one led to another. Should we try to recover the badly distorted bullets from the sand backstop? Should we separate our "blow-up's" from our "glances"? Should we angle the panels in a single direction to "influence a glance" and then mea-

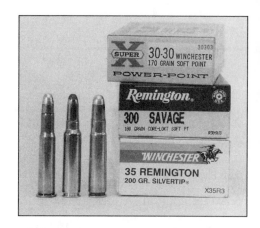

Three traditional brush loads delivered consistent results — they all failed to hit the target enough times.

sure that? How about tracking bullets by their RPM rates? Should the premium bullets be a separate test?

In the end, I was reminded this was not a forensic study and only a dozen calibers were needed. What mattered was hits on target and leave the rest to the number-crunchers. Once we got started shooting it was hard to stop, it wasn't science but it sure was a hoot. The calibers, bullets, and hits are all on the chart.

When nobody was looking, I had one brief bout of "wishful thinking," firing 280 Remingtons through the brushpile. The 280 is my all-around favorite cartridge and I wondered if one weight or style of bullet would test superior to the others. Of the two Federal Premium loads I had, the 140-grain Bearclaw and 150 Nosler bullets combined for 5 center hits out of 12 shots fired. The Norma 150-grain H-Mantle bullet keyholed four of six times and scored two hits, the 162-grain Silvertip Boattail one, and the 160-grain Failsafe three while creating a decent 8-inch group low and right.

So take your pick, but don't take your chances in brush. A 35 Remington and a 30-06 are equal failures. There is no magic in a 44 Magnum. Solid-copper bullets keyholed everytime and looked like bent solids out of a dead Cape buffalo. In a sleeting Lake Superior wind I fired the 375 H&H— and it's a lousy brush caliber as Jack O'Connor said it was. The 404 Jeffrey makes a great brush cartridge as Jim Carmichel suggested, but who cares? If the leafy crud you shoot into is thick enough to deflect a 243, it's going to do the same for the 270, or a 280. The 405-grain flatnose 45-70 is a pretty good grouper, maybe if..... nah, I'm not leaving that door open even a crack.

I'll just keep the 35 Remington. There are no brush bullets, only brush rifles, and it's a brush rifle. ●

Early on, both Keith and O'Connor recommended big heavy bullets in brush. Older, they changed their minds.

TROPICAL CARABINAS

by Carlos Schmidt

THAT A SHORT, light, handy rifle is a mighty useful tool there can be no doubt. Something that points quickly, shoots an adequate weight bullet with enough accuracy to hit what it is aimed at is what I consider a proper *tropical carabina*. For years I have tried different rifles, mostly in the tropical forest and jungles of Nicaragua, where a shot over 50 yards is an exception. Unfortunately, probably due to age, I cannot make up my mind about which rifle, or carabina, is the best. But I have narrowed the field to the three rifles I now use.

A dozen or so years ago I was offered a beat-up Czech VZ-24 Mauser in 8mm. Since the price was 'zero' I accepted the rifle. Someone had shot it with an obstruction in the barrel, resulting in a bulge about six inches behind the muzzle. The bore was rotted out from corrosive ammunition, and the military stock had been "sporterized" by a less-than-expert woodworker. It had a 10-pound trigger pull. Worst of all, there was no 8mm ammunition to be found anywhere in Nicaragua. On the plus side, I had a genuine VZ-24 action in decent shape – except for some surface rust – and therefore, with a bit of ingenuity, a base for building a powerful jungle carabina.

Some years later I ran across a new Israeli barrel for the VZ 24 chambered for the 7.62mm NATO/308 Winchester. In the early stages of the Contra War, the guerrillas were given VZ 24 rifles rebarreled to 7.62mm NATO – maybe that is where that new barrel came from. In any event, the rebarreling changed the rifle completely. As a result of informal military assistance, from many nations to both sides of that war, that included many G3s and FALs, there still is a considerable amount of 7.62mm

The distillation of years of experience and experiment, these are the three rifles author Schmidt considers *tropical carabinas*: Rossi Model 92, "*Afrikaaner*" VZ24 Mauser and the Mosin Nagant 1944 carbine.

Travel through vast tropical forests is best done with an experienced mountain guide; here, mine looks out over the jungle-covered mountains of the Bosawas National Forest Reserve which, at some 8,000 square kilometers, approaches the size of El Salvador.

ammo floating around; surprisingly, mostly tracer ammunition. The last task to be addressed was the weather-proofing of the rifle. I did not do much with the stock as it still oozed cosmoline whenever exposed to direct sunlight.

The metal was a different story. Though I had the action blued when I rebarreled the rifle, the metal parts started to rust immediately. The solution was to boil the action and then apply Brownell's Teflon spray. A friendly hotel owner friend of mine agreed to let me do a little "cooking" in his kitchen. I told him I was going to prepare something exotic. The barreled action fit nicely into his large rice cooker where all the grease was boiled off. It also fit nicely into his industrial-size chicken roaster. When he saw the barreled action come out of the chicken roaster, he just smiled.

I made three more additions. I replaced the military trigger with an adjustable trigger which reduced the trigger pull to the three-pound class. I then threw away the stamped arctic trigger guard, replaced it with an original one and added Gibbs Rifle Company's removable clip. Reassembled, the VZ 24 looks like it has a glass-bead finish and does not rust anymore.

As for accuracy I found that, by pulling the tracer bullets from the old Remington ammunition and replacing them with 150-grain Hornady spitzers, on most days I could shoot one-inch groups at 50 meters using the military iron sights, my progressive tri-focals notwithstanding.

Lastly, I decided to put a light-gathering scope on the rifle as the jungle can be a very shady, almost dark place. The Simmons Pro 50 that I scrounged proved up to the task. Mounting the scope was more of a challenge as there is no one in Nicaragua that will bend the bolt correctly or drill and tap the receiver for top mounts. I tried one of the advertised mounts that clamps onto the front

and back receiver rings and leaves no permanent change, except the need to relieve the stock a bit for the bottom of the receiver clamps. Elegant and svelt this mounting system is not; but it does not lose its zero and it does allow me to hunt in the jungle where sometimes the canopy makes it too dark to see my iron sights.

When I finally found a woodworker, an old carpenter friend of mine, to

Petunia carries author Schmidt across yet another river, the Bocay, into the Bosawas National Reserve. The Rossi Model 92 is in a scabbard under the author's left leg, where it should be. Since there are no roads, jungle travel is by dugout canoe, by foot – or on the back of a mule. Schmidt much prefers the latter, reporting Petunia's ride "as smooth as that of a Cadillac."

make a few changes to the stock, the rifle took on an appearance much like those Mausers marketed in Africa after World War I. The rifle points well and, with its easy trigger pull, makes a fine deer rifle. The capabilities of the 7.62mmNATO/308 Winchester round need little introduction and certainly allow that rifle to kill deer much farther than I will shoot at one. On the deer I have shot with it, using the 150-grain Hornady spire point, no searching was necessary after I pulled the trigger as the animals didn't travel very far after being hit by the Hornady bullet. I am mighty satisfied with that Czech Mauser and find it handy as a general-use rifle just as settlers of post-World War I Africa must have found many of the converted Mausers that Finn Aagard and Ross Seyfried write about so passionately. Half-sporterized, it even looks the part of an *Africanized* Mauser, circa 1924. It is some rifle.

One day, the manager of the finest shooting range in Nicaragua and major promotor of organized shooting in Nicaragua, Salvador Luna, and the General, watching me work on the VZ 24 Mauser, suggested I try the Moisin Nagant carbine and that I might be surprised by its power and accuracy. Moreover, in the interests of science, the General offered to assign me two Moisin Nagants and a sufficient amount of ammunition to use to write this article. I decided to take the General's suggestion and soon had two Moisin Nagants, Model 1944, caliber 7.52mmx54R – and a couple of hundred rounds of ammunition.

The General, Major General Roberto Calderón, Inspector General and General number three of the Army of Nicaragua, is an old shooting acquaintance. A first-rate shot in both Bianchi Cup and IPSC competition, he has always had the honor of bettering my scores by enough points to put me several places behind him in organized shoots. No matter, he is the consummate gentleman, much like some of the characters that Skeeter Skelton and Sheriff Jim Wilson have written about on the borderlands of Texas and Mexico. With General Calderón a smile, a verbal agreement and a handshake have the same authority as an army division.

The General gained his military experience by spending several years in the mountains fighting the Somoza regime. I think he still has a damaged thumbnail from loading his old Garand in haste during those years. Afterward, his organizational and administrative skills allowed him to rapidly rise in the Army to his present position. Hence, I did not think he would have too much trouble obtaining the rifles he offered.

Both Mosin Nagant rifles were build during World War II. One had been rebuilt and reblued and was in 'new' condition. The other showed some slight darkening of the bore, but otherwise was in the same, almost new, condition. Both showed the usual stacking dents and scratches. Both were still covered with cosmoline. The ammunition was the steel casing washed in copper variety.

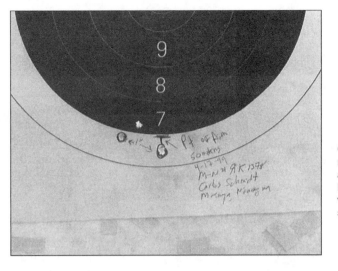

Once the front sight was moved and the rear sight adjusted properly, the Mosin Nagant carbine would reliably deliver this sort of group at fifty meters.

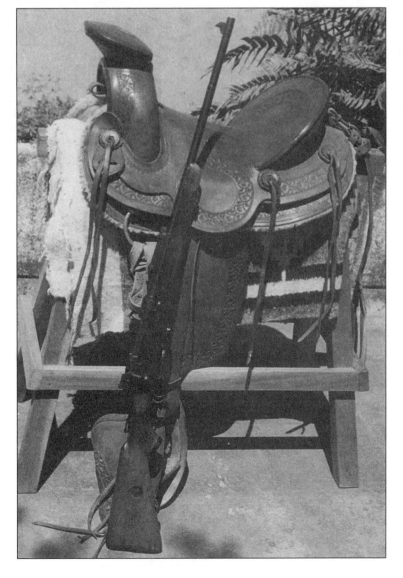

The first of the line, evolving over the years, is this rebarreled and generally refurbished Mauser. Here it rests, without scope, against author's old Sosa Brothers saddle.

The true *tropical carabina* comes naturally to the shoulder for offhand shooting, as this Mosin Nagant does for General Calderón.

meters. When I then sat down to carefully shoot the rifle for group with the military ammo, I got quite a surprise: at 50 meters and with the military sights it was no big deal to shoot consistent one-inch groups. At 100 meters most three-shot groups went into two inches. I shot three groups in a row at 50 meters – and quit shooting. Obviously whoever re-built that rifle in 1944 knew what they were doing.

A good rifle is a joy to an experienced marksman. General Roberto Calderón likes what he feels in the Mosin Nagant carbine.

The first trip to the range held some surprises. After a few rounds it was clear the ammunition was loaded to full power. The General's new Toyota LandCruiser II was parked 30 yards from the firing line. The first shot set off the burglar alarm, testifying to the considerable muzzle blast of the Moisin carbine. The second characteristic of the Moisin is that, with its permanently-attached bayonet on the right side of the barrel, it shot 18 inches to the left at 100 yards. With the supplied ammunition, and with the rear sight setting adjusted to its lowest setting, the carbine also shot about a foot low at the same distance. Clearly something had to be done.

The armorers who put together the rifle at Tula had marked the front sight ramp with a central stamp that gave me a reference point to use to move the front sight dovetailed into the front sight base. With a brass hammer and brass punch, sufficient ammunition – and a bit of luck – I moved the point of impact to the center of point of aim. I placed the sight ramp on 400 meters and the carbine was sighted in for 100

I tried the other rifle and the results were the same – better accuracy than I had any right to expect from such a crude-looking rifle. What is obvious from the outside is that the barrel bands are tightly clamped around the stock and handguard. The laminated stock is heavy, and not very well inletted around the action, but holds the barrel very tightly between the stock and handguard.

I did not disassemble either of the Moisin carbines as the barrel bands are clamped on tightly and I decided to leave them alone. So what is under the handguard is still the secret of the armorers who rebuilt those carbines 54 years ago. It would not surprise me to find shims under the barrel to dampen its vibrations, for example. But, for whatever reason, both rifles shoot as well as a $600 new factory bolt-action rifle.

Mechanically, obvious care was taken machining parts, such as the bolt, where tolerances had to be strictly maintained; in other areas the rifle is put together a bit crudely. But it is also true that the rifle is just about indestructible. It weighs a hefty 8 pounds and the stock is at least as strong as the Garand stock. I have little doubt that should my favorite mule, Petunia, a big jack of 1200 pounds, decide to dust off and roll over, as horses and mules are wont to do, with the Moisin strapped to the saddle in its scabbard, the only effect on the Moisin Nagant would be that the carbine would get dusty. With almost any other rifle, including the other two noted in this article, the effect would be complete disaster.

Part of the fine accuracy of the Moisin must be attributed to the ammunition. I never did slug the bore of either rifle but I did pull the bullets from several rounds. The casings are headstamped *80* and *96*. The bullets averaged 147.1 grains and are 1.27-inches long. More importantly, they measure a full 0.313-inches in diameter. The powder charge averaged 48.6 grains of some extruded powder, resembling 4350. Out to 400 meters it was not very difficult to hit a man-sized or deer-sized figure. To date I have only killed one fox with the Moisin; shot in the chest, it did not suffer long.

After getting used to the Mannlicher-type bolt action and loading the magazine, the Moisin carbine is actually quite handy, if a bit heavy. It does have two drawbacks: a heavy trigger pull and a safety that is slow both to set and to release. But these qualities of the Moisin can be dealt after a bit of practice.

In sum, the Moisin Nagant Model 1944 carbine must rate as one of the ruggedest bolt-action rifles ever made. It is short, powerful and more accurate than anyone would ever think. Its bolt works smoothly and, for a knockabout rifle, it probably has no peer. It will accompany me on my next mining trip to the northern mountains. I will not be undergunned.

The first deer rifle I used as a boy was a lever action, a Savage Model 99 in 358 Winchester. It shot 250-grain bullets best and so I shot many deer and some elk with the Hornady 250-grain roundnose. When I weighed 128 pounds, dripping wet, the recoil of that six-pound Model 99 Featherweight was no joke, but nothing ever escaped once I pulled the trigger and I came to have the greatest affection for the lever-action rifle. Now my game is much smaller, 10-30 pounds, and the occasional tropical turkey and rabbit I run into; usually while doing something other than hunting.

A light lever action, that kills but does not tear up the meat, is particularly useful when travelling in a dugout canoe and generally knocking about. I picked a replica of the Winchester M 92, made by Rossi, in 44 Magnum, and found it a most handy rifle. As to its caliber, a wrong assumption made by many people is that the 44 Magnum must always be shot with magnum-powered loads. Nothing could be farther from the truth. When I first obtained the Rossi I put a Williams peep sight on it, lightened the trigger pull and baked on a coat of teflon in the same kitchen where I cooked the VZ 24 Mauser. I admit I tried it with my magnum load of 22.9 grains of Bulgarian Ball powder (which burns like H110) and a 240-grain softpoint bullet. It shot amazingly well, grouping into that mythical inch at 50 yards. On small game it was worse than useless; in one instance, blowing a large (*and succulent*) iguana in two. Clearly something had to be done.

As the late Francis Sell noted in several of his articles, an accurate, iron-sighted light lever-action rifle of medium power is a useful tool, with much more application than a high-powered rifle that fires only one or two shots a year. I

started with cast bullets, and soon found the Lyman #429215, weighing about 215 grains cast medium-hard and sized 0.430-inch, to be a good bullet that worked through the action of the Rossi and shot into the mythical one inch at 50 yards with 10.5 grains of DuPont 4756. Velocity? Probably about 1100-1200 fps.

Sighted in at 50 yards, it takes a little hold-over past 100 yard to hit something. But, used on game, it destroyed no meat and punched a 44-caliber hole though anything it hit. With rabbits, the *pizote* (a racoon-like animal with a long, movable nose), and even the *thicket tinamou* (a native gamebird about the size of the ruffed grouse and related to the ostrich), the animal was anchored with the first shot, and no meat wasted. Actually, what I developed nearly duplicates the old factory load for the 44-40 Winchester, but utilizing smokeless powder and a modern brass casing, that of the 44 Magnum. With this load, case life is indefinite; something not true with the 44-40.

I took this rifle, in a scabbard strapped to my saddle, to the edge of the huge National Reserve Bosawás in northern Nicaragua on the Honduran border last May. On my favorite mule, Petunia, the weight

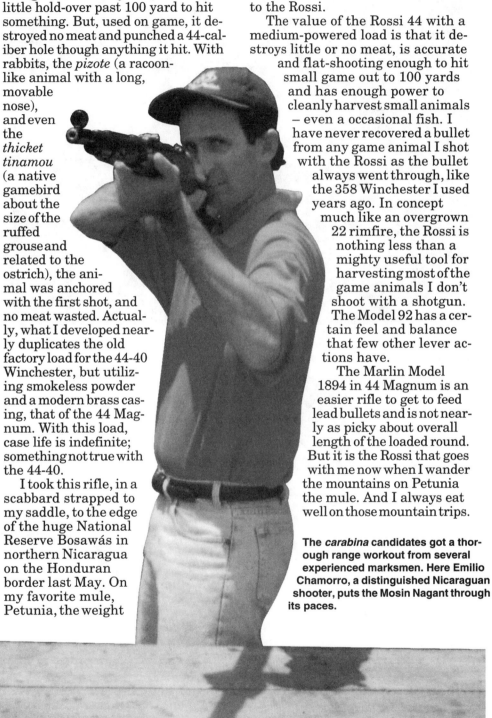

of the Rossi was of no consequence and I had a good ride and a good hunt with the Rossi, using lead bullets. I even tried "barking" some of the tropical fish called the *guapote*, which weigh a couple of pounds and resemble the largemouth bass in appearance and walleye pike in flavor. I spent one night frying fish by the side of an unnamed stream, thanks to the Rossi.

The value of the Rossi 44 with a medium-powered load is that it destroys little or no meat, is accurate and flat-shooting enough to hit small game out to 100 yards and has enough power to cleanly harvest small animals – even a occasional fish. I have never recovered a bullet from any game animal I shot with the Rossi as the bullet always went through, like the 358 Winchester I used years ago. In concept much like an overgrown 22 rimfire, the Rossi is nothing less than a mighty useful tool for harvesting most of the game animals I don't shoot with a shotgun. The Model 92 has a certain feel and balance that few other lever actions have.

The Marlin Model 1894 in 44 Magnum is an easier rifle to get to feed lead bullets and is not nearly as picky about overall length of the loaded round. But it is the Rossi that goes with me now when I wander the mountains on Petunia the mule. And I always eat well on those mountain trips.

The *carabina* candidates got a thorough range workout from several experienced marksmen. Here Emilio Chamorro, a distinguished Nicaraguan shooter, puts the Mosin Nagant through its paces.

The Rossi Model 92 wins yet another admirer, resting lightly in the hands of archaeologist Edgard Guerrero as he prepares for his jungle travel.

Yet another noted Nicaraguan shooter, Salvador Luna, fired both the Rossi M92 and the Mosin Nagant.

I have not tried this 44 load on the Central American caiman, the bad-tempered alligator-type animal still common in some locales, that frequents the calm waters below the rapids on many large rivers. Hunting the caiman is permitted, mostly for the hides. I have had the opportunity on several occasions to shoot one, but I have just never pulled the trigger even though the meat in the tail is first-rate. After many years I still get a thrill out of seeing a large caiman sunning itself by the edge of a river, knowing that this is the real jungle and not Disneyworld. Some day if I get too close to one in a swamped dugout canoe I will find out if the bullet will penetrate a caiman's skull. It probably will. But I can wait until that day comes.

In the meantime, I sometimes harvest almost as much meat with the Rossi as I do with my Brno double barrel, a sidelock ejector model made during the bad old days of the Iron Curtain, in large part due to the very fine Central American upland game hunting for dove, spot-bellied bobwhite quail and clouds of migratory teal. But there is no question, a centerfire lever-action rifle of medium power is a useful tool all out of proportion with the treatment such an arm gets in the sporting journals. And the Rossi 44 Magnum firing a 215-grain lead bullet at 1200 fps is as useful as any such medium-powered centerfire lever-action rifle, bar none.

Which rifle is my favorite? Hard to say, as I tend to think of each rifle as a tool with a specific use. But I can say this: for rough usage packing into the old Spanish mines close by the Honduran border where everything is done from the back of a mule, the Moisin Nagant has no peer and it shoots as well as the other two. The VZ 24 makes an attractive, almost elegant rifle to use to hunt deer in western Nicaragua. But the Rossi with lead bullets goes almost everywhere with me, except mining. I harvest more game with the Rossi than I ever have with any other rifle, with the exception of the big boomers I used to use for elk. Perhaps, in the end, it is habit; I started hunting deer with a lever-action rifle at the tender age of 14 and I shall continue to use lever actions as my first choice for as long as I care to hunt.

Life With Lil' Lightning

by Norm Nelson

Although not a sales success, the Savage Model 170 slide-action rifle became the author's favorite timber rifle – after a few carefully considered changes.

FOR 58 YEARS I've hunted forests east and west for whitetails, blacktails and mule deer. Of the 20 rifles I've used (six lever guns, ten bolt actions, two slide actions, and two autoloaders), which one have I found best for woodland deer hunting?

Answer – the little-known Savage 170 slide-action in 30-30 Winchester – basically a Savage-Stevens pump shotgun action with a 22-inch barrel and a tubular magazine. It has these important timber hunting characteristics: (1) fairly light and compact; (2) fast-handling for that vital first shot; (3) quick and non-distractive in repeat shots; (4) reliable in operation; (5) a sighting system useable in any weather and under adverse light conditions; (6) holding zero despite changes in weather. Lots of rifles are satisfactory for open country. But a really good one

▲ **Lil' Lightning, timber rifle.**

for forest deer (the most common quarry of U.S. big-game hunters) should have the above features for reasons cited later. Unless also to be used on elk or moose, a timber deer rifle need not be a ballistic barn-burner.

Unlike the century-long production lives of classic deer rifles like the Winchester and Savage lever guns, the Savage Model 170 was made only for 11 years: 1970-81.

Why did it flop? First, the Model 170 failed to make the grade at the keyboards of gun writers, most of whom were obsessed with bolt-action rifles. So their readers often assume non-bolt action big-game rifles are either junk or playthings for nostalgia nuts. Second, Savage Arms in the 70s was not a marketing fireball. They promised to add the 35 Remington chambering to the Model 170 line, yet I'm told the 35 Remington option never appeared. The company tried to jump-start Model 170 sales by adding an 18 1/2-inch-barreled carbine in 1974. But that didn't save the baby either.

A short snippet in GUN DIGEST years ago reported that Savage planned to also chamber the Model 170 in the unsung but excellent 358 Winchester. That, too, was still-born. One wonders how many luncheon martinis made the sales folks clean forget the

little problem of spitzer bullets in tubular magazines! But maybe they had in mind a clip version that was later axed by the cost accountants.

Despite missing fire at the sales counter, the Model 170 scores in the X-ring as a forest deer rifle. At only 6-3/4 pounds (a pound under modern Remington pump rifles), it's user-friendly in the thick woods and brush so beloved by bucks of all three species. That's where heavier, longer rifles are simply not as functional. I've found the Model 170 is very quick at what old-timers called *pointing out* and what the modern military calls *target acquisition*. Aided by a handy tang safety, this means fast first-shot capability, a real plus in timber snap-shooting.

The standard 170 (but not the carbine version) was made with a modestly raised stock comb good for scope use. This is a virtue forgotten in too many modern throwbacks to the low-comb "classic stock" offered today by some gunmakers

In forest deer hunting, fast, well-aimed repeat fire is often where the rubber meets the road. The speed demons are autoloaders and slide-actions. Lever guns come in third. That leaves the vaunted bolt action circling the drain. The late, great Col. Charley Askins (who loved bolt guns for certain work) admitted "The fact is that (the turnbolt action) is by far the slowest of the lot .... only a single shot is more molasses-slow." Of course the

On stand. Author Nelson and, in the crook of his arm, Lil' Lightning.

autoloader is fastest, but a pump gun is almost as quick and theoretically has an edge in reliability, particularly with handloads. Nailing deer back in the pines and puckerbrush is too chancy a sport to blow opportunities because a gun jams.

Here's a rarely discussed but important factor. In repeat fire, both pump guns and autoloaders also have the great advantage of minimal distraction of the shooter. This leaves him free to better "process the data" on where that bounding buck is going and to develop a correct sight picture for the next shot. Don't underestimate the value of concentrating on your aim and the game, not on the seven (count them yourself) distinct hand operations which the clumsy turnbolt action demands. (And for efficient fire control, the wrong hand at that.)

The Model 170 can be surprisingly accurate. Gun guru Jim Carmichael,

in his definitive *Book Of The Rifle*, describes extensive accuracy tests of two dozen non-bolt-action big-game rifles (pumps, autoloaders, lever guns) with 20 five-shot groups per gun and factory ammo. All did well. The best, Big Jim found, was a Savage 170 that ran off with the bone by producing two groups under an inch and averaging under two inches for all 20 groups. He added, "How many bolt-action big-game rifles have you tried that will do that?" (It's hilarious that Jim's original report in *Outdoor Life* on non-bolt action accuracy drew sacks of hate mail from hysterical bolt action devotees! Someone should write a book on "Religious Fervor In The Shooting Sports.")

With handloads, my Model 170 will do that well or a tad better. But tight groups from a benchrest are irrelevant at timber hunting's close ranges. Hairsplitting accuracy (supposedly the great alibi for enduring bolt action clumsiness) has been absurdly over-

valued in recent decades. Truth is, accuracy of two and three minutes of angle will pile up big game regularly. If you have the 1983 GUN DIGEST on hand, look up ballistic/statistic expert David Leestma's landmark article, *"Computers Look At Rifle Accuracy For You."* He reveals that if you average an 8-inch, 5-shot group at 200 yards (4 minutes-of-angle), your chances "....of hitting a 10-inch diameter 'kill zone' in a deer are better than 99 out of 100 at 100 yards, a hefty 83 out of 100 at 200 yards." For perspective, a Minnesota study showed average deer-killing range in brushy northern forests to be about 40 yards. Leestma added that if you are a bad shot from a field position (which in timber is typically offhand), an accurate rifle won't help you. And if you are an average shot who rarely practices and lacks ambition to improve your shooting, a 3 to 5 minute-of-angle rifle is about all you need. To put it bluntly, MOA accuracy in forest deer shooting is like chrome trim on an all-terrain vehicle. It may warm your heart but adds nothing to practical performance.

My secondhand Savage 170, a Father's Day gift from my firstborn hunting partner, triggered a labor of love in customizing it. First, factory finish was stripped from buttstock and forend. Next, the pistol grip was slenderized (better for a gloved hand). Then came 20-line checkering and a carved maple leaf pattern (for better wet weather grasp) hugging the grip's contours.

The stock's walnut grain was pleasingly enhanced with selective staining plus LP torch-flaming, both done as porcupines copulate—delicately. Torching the forearm revealed so much previously invisible wood figure that I ruled out checkering the underside. Fine wood figure is hard to come by these days, and mutilating it with

This woodsman's rifle now has a trap buttplate which holds two cartridges, waterproofed matches, fluorescent tape and spare compass. Just in case.

Customizing of the Savage slide-action woods rifle included jeweling the bolt, plus combined checkering and carving of the slimmed stock wrist. Worn anodizing was removed from the aluminum trigger guard, resulting in a pleasing silver matte finish. Scope is a Nikon 2-7x.

Now for the skeleton in the Savage 170's closet. The forearms rattle, a no-no in the woods. I simply carry mine draped in the crook of my elbow to keep it quiet. Savage later re-engineered the rifle with a simple T-bar and spring that eliminated the rattling. One of these days I'll so modify mine.

checkering is not to be done – at least, not by me. I disliked the forend finger grooves but decided they'd look better if checkered, which they did. Final stock finish was with many rubbed-down coats of Linspeed for a soft gloss.

This is a woodsman's rifle. For those 'bad hair' days in the far-back boonies, a trap buttplate (from an old Mossberg 22 rimfire) holds two extra cartridges, moisture-proof matches, spare compass and kill site marking ribbon. The trapdoor's inside is sandpaper-lined for match-striking when the world is wet.

Metal work was minimal. Pending future hot-bluing, cold blue touch-up was good enough for now. Worn black anodizing on the trigger guard was polished off, and the bare aluminum given a matte finish. I polished the bolt prior to damascening, not just for looks but to help hold a protective oil film.

A fine rifle, which my Savage Model 170 had now become, deserves a fine scope. A 2-7X Nikon does the honors. Weaver top mounts (also given a silver matte finish to match the trigger guard) are sturdy, light and quickly detachable—which permits iron sight use when a wet snowstorm puts even a good scope out of business. Safety-lock QD swivels (Michael's of Oregon) anchor a stout sling.

A fellow gun nut looked at my refurbished Model 170 and sighed, "All that work, and you still have only a 30-30." I shot back, "And how many tens of millions of deer have 30-30s hung on American meat poles?" In any event, I'm handloading this 30-30 to 300 Savage performance levels, with no high pressure problems. The real limitation on 30-30 factory ammo pressure is not so much aged lever guns' strength, but the fact that typical toggle-joint lever actions

The Savage 170 pump 30-30, here gone huntin' with author's son Peter, is an excellent rifle for hunting typically dense forest and brush hideaways so favored by buck deer.

don't have enough extractive *pizzazz*. Hence they must be loaded to low pressures – or have empties driven out with a cleaning rod. But the Model 170's wedged-up breech locking stores energy that is abruptly released by working the action. This provides good primary case extraction, missing from those toggle-joint lever guns.

In today's liability climate, I won't reveal my souped-up 30-30 handload data. I will say that my favorite load – only for the Model 170, mind you – is with 130-grain flat-nose Speers at 2700 fps. This makes a credible 200 yard deer load, still retaining well over 1,000 foot-pounds of *buck tranquilizer*. But only twice in my life have I gotten that long a shot at timber country deer, east or west.

That minor glitch notwithstanding, the Savage 170 has many things going for it in addition to fast follow-up shots. One case history (of several) – caught off guard when a western whitetail buck rocketed out of concealment, I missed my first shot. As always, I wasn't conscious of working the slide action – that's pure reflex action, and a fast one. He leaped for thick conifer cover. The second shot nailed him while airborne, a fraction of a second short of vanishing.

After field-dressing the buck, I hiked out to the road, looking for my son to help drag it. Glancing at my blood-stained hands, Peter grinned and said, "When I heard a rifle go *blam-blam* real fast, I knew darned well it had to be you, Lil' Lightning, and a dead deer." ●

"SOMETIMES SECOND PLACE WINS"

by Roderick T. Halvorsen

THE INTRODUCTION OF the Sako 75 ushered in a new era for the Finnish arms maker. No longer would that great company be producing a Mauser-inspired bolt action for big game calibers.

The Series 90 (S491, M591, L691) and the AI, AII and AV actions helped to build Sako's well-earned reputation. While no longer produced, the rifles built around these actions exist in quantity on the used market and indeed some may still be found new-in-the-box. They are not to be ignored, and deserve a place with the Mauser 98, pre-64 Winchester Model 70, and Remington 700 actions for reliability and accuracy. The following article tells why.

It was a thing of beauty. The stock was well-figured, oil-finished walnut. Overall styling was English Classic with barrel-mounted front swivel, express sights and deep lustrous bluing. It just looked like a rifle should. A 2 3/4-power Leupold sat up top, chosen as a suitably traditional accompaniment to the rifle's chambering: the incomparable 375 Holland and Holland Magnum. Built by a well-respected European gunmaker, I had the highest hopes for the rifle.

Two months later I could think of several more colorful but none more truthful three-word descriptions for it: *piece of junk*. The "oil-finished" stock had never been properly sanded and sealed and consequently grew "hair" when taken out in the rain. Upon closing the bolt, the striker would occasionally drop onto a loaded round, and then I received a recall notice in the mail stating that, with vigorous use, the bolt handle could snap off.

My silk purse had just turned into a sow's ear.

A call to the "exclusive" (why would anyone else want to market such a cob?) distributor of my fifteen-hundred dollar crowbar revealed my ex-periences were not uncommon. Yes, they would be happy to take it back. Subsequently, the salesman somewhat sheepishly suggested an exchange for another European arm. He described the Finnish Sako Finnbear.

The stock was epoxy-finished (no hair!). The bolt was a single steel forging (no embarrassment!). The trigger was safe and reliable (no excuses!). Styling was anything but English Classic, but then, under the circumstances ...

Begging off an immediate answer, I spent the next week researching the offer. Catalogues were obtained and calls made. Indeed, it appeared the salesman's representations were, if anything, understated. All indications pointed to a rugged product, one that would do its maker and owner proud. I'd try it.

Since I'd been offered a swap for the "Big Disaster", and the "Big Finn" was somewhat less expensive, I specified some additions and changes to even up the score. Further review of the 375's ballistics prompted me to order a Leupold 4-power scope, an increase in magnification that has

A large cow taken at 150 paces with the author's favorite load, the big Hornady 300 RN and 76 grains IMR 4350.

since been greatly appreciated. To get to the iron sights, a set of EAW detachable mounts were fitted. A single standing rear and band-mounted front sight completed the package.

Years later, the stock finish has proved virtually bulletproof. The deep bluing is now worn off in great gaping patches; the result of years of near abuse, certainly not a factory fault. The trigger is nothing short of perfection. With a 3-pound pull, release feels like snapping off an icicle from a Karelian sauna roof in January!

After gobbling up 2000 rounds of full-power ammunition and enduring 10 years of use in all weather conditions, and with all-too-frequent stretches of time without well-deserved maintenance, accuracy remains superb. Several 3-shot groups have measured less than 1-inch center-to-center at 200 yards. While hardly necessary for big game, such performance inspires tremendous confidence.

With twenty-three-inch barrel, ample cheekpiece and palmswell grip, the rifle fits me like a hug from momma. English Classic is not missed. Stock design and scope mounting make for a "heads-up" shooting stance, minimizing recoil sensation and assisting repeat shots while working the bolt with rifle shouldered. Some proclaim the mounting of a front swivel on a three-seven-five should be accomplished on the barrel, to elimi-

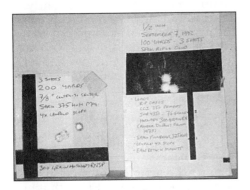

Off the bench, the Big Finn performs superbly, whether at 100 or 200 yards.

Trophy blue wildebeest taken in Northern Zululand, load used: Hornady 300-grain RN, 76 grains IMR 4350.

nate the possibility of a stock-mounted stud cutting the hand in recoil. Never have I experienced this.

I have used this rifle in the U.S. South, Pacific Northwest and in southern Africa, taking animals ranging in size from ruffed grouse to bull elk and blue wildebeest. The rifle and cartridge combination are certainly not instant death to anything tagged just anywhere. No rifle is. It is, however, exactly what its designers hoped it would be: a reliable tool built for the very demanding purpose of killing game animals.

A variety of loads have passed through the gullet of the Big Finn. Early on I had a thing for the Speer 235-grain semi-spitzer over 75 grains of IMR 4064. I didn't have a chronograph in those days but I know those little pellets flew fast, and generally caught up to what they were chasing. But what they did when they got there was not always impressive. Two blew to atoms on small deer and accuracy was a bit fickle. At 100 yards, 3-shot groups comprised two rubbing shoulders while the third stood like a wallflower as much as two inches away. Nevertheless, for some time I fell prey to the traditional reasoning that the 235-grain was meant for game like deer and using anything else on them was tantamount to drinking tequila at the Highland games. Just not done!

Eventually, I relaxed.

There are no flies on the 270-grain Hornady Spire Point and I found them useful. On top of 70 grains of IMR 4064 it delivered good accuracy and fine performance on game. Zebra and smaller African game have fallen to this load, with one notable experience occurring in northern Zululand. I shot a medium-sized impala as he quartered away from me. Impact was on the shoulder and the bullet hop-scotched from vertebrae to vertebrae, shattering them all till it drilled through the skull. The *inkonka* dropped, of course, with the slug lodged under the hide just below the forehead.

Another bullet I tried with what I considered limited success was the 300-grain Sierra boat-tail soft-point. While it is certainly

At 40 yards, many other calibers would have nicely dropped this big herd stallion. Placed high on the shoulder, the 270-grain Hornady spire point whistled clean through.

a fine choice for some rifles it was not a sterling performer in mine. The Sierra had to be seated deeply for the cartridge to feed from the magazine, leaving inadequate space for fuel. At best, upper-end 35 Whelen velocities were obtained, about 2250 fps. Still, I used it to take one small canyon country whitetail at 250 long paces. With a 3/8-inch hole in and same out I had no reason to expect the little ungulate to drop in his tracks, and he didn't. From the rimrock I could see him dive into the sagebrush where he covered some 200 yards before he gave up.

My favorite load, which I now use exclusively, I discovered early on. Nevertheless, for some years I bowed to convention and reserved it for only the big and beefy. I harbor no such scruples today. The 300-grain Hornady round nose, over 76 grains of IMR 4350, chugs along at 2450 fps and groups amazingly. It is my most accurate load, and performance at the sharp end ain't shabby, either! Whether *biggish* stuff in Africa or elk or deer here, it makes them all meat.

While I understand that field comparisons of bullet performance rank with voodoo for scientific accuracy, a pair of experiences drive home the excellence of the Hornady 300-grain Round Nose. Two deer were shot in different seasons. Both were below, and facing me at 60 paces. Both had their heads down, feeding. This exposed the spine at the withers and that is where the bullets went, angling down and toward the rear. Both deer crumpled at the shot, lights out.

Only the bullet performance was different. The first animal was hit

Sometimes a four-shot magazine does help. This doe fell to round number five from the big Sako. Bullet was the Speer 235-grain semi-spitzer backed by 75 grains of IMR 4064.

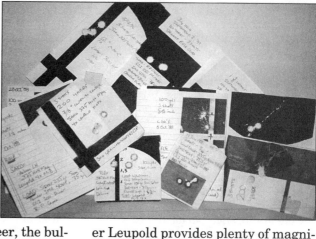

Fine groups shot over the years instill great confidence in a rifle.

with a 235-grain Speer, the bullet exploding on the spine, penetrating at most six inches. The second deer took the 300-grain Hornady. That slug mushed the spine and then went on to traverse the length of the deer. I found it embedded in the right ham. The bullet had bored through nearly three feet of flesh and bone. I have taken deer, elk and wildebeest with the 300-grain Hornady RN – it works.

A hunting rifle is both carried and shot. Because of that, unfortunate compromises are sometimes made. Many are the rifles I have seen and handled which lean heavily one way or the other. Mine does not. It is easy to carry and just as enjoyable to shoot. The Big Finn weighs 9.5 pounds with scope, empty. That is not too much to carry but is enough to soak up a bit of kick. With the scope removed, the rifle recoils a bit more noticeably though the stock design takes all the hurt out of it.

The balance is superb, barrel length optimal and sights wholly appropriate. Though the trajectory of the 375 Holland and Holland warrants a fine scope, many so-chambered rifles sport obese, blocky, bulky variables neither necessary nor even desirable on a big game rifle. The 4-power Leupold provides plenty of magnification for distance shooting and enough field of view for just-off-the-prow poking. Balance is not disturbed and mounting is secure and safe. I have never been "bit" by the scope whether shooting offhand, from the bench or from prone. A rifle is meant for the spilling of blood, but preferably not the shooter's! I have a lightweight 30-06 with a large variable that needs to learn this!

The quick-detachable EAW mounts maintain zero consistently. Truthfully, I have never had to remove the scope for a shot at game, but knowing I can do so speedily and without tools is a further confidence-builder.

The bolt handle will not peel off (!) and is easily grasped for fast repeat shots. I have never understood why Sako stands virtually alone in providing an ample bolt handle for grasping. Many bolt guns require canting or some other odd movement to open the action. Not so with the bolt handle on the Big Finn—that big hunk of steel just sticks out and shakes hands with you.

Another feature somewhat unique to the Sako AV is its magazine capacity. Though not advertised, my rifle holds four rounds in the box and I have had use for all of them. One memorable experience occurred in Kentucky soon after the rifle was purchased. All five cartridges were expended at a fleeing whitetail. Five were needed, too, as it was the last bullet out that brought home the bacon!

I have slung, dragged, toted and aimed this rifle on many adventures in many far-flung places. It was not my first pick, but I have never been sorry I tried it. In the words of Chris Wex, a professional with whom I hunted in South Africa years ago, "It just puts 'em down".

What more could I ask?

Big elk and Big Finn make a perfect match. Load? The 300-grain Hornady RN over 76 grains IMR 4350, of course.

ONE GOOD GUN

A Small Problem

by Danny Arnold

BEING BLESSED WITH several smaller-sized people in my family, I've had the experience, as many of us have, of trying to find a gun to fit a smaller person, be it a child, spouse, or friend. While the major gunmakers have started producing rifles for smaller-stature shooters, the end result is not necessarily attractive, or fit and handle well. More importantly, the cost is comparable to the full-sized version.

Most attempts at fitting a full-size gun to a small shooter, by the well-intentioned novice, make things worse because most simply shorten the buttstock. The result doesn't have the grace or handling of a really fine gun because the rifle's balance point is now somewhere forward of the action, and the remaining areas of the rifle are still full-sized, which doesn't fit the shooter's hands.

If one is to cut down or re-make a rifle to fit a small person there are several qualities the subject rifle should have: adequate ballistics, price, ease of modification, price, availability, and price. Yes, that's right. Price figures predominately in this endeavor. If this rifle is for a growing child, it will probably be outgrown and passed down to another beginner, or at least no longer be used, so we don't want to spend too much. This leaves us with a single-shot or bolt-action rifle, chambered for the 243 Winchester or larger cartridge, commonly available, and affordably-priced. If your mental list seems darned short it is because, outside of military surplus rifles, there aren't many rifles that fit these criteria.

My list has only one rifle on it. Actually it only *needs* one rifle, the Savage 340, also known as the Stevens 325, one of the most under-appreciated rifles made.

Why the Savage? Consider its attributes: a re-shapeable solid wood stock, 30-30 Winchester chambering,

ability to be scoped, and wide availability thanks to a production run of over 30 years. Oh, also price, price, price!

Now, permit me to tell you a tale for I, too, have tried to fit a gun to a small person.

My mother, at the tender age of fifty-something, decided she would like to take up deer hunting and see what all the fuss was about. Right away my Dad and I knew we had a problem. At five-foot, two-inches and a little over a hundred pounds, Mom was going to be trouble to fit with a rifle. She already shoots a little informal skeet with a Mossberg 500 youth model in 20 gauge; might a slug barrel be the answer? Unfortunately no. Accuracy with traditional Foster-type slugs or sabots was good, but not confidence-inspiring. One of the Chinese SKSs perhaps? The fit was good, the price was right, but the accuracy from this specimen was abysmal, groups being measured with the entire ruler instead of just the first two or three inches. Another problem: too much weight. At this point, frustration set in. So, like most good gun traders, Dad and I escaped to the peace and quiet of a local gun show. That's where I saw it–the perfect rifle–a Savage model 340 chambered for the 30-30 round.

Most of you are probably thinking, what is a Savage 340? Unless you are already a fan of the rifle, a little description is in order. The Savage 340 was a bolt-action, clip-fed rifle introduced in 1950 chambered

in 22 Hornet, 222 Remington, and 30-30 Winchester. It is a basic rifle, an affordable, well-made rifle for Mr. Average Workingman, or the beginning hunter. Savage made thousands of them and they can now be had very reasonably. Why? Who knows, maybe the hunter's desire to upgrade to the latest rifle/cartridge combination, or a newer, sexier rifle? The Savage 340 is not a head-turner, but someone else's loss is your gain.

Dad took some persuading to see the possibilities. Admittedly the gun had

Proper modification of the Savage 340 resulted in this well-proportioned hunting rifle.

seen use, but not abuse. The finish was worn, the stock scratched and discolored, but the action was sound and, like most guns that are carried much and used little, had a flawless bore. The final persuader for Dad was the price: $80.00 asking haggled down to $75.00.

Now, how to make a proper-fitting and handling rifle out of the 340. I dropped off the 340 at a gunsmith friend's place of business to have the barrel cut down to 19 inches, recrowned and the front sight re-mounted. The stock was shortened and a recoil pad added to bring the length of pull down to 11 inches. The recoil pad chosen was smooth so as to be quick-mounting. The action was drilled and tapped for a Weaver scope mount. The 340 has a split bridge receiver which necessitates a side-mounted scope mount. As a bonus, he polished and re-blued the rifle. All for the whopping cost of $120.00.

The woodwork would be my job. I shortened the forend by two inches and reshaped the tip. The area from tip to magazine well was slimmed to keep a petite appearance. The grip was shortened by a half-inch and some wood around the entire grip area was removed to better fit Mom's hand. Several hours sanding and many coats of tung oil later, the stock looks like it came that way from the factory. Another bonus—many older guns have nice wood under all that old finish. Sanding revealed a pleasing grain and color hard to find in newer guns. A sling with quick detachable swivels and a Tasco Pronghorn 4x32 scope top off the package.

The proof of the modification project shows in the results delivered: Mom with her 12-pointer, November 1995.

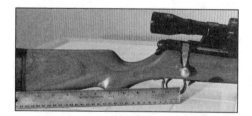

This measurement shows just how short that length of pull really is.

So how does it all work? I didn't expect great accuracy. Theoretically the rifle's potential is handicapped by a barrel band and screw arrangement holding the barreled action in the stock. I expected accuracy to be in the 2 minute area, kind of *ho hum*, but adequate for the 125 yard or less shots offered here in the blackjack forests of Oklahoma. Surprise! Accuracy with factory 150-grain or handloads runs right about 1 MOA, or 1 inch at 100 yards for a three-shot group. So much for theories. The rifle fits Mom like a glove; a quick-handling rifle of 36 inches overall that she handles better than her shotgun.

In three years of hunting Mom has taken three deer, one a magnificently racked 12-pointer which beats both Dad and I. Two of her deer needed one shot each. The other deer took two shots; the first was fatal but the deer,

being somewhat ignorant of terminal ballistics, required another shot to persuade him to stay put. This is the ultimate proof of effectiveness of hunter and weapon.

Inexpensive, effective, fun—that is the Savage 340. Since finishing this project, I have run into a couple of 340 fans at our gun club. They have gone so far as to totally restock their guns, one in a well-executed Mannlicher-style stock. They report accuracy on par with Mom's rifle, but affected by the tightness of the front band mounting screw. A tip: Tighten or loosen the barrel band and see what happens to accuracy, then make some witness marks so you can verify the tightness of the front band with a glance.

My next project is a Savage 340 for my son. He won't be able to use it for a while, so I might just play with it—until he's out of pre-school!   •

Reduction in size and proportion is clear in this side-by-side comparison of the modified Savage 340 (foreground) and the author's full-size Remington 700.

A SURVIVAL TALE:

THE AR-7 EXPLORER

Born of a military need that preceded its debut by nearly twenty years, the AR-7 has endured the winds of change to maintain its unique position as perhaps the most ingenious gun ever designed specifically as a survival tool.

by W. E. Sprague

THE 22 AR-7 Explorer — doubtless familiar to many as a trim little takedown rifle that, when disassembled, stores its components in its buttstock — occupies a unique position in firearms history. It is a "survival" gun that is itself a survivor. Born of a military need that preceded its debut by nearly twenty years, it was commercially introduced in 1959, and has since endured not only the rigors of the marketplace, but the vagaries of the business world to retain its singular position as perhaps the most ingenious gun ever designed specifically as a survival tool.

It could be argued, of course, that every gun is a survival tool since, obviously, in a survival situation, any gun is better than none. But the validity of the argument begins to fade as the likelihood of need approaches the

highly probable. And this — the high probability of needing a specialized survival gun — was the situation confronting the Army Air Corps at the beginning of World War II, the point at which the AR-7 story actually begins.

Aware that bail-outs and crash-landings behind enemy lines were likely to be a part of modern aerial warfare, the Army sought to find a gun meant only for survival use, that would improve the chances of airmen downed in hostile territory. The small arms carried by aircrews were deemed to be less than ideal in conditions such as those in the South Pacific jungles where a lack of food might prove to be a much greater threat to survival than the presence of enemy troops.

The process of military procurement being what it is, though, it was quite late in the war before the Air

Force now found what it thought it was looking for. In April of 1944, according to the Record of Army Ordnance Research and Development for 1946, it opted for the commercially available Stevens (later Savage) 22/410 rifle/shotgun for use with its emergency kits.

A problem, however, soon arose regarding suitable ammunition. When the Air Force asked Ordnance to procure a large supply of 22 hollow point rifle ammunition and 410 rifled slugs, Ordnance in turn asked the Assistant Chief of Staff G-2 to furnish an opinion as to what retaliation the enemy might take against U.S. aircrew members who were captured with such ammunition in their possession. Earlier decisions by the Judge Advocate General held that, since they were obviously meant for the taking of small game or defending against animal attack, hollowpoints and rifled slugs were clearly not against the rules of warfare.

"Use against (enemy) personnel, however," the JAG cautioned, "might be considered a violation of Article 23e of the Hague Regulations, which states that 'it is specifically forbidden to employ arms, projectiles, or materials calculated to cause unnecessary injury.'"

On the basis of this caution, the Assistant Chief of Staff G-2 strongly advised against issuing hollowpoints and rifled slugs, fearing that the Japanese would not only use airmen captured with such ammunition for adverse propaganda purposes, but would also "impose brutalities more severe than those inflicted upon other captured American air personnel."

As a result, the AAF immediately banned the use of both items in all combat areas, and in place of the rifled slug, it selected a .410 shotshell loaded with number 7-1/2 shot. Replacing the hollowpoints, however, proved to be more of a problem, presumably because even solid lead 22 bullets were thought to be in violation of Article 23e. In any case, the AAF asked the Ordnance Department to develop and test a caliber 22 Long Rifle cartridge employing a jacketed bullet, a request that resulted in still further delays. In fact, it was not until May of 1945 that the Ordnance Committee finally adopted the newly developed round as Standard, giving it the nomenclature, "Cartridge, Ball, Caliber 22, Long Rifle, M24."

A "CONVENTIONAL" AR-7

In 1959, when Armalite first introduced the AR-7 Explorer, it also offered with a traditional wooden stock, giving it a more conventional appearance. Exactly why is a matter of conjecture, since doing so deprived the little rifle of two of its major selling points, its capacity to float, and to store its disassembled components in its buttstock. Perhaps it felt that a more conventional appearance might better appeal to the more traditional types among its potential buyers.

Whatever the reason, Armalite did little to promote its wooden-stocked offering and, by the time Charter Arms acquired the rights to the AR-7, it was virtually forgotten. In the interim, however, a few other firms offered wooden stocks for the rifle as an aftermarket accessory. For the most part, though, these tended to be inferior in both finish and design. It was only when Survival Arms acquired the AR-7 that a quality wooden stock reappeared. Along with a model called the Sporter that featured a telescoping metal stock and a 25-round magazine, there was the Wildcat, fitted with a conventional walnut stock.

Interestingly enough, neither the Sporter model nor the Wildcat were listed in Survival's literature.

Delays notwithstanding, during the course of the war, the AAF bought some 10,000 Stevens 22/410s. Just how many were used for survival purposes is unknown, but it would seem that Stevens (Savage) was the very first supplier of an official U.S. survival gun. It was not, however, the only one.

Toward the end of the war, O.F. Mossberg & Sons, Inc., came up with a wide variety of barrels in different lengths and bores — some smooth, some choked, some rifled, and some partly rifled — for the M1911A1 45 service pistol. The idea was to find a replacement for the issue barrel that would optimize the use of 45 shot cartridges for taking small game under survival conditions. The various barrels were duly tested at Aberdeen Proving Ground, and by September of 1945, a 10-inch barrel with a cylinder bore was adopted for issue to AAF personnel. But by then, the war was over, and it thus seems highly unlikely that the Mossberg barrel ever saw actual use.

In 1947, the Army Air Force became the U.S. Air Force, an independent branch of service. And some two years later — perhaps because it

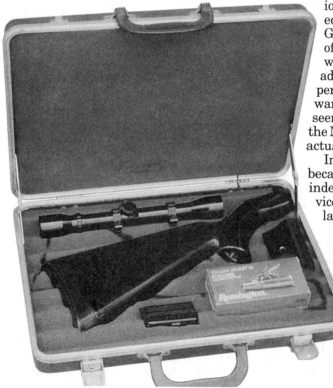

A converted four-gun pistol case accommodates the author's AR-7, along with a scope and mount, extra magazines and a "brick" (500 rounds) of ammo, comprising a handy "survival kit." No doubt similar kits can be found on board countless RVs, boats and light planes.

felt that something better than its predecessor's choice of a 22 LR cartridge fired by the Stevens was needed for taking game in a survival situation — the Air Force came up with its own "in-house" design, one that was both a bit more potent and compact, and one that, quite unwittingly, would lead to the development of the AR-7.

The new gun, initially labeled as the T-38, and designed primarily for use by the Strategic Air Command, was the brainchild of then Major (later Colonel) Burton T. Miller. Weighing in at just under four pounds, it was a bolt-action, centerfire rifle with a detachable four-shot magazine, a telescoping wire stock, and a detachable 14-inch barrel. Omitting the .410 capability of the Stevens (perhaps because a Mossberg barrel used with an airman's 45 would satisfy any shotshell needs), it replaced the 22 LR with the 22 Hornet. Following its development and testing, its official designation became "Rifle, Survival, Cal. .22, M4," and the next year — 1950 — over 29,000 units were made by Harrington & Richardson.

About that time, another ordnance request was made — apparently as an option for those who felt that the 45 shot cartridge was inadequate for survival needs. In any case, it called for a folding over/under gun, to be chambered for the .410 and 22 Hornet. First designated "Weapon, Survival T-39," and later "Rifle-Shotgun, Survival M6," a trial batch of some 30 units were made by H&R, but the Ithaca Gun Company scored the major contract, producing more than 66,000 guns in all.

(An "improved" version of the M6, called the M6 Scout, was introduced late in 1981 by Springfield Armory. To

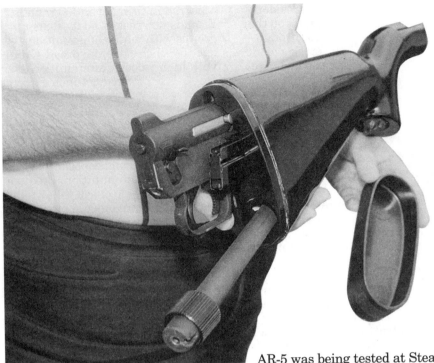

The AR-7's stock readily accommodates its disassembled action, barrel and eight-round magazine, each in its own compartment. With butt cap in place, the rifle will float either assembled or with its components stowed.

make it legal for civilian use, Springfield has added four inches to the original 14-inch barrel and, to forestall liability claims, it has fitted the original grip trigger with a guard. Other changes include a choice of rifle chamberings — either 22LR or 22 Hornet — and a removable pivot pin that allows the gun to be disassembled for storage. It folds down to 19 inches, and measures 32 inches when extended. And, like the original USAF design, it stores a mix of rifle cartridges and shotshells in a stock comb trap.)

By 1951, the USAF, apparently satisfied with its supply of M4s and M6s, turned its attention to specialized handguns — specifically Colt and Smith & Wesson 38 Special revolvers made with aluminum frames and cylinders. Designed as light-weight, anti-personnel defense guns rather than strictly survival guns, a goodly number of these were made. Subsequently judged to be unsafe, they were recalled, with most of them ending up as scrap.

Interest in survival guns was not abandoned, however, and in the mid-1950s, the Air Force, with Major Miller again leading the way, asked the Armalite division of Fairchild Engine and Airplane Corporation to develop one that was capable of floating. Armalite obliged, and before the close of 1955 a trial lot of what Armalite called the

AR-5 was being tested at Stead Air Force Base near Las Vegas, Nevada.

Based on the T-38/M4 design, the AR-5 was also a bolt-action rifle with a detachable box magazine and a detachable 14-inch barrel, and was also chambered for the 22 Hornet. It was quite a bit lighter, however, weighing in at 2-1/2 pounds, thanks to an aluminum receiver and an aluminum barrel with stainless steel liner. But, in place of the M4's telescoping wire stock, it had a detachable fiberglass stock, a hollow affair that not only made it capable of floating, but accepted both barrel and receiver (with magazine in place) when the gun was broken down for storage.

Advanced in design though it was, the AR-5 was not without its trials and tribulations. First, a minor problem arose in its sustained fire test at Stead AFB, caused by a difference in the coefficient of expansion between the aluminum barrel and its stainless liner when the barrel got hot. Corrections

were duly made by Armalite, of course, but the road ahead presented another problem of a less mechanical kind.

In 1957, its tests apparently completed without further difficulties, the specifications for the AR-5 were finalized at Wright-Patterson AFB. But while the specs were taken from Armalite drawings, Armalite never received the final specification package. Under the Eisenhower administration, the prime focus of Cold War military preparedness had begun to shift away from the idea of manned bombers to the idea of massive retaliation with the use of nuclear missiles. As a result, no procurement of the AR-5 — officially adopted as the MA-1 — was ever made. (Presumably, though, the Air Force still has access to the design, should ever a need for it arise.)

While the AR-5 was never produced in volume, its ability to float, whether assembled or disassembled, and store its disassembled components in its buttstock, were apparently just too good to be forgotten or ignored. In any event, two years later, they found their full expression in a slightly different design when Armalite, perhaps in a move to recoup the time and money spent developing the AR-5, introduced the AR-7 Explorer to the civilian marketplace.

Retaining the basic features of the AR-5 — buttstock storage capacity and flotation capability — the AR-7 departed from its bolt-action theme and center-fire caliber. Instead, the Explorer was a semi-automatic, chambered for the 22 LR, a much less costly and far more popular cartridge than the 22 Hornet. The smaller rimfire cartridge also endowed its detachable magazine with a greater capacity — eight rounds instead of five — without a significant increase in overall size.

The action itself was a conventional blowback type that fired from the closed bolt position. Its frame, however, along with its receiver

A simple but ingenious scope mount was introduced by Charter Arms soon after it acquired the rights to the AR-7. Matching the contour of the receiver 's side-plate, it's held in place by a longer side-plate screw (furnished with the mount) and a pair of hex-head screws that bear against the top of the receiver. It accommodates standard scope rings and virtually any kind of scope.

With the action secured to the stock, the barrel is aligned by a lug that engages a matching recess in the frame and is then secured by tightening its knurled collar.

ening a "resident" wing-nut bolt that ran up through the stock's pistol grip. The barrel — properly aligned by a lug that engaged a matching recess in the frame — was then fitted to the action, and secured by tightening its knurled collar. Next, the magazine, loaded with up to eight rounds, was inserted into the frame. And, lastly, a quick pull and release of a retractable charging handle on the right side of the receiver chambered the first round, making the rifle ready to fire.

With some shooters, takedown rifles do not inspire confidence, since the mating of their components can be critical to their function and performance. Any doubts about the AR-7 were quickly dispelled by test reports that soon appeared in various gun magazines, such as the following from the September, 1960, issue of the *American Rifleman*:

"...The sample (AR-7) was function - and accuracy - tested with several brands of both regular and high-velocity ammunition. Not one malfunction

occurred in firing over 300 rounds. From bench rest at 50 ft., 8-shot groups with match ammunition averaged 5/8-inch extreme spread. Groups with high-velocity ammunition averaged 3/4-inch extreme spread. Ejection is to the right and empties are not thrown into the face of the left-handed shooter.

"The barrel collar tended to work loose during firing, especially with high-velocity ammunition. Frequent precautionary checks of collar tightness are recommended if much shooting is done, as groups enlarge noticeably when the collar loosens. However, headspace adjustment is not critical as the fit of bolt to barrel is not altered . . . .

"The rifle will float in both stowed and assembled condition, provided the (butt cap) is attached. Air bubbles rose to the surface when the stowed rifle was completely immersed in water but it is doubtful if sufficient water could enter the stock to displace enough air to cause the rifle to sink."

In all, the *Rifleman* concluded, the AR-7 was "quite suitable for plinking and small game shooting."

This "suitability," together with its compactness (when stowed, its overall length was only 16-3/4 inches) soon made the AR-7 a popular choice with light plane pilots, boaters, fishermen, and campers. Despite its initial success, by the turn of the decade the AR-7 seemed headed for hard times.

Exactly why is a matter of speculation, but the chief reason seems to have been that Armalite — no longer part of Fairchild, but owned

side-plate, was still made of aluminum, and like the AR-5, its barrel (lengthened to a minimally legal 16 inches) was the same composite affair — an aluminum body with a rifled steel liner — that attached to the action by way of a knurled collar that threaded onto the frame.

Its buttstock, too, differed from that of its predecessor's, if only slightly. While both were made of high-strength fiberglass, the AR-5 had a textured finish that was uniformly dark. By contrast, the Explorer's had a glossy, brown finish that was "marbled" with a rather garish and fanciful pattern that was meant, perhaps, to simulate wood grain. There were also minor differences in its shape and dimensions, owing, of course, to corresponding differences in the size and shape of the AR-7's detachable metal components.

Assembling the AR-7 proved to be quick and easy, taking less than a minute. When stowed, its components were sealed inside its buttstock by a butt cap made of a relatively soft, resilient plastic that was formed with an integral bead lock that snapped over the end of the stock. A tug at the toe of the butt cap freed it from the buttstock, allowing the barrel, action, and magazine to be removed.

After replacing the butt cap, the action was slipped into the yoke of the stock, then secured in place by tight-

The last step in assembling the AR-7 is a matter of simply inserting its magazine, which can be loaded with up to eight rounds. Pulling back and releasing its retractable charging handle makes the rifle ready to fire.

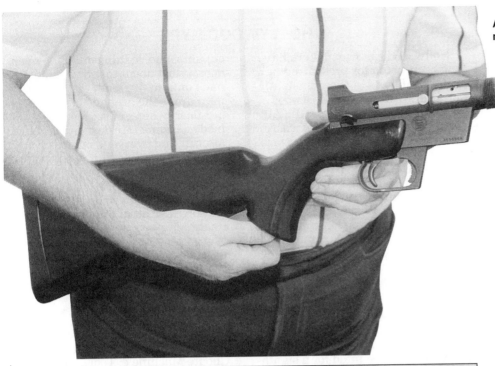

instead by a group of investors who had acquired it in the mid-1960s — may have been more concerned with promoting its military arms than in promoting the AR-7. Such, at least, is the implication inherent in the fact that, in 1973, Armalite sold rights to the AR-7 to Charter Arms — a move dictated, according to some, by Armalite's need for cash to keep itself afloat.

While the Charter AR-7 was essentially the same as the one produced by Armalite, there were some minor differences. According to CHARCO, Charter's eventual heir, the side-plate was slightly redesigned, as were the trigger and hammer. But perhaps the most notable change was in the appearance of the buttstock. Charter got rid of Armalite's fanciful "graining," and switched from brown as a basic color to black.

Charter also introduced a pair of aftermarket accessories, one of them being a "soft" carrying case that resembled an oversized pistol rug, and the other a simple but ingenious scope mount. The latter, formed to fit the receiver's side-plate, was firmly held in place by replacing the side-plate screw with a slightly longer one that was furnished with the mount, and by a pair of hex-head screws that bore down against the top of the receiver just ahead of the rear sight.

Under the Charter banner, the AR-7 prospered. In part, this was no doubt due to Charter's promotional efforts. But it could be successfully argued that it was also due to what, in retrospect, some have chosen to call the Survivalist Movement, a social phenomenon of the '70s and '80s that gave a new twist to the idea of a specialized survival gun. While the original idea was that of a gun meant to be used for taking game in an emergency survival situation, the new twist, born of mounting Cold War fears, added the element of self-defense in a post-apocalyptic world.

The idea of using a 22 for personal defense might seem ludicrous to anyone accustomed to thinking of self-defense in terms of a big bore handgun. But as many survivalist writers argued in their various books and articles on the subject, multiple hits with a 22 could be equally effective in halting an aggressor — especially since

Shown here with Ram-Line's extended magazine, Eagle International's AR-7 "conversion kit," another Cold War inspiration, featured a telescoping pistol-grip stock and a full-length barrel shroud with an H&K-type ring-and-post front sight. These items, too, have been discontinued by their manufacturers.

THE EXPLORER II

In 1981, Charter Arms introduced a pistol version of the AR-7 Explorer. Called the Explorer II, it used the same magazine and action as the AR-7, along with a shortened version of the same composite aluminum-steel barrel. Available in lengths of either six, eight, or ten inches, the barrel was attached to the action with the same knurled-collar arrangement that was used with the AR-7. However, to keep the shorter pistol barrels from being used with the AR-7 — which, of course, would have made it an illegal "sawed-off" rifle — their alignment lugs were radically redesigned.

The pistol configuration was achieved by replacing the rifle's buttstock with a wooden pistol grip that jutted down just behind the trigger guard and action, much like that of the classic 1896-pattern Mauser military pistol. In fact, its overall design bore such a strong resemblance to that famous pistol that, given its modest price, it was often called "the poor man's broom handle Mauser." Despite such nostalgic appeal, however, it would seem that it was less than a stunning success, and was offered by neither of Charter Arms' successors.

they could be delivered in less time than it took to launch a couple of hard-recoiling big bore rounds. And, as they also pointed out, a thousand rounds of 22s were a whole lot easier to carry around than a couple of hundred rounds of big bore, and would last a whole lot longer.

Possibly inspired by such thinking, several firms came up with appropriate AR-7 accessories. Ram-Line, Inc., for one, introduced a 25-round magazine. Made of a tough transparent plastic, it allowed the AR-7 shooter to keep easy track of his remaining rounds, and it more than tripled the rifle's magazine capacity. Choate Machine & Tool Co., Inc., for still another example, offered a "conversion kit," consisting of one of its popular Zytel™ pistol-grip stocks, and a half-length, ventilated barrel shroud. A similar kit, comprised of a full-length ventilated shroud (complete with its own H&K-type sighting system) and a telescoping pistol-grip stock, was likewise offered by Eagle International, Inc.

Granted, the use of such accessories defeated the AR-7's "floatability" and buttstock storage capacity. But since they gave the rifle an intimidating look and substantially increased its immediate firepower, they found favor with many AR-7 owners who subscribed to the nuclear-holocaust, head-for-the-

HOLLYWOOD HYPE

Hollywood's movie makers have long been noted for presenting new or unusual guns in their cinematic epics, as witness Clint Eastwood's S&W Model 29 (and, later, the Auto Mag) in his Dirty Harry movies. And while the AR-7 is hardly in a class with a 44 Magnum, thanks to the ingenuity of it's design it, too, has been featured in a couple of films.

In one, the always intrepid James Bond, out in the open and under attack by a marauding helicopter, produces an AR-7 from his attaché case and, quickly assembling it, employs the little rifle in a most remarkable fashion. He brings down the harassing aircraft by wounding one of its oc-

cupants who, leaning out of an open door, is just about to drop a hand grenade on him. Instead, the wounded man drops the grenade on the chopper floor, where, of course, it explodes, completely destroying the aircraft and everyone on board.

In yet another film, George C. Scott, as a rancher bent on revenge against some Big Brother types who had callously, if accidently, killed his son in an errant nerve gas experiment, employs an AR-7, again in typical cinematic fashion, to intimidate, devastate, and decimate a succession of antagonists in his ultimately tragic and unsuccessful quest for vengeance.

hills philosophy of the times. And, too, they probably accounted for a significant increase in AR-7 sales to like-minded folks who opted to add an Explorer to their other survival gear.

With the fall of the Berlin Wall in 1989 and the subsequent end of the Cold War, the popularity of such accessories, as well as that of the Survivalist Movement, began to fade, and long before the rise of anti-gun hysteria over anything with a pistol-grip

stock or an extended magazine, both Choate Machine & Tool and Eagle International discontinued their AR-7 offerings, as did Ram-Line. Many of these accessories, manufactured prior to the passage of any prohibitive legislation, were acquired by other manufacturers and suppliers, and are still available; the legality of their use, though, may be questionable.

Whether declining interest in the survivalist philosophy also led to declining sales of the AR-7, itself, is a matter of conjecture. But, in 1992, when the new firm of CHARCO acquired and reintroduced the Charter line of products, the AR-7 was not among them. Far from becoming extinct, it soon appeared in the marketplace, bearing the brand of yet another new firm, Survival Arms, Inc.

Survival offered the AR-7 in three basic but near-identical models — the AR-7, the AR-7S, and the AR-7C — with the differences between them being largely cosmetic. The first is the familiar all-black model, while the AR-7S has the same black stock but a silver-finished barrel and action, and the AR-7C is, as the "C" designation implies, completely finished — buttstock, barrel, and action — in camouflage.

Since first introduced by Armalite, an estimated 350,000 AR-7s have been sold. What the future holds for this unique little takedown rifle is, of course, anyone's guess; it may yet meet its marketplace demise. But given its proven record as a survivor, and that it is still perhaps the most ingenious gun ever designed specifically as a survival tool, the chances are it will live substantially beyond that 350,000 mark. ●

The AR-7 is just as quickly disassembled. Remove the magazine by pressing the release located inside the front of the trigger guard. Then clear the chamber, undo the barrel collar and the stock's "resident" wing-nut bolt, and the components are ready for storage in the buttstock.

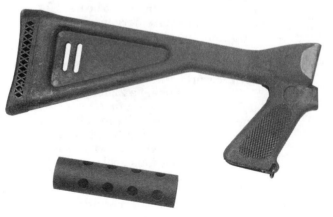

Designed to adapt the AR-7 for personal defense, Choate's Zytel ™ pistol-grip stock and short barrel shroud, along with Ram-Line's extended magazine, were among a number of "after-market" accessories inspired by the Cold War fears of the 70s and 80s; all three items were discontinued soon after the end of the Cold War.

by JOHN MALLOY

HANDGUNS TODAY:

AUTOLOADERS

"IT WAS THE best of times, it was the worst of times ... This introduction from Dickens' *TALE OF TWO CITIES* seems somehow appropriate for a discussion of autoloading handguns.

On one hand, handguns have been made and sold in record numbers. On the other, semiautomatic pistols have been under attack as never before.

Several factors contributed to the reported record sales of handguns. Reaction of some politicians to the Columbine school shootings of April, 1999 was to "do something" to demonstrate their concern. Much of this "something" was to introduce anti-gun legislation. Gun shows came under legislative attack in many places. Many people, fearing that some firearms--or some rights--might no longer be available, bought guns in record numbers.

Added to this was growing concern in 1999 of potential Year 2000 (Y2K) computer problems. Prudent people reasoned that if Y2K problems caused disruptions in basic services, then social unrest (riots and assaults) could ensue. Firearms were purchased as protection against such problems, many by first-time gunowners. As we now know, civilization did not collapse on January 1, 2000. Many new gunowners found they liked the fun and the self-discipline of shooting

and became dedicated members of the shooting sports community.

Along with the agitation for legislation, litigation by city governments against manufacturers of autoloading handguns was initiated as a weapon. Small companies, in particular, could not bear the cost of defending themselves against multiple lawsuits. By late 1999, it was rumored that several companies--among them Lorcin and Davis--had gone bankrupt. The good news, as we shall see, is that this is only partially true. The bad news is that this is partially true.

Many manufacturers are offering key locks to disable the mechanism of the pistols they offer. Many shooters feel that this concept seems to have some merit, as it can be used or not used at the option of the owner.

With woeful deception involved in the misnaming, so-called "smart guns" are also being developed. The favored concept seems to be an electronic device that would not allow the trigger to be pulled unless the gun received a signal from a transmitter worn by an authorized person. The concept has received more attention following the tragic school shootings, but apparently was originally developed to keep police officers from being shot with

their own guns. Some officers, however, contend that training is preferable to complex gadgetry.

Still, not all the news is related to the political situation and, very definitely, not all of it is bad.

True, some manufacturers are gone, and a surprising number of models of semiautomatic handguns have been discontinued within the past year.

However, new manufacturers have entered the autoloading handgun field, and interesting new ideas and new models from existing manufacturers are being introduced. Importers are bringing in new models from abroad.

The effect of expanding, lawful concealed carry is evident as more people in our country choose to exercise their right to bear arms. The autoloading handgun lines of many companies have grown smaller and lighter. Polymer frames grow in popularity, and several manufacturers

have introduced new pistols with such frames. Titanium, introduced for revolvers within the past few years, is now being used for autoloaders.

Several powerful new centerfire cartridges have been introduced for big-bore semiautomatics. At the same time, conversion kits to adapt centerfire autoloaders to use the 22 Long Rifle (22 LR) cartridge are in demand; several new ones are offered by pistol manufacturers and aftermarket suppliers.

The 1911 Colt/Browning pistol design remains a favorite. New variations of models made by traditional manufacturers are offered. Also, new manufacturers have appeared on the handgun scene to offer their versions of the 1911.

To celebrate their company anniversaries or the anniversary of a particular pistol's introduction, several manufacturers have introduced new models recently. Other manufacturers

Petite Kathy Gilliam displays the small Accu-Tek XL-9 subcom-pact pistol, a stainless-steel double-action in 9mm.

seem to have timed new models to coincide with the turnover of the calendar. Note how many models bear the designation "Millennium" or the number "2000."

Indeed, the current autoloading handgun scene is an active one, with much going on.

Let's take a look at what the companies are doing:

ACCU-TEK

Excel Industries, the manufacturer of Accu-Tek firearms, is offering a new 9mm double-action only (DAO) pistol. The stainless-steel pistol, dubbed the XL-9, measures only 3.6x5.6 inches, easily placing it in the subcompact category. With its 3-inch barrel, weight is 24 ounces and capacity is 5+1. It comes with two magazines, one flush and one with a finger-rest extension.

New compact single-action Accu-Tek pistols in 9mm, 40 and 45 calibers are presently in development. The new stainless-steel All-Star pistols will be the company's largest-caliber offerings. Scheduled availability for the new guns was set for mid-2000.

ALCHEMY ARMS

Shown for the first time at the January 2000 SHOT Show was the Alchemy Arms

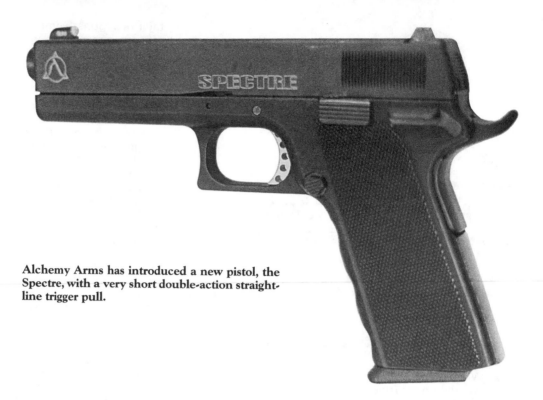

Alchemy Arms has introduced a new pistol, the Spectre, with a very short double-action straight-line trigger pull.

Spectre pistol. Looking a little bit like a 1911, the Spectre can be considered a full-size pistol, and comes with a 4 1/2-inch barrel. The frame is aluminum alloy, and slides in both carbon steel and stainless are offered. The locking system is of a conventional tilting-barrel type. The gun has a beavertail tang grip safety and a frame-mounted thumb safety.

What makes the new pistol stand out is the trigger mechanism. The striker-fired pistol is double-action only (DAO) yet it has a straight-line trigger pull, like a 1911, with only .155-inch of travel. If your decimals are rusty, .155-inch is right between 1/8 and 3/16-inch.

The pistol is offered in 9mm, 40 S&W and 45 ACP. Three versions are planned—

a standard 32-ounce black (SI) model with a carbon-steel slide, a two-tone (SG) model with a stainless-steel slide and a 27-ounce titanium (TI) model. Production of these three models was scheduled to begin in February 2000. A compact variant with a 3-inch barrel will come later.

Alchemy began about 12 years ago as a supplier of aftermarket pistol parts, and now the new firearms manufacturer offers this new pistol design. The company feels that the Spectre offers the straight trigger movement and the feel of a 1911, combined with the striker fire and trigger action that Glock has made popular.

BERETTA

Beretta has introduced a new 9000S pistol. This is a new look and a new concept for Beretta, as the pistol is a polymer-frame compact. Available in 9mm and 40 S&W calibers, it is hammer-fired and retains the traditional Beretta open-top slide. However, the slide opening is relatively narrow and has a definite ejection "scallop" and the locking system is of the tilting-barrel type, with the locking surfaces toward the sides instead of on the top. The 9000S measures 4.8x6.6 inches and weighs about 27

The 9000S guns are a real departure for Beretta— polymer frames and tilting-barrel locking system, among other things. This is the Type D, which has a double-action-only trigger mechanism.

Century International Arms is now the importer of the South African Republic Arms pistols. Century's Steve Kehaya shows the latest model, the 40-caliber RAP 440.

ounces. Two variants will be made. The type F is a conventional double-action (DA) and the Type D is DAO.

To commemorate the millennium, Beretta has introduced the Elite 2000 pistol as a limited-production item. Based on the Model 92 pistol, the new gun has a matte black finish and laminated rosewood grips with a Beretta logo medallion inset. Serial numbers will be Y2K-0001 to Y2K-2000.

With little fanfare, Beretta has added a titanium version to its Bobcat 32 ACP pistol line. Although it is a catalog item, it has been reported that only a limited run will be made.

CENTURY INTERNATIONAL

Century International Arms is now the importer of the South African Republic Arms pistols. New in that line is the 40 S&W caliber RAP 440. The steel pistol is 6 inches long and weighs 31 ounces. It has a 3 1/2-inch barrel, and a capacity of 8+1.

Century also is offering the new compact Hungarian pistol, the FEG P9RZ. This scaled-down 9mm FEG has a bobbed hammer, a 3.6-inch barrel and is 7 inches long. It weighs about 30 ounces and has 10+1 capacity.

CHARLES DALY

The Charles Daly name was first applied to handguns only a short time ago, when a 1911-type pistol was introduced in 1998. Now, the pistol offerings have been expanded.

Completely new pistols of new design have polymer frames and are conventional DA. The designation is DDA, for Daly Double Action. The guns are made by Bul Transmark of Israel and are similar to, but not the same as, ones that Bul now markets elsewhere. The internal mechanism is similar to that of the CZ-75. Calibers are 40 S&W and 45 ACP.

Two DDA variants are offered. A compact version has a 3 5/8-inch barrel, and is 7 3/8 inches long, weighing 26 ounces. The full-size model has a 4 1/2-inch barrel, with an overall length of 8 1/4 inches. It weighs 28.5 ounces. Both variants have 10+1 capacity.

Actually, a number of other variants could be said to exist, as the polymer frames are available in several different colors.

CIENER

A new 22 Long Rifle (22 LR) conversion kit for the Glock pistols has been introduced by Jonathan Arthur Ciener. The new conversion unit has the exact dimensions and appearance of the original Glocks. That factor alone is important to some people. However, converted pistols can also use holsters and some other accessories that work with the Glock, a nice plus. The Ciener conversions are offered in two different sizes, and will work with most of Glock's 9mm and 40-caliber pistols.

COLT

There were rampant Colt rumors in the air prior to the 2000 SHOT Show. At that time, Colt spokesmen verified that most of the guns in the previous handgun line, including all the new models introduced last year, have been discontinued. This means that all double-action (DA) revolvers are gone, including the new multi-caliber models. All the Mustang/Pony 380 semiautos are gone. The new 9mm DAO autoloaders introduced just last year are also gone.

Still in the line are the single-action revolvers and the 1911-style 45s. The 1911s, however, are pretty much limited to Government- and Commander-size pistols, and only in 45 ACP caliber. The smaller Officers variant is gone, but the recently-introduced Defender is still in the catalog. The 1991-series 45s are also still listed.

The Colt Custom Shop is still making custom guns.

There has been another reorganization of Colt's leadership. Colt now has a new CEO, Lt. Gen. William Keys. Keys replaces Stephen Sliwa, who briefly headed up iColt, a now-defunct subsidiary formed to develop "smart gun" technology.

CZ

A new DAO version of the CZ-75 has been introduced. The new variant has a bobbed hammer. The trigger mechanism is such that the hammer can be activated again in case of a misfire. The new CZ will be available in 9mm and 40 calibers.

CZ is going the other way, too. Also offered is a new single-action-only version of the CZ-75. This one can be carried cocked-and-locked, and is designed to appeal to those who use such pistols in competition. It has a distinctive appearance because of its straight trigger.

The CZ-75 PCR model is being offered in the U. S. now. PCR stands for "Police of the Czech Republic", and the pistol is of the same type as designed for that law-enforcement group. It is an alloy-frame compact, with a decocking lever and rubber grips.

Begun in 1968, the Dan Wesson firm offered interchangeable-barrel revolvers, such as this early Dll used by Malloy. Now, the reorganized company offers 1911-type semiautomatics as well as revolvers.

DAVIS INDUSTRIES

Jim Davis (right) and his son Aaron Davis were at the 2000 SHOT Show to prove that rumors of the company's demise were false. Davis Industries displayed their line of affordable derringers and semiautomatic pistols.

To commemorate the CZ-75's 25th anniversary (and a total of over 2 million pistols made), CZ is introducing a special 25th Anniversary model. It is a high-polish pistol with walnut grips and special markings. Only 1000 will be made, with 500 allotted for the United States market.

A 22LR conversion kit is now available for the CZ-75 from the company.

DAN WESSON

Known for its interchangeable-barrel revolver design since 1968, Dan Wesson has been under new ownership since 1996, and the company is now in the autoloading pistol business. Based on the 1911 design, Dan Wesson's new "PointMan" pistols will be offered in Government and Commander sizes. A variety of features will make the variants suitable for Bullseye, IDPA, IPSC or other types of pistol shooting in which revolvers seem to be playing second fiddle to semiautos.

DAVIS

Davis is still in business! The Davis display at the 2000 SHOT Show was welcome proof that rumors of the company's demise were greatly exaggerated. Davis quietly continues to make their affordable line of derringers and semiautomatic 32 and 380 pistols. In business since 1982, Davis offers a lifetime warranty on its products, so Davis customers certainly want the company to remain in business.

EAA

European American Armory is now offering a 22LR conversion kit for their Witness series of pistols.

Also, the company has introduced the Tanfoglio-developed F.A.R. system for semiautomatic pistols. (F.A.R. stands for "Fast, Accurate, Reliable" in company literature). Essentially, this system uses a Witness pistol redesigned to be blowback operated, with a fixed barrel. Chamber pressure is controlled by using a much-longer cartridge case of an as-yet unnamed cartridge. The case is slightly longer than that of a 38 Super, but has the smaller internal capacity of a 9mm Luger case. Thus, the rear of the case has a very large solid section. So, as the case moves rearward out of the chamber, the solid rear portion leaves first, and is unaffected by the pressure in the chamber. By the time the thin case walls move out of the chamber, the bullet has exited from the barrel and pressure has dropped.

EAA claims that the advantages of the system are a straight-line, fixed barrel for better potential accuracy, faster cycle time without a locking system, and the ability to use a longer, gentler ramp into the chamber for more reliable feeding.

FIRESTORM

A new line of imported semiautomatic pistols was introduced at the January 2000 SHOT Show. Although the first ones will probably be 1911-style 45s, the Firestorm pistols fall into three general categories.

The Firestorm 380 is a conventional DA blowback of the pocket pistol type. With a 3 1/2-inch barrel and 23-ounce weight, its size of about 6 1/2x4 3/4 inches places it in the compact class. It has a slide-mounted safety that blocks the firing pin. Capacity is 7+1.

The Mini-Firestorm 9mm and 40 pistols are locked-breech pistols. Trigger mechanism is conventional DA, and the thumb safety is frame-mounted. A barrel length of 3 1/2 inches gives dimensions of 7x4 1/2 inches. Although larger than the 380, the Mini is still in the compact class. Weight is 24.5 ounces, and capacity is 10+1.

The Firestorm 45s are steel-frame 1911-style pistols, in three sizes. The full-size Government pistols have 5 1/8-inch barrels and weigh 36 ounces. Similar to the 1911 design, they have grip safeties and frame-mounted thumb safeties. Capacity is 7+1. The Compact 45 has a 4 1/4-inch barrel, reducing the length and cutting weight to 34 ounces. The 45 Mini-Compact is a smaller pistol with a double-column magazine. Barrel length is 3 1/8 inches. Weight is 31 ounces and capacity goes up to 10+1.

Firestorm pistols are imported by SGS Importers of Wanamassa, New Jersey.

GALENA/AMT

Recall that Galena Industries took over production of the AMT firearms line last year. Galena

FireStorm is a new name in the autoloading pistol field. Several different types will be offered, this one a full-size 45-caliber Government style.

now makes the line of Backups, Automags and 1911-style pistols previously manufactured by AMT. In mid-1999, production of those guns was moved from Irwindale, California to Sturgis, South Dakota.

Since the move, the company has been retooling for all the product lines, a process they anticipated to last into late 2000. The company believes this retooling will result in better reliability and better accuracy for all the Galena guns.

Galena points out that all their firearms carry a lifetime warranty.

GLOCK

Glock's single-column compact 45, the Model 36, introduced last year, is now in production. First shipment of the slimline production pistols was scheduled for the Spring of 2000.

Noticeably thinner than the Glock 30, (its double-column counterpart), the 36 has a 3 3/4" barrel, measures 6.7x4.7 inches, and weighs 22.5 ounces. It has 6+1 capacity.

GRIFFON

Griffon USA, the importer of the South African Griffon pistols, is offering the Griffon 1911A1 Combat model, a designation which leaves little doubt as to the origin of the design. For now at least, all Griffon pistols are Commander-size 45s. They have 4 1/8-inch barrels, and weigh 36.5 ounces. Capacity is 7+1. The Griffon pistols have

The Griffon 1911A1 Combat pistol is being imported from South Africa. The Commander-size pistol is offered in 45 ACP.

distinctive portholes on the front of the slide.

The Griffon 9mm pistol, based on a modified Tokarev design, was originally scheduled to come in along with the 45, but will not be imported.

HECKLER & KOCH

The year 2000 marked HK's 50th anniversary. To commemorate the event, a special series of 1000 USP Compact 45-caliber pistols have been made. The pistols have the HK 50th Anniversary logo on the slide and are numbered "- of 1000". They come cased with a commemorative coin and an extra magazine and a key for the lockout device. Number 1

of 1000 was displayed at the January 2000 SHOT Show.

Rumors were circulating prior to the SHOT Show that Colt was planning to buy Heckler & Koch. At the show, an HK spokesman reported that HK's parent company had signed a letter of intent with Colt, and that negotiations were under way. Later information, however, indicated that the arrangements were being made with one of Colt's principal owners, and not with the Colt company.

HIGH STANDARD

Lots of things are going on at High Standard.

A joint venture has been established between High

Standard, Firearms International (FI) and Olympic Arms. A number of new things are being offered. Even more are being planned.

The High Standard line of 22-caliber target pistols remains a mainstay, and the guns continue to use the familiar High Standard names from the past. The target 22s now feature Herrett grips.

New is a full line of 1911-style 45 pistols, and the company has resurrected the "Crusader" name for their custom series 45s, with 4- or 5-inch barrels. Match versions will be made with 5- or 6-inch barrels, and there will be military-style variants offered also. A 5-inch barrel, 26-ounce titanium variant will also be

Glock's new slimline Model 36--the company's first pistol with a single-column magazine--is now in production.

Heckler & Koch's Jennifer Golisch holds the cased Number 1 of 1000 commemorative USP pistol. The series of 1000 guns will recognize the company's 50th anniversary.

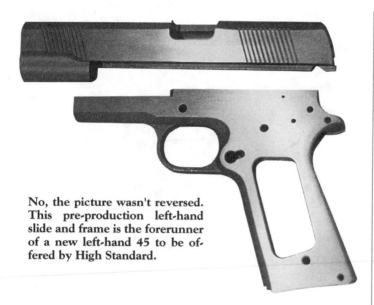

No, the picture wasn't reversed. This pre-production left-hand slide and frame is the forerunner of a new left-hand 45 to be offered by High Standard.

made. "Sharpshooter" conversion kits to convert the 45s to use 22 LR ammunition are also offered.

The Olympic name will now be used primarily on guns made for export—the High Standard name will be phased in on all the new 45s.

By mid-2000, the company also planned to introduce a left-hand 1911-type 45. Olympic had bought the tooling for the departed Randall pistols, including the left-hand models, and the time may be right to offer pistols for the southpaws among us again.

Bob Shea helped man the High Standard booth at the 2000 SHOT Show. Shea, who started his working career with High Standard in 1942, now works part-time for the company, and still works on the 22 semiautomatics.

Sure to catch attention is the new P51 50-caliber pistol designed by Robert Pauza. Pauza's big rifle chambered for the 50 BMG (50 Browning Machine Gun) cartridge is a prominent item in the FI catalog. A prototype of the 1911-style, tilting-barrel pistol was demonstrated at the January 2000 SHOT Show. Pauza points out that the new 50 has 24% more frontal area than a 45. The prototype pistol is said to be controllable while pushing a 300-grain bullet out at 1250 feet per second. High Standard hoped to have the P51 in production during the year 2000.

HI-POINT

The Hi-Point 9mm Comp pistol, announced last year, is now in production. It is available from the company with an optional laser.

Hi-Point has a tradition of introducing new features into the line without much fanfare. For 2000, all models will have a trigger lock and adjustable sights. Of special interest, all models will also come with an additional aperture rear sight. Aperture sights, also called "peep" sights or "ghost rings," have been installed on custom handguns before, but the new Hi-Points may be the first

Firearms designer Robert Pauza displays his new P51 pistol and the 50-caliber cartridge it shoots.

Two new cartridges for semiautomatic pistols were recently introduced. The 50 Pauza, for the Pauza P51 pistol, is at left. In the center is the high-velocity 40 Super cartridge. A 45 ACP is shown at the right for comparison.

Charles Brown (left) explains features of the new Hi-Point pistols to Malloy. The first factory offering of pistols with aperture sights is being made by Hi-Point.

Kahr has introduced a polymer-frame pistol. The new Kahr P9 is a double-action-only 9mm with a capacity of 7+1.

factory offering of pistols so equipped. The notch and aperture sights can be easily switched by the owner.

HS AMERICA

A new company, HS America, has been formed to market a new pistol from Croatia. The 2000 SHOT Show was its first public showing. The new HS 2000 has a polymer frame with steel rails. The pistol, now available in 9mm and 40, locks by means of a cam-operated tilting-barrel system. Trigger action is similar to that of the Glock.

With a 4-inch barrel, the pistol measures 5.7x7.2 inches (just outside our arbitrary 5x7 "compact" category) and weighs only 23 ounces. It can be supplied with a 15-round magazine for law enforcement or a standard 10-round magazine for the common folk. The magazine is of Beretta dimensions; although the catch hole is in a different position, pre-ban Beretta magazines can be adapted.

The HS 2000 has a true ambidextrous magazine release, a grip safety as well as trigger safety and internal

firing pin block, and an external slide release. Planned for the future are versions in 357 SIG and 45 ACP. A smaller compact variant is also in the works.

HS 2000 pistols are imported by Intrac Arms of Knoxville, Tennessee.

KAHR

Kahr, one of the early leaders in the small 9mm pistol field, has now introduced a polymer-frame model. The new P9 is a 9mm DAO pistol with a 3 1/2-inch barrel, weighs about 16 ounces and measures 4 1/2x6

inches. Capacity is 7+1. Only a single polymer version is available, but everyone who handled it at the SHOT Show seemed to like it, so perhaps Kahr will offer variants in the future.

Recall that Kahr acquired Auto-Ordnance (A-O) last year. Kahr plans to make 45-caliber Auto-Ordnance/Thompson 1911A1 pistols standardized on the appearance of the World War II GI model, complete with brown plastic grips and lanyard loop on the butt. Previous A-O pistols used parts from different suppliers, and features varied from lot to lot.

In addition to the military model, Thompson 1911A1 offerings include Standard and Deluxe models, with no lanyard loop and different finishes and grips.

The Thompson 1927A1 and M1 semiautomatic "Tommy Gun" carbines are in Kahr's lineup, but the 1927A5 Thompson semiautomatic pistol was not in the new catalog. That model never sold very well for A-O and it is cumbersome, but it was fun to shoot.

KEL-TEC

The new 6 1/2-ounce 32-caliber P-32 reached full production in November of 1999, and by January 2000, Kel-Tec had shipped over 10,000 pistols.

In the near future, the company plans to offer hard chrome and Parkerized

The new HS2000 pistol, available initially in 9mm and 40 S&W, features a polymer frame and a Glock-type trigger safety. It also has a grip safety.

Kel-Tec's light little 32-caliber polymer-frame P-32, introduced last year, is now in full production.

Kimber now claims to be first in the number of 1911-type pistols made and sold. Among its new offerings is the CDP series, designed for concealed carry and personal protection. This one is the Ultra, with 3-inch barrel and 6+1 capacity. 45 ACP, of course.

versions. In addition, the polymer frames may be offered in a rainbow of colors.

KIMBER

Kimber's Dwight van Brunt reports that the company, in sheer numbers of pistols sold, has become the number one maker of 1911-style pistols. There should be something in their line that should suit most shooters--they offer 54 different variations.

New for 2000 was a line of custom shop-pistols designed for concealed carry. These guns are designated "CDP" for "Custom Defense Package." Assembly is of matte black aluminum frames and stainless-steel slides. Chambering is 45 ACP.

They feature the rounding of all edges and corners, 3-dot Tritium night sights, checkered front strap, aluminum match trigger, ambidextrous safety and special "double diamond" rosewood grips.

CDP pistols come in three sizes. The Ultra, at 25 ounces, has a 3-inch barrel and 6+1 capacity. The Compact, with a longer slide, goes 28 ounces, has a 4-inch barrel and also has 6+1 capacity. The Pro, also with a 4-inch barrel, has the longer grip frame, giving it 7+1 capacity.

LES BAER

New from Les Baer is the Monolith, a 1911-type competition pistol with a 5-inch

barrel. The new pistol has a special frame with the forward section, generally called the dust cover, lengthened to the front of the special matching slide. Rail contact is therefore along the entire length of the slide and frame, in a fashion similar to that of the early pre-1911 Colt 38 autos. The Monolith's extended frame puts more weight forward, reducing muzzle rise. Les Baer guarantees 3-inch groups at 50 yards. Calibers offered are 45 ACP and 400 Cor-Bon, and also 40, 9mm and 38 Super.

LORCIN

Lorcin Engineering Company, of Mira Loma, California, has gone out of business. In the company's twelve years of business, it reportedly became the largest maker of 380-caliber pistols in the United States.

Numrich Gun Parts Corporation has bought all the existing Lorcin parts.

MAGNUM RESEARCH

New for 2000 was the Baby Eagle in 45 ACP caliber. The Baby Eagle pistols are made by Israeli Military Industries (IMI). Recall that the Baby Eagle was gone from the Magnum Research line for several years. When it returned in 1999, it was available in 9mm and 40, with a 45 scheduled for later. Now the promised 45 has arrived. The new 45 has a full-size frame and a shorter 3.7 inch barrel. Overall length is 7.75 inches. Although the frame will hold the larger law-enforcement magazine, capacity for ordinary people is 10+1.

NORTH AMERICAN ARMS

NAA now has a custom shop. This means that their little 32-caliber Guardian, normally available in stainless with flat black grips, can now be had in a number of different finishes and grips. They also offer alternate sights, porting and other modifications.

Les Baer Custom has introduced their new Monolith pistol. Based on the 1911 design, the Monolith has an extended forward frame section and full-length frame/slide rails.

Magnum Research's new 45-caliber Baby Eagle pistol is offered with a full-size grip frame and a short slide to match its 3.7-inch barrel.

Two magazines are now furnished with each NAA Guardian pistol. One has the original flat base, while the second has a finger rest, giving the owner a choice. As another incentive to buy one, North American has reduced the retail price of the Guardian.

NORTHWEST ARMS

A new company, Northwest Arms, recently purchased the factory operation formerly known as Wilkinson Arms. Designer Ray Wilkinson had named his guns after his daughters, and the guns made by Northwest carry those same names.

The Linda was a large tubular-receiver 9mm pistol with an extended magazine. Northwest has finished the remaining receivers as carbines with 16 3/16-inch barrels which, with BATF approval, come with pre-ban 31-round magazines.

The Sherry was a little 22 LR-caliber pocket pistol.

Northwest has revised the design somewhat with a new magazine and a redesigned firing pin. While the original pistols used top ejection, the new version features ejection angled to the right.

The little Sherry weighs 9 1/4 ounces, has a 2 1/2-inch barrel, and measures 3x4 3/8 inches, hiding easily under a 3x5 note card. It comes with an 8-round magazine.

Northwest says that, for a limited time, a free Sherry 22 pistol will be included with the purchase of a Linda carbine.

PARA-ORDNANCE

Para-Ordnance proudly points out that their new double-action LDA (Light Double Action) pistol, introduced last year, was named "Gun of the Year" by *Guns & Ammo* magazine.

A new variant of that system, the P12 LDA, has now been introduced. It features the same light DAO trigger, but is made with a spurless hammer, in the small "Officer's" size, with a 3 1/2-inch barrel. At this time, it is available in 45 ACP only. An interesting feature is that the slide will not open if the grip safety is not activated. Availability was planned for the Spring of 2000.

Something different coming up. A new departure for Para-Ordnance, which began with and gained fame for its high-capacity double-column pistol frames, is its planned first-ever single-column-magazine pistol. This slimmer variant will be called the 745 LDA.

PHOENIX

Phoenix has introduced a neat little pistol kit. Called the Deluxe Rangemaster Target Kit, it contains an impressive group of items in a lockable plastic case.

Included are the Phoenix HP 22 pistol with 3-inch barrel

North American Arms' little Guardian 32 now comes with two magazines—the original version, which is flat on the bottom, and the new finger-rest version shown.

Originally offered by Wilkinson Arms, the little 22-caliber Sherry pistol is now available again, in slightly redesigned form, from Northwest Arms.

Looking a bit like a 1911 on steroids, the prototype Pauza P51 pistol is chambered for a powerful new 50-caliber cartridge.

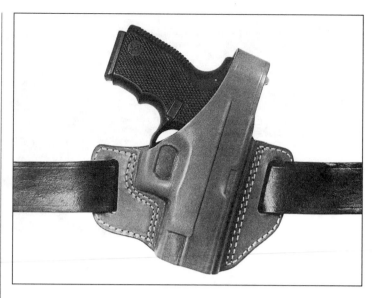

Sometimes it is hard to find suitable holsters for pistols that aren't 1911s. Republic Arms of Chino, CA has addressed the problem by offering a line of holsters for the company's 45-caliber Patriot pistol.

and flush magazine, and also a 5-inch barrel and extended grip magazine to convert the compact pistol into an informal target pistol. Also included are a basic cleaning kit, a cable lanyard to fasten the gun to a fixed object, and a magazine well lock that disables the pistol when installed. As a nice touch, the magazine well lock and the carrying case are keyed alike.

The pistol lock/cable lanyard are shipped with all new Phoenix pistols. Phoenix also offers them to owners of older pistols simply for the cost of the shipping charge.

REPUBLIC ARMS (U.S.)

Republic Arms, of Chino, California, has made note of their customers' requests for a holster specifically designed for their Patriot pistol. Republic now offers such a line of holsters. The holsters are made by Gould & Goodrich, and are available in belt and paddle varieties.

At the 2000 SHOT Show, Republic displayed some pistols made up with express-type sights--a large bead front sight, and a shallow V-notch rear--that may be considered as an option later.

REPUBLIC ARMS (South Africa)

The South African Republic Arms line of steel-frame 9mm and 40 pistols is now being imported by Century International Arms of St. Albans, Vermont.

RUGER

Sturm, Ruger & Co., having made a big splash during its 50th anniversary in

1999, had no new offerings in the semiautomatic pistol field for 2000.

However, the company made the news. Ruger sent out a memo that was the subject of a January 2000 Associated Press (AP) news story. A *Denver Post* reporter became aware of a December 1999 instruction from Ruger to its distributors. It stated that guns be shipped only to Federal Firearms License (FFL) dealers "selling exclusively from their regular place of business." This instruction was interpreted as banning sales of Ruger guns at gun shows.

The resulting flap caused Ruger to issue, in late January, a clarification. It stated that Ruger policy since 1985 has been to instruct distributors to sell only to dealers who sell

from retail stores. It explained that the word "exclusively" was added in December 1999 only to stop mail-order sales to individual FFL holders. The company has no objection to Ruger firearms being legally sold at a gun show by a stocking retail dealer. The letter concluded that gun shows "occupy a special and legitimate niche in the lawful enjoyment of firearms."

SIG

Last year SIG Arms introduced their Trailside 22 pistol, basically a Hammerli

dressed down for use as a field or plinking pistol. Now, the Trailside itself has been dressed up, and the result is the Trailside Competition pistol. The new match pistol has adjustable sights, adjustable grips and a steel weight balance system. To prove that they are good shooters, SIG includes a factory target center in a medallion that comes with each pistol.

Also new is the SIG E.P.L.S. pistol, which will begin limited shipments during 2000. The initials stand for Electronic

The introduction of SIG's new EPLS (Electronic Personal Locking System) pistol—the first to have a built-in composite electronic/mechanical locking system—has created considerable discussion.

After a long period of limited production, the beautifully made single-action SIG Model P 210 pistol has been officially discontinued.

Personal Locking System. The pistol has an electronic/mechanical device that locks the trigger. It is powered by a small lithium battery to operate a tiny electric servo motor that can lock or unlock the trigger. The device sits forward of the trigger guard and has buttons that allow the owner to program the system, assigning his own code. The E.P.L.S. can also be preprogrammed in unlocked or locked modes, or with time delays of one hour or eight hours, after which, the gun will revert to a locked condition. The pistol itself is a modified P229 and is available in 9mm, 357 SIG and 40 S&W.

Something old gone: The beautifully-made SIG P210, the single-action 9mm that has been in only limited production in recent years, is now dropped from the line and gone for good.

Something new: SIG of Switzerland reportedly has purchased the Mauser trade name and SIG Arms will handle the importing of a new Mauser M2 pistol, made in Germany. It is a DAO, with a rotating barrel locking system, and will be chambered for 357 SIG, 40 S&W and 45 ACP.

SMITH & WESSON

S&W and Walther have an arrangement, and one of the results is the SW99 pistol offered by the American company. The polymer frame is made in Germany by Walther, and the slide and barrel are made in the U. S. by S&W. Although at first glance it is difficult to distinguish between the SW99 and the Walther P99, there are subtle differences. The SW99's trigger guard is rounded, not squared. The S&W slide is contoured differently and has slide serrations front and rear.

Features such as the interchangeable backstrap system and the flush decocking control are included in the SW99. It is a conventional DA pistol, offered in 9mm and 40, with about a 4-inch barrel. The length is 7 1/4 inches and the weight is about 25 ounces.

The TSW (Tactical Smith & Wesson) series of pistols has been expanded, and the pistols have some new features, including an accessory rail on the frame's forward extension, often called the dust cover. The other remaining pistols now in the line are all in the Sigma, Chiefs Special or Value series. Long-time standby full-size guns, such as the 4506, have been discontinued. The longest barrel cataloged for an S&W centerfire autoloader now is 4 1/4 inches.

Special pistols are still available from the S&W Performance Center.

SPRINGFIELD

Compact 45s with 10-shot magazines caught the attention of the shooting world in the last couple of years. Springfield, claiming to have the greatest selection of 1911-type pistols has one, of course, in their line. Actually, the pistol can use a 12-shot magazine, but is sold with a 10-rounder except to law enforcement and sales outside the U. S. The diminutive 1911-style 45 has a 3.5-inch barrel and weighs 31

The S&W Model 4586TSW pistol demonstrates the features of the new Tactical pistol line. Noticeable is the new accessory or equipment rail on the forward dust cover of the frame. This version is an 8+1 stainless-steel 45 with a 4 1/4-inch barrel.

S&W's Performance Center offers non-catalog items such as the 945, a single-action 45 with a 3.75-inch barrel and a weight of 28 ounces. Unlike most S&W autos, the 945 can be carried cocked-and-locked.

ounces. It is available in stainless or Parkerized finish, and a V-10 ported version is available.

Springfield offers a Parkerized 1911A1 that essentially recreates a military-specification '11A1. All other Springfield 1911-type pistols now come, in the company's term, "loaded." They have beavertail grip safeties, extended thumb safeties, front and rear slide serrations, special sights and

other niceties that are currently popular.

STANDARD ARMS

A new company, Standard Arms of Nevada, had the first showing of its new SA-9 9mm pistol at the 2000 SHOT Show. The DAO pistol has a polymer frame and 4140 steel slide. It has a pronounced projection on the front of the trigger guard for those who favor placing a finger there in a two-handed hold. The pistol's size

of 4.3x6 inches squeezes it into the subcompact class. Capacity is 10+1. However, the grip can accommodate a 13-round magazine, which is available for law enforcement.

A 380-caliber Standard pistol was scheduled for availability in mid-2000. A 40-caliber variant was anticipated by the beginning of 2001.

STEYR

Steyr made a splash with its interesting polymer-frame M9 and M40 pistols last year. For 2000, they introduced S-series (small size) variants. The new S9 and S40 pistols are about 1/2-inch shorter in both directions, measuring 4.6x6.5 inches. They weigh about 22.5 ounces. Barrel length in either caliber is about 3 1/2 inches, also about 1/2-inch shorter. The new S-series pistols were scheduled for full production by mid-2000.

Also, a new M-series pistol in 357 SIG was planned for introduction by the end of 2000.

STI

STI International has introduced a new Xcaliber 450 pistol with a single-column frame and the Xcaliber 450+ with a double-column frame. The guns have 6-inch bull barrels with V-10 porting. The barrels are bored and rifled for 45 caliber. A change of recoil springs allows the use of cartridges of different power levels--45 ACP, +P and +P+ loads, and 45 Super.

STI also introduced pistols chambered for the new 40 Super cartridge. Developmental work for this cartridge began by necking down the 45 Super and then the 45 Winchester Magnum (45 WM) cartridge. The final form is a bottleneck case of 45 ACP base diameter and the .992-inch length of the 10mm

The SW99 pistol is Smith & Wesson's slightly-revised version of the Walther P99. The double-action SW99 is offered in 9mm and 40 S&W calibers.

The big Smith & Wesson 4506, here being shot by Malloy, and other full-size pistols have been dropped from the S&W line, replaced by an extended line of TSW, Value, Sigma and Chiefs Special pistols.

Lots of people like high-capacity compact 45s. Vickie Lawrence demonstrates Springfield Armory's offering in that category.

chamberings. As the Taurus catalog cutely puts it, it took "only a few fractions of an inch here and there" to make the Millennium into a 45. Actually, the overall length of the PT-145, as the new 45 is designated, is given as an even 6 inches--actually 1/8-inch shorter than the original 9mm. The PT-145 has standard Millennium features, including the thumb safety.

During 2000, Taurus began to phase in a key-locking system for its semiautomatic pistols. Similar to the system used successfully on its revolvers the key lock, once locked, would make the pistol inoperable until manually unlocked again. Two keys will come with each gun. This is a nice extra, so that your wife can unlock the gun when you're away and things go bump in the night.

One gun is back in the Taurus lineup. The 40-caliber versions of the PT-92 and PT-99 had been previously dropped from the line. Now, the redesigned 40 is back as the PT-100. Several finish options are offered.

VEKTOR

Last year, Vektor USA created some sensation with its futuristic-looking 9mm CPI polymer pistol. Recall that the sleek-looking compact pistol was a South African design, using a gas-delay blowback system.

The new Standard Arms SA-9 is a compact polymer-frame pistol, offered in 9mm. The trigger mechanism is double-action-only. A new gun from a new company.

Auto cartridge case. Overall length is 1.25 inches, so that the 40 Super will work through a standard 45 magazine. STI offers a combo pistol with barrels for both 45 and 40 Super. 40 Super ammunition is available from Triton. In testing, 135-grain bullets were pushed to about 1800 feet per second—pretty zippy. (As an aside, it is rumored that the CZ97B will be offered in 40 Super next year.)

Also of interest in the STI line is the LS pistol in 9mm and 40 S&W. The pistol takes the 1911 design and squeezes it down until the dimensions are suited to the 9mm and 40 S&W cartridges. The thickness is .765-inch across the metal, 1-inch across the grips. With a 3.4-inch barrel, dimensions are 4.25x7 inches. Capacity is 6+1 in 40, 7+1 in 9mm. A longer-grip variant, the BLS, which increases the capacity to 8+1 and 9+1, is also available.

TAURUS

Taurus was in the forefront of the recent introduction of Titanium revolvers. Now, the company is offering its Millennium PT-111 as a titanium-slide autoloader. The frame is the original polymer, but the lighter slide reduces weight to 16 ounces. The Titanium Millennium remains a 10+1 9mm and, although it is a DAO, has a frame-mounted thumb safety.

The Millennium series, previously 9mm, 40 and 380, now has added 45 ACP to its

The Steyr M-series pistol, introduced last year, now has a shortened variant available. The new S-series pistols have barrels about 3-1/2 inches long, and are offered in 9mm and 40 S&W chamberings.

The January 2000 SHOT Show marked the debut of the 40-caliber CP2. At first glance, it looks similar to the CP1. However, the pistol displayed was a functional prototype, and mechanically differed markedly from the CP1. The new pistol was built to develop concepts that may (or may not) appear in future Vektor variants. It has, instead of the gas-delay system, a more-or-less traditional cam-actuated tilting-barrel locking arrangement. The trigger is of the pivoting, rather than the

STI's new Xcaliber 450 can handle 45-caliber cartridges of various power levels by changing the recoil springs.

The new 40-caliber Vektor CP2 is styled in the futuristic styling of the CP1, but the internal mechanism may be different. This is a functional prototype, with different trigger, safety and locking mechanism.

sliding, type. It has an external slide release and a frame-mounted manual safety.

Whatever final form the new CP2 takes, it will probably be ready for production in 2001.

Vektor has also expanded its line of full-size 9mm and 40 S&W service pistols to include variants suitable for many types of sport and competition, including some designed for IPSC open class.

WALTHER

The previous importer of Walther pistols, Interarms, is no longer in business. A new company, Walther USA, has been formed to handle importation of Walther products. We are reminded of the previously-discussed relationship with Smith & Wesson, for Walther USA uses the same corporate mailing address.

The Walther line coming in is much smaller, but has some interesting offerings. The original conventional-DA P99 has been changed to the P99QA ("Quick Action"). Described as a single-action trigger mechanism, it is actually a Glock-type trigger. The striker is partially cocked by the movement of the slide, then the cocking is completed by the action of the trigger. To accomplish this, the trigger moves about 1/4-inch. Some customers require the trigger pressure to be of certain specifications for all shots, so Walther has phased out the original P99 and P990 in favor of the P99QA.

One special version of the outgoing standard P99 was scheduled for availability during the year 2000. A Year 2000 commemorative version was planned, engraved with Year 2000 markings and special serial numbers. Each pistol came with a case, a special certificate and a fascinating 150-minute

Disassembled, the Vektor CP2 prototype can be seen to have a cam-actuated tilting-barrel locking system, a system very different from that of the CP1.

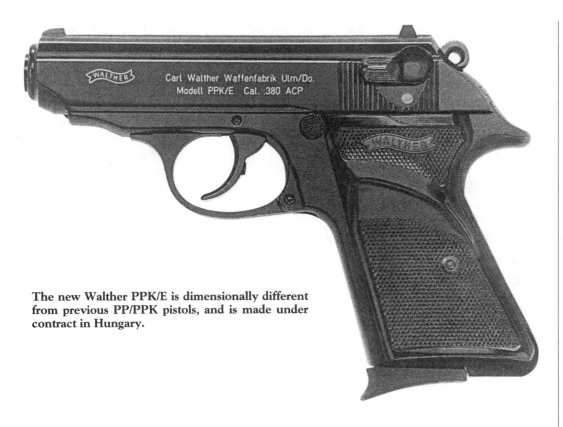

The new Walther PPK/E is dimensionally different from previous PP/PPK pistols, and is made under contract in Hungary.

After seven decades of production (1929-1999), all models of the original Walther PP and PPK pistols, such as this 22-caliber PPK, have been discontinued.

videotape of the history of the Walther firm.

Also only available as commemoratives are the last 500 PP and PPK pistols made. The design dates back to 1929, and after 70 years the PP/PPK series was retired. The 500 "Last Edition" guns were engraved and cased, each with a certificate and the Walther video.

One would hope that the PPK/S would still be in the line, but that little pistol is also gone, replaced by a similar, but not the same, new model, the PPK/E. Parts are not necessarily interchangeable with the earlier models, as the PPK/E is made by a different European manufacturer (FEG) to slightly different dimensions. The most noticeable difference is the larger grip, which gives a capacity of 7+1 for the 380 and 8+1 for the 32. The 32 and 380 versions were planned for March 2000 availability, while a 22LR variant was scheduled for September 2000. The PPK/E is offered in blued finish only.

WILSON

New for the year 2000, Wilson Combat offers a 1911-style 45 called the Millennium Protector. With its black Parkerized finish, it is Wilson's lowest-price custom pistol. Yet it comes with features such as a high-ride beavertail grip safety, speed hammer, front and rear slide serrations, beveled magazine well and other things currently in vogue. The black rubber grips have a large-diamond checkering pattern. The Millennium Protector is guaranteed to shoot groups of 1 1/2 inches or less at 25 yards.

Wilson makes a 22 LR conversion unit for 1911-type pistols and, also offers a complete 22 pistol built on a Wilson frame. It also is guaranteed to shoot within 1 1/2 inches at 25 yards. ●

POSTSCRIPT

Today, our entire firearms industry is facing challenges.
It is vital to continue our fight against those who would deprive us of our rights. But this is never-ending work. Every now and then, take a break and enjoy yourself. Buy a new gun. Go shooting.

by HAL SWIGGETT

HANDGUNS TODAY:

SIXGUNS AND OTHERS

THE ANNUAL SHOT Show is the "biggie" as far as the shooting sports market is concerned. Each year, thousands of firearms dealers walk the aisles to inspect — and order — the latest in firearms, optics, ammunition and such. This year, the show was held in Las Vegas and enjoyed record attendance. Happily, there is plenty of handgun news to report.

I'll begin my review with the oldest handgun manufacturing company in the United States. A company founded in 1857 and still going strong today in the same location. That company is...

SMITH & WESSON

Their new catalog lists thirty-two (32) models of double-action revolvers with barrel lengths from 1 7/8-inch to 8 3/8-inches. Here's the rundown:

Models 317/317LS, in 22LR, are made of aluminum alloy and stainless steel, have an 8-round capacity and 1 7/8-inch barrels. The Model 317 Kit Gun wears a 3-inch barrel and an adjustable rear sight. Same capacity and construction as above.

On page 12 of the new S&W catalog is a model I have owned for many, many years — and used extensively — the K-22. Mine

is engraved by Charlie Price, an engraver who was shot down during WWII and survived. He very fancifully engraved the back portion of the frame and, on the right side, inlaid a gold coiled ready-to-strike rattlesnake. S&W's "modern" K-22 is machined from stainless steel, offered with barrel lengths of 4-,6- or 8 3/8-inches and your choice of 6- or 10-shot cylinders.

Models 331 and 332 have fixed sights, 6-round cylinders chambered for the 32 H&R Magnum and 1 7/8-inch barrels. Their only difference: M331 is single- or double-action and M332 double-action-only. Weight: M331 - 11.9 ounces; M332 - a full 12 ounces.

S&W offers eight models chambered in 38 Special. Barrel lengths range from 1 7/8-inches to 3.2-inches, with three models in double-action-only. Weights vary from 10.8 ounces to 20 ounces. Their only common feature is cylinder capacity - all are 5 rounds.

Model 60/60LS is chambered 38 Special/357 Magnum with choice of 2 1/8- or 3-inch barrels. Model 640 likewise, but DAO (double-action-only).

S&W's catalog lists eight more double-action revolvers chambered 38 Special/357 Magnum.

Model 610 is stainless steel (S/S), chambered for the 10mm; Model 657, chambered 41 Magnum and Model 625, 45

ACP. This model is among my "acquirements not for sale"! It belonged to a San Antonio police officer who was into competitive shooting and won a lot of matches. When he retired, he wouldn't sell it but, one afternoon, he drove by my home and gave it to me.

COLT

This Hartford, CT-based company offers a pair of single action revolvers. First is the Cowboy, chambered for the 45 Colt, with a barrel length of 5 1/2-inches and six-round capacity. The new lockwork design includes a transfer bar safety, meaning the revolver can safely utilize all six chambers. Grips are First Generation as is the blued barrel and color-cased frame.

Second is the Single Action Army in blue & color-case or nickel finish, chambered in your choice of 44-40 or 45 Colt. Barrel lengths are 4 3/4- or 5 1/2-inch, your choice. One of my all-time favorite six-guns is a 7 1/2-inch Colt SAA with blued barrel and cylinder, color-cased frame and stag grips. Plus, I'd best add, an adjustable rear sight. The barrel reads, left side, "COLT NEW FRONTIER S.A.A. .45".

Two more Colt favorites — make that three — no longer in production, all double-action: a stainless steel ANACONDA chambered for the 45 Colt, a 7 1/2-inch New Service in 45 Colt and, third, a blued 6-inch Officers Model Match marked "CAL. 22 MAGNUM CTG". I was told by one of Colt's top

Add a longer barrel and adjustable rear sight to this S&W Model 317 and you have the easy-carrying Model 317 Kit Gun and 8 rounds of 22LR available.

More horsepower in lightweight carry-guns, S&W's Models 331 (shown) and 332 make snag-proof pocket carry easy and deliver the potent 32 H&R Magnum round.

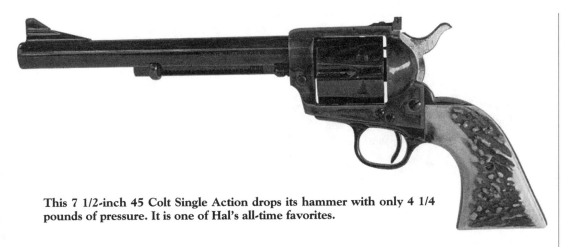

This 7 1/2-inch 45 Colt Single Action drops its hammer with only 4 1/4 pounds of pressure. It is one of Hal's all-time favorites.

executives, during an NSGA Show held in Chicago's McCormick Place (before the SHOT Show came into existence), that 500 of these had been manufactured but only 88 ever left the factory.

RUGER

Would you believe a double-action six-shooter chambered for the 454 Casull? On the right side of the barrel, in big capital letters, is "SUPER REDHAWK". Ruger's chambering specification is stamped on the frame's right side and that same "designation" is on its cylinder - two lines, in two places: ".45 COLT CAL. "(top line) then ".454 CASULL CAL."

Barrel length is 7 1/2 inches. The rear sight has a white-outlined notch and is fully adjustable. The front sight is a field ramp design, with a red insert. This Super Redhawk is designed with integral scope bases and delivered with 1-inch rings. This Super Redhawk's finish is, for lack of a better way to put it, unusual. The best way I can describe it is simply "gray". *Ruger calls the finish 'Target Grey'/Ed.*

Trigger pull on my evaluation sample is surprisingly crisp for a straight-from-the-factory revolver and breaks, consistently, at 4 3/4 pounds. Weight? With Leupold's 2-8x scope aboard in Ruger's rings, the rig weighs 4 pounds, 2 1/2 ounces.

How does it shoot? At 50 yards my five-shot groups consistently measured 1 3/4- to 2 1/2-inches with Winchester ammunition (the only manufacturer of 454 Casull factory ammunition I

know about). I couldn't see any difference, in accuracy, between their 250-grain JHPs and 260-grain Partition Gold cartridges. I did try two full cylinders of Winchester's 225-grain Silvertip Hollow Point 45 Colt ammo but, honestly, can't imagine anyone underpowering a 454 Casull revolver to this extent.

As most of my readers know, I am a dedicated single-action shooter and, although a double-action, this Ruger Super Redhawk 45 Colt/454 Casull just may have found a home.

THOMPSON/CENTER ARMS

T/C's Encore single shot pistol is delivered in more barrel lengths, finishes and chamberings than you would believe possible - plus an Encore package.

These pistols come in your choice of blued or stainless steel. There is another decision to make - solid American walnut or rubber finger-grooved grips. Barrel lengths are 10, 12 and 15 inches. Chamberings offered: 223 Remington, 22-250 Remington, 243 Winchester, 260 Remington, 270 Winchester, 7mm-08 Remington, 308 Winchester, 30-06 Springfield, 44 Remington Magnum, 454 Casull, 45/70 Govt. and 45 Colt/.410-bore (3" chamber). My Thompson/Center Encore pistol - as described below - weighs an even five pounds on my postal scale.

I used an Encore chambered in 308 Winchester, with T/C's 2.5-7x scope on a 15-inch barrel, and one of Peter Pi's Cor-Bon cartridges to tag the most unusual deer I've ever killed in my 72 years of hunting.

Why so unusual? By the taxidermist's estimate, the buck had between 200 and 300 yards of electric fence wire around his antlers, pinning his ears tight — plus 21 strands around his neck. A single round of Cor-Bon's 150-grain Bonded Spitzer SP took off the top of his heart, at 99 yards according to Bushnell's newest rangefinder.

Sighting-in with Cor-Bon's 308 Winchester 150-grain cartridges before I left Texas, I was able to put two, 3-shot

Winchester's 454 Casull cartridges do in fact "fill" this Ruger's six chambers.

Ruger's double action .454 Casull, with a Leupold 2x-6x scope, will serve any handgun hunter well.

Thompson/Center's "ENCORE", chambered 308 Win., with T/Cs 2.5-7x scope took, with a single shot, a mighty unusual deer this past season - in Wyoming.

groups 2 1/2 inches high at 100 yards into, believe it or not, 1 3/4- and 1 1/2-inches. Now you know why I am so high on T/C's 308 Winchester-chambered Encore pistol and Peter Pi's Single Shot Hunter hunting pistol ammunition. Cor-Bon lists muzzle velocity for this particular load at 2625 fps with the warning: Not for use in lever-action rifles.

FREEDOM ARMS, INC.

FA now offers two versions of their Model 83: Premier Grade and Field Grade; both with adjustable sights. Both five-shot, single-action revolvers are available in 50 Action Express, 475 Linebaugh, 454 Casull, 44

Remington Magnum, 41 Remington Magnum and 357 Remington Magnum.

Barrel lengths of the 50, 454, 44 RM and 41 RM are 4 3/4-, 6-7 1/2- and 10-inches. The 475 lists only 4 3/4-, 6- and 7 1/2-inch barrels; their 357 Magnum, those same lengths, plus 9-inch. FA also catalogs a Model 97 (a five- or six-shot revolver), listed as a five-shot when chambered in 45 Colt and 41 Remington Magnum; a six-shot in 357 Magnum.

Also from Freedom Arms: Two models chambered in 22 Long Rifle - one with a 10-inch barrel called "Silhouette Class" wearing silhouette competition sights, black micarta grips and trigger over-

travel screw. The "Varmint Class" 22 LR offers a choice of 5 1/8- or 7 1/2-inch barrel, express sights, black and green laminated hardwood grips and a trigger over-travel screw. Both of these 22s are matte-finish stainless steel, as are all of FA's single-actions.

I have been shooting, for many years, a Freedom Arms 454 Casull with a 9 1/4-inch barrel (including SSK Industries' muzzle brake - fitted so perfectly even a trained eye cannot distinguish where the brake starts and the original barrel ends), topped with a Simmons 1.5-4x scope in SSK's 4-ring mount. This one will be back in South Africa

with me in June. I believe the customs agents at Johannesburg's Jan Smuts International Airport have its serial number memorized; they actually smile every time they see it.

In South Africa (I've been there many times) my Freedom Arms 454 Casull with 4 3/4-inch barrel is always on my right hip - fully loaded - in a holster made for me years ago with cartridge loops on the outside. Never have needed it but sure as I don't wear it I will need it — badly.

COMPETITOR CORP.

Al Straitiff continues on with his cannon-breech single-shot pistol, available in a wide array of chamberings. The one I have been shooting for a good many years is chambered 284 Winchester with a Leupold 2.5-8x scope on top. With its one-piece stock and 14-inch barrel (including muzzle brake) my Competitor's overall length is 16 inches and it weighs - scope, mount and all - 5 1/4 pounds.

How does it work? Twist its "breech" to the right to open - insert a cartridge - back to the left to close - then gently, very gently touch the trigger. Why so gently? There is an "insert" in Competitor's trigger. Mine breaks at 1 1/4-pounds of "touch" - not, really, a "pull".

True, with its cannon-breech, it looks a bit strange. Also true, once the shooter has become accustomed to firing the Competitor a second, or even a third, shot can be fired muy pronto when extra cartridges are held in a wrist band. Mine will be in South Africa with me, again, in June. It is zeroed 3 inches high at 100 yards. This means any "critter" within 200 yards is in serious trouble.

M.O.A. Corporation

Richard Mertz takes his single-shot pistol business mighty serious. He will chamber almost any cartridge you can dream up and put it into your choice of 8 3/4-, 10 1/2- or 14-inch barrels. Special barrel lengths are available at extra charge and must be approved by Richard Mertz himself. And, I'd best add, his Maximum barrels are free-floated.

Freedom Arms "pair"—their 4 5/8-inch and 9 1/2-inch, both chambered 454 Casull. These have become one of this writer's all-time favorites for hunting - both stateside and in South Africa.

Taurus' new Police Model 85 is a 5-shooter, hammerless (meaning double-action-only), weighing 13 ounces and chambered 38 Special. Model 617 is 357 Magnum, 7-shot, double-action (as are all of these next offerings). Model 415 is chambered 41 Magnum and, like all of these except Model 617, a 5-shooter.

Model 450 is chambered 45 Colt (for reasons unknown - Taurus added the word "LONG" before Colt). There is no such cartridge listed in *Cartridges of the World*.

Model 445 is chambered 44 Special. Models 85 MULTI and 85 CHULT are chambered 38 Special with the latter (CHULT) listed as double-action-only (DAO).

All of the above carry two-inch barrels and are made of "Total Titanium".

Taurus lists, on page six of their new catalog, eight 22 Short/Long/Long Rifle-chambered, double-action 9-shot revolvers. Plus, eight models offering 22 Magnum (WMR) as eight-shooters. Page seven lists sixteen models of two- and three-inch 38 Special double-action revolvers, with four of those sixteen as DAO (double action only).

Wherever Hal's scoped 454 Casull goes hunting, his iron-sighted 4 5/8-inch FA rig is always on his hip to better handle close encounters.

The product literature reports 1/2-minute-of-angle accuracy from the 22-250, 6PPC and 250 Savage chamberings. The Maximum pistol is widely used in IHMSA silhouette and has won championships every year since 1986. Of interest to handgun hunters, there are nine color photographs in his catalog showing "critters" from

wild hogs to elk — even Greater Kudu — taken by hunters.

The Maximum is available in either blued or stainless steel. Options include a muzzle brake, fluted barrel (stainless only) and most any chambering you might desire. Delivery time averages three to four months.

TAURUS

This Florida-based company extols, for all the shooting world to hear, TITANIUM. New for 2000, they offer their Model 627 Tracker, a 7-shot 357 Magnum or 5-shot 41 Magnum, with 4-inch barrel, in their "Total Titanium Shadow Gray" finish.

▲ The Competitor is a bit "unusual" with its "cannon-like" breech - but - once understood.....

◄ ..... it is mighty fast to eject the empty and get a fresh cartridge chambered.

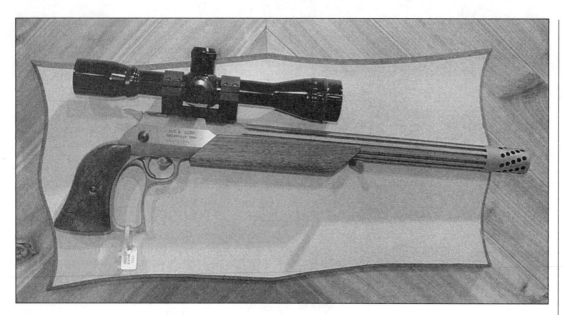

M.O.A.'s "Maximum" has captured more than a few silhouette championships, and is equally successful in the hunting field.

Page eight and nine details a 7-shot +P 38 Special as well as five- and seven-shot 357 Magnum double action revolvers.

Page 10 and 11 are back on twenty (20) models of Total Titanium double action revolvers chambered 357 Magnum, 44 Special, 41 Magnum and 45 Colt.

Pages 12 through 14 are, by far, most interesting to big-bore shooters. Here are displayed b-i-g 6 1/2-inch to 8 3/8-inch double-action revolvers chambered 44 Magnum, 45 Colt and 454 Casull.

Page 15 will interest more than a few handgunners. Why?

Taurus starts off the page with b-i-g black letters reading "VARMINTS BEWARE". This one is 8-shot - with 10-inch heavy vent-rib barrel, designed to accept 22 Hornet cartridges. It is delivered with a scope mounting base installed and, yes, the shooter will have to pull the trigger eight times before it has to be reloaded. Recoil? There should be very little, if any, because this Raging Hornet weighs 50 ounces (minus scope).

There is no way, on these pages, their entire catalog be properly described, so see your nearest firearms dealer, or order your own copy.

SAVAGE ARMS

This company is far better known for its excellent, reasonably priced rifles. However, they do turn out some mighty fine bolt-action pistols, with the bolt on the proper side for right-handed shooters (meaning left-side), with right-side ejection. I have been shooting one chambered 22-250

Remington, topped with a Burris 3-9x scope. This rig did, in fact, cause the demise of more than a few Kansas prairie dogs a few months back. Trigger pull, from their factory, is clean as breaking glass - at 2 1/8 pounds. Their new catalog lists six models:

516SAK is chambered 22-250 Remington, 243 Winchester, 7mm-O8 Remington, 260 Remington and 308 Winchester, all with a 12-inch barrel AND their very efficient muzzle brake.

Model 516FSS carries a 14-inch barrel with no muzzle brake, chambered 223 Remington, 22-250 Remington, 243 Winchester, 7mm-08 Remington, 260 Remington and 308 Winchester. Both of the foregoing have stainless-steel barrels.

Model 510F is blued and chambered for 223 Remington, 22-250 Remington, 243 Winchester, 7mm-08 Remington, 260 Remington and 308 Winchester.

Sport Striker carries 10 inches of barrel with choice of two chamberings: 501F - 22 Long Rifle; 502F - 22 WMR.

Still more: Super Striker is offered in two models - 516BSAK, with 12 inches of fluted stainless steel barrel, with muzzle brake, chambered to accept 223 Remington, 22-250 Rem., 243 Win., 7mm-08 Rem., 260 Remington and 308 Winchester. Model 516BSS is 14 inches of fluted stainless steel barrel, minus the muzzle brake. Chamberings are same as listed above.

These last two wear thumb-hole laminated stocks with dual pillar-bedding. And, I'd best add, all are drilled and tapped for scope mounting.

HARRINGTON & RICHARDSON / NEW ENGLAND FIREARMS

Harrington & Richardson and New England Firearms have decided to sit out this year in terms of handgun manufacturing. Neither company will manufacture handguns during 2000. However, I'm told both plan to resume production of their revolvers next year - 2001.

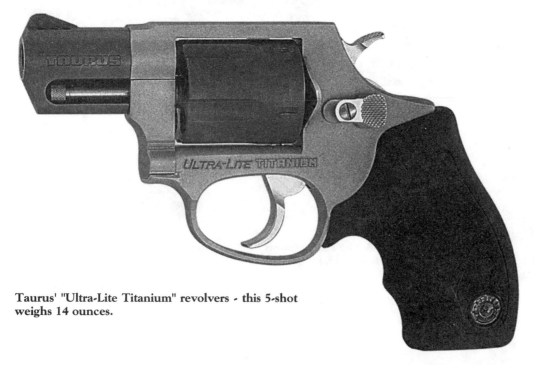

Taurus' "Ultra-Lite Titanium" revolvers - this 5-shot weighs 14 ounces.

Taurus' big Raging Bull 454 Casull is still doing its more-than-creditable job.

CHARTER ARMS

Charter Arms is offering two double-action revolvers - both with 5-round cylinders and stainless steel construction. Undercover is chambered 38 Special and weighs 19 1/2 ounces; Bulldog is chambered for the 44 Special and is a bit heavier at 21 ounces. Each with 2-inch barrels. Both lock up in three places: at the hand, cylinder stop and ejector-rod collar.

I've often carried an earlier model, no longer manufactured, called Bulldog Pug, chambered for the 44 Special. Its hammer is "bobbed", meaning double-action-only. Charter also offers the Compact with a standard hammer and the Super Compact hammerless (like mine).

AMERICAN DERRINGER

This company has been around for many, many years. My very own stainless steel derringer – 45 Colt, three-inch barrels; weight: (both barrels filled with 255-grain SWC cartridges) 1pound, 1/2-ounce, is here on my desk as these words are typed.

BOND ARMS

Greg Bond manufactures single-action, high-quality derringers with interchangeable barrels. Chamberings are 9mm, 357 Magnum/38 Special, 40, 44 Magnum/44 Special, 45 Colt/.410-bore and 45 ACP. Bond Arms is a fairly young company but does manufacture a very fine product. If that was not the case, the company would not be mentioned here.

MANURHIN

A few years back I visited the Manurhin plant in Mulhouse, France. In fact - I spent 8 1/2 hours in their facility - about half with the international sale manager and an interpreter.

The interpreter took me through their manufacturing department then to the range, in a basement, where all Manurhin handguns were test-fired before shipping. The rangemaster asked if I would like to shoot one of their guns and handed me one of their 357 Magnum DAs and a box of ammunition. Loading five in its 6-shot cylinder I, carefully as I could, fired them at the 25-yard target. He looked, very closely, then asked, "Sir, would you do that again?" I placed another five in the cylinder then touched them off. He watched every one - then turned to me and said, "Sir, you shoot better than our guns!" All of you reading this know that to be totally impossible.

Once back in the United States I received a Manurhin MR 73 double-action revolver, with excellent target sights, chambered 32 Long. These are, by far, the best-finished handguns I've seen anyplace in the world. Immaculate might be a better description. The entire metal finish is polished and deeply blued to perfection.

The factory trigger pull is 3 1/4 pounds. Another desirable feature not commonly offered by American manufacturers is the trigger stop screw which adjusts so that no trigger over-travel is felt. Actual trigger movement is the tiniest fraction of an inch - barely visible to even a practiced eye.

SSK INDUSTRIES

J.D. Jones, founder of SSK Industries, is a long, long-time friend. How long? His youngest daughter still calls me "My Pal Hal" and she is now a schoolteacher with children of her own.

All that to say this: I have a Ruger Super Redhawk 44 Magnum that he rebuilt. Its octagon barrel reads: "Custom Crafted For Hal Swiggett By J.D. Jones". On that same side, the frame reads (over Super Redhawk) "SSK Custom". Over .44 MAGNUM CAL. on that same portion of the frame, it reads: "Beauty and the Beast". Beast's barrel is 6 1/8-inches long but only 3 1/2-inches protrudes from the frame -

Savage Arms bolt-action pistol, with its bolt on the left side, is the one Hal likes best.

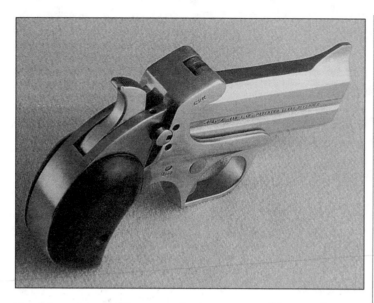

Bond Arms is one of the newer, but very successful, manufacturers of pocket pistols. Shown here is their newest 45 Colt/.410 3-inch pistol.

with a cavernous hole beneath its red front sight.

J.D. - and his SSK Industries - can and will build anything within semi-reason should you have custom-work desires.

DAVIS DERRINGERS

This California-based company offers three versions of their derringers: Standard D-Series is chambered 22 LR, 22 WMR, 25 Auto or 32 Auto. Barrel length is 2.4 inches. Weight empty, 9.5 ounces. Grips unbreakable pearl on their 22 LR and 25 Auto.

The Big Bore Series is chambered 22 WMR, 32 H&R Magnum, 9mm or 38 Special.

Barrel length is 2.75 inches and weight empty, is 14 ounces. Grips are molded black synthetic, laminated oak or laminated rosewood. Metal finish is your choice of chrome or black Teflon.

The Long Bore Series is chambered 22 WMR, 9mm or 38 Special. Barrel length is 3.5 inches and it weighs, empty, 16 ounces. Grips are molded black synthetic, laminated oak or laminated rosewood. Metal finish is your choice of chrome or black Teflon.

DAN WESSON

On my desk, as these words are typed, are two DWs I've hung onto for years: one is a

very heavy 45 Colt, with a 6-inch barrel and immaculately blued finish. It weighs, on my postal scale, 3 1/2 pounds. Trigger pull is 2 1/2 pounds. The other is a stainless steel 6-inch, chambered 22 Winchester Magnum. Trigger pull is exactly 3 pounds. Both are fitted with adjustable rear sights. The 45 has a yellow insert up front and my 22 Winchester Magnum has a red insert.

ANSCHUTZ

Anschütz bolt-action pistols are known world-wide. Dieter Anschutz' two newest offerings are: the Model 64 P chambered 22 Long Rifle (5 round capacity) and the Model 64 P Magnum for the larger 22 WMR cartridge (4 round capacity).

The well-proven barreled actions of these two are seated in a black – ergonomic, weather-proof and non-slip – synthetic stock. Both weigh 3 1/2 pounds, have two-stage triggers and are drilled and tapped for scope mounting.

BOWEN CLASSIC ARMS CORP.

I have two examples of Hamilton Bowen's expertise on my desk. One a rechambered stainless steel Smith & Wesson 5-inch that started life chambered 10mm. The other is built on a Ruger 44 Magnum New Model Super Blackhawk

frame - but no longer feeds on those little 44 Magnum "cattiges", as one of my gunsmith friends called them.

First, the S&W: It started life as the Model 610, chambered 10mm, with S&W's full lug barrel. Approximately 5,000 were manufactured in 1990 only, then the model was reintroduced in 1998.

Stamped on the right side its barrel, where 10mm used to be, now appears 38-40. I showed this to Ross Seyfried at one of Winchester's meetings. He sort of ho-hummed and, more than likely, wondered why I was wasting his time. I suggested turning it over and looking at its "other" side. Soon as he saw ".38-40 CAL." he looked me in the eye and said, "Hal, I think you have something here!" I already knew I did.

Hamilton's "other" work of gunsmithing art started life as a Ruger 44 Magnum New Model Super Blackhawk. It now wears a 7 1/2-inch octagon barrel that reads "BOWEN CLASSIC ARMS CORP." on its left side and ".500 MAGNUM CAL." on that opposite side, and measures .745-inches across the "flats".

My rather heavy single-action Ruger weighs, on my postal scale, 3 pounds, 1 ounce. Trigger pull on this highly customized single action is a mighty crisp 3 1/2 pounds, with no take-up slack.

The load Hamilton gave me uses H110 under a 420-grain cast .512-inch bullet launched by one of Winchester's Large Rifle primers. The case, originally 348 Winchester, is shortened to 1.39-inches, making a loaded cartridge measure 1.8-inches overall. The loaded cartridge weight is a fraction short of 1 1/2 ounces.

E.M.F.

This California-based importer lists more than a few single-action revolvers. You will need their catalog to see them all - but - I'll do my best to describe a few - the rest will be up to you. All are listed as "HARTFORD MODEL".

1873 Single Action Army - Their 1873 Single Action Army's barrel length is 7 1/2-inches and is chambered for six cartridges: 45 Colt, 357 Magnum and 44-40 as

Manurhin revolvers are manufactured in France. Though offered in several chamberings, the one shown here is chambered for the 32 Long.

One of my favorite revolvers is this stainless Dan Wesson chambered 22 WMR.

work with their 22 LR-chambered single-actions a few months back and they performed right well.

HERITAGE MANUFACTURING

Manufactured here in good ol' USA, this Florida-based company turns out (in the revolver category) only 22 Long Rifle and 22 WMR single-action revolvers with two grip configurations - bird head and traditional. Two finishes also - blue or nickel - with barrel lengths 3 1/2-, 4 3/4-, 6- and 9-inches.

I've said it before - but here it is again - for honest-to-goodness fun with any handgun, it has to be - must be - a rimfire single action.

EUROPEAN AMERICAN ARMORY

This Florida-based importer offers one double-action revolver and three single-action revolvers manufactured in Germany.

"Windicator" is their 38 Special/357 Magnum 6-shot double-action revolver. Barrel lengths are 2 or 4 inches. Finish is blue with a choice of fixed or adjustable sights.

Two of EAA's single-actions are chambered 357 Magnum, 44-40, 44 Remington Magnum or 45 Colt. Barrel lengths are 4 1/2 or 7 1/2 inches with fixed sights, 6-shot cylinders and deep bluing with color case frames, or nickel finish. Weight of their shorter

standard, plus "special" chamberings of 38-40, 32-20 and 44 Special.

1873 Frontier - The Hartford Single Action Revolver is the most prized of all Cowboy revolvers. Barrel length is 5 1/2-inches and, quoting their literature, "Great Attention Has Been Given to Every Detail to insure That it Truly is Identical to the Original Colt Single Action Revolver in Authenticity as Well as Quality. All Parts are Interchangeable with the Original 1st and 2nd Generation Colts." All those "capital letters" are theirs - not mine.

1873 Sixshooter - This 4 3/4-inch barrel single-action is listed as "The New Hartford Model Revolver", available with either the Old Model or New Model frames. And yes, there is more. Old Model frames are chambered 45 Colt, 38-40, 32-20 and 44-40. New Model frames are chambered 45 Colt, 357 Magnum and 44 Special. They offer engraved models with what they call "Class 'A' Engraving and Custom Blue Finish".

E.M.F. also lists a Cavalry Model (7 1/2-inch) and Artillery Model (5 1/2-inch) - both chambered for what they call 45 Long Colt (it is still, correctly, the 45 Colt

cartridge). There are more - a lot more - including Lightning or Express models with 4-, 4 3/4- and 5 1/2-inch barrels. You really will need their catalog.

I A R

This California-based importer of Italian-manufactured single-action revolvers offers three versions - the 1873 Six Shooter (22 Long Rifle/22 WMR combo) with a 5 1/2-inch barrel, the 1873 Frontier Marshall (357 Magnum or 45 Colt) with 7 1/2-inch barrel and the 1873 Frontier 22 (22 Long Rifle only), with a 4 1/2-inch barrel. I had reason to

What you see here is the first Anschütz pistol chambered 22 WMR. Proof? it is the only early Anschütz pistol with the bolt on the right side. Dieter built this one specifically for me using one of his rifle actions.....

Hamilton Bowen built this octagon-barreled 500 Magnum on a Ruger frame.

version is 2.45 pounds and 2.7 pounds for their longer-barreled six-gun. New to EAA's line is a 6- or 8-shot 22 Long Rifle/ 22 WMR single-action in two barrel lengths: 4 3/4- or 6 3/4 inches. Your choice of deep blue or nickel finish. Grips on all three are European walnut and sights are fixed.

CIMARRON ARMS

Cimarron imports replicas any of you would be hard-pressed to differentiate from an original, except for the finish. Elderly, original six-guns would be well-worn.

Should you be interested I can fully recommend your looking into Cimarron's line of brand-spankin' new "Oldtimers".

Not a gun, but a fine book about...single action revolvers. Three hundred twenty pages filled with information about single-action revolvers. Devoted - entirely - to Action Shooting Cowboy Style (the title). Written by John Taffin and published by Krause Publications, the book goes into detail about Cowboy Action Shooting and the guns and loads used - including cap-and-ball six-guns. Though I

have never become involved in this sort of shooting I will support anything that speaks favorably about my all-time favorite hunting firearm. As most of you know - I hunt over a lot of the world and only with handguns!

How long have I been shooting handguns? My grandfather started me with a Colt's Single Action revolver on my sixth birthday - July 22, 1927. And I am still at it!

PHELPS MFG. CO.

I have owned, for many years, one of Gene Phelps' humongous six-guns -

chambered for the 45-70 Government. Barrel length is 8 inches - weight an even six pounds on my Remington Game Scale. Cylinder length is 2 1/4 inches with 6-shot capacity. Yes! With adjustable sights, too. The one here on my desk (which came from Gene himself) reads, on its right-side frame below the cylinder, "Heritage 1". Trigger pull is 3 1/2 pounds.

Phelps first manufactured his b-i-g single actions in 1978 - all chambered 45-70. Later he added 444 Marlin, 375 Winchester and, last, 50-70 Government. These six-guns are no longer manufactured so you'll have to watch the classified ads and check the gun shows to find one.

CLASSIC OLD WEST STYLES

Based in El Paso, Texas this company offers anything any of you "Westerners" might think of concerning how, and where, to carry your single- and double-action revolvers.

Their catalog offers more gunleather styles than you might imagine. In other words "nothing has been left out". That includes clothing, etc.

This includes gun inlays (A) United States Marshall, (B) Texas Ranger, (C) Rattlesnake, (D) Tombstone Marshall, (E) Deputy Sheriff, (F) Wyatt Earp and (G) Texas Star. Plus imitation ivory grips with Mexican Eagle, Liberty Cap,

Gene Phelps' 45-70 six-shooter is not really intended for quick-draw competition. Why? It weighs an even six pounds.

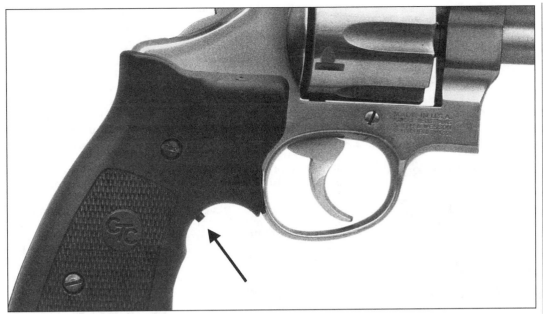

Lasergrips are black, nicely checkered for a firm grip and look like any other handgun grip except for a tiny, almost invisible, protrusion on the upper right side. Gripping the revolver automatically activates a red laser beam, which indicates exactly where a bullet will go.

Kirkpatrick Leather's "Hal Swiggett" shoulder holster for big hunting handguns. This one was built for Hal's 454 Casull Freedom Arms single action with its 1.5-4x Simmons scope.

beam hits them right where a bullet could instantly follow.

C-MORE SYSTEMS

I have one of these sights on an 8 1/2-inch Mag-na-Ported STALKER 44 Magnum Ruger New Model SUPER BLACKHAWK and it is, by far, the "fastest" sight on any of my handguns. Simply put the red dot on where you want your bullet to go, then touch it off! A bit bulky - but it does everything C-More says it will.

GARRETT CARTRIDGES

Though Randy Garrett does not manufacture "Sixguns and Others" firearms, he does load the finest ammunition for 44 Remington Magnum-chambered Ruger Redhawk and Super Redhawk double-action revolvers. By "finest" I mean "most powerful" - designed specifically for Ruger's b-i-g double-action six-guns.

KIRKPATRICK LEATHER

I found this Laredo (Texas)-based company many years back. He designed a shoulder holster specifically for my Freedom Arms 454 Casull single-action with its 9 1/4-inch barrel (including muzzle brake) and its 1.5-4x Simmons scope on top. He made another to fit my Thompson/Center Encore 308 Winchester - with its 15-inch barrel and T/C's 2.5-7x scope. My name is stamped on each and every shoulder holster he has sold.

Should you have one of the above handgun models, he can build a holster for you, too. Or you can lay your handgun (scoped or not) on a large sheet of paper, draw an outline around it - mail it to him - and he will tell you exactly what the cost will be before he starts his expert leather workers on it.

MICHAELS OF OREGON

Home of the "World's Fastest Gun Bore Cleaner". Mine measures 22 inches and includes an end-weighted cord to get it through the barrel. It does what it says in the literature - "Cleans Gun Bores in 10 Seconds". For 44/45-caliber pistol, 30-caliber rifle or 12 gauge.

Liberty Eagle, Checkered, Checkered with Star, Steer Skull, Schofield, Navy Eagle, Ruger Vaquero Plain and Ruger Vaquero Bull. There is more, much more - so - send for their catalog.

COR-BON

Peter Pi's Cor-Bon ammunition company turns out, by far, the best specialty ammunition offered today. I say "specialty" because his company does not load for every caliber/cartridge. His company also turns out what he calls "Bee Safe Pre-Fragmented Safety Ammunition" in eight different chamberings.

I used his 308 Super Mag in my Thompson/Center Encore pistol to take the most unusual deer I've ever tagged. He has two loadings for the 308 Winchester cartridge: 165-grain SPBT and 180-grain SPBT. The cartridge that "tagged" my trophy was one of his 165-grainers. A one-shot kill, top of the heart shot at, according to Bushnell's new rangefinder, 99 yards.

LASERGRIPS

I have these on one of my Smith & Wesson stainless steel double-actions. Other than the tiny "hump" on the right grip, topside, no one would ever notice anything different until the red laser

by **RAYMOND CARANTA**

THE GUNS OF EUROPE

The European Single Shot Centerfire Rifle.

DURING THE MUZZLELOADING era, most rifles were single shot, in order to optimize their long range accuracy, reduce their weight and cost.

The introduction of efficient metallic cartridges, during the second half of the nineteenth century, enabled manufacturers to economically produce repeating rifles which, by 1900, had conquered the military market and a significant share of the commercial one.

Then, only four minor classes of users resisted the lure of fire-power: the target shooters, for whom it was of no significance, the *"Pirschell"* and mountain hunters, looking for light and highly accurate guns and some rural hunters, extremely cost-sensitive, for economical reasons.

At the turn of the twentieth century current or obsolescent military rifle calibers were often used, in bolt-action guns, both for big game hunting and target shooting.

For instance, in the French colonial empire, the former 11mm Gras (385-grain lead bullet @ 1500 fps) service round was very popular for hunting up to World War I, together with the new 8mm Lebel (198-grain jacketed or soft point bullet @ 2380 fps).

The 8mm Rival was similar to the latter loading.

Likewise, the Italians used both their 10.4mm "M70" Vetterli round (313-grain lead bullet @ 1345 fps) and, for long range chamois hunting, the 6.5mm Carcano service caliber (160-grain jacketed or soft-point bullet @ 2300 fps); the Swiss, a similar Vetterli loading and, still for chamois, the 7.5mm Schmidt-Rubin cartridge (190-grain bullet @ 2500 fps)and, the British, several variations of their Martini-Henry 450 and 303 British calibers.

For target shooting, in France, the 6mm rimfire calibers ("Bosquette" at 12 meters and "Long" up to 100 meters) were kings, with a smaller following for the American 22 rimfires (Short, Long and the then-new "Long Rifle").

For hunting wolves, foxes and small to medium game under 100 yards, single shot rifles chambered in 22 WCF (45-grain lead bullet @ 1540 fps), 8mm service Model 1892 revolver (117-grain jacketed bullet @ 1150 fps in rifle barrels) and 32 WCF (115-grain bullet @ 1177 fps) were in widespread use.

In central Europe, the situation was more sophisticated as, beside the usual service rifle calibers such as the German 7.9mm Model 1888 (226-grain bullets @ 2100 fps), a dozen special commercial calibers were in use for single shot rifles.

Among them, the 8.15x46mm (151-grain soft-point bullet @ 1800 fps) was extremely popular for both

Before World War II, the "Simplex-Express", made by Manufrance, was a popular single shot rifle in the French colonial empire (weight 9.2 pounds approximately).

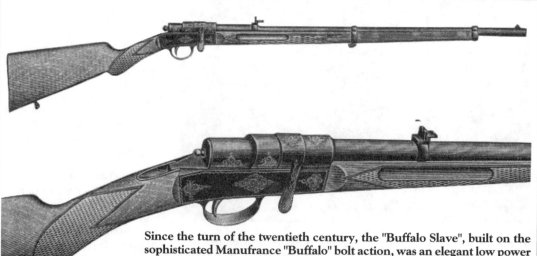

Since the turn of the twentieth century, the "Buffalo Slave", built on the sophisticated Manufrance "Buffalo" bolt action, was an elegant low power single shot centerfire rifle (length overall - 42 inches. Weight - 4.85 lbs.).

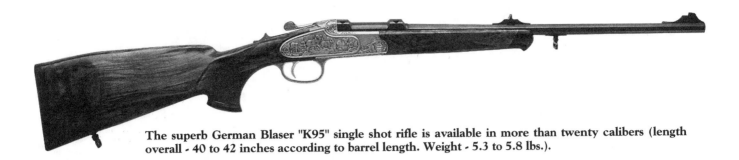

The superb German Blaser "K95" single shot rifle is available in more than twenty calibers (length overall - 40 to 42 inches according to barrel length. Weight - 5.3 to 5.8 lbs.).

target shooting and hunting, and a 9.3x4mm Mauser caliber was also used.

Classic German hunting calibers, chambered in single shot rifles of the period, were the 6.5x27mm Mauser (82-grain soft-point bullet @ 1570 fps), 6.5x4mm Sauer (126-grain lead bullet @ 1150 fps), 8x48mm Sauer (196-grain soft-point bullet @ 1685 fps), 9.3x72mm Sauer (186-grain soft-point bullet) and the 11.15x65mm Express (ballistics unknown to this writer).

In France, before World War II, the 22 Long Rifle had definitely superseded the former 6mm rimfires for target shooting and, for big game hunting, the 8mm Lebel (see above), 375 H&H Magnum (270- or 300-grain soft- point bullet @ 2700/2500 fps) and 405 Winchester (300-grain soft point bullet @ 1970 fps) were standard. For smaller game, the single shot 8mm Model 1892 and 32 WCF carbines, previously mentioned, remained in use.

While fixed-barrel single shot hunting centerfire carbines had been relatively common, the current European production is mostly based on the German folding-barrel *Kipplauf* type, with some rare exceptions, such as the Furtschegger *Heeren-Blockbuchse,* or the Heym-Ruger *Blockbuchse,* based on an American Ruger action.

These modern single shot hunting rifles are principally manufactured in Germany (Blaser, Heym and Krieghoff), Austria (Ferlach, Furtschegger and Franz Sodia), Italy (Renato Gamba, Pedretti, Perugini & Visini and Zanardini), Czech Republic (Zbrojovka Brno) or France (Chapuis Armes).

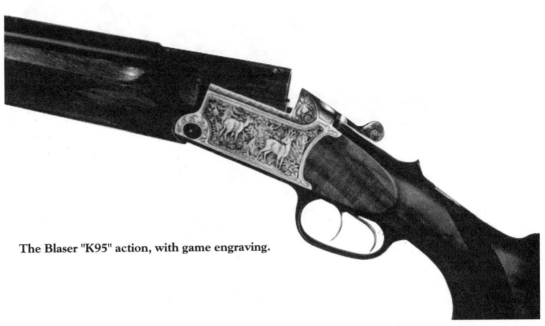

The Blaser "K95" action, with game engraving.

Blaser Jagdwaffen

This German company is mostly known for its expensive "RG3" repeating bolt action rifle of original design, but Blaser also makes combination guns, Drillings and I.S.U. 300-meter "Standard" target rifles.

The Blaser K95 *Kipplauf-Buchsell* is available in the following calibers: - 22 Hornet - 222 Remington - 5.6x50R Magnum - 5.6x52R - 243 Winchester - 6.5x57R - 6.5x65R RWS - 6.5x68R - 270

Winchester - 7x57R - 7x65R - 7mm Remington Mag - 30R Blaser, 300 Winchester Magnum - 300 Weatherby Magnum - 8x57JRS - 8x68S and 9.3x74R.

Barrel lengths are 23.6 inches for standard calibers and 25.6 inches for Magnums. Weight is 5.3 to 5.74 pounds, depending on calibers.

The "Luxus" is the basic model, followed by the engraved "Diplomat" and the "Baronessell" with sideplates and octagonal barrel.

A "Mag-na-Port" muzzle brake and "kickstop" stock recoil absorber are optional.

Prices (from $2,400.00 to $8,300.00 in France) are in direct relation with the "K95" origin and quality.

Brno Arms ("Zbrojovka Brno")

A traditional Czech company justly famous since the 1920s for the quality of their materials and workmanship.

They are now making a classic "ZBK110" top-lever

The inexpensive Czech Brno "ZBK 110" hunting rifle is easily convertible into a 12 gauge Magnum shotgun by changing its barrel (length overall - 40 inches. Weight - 6 lb.). For next year, the factory announces a more sophisticated "ZK99" *Kipplauf,* available in 12 different calibers, from 22 Hornet to 30-06 Springfield.

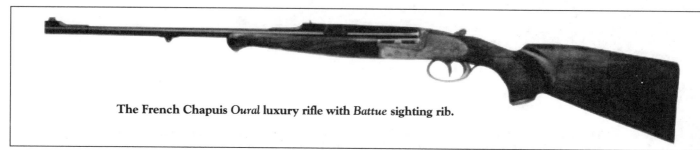

The French Chapuis *Oural* luxury rifle with *Battue* sighting rib.

A Chapuis *Oural* rifle with it's action opened.

folding-barrel single shot rifle chambered in 22 Hornet - 222 Remington - 5.6x50R Magnum - 5.6x52R - 7x57R - 7x65R and 8x57JRS with 23.6-inch barrel, weighing 6 pounds, at a very attractive price (from $224.00 to $306.00 in France).

The matching 12 gauge shotgun is the "ZBK100", with a 27.5-inch, or 31.5-inch, barrel (weight is 5.5 or 5.7 pounds), interchangeable with the whole rifled range (price of combo $383.00 in France).

Chapuis Armes

This is a French shotgun manufacturer located at Saint-Bonnet-le-Chateau, near Saint-Etienne, who also produces double express rifles and a very nice *Oural Kipplauf*, available in 6.5x57R - 7x65R - 270 Winchester and 300 Winchester Magnum; with the standard 23.6-inch barrel, at 6 pounds approximately. Three grades, "Exel", "Luxe" and "Elite", are offered at, respectively, $3,700.00, $6,300.00 and $9,800.00.

Ferlach

These aristocrats of Austrian gunmakers list a wonderful line of traditional shotguns and rifles, including a luxury Model 70 *Kipplaufbuchse,* with "Rasant" steel,, 26- to 28-inch barrels, chambered in any classic caliber, as required. Lower weight is 7 pounds. Bohler "Antinit NG"/ or "Super Blitz" steel are optional for barrels. Sideplates are also optional. Price and lead-time on request, in accordance with specific requirements.

W. Furtschegger

Another prestigious Austrian gunmaker from Kufstein (Tirol) who offers a line of custom shotguns and rifles, including a marvelous

Heeren-Blockbuchse fixed barrel, in "Standard" and "Exclusive" grades.

Weights are from 5.3 to 6.4 pounds as per specifications. Barrels are available in Bohler "Rasant" or "Super Blitz" steel.

Price and lead-time on request.

Renato-Gamba

This flamboyant Italian gunmaker has produced for many years a luxury "Mustang" rifle of *Kipplauf* style, chambered in 243 Winchester - 6.5x57R - 7x65mm and 30/06 Springfield, with 24.5- and 25.5-inch demi-bloc barrels. This gun features an H&H sidelock with set-trigger and treble Greener locks. Average weight is listed as 6.2 pounds. Price on request.

Heym-Waffenfabrik GmbH

This company, founded in 1865, is also famous in Europe for its luxury rifles and shotguns.

In the field of single shot hunting rifles Heym has built, for years, custom guns on the Ruger Number 1 action.

Now, they are producing their own *Kipplauf-Buchsell* Model "44B", chambered in a host of calibers: 22 Hornet - 222 Remington - 222 Remington Magnum - 22-250 Remington - 243 Winchester - 308 Winchester - 30-06 Springfield - 30R Blaser - 5.6x50R Magnum - 5.6x52R - 5.6x57R - 6x62R Freres - 6.5x55SM - 6.565R RWS - 6.5x57 R - 7x57R - 7x65R - 8x57IRS - 8x75RS - 9.3x74 R - 10.3x60R Swiss.

The standard barrel length is 23.6 inches and weight is 6 pounds, approximately. Price on request.

Krieghoff

A particularly innovative German gunmaker who lists, since 1997, a beautiful "Hubertus" single barrel rifle

The nice Austrian Model 70 *Kipplaufbuchse*, from Ferlach.

The Austrian *Heeren-Blockbuchse* from W. Furtschegger is a magnificent fixed-barrel single shot hunting rifle available in several grades of engraving.

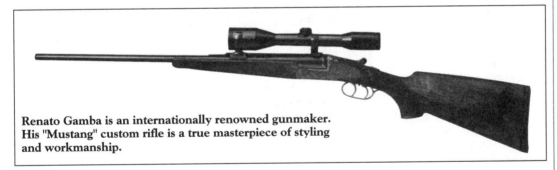

The German gunmaker, Heym, has been famous in Europe for several years, with his beautiful single shot "HR30/38" fixed-barrel rifles built around a Ruger action.

Renato Gamba is an internationally renowned gunmaker. His "Mustang" custom rifle is a true masterpiece of styling and workmanship.

Winchester - 30-06 Springfield - 270 Weatherby Magnum - 7mm Remington Magnum - 300 Winchester Magnum. Prices, in France, range from $2,500.00 to 3,500.00 as per specifications and style.

Armi-Pedretti-di-Enrico

This Italian company, founded in 1948 in Gardone VT by Giuseppe Pedretti, is specialized, among others, in the production of folding single barrel shotguns.

They make also a small top-lever rifle Model "FP105LR", chambered in 22 rimfire, 22 Hornet, 5.6x52R, 222 Remington, 357 Magnum and 44 Magnum.

This nice gun is fitted with open adjustable sights and features a rail for scope mounting. The silver-gray action is scroll engraved.

with steel, or light alloy, top-lever action.

The hammerless "Hubertus" rifle is fitted with the Krieghoff patented universal trigger set at 3.5 pounds, and hand-cocking device.

Optional sideplates and engravings. Barrel length: 23.6 inches. Weight: 6.4 pounds with the steel action and 5.5 pounds with the light alloy one. Double locks. The following calibers are

available: 5.6x50R Magnum - 5.6x52R - 6.2X62R Freres - 6.5x57 - 6.5x57R - 6.5x65R - 7x57 - 7x57R - 4x64 - 7x65R - 8x57IRS - 8x57RS - 222 Remington - 243 Winchester - 270 Winchester - 308

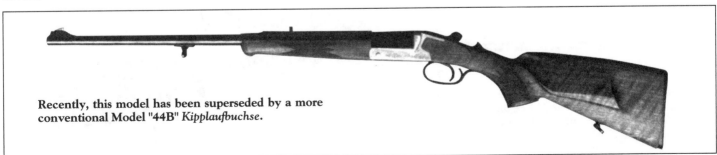

Recently, this model has been superseded by a more conventional Model "44B" *Kipplaufbuchse*.

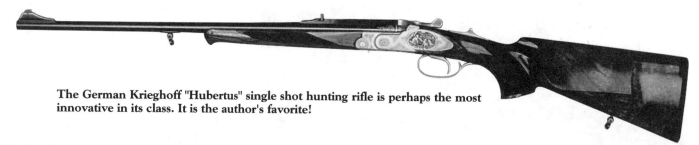

The German Krieghoff "Hubertus" single shot hunting rifle is perhaps the most innovative in its class. It is the author's favorite!

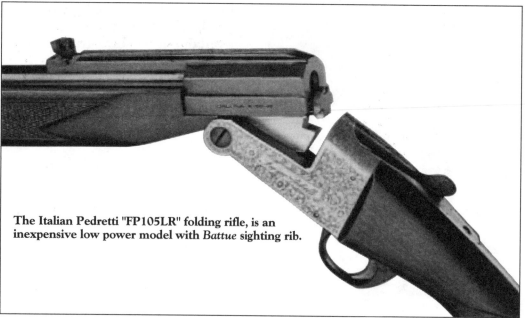

The Italian Pedretti "FP105LR" folding rifle, is an inexpensive low power model with *Battue* sighting rib.

Perugini & Visini

Another Italian company, founded in 1968 in Nuvolera, Brescia province, offering a complete line of hunting rifles and double shotguns.

Perugini & Visini are also manufacturing an ejector single barrel *Kipplauf* rifle, the "Eagle", featuring a patented action, Bohler steel barrel and fine European walnut stock. Set trigger is basic. Interchangeable smoothbore 20 gauge and .410 barrels are optional.

Available calibers are: 17 Remington - 222 Remington - 22/250 Remington - 243 Winchester - 270 Winchester - 30-06 Springfield - 7mm Remington Magnum - 300 Winchester Magnum - 5.6x50R - 5.6x57R - 6.5x57R - 6.5x68R - 7x57R - 7x65R - 9.3x74R and 10.3x60R.
Price on request.

Franz-Sodia

This is a famous Austrian gunmaker from Ferlach with a prestigious line of express rifles, mountain double rifles and shotguns.

The Franz-Sodia *Kipplauf-Buchsell* is their luxury model "150AN", richly engraved, with Kersten dual locking lugs, chambered in: 5.6x50R - 5.6x57R - 6.5x57R - 6.5x68R - 9.3x74R - 222 Remington - 243 Winchester - 270 Winchester - 308 Winchester - 30-06 Springfield and 7mm Remington Magnum. Available barrel lengths are 23.6- and 25.6-inches. Barrels are octagonal, made of Bohler "Rasant" steel. Price as per specifications requested.

Zanardini

M.A.Pl.Z. Zanardini is an Italian company, founded in 1946 at Gardone VT, specialized in the manufacture of top quality hunting rifles and shotguns.

Their line includes two folding-barrel single shot rifles, the "Fuchs B", with locking lever under the trigger guard, and the "Prinz 401", a classical *Kipplauf*. Both are beautiful guns.

The "Fuchs B" is available with 18-inch, 21-inch, 23.6-inch and 25.6-inch barrels fitted with adjustable open sights on a *Battue* rib. Scope mounting is provided. This gun can be completely folded to barrel, or stocked action, length.

Available calibers are: 243 Winchester - 6.62 Freres - 6.5x65R - 308 Winchester - 30-06 Springfield - 8x57JRS - 9.3x74R - 10.3x60R - 22 Hornet - 222 Remington - 5.6x50R Mag - 5.6x52R - 6.5x57R - 7x65R - 22/250 Remington.

The "DeLuxe" model is hammerless, with Kersten dual lugs and a patented safety device. The barrel can be round or octagonal, within the same range of lengths as the "Fuchs B". H&H-type side-locks are optional. The following calibers are available: 22 Hornet - 222 Remington - 5.6x50R Magnum - 5.6x52R - 6.5x57R - 22/250 Remington - 270 Winchester - 270 Winchester Magnum - 6.5x57R - 6.5x68R - 7x65R - 7x57R - 243 Winchester - 240 Weatherby Magnum - 6.62 Freres - 257 Weatherby Mag - 6.5x65R - 25-06 Remington - 308 Winchester - 30-06 Springfield - 9.3x74R - 8x57JRS - 7x75R Von Hof - 10.3x60 and 223 Remington.

Zanardini makes also a "Prinz 401 Super DeLuxe" gun, which creates a

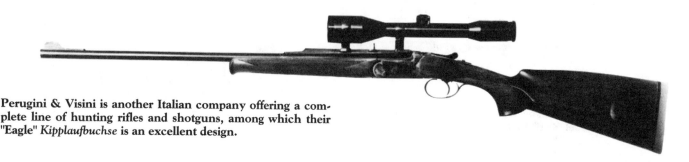

Perugini & Visini is another Italian company offering a complete line of hunting rifles and shotguns, among which their "Eagle" *Kipplaufbuchse* is an excellent design.

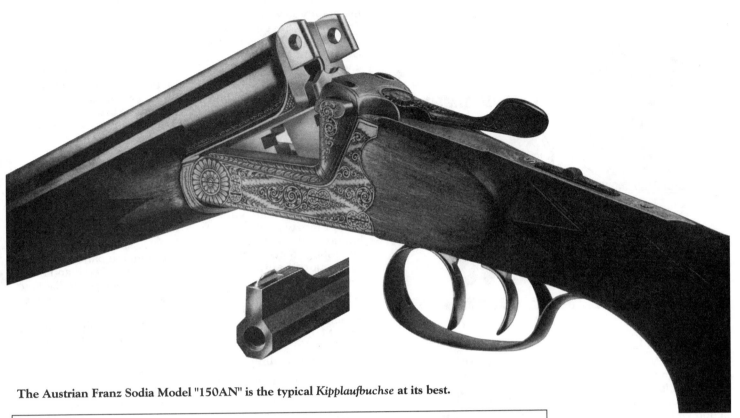

The Austrian Franz Sodia Model "150AN" is the typical *Kipplaufbuchse* at its best.

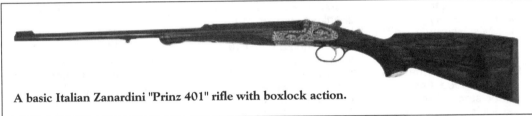

A basic Italian Zanardini "Prinz 401" rifle with boxlock action.

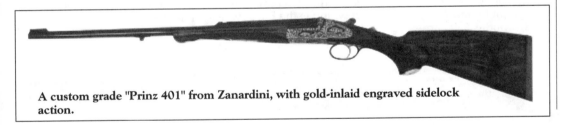

A custom grade "Prinz 401" from Zanardini, with gold-inlaid engraved sidelock action.

confusion, as it is an external-hammer double express rifle, not falling within the field of this article.

In short, with the exception of the Brno "ZKB110" and Pedretti rifles, all the others are luxury guns, built more or less to custom requirements for wealthy hunters.

In France, their prices range from about $2,400.00 for a good basic model, to more than $10,000.00 for true collector's pieces. ●

Manufacturers Addresses

BLASER JAGDWAFFEN
GmbH Ziegelstadel, 1
D - 88316 ISNY IM ALLGAU, Deutschland

BRNO A.S. Arms Division
P.O. Box 17,
Lazaretni 7
65617 BRNO,
Czech Republic

CHAPUIS ARMES - ZI La
JAGDWAFFEN AUS FERLACH -
Postfach 59,
A-9170 FERLACH, Austria

W. FURTSCHEGGER
- Kreuzgasse 2,
KUFSTEIN/TIROL, Austria

RENATO GAMBA (Societa Armi Bresciane)
- Via Artigiani, 93,
I-25063 GARDONE,
Val Trompia (BS), Italy

HEYM WAFFENFABRIK GmbH - Am Aschenbach, 2
D-98646 GLEICHAMBERG,
Deutschland

KRIEGHOFF GmbH
Postfach 2610,
D-89016 ULM/DONAU,
Deutschland

F. PEDRETTI di ENRICO
Via G. Pascoli, 154
1-25063 GARDONE VT
Brescia, Italy

PERUGINI & VISINI
Via Camprelle, 126
I-25080 NUVOLERA
Brescia, Italy

FRANZ SODIA JAGDEWEHRFABRIK -
9170 FERLACH/KARNTEN, Austria

ZANARDINI P & C SNC MAPIZ - Via C. Goldoni, 34
I-25063 GARDONE VT BS, Italy

by LAYNE SIMPSON

RIFLE REVIEW

Anschütz

THE NEW MODEL 1710D Classic Signature rifle in 22 Long Rifle is built around the famous Anschütz Model 54 action with all metal parts highly polished to create a blue job you'll need sun glasses to look at. Limited to a production of 200 units during the year 2000, the trigger guard of each rifle has Dieter Anschutz's signature along with a 1-of-X serial number and "2000", all in 24 karat gold. As a bonus, it will shoot as good as it looks.

Beretta

A few months before writing this, I spent a couple of fun days shooting various clay target games with a new Beretta AL391 autoloader at the a very nice facility near Tunica, Mississippi called The Willows. While there, I learned that Beretta's family of Mato centerfire rifles has grown to include a new synthetic-stocked version. The stock is made up of Kevlar-reinforced fiberglass and graphite and, like Henry Ford's Model T, it comes in any color you want so long as the color you want is black. The rifle weighs eight pounds and has a 23 1/2-inch barrel. Other features include controlled-round cartridge feeding, fully adjustable trigger, detachable magazine box and Model 70-style safety on the bolt shroud.

Synthetic stocks are nice to have for some applications but the older I get the more I appreciate fine wood, which goes a long way toward explaining why the Deluxe version of the Mato with its fancy Claro walnut stock and hand-cut checkering is so appealing to me. It and the synthetic rifle are available in 270, 280, 30-06, 7mm Remington Magnum, 300 Winchester Magnum, 338 Winchester Magnum and 375 H&H Magnum.

Browning

While hunting pheasant, sharp-tail grouse, prairie chicken, chukar and clay targets in South Dakota with spanking new Browning Citori Lightning Feather shotguns in 12, 20 and 28 and .410, I learned that the company planned to introduce a composite-barrel version of its A-Bolt Stainless Stalker in 22-250 and 300 Winchester Magnum. Also new from Browning is the European-designed Acera with a straight-pull action in 30-06 and 300 Winchester Magnum.

Dakota

The Dakota family of wood-stocked rifles now includes Model 76 variants called Classic, Safari and Traveler, the latter a takedown version. Action lengths available are standard, short magnum and short-fat magnum. Then we have the Hunter with its synthetic stock and the Model 10, America's most handsome single shot rifle. Which Dakota would I rather own? That's an easy one — the Legend, an $18,000 side-by-side boxlock shotgun, the parts for which are made by Ferlib and the finishing touches applied by Dakota — the Legend's grace and beauty is something to behold. Make mine with double triggers, a straight-grip buttstock, beavertail forearm, and in 28-gauge with 28-inch barrels choked at five and 15 points. And don't forget to extend the consignment period until 2075!

Ed Brown Custom

Seems like everyone who owns a machine shop these days is building rifles from scratch. One of the latest is 1911 pistol guru Ed Brown who recently introduced an entire family of rifles built around an action that closely

Browning Citori Lightning Feather.

Composite-barrel version of Browning's A-Bolt Stainless Stalker.

Also new from Browning is the European-designed Acera with a straight-pull action in 30-06 and 300 Winchester Magnum.

resembles the Remington Model 700 action. There is one major exception— the bolt shroud-mounted three-position safety is a Winchester Model 70-type. Called the Model 702, a number of long-action variations are slated to become available, including the relatively light Savanna, the slightly heavier Ozark and a rifle for Africa called Bushveld. To mention but a few of the available chamberings, 257 Ackley Improved, 25-06, 257 STW, 264 Winchester Magnum, 6.5 STW, 280 Ackley Improved, 7mm STW, 416 Remington Magnum, 404 Jeffery and 416 Rigby. The short action rifle will be offered in shorter chamberings such as 222, 22-250, 220 Swift, 6mm BR Remington, 243 Winchester, 6.5-284, 7mm-08, 308 Winchester. Extra cost options include McMillan stocks and Jewell triggers.

Kimber

During 1999 Kimber was too busy turning out high-quality 1911 pistols to build more than a few prototype Model 82C rifles but, take it from one who has closely examined them all, the new rifle will be worth the wait. By the time you read this I will probably have shot a production gun so stay tuned

for a more detailed report next year.

Marlin

Biggest news from 100 Kenna Drive up in North Haven, CT is the 450 Marlin chambering. Developed with the assistance of Hornady (who is loading the ammo), the new cartridge might best be described as a slightly lengthened version of the old 458x2-inch wildcat which was made by shortening the 458 Winchester case to two inches. The biggest difference between the two is a wider belt on the 450 Marlin which serves to increase headspace length by about .030-inch, thereby preventing the cartridge from being chambered in rifles reamed for other Holland & Holland-style belted cartridges. Loaded with a 350-grain soft-nose bullet, the cartridge comes with respective muzzle velocity and energy ratings of 2100 fps and 3427 foot-pounds when fired in a 24-inch barrel; a bit optimistic at this early date since Marlin is presently offering the new chambering only in its Model 1895M with 18 1/2-inch barrel. This level of performance, by the way, is about what handloaders have been squeezing from New Model 1895s in 45-70 but it is the first

time such power is available to those who stick with factory loads. While the Guide Gun concept with its snub-nosed barrel has proven to be quite successful for Marlin, I'd personally like to see the new chambering offered in the standard-length Model 1895 with 22-inch barrel.

While old-fashioned conservatives like me are shocked to see Marlin carve the barreled action of its Model 336 deer rifle from stainless steel it had to happen simply because that material has become so popular among hunters. Available only with a 20-inch barrel in 30-30, all major metal parts of the Model 336M: receiver, bolt, barrel and finger lever are stainless steel while some of its smaller parts are regular nickel-plated carbon steel. The seven-pound rifle has an American walnut buttstock and forearm with cut checkering and Marlin's tough Mar-Shield finish.

Marlin's first Guide Gun version of its Model 1894 is the P-model in 44 Magnum/44 Special. It has a 16 1/4-inch ported barrel, measures 33 1/4 inches overall and weighs only 5 3/4 pounds. In the 22 rimfire department, other new items are the Model 25NC bolt gun and the Model 60C autoloader, both

with their stocks hidden from view by Mossy Oak's Break-up camo finish.

Mossberg

Long known for producing economy-grade repeating shotguns, Mossberg recently unveiled the SSi-ONE which they say is short for "single shot interchangeable". Interchangeable 24-inch barrels available in 223, 243, 270, 308, 30-06 and 12 gauge slug (the latter fully rifled) make it an extremely versatile firearm for those who enjoy the challenge of being in the field with a single-shot firearm. Also available is a heavy barrel in 22-250. Of underlever break-action design, its many features include an ambidextrous tang-mounted safety, cocked firing pin indicator, single-stage trigger, auto-ejector, quick-detach sling swivel posts and satin-finished stock and forearm with cut checkering. The receiver is drilled and tapped for scope mounting and each rifle leaves the factory with a Weaver-style base. Weight ratings run from eight to 10 pounds.

New England Firearms

Built on the same side-lever action as other single-shot rifles and shotguns

Reputed to be extremely accurate, the Savannah from Ed Brown Products is available in a variety of standard and wildcat chamberings.

produced by New England Firearms, a special edition called the Wesson & Harrington features such nice details as case-colored and engraved receiver and fancy walnut with cut checkering. The Buffalo Classic weighs eight pounds and is in 45-70 Government while the Target Model is the same except chambered to 38-55 Winchester. Both models have curved steel buttplates and, like all New England firearms, are made in the good old U.S. of A.

Prairie Gun Works

Last time we sat by the old campfire I mentioned I had commissioned Prairie Gun Works to build the first rifle ever in 6.5 STW. Nothing more or less than my old 7mm STW necked down, this particular offspring is about 200 feet per second faster with all bullet weights than the 264 Winchester Magnum. The new cartridge is housed in the latest M18-Ti rifle from PGW and the entire outfit weighs only six pounds. The rifle has a titanium receiver, extremely light synthetic stock, a 26-inch barrel and averages less than an inch at 100 yards with a variety of full-power handloads.

For quite some time Bob Nosler and I had planned to hunt the giant black bears on Vancouver Island and, when the opportunity came along to do just that with outfitter Jim Shockey, I decided the new PGW rifle in 6.5 STW would be the right bruin medicine to take along. Bob scored first; using Federal Premium 300 Winchester Magnum factory ammo loaded with his 180-grain Partition, he took a nice boar at less than 100 yards. As it turned out, three bruins were taken with my rifle on that hunt, one by me and two others by Bob Chuisano who had traveled to British Columbia from Cedar Rapids, Iowa. All were one-shot kills at distances ranging from 114 to 166 yards as measured by a Bushnell laser rangefinder. The load we used consisted of the 6.5 STW case formed from Federal 7mm STW brass, Federal 215 primer and the Nosler 140-grain Partition seated atop 88.0 grains of H870 for just over 3300 feet per second at the muzzle. Nice rifle, nice cartridge and nice bear hunt.

The latest rifle from PGW is the LRT-2 which is available in really big numbers such as Weatherby's 30-378, 378, 416 and 460 as well as the 416 Rigby and 505 Gibbs. It is also available in 409 Chevy, a .416-caliber wildcat that shoves a 400-grain bullet out the muzzle at 3000 fps. To name but a few of the features of this action: cone breech, one-piece bolt body, four-round magazine and dual extractors.

Remington

Regular readers of this column might recall that several years ago I described how much fun it was to shoot a prototype version of an electronic rifle being developed by Remington. At the time it was uncertain whether or not the concept would actually see production but I am now told that EtronX rifles will begin to appear on dealer's shelves sometime during 2000. Simply described, the new rifle is nothing more or less than Remington's ever-popular Model 700 with electronic ignition. Its first chamberings will be 220 Swift, 22-250 and 243 Winchester. While the system requires the use of a special primer, it utilizes standard cartridge cases—good news to handloaders. This assumes, of course, that Remington will eventually sell the primer as an individual component. Think of the trigger on this one as a light switch on the wall of your home and you've got the idea; squeezing it allows electrical current from a standard 9-volt battery (housed in the buttstock) to flow through a spring-loaded contact pin(which replaces the conventional firing pin in the bolt)and into the special primer. Lock time is about as close to instantaneous as we'll ever get with today's technology. Light-emitting diodes located at the top of the grip indicate the status of the system, like whether the manual safety is on or off and whether the chamber is loaded. The new EtronX rifle has a heavy 26-inch barrel of Type 416 steel, a Kevlar-

Remington Model 700 Classic.

Remington's EtronX rifle (center); EtronX rifle with cutaway views.

Remington 7LS.

reinforced synthetic stock and weighs around nine pounds.

Last year I told about toting a Model 700 chambered for the new 300 Ultra Mag in Alaska where I bagged black bear, moose and a brown bear that squared close to ten feet, all with factory ammo loaded with the Nosler 180-grain Partition bullet. Southpaw hunters should be pleased to learn the chambering is now available in the Model 700 BDL/LH. During the hunt in Alaska, a Remington official and I discussed various calibers that would work on the new case and my vote went to the 338 as the next to be in line. Which is exactly what has happened. Loaded with a 250-grain A-Frame bullet at an advertised muzzle velocity of 2900 fps, the new 338 Ultra Mag virtually duplicates the performance of Roy Weatherby's fine old 340 Magnum. Model 700 variations slated for the new chambering during 2000 are BDL, BDL/SS, LSS, Sendero SF, APR, AWR, Custom KS Mountain and Custom KS Stainless Mountain. My crystal ball says the next calibers in line are the 375 Ultra Mag, which should duplicate the performance of the 375 Weatherby Magnum, and the

7mm Ultra Mag, which is basically a 7mm STW without a belt on its case.

The first limited-edition Model 700 Classic introduced by Remington back in 1981 was chambered for the 7x57mm Mauser. It was followed by the 257 Roberts, 300 H&H Magnum, 250-3000 Savage, 350 Remington Magnum, 264 Winchester Magnum, 338 Winchester Magnum, 35 Whelen, 300 Weatherby Magnum, 25-06 Remington, 7mm Weatherby Magnum, 220 Swift, 222 Remington, 6.5x55 Swedish, 300 Winchester Magnum, 375 H&H Magnum, 280 Remington and the 8mm Remington Magnum, in that order. For 2000 it is the 223 Remington, a cartridge that most certainly has become a classic since its introduction in 1964. The latest 'classic' Classic is on the short Model 700 action and has a 24-inch barrel.

Much to the disappointment of no small number of varmint shooters, Remington dropped its popular Model 700 Varmint Synthetic a few seasons ago. It is now back in 223, 22-250 and 308 with a 26-inch heavy barrel, Kevlar-reinforced composite stock and a nominal weight of nine pounds.

As Remington's 22 rimfire lineup goes, the latest Model 597 autoloader variation is the Stainless Sporter replete with hardwood stock and 20-inch stainless steel barrel. Nominal weight is 5-1/2 pounds.

Ever since its introduction, the Remington Model Seven carbine has been one of my favorites for use in the sometimes-cramped quarters of a tree stand and three new variations are sure to make it a favorite of other deer hunters as well. They are the Seven LS with stainless steel barreled action and brown laminated wood stock, Seven LS with blued steel and the same type of stock, and Seven Youth also with blued steel but with the length of pull of its hardwood stock reduced for shorter arms. The latter weighs 6-1/4 pounds while the two grownup versions peg the scale at a quarter-pound more. All have 20-inch barrels. The LSS version is available in 22-250, 243 and 7mm-08 while you can buy its LS mate in those chamberings as well as 260 and 308. Available Youth variant chamberings are 223, 243, 260 and 7mm-08.

While Remington's Model 700 Composite rifle is not new, its performance was new to me

when I only recently got around to working with one in 223 caliber. Varmint shooters who read this might be interested in the results of barrel heat-up and cool-down comparison tests I performed with that rifle and a Model 700 Varmint Special with a heavy all-steel barrel. Use of a digital thermometer revealed that it took 19 consecutive five-shot groups (90 shots) to increase the exterior surface temperature of the composite barrel to 155 degrees Fahrenheit while it took only 11 groups or 55 rounds to heat the all-steel barrel to the same temperature. During the cool-down part of my tests I found that it took just over 35 minutes for the surface temperature of the all-steel barrel to drop down to 90 degrees compared to 32 seconds for the composite barrel. As for accuracy, the Composite rifle chalked up an overall average of 1.03 inches for 19 five-shot groups fired with Black Hills 52-grain HP match ammo whereas the other rifle averaged 0.982-inch for 11 five-shot groups. *Velly intellesting*, don't you think?

During the past few years I have been compiling data on the effectiveness of various

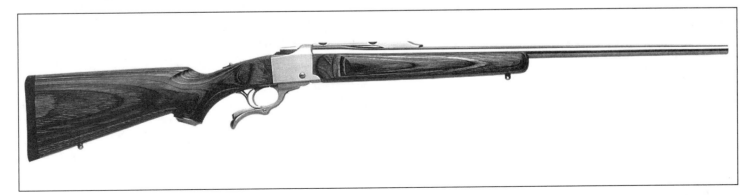

The Ruger No. 1 Stainless Standard.

Savage's new Model 12VSS may be just what every varmint hunter has been waiting for.

22-caliber centerfire cartridges loaded with the latest generation of premium-grade, controlled-expansion bullets on deer-size game. The best whitetail buck I have taken to date with one of the 22s fell victim to a Model 700 VS in 220 Swift and Federal's factory ammo loaded with the 55-grain Trophy Bonded Bear Claw bullet. One shot at just over 200 yards did the trick; leaving quite a blood trail, the buck ran no more than 30 yards before piling up. That particular load in that particular rifle, by the way, averaged 1.18 inches for several five-shot groups at 100 yards with the smallest group measuring only 0.421-inch.

Ruger

Ruger's No. 1, the rifle we all have learned to love due to its smooth lines and classical beauty, is now available in stainless steel and laminated wood. Called, aptly enough, the Ruger No. 1 Stainless Standard or K1-B-BBZ in Ruger catalog talk, it is best described as a 21st century version of the 20th century No. 1B, has a 26-inch barrel, weighs eight pounds and is available in 25-06, 7mm Remington Magnum, 7mm STW and 300 Weatherby Magnum. This is, by the way, is the first time Ruger has chambered a rifle in 7mm STW. Another variant called the No. 1 Stainless Varminter has a heavier 24-inch barrel, weighs nine pounds and is presently available only in 22-250.

Sako/Tikka

I consider the Sako Model 75 one of the best rifle designs of the 20th century and a new-for-2000 variant with a keyed activating/deactivating device in the rear of its bolt should make it even more popular among those who see a need for storing a rifle so it cannot possibly be fired by unauthorized persons. Sako calls it the Key Concept and it works. Also new from my Finnish moose-hunting buddies is the 300 Ultra Mag chambering in the Model 75 Hunter and a left-hand version of the Tikka Whitetail Hunter in several chamberings. Last but certainly not least, Sako's Finnfire bolt gun in 22 Long Rifle has a new stock that more closely resembles the lines of the Model 75 stock.

Savage

Latest varmint rifle from Savage is the Model 112VSS in 223 and 22-250. Weighing 15 pounds, the new introduction has a blued receiver, heavy 26-inch stainless steel barrel, Sharp-Shooter adjustable trigger and Choate synthetic stock with adjustable cheek rest. The Model 112VSS in 22-250 I used on a Montana prairie dog shoot wore a Sightron 6-24x scope and was delightfully accurate; not to mention an excellent trigger which has been a long time coming on Savage rifles.

The Savage centerfire receiver has always been long enough for full-length Holland & Holland-style cartridges but its magazine length has always restricted it to the use of short magnums and standard non-belted cartridges. Realizing that the popularity of longer cartridges is growing by leaps and bounds, Savage has lengthened the magazine box to accommodate the first full-length chamberings to be offered in the Model 110/112 series, the 375 H&H Magnum and my own 7mm STW. The former is now available in the Model 116SE (Safari Express) while the latter is offered in the Model 114U which just happens to be my favorite Savage rifle. It has a blued steel barreled action nestled in an American walnut stock replete with cut checkering and ebony forearm tip. The longer magazine will also allow Savage to add other chamberings, such as the 300 and 340 Weatherby magnums as well as the 300 and 338 Ultra Mags, to its list of options.

Thompson/Center

Back in January I examined a pre-production version of T/C's new Classic 22 rimfire autoloader and was impressed by what I saw. Among other nice things, its 22-inch barrel is screwed into a steel receiver and its Monte Carlo-style stock is genuine walnut. Other features include quick-detach sling swivel posts, receiver drilled and tapped for scope mounting, eight-round detachable magazine, fully adjustable rear sight and a two-position safety located on the right-hand side of the receiver. Overall length is 39 1/2 inches and weight is a nominal 5 1/2 pounds.

Latest from T/C is this autoloading rifle in 22 Long Rifle.

The Coyote, the latest variation of the Model 70 Winchester.

USRAC Model 1886 Extra Light Grade 1.

Model 70 Classic Sporter fron Winchester.

Considering the amount of beef in the steel receiver plus the great amount of interest in the 22 WMR, I won't be surprised to see the T/C rifle eventually become available in that chambering.

U.S. Repeating Arms

One of the most enjoyable big-game hunts I participated in during the 1999 season was for pronghorn antelope in New Mexico. The rifle I used to take a rather decent buck with a single shot at about 200 yards was a Winchester Model 70 Classic Sporter in 7mm STW. The rifle worked great, as did the Winchester Supreme ammo loaded with the 140-grain Ballistic Silvertip bullet. The 7mm STW is also available in the left-hand

version of that same rifle, as well as the right-hand Classic Stainless which is a new chambering for that rifle in 2000.

Latest Model 70 variation is the Coyote with laminated wood stock, blued-steel action, 24-inch medium-heavy stainless steel barrel in 223, 22-250 and 243, all at a weight of nine pounds.

Great news from USRAC in lever guns is the 405 Winchester chambering in the Japanese-made Winchester Model '95. Grade I is blued steel and walnut while the High Grade has deer and elk romping about its white receiver. Rifling twist rate of the 24-inch barrel is 1:10 inches and the rifle weighs around eight pounds.

Actually, my pick of the best lever gun news from USRAC is the Extra Light version of the 45-70 caliber Model 1886. Also available in Grade I and High Grade versions, it has a lightweight 22-inch barrel and since it weighs only 7 1/4-pounds it will kick like an enraged mule with heavy loads but I really must have one. Continuing in the lever gun department, the Model 94 Pack Rifle in 30-30 and 44 Magnum with its curved-grip buttstock, hand-filling forearm, 3/4-length magazine tube and 18-inch barrel is sure to be a winner among those who have grown weary of the more common saddle rifle look. I am amazed at how many different Model 94 variations are now available.

Counting the new Pack Rifle, there are 12 styles and six chamberings, 30-30, 357 Magnum, 44-40, 44 Magnum, 444 Marlin and 45 Colt. Sadly enough, though, the fine 307 Winchester is now missing from the list of options.

Last but certainly not least to me, USRAC was the first major company to offer a rifle chambered for my 7mm STW and in 1999 became the first major to offer the 358 STA, one of my family of wildcats on the 8mm Remington Magnum case. The 358 STA chambering is now available in two Custom Shop Model 70s, the Custom African Express and the new-for-2000 Classic Custom Safari Express. In addition to the 358 STA, both are available in 375 H&H Magnum, 416 Remington

Winchester 70 Classic Stainless.

Model 1895 Grade 1.

Winchester Model 94 Pack Rifle.

Magnum, 458 Winchester Magnum and another wildcat called the 458 Lott. Another new Custom Shop Model 70 offering is the Custom Shop Short Action in 243, 257 Roberts, 260 Remington, 7mm-08, 308 and, believe it or not, 358 Winchester. Continuing on with Model 70s we all would love to own, there's the Custom Ultra Light with full-length, Mannlicher-style stock and 19-inch barrel in 260, 7mm-08 and 308 and the Custom Extreme Weather with stainless steel barreled action and McMillan synthetic stock in five different chambers from 25-06 to 338 Winchester Magnum. One of the most handsome new Custom Shop offerings is the Model 94 Custom Limited Edition with its high-grade wood, engraved receiver and 24-inch octagon barrel in 44-40 Winchester.

USRAC's Winchester Model 1885 single shot family keeps growing with a new 22 Long Rifle version added in 2000. Two grades are available, both with 24 1/2-inch barrels and weights of eight pounds.

Volquartsen

Tom Volquartsen carves the action of his 22 WMR autoloader from a block of stainless steel. He then screws in a match-grade stainless steel barrel, precision-beds the barreled action into a laminated wood stock or a McMillan synthetic stock and what he comes up with is a quick-shooting rifle that uses the rotary magazine Ruger makes for its 10/22 and 77/22. His rifles will consistently squeeze five bullets inside an inch at 100 yards with accurate ammo, such as Federal's

Premium recipe with the 30-grain Sierra bullet. Anyone who hasn't tried a Volquartsen rifle on targets such as prairie dogs, ground squirrels, flickertails, starlings or tin cans is missing out on a lot of fun. I own three Volquartsen rifles in 22 WMR, 22 Long Rifle and 22 Short, the latter called the Firefly. I also own one of his custom pistols in 22 Long Rifle. With all that accuracy at my fingertips you can just imagine how much fun I have.

Weatherby

If memory serves me correctly, the most consistently accurate centerfire factory rifle I worked with during 1999 was a Mark V SVM (Super Varmint Master).

This recent introduction from Weatherby is built on the lightweight Mark V action and has a Krieger match-grade,

button-rifled barrel of Type 400 stainless steel. Relatively heavy, the free-floating barrel is 26 inches long, tapers to a muzzle diameter of .823-inch and has an 11 degree concave crown. The barrel is cryogenically stress relieved at minus 300 degrees Fahrenheit and has six deep cooling flutes with black accent stripes. The Kevlar-reinforced fiberglass stock of the Mark V SVM has a CNC-machined aluminum bedding block and its beavertail-style forearm is just the ticket for shooting over a sandbag. Sear engagement of the fully-adjustable trigger is factory preset at .012- to .015-inch and a pull weight of about four pounds.

The Mark V SVM is rated at 8 1/2 pounds and is available in 223, 22-250, 220 Swift, 243 Winchester, 7mm-08 and 308.

Winchester's Custom Ultra Light with full-length, Mannlicher-style stock.

After adjusting the trigger of a 22-250 caliber rifle to 20 ounces and outfitting it with a new Weaver Grand Slam 6-20X scope, I checked it out with a variety of factory ammo and handloads at the 100-yard benchrest. An overall average of .517-inch for just over 50 five-shot groups proved what I already knew only too well — the fellows at Weatherby know what it takes to build a superbly accurate rifle at an affordable price.

During the 1999 season I hunted deer, wild hog and ground squirrels in California with a new Weatherby Mark V rifle in 240 Weatherby Magnum. I used Weatherby factory ammo loaded with the Nosler 100-grain Partition at 3400 fps and cartridge and rifle proved so impressive in performance that I soon thereafter added the Deluxe version of the Mark V in that chambering to my hunting battery. Mine wears a Leupold 3-9x Compact scope and its size and weight are perfect for the lightweight Weatherby rifle. For the benefit of those who are not familiar with the Weatherby centerfire rifle lineup I'll mention that the 240 Magnum — along with non-

belted chamberings ranging in calibers from the 223 to the 30-06 — are built around a stretched version of the old Varmintmaster action. The 257, 270, 7mm, 300, 340, 416 and 460 Weatherby chamberings — along with other belted magnums such as the 7mm Remington and 300 Winchester — are on the heavier standard Mark V action.

And speaking of rifles built on the standard Mark V action, Weatherby's new Mark V Ultra Lightweight tips the scale at 6 3/4 pounds, has a 26-inch barrel replete with lightening flutes and wears a

Kevlar/fiberglass stock replete with precision-machined bedding block. Some of the weight reduction comes from the use of deeper and wider flutes in the bolt body, skeletonized bolt handle and fluted bolt shroud, along with the use of aluminum in non-stress areas such as the cartridge follower, floorplate and trigger guard.

In the past, the Weatherby custom shop focused its efforts on high-dollar rifles for the rich and famous and, while that type of work is still available, a considerable amount of emphasis is now

Tom Volquartsen holds one of his super-accurate 22 WMR autoloaders.

A Weatherby Mark V Sporter in 240 Weatherby Magnum worked great on this California deer.

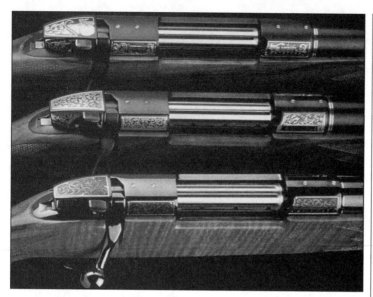

In addition to building high-grade rifles like these, Weatherby's Custom Shop is now offering many other less expensive services.

placed on downrange performance as well as a few other things that appeal to a larger segment of America's hunters and shooters: upgraded wood, special checkering patterns, personalized metal engraving, various paint schemes for synthetic stocks, special metal finishes and barrels of various weights and lengths and with various rifling twists from various makers such as Shilen and Hart.

Moving back to upscale rifles, I recently examined a leather-cased custom shop Safari Classic in 375 Weatherby Magnum. The French walnut stock, flawless cut checkering, engraved crossbolts, steel trapdoor-style grip cap, ebony forearm tip, leather-covered rubber recoil pad, Model 70 Super Grade-style quick-detach sling swivels, express rear sight, barrel-band style front sight with interchangeable daytime and night sights and quick-detach scope mount really made the rifle something special. I'd love to hunt Cape buffalo with it.

Wilson Combat

Heretofore known worldwide for building extremely accurate and totally reliable 1911-style pistols, Bill Wilson is now in the AR-15 business with three models, all with flat-top-style receivers and all in 223 Remington for now. The TPR-15 Tactical Precision Rifle has all the bells and whistles action rifle competitors like, including a 18-inch match-grade barrel and free-floating tubular aluminum handguard. Chop its barrel back to 16 1/4-inches, add a front sight and compensator and you have the UT-15 Urban Tactical. Both are guaranteed to shoot three bullets into an inch at 100 yards with one of several factory loads specified by Wilson. I shot a UT-15 rather extensively and its overall average accuracy was 1.09 inches for three, three-shot groups with seven factory recipes and four handloads. Best accuracy at 0.68-inch was with Norma 55-grain hollowpoint ammo and second best at 0.83-inch was my handload with Hodgdon's H335 and Walt Berger's 52-grain hollowpoint. Not bad for an ugly old military-style autoloader. For a bit less money Wilson also offers the M4-T Tactical Carbine which is similar to his UT-15 except for its standard two-piece handguard and two minute-of-angle guarantee. ●

Editor's note; Layne is field editor of *Shooting Times* magazine.

Mike Jordan (right) and Winchester sponsored Layne and four other gun writers at the 100th anniversary Grand American Trap Shoot.

100th Anniversary Grand American

One of the highlights for me during 1999 was competing in the Grand American Trap Shoot in Vandalia, Ohio as a guest of Mike Jordan of Winchester. Actually, Winchester sponsored an entire squad of gun writers at the event and I was one of five to attend. What made the '99 shoot so special was the fact that it was the 100th anniversary of the Grand. Over 7,000 shooters were there, making it quite a spectacular shooting experience. To give you some idea of its size, the trap line is over a mile long and consists of 100 trap fields in a row. Somewhere between five and six million targets are thrown during the shoot. I used my Remington 90-T trap gun and Winchester AA target ammo with an ounce of No. 8 shot and did okay for a first-timer. Any shotgunner who has not attended the Grand owes it to himself (or herself) to do so simply because there is nothing like it anywhere else in the world. Vendor row is over a mile long and everybody who is anybody in the world of shotguns is there with their latest goods.

For entry forms contact the Amateur Trapshooting Association at 937-898-4638.

THE 2001 GUN DIGEST WEB DIRECTORY

by Holt Bodinson

WHO WOULD HAVE ever thought that a "mouse" would be an essential tool in the firearms field? Yet, today, that simple tool combined with the Internet opens up a world of firearms-related information for the consumer. Need a catalog? A part? Just imagine having Brownells' complete 440 page Internet catalog at your fingertips. Ammunition? Ballistic data? Well, tap right into the four-color catalogs of Winchester, Federal, Remington and others. Concerned about Second Amendment rights? Visit the web pages of NRA's ILA, the Second Amendment Foundation, or the Citizens Committee for the Right to Keep and Bear Arms.

Our *Gun Digest* Web Directory is in its second year of publication, and it continues to grow at Mach speed. During the past year, firearm manufacturers and purveyors, organizations and forums—even enthusiastic private parties—have added new sites, improved existing sites, increased security protection and converted E-mail addresses into full-blown web pages.

It is estimated that by the end of 2001, there will be over 175 million users on the Internet with tens of thousands of new users being added daily. Internet purchases alone are expected to exceed $220

billion by this year. And the international firearms industry is doing an excellent job of keeping up with the times.

One of the more interesting developments this past year is the growing success of firearm-related auction and dealer sites. One can literally scour the world to find a particular firearm, modern or antique, or firearm-related accessory. For a sophisticated auction site, try Auction Arms at **www.auctionarms.com**; for an interesting example of a multiple dealer site click on **www.doublegun.com**; and for up-to-the-minute information on firearms and accessories for sale, try our own **www.gunlist.com**.

The following index of current Web sites is offered to our readers as a convenient jumping-off point. The Internet is such a dynamic and changing environment that half the fun is just exploring what's out there. Considering that most of the Web sites have hot links to other firearm-related Web sites, the Internet trail just goes on-and-on once you've taken the initial step to go online.

Here are a few pointers:

If the web site you desire is not listed, try using the full name of the company or product, typed without spaces, between **www.-and-.com**, for example, **www.krause.com**. Probably

95% of current Web sites are based on this simple, self-explanatory format.

Try a variety of search engines like *Microsoft Internet Explorer*, *GoTo.com*, *Yahoo*, *HotBot*, *AltaVista*, *Lycos*, *Excite*, *InfoSeek*, *Looksmart*, *Google*, and *WebCrawler* while using key words such as gun, firearm, rifle, pistol, blackpowder, shooting, hunting— frankly, any word that relates to the sport. Each search engine seems to comb through the World Wide Web in a different fashion and produces different results. While the Internet has been a bastion of freedom without censors, AOL did eliminate some firearm sites last year and often seems to search without luck for firearm-related information. That's why having the option to use alternative search engines is so important. Accessing the various search engines is simple. Just type **www.yahoo.com** for example, and you're on your way.

Finally, the best introduction to firearms-related Web sites is a large, specialized Web site like Shooter's Online Services located at **www.shooters.com**. There are enough firearm-related links at **www.shooters.com** to make your initial trips down the Internet highway a rewarding adventure.

A whole world is just a "click" away. Enjoy our Directory!

WEB DIRECTORY

AMMUNITION AND COMPONENTS

3D Ammunition www.3dammo.com
Accurate Arms Co. Inc www.accuratepowder.com
ADCO/Nobel Sport Powder www.adcosales.com
Aguila Ammunition www.aguilaammo.com
All Purpose Ammunition www.dragonbreath.com
Alliant Powder www.alliantpowder.com
Ammo Depot www.ammodepot.com
Arizona Ammunition, Inc. www.arizonaammunition.com
A-Zoom Ammo www.a-zoom.com
Ballard Rifle & Cartridge LLC www.ballardrifles.com
Ballistic Products, Inc. www.ballisticproducts.com
Barnes Bullets www.barnesbullets.com
Baschieri & Pellagri www.baschieri-pellagri.com
Berger Bullets, Ltd. www.bergerbullets.com
Berry's Mfg., Inc. www.berrysmfg.com
Big Bore Bullets of Alaska www.awloo.com/bbb/index.htm
Bismuth Cartridge Co. www.bismuth-notox.com
Black Hills Ammunition, Inc. www.black-hills.com
Brenneke of America Ltd. turpin@theriver.com
Bull-X inc. www.bull-x.com
Calhoon, James, Bullets www.jamescalhoon.com
CCI-Blount www.blount.com
Century Arms www.centuryarms.com
Cheaper Than Dirt www.cheaperthandirt.com
Claybuster Wads www.claybuster.com
Clean Shot Powder www.cleanshot.com
Cole Distributing www.cole-distributing.com
Cor-Bon www.cor-bon.com
Denver Bullet Co. denbullets@aol.com
Dillon Precision www.dillonprecision.com
DKT, Inc. www.dktinc.com
Dynamit Nobel RWS Inc. www.dnrws.com
Elephant Black Powder www.elephantblackpowder.com
Eley Ammunition www.shooters.com/eley
Eley Hawk Ltd. www.eleyhawk.com
Eley Limited www.eley.co.uk
Federal Cartridge Co. www.federalcartridge.com
Fiocchi of America www.fiocchiusa.com
Fowler Bullets www.benchrest.com/fowler
Glaser Safety Slug, Inc. www.safetyslug.com
GOEX Inc. www.goexpowder.com
Graf & Sons graf@email-pinet.net
Hi-Tech Ammunition www.iidbs.com/hitech
Hirtenberger kengsfirearms@mindspring.com
Hodgdon Powder www.hodgdon.com
Hornady www.hornady.com
Hull Cartridge www.hullcartridge.com
Huntington Reloading Products www.huntingtons.com

Impact Bullets www.impactbullets.com
IMR Smokeless Powders www.imrpowder.com
ION Industries, Inc. www.trutracer.com
Keng's Firearms Specialty kengsfirearms@mindspring.com
Kent Cartridge America www.kentgamebore.com
Kynoch Ammunition kynamco@aol.com
Lapua www.lapua-usa.com
Laser-Cast www.laser-cast.com
Lawrence Brand Shot www.metalico.com
Lazzeroni Arms Co. www.lazzeroni.com
Lightfield Slug Group slugrp@bedford.net
Lomont Precision Bullets www.klomont.com/kent
Lyman www.lymanproducts.com
Magnus Bullets www.magnusbullets.com
Mast Technology www.bellammo.com
Midway USA www.midwayusa.com
Miltex, Inc. www.miltexusa.com
MK Ballistic Systems www.mkballistics.com
Mullins Ammunition www.mullinsammunition.com
National Bullet Co. www.nationalbullet.com
Nobel Sport www.adcosales.com
Nosler Bullets Inc www.nosler.com
Old Western Scrounger www.snowcrest.net/oldwest
Oregon Trail/Laser-Cast Bullets www.shooters.com/lasercast
Pattern Control www.patterncontrol.com
PMC-Eldorado Cartridge www.pmcammo.com
Primex Technologies Inc. ksstase11@primextech.com
Pro Load Ammunition www.proload.com
Rainier Ballistics www.rainierballistics.com
Reloading Specialties Inc. www.reloadingspecialties.com
Remington www.remington.com
Sauvestre Slug kengsfirearms@mindspring.com
Sellier & Bellot USA Inc. www.sb-usa.com
Shilen www.shilen.com
Sierra www.sierrabullets.com
Slug Group Inc. slugrp@bedford.net
Speer-Blount www.blount.com
Sporting Supplies Int'l Inc. www.ssiintl.com
Starline www.starlinebrass.com
Triton Cartridge www.triton-ammo.com
Tru-Tracer www.trutracer.com
Vihtavuori Lapua kaltron@concentric.net
Western Powders Inc. www.westernpowders.com
Widener's Reloading & Shooters Supply www.wideners.com
Winchester Ammunition www.winchester.com
Wolf Ammunition www.wolfammo.com
Woodleigh Bullets zedfield@apollo.ruralnet.net.au
Zanders Sporting Goods www.gzanders.com

CASES, SAFES, GUN LOCKS, AND CABINETS

Ace Case Co. www.acecase.com
AG English Sales Co. www.agenglish.com
All Americas' Outdoors www.innernet.net/gunsafe
Alpine Cases www.0800.co.za/alpine
Aluma Sport by Dee Zee www.deezee.com

American Security Products www.amsecusa.com
Americase www.americase.com
Avery Outdoors, Inc. www.averyoutdoors.com
Bear Track Cases www.beartrackcases.com
Boyt Harness Co. www.boytharness.com

WEB DIRECTORY

Bulldog Gun Safe Co. www.gardall.com
Cannon Safe Co. www.cannonsafe.com
CCL Security Products www.cclsecurity.com
Concept Development Corp. www.saf-t-blok.com
Fort Knox Safes www.ftknox.com
Franzen Security Products www.securecase.com
Frontier Safe Co. www.frontiersafe.com
Granite Security Products www.granitesafe.com
Gunlocker Phoenix USA Inc. www.gunlocker.com
GunVault www.gunvault.com
Hakuba USA Inc. www.hakubausa.com
Heritage Safe Co. www.heritagesafecompany.com
Hide-A-Gun www.hide-a-gun.com
Hunter Company www.huntercompany.com
Knouff & Knouff, Inc. www.kkair.com
Kolpin Mfg. Co. www.kolpin.com
Liberty Safe & Security www.libertysafe.com
New Innovative Products www.starlightcases
Noble Security Systems Inc. www.noble.co.ll

Phoenix USA Inc. www.gunlocker.com
Rhino Gun Cases www.rhinoguns.com
Rocky Mountain Safe Inc. www.rockymountainsafe.com
Safe Tech, Inc. www.safrgun.com
Saf-T-Hammer www.saf-t-hammer.com
Saf-T-Lok Corp. www.saf-t-lok.com
San Angelo All-Aluminum Products Inc.
    sasptuld@x.netcom.com
Securecase www.securecase.com
Shot Lock Corp. www.shotlock.com
Smart Lock Technology Inc. www.smartlock.com
Sportsmans Steel Safe Co. www.sportsmansteelsafes.com
Stack-On Products Co. www.stack-on.com
T.Z. Case Int'l www.tz-case.com
Treadlock Security Safes www.treadlok.com
Versatile Rack Co. www.versatilegunrack.com
V-Line Industries www.vlineind.com
Winchester Safes www.fireking.com
Ziegel Engineering ziegel@aol.com

CHOKE DEVICES, RECOIL REDUCERS, AND ACCURACY DEVICES

100 Straight Products www.100straight.com
Answer Products Co. www.answerrifles.com
Briley Mfg www.briley.com

Carlson's www.carlsonschokes.com
Colonial Arms www.colonialarms.com
Mag-Na-Port Int'l Inc. www.magnaport.com

CHRONOGRAPHS

Competition Electronics www.competitionelectronics.com
Competitive Edge Dynamics www.cedhk.com
Oehler Research Inc. www.oehler-research.com

PACT www.pact.com
ProChrony www.competitionelectronics.com
Shooting Chrony Inc www.pathcom.com/~chrony

CLEANING PRODUCTS

Accupro www.accupro.com
Ballistol USA www.ballistol.com
Birchwood Casey www.birchwoodcasey.com
Bore Tech www.boretech.com
Break-Free, Inc. break-free@worldnet.att.net
Bruno Shooters Supply www.brunoshooters.com
Butch's Bore Shine www.bbsindustries.com
Clenzoil www.clenzoil.com
Corrosion Technologies www.corrosionx.com
Dewey Mfg. www.deweyrods.com
Eezox Inc. www.xmission.com
G 96 www.g96.com
Hoppes www.hoppes.com
KG Industries www.kgproducts.com

Kleen-Bore Inc. www.kleen-bore.com
L&R Mfg. www.lrultrasonics.com
Mpro7 Gun Care www.mp7.com
Otis Technology, Inc. www.otisgun.com
Outers www.outers-guncare.com
Ox-Yoke Originals Inc. www.oxyoke.com
ProTec Lubricants www.proteclubricants.com
Sagebrush Products www.sagebrushproducts.com
Sentry Solutions Ltd. www.sentrysolutions.com
Shooters Choice Gun Care www.shooters-choice.com
Silencio www.silencio.com
Stony Point Products www.stoneypoint.com
Tetra Gun www.tetraproducts.com
World's Fastest Gun Bore Cleaner www.michaels-oregon.com

FIREARM MANUFACTURERS AND IMPORTERS

AAR, Inc. www.iar-arms.com
Ace Custom 45's www.acecustom45.com
Advanced Weapons Technology www.AWT-Zastava.com
Airgun Express www.airgunexpress.com
Alchemy Arms www.alchemyltd.com
Aldo Uberti & Co. uberti@lumetel.it
American Derringer Corp. www.amderringer.com
AMT www.amtguns.com

Answer Products Co. www.thewild.com/answer/
AR-7 Industries, LLC www.ar-7.com
Armalite www.armalite.com
Arms Corp. of the Philippines armscor@info.com.ph
Arnold Arms www.arnoldarms.com
Arthur Brown Co. www.eabco.com
Autauga Arms, Inc. autaugaarms@mindspring.com
Auto-Ordnance Corp. www.auto-ordnance.com

WEB DIRECTORY

Axtell Rifle Co. **www.riflesmith.com**
Aya **www.webstudio.net/aya**
Ballard Rifle & Cartridge LLC **www.ballardrifles.com**
Barrett Firearms Mfg. **www.barrettrifles.com**
Beeman Precision Airguns **www.beeman.com**
Benelli USA Corp. **www.benelliusa.com**
Benjamin Sheridan **www.crosman.com**
Beretta U.S.A. Corp. **www.berettausa.com**
Bill Hanus Birdguns **www.billhanusbirdguns.com**
Blackstar **www.benchrest.com/blackstar**
Bond Arms **www.bondarms.com**
Borden's Rifles, Inc. **www.bordensrifles.com**
Bowen Classic Arms **www.bowenclassicarms.com**
Briley Mfg **www.briley.com**
BRNO Arms **www.zbrojouka.com**
Brolin Arms **www.shooters.com/brolin/**
Brown, Ed Products **www.edbrown.com**
Browning **www.browning.com**
BUL Transmark, Ltd. **www.aquanet.co.il/bul_m5**
Bushmaster Firearms/Quality Parts **www.bushmaster.com**
Cape Outfitters **www.doublegun.com**
Carbon 15 **www.professional-ordnance.com**
Casull Arms Corp. **www.casullarms.com**
Century Arms **www.centuryarms.com**
Chadick's Ltd. **www.chadicks-ltd.com**
Charles Daly **www.charlesdaly.com**
Charter2000, Inc. **www.charterfirearms.com**
Christensen Arms **www.christensenarms.com**
Cimarron Firearms Co. **www.cimarron-firearms.com**
Clark Custom Guns **www.clarkcustomguns.com**
Colt Mfg Co. **www.colt.com**
Connecticut Valley Arms **www.cva.com**
Coonan Arms **www.uslink.net/~cruzer/main/htm**
Cooper Firearms **www.cooperfirearms.com**
Crosman **www.crosman.com**
Crossfire, L.L.C. **www.crossfirelle.com**
CZ USA **www.cz-usa.com**
Daisy Mfg Co. **www.daisy.com**
Dakota Arms Inc. **www.dakotaarms.com**
Davis Industries **www.davisindguns.com**
Dixie Gun Works **www.dixiegun.com**
Dlask Arms Corp. **www.dlask.com**
D.S. Arms, Inc. **www.dsarms.com**
DZ Arms **www.tool-fix.com/dzarms.html**
Eagle Imports, Inc. **www.bersa-llama.com**
Enterprise Arms **www.enterprise.com**
European American Armory Corp. **www.eaacorp.com**
Fabarm **www.fabarm.com**
Freedom Arms **www.freedomarms.com**
Gamo **www.gamo.com**
Gary Reeder Custom Guns **www.reeder-customguns.com**
Gibbs Rifle Company **www.gibbsrifle.com**
Glock **www.glockworks.com**
Griffin & Howe **www.griffinhowe.com**
Griffon USA, Inc. **griffonusa@aol.com**
Grizzly Big Boar Rifle **www.largrizzly.com**

GSI Inc. **www.gsifirearms.com**
H&R 1871, Inc., New England Firearms, H&R **hr1871@hr1871.com**
Hammerli **www.hammerli.com**
Harris Gunworks **www.harrisgunworks.com**
Heavy Express, Inc. **www.heavyexpress.com**
Heckler and Koch **www.hecklerkoch-usa.com**
Henry Repeating Arms Co. **www.henryrepeating.com**
High Standard Mfg. **www.highstandard.com**
Hi-Point Firearms **www.hi-pointfirearms.com**
H-S Precision **www.hsprecision.com**
IAR Inc. **www.iar-arms.com**
Imperial Miniature Armory **www.1800miniature.com**
Interarms **www.interarms.com**
Inter Ordnance **www.inter-ordnance.com**
Intrac Arms International LLC **defence@dldnet.com**
Israel Arms **www.israelarms.com**
Ithaca Gun Co. **www.ithacagun.com**
JP Enterprises, Inc. **www.jpar15.com**
Kahr Arms **www.kahr.com**
Kel-Tec CNC Ind., Inc. **www.kel-tec.com**
Kimber **www.kimberamerica.com**
Knight's Mfg. Co. **kacsr25@aol.com**
Knight Rifles **www.knightrifles.com**
Krieghoff GmbH **www.krieghoff.de**
Krieghoff Int'l **www.shootingsports.com**
L.A.R Mfg **www.largrizzly.com**
Lazzeroni Arms Co. **www.lazzeroni.com**
Les Baer Custom, Inc. **www.lesbaer.com**
Lone Star Rifle Co. **www.lonestarrifle.com**
Magnum Research **www.magnumresearch.com**
Marksman Products **www.marksman.com**
Marlin **www.marlinfirearms.com**
McMillan Bros Rifle Co. **www.mcfamily.com**
Merkel **www.gsifirearms.com**
Miltex, Inc. **www.miltexusa.com**
Navy Arms **www.navyarms.com**
Nesika Actions **www.nesika.com**
North American Arms **www.naaminis.com**
Nowlin Mfg. Inc. **www.nowlinguns.com**
O.F. Mossberg & Sons **www.mossberg.com**
Olympic Arms **www.olyarms.com**
Para-Ordnance **www.paraord.com**
Pedersoli Davide & Co. **www.davide-pedersoli.com**
Remington **www.remington.com**
Republic Arms Inc. **www.republicarmsinc.com**
Rizzini Di Rizzini **www.rizzini.it**
Robar Companies, Inc. **www.robarguns.com**
Robinson Armament Co. **www.robarm.com**
Rock River Arms, Inc. **www.rockriverarms.com**
Rogue Rifle Co. Inc. **www.chipmunkrifle.com**
Rossi Arms **www.rossiusa.com**
RPM **www.rpmxlpistols.com**
Sabatti SpA **info@sabatti.it**
Safari Arms **www.olyarms.com**
Samco Global Arms Inc. **www.samcoglobal.com**

WEB DIRECTORY

Savage Arms Inc. **www.savagearms.com**
Scattergun Technologies Inc. **www.scattergun.com**
SIG Arms, Inc. **www.sigarms.com**
Simpson Ltd. **www.simpsonltd.com**
SKB Shotguns **www.skbshotguns.com**
Slug Group Inc. **slugrp@bedford.net**
Smith & Wesson **www.smith-wesson.com**
Springfield Armory **www.springfield-armory.com**
SSK Industries **www.sskindustries.com**
Steyr Mannlicher **www.gsifirearms.com**
STI Int'l **sales@sti-guns.com**
Strayer-Voigt Inc. **www.sviguns.com**
Sturm, Ruger & Company **www.ruger-firearms.com**
Tar-Hunt Slug Guns, Inc. **www.tar-hunt.com**
Taurus **www.taurususa.com**

Tennessee Guns **www.tennesseeguns.com**
The 1877 Sharps Co. **www.1877sharps.com**
Thompson Center Arms **www.tcarms.com**
Traditions **www.traditionsmuzzle.com**
Uberti USA, Inc. **www.uberti.com**
United States Fire Arms Mfg. Co. **www.usfirearms.com**
Vektor USA **vektorusa@series2000.com**
Volquartsen Custom Ltd. **www.volquartsen.com**
Weatherby **www.weatherby.com**
Webley Scott Ltd. **www.webley.g.uk**
Wild West Guns **www.wildwestguns.com**
William Larkin Moore & Co. **www.doublegun.com**
Wilson Combat **www.wilsoncombat.com**
Wilson's Gun Shop Inc. **www.wilsoncombat.com**
Winchester Firearms **www.winchester-guns.com**

GUN PARTS, BARRELS, AFTER-MARKET ACCESSORIES

300 Below **www.300below.com**
Accuracy Speaks, Inc. **www.accuracyspeaks.com**
American Spirit Arms Corp. **www.gunkits.com**
Badger Barrels, Inc. **www.badgerbarrels.com**
Bar-Sto Precision Machine **www.barsto.com**
Belt Mountain Enterprises **www.beltmountain.com**
Blackstar **www.benchrest.com/blackstar**
Buffer Technologies **www.buffertech.com**
Bullberry Barrel Works **www.bullberry.com**
Bushmaster Firearms/Quality Parts **www.bushmaster.com**
Butler Creek Corp **www.butler-creek.com**
Caspian Arms Ltd. **caspianarm@aol.com**
Cheaper Than Dirt **www.cheaperthandirt.com**
Chesnut Ridge **www.chestnutridge.com/**
Chip McCormick Corp **www.chipmccormickcorp.com**
Colonial Arms **www.colonialarms.com**
Cylinder & Slide Shop **www.cylinder-slide.com**
Dixie Gun Works **www.dixiegun.com**
DPMS **www.dpmsinc.com**
D.S.Arms, Inc. **www.dsarms.com**
Ed Brown Products **www.edbrown.com**
EFK Marketing/Fire Dragon Pistol Accessories
   www.flmfire.com
Federal Arms **www.fedarms.com**
Gun Parts Corp. **www.gunpartscorp.com**
Hastings Barrels **www.hastingsbarrels.com**
Heckman Specialties **www.members.tripod.com/~heckspec**
Heine Specialty Products **www.heine.com**
Interntional Training Concepts Inc. **isub4itc@gvi.net**
Jarvis, Inc. **www.jarvis-custom.com**
J&T Distributing **www.jtdistributing.com**
Jonathan Arthur Ciener, Inc. **www.22lrconversions.com**
JP Enterprises **www.jpar15.com**
King's Gunworks **www.kingsgunworks.com**
Les Baer Custom, Inc. **www.lesbaer.com**
Lilja Barrels **www.riflebarrels.com**

Lothar Walther Precision Tools Inc. **www.lothar-walther.de**
M&A Parts, Inc. **www.m-aparts.com**
Marvel Products, Inc. **www.marvelprod.com**
MEC-GAR SrL **www.mec-gar.it**
Michaels of Oregon Co. **www.michaels-oregon.com**
Pachmayr **www.pachmayr.com**
Pac-Nor Barreling **www.pac-nor.com**
Para Ordnance Pro Shop **www.ltms.com**
Point Tech Inc. **pointec@ibm.net**
Promag Industries **www.promagindustries.com**
Power Custom, Inc. **www.powercustom.com**
Rocky Mountain Arms **www.rockymountainarms.com**
Royal Arms Int'l **www.royalarms.com**
R.W. Hart **www.rwhart.com**
Sarco Inc. **www.webspan.net/~sarco/**
Scattergun Technologies Inc. **www.scattergun.com**
Shilen **www.shilen.com**
Smith & Alexander Inc. **www.smithandalexander.com**
Speed Shooters Int'l **www.shooternet.com/ssi**
Sprinco USA Inc. **sprinco@primenet.com**
SSK Industries **www.shooters.com/apg/members.htm**
Tapco **www.tapco.com**
Trapdoors Galore **www.trapdoors.com**
Triple K Manufacturing Co. Inc. **www.triplek.com**
U.S.A. Magazines Inc. **www.usa-magazines.com**
Verney-Carron SA **www.verney-carron.com**
Volquartsen Custom Ltd. **www.volquartsen.com**
W.C. Wolff Co. **www.gunsprings.com**
Waller & Son **www.wallerandson.com**
Weigand Combat Handguns **www.weigandcombat.com**
Western Gun Parts **www.westerngunparts.com**
Wilson Combat **www.wilsoncombat.com**
Wisner's Inc. **www.localaccess.com/gunparts/**
Z-M Weapons **www.zmweapons.com/home.htm**

WEB DIRECTORY

GUNSMITHING SUPPLIES AND INSTRUCTION

American Gunsmithing Institute www.americangunsmith.com
Brownells, Inc. www.brownells.com
B-Square Co. www.b-square.com
Clymer Mfg. Co. www.clymertool.com
Craftguard Metal Finishing crftgrd@aol.com
Du-Lite Corp. www.dulite.com

Dvorak Instruments www.dvorakinstruments.com
Gradiant Lens Corp. www.gradientlens.com
JGS Precision Tool Mfg. LLC www.jgstools.com
Midway www.midwayusa.com
Olympus America Inc. www.olympus.com

HANDGUN GRIPS

Ajax Custom Grips, Inc. www.ajaxgrips.com
Altamont Co. altamont@net66.com
Barami Corp. www.baramihipgrip.com
Eagle Grips www.eaglegrips.com
Fitz Pistol Grip Co. johnpaul@snowcrest.net
Hogue Grips www.getgrip.com

Lasergrips www.crimsontrace.com
Lett Custom Grips www.lettgrips.com
Pachmayr www.pachmayr.com
Pearce Grips www.pearcegrip.com
Trausch Grips Int.Co. www.erausch.com
Uncle Mike's: www.uncle-mikes.com

HOLSTERS AND LEATHER PRODUCTS

Aker Leather Products www.akerleather.com
Alessi Distributor R&F Inc. www.alessiholsters.com
Bianchi www.bianchiint.com
Blackhills Leather www.blackhillsleather.com
BodyHugger Holsters www.nikolais.com
Brigade Gun Leather www.brigadegunleather.com
Chimere www.chimere.com
Classic Old West Styles www.cows.com
Conceal It www.conceal-it.com
Conceal 'N Draw www.themetro.om/03/fempro
Coronado Leather Co. www.coronadoleather.com
Creedmoor Sports, Inc. www.creedmoorsports.com
Custom Leather Wear www.customleatherwear.com
Defense Security Products www.thunderwear.com
DeSantis Holster www.desantisholster.com
Dillon Precision www.dillonprecision.com
Don Hume Leathergoods, Inc. www.donhume.com
Ernie Hill International www.erniehill.com
Fist www.fist-inc.com
Front Line Ltd. frontlin@internet-zahav.net
Galco www.usgalco.com
Gilmore's Sports Concepts www.gilmoresports.com
Gould & Goodrich www.goulduse.com
Gunmate Products www.gun-mate.com
Hellweg Ltd. www.hellwegltd.com

Hide-A-Gun www.hide-a-gun.com
Hunter Co. www.huntercompany.com
Kirkpatrick Leather Company www.kirkpatrickleather.com
Kramer Leather www.kramerleather.com
Law Concealment Systems www.handgunconcealment.com
Levy's Leathers Ltd. www.levysleathers.com
Michaels of Oregon Co. www.michaels-oregon.com
Milt Sparks Leather www.miltsparks.com
Mitch Rosen Extraordinary Gunleather www.mitchrosen.com
Old World Leather www.gun-mate.com
Pager Pal www.pagerpal.com
Phalanx Corp. www.phalanxarms.com
PWL www.pwlusa.com
Rumanya Inc. www.rumanya.com
Safariland Ltd. Inc. www.safariland.com
Shooting Systems Group Inc. www.shootingsystems.com
Strictly Anything Inc. www.strictlyanything.com
Strong Holster Co. www.strong-holster.com
The Belt Co. www.conceal-it.com
The Leather Factory Inc. lflandry@flash.net
The Outdoor Connection www.outdoorconnection.com
Top-Line USA Inc. www.toplineusa.com
Triple K Manufacturing Co. www.triplek.com
Wilson Combat www.wilsoncombat.com

MISCELLANEOUS SHOOTING PRODUCTS

10X Products Group www.10Xwear.com
Aero Peltor www.aearo.com
Beartooth www.beartoothproducts.com
Dalloz Safety www.cdalloz.com
Deben Group Industries Inc. www.deben.com
E.A.R., Inc. www.earinc.com

Johnny Stewart Wildlife Calls www.stewartoutdoors.com
North Safety Products www.northsafety-brea.com
Second Chance Body Armor Inc. email@secondchance.com
Silencio www.silencio.com
Smart Lock Technologies www.smartlock.com
Walker's Game Ear Inc. www.walkersgameear.com

MUZZLELOADING FIREARMS AND PRODUCTS

Austin & Halleck, Inc. austinhal@aol.com
CVA www.cva.com
Dixie Gun Works, Inc. www.dixiegun.com
Elephant Black Powder www.fastlane.net/~petro

Goex Black Powder www.goexpowder.com
Jedediah Starr Trading Co. www.jedediah-starr.com
Jim Chambers Flintlocks www.flintlocks.com
Knight Rifles www.knightrifles.com

WEB DIRECTORY

Log Cabin Shop www.logcabinshop.com
Lyman www.lymanproducts.com
Millennium Designed Muzzleloaders
  www.m2kmuzzleloaders.com
Mountain State Muzzleloading
  www.mtnstatemuzzleloading.com
MSM, Inc. www.msmfg.com

Muzzleloading Technologies, Inc. www.mtimuzzleloading.com
October Country Muzzleloading www.oct-country.com
Ox-Yoke Originals Inc. www.oxyoke.com
Rightnour Mfg. Co. Inc. www.rmcsports.com
Thompson Center Arms www.tcarms.com
Traditions Performance Muzzleloading
  www.traditionsmuzzle.com

PUBLICATIONS, VIDEOS, AND CD'S

Airgun Letter www.airgunletter.com
American Firearms Industry www.amfire.com
American Handgunner www.americanhandgunner
American Shooting Magazine www.americanshooting.com
Blacksmith bcbooks@glasscity.net
Blackpowder Hunting www.blackpowderhunting.com
Black Powder Journal www.blackpowderjournal.com
Blue Book Publications www.bluebookinc.com
Combat Handguns www.combathandguns.com
Countrywide Press www.countrysport.com
DBI Books/Krause Publications www.krause.com
Delta Force www.infogo.com/delta
Discount Gun Books www.discountgunbooks.com
Gun List www.gunlist.com
Gun Video www.gunvideo.com
GUNS Magazine www.gunsmagazine.com
Gunweb Magazine WWW Links www.imags.com
Harris Publications www.harrispublications.com
Heritage Gun Books www.gunbooks.com
Krause Publications www.krause.com
Moose Lake Publishing MooselakeP@aol.com
Munden Enterprises Inc. www.bob-munden.com
Outdoor Videos www.outdoorvideos.com
Precision Shooting www.precisionshooting.com

Ray Riling Arms Books Co., Inc.
  www.rayrilingarmsbooks.com
Rifle and Handloader Magazines www.riflemagazine.com
Rifle and Shotgun Magazine/Gun Journal
  www.natcom-publications.com
Safari Press Inc. www.safaripress.com
Shooters News www.shootersnews.com
Shooting Industry www.shootingindustry.com
Shooting Sports Retailer ssretailer@ad.com
Shotgun News www.shotgunnews.com
Shotgun Report www.shotgunreport.com
Shotgun Sports Magazine www.shotgun-sports.com
Small Arms Review www.smallarmsreview.com
Sporting Clays Web Edition www.sportingclays.com
Sports Afield www.sportsafield.comm
Sports Trend www.sportstrend.com
Sportsmen on Film www.sportsmenonfilm.com
Tactical Shooter www.tacticalshooter.com
The Gun Journal www.shooters.com
The Shootin Iron www.off-road.com/4x4web/si/si.html
The Single Shot Exchange Magazine singleshot@earthlink.net
Voyageur Press www.voyageurpress.com
VSP Publications www.gunbooks.com
Vulcan Outdoors Inc. www.vulcanpub.com
Wolfe Publishing Co. wolfepub@bslnet.com

RELOADING TOOLS AND SUPPLIES

Ballisti-Cast Mfg. www.powderandbow.com/ballist
Bruno Shooters Supply www.brunoshooters.com
Bullet Moulds www.bulletmolds.com
CH Tool & Die www.cdhd.com
Corbin Mfg & Supply Co. www.corbins.com
Dillon Precision www.dillonprecision.com
Forster Precision Products www.forsterproducts.com
Hanned Line www.hanned.com
Harrell's Precision www.harrellsprec.com
Hornady www.hornady.com
Huntington Reloading Products www.huntingtons.com
J & J Products Co. www.jandjproducts.com
Lee Precision, Inc. www.leeprecision.com
Lyman www.lymanproducts.com
Mayville Engineering Co. (MEC) www.mayvl.com

Midway www.midwayusa.com
Moly-Bore www.molybore.com
MTM Case-Guard www.mtmcase-guard.com
NECO www.neconos.com
Neil Jones Custom Products www.neiljones.com
Ponsness/Warren www.reloaders.com
Ranger Products
  www.pages.prodigy.com/rangerproducts.home.htm
Rapine Bullet Mold Mfg Co. www.bulletmolds.com
RCBS www.rcbs.com
Redding Reloading Equipment www.redding-reloading.com
Russ Haydon's Shooting Supplies www.shooters-supply.com
Sinclair Int'l Inc. www.sinclairintl.com
Stony Point Products Inc www.stonypoint.com
The Hanned Line www.hanned.com
Thompson Bullet Lube Co. www.vipersites.com/tbl

RESTS— BENCH, PORTABLE, ATTACHABLE

B-Square www.b-square.com
Desert Mountain Mfg. www.bench-master.com

Harris Engineering Inc.
  www.cyberteklabs.com/harris/main/htm

WEB DIRECTORY

L Thomas Rifle Support www.ltsupport.com
Level-Lok www.levellok.com
Midway www.midwayusa.com
Ransom International www.ransom-intl.com

R.W. Hart www.rwhart.com

Sinclair Intl, Inc. www.sinclairintl.com

Versa-Pod www.versa-pod.com

SCOPES, SIGHTS, MOUNTS AND ACCESSORIES

Accusight www.accusight.com
ADCO www.shooters.com/adco/index/htm
Aimpoint www.aimpointusa.com
Aim Shot, Inc. www.hi-techoptics.com
Aimtech Mount Systems www.aimtech-mounts.com
Alpec Team, Inc. www.alpec.com
American Technologies Network, Corp. www.atncorp.com
Ashley Outdoors, Inc. www.ashleyoutdoors.com
ATN www.atncorp.com
BSA Optics bsaoptics@bellsouth.net
B-Square Company, Inc. www.b-square.com
Burris www.burrisoptics.com
Bushnell Corp. www.bushnell.com
Carl Zeiss Optical Inc. www.zeiss.com
C-More Systems www.cmore.com
Conetrol Scope Mounts www.conetrol.com
Crossfire L.L.C. www.amfire.com/hesco/html
DCG Supply Inc. www.dcgsupply.com
Decot Hy-Wyd Sport Glasses www.sportglasses.com
EasyHit, Inc. www.easyhit.com
Electro-Optics Technologies www.eotechmdc.com/holosight
Europtik Ltd. www.europtik.com
Gilmore Sports www.gilmoresports.com
Hakko Co. Ltd. hakko@hakko-japan.co.jp
Hesco www.hescosights.com
Hitek Industries www.nightsight.com
HIVIZ www.northpass.com
Innovative Weaponry, Inc. www.ptnightsights.com
Ironsighter Co. www.ironsighter.com
ITT Night Vision www.ittnightvision.com
Kowa Optimed Inc. www.kowascope.com
Laser Bore Sight www.laserboresight.com
Laser Devices Inc. www.laserdevices.com
Lasergrips www.crimsontrace.com
LaserLyte www.laserlyte.com

LaserMax Inc. www.lasermax-inc.com
Laser Products www.surefire.com
Leapers, Inc. www.leapers.com
Leica Camera Inc. carleica@aol.com
Leupold www.leupold.com
Lyman www.lymanproducts.com
Millett www.millettsights.com
Miniature Machine Corp. www.mmcsight.com
NAIT www.nait.com
Newcon International Ltd. newconsales@newcon-optik.com
Night Owl Optics www.jnltrading.com
Nikon Inc. www.nikonusa.com
North American Integrated Technologies www.nait.com
O.K. Weber, Inc. www.okweber.com
Pentax Corp. www.pentaxsportoptics.com
Premier Reticle www.premierreticles.com
R&R Int'l Trade www.nightoptic.com
Schmidt & Bender www.schmidt-bender.com
Scopecoat www.scopecoat.com
Scopelevel www.scopelevel.com
Segway Industries www.segway-industries.com
Shepherd Scope Ltd. www.shepherdscopes.com
Simmons-Blount www.blount.com
S&K www.sandkmfg.com
Springfield Armory www.springfield-armory.com
Sure-Fire www.surefire.com
Swarovski/Kahles www.swarovskioptik.com
Swift Instruments Inc. www.swift-optics.com
Tasco www.tascosales.com
Trijicon Inc. www.trijicon-inc.com
Truglo Inc. www.truglosights.com
U.S. Optics Technologies Inc. www.usoptics.com
Weaver-Blount www.blount.com
Wilcox Industries Corp www.wilcoxind.com
Williams Gun Sight Co. www.williamsgunsight.com

SHOOTING ORGANIZATIONS, SCHOOLS AND RANGES

Amateur Trapshooting Assoc. www.shootata.com
American Gunsmithing Institute www.americangunsmith.com
American Shooting Sports Council www.assc.com
BATF www.atf.ustreas.gov
Blackwater Lodge and Training Center
    www.blackwaterlodge.com
Boone and Crockett Club www.boone-crockett.org
Buckmasters, Ltd. www.buckmasters.com
Citizens Committee for the Right to Keep & Bear Arms
    www.ccrkba.org
Civilian Marksmanship Program www.odcmp.com
Ducks Unlimited www.ducks.org
Front Sight Firearms Training Institute www.frontsight.com

Gun Clubs www.associatedgunclubs.org
Gun Owners' Action League www.goal.org
Gun Owners of America www.gunowners.org
Gun Trade Assoc. Ltd. www.brucepub.com/gta
Gunsite Training Center, Inc. www.gunsite.com
International Defense Pistol Assoc. www.idpa.com
International Hunter Education Assoc. www.ihea.com
National 4-H Shooting Sports kesabo@nmsu.edu
National Benchrest Shooters Assoc. www.benchrest.com
National Muzzle Loading Rifle Assoc. www.nmlra.org
National Reloading Manufacturers Assoc
    www.reload-nrma.com
National Rifle Assoc. www.nra.org

WEB DIRECTORY

National Shooting Sports Foundation www.nssf.org
National Skeet Shooters Association www.nssa-nsca.com
National Sporting Clays Assoc. www.nssa-nsca.com
National Wild Turkey Federation www.hooks.com/nwtf
North American Hunting Club www.huntingclub.com
Pennsylvania Gunsmith School www.pagunsmith.com
Quail Unlimited www.qu.org
Right To Keep and Bear Arms www.rkba.org
Rocky Mountain Elk Foundation www.rmef.org
S&W Academy and Nat'l Firearms Trng. Center
   www.smith-wesson.com/academy/index.html
Second Amendment Foundation www.saf.org
Shooting Ranges Int'l www.shootingranges.com

Single Action Shooting Society www.sassnet.com
Ted Nugent United Sportsmen of America
   www.outdoors.net/tednugent
Thunder Ranch www.thunderranchinc.com
Trapshooters Homepage www.trapshooters.com
Trinidad State Junior College www.tsjc.cccoes.edu
U.S. Int'l Clay Target Assoc. www.usicta.com
United States Fish and Wildlife Service www.fws.gov
U.S. Practical Shooting Assoc. www.uspsa.org
USA Shooting Home Page www.usashooting.edu
USA Shooting www.usashooting.org
Wildlife Legislative Fund of America www.wlfa.org
Women's Shooting Sports Foundation wssf@worldnet.att.net

STOCKS

Bell & Carlson, Inc. www.users.pld.com/bacinc
Boyd's Gunstock Industries, Inc. www.boydboys.com
Butler Creek Corp www.butler-creek.com
Calico Hardwoods, Inc. www.calicohardwoods.com
Choate Machine www.riflestock.com
Great American Gunstocks www.gunstocks.com

M L Greene Precision Products www.henge.com/~mlgreene
McMillan Fiberglass Stocks www.mcmfamily.com
Ram-Line- Blount Inc. www/blount.com
Rimrock Rifle Stock www.rimrockstocks.com
Royal Arms Gunstocks www.imt.net/~royalarms

TARGETS AND RANGE EQUIPMENT

Action Target Co. www.actiontarget.com
Advanced Interactive Systems www.ais-sim.com
Birchwood Casey www.birchwoodcasey.com
Caswell Detroit Armor Companies www.bullettrap.com
MTM Products www.mtmcase-gard.com
Newbold Target Systems www.newboldtargets.com
Range Management Services Inc. www.casewellintl.com

Reactive Target Systems Inc. chrts@primenet.com
Super Trap Bullet Containment Systems www.supertrap.com
Thompson Target Technology
   www.cantorweb.com/thompsontargets
Visible Impact Targets www.crosman.com
White Flyer www.whiteflyer.com

TRAP AND SKEET SHOOTING EQUIPMENT AND ACCESSORIES

Auto-Sporter Industries www.auto-sporter.com
10X Products Group 10X@10xwear.com
Claymaster Traps www.claymaster.com
Do-All Traps, Inc. www.do-alltraps.com

Laporte USA www.laporte-shooting.com
Outers www.blount.com
Trius Products Inc. www.triustraps.com

TRIGGERS

Shilen www.shilen.com
Timney Triggers www.timneytrigger.com

Brownells www.brownells.com

MAJOR SHOOTING WEB SITES AND LINKS

All Outdoors www.alloutdoors.com
Alphabetic Index of Links www.gunsgunsguns.com
Auction Arms www.auctionarms.com
Firearms Internet Database www.savannahlane.com
Gun Broker Auctions www.gunbroker.com
Gun Games Online www.gungames.com
Gun Index www.gunindex.com
Gun Talk www.shooters.com/guntalkactivitiesframe.html
GunLinks www.gunlinks.com
Guns For Sale www.gunsamerica.com
Gunweb www.gunweb.com
GunXchange www.gunxchange.com

Hunting Digest www.huntingdigest.com
Hunting Information (NSSF) www.huntinfo.com
Rec.Guns www.recguns.com
Shooters' Gun Calendar www.guncalendar.com/index.cfm
Shooter's Online Services www.shooters.com
Shooters Search www.shooterssearch.com
Shotgun Sports Resource Guide www.shotgunsports.com
The Hunting Net www.huntingnet.com
The Sportsman's Web www.sportsmansweb.com
TUCO's Firearms Forums www.paradise-web.com/plus/
   plus.mirage?who=tuco10&all=yes
Where To Shoot www.wheretoshoot.com

by BILL HANUS

SHOTGUN REVIEW

IF LAST YEAR was designated as the "Year of the Magnum", then 2K has to be built around the theme of letting the good times roll. As the baby boom generation quick-marches toward its peak spending years, they have become increasingly aware of shotgun deficiencies in their gun cabinets.

It did not take a mint to fall on some of the shotgun makers for them to figure out the that there is a market for shootable art - "shoulder candy" in the parlance of the day - among the boomers. These five-figure confections will, no doubt, be chronicled in the coffee table magazines designed to whet the appetites of this new class of shotgun "collector/investor."

Among those who feel the best return on a shotgun investment is not missing a bird off point all season - equally nifty and exciting things are happening in shotgunning. So lean back, take a deep breath and prepare to join shotgun makers, dealers, shooters and collectors in another chorus of: "*Happy Days Are Here Again!*"

Start this year's taste-testing with these three dandies:

"Cutting edge, outside the box" and "pushing the envelope" are hardly cliches that one would think of applying to the shotgun industry. Indeed, in a business where a coat of camouflage paint on a goose gun can be passed off as a "new" turkey gun; and some of the nicest birdgun doubles on today's market are reproductions of designs that have since celebrated their Diamond Jubilee anniversaries - the technology that **FABARM** puts into its doubles, over/unders and semi-automatics makes them the most technically advanced shotguns on the market. The 12 gauge FABARM Classic Lion Grade

FABARM Classic Lion Grade II, $2,249 cased.

11 side-by-side has all the usual amenities that you'd expect - a single selective trigger, 3-inch chambers, chrome-lined bores, screw-in chokes, etc. But it's what you get that you didn't expect that explain why it deserves your special attention this year.

The FABARM TriBore Barrel System has all the advantages of back-boring - something competition target shooters have been doing for years. It's benefits? Softer recoil, increased velocity and optimum patterning. The first over-bored region, just ahead of the chamber and lengthened forcing cones has an internal diameter of 18.8mm. This softens recoil without sacrificing velocity. In the middle of the barrel the "first choking" area begins with an internal bore diameter of 18.4 mm, increasing velocity. About 6 inches from the end of the muzzle the bore tapers into the screw-in choke. The final choke constriction takes place about 1 1/2 inches from the muzzle, with the selected choke dimensions consistent to the muzzle – ensuring uniform distribution and patterning.

Five standard chokes (C, IC, M, IM, F) are standard with a rifled choke, which functions as a "spreader", available that would be perfect for bobwhite, woodcock and station 8 on the skeet field. The gun is steel shot-friendly (in the open chokes).

The Grade II Classic Lion has so many other "nice touches" in addition to the palm swell grip that it's hard to know where to begin. It has nicely upgraded dark wood that contrasts with the white metal finish. Good wood-to-metal fit. The sideplates are engraved and detachable (and you'll discover coiled hammer springs inside). It has a checkered trigger. A pierced opening lever. The screw-in chokes are inletted so that there is a built-in stop, making it hard to over-tighten the chokes. It comes in a deluxe, fitted case. And, rarest of all - a Lifetime Warranty backed by

Heckler & Koch, the importer of this line of fine guns.

You might expect to pay $4,000 for a side-by-side of this quality, but the Year 2000 price is only $2,249!

Sturm, Ruger seems to have this knack of inventing the obvious. The idea of adding the option of .410 barrel inserts to their 28-gauge gun is a wonderful one.

As luck would have it, I had borrowed a 50th Anniversary (1949-1999) Limited Edition of Ruger's Red Label 28-gauge for review when Ruger announced the availability of .410 barrel inserts. It took only a phone call to be allowed to have all the fun I wanted in .41 0 on top of the joy of 28 gauge!

The insert tubes themselves are made of red anodized aircraft aluminum alloy, *NOT STEEL*. The chambers are made from grade 6 titanium alloy. They weigh about 10 ounces - but the added weight on the front end of this gun does nothing but enhance the swing on the skeet field.

These .410 conversion sets are available in either 26- or 28-inch lengths with 2 stainless steel Skeet choke tubes and a suggested retail price of $525 from the Product Service Department of Sturm, Ruger & Co., Inc. Newport, NH 603/865-2442.

Baschieri & Pellagri Shotgun Shells

In the period between World War I and World War II live pigeon shooting emerged as a high-stakes spectator sport for the rich and famous. Shotgun manufacturers developed special models (AYA's heavy frame Model 56, for example) that set new standards for accuracy, reliability and excellence. Price was no object. Performance was everything. "Pigeon Grade" described the best of the best.

In 1940, Baschieri & Pellagri shotshells were used to win the first of 22 World Live Pigeon Championships. Plus five Olympic Gold Medals, including Atlanta in 1996. It's clear that B&P makes superb

Benelli Nova Pump Rifled Slug Model expands Benelli's superb Nova Pump line introduced last year.

Benelli Montefeltro Short Stock 20-gauge with 12 1/2-inch length of pull with 24- or 26-inch barrel and weighing under 5-1/2 pounds.

shotgun shells - "Pigeon Grade" ammunition, you might say.

After discovering their 29-gram, 1,325 fps 16-gauge load (think of lightning striking), which I was pleased to recommend last year, I learned that Bob Brister (who literally wrote the book: *Shotgunning*) had asked Mike Dotson of B&P America to make up some shells that would reliably break sporting clays targets out to 60 yards. I can confirm Larry Nailon's (ace shotshell ballistician and writer on the subject) findings: they work just as Bob Brister wanted.

The secret: it's a 28-gram (1 oz.) load, in a Gordon System case using B&P components to exit at 1,409 fps, measured one meter from the muzzle. The best 5% antimony pellets in the world are polished super-smooth (they look like they are nickel-plated) and dry-lubricated.

New for the millennium from B&P:

*The 28-gram load described above, designated F2 Ultra Velocity Sporting Clay, will be a stock item;

*Photodegradeable wads will be used in all versions of the F2 Sporting Clays shotshells;

*The Gordon System case will also be used on all 16-and 20-gauge shotshells instead of just 12-gauge loads. Briefly, the Gordon case with its collapsible base wad cushions felt recoil by spreading out the recoil over about a 20% longer time period.

*A 28-gauge shotshell based on the Fiocchi (reloadable) case. First call on this newcomer to the lineup is 3/4 oz. @ 1,230 fps in No. 7-1/2 and No. 8 shot of polished shot - the same used in the Ultra Velocity load - delivered with an amazingly low pressure of 8550 P.S.I.

Call Mike Dotson, B&P America, at 972/726-9073 and identify yourself "*as a friend of Bill Hanus*" and put yourself in touch with the good stuff.

Like the appetizers? Here comes the meat-and-potatos!

Benelli

For decades, autoloading shotguns have used one of four operating systems. Long-recoil guns were the first, beginning with Browning's 1903 invention. Short-recoil guns appeared in the 1950s, followed by short- and long-stroke piston gas operation in the 1960s. All these systems have been successful, with millions of guns using them.

The Benelli uses a unique inertia recoil system - with only seven moving parts, entirely contained in the receiver of the gun - and will operate with all sorts of ammunition interchangeably, without adjustment. Benelli's 20-gauge semi-automatics

are among the lightest 20-gauge guns on the market — all weighing under 6 pounds. All sporting models come with a set of shims to adjust the amount of drop and/or the length of pull to a limited degree.

Benelli Limited Edition Legacy in 12 and 20-gauge (250 of each) with game scene engraving and gold accents and upgraded fancy walnut.

Beretta

As one of the Honors Graduates from the "if it ain't broke, don't fix it" School of Life, it boggled my mind when Beretta announced they were replacing their AL-390 with the Model AL-391. What they've added is well worth noting. The improvements include:

Most important - a system of shims and spacers that allows the shooter to adjust the drop and cast, while interchangeable recoil pads allow for adjustment in length of pull. This may be old stuff to competitive shooters, but this is big news to hunters.

Significant others - the AL-391 has a little plastic bumper in the back of the receiver that helps soak up recoil and vibration when the bolt slams into the receiver -a "no-brainer" kind of idea; a larger opening in the trigger guard making it easier to get at the trigger wearing a glove; plus a

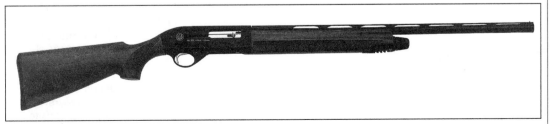

Beretta AL391 Urika Gold Field is available in both 12 and 20-gauge with a variety of barrel lengths with screw-in chokes.

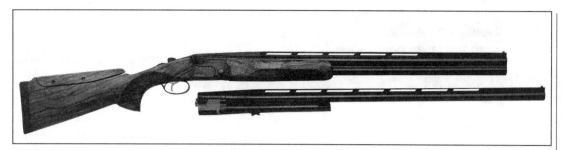

Beretta DT 10 Trident, the new top-of-the-line 12-gauge competition gun from Beretta

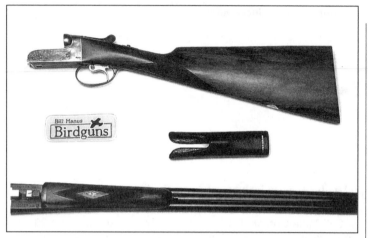

Bill Hanus Birdgun by AYA - new single selective trigger model in 16, 20, or 28 gauge with select wood, leather hand-guard and available stocked for left-handers.

Browning Citori Privilege. Browning's first side plate in over a decade, lavishly engraved with high-grade walnut. 12 gauge only.

Browning Auto-5 Final Tribute special edition of 1000 guns with distinctive white, engraved receiver, high-grade select walnut. 12 gauge only.

Browning BPS 12 Gauge Stalker Combo. The 3 1/2-inch Stalker is available in a combo that includes a 22-inch rifled barrel or 20.5-inch standard barrel with an Extra-Full Turkey choke tube.

weatherproof coating that provides protection against humidity and harsh weather conditions. I count over 30 different models of the AL-391, about a third of which are 20-gauge guns.

On top of the AL-391 Urika, about which paeans are yet to be writ, comes the all-new DT 10 Trident, which they describe as "the technology of victory." The "DT" in the model description stands for Detachable Trigger - which quickly conveys the message that what we are looking at is another phrase they use in describing this gun - "professional perfection."

Bill Hanus Birdguns by AYA

These elegant small gauge doubles duplicate the style and handling characteristics of traditional, ejector-grade English game guns. Made only in 16, 20 and 28 gauge with each mounted on frames proportionate to the gauge. Standard stock dimensions are 1 1/2 x 2 3/8 x 14 3/8 inches with about 3/16-inch cast-off. Stocks set with 3/16-inch cast-on for left-handed shooters may be ordered at no extra charge.

These guns have longer barrels, open chokes, English grips, splinter forends, upgraded wood, fit and finish, and come with an English leather-covered hand-guard.

Briley

Long known for their excellence with screw-chokes and small gauge conversion tubes for 12 gauge skeet guns, Briley has expanded big-time into the small gauge area with such offerings as: 28 gauge and .410 conversion sets for 20 gauge guns; 28 gauge and .410 inserts for 16 gauge and .410 tubes for 28 gauge guns. Give your old side-by-side or over/under new life with a set of small gauge tubes. Available in both standard and "Ultralite" weights, prices per pair start at $350 for the standard tubes and include 4 choke tubes per set. 800/331-5718 (outside Texas) or 713/932-6996 in the Lone Star.

Browning

Browning introduced some new high grade Citoris with Privilege, BG, VI and BG, III nameplates, which vie with one another for beauty. The Citori Ultra XS/XT and Citori Feather XS skeet and sporting clays guns, like all Browning target guns (but with the exception of 28 gauge and .410 bores) are ported, to reduce recoil and muzzle jump. Gauge for gauge the Feather models appear to be lighter than the Ultras by about 10 ounces in the 28 gauges. One of Browning's nice touches is their Triple Trigger system that comes standard on all sporting clays guns. This consists of three interchangeable trigger shoes (wide-smooth, wide-checkered and narrow-smooth) each of which is adjustable to three positions for length of pull or, more accurately, adjusting the radius of the pistol grip to the length of the shooter's finger.

Browning's Gold guns — except for the rifled slug barrel guns — are back-bored. This reduces the friction of the shot pellets - resulting in more shot pellets in the target zone.

Charles Daly

What the world needs is a good .410 double that doesn't cost an arm and a leg. Well, Charles Daly has found a small Italian maker that

Charles Daly Country Squire Over & Under built from the ground up as a .410 with 26-inch barrels, fixed Full/Full chokes and raised ventilated rib.

Charles Daly Country Squire Side by Side sculpted to .410 dimensions with Chrome-Moly steel barrels, internally honed and chromed. 26-inch barrels, fixed F/F chokes.

charge against the barrel wall, which reduces the pressure or constriction of the barrel walls on the shot charge. This means fewer deformed shot

produces an underlever over/under and side-by-side, both of which are a joy to hold and behold. Slim English grips, nice wood, a red rubber pad with case color receiver and opening lever/trigger guards. These are extractor guns with gold-plated double triggers and priced in the $700 range.

F.A.I.R./I.Rizzini

There are several members of the Rizzini family who make shotguns, so confusion comes easily when referring to a "Rizzini" shotgun. F.A.I.R. is the acronym for *Fabbrica Armi Isidoro Rizzini*. The hot item in this line is a 16 gauge over/under with screw-in chokes, available with a half-pistol grip or English grip, in four trim lines.

The 16 gauge is built on a true 16-gauge frame, not 16-gauge barrels on a 12-gauge frame. Higher grades offer more gold accents, better wood, fitted cases.

A 28 gauge over/under built on a true 28-gauge frame with screw-in chokes has been announced for year 2000. It will be available in all four grades and priced slightly higher than the 16 gauge guns.

Fausti Stefano

Makes a pretty complete line of side-by-side and over/under shotguns that are imported by **Traditions Performance Firearms**. The over/unders come in three grades, all of which have single selective triggers, mechanical triggers and recoil pads. The Field I has fixed chokes and extractors and is available in 12, 20, 28 and .410. Field II adds screw-in chokes and automatic ejectors. Field III is the top-of-the-line with some gold appointments, but is available in 12 gauge only.

The Elite side-by-side series has two models, each of which is offered in 12, 20, 28 and .410. Elite ST is a single trigger model with pistol grip and beavertail forend. The Elite DT has double triggers, pistol grip and splinter forend.

Federal Ammunition

Several new shotshell products of interest at Federal this year: (1) A Federal Gold Medal Spreader Load in 12 gauge with 1-1/8 ounce of #8 or #8-1/2 shot which promises wide, even patterns as close as 15 yards; (2) new Tungsten-Polymer loads in 3 1/2-inch for 10 and 12 gauge, plus a 3- and 2 3/4-inch for 20 gauge, all in #4 and #6 shot; (3) new high-velocity - 1,500 fps - steel loads in 12 and 20 gauge; and (4) a non-toxic shell which combines tungsten-iron and steel pellets — two sizes of shot with two different metals — recommended as an upgrade from all-steel loads.

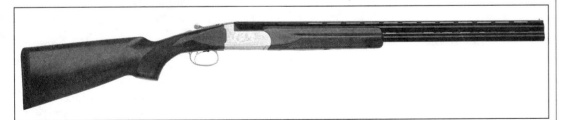

Fausti Stefano Field II moderately priced, full-featured over/under available in all four popular gauges.

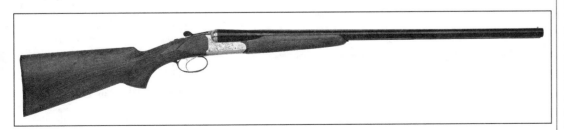

Fausti Stefano Elite ST moderately priced side-by-sides in all popular gauges and available in both single and double trigger models.

Franchi

Now owned by Benelli, Franchi is operated as a separate division and continues to offer its line of Alcione Field and Light Field over/unders and long-recoil AL 48 semi-autos built on the John Browning design, now almost a century old. New this year is the AL 48 Deluxe with high-polish blued finish and upgraded walnut on butt stock and forend. All AL 48 models come with a set of shims to add cast-on, cast-off as well as move the butt stock up and down. All AL 48 models are available in 12, 20 and 28 gauge.

▼Franchi 612 Sporting in 12 gauge with 5 extended choke tubes, select walnut and 30-inch barrels.

◀Franchi AL 48 Deluxe special treatment is available only on their 5.6-pound 20 gauge and 5.4-pound 28 gauge semi-autos, both with C, IC and M choke tubes.

The Alcione Field has, new this year, a left-hand model 12 gauge with 26- or 28-inch barrels.

H&R 1871

They've introduced the Trigger Guardian Trigger Locking System for their long guns. This device is not simply a trigger lock but a lockable trigger-immobilizing device.

Owners of New England Firearms-, Harrington & Richardson-, Wesson & Harrington- or H&H 1871-brand guns shipped before 12/I/99, may buy Trigger Guard units for $5.95 each from: Trigger Guard Offer, H&R 1871R, Inc., 60 Industrial Rowe, Gardner, MA 01440.

HK/FABARMS

Heckler & Koch, a well-known military and police firearms manufacturer, joined forces with FABARM — *Fabbrica Bresciana Armi S.p.A.* — a direct descendant of the Galesi family, a 100-year-old gunsmithing dynasty. Although well-known in Europe, they are virtually unknown in the U.S. They bring innovative technology to the American marketplace — like their patented TriBore Barrel System — and they offer the industry's only Lifetime Warranty.

In addition to TriBore barrels, FABARM makes extensive use of palm swell grips, barrel porting, double sets of locking lugs on over/under and side-by-side shotguns, inertial single selective triggers, carbon fiber protective coating on some models, better-than-average polished oil-finished walnut, diamond fine-hand-checkering, fitted cases and moderate prices. They are full-line shotgun makers, offering semi-automatic, pump (although thse are primarily police/military types), over/under and side-by-side models.

Several innovative examples stand out and are illustrated in this article.

FABARM Max Lion Light 12 or 20 Gauge feature 24-inch TriBore ported barrels (this includes 20 gauge models), adjustable trigger, palm swell grip, C-IC-M-IM-F choke tubes,

FABARM Monotrap 12 Gauge - built on a 20 gauge frame (for quick handling) with adjustable comb, adjustable trigger, palm swell grip, TriBore ported 30-inch barrel with M-IM-F choke tubes.

FABARM Sporting Clays Extra 12 Gauge 28-inch ported (30-inch available), recoil deduction system installed, adjustable comb, carbon fiber finish, eight competition tubes, palm swell grip, olive wood grip cap and leather-faced recoil pad.

FABARM Sporting Clays Competition Lion Extra competition buttstock with adjustable comb, durable carbon fiber finish, set of eight competition choke tubes and 30-inch TriBore ported barrels.

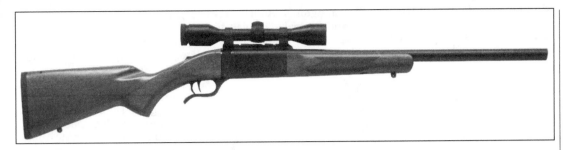

Mossberg SSi - One 12 Gauge Slug Gun, a new "Single Shot Interchangeable" model with numerous rifle calibers ranging from varmint to big game.

Mossberg M835 Ulti-Mag® pump action shoots 2 3/4-inch, 3-inch and 3 1/2-inch loads interchangeably. Shown with Realtree Hardwoods camo.

manual safety, leather-faced rubber recoil pad. The 20 gauge model tested weighed under six pounds!

Kent Cartridge America

Kent Cartridge claims their IMPACT Tungsten MatriX non-toxic waterfowl loads have been field-tested and proven the most effective shot shell you can buy. They say that you can put 90% of the pellets in a 30-inch circle at 40 yards - and that "it is solidly lethal at 65 yards." These Waterfowl loads in 12 and 20 gauge are mostly between 1,350 and 1,400 fps with #1, #3 and #5 shot sizes. There's a new 3 1/3-inch 12 gauge 2 1/4 oz. version with #1 or #3 shot.

The IMPACT Pheasant/Game loads in 12, 16 and 20 gauge range from 1,200 to 1,350 fps with #5 and #6 shot sizes offered.

Non-toxic IMPACT Tungsten MatriX shotshells satisfy environmental and conservation requirements and can be used in any nitro-proofed shotgun with the same chokes one would normally use for lead shot.

Mossberg

Factory porting and over-bored barrels are standard on Mossberg's Model 835 Ulti-Mag 12 gauge 3 1/2-inch repeater shotgun. M835 are overbored

faster target acquisition on repeat shots.

Merkel

Merkel is enhancing their fine line of side-by-side shotgun and over/under shotguns with Luxury Grade Wood and fitted cases. The well-known model 147E, for example, becomes Model 147EL with luxury grade wood - a $1,000 option for all gauges.

New models this year are the M280EL in 28 gauge, M360EL in .410 bore (built on the 28-gauge frame) and the

to $20,000 and available in 12, 20, and 28 gauge.

Left-hand stocking is offered as an $895 option and guns stocked to customer's specifications add $1,395.

Perazzi

Perazzi introduced a MX5 model in 20 and 28 gauge, as well as a two-gauge MX5/20-28 set. These are available in four different barrel lengths, from 26 3/4-inch to 29 1/2-inch, fixed or screw-in chokes and single selective trigger. These guns extend Perazzi's offerings in the MX5 game gun line, which last year saw the introduction of a 16 gauge over/under.

Poly-Wad

Jay Menefee of Spred-R Wad fame has introduced a line of low pressure 12 and 16 gauge 2 1/2-inch loads — called "The Vintager" — for people who shoot older model guns. These are 7/8 oz. loads of #6 or #7-1/2 magnum shot with pressure readings of 6,300 and 7,000 P.S.I. Low recoil with just enough oomph to get the job done. 800/998-0669.

Remington

Lots of new and exciting things at Remington this year. The Model 300 Ideal heads the list - a new 12 gauge over/

◄Merkel Model 147SL side-by-side H&H style sidelocks with cocking indicators, side clips and double triggers in 12, 16, 20 or 28 gauge with luxury wood.

▲ Merkel Model 2001 EL Sporter boxlock, single or double triggers, English or pistol grip, ventilated forend, luxury wood in 12, 20 or 28 gauge.

to .775-inch, which compares to .731-inch for their standard M500, hence require oversized choke tubes to accommodate the larger bore diameter at the muzzle. Mossberg claims the ported barrels and over-bored barrels significantly reduce recoil in the 3 1/2-inch magnum loads and reduce muzzle jump and make for

M280/360EL two-barrel set, all with luxury grade wood and fitted cases. Similarly, the M280SL, M360SL and M280/360SL two-barrel 28/410 sets have silver-greyed sidelocks, with luxury grade wood in fitted cases.

Merkel does not have a bottom-of-the-line over/under. Every model offered has luxury grade wood and comes with a fitted case and are priced from about $5,200

under chambered for 2 3/4- and 3-inch shells and available in 26-, 28- and 30-inch barrel lengths, pistol grip, Rem Chokes, single mechanical trigger and automatic ejectors. This gun has a straight comb and a drop at heel of 2 inches, "to keep recoil in a straighter line."

The Model 11-87 Super Magnum autoloader handles all 12 gauge loads up to the 3 1/2-inch and is available with either a cut-checkered

▼**Remington Model 300 Ideal Over/Under** - a new 12 gauge chambered for 2 3/4- and 3-inch shells.

▼**Remington SP-10 Synthetic** - the 10 gauge semi-auto designed to function under adverse weather conditions.

▼**Remington Model 11-87 Upland Special** - a quick-handling upland game gun available in either 12 or 20 gauge.

◄**Remington Model 1100 Sporting 12** with a 28-inch target barrel and four extended Rem Choke constrictions.

walnut stock or a tough black synthetic model. The Model 11-87 Premier includes a variety of options including cantilever scope mount, which may be used to convert the Model 11-87 to a deer gun. These scope mounts are also made for M870 and M1100shotguns. The Model 11-87 Premier handles 2 3/4- and 3-inch shells interchangeably. Upland Special Model 11-87 has English grips, a 23-inch barrel and is available in both 12 and 20 gauge.

The Model 1100 line appears to be more focused on competitive shooting with two new models introduced - the Model 1100 Sporting 12 and the Classic Trap. The Model 1100 .410 semi-auto is not cataloged by Remington this year.

Remington's Special Purpose Waterfowl Guns include both 10 and 12 gauge guns with the 10 gauge on Remington's proven SP-10 model and the 12 gauge on the 11-87.

The 870 Express Super Magnum heads Remington's line-up for pump action fans. This is the 3 1/2-inch model and available in a variety of finishes for both turkey, waterfowl and upland game plus a model with an extra rifled barrel for deer. A new Model 870 Classic Trap is introduced this year, while the Model 870 Express continues to offer a wide variety of turkey, deer, waterfowl, upland game, youth, left-hand and self-defense models in 12 and 20 gauge. Model 870 Wingmaster pumps are offered in Super Magnum (3 1/2-inch chamber) and in regular 12, 20, 28 and .410 models.

Ruger

Ruger has taken a bold new step into the world of competitive shooting with their new Ruger Trap Model for competitive trap shooters. The new gun features a fully

Ruger Model KTS-1 234-BRE Trap Model - Ruger's all-new trap gun for competitive shooters.

▲SIG Apollo TR-40 Gold with case-colored sideplates and discreet gold game scenes.

▶SIG Apollo TR-40 Silver with polished chrome receiver and gold accents.

◀SIG Apollo TR-30 with case-colored sideplates.

adjustable rib for pattern position (with 3/8-inch height adjustment) and a select walnut checkered stock, adjustable for length of pull from 13 1/2 to 15 1/2 inches. The comb of the stock is adjustable for height and cast for right-hand or left-handed shooters. The target trigger is adjustable for weight of pull and the pattern-control barrel is manufactured with straight grooves running the full length to prevent the wad from rotating in its passage down the barrel. The chrome-molybdenum monoblock is mated to the stainless steel receiver and 34" stainless steel barrel. Full and modified tubes are provided with the gun.

The engraved series of Ruger Red Labels introduced for Ruger's 50th Anniversary in 1999 proved so popular that the line is now available with special scroll engraving and a 24-carat gold game bird appropriate to each gauge.

S. I. A. C. E.

A modern-day 20 gauge side-by-side hammer gun emulating a "Best" grade English gun of a by-gone

◀SIG Apollo TT-25 Competition Shotgun dimensioned and balanced for the American sporting clays shooter.

era. This gun has a top-mounted safety so that the gun may be carried with the hammers fully cocked, and fired only when the safety is released.

S.I.A.C.E. "Vintager" 20 gauge hammer gun available with extractors, English grip and fixed chokes.

SKB

SKB makes very nice side-by-side and over/under shotguns. The side-by-side models are on the 12 gauge production cycle, so 20 gauge guns and the smaller gauges based on the 20 gauge side-by-side frame are in limited supply this year.

In their 12 gauge over/under line, SKB has been a pioneer in over-bored barrels, longer forcing cones and, more recently in their target models, competition chokes and porting by Pro-port.

SIG Arms

SIG Arms has joined with the Italian maker B. Rizzini to produce the Apollo line of over/under shotguns in two distinct product groups: Apollo TR Field Shotguns - Nice shotguns made in two frame weights and four forend sizes to accommodate 12, 20, 28 and .410 barrel sizes. There are five trim levels in all four gauges. These are full-feature guns, with single selective triggers, full set of chokes tubes (in 12 and 20 gauge), select Turkish walnut, 20-line checkering and a rubber recoil pad. This pad is of the non-skid variety and the length of pull is 14 3/4 inches, which hung up on my sweater every time I tried to shoulder the gun, so try before you buy. The small gauge guns have fixed chokes and the radius of the 28 gauge forend is smaller than the 20 and the .410 forend is smaller than the 28 — an illusion that fools your left hand into thinking you are shooting a smaller gun than one mounted on a 20 gauge frame.

Weatherby SAS Superflauge features M.L. Lynch Superflauge camo, the ultimate camo concealment pattern.

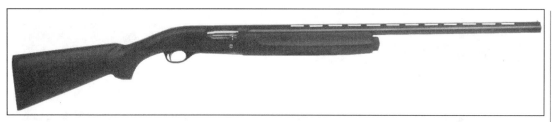

Weatherby SAS Synthetic fiberglass black synthetic stock is lightweight and exceptionally durable.

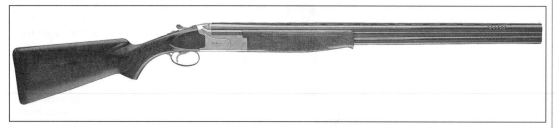

Winchester Supreme Sporting new Belgian-made 12 gauge over/under ported and back-bored with adjustable trigger for length of pull with 28- or 30-inch barrels.

Winchester Supreme Field new Belgian-made 12 gauge over/under back-bored with the Invector Plus choke system and 28-inch barrels.

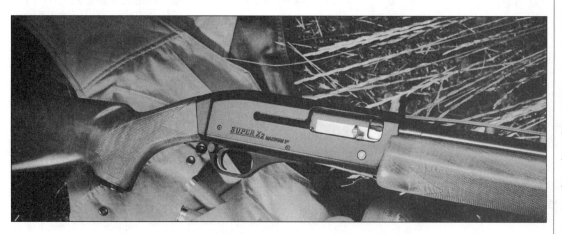

Winchester Super 2X Field 3-inch with traditional satin walnut stock and low luster barrel and receiver this gun goes from pheasant to clay birds without a hitch.

The Apollo TT 25 Competition shotguns are offered in 12 and 20 gauge, 28-, 30- and 32-inch barrels in 12 gauge; 28- and 30-inch in 20 gauge. Four interchangeable chokes are provides - F-M-IC-SK - and five-inch forcing cones are standard.

Weatherby

The big news at Weatherby this year is the introduction of their SAS - semiautomatic shotgun. It comes in four basic sub-models - Field, SAS Shadow Grass, SAS Superflauge and SAS Synthetic. It is chambered for 2 3/4- and 3-inch 12 gauge shells and comes with five standard Briley chokes.

Weatherby's well-established over/under line all come with Briley choke tubes as standard. Forcing cones have been lengthened and the Orion Sporting Clays SSC Model has ported barrels, comes with cast-off and has an adjustable trigger to accommodate different finger lengths.

Winchester

Finding an encore for their introduction of the 3 1/2-inch Super X2 last year would be a daunting task for any maker - but Winchester is up to the job. This year they've come back with a Belgian-made 12 gauge over/under called the Supreme that's available in two models - Field and Sporting. Both models back-bored but the Sporting model is also ported and comes with an adjustable trigger shoe to customize the length of pull. Winchester also back-bored their new-last-year Super X2 line 3- and 3 1/2-inch semi-automatics.

The Model 1300R Speed Pump deserves some comment. Winchester shotguns have been equipped with rotary bolts for years. Winchester says it is the key to its tight lockup and uncommon strength and — they say — it's the reason you get inertia-assisted pumping for faster second and third shots.

Winchester Model 1300 Speed Pump now available in 12 or 20 gauge, 3-inch chambers, English grip and WinChoke tubes. ●

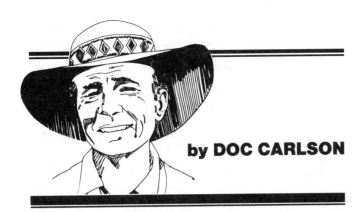

by DOC CARLSON

BLACKPOWDER REVIEW

IT WAS NOT very many years ago when the selection of newly made firearms and accessories of interest to the blackpowder shooter was pretty slim. One or two companies were either importing or making a very few replicas of the old time guns. As a result, there was very little interest in the blackpowder-oriented shooting sports. Interest lived in re-enactors, a few target shooters and the die-hard muzzleloading hunter. I guess I qualified for all three categories. Then, in the 1960s, the Civil War Centennial came

along and interest picked up— at least among the Civil War re-enactor groups. The average citizen became aware of the fun and challenge of shooting and hunting with the guns of our ancestors. More companies got into the market and several states set up primitive weapon seasons. Suddenly, muzzleloading guns were back.

Today, the blackpowder shooter has a plethora of guns and accessories available. Many companies, old and new, are supplying the varied interests and activities of the muzzleloader: hunting,

reenacting, target shooting, black powder cartridge silhouette, cowboy action shooting — or just plinking with a gun that's fun to load and shoot.

The tremendous interest in the in-line muzzleloader over the past few years seems to have slowed, although there are many models out there in all sizes and shapes. There is still plenty of interest in this area and upgrading and improving the breed continues. But, there does seem to be more traditional blackpowder firearms being introduced. Some hunters and casual shooters who started with the in-lines are now getting into the traditional sidehammer gun.   We'll see where this goes in the next couple of years.

Modern Muzzleloading Inc., the maker of the well-known **Knight Muzzleloading** line of in-line guns, has upgraded their very successful Disc Rifle by adding a laminated thumbhole Monte Carlo stock with palm swell grip and fluted stainless barrel. Called the Master Hunter, the rifle has a jeweled bolt, gold-plated trigger and a satin-finished metal ramrod added to make this a very nice-looking rifle. Too nice to take into the woods and risk scratching the stock? Knight has the answer. They include a black thumbhole

synthetic stock so the hunter can change stocks before he takes to the woods and save the fancy stock for display in the home gun rack or at the range, where the environment is a little more controllable. A nice idea.

Knight's entire rifle line is available with Realtree camouflage over hardwood or with black synthetic stocks. All their rifles now come with a Magnum Cross Fire breech plug. This plug has a cross machined in its face to direct the fire in four directions around the bottom of the powder charge to ensure good ignition. This design is aimed at eliminating misfires when using Pyrodex or the newer Pyrodex pellets. Also, many of the Knight guns are available with Tru-Glo fiber-optic sights, including the Master Hunter series of Disc Rifle.

White Rifles, another well-known in-line manufacturer, has added a 41-caliber to their line for this year. The company that makes these fine rifles, Muzzleloading Technologies, has designed the rifle in line with the bore axis to improve pointing and recoil management, important in a rifle intended to launch bullets weighing up to 600 grains.

The White system uses an easy-loading undersize bullet. On firing, inertia causes the bullet to shorten and fill the rifling along its entire length

For 2000, Modern Muzzleloading has expanded their DISC rifle line with this Master Hunter model featuring a laminated thumbhole stock, fluted stainless steel barrel and other trimmings.

DISC rifles are now available with synthetic thumbhole stock, stainless steel action and barrel.

The Magnum Cross-Fire Breech Plug, designed to ignite Pyrodex pellets reliably, now standard on all rifles from Modern Muzzle-loading.

for superb accuracy. They also now are offering sabot loads. These are not pistol bullets but a harder lead bullet that carries a great deal of weight and, due to its hardness, penetrates well in large and/or dangerous game. The patented sabot features two grooves that can be filled with lubricant to keep fouling soft and facilitate loading.

This system was developed by Dr. Gary White during a lifetime of hunting all over the world. It's a good system and worth a look by any serious hunter.

Millennium-Designed Muzzleloaders is relatively new to the muzzleloading marketplace, having been making in-line guns for about three years, if memory serves.

They have a new muzzleloading firearm this year that is a bit different — but will be very familiar to many shooters. They have taken the familiar single barrel shotgun and adapted it to muzzleloading use. The result is a break-open, center-hammer muzzleloader offered in 50-caliber and 12 gauge. It features a transfer bar system that blocks firing of the gun unless the trigger is held back. This precludes firing by a blow on the hammer in its at-rest position. The gun cannot be opened with the hammer cocked, nor can the hammer be cocked if the breech is open, to prevent inadvertent discharge. The gun uses #209 shotgun primers but can also use #11 or musket caps, if desired. The breech is a closed system but the guns are also available with a modified breech for those states requiring an exposed ignition system. Easily used by right-or left-handers, the gun retails for under $300. Certainly a familiar feel for those of us who learned to shoot using the venerable single-shot shotgun.

Austin and Halleck makes possibly the best-looking in-line bolt action on the market. Their top-of-the-line gun features high gloss blue, gloss-finished Exhibition-grade wood stock with cut checkering and a half-octagon to round barrel. These are very nice-looking rifles. They look

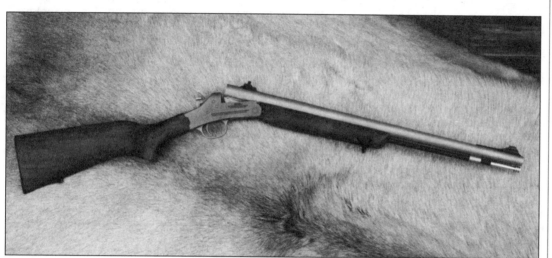

The Buckwacka percussion rifle or shotgun, from Millennium-Designed Muzzleloaders.

Austin & Halleck's new halfstock traditional rifle, in 50-caliber, percussion or flint and several grades of wood.

The Buckhunter, from Traditions, is an affordable first in-line muzzleloader.

Tradition's new in-line rifle series, the Lightning Lightweight, is designed for the serious hunter.

custom — top quality all the way. The guns can also be had with hand-selected wood, only slightly less-figured than the Exhibition grade. They have now added Fancy and Standard rifle grades, at lower prices. The difference is the grade of wood used. The Standard stock is straight-grained, while the Fancy shows a bit more figure but not in the realm of the Exhibition or Hand-Select grades. I did a test-fire report of these guns some time back and they shoot as good as they look. Also new this year is a Monte Carlo-style stock that is intended for use with scopes. Along with the classic style of the other rifles, this makes a pretty complete line.

Another new product this year is the classic style in synthetic stocks. These guns are the same Austin and Halleck action and barrel as

their higher-priced offerings but are stocked with the very practical synthetic gun handle. Actions and barrels of these rifles are octagon to round and available in either blued or stainless steel. These new offerings will come in well under $400 retail. A good, practical hunting gun at a good price.

Along with the in-line rifles, the Austin and Halleck folks are bringing out a very traditional half-stock rifle with styling similar to the Hatfield rifle of a few years back. This Kentucky-style rifle uses all iron hardware with a browned barrel. Sights are traditional rear notch and blade front. Caliber is 50 with either a 1-in-66-inch twist for round ball or 1-in-28 for slug shooting. Stocks can be had in either Standard or Select wood, with the Select being very nicely figured. Ignition is by either

caplock or flintlock, your choice. The triggerguard and forend tip are reminiscent of the Hawken rifles of yesteryear but the overall style is half-stock Kentucky. The lock, in either flint or percussion, features a fly on the tumbler for use with the standard double-set triggers. I can't wait to get my hands on one of these.

Traditions Performance Firearms, a company that has been in the muzzleloading business for some time, has added to their Buckhunter series of in-line guns. This gun is now available with a black synthetic stock and a C-Nickel action and barrel. The C-Nickel is their name for a matte-finish nickel plate that imitates the more expensive stainless steel. Supplied in 50-caliber with a stainless steel breech plug and adjustable sights, this is a solid, plain Jane, no-

nonsense gun. Priced at under 160 bucks, it is an ideal first-time in-line rifle for the muzzleloading hunter, or a youth starter gun.

Traditions also expanded their bolt action in-line guns with the addition of the Lightning Lightweight series. These guns use a synthetic stock with a spiderweb pattern and a 22-inch fluted barrel in blue, stainless or nickel plate. Tru-Glo fiber-optic sights and an ignition system that can use either standard #11 caps or the hotter musket caps, along with a built-in weather shroud, make this a serious hunting gun. The gun is rated for up to three Pyrodex pellets or 150 grains of powder behind a pistol bullet/sabot combination.

Of interest to the Cowboy Action shooters is the addition of a carbine version to the popular 1892 Lever Action line

Rounding out Tradition's growing line of cartridge guns, the Model 1892 lever-action is now also available in carbine form.

Smith & Wesson's new Schofield 2000 revolver is for the cowboy action shooter.

of rifles. These guns look good with their color case-hardened receivers, crescent butt plate and barrels that are octagon on the 24-inch rifle and round on the 20-inch carbine. These rifles compliment Tradition's line of 1873 single-action cartridge revolvers and the 38 Special cartridge conversions based on the Colt and Remington Army and Navy cap and ball guns.

Also new this year for the Cowboy Action shooters, **Smith and Wesson** is reintroducing the Model 3 Schofield revolver. Designed by Brevet Lieutenant Colonel George W. Schofield and accepted by the U. S. Military in 1874, Smith and Wesson produced nearly 9,000 of the guns before production ceased in 1879. Now, after 125 years, the Smith and Wesson Schofield is back. Chambered in 45 S&W, the blued steel revolver features walnut grips and case-hardened hammer, trigger and latch. The 7-inch

barrel is the same length as was standard on the Cavalry Model of 1875. The gun is a top-break design that was, and still is, an ideal system for fast reloading by a mounted man. Horse soldiers of the time could reload the Schofield seven times while the competing Colt 1873 single-action was reloaded once. This Smith and Wesson single-action revolver was considered by many to be the best available on the American frontier.

The new gun, called the Schofield 2000 by S&W, uses better steel than the original and incorporates a couple of safety features to make the gun compatible with our litigious society, something the original designers of the revolver didn't have to deal with. Every one of that simpler time was expected to know how to use their possessions correctly. At any rate, instead of the fixed firing pin on the hammer, the newly

designed gun uses a spring-loaded, frame-mounted, rebounding firing pin. It also incorporates a hammer block safety that will not allow the gun to fire unless the trigger is held full back.

Interestingly, the S&W folks say the decision to reintroduce this classic firearm came from the clamoring of the Cowboy Action shooters and aficionados. Nice to know that the major companies still listen to their customers. It's good to see this old classic back.

Connecticut Valley Arms has added a three-way breech plug to their in-line guns that will allow the hunter to use #11 caps, musket caps or #209 shotgun primers. This allows

the shooter to use whatever igniter he feels is best for the prevailing conditions. It also allows one to try the different primers when working up a load. This seems to be a trend among the in-line makers, probably brought on by field reports of misfires. They are also selling the breech plug separately so that owners of older CVA guns may update their rifles.

CVA is now marketing a bore-diameter lead bullet, with a snap-on plastic skirt. These are similar to the Black Belt bullets that may be familiar to some. The idea is that the bullet loads easily, even after several shots, and the skirt effectively seals the bore behind the bullet to ensure best accuracy. I have used the Black Belt bullet for some time and find them to be very accurate and effective on game, due to the heavyweight bullet. These should produce much the same results. These bullets, legal in Colorado by the way, are available in 50- and 54-caliber and either copper-coated for deeper penetration, or pure lead.

For the youth or petite woman shooter or hunter, CVA has their Youth Hunter Rifle. With an overall length of 38 inches, a shorter length of pull and a 24-inch barrel with a 1-in-48-inch twist, this is a light, handy rifle for the

CVA copper-plated 50-caliber PowerBelt Bullets, 295- or 348-grains.

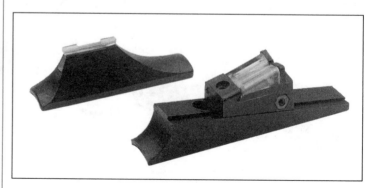

CVA US Illuminator II Sight System.

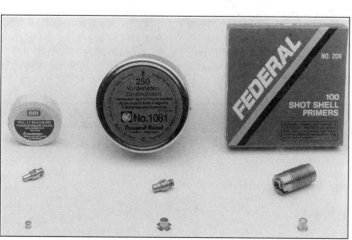

CVA MusketMag 3-Way Ignition System.

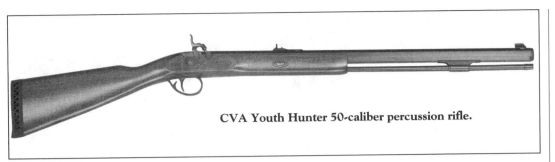

CVA Youth Hunter 50-caliber percussion rifle.

smaller person. It will handle either conical bullets or patched roundball with equal aplomb. This is a traditional style, sidelock rifle for those who prefer them to the in-lines. The hardwood stock has a recoil pad softer than the usual ones. A synthetic ramrod, very resistant to breaking, completes the unit. This is a good beginner rifle that is equally at home plinking, target shooting or hunting. At a price of less than $130.00 retail, I suspect these will be very popular.

Thompson/Center Arms is an outfit that never ceases to amaze me with their continual innovation. Their latest is a traditional flintlock rifle that will shoot Pyrodex pellets as well as standard blackpowder and even loose Pyrodex. What makes this gun work is an innovative breech plug that has a cone-shape at the front

that holds the pellet slightly above the breech plug. This allows the priming powder to ignite all around the base of the pellet for good ignition. The touch hole is large enough that 4Fg priming powder will infiltrate around the edge of the breech plug cone making, in effect, a small booster charge that helps ignite the pellets or loose Pyrodex. Pyrodex must be under pressure to burn well and simultaneous ignition of the pellet raises this pressure quickly and it then delivers velocities that are similar to a percussion gun. My testing with one of the guns showed that, if one is careful to get some of the priming powder worked through the touch hole as the pan is primed, ignition is instantaneous and accuracy is good. This rifle is very good news for those who shoot flintlocks, either from

preference or because of law, and have trouble buying blackpowder. Pyrodex is carried almost universally by dealers who carry muzzleloading supplies whereas blackpowder is difficult to find in many areas, due to regulations on the local level and shipping difficulties.

The new rifle is called the Firestorm. It is offered in 50-caliber with a 1-turn-in-48-inch barrel to handle either conical bullets, sabot bullets or patched roundball with equal accuracy. The 26-inch barrel has the popular QLA loading system; a counterbore extending about an inch inside the muzzle. This makes it much easier to center and load both slugs and sabots. The stock is a black synthetic with a black recoil pad. The lock is, of course, a typical sidelock flintlock fired by a single trigger and the ramrod is aluminum. Overall, a no-nonsense hunting rifle conforming to the law in those states that require flintlocks firing patched roundball for hunting. The gun is recommended for use with heavy magnum 150 grain loads.

A companion rifle in percussion is also available. This gun has a special breech that uses #209 shotgun primers instead of caps for

surer ignition. Called the Firestorm 209 Caplock, the major difference between this and the flintlock rifle — other than the percussion ignition — is the barrel uses a 1-in-28-inch twist for conicals and sabot loads. Both guns are fitted with fully adjustable fiber-optic sights, appreciated by hunters in bad light situations. The percussion rifle is also recommended for use with 150 grain magnum loadings. Both guns feature a heavy recoil lug welded under the barrel for solid and consistent barrel-to-stock fit, which contributes to uniform accuracy.

There is very good news for the traditional gun lovers out there. **Dixie Gun Works**, well known for traditional reproductions as well as parts and accessories for those guns, has a new Early American Jaeger Rifle. Patterned after the early forerunners to the graceful Kentucky Rifle, this Germanic rifle is a delight for those who are oriented toward a more historically correct firearm.

The first impression of this Italian-made replica is that one is looking at a custom-made firearm. It has the custom look and feel. The walnut stock carries what looks like a satin oil finish that sets off the browned steel furniture. The 54-caliber, 1-inch octagon barrel is just under 28 inches long. The twist is 1-in-24-inches. This gun is obviously intended for use with conicals or sabot loads but, I'm told by the Dixie folks, it shoots patched roundball surprisingly well. The butt plate is a typical flat-type that, along with the Jaeger-style butt design, will distribute recoil very well. A U-shape attachment for an

This new breechplug design from T/C delivers even ignition to the base of Pyrodex pellets.

T/C's new Firestorm flintlock rifle handles Pyrodex, either pellets or loose, thanks to the newly-designed breechplug. A percussion model is also available.

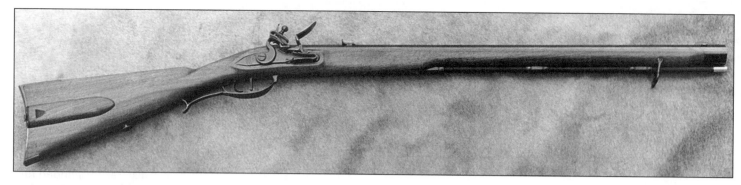

Early American Jaeger flintlock rifle, from Dixie Gunworks.

original-type sling is installed in the full stock forearm and a butt-mounted button completes the sling system. The forend is tipped with a simulated horn cap that looks very nice. A wood ramrod hangs in two thimbles, which are browned as is the entry pipe. Sights are typical open rear and blade front.

The thing that really gets one's attention when viewing this gun is the presence of a sliding wood patch box cover, a feature many of the original guns had but which is never seen on production firearms. This is really a nice touch. The fit of the wood lid is very good, as is all the insetting. Overall fit and finish is just outstanding for a mass-produced gun.

The rifle is offered in right-hand only, with either flint or percussion ignition. Double-set triggers are standard with the front trigger functional if unset. Lock and trigger quality is good. The flintlock throws good sparks and should be a reliable shooter. Priced at about half what a basic custom rifle would cost, this hunting rifle should find many friends out there. I'm told that the Jaeger may be available with traditional carving on the

stock later. This is going to be a winner, in my opinion.

A new cartridge reproduction gun is on the horizon for the Cowboy Action shooters and the Civil War re-enactors. **Taylor's and Company** will have a reproduction of the Spencer Carbine out by mid-year, I'm told. Having seen the prototype action, it appears this will be a top-quality gun. Calibers planned are 45 Schofield, 44 Russian and 56/50.

Also new this year, from the Taylor's people, is the reproduction Starr revolver of Civil War fame. These 44-caliber revolvers will be offered in both double- and single-action.

These additions will fit nicely in their very complete line of Civil War-era reproductions and their line of Sharps rifles and sights, early Winchester lever guns and single-action Colt repros for the Cowboy Action crowd.

Goex, Inc. is making a new non-fouling, non-corrosive blackpowder replica propellant that is intended as a Pyrodex-type replacement powder. It can be loaded on a weight or volume basis to replace blackpowder loadings

and produces consistent shot-to-shot ballistics. It leaves very little residue and can be cleaned up with tap water. Called Clear Shot, it is a ball-type powder and is available in 2Fg and 3Fg granulations.

Also, along the propellant line, **Elephant Brand** blackpowder continues to improve their already top quality product. It is giving very consistent burn rates and somewhat higher velocities, load for load. This powder is well known for very little velocity variation shot-to-shot and is considered to be a top quality propellant for blackpowder firearms.

Petro-Explo Company, the importer of Elephant Black Powder, is also bringing in Swiss blackpowder. This powder gets high ratings from the blackpowder cartridge shooters, especially those shooting the long range competitions such as Black Powder Cartridge Silhouette. It looks as if powder supplies for shooters who glory in clouds of white smoke will be in good shape for the future.

The fiber-optic sight is increasingly seen on muzzle-loading hunting arms in the past couple of years. **Tru-Glo, HiViz, Williams** and others have these sights available to install on most any muzzle loader, as well as modern firearms. The more fragile plastic sights are being replaced by metal sights, which stand the rigors of the hunting field much better. Fiber-optic sights give a much better sight picture in poor light or for those of us whose "over 40" eyes do not see open sights as well as we used to. It really helps those folks hunting in states that do not allow anything but open sights on muzzle-loaders.

Many of the muzzleloader manufacturers are installing these sights as standard equipment on their hunting guns also.

While on the subject of sights, aperture sights have long been an answer when focusing over the open sights becomes a problem. Until now, most aperture sights looked too modern to blend in on traditional muzzleloading guns. **Ashley Outdoors** has cured that problem. They make a line of small good-looking aperture sights that are unobtrusive on traditional guns. They closely resemble sights that I have seen on 15th century cross-bows in the Tower of London collections. That should be authentic enough for anybody. They also make a ramrod with a folding "T" handle that fits in the ferrules of an ML gun and is indistinguishable from the standard rod, but gives the shooter a steel ramrod with a "T" handle for loading and cleaning. Really a very innovative and handy accessory in the hunting field or at the range. They also make the same ramrod in a threaded take-down version that can be carried in your possibles bag or, certainly, in your luggage when you go on a hunting trip, it being only 6 1/2-inches long and 1-inch in diameter when broken down in its carrying bag with all tips, etc.

With all the new stuff coming onto the market, a trip to your local blackpowder shooters supply store is certainly in order. If he isn't carrying some of the aforementioned products, tell him to contact the manufacturer or importer and get them in stock. It sure looks as this blackpowder game is here to stay.

•

Aperture rear sight, from Ashley Outdoors.

by BOB BELL

SCOPES AND MOUNTS

Don't Overlook That Reticle!

GREAT LENSES PROPERLY located according to a carefully worked out optical formula and immovably installed within a strong metal tube, are automatically assumed by many users to be the most important part of a telescope. Perhaps they are, if your only goal is to get the best target image possible. But a hunter wants something else. His main objective is to put a killing bullet into a game animal. Sure, he wants the image his scope delivers to be as clear, detailed and bright as possible, but none of that means anything to him unless that scope also helps him properly place his bullet. To do that, it must have an aiming point whose location closely coincides with his bullet's path, in effect showing him where the bullet will strike anywhere within its effective range. In a scope, this aiming point is called a reticle.

To be visible from the rear (or aiming end) of a scope, the reticle must be placed in either of two focal planes - the first plane, which is where the objective unit creates an upside down, right-to-left image — or the second plane, which is where the erector lenses create an image which is now positioned as the eye expects to see it. That is, the reversed image itself has been reversed, bringing it back to what we think of as "normal." The light rays then pass through the ocular lens or eyepiece and out the rear end of the scope.

If the eye is positioned at its optimum distance behind the scope to obtain a full field of view... that is, where the ocular lens is entirely bright and surrounded by only a thin black circle which is the rear end of the scope tube...it is at the ideal "eye relief" which the scope designers have intended. This difference can be somewhat different with each model scope, but it is almost always from 3 to 4 inches. A certain minimum is required so that a heavy recoiling rifle will not slam the rear of the scope into the eyebrow. Scopes with longer-than-normal eye relief can be designed, but only at the expense of other desirable optical characteristics — a wide field of view, for instance. There are no free lunches in optics; you improve one thing only at the expense of another.

It might be worth mentioning that the eye — either unaided or when using a rifle scope, binoculars, spotting scope or whatever — does not look outward and "see" an object where it actually is located. It sees something - anything - only because an infinite number of reflected light rays travel from that object and some of them enter the eye's pupil; here they excite nerve endings on the retina,

impulses travel through the optic nerve, and somehow these are interpreted as visual images by the brain. These light rays originate in an incandescent source such as the sun, or they can be reflected from such a source into the eye. Thus it's obvious that any "seeing" we do actually takes place within our brains, and that there's always a time lag in the process; that is, everything we see is actually in the past, as it takes time for those light rays to reach our brains from the object which bounced them toward us. Not a long time, of course. When we see a deer 60 yards away, light reflected from him to us is arriving at a bit more than 186,000 miles per second, so it doesn't take long to get here. It'd take a pretty good pocket calculator to figure what percentage of a second is used up. But there is a percentage, there is a time lag, so everything we see is in the past.

This is easier to understand if we consider the stars we see in a night sky. They're light-years away. Even at 186,000 miles per second, it takes years for their light to reach us. Some of them might have burned out before we were born, but we're still seeing the light sent out when they were functioning normally... if anyone knows what's normal for a star.

Anyway, it's important to understand that light comes to us rather than our eyes somehow reaching out to distant objects, for this allows us to position a series of lenses between the incoming light rays and our eyes and thus affect the paths the rays follow. These lenses can be in a scope, binoculars or whatever, and when properly designed and positioned they present an enlarged view to the user. For hundreds of years now, experimenters and very smart optical engineers have been researching what kinds of glass are best for lenses, its grinding, polishing, coating, spacing, etc. But ultimately an adjustable reticle must be installed somewhere in the system, for that's what makes it worthwhile for a shooter to

use a scope. It has to be adjustable because its position must be closely related to the bullet's path. You don't alter the bullet path to coincide with the reticle, you move the reticle to agree with the bullet path. (Or in most modern scopes the target image is moved to where you want it, but again the bullet path stays as-is.)

Scopes had been used by a few Civil War snipers and Western buffalo hunters in the late 1800s — even by ballistic experimenters long before that — but it was not until the 1930s and '40s that scopes started to catch on with the more advanced American shooters. Most of these were big game hunters, and their favored scopes were of low power, 2x to 4x, to get a large field of view, and they had what might be called conventional reticles: simple crosshairs, as in a surveyor's transit, or a flat-top post with a horizontal crosshair which was intended to prevent canting.

The post was liked by military riflemen/hunters, some of whom were then among our most popular gunwriters. The post resembled the metallic front sight of an '03 Springfield or '17 Enfield and so looked familiar, I suppose. At the short ranges where almost all big game was shot then - rarely over a couple of hundred yards - these served perfectly. The post was favored in the woods as it was conspicuous, and the crosshair reticle for more open shooting, where it was easily seen.

A few hunters chose T. K. Lee's famous Floating Dot reticle, which he could make in almost any desired size and place in any location. It got the moniker "floating" because it was installed on such fine crosshairs, allegedly the silk of black widow spiders, that they were almost invisible. Numerous other reticle designs for conventional rifles were developed, probably culminating in today's popular Plex reticle, with its crosshair intersection and conspicuous posts entering the field from the four cardinal compass points.

But there's always a certain percentage of shooters who

are never satisfied with the cartridges that have been around awhile, so they are always trying to improve them. The most obvious way to do this was to make bullets of a given diameter and weight go faster, thus making them more effective at greater range. Consider the progression from 30-40 to 30-06 to 300 H&H to 300 Winchester Magnum. Such increasingly larger cases could use more propellant at a safe pressure, thereby boosting velocity with a given bullet, so a number of experimenters kept increasing case size. But there was a limit as to how far they could go; after all, the cartridge had to fit into a rifle which could be handled by a shooter.

Many lines of cartridges grew to about the same number and gave about the same ballistics, though each experimenter tried to convince shooters that his cartridges had some magical properties that set it apart. Lines which gained some followings, at least for a time, included the PMVF (Powell-Miller-Venturi-Freebored), CCC (Controlled Combustion Chambrage), bulletmaker Fred Barnes' BJ (Barnes-Johnson) cartridges, the OKH series from Charley O'Neil, Elmer Keith and Don Hopkins, P. O. Ackley's "improved" loads, Roy Weatherby's line, on up to today's entries from Dakota and Lazzeroni. There were many more but you get the idea.

With a rifle/cartridge that's effective much farther than an '06, say, provided it can be hit with, scopes kept increasing in magnification to improve aiming ability, with high-grade variables becoming most popular. (Even if top magnification might be chosen for the long-range chance that this type of shooter dreamed about, he also wanted to be prepared for any real trophy that showed up at short or medium range, perhaps 200-500 yards; thus something in the 6-24x class was often used.)

Scopes of this power range were best served by reticles of more complex design than woods scopes. They didn't have to be simple and

conspicuous as they didn't have to be used in a fraction of a second. Animals at long range didn't even know a hunter was in the area, so were usually shot at when motionless or moving slowly. In such a situation the hunter had time to get into a shooting position with rest, calculate range, wind and perhaps mirage, check the table taped to his stock which listed his previously determined points of impact at 50- or 100-yard intervals, aim and fire.

The biggest problem in this whole setup was determining the range. Military rangefinders could be found occasionally, and they were very accurate when calibrated properly, but they were too big, too heavy and too expensive for most hunters. Small laser units were not yet commonly available. But there was one unit that was immediately available, weighed and cost nothing, and was accurate enough for the shooter's purposes if he did his part — the reticle.

Assuming he knew how much a reticle, or part of it, subtended at a given range, and he had a fairly good idea of his target's dimensions, by directly comparing the reticle to the target he could get a good idea of range. For example, if a center dot subtended 3 moa (3 inches per hundred yards) and it just

equaled a deer's withers-to-brisket depth of approximately 18 inches, the range would equal 18 divided by 3 or 600 yards. Anyone who's tried it knows it's not real easy to make such a comparison - ambient light, lens quality, eye efficiency, rifle movement, etc. affect resolution — but it's usually possible to do much better than with the eye alone. In fact, most shooters have no realistic estimate of range if it's more than a couple of hundred yards, so they need some help.

Many reticles based on this direct comparison method have been devised. Decades ago the late Tackhole Lee could install a series of Floating Dots on the bottom half of the vertical crosshair if someone would tell him the bullet's drop in inches at 100-yard intervals. (That would be determined by actual shooting, of course.) And today's Mil-Dot reticle can be thought of as a variation of Lee's system. Instead of matching the dot spacing to a given load's actual bullet drop, the Mil-Dot reticle has dots of a known size and regular spacing, so they can be used with bullets of different trajectories once the correlation is known.

Other complex reticles such as supplied by Nightforce, Springfield Armory and others have

layouts of lines and dots or circles of various sizes and spacings which can be used the same way. And Dan Shepherd's system of open circles vertically spaced so each encloses an average deer's body depth at 100-yard intervals works the same way. Elk hunters can get the Shepherd with 24-inch instead of 18-inch aiming circles.

There are other long-range reticles, but you get the idea. All of these are photo-deposited or otherwise applied to a plane lens (one that neither converges nor expands light rays). These are exceedingly accurate because they are mathematically constructed to a large format and then photographically reduced to fit on the lens. It's claimed that because such a reticle is on a solidly installed lens it's stronger than an early style crosshair which actually consisted of thin wires soldered to a metal ring. This might be true, but putting the reticle on an added lens means it reduces light transmission a trifle (which admittedly is unimportant in today's scopes that pass more than 90% of the light that hits their objectives), and the reticle-lens must be absolutely clean — no stray fingerprints from the assembly process nor specks of dust floating around inside the tube; these inevitably

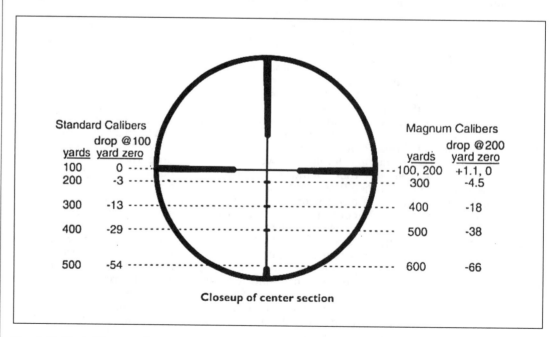

Standard Calibers		Magnum Calibers	
drop @100		drop @200	
yards	yard zero	yards	yard zero
100	0	100, 200	+1.1, 0
200	-3	300	-4.5
300	-13	400	-18
400	-29	500	-38
500	-54	600	-66

Closeup of center section

Burris Ballistic Plex reticle shows approximate long-range drops when zeroed at 100 yards.

New Burris Black Diamond is an 8-32x50 with target knobs.

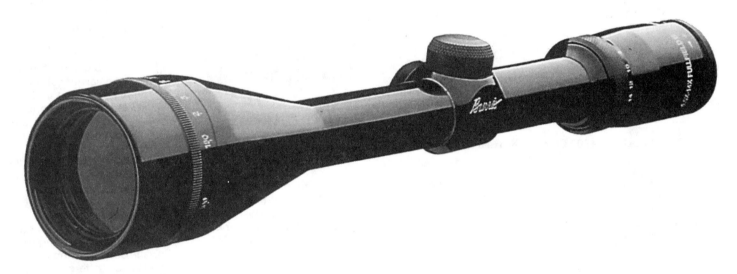

The 4.5-14x42 Fullfield II is the highest power of the new Burris line.

wind up where they're not wanted... in full view because they're right on a focal plane.

Many of today's reticles also can be illuminated when desired, even in color, and this is helpful at times.

In the end, today's super-efficient cartridges and rifles are made practicable only by scopes that make it possible to take advantage of their ballistics and accuracy. But don't forget that such scopes are so efficient only because of their reticles.

This year's new stuff follows, in alphabetical order for a change:

BSA has several lines of new scopes this year. Tops are the Catseyes, which are made in 1.5-4.5x32, 3-10x44, 3.5-10x50, (also with

illuminated reticles), 4-16x50, and 6-24x50. These range from 11.2 to 16 in. and 12 to 23 oz. Eye relief is unusually long at 4.5 to 5 inches, which is comforting to know when mounted on a hard-kicking magnum — if installed far enough forward to take advantage of it.

There's also the Deer Hunter series, which has several straight low powers, 3-9s with 32, 40 or 50mm objectives, a 2.5-10x44 and a 1.5-4.5x32. Then the Contender and Platinum lines each have a 24x or 36x with 40, 44 or 50mm objectives, various medium-power variables, even a 10-50x60 for those special occasions when ultra-high magnification is usable. The 10-50x has a "Big

Wheel" parallax adjustment on the left side of the turret, which is more convenient than screwing the objective unit in or out. Reticle in the above scopes is the European style of 3 pointed posts overlying crosshairs. Some tubes have a thin tough rubber coating. Eyepieces focus quickly from -4 to +4 diopters and adjustments are 1/8-moa clicks.

BSA also has several air rifle scopes and red dot scopes with 30, 42 or 50mm lenses; these are primarily for handguns or shotguns but they're also fast on woods rifles where shots can be at short range and sudden.

Burris has added several scopes to the Black Diamond line, the 6x50, 8-32x50 and the

Mr. T. Titanium 2.5-10x50. The latter has scratch-proof T-Plate coating on external lens surfaces; according to the manufacturer, hunters in the toughest environments won't have to worry about having a "soft clean lens cloth" in a baggie after a slip down a muddy sidehill; just swipe the mud off Mr. T's lenses and wipe them clean with your dirty shirttail, they say, it won't hurt anything. Sure'n we've come a long ways from the soft lens coatings of the post-WWII years.

Titanium is a most interesting material for scope tubes. It's lighter than steel and on these models is coated with a nitride that's harder than carbide or hard chrome. Use of titanium nitride,

This 3-9x Sportview from Bushnell has an extremely large objective, 60mm, for great light even at top magnification.

The 6-24x40 Bushnell 4200 Elite can be used for varmints at any range, much benchrest shooting.

aluminum titanium nitride or chrome nitride allows these Mr. Ts to be made in several finishes ... what Burris calls Carbon Black, Titanium Gray or Autumn Gold. Think the latter might induce some gunmaker to bring out a gold-plated barrel and action to go with the scope? Talk about flamboyant!

There's also a new line called the Fullfield II series, in 1.75-5x, 3-9x40, 3.5-10x50 and 4.5-14x42. These are made with several finishes to complement your rifle. As you might know, the Fullfields have a somewhat larger eyepiece than normal, so they give an enlarged field of view. Unlike other scope makers, the Fullfields have a conventional round field rather than a TV-view. The Fullfield IIs have been updated somewhat: eye relief is almost 4 inches, eyepiece and power ring are one-piece, potential leak paths have special seals, and the adjusting system is closer to the center of the scope to better accommodate mounting.

The 3-9x40 Fullfield II is available with the new Ballistic Plex reticle, which has short horizontal lines on the lower vertical hair to use as aiming points at 100-500 yards with many of today's high velocity cartridges. A similar ballistic Mil-Dot design is offered in various other Burris scopes; like other Mil-Dot reticles, it's useful as a rangefinder and has aiming points up to 700 yards.

Bushnell/Bausch & Lomb is how this manufacturer can be referred to this year, and probably just Bushnell next year, for market research has shown the Bushnell name has greater recognition among scope buyers than B&L. Performance standards that always distinguished B&L products will be carried on in Bushnell's new top-of-the-line scopes.

The Elite 3200 series is now offered with the RainGuard water repellant system which had been offered only on the 4200s last year. This is a real advance for big game hunters who, unlike varmint shooters, often have to be out in the worst weather conditions. Rain and snow are often the norm when elk or moose or bears are on your license.

An 8-32x40 has been added to the 4200 Elites, and it should handle any varmint that isn't running too fast, and do it at any range. Its 1/8-minute clicks make it suitable for most any benchrest shooting too. For all-round hunting use, a 3-9x50 is now offered with a Command Post reticle, an answer to varying light conditions that Bushnell came up with many years ago and has brought back in an improved version. Simple crosshairs are used when light is no problem, then turning a ring brings three posts (conspicuous posts) into view (none at 12 o'clock) for use at dawn or dusk.

A new 4-16x50 in the Trophy series will take care of most hunters' demands and can take the unusual recoil effects of an airgun; for such use it can be focused as near as 10 meters. Then in the Sportview line there's a 3-9x with an unusually large objective, 60mm. This will transmit all of the light the eye can take in, even at 9x, which is unusual at that high a magnification. The Banner line hasn't been forgotten,

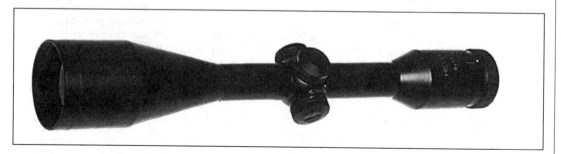

The Kahles 8x50 is available with illuminated reticle, from Swarovski.

either. A 4x32 and two variables - 3-9x50 and 1-4x32 - have been added.

For brush hunters, Bushnell's non-magnifying HOLOsight has been updated. This 2nd generation unit weighs only 6 1/2 ounces and measures just over 4 inches. With its unlimited eye relief and field, and a reticle pattern that's seen right on the target, the HOLOsight is awfully fast to use. Just what's needed when a buck explodes from a nearby tangle.

Kahles was a family-owned optical company from its founding in 1898 until 1974, when it was sold to Swarovski as there was no heir in the family to take it over. Always known for its high quality scopes and binoculars, Kahles made sniper scopes during both World Wars. In 1989 Kahles Ltd. G.M.B.H. was registered as an independent company within the Swarovski Group.

One series of Kahles scopes is built on 30mm tubes, another on 1-inch diameter, both of hardened aluminum. There are Tactical 6x42 and 10x42 steel tube models with Mil-Dot reticles. Numerous other styles are available in the first two series. A 1.1-4x24, 1.5-6x42, 2.5-10x50, and 3-12x56 make up the Helia Series, new this spring. Illuminated reticles are available for most.

Leica's Ultravid scopes come in only three models — 1.75-6x32, 3.5-10x42 and 4.5-14x42 — but it's hard to see any real need for more. Their one-piece 30mm tubes are machined from a block of aircraft-grade aluminum and have a hard black matte finish, adjustment turrets are about centered for easy mounting, they have rapid-focusing diopter eyepieces and 1/4-moa clicks, and their optics - well, who has a better reputation than Leica?

Leupold now has illuminated reticles in five of their Vari-X III scopes, the 1.5-5x20, 3.5-10x50, 3.5-10x40 Long Range MI, 3.5-10x40 Long Range M3, and 4.5-14x50 AO. There's also a new M8 6x42 with adjustable objective and target adjustment knobs. The illumination has 11 brightness settings, so can be adapted to any ambient conditions without overpowering the target or affecting the shooter's low-light vision.

Altogether, Leupold offers a choice of 14 reticle styles, but all of these are not available in all scopes. In the Vari-X IIIs mentioned above, most can be had with a Duplex, Mil-Dot, or German #4, which has crosshairs for precise aiming and three posts entering the field from 3, 6, and 9 o'clock to aid target acquisition in dim light.

Two Leupold scopes offer bullet drop compensation. The Mark 4 M3-10x40 and the Vari-X III 3.5-10x40 Long Range M3 have an elevation adjustment that compensates for bullet drop from 100 to 1000 yards. This will work only for cartridges having similar trajectories, of course, such as the 5.56mm (223 Rem.) 55-grain @ 3200 fps, 308 Winchester 168-grain @ 2600 fps, 30-06 180-grain @ 2700 fps, or 300 Winchester Magnum 220 grain @ 2650 fps.

The new M8 6x42 will be popular with benchresters in Hunter Class, undoubtedly, but I expect it will also find favor with many hunters. The trend toward higher magnification has been growing for decades, even for woods use, and many hunters who would have mounted a 4x a generation ago now opt for a 6x. The higher power is handicapped by its smaller field of view, but this is not so important to the man who does a lot of waiting and watching rather than walking. A moving hunter often bumps game, so has a running shot and a big field of view helps; but a guy on stand routinely gets a chance at standing or walking game, and the extra power allows him to aim precisely and avoid tiny obstructions in the bullet's path.

Nikon has a new 2-scope line called the Titanium. Made in 3.3-10x44 and 5.5-16x44, both of these scopes use titanium for their ocular and objective bells, to get the maximum protection for the enclosed lenses. The objective units are adjustable for range to eliminate parallax, of course. The Titaniums have 1/4-moa clicks and 1-inch center tubes.

A new entry in Nikon's Buckmaster line is a 4.5-14x40. It doesn't have quite as much light transmission as their Monarch UCC scopes (88 vs 95 percent), but I don't think that's enough to bother

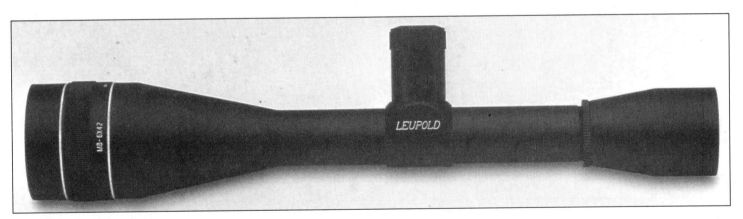

This M8 6x42 from Leupold will doubtless be popular with many hunters who like to sit in the woods and watch.

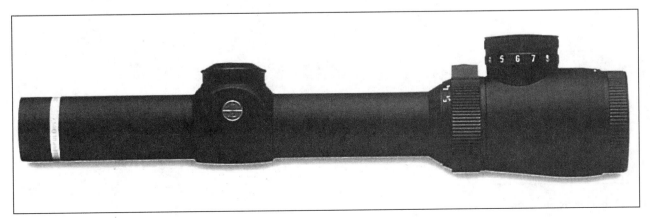

Leupold's new Vari-X III 1.5-5x20 has a lighted reticle for even better use in dark woods where its low-power magnification range pays off.

The Leupold 3.5-10x40 Long Range M1 scope has an illuminated reticle for dim light situations.

anyone. Experts in the field of optics have told me there has to be a change of about 10 percent in light transmission for the human eye to recognize a difference, so in the real world these are almost the same. Any improvement in anything has to have some value, of course - that's how

progress comes about - but at times a hunter might not want to pay the extra cost. The new scope is just under 15 inches long and weighs 19 ounces.

Nightforce Extreme Scope, or NXS, is the name given to this company's new entry. It's a 5.5-22x with a triple-element 56mm

objective unit, built on a 30mm hardened aluminum tube. Eye relief is long, almost 4 inches, clicks are 1/4-minute, and lenses have 4-layer broadband coating. Parallax adjustment is in a third turret on the left side, which is more convenient to anyone in shooting position

than an adjustable objective. Six reticle designs are offered. The rangefinders look complex at first but a few minutes' study clears that up, then it becomes obvious how efficient they are. All can be illuminated. The NXS is 15 1/4 in. long and weighs 32 ounces, so requires a strong mounting system, preferably one with a recoil shoulder on the base. (Personally, I think all mounts should be made that way; otherwise all recoil force must be absorbed by the base-mounting screws, and that seems a lot to ask with scopes getting heavier all the time.)

Most Nightforce scopes are obviously intended for long- or ultralong-range shooting, the kind where you can run out of vertical adjustment before you get zeroed. So they offer 2-piece custom tapered steel bases made by Bruce Baer. These add at least 20 minutes-of-angle to the up travel of internal adjustments. Currently they're made for Remington, Winchester, Savage and Weatherby actions.

Schmidt & Bender is located in a small city in about the middle of Germany's

Nikon's new Titanium models use this metal for their ocular and objective bells.

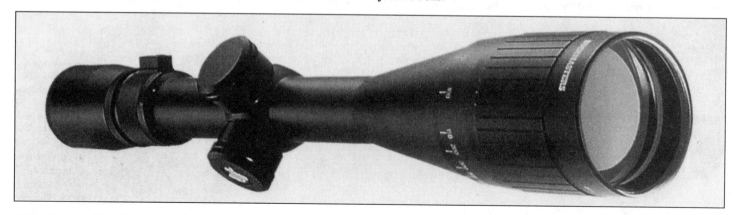

The 4.5-14x40 Buckmaster from Nikon.

RETICLE OPTIONS

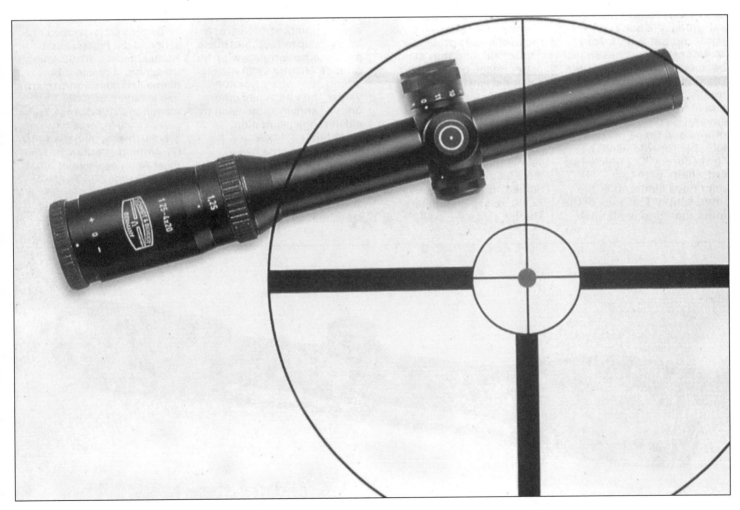

| NP-1 | NP-200 | NP-1RR | NP-R2 | MIL-DOT | CH-1,2,3 & 4 |

These are the reticle options in the new Nightforce NXS

famed optical region. They make rifle scopes. Not cameras or binoculars or astronomical telescopes, just rifle scopes. You might say that keeps their attention tightly focused. At the moment they offer about a score of models, some with illuminated steel reticles. Straight powers are on 1-inch steel tubes, variables on hardened aluminum 30mm tubes, except for the PM (Police/Marksman) series which has 34mm diameter to give more room for adjustments. S&B isn't fascinated with extreme power, top magnification being in a couple of 4-16x50s named the Long Range and Varmint models. Except for reticle designs there's no obvious difference. Long Range has three variations of the Plex style, while the Varmint comes with either extremely fine (less than 1/16-moa) crosshairs or their No. 8 Dot; this one has 1/3-minute dots on the lower half of the vertical crosshair, spaced to closely correspond with a high velocity bullet's impact at hundred-yard intervals up to 700 yards. The focusing unit to eliminate parallax at any range is in the turret.

Also available is a 4-16x50 Precision Hunter. At bottom power the reticle looks like any other Plex, but as power is turned up to 16x the fine crosshairs are seen to have Mil-Dots, so can be used for range and windage calculations. And the little

Here's a close-up of Schmidt & Bender's 1.25-4x20 woods scope with on-off red Flash Dot reticle.

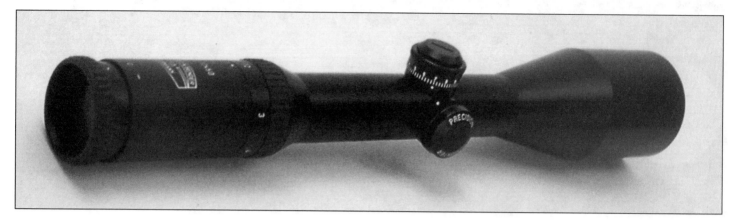

Schmidt & Bender's 3-12x50 Precision Hunter has a Mil-Dot reticle, is parallax-free at 200 meters.

1.25-4x20 big game scope now has an adjustable-intensity red dot reticle called the Flash Dot. This size scope has always been my favorite for normal hunting, but S&B says the 3-12x50 is their most popular variable, so I guess I'm in the minority. Again.

Sightron makes a bunch of scopes in most conventional magnifications, including models for handguns and shotguns. We had one of the latter but put it on a 7mm Magnum. It was chosen just because it had their Double Diamond reticle. Viewed totally, this is large, for quick aim at flying game, but it has several distinct aiming points and these make it suitable for rifle use. The "transparent" DD reticle has crosshairs with two diamonds centered at the intersection. The apex of the inner diamond is about 4-

moa above center, which gives a long range zero, while the bottom tip of the diamond can be used for extreme range shots after you check out where your bullet will intersect it. Or maybe you'll just mount it on a shotgun.

Simmons' Whitetail Expedition scopes are their latest with the aspherical lens system they introduced a few years ago in the Aetecs. For anyone unfamiliar with this, the asphericals provide a flatter field, and thus slightly better image quality, than spherical lenses at their extreme outer edges. Whitetail Expeditions are made in 1.5-6x32, 3-9x42, 4-12x42 and 6-18x42.

A new Simmons line this year is the 8-Point. As usual, the 3-9x models are most numerous, with objectives of 32, 40 and 50 millimeters. There's also a 4-12x40

adjustable objective and 4x32s for both rifle and shotgun.

Springfield Armory is now on the 3rd generation of their 4-14x56 Govt. Model 7.62mm scope. It differs from the 2nd generation only in that the rangefinding reticle is illuminated in green. It has seven brightness settings, so it can be adjusted to give good contrast under any ambient light conditions. Its reticle has aiming points at 100-yard intervals up to 1000, and these are placed to correlate with the drop of 7.62mm (308) match ammo after zeroing at 100 yards. The reticle has other units of known subtension to aid in range estimation.

Another 4-14x56 Springfield scope has a similar reticle on the bottom half of the vertical crosshair, with Mil-Dots on the top half and on the horizontal crosshair. These are intended

to aid in rapid range and wind estimation, of course. Then there's a fixed power 10x56 with full Mil-Dot reticle, target windage and elevation knobs and adjustable objective. All 4-14x56 models except the 1st generation scope have range-adjustable objectives, target knobs, and an internal bubble level in the bottom of the field to help the shooter eliminate canting, as does a 6-20x56 Mil-Dot Govt. Model.

Swarovski has added one scope to the Professional Hunter line, a 4-16x50. Like all the others, its main tube diameter is 30mm and it can be had in either steel or aluminum. This diameter tube gives space for greater w. and e. adjustments than the 1-inch (25.4mm) that's standard in most American scopes. That can be helpful - in fact, necessary - when shooting at a distance which 16x makes possible. Personally, I'm

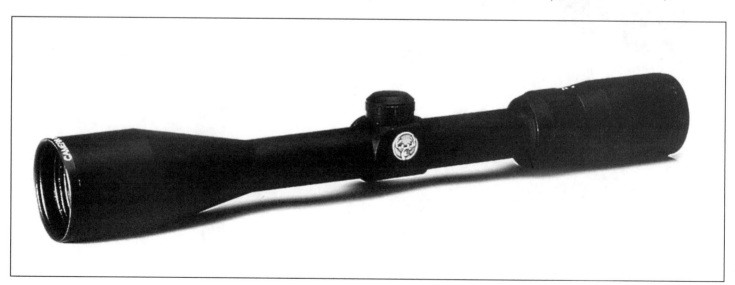

This new Whitetail Expedition scope from Simmons is a 3-9x42, to handle most hunting situations.

One of Springfield Armory's 4-14x56 Govt. Model scopes. Various rangefinding reticles are available.

opposed to such shooting, but on rare occasions when wounded game is fleeing, high magnification might be useful in placing a killing shot. The adjustment housing of the 4-16x has four-point coil spring suspension and its reticle is electro-chemically etched from a stainless steel wafer.

Swarovski straight power scopes are made with either 1-inch or 30mm tubes, and their AV 1-inch variable comes in several medium magnification brackets. Then there's the big 3-12x50 LRS. This is the only scope I can think of that has a built-in laser rangefinder. This is a logical development that provides both aiming capability and near-exact rangefinding in a single optical unit. Much more work will be done in this area by various manufacturers (including governments whose military recognizes the value and cost-effectiveness of long-range snipers), and size will go down and efficiency up. The LRS is 15 1/2 inches long and weighs 40 ounces, so requires a very strong mounting system if it's to remain in zero. And to me it has a weird appearance for a scope. Nevertheless, it's a sign of which way things are going.

Weaver's new scopes this year are the Grand Slams (could there be a connection with Speer Bullets?) and the Tacticals. There are half a dozen Grand Slams - I.5-5x32, 3-10x40, 3.5-10x50, 4.5-14x40 and 6-20x40 variables and a 4.75x40. All have quarter-

Swarovski introduced this 4-16x50/to their Professional Hunter line this year. Its 30mm tube can be had in either steel or aluminum.

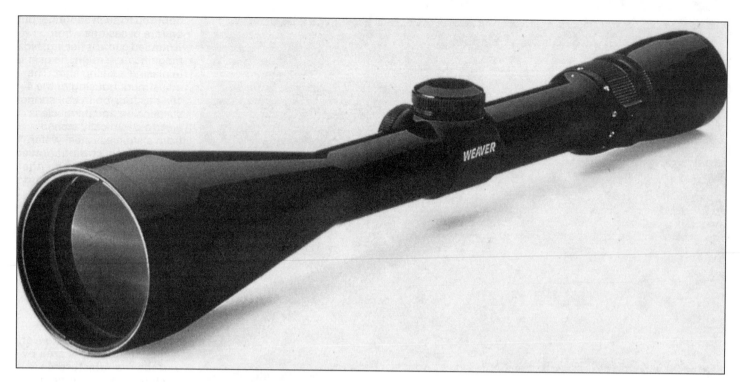

The Weaver 3-9x Classic has a 50mm objective.

The new Weaver 3-10x40 is called the Grand Slam.

minute clicks except the 4.5-14x, which has 1/8. Don't ask me why; I wish someone would explain it to me. Maybe if you want to hit a chicken egg at 500 yards, but then 14x doesn't seem like enough magnification. So... ?

There are only two Tacticals, 3-9x and 4.5-14x, both with 40mm objectives. The name suggests these are intended for military snipers and law enforcement SWAT teams, and their design furthers that idea. Most American variables have the reticle in the second focal plane, so it appears smaller as the

magnification is increased, or vice versa. Europeans have always preferred the reticle in the first focal plane, where its size varies directly with magnification (rather than inversely) so always subtends the same amount of the target. This prevents the point of impact from wandering due to minute reticle movement when power is switched; this simplifies using the reticle as a rangefinder by comparing its subtension with the known size of a target. All snipers use this method routinely, so the Tacticals make things easier

when the situation is stressful.

The Tactical reticle is a Plex design with a 1-inch open diamond at the intersection and tiny stadia lines of known dimensions and spacing on the vertical and horizontal crosshairs. These give references for holdoffs for both range and wind.

The Weaver K and V series are now called Classics - which seems logical for anything that's been around so long - but the target models are still referred to as the T Series. Most have the excellent Micro-Trac 1/4-minute

adjustments, some high powers 1/8-minute.

Zeiss has no new scopes for U.S. hunters this year. (Why should they, they had half a dozen new ones last year and whole lines of top grade older models.) Most Zeiss variables have the European reticle placement, as described earlier, but in the 1.1-4x24 Varipoint which was introduced a few years ago, the battery-powered red dot gets smaller as the magnification is increased or larger as it's lowered. Which makes sense to me. ●

HANDLOADING UPDATE

by LARRY S. STERETT

INTEREST IN HANDLOADING continues to grow and so does the number of new handloading products. Handloaders are always looking for ways to increase the quality of the ammunition they produce, and to reload faster and more economically. This seems to be particularly so with varmint hunters, trapshooters, cowboy action shooters, 'combat' shooters and, more recently, the 50 BMG shooters.

Dillon Precision Products, home of the 'Big Blue' machines, still has a great line for loading metallic cartridges, and last year the firm introduced the Model SL 900 Shotshell Reloader in 12 gauge. Now they've gone a step, actually two steps, further with the introduction of the SL 900 in 20 and 28 gauges. The electric case feeding, automatic positive-feed priming system and a 25-pound shot hopper are

standard, just as on the 12 gauge 900. (Skeet shooters should welcome this news.) Conversion units in these gauges are available for those handloaders who already are the proud owners of an SL 900 in 12 gauge. (A .410-bore SL 900 is not available as this is written, but it is in the works.)

Back in the thirties and late forties there were a number of shooters experimenting with 20- and 23-caliber rifles. In the next couple of decades it seemed to be with 14-, 17- and 19-calibers. (This handloader has shot most of them from the 14- to 50-caliber, but never a 19.) For those shooters unaware of the 19-caliber, it's literally the same as the 4.85mm which the British and some other countries were testing in the early 1970's. (The 4.85mm apparently won the trials out to 400 meters, but lost the battle to the 5.56mm (223) due to the need for a one-piece cleaning rod in the small bore.) For those shooters owning a 19-caliber rifle, **James Calhoon** has loading dies, both bench-rest and neck-sizing, and components in this caliber and others. Calhoon also has a 'rebarrel kit' for the 19 Calhoon and 19-223 Calhoon cartridges.

Last year **Forster Products** introduced two case trimmers for the big cases, the "Classic" for those blackpowder and English cases up to 4 1/8-inches long, and the 50 BMG set up specifically to trim the big Browning. (The Forster trimmers use Brown & Sharpe-style collets to retain the cases during trimming, but the 50 BMG trimmer does not use a collet, using a rim holder instead. Also new was a Hand Outside Neck Turner for the 50 BMG. This year twenty-seven (27) additional calibers have been added to this Neck Turner line. Using centerless ground pilots in calibers from 17 to 60, this Neck Turner features a micrometer adjustment knob and the industry's only carbide neck thickness cutter. (Forster currently has three hand-operated case trimmers in their line, plus a powder adapter, and a "Power" Trimmer.)

Forster continues to manufacture a line of Bench Rest Competition Dies, powder measure, the Co-Ax reloading press, and the Co-Ax Case and Cartridge Inspector, along with a number of other products for handloaders. One handy item is a Stuck Case Remover for

Handloaders of 19-caliber cartridges can find loading dies and components at James Calhoon, whose 19-223 and 19 Calhoon cartridges are shown here with parent 223 Remington and 22 Hornet cartridges.

Forster Products has case trimmers which will easily handle the 50-calibers, such as the 50 BMG, 50-140, and 500 Jeffrey, shown here with fired 50 BMG and 50 Spotter cases.

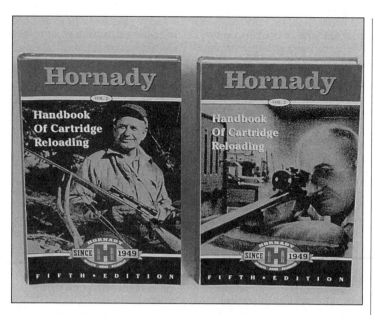

Hornady's new *Handbook of Cartridge Reloading, 5th Edition*, consists of two volumes, featuring thousands of tested loads, with new powders and new bullets.

those rare times when a case becomes stuck in a die and the rim pulls off.

All the major powder companies have new abbreviated or full scale loading manuals and/or handbooks available, plus **Hornady** has a new two-volume, *Handbook of Cartridge Reloading*. Dealers handling Vectan powders by **NobelSport** through ADCO should have copies of *Reloading Charges* which provides reloading data for both metallic and shotgun cartridges, including several European calibers. (There's a load for the 7.5x54mm MAS and, by the time this appears in print, Starline should have new brass cases available for this cartridge, complete with Boxer primer pocket.) One 50 BMG load is listed for a 656-grain bullet, and a powder charge that's nearly four times as heavy as one for the 458 Winchester Magnum. Shotshell loads are primarily for the 12 gauge. **Alliant Powders'** new magazine-size guide features loading data for the latest Steel and Reloder 25 powders for both shotshells and metallic cartridges, along with technical data, reference tables and handloading precautions.

Ramshot Powders, the Montana brand, has a new *Load Guide, Edition One*, with a number of handgun and rifle cartridge loads, including one for the 50 BMG, plus some 12 gauge loads. The Guide features a 'powder bushing' listing for MEC, P/W and Hornady presses, plus several worksheet pages.

Hodgdon Powder, 'The Brand That's True,' introduced their new comprehensive, loose-leaf Data Manual No. 27 last year. This year they have a softbound *Basic Reloaders Manual 2000* containing the very latest loads from the Hodgdon Laboratory. Featured are loads using the new Benchmark powder for rifles and the Longshot for shotshells, in addition to the regular Hodgdon line of powders.

Accurate Arms not only has a new softbound *2000 Reloaders Guide Millennium*, but a much larger *Loading Guide Number Two*. The first features the overall length of all metallic cartridges, data on the 300 Remington Ultra Mag and updated data on the 45-70, 45-120, and 25-06, plus shotshells. The larger (book-size) Guide contains 50 more pages than the first edition, with data for the 4064 and 5744 powders, a section on Cowboy Action Shooting, reduced load data and data on new cartridges, such as the 300 Whisper, 400 Cor-Bon, 357 SIG, etc.

Battenfield Technologies, Inc. may be a new name on the reloading scene, but it's really a combination of product lines, including **Fajen, PAST** and **Winchester Shooting Products**, brought to us by the **Midway** people of Columbia, Missouri. Under the **Frankford Arsenal** label there's the Model SS-99 (Midway 2009) single-stage press capable of handling cases such as the 470 N.E., 460 Weatherby Magnum, Sharps 31/4-inch. A Super Charger Powder Measure Kit, Reloading Stand and Case Tumbler and accessories also bear the Frankford label. There's also a neat battery-operated Jiffy Trickler, plus Bullet Puller, Case Neck Lubricator, two calipers and two micrometers. (All handloaders should have at least one caliper available for measuring case length, neck diameter, bullet diameter, and overall cartridge length.) The press and powder measure are not available under the Winchester Shooting Products label, but the Reloading Stand, Case Tumbler, and Bullet Puller are, in addition to some other items such as forearm rest, shooting box and caliper.

Handloaders in need of additional ballistic information may find it in *Ammo & Ballistics* by Bob Forker from **Safari Press**. This softbound volume contains ballistic data for 75 small, medium and big bore centerfire rifle cartridges from the 17 Remington to the 50 BMG. A dimensioned case drawing is provided for each cartridge, along with several different bullet weights. Similar data is provided for 18 African calibers from the 416 Remington Magnum to the 700 Nitro Express. A total of 29 handgun cartridges from the 25 ACP 50 Action Express are covered, which takes care of most, but not all, such cartridges in current production. In addition, there are several articles relating to the various types of cartridges. While the rimfires are not readily reloadable without difficulty, information on them, complete with dimensioned drawings, is provided from the 22 Short to the 22 WRM Shotshell.

Ammo & Ballistics provides case dimensions and ballistics for 75 cartridges from the 17 Remington to the 50 BMG.

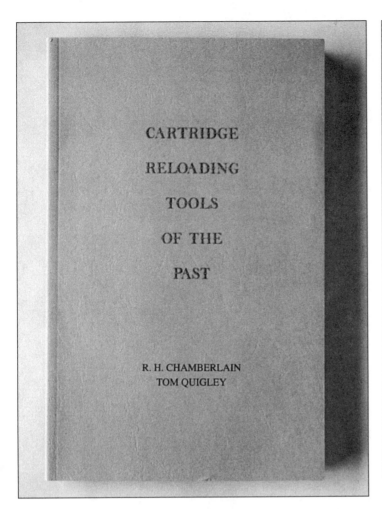

Cartridge Reloading Tools of the Past is an excellent reference source on older 'tong' tools of the type currently popular with Cowboy Action Shooters.

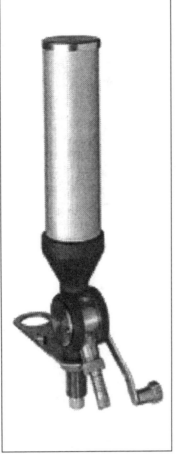

Hornady's new anti-static black powder measure for black powder cartridges and Cowboy Action Shooting.

Hornady's Lock-N-Load die bushing for the 50 BMG press permits the loading of regular smaller bore cartridges.

Handloaders who reload their cases repeatedly will appreciate the new Hornady Anneal Kit, which comes complete with three holders for small, medium and magnum-size cases.

The **Lyman Products Corporation** is entering its third century, with some of the line, such as the Ideal 'Tong Tool', having originated in the 1800s. Last year saw the introduction of the Classic 55 Black Powder Measure with the 24-inch drop tube, and the redesigned T-Mag Turret Press and Crusher II single-stage press with 'silver hammertone' powder coat finish in place of orange. Both presses feature flat machined bases for solid mounting, and left or right-hand operation. The Crusher II will handle cases up to 4 1/2 inches length, and the T-Mag turret has six stations. Optional turret heads are available and the indexing handles double as a wrench to remove the turret.

A couple of old calibers, 38-55 and 40-65 Winchester, have been reintroduced in the Ideal 310 Tool, mainly due to interest from cowboy action shooters. Currently the 310 is available for 21 different cartridges, although some may be discontinued at any time. (The 310 dies will also work in the older Lyman Tru-Line Junior Press for handloaders owning this model.)

In the regular die line there are nine additions, including the 300 and 338 Remington Ultra Mags, 40-65, 40-70, 45-90, 45-100, 45-120 and 50-90. Again, cowboy action shooters have created a demand for many of the old blackpowder cartridges. (Lyman has four cast bullet moulds specially designed for cowboy action shooting, plus a new mould for casting 335-grain bullets for the 38-55. Another new mould will produce 150-grain bullets for use in the 260 Remington or 6.5x55mm cartridges.

Lyman currently has five case trimmers, including one for the 50 BMG cartridge, plus a power adapter. A variety of deburring tools is available to handle cases up to 60 caliber;

new is a Power Deburring Set usable in a power screwdriver. Another useful item is the Universal Inside/Outside Tool which will handle cases from 22- to 45-caliber via an adjustable cutting blade.

Cowboy action shooters and handloaders interested in the reloading tools of yesteryear may find *Cartridge Reloading Tools of the Past* by R. H. Chamberlain and Tom Quigley a handy reference. Following a brief history of handloading, it covers most of the older tools, many of which were 'tong tools', by such firms as Winchester, Remington, Marlin, Browning, Sharps, Savage, Smith & Wesson, Ideal, Stevens, Ballard and U.M.C. The tools, powder measures and moulds are mainly for loading metallic cartridges, although shot may have been loaded in some instances. The book, which is available from Tom Quigley, also features an appendix filled

with patent drawings for loading tools from the late 1800's.

Hornady Manufacturing Co. has been producing 750-grain A-MAX bullets for several years for reloading the 50 BMG cartridge. Now, if a handloader has the cases, primers and powder, the rest—bullets, press and dies, etc. can be ordered from a Hornady dealer. New is the 50 Caliber BMG Press, available separately, or as a kit, complete with dies. The single-stage press, with three heavy supporting posts, features the Hornady Lock-N-Load die bushing. A separate conversion bushing is

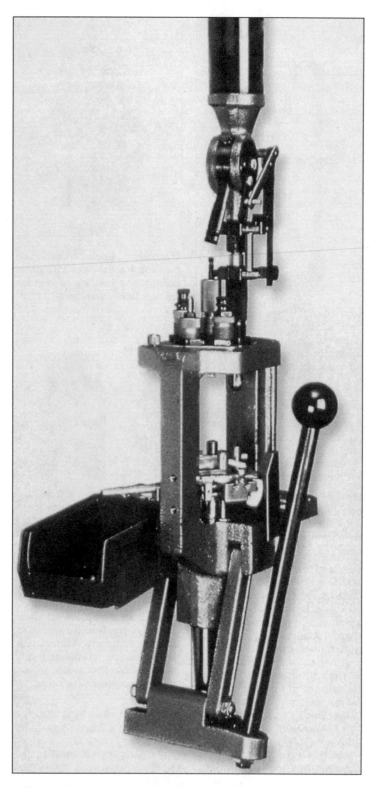

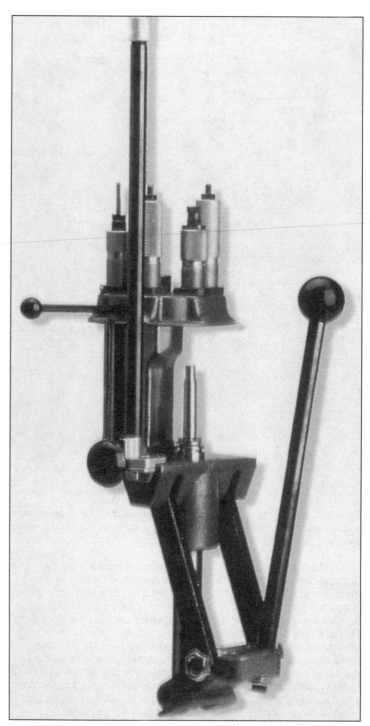

The RCBS Turret Press features a cast iron turret with six stations and toggle lock. The turret heads are interchangeable, with the indexing handle used as a wrench. Tube feed priming is standard with the Turret Press.

RCBS's new Pro 2000 Progressive Press features five stations, and utilizes the APS Priming System.

available to permit the use of a standard shell holder for loading other calibers on the 50 BMG Press. Also new is a 50 BMG Powder Measure with a 265 grain capacity metering unit and an extended drop tube.

Handloaders having a Hornady powder measure with limited metering capacity can now obtain a High Capacity Kit. The Kit contains two metering units having capacities of 80 to 180 grains and 165 to 265 grains. A clear drop tube and an extended hopper tube are included. (Hornady has six other metering inserts available, including a new Lock-N-Load Fine Adjust insert.)

Another new product from the Grand Island firm is an Anneal Kit for metallic cases. Annealing once-fired cases can extend case reloading life by reducing brittleness, and provide more uniform bullet pull for increased accuracy. The kit comes complete with three holders for small, medium and large or magnum-size cases.

Hornady powder measures and scales have been available for many years, but new is a battery (9-volt) powered Digital Reloading Scale. Accurate to +/- 0.1 grain, the scale comes with two calibration weights. The unit is compatible with an optional AC adapter, which can be purchased separately.

In the reloading die lineup, Hornady has all the most

The Turret Head for the new RCBS Press has six stations and permits rapid changing of calibers.

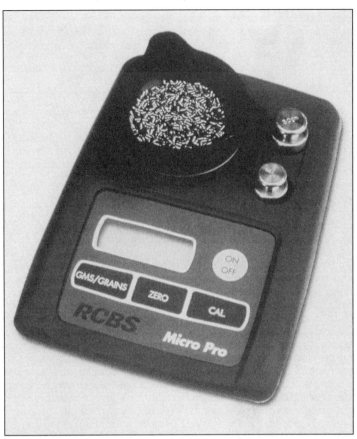

The new RCBS Micro Pro Electronic Scale will operate on a 9-volt battery or optional 110/220 VAC. It has a 750 grain capacity, and (+/-)0.1 grain accuracy at the lower range. It comes complete with two brass calibration weights.

common, and many not so common cartridges covered from the 17/222 to the 460 Weatherby Magnum, including a number of European calibers, such as the 7.5mm Swiss and 10.3x60mm and several wildcats, including the 7mm Merrill and 25/284. The handgun line ranges from the 25 ACP to the 50 Action Express and includes the 400 Cor-Bon, 44 Auto Mag and 475 Linebaugh. Others may have been added before this sees print.

Another welcome addition to the Hornady line is the *Fifth Edition* of the *Hornady Handbook of Cartridge Reloading*. This updated two volume set, which pictures the late Joyce Hornady on the covers, features thousands of tested loads with new powders and new bullets for 188 rifle and handgun cartridges. These hardbound volumes provide trajectory, energy, and sighting data for more than 200 Hornady bullets. It belongs on every handloader's reference shelf.

For shotshell reloaders the Model 366 progressive is available in 12, 20, and 28

gauge, plus .410-bore for 2 1/2-inch shells, but the Apex 3.1 is no longer cataloged. Gauge conversion kits and magnum conversion kits, up to 3-inch, are available for the 366, but no kits to handle the 3 1/2-inch 12 gauge shells.

Blount's **RCBS** has two new reloading presses for metallics, the Pro 2000 Progressive Press and the Turret Press. Both feature cast-iron frames, and the Pro 2000 has cast links and toggle block. The Turret feature cast-iron turret and toggle block. Both presses utilize standard 7/8x14 dies, with the Turret featuring six stations and the Pro 200, five stations. The Pro 2000 utilizes the APS Priming System, with tube priming optional, while the Turret model uses the tube feed priming system. Turret heads are interchangeable, and the indexing handle can be used to remove the turret head.

The Rock Chucker, Reloader Special-5, and Partner presses are still in the RCBS line, as is the AmmoMaster Single Stage press and the 50 BMG Pack. The AmmoMaster Progressive is no longer

cataloged, but the Piggyback II unit can be used to turn the single stage Rock Chucker, or one of the Reloader Specials into a five-station, auto-indexing progressive unit.

The Trim Pro 3-Way Cutter was introduced in seven calibers last year. Now 3-Way Pilot/Chamfers have been added in the same calibers. The APS Hand-Priming Tool was announced last year, but it's actually available now, as is a new Micro Pro Electronic Scale. The Scale, which will operate on a 9-volt battery, or optional 110 or 220 VAC, has a 750 grain capacity. Accuracy is +/- 0.1 grain from 0 to 350 grains and +/- .2 grain from 350 to 750 grains. It comes with two brass calibration weights.

The X-Dies, which eliminate the need for case trimming once a standardization trim is done, by reducing case growth (or stretching) during sizing. Dies for 13 additional cartridges have been added, bringing the total to 25, ranging from the 22 Hornet to the 338

Winchester Magnum. Cases such as the 50 BMG still require trimming.

Cowboy action shooting has prompted RCBS to add two additional cartridges, 40-65 Winchester and 45-70 Gov't., to the Cowboy die line. Three new cast bullet designs have been added to the rifle bullet mould line. These include a 170-grain FN .321-inch, a 120-grain round nose for the 310 Cadet, and a 370-grain flat nose .446-inch for 11mm cartridges. All are double cavity moulds.

The SPEER *Reloading Manual #13*, with over 9,000 powder loads, bullet data and ballistics tables, etc., mentioned last year is available, as is the computer program RCBS.LOAD. The PC program, which requires Windows 95 to run, contains an electronic version of *Manual #13*, plus the RCBS *Cast Bullet Manual* and *Accurate Loading Guide #1*.

Handloaders who are loading big time or for club use might consider the ProCast, high-volume, low-

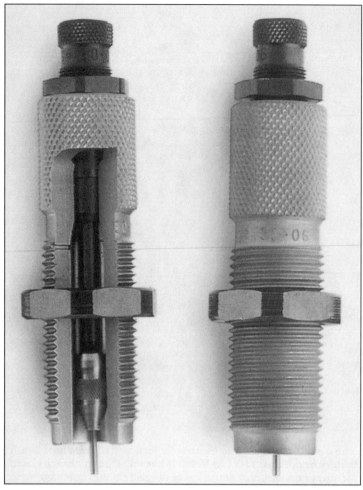

The X-Dies from RCBS practically eliminate the need for case trimming by reducing case growth during sizing. Dies for 13 additional calibers are now available, bringing the total to 25, ranging from the 22 Hornet to the 338 Winchester Magnum.

maintenance bullet casting machine by **Kohart Mfg., Inc.** The ProCast can produce up to 6,000 bullets per hour, using ten dual-cavity moulds mounted between two #50 roller chains to provide precise positioning and isolation for each mould. A safety switch shuts the machine down if any mould should remain open and an automatic lubrication system lightly greases the guide rails to prevent mould contamination. Currently 35 different JDH mould designs are available for the ProCast to turn out bullets from a 100 grain 32 wadcutter to a 405-grain bevel base, flat-pointed slug for the 45-70. The balance of the designs are for handloading the various 9mm, 10mm, 38, 41, 44, and 45 handgun cartridges.

Lee Precision, Inc. always manages to come up with something new for handloaders, and this year it's the Zip Trim. In principle it works much the same way as the recoil starter on many lawn mowers, or the string starter for a spinning top.

It's literally a miniature hand-powered lathe which rotates the cartridge case. Slip the head of the case into the shell holder, insert the pilot of the trimmer into the mouth of the case until it makes contact and pull the handle on the Zip-Trim. Remove the trimmer, pick up the chamfer tool and remove the burrs, inside and out in seconds, by touching it to the case mouth as the handle on the Zip-Trim is pulled. Fine steel wool or Scotch-Brite can be touched to the rotating case to polish it, if needed, and the whole thing can be accomplished in 12 seconds, according to Lee. It comes with mounting hardware, and will handle cases from the 25 ACP up to the 460 Weatherby Magnum, with the proper shell holder. Shell holders, Chamfer Tool and Case Trimmers are not included.

Lee continues to add to their line of handgun and rifle cartridge dies in Deluxe and standard types. Among the newest are ones for the 454 Casull and the 50 Action Express. There are also Taper

Crimp dies available for several different cartridges, including the 7.62x39mm Russian and the Casull, plus a number of dies for foreign rifle calibers such as the 7.5x55mm Swiss and the 7.5x54mm French.

Redding Reloading Equipment manufactures an extensive line of reloading dies. New are the Competition Bullet Seating Die for straight wall handgun and rifle cartridges. Featuring micrometer adjustment and spring loaded seating stem, the new die is available for eight handgun cartridges from the 9mm Luger to the 45 Colt/454 Casull, and five rifle cartridges from the 38-40 Winchester to the 45-70 Government. Redding has also added the 30-06 Springfield to their list of Small Bore Body Dies.

In their Competition Bushing Neck Die Sets, Redding has six additional cartridges available, including the 338 Winchester and 338 Remington Ultra Magnums, the 6mm Remington Improved 40

degrees, 25-06 Remington Improved 40 degrees, 6.5mm/06 and 338/06, plus the 338 Remington Ultra Mag in the more conventional Series B dies, which are costly to produce.

Redding continues to produce both Profile Crimp and Taper Crimp dies in Series A-D with six additional cartridges added to the Profile Crimp series. These cartridges, 32-20, 38-55, 38-40, 40-65, 44-40, and 45-70 are enjoying a new surge in popularity due to Cowboy Action Shooting. Similarly this type of shooting has brought about an increase in the number of SAECO bullet moulds in the Redding line. The 'black powder/CAS' line features 21 different designs from 30 to 45 caliber, with the smallest being a 140-grain flat point for the 30-30 Winchester and the largest being a 525-grain round nose for the 45-70 Gov't.

Two other new items for the handloader are the "Instant Indicator" Headspace & Bullet Comparator, and the Competition Model 10-X Pistol and Small Rifle Powder Measure. The latter is similar to the regular BR-30 measure, but with the diameter of the metering cavity reduced to provide a charge weight range from 1 to 25 grains. The operating handle can be changed for use by left-handed reloaders by removing the micrometer unit and reorienting the drum.

The "Instant Indicator" can compare headspace and bullet seating depths within 0.001-inch. It checks the headspace from the case shoulder to the base, and comes complete with one bore diameter bushing and instructions to quickly compare overall case length and bullet base to give. Currently headspace bushings are available for 25 different cartridges from the 222 Remington to the 338 Winchester Magnum. (The "Instant Indicator" may be used for a family of cartridges with the same shoulder angle.) To compare bullet seating depths, a standard Redding sizing bushing of the proper bore diameter for the

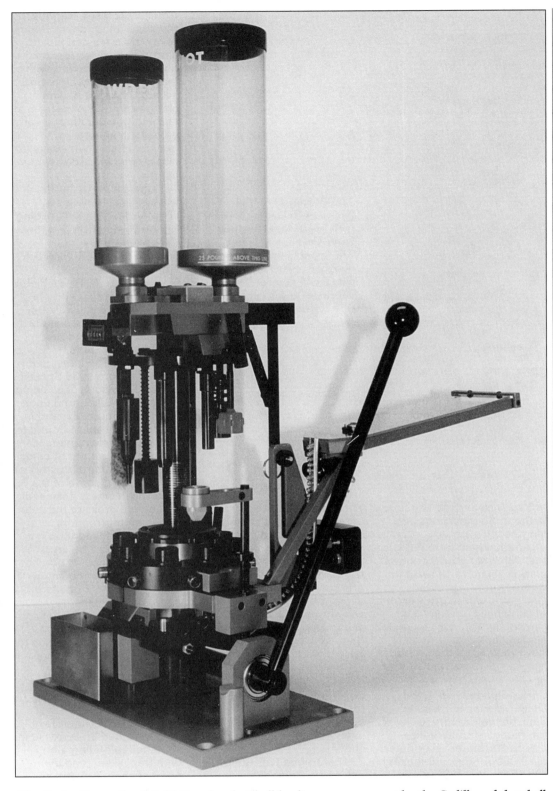

The Spolar Power Load Gold Premier shotshell loading press may not be the Cadillac of shotshell loaders, but it's close. Precision machined from steel and aluminum, it's available in 12, 20 and 28 gauges, plus .410-bore, and a change of gauges can be accomplished in five minutes or less.

designed an Automatic Shell Feed System that cuts the reloading time virtually in half. The hopper holds 500 empty shells and feeds them brass head down onto the shell feed seating assembly. An electric motor, which turns the sorting disc in the hopper, utilizes an infrared laser light to stop the motor automatically when the feed tube is full. This new system, available from P/W. can be installed quickly on all P/W Platinum 2000, 950, 900, L/S-1000 and 800 series reloaders.

In addition to the new, improved loader, the Platinum 2000 Series, which is available in 12, 20, and 28 gauge, plus .410-bore, P/W has a new External Adjusting Primer Feed Assembly, and a Die Removal System which can be retro-fitted to earlier models. The fully progressive 2000 has these features, plus a shot tube holding 25 pounds, and a 19-inch tall powder tube. For less than nine C-notes, the Platinum 2000 automatically decaps, primes, charges powder, seats the wad, charges the shot, pre-crimps, taper final crimps and ejects the complete shells, indexing between each station.

For a couple of C-notes over a Grand, shotshell handloaders can own a **Spolar** Power Load Gold Premier, precision machined from steel and billet aluminum. Available in 12, 20, and 28 gauge, plus .410-bore, the Spolar features an electronic shot, powder and primer settling system, two final crimps and a change of gauges in five minutes or less. The shot hopper holds 25 pounds, and the powder and shot bushings cam be changed easily. (The powder and shot hoppers are threaded for increased stability.) Right- or left-hand operation, with hydraulic capability, are standard features as is the ability to remove a shell for examination at any time from any station. Shot and wad are dropped simultaneously, reducing the possibility of cocked wads, or wads which pop back up out of the shells. Sealed ball bearings, die lube and a counter are standard

caliber being used is inserted. Eight such bushings are available, from .224-inch to .338-inch, with additional ones possibly later.

In addition to regular sizing and seating dies, Redding has available nearly three dozen forming die sets to form

everything from the 17 Ackley Hornet, using regular 22 Hornet cases, to the 40-70 Gov't. using the 45-70 Gov't. case. These are in addition to dozens of Form and Trim Dies for other cartridges. (Owners of the IAI M1 Carbines chambered for the 5.7mm

MMJ cartridge may appreciate knowing Redding has forming dies.)

Olympic Gold Medalist Kim Rhode uses thousands of shotshells each year loaded on a **Ponsness/Warren** 12 gauge press. To increase production, Kim's father

The Oregon Trail Bullet Co. has a new Reloading Manual with lots of loads for their Laser-Cast line of bullets. The spiral bound volume, designed to lay flat, contains data for 25 popular handgun cartridges and 13 popular rifle cartridges.

from the 32 H & R Magnum to the 45 Colt in modern Ruger revolvers are listed. Each cartridge covered has a dimensioned drawing, with at least one bullet weight and several different powder charges. Data is in the form of starting powder charge with velocity, a never-exceed powder charge with velocity and overall loaded cartridge length.

Spiral-bound to lay flat this volume also contains a chapter devoted to "Loading for the Competitor." For those shooters in the various competitions, IPSC/USPSA, NRA Action Shooting, Cowboy Action, Police Pistol Combat, etc., this volume could be especially useful.

Midway USA has a fourth volume of the LoadMAP series of reloading handbooks. The latest is for the 357 Magnum/38 Special, with the previous ones being for the 45 ACP, 9mm Luger, and 44 Magnum. Printed in full color and spiral-bound to lay flat, the latest manual follows the method of color graphs. It contains a history of the cartridge, some of the firearms in which it is used, and over a gross of full color pages of information, including the Hodgdon Titegroup and Lil'Gun powders. Measured 10-shot group sizes are shown for each projectile/propellant combination, and 74 projectiles and 18 propellants are covered.

Handloading continues to grow in popularity in every area. Cowboy Action Shooting has prompted an increase of interest in many of the older black powder cartridges, Sporting Clays has prompted an increase in shotshell reloading along with trap, skeet, and even combat shooting, and of course the increase in the number of rifles chambered for the 50 BMG cartridge has increased the number loading tools being manufactured for this big bore cartridge, along with components. If enough handloaders ask for new, improved equipment, the manufacturers will produce it. It doesn't get much better than that. ●

features, as is a locking system which can be used to prevent unauthorized operation. Theoretically, with the hydraulic system installed, the Gold Premier can turn out 1,200 loaded shells per hour, with 800 being more realistic. (Back in the early 1960s the old Hollywood progressive was advertised as being capable of turning out 1,800 loaded shells per hour, via hand operation, but to accomplish this would have required a crew to keep the hoppers filled.)

With steel shot becoming easier to obtain and powders specially tailored for use with steel shot, loading data also becomes more readily available. One of the latest is *Volume VII* of the R.S.I. *Steel Shotshell Reloading Handbook* from **Reloading Specialties Inc.** There are 57+ new loads using Alliant "Steel" powder, with ones tailored for use with steel shot, plus 17 loads for Bismuth shot. There are no 16 gauge loads included, but the 20 gauge in 3-inch, 10 gauge

in 3 1/2-inch and the 12 gauge in the three most common lengths.

Another item from R.S.I. is the "All Seal," a primer and crimp sealant to be used for weatherproofing reloads. One bottle will seal hundreds of shotshells or metallic cartridges. R.S.I. also handles shotshell reloading components, including the "Super Sam" steel shot made of soft, low carbon steel.

Handloaders using the **Oehler** Model 43 Personal Ballistics Laboratory to check their loads should realize there are a number of updates available. Anyone purchasing after February 1999 would automatically have received the Windows version of the Model 43 software, but Windows Software (upgrade from DOS version) is available for older Model 43 systems, as is Ballistic Explorer for Windows, an improved Downrange Amplifier, Downrange Skyscreen III (3 ea.) and wide Diffusers and Hooded Shells for the three Skyscreen IIIs. Improvements in the

Windows include an improved battery charger circuit to prevent overcharge, color printing, notes can be added at any time during the test or during replay, pressure can be measured without using muzzle screens, and bullet holes are shown to scale on target plots (they look like your paper target), and the program supports longer test, gun, and load record names. (The test directory allows several ways to sort tests, showing the type of measurement, gun name, load name, and number of shots.)

The Oregon Trail Bullet Co. has a new *Reloading Manual* with loads using their Laser-Cast line of bullets. Rifle loads range from the 30 Carbine to the 45-70 Gov't., with separate loads for modern 45-70 rifles. While some of the cartridges, such as the 32-20 Winchester, 44 Magnum, 45 Colt, etc. are considered handgun cartridges, loads for use when such cartridges are used in carbines or rifles are provided. Loads for 25 popular handgun cartridges,

by **HOLT BODINSON**

AMMUNITION, BALLISTICS AND COMPONENTS

MAYBE IT'S THE wealth effect or maybe it's the growing sophistication of a more demanding group of shooters, but what's been impressive in the ammunition field is the expansion of premium lines featuring higher quality custom bullets and harder shot at faster and faster velocities. As innovation goes, Remington stole the show with their introduction of electronically primed ammunition; Winchester with its totally redesigned "AA" case; Hornady/Marlin with their belted levergun cartridge, the 450 Magnum; and SSK with their .50-caliber Peacekeeper. And where's "moly" going when Nosler brings out a new line of completely "Moly-Free" bullets? Then there's FN's new 5.7x28mm military small arms cartridge propelling a wee 31-grain projectile at 2346 fps and rumored to have tremendous terminal ballistics. If that whets one's interest, see the new 5mm-centerfire cartridge description under "Schroeder" and the .12-caliber under "Eichelberger" in our text. From all points of view, it's been a busy and fascinating year in the wonderful world of ammunition, ballistics and components.

AFSCO Ammunition

Advertising as a one-stop source for "American, foreign, obsolete and African" ammunition, Anthony Sailer of AFSCO is just that. I haven't stumped him yet. Try him for everything from 17 BumbleBee to 500 Jeffery. If he doesn't stock it, he will create it overnight.

Tel: (715) 229-2516

Ammo Depot

This is a general supply company for ammunition, components and reloading tools that is impressive because of its diverse offerings, including Pyrodex loaded ammunition for all of the cowboy and obsolete Winchester rifle calibers. Well worth knowing. www.ammodepot.com

Ballard Rifle & Cartridge

Need cases for the 25-20 Single Shot, 25-21 Stevens, 577 Snider, 577-450 Martini Henry, 50 Rem Pistol, or most other obsolete cases? Check Ballard. This unique firm that is manufacturing classic, and I might add, stunning, Ballard rifles and original replacement parts, also offers a very complete line of lathe-turned cases. I've used their 577-450 cases. Quality products. Nice to deal with. www.ballardrifles.com

Ballistic Products, Inc.

When I go looking for the most technologically advanced and diverse selection of shotshell components and reloading data, Ballistic Products is where I head. Their catalogs and extensive offering of proprietary reloading manuals are mind-bending. The quality of their products and service is superior. Four updated reloading manuals are rolling off the press— *Status of Steel 2001*; *Handloading Bismuth 2001*; the *Sixteen-Gauge*; and the *Powder Manual*. Special attention is being given this year to expanding their lines of wads for the smaller bores including 20-gauge steel shot, spreader and trap wads; and two, new .410 wads--the "Stump" brush wad and the "Stretch" mid-to-long range wad. If you need to make a 2-2 1/2-inch shell for one of those fine European doubles, Ballistic Products has introduced a neat hand-operated trimmer—the Trim Doctor—that will do just that. This house is also a good source for Kent Tungsten Matrix and FASTEEL and the Bismuth lines of non-toxic ammunition. www.ballisticproducts.com

Barnes

Barnes' baked-on, high-tech, dry film bullet lubricant is proving increasingly popular as an alternative to moly, so they're applying it to a variety of existing X-Bullets this year in calibers .224, .308, .375, .416, .470 and .500. With renewed interest in the 45/70 and this year's introduction of the 450 Magnum from Hornady, Barnes' latest 250- and 300-grain FNSP X-Bullets are right on target. www.barnesbullet.com

Beartooth Bullets

Offering an extensive selection of LBT bullet designs in calibers from .22 to .600 Nitro that are cast and sized specifically to the customer's requirements, Beartooth Bullets also offers a "*Technical Manual*" on the loading and performance of cast bullets. Bullet prices are reasonable; quality is exceptional; and Beartooth's website is first rate. www.beartoothbullets.com

Bell Brass

Advertising as "The toughest brass in the business," Bell isn't kidding if my experience with their Lazzeroni magnum cases is any indication. New this year for British fans are the 450/400 3 1/4" and 450 Basic cases. In the black powder category,

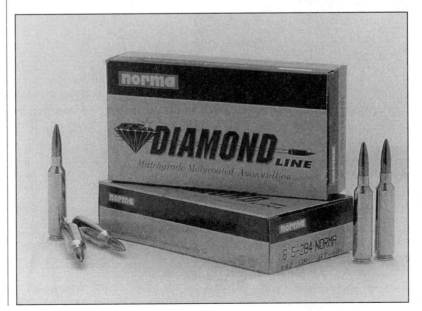

Norma's popular 6.5-284 match cartridge is being loaded by Black Hills.

new cases include the 44 Sharps Basic, 43 Mauser, 43 Spanish, and 50 Sharps Cylindrical 3-inch. Rounding out the 2001 offerings are the 458 Lott and the 416 Remington with a company promise to draw the 505 Gibbs, 405 Win., and 500/465 NE sometime in the near future. Finally, as a builder and re-builder of arsenal-quality loading machinery, Bell is offering production-style gauges for the serious handloader.
www.bellammo.com

Black Hills Ammunition

If you see boxes of Norma Diamond Line ammunition in 6.5-284 Norma, 6mm Norma BR or 338 Lapua on your dealer's shelves, be advised that it's being loaded this year right here in the USA by Black Hills Ammunition. Black Hills already loads the .223/69-grain BTHP and .308/ 168-grain BTHP in the Norma Diamond Line, and the latest Norma contract follows on the heels of Black Hills' continuing contracts to supply our US military shooting teams with a variety of high quality match ammunition. Also new in the Black Hill lineup this year are a 32 H&R Magnum load featuring Hornady's 85-grain XTP bullet at 1100 fps; two 357 SIG loads with either the

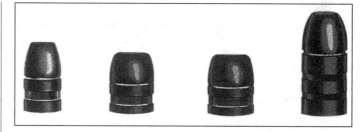

Given the popularity of cowboy action shooting, Speer has introduced a complete line of authentic looking, Old West-type bullets.

Speer 125-grain TMJ or Gold Dot bullet at 1350 fps; a heavy 223 match loading featuring the 77- grain Sierra MatchKing at 2750 fps; and a new 308 Winchester loading with the 165-grain Nosler Ballistic Tip at 2650 fps. By all means, order Black Hills' year 2000 catalog. It's informative, graphically stunning and refreshingly humorous.
www.black-hills.com

Buffalo Bore Ammunition

Here is a fairly new company that has focused on assembling high velocity, high performance, hunting ammunition for modern rifles and revolvers. Loading jacketed and hard cast lead bullets, Buffalo Bore has pushed velocities to the max. For example, in the 45/70 lever gun category, they offer a 405-grain Remington bullet at 2000 fps; a 350-grain Speer at 2100 fps; and a 430-grain lead load at 1925 fps. The company has a complete selection of heavy hunting loads for the 475 and 500 Linebaugh, 45 Colt, 454 Casull and 44 Magnum while a new line of +P tactical/defensive ammunition has been added this year for calibers from 32 ACP through 45 ACP. Two unusual loadings being offered are the 38/55 Winchester with bullets properly sized to fit those generous, old Winchester Model '94 bores and a heavy 348 Winchester load consisting of a 250-grain JFN at 2250 fps. Buffalo Bore also catalogs a complete selection of hard cast bullets for sale featuring many of the excellent LBT designs.
www.sixgunner.com

James Calhoon

Covered in detail last year, one of Calhoon's proprietary cartridges, the 19 Calhoon, a .19-caliber wildcat based on an improved Hornet case, received quite a bit of attention by some of the "majors" at the last SHOT Show. This wee cartridge propels a 27-grain bullet at 3600 fps and a 32-grain at 3400 fps with a miserly 12-15 grains of powder. Stay tuned. It may be coming to your dealer's shelves.
www.jamescalhoon.com

Cast Performance Bullet Company

As a measure of their quality, this company provides the heat-treated LBT designs that are loaded by both Federal and Cor-Bon in their premium handgun ammunition lines. Fortunately for the handloader, the company offers a very complete and economical retail selection of LBT bullets in .38, .41, .44,

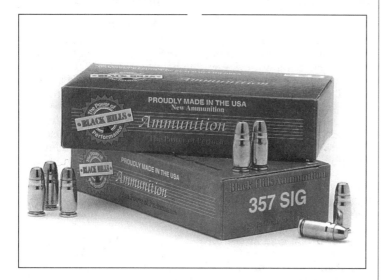

The hot and sensational 357 SIG has been added to the Black Hills line this year.

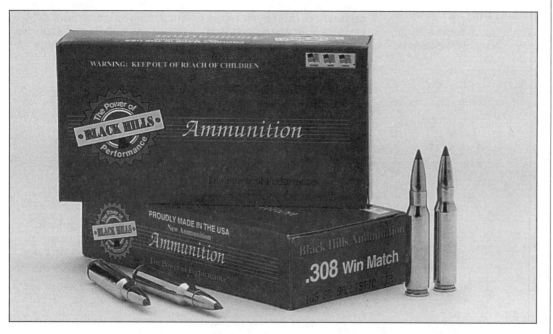

Nosler's accurate Ballistic Tips are appearing in most commercial lines, like this 308 Winchester match load by Black Hills.

Speer's new sintered copper bullet for indoor ranges fragments upon impact into a pile of copper dust.

swaged lead bullets in 38, 44, 45 and 45/70 caliber has been introduced that features a revolutionary lubricant that virtually eliminates leading. www.cci-ammunition.com and www.speer-bullets.com

Clean Shot Powder

A volume-to-volume replacement for black powder without the latter's fouling and sulfur corrosion, Clean Shot powder can now be obtained in pellet form for the 44/45 cap-and-ball revolver and 50/54-caliber rifles.
www.cleanshot.com

Cole Distributing

A major importer and distributor of the IMI and Aguila brands plus a good deal of surplus military ammunition, Cole has announced that they will be importing non-corrosive, boxer-primed, 7.5 MAS and 7.5 Swiss ammunition from FNM in Portugal. This will be the best of news to all of the owners of the 1000's of French MAS rifles that have been imported into the USA during the last few years. Surplus French military ball has been scarce, expensive and corrosive.
www.cole distributing.com

Eichelberger

If sub-sub calibers like the .12 and .14 sound intriguing, W.A. Eichelberger is man who keeps them shooting. Eichelberger is THE source for .12-,.14-, and .20-caliber bullets, cases, cleaning rods and loading manuals. Even if you never intend to shoot

these tiny bores, you may be interested in one of his many cartridge collector sets, including one consisting of the Long Rifle case formed and loaded with bullets from .12-to-.20-caliber. His brochure is also an excellent reference source for sub-caliber barrels, reamers, dies, rifles and journals. Address: 158 Crossfield Rd., King of Prussia,PA 19406

Estate Cartridge

Known for their high quality and custom shotgun ammunition, Estate Cartridge is adding a Buffered Magnum Hunting load in 12- and 20-gauge with extra-hard #4 or #6 shot as well as a new 3 1/2-inch High Velocity Magnum Steel loading with 1 1/2 ounces of BBB,BB,1,2,3,4,6 shot at 1400 fps. Tel: 409-856-7277

Federal

Federal has designed a new rifle bullet. Called the "Deep-Shok," this spitzer boattail features a core that is mechanically locked into the jacket, providing 85% weight retention upon impact and reliable expansion at velocities from 1800-to-3000 fps. The Deep-Shok will be loaded in most popular hunting calibers from the 243 to the 300 Win. Mag. Added this year to the Premium Safari Rifle line is the 300 Rem. Ultra Mag. loaded with a 180-grain Trophy Bonded Bear Claw. Featuring a 300-grain Trophy Bonded HP, the 454 Casull cartridge its appearance in

.458(rifle), .475 and .500 (Linebaugh) calibers. Their spec sheets also contain recommended loading data. Check 'em out at www.castperformance.com

CCI/Speer

The 22 Magnum is certainly on the comeback trail, and CCI has added a 5th loading to their 22 Win.Mag. line. The new loading labeled the "TNT" features a 30-grain bullet with a cavernous hollowpoint at a velocity of 2200 fps. Missing from the handgun shotshell line has been the old 45 Colt. This year CCI has corrected that with a load of one hundred and fifty #9 shot at 1000 fps. In response to the need for lead-free, non-toxic range loads, Speer has introduced Lawman RHT ammunition for the 9mm, 40 S&W and 45 ACP. The new

loading consists of a sintered copper bullet that breaks up into small particles when it impacts the backstop. Comes with lead-free primers, too. The nose of the RHT bullet carries a raised cruciform brand that signals to the range master that it's O.K. ammo and to the police officer that it's not regular duty ammunition. To please the handgun hunting community, Speer is introducing a 240-grain Gold Dot 44 Magnum load at 1400 fps. Added to the Speer jacketed bullet component line are the 400-grain .475 Linebaugh Gold Dot; 85-grain .32 JHP; 225-grain .338 Grand Slam SP; 300-grain .375 African Grand Slam SP; 90-grain 6.5mm TNT HP; and 130-grain 7-30 Waters FNSP. And to keep the cowboys and cowgirls shooting, a new line of

Federal has a new hunting bullet--the Deep-Shok--providing improved penetration and expansion on big game.

Combining steel and tungsten-iron shot gives the duck hunter an added edge over decoys.

Federal's new 20-gauge steel loads are a welcome response to increased lead shot restrictions for upland game.

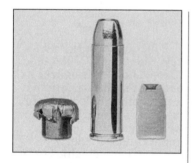

Federal's 454 Casull load features a tough 300-grain Trophy Bonded Bear Claw bullet for the largest game.

the Premium Handgun Hunting line. Combining #4 Tungsten-Iron and #2 steel pellets in the same shot column, Federal has designed a 12-gauge 3 1/2-inch non-toxic shell that costs less than Tungsten-Iron and Tungsten-Polymer and provides excellent patterning performance for near or far targets. New also to Federal's shotgun ammunition line are a 12-gauge spreader load with #8 or #8 1/2 shot; 12- and 20-gauge high velocity upland game steel loads for areas mandating the use of non-toxic shot; high velocity turkey loads for the 3-inch and 3 1/2-inch 10- and 12-gauges with buffered #4,5 and 6 copper-plated shot. In the handgun ammunition area, Federal has added to their American Eagle line reduced-lead target loads for the 9mm, 40 S&W and 45 Auto.
www.federalcartridge.com

Fiocchi

Fiocchi is well known for their hard nickel-plated shot loads that deliver exceptional patterns. This year Fiocchi is expanding the line with a three-inch 20-gauge 1 1/4 ounce load of #4,5 and 6; a Live Pigeon/FITASC 12-gauge load with 1 1/4 ounce of #7 1/2 or 8's at 1225 fps as well as a high velocity hunting load with 1 1/4 ounce of #4,5,6 and 7 at 1330. The steel shot line has been expanded greatly, and particularly intriguing are the 20-gauge loadings that include in the 3-inch case, 7/8-ounce of #2,3 and 4 steel at a sizzling 1500 fps.
www.fiocchiusa.com

Garrett Cartridges

Like to hunt with the 45/70 or 44 Magnum? Randy Garrett's custom ammunition for both calibers is legendary in big game circles for its ability to penetrate bone-and-body through-and-through. His latest 45/70 loading consists of a super-hard-cast, gas-checked, 530-grain bullet with a .360-inch meplat that moves out at 1550 fps from a 22" barrel. Normal accuracy for 3-shot groups at 100 yards from a lever gun is 1-1.5 inches. Complementing the 45/70 load is a new +P loading for the 44 Mag. featuring a 330-grain hard cast Hammerhead bullet at 1385 fps. Because of its length and chamber pressure, the new 44 Mag. loading is suitable only for Ruger Redhawks and Super Redhawks.
www.garrettcartridge.com

Hi-Tech Ammunition

Simply the best source I know of for surplus .223, .30, and .50 military bullets, brass, and powder. They have it all—FMJ, tracer, APIT--even military reference manuals on loading data and performance.
www.hi-techammo.com

Hodgdon Powder Co., Inc.

The Powder Meisters have done it again--two new powders for the reloading bench. LONGSHOT, a spherical shotgun powder, will definitely turn some heads. Due to its slow burning rate and long peak time, LONGSHOT is capable of propelling 1 1/8 ounces of lead shot to 1585 fps from a 2 3/4-inch 12-gauge hull. Suitable for all gauges other than the .410, it establishes a new benchmark for high performance shotgun propellants. And speaking about benchmarks,

Fiocchi is expanding it's line of hard nickel-plated shot loads for the coming hunting season.

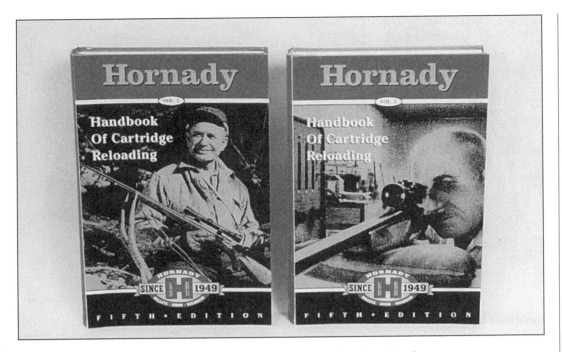

Hornady's fifth edition of its loading manual has been completely updated.

Hodgdon's other new powder is BENCHMARK—a small-grained, temperature-tolerant propellant for accurate little cases like the 22 PPC, 6mm BR, 222 and 223. BENCHMARK also turns in sterling performance in the 308 with 147-155-grain bullets. Hodgdon reports excellent results in the 7mm-08, 7x57, 30-30 and 35 Rem as well. To tailor their reloading data to the needs of computer fans, Hodgdon has released a new computer reloading program titled, BLAST ELECTRONIC MANUAL VERSION TWO. The program contains updated data from Hodgdon's *#27 Data Manual*, extensive shotshell and cowboy action data plus a condensed version of the Barnes external ballistics program. I found the shotshell portion of the program especially useful. For those without a computer, Hodgdon has also issued the *Basic Reloading Manual 2000* in printed form that covers 1,100 loads for 105 metallic cartridges and more than 1,400 of the latest shotshell recipes. www.hodgdon.com

Hornady

Hornady and Marlin joined together to bring shooters a new belted .45-caliber cartridge, the 450 Marlin. Chambered in Marlin's fast-handling 1895M Guide Gun, the 450 Marlin case launches a 350-grain FP bullet at 2100 fps from a 24 inch barrel. While many handloaders reach that level of performance with the 45/70 cartridge in modern rifles, the 450 Marlin permits ammunition companies to load and market what amounts to a +P 45/70 load without the concern that it will be accidentally fired in one of the many older and weaker 45/70s still in circulation. This is a banner year for Hornady and new cartridges with the introduction of loadings and new component bullets for the 376 Steyr, 475 Linebaugh, and 454 Casull. For slug gunners, there is a hot new factory load consisting of a 300-grain XTP bullet loaded to 2000 fps in a 2 3/4-inch case. Even Hornady's "Light Magnum" series has been expanded with the addition of 150-grain Super Shock Tip (SST) bullets in the 308 Win. and 30-06. Finally, Hornady's excellent two-volume reloading manual has been completely updated and should be available by the time you read this. www.hornady.com

Lazzeroni

What may be the ultimate 7mm long-range hunting cartridge, John Lazzeroni has introduced the 7.21 Firebird. Basically the large capacity 7.82(.308) Warbird case necked down to 7mm, the Firebird delivers a scorching 3,724 fps with a plated 140-grain Nosler Partition bullet. www.lazzeroni.com

Mountain State Muzzleloading Supplies, Inc.

Here's the one-stop shop for muzzleloading projectiles and components par excellence. If they don't have it, they can probably get it. Their massive new catalog sells for $4.00 and the price is refundable. www.mtnstatesmuzzle loading.com

Noble Sport

Imported by ADCO of Woburn, Massachusetts, Noble Sport now offers a complete line of 16 Vectan propellants for rifle, pistol and shotgun cartridges. More importantly, Nobel Sport has issued a comprehensive handloading manual in English that covers both U.S. and European calibers in depth. The manual is well written and includes valuable data that does not typically appear in U.S. manuals. The U.S. importer, ADCO, can be reached at (781) 935-1799. www.snpe.com

Norma

Remember Norma's Magnum Rifle Powder(MRP)? Well, this year Norma's given us a new blend called MRP-2 that is even slower and designed specifically for the big boomers—like the 30-387 Weatherby and 7mm STW. Norma reports MRP-2 is also ideal for extracting the utmost velocity from their new 6.5-284 case. www.norma.cc

Northern Precision

If you own one of Marlin's 45/70 or 450 Guide Guns, Northern Precision, working with Ken Waters, has developed a 400-grain, flat point, bonded-core bullet designed specifically for these great big game cartridges. Also new this year are a bonded-core, fast-expanding, 30-caliber White-Tail bullet in weights from 150-220-grains

Nosler's .224-caliber 60-grain Partition is designed specifically for hunting deer and antelope with high velocity .224s.

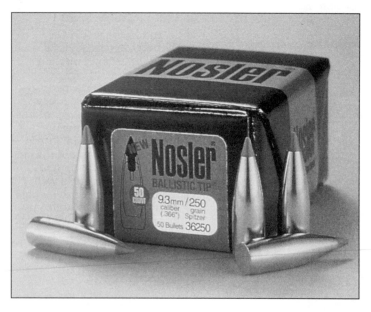

European and African hunters who shoot a lot of 9.3s now have a modern Ballistic Tip to work with.

PMC has integrated the famous Brenneke slug into its shotgun ammunition line.

made with J-4 jackets treated with Fastex to minimize fouling, and a series of bonded-core .375 pistol and rifle bullets in a variety of weights and tip forms. Tel: 315-493-1711

Nosler

Whether you agree with it or not, a lot of deer and antelope are successfully taken each year with high velocity .224 varmint rifles. A few years ago, Winchester introduced its 64-grain "deer" bullet in the 223, and this year, Nosler has introduced its smallest Partition bullet yet— a 60-grain .224-inch pill designed specifically for taking light big game with rifles in the 22-250 and 220 Swift class. At the other caliber extreme, Nosler has introduced a .416/400-grain Partition designed for heavy North American and African big game. In a very interesting move, Nosler has fielded "Moly-Free" Partition Gold bullets in .270/150-grain; 7mm/160-grain; .308/150- and 180-grain, and .338/250-grain. Moly has not been found to be a cure-all. Many members of the benchrest fraternity have stopped using moly-coated match bullets entirely while some custom barrel makers will not guarantee their products if used with moly-coated bullets. Expanding their J4 Competition line, Nosler has fielded a 30-caliber 155-grain HPBT. New Ballistic

Tip offerings this year include a 9.3mm/250-grain; 8mm/180-grain; 6mm/80-grain; and a .224/55-grain Ballistic Silvertip varmint bullet. www.nosler.com

Old Western Scrounger

Entering the millennium with the slogan "The impossible comes off the shelf; the miracle takes a bit longer," the OWS is at it again. With the reintroduction of the Model 1895 Winchester in 405 Winchester, everyone has been asking, "Who will be making the ammunition?" The Scrounger already does, of course, but this year he is introducing a loading featuring Woodleigh's terrific 300-grain, bonded-core SP/RN in Bertram brass headstamped "O.W.S. 405 Win." Just in time for the African big game season! And the good news continues. Also new this year are 2 7/8-inch 10-gauge smokeless and blackpowder shells plus some new 8-gauge loads from GameBore. And if you have a gun but no ammunition, the OWS is bringing back the 41 Remington derringer cartridge, the 221 Fireball, 222 Rem. Mag., 7.92x33 Kurz, 350 Rem. Mag., 357 Maximum, 401 Herter's Power Mag., and is importing S&B's 22 Savage H.P., 25-35 Win, and 7.62x25 Tokarev ammunition. Bullet casters, need pure tin? The OWS has it in 1-lb. blocks. Finally, the OWS has taken on

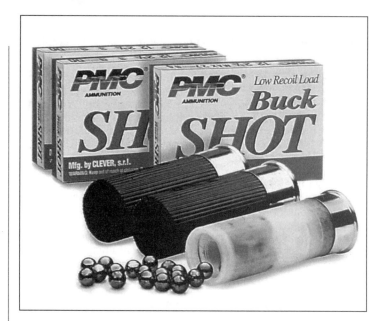

PMC's low recoil buckshot load is a favorite for tactical and home defense use.

The 22 Winchester Magnum is undergoing a sensational revival and PMC is offering their new SP and FMJ loads this year.

J. D. Jones' new 50 Peacekeeper cartridge provides 88% of the ballistics of the 50 BMG in a 13-pound rifle.

the whole Kynoch line of big bore ammunition. www.snowcrest.net/oldwest

PMC Ammunition

PMC has greatly expanded its shotshell line with low recoil 12-gauge loads for cowboy action shooting; heavy field loads for the 16-, 28- and .410-bores; clay target loads for the 28-gauge and .410; a 3-inch 12-gauge turkey load pushing #4 or #6 shot at 1210 fps; a 1 ounce Brenneke slug

load for the 12-gauge doing 1600 fps; high velocity 00 and #4 buck, and low recoil OO buck shells for the 12-gauge. In the rifle line, there's two new 22 Mag. loadings featuring either a 40- grain SP or FMJ at 1910 fps; a 180-grain SP and 174-grain FMJ load for the grand old 303 British; and a 170-grain SP loading for the 7x64 Brenneke. Finally, PMC is offering the increasingly popular 357 SIG with either a Starfire or FMJ 124-grain

bullet at 1350 fps. www.pmcammo.com

Precision Reloading, Inc.

Simply a great source for reloading components with a particular bent toward smoothbores. Beautiful catalog. www.precisionreloading.com

Ramshot

The Western Powders company of Miles City, Montana has come on line with nine handloading propellants for rifle, pistol and shotgun.

They're not widely distributed yet so see their data at: www.westernpowders.com

RCBS

For the owners of 310 Cadet Martinis or 310s that have been rechambered to 32/20—owners who have been frustrated in their search for accurate bullets— RCBS brings great news. They have catalogued a mould that was formerly supplied only to N.D.F.S. in England. The actual specifications for the new 310 Cadet mould are .323-inch nose and .312-inch heel—not the .310-inch

diameter as reflected in the new catalog. www.rcbs.com

Remington

The millennium innovation award in components has to go to Remington for the commercial introduction of their large rifle electronic primer—the EtronX. We've seen electronic primers in caseless sporting ammunition but not as reloading components. Better yet, the EtronX primer provides the handloader with the same performance and pressure level achieved with standard 9 1/2s. It was only a matter of time until Big Green necked its Ultra Mag case up and down. This year it's UP as the 338 Ultra Mag loaded with a 250-grain Swift A-Frame bullet at 2900 fps. There are two new loadings for the 300 Utra Mag—a 200-grain Nosler Partition at 3075 and a 180-grain Swift Scirocco at 3250 fps. The little green-tipped 22 Win. Mag. load featuring a 33-grain Hornady V-Max boat-tail bullet at 2000 fps is here--it's good-looking and accurate. Speaking about rimfire, Remington and Eley, Ltd. are partnering to

SSK's complete lineup of .50-caliber offerings, from the diminutive 50 American Eagle to the 50 Sharps 3 1/4-inch.

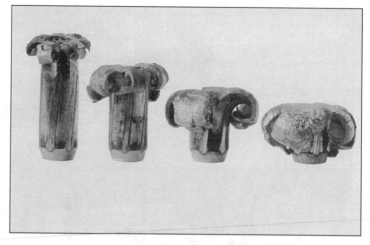

Remington is already loading Swift's bonded-core, polymer-tipped Scirocco bullet.

Swift's Scirocco bullet exhibits excellent expansion over a wide range of velocities while maintaining jacket/core integrity.

provide three grades of target 22 rimfire ammunition for serious competitors. Finally, Remington is fielding a much needed 20-gauge Copper Solid Sabot Slug weighing 5/8-ounce and driven at a velocity of 1500 fps.
www.remington.com

Schroeder

For the owners of Model 591/592 Remingtons chambered for the utterly obsolete 5mm Remington rimfire cartridge, there is hope. Steve Schroeder is offering a simple conversion kit, cases and three bullet types to convert those rimfires into delightful 5mm centerfires. I've done the

conversion, and it works perfectly. Taking only 4.5-5.0 grains of Win. 296 powder, the new little 5mm centerfire at 2000 fps is a real hoot--the perfect suburban varmint cartridge. Schroeder also offers a complete selection of obsolete jacketed bullet forms for oddballs like the 7mm and 8mm Nambu's and 351 Win. Tel: (619) 423-8124

Sierra

Combining their MatchKing jackets with an explosive acetyl resin tip, Sierra has expanded its BlitzKing varmint bullet line to include a 6mm 55-grain flat base; a 6mm 70-grain boattail; and in .224-caliber, boattail BlitzKings in 50-grain

and 55-grain and a 40-grain flat base. Available in bulk boxes of 100 and 500, the BlitzKings can be ordered with a moly-coating in the 500 bulk pack. Speaking of bulk packs, the whole range of Sierra MatchKings can now be ordered in boxes of 500 with many of the more popular bullets available with moly-coating. To clarify a vital issue, the new catalog clearly indicates the best barrel twists required to stabilize Sierra's superb long-range specialty bullets.
www.sierrabullets.com

SSK Industries

J.D. Jones has been as creative as ever during the last twelve months. His latest

brainchild is the 50 Peacekeeper—the 460 Weatherby opened up to .50-caliber and set-up for .50-caliber BMG and hunting bullets. Performance of this new cartridge is sensational in a 13-pound gun with a 23-inch barrel giving fully 88% of the velocity normally obtained in a full 50 BMG chambering; for example, 2400 fps with a 650-grain bullet and 2206 fps with a 750-grain. SSK currently offers a complete selection of .50-caliber cartridges from the diminutive 50 American Eagle through the 50x3 1/4-inch Sharps, and for big things that need killing, the 700 JDJ and the 950 JDJ--the latter slinging a 3200-grain bullet. Great new web site at www.sskindustries.com

Swift Bullet Company

Combining a pure copper jacket, a bonded lead core, a polymer tip, a 15-degree boattail and a secant ogive, Swift's new Scirocco bullet is being offered in a .30-caliber 180- and 165-grain form; a .270-caliber 130-grain; 7mm 150-grain; and a .338-caliber weight that is yet to be determined. Swift plans on offering the Scirocco line in every caliber from .224 through .338, and as we've seen Remington is already loading the new bullet in their .300 Ultra Mag. Tel: (785) 754-3959

VihtaVuori/Lapua

Imported by Kaltron/Pettibone of Bensenville,

Winchester's component bullets and brass are now bulk-packed for added convenience and cost savings to the handloader.

Winchester's redesigned "AA" hull, featured in loads like these Super Handicaps, will give extended life at the reloading bench.

Winchester's Supreme surface coating technology delivers superior ballistic performance and higher velocities in its Power Point Plus ammunition.

Illinois, VihtaVuori has just released the 3rd edition of its reloading manual. The manual has been thoroughly updated and includes data for newer cartridges like the 30-378 Weatherby, 357 SIG and 50 AE. The manual is an entertaining and informative read with information about Scandinavian wildcat cartridges unavailable elsewhere. Lapua has some interesting new "extra-long range shooting cartridges" that include the 6mm BR Norma, the 308 Win, and the 338 Lapua Mag. Reach Kaltron/Pettibone at ((630) 350-1116. VihtaVuori-www.nammo.fi and Lapua www.lapua.com

Winchester

Labeling the line, the "Official Ammunition of the New Millennium," Winchester has been busy. The justifiably famous "AA" hull just got a face-lift. No longer is it "compression-formed." Searching for a way to improve its durability as a highly prized case for reloading, the new "AA 2000" is made from an extruded tube of super high strength plastic and a separate polymer base wad and head. The internal volume of the new AA hull is identical to the old so identical reloading data can be used. Most importantly, Winchester claims the new hull will stand up to more sizing and reloading than any hull currently on the market. There are some surprises not even reflected in the current catalog. The AA Super-Handicap load has been souped up to 1290 fps featuring hard shot with a 6% antimony content. The AA Super-Sport sporting clays loads have been given a shot of adrenaline with the 12-gauge one ounce #7 1/2 and #8 loads doing 1350 fps and the 20-gauge one ounce loads achieving 1165 fps. Gone from the line is the "Upland Game" loads that this year are replaced by the return of the "Super-X" brand. The shells are improved, too, featuring AA wads and base wads. Winchester and Bismuth have split the blanket, so Bismuth will disappear from the line. In the Supreme rifle area, Power-Point Plus loads for the 270 Winchester and 7mm-08 Remington have been added as well as a 168-grain match load for the 308 Winchester. Lots of interesting new handgun ammunition including WinClean loads for the 380 Auto and 357 Mag. Bowing to the wishes of the handloading community, Winchester is marketing bulk "consumer packs" (read "plastic bags") full of handgun and rifle bullets as well as a complete selection of unprimed handgun and rifle brass. Finally, the component powder line has been streamlined to include only Win. 231, 296, Super-Target, Super-Field, 748, 760 and WXR(replacing Magnum Rifle powder). If you load Action Pistol, AA Plus, Super-Lite, 540 or Magnum Rifle powder, you better stock-up now. ●

AVERAGE CENTERFIRE RIFLE CARTRIDGE BALLISTICS AND PRICES

Many manufacturers do not supply suggested retail prices. Others did not get their pricing to us before press time. All pricing can vary dependent on the exact brand and style of ammo selected and/or the retail outlet from which you make your purchase. Pricing has been rounded to the nearest dollar and represents our best estimate of average pricing. An * after the cartridge means these loads are available with Nosler Partition or Swift A-Frame bullets. Listed pricing may or may not reflect this bullet type. ** = these are packed 50 to box, all others are 20 to box. Wea. Mag.= Weatherby Magnum. Spfd. = Springfield. A-A-Sq. = A-Square. N.E.=Nitro Express.

Cartridge	Bullet Weight Grains	VELOCITY (fps)					ENERGY (ft. lbs.)					TRAJ. (in.)				Approx. Price per box
		Muzzle	100 yds.	200 yds.	300 yds.	400 yds.	Muzzle	100 yds.	200 yds.	300 yds.	400 yds.	100 yds.	200 yds.	300 yds.	400 yds.	
17 17 Remington	25	4040	3284	2644	2086	1606	906	599	388	242	143	+2.0	+1.7	-4.0	-17.0	$17
221 Fireball	50	2800	2137	1580	1180	988	870	507	277	155	109	+0.0	-7.0	-28.0	NA	$14
22 22 Hornet	34	3050	2132	1415	1017	852	700	343	151	78	55	+0.0	-6.6	-15.5	-29.9	NA
22 Hornet	35	3100	2278	1601	1135	929	747	403	199	100	67	+2.75	0.0	-16.9	-60.4	NA
22 Hornet	45	2690	2042	1502	1128	948	723	417	225	127	90	+0.0	-7.7	-31.0	NA	$27**
218 Bee	46	2760	2102	1550	1155	961	788	451	245	136	94	+0.0	-7.2	-29.0	NA	$46**
222 Remington	40	3600	3117	2673	2269	1911	1151	863	634	457	324	++1.07	0.0	-6.13	-18.9	NA
222 Remington	50	3140	2602	2123	1700	1350	1094	752	500	321	202	++2.0	-0.4	-11.0	-33.0	$11
222 Remington	55	3020	2562	2147	1773	1451	1114	801	563	384	257	+2.0	-0.4	-11.0	-33.0	$12
22 PPC	52	3400	2930	2510	2130	NA	1335	990	730	525	NA	+2.0	1.4	-5.0	NA	NA
223 Remington	40	3650	3010	2450	1950	1530	1185	805	535	340	265	+2.0	+1.0	-6.0	-22.0	$14
223 Remington	40	3800	3305	2845	2424	2044	1282	970	719	522	371	0.84	0.0	-5.34	-16.6	NA
223 Remington	50	3300	2874	2484	2130	1809	1209	917	685	504	363	1.37	0.0	-7.05	-21.8	NA
223 Remington	52/53	3330	2882	2477	2106	1770	1305	978	722	522	369	+2.0	+0.6	-6.5	-21.5	$14
223 Remington	55	3240	2748	2305	1906	1556	1282	922	649	444	296	+2.0	-0.2	-9.0	-27.0	$12
223 Remington	60	3100	2712	2355	2026	1726	1280	979	739	547	397	+2.0	+0.2	-8.0	-24.7	$16
223 Remington	64	3020	2621	2256	1920	1619	1296	977	723	524	373	+2.0	-0.2	-9.3	-23.0	$14
223 Remington	69	3000	2720	2460	2210	1980	1380	1135	925	750	600	+2.0	+0.8	-5.8	-17.5	$15
223 Remington	75	2790	2554	2330	2119	1926	1296	1086	904	747	617	2.37	0.0	-8.75	-25.1	NA
223 Remington	77	2750	2584	2354	2169	1992	1293	1110	948	804	679	1.93	0.0	-8.2	-23.8	NA
222 Rem. Mag.	55	3240	2748	2305	1906	1556	1282	922	649	444	296	+2.0	-0.2	-9.0	-27.0	$14
225 Winchester	55	3570	3066	2616	2208	1838	1556	1148	836	595	412	+2.0	+1.0	-5.0	-20.0	$19
224 Wea. Mag.	55	3650	3192	2780	2403	2057	1627	1244	943	705	516	+2.0	+1.2	-4.0	-17.0	$32
22-250 Rem.	40	4000	3320	2720	2200	1740	1420	980	660	430	265	+2.0	+1.8	-3.0	-16.0	$14
22-250 Rem.	50	3725	3264	2641	2455	2103	1540	1183	896	669	491	0.89	0.0	-5.23	-16.3	NA
22-250 Rem.	52/55	3680	3137	2656	2222	1832	1654	1201	861	603	410	+2.0	+1.3	-4.0	-17.0	$13
22-250 Rem.	60	3600	3195	2826	2485	2169	1727	1360	1064	823	627	+2.0	+2.0	-2.4	-12.3	$19
220 Swift	40	4200	3678	3190	2739	2329	1566	1201	904	666	482	+0.51	0.0	-4.0	-12.9	NA
220 Swift	50	3780	3158	2617	2135	1710	1586	1107	760	506	325	+2.0	+1.4	-4.4	-17.9	$20
220 Swift	50	3850	3396	2970	2576	2215	1645	1280	979	736	545	0.74	0.0	-4.84	-15.1	NA
220 Swift	55	3800	3370	2990	2630	2310	1765	1390	1090	850	650	0.8	0.0	-4.7	-14.4	NA
220 Swift	55	3650	3194	2772	2384	2035	1627	1246	939	694	506	+2.0	+2.0	-2.6	-13.4	$19
220 Swift	60	3600	3199	2824	2475	2156	1727	1364	1063	816	619	+2.0	+1.6	-4.1	-13.1	$19
22 Savage H.P.	71	2790	2340	1930	1570	1280	1225	860	585	390	190	+2.0	-1.0	-10.4	-35.7	NA
6mm (24) 6mm BR Rem.	100	2550	2310	2083	1870	1671	1444	1185	963	776	620	+2.5	-0.6	-11.8	NA	$22
6mm Norma BR	107	2822	2667	2517	2372	2229	1893	1690	1506	1337	1181	+1.73	0.0	-7.24	-20.6	NA
6mm PPC	70	3140	2750	2400	2070	NA	1535	1175	895	665	NA	+2.0	+1.4	-5.0	NA	NA
243 Winchester	55	4025	3597	3209	2853	2525	1978	1579	1257	994	779	+0.6	0.00	-4.0	-12.2	NA
243 Winchester	60	3600	3110	2660	2260	1890	1725	1285	945	680	475	+2.0	+1.8	-3.3	-15.5	$17
243 Winchester	70	3400	3040	2700	2390	2100	1795	1435	1135	890	685	1.1	0.0	-5.9	-18.0	NA
243 Winchester	75/80	3350	2955	2593	2259	1951	1993	1551	1194	906	676	+2.0	+0.9	-5.0	-19.0	$16
243 Winchester	85	3320	3070	2830	2600	2380	2080	1770	1510	1280	1070	+2.0	+1.2	-4.0	-14.0	$18
243 Winchester	90	3120	2871	2635	2411	2199	1946	1647	1388	1162	966	1.4	0.0	-6.4	-18.8	NA
243 Winchester*	100	2960	2697	2449	2215	1993	1945	1615	1332	1089	882	+2.5	+1.2	-6.0	-20.0	$16
243 Winchester	105	2920	2689	2470	2261	2062	1988	1686	1422	1192	992	+2.5	+1.6	-5.0	-18.4	$21
243 Light Mag.	100	3100	2839	2592	2358	2138	2133	1790	1491	1235	1014	+1.5	0.0	-6.8	-19.8	NA
6mm Remington	80	3470	3064	2694	2352	2036	2139	1667	1289	982	736	+2.0	+1.1	-5.0	-17.0	$16
6mm Remington	100	3100	2829	2573	2332	2104	2133	1777	1470	1207	983	+2.5	+1.6	-5.0	-17.0	$16
6mm Remington	105	3060	2822	2596	2381	2177	2105	1788	1512	1270	1059	+2.5	+1.1	-3.3	-15.0	$21
6mm Rem. Light Mag.	100	3250	2997	2756	2528	2311	2345	1995	1687	1418	1186	1.59	0.0	-6.33	-18.3	NA
6.17(.243) Spitfire	100	3350	3122	2905	2698	2501	2493	2164	1874	1617	1389	2.4	3.20	0	-8	NA
240 Wea. Mag.	87	3500	3202	2924	2663	2416	2366	1980	1651	1370	1127	+2.0	+2.0	-2.0	-12.0	$32
240 Wea. Mag.	100	3395	3106	2835	2581	2339	2559	2142	1785	1478	1215	+2.5	+2.8	-2.0	-11.0	$43
25 25-20 Win.	86	1460	1194	1030	931	858	407	272	203	165	141	0.0	-23.5	NA	NA	$32**
25-35 Win.	117	2230	1866	1545	1282	1097	1292	904	620	427	313	+2.5	-4.2	-26.0	NA	$24
250 Savage	100	2820	2504	2210	1936	1684	1765	1392	1084	832	630	+2.5	+0.4	-9.0	-28.0	$17

Many manufacturers do not supply suggested retail prices. Others did not get their pricing to us before press time. All pricing can vary dependent on the exact brand and style of ammo selected and/or the retail outlet from which you make your purchase. Pricing has been rounded to the nearest dollar and represents our best estimate of average pricing. An * after the cartridge means these loads are available with Nosler Partition or Swift A-Frame bullets. Listed pricing may or may not reflect this bullet type. ** = these are packed 50 to box, all others are 20 to box. Wea. Mag.= Weatherby Magnum. Spfd. = Springfield. A-A-Sq. = A-Square. N.E.=Nitro Express.

Cartridge	Bullet Weight Grains	VELOCITY (fps)					ENERGY (ft. lbs.)					TRAJ. (in.)				Approx. Price per box
		Muzzle	100 yds.	200 yds.	300 yds.	400 yds.	Muzzle	100 yds.	200 yds.	300 yds.	400 yds.	100 yds.	200 yds.	300 yds.	400 yds.	
257 Roberts	100	2980	2661	2363	2085	1827	1972	1572	1240	965	741	+2.5	-0.8	-5.2	-21.6	$20
257 Roberts+P	117	2780	2411	2071	1761	1488	2009	1511	1115	806	576	+2.5	-0.2	-10.2	-32.6	$18
257 Roberts+P	120	2780	2560	2360	2160	1970	2060	1750	1480	1240	1030	+2.5	+1.2	-6.4	-23.6	$22
257 Roberts	122	2600	2331	2078	1842	1625	1831	1472	1169	919	715	+2.5	0.0	-10.6	-31.4	$21
257 Light Mag.	117	2940	2694	2460	2240	2031	2245	1885	1572	1303	1071	+1.7	0.0	-7.6	-21.8	NA
25-06 Rem.	87	3440	2995	2591	2222	1884	2286	1733	1297	954	686	+2.0	+1.1	-2.5	-14.4	$17
25-06 Rem.	90	3440	3043	2680	2344	2034	2364	1850	1435	1098	827	+2.0	+1.8	-3.3	-15.6	$17
25-06 Rem.	100	3230	2893	2580	2287	2014	2316	1858	1478	1161	901	+2.0	+0.8	-5.7	-18.9	$17
25-06 Rem.	117	2990	2770	2570	2370	2190	2320	2000	1715	1465	1246	+2.5	+1.0	-7.9	-26.6	$19
25-06 Rem.*	120	2990	2730	2484	2252	2032	2382	1985	1644	1351	1100	+2.5	+1.2	-5.3	-19.6	$17
25-06 Rem.	122	2930	2706	2492	2289	2095	2325	1983	1683	1419	1189	+2.5	+1.8	-4.5	-17.5	$23
257 Wea. Mag.	87	3825	3456	3118	2805	2513	2826	2308	1870	1520	1220	+2.0	+2.7	-0.3	-7.6	$32
257 Wea. Mag.	100	3555	3237	2941	2665	2404	2806	2326	1920	1576	1283	+2.5	+3.2	0.0	-8.0	$32
257 Scramjet	100	3745	3450	3173	2912	2666	3114	2643	2235	1883	1578	+2.1	+2.77	0.0	-6.93	NA
6.5x50mm Jap.	139	2360	2160	1970	1790	1620	1720	1440	1195	985	810	+2.5	-1.0	-13.5	NA	NA
6.5x50mm Jap.	156	2070	1830	1610	1430	1260	1475	1155	900	695	550	+2.5	-4.0	-23.8	NA	NA
6.5x52mm Car.	139	2580	2360	2160	1970	1790	2045	1725	1440	1195	985	+2.5	-1.0	-13.9	NA	NA
6.5x52mm Car.	156	2430	2170	1930	1700	1500	2045	1630	1285	1005	780	+2.5	0.0	-8.2	-23.9	NA
6.5x55mm Light Mag.	129	2750	2549	2355	2171	1994	2166	1860	1589	1350	1139	+2.0	0.0	-8.2	-23.9	NA
6.5x55mm Swe.	140	2550	NA	NA	NA	NA	2020	NA	NA	NA	NA	NA	NA	NA	NA	$18
6.5x55mm Swe.*	139/140	2850	2640	2440	2250	2070	2525	2170	1855	1575	1330	+2.5	+1.6	-5.4	-18.9	$18
6.5x55mm Swe.	156	2650	2370	2110	1870	1650	2425	1950	1550	1215	945	+2.5	0.0	-10.3	-30.6	NA
260 Remington	125	2875	2669	2473	2285	2105	2294	1977	1697	1449	1230	1.71	0.0	-7.4	-21.4	NA
260 Remington	140	2750	2544	2347	2158	1979	2351	2011	1712	1448	1217	+2.2	0.0	-8.6	-24.6	NA
6.5-284 Norma	142	3025	2890	2758	2631	2507	2886	2634	2400	2183	1982	1.13	0.0	-5.7	-16.4	NA
6.71 (264) Phantom	120	3150	2929	2718	2517	2325	2645	2286	1969	1698	1440	+1.3	0.0	-6.0	-17.5	NA
6.5 Rem. Mag.	120	3210	2905	2621	2353	2102	2745	2248	1830	1475	1177	+2.5	+1.7	-4.1	-16.3	Disc.
264 Win. Mag.	140	3030	2782	2548	2326	2114	2854	2406	2018	1682	1389	+2.5	+1.4	-5.1	-18.0	$24
6.71 (264) Blackbird	140	3480	3261	3053	2855	2665	3766	3307	2899	2534	2208	+2.4	+3.1	0.0	-7.4	NA
270 Winchester	100	3430	3021	2649	2305	1988	2612	2027	1557	1179	877	+2.0	+1.0	-4.9	-17.5	$17
270 Winchester	130	3060	2776	2510	2259	2022	2702	2225	1818	1472	1180	+2.5	+1.4	-5.3	-18.2	$17
270 Win. Supreme	130	3150	2881	2628	2388	2161	2865	2396	1993	1646	1348	1.3	0.0	-6.4	-18.9	NA
270 Winchester	135	3000	2780	2570	2369	2178	2697	2315	1979	1682	1421	+2.5	+1.4	-6.0	-17.6	$23
270 Winchester*	140	2940	2700	2480	2260	2060	2685	2270	1905	1590	1315	+2.5	+1.8	-4.6	-17.9	$20
270 Win. Light Magnum	130	3215	2998	2790	2590	2400	2983	2594	2246	1936	1662	1.21	0.0	-5.83	-17.0	NA
270 Winchester*	150	2850	2585	2336	2100	1879	2705	2226	1817	1468	1175	+2.5	+1.2	-6.5	-22.0	$17
270 Win. Supreme	150	2930	2693	2468	2254	2051	2860	2416	2030	1693	1402	1.7	0.0	-7.4	-21.6	NA
270 Wea. Mag.	100	3760	3380	3033	2712	2412	3139	2537	2042	1633	1292	+2.0	+2.4	-1.2	-10.1	$32
270 Wea. Mag.	130	3375	3119	2878	2649	2432	3287	2808	2390	2026	1707	+2.5	-2.9	-0.9	-9.9	$32
270 Wea. Mag.*	150	3245	3036	2837	2647	2465	3507	3070	2681	2334	2023	+2.5	+2.6	-1.8	-11.4	$47
7mm BR	140	2216	2012	1821	1643	1481	1525	1259	1031	839	681	+2.0	-3.7	-20.0	NA	$23
7mm Mauser*	139/140	2660	2435	2221	2018	1827	2199	1843	1533	1266	1037	+2.5	0.0	-9.6	-27.7	$17
7mm Mauser	145	2690	2442	2206	1985	1777	2334	1920	1568	1268	1017	+2.5	+0.1	-9.6	-28.3	$18
7mm Mauser	154	2690	2490	2300	2120	1940	2475	2120	1810	1530	1285	+2.5	+0.8	-7.5	-23.5	$17
7mm Mauser	175	2440	2137	1857	1603	1382	2313	1774	1340	998	742	+2.5	-1.7	-16.1	NA	$17
7x57 Light Mag.	139	2970	2730	2503	2287	2082	2722	2301	1933	1614	1337	+1.6	0.0	-7.2	-21.0	NA
7x30 Waters	120	2700	2300	1930	1600	1330	1940	1405	990	685	470	+2.5	-0.2	-12.3	NA	$18
7mm-08 Rem.	120	3000	2725	2467	2223	1992	2398	1979	1621	1316	1058	+2.0	0.0	-7.6	-22.3	$18
7mm-08 Rem.*	140	2860	2625	2402	2189	1988	2542	2142	1793	1490	1228	+2.5	+0.8	-6.9	-21.9	$18
7mm-08 Rem.	154	2715	2510	2315	2128	1950	2520	2155	1832	1548	1300	+2.5	+1.0	-7.0	-22.7	$23
7mm-08 Light Mag.	139	3000	2790	2590	2399	2216	2777	2403	2071	1776	1515	+1.5	0.0	-6.7	-19.4	NA
7x64mm Bren.	140	Not Yet Announced														$17
7x64mm Bren.	154	2820	2610	2420	2230	2050	2720	2335	1995	1695	1430	+2.5	+1.4	-5.7	-19.9	NA
7x64mm Bren.*	160	2850	2669	2495	2327	2166	2885	2530	2211	1924	1667	+2.5	+1.6	-4.8	-17.8	$24
7x64mm Bren.	175	Not Yet Announced														$17

25 cont.

6.5

27

7mm

Many manufacturers do not supply suggested retail prices. Others did not get their pricing to us before press time. All pricing can vary dependent on the exact brand and style of ammo selected and/or the retail outlet from which you make your purchase. Pricing has been rounded to the nearest dollar and represents our best estimate of average pricing. An * after the cartridge means these loads are available with Nosler Partition or Swift A-Frame bullets. Listed pricing may or may not reflect this bullet type. ** = these are packed 50 to box, all others are 20 to box. Wea. Mag. = Weatherby Magnum. Spfd. = Springfield. A-A-Sq. = A-Square. N.E.=Nitro Express.

Cartridge	Bullet Weight Grains	VELOCITY (fps)					ENERGY (ft. lbs.)					TRAJ. (in.)				Approx. Price per box
		Muzzle	100 yds.	200 yds.	300 yds.	400 yds.	Muzzle	100 yds.	200 yds.	300 yds.	400 yds.	100 yds.	200 yds.	300 yds.	400 yds.	
284 Winchester	150	2860	2595	2344	2108	1886	2724	2243	1830	1480	1185	+2.5	+0.8	-7.3	-23.2	$24
280 Remington	120	3150	2866	2599	2348	2110	2643	2188	1800	1468	1186	+2.0	+0.6	-6.0	-17.9	$17
280 Remington	140	3000	2758	2528	2309	2102	2797	2363	1986	1657	1373	+2.5	+1.4	-5.2	-18.3	$17
280 Remington*	150	2890	2624	2373	2135	1912	2781	2293	1875	1518	1217	+2.5	+0.8	-7.1	-22.6	$17
280 Remington	160	2840	2637	2442	2556	2078	2866	2471	2120	1809	1535	+2.5	+0.8	-6.7	-21.0	$20
280 Remington	165	2820	2510	2220	1950	1701	2913	2308	1805	1393	1060	+2.5	+0.4	-8.8	-26.5	$17
7x61mm S&H Sup.	154	3060	2720	2400	2100	1820	3200	2520	1965	1505	1135	+1.8	-5.0	-19.8		NA
7mm Dakota	160	3200	3001	2811	2630	2455	3637	3200	2808	2456	2140	+2.1	+1.9	-2.8	-12.5	NA
7mm Rem. Mag.*	139/140	3150	2930	2710	2510	2320	3085	2660	2290	1960	1670	+2.5	+2.4	-2.4	-12.7	$21
7mm Rem. Mag.	150/154	3110	2830	2085	2320	2085	3221	2667	2196	1792	1448	+2.5	+1.6	-4.6	-16.5	$21
7mm Rem. Mag.*	160/162	2950	2730	2520	2320	2120	3090	2650	2250	1910	1600	+2.5	+1.8	-4.4	-17.8	$34
7mm Rem. Mag.	165	2900	2699	2507	2324	2147	3081	2669	2303	1978	1689	+2.5	+1.2	-5.9	-19.0	$28
7mm Rem Mag.	175	2860	2645	2440	2244	2057	3178	2718	2313	1956	1644	+2.5	+1.0	-6.5	-20.7	$21
7mm Wea. Mag.	140	3225	2970	2729	2501	2283	3233	2741	2315	1943	1621	+2.5	+2.0	-3.2	-14.0	$35
7mm Wea. Mag.	154	3260	3023	2799	2586	2382	3539	3044	2609	2227	1890	+2.5	+2.8	-1.5	-10.8	$32
7mm Wea. Mag.*	160	3200	3004	2816	2637	2464	3637	3205	2817	2469	2156	+2.5	+2.7	-1.5	-10.6	$47
7mm Wea. Mag.	165	2950	2747	2553	2367	2189	3188	2765	2388	2053	1756	+2.5	+1.8	-4.2	-16.4	$43
7mm Wea. Mag.	175	2910	2693	2486	2288	2098	3293	2818	2401	2033	1711	+2.5	+1.2	-5.9	-19.4	$35
7.21(.284) Tomahawk	140	3300	3118	2943	2774	2612	3386	3022	2693	2393	2122	2.3	3.20	0.0	-7.7	NA
7mm STW	140	3325	3064	2818	2585	2364	3436	2918	2468	2077	1737	+2.3	+1.8	-3.0	-13.1	NA
7mm STW Supreme	160	3150	2894	2652	2422	2204	3526	2976	2499	2085	1727	1.3	0.0	-6.3	-18.5	NA
7mm Firehawk	140	3625	3373	3135	2909	2695	4084	3536	3054	2631	2258	+2.2	+2.9	0.0	-7.03	NA
7.21 (.284) Firebird	140	3750	3522	3306	3101	2905	4372	3857	3399	2990	2625	1.6	2.4	0.0	-6	NA
30 Carbine	110	1990	1567	1236	1035	923	977	600	373	262	208	0.0	-13.5	NA	NA	$28**
303 Savage	190	1890	1612	1327	1183	1055	1507	1096	794	591	469	+2.5	-7.6	NA	NA	$24
30 Remington	170	2120	1822	1555	1328	1153	1696	1253	913	666	502	+2.5	-4.7	-26.3	NA	$20
7.62x39mm Rus.	123/125	2300	2030	1780	1550	1350	1445	1125	860	655	500	+2.5	-2.0	-17.5	NA	$13
30-30 Win.	55	3400	2693	2085	1570	1187	1412	886	521	301	172	+2.0	0.0	-10.2	-35.0	$18
30-30 Win.	125	2570	2090	1660	1320	1080	1830	1210	770	480	320	-2.0	-2.6	-19.9	NA	$13
30-30 Win.	150	2390	1973	1605	1303	1095	1902	1296	858	565	399	+2.5	-3.2	-22.5	NA	$13
30-30 Win. Supreme	150	2480	2095	1747	1446	1209	2049	1462	1017	697	487	0.0	-6.5	-24.5		NA
30-30 Win.	160	2300	1997	1719	1473	1268	1879	1416	1050	771	571	+2.5	-2.9	-20.2	NA	$18
30-30 PMC Cowboy	170	1300	1198	1121			638	474				0.0	-27.0			NA
30-30 Win.*	170	2200	1895	1619	1381	1191	1827	1355	989	720	535	+2.5	-5.8	-23.6	NA	$13
300 Savage	150	2630	2354	2094	1853	1631	2303	1845	1462	1143	886	+2.5	-0.4	-10.1	-30.7	$17
300 Savage	180	2350	2137	1935	1754	1570	2207	1825	1496	1217	985	+2.5	-1.6	-15.2	NA	$17
30-40 Krag	180	2430	2213	2007	1813	1632	2360	1957	1610	1314	1064	+2.5	-1.4	-13.8	NA	$18
7.65x53mm Arg.	180	2590	2390	2200	2010	1830	2685	2280	1925	1615	1345	+2.5	0.0	-27.6	NA	NA
307 Winchester	150	2760	2321	1924	1575	1289	2530	1795	1233	826	554	+2.5	-1.5	-13.6	NA	Disc.
307 Winchester	180	2510	2179	1874	1599	1362	2519	1898	1404	1022	742	+2.5	-1.6	-15.6	NA	$20
7.5x55 Swiss	180	2650	2450	2250	2060	1880	2805	2390	2020	1700	1415	+2.5	+0.6	-8.1	-24.9	NA
308 Winchester	55	3770	3215	2726	2286	1888	1735	1262	907	638	435	-2.0	+1.4	-3.8	-15.8	$22
308 Winchester	150	2820	2533	2263	2009	1774	2648	2137	1705	1344	1048	+2.5	+0.4	-8.5	-26.1	$17
308 Winchester	165	2700	2440	2194	1963	1748	2670	2180	1763	1411	1199	+2.5	0.0	-9.7	-28.5	$20
308 Winchester	168	2680	2493	2314	2143	1979	2678	2318	1998	1713	1460	+2.5	0.0	-8.9	-25.3	$18
308 Winchester	178	2620	2415	2220	2034	1857	2713	2306	1948	1635	1363	+2.5	0.0	-9.6	-27.6	$23
308 Winchester*	180	2620	2393	2178	1974	1782	2743	2288	1896	1557	1269	+2.5	-0.2	-10.2	-28.5	$17
308 Light Mag.*	150	2980	2703	2442	2195	1964	2959	2433	1986	1606	1285	+1.6	0.0	-7.5	-22.2	NA
308 Light Mag.	165	2870	2658	2456	2263	2078	3019	2589	2211	1877	1583	+1.7	0.0	-7.5	-21.8	NA
308 High Energy	165	2870	2600	2350	2120	1890	3020	2485	2030	1640	1310	+1.8	0.0	-8.2	-24.0	NA
308 Light Mag.	168	2870	2658	2456	2263	2078	3019	2589	2211	1877	1583	+1.7	0.0	-7.5	-21.8	NA
308 High Energy	180	2740	2550	2370	2200	2030	3000	2600	2245	1925	1645	+1.9	0.0	-8.2	-23.5	NA
30-06 Spfd.	55	4080	3485	2965	2502	2083	2033	1483	1074	764	530	+2.0	+1.9	-2.1	-11.7	$22
30-06 Spfd.	125	3140	2780	2447	2138	1853	2736	2145	1662	1279	953	+2.0	+1.0	-6.2	-21.0	$17

7mm cont.

30

Many manufacturers do not supply suggested retail prices. Others did not get their pricing to us before press time. All pricing can vary dependent on the exact brand and style of ammo selected and/or the retail outlet from which you make your purchase. Pricing has been rounded to the nearest dollar and represents our best estimate of average pricing. An * after the cartridge means these loads are available with Nosler Partition or Swift A-Frame bullets. Listed pricing may or may not reflect this bullet type. ** = these are packed 50 to box, all others are 20 to box. Wea. Mag.= Weatherby Magnum. Spfd. = Springfield. A-A-Sq. = A-Square. N.E.=Nitro Express.

Cartridge	Bullet Weight Grains	VELOCITY (fps)					ENERGY (ft. lbs.)					TRAJ. (in.)				Approx. Price per box
		Muzzle	100 yds.	200 yds.	300 yds.	400 yds.	Muzzle	100 yds.	200 yds.	300 yds.	400 yds.	100 yds.	200 yds.	300 yds.	400 yds.	
30-06 Spfd.	150	2910	2617	2342	2083	1853	2820	2281	1827	1445	1135	+2.5	+0.8	-7.2	-23.4	$17
30-06 Spfd.	152	2910	2654	2413	2184	1968	2858	2378	1965	1610	1307	+2.5	+1.0	-6.6	-21.3	$23
30-06 Spfd.*	165	2800	2534	2283	2047	1825	2872	2352	1909	1534	1220	+2.5	+0.4	-8.4	-25.5	$17
30-06 Spfd.	168	2710	2522	2346	2169	2003	2739	2372	2045	1754	1497	+2.5	+0.4	-8.0	-23.5	$18
30-06 Spfd.	178	2720	2511	2311	2121	1939	2924	2491	2111	1777	1486	+2.5	+0.4	-8.2	-24.6	$23
30-06 Spfd.*	180	2700	2469	2250	2042	1846	2913	2436	2023	1666	1362	-2.5	0.0	-9.3	-27.0	$17
30-06 Spfd.	220	2410	2130	1870	1632	1422	2837	2216	1708	1301	988	+2.5	-1.7	-18.0	NA	$17
30-06 Light Mag.	150	3100	2815	2548	2295	2058	3200	2639	2161	1755	1410	+1.4	0.0	-6.8	-20.3	NA
30-06 Light Mag.	180	2880	2676	2480	2293	2114	3316	2862	2459	2102	1786	+1.7	0.0	-7.3	-21.3	NA
30-06 High Energy	180	2880	2690	2500	2320	2150	3315	2880	2495	2150	1845	+1.7	0.0	-7.2	-21.0	NA
7.82 (308) Patriot	150	3250	2999	2762	2537	2323	3519	2997	2542	2145	1798	+1.2	0.0	-5.8	-16.9	NA
308 Norma Mag.	180	3020	2820	2630	2440	2270	3645	3175	2755	2385	2050	+2.5	+2.0	-3.5	-14.8	NA
300 Dakota	200	3000	2824	2656	2493	2336	3996	3542	3131	2760	2423	+2.2	+1.5	-4.0	-15.2	NA
300 H&H Magnum*	180	2880	2640	2412	2196	1990	3315	2785	2325	1927	1583	+2.5	+0.8	-6.8	-21.7	$24
300 H&H Magnum	220	2550	2267	2002	1757	NA	3167	2510	1958	1508	NA	-2.5	-0.4	-12.0	NA	NA
300 Peterson	180	3500	3319	3145	2978	2817	4896	4401	3953	3544	3172	+2.3	+2.9	0.0	-6.8	$22
300 Win. Mag.	150	3290	2951	2636	2342	2068	3605	2900	2314	1827	1424	+2.5	+1.9	-3.8	-15.8	$24
300 Win. Mag.	165	3100	2877	2665	2462	2269	3522	3033	2603	2221	1897	+2.5	+2.4	-3.0	-16.9	$29
300 Win. Mag.	178	2900	2760	2568	2375	2191	3509	3030	2606	2230	1897	+2.5	+1.4	-5.0	-17.6	$22
300 Win. Mag.*	180	2960	2745	2540	2344	2157	3501	3011	2578	2196	1859	+2.5	+1.2	-5.5	-18.5	NA
300 W.M. High Energy	180	3100	2830	2580	2340	2110	3840	3205	2660	2190	1790	+1.4	0.0	-6.6	-19.7	NA
300 W.M. Light Mag.	180	3100	2879	2668	2467	2275	3840	3313	2845	2431	2068	+1.39	0.0	-6.45	-18.7	NA
300 Win. Mag.	190	2885	1691	2506	2327	2156	3511	3055	2648	2285	1961	+2.5	+1.2	-5.7	-19.0	$26
300 W.M. High Energy	200	2930	2740	2550	2370	2200	3810	3325	2885	2495	2145	+1.6	0.0	-6.9	-20.1	NA
300 Win. Mag.*	200	2825	2595	2376	2167	1970	3545	2991	2508	2086	1742	-2.5	+1.6	-4.7	-17.2	$36
300 Win. Mag.	220	2680	2448	2228	2020	1823	3508	2927	2424	1993	1623	+2.5	0.0	-9.5	-27.5	$23
300 Rem. Ultra Mag.	180	3250	3037	2834	2640	2454	4221	3686	3201	2786	2407	2.4		-3.0	-12.7	NA
300 Rem. Ultra Mag.	200	3025	2826	2636	2454	2279	4063	3547	3086	2673	2308	2.4	0.0	-3.4	-14.6	NA
300 Wea. Mag.	100	3900	3441	3038	2652	2305	3714	2891	2239	1717	1297	+2.0	+2.6	-0.6	-8.7	$32
300 Wea. Mag.	150	3600	3307	3033	2776	2533	4316	3642	3064	2566	2137	+2.5	+3.2	0.0	-8.1	$32
300 Wea. Mag.	165	3450	3210	3000	2792	2593	4360	3796	3297	2855	2464	+2.5	+3.2	0.0	-7.8	NA
300 Wea. Mag.	178	3120	2902	2695	2497	2308	3847	3329	2870	2464	2104	+2.5	-1.7	-3.6	-14.7	$43
300 Wea. Mag.	180	3330	3110	2910	2710	2520	4430	3875	3375	2935	2540	+1.0	0.0	-5.2	-15.1	NA
300 Wea. Mag.	190	3030	2830	2638	2455	2279	3873	3378	2936	2542	2190	+2.5	+1.6	-4.3	-16.0	$38
300 Wea. Mag.	220	2850	2541	2283	1964	1736	3967	3155	2480	1922	1471	+2.5	+0.4	-8.5	-26.4	$35
300 Warbird	180	3400	3180	2971	2772	2582	4620	4042	3528	3071	2664	+2.59	+3.25	0.0	-7.95	NA
300 Pegasus	180	3500	3319	3145	2978	2817	4896	4401	3953	3544	3172	+2.28	+2.89	0.0	-6.79	NA
32-20 Win.	100	1210	1021	913	834	769	325	231	185	154	131	0.0	-32.3	NA	NA	$23**
303 British	150	2685	2441	2210	1992	1787	2401	1984	1627	1321	1064	+2.5	+0.6	-8.4	-26.2	$18
303 British	180	2460	2124	1817	1542	1311	2418	1803	1319	950	687	+2.5	-1.8	-16.8	NA	$18
303 Light Mag.	150	2830	2570	2325	2094	1884	2667	2199	1800	1461	1185	+2.0	0.0	-8.4	-24.6	NA
7.62x54mm Rus.	146	2950	2730	2520	2320	NA	2820	2415	2055	1740	NA	+2.5	+2.0	-4.4	-17.7	NA
7.62x54mm Rus.	180	2580	2370	2180	2000	1820	2650	2250	1900	1590	1100	+2.5	0.0	-9.8	-28.5	NA
7.7x58mm Jap.	180	2500	2300	2100	1920	1750	2490	2105	1770	1475	1225	+2.5	0.0	-10.4	-30.2	NA
8x57mm JS Mau.	165	2850	2520	2210	1930	1670	2965	2330	1795	1360	1015	+2.5	+1.0	-7.7	NA	NA
32 Win. Special	170	2250	1921	1626	1372	1175	1911	1393	998	710	521	+2.5	-3.5	-22.9	NA	$14
8mm Mauser	170	2360	1969	1622	1333	1123	2102	1464	993	671	476	+2.5	-3.1	-22.2	NA	$18
8mm Rem. Mag.	185	3080	2761	2464	2186	1927	3896	3131	2494	1963	1525	+2.5	+1.4	-5.5	-19.7	$30
8mm Rem. Mag.	220	2830	2581	2346	2123	1913	3912	3254	2688	2201	1787	+2.5	+0.6	-7.6	-23.5	Disc.
338-06	200	2750	2553	2364	2184	2011	3358	2894	2482	2118	1796	+1.9	0.0	-8.22	-23.6	NA
330 Dakota	250	2900	2719	2545	2378	2217	4668	4103	3595	3138	2727	+2.3	+1.3	-5.0	-17.5	NA
338 Lapua	250	2963	2795	2640	2493	NA	4842	4341	3881	3458	NA	+1.9	0.0	-7.9	NA	NA
338 Win. Mag.	200	2960	2658	2375	2110	1862	3890	3137	2505	1977	1539	+2.5	+1.0	-6.7	-22.3	$27
338 Win. Mag.*	210	2830	2590	2370	2150	1940	3735	3130	2610	2155	1760	+2.5	+1.4	-6.0	-20.9	$33
338 Win. Mag.*	225	2785	2517	2266	2029	1808	3871	3165	2565	2057	1633	+2.5	+0.4	-8.5	-25.9	$27

30

30 Mag.

31

8mm

33

Many manufacturers do not supply suggested retail prices. Others did not get their pricing to us before press time. All pricing can vary dependent on the exact brand and style of ammo selected and/or the retail outlet from which you make your purchase. Pricing has been rounded to the nearest dollar and represents our best estimate of average pricing. An * after the cartridge means these loads are available with Nosler Partition or Swift A-Frame bullets. Listed pricing may or may not reflect this bullet type. ** = these are packed 50 to box, all others are 20 to box. Wea. Mag.= Weatherby Magnum. Spfd. = Springfield. A-A-Sq. = A-Square. N.E.=Nitro Express.

Cartridge	Bullet Weight Grains	VELOCITY (fps)					ENERGY (ft. lbs.)					TRAJ. (in.)				Approx. Price per box
		Muzzle	100 yds.	200 yds.	300 yds.	400 yds.	Muzzle	100 yds.	200 yds.	300 yds.	400 yds.	100 yds.	200 yds.	300 yds.	400 yds.	
338 W.M. Heavy Mag.	225	2920	2678	2449	2232	2027	4259	3583	2996	2489	2053	+1.75	0.0	-7.65	-22.0	NA
338 W.M. High Energy	225	2940	2690	2450	2230	2010	4320	3610	3000	2475	2025	+1.7	0.0	-7.5	-22.0	NA
338 Win. Mag.	230	2780	2573	2375	2186	2005	3948	3382	2881	2441	2054	+2.5	+1.2	-6.3	-21.0	$40
338 Win. Mag.*	250	2660	2456	2261	2075	1898	3927	3348	2837	2389	1999	+2.5	+0.2	-9.0	-26.2	$27
338 W.M. High Energy	250	2800	2610	2420	2250	2080	4350	3775	3260	2805	2395	+1.8	0.0	-7.8	-22.5	NA
338 Ultra Mag.	250	2860	2645	2440	2244	2057	4540	3882	3303	2794	2347	1.7	0.0	-7.6	-22.1	NA
8.59(.338) Galaxy	200	3100	2899	2707	2524	2347	4269	3734	3256	2829	2446	3	3.80	0.0	-9.3	NA
340 Wea. Mag.*	210	3250	2991	2746	2515	2295	4924	4170	3516	2948	2455	+2.5	+1.9	-1.8	-11.8	$56
340 Wea. Mag.*	250	3000	2806	2621	2443	2272	4995	4371	3812	3311	2864	+2.5	+2.0	-3.5	-14.8	$56
338 A-Square	250	3120	2799	2500	2220	1958	5403	4348	3469	2736	2128	+2.5	+2.7	-1.5	-10.5	NA
338-378 Wea. Mag.	225	3180	2974	2778	2591	2410	5052	4420	3856	3353	2902	3.1	3.80	0.0	-8.9	NA
338 Titan	225	3230	3010	2800	2600	2409	5211	4524	3916	3377	2898	+3.07	+3.80	0.0	-8.95	NA
338 Excalibur	200	3600	3361	3134	2920	2715	5755	5015	4363	3785	3274	+2.23	+2.87	0.0	-6.99	NA
338 Excalibur	250	3250	2922	2618	2333	2066	5863	4740	3804	3021	2370	+1.3	0.0	-6.35	-19.2	NA
348 Winchester	200	2520	2215	1931	1672	1443	2820	2178	1656	1241	925	+2.5	-1.4	-14.7	NA	$42
357 Magnum	158	1830	1427	1138	980	883	1175	715	454	337	274	0.0	-16.2	-33.1	NA	$25**
35 Remington	150	2300	1874	1506	1218	1039	1762	1169	755	494	359	+2.5	-4.1	-26.3	NA	$16
35 Remington	200	2080	1698	1376	1140	1001	1921	1280	841	577	445	+2.5	-6.3	-17.1	-33.6	$16
356 Winchester	200	2460	2114	1797	1517	1284	2688	1985	1434	1022	732	+2.5	-1.8	-15.1	NA	$31
356 Winchester	250	2160	1911	1682	1476	1299	2591	2028	1571	1210	937	+2.5	-3.7	-22.2	NA	$31
358 Winchester	200	2490	2171	1876	1619	1379	2753	2093	1563	1151	844	+2.5	-1.6	-15.6	NA	$31
358 STA	275	2850	2562	2292	2039	NA	4958	4009	3208	2539	NA	+1.9	0.0	-8.6	NA	NA
350 Rem. Mag.	200	2710	2410	2130	1870	1631	3261	2579	2014	1553	1181	+2.5	0.0	-10.0	-30.1	$33
35 Whelen	200	2675	2378	2100	1842	1606	3177	2510	1958	1506	1145	+2.5	-0.2	-10.3	-31.1	$20
35 Whelen	225	2500	2300	2110	1930	1770	3120	2650	2235	1870	1560	+2.6	0.0	-10.2	-29.9	NA
35 Whelen	250	2400	2197	2005	1823	1652	3197	2680	2230	1844	1515	+2.5	-1.2	-13.7	NA	$20
358 Norma Mag.	250	2800	2510	2230	1970	1730	4350	3480	2750	2145	1655	+2.5	+1.0	-7.6	-25.2	NA
358 STA	275	2850	2562	229*2	2039	1764	4959	4009	3208	2539	1899	+1.9	0.0	-8.58	-26.1	NA
9.3x57mm Mau.	286	2070	1810	1590	1390	1110	2710	2090	1600	1220	955	+2.5	-2.6	-22.5	NA	NA
9.3x62mm Mau.	286	2360	2089	1844	1623	NA	3538	2771	2157	1670	1260	+2.5	-1.6	-21.0	NA	NA
9.3x64mm	286	2700	2505	2318	2139	1968	4629	3984	3411	2906	2460	+2.5	+2.7	-4.5	-19.2	NA
9.3x74Rmm	286	2360	2089	1844	1623	NA	3538	2771	2157	1670	NA	+2.5	-2.0	-11.0	NA	NA
38-55 Win.	255	1320	1190	1091	1018	963	987	802	674	587	525	0.0	-23.4	NA	NA	$25
375 Winchester	200	2200	1841	1526	1268	1089	2150	1506	1034	714	527	+2.5	-4.0	-26.2	NA	$27
375 Winchester	250	1900	1647	1424	1239	1103	2005	1506	1126	852	676	+2.5	-6.9	-33.3	NA	$27
376 Steyr	225	2600	2331	2078	1842	1625	3377	2714	2157	1694	1319	2.5	0.0	-10.6	-31.4	NA
376 Steyr	270	2600	2372	2156	1951	1759	4052	3373	2787	2283	1855	2.3	0.0	-9.9	-28.9	NA
375 Dakota	300	2600	2316	2051	1804	1579	4502	3573	2800	2167	1661	+2.4	0.0	-11.0	-32.7	NA
375 N.E. 2-1/2"	270	2000	1740	1507	1310	NA	2398	1815	1362	1026	NA	+2.5	-6.0	-30.0	NA	NA
375 Flanged	300	2450	2150	1886	1640	NA	3998	3102	2369	1790	NA	+2.5	-2.4	-17.0	NA	NA
375 H&H Magnum	250	2670	2450	2240	2040	1850	3955	3335	2790	2315	1905	+2.5	-0.4	-10.2	-28.4	NA
375 H&H Magnum	270	2690	2420	2166	1928	1707	4337	3510	2812	2228	1747	+2.5	0.0	-10.0	-29.4	$28
375 H&H Magnum*	300	2530	2245	1979	1733	1512	4263	3357	2608	2001	1523	+2.5	-1.0	-10.5	-33.6	$28
375 H&H Hvy. Mag.	270	2870	2628	2399	2182	1976	4937	4141	3451	2150	1845	+1.7	0.0	-7.2	-21.0	NA
375 H&H Hvy. Mag.	300	2705	2386	2090	1816	1568	4873	3793	2908	2195	1637	+2.3	0.0	-10.4	-31.4	NA
375 Wea. Mag.	300	2700	2420	2157	1911	1685	4856	3901	3100	2432	1891	+2.5	-.04	-10.7	-	NA
378 Wea. Mag.	270	3180	2976	2781	2594	2415	6062	5308	4635	4034	3495	+2.5	+2.6	-1.8	-11.3	$71
378 Wea. Mag.	300	2929	2576	2252	1952	1680	5698	4419	3379	2538	1881	+2.5	+1.2	-7.0	-24.5	$77
375 A-Square	300	2920	2626	2351	2093	1850	5679	4594	3681	2917	2281	+2.5	+1.4	-6.0	-21.0	NA
38-40 Win.	180	1160	999	901	827	764	538	399	324	273	233	0.0	-33.9	NA	NA	$42**
450/400-3"	400	2150	1932	1730	1545	1379	4105	3316	2659	2119	1689	+2.5	-4.0	-9.5	-30.0	NA
416 Dakota	400	2450	2294	2143	1998	1859	5330	4671	4077	3544	3068	+2.5	-0.2	-10.5	-29.4	NA
416 Taylor	400	2350	2117	1896	1693	NA	4905	3980	3194	2547	NA	+2.5	-1.2	15.0	NA	NA
416 Hoffman	400	2380	2145	1923	1718	1529	5031	4087	3285	2620	2077	+2.5	-1.0	-14.1	NA	NA
416 Rigby	350	2600	2449	2303	2162	2026	5253	4661	4122	3632	3189	+2.5	-1.8	-10.2	-26.0	NA

33 cont.

34 35

9.3 mm

375

40 41

Many manufacturers do not supply suggested retail prices. Others did not get their pricing to us before press time. All pricing can vary dependent on the exact brand and style of ammo selected and/or the retail outlet from which you make your purchase. Pricing has been rounded to the nearest dollar and represents our best estimate of average pricing. An * after the cartridge means these loads are available with Nosler Partition or Swift A-Frame bullets. Listed pricing may or may not reflect this bullet type. ** = these are packed 50 to box, all others are 20 to box. Wea. Mag.= Weatherby Magnum. Spfd. = Springfield. A-A-Sq. = A-Square. N.E.=Nitro Express.

Cartridge	Bullet Weight Grains	VELOCITY (fps)					ENERGY (ft. lbs.)					TRAJ. (in.)				Approx. Price per box
		Muzzle	100 yds.	200 yds.	300 yds.	400 yds.	Muzzle	100 yds.	200 yds.	300 yds.	400 yds.	100 yds.	200 yds.	300 yds.	400 yds.	
416 Rigby	400	2370	2210	2050	1900	NA	4990	4315	3720	3185	NA	+2.5	-0.7	-12.1	NA	NA
416 Rigby	410	2370	2110	1870	1640	NA	5115	4050	3165	2455	NA	+2.5	-2.4	-17.3	NA	$110
416 Rem. Mag.*	350	2520	2270	2034	1814	1611	4935	4004	3216	2557	2017	+2.5	-0.8	-12.6	-35.0	$82
416 Rem. Mag.*	400	2400	2175	1962	1763	1579	5115	4201	3419	2760	2214	+2.5	-1.5	-14.6	NA	$80
416 Wea. Mag.*	400	2700	2397	2115	1852	1613	6474	5104	3971	3047	2310	+2.5	0.0	-10.1	-30.4	$96
10.57 (416) Meteor	400	2730	2532	2342	2161	1987	6621	5695	4874	4147	3508	+1.9	0.0	-8.3	-24.0	NA
404 Jeffrey	400	2150	1924	1716	1525	NA	4105	3289	2614	2064	NA	+2.5	-4.0	-22.1	NA	NA
425 Express	400	2400	2160	1934	1725	NA	5115	4145	3322	2641	NA	+2.5	-1.0	-14.0	NA	NA
44-40 Win.	200	1190	1006	900	822	756	629	449	360	300	254	0.0	-33.3	NA	NA	$36**
44 Rem. Mag.	210	1920	1477	1155	982	880	1719	1017	622	450	361	0.0	-17.6	NA	NA	$14
44 Rem. Mag.	240	1760	1380	1114	970	878	1650	1015	661	501	411	0.0	-17.6	NA	NA	$13
444 Marlin	240	2350	1815	1377	1087	941	2942	1753	1001	630	472	+2.5	-15.1	-31.0	NA	$22
444 Marlin	265	2120	1733	1405	1160	1012	2644	1768	1162	791	603	+2.5	-6.0	-32.2	NA	Disc.
45-70 Govt.	300	1810	1497	1244	1073	969	2182	1492	1031	767	625	0.0	-14.8	NA	NA	$21
45-70 Govt. Supreme	300	1880	1558	1292	1103	988	2355	1616	1112	811	651	0.0	-12.9	-46.0	-105	NA
45-70 Govt. CorBon	350	1800	1526	1296			2519	1810	1307			0.0	-14.6			NA
45-70 Govt.	405	1330	1168	1055	977	918	1590	1227	1001	858	758	0.0	-24.6	NA	NA	$21
45-70 Govt. PMC Cowboy	405	1550	1193				1639	1280				0.0	-23.9			NA
45-70 Govt. Garrett	415	1850					3150					3.0	-7.0			NA
45-70 Govt. Garrett	530	1550	1343	1178	1062	982	2828	2123	1633	1327	1135	0.0	-17.8			NA
450 Marlin	350	2100	1774	1488	1254	1089	3427	2446	1720	1222	922	0.0	-9.7	-35.2		NA
458 Win. Magnum	350	2470	1990	1570	1250	1060	4740	3065	1915	1205	870	+2.5	-2.5	-21.6	NA	$43
458 Win. Magnum	400	2380	2170	1960	1770	NA	5030	4165	3415	2785	NA	+2.5	-0.4	-13.4	NA	$73
458 Win. Magnum	465	2220	1999	1791	1601	NA	5088	4127	3312	2646	NA	+2.5	-2.0	-17.7	NA	NA
458 Win. Magnum	500	2040	1823	1623	1442	1237	4620	3689	2924	2308	1839	+2.5	-3.5	-22.0	NA	$61
458 Win. Magnum	510	2040	1770	1527	1319	1157	4712	3547	2640	1970	1516	+2.5	-4.1	-25.0	NA	$41
450 Dakota	500	2450	2235	2030	1838	1658	6663	5544	4576	3748	3051	+2.5	-0.6	-12.0	-33.8	NA
450 N.E. 3-1/4"	465	2190	1970	1765	1577	NA	4952	4009	3216	2567	NA	+2.5	-3.0	-20.0	NA	NA
450 N.E. 3-1/4"	500	2150	1920	1708	1514	NA	5132	4093	3238	2544	NA	+2.5	-4.0	-22.9	NA	NA
450 No. 2	465	2190	1970	1765	1577	NA	4952	4009	3216	2567	NA	+2.5	-3.0	-20.0	NA	NA
450 No. 2	500	2150	1920	1708	1514	NA	5132	4093	3238	2544	NA	+2.5	-4.0	-22.9	NA	NA
458 Lott	465	2380	2150	1932	1730	NA	5848	4773	3855	3091	NA	+2.5	-1.0	-14.0	NA	NA
458 Lott	500	2300	2062	1838	1633	NA	5873	4719	3748	2960	NA	+2.5	-1.6	-16.4	NA	NA
450 Ackley Mag.	465	2400	2169	1950	1747	NA	5947	4857	3927	3150	NA	+2.5	-1.0	-13.7	NA	NA
450 Ackley Mag.	500	2320	2081	1855	1649	NA	5975	4085	3820	3018	NA	+2.5	-1.2	-15.0	NA	NA
460 Short A-Sq.	500	2420	2175	1943	1729	NA	6501	5250	4193	3319	NA	+2.5	-0.8	-12.8	-	NA
460 Wea. Mag.	500	2700	2404	2128	1869	1635	8092	6416	5026	3878	2969	+2.5	+0.6	-8.9	-28.0	$72
500/465 N.E.	480	2150	1917	1703	1507	NA	4926	3917	3089	2419	NA	+2.5	-4.0	-22.2	-	NA
470 Rigby	500	2150	1940	1740	1560	NA	5130	4170	3360	2695	NA	+2.5	-2.8	-19.4	NA	NA
470 Nitro Ex.	480	2190	1954	1735	1536	NA	5111	4070	3210	2515	NA	+2.5	-3.5	-20.8	NA	NA
470 Nitro Ex.	500	2150	1890	1650	1440	1270	5130	3965	3040	2310	1790	+2.5	-4.3	-24.0	NA	$177
475 No. 2	500	2200	1955	1728	1522	NA	5375	4243	3316	2573	NA	+2.5	-3.2	-20.9	NA	NA
505 Gibbs	525	2300	2063	1840	1637	NA	6166	4922	3948	3122	NA	+2.5	-3.0	-18.0	NA	NA
500 N.E.-3"	570	2150	1928	1722	1533	NA	5850	4703	3752	2975	NA	+2.5	-3.7	-22.0	NA	NA
500 N.E.-3"	600	2150	1927	1721	1531	NA	6158	4947	3944	3124	NA	+2.5	-4.0	-22.0	NA	NA
495 A-Square	570	2350	2117	1896	1693	NA	5850	4703	3752	2975	NA	+2.5	-1.0	-14.5	NA	NA
495 A-Square	600	2280	2050	1833	1635	NA	6925	5598	4478	3562	NA	+2.5	-2.0	-17.0	NA	NA
500 A-Square	600	2380	2144	1922	1766	NA	7546	6126	4920	3922	NA	+2.5	-3.0	-17.0	NA	NA
500 A-Square	707	2250	2040	1841	1567	NA	7947	6530	5318	4311	NA	+2.5	-2.0	-17.0	NA	NA
500 BMG PMC	660	3080	2854	2639	2444	2248	13688	500 yd. zero				+3.1	+3.90	+4.7	+2.8	NA
577 Nitro Ex.	750	2050	1793	1562	1360	NA	6990	5356	4065	3079	NA	+2.5	-5.0	-26.0	NA	NA
577 Tyrannosaur	750	2400	2141	1898	1675	NA	9591	7633	5996	4671	NA	+3.0	0.0	-12.9	NA	NA
600 N.E.	900	1950	1680	1452	NA	NA	7596	5634	4212	NA	NA	+5.6	0.0	NA	NA	NA
700 N.E.	1200	1900	1676	1472	NA	NA	9618	7480	5774	NA	NA	+5.7	0.0	NA	NA	NA

40

425
44

45

475

50
58

600
700

Notes: Blanks are available in 32 S&W, 38 S&W and 38 Special. "V" after barrel length indicates test barrel was vented to produce ballistics similar to a revolver with a normal barrel-to-cylinder gap. Ammo prices are per 50 rounds except when marked with an ** which signifies a 20 round box; *** signifies a 25-round box. Not all loads are available from all ammo manufacturers. Listed loads are those made by Remington, Winchester, Federal, and others. DISC. is a discontinued load. Prices are rounded to nearest whole dollar and will vary with brand and retail outlet. † = new bullet weight this year; "c" indicates a change in data.

	Cartridge	Bullet Wgt. Grs.	VELOCITY (fps)			ENERGY (ft. lbs.)			Mid-Range Traj. (in.)		Bbl. Lgth. (in.)	Est. Price/ box
			Muzzle	50 yds.	100 yds.	Muzzle	50 yds.	100 yds.	50 yds.	100 yds.		
22	221 Rem. Fireball	50	2650	2380	2130	780	630	505	0.2	0.8	10.5"	$15
25	25 Automatic	35	900	813	742	63	51	43	NA	NA	2"	$18
	25 Automatic	45	815	730	655	65	55	40	1.8	7.7	2"	$21
	25 Automatic	50	760	705	660	65	55	50	2.0	8.7	2"	$17
30	7.5mm Swiss	107	1010	NA	NA	240	NA	NA	NA	NA	NA	NEW
	7.62mmTokarev	87	1390	NA	NA	365	NA	NA	0.6	NA	4.5"	NA
	7.62 Nagant	97	1080	NA	NA	350	NA	NA	NA	NA	NA	NEW
	7.63 Mauser	88	1440	NA	NA	405	NA	NA	NA	NA	NA	NEW
	30 Luger	93†	1220	1110	1040	305	255	225	0.9	3.5	4.5"	$34
	30 Carbine	110	1790	1600	1430	785	625	500	0.4	1.7	10"	$28
32	32 S&W	88	680	645	610	90	80	75	2.5	10.5	3"	$17
	32 S&W Long	98	705	670	635	115	100	90	2.3	10.5	4"	$17
	32 Short Colt	80	745	665	590	100	80	60	2.2	9.9	4"	$19
	32 H&R Magnum	85	1100	1020	930	230	195	165	1.0	4.3	4.5"	$21
	32 H&R Magnum	95	1030	940	900	225	190	170	1.1	4.7	4.5"	$19
	32 Automatic	60	970	895	835	125	105	95	1.3	5.4	4"	$22
	32 Automatic	60	1000	917	849	133	112	96			4"	NA
	32 Automatic	65	950	890	830	130	115	100	1.3	5.6	NA	NA
	32 Automatic	71	905	855	810	130	115	95	1.4	5.8	4"	$19
	8mm Lebel Pistol	111	850	NA	NA	180	NA	NA	NA	NA	NA	NEW
	8mm Steyr	112	1080	NA	NA	290	NA	NA	NA	NA	NA	NEW
	8mm Gasser	126	850	NA	NA	200	NA	NA	NA	NA	NA	NEW
9mm 38	380 Automatic	60	1130	960	NA	170	120	NA	1.0	NA	NA	NA
	380 Automatic	85/88	990	920	870	190	165	145	1.2	5.1	4"	$20
	380 Automatic	90	1000	890	800	200	160	130	1.2	5.5	3.75"	$10
	380 Automatic	95/100	955	865	785	190	160	130	1.4	5.9	4"	$20
	38 Super Auto +P	115	1300	1145	1040	430	335	275	0.7	3.3	5"	$26
	38 Super Auto +P	125/130	1215	1100	1015	425	350	300	0.8	3.6	5"	$26
	38 Super Auto +P	147	1100	1050	1000	395	355	325	0.9	4.0	5"	NA
	9x18mm Makarov	95	1000	NA	NA	NA	NA	NA	NA	NA	NA	NEW
	9x18mm Ultra	100	1050	NA	NA	240	NA	NA	NA	NA	NA	NEW
	9x23mm Largo	124	1190	1055	966	390	306	257	0.7	3.7	4"	NA
	9x23mm Win.	125	1450	1249	1103	583	433	338	0.6	2.8	NA	NA
	9mm Steyr	115	1180	NA	NA	350	NA	NA	NA	NA	NA	NEW
	9mm Luger	88	1500	1190	1010	440	275	200	0.6	3.1	4"	$24
	9mm Luger	90	1360	1112	978	370	247	191	NA	NA	4"	$26
	9mm Luger	95	1300	1140	1010	350	275	215	0.8	3.4	4"	NA
	9mm Luger	100	1180	1080	NA	305	255	NA	0.9	NA	4"	NA
	9mm Luger	115	1155	1045	970	340	280	240	0.9	3.9	4"	$21
	9mm Luger	123/125	1110	1030	970	340	290	260	1.0	4.0	4"	$23
	9mm Luger	140	935	890	850	270	245	225	1.3	5.5	4"	$23
	9mm Luger	147	990	940	900	320	290	265	1.1	4.9	4"	$26
	9mm Luger +P	90	1475	NA	NA	437	NA	NA	NA	NA	NA	NA
	9mm Luger +P	115	1250	1113	1019	399	316	265	0.8	3.5	4"	$27
	9mm Federal	115	1280	1130	1040	420	330	280	0.7	3.3	4"V	$24
	9mm Luger Vector	115	1155	1047	971	341	280	241	NA	NA	4"	NA
	9mm Luger +P	124	1180	1089	1021	384	327	287	0.8	3.8	4"	NA
38	38 S&W	146	685	650	620	150	135	125	2.4	10.0	4"	$19
	38 Short Colt	125	730	685	645	150	130	115	2.2	9.4	6"	$19
	39 Special	100	950	900	NA	200	180	NA	1.3	NA	4"V	NA
	38 Special	110	945	895	850	220	195	175	1.3	5.4	4"V	$23

Notes: Blanks are available in 32 S&W, 38 S&W and 38 Special. "V" after barrel length indicates test barrel was vented to produce ballistics similar to a revolver with a normal barrel-to-cylinder gap. Ammo prices are per 50 rounds except when marked with an ** which signifies a 20 round box; *** signifies a 25-round box. Not all loads are available from all ammo manufacturers. Listed loads are those made by Remington, Winchester, Federal, and others. DISC. is a discontinued load. Prices are rounded to nearest whole dollar and will vary with brand and retail outlet. † = new bullet weight this year; "c" indicates a change in data.

Cartridge	Bullet Wgt. Grs.	VELOCITY (fps)			ENERGY (ft. lbs.)			Mid-Range Traj. (in.)		Bbl. Lgth. (in).	Est. Price/ box
		Muzzle	50 yds.	100 yds.	Muzzle	50 yds.	100 yds.	50 yds.	100 yds.		
38 Special	110	945	895	850	220	195	175	1.3	5.4	4"V	$23
38 Special	130	775	745	710	175	160	120	1.9	7.9	4"V	$22
38 Special Cowboy	140	800	767	735	199	183	168			7.5" V	NA
38 (Multi-Ball)	140	830	730	505	215	130	80	2.0	10.6	4"V	$10**
38 Special	148	710	635	565	165	130	105	2.4	10.6	4"V	$17
38 Special	158	755	725	690	200	185	170	2.0	8.3	4"V	$18
38 Special +P	95	1175	1045	960	290	230	195	0.9	3.9	4"V	$23
38 Special +P	110	995	925	870	240	210	185	1.2	5.1	4"V	$23
38 Special +P	125	975	929	885	264	238	218	1	5.2	4"	NA
38 Special +P	125	945	900	860	250	225	205	1.3	5.4	4"V	#23
38 Special +P	129	945	910	870	255	235	215	1.3	5.3	4"V	$11
38 Special +P	130	925	887	852	247	227	210	1.3	5.50	4"V	NA
38 Special +P	147/150(c)	884	NA	NA	264	NA	NA	NA	NA	4"V	$27
38 Special +P	158	890	855	825	280	255	240	1.4	6.0	4"V	$20
357 SIG	115	1520	NA	NA	593	NA	NA	NA	NA	NA	NA
357 SIG	124	1450	NA	NA	578	NA	NA	NA	NA	NA	NA
357 SIG	125	1350	1190	1080	510	395	325	0.7	3.1	4"	NA
357 SIG	150	1130	1030	970	420	355	310	0.9	4.0	NA	NA
356 TSW	115	1520	NA	NA	593	NA	NA	NA	NA	NA	NA
356 TSW	124	1450	NA	NA	578	NA	NA	NA	NA	NA	NA
356 TSW	135	1280	1120	1010	490	375	310	0.8	3.50	NA	NA
356 TSW	147	1220	1120	1040	485	410	355	0.8	3.5	5"	NA
357 Mag., Super Clean	105	1650									NA
357 Magnum	110	1295	1095	975	410	290	230	0.8	3.5	4"V	$25
357 (Med.Vel.)	125	1220	1075	985	415	315	270	0.8	3.7	4"V	$25
357 Magnum	125	1450	1240	1090	585	425	330	0.6	2.8	4"V	$25
357 (Multi-Ball)	140	1155	830	665	420	215	135	1.2	6.4	4"V	$11**
357 Magnum	140	1360	1195	1075	575	445	360	0.7	3.0	4"V	$25
357 Magnum	145	1290	1155	1060	535	430	360	0.8	3.5	4"V	$26
357 Magnum	150/158	1235	1105	1015	535	430	360	0.8	3.5	4"V	$25
357 Mag. Cowboy	158	800	761	725	225	203	185				NA
357 Magnum	165	1290	1189	1108	610	518	450	0.7	3.1	8-3/8"	NA
357 Magnum	180	1145	1055	985	525	445	390	0.9	3.9	4"V	$25
357 Magnum	180	1180	1088	1020	557	473	416	0.8	3.6	8"V	NA
357 Mag. CorBon F.A.	180	1650	1512	1386	1088	913	767	1.66	0.0		NA
357 Mag. CorBon	200	1200	1123	1061	640	560	500	3.19	0.0		NA
357 Rem. Maximum	158	1825	1590	1380	1170	885	670	0.4	1.7	10.5"	$14**
40 S&W	135	1140	1070	NA	390	345	NA	0.9	NA	4"	NA
40 S&W	155	1140	1026	958	447	362	309	0.9	4.1	4"	$14***
40 S&W	165	1150	NA	NA	485	NA	NA	NA	NA	4"	$18***
40 S&W	180	985	936	893	388	350	319	1.4	5.0	4"	$14***
40 S&W	180	1015	960	914	412	368	334	1.3	4.5	4"	NA
400 Cor-Bon	135	1450	NA	NA	630	NA	NA	NA	NA	5"	NA
10mm Automatic	155	1125	1046	986	436	377	335	0.9	3.9	5"	$26
10mm Automatic	170	1340	1165	1145	680	510	415	0.7	3.2	5"	$31
10mm Automatic	175	1290	1140	1035	650	505	420	0.7	3.3	5.5"	$11**
10mm Auto. (FBI)	180	950	905	865	361	327	299	1.5	5.4	4"	$16**
10mm Automatic	180	1030	970	920	425	375	340	1.1	4.7	5"	$16**
10mm Auto H.V.	180†	1240	1124	1037	618	504	430	0.8	3.4	5"	$27
10mm Automatic	200	1160	1070	1010	495	510	430	0.9	3.8	5"	$14**
10.4mm Italian	177	950	NA	NA	360	NA	NA	NA	NA	NA	NEW

38 cont.

357

40, 10mm

Notes: Blanks are available in 32 S&W, 38 S&W and 38 Special. "V" after barrel length indicates test barrel was vented to produce ballistics similar to a revolver with a normal barrel-to-cylinder gap. Ammo prices are per 50 rounds except when marked with an ** which signifies a 20 round box; *** signifies a 25-round box. Not all loads are available from all ammo manufacturers. Listed loads are those made by Remington, Winchester, Federal, and others. DISC. is a discontinued load. Prices are rounded to nearest whole dollar and will vary with brand and retail outlet. † = new bullet weight this year; "c" indicates a change in data.

Cartridge	Bullet Wgt. Grs.	VELOCITY (fps)			ENERGY (ft. lbs.)			Mid-Range Traj. (in.)		Bbl. Lgth. (in).	Est. Price/ box
		Muzzle	50 yds.	100 yds.	Muzzle	50 yds.	100 yds.	50 yds.	100 yds.		
40, 10mm cont.											
41 Action Exp.	180	1000	947	903	400	359	326	0.5	4.2	5"	$13**
41 Rem. Magnum	170	1420	1165	1015	760	515	390	0.7	3.2	4"V	$33
41 Rem. Magnum	175	1250	1120	1030	605	490	410	0.8	3.4	4"V	$14**
41 (Med. Vel.)	210	965	900	840	435	375	330	1.3	5.4	4"V	$30
41 Rem. Magnum	210	1300	1160	1060	790	630	535	0.7	3.2	4"V	$33
44											
44 S&W Russian	247	780	NA	NA	335	NA	NA	NA	NA	NA	NA
44 S&W Special	180	980	NA	NA	383	NA	NA	NA	NA	6.5"	NA
44 S&W Special	180	1000	935	882	400	350	311	NA	NA	7.5"V	NA
44 S&W Special	200†	875	825	780	340	302	270	1.2	6.0	6"	$13**
44 S&W Special	200	1035	940	865	475	390	335	1.1	4.9	6.5"	$13**
44 S&W Special	240/246	755	725	695	310	285	265	2.0	8.3	6.5"	$26
44-40 Win. Cowboy	225	750	723	695	281	261	242				NA
44 Rem. Magnum	180	1610	1365	1175	1035	745	550	0.5	2.3	4"V	$18**
44 Rem. Magnum	200	1400	1192	1053	870	630	492	0.6	NA	6.5"	$20
44 Rem. Magnum	210	1495	1310	1165	1040	805	635	0.6	2.5	6.5"	$18**
44 (Med. Vel.)	240	1000	945	900	535	475	435	1.1	4.8	6.5"	$17
44 R.M. (Jacketed)	240	1180	1080	1010	740	625	545	0.9	3.7	4"V	$18**
44 R.M. (Lead)	240	1350	1185	1070	970	750	610	0.7	3.1	4"V	$29
44 Rem. Magnum	250	1180	1100	1040	775	670	600	0.8	3.6	6.5"V	$21
44 Rem. Magnum	250	1230	1132	1057	840	711	620	0.8	2.9	6.5"V	NA
44 Rem. Magnum	275	1235	1142	1070	931	797	699	0.8	3.3	6.5"	NA
44 Rem. Magnum	300	1200	1100	1026	959	806	702	NA	NA	7.5"	$17
44 Rem. Magnum	330	1385	1297	1220	1406	1234	1090	1.83	0.00	NA	NA
440 CorBon	260	1700	1544	1403	1669	1377	1136	1.58	NA	10	NA
45, 50											
450 Short Colt/450 Revolver	226	830	NA	NA	350	NA	NA	NA	NA	NA	NEW
45 S&W Schofield	180	730	NA	NA	213	NA	NA	NA	NA	NA	NA
45 S&W Schofield	230	730	NA	NA	272	NA	NA	na			
45 Automatic	165	1030	930	NA	385	315	NA	1.2	NA	5"	NA
45 Automatic	185	1000	940	890	410	360	325	1.1	4.9	5"	$28
45 Auto. (Match)	185	770	705	650	245	204	175	2.0	8.7	5"	$28
45 Auto. (Match)	200	940	890	840	392	352	312	2.0	8.6	5"	$20
45 Automatic	200	975	917	860	421	372	328	1.4	5.0	5"	$18
45 Automatic	230	830	800	675	355	325	300	1.6	6.8	5"	$27
45 Automatic	230	880	846	816	396	366	340	1.5	6.1	5"	NA
45 Automatic +P	165	1250	NA	NA	573	NA	NA	NA	NA	NA	NA
45 Automatic +P	185	1140	1040	970	535	445	385	0.9	4.0	5"	$31
45 Automatic +P	200	1055	982	925	494	428	380	NA	NA	5"	NA
45 Super	185	1300	1190	1108	694	582	504	NA	NA	5"	NA
45 Win. Magnum	230	1400	1230	1105	1000	775	635	0.6	2.8	5"	$14**
45 Win. Magnum	260	1250	1137	1053	902	746	640	0.8	3.3	5"	$16**
45 Win. Mag. CorBon	320	1150	1080	1025	940	830	747	3.47			NA
455 Webley MKII	262	850	NA	NA	420	NA	NA	NA	NA	NA	NA
45 Colt	200	1000	938	889	444	391	351	1.3	4.8	5.5"	$21
45 Colt	225	960	890	830	460	395	345	1.3	5.5	5.5"	$22
45 Colt + P CorBon	265	1350	1225	1126	1073	884	746	2.65	0.0		NA
45 Colt + P CorBon	300	1300	1197	1114	1126	956	827	2.78	0.0		NA
45 Colt	250/255	860	820	780	410	375	340	1.6	6.6	5.5"	$27
454 Casull	250	1300	1151	1047	938	735	608	0.7	3.2	7.5"V	NA
454 Casull	260	1800	1577	1381	1871	1436	1101	0.4	1.8	7.5"V	NA
454 Casull	300	1625	1451	1308	1759	1413	1141	0.5	2.0	7.5"V	NA
454 Casull CorBon	360	1500	1387	1286	1800	1640	1323	2.01	0.0		NA
475 Linebaugh	400	1350	1217	1119	1618	1315	1112	NA	NA	NA	NA
50 Action Exp.	325	1400	1209	1075	1414	1055	835	0.2	2.3	6"	$24**

Note: The actual ballistics obtained with your firearm can vary considerably from the advertised ballistics. Also, ballistics can vary from lot to lot with the same brand and type load.

Cartridge	Bullet Wt. Grs.	Velocity (fps) 22-1/2" Bbl.		Energy (ft. lbs.) 22-1/2" Bbl.		Mid-Range Traj. (in.)	Muzzle Velocity
		Muzzle	100 yds.	Muzzle	100 yds.	100 yds.	6" Bbl.
22 Short Blank	—	—	—	—	—	—	—
22 Short CB	29	727	610	33	24	NA	706
22 Short Target	29	830	695	44	31	6.8	786
22 Short HP	27	1164	920	81	50	4.3	1077
22 Colibri	20	375	183	6	1	NA	NA
22 Long CB	29	727	610	33	24	NA	706
22 Long HV	29	1180	946	90	57	4.1	1031
22 LR Ballistician	25	1100	760	65	30	NA	NA
22 LR Pistol Match	40	1070	890	100	70	4.6	940
22 LR Sub Sonic HP	38	1050	901	93	69	4.7	NA
22 LR Standard Velocity	40	1070	890	100	70	4.6	940
22 LR HV	40	1255	1016	140	92	3.6	1060
22 LR Silhoutte	42	1220	1003	139	94	3.6	1025
22 SSS	60	950	802	120	86	NA	NA
22 LR HV HP	40	1280	1001	146	89	3.5	1085
22 LR Hyper HP	32/33/34	1500	1075	165	85	2.8	NA
22 LR Stinger HP	32	1640	1132	191	91	2.6	1395
22 LR Hyper Vel	30	1750	1191	204	93	NA	NA
22 LR Shot #12	31	950	NA	NA	NA	NA	NA
22 Win. Mag.	30	2200	1373	322	127	1.4	1610
22 Win. Mag. V-Max BT	33	2000	1495	293	164	0.60	NA
22 Win. Mag. JHP	34	2120	1435	338	155	1.4	NA
22 Win. Mag. JHP	40	1910	1326	324	156	1.7	1480
22 Win. Mag. FMJ	40	1910	1326	324	156	1.7	1480
22 Win. Mag. JHP	50	1650	1280	300	180	1.3	NA
22 Win. Mag. Shot #11	52	1000	—	NA	—	—	NA

SHOTSHELL LOADS & PRICES

NOTES: * = 10 rounds per box. ** = 5 rounds per box. Pricing variations and number of rounds per box can occur with type and brand of ammunition. Listed pricing is the average nominal cost for load style and box quantity shown. Not every brand is available in all shot size variations. Some manufacturers do not provide suggested list prices. All prices rounded to nearest whole dollar. The price you pay will vary dependent upon outlet of purchase. # = new load spec this year; "C" indicates a change in data.

Dram Equiv.	Shot Ozs.	Load Style	Shot Sizes	Brands	Avg. Price/box	Velocity (fps)
10 Gauge 3-1/2" Magnum						
4-1/2	2-1/4	premium	BB, 2, 4, 5, 6	Win., Fed., Rem.	$33	1205
Max	2	premium	4, 5, 6	Fed., Win.	NA	1300
4-1/4	2	high velocity	BB, 2, 4	Rem.	$22	1210
4-1/2	2-1/4	duples	4x6	Rem.	$14*	1205
Max	18 pellets	premium	00 buck	Fed., Win.	$7**	1100
Max	1-7/8	Bismuth	BB, 2, 4	Win., Bis.	NA	1225
Max	1-3/4	Tungsten-Polymer	4, 6	Fed.	NA	1325
4-1/4	1-3/4	steel	TT, T, BBB, BB, 1, 2, 3	Win., Rem.	$27	1260
Mag	1-5/8	steel	T, BBB	Win.	$27	1285
4-5/8	1-5/8	steel	F, T, BBB	Fed.	$26	1350
Max	1-5/8	Tungsten - Iron	BBB, BB, 2, 4	Fed.		1300
Max	1-5/8	Bismuth	BB, 2, 4	Bismuth	NA	1375
Max	1-3/8	steel	T, BBB, BB, 2	Fed., Win.	NA	1450
Max	1-3/8	Tungsten - Iron	BBB, BB, 2, 4	Fed.		1450
Max	1-3/4	slug, rifled	slug	Fed.	NA	1280
Max	54 pellets	Super-X	4 Buck	Win.	NA	1150
12 Gauge 3-1/2" Magnum						
Max	2/14	premium	4, 5, 6	Fed., Rem., Win.	$13*	1150
Max	2	Lead	4, 5, 6	Fed.	NA	1275
Max	18 pellets	premium	00 buck	Fed., Win., Rem.	$7**	1100
Max	1-7/8	Bismuth	BB, 2, 4	Win., Bis.	NA	1225
Max	1-3/4	Tungsten-Polymer	4, 6	Fed.	NA	1275
4 -1/8	1-9/16	steel	TT, F, T, BBB, BB, 1, 2	Rem., Win., Fed.	$22	1335
Max	1-3/8	steel	T, BBB, BB, 2, 4	Fed., Win.	NA	1450
Max	1-3/8	Tungsten - Iron	BBB, BB, 2, 4	Fed.	NA	1450
Max	24 pellets	Premium	1 Buck	Fed.	NA	1100
Max	54 pellets	Super-X	4 Buck	Win.	NA	1050
12 Gauge 3" Magnum						
4	2	premium	BB, 2, 4, 5, 6	Win., Fed., Rem.	$9*	1175
4	2	duplex	4x6	Rem.	$10	1175
4	1-7/8	premium	BB, 2, 4, 6	Win., Fed., Rem.	$19	1210
4	1-7/8	duplex	4x6	Rem., Fio.	$9*	1210
Max	1-3/4	turkey	4, 5, 6	Fed., Fio., Win.	NA	1300
4-1/2	1-3/4	duplex	2x4, 4x6	Fio.	NA	1150
4	1-5/8	premium	2, 4, 5, 6	Win., Fed., Rem.	$18	1290
Max	1-5/8	Bismuth	BB, 2, 4, 5, 6	Win., Bis.	NA	1250
4	24 pellets	buffered	1 buck	Win., Fed., Rem.	$5**	1040
4	15 pellets	buffered	00 buck	Win., Fed., Rem.	$6**	1210
4	10 pellets	buffered	000 buck	Win., Fed., Rem.	$6**	1225
4	41 pellets	buffered	4 buck	Win., Fed., Rem.	$6**	1210
Max	1-3/8	Tungsten - Polymer	4, 6	Fed.	NA	1330
Max	1-3/8	Tungsten-Iron	4	Fed.	NA	1300
Max	1-3/8	slug	slug	Bren.	NA	1476
Max	1-1/4	slug, rifled	slug	Fed.	NA	1600

Dram Equiv.	Shot Ozs.	Load Style	Shot Sizes	Brands	Avg. Price/box	Velocity (fps)
12 Gauge 3" Magnum (cont.)						
Max	1-3/16	saboted slug	copper slug	Rem.	NA	1500
Max	1-1/8	Tungsten - Iron	BBB, BB, 2, 4	Fed.	NA	1400
Max	1	steel	4, 6	Fed.		1330
Max	1	slug, rifled	slug, magnum	Win., Rem.	$5**	1760
Max	1	saboted slug	slug	Rem., Win., Fed.	$10**	1550
3-5/8	1-3/8	steel	TT, F, T, BBB, BB, 1, 2, 3, 4	Win., Fed., Rem.	$19	1275
Max	1-1/8	steel	T, BBB, BB, 2, 4, 5, 6	Fed., Win.	NA	1450
Max	1-1/8	steel	BB, 2	Fed.	NA	1400
4	1-1/4	steel	TT, F, T, BBB, BB, 1, 2, 3, 4, 6	Win., Fed., Rem.	$18	1375
Max	1-1/4	Tungsten-Iron and Steel	4x2	Fed.	NA	1400
Max	1-1/8	Tungsten-Polymer	4, 6	Fed.	NA	1375
Max	1-3/8	Tungsten-Polymer	4, 6	Fed.	NA	1330
12 Gauge 2-3/4"						
Max	1-5/8	magnum	4, 5, 6	Win., Fed.	$8*	1250
Max	1-3/8	turkey	4, 5, 6	Fio.	NA	1250
Max	1-3/8	duplex	2x4, 4x6	Fio.	NA	1200
Max	1-3/8	Bismuth	BB, 2, 4, 5, 6	Win., Bis.	NA	1280
3-3/4	1-1/2	magnum	BB, 2, 4, 5, 6	Win., Fed., Rem.	$16	1260
3-3/4	1-1/2	duplex	BBx4, 2x4, 4x6	Rem., Fio.	$9*	1260
Max	1-1/4	Supreme H-V	4, 6, 7-1/2	Win.	NA	1400
3-3/4	1-1/4	high velocity	BB, 2, 4, 5, 6, 7-1/2, 8, 9	win., Fed., Rem., Fio.	$13	1330
Max	1-1/4	Tungsten-Polymer	4, 6	Fed.	NA	1330
3-1/2	1-1/4	mid-velocity	7, 8, 9	Win.	Disc.	1275
3-1/4	1-1/4	standard velocity	6, 7-1/2, 8, 9	Win., Fed., Rem., Fio.	$11	1220
Max	1-1/4	Bismuth	4, 6	Win.		1220
3-1/4	1-1/8	standard velocity	4, 6, 7-1/2, 8, 9	Win., Fed., Rem., Fio.	$9	1255
Max	1	steel	BB, 2	Fed.	NA	1450
Max	1	Tungsten - Iron	BB, 2, 4	Fed.	NA	1450
3-1/4	1	standard velocity	6, 7-1/2, 8	Rem., Fed., Fio., Win.	$6	1290
3-1/4	1-1/4	target	7-1/2, 8, 9	Win., Fed., Rem.	$10	1220
3	1-1/8	spreader	7-1/2, 8, 8-1/2, 9	Fio.	NA	1200
3	1-1/8	duplex target	7-1/2x8	Rem.	NA	1200
3	1-1/8	target	7-1/2, 8, 9, 7-1/2x8	Win., Fed., Rem., Fio.	$7	1200
3	1-1/8	duplex clays	7-1/2x8-1/2	Rem.	NA	1200
2-3/4	1-1/8	target	7-1/2, 8, 8-1/2, 9, 7-1/2x8	Win., Fed., Rem., Fio.	$7	1145
2-3/4	1-1/8	duplex target	7-1/2x8	Rem.	NA	1145
2-3/4	1-1/8	low recoil	7-1/2, 8	Rem.	NA	1145
2-1/2	26 grams	low recoil	8	Win.	NA	980
2-1/4	1-1/8	target	7-1/2, 8, 8-1/2, 9	Rem., Fed.	$7	1080
Max	1	spreader	7-1/2, 8, 8-1/2, 9	Fio.	NA	1300

SHOTSHELL LOADS & PRICES, *continued*

Dram Equiv.	Shot Ozs.	Load Style	Shot Sizes	Brands	Avg. Price/box	Velocity (fps)
12 Gauge 2-3/4" (cont.)						
3-1/4	28 grams (1 oz)	target	7-1/2, 8, 9	Win., Fed., Rem., Fio.	$8	1290
3	1	target	7-1/2, 8, 8-1/2, 9	Win., Fio.	NA	1235
2-3/4	1	target	7-1/2, 8, 8-1/2, 9	Fed., Rem., Fio.	NA	1180
3-1/4	24 grams	target	7-1/2, 8, 9	Fed., Win., Fio.	NA	1325
3	7/8	light	8	Fio.	NA	1200
3-3/4	8 pellets	buffered	000 buck	Win., Fed., Rem.	$4**	1325
4	12 pellets	premium	00 buck	Win., Fed., Rem.	$5**	1290
3-3/4	9 pellets	buffered	00 buck	Win., Fed., Rem., Fio.	$19	1325
3-3/4	12 pellets	buffered	0 buck	Win., Fed., Rem.	$4**	1275
4	20 pellets	buffered	1 buck	Win., Fed., Rem.	$4**	1075
3-3/4	16 pellets	buffered	1 buck	Win., Fed., Rem.	$4**	1250
4	34 pellets	premium	4 buck	Fed., Rem.	$5**	1250
3-3/4	27 pellets	buffered	4 buck	Win., Fed., Rem., Fio.	$4**	1325
Max	1	saboted slug	slug	Win., Fed., Rem.	$10**	1450
Max	1-1/4	slug, rifled	slug	Fed.	NA	1520
Max	1-1/4	slug	slug	Lightfield		1440
Max	1	slug, rifled	slug, magnum	Rem., Fio.	$5**	1680
Max	1	slug, rifled	slug	Win., Fed., Rem.	$4**	1610
Max	1	sabot slug	slug	Sauvestre		1640
3	1-1/8	steel target	6-1/2, 7	Rem.	NA	1200
2-3/4	1-1/8	steel target	7	Rem.	NA	1145
3	1#	steel	7	Win.	$11	1235
3-1/2	1-1/4	steel	T, BBB, BB, 1, 2, 3, 4, 5, 6	Win., Fed., Rem.	$18	1275
3-3/4	1-1/8	steel	BB, 1, 2, 3, 4, 5, 6	Win., Fed., Rem., Fio.	$16	1365
3-3/4	1	steel	2, 3, 4, 5, 6, 7	Win., Fed., Rem., Fio.	$13	1390
Max	7/8	steel	7	Fio.	NA	1440
16 Gauge 2-3/4"						
3-1/4	1-1/4	magnum	2, 4, 6	Fed., Rem.	$16	1260
3-1/4	1-1/8	high velocity	4, 6, 7-1/2	Win., Fed., Rem., Fio.	$12	1295
Max	1-1/8	Bismuth	4, 5	Win., Bis.	NA	1200
2-3/4	1-1/8	standard velocity	6, 7-1/2, 8	Fed., Rem., Fio.	$9	1185
2-1/2	1	dove	6, 7-1/2, 8, 9	Fio., Win.	NA	1165
2-3/4	1		6, 7-1/2, 8	Fio.	NA	1200
Max	15/16	steel	2, 4	Fed., Rem.	NA	1300
Max	7/8	steel	2, 4	Win.	$16	1300
3	12 pellets	buffered	1 buck	Win., Fed., Rem.	$4**	1225
Max	4/5	slug, rifled	slug	Win., Fed., Rem.	$4**	1570
Max	.92	sabot slug	slug	Sauvestre		1560
20 Gauge 3" Magnum						
3	1-1/4	premium	2, 4, 5, 6, 7-1/2	Win., Fed., Rem.	$15	1185
Max	1-1/4	Tungsten-Polymer	4, 6	Fed.	NA	1185
3	1-1/4	turkey	4, 6	Fio.	NA	1200
Max	18 pellets	buck shot	2 buck	Fed.	NA	1200

Dram Equiv.	Shot Ozs.	Load Style	Shot Sizes	Brands	Avg. Price/box	Velocity (fps)
20 Gauge 3" Magnum (cont.)						
Max	24 pellets	buffered	3 buck	Win.	$5**	1150
2-3/4	20 pellets	buck	3 buck	Rem.	$4**	1200
3-1/4	1	steel	1, 2, 3, 4, 5, 6	Win., Fed., Rem.	$15	1330
Max	1-1/16	Bismuth	2, 4, 5, 6	Bismuth	NA	1250
Max	7/8	Tungsten-Iron	2, 4	Fed.	NA	1375
Mag	5/8	saboted slug	275 gr.	Fed.	NA	1450
20 Gauge 2-3/4"						
2-3/4	1-1/8	magnum	4, 6, 7-1/2	Win., Fed., Rem.	$14	1175
Max	1-1/8	Tungsten-Polymer	4, 6	Fed.	NA	1175
2-3/4	1	high velocity	4, 5, 6, 7-1/2, 8, 9	Win., Fed., Rem., Fio.	$12	1220
Max	1	Bismuth	4, 6	Win., Bis.	NA	1200
Max	1	Supreme H-V	4, 6, 7-1/2	Win.	NA	1300
Max	7/8	Steel	2, 3, 4	Fio.	NA	1500
2-1/2	1	standard velocity	6, 7-1/2, 8	Win., Rem., Fed., Fio.	$6	1165
2-1/2	7/8	clays	8	Rem.	NA	1200
2-1/2	7/8	promotional	6, 7-1/2, 8	Win., Rem., Fio.	$6	1210
2-1/2	1	target	8, 9	Win., Rem.	$8	1165
2-1/2	7/8	target	8, 9	Win., Fed., Rem.	$8	1200
2-1/2	7/8	steel - target	7	Rem.		1200
Max	5/8	Saboted Slug	Copper Slug	Rem.	NA	1500
Max	20 pellets	buffered	3 buck	Win., Fed.	$4	1200
Max	5/8	slug, saboted	slug	Win.,	$9**	1400
2-3/4	5/8	slug, rifled	slug	Rem.	$4**	1580
Max	3/4	saboted slug	copper slug	Fed., Rem.	NA	1450
Max	3/4	slug, rifled	slug	Win., Fed., Rem., Fio.	$4**	1570
Max	.9	sabot slug	slug	Sauvestre		1480
Max	3/4	steel	2, 3, 4, 6	Win., Fed., Rem.	$14	1425
28 Gauge 2-3/4"						
2	1	high velocity	6, 7-1/2, 8	Win.	$12	1125
2-1/4	3/4	high velocity	6, 7-1/2, 8, 9	Win., Fed., Rem., Fio.	$11	1295
2	3/4	target	8, 9	Win., Fed., Rem.	$9	1200
Max	5/8	Bismuth	4, 6	Win., Bis.	NA	1250
410 Bore 3"						
Max	11/16	high velocity	4, 5, 6, 7-1/2, 8, 9	Win., Fed., Rem., Fio.	$10	1135
Max	9/16	Bismuth	4	Win., Bis.	NA	1175
410 Bore 2-1/2"						
Max	1/2	high velocity	4, 6, 7-1/2	Win., Fed., Rem.	$9	1245
Max	1/5	slug, rifled	slug	Win., Fed., Rem.	$4**	1815
1-1/2	1/2	target	8, 8-1/2, 9	Win., Fed., Rem., Fio.	$8	1200

SHOOTER'S MARKETPLACE

INTERESTING PRODUCT NEWS FOR THE ACTIVE SHOOTING SPORTSMAN.

The companies represented on the following pages will be happy to provide additional information – feel free to contact them.

SOLID STEEL RINGS & BASES

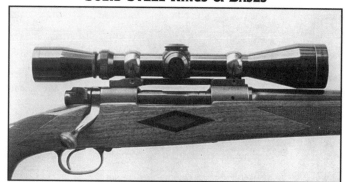

The World's Sleekest System! The only projectionless split-ring scope mount in the world. Cut from the solid. Not a cookie-cutter, detach-and-duck perversion of Conetrol's splendid concept, but the genuine original machine-cut rendition of a pristine one-of-a-kind product. The strongest because muscle is packed into both rings. Others limit strength to one ring. Dual ring movement allows scope to be centered over gun after adjustment, not possible for other mount designs. Conetrol fits more high-power firearms than any other mount-maker - can provide mounting even for guns long obsolete.

Three basic styles - from matte to streamlined high gloss. Fluted bases. Teflon. Stainless steel or electroless nickel. Metric ring sizes.

CONETROL SCOPE MOUNTS
10225 Hwy. 123 South, Seguin, TX 78155
Phone: (800) CONETROL • Web: www.conetrol.com

NYLON COATED GUN CLEANING RODS

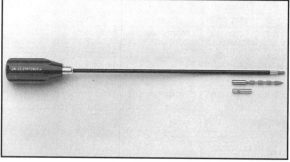

J. Dewey cleaning rods have been used by the U.S. Olympic shooting team and the benchrest community for over 20 years. These one-piece, spring-tempered, steel-base rods will not gall delicate rifling or damage the muzzle area of front-cleaned firearms. The nylon coating eliminates the problem of abrasives adhering to the rod during the cleaning operation. Each rod comes with a hard non-breakable plastic handle supported by ball-bearings, top and bottom, for ease of cleaning.

The brass cleaning jags are designed to pierce the center of the cleaning patch or wrap around the knurled end to keep the patch centered in the bore.

Coated rods are available from 17-caliber to shotgun bore size in several lengths to meet the needs of any shooter. Write for more information.

J. DEWEY MFG. CO., INC.
P.O. Box 2014, Southbury, CT 06488
Phone: 203-264-3064 • Fax: 203-262-6907
www.deweyrods.com

PRECISION RIFLE REST

Bald Eagle Precision Machine Co. offers a rifle rest perfect for the serious benchrester or dedicated varminter.

"The Slingshot" or Next Generation has 60° front legs. The rest is constructed of aircraft-quality aluminum or fine grain cast iron and weighs 12 to 20 lbs. The finish is 3 coats of Imron clear. Primary height adjustments are made wtih a rack and pinion gear. Secondary adjustment uses a mariner wheel with thrust bearings for smooth operation. A hidden fourth leg allows for lateral movement on the bench.

Bald Eagle offers approximately 150 rest combinations to choose from, including windage adjustable, right or left hand, cast aluminum or cast iron.

Prices: $165.00 to $335.00.

BALD EAGLE PRECISION MACHINE CO.
101-K Allison Street, Lock Haven, PA 17745
Phone: 570-748-6772 • Fax: 570-748-4443
Web: www.baldeaglemachine.com

SHOOTER'S MARKETPLACE

THE JACKASS RIG RETURNS

First introduced in 1969, this shoulder system features a horizontal holster with patented swivel connectors, a streamlined ammo carrier and a genuine suede leather harness for unparalleled concealment suitability. The suede harness has our trademarked clover-shaped flexalon backplate that allows greater adjustment and comfort. The Original Jackass Rig comes in Havana Brown, is available in right or left-handed designs and sells for $114.00 + S&H. All components also may be purchased separately. Tie downs are also available.

GALCO INTERNATIONAL

2019 W. Quail Ave. • Phoenix, AZ 85027

Phone: 602-258-8295 • 800-US-Galco (874-2526)

Fax: 800-737-1725 • Web: www.usgalco.com

TOP-QUALITY BULLET LUBE

Rooster Laboratories offers consistently high performance, professional high-melt cannelure bullet lubricants in a choice of two hardnesses. Both are available in 2"x 6"sticks for the commercial reloader, and 1"x 4" hollow and solid sticks.

With a 230°F melting point, both are ideal for indoor and outdoor shooting. Both bond securely to the bullet, remaining intact during shooting.

Zambini is a hard, tough lubricant designed primarily for pistols. HVR is softer, but still firm. Designed primarily for high-velocity rifles, HVR is easier to apply, and also excellent for pistols. Application requires that the lubesizer be heated.

Prices: 2"x6" sticks $4.00; 1"x4" sticks $135.00 per 100. Contact Rooster Laboratories for more information.

ROOSTER LABORATORIES

P.O. Box 412514, Kansas City, MO 64141

Phone: 816-474-1622

FINE GUN STOCKS

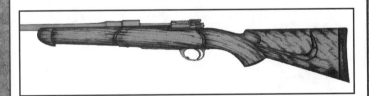

Manufacturing custom and production gunstocks for hundreds of models of rifles and shotguns—made from the finest stock woods and available in all stages of completion.

GREAT AMERICAN GUNSTOCK COMPANY

3420 Industrial Drive

Yuba City, CA 95993

Phone: 530-671-4570

Fax: 530-671-3906

Gunstock Hotline: 800-784-GUNS (4867)

Web: www.gunstocks.com

Email: gunstox@oro.net

FOLDING BIPODS

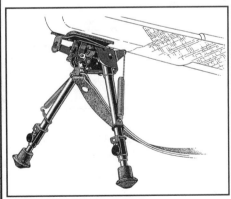

Harris Bipods clamp securely to most stud-equipped bolt-action rifles and are quick-detachable. With adapters, they will fit some other guns. On all models except the Model LM, folding legs have completely adjustable spring-return extensions. The sling swivel attaches to the clamp. This time-proven design is manufactured with heat-treated steel and hard alloys and has a black anodized finish.

Series S Bipods rotate 35° for instant leveling on uneven ground. Hinged base has tension adjustment and buffer springs to eliminate tremor or looseness in crotch area of bipod. They are otherwise similar to non-rotating Series 1A2.

Thirteen models are available from Harris Engineering; literature is free.

HARRIS ENGINEERING INC.

Dept: GD54, Barlow, KY 42024

Phone: 502-334-3633 • Fax: 502-334-3000

Web: www.cyberteklabs.com/harris/main/htm

SHOOTER'S MARKETPLACE

SPORTSMAN'S UTILITY CASE

Introducing the multi-purpose Sportsman's Utility Case from MTM Case-Gard. Designed to carry and protect just about any type of field gear that sportsmen need for a great day outdoors. The foam-padded lift-out tray, 18.5" x 10.5", has two height positions. The large open section can be used many ways. The locking tab has been sized for the standard Master Lock combination lock. Send $2 for our catalog or visit our Web site.

MTM MOLDED PRODUCTS CO.

P. O. Box 14117 • Dayton, OH 45413

Web: www.mtmcase-gard.com

CHEYENNE PIONEER PRODUCTS
Presents
CHEYENNE CRT'G. BOXES ™

Authentic antique-looking cartridge boxes styled and constructed like the boxes produced from 1873 to the 1950s—only better. Using the same materials, colors and graphics, Cheyenne Pioneer Products produces a line of cartridge boxes that capture the details of the old-time originals, but are tougher and more durable.

1880 CLASSICS™ provide Cowboy Action Shooters, Old West enthusiasts and re-enactors with an alternative to modern factory ammunition packaging or plastic after-market boxes.

20th CENTURY CLASSICS™ satisfy the demands of modern shooting & reloading aficionados with many favorites like 44 magnum and 38 special.

For more information, contact

CHEYENNE PIONEER PRODUCTS

P. O. Box 28425. • Kansas City, MO 64188
Phone: 816-413-9196 • Fax: 816-455-2859
Web: www.cartridgeboxes.com • Email: cheyennepp@aol.com

M888
M1 CARBINE

The new M888 M1 Carbine is manufactured in the USA. It has a new receiver, match grade barrel and wood stock, all made by iai and assembled with original unused Mil-Spec parts to produce a light-weight, low-recoil rifle. Firing is very controllable, so that the M888 is ideal for anyone who needs a firearm that is easy to use, including law enforcement.

The M888 will be available in 5.7mm Johnson, a standard 30 Carbine case necked down to 22 caliber.

During this year, iai will offer the M1 Garand and a line of 1911-A1 45 ACP pistols.

IAI INC.

5709 Hartsdale
Houston, TX 77036
Phone: 713-789-0745
Fax: 713-789-7513
Web: www.israelarms.com
Email: iaipro@wt.net

CUSTOM RESTORATION/CASE COLORING

Doug Turnbull Restoration continues to offer bone charcoal case hardening work, matching the original case colors produced by Winchester, Colt, Marlin, Parker, L.C. Smith, Fox and other manufacturers. Also available is charcoal blue, known as Carbona or machine blue, a prewar finish used by most makers. "Specializing in the accurate recreation of historical metal finishes on period firearms, from polishing to final finishing. Including Bone Charcoal Color Case Hardening, Charcoal Bluing, Rust Blue, and Nitre Blue".

DOUG TURNBULL RESTORATION

P.O. Box 471, 6680 Rt 5&20, Dept SM2000
Bloomfield, New York 14469 • Phone/Fax: 716-657-6338
Email: turnbullrest@mindspring.com
Web: www.turnbullrestoration.com

SHOOTER'S MARKETPLACE

FIREARMS RESPONSIBILITY CONTRACT

Our children and our families are of primary importance when it comes to firearms safety in the home. At H&R 1871®, Inc. we have taken this very, very seriously. That is why, in 1993 we began shipping, with every firearm we sell, our Family Firearms Responsibility Contract. It provides a framework and a guide for the family to discuss firearms issues within the home. It offers a meaningful blueprint for the responsible actions of both parent and child alike, and the signature lines for parents and children create a tangible commitment to safety.

The contract discusses handling, storage and a range of safety precautions for the parents. It also educates younger members of the family on how to treat and respect firearms within their own home, and what to do if a firearm is encoutered outside of the home.

Free copies are available by sending a SASE to:

H&R 1871®, INC.

60 Industrial Rowe, Gardner, MA 01440
Phone: 978-632-9393 • Fax: 978-632-2300
Email: hr1871@hr1871.com

TRIGGER LOCKING SYSTEM

H&R 1871®, Inc. now offers a unique trigger locking system to owners of its long guns shipped before December 1, 1999.

The *Trigger Guardian*™ is specifically designed to completely fill the trigger guard of any H&R 1871®, Inc. long gun and immobilize the trigger.

For a limited time, current owners of New England Firearms®, Harrington & Richardson® or Wesson & Harrington® brand rifles and shotguns can directly purchase *Trigger Guardian*™ systems from H&R 1871®, Inc. The price per unit is $5.95 including shipping. Send check or money order, shipping address and a daytime phone humber to:

H&R 1871®, INC.

60 Industrial Rowe, Gardner, MA 01440
Phone: 978-632-9393 • Fax: 978-632-2300
Email: hr1871@hr1871.com

NEW ENGLAND FIREARMS®
10 GA. 3-1/2" CAMO TURKEY SHOTGUN

This year's highlight is a new 10 ga. 3-1/2" offering with a camo stock and forend finish, and a screw-in Turkey extra full choke tube.

The new NEF "10 ga. Camo Turkey" shotguns have a 24" barrel, extra-full screw-in choke tube and a 3-1/2" chamber for the heaviest loads. The finish on the American hardwood stock and forend is green and black camo which, along with a matte black metal finish assures low visibility. Standard features include a ventilated recoil pad, sling swivels and a camo sling. The stock includes a steel counterweight to help moderate recoil from the heaviest 10 ga. turkey loads. It also uses the patented NEF transfer bar system for a high level of hammer down safety when in the field. This model also participates in the NEF additional barrel program allowing it to be factory-retrofitted with other 10 ga. shotgun barrels for a wide variety of uses.

For more information about the new "10 ga. Camo Turkey" shotgun, see your New England Firearms® stocking, Gold Star Dealer or write:

H&R 1871®, INC.

60 Industrial Rowe, Gardner, MA 01440
Phone: 978-632-9393 • Fax: 978-632-2300
Email: hr1871@hr1871.com

NEW ENGLAND FIREARMS®
ENDOWMENT EDITION SHOTGUNS

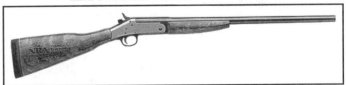

Through a unique partnership with the National Rifle Association Foundation, New England Firearms® will produce three very special new youth shotguns. The sale of which will provide funding to the Foundation's Youth Education Endowment.

These new NEF youth shotguns are based on the current Pardner® Youth shotguns in 20 ga., 28 ga., and 410, featuring polished blue receivers and real American black walnut stocks and forends. The engraving has both the NRA Foundation's logo and the inscription "Youth Endowment Edition."

This unique youth shotgun will provide an excellent beginning for your young hunters and at the same time help build a lasting future for the shooting sports.

See your New England Firearms® stocking, Gold Star Dealer or write:

H&R 1871®, INC.

60 Industrial Rowe, Gardner, MA 01440
Phone: 978-632-9393 • Fax: 978-632-2300
Email: hr1871@hr1871.com

SHOOTER'S MARKETPLACE

GLASER SAFETY SLUG

For over 25 years Glaser has provided a state-of-the-art personal defense ammunition used by the law enforcement and civilian communities. Available in two bullet styles, the Glaser Blue is offered in a full range of handgun calibers from 25ACP to 45 Colt (including the 9MM Makarov and 357 Sig) and four rifle cailbers: .223, 308, 30-06 and 7.62x39. The Glaser Silver is available in all handgun calibers from 380ACP to 45 Colt.

A complete brochure is available on the internet.

GLASER SAFETY SLUG, INC.

P.O. Box 8223, Foster City, CA 94404
www.safetyslug.com

QUALITY GUNSTOCK BLANKS

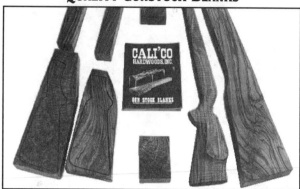

Cali'co Hardwoods has been cutting superior-quality shotgun and rifle blanks for more than 31 years. Cali'co supplies blanks to many of the major manufacturers—Browning, Weatherby, Ruger, Holland & Holland, to name a few—as well as custom gunsmiths the world over.

Profiled rifle blanks are available, ready for inletting and sanding. Cali'co sells superior California hardwoods in Claro walnut, French walnut, Bastogne, maple and myrtle.

Cali'co offers good, serviceable blanks and some of the finest exhibition blanks available. Satisfaction guaranteed.

Color catalog, retail and dealer price list (FFL required) free upon request.

CALI'CO HARDWOODS, INC.

3580 Westwind Blvd., Santa Rosa, CA 95403
Phone: 707-546-4045 • Fax: 707-546-4027

CUSTOM HUNTING HANDGUNS

Gary Reeder Custom Guns, builder of full custom guns, including custom cowboy guns, hunting handguns, hunting rifles, custom Contenders and Contender barrels, custom Encores and Encore barrels has a brochure available, or you can check out our web site at www.reedercustomguns.com. One of the most popular custom hunting handguns is our Ultimate Back Up 2. This little 5 shot beauty comes chambered in 475 Linebaugh or 500 Linebaugh. The UBU 2 is a 3-1/2 inch, all stainless revolver with our popular Gunfighter Grip, and is ported for less recoil. For more info contact:

GARY REEDER CUSTOM GUNS

2710 N Stevens Blvd., #22, Flagstaff, AZ 86004
Phone: 520-526-3313

CUSTOM COWBOY HANDGUNS

Gary Reeder Custom Guns, builder of full custom guns, hunting handguns, custom Contenders and Contender barrels and custom Encores and Encore barrels, would be happy to build a custom gun for you. See our web site at www.reedercustomguns.com, or call Gary Reeder. One of our most popular cowboy guns since 1991 has been our Tombstone Classic. This little beauty has our own birdhead grip, comes in full hi polished stainless, Black Chromex finish or two-toned. The Tombstone is fully engraved and highly slicked up inside, and is only one of a series of close to 20 custom cowboy guns.

GARY REEDER CUSTOM GUNS

2710 N Stevens Blvd., #22, Flagstaff, AZ 86004
Phone: 520-526-3313

SHOOTER'S MARKETPLACE

NEW SCOPES FROM SWIFT

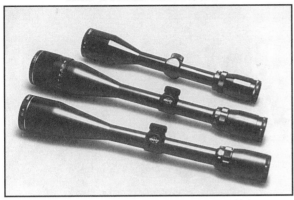

Swift reports that the new Swift Premier Line is brighter than comparable scopes, with generous eye relief. All are hard anodized, waterproof and have the Swift self-centering Quadraplex reticle.

This new line features objective adjustments for parallax, full saddle construction for strength, elevation and windage adjustments, multi-coated optics and Speed Focus, a feature that makes it quicker to focus.

Included are six new riflescope models: five 50mm scopes with variable power ranges from 2.5x to 18x, and a 40mm scope with a 3-9x zoom, plus one new pistolscope, (Model 679M) a 1.25 - 4x, 28mm.

SWIFT INSTRUMENTS, INC.
952 Dorchester Avenue, Dept: GD, Boston, MA 02125
Phone: 617-436-2960 • Fax: 617-436-3232
Email: swift1@tiac.net • Web: www.swift-optics.com

NEW BINOCULARS FOR HUNTERS

Swift 818R Trilyte: this 12 ounce roof prism, rubber armored, camouflage binocular is light enough to carry all day. Prisms use both BaK-4 and BaK-7 optical glass with magenta and aluminum coating. Multi-coating (green) is used on exterior objective and ocular lenses. It is supplied with both objective and eyepiece lens caps and a padded pouch-type case with belt strap.

For more information, contact:

SWIFT INSTRUMENTS, INC.
952 Dorchester Avenue, Dept. GD, Boston, MA 02125
Phone: 617-436-2960 • Fax: 617-436-3232
Email: swift1@tiac.net • Web: www.swift-optics.com

CART-RIGHT GUN CARTS:
NOT JUST ANOTHER GUN CART!

Carts are designed for quick and easy disassembly. Will fit into a car as small as a Mazda Miata. No tools required. The cart has a swing-down handle, removable ammo box and cargo box, with dovetail joint construction, five long gun racks with locking bar and padlock, removable 16" wheels and axle. Several wheel types and sizes to choose from. Other gun cart models available. All cabinet grade construction and lifetime warranty.

LONGHORN LEATHER & CARTS
2 Hudson Street, Annapolis, MD 21401
Phone: 410-573-1622
Web: www.cartrightguncarts.com

NEW MANUAL AVAILABLE

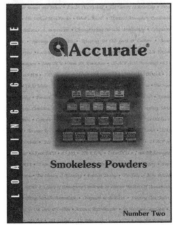

Accurate Powder's newest manual, Number Two, contains new data on powders XMR 4064 and XMP 5744, as well as a special section on Cowboy Action Shooting. In addition, the 400 page manual has loads for new cartridges, such as the .260 Rem., .300 Rem. Ultra Mag., .338 Rem. Ultra Mag., .357 Sig., .300 Whisper, .400 Corbon and more. It also includes many new bullets for the most popular cartridges as well as data for sabots in selected calibers. The price for the book is $16.95, plus $2.00 for shipping and handling in the continental U.S. To order a copy, call or write:

ACCURATE ARMS
5891 Hwy. 230 W., McEwen, TN 37101
Phone: 1-800-416-3006
Web: www.accuratepowder.com

SHOOTER'S MARKETPLACE

10-22® HAMMER AND SEAR PAC

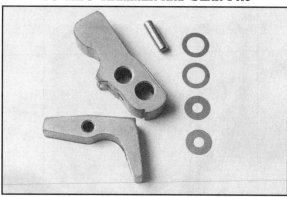

Power Custom introduces a new Ruger 10-22® Matched Hammer & Sear to reduce the trigger pull weight for your 10-22® & 10-22 Magnum. This allows for a 2 1/2lb. trigger pull. Manufactured by the E.D.M. process out of carbon steel and heat treated to a 56-58 Rc and precision ground with honed engagement surfaces. Kit includes extra power hammer & sear disconnector spring, 2 precision trigger shims, 2 precision hammer shims, and a replacement trigger return spring. Price $55.95.

10-22® is a registered trademark of Sturm, Ruger & Co. Inc.

POWER CUSTOM, INC.
29739 Hwy J, Dept GD,
Gravois Mills, MO 65037
Phone: 573-372-5684 • Fax: 573-372-5799
Website: www.powercustom.com

PRESSURE ◆ VELOCITY ◆ ACCURACY

You must know all three. For over thirty years, Oehler ballistic test equipment and software have been the standard for precision measurements. We invite comparison. and even make our systems compare to themselves. The patented *Proof Channel*™ uses three screens to make two velocity measurements on each shot. The Model 43 Personal Ballistics Lab provides shooters with accurate measurements of pressure, velocity, ballistic coefficient, and target information. Oehler instruments are used by military proving grounds and all major ammunition makers.

Phone for free catalog or technical help.

OEHLER RESEARCH, INC.
P.O. Box 9135, Austin, TX 78766
Phone: 800-531-5125 or 512-327-6900
Web: www.oehler-research.com

LIGHT WEIGHT COVER-UP

Light weight cover-up, the first vest specifically designed for concealed carry. Light weight and airy fabric for all year-round wear. Casual or dress, travels, well, wrinkle resistant. E-Z care wash and wear. Generous fit to avoid any imprinting, firearm can be accessed with vest buttoned. Three outside patch pockets and one inside breast pocket. All seams and facings double stitched with fusing for strength and resilience. Available in black, tan, and stonewashed blue. Small to 3XL: $38.00. 4XL to 7XL: $44.00. Designed and manufactured by Smith & Alexander in the U.S.A.

SMITH & ALEXANDER, INC.
P.O. Box 496208, Garland, TX 75049
Phone: 1-800-722-1911 • Fax: 1-972-840-6176
Email: sa1911@gte.net • Website: wwwsmithandalexander.com

S&A MAG GUIDE

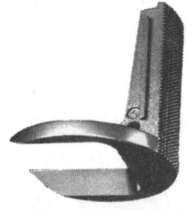

The S&A Mag Guide is the only one-piece magazine guide in the marketplace for 1911 pistols. It's the most popular and practical addition to the 1911 firearm. No frame modification, installs in minutes. Increases magazine opening 100%. 20LPI checkering for maximum grip, adds 1/4" length for extra leverage and recoil control. Will fit most 1911 clones, Colt, Springfield, Kimber, Auto-Ordnance, Norinco and Para Ordnance. Available in stainless steel or blued. Government and officer's models now available in hard anodized aluminum, neutral or black. $74.95 each.

SMITH & ALEXANDER, INC.
P.O. Box 496208, Garland, TX 75049
Phone: 1-800-722-1911 • Fax: 1-972-840-6176
Email: sa1911@gte.net • Website: wwwsmithandalexander.com

SHOOTER'S MARKETPLACE

THE SAVANNA, MODEL 702

Ed Brown, famous for 1911 custom handguns, introduces a complete line of custom bolt action rifles. The Savanna is a superbly accurate hunting rifle intended for long ranges around the world. It is based on Ed Brown's own custom action, crafted completely in-house, for the upmost in precision. The Savanna includes a steel floor plate and trigger guard, match quality, hand lapped barrel, and Talley scope mounts. The finest quality fiberglass or wood stocks, as well as other options are available. For a complete color catalog of our entire line of rifles and handguns, send $2.00 to:

ED BROWN PRODUCTS, INC.
43825 Muldrow Trail, Perry, MO 63462
Phone: (573) 565-3261 • Web: www.edbrown.com

FRIENDLY CLAY TARGET THROWERS

Model ST1

Trius Traps offer shooters supeior quality, easy cocking, manual clay target traps. Singles, doubles plus piggy back doubles. Traps are factory-assembled and tested. Add mount, attach main spring and you're ready to shoot. All adjustments made without tools. Birdshooter — quality at a budget price. Trius Model 92 — the original "Foot trap." Trapmaster — sit down comfort with pivoting action. The innovative 1-Step (shown) almost effortless to use. Set arm without tension, place targets on arm and step on pedal to put tension on main spring and release target. High angle target retainer on all traps.

TRIUS TRAPS, INC.
Attn: Dept. SM'2001, P.O. Box 25 • Cleves, OH 45002
Phone: 513-941-5682 • Fax: 513-941-7970

RIFLE AND PISTOL MAGAZINES

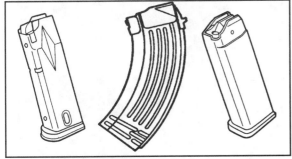

Forrest Inc. offers shooters one of the largest selections of standard and extended high-capacity magazines in the United States. Whether you're looking for a few spare magazines for that obsolete 22 rifle or pistol, or wish to replace a reduced-capacity ten-shot magazine with the higher-capacity pre-ban original, all are available from this California firm. They offer competitive pricing especially for dealers wanting to buy in quantity. Gun show dealers are our specialty.

Forrest Inc. also stocks parts and accessories for the Colt 1911 45 Auto pistol, the SKS and MAK-90 rifles as well as many U.S. military rifles. One of their specialty parts is firing pins for obsolete weapons.

Call or write Forrest Inc. for more information and a free brochure. Be sure and mention *Shooter's Marketplace*.

FORREST INC.
P.O. Box 326, Dept: #100, Lakeside, CA 92040
Phone: 619-561-5800 • Fax: 888-GUNCLIP
Website: www.gunmags.com

ASHLEY OUTDOORS LEVER SCOUT™ MOUNT

Scout Scope Mount for lever guns w/8" Weaver-style rail and cross slots on 1/2" centers. Mounts scope 1/8" lower than previously possible for Marlin 1895 Guide Gun. Positions intermediate eye relief scope forward for extremely fast reticle acquisition, facilitates both eyes wide open for better target acquisition, and allows use of AO Ghost-Ring Sights without scope. Simple installation, no gunsmithing required, uses existing rear dovetail and front two mounting holes on receiver. Ashley Outdoors: makers of Ashley Express / Pro Express Sights.

Price: Lever Scout™ Mount: $50.00

ASHLEY OUTDOORS, INC.
2401 Ludelle, Fort Worth, TX 76105
Phone: 817-536-0136 • Fax: 800-734-7939

SHOOTER'S MARKETPLACE

BUTCH'S BORE SHINE

Butch's Bore Shine is the revolutionary new gun solvent competitive shooters have been switching to. Butch's is a true "All-In-One" Cleaning Solvent formulated to remove powder, copper and lead fouling as well as control Moly buildup. It's non-abrasive and barrel safe. There is nothing that cleans as well as Butch's. Try it! You wil never use anything else!

Butch's Natural High Pressure Gun Oil inhibits fouling and protects against corrosion. It is an excellent bore conditioner. Best used with Butch's Bore Shine.

Butch's is distributed by Lyman Products. For information call 1-800-22-LYMAN.

LYMAN PRODUCTS CORPORATION
Dept. 283, 475 Smith Street, Middletown, CT 06457

M27/33 PLUSONE™ EXTENSION

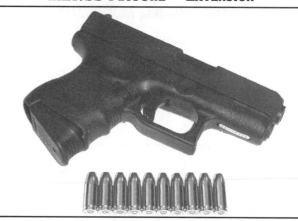

Pearce Grip Inc., originators of the popular grip extension line for the Glock® sub-compact auto pistols, introduces a M27/33 PlusOne™ extension. This unit converts the Glock® model 27 (40SW) or model 33 (357SIG) factory nine round magazine to the legal maximun of ten as well as provides the extra finger groove for shooting comfort and control. The PlusOne™ replaces the factory magazine floor plate and is held securely to the magazine body with a supplied internal locking insert. This new extension is made from a high impact polymer and incorporates the same texture and checkering pattern found on the pistol frame for a factory appearance. For more information or for a dealer near you contact:

PEARCE GRIP, INC.
P.O. Box 40367, Fort Worth, TX 76140
Phone: 800-390-9420 • Fax: 817-568-9707

PROTECTIVE METAL CASES

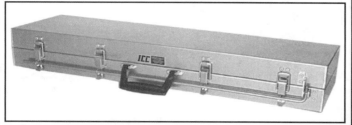

A complete line of 2 pc. and 3 pc. "Flat Style" and "Trunk Style" aluminum transport / shipping cases are offered by KK AIR / ICC. 40 different standard sizes offered, with "Special" cases built to customer requirements. These cases are made of .063 and .080 aluminum, built for strength with the "Traveling Sportsman" in mind. NEW CONCEALMENT DUFFELS and case jackets are available for all case models, including special cases and cases built by other companies. Write or call KK AIR / ICC for more information and pricing.

You can pay more but you can't buy better.

KK AIR / ICC CASE PRODUCTS
P.O. Box 9912, Spokane, WA 99209
Phone: 800-262-3322 • Fax: 509-326-5436
Email: info@kkair.com • Web: www.kkair.com
LIFETIME WARRANTY

HIGH QUALITY OPTICS

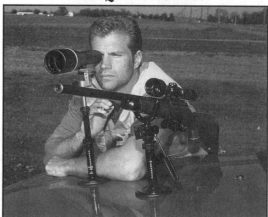

One of the best indicators of quality is a scope's resolution number. The smaller the number, the better. Our scope has a resolution number of 2.8 seconds of angle. This number is about 20% smaller (better) than other well-known scopes costing much more. It means that two .22 caliber bullets can be a hair's breath apart and edges of each still be clearly seen. With a Shepherd at 800 yards, you will be able to tell a four inch antler from a four inch ear and a burrowing owl from a prairie dog. Bird watchers will be able to distinguish a Tufted Titmouse from a Ticked-Off Field Mouse. Send for free catalog.

SHEPHERD ENTERPRISES, INC.
Box 189, Waterloo, NE 68069
Phone: 402-779-2424 • Fax: 402-779-4010
Email: shepherd@shepherdscopes.com • Web: www.shepherdscopes.com

SHOOTER'S MARKETPLACE

COMBINATION RIFLE AND OPTICS REST

The Magna-Pod weighs less than two pounds, yet firmly supports more than most expensive tripods. It will hold 50 pounds at its low nine inch height and over 10 pounds extended to 17 inches. It sets up in seconds where there is neither time nor space for a tripod and keeps your expensive equipment safe from knock-overs by kids, pets, pedestrians, or even high winds. It makes a great mono-pod for camcorders, etc., and its carrying box is less than 13" x 13" x 3-1/4" high for easy storage and access.

Attached to its triangle base it becomes an extremely stable table pod or rifle bench rest. The rifle yoke pictured in photo at left is included.

It's 5 pods in 1: Magna-Pod, Mono-Pod, Table-Pod, Shoulder-Pod and Rifle Rest. Send for free catalog.

SHEPHERD ENTERPRISES, INC.
Box 189, Waterloo, NE 68069
Phone: 402-779-2424 • Fax: 402-779-4010
Email: shepherd@shepherdscopes.com • Web: www.shepherdscopes.com

6x18x40 VARMINT/TARGET SCOPE

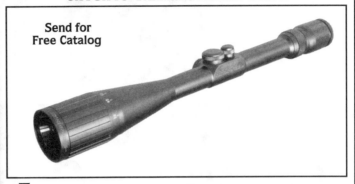

Send for Free Catalog

The Shepherd 6x18x40 Varmint/Target Scope makes long-range varmint and target shooting child's play. Just pick the ranging circle that best fits your target (be it prairie dogs, coyotes or paper varmints) and Shepherd's exclusive, patented Dual Reticle Down Range System does the rest. You won't believe how far you can accurately shoot, even with rimfire rifles.

Shepherd's superior lens coating mean superior light transmission and tack-sharp resolution.

This new shockproof, waterproof scope features 1/4 minute-of-angle clicks on the ranging circles and friction adjustments on the crosshairs that allow fine-tuning to 0.001 MOA. A 40mm adjustable objective provides a 5.5-foot field of view at 100 yards (16x setting). 16.5 FOV @ 6X.

SHEPHERD ENTERPRISES, INC.
Box 189, Waterloo, NE 68069
Phone: 402-779-2424 • Fax: 402-779-4010
Email: shepherd@shepherdscopes.com • Web: www.shepherdscopes.com

FINE CAST RIFLE AND HANDGUN BULLETS

The shooters at Oregon Trail Bullet Company set out five years ago with one goal: to make the finest cast rifle and handgun bullets available. Their ongoing R&D program led them to develop their ultra-hard 24BHN 7-element LASER-CAST Silver Alloy, specialized production tooling and quality-control procedures, with the LASER-CAST bullet line now widely recognized as an industry leader. Over 60 advanced designs are now catalogued with more in development, producing a top-performing bullet for any application like IPSC, Cowboy or Silhouette, all backed by their money back guarantee and friendly customer service. Call for a free sample and "Shoot The REAL Silver Bullet."

OREGON TRAIL BULLET COMPANY
Box 529-GD, Baker City, Oregon 97814-0529
Phone: 800-811-0548
Web: www.laser-cast.com

BUY & SELL GUNS

Gun List is the nation's only indexed firearm paper devoted to helping the gun enthusiast find guns, parts, supplies & ammunition for most firearms. Gun List is an essential publication for buyers & sellers because it contains advertisements from the nation's top gun dealers and an extensive list of alphabetized classifieds. Every issue features over 40,000 firearms for sale.

1 year (26 issues)................... $36.98
2 years (52 issues)................... $65.98
3 years (78 issues)................... $91.98
write for foreign rates

KRAUSE PUBLICATIONS, DEPT. ABAZFK
700 E. State Street, Iola, WI 54990-0001
Phone: 800/258-0929 • Fax: 715/445-4087
www.gunlist.net

2001 GUN DIGEST Complete Compact CATALOG

GUNDEX

GUNDEX

HANDGUNS

RIFLES

SHOTGUNS

BLACKPOWDER

AIRGUNS

ACCESSORIES

REFERENCE

DIRECTORY OF THE ARMS TRADE

GUNDEX

GUNDEX

GUNDEX

Includes models suitable for several forms of competition and other sporting purposes.

Accu-Tek BL-9

Accu-Tek CP-45

Accu-Tek AT-380

Accu-Tek HC-380

AA ARMS AP9 MINI PISTOL

Caliber: 9mm Para., 10-shot magazine. **Barrel:** 3". **Weight:** 3.5 lbs. **Length:** 12" overall. **Stocks:** Checkered black synthetic. **Sights:** Post front adjustable for elevation, rear adjustable for windage. **Features:** Ventilated barrel shroud; blue or electroless nickel finish. Made in U.S. by AA Arms.

Price: 3" barrel, blue $239.00
Price: 3" barrel, electroless nickel $259.00
Price: Mini/5, 5" barrel, blue $259.00
Price: Mini/5, 5" barrel, electroless nickel................. $279.00

ACCU-TEK BL-9 AUTO PISTOL

Caliber: 9mm Para., 5-shot magazine. **Barrel:** 3". **Weight:** 22 oz. **Length:** 5.6" overall. **Stocks:** Black pebble composition. **Sights:** Fixed. **Features:** Double action only; black finish. Introduced 1997. Price includes cleaning kit and gun lock, two magazines. Made in U.S. by Accu-Tek.

Price: $232.00

Accu-Tek Model AT-32SS Auto Pistol

Same as the AT-380SS except chambered for 32 ACP. Introduced 1991. Price includes cleaning kit and gun lock.

Price: Satin stainless $221.00

ACCU-TEK MODEL AT-380 AUTO PISTOL

Caliber: 380 ACP, 5-shot magazine. **Barrel:** 2.75". **Weight:** 20 oz. **Length:** 5.6" overall. **Stocks:** Grooved black composition. **Sights:** Blade front, rear adjustable for windage. **Features:** Stainless steel frame and slide. External hammer; manual thumb safety; firing pin block, trigger disconnect. Introduced 1991. Price includes cleaning kit and gun lock. Made in U.S. by Accu-Tek.

Price: Satin stainless $221.00

ACCU-TEK CP-45 AUTO PISTOL

Caliber: 45 ACP, 6-shot magazine. **Barrel:** 3-1/4 inches. **Weight:** 31 oz. **Length:** 6-3/8 inches overall. **Grips:** Checkered black nylon. **Sights:** Fully adjustable rear, three-dot; blade front. **Features:** Stainless steel frame and slide; single action with external hammer and firing pin block, manual thumb safety; last-shot hold open. Includes gun lock and cleaning kit. Introduced 2000. Made in U.S. by Excel Industries Inc.

Price: $425.00

ACCU-TEK MODEL HC-380 AUTO PISTOL

Caliber: 380 ACP, 10-shot magazine. **Barrel:** 2.75". **Weight:** 26 oz. **Length:** 6" overall. **Stocks:** Checkered black composition. **Sights:** Blade front, rear adjustable for windage. **Features:** External hammer; manual thumb safety with firing pin and trigger disconnect; bottom magazine release. Stainless steel construction. Introduced 1993. Price includes cleaning kit and gun lock. Made in U.S. by Accu-Tek.

Price: Satin stainless $231.00

ACCU-TEK XL-9 AUTO PISTOL

Caliber: 9mm Para., 5-shot magazine. **Barrel:** 3". **Weight:** 24 oz. **Length:** 5.6" overall. **Stocks:** Black pebble composition. **Sights:** Three-dot system; rear adjustable for windage. **Features:** Stainless steel construction; double-action-only mechanism. Introduced 1999. Price includes cleaning kit and gun lock, two magazines. Made in U.S. by Accu-Tek.

Price: $248.00

Accu-Tek XL9

Auto-Ordnance 1911A1 Standard

AMT Backup

AMERICAN ARMS MATEBA AUTO/REVOLVER

Caliber: 357 Mag., 6-shot. **Barrel:** 4", 6", 8". **Weight:** 2.75 lbs. **Length:** 8.77" overall. **Stocks:** Smooth walnut. **Sights:** Blade on ramp front, adjustable rear. **Features:** Double or single action. Cylinder and slide recoil together upon firing. All-steel construction with polished blue finish. Introduced 1995. Imported from Italy by American Arms, Inc.

Price: $1,295.00
Price: 6" $1,349.00

AMT AUTOMAG II AUTO PISTOL

Caliber: 22 WMR, 9-shot magazine (7-shot with 3-3/8" barrel). **Barrel:** 3-3/8", 4-1/2", 6". **Weight:** About 32 oz. **Length:** 9-3/8" overall. **Stocks:** Grooved carbon fiber. **Sights:** Blade front, adjustable rear. **Features:** Made of stainless steel. Gas-assisted action. Exposed hammer. Slide flats have brushed finish, rest is sandblast. Squared trigger guard. Introduced 1986. From Galena Industries, Inc.

Price: $429.00

AMT AUTOMAG III PISTOL

Caliber: 30 Carbine, 8-shot magazine. **Barrel:** 6-3/8". **Weight:** 43 oz. **Length:** 10-1/2" overall. **Stocks:** Carbon fiber. **Sights:** Blade front, adjustable rear. **Features:** Stainless steel construction. Hammer-drop safety. Slide flats have brushed finish, rest is sandblasted. Introduced 1989. From Galena Industries, Inc.

Price: $529.00

AMT AUTOMAG IV PISTOL

Caliber: 45 Winchester Magnum, 6-shot magazine. **Barrel:** 6.5". **Weight:** 46 oz. **Length:** 10.5" overall. **Stocks:** Carbon fiber. **Sights:** Blade front, adjustable rear. **Features:** Made of stainless st3578eel with brushed finish. Introduced 1990. Made in U.S. by Galena Industries, Inc.

Price: $599.00

AMT 45 ACP HARDBALLER II

Caliber: 45 ACP. **Barrel:** 5". **Weight:** 39 oz. **Length:** 8-1/2" overall. **Stocks:** Wrap-around rubber. **Sights:** Adjustable. **Features:** Extended combat safety, serrated matte slide rib, loaded chamber indicator, long grip safety, beveled magazine well, adjustable target trigger. All stainless steel. From Galena Industries, Inc.

Price: $425.00
Price: Government model (as above except no rib, fixed sights) . $399.00
Price: 400 Accelerator (400 Cor-Bon, 7" barrel) $549.00
Price: Commando (40 S&W, Government Model frame) $435.00

AMT 45 ACP HARDBALLER LONG SLIDE

Caliber: 45 ACP. **Barrel:** 7". **Length:** 10-1/2" overall. **Stocks:** Wrap-around rubber. **Sights:** Fully adjustable rear sight. **Features:** Slide and barrel are 2" longer than the standard 45, giving less recoil, added velocity, longer sight radius. Has extended combat safety, serrated matte rib, loaded chamber indicator, wide adjustable trigger. From Galena Industries, Inc.

Price: $529.00

AMT BACKUP PISTOL

Caliber: 357 SIG (5-shot); 38 Super, 9mm Para. (6-shot); 40 S&W, 400 Cor-Bon; 45 ACP (5-shot). **Barrel:** 3". **Weight:** 23 oz. **Length:** 5-3/4" overall. **Stocks:** Checkered black synthetic. **Sights:** None. **Features:** Stainless steel construction; double-action-only trigger; dust cover over the trigger transfer bar; extended magazine; titanium nitride finish. Introduced 1992. Made in U.S. by Galena Industries.

Price: 9mm, 40 S&W, 45 ACP $319.00
Price: 38 Super, 357 SIG, 400 Cor-Bon $369.00

AMT 380 DAO Small Frame Backup

Similar to the DAO Backup except has smaller frame, 2-1/2" barrel, weighs 18 oz., and is 5" overall. Has 5-shot magazine, matte/stainless finish. Made in U.S. by Galena Industries.

Price: $319.00

AUTO-ORDNANCE 1911A1 AUTOMATIC PISTOL

Caliber: 45 ACP, 7-shot magazine. **Barrel:** 5". **Weight:** 39 oz. **Length:** 8-1/2" overall. **Stocks:** Checkered plastic with medallion. **Sights:** Blade front, rear adjustable for windage. **Features:** Same specs as 1911A1 military guns—parts interchangeable. Frame and slide blued; each radius has non-glare finish. Made in U.S. by Auto-Ordnance Corp.

Price: 45 ACP, blue $447.00
Price: 45 ACP, Parkerized $462.00
Price: 45 ACP Deluxe (three-dot sights, textured rubber wraparound grips) $455.00

Auto-Ordnance 1911A1 Custom High Polish Pistol

Similar to the standard 1911A1 except has a Videki speed trigger, extended thumb safety, flat mainspring housing, Acurod recoil spring guide system, rosewood grips, custom combat hammer, beavertail grip safety. High-polish blue finish. Introduced 1998. Made in U.S. by Auto-Ordnance Corp.

Price: $585.00

Auto-Ordnance Deluxe

Baer Custom Carry

Auto-Ordnance Pit Bull

Baer Premium II

Auto-Ordnance ZG-51 Pit Bull Auto

Same as the 1911A1 except has 3-1/2" barrel, weighs 36 oz. and has an over-all length of 7-1/4". Available in 45 ACP only; 7-shot magazine. Introduced 1989.

Price: **$470.00**

AUTAUGA 32 AUTO PISTOL

Caliber: 32 ACP, 6-shot magazine. **Barrel:** 2". **Weight:** 11.3 oz. **Length:** 4.3" overall. **Stocks:** Black polymer. **Sights:** Fixed. **Features:** Double-action-only mechanism. Stainless steel construction. Uses Winchester Silver Tip ammunition.

Price: .... **NA**

BAER 1911 CUSTOM CARRY AUTO PISTOL

Caliber: 45 ACP, 7- or 10-shot magazine. **Barrel:** 5". **Weight:** 37 oz. **Length:** 8.5" overall. **Stocks:** Checkered walnut. **Sights:** Baer improved ramp-style dovetailed front, Novak low-mount rear. **Features:** Baer forged NM frame, slide and barrel with stainless bushing; fitted slide to frame; double serrated slide (full-size only); Baer speed trigger with 4-lb. pull; Baer deluxe hammer and sear, tactical-style extended ambidextrous safety, beveled magazine well; polished feed ramp and throated barrel; tuned extractor; Baer extended ejector, checkered slide stop; lowered and flared ejection port, full-length recoil guide rod; recoil buff. Made in U.S. by Les Baer Custom, Inc.

Price: Standard size, blued. **$1,620.00**
Price: Standard size, stainless **$1,690.00**
Price: Comanche size, blued **$1,640.00**
Price: Comanche size, stainless. **$1,690.00**
Price: Comanche size, aluminum frame, blued slide **$1,890.00**
Price: Comanche size, aluminum frame, stainless slide **$1,995.00**

Baer 1911 Concept III Auto Pistol

Same as the Concept I except has forged stainless frame with blued steel slide, Bo-Mar rear sight, 30 lpi checkering on front strap. Made in U.S. by Les Baer Custom, Inc.

Price: **$1,520.00**
Price: Concept IV (with Baer adjustable rear sight) **$1,499.00**
Price: Concept V (all stainless, Bo-Mar sight, checkered front strap)
.... **$1,558.00**
Price: Concept VI (stainless, Baer adjustable sight, checkered front strap) **$1,558.00**

BAER 1911 PREMIER II AUTO PISTOL

Caliber: 9x23, 38 Super, 400 Cor-Bon, 45 ACP, 7- or 10-shot magazine. **Barrel:** 5". **Weight:** 37 oz. **Length:** 8.5" overall. **Stocks:** Checkered rosewood, double diamond pattern. **Sights:** Baer dovetailed front, low-mount Bo-Mar rear with hidden leaf. **Features:** Baer NM forged steel frame and barrel with stainless bushing; slide fitted to frame; double serrated slide; lowered, flared ejection port; tuned, polished extractor; Baer extended ejector, checkered slide stop, aluminum speed trigger with 4-lb. pull, deluxe Commander hammer and sear, beavertail grip safety with pad, beveled magazine well, extended ambidextrous safety; flat mainspring housing; polished feed ramp and throated barrel; 30 lpi checkered front strap. Made in U.S. by Les Baer Custom, Inc.

Price: Blued **$1,428.00**
Price: Stainless. **$1,558.00**
Price: 6" model, blued, from **$1,595.00**

BAER 1911 S.R.P. PISTOL

Caliber: 45 ACP. **Barrel:** 5". **Weight:** 37 oz. **Length:** 8.5" overall. **Stocks:** Checkered walnut. **Sights:** Trijicon night sights. **Features:** Similar to the F.B.I. contract gun except uses Baer forged steel frame. Has Baer match barrel with supported chamber, Wolff springs, complete tactical action job. All parts Mag-na-fluxed; deburred for tactical carry. Has Baer Ultra Coat finish. Tuned for reliability. Contact Baer for complete details. Introduced 1996. Made in U.S. by Les Baer Custom, Inc.

Price: Government or Comanche length **$2,990.00**

BAER 1911 CONCEPT I AUTO PISTOL

Caliber: 45 ACP, 7-shot magazine. **Barrel:** 5". **Weight:** 37 oz. **Length:** 8.5" overall. **Stocks:** Checkered rosewood. **Sights:** Baer dovetail front, Bo-Mar deluxe low-mount rear with hidden leaf. **Features:** Baer forged steel frame, slide and barrel with Baer stainless bushing; slide fitted to frame; double serrated slide; Baer beavertail grip safety, checkered slide stop, tuned extractor, extended ejector, deluxe hammer and sear, match disconnector; lowered and flared ejection port; fitted recoil link; polished feed ramp, throated barrel; Baer fitted speed trigger, flat serrated mainspring housing. Blue finish. Made in U.S. by Les Baer Custom, Inc.

Price: $1,390.00
Price: Concept II (with Baer adjustable rear sight) $1,390.00

Baer 1911 Concept VII Auto Pistol

Same as the Concept I except reduced Comanche size with 4.25" barrel, weighs 27.5 oz., 7.75" overall. Blue finish, checkered front strap. Made in U.S. by Les Baer Custom, Inc.

Price: $1,495.00
Price: Concept VIII (stainless frame and slide, Baer adjustable rear sight) $1,547.00

Baer 1911 Concept IX Auto Pistol

Same as the Comanche Concept VII except has Baer lightweight forged aluminum frame, blued steel slide, Baer adjustable rear sight. Chambered for 45 ACP, 7-shot magazine. Made in U.S. by Les Baer Custom, Inc.

Price: $1,655.00
Price: Concept X (as above with stainless slide) $1,675.00

Baer 1911 Prowler III Auto Pistol

Same as the Premier II except also has full-length guide rod, tapered cone stub weight and reverse recoil plug. Made in U.S. by Les Baer Custom, Inc.

Price: Standard size, blued.......... $1,795.00

BERETTA MODEL 92FS PISTOL

Caliber: 9mm Para., 10-shot magazine. **Barrel:** 4.9". **Weight:** 34 oz. **Length:** 8.5" overall. **Stocks:** Checkered black plastic. **Sights:** Blade front, rear adjustable for windage. Tritium night sights available. **Features:** Double action. Extractor acts as chamber loaded indicator, squared trigger guard, grooved front- and backstraps, inertia firing pin. Matte or blued finish. Introduced 1977. Made in U.S. and imported from Italy by Beretta U.S.A.

Price: With plastic grips $655.00
Price: Stainless, rubber grips $718.00

Beretta Model 92FS/96 Brigadier Pistols

Similar to the Model 92FS/96 except with a heavier slide to reduce felt recoil and allow mounting removable front sight. Wrap-around rubber grips. Three-dot sights dovetailed to the slide, adjustable for windage. Weighs 35.3 oz. Introduced 1999.

Price: 9mm or 40 S&W, 10-shot.......... $702.00

Beretta Model 92FS 470th Anniversary Limited Edition

Similar to the Model 92FS stainless except has mirror polish finish, smooth walnut grips with inlaid gold-plated medallions. Special and unique gold-filled engraving includes the signature of Beretta's president. The anniversary logo is engraved on the top of the slide and the back of the magazine. Each pistol identified by a "1 of 470" gold-filled number. Special chrome-plated magazine included. Deluxe lockable walnut case with teak inlays and engraving. Only 470 pistols will be sold. Introduced 1999.

Price: $2,082.00

Beretta Model 92FS Compact and Compact Type M Pistol

Similar to the Model 92FS except more compact and lighter: overall length 7.8"; 4.3" barrel; weighs 30.9 oz. Has Bruniton finish, chrome-lined bore, combat trigger guard, ambidextrous safety/decock lever. Single column 8-shot magazine (Type M), or double column 10-shot (Compact), 9mm only. Introduced 1998. Imported from Italy by Beretta U.S.A.

Price: Compact (10-shot) $655.00
Price: Compact Type M (8-shot).......... $655.00

Beretta 96

Beretta 950 Jetfire

Beretta Model 96 Pistol

Same as the Model 92FS except chambered for 40 S&W. Ambidextrous safety mechanism with passive firing pin catch, slide safety/decocking lever, trigger bar disconnect. Has 10-shot magazine. Available with three-dot sights. Introduced 1992.

Price: Model 96, plastic grips $655.00
Price: Stainless, rubber grips $718.00

Beretta M9 Special Edition Pistol

Copy of the U.S. M9 military pistol. Similar to the Model 92FS except has special M9 serial number range; one 15-round (pre-ban) magazine; dot-and-post sight system; special M9 military packaging; Army TM 9-1005-317-10 operator's manual; M9 Special Edition patch; certificate of authenticity; Bianchi M12 holster, M1025 magazine pouch, and M1015 web pistol belt. Introduced 1998. From Beretta U.S.A.

Price: $861.00

BERETTA MODEL 80 CHEETAH SERIES DA PISTOLS

Caliber: 380 ACP, 10-shot magazine (M84); 8-shot (M85); 22 LR, 7-shot (M87). **Barrel:** 3.82". **Weight:** About 23 oz. (M84/85); 20.8 oz. (M87). **Length:** 6.8" overall. **Stocks:** Glossy black plastic (wood optional at extra cost). **Sights:** Fixed front, drift-adjustable rear. **Features:** Double action, quick takedown, convenient magazine release. Introduced 1977. Imported from Italy by Beretta U.S.A.

Price: Model 84 Cheetah, plastic grips.......... $565.00
Price: Model 84 Cheetah, wood grips $595.00
Price: Model 84 Cheetah, wood grips, nickel finish $639.00
Price: Model 85 Cheetah, plastic grips, 8-shot.......... $533.00
Price: Model 85 Cheetah, wood grips, 8-shot $566.00
Price: Model 85 Cheetah, wood grips, nickel, 8-shot.......... $596.00
Price: Model 87 Cheetah, wood, 22 LR, 7-shot $565.00

Beretta Model 86 Cheetah

Similar to the 380-caliber Model 85 except has tip-up barrel for first-round loading. Barrel length is 4.4", overall length of 7.33". Has 8-shot magazine, walnut grips. Introduced 1989.

Price: $566.00

BERETTA MODEL 950 JETFIRE AUTO PISTOL

Caliber: 25 ACP, 8-shot. **Barrel:** 2.4". **Weight:** 9.9 oz. **Length:** 4.7" overall. **Stocks:** Checkered black plastic or walnut. **Sights:** Fixed. **Features:**

Beretta M8000/8040 Cougar

Bersa Thunder 380

Single action, thumb safety; tip-up barrel for direct loading/unloading, cleaning. From Beretta U.S.A.

Price: Jetfire plastic, blue **$220.00**
Price: Jetfire plastic, nickel **$300.00**
Price: Jetfire wood, EL **$337.00**
Price: Jetfire plastic, matte finish **$220.00**

Beretta Model 21 Bobcat Pistol

Similar to the Model 950 BS. Chambered for 22 LR or 25 ACP. Both double action. Has 2.4" barrel, 4.9" overall length; 7-round magazine on 22 cal.; 8 rounds in 25 ACP, 9.9 oz., available in nickel, matte, engraved or blue finish. Plastic or walnut grips. Introduced in 1985.

Price: Bobcat, 22-cal., blue............................... **$279.00**
Price: Bobcat, nickel, 22-cal. **$322.00**
Price: Bobcat, 25-cal., blue............................... **$279.00**
Price: Bobcat, nickel, 25-cal. **$322.00**
Price: Bobcat EL, 22 or 25 .... **$356.00**
Price: Bobcat plastic matte, 22 or 25 .... **$246.00**

BERETTA MODEL 3032 TOMCAT PISTOL

Caliber: 32 ACP, 7-shot magazine. **Barrel:** 2.45". **Weight:** 14.5 oz. **Length:** 5" overall. **Stocks:** Checkered black plastic. **Sights:** Blade front, drift-adjustable rear. **Features:** Double action with exposed hammer; tip-up barrel for direct loading/unloading; thumb safety; polished or matte blue finish. Imported from Italy by Beretta U.S.A. Introduced 1996.

Price: Blue **$362.00**
Price: Matte **$333.00**

BERETTA MODEL 8000/8040/8045 COUGAR PISTOL

Caliber: 9mm Para., 10-shot, 40 S&W, 10-shot magazine; 45 ACP, 8-shot. **Barrel:** 3.6". **Weight:** 33.5 oz. **Length:** 7" overall. **Stocks:** Checkered plastic. **Sights:** Blade front, rear drift adjustable for windage. **Features:** Slide-mounted safety; rotating barrel; exposed hammer. Matte black Bruniton finish. Announced 1994. Imported from Italy by Beretta U.S.A.

Price: **$695.00**
Price: D model, 9mm, 40 S&W **$672.00**
Price: D model, 45 ACP **$724.00**

BERETTA MODEL 9000S COMPACT PISTOL

Caliber: 9mm Para., 40 S&W; 10-shot magazine. **Barrel:** 3.4". **Weight:** 26.8 oz. **Length:** 6.6". **Grips:** Soft polymer. **Sights:** Windage-adjustable white-dot rear, white-dot blade front. **Features:** Glass-reinforced polymer frame; patented tilt-barrel, open-slide locking system; chrome-lined barrel; external serrated hammer; automatic firing pin and manual safeties. Introduced 2000. Imported from Italy by Beretta USA.

Price: 9000S Type F (single and double action, external
hammer) **$551.00**
Price: 9000S Type D (double-action only, no external
hammer or safety). **$551.00**

Beretta Model 8000/8040/8045 Mini Cougar

Similar to the Model 8000/8040 Cougar except has shorter grip frame and weighs 27.6 oz. Introduced 1998. Imported from Italy by Beretta U.S.A.

Price: 9mm or 40 S&W................................... **$695.00**
Price: 9mm or 40 S&W, DAO............................. **$672.00**
Price: 45 ACP, 6-shot.................................... **$724.00**
Price: 45 ACP DAO **$724.00**

BERSA THUNDER 380 AUTO PISTOLS

Caliber: 380 ACP, 7-shot (Thunder 380 Lite), 9-shot magazine (Thunder 380 DLX). **Barrel:** 3.5". **Weight:** 25.75 oz. **Length:** 6.6" overall. **Stocks:** Black polymer. **Sights:** Blade front, notch rear adjustable for windage; three-dot system. **Features:** Double action; firing pin and magazine safeties. Available in blue or nickel. Introduced 1995. Distributed by Eagle Imports, Inc.

Price: Thunder 380, 7-shot, deep blue finish **$234.95**

BROWNING FORTY-NINE AUTOMATIC PISTOL

Caliber: 40 S&W, 10-shot magazine. **Barrel:** 4.25". **Weight:** 26 oz. **Length:** 7.75" overall. **Stocks:** Integral; black nylon with pebble-grain texture. **Sights:** Dovetailed three-dot. **Features:** Has FN's patented RSS (Repeatable Secure Striker) firing system; extended modular slide rails; reversible magazine catch; stainless slide, black nylon frame. Introduced 1999. Imported by Browning.

Price: **$440.00**

BROWNING HI-POWER 9mm AUTOMATIC PISTOL

Caliber: 9mm Para., 40 S&W, 10-shot magazine. **Barrel:** 4-21/32". **Weight:** 32 oz. **Length:** 7-3/4" overall. **Stocks:** Walnut, hand checkered, or black Polyamide. **Sights:** 1/8" blade front; rear screw-adjustable for windage and elevation. Also available with fixed rear (drift-adjustable for windage). **Features:** External hammer with half-cock and thumb safeties. A blow on the hammer cannot discharge a cartridge; cannot be fired with magazine removed. Fixed rear sight model available. Imported from Belgium by Browning.

Price: Fixed sight model, walnut grips **$615.00**
Price: 9mm with rear sight adj. for w. and e., walnut grips **$668.00**
Price: Mark III, standard matte black finish, fixed sight, moulded grips,
ambidextrous safety **$579.00**
Price: Silver chrome, adjustable sight, Pachmayr grips **$684.00**

Browning 40 S&W Hi-Power Mark III Pistol

Similar to the standard Hi-Power except chambered for 40 S&W, 10-shot magazine, weighs 35 oz., and has 4-3/4" barrel. Comes with matte blue finish, low profile front sight blade, drift-adjustable rear sight, ambidextrous safety, moulded polyamide grips with thumb rest. Introduced 1993. Imported from Belgium by Browning.

Price: Mark III **$579.00**

NEW!

Browning Capitan Hi-Power   **Browning Micro Buck Mark Standard**   **Browning Buck Mark Challenge**   **Browning Buck Mark Varmint**

Browning Capitan Hi-Power Pistol

Similar to the standard Hi-Power except has adjustable tangent rear sight authentic to the early-production model. Also has Commander-style hammer. Checkered walnut grips, polished blue finish. Reintroduced 1993. Imported from Belgium by Browning.

Price: 9mm only **$728.00**

Browning Hi-Power HP-Practical Pistol

Similar to the standard Hi-Power except has silver-chromed frame with blued slide, wrap-around Pachmayr rubber grips, round-style serrated hammer and removable front sight (drift-adjustable for windage). Available in 9mm Para. or 40 S&W. Introduced 1991.

Price: **$662.00**
Price: With fully adjustable rear sight **$717.00**

BROWNING BUCK MARK 22 PISTOL

Caliber: 22 LR, 10-shot magazine. **Barrel:** 5-1/2". **Weight:** 32 oz. **Length:** 9-1/2" overall. **Stocks:** Black moulded composite with checkering. **Sights:** Ramp front, Browning Pro Target rear adjustable for windage and elevation. **Features:** All steel, matte blue finish or nickel, gold-colored trigger. Buck Mark Plus has laminated wood grips. Made in U.S. Introduced 1985. From Browning.

Price: Buck Mark, blue **$265.00**
Price: Buck Mark, nickel finish with contoured rubber stocks. . . . **$312.00**
Price: Buck Mark Plus **$324.00**

Browning Buck Mark Camper

Similar to the Buck Mark except 5-1/2" bull barrel. Weight is 34 oz. Available in matte blue. Introduced 1999. From Browning.

Price: **$234.00**

Browning Buck Mark Challenge, Challenge Micro

Similar to the Buck Mark except has a lightweight barrel and smaller grip diameter. Barrel length is 5-1/2", weight is 25 oz. Introduced 1999. From Browning.

Price: **$296.00**
Price: Challenge Micro (4" barrel) **$296.00**

Calico M-110

Browning Micro Buck Mark

Same as the standard Buck Mark and Buck Mark Plus except has 4" barrel. Available in blue or nickel. Has 16-click Pro Target rear sight. Introduced 1992.

Price: Blue **$265.00**
Price: Nickel **$312.00**
Price: Buck Mark Micro Plus **$324.00**
Price: Buck Mark Micro Plus Nickel **$354.00**

Browning Buck Mark Varmint

Same as the Buck Mark except has 9-7/8" heavy barrel with .900" diameter and full-length scope base (no open sights); walnut grips with optional forend, or finger-groove walnut. Overall length is 14", weighs 48 oz. Introduced 1987.

Price: **$403.00**

CALICO M-110 AUTO PISTOL

Caliber: 22 LR. **Barrel:** 6". **Weight:** 3.7 lbs. (loaded). **Length:** 17.9" overall. **Stocks:** Moulded composition. **Sights:** Adjustable post front, notch rear. **Features:** Aluminum alloy frame; compensator; pistol grip compartment; ambidextrous safety. Uses same helical-feed magazine as M-100 Carbine. Introduced 1986. Made in U.S. From Calico.

Price: **$570.00**

Carbon-15

Colt 1991 Model O Compact

Charles Daly M-1911-A1P

Colt XS Model O Commander

CARBON-15 (Type 97) PISTOL

Caliber: 223, 10-shot magazine. **Barrel:** 7.25". **Weight:** 46 oz. **Length:** 20" overall. **Stock:** Checkered composite. **Sights:** Ghost ring. **Features:** Semi-automatic, gas-operated, rotating bolt action. Carbon fiber upper and lower receiver; chromemoly bolt carrier; fluted stainless match barrel; mil. spec. optics mounting base; uses AR-15-type magazines. Introduced 1992. From Professional Ordnance, Inc.

Price: **$1,600.00**
Price: Type 20 pistol (light-profile barrel, no compensator, weighs
40 oz.). **$1,500.00**

CHARLES DALY M-1911-A1P AUTOLOADING PISTOL

Caliber: 45 ACP, 7- or 10-shot magazine. **Barrel:** 5". **Weight:** 38 oz. **Length:** 8-3/4" overall. **Stocks:** Checkered. **Sights:** Blade front, rear drift adjustable for windage; three-dot system. **Features:** Skeletonized combat hammer and trigger; beavertail grip safety; extended slide release; over-size thumb safety; Parkerized finish. Introduced 1996. Imported from the Philippines by K.B.I., Inc.

Price: **$469.95**

COLT MODEL 1991 MODEL O AUTO PISTOL

Caliber: 45 ACP, 7-shot magazine. **Barrel:** 5". **Weight:** 38 oz. **Length:** 8.5" overall. **Stocks:** Checkered black composition. **Sights:** Ramped blade front, fixed square notch rear, high profile. **Features:** Parkerized finish. Continuation of serial number range used on original G.I. 1911 A1 guns. Comes with one magazine and moulded carrying case. Introduced 1991.
Price: **$573.00**
Price: Stainless. **$628.00**

Colt Model 1991 Model O Compact Auto Pistol

Similar to the Model 1991 A1 except has 3-1/2" barrel. Overall length is 7", and gun is 3/8" shorter in height. Comes with one 6-shot magazine, moulded case. Introduced 1993.
Price: **$556.00**

COLT XS SERIES MODEL O AUTO PISTOLS

Caliber: 45 ACP, 8-shot magazine. **Barrel:** 4.25", 5". **Weight:** N/A. **Length:** N/A. **Grips:** Checkered, double diamond rosewood. **Sights:** Drift-adjust-able three-dot combat. **Features:** Brushed stainless finish; adjustable, two-cut aluminum trigger; extended ambidextrous thumb safety; upswept beavertail with palm swell; elongated slot hammer; beveled magazine well. Introduced 1999. From Colt's Manufacturing Co., Inc.
Price: XS Government (5" barrel) **$750.00**
Price: XS Commander (4.25" barrel) **$750.00**

COLT XS LIGHTWEIGHT COMMANDER AUTO PISTOL

Caliber: 45 ACP, 8-shot. **Barrel:** 4-1/4". **Weight:** 26 oz. **Length:** 7-3/4" overall. **Stocks:** Double diamond checkered rosewood. **Sights:** Fixed, glare-proofed blade front, square notch rear; three-dot system. **Features:** Brushed stainless slide, nickeled aluminum frame; McCormick elongated-slot enhanced hammer, McCormick two-cut adjustable aluminum ham-mer. Made in U.S. by Colt's Mfg. Co., Inc.
Price: 45, stainless **$750.00**

Colt Model 1991 Model O Commander Auto Pistol

Similar to the Model 1991 Model O except has 4-1/4" barrel. Parkerized finish. 7-shot magazine. Comes in moulded case. Introduced 1993.
Price: **$556.00**

Colt XS Lightweight Commander

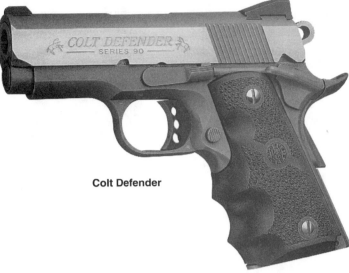

Colt Defender

Colt Lightweight Commander

Coonan 357 Magnum

COLT DEFENDER
Caliber: 40 S&W, 45 ACP, 7-shot magazine. **Barrel:** 3". **Weight:** 22-1/2 oz. **Length:** 6-3/4" overall. **Stocks:** Pebble-finish rubber wraparound with finger grooves. **Sights:** White dot front, snag-free Colt competition rear. **Features:** Stainless finish; aluminum frame; combat-style hammer; Hi Ride grip safety, extended manual safety, disconnect safety. Introduced 1998. Made in U.S. by Colt's Mfg. Co.
Price: **$840.00**

COONAN 357 MAGNUM, 41 MAGNUM PISTOLS
Caliber: 357 Mag., 41 Magnum, 7-shot magazine. **Barrel:** 5". **Weight:** 42 oz. **Length:** 8.3" overall. **Stocks:** Smooth walnut. **Sights:** Interchangeable ramp front, rear adjustable for windage. **Features:** Stainless steel construction. Unique barrel hood improves accuracy and reliability. Linkless barrel. Many parts interchange with Colt autos. Has grip, hammer, half-cock safeties, extended slide latch. Made in U.S. by Coonan Arms, Inc.
Price: 5" barrel, from. **$735.00**
Price: 6" barrel, from. **$768.00**
Price: With 6" compensated barrel **$1,014.00**
Price: Classic model (Teflon black two-tone finish, 8-shot magazine, fully adjustable rear sight, integral compensated barrel) **$1,400.00**
Price: 41 Magnum Model, from **$825.00**

Coonan Compact Cadet 357 Magnum Pistol
Similar to the 357 Magnum full-size gun except has 3.9" barrel, shorter frame, 6-shot magazine. Weight is 39 oz., overall length 7.8". Linkless bull barrel, full-length recoil spring guide rod, extended slide latch. Introduced 1993. Made in U.S. by Coonan Arms, Inc.
Price: **$855.00**

CZ 75B 9mm

CZ 75B AUTO PISTOL
Caliber: 9mm Para., 40 S&W, 10-shot magazine. **Barrel:** 4.7". **Weight:** 34.3 oz. **Length:** 8.1" overall. **Stocks:** High impact checkered plastic. **Sights:** Square post front, rear adjustable for windage; three-dot system. **Features:** Single action/double action design; firing pin block safety; choice of black polymer, matte or high-polish blue finishes. All-steel frame. Imported from the Czech Republic by CZ-USA.

CZ 75B Decocker

CZ 85

CZ 75D Compact

CZ 83B

Price: Black polymer. **$472.00**
Price: Glossy blue. **$486.00**
Price: Dual tone or satin nickel. **$486.00**
Price: 22 LR conversion unit. **$279.00**

CZ 75B Decocker

Similar to the CZ 75B except has a decocking lever in place of the safety lever. All other specifications are the same. Introduced 1999. Imported from the Czech Republic by CZ-USA.
Price: 9mm, black polymer. **$467.00**

CZ 75B Compact Auto Pistol

Similar to the CZ 75 except has 10-shot magazine, 3.9" barrel and weighs 32 oz. Has removable front sight, non-glare ribbed slide top. Trigger guard is squared and serrated; combat hammer. Introduced 1993. Imported from the Czech Republic by CZ-USA.
Price: 9mm, black polymer. **$499.00**
Price: Dual tone or satin nickel. **$513.00**
Price: D Compact, black polymer. **$526.00**

CZ 85B Auto Pistol

Same gun as the CZ 75 except has ambidextrous slide release and safety-levers; non-glare, ribbed slide top; squared, serrated trigger guard; trigger stop to prevent overtravel. Introduced 1986. Imported from the Czech Republic by CZ-USA.

Price: Black polymer. **$483.00**
Price: Combat, black polymer **$540.00**
Price: Combat, dual tone **$487.00**
Price: Combat, glossy blue. **$499.00**

CZ 85 Combat

Similar to the CZ 85B (9mm only) except has an adjustable rear sight, adjustable trigger for overtravel, free-fall magazine, extended magazine catch. Does not have the firing pin block safety. Introduced 1999. Imported from the Czech Republic by CZ-USA.
Price: 9mm, black polymer. **$540.00**
Price: 9mm, glossy blue **$561.00**
Price: 9mm, dual tone or satin nickel **$561.00**

CZ 83B DOUBLE-ACTION PISTOL

Caliber: 9mm Makarov, 32 ACP, 380 ACP, 10-shot magazine. **Barrel:** 3.8". **Weight:** 26.2 oz. **Length:** 6.8" overall. **Stocks:** High impact checkered plastic. **Sights:** Removable square post front, rear adjustable for windage; three-dot system. **Features:** Single action/double action; ambidextrous magazine release and safety. Blue finish; non-glare ribbed slide top. Imported from the Czech Republic by CZ-USA.
Price: Blue **$378.00**
Price: Nickel **$378.00**

CZ 97B

CZ 100

CZ 75/85 Kadet

Davis P-380

Davis P-32

CZ 97B AUTO PISTOL

Caliber: 45 ACP, 10-shot magazine. **Barrel:** 4.85". **Weight:** 40 oz. **Length:** 8.34" overall. **Stocks:** Checkered walnut. **Sights:** Fixed. **Features:** Single action/double action; full-length slide rails; screw-in barrel bushing; linkless barrel; all-steel construction; chamber loaded indicator; dual transfer bars. Introduced 1999. Imported from the Czech Republic by CZ-USA.
Price: Black polymer.................................... **$607.00**
Price: Glossy blue....................................... **$621.00**

CZ 75/85 KADET AUTO PISTOL

Caliber: 22 LR, 10-shot magazine. **Barrel:** 4.88". **Weight:** 36 oz. **Length:** NA. **Stocks:** High impact checkered plastic. **Sights:** Blade front, fully adjustable rear. **Features:** Single action/double action mechanism; all-steel construction. Duplicates weight, balance and function of the CZ 75 pistol. Introduced 1999. Imported from the Czech Republic by CZ-USA.
Price: Black polymer.................................... **$486.00**

CZ 100 AUTO PISTOL

Caliber: 9mm Para., 40 S&W, 10-shot magazine. **Barrel:** 3.7". **Weight:** 24 oz. **Length:** 6.9" overall. **Stocks:** Grooved polymer. **Sights:** Blade front with dot, white outline rear drift adjustable for windage. **Features:** Double action only with firing pin block; polymer frame, steel slide; has laser sight mount. Introduced 1996. Imported from the Czech Republic by CZ-USA.
Price: 9mm Para....................................... **$405.00**
Price: 40 S&W **$405.00**

DAVIS P-380 AUTO PISTOL

Caliber: 380 ACP, 5-shot magazine. **Barrel:** 2.8". **Weight:** 22 oz. **Length:** 5.4" overall. **Stocks:** Black composition. **Sights:** Fixed. **Features:** Choice of chrome or black Teflon finish. Introduced 1991. Made in U.S. by Davis Industries.
Price: **$98.00**

DAVIS P-32 AUTO PISTOL

Caliber: 32 ACP, 6-shot magazine. **Barrel:** 2.8". **Weight:** 22 oz. **Length:** 5.4" overall. **Stocks:** Laminated wood. **Sights:** Fixed. **Features:** Choice of black Teflon or chrome finish. Announced 1986. Made in U.S. by Davis Industries.
Price: **$107.00**

Desert Eagle Mark XIX

E.A.A. Witness

Desert Eagle Baby Eagle

Entréprise Elite P500

DESERT EAGLE MARK XIX PISTOL

Caliber: 357 Mag., 9-shot; 44 Mag., 8-shot; 50 Magnum, 7-shot. **Barrel:** 6", 10", interchangeable. **Weight:** 357 Mag.—62 oz.; 44 Mag.—69 oz.; 50 Mag.—72 oz. **Length:** 10-1/4" overall (6" bbl.). **Stocks:** Rubber. **Sights:** Blade on ramp front, combat-style rear. Adjustable available. **Features:** Interchangeable barrels; rotating three-lug bolt; ambidextrous safety; adjustable trigger. Military epoxy finish. Satin, bright nickel, hard chrome, polished and blued finishes available. 10" barrel extra. Imported from Israel by Magnum Research, Inc.

Price: 357, 6" bbl., standard pistol **$1,199.00**
Price: 44 Mag., 6", standard pistol **$1,199.00**
Price: 50 Magnum, 6" bbl., standard pistol **$1,199.00**
Price: 440 Cor-Bon, 6" bbl. **$1,389.00**

DESERT EAGLE BABY EAGLE PISTOLS

Caliber: 9mm Para., 40 S&W, 45 ACP, 10-round magazine. **Barrel:** 3.5", 3.7", 4.72". **Weight:** NA. **Length:** 7.25" to 8.25" overall. **Grips:** Polymer. **Sights:** Drift-adjustable rear, blade front. **Features:** Steel frame and slide; polygonal rifling to reduce barrel wear; slide safety; decocker. Reintroduced in 1999. Imported from Israel by Magnum Research Inc.

Price: Standard (9mm or 40 cal.; 4.72" barrel, 8.25" overall) . . . **$449.00**
Price: Semi-Compact (9mm, 40 or 45 cal.; 3.7" barrel,
   7.75" overall) **$449.00**
Price: Compact (9mm or 40 cal.; 3.5" barrel, 7.25" overall) **$449.00**
Price: Polymer (9mm or 40 cal; polymer frame; 3.25" barrel,
   7.25" overall) **$449.00**

E.A.A. WITNESS DA AUTO PISTOL

Caliber: 9mm Para., 10-shot magazine; 38 Super, 40 S&W, 10-shot magazine; 45 ACP, 10-shot magazine. **Barrel:** 4.50". **Weight:** 35.33 oz.

Length: 8.10" overall. **Stocks:** Checkered rubber. **Sights:** Undercut blade front, open rear adjustable for windage. **Features:** Double-action trigger system; round trigger guard; frame-mounted safety. Introduced 1991. Imported from Italy by European American Armory.

Price: 9mm, blue **$351.00**
Price: 9mm, Wonder finish **$366.00**
Price: 9mm Compact, blue, 10-shot **$351.00**
Price: As above, Wonder finish **$366.60**
Price: 40 S&W, blue **$366.60**
Price: As above, Wonder finish **$366.60**
Price: 40 S&W Compact, 9-shot, blue **$366.60**
Price: As above, Wonder finish **$366.60**
Price: 45 ACP, blue **$351.00**
Price: As above, Wonder finish **$366.60**
Price: 45 ACP Compact, 8-shot, blue **$351.00**
Price: As above, Wonder finish **$366.60**

E.A.A. EUROPEAN MODEL AUTO PISTOLS

Caliber: 32 ACP or 380 ACP, 7-shot magazine. **Barrel:** 3.88". **Weight:** 26 oz. **Length:** 7-3/8" overall. **Stocks:** European hardwood. **Sights:** Fixed blade front, rear drift-adjustable for windage. **Features:** Chrome or blue finish; magazine, thumb and firing pin safeties; external hammer; safety-lever takedown. Imported from Italy by European American Armory.

Price: Blue **$132.60**
Price: Wonder finish **$163,80**

ENTRÉPRISE ELITE P500 AUTO PISTOL

Caliber: 45 ACP, 10-shot magazine. **Barrel:** 5". **Weight:** 40 oz. **Length:** 8.5" overall. **Stocks:** Black ultra-slim, double diamond, checkered synthetic. **Sights:** Dovetailed blade front, rear adjustable for windage; three-dot system. **Features:** Reinforced dust cover; lowered and flared ejection

Entréprise Boxer P500

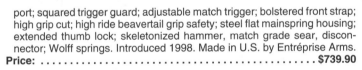

Entréprise Tactical 500

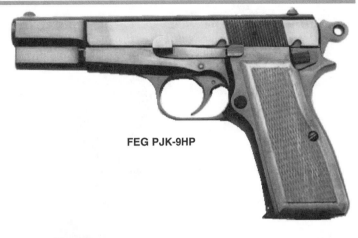

FEG PJK-9HP

Felk MTF 450

port; squared trigger guard; adjustable match trigger; bolstered front strap; high grip cut; high ride beavertail grip safety; steel flat mainspring housing; extended thumb lock; skeletonized hammer, match grade sear, disconnector; Wolff springs. Introduced 1998. Made in U.S. by Entréprise Arms.
Price: $739.90

Entréprise Boxer P500 Auto Pistol

Similar to the Medalist model except has adjustable Competizione "melded" rear sight with dovetailed Patridge front; high mass chiseled slide with sweep cut; machined slide parallel rails; polished breech face and barrel channel. Introduced 1998. Made in U.S. by Entréprise Arms.
Price: $1,399.00

Entréprise Medalist P500 Auto Pistol

Similar to the Elite model except has adjustable Competizione "melded" rear sight with dovetailed Patridge front; machined slide parallel rails with polished breech face and barrel channel; front and rear slide serrations; lowered and flared ejection port; full-length one-piece guide rod with plug; National Match barrel and bushing; stainless firing pin; tuned match extractor; oversize firing pin stop; throated barrel and polished ramp; slide lapped to frame. Introduced 1998. Made in U.S. by Entréprise Arms.
Price: 45 ACP.. $979.00
Price: 40 S&W $1,099.00

Entréprise Tactical P500 Auto Pistol

Similar to the Elite model except has Tactical2 Ghost Ring sight or Novak lo- mount sight; ambidextrous thumb safety; front and rear slide serrations; full-length guide rod; throated barrel, polished ramp; tuned match extractor; fitted barrel and bushing; stainless firing pin; slide lapped to frame; dehorned. Introduced 1998. Made in U.S. by Entréprise Arms.
Price: $979.90
Price: Tactical Plus (full-size frame, Officer's slide) $1,049.00

ERMA KGP68 AUTO PISTOL

Caliber: 32 ACP, 6-shot, 380 ACP, 5-shot. **Barrel:** 4". **Weight:** 22-1/2 oz. **Length:** 7-3/8" overall. **Stocks:** Checkered plastic. **Sights:** Fixed. **Features:** Toggle action similar to original "Luger" pistol. Action stays open after last shot. Has magazine and sear disconnect safety systems.
Price: $499.95

FEG PJK-9HP AUTO PISTOL

Caliber: 9mm Para., 10-shot magazine. **Barrel:** 4.75". **Weight:** 32 oz. **Length:** 8" overall. **Stocks:** Hand-checkered walnut. **Sights:** Blade front, rear adjustable for windage; three dot system. **Features:** Single action; polished blue or hard chrome finish; rounded combat-style serrated hammer. Comes with two magazines and cleaning rod. Imported from Hungary by K.B.I., Inc.
Price: Blue $259.95
Price: Hard chrome $259.95

FEG SMC-380 AUTO PISTOL

Caliber: 380 ACP, 6-shot magazine. **Barrel:** 3.5". **Weight:** 18.5 oz. **Length:** 6.1" overall. **Stocks:** Checkered composition with thumbrest. **Sights:** Blade front, rear adjustable for windage. **Features:** Patterned after the PPK pistol. Alloy frame, steel slide; double action. Blue finish. Comes with two magazines, cleaning rod. Imported from Hungary by K.B.I., Inc.
Price: $224.95

FELK MTF 450 AUTO PISTOL

Caliber: 9mm Para. (10-shot); 40 S&W (8-shot); 45 ACP (9-shot magazine). **Barrel:** 3.5". **Weight:** 19.9 oz. **Length:** 6.4" overall. **Stocks:** Checkered. **Sights:** Blade front; adjustable rear. **Features:** Double-action-only trigger; striker fired; polymer frame; trigger safety, firing pin safety, trigger

Glock 17C

Glock 22

Glock 26

bar safety; adjustable trigger weight; fully interchangeable slide/barrel to change calibers. Introduced 1998. Imported by Felk Inc.

Price: **$395.00**
Price: 45 ACP pistol with 9mm and 40 S&W slide/barrel
assembly **$999.00**

GLOCK 17 AUTO PISTOL

Caliber: 9mm Para., 10-shot magazine. **Barrel:** 4.49". **Weight:** 22.04 oz. (without magazine). **Length:** 7.32" overall. **Stocks:** Black polymer. **Sights:** Dot on front blade, white outline rear adjustable for windage. **Features:** Polymer frame, steel slide; double-action trigger with "Safe Action" system; mechanical firing pin safety, drop safety; simple takedown without tools; locked breech, recoil operated action. Adopted by Austrian armed forces 1983. NATO approved 1984. Imported from Austria by Glock, Inc.
Price: Fixed sight, with extra magazine, magazine loader, cleaning kit

.... **$641.00**
Price: Adjustable sight **$671.00**
Price: Model 17L (6" barrel) **$800.00**
Price: Model 17C, ported barrel (compensated) **$646.00**

Glock 19 Auto Pistol

Similar to the Glock 17 except has a 4" barrel, giving an overall length of 6.85" and weight of 20.99 oz. Magazine capacity is 10 rounds. Fixed or adjustable rear sight. Introduced 1988.
Price: Fixed sight **$641.00**
Price: Adjustable sight **$671.00**
Price: Model 19C, ported barrel **$646.00**

Glock 20 10mm Auto Pistol

Similar to the Glock Model 17 except chambered for 10mm Automatic cartridge. Barrel length is 4.60", overall length is 7.59", and weight is 26.3 oz. (without magazine). Magazine capacity is 10 rounds. Fixed or adjustable rear sight. Comes with an extra magazine, magazine loader, cleaning rod and brush. Introduced 1990. Imported from Austria by Glock, Inc.
Price: Fixed sight **$700.00**
Price: Adjustable sight **$730.00**

Glock 21 Auto Pistol

Similar to the Glock 17 except chambered for 45 ACP, 10-shot magazine. Overall length is 7.59", weight is 25.2 oz. (without magazine). Fixed or adjustable rear sight. Introduced 1991.
Price: Fixed sight **$700.00**
Price: Adjustable sight **$730.00**

Glock 22 Auto Pistol

Similar to the Glock 17 except chambered for 40 S&W, 10-shot magazine. Overall length is 7.28", weight is 22.3 oz. (without magazine). Fixed or adjustable rear sight. Introduced 1990.
Price: Fixed sight **$641.00**
Price: Adjustable sight **$671.00**
Price: Model 22C, ported barrel **$646.00**

Glock 23 Auto Pistol

Similar to the Glock 19 except chambered for 40 S&W, 10-shot magazine. Overall length is 6.85", weight is 20.6 oz. (without magazine). Fixed or adjustable rear sight. Introduced 1990.
Price: Fixed sight **$641.00**
Price: Model 23C, ported barrel **$646.00**
Price: Adjustable sight **$671.00**

GLOCK 26, 27 AUTO PISTOLS

Caliber: 9mm Para. (M26), 10-shot magazine; 40 S&W (M27), 9-shot magazine. **Barrel:** 3.46". **Weight:** 21.75 oz. **Length:** 6.29" overall. **Stocks:** Integral. Stippled polymer. **Sights:** Dot on front blade, fixed or fully adjustable white outline rear. **Features:** Subcompact size. Polymer frame, steel slide; double-action trigger with "Safe Action" system, three safeties. Matte black Tenifer finish. Hammer-forged barrel. Imported from Austria by Glock, Inc. Introduced 1996.
Price: Fixed sight **$641.00**
Price: Adjustable sight **$671.00**

GLOCK 29, 30 AUTO PISTOLS

Caliber: 10mm (M29), 45 ACP (M30), 10-shot magazine. **Barrel:** 3.78". **Weight:** 24 oz. **Length:** 6.7" overall. **Stocks:** Integral. Stippled polymer. **Sights:** Dot on front, fixed or fully adjustable white outline rear. **Features:** Compact size. Polymer frame steel slide; double-recoil spring reduces recoil; Safe Action system with three safeties; Tenifer finish. Two magazines supplied. Introduced 1997. Imported from Austria by Glock, Inc.
Price: Fixed sight **$700.00**
Price: Adjustable sight **$730.00**

Glock 30

Glock 35

Glock 31

Hammerli Trailside PL 22

Glock 31/31C Auto Pistols

Similar to the Glock 17 except chambered for 357 Auto cartridge; 10-shot magazine. Overall length is 7.32", weight is 23.28 oz. (without magazine). Fixed or adjustable sight. Imported from Austria by Glock, Inc.

Price: Fixed sight **$641.00**
Price: Adjustable sight **$671.00**
Price: Model 31C, ported barrel **$646.00**

Glock 32/32C Auto Pistols

Similar to the Glock 19 except chambered for the 357 Auto cartridge; 10-shot magazine. Overall length is 6.85", weight is 21.52 oz. (without magazine). Fixed or adjustable sight. Imported from Austria by Glock, Inc.

Price: Fixed sight **$616.00**
Price: Adjustable sight **$644.00**
Price: Model 32C, ported barrel **$646.00**

Glock 33 Auto Pistol

Similar to the Glock 26 except chambered for the 357 Auto cartridge; 9-shot magazine. Overall length is 6.29", weight is 19.75 oz. (without magazine). Fixed or adjustable sight. Imported from Austria by Glock, Inc.

Price: Fixed sight **$641.00**
Price: Adjustable sight **$671.00**

GLOCK 34, 35 AUTO PISTOLS

Caliber: 9mm Para. (M34), 40 S&W (M35), 10-shot magazine. **Barrel:** 5.32". **Weight:** 22.9 oz. **Length:** 8.15" overall. **Stocks:** Integral. Stippled polymer. **Sights:** Dot on front, fully adjustable white outline rear. **Features:** Polymer frame, steel slide; double-action trigger with "Safe Action" system; three safeties; Tenifer finish. Imported from Austria by Glock, Inc.

Price: Model 34, 9mm. **$770.00**
Price: Model 35, 40 S&W **$770.00**

GLOCK 36 AUTO PISTOL

Caliber: 45 ACP, 6-shot magazine. **Barrel:** 3.78". **Weight:** 20.11 oz. **Length:** 6.77" overall. **Stocks:** Integral. Stippled polymer. **Sights:** Dot on front, fully adjustable white outline rear. **Features:** Polymer frame, steel slide; double-action trigger with "Safe Action" system; three safeties; Tenifer finish. Imported from Austria by Glock, Inc.

Price: Fixed sight **$700.00**
Price: Adj. sight **$730.00**

HAMMERLI TRAILSIDE PL 22 TARGET PISTOL

Caliber: 22 LR, 10-shot magazine. **Barrel:** 4.5", 6". **Weight:** 28 oz. (4.5" barrel). **Length:** 7.75" overall. **Stocks:** Wood target-style. **Sights:** Blade front, rear adjustable for windage. **Features:** One-piece barrel/frame unit; two-stage competition-style trigger; dovetail scope mount rail. Introduced 1999. Imported from Switzerland by SIGARMS, Inc.

Price: . . . . **NA**

HECKLER & KOCH USP AUTO PISTOL

Caliber: 9mm Para., 10-shot magazine, 40 S&W, 10-shot magazine. **Barrel:** 4.25". **Weight:** 28 oz. (USP40). **Length:** 6.9" overall. **Stocks:** Non-slip stippled black polymer. **Sights:** Blade front, rear adjustable for windage. **Features:** New HK design with polymer frame, modified Browning action with recoil reduction system, single control lever. Special "hostile environment" finish on all metal parts. Available in SA/DA, DAO, left- and right-hand versions. Introduced 1993. Imported from Germany by Heckler & Koch, Inc.

Price: Right-hand **$699.00**
Price: Left-hand **$714.00**
Price: Stainless steel, right-hand **$749.00**
Price: Stainless steel, left-hand **$799.00**

Heckler & Koch USP Compact

Heckler & Koch USP45

Heckler & Koch USP45 Tactical

Heckler & Koch USP Expert

Heckler & Koch USP Compact Auto Pistol

Similar to the USP except has 3.58" barrel, measures 6.81" overall, and weighs 1.60 lbs. (9mm). Available in 9mm Para. or 40 S&W with 10-shot magazine. Introduced 1996. Imported from Germany by Heckler & Koch, Inc.

Price: Blue $719.00
Price: Blue with control lever on right $744.00
Price: Stainless steel $769.00
Price: Stainless steel with control lever on right $794.00

Heckler & Koch USP45 Auto Pistol

Similar to the 9mm and 40 S&W USP except chambered for 45 ACP, 10-shot magazine. Has 4.13" barrel, overall length of 7.87" and weighs 30.4 oz. Has adjustable three-dot sight system. Available in SA/DA, DAO, left- and right-hand versions. Introduced 1995. Imported from Germany by Heckler & Koch, Inc.

Price: Right-hand $759.00
Price: Left-hand $784.00
Price: Stainless steel right-hand $799.00
Price: Stainless steel left-hand $724.00

Heckler & Koch USP45 Compact

Similar to the USP45 except has stainless slide; 8-shot magazine; modified and contoured slide and frame; extended slide release; 3.80" barrel, 7.09" overall length, weighs 1.75 lbs.; adjustable three-dot sights. Introduced 1998. Imported from Germany by Heckler & Koch, Inc.

Price: With control lever on left, stainless. $789.00
Price: As above, blue $739.00
Price: With control lever on right, stainless. $814.00
Price: As above, blue $739.00

HECKLER & KOCH USP45 TACTICAL PISTOL

Caliber: 45 ACP, 10-shot magazine. **Barrel:** 4.92". **Weight:** 2.24 lbs. **Length:** 8.64" overall. **Stocks:** Non-slip stippled polymer. **Sights:** Blade front, fully adjustable target rear. **Features:** Has extended threaded barrel with rubber O-ring; adjustable trigger; extended magazine floorplate; adjustable trigger stop; polymer frame. Introduced 1998. Imported from Germany by Heckler & Koch, Inc.
Price: $999.00

HECKLER & KOCH MARK 23 SPECIAL OPERATIONS PISTOL

Caliber: 45 ACP, 10-shot magazine. **Barrel:** 5.87". **Weight:** 43 oz. **Length:** 9.65" overall. **Stocks:** Integral with frame; black polymer. **Sights:** Blade front, rear drift adjustable for windage; three-dot. **Features:** Polymer frame; double action; exposed hammer; short recoil; modified Browning action. Civilian version of the SOCOM pistol. Introduced 1996. Imported from Germany by Heckler & Koch, Inc.
Price: $2,169.00

Heckler & Koch USP Expert Pistol

Combines features of the USP Tactical and HK Mark 23 pistols with a new slide design. Chambered for 45 ACP; 10-shot magazine. Has adjustable target sights, 5.20" barrel, 8.74" overall length, weighs 1.87 lbs. Match-grade single- and double-action trigger pull with adjustable stop; ambidextrous control levers; elongated target slide; barrel O-ring that seals and centers barrel. Suited to IPSC competition. Introduced 1999. Imported from Germany by Heckler & Koch, Inc.
Price: $1,369.00

HECKLER & KOCH P7M8 AUTO PISTOL

Caliber: 9mm Para., 8-shot magazine. **Barrel:** 4.13". **Weight:** 29 oz. **Length:** 6.73" overall. **Stocks:** Stippled black plastic. **Sights:** Blade front, adjustable rear; three dot system. **Features:** Unique "squeeze cocker" in frontstrap cocks the action. Gas-retarded action. Squared combat-type trigger guard. Blue finish. Compact size. Imported from Germany by Heckler & Koch, Inc.
Price: P7M8, blued $1,229.00

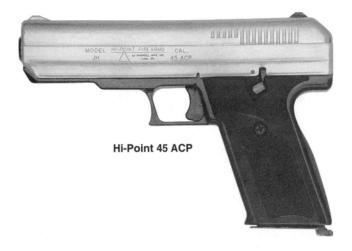

Heckler & Koch P7M8

Hi-Point 45 ACP

Heritage Stealth

Hi-Point 9MM Comp

HERITAGE STEALTH AUTO PISTOL

Caliber: 9mm Para., 40 S&W, 10-shot magazine. **Barrel:** 3.9". **Weight:** 20.2 oz. **Length:** 6.3" overall. **Stocks:** Black polymer; integral. **Sights:** Blade front, rear drift adjustable for windage. **Features:** Gas retarded blowback action; polymer frame, 17-4 stainless slide; frame mounted ambidextrous trigger safety, magazine safety. Introduced 1996. Made in U.S. by Heritage Mfg., Inc.

Price: **$289.95**
Price: Stainless or stainless/black **$329.95**

HERITAGE H25S AUTO PISTOL

Caliber: 25 ACP, 6-shot magazine. **Barrel:** 2.25". **Weight:** 13.5 oz. **Length:** 4.5" overall. **Stocks:** Smooth hardwood. **Sights:** Fixed. **Features:** Frame-mounted trigger safety, magazine disconnect safety. Made in U.S. by Heritage Mfg. Inc.

Price: Blue **$149.95**
Price: Nickel **$159.95**

HI-POINT FIREARMS 40 S&W AUTO

Caliber: 40 S&W, 8-shot magazine. **Barrel:** 4.5". **Weight:** 39 oz. **Length:** 7.72" overall. **Stocks:** Checkered acetal resin. **Sights:** Adjustable; low profile. **Features:** Internal drop-safe mechanism; alloy frame. Introduced 1991. From MKS Supply, Inc.

Price: Matte black. **$159.00**

HI-POINT FIREARMS 45 CALIBER PISTOL

Caliber: 45 ACP, 7-shot magazine. **Barrel:** 4.5". **Weight:** 39 oz. **Length:** 7.95" overall. **Stocks:** Checkered acetal resin. **Sights:** Adjustable; low

profile. **Features:** Internal drop-safe mechanism; alloy frame. Introduced 1991. From MKS Supply, Inc.

Price: Matte black. **$159.00**
Price: Chrome slide, black frame **$169.00**

HI-POINT FIREARMS 9MM COMP PISTOL

Caliber: 9mm, Para., 10-shot magazine. **Barrel:** 4". **Weight:** 39 oz. **Length:** 7.72" overall. **Stocks:** Textured acetal plastic. **Sights:** Adjustable; low profile. **Features:** Single-action design. Scratch-resistant, non-glare blue finish, alloy frame. Muzzle brake/compensator. Compensator is slotted for laser or flashlight mounting. Introduced 1998. From MKS Supply, Inc.

Price: Matte black. **$159.00**

HI-POINT FIREARMS MODEL 9MM COMPACT PISTOL

Caliber: 9mm Para., 8-shot magazine. **Barrel:** 3.5". **Weight:** 29 oz. **Length:** 6.7" overall. **Stocks:** Textured acetal plastic. **Sights:** Combat-style adjustable three-dot system; low profile. **Features:** Single-action design; frame-mounted magazine release; polymer or alloy frame. Scratch-resistant matte finish. Introduced 1993. From MKS Supply, Inc.

Price: Black, alloy frame **$137.00**
Price: With polymer frame (29 oz.), non-slip grips **$137.00**
Price: Aluminum with polymer frame **$137.00**

Hi-Point Firearms Model 380 Polymer Pistol

Similar to the 9mm Compact model except chambered for 380 ACP, 8-shot magazine, adjustable three-dot sights. Weighs 29 oz. Polymer frame. Introduced 1998. Made in U.S. From MKS Supply.

Price: **$99.95**

Kahr MK40

Kel-Tec P-11

Kahr K9

Kel-Tec P-32

HS AMERICA HS 2000 PISTOL

Caliber: 9mm Para., 357 SIG, 40 S&W, 10-shot magazine. **Barrel:** 4.08 inches. **Weight:** 22.88 oz. **Length:** 7.2 inches overall. **Grips:** Integral black polymer. **Sights:** Drift-adjustable white dot rear, white dot blade front. **Features:** Incorporates trigger, firing pin, grip and out-of-battery safeties; firing-pin status and loaded chamber indicators; ambidextrous magazine release; dual-tension recoil spring with stand-off device; polymer frame; black finish with chrome-plated magazine. Imported from Croatia by HS America.
Price: $419.00

KAHR K9, K40 DA AUTO PISTOLS

Caliber: 9mm Para., 7-shot, 40 S&W, 6-shot magazine. **Barrel:** 3.5". **Weight:** 25 oz. **Length:** 6" overall. **Stocks:** Wrap-around textured soft polymer. **Sights:** Blade front, rear drift adjustable for windage; bar-dot combat style. **Features:** Trigger-cocking double-action mechanism with passive firing pin block. Made of 4140 ordnance steel with matte black finish. Contact maker for complete price list. Introduced 1994. Made in U.S. by Kahr Arms.
Price: E9, black matte finish $399.00
Price: Matte black, night sights 9mm $640.00
Price: Matte stainless steel, 9mm. $580.00
Price: 40 S&W, matte black $550.00
Price: 40 S&W, matte black, night sights $640.00
Price: 40 S&W, matte stainless $580.00
Price: K9 Elite 98 (high-polish stainless slide flats, Kahr combat
trigger), from $631.00
Price: As above, MK9 Elite 98, from. $631.00
Price: As above, K40 Elite 98, from $631.00

Kahr K9 9mm Compact Polymer Pistol

Similar to K9 steel frame pistol except has polymer frame, matte stainless steel slide. Barrel length 3.5"; overall length 6"; weighs 17.9 oz. Includes two 7-shot magazines, hard polymer case, trigger lock. Introduced 2000. Made in U.S. by Kahr Arms.
Price: $527.00

Kahr MK9/MK40 Micro Pistol

Similar to the K9/K40 except is 5.5" overall, 4" high, has a 3" barrel. Weighs 22 oz. Has snag-free bar-dot sights, polished feed ramp, dual recoil spring system, DA-only trigger. Comes with 6- and 7-shot magazines. Introduced 1998. Made in U.S. by Kahr Arms.
Price: Matte stainless $580.00
Price: Elite 98, polished stainless, tritium night sights $721.00

KEL-TEC P-11 AUTO PISTOL

Caliber: 9mm Para., 10-shot magazine. **Barrel:** 3.1". **Weight:** 14 oz. **Length:** 5.6" overall. **Stocks:** Checkered black polymer. **Sights:** Blade front, rear adjustable for windage. **Features:** Ordnance steel slide, aluminum frame. Double-action-only trigger mechanism. Introduced 1995. Made in U.S. by Kel-Tec CNC Industries, Inc.
Price: Blue $309.00
Price: Hard chrome $363.00
Price: Parkerized $350.00

KEL-TEC P-32 AUTO PISTOL

Caliber: 32 ACP, 7-shot magazine. **Barrel:** 2.68". **Weight:** 6.6 oz. **Length:** 5.07" overall. **Stocks:** Checkered composite. **Sights:** Fixed. **Features:** Double-action-only mechanism with 6-lb. pull; internal slide stop. Textured composite grip/frame. Made in U.S. by Kel-Tec CNC Industries, Inc.
Price: $295.00

Kimber Custom 45

Kimber Ultra Carry

Kimber Compact Custom

Kimber High Capacity Polymer

KIMBER CUSTOM AUTO PISTOL

Caliber: 45 ACP, 7-shot magazine. **Barrel:** 5", match grade. **Weight:** 38 oz. **Length:** 8.7" overall. **Stocks:** Checkered black rubber (standard), or rosewood. **Sights:** McCormick dovetailed front, low combat rear. **Features:** Slide, frame and barrel machined from steel forgings; match-grade barrel, chamber, trigger; extended thumb safety; beveled magazine well; beveled front and rear slide serrations; high-ride beavertail safety; checkered flat mainspring housing; kidney cut under trigger guard; high cut grip design; match-grade stainless barrel bushing; Commander-style hammer; lowered and flared ejection port; Wolff springs; bead blasted black oxide finish. Made in U.S. by Kimber Mfg., Inc.

Price: Custom **$723.00**
Price: Custom Walnut (double-diamond walnut grips) **$745.00**
Price: Custom Stainless **$823.00**
Price: Custom Stainless 40 S&W **$861.00**
Price: Custom Stainless Target 45 ACP (stainless, adj. sight) **$935.00**
Price: Custom Stainless Target 40 S&W **$968.00**

Kimber Compact Auto Pistol

Similar to the Custom model except has 4" bull barrel fitted directly to the slide without a bushing; full-length guide rod; grip is .400" shorter than full-size gun; no front serrations. Steel frame models weigh 34 oz., aluminum 28 oz. Introduced 1998. Made in U.S. by Kimber Mfg., Inc.

Price: 45 ACP, matte black **$757.00**
Price: Compact Stainless 45 ACP **$863.00**
Price: Compact Stainless 40 S&W **$893.00**
Price: Compact Stainless Aluminum 45 ACP (aluminum frame,
stainless slide) **$829.00**
Price: Compact Stainless Aluminum 40 S&W **$864.00**

Kimber Pro Carry Auto Pistol

Similar to the Compact model except has aluminum frame with full-length grip. Has 4" bull barrel fitted directly to the slide without bushing. Introduced 1998. Made in U.S. by Kimber Mfg., Inc.

Price: 45 ACP **$758.00**
Price: 40 S&W **$792.00**
Price: Stainless Pro Carry 45 ACP **$829.00**
Price: Stainless Pro Carry 40 S&W **$864.00**

Kimber Ultra Carry Auto Pistol

Similar to the Compact Aluminum model except has 3" balljoint spherical bushingless cone barrel; aluminum frame; beveling at front and rear of ejection port; relieved breech face; tuned ejector; special slide stop; dual captured low-effort spring system. Weighs 25 oz. Introduced 1999. made in U.S. by Kimber Mfg., Inc.

Price: 45 ACP **$792.00**
Price: 40 S&W **$822.00**
Price: Stainless, 45 ACP **$868.00**
Price: Stainless, 40 S&W **$904.00**

KIMBER HIGH CAPACITY POLYMER PISTOL

Caliber: 45 ACP, 14-shot magazine. **Barrel:** 5". **Weight:** 34 oz. **Length:** 8.7" overall. **Stocks:** Integral; checkered black polymer. **Sights:** McCormick low profile front and rear. **Features:** Polymer frame with steel insert. Comes with pre-ban magazine. Checkered front strap and mainspring housing; polymer trigger; stainless high ride beavertail grip safety; hooked trigger guard. Introduced 1997. Made in U.S. by Kimber Mfg., Inc.

Price: Matte black finish **$904.00**
Price: Polymer Stainless (satin-finish stainless slide) **$973.00**
Price: Polymer Pro Carry (compact slide, 4" bull barrel) **$924.00**
Price: Polymer Pro Carry Stainless **$993.00**

Kimber Pro CDP

Kimber Ultra CDP

Llama Micromax

Kimber Gold Match Auto Pistol

Similar to the Custom model except has Kimber adjustable sight with rounded and blended edges; stainless steel match-grade barrel hand-fitted to spherical barrel bushing; premium aluminum trigger; extended ambidextrous thumb safety; hand-checkered double diamond rosewood grips. Hand-fitted by Kimber Custom Shop. Made in U.S. by Kimber Mfg., Inc.

Price: Gold Match 45 ACP **$1,135.00**
Price: Stainless Gold Match 45 ACP (highly polished flats) **$1,277.00**
Price: Stainless Gold Match 40 S&W **$1,306.00**

Kimber Polymer Gold Match Auto Pistol

Similar to the Polymer model except has Kimber adjustable sight with rounded and blended edges; stainless steel match-grade barrel hand-fitted to spherical barrel bushing; premium aluminum trigger; extended ambidextrous thumb safety. Hand-fitted by Kimber Custom Shop. Introduced 1999. Made in U.S. by Kimber Mfg., Inc.

Price: **$1,183.00**
Price: Polymer Stainless Gold Match (polished stainless slide) . **$1,337.00**

Kimber Gold Combat Auto Pistol

Similar to the Gold Match except designed for concealed carry. Has two-piece extended and beveled magazine well, tritium night sights; premium aluminum trigger; 30 lpi front strap checkering; special Custom Shop markings; Kim Pro black finish. Introduced 1999. Made in U.S. by Kimber Mfg., Inc.

Price: 45 ACP **$1,633.00**
Price: Gold Combat Stainless (satin-finished stainless frame and slide, special Custom Shop markings) **$1,576.00**

KIMBER PRO CDP AUTO PISTOL

NEW! **Caliber:** 45 ACP, 7-shot magazine. **Barrel:** 4". **Weight:** 28 oz. **Length:** 7.7" overall. **Grips:** Hand-checkered. double diamond rosewood. **Sights:** Tritium three-dot. **Features:** Matte black, machined aluminum frame; satin stainless steel slide; match-grade barrel and chamber; beveled magazine well; extended ejector; high-ride beavertail grip safety; match-grade trigger group; ambidextrous safety; checkered frontstrap; meltdown treatment. Introduced 2000. Made in U.S. by Kimber.

Price: **$1,086.00**

KIMBER ULTRA CDP AUTO PISTOL

Caliber: 45 ACP, 6-shot magazine. **Barrel:** 3". **Weight:** 25 oz. **Length:** 6.8" overall. **Grips:** Hand-checkered. double diamond rosewood. **Sights:** Tritium three-dot. **Features:** Matte black, machined aluminum frame; satin stainless steel slide; match-grade barrel and chamber; beveled magazine well and ejection port; dual recoil spring system for reliability and ease of manual slide operation; match-grade barrel, chamber and trigger; ambi-

dextrous safety; checkered frontstrap; meltdown treatment. Introduced 2000. Made in U.S. by Kimber.

Price: **$1,086.00**

LLAMA MICROMAX 380 AUTO PISTOL

Caliber: 32 ACP, 8-shot, 380 ACP, 7-shot magazine. **Barrel:** 3-11/16". **Weight:** 23 oz. **Length:** 6-1/2" overall. **Stocks:** Checkered high impact polymer. **Sights:** 3-dot combat. **Features:** Single-action design. Mini custom extended slide release; mini custom extended beavertail grip safety; combat-style hammer. Introduced 1997. Imported from Spain by Import Sports, Inc.

Price: Matte blue **$246.95**
Price: Satin chrome (380 only) **$281.95**

LLAMA MINIMAX SERIES

Caliber: 9mm Para., 8-shot; 40 S&W, 7-shot; 45 ACP, 6-shot magazine. **Barrel:** 3-1/2". **Weight:** 35 oz. **Length:** 7-1/3" overall. **Stocks:** Checkered rubber. **Sights:** Three-dot combat. **Features:** Single action, skeletonized combat-style hammer, extended slide release, cone-style barrel, flared ejection port. Introduced 1996. Imported from Spain by Import Sports, Inc.

Price: Blue **$308.95**
Price: Duo-Tone finish (45 only) **$314.95**
Price: Satin chrome **$314.95**

Lorcin L9MM

Llama Minimax

Llama Max-1

North American
Arms Guardian

Llama Minimax Sub Compact Auto Pistol

Similar to the Minimax except has 3.14" barrel, weighs 31 oz.; 6.8" overall length; has 10-shot magazine with finger extension; beavertail grip safety. Introduced 1999. Imported from Spain by Import Sports, Inc.

Price: 9mm Para., 40 S&W, 45 ACP, matte blue **$314.95**
Price: As above, satin chrome **$324.95**
Price: Duo-Tone finish (45 only) **$341.95**

LLAMA MAX-I AUTO PISTOLS

Caliber: 45 ACP, 7-shot. **Barrel:** 5-1/8". **Weight:** 36 oz. **Length:** 8-1/2" overall. **Stocks:** Black rubber. **Sights:** Blade front, rear adjustable for windage; three-dot system. **Features:** Single-action trigger; skeletonized combat-style hammer; steel frame; extended manual and grip safeties. Introduced 1995. Imported from Spain by Import Sports, Inc.

Price: 45 ACP, 7-shot, Government model **$298.95**
Price: As above, satin chrome finish **$314.95**

LORCIN L-22 AUTO PISTOL

Caliber: 22 LR, 9-shot magazine. **Barrel:** 2.5". **Weight:** 16 oz. **Length:** 5.25" overall. **Stocks:** Black combat, or pink or pearl. **Sights:** Fixed three-dot system. **Features:** Available in chrome or black Teflon finish. Introduced 1989. From Lorcin Engineering.

Price: About **$89.00**

LORCIN L9MM AUTO PISTOL

Caliber: 9mm Para., 10-shot magazine. **Barrel:** 4.5". **Weight:** 31 oz. **Length:** 7.5" overall. **Stocks:** Grooved black composition. **Sights:** Fixed; three-dot system. **Features:** Matte black finish; hooked trigger guard; grip safety. Introduced 1994. Made in U.S. by Lorcin Engineering.

Price: **$159.00**

LORCIN L-25, LT-25 AUTO PISTOLS

Caliber: 25 ACP, 7-shot magazine. **Barrel:** 2.4". **Weight:** 14.5 oz. **Length:** 4.8" overall. **Stocks:** Smooth composition. **Sights:** Fixed. **Features:** Available in choice of finishes: chrome, black Teflon or camouflage. Introduced 1989. From Lorcin Engineering.

Price: L-25 . . . . **$69.00**
Price: LT-25 . . . . **$79.00**

LORCIN L-32, L-380 AUTO PISTOLS

Caliber: 32 ACP, 380 ACP, 7-shot magazine. **Barrel:** 3.5". **Weight:** 27 oz. **Length:** 6.6" overall. **Stocks:** Grooved composition. **Sights:** Fixed. **Features:** Black Teflon or chrome finish with black grips. Introduced 1992. From Lorcin Engineering.

Price: L-32 32 ACP. **$89.00**
Price: L-380 380 ACP. **$100.00**

NORTH AMERICAN ARMS GUARDIAN PISTOL

Caliber: 32 ACP, 6-shot magazine. **Barrel:** 2.1". **Weight:** 13.5 oz. **Length:** 4.36" overall. **Stocks:** Black polymer. **Sights:** Fixed. **Features:** Double-action-only mechanism. All stainless steel construction; snag-free. Introduced 1998. Made in U.S. by North American Arms.

Price: **$359.00**

OLYMPIC ARMS OA-96 AR PISTOL

Caliber: 223. **Barrel:** 6", 8", 4140 chrome-moly steel. **Weight:** 5 lbs. **Length:** 15-3/4" overall. **Stocks:** A2 stowaway pistol grip; no buttstock or receiver tube. **Sights:** Flat-top upper receiver, cut-down front sight base. **Features:** AR-15-type receivers with special bolt carrier; short aluminum hand guard; Vortex flash hider. Introduced 1996. Made in U.S. by Olympic Arms, Inc.

Price: **$858.00**

One Pro .45

Para-Ordnance P12.45

Para-Ordnance LDA

Peters Stahl High Capacity

Olympic Arms OA-98 AR Pistol

Similar to the OA-93 except has removable 7-shot magazine, weighs 3 lbs. Introduced 1999. Made in U.S. by Olympic Arms, Inc.

Price: **$990.00**

ONE PRO .45 AUTO PISTOL

Caliber: 45 ACP or 400 Cor-Bon, 10-shot magazine. **Barrel:** 3.75" **Weight:** 31.1 oz. **Length:** 7.04" overall. **Stocks:** Textured composition. **Sights:** Blade front, drift-adjustable rear; three-dot system. **Features:** All-steel construction; decocking lever and automatic firing pin lock; DA or DAO operation. Introduced 1997. Imported from Switzerland by Magnum Research, Inc.

Price: **$649.00**
Price: Conversion kit, 45 ACP/400, 400/45 ACP **$249.00**

ONE PRO 9 AUTO PISTOL

Caliber: 9mm Para., 10-shot magazine. **Barrel:** 3.01". **Weight:** 25.1 oz. **Length:** 6.06" overall. **Stocks:** Smooth wood. **Sights:** Blade front, rear adjustable for windage. **Features:** Rotating barrel; short slide; double recoil springs; double-action mechanism; decocking lever. Introduced 1998. Imported from Switzerland by Magnum Research.

Price: **$649.00**

PARA-ORDNANCE P-SERIES AUTO PISTOLS

Caliber: 9mm Para., 40 S&W, 45 ACP, 10-shot magazine. **Barrel:** 3", 3-1/2", 4-1/4", 5". **Weight:** From 24 oz. (alloy frame). **Length:** 8.5" overall. **Stocks:** Textured composition. **Sights:** Blade front, rear adjustable for windage. High visibility three-dot system. **Features:** Available with alloy, steel or stainless steel frame with black finish (silver or stainless gun). Steel and stainless steel frame guns weigh 40 oz. (P14.45), 36 oz. (P13.45), 34 oz. (P12.45). Grooved match trigger, rounded combat-style hammer. Beveled magazine well. Manual thumb, grip and firing pin lock

safeties. Solid barrel bushing. Contact maker for full details. Introduced 1990. Made in Canada by Para-Ordnance.

Price: P14.45ER (steel frame) **$775.00**
Price: P14.45RR (alloy frame) **$740.00**
Price: P12.45RR (3-1/2" bbl., 24 oz., alloy) **$740.00**
Price: P13.45RR (4-1/4" barrel, 28 oz., alloy) **$740.00**
Price: P12.45ER (steel frame) **$750.00**
Price: P16.40ER (steel frame) **$875.00**
Price: P10-9RR (9mm, alloy frame) **$740.00**

Para-Ordnance Limited Pistols

Similar to the P-Series pistols except with full-length recoil guide system; fully adjustable rear sight; tuned trigger with overtravel stop; beavertail grip safety; competition hammer; front and rear slide serrations; ambidextrous safety; lowered ejection port; ramped match-grade barrel; dovetailed front sight. Introduced 1998. Made in Canada by Para-Ordnance.

Price: 9mm, 40 S&W, 45 ACP .... **$865.00** to **$899.00**

Para-Ordnance LDA Auto Pistols

Similar to the P-series except has double-action trigger mechanism. Steel frame with matte black finish, checkered composition grips. Available in 9mm Para., 40 S&W, 45 ACP. Introduced 1999. Made in Canada by Para-Ordnance.

Price: **$775.00**

PETERS STAHL AUTOLOADING PISTOLS

Caliber: 9mm Para., 45 ACP. **Barrel:** 5" or 6". **Weight:** NA. **Length:** NA. **Grips:** Walnut or walnut with rubber wrap. **Sights:** Fully adjustable rear, blade front. **Features:** Stainless steel extended slide stop, safety and extended magazine release button; speed trigger with stop and approx. 3-lb. pull; polished ramp. Introduced 2000. Imported from Germany by Phillips & Rogers.

Price: High Capacity (accepts 15-shot magazines in 45 cal.; includes 10-shot magazine) **$1,695.00**

Peters Stahl Trophy Master

Peters Stahl Millenium

Phoenix Arms HP22

PSA-25 Auto

Republic Patriot

Price: Trophy Master (blued or stainless, 7-shot in 45,
8-shot in 9mm) **$1,995.00**
Price: Millenium Model (titanium coating on receiver and slide). **$2,195.00**

PHOENIX ARMS HP22, HP25 AUTO PISTOLS

Caliber: 22 LR, 10-shot (HP22), 25 ACP, 10-shot (HP25). **Barrel:** 3".
Weight: 20 oz. **Length:** 5-1/2" overall. **Stocks:** Checkered composition.
Sights: Blade front, adjustable rear. **Features:** Single action, exposed
hammer; manual hold-open; button magazine release. Available in satin
nickel, polished blue finish. Introduced 1993. Made in U.S. by Phoenix
Arms.
Price: With gun lock **$116.00**

PSA-25 AUTO POCKET PISTOL

Caliber: 25 ACP, 6-shot magazine. **Barrel:** 2-1/8". **Weight:** 9.5 oz. **Length:**
4-1/8" overall. **Stocks:** Checkered black polymer, ivory, checkered transparent carbon fiber-filled polymer. **Sights:** Fixed. **Features:** All steel construction; striker fired; single action only; magazine disconnector; cocking
indicator. Introduced 1987. Made in U.S. by Precision Small Arms, Inc.
Price: Traditional (polished black oxide). **$269.00**
Price: Nouveau - Satin (brushed nickel) **$269.00**
Price: Nouveau - Mirror (highly polished nickel) **$309.00**
Price: Featherweight (aluminum frame, nickel slide) **$405.00**
Price: Diplomat (black oxide with gold highlights, ivory grips) **$625.00**
Price: Montreaux (gold plated, ivory grips) **$692.00**
Price: Renaissance (hand engraved nickel, ivory grips). **$1,115.00**
Price: Imperiale (inlaid gold filigree over blue, scrimshawed
ivory grips) **$3,600.00**

REPUBLIC PATRIOT PISTOL

Caliber: 45 ACP, 6-shot magazine. **Barrel:** 3". **Weight:** 20 oz. **Length:** 6"
overall. **Stocks:** Checkered. **Sights:** Blade front, drift-adjustable rear.
Features: Black polymer frame, stainless steel slide; double-action-only

trigger system; squared trigger guard. Introduced 1997. Made in U.S. by
Republic Arms, Inc.
Price: About **$325.00**

ROCK RIVER ARMS STANDARD MATCH AUTO PISTOL

Caliber: 45 ACP. **Barrel:** NA. **Weight:** NA. **Length:** NA. **Grips:** Cocobolo,
checkered. **Sights:** Heine fixed rear, blade front. **Features:** Chrome-moly
steel frame and slide; beavertail grip safety with raised pad; checkered
slide stop; ambidextrous safety; polished feed ramp and extractor; aluminum speed trigger with 3.5 lb. pull. Made in U.S. From Rock River Arms.
Price: **$1,025.00**

Rock River Standard Match

Ruger P89

Ruger P93DAO

Ruger P90

ROCKY MOUNTAIN ARMS PATRIOT PISTOL

Caliber: 223, 10-shot magazine. **Barrel:** 7", with muzzle brake. **Weight:** 5 lbs. **Length:** 20.5" overall. **Stocks:** Black composition. **Sights:** None furnished. **Features:** Milled upper receiver with enhanced Weaver base; milled lower receiver from billet plate; machined aluminum National Match handguard. Finished in DuPont Teflon-S matte black or NATO green. Comes with black nylon case, one magazine. Introduced 1993. From Rocky Mountain Arms, Inc.
Price: With A-2 handle top . . . . **$2,500.00** to **$2,800.00**
Price: Flat top model. **$3,000.00** to **$3,500.00**

RUGER P89 AUTOLOADING PISTOL

Caliber: 9mm Para., 10-shot magazine. **Barrel:** 4.50". **Weight:** 32 oz. **Length:** 7.84" overall. **Stocks:** Grooved black Xenoy composition. **Sights:** Square post front, square notch rear adjustable for windage, both with white dot inserts. **Features:** Double action with ambidextrous slide-mounted safety-levers. Slide is 4140 chrome-moly steel or 400-series stainless steel, frame is a lightweight aluminum alloy. Ambidextrous magazine release. Blue or stainless steel. Introduced 1986; stainless introduced 1990.
Price: P89, blue, with extra magazine and magazine loading tool, plastic case with lock **$430.00**
Price: KP89, stainless, with extra magazine and magazine loading tool, plastic case with lock **$475.00**

Ruger P89D Decocker Autoloading Pistol

Similar to the standard P89 except has ambidextrous decocking levers in place of the regular slide-mounted safety. The decocking levers move the firing pin inside the slide where the hammer can not reach it, while simultaneously blocking the firing pin from forward movement—allows shooter to decock a cocked pistol without manipulating the trigger. Conventional thumb decocking procedures are therefore unnecessary. Blue or stainless steel. Introduced 1990.

Price: P89D, blue with extra magazine and loader, plastic case with lock **$430.00**
Price: KP89D, stainless, with extra magazine, plastic case with lock **$475.00**

Ruger P89 Double-Action-Only Autoloading Pistol

Same as the KP89 except operates only in the double-action mode. Has a spurless hammer, gripping grooves on each side of the rear of the slide; no external safety or decocking lever. An internal safety prevents forward movement of the firing pin unless the trigger is pulled. Available in 9mm Para., stainless steel only. Introduced 1991.
Price: With lockable case, extra magazine, magazine loading tool **$475.00**

RUGER P90 MANUAL SAFETY MODEL AUTOLOADING PISTOL

Caliber: 45 ACP, 7-shot magazine. **Barrel:** 4.50". **Weight:** 33.5 oz. **Length:** 7.87" overall. **Stocks:** Grooved black Xenoy composition. **Sights:** Square post front, square notch rear adjustable for windage, both with white dot inserts. **Features:** Double action with ambidextrous slide-mounted safety-levers which move the firing pin inside the slide where the hammer can not reach it, while simultaneously blocking the firing pin from forward movement. Stainless steel only. Introduced 1991.
Price: KP90 with extra magazine, loader, plastic case with lock **$513.00**
Price: P90 (blue). **$476.00**

Ruger KP90 Decocker Autoloading Pistol

Similar to the P90 except has a manual decocking system. The ambidextrous decocking levers move the firing pin inside the slide where the ham-

Ruger 22/45

Ruger KMK-4

Ruger KP95DAO

Ruger KP512

mer can not reach it, while simultaneously blocking the firing pin from forward movement—allows shooter to decock a cocked pistol without manipulating the trigger. Available only in stainless steel. Overall length 7.87", weighs 34 oz. Introduced 1991.

Price: KP90D with lockable case, extra magazine, and magazine
loading tool **$513.00**

RUGER P93 COMPACT AUTOLOADING PISTOL

Caliber: 9mm Para., 10-shot magazine. **Barrel:** 3.9". **Weight:** 31 oz. **Length:** 7.3" overall. **Stocks:** Grooved black Xenoy composition. **Sights:** Square post front, square notch rear adjustable for windage. **Features:** Front of slide is crowned with a convex curve; slide has seven finger grooves; trigger guard bow is higher for a better grip; 400-series stainless slide, lightweight alloy frame; also in blue. Decocker-only or DAO-only. Introduced 1993. Made in U.S. by Sturm, Ruger & Co.

Price: KP93DAO, double-action-only **$520.00**
Price: KP93D ambidextrous decocker, stainless **$520.00**
Price: P93D, ambidextrous decocker, blue **$445.00**

Ruger KP94 Autoloading Pistol

Sized midway between the full-size P-Series and the compact P93. Has 4.25" barrel, 7.5" overall length and weighs about 33 oz. KP94 is manual safety model; KP94DAO is double-action-only (both 9mm Para., 10-shot magazine); KP94D is decocker-only in 40-caliber with 10-shot magazine. Slide gripping grooves roll over top of slide. KP94 has ambidextrous safety-levers; KP94DAO has no external safety, full-cock hammer position or decocking lever; KP94D has ambidextrous decocking levers. Matte finish stainless slide, barrel, alloy frame. Also available in blue. Introduced 1994. Made in U.S. by Sturm, Ruger & Co.

Price: P94, P944, blue (manual safety) **$445.00**
Price: KP94 (9mm), KP944 (40-caliber) (manual
safety-stainless) **$520.00**
Price: KP94DAO (9mm), KP944DAO (40-caliber) **$520.00**
Price: KP94D (9mm), KP944D (40-caliber) - decock only **$520.00**

RUGER P95 AUTOLOADING PISTOL

Caliber: 9mm Para., 10-shot magazine. **Barrel:** 3.9". **Weight:** 27 oz. **Length:** 7.3" overall. **Stocks:** Grooved; integral with frame. **Sights:** Blade front, rear drift adjustable for windage; three-dot system. **Features:** Moulded polymer grip frame, stainless steel or chrome-moly slide. Suitable for +P+ ammunition. Decocker or DAO. Introduced 1996. Made in U.S. by Sturm, Ruger & Co. Comes with lockable plastic case, spare magazine, loading tool.

Price: P95 DAO double-action-only **$388.00**
Price: P95D decocker only **$388.00**
Price: KP95 stainless steel **$431.00**
Price: KP95DAO double-action only, stainless steel **$431.00**

RUGER P97 AUTOLOADING PISTOL

Caliber: 45ACP 8-shot magazine. **Barrel:** 4-1/8". **Weight:** 30-1/2 oz. **Length:** 7-1/4" overall. **Grooved:** Integral with frame. **Sights:** Blade front, rear drift adjustable for windage; three dot system. **Features:** Moulded polymer grip frame, stainless steel slide. Decocker or DAO. Introduced 1997. Made in U.S. by Sturm, Ruger & Co. Comes with lockable plastic case, spare magaline, loading tool. .

Price: (KP97D decock-only) **$460.00**
Price: (KP97DAO double-action only) **$460.00**

RUGER MARK II STANDARD AUTOLOADING PISTOL

Caliber: 22 LR, 10-shot magazine. **Barrel:** 4-3/4" or 6". **Weight:** 25 oz. (4-3/4" bbl.). **Length:** 8-5/16" (4-3/4" bbl.). **Stocks:** Checkered plastic. **Sights:** Fixed, wide blade front, fixed rear. **Features:** Updated design of the original Standard Auto. Has new bolt hold-open latch. 10-shot magazine, magazine catch, safety, trigger and new receiver contours. Introduced 1982.

Price: Blued (MK 4, MK 6) **$278.00**
Price: In stainless steel (KMK 4, KMK 6) **$364.00**

Ruger 22/45 Mark II Pistol

Similar to the other 22 Mark II autos except has grip frame of Zytel that matches the angle and magazine latch of the Model 1911 45 ACP pistol. Available in 4", 4-3/4" standard and 5-1/2" bull barrel. Comes with extra magazine, plastic case, lock. Introduced 1992.

Price: P4, 4", adjustable sights **$265.00**
Price: KP 4 (4-3/4" barrel), fixed sights **$294.00**
Price: KP512 (5-1/2" bull barrel), stainless steel, adj. sights **$347.00**
Price: P512 (5-1/2" bull barrel), all blue), adj. sights **$265.00**

SAFARI ARMS ENFORCER PISTOL

Caliber: 45 ACP, 6-shot magazine. **Barrel:** 3.8", stainless. **Weight:** 36 oz. **Length:** 7.3" overall. **Stocks:** Smooth walnut with etched black widow spider logo. **Sights:** Ramped blade front, LPA adjustable rear. **Features:** Extended safety, extended slide release; Commander-style hammer; beavertail grip safety; throated, polished, tuned. Parkerized matte black or satin stainless steel finishes. Made in U.S. by Safari Arms.
Price: $630.00

SAFARI ARMS GI SAFARI PISTOL

Caliber: 45 ACP, 7-shot magazine. **Barrel:** 5", 416 stainless. **Weight:** 39.9 oz. **Length:** 8.5" overall. **Stocks:** Checkered walnut. **Sights:** G.I.-style blade front, drift-adjustable rear. **Features:** Beavertail grip safety; extended thumb safety and slide release; Commander-style hammer. Parkerized finish. Reintroduced 1996.
Price: $439.00

SAFARI ARMS CARRIER PISTOL

Caliber: 45 ACP, 7-shot magazine. **Barrel:** 6", 416 stainless steel. **Weight:** 30 oz. **Length:** 9.5" overall. **Stocks:** Wood. **Sights:** Ramped blade front, LPA adjustable rear. **Features:** Beavertail grip safety; extended controls; full-length recoil spring guide; Commander-style hammer. Throated, polished and tuned. Satin stainless steel finish. Introduced 1999. Made in U.S. by Safari Arms, Inc.
Price: $714.00

SAFARI ARMS COHORT PISTOL

Caliber: 45 ACP, 7-shot magazine. **Barrel:** 3.8", 416 stainless. **Weight:** 37 oz. **Length:** 8.5" overall. **Stocks:** Smooth walnut with laser-etched black widow logo. **Sights:** Ramped blade front, LPA adjustable rear. **Features:** Combines the Enforcer model, slide and MatchMaster frame. Beavertail grip safety; extended thumb safety and slide release; Commander-style hammer. Throated, polished and tuned. Satin stainless finish. Introduced 1996. Made in U.S. by Safari Arms, Inc.
Price: $654.00

SAFARI ARMS MATCHMASTER PISTOL

Caliber: 45 ACP, 7-shot. **Barrel:** 5" or 6", 416 stainless steel. **Weight:** 38 oz. (5" barrel). **Length:** 8.5" overall. **Stocks:** Smooth walnut. **Sights:** Ramped blade, LPA adjustable rear. **Features:** Beavertail grip safety; extended controls; Commander-style hammer; throated, polished, tuned. Parkerized matte-black or satin stainless steel. Made in U.S. by Olympic Arms, Inc.
Price: 5" barrel $594.00
Price: 6" barrel $654.00

Safari Arms Carry Comp Pistol

Similar to the Matchmaster except has Wil Schueman-designed hybrid compensator system. Made in U.S. by Olympic Arms, Inc.
Price: $1,067.00

SEECAMP LWS 32 STAINLESS DA AUTO

Caliber: 32 ACP Win. Silvertip, 6-shot magazine. **Barrel:** 2", integral with frame. **Weight:** 10.5 oz. **Length:** 4-1/8" overall. **Stocks:** Glass-filled nylon. **Sights:** Smooth, no-snag, contoured slide and barrel top. **Features:** Aircraft quality 17-4 PH stainless steel. Inertia-operated firing pin. Hammer fired double-action-only. Hammer automatically follows slide down to safety rest position after each shot—no manual safety needed. Magazine safety disconnector. Polished stainless. Introduced 1985. From L.W. Seecamp.
Price: $425.00

SIG SAUER P220 SERVICE AUTO PISTOL

Caliber: 45 ACP, (7- or 8-shot magazine). **Barrel:** 4-3/8". **Weight:** 27.8 oz. **Length:** 7.8" overall. **Stocks:** Checkered black plastic. **Sights:** Blade front, drift adjustable rear for windage. Optional Siglite nightsights. **Features:** Double action. Decocking lever permits lowering hammer onto locked firing pin. Squared combat-type trigger guard. Slide stays open after last shot. Imported from Germany by SIGARMS, Inc.
Price: Blue SA/DA or DAO $790.00
Price: Blue, Siglite night sights $880.00
Price: K-Kote or nickel slide $830.00
Price: K-Kote or nickel slide with Siglite night sights $930.00

SIG Sauer P220

SIG Arms P245 Compact

SIG Sauer P220 Sport Auto Pistol

Similar to the P220 except has 4.9" barrel, ported compensator, all-stainless steel frame and slide, factory-tuned trigger, adjustable sights, extended competition controls. Overall length is 9.9", weighs 43.5 oz. Introduced 1999. From SIGARMS, Inc.
Price: $1,320.00

SIG Sauer P245 Compact Auto Pistol

Similar to the P220 except has 3.9" barrel, shorter grip, 6-shot magazine, 7.28" overall length, and weighs 27.5 oz. Introduced 1999. From SIGARMS, Inc.
Price: Blue $780.00
Price: Blue, with Siglite sights $850.00
Price: Two-tone $830.00
Price: Two-tone with Siglite sights $930.00
Price: With K-Kote finish.............................. $830.00
Price: K-Kote with Siglite sights $930.00

SIG Sauer P229 DA Auto Pistol

Similar to the P228 except chambered for 9mm Para., 40 S&W, 357 SIG. Has 3.86" barrel, 7.08" overall length and 3.35" height. Weight is 30.5 oz. Introduced 1991. Frame made in Germany, stainless steel slide assembly made in U.S.; pistol assembled in U.S. From SIGARMS, Inc.
Price: $795.00
Price: With nickel slide $890.00
Price: Nickel slide Siglite night sights..................... $935.00

SIG PRO AUTO PISTOL

Caliber: 9mm Para., 40 S&W, 10-shot magazine. **Barrel:** 3.86". **Weight:** 27.2 oz. **Length:** 7.36" overall. **Stocks:** Composite and rubberized one-piece. **Sights:** Blade front, rear adjustable for windage. Optional Siglite night sights. **Features:** Polymer frame, stainless steel slide; integral frame accessory rail; replaceable steel frame rails; left- or right-handed magazine release. Introduced 1999. From SIGARMS, Inc.

SIG Arms Pro 2009

SIG Sauer P229S

SIG Sauer P232

Smith & Wesson 457

Price: SP2340 (40 S&W) **$596.00**
Price: SP2009 (9mm Para.) **$596.00**
Price: As above with Siglite night sights **$655.00**

SIG Sauer P226 Service Pistol

Similar to the P220 pistol except has 4.4" barrel, and weighs 28.3 oz. 357 SIG or 40 S&W. Imported from Germany by SIGARMS, Inc.

Price: Blue SA/DA or DAO **$830.00**
Price: With Siglite night sights **$930.00**
Price: Blue, SA/DA or DAO 357 SIG **$830.00**
Price: With Siglite night sights **$930.00**
Price: K-Kote finish, 40 S&W only or nickel slide **$830.00**
Price: K-Kote or nickel slide Siglite night sights **$930.00**
Price: Nickel slide 357 SIG. **$875.00**
Price: Nickel slide, Siglite night sights **$930.00**

SIG Sauer P229 Sport Auto Pistol

Similar to the P229 except available in 357 SIG only; 4.8" heavy barrel; 8.6" overall length; weighs 40.6 oz.; vented compensator; adjustable target sights; rubber grips; extended slide latch and magazine release. Made of stainless steel. Introduced 1998. From SIGARMS, Inc.
Price: **$1,320.00**

SIG SAUER P232 PERSONAL SIZE PISTOL

Caliber: 380 ACP, 7-shot. **Barrel:** 3-3/4". **Weight:** 16 oz. **Length:** 6-1/2" overall. **Stocks:** Checkered black composite. **Sights:** Blade front, rear adjustable for windage. **Features:** Double action/single action or DAO. Blowback operation, stationary barrel. Introduced 1997. Imported from Germany by SIGARMS, Inc.

Price: Blue SA/DA or DAO **$505.00**
Price: In stainless steel. **$545.00**
Price: With stainless steel slide, blue frame **$525.00**
Price: Stainless steel, Siglite night sights, Hogue grips **$585.00**

SIG SAUER P239 PISTOL

Caliber: 9mm Para., 8-shot, 357 SIG 40 S&W, 7-shot magazine. **Barrel:** 3.6". **Weight:** 25.2 oz. **Length:** 6.6" overall. **Stocks:** Checkered black composite. **Sights:** Blade front, rear adjustable for windage. Optional Siglite night sights. **Features:** SA/DA or DAO; blackened stainless steel slide, aluminum alloy frame. Introduced 1996. Made in U.S. by SIGARMS, Inc.

Price: SA/DA or DAO **$620.00**
Price: SA/DA or DAO with Siglite night sights **$720.00**
Price: Two-tone finish. **$665.00**
Price: Two-tone finish, Siglite sights. **$765.00**

SMITH & WESSON MODEL 22A SPORT PISTOL

Caliber: 22 LR, 10-shot magazine. **Barrel:** 4", 5-1/2", 7". **Weight:** 29 oz. **Length:** 8" overall. **Stocks:** Two-piece polymer. **Sights:** Patridge front, fully adjustable rear. **Features:** Comes with a sight bridge with Weaver-style integral optics mount; alloy frame; .312" serrated trigger; stainless steel slide and barrel with matte blue finish. Introduced 1997. Made in U.S. by Smith & Wesson.

Price: 4" **$230.00**
Price: 5-1/2" **$255.00**
Price: 7" **$289.00**

SMITH & WESSON MODEL 457 TDA AUTO PISTOL

Caliber: 45 ACP, 7-shot magazine. **Barrel:** 3-3/4". **Weight:** 29 oz. **Length:** 7-1/4" overall. **Stocks:** One-piece Xenoy, wrap-around with straight backstrap. **Sights:** Post front, fixed rear, three-dot system. **Features:** Aluminum alloy frame, matte blue carbon steel slide; bobbed hammer; smooth trigger. Introduced 1996. Made in U.S. by Smith & Wesson.
Price: **$563.00**

Smith & Wesson 4013 TSW

Smith & Wesson 3913 LadySmith

SMITH & WESSON MODEL 908 AUTO PISTOL

Caliber: 9mm Para., 8-shot magazine. **Barrel:** 3-1/2". **Weight:** 26 oz. **Length:** 6-13/16". **Stocks:** One-piece Xenoy, wrap-around with straight backstrap. **Sights:** Post front, fixed rear, three-dot system. **Features:** Aluminum alloy frame, matte blue carbon steel slide; bobbed hammer; smooth trigger. Introduced 1996. Made in U.S. by Smith & Wesson.
Price: **$509.00**

SMITH & WESSON 9mm RECON AUTO PISTOL MODEL

Caliber: 9mm Para. **Barrel:** 3-1/2". **Weight:** 27 oz. **Length:** 7" overall. **Stocks:** Hogue wrap-around, finger-groove rubber. **Sights:** Three-dot Novak Low Mount, drift adjustable. **Features:** Traditional double-action mechanism. Tuned action, hand-crowned muzzle, polished feed ramp, hand-lapped slide, spherical barrel bushing. Checkered frontstrap. Introduced 1999. Made by U.S. by Smith & Wesson.
Price: **$1,150.00**

SMITH & WESSON MODEL 2213, 2214 SPORTSMAN AUTOS

Caliber: 22 LR, 8-shot magazine. **Barrel:** 3". **Weight:** 18 oz. **Length:** 6-1/8" overall. **Stocks:** Checkered black polymer. **Sights:** Patridge front, fixed rear; three-dot system. **Features:** Internal hammer; serrated trigger; single action. Model 2213 is stainless with alloy frame, Model 2214 is blued carbon steel with alloy frame. Introduced 1990. Made in U.S. by Smith & Wesson.
Price: Model 2213. .... **$340.00**
Price: Model 2214. .... **$292.00**

SMITH & WESSON MODEL 4013, 4053 TSW AUTOS

Caliber: 40 S&W, 9-shot magazine. **Barrel:** 3-1/2". **Weight:** 26.4 oz. **Length:** 6-7/8" overall. **Stocks:** Xenoy one-piece wrap-around. **Sights:** Novak three-dot system. **Features:** Traditional double-action system; stainless slide, alloy frame; fixed barrel bushing; ambidextrous decocker; reversible magazine catch. Introduced 1997. Made in U.S. by Smith & Wesson.
Price: Model 4013 TSW **$844.00**
Price: Model 4053 TSW, double-action-only **$844.00**

Smith & Wesson Model 22S Sport Pistols

Similar to the Model 22A Sport except with stainless steel frame. Available only with 5-1/2" or 7" barrel. Introduced 1997. Made in U.S. by Smith & Wesson.
Price: 5-1/2" standard barrel. **$312.00**
Price: 5-1/2" bull barrel, wood target stocks with thumbrest. **$379.00**
Price: 7" standard barrel. **$344.00**
Price: 5-1/2" bull barrel, two-piece target stocks with thumbrest .. **$353.00**

SMITH & WESSON MODEL 410 DA AUTO PISTOL

Caliber: 40 S&W, 10-shot magazine. **Barrel:** 4". **Weight:** 28.5 oz. **Length:** 7.5 oz. **Stocks:** One-piece Xenoy, wrap-around with straight backstrap. **Sights:** Post front, fixed rear; three-dot system. **Features:** Aluminum alloy frame; blued carbon steel slide; traditional double action with left-side

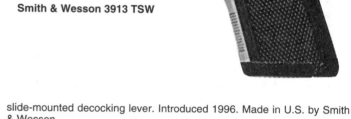

Smith & Wesson 3913 TSW

slide-mounted decocking lever. Introduced 1996. Made in U.S. by Smith & Wesson.
Price: **$563.00**

SMITH & WESSON MODEL 910 DA AUTO PISTOL

Caliber: 9mm Para., 10-shot magazine. **Barrel:** 4". **Weight:** 28 oz. **Length:** 7-3/8" overall. **Stocks:** One-piece Xenoy, wrap-around with straight backstrap. **Sights:** Post front with white dot, fixed two-dot rear. **Features:** Alloy frame, blue carbon steel slide. Slide-mounted decocking lever. Introduced 1995.
Price: Model 910 .... **$509.00**

SMITH & WESSON
MODEL 3913 TRADITIONAL DOUBLE ACTION

Caliber: 9mm Para., 8-shot magazine. **Barrel:** 3-1/2". **Weight:** 26 oz. **Length:** 6-13/16" overall. **Stocks:** One-piece Delrin wrap-around, textured surface. **Sights:** Post front with white dot, Novak LoMount Carry with two dots, adjustable for windage. **Features:** Aluminum alloy frame, stainless slide (M3913) or blue steel slide (M3914). Bobbed hammer with no half-cock notch; smooth .304" trigger with rounded edges. Straight backstrap. Extra magazine included. Introduced 1989.
Price: **$662.00**

Smith & Wesson Model 3913-LS LadySmith Auto

Similar to the standard Model 3913 except has frame that is upswept at the front, rounded trigger guard. Comes in frosted stainless steel with matching gray grips. Grips are ergonomically correct for a woman's hand. Novak LoMount Carry rear sight adjustable for windage, smooth edges for snag resistance. Extra magazine included. Introduced 1990.
Price: **$744.00**

Smith & Wesson 4506

Smith & Wesson 4553 TSW

Smith & Wesson Sigma SW40V

Smith & Wesson Model 3953 DAO Pistol

Same as the Model 3913 except double-action-only. Model 3953 has stainless slide with alloy frame. Overall length 7"; weighs 25.5 oz. Extra magazine included. Introduced 1990.
Price: $724.00

Smith & Wesson Model 3913TSW/3953TSW Auto Pistols

Similar to the Model 3913 and 3953 except TSW guns have tighter tolerances, ambidextrous manual safety/decocking lever, flush-fit magazine, delayed-unlock firing system; magazine disconnector. Compact alloy frame, stainless steel slide. Straight backstrap. Introduced 1998. Made in U.S. by Smith & Wesson.
Price: Single action/double action $724.00
Price: Double action only $724.00

SMITH & WESSON MODEL 4006 TDA AUTO

Caliber: 40 S&W, 10-shot magazine. **Barrel:** 4". **Weight:** 38.5 oz. **Length:** 7-7/8" overall. **Stocks:** Xenoy wrap-around with checkered panels. **Sights:** Replaceable post front with white dot, Novak LoMount Carry fixed rear with two white dots, or micro. click adjustable rear with two white dots. **Features:** Stainless steel construction with non-reflective finish. Straight back-strap. Extra magazine included. Introduced 1990.
Price: With adjustable sights $899.00
Price: With fixed sight.................................. $864.00
Price: With fixed night sights $991.00

Smith & Wesson Model 4043, 4046 DA Pistols

Similar to the Model 4006 except is double-action-only. Has a semi-bobbed hammer, smooth trigger, 4" barrel; Novak LoMount Carry rear sight, post front with white dot. Overall length is 7-1/2", weighs 28 oz. Model 4043 has alloy frame. Extra magazine included. Introduced 1991.
Price: Model 4043 (alloy frame) $844.00
Price: Model 4046 (stainless frame)...................... $864.00
Price: Model 4046 with fixed night sights $991.00

SMITH & WESSON MODEL 4500 SERIES AUTOS

Caliber: 45 ACP, 8-shot magazine. **Barrel:** 5" (M4506). **Weight:** 41 oz. (4506). **Length:** 8-1/2" overall. **Stocks:** Xenoy one-piece wrap-around, arched or straight backstrap. **Sights:** Post front with white dot, adjustable or fixed Novak LoMount Carry on M4506. **Features:** M4506 has serrated hammer spur. All have two magazines. Contact Smith & Wesson for complete data. Introduced 1989.
Price: Model 4506, fixed sight $822.00
Price: Model 4506, adjustable sight $855.00
Price: Model 4566 (stainless, 4-1/4", traditional DA, ambidextrous safety, fixed sight)....................................... $897.00
Price: Model 4586 (stainless, 4-1/4", DA only).............. $897.00

SMITH & WESSON MODEL 4513TSW/4553TSW PISTOLS

Caliber: 45 ACP, 6-shot magazine. **Barrel:** 3-3/4". **Weight:** 28 oz. (M4513TSW). **Length:** 6-7/8 overall. **Stocks:** Checkered Xenoy; straight backstrap. **Sights:** White dot front, Novak Lo Mount Carry 2-Dot rear. **Features:** Model 4513TSW is traditional double action, Model 4553TSW is double action only. TSW series has tighter tolerances, ambidextrous manual safety/decocking lever, flush-fit magazine, delayed-unlock firing system; magazine disconnector. Compact alloy frame, stainless steel slide. Introduced 1998. Made in U.S. by Smith & Wesson.
Price: Model 4513TSW $880.00
Price: Model 4553TSW $837.00

SMITH & WESSON MODEL 5900 SERIES AUTO PISTOLS

Caliber: 9mm Para., 10-shot magazine. **Barrel:** 4". **Weight:** 28-1/2 to 37-1/2 oz. (fixed sight); 38 oz. (adjustable sight). **Length:** 7-1/2" overall. **Stocks:** Xenoy wrap-around with curved backstrap. **Sights:** Post front with white dot, fixed or fully adjustable with two white dots. **Features:** All stainless, stainless and alloy or carbon steel and alloy construction. Smooth .304" trigger, .260" serrated hammer. Introduced 1989.
Price: Model 5906 (stainless, traditional DA, adjustable sight, ambidextrous safety) $861.00
Price: As above, fixed sight $822.00
Price: With fixed night sights $948.00
Price: Model 5946 DAO (as above, stainless frame and slide) .. $822.00

SMITH & WESSON ENHANCED SIGMA SERIES PISTOLS

Caliber: 9mm Para., 40 S&W, 10-shot magazine. **Barrel:** 4". **Weight:** 26 oz. **Length:** 7.4" overall. **Stocks:** Integral. **Sights:** White dot front, fixed rear; three-dot system. Tritium night sights available. **Features:** Ergonomic polymer frame; low barrel centerline; internal striker firing system; corrosion-resistant slide; Teflon-filled, electroless-nickel coated magazine. Introduced 1994. Made in U.S. by Smith & Wesson.

Springfield 1911A1 Standard

Springfield Full-Size 1911A1

Springfield N.R.A. PPC

Price: SW9E, 9mm, 4" barrel, black finish, fixed sights **$657.00**
Price: SW9V, 9mm, 4" barrel, satin stainless, fixed night sights . **$447.00**
Price: SW40E, 40 S&W, 4" barrel, black finish, fixed sights..... **$657.00**
Price: SW40V, 40 S&W, 4" barrel, black polymer, fixed sights .. **$447.00**

SMITH & WESSON SIGMA SW380 AUTO
Caliber: 380 ACP, 6-shot magazine. **Barrel:** 3". **Weight:** 14 oz. **Length:** 5.8" overall. **Stocks:** Integral. **Sights:** Fixed groove in the slide. **Features:** Polymer frame; double-action-only trigger mechanism; grooved/serrated front and rear straps; two passive safeties. Introduced 1995. Made in U.S. by Smith & Wesson.
Price: **$328.00**

Smith & Wesson Model 6906 Double-Action Auto
Similar to the Model 5906 except with 3-1/2" barrel, 10-shot magazine, fixed rear sight, .260" bobbed hammer. Extra magazine included. Introduced 1989.
Price: Model 6906, stainless............................ **$720.00**
Price: Model 6906 with fixed night sights **$836.00**
Price: Model 6946 (stainless, DA only, fixed sights).......... **$720.00**

SMITH & WESSON MODEL CS9 CHIEFS SPECIAL AUTO
Caliber: 9mm Para., 7-shot magazine. **Barrel:** 3". **Weight:** 20.8 oz. **Length:** 6-1/4" overall. **Stocks:** Hogue wrap-around rubber. **Sights:** White dot front, fixed two-dot rear. **Features:** Traditional double-action trigger mechanism. Alloy frame, stainless or blued slide. Introduced 1999. Made in U.S. by Smith & Wesson.
Price: Blue or stainless................................ **$648.00**

Smith & Wesson Model CS40 Chiefs Special Auto
Similar to the CS9 except chambered for 40 S&W (7-shot magazine), has 3-1/4" barrel, weighs 24.2 oz., and measures 6-1/2" overall. Introduced 1999. Made in U.S. by Smith & Wesson.
Price: Blue or stainless................................ **$683.00**

Smith & Wesson Model CS45 Chiefs Special Auto
Similar to the CS40 except chambered for 45 ACP, 6-shot magazine, weighs 23.9 oz. Introduced 1999. Made in U.S. by Smith & Wesson.
Price: Blue or stainless................................ **$683.00**

SPRINGFIELD, INC. FULL-SIZE 1911A1 AUTO PISTOL
Caliber: 9mm Para., 9-shot; 38 Super, 9-shot; 45 ACP, 8-shot. **Barrel:** 5". **Weight:** 35.6 oz. **Length:** 8-5/8" overall. **Stocks:** Checkered plastic or walnut. **Sights:** Fixed three-dot system. **Features:** Beveled magazine well; lowered and flared ejection port. All forged parts, including frame, barrel, slide. All new production. Introduced 1990. From Springfield, Inc.
Price: Mil-Spec 45 ACP, Parkerized...................... **$610.00**
Price: Standard, 45 ACP, blued.......................... **$669.00**
Price: Standard, 45 ACP, stainless **$719.00**
Price: Lightweight (28.6 oz., matte finish)................. **$695.00**
Price: Standard, 9mm, 38 Super, blued................... **$549.00**
Price: Standard, 9mm, stainless steel **$599.00**

Springfield, Inc. N.R.A. PPC Pistol
Specifically designed to comply with NRA rules for PPC competition. Has custom slide-to-frame fit; polished feed ramp; throated barrel; total internal honing; tuned extractor; recoil buffer system; fully checkered walnut grips; two fitted magazines; factory test target; custom carrying case. Introduced 1995. From Springfield, Inc.
Price: **$1,469.00**

Springfield, Inc. TRP Pistols
Similar to the 1911A1 except 45 ACP only; has checkered front strap and mainspring housing; Novak combat rear sight and matching dovetailed front sight; tuned, polished extractor; oversize barrel link; lightweight speed trigger and combat action job; match barrel and bushing; extended ambidextrous thumb safety and fitted beavertail grip safety; Carry bevel on entire pistol; checkered cocobolo wood grips; comes with two Wilson 8-shot magazines. Frame is engraved "Tactical," both sides of frame with "TRP." Introduced 1998. From Springfield, Inc.
Price: Standard with Armory Kote finish................... **$1,299.00**
Price: Standard, stainless steel **$1,289.00**
Price: Champion, Armory Kote.......................... **$1,349.00**

Springfield, Inc. 1911A1 High Capacity Pistol
Similar to the Standard 1911A1 except available in 45 ACP with 10-shot magazine. Has Commander-style hammer, walnut grips, beveled magazine well, plastic carrying case. Introduced 1993. From Springfield, Inc.
Price: Mil-Spec 45 ACP **$733.00**
Price: 45 ACP Factory Comp........................... **$1,198.00**
Price: 45 ACP Compact, Ultra **$759.00**
Price: As above, stainless steel **$859.00**

Springfield, Inc. 1911A1 Custom Carry Gun
Similar to the standard 1911A1 except has Novak low-mount sights, Videki speed trigger, match barrel and bushing; extended thumb safety, beavertail grip safety; beveled, polished magazine well, polished feed ramp

Springfield TRP

Stoeger American Eagle Luger

Springfield V10 Ultra Compact

Taurus PT 22

and throated barrel; match Commander hammer and sear, tuned extractor; lowered and flared ejection port; recoil buffer system, full-length spring guide rod; walnut grips. Comes with two magazines with slam pads, plastic carrying case. Available in all popular calibers. Introduced 1992. From Springfield, Inc.

Price: **$1,299.00**

Springfield, Inc. 1911A1 Factory Comp

Similar to the standard 1911A1 except comes with bushing-type dual-port compensator, adjustable rear sight, extended thumb safety, Videki speed trigger, and beveled magazine well. Checkered walnut grips standard. Available in 45 ACP, blue only. Introduced 1992.

Price: 45 ACP.. **$1,158.00**

Springfield, Inc. 1911A1 Champion Pistol

Similar to the standard 1911A1 except slide is 4.025". Novak sight system. Comes with Delta hammer and cocogrips. Available in 45 ACP only; Parkerized or stainless. Introduced 1989.

Price: Parkerized **$669.00**
Price: Stainless.. **$739.00**

Springfield, Inc. V10 Ultra Compact Pistol

Similar to the 1911A1 Compact except has shorter slide, 3.5" barrel, recoil reducing compensator built into the barrel and slide. Beavertail grip safety, beveled magazine well, "hi-viz" combat sights, Videki speed trigger, flared ejection port, stainless steel frame, blued slide, match grade barrel, walnut grips. Introduced 1996. From Springfield, Inc.

Price: V10 45 ACP **$769.00**
Price: Ultra Compact (no compensator), 45 ACP............. **$1069.00**

STEYR M & S SERIES AUTO PISTOLS

Caliber: 9mm Para., 40 S&W, 357 SIG; 10-shot magazine. **Barrel:** 4" (3.58" for Model S). **Weight:** 28 oz. (22.5 oz. for Model S). **Length:** 7.05" overall (6.53" for Model S). **Grips:** Ultra-rigid polymer. **Sights:** Drift-adjustable, white-outline rear; white-triangle blade front. **Features:** Polymer frame; trigger-drop firing pin, manual and key-lock safeties; loaded chamber indicator; 5.5-lb. trigger pull; 111-degree grip angle enhances natural pointing. Introduced 2000. Imported from Austria by GSI Inc.

Price: Model M (full-sized frame with 4" barrel) **$609.95**
Price: Model S (compact frame with 3.58" barrel) **$609.95**
Price: Extra 10-shot magazines (Model M or S) **$39.00**

STOEGER AMERICAN EAGLE LUGER

Caliber: 9mm Para., 7-shot magazine. **Barrel:** 4", 6". **Weight:** 32 oz. **Length:** 9.6" overall. **Stocks:** Checkered walnut. **Sights:** Blade front, fixed rear. **Features:** Recreation of the American Eagle Luger pistol in stainless steel. Chamber loaded indicator. Introduced 1994. From Stoeger Industries.

Price: 4", or 6" Navy Model **$720.00**
Price: With matte black finish............................... **$798.00**

TAURUS MODEL PT 22/PT 25 AUTO PISTOLS

Caliber: 22 LR, 8-shot (PT 22); 25 ACP, 9-shot (PT 25). **Barrel:** 2.75". **Weight:** 12.3 oz. **Length:** 5.25" overall. **Stocks:** Smooth rosewood. **Sights:** Blade front, fixed rear. **Features:** Double action. Tip-up barrel for loading, cleaning. Blue or stainless. Introduced 1992. Made in U.S. by Taurus International.

Price: 22 LR or 25 ACP, blue, nickel or with duo-tone finish
with rosewood grips **$203.00**

Taurus PT92B   **Taurus PT-911**   **Taurus PT-945**   **Taurus PT-957**

Price: 22 LR or 25 ACP, blue with gold trim, rosewood grips.... **$219.00**
Price: 22 LR or 25 ACP, blue, nickel or duo-tone finish with checkered
  wood grips **$180.00**
Price: 22 LR or 25 ACP, blue with gold trim, mother of pearl grips
  .... **$219.00**

TAURUS MODEL PT92B AUTO PISTOL

Caliber: 9mm Para., 15-shot magazine. **Barrel:** 5". **Weight:** 34 oz. **Length:** 8.5" overall. **Stocks:** Black rubber. **Sights:** Fixed notch rear. Three-dot sight system. **Features:** Double action, exposed hammer, chamber loaded indicator, ambidextrous safety, inertia firing pin. Imported by Taurus International.
Price: Blue **$508.00**
Price: Stainless steel **$523.00**
Price: Blue with gold trim, rosewood grips **$550.00**
Price: Stainless steel with gold trim, rosewood grips **$570.00**

Taurus Model PT99 Auto Pistol

Similar to the PT92 except has fully adjustable rear sight, smooth Brazilian walnut stocks and is available in stainless steel or polished blue. Introduced 1983.
Price: Blue **$531.00**
Price: Stainless steel **$547.00**

TAURUS MODEL PT-111 MILLENNIUM AUTO PISTOL

Caliber: 9mm Para., 10-shot magazine. **Barrel:** 3.25". **Weight:** 18.7 oz. **Length:** 6.0" overall. **Stocks:** Polymer. **Sights:** Fixed. Low profile, three-dot combat. **Features:** Double action only. Firing pin lock; polymer frame; striker fired; push-button magazine release. Introduced 1998. Imported by Taurus International.
Price: Blue **$367.00**
Price: Stainless.. **$383.00**

Taurus Model PT-111 Millennium Titanium Pistol

Similar to the PT-111 except with titanium slide, night sights.
Price: **$547.00**

TAURUS MODEL PT-911 AUTO PISTOL

Caliber: 9mm Para., 10-shot magazine. **Barrel:** 4". **Weight:** 28.2 oz. **Length:** 7" overall. **Stocks:** Black rubber. **Sights:** Fixed. Low profile, three-dot combat. **Features:** Double action, exposed hammer; ambidextrous hammer drop; chamber loaded indicator. Introduced 1997. Imported by Taurus International.
Price: Blue **$453.00**
Price: Stainless.. **$469.00**
Price: Blue with gold accents **$504.00**
Price: Stainless with gold accents **$508.00**

Taurus Model PT-138 Auto Pistol

Similar to the PT-911 except chambered for 380 ACP, with 10-shot magazine. Double-action-only mechanism. Has black polymer frame with blue or stainless slide. Introduced 1999. Imported by Taurus International.
Price: Blue **$367.00**
Price: Stainless.. **$383.00**

TAURUS MODEL PT-945 AUTO PISTOL

Caliber: 45 ACP, 8-shot magazine. **Barrel:** 4.25". **Weight:** 29.5 oz. **Length:** 7.48" overall. **Stocks:** Black rubber. **Sights:** Drift-adjustable front and rear; three-dot system. **Features:** Double-action mechanism. Has manual ambidextrous hammer drop safety, intercept notch, firing pin block, chamber loaded indicator, last-shot hold-open. Introduced 1995. Imported by Taurus International.
Price: Blue **$484.00**
Price: Stainless.. **$500.00**
Price: Blue, ported **$523.00**
Price: Stainless, ported **$539.00**

TAURUS MODEL PT-957 AUTO PISTOL

Caliber: 357 SIG, 10-shot magazine. **Barrel:** 3-5/8". **Weight:** 28 oz. **Length:** 7" overall. **Stocks:** Checkered rubber. **Sights:** Fixed, low profile, three-dot combat. **Features:** Double action mechanism; exposed hammer; ported barrel/slide; three-position safety with decocking lever and ambidextrous safety. Introduced 1999. Imported by Taurus International.
Price: Blue **$508.00**
Price: Stainless.. **$523.00**
Price: Blue with gold accents, rosewood grips **$553.00**
Price: Stainless with gold accents, rosewood grips **$568.00**

HANDGUNS

Taurus PT-938

Vektor Ultra with Tasco Scope

Taurus PT-940

Vektor SP1

TAURUS MODEL PT-938 AUTO PISTOL

Caliber: 380 ACP, 10-shot magazine. **Barrel:** 3.72". **Weight:** 27 oz. **Length:** 6.5" overall. **Stocks:** Black rubber. **Sights:** Fixed. Low profile, three-dot combat. **Features:** Double-action only. Chamber loaded indicator; firing pin block; ambidextrous hammer drop. Introduced 1997. Imported by Taurus International.

Price: Blue **$453.00**
Price: Stainless....................................... **$469.00**

TAURUS MODEL PT-940 AUTO PISTOL

Caliber: 40 S&W, 10-shot magazine. **Barrel:** 3.35". **Weight:** 28.2 oz. **Length:** 7.05" overall. **Stocks:** Black rubber. **Sights:** Drift-adjustable front and rear; three-dot combat. **Features:** Double action, exposed hammer; manual ambidextrous hammer-drop; inertia firing pin; chamber loaded indicator. Introduced 1996. Imported by Taurus International.

Price: Blue **$469.00**
Price: Stainless steel **$484.00**
Price: Blue with gold accents, rosewood grips **$540.00**
Price: Stainless with gold accents, rosewood grips **$555.00**

VEKTOR SP1 SPORT PISTOL

Caliber: 9mm Para., 10-shot magazine. **Barrel:** 5 ". **Weight:** 38 oz. **Length:** 9-3/8" overall. **Stocks:** Checkered black composition. **Sights:** Combat-type blade front, adjustable rear. **Features:** Single action only with adjustable trigger stop; three-chamber compensator; extended magazine release. Introduced 1999. Imported from South Africa by Vektor USA.

Price: **$829.95**

Vektor SP1 Tuned Sport Pistol

Similar to the Vektor Sport except has fully adjustable straight trigger, LPA three-dot sight system, and hard nickel finish. Introduced 1999. Imported from South Africa by Vektor USA.

Price: **$1,199.95**

VEKTOR SP1 Target Pistol

Similar to the Vektor Sport except has 5-7/8" barrel without compensator; weighs 40-1/2 oz.; has fully adjustable straight match trigger; black slide, bright frame. Introduced 1999. Imported from South Africa by Vektor USA.

Price: **$1,299.95**

Vektor SP1, SP2 Ultra Sport Pistols

Similar to the Vektor Target except has three-chamber compensator with three jet ports; strengthened frame with integral beavertail; lightweight polymer scope mount (Weaver rail). Overall length is 11", weighs 41-1/2 oz. Model SP2 is in 40 S&W. Introduced 1999. Imported from South Africa by Vektor USA.

Price: SP1 (9mm)..................................... **$2,149.95**
Price: SP2 (40 S&W) **$2,149.95**

VEKTOR SP1 AUTO PISTOL

Caliber: 9mm Para., 40 S&W (SP2), 10-shot magazine. **Barrel:** 4-5/8". **Weight:** 35 oz. **Length:** 8-1/4" overall. **Stocks:** Checkered black composition. **Sights:** Combat-type fixed. **Features:** Alloy frame, steel slide; traditional double-action mechanism; matte black finish. Introduced 1999. Imported from South Africa by Vektor USA.

Price: SP1 (9mm)..................................... **$599.95**
Price: SP1 with nickel finish **$629.95**
Price: SP2 (40 S&W) **$649.95**

Vektor SP1, SP2 Compact General's Model Pistol

Similar to the 9mm Para. Vektor SP1 except has 4" barrel, weighs 31-1/2 oz., and is 7-1/2" overall. Recoil operated. Traditional double-action mechanism. SP2 model is chambered for 40 S&W. Introduced 1999. Imported from South Africa by Vektor USA.

Price: SP1 (9mm Para.) **$649.95**
Price: SP2 (40 S&W) **$649.95**

Walther PP

Walther PPK

Walther PPK/S

Walther P99

Walther TPH

VEKTOR CP-1 COMPACT PISTOL

Caliber: 9mm Para., 10-shot magazine. **Barrel:** 4". **Weight:** 25.4 oz. **Length:** 7" overall. **Stocks:** Textured polymer. **Sights:** Blade front adjustable for windage, fixed rear; adjustable sight optional. **Features:** Ergonomic grip frame shape; stainless steel barrel; delayed gas-buffered blowback action. Introduced 1999. Imported from South Africa by Vektor USA.

Price: With black slide	**$479.95**
Price: With nickel slide	**$499.95**
Price: With black slide, adjustable sight	**$509.95**
Price: With nickel slide, adjustable sight.	**$529.95**

WALTHER PP AUTO PISTOL

Caliber: 380 ACP, 7-shot magazine. **Barrel:** 3.86". **Weight:** 23-1/2 oz. **Length:** 6.7" overall. **Stocks:** Checkered plastic. **Sights:** Fixed, white markings. **Features:** Double action; manual safety blocks firing pin and drops hammer; chamber loaded indicator on 32 and 380; extra finger rest magazine provided. Imported from Germany by Carl Walther USA.

Price: 380 .... **$999.00**

Walther PPK/S American Auto Pistol

Similar to Walther PP except made entirely in the United States. Has 3.27" barrel with 6.1" length overall. Introduced 1980.

Price: 380 ACP only, blue. **$540.00**
Price: As above, 32 ACP or 380 ACP, stainless **$540.00**

Walther PPK American Auto Pistol

Similar to Walther PPK/S except weighs 21 oz., has 6-shot capacity. Made in the U.S. Introduced 1986.

Price: Stainless, 32 ACP or 380 ACP. **$540.00**
Price: Blue, 380 ACP only **$540.00**

WALTHER MODEL TPH AUTO PISTOL

Caliber: 22 LR, 25 ACP, 6-shot magazine. **Barrel:** 2-1/4". **Weight:** 14 oz. **Length:** 5-3/8" overall. **Stocks:** Checkered black composition. **Sights:** Blade front, rear drift-adjustable for windage. **Features:** Made of stainless steel. Scaled-down version of the Walther PP/PPK series. Made in U.S. Introduced 1987. From Carl Walther USA.

Price: Blue or stainless steel, 22 or 25 .... **$440.00**

WALTHER P88 COMPACT PISTOL

Caliber: 9mm Para., 10-shot magazine. **Barrel:** 3.93". **Weight:** 28 oz. **Length:** NA. **Stocks:** Checkered black polymer. **Sights:** Blade front, drift adjustable rear. **Features:** Double action with ambidextrous decocking lever and magazine release; alloy frame; loaded chamber indicator; matte blue finish. Imported from Germany by Carl Walther USA.

Price: **$900.00**

WALTHER P99 AUTO PISTOL

Caliber: 9mm Para., 9x21, 40 S&W, 10-shot magazine. **Barrel:** 4". **Weight:** 25 oz. **Length:** 7" overall. **Stocks:** Textured polymer. **Sights:** Blade front (comes with three interchangeable blades for elevation adjustment), micrometer rear adjustable for windage. **Features:** Double-action mechanism with trigger safety, decock safety, internal striker safety; chamber loaded indicator; ambidextrous magazine release levers; polymer frame

HANDGUNS

Dan Wesson Pointman Major

Dan Wesson Pointman Guardian

Dan Wesson Pointman Seven

Wilkinson Sherry

with interchangeable backstrap inserts. Comes with two magazines. Introduced 1997. Imported from Germany by Carl Walther USA.
Price: **$799.00**

Walther P990 Auto Pistol

Similar to the P99 except is double action only. Available in blue or silver tenifer finish. Introduced 1999. Imported from Germany by Carl Walther USA.
Price: **$749.00**

WALTHER P-5 AUTO PISTOL

Caliber: 9mm Para., 8-shot magazine. **Barrel:** 3.62". **Weight:** 28 oz. **Length:** 7.10" overall. **Stocks:** Checkered plastic. **Sights:** Blade front, adjustable rear. **Features:** Uses the basic Walther P-38 double-action mechanism. Blue finish. Imported from Germany by Carl Walther USA.
Price: **$900.00**

DAN WESSON POINTMAN MAJOR AUTO PISTOL

Caliber: 45 ACP. **Barrel:** 5". **Weight:** NA. **Length:** NA. **Grips:** Rosewood checkered. **Sights:** **Features:** Stainless steel frame and serrated slide; Chip McCormick match-grade trigger group, sear and disconnect; match-grade barrel; high-ride beavertail safety; checkered slide release; high rib; interchangeable sight system; laser engraved. Introduced 2000. Made in U.S. by Dan Wesson Firearms.
Price: Model PM1 .... **$779.00**

Dan Wesson Pointman Minor Auto Pistol

Similar to Pointman Major except has blued frame and slide with fixed rear sight. Introduced 2000. Made in U.S. by Dan Wesson Firearms.
Price: Model PM2 .... **$599.00**

Dan Wesson Pointman Seven Auto Pistols

Similar to Pointman Major except has dovetail adjustable target rear sight and dovetail target front sight. Available in blued or stainless finish. Introduced 2000. Made in U.S. by Dan Wesson Firearms.
Price: PM7 (blued frame and slide) **$999.00**
Price: PM7S (stainless finish) **$1,099.00**

Dan Wesson Pointman Guardian Auto Pistols

Similar to Pointman Major except has a more compact frame with 4.25" barrel. Avaiable in blued or stainless finish with fixed or adjustable sights. Introduced 2000. Made in U.S. by Dan Wesson Firearms.
Price: PMG-FS (blued frame and slide, fixed sights) **$769.00**
Price: PMG-AS (blued frame and slide, adjustable sights) **$779.00**
Price: PMGD-FS Guardian Duce (stainless frame and blued slide, fixed sights) **$829.00**
Price: PMGD-AS Guardian Duce (stainless frame and blued slide, adj. sights) **$839.00**

WILKINSON SHERRY AUTO PISTOL

Caliber: 22 LR, 8-shot magazine. **Barrel:** 2-1/8". **Weight:** 9-1/4 oz. **Length:** 4-3/8" overall. **Stocks:** Checkered black plastic. **Sights:** Fixed, groove. **Features:** Cross-bolt safety locks the sear into the hammer. Available in all blue finish or blue slide and trigger with gold frame. Introduced 1985.
Price: **$195.00**

WILKINSON LINDA AUTO PISTOL

Caliber: 9mm Para. **Barrel:** 8-5/16". **Weight:** 4 lbs., 13 oz. **Length:** 12-1/4" overall. **Stocks:** Checkered black plastic pistol grip, walnut forend. **Sights:** Protected blade front, aperture rear. **Features:** Fires from closed bolt. Semi-auto only. Straight blowback action. Cross-bolt safety. Removable barrel. From Wilkinson Arms.
Price: **$533.33**

Includes models suitable for several forms of competition and other sporting purposes.

Baer 1911 Ultimate Master

Baer 1911 Bullseye Wadcutter

Beretta Model 89

Beretta Model 96 Combat

BAER 1911 ULTIMATE MASTER COMBAT PISTOL

Caliber: 9x23, 38 Super, 400 Cor-Bon 45 ACP (others available), 10-shot magazine. **Barrel:** 5", 6"; Baer NM. **Weight:** 37 oz. **Length:** 8.5" overall. **Stocks:** Checkered rosewood. **Sights:** Baer dovetail front, low-mount Bo-Mar rear with hidden leaf. **Features:** Full-house competition gun. Baer forged NM blued steel frame and double serrated slide; Baer triple port, tapered cone compensator; fitted slide to frame; lowered, flared ejection port; Baer reverse recoil plug; full-length guide rod; recoil buff; beveled magazine well; Baer Commander hammer, sear; Baer extended ambidextrous safety, extended ejector, checkered slide stop, beavertail grip safety with pad, extended magazine release button; Baer speed trigger. Made in U.S. by Les Baer Custom, Inc.
Price: Compensated, open sights. $2,560.00
Price: 6" Model 400 Cor-Bon $2,590.00
Price: Compensated, with Baer optics mount. $3,195.00

Baer 1911 Ultimate Master Steel Special Pistol

Similar to the Ultimate Master except chambered for 38 Super with supported chamber (other calibers available), lighter slide, bushing-type compensator; two-piece guide rod. Designed for maximum 150 power factor. Comes without sights—scope and mount only. Hard chrome finish. Made in U.S. by Les Baer Custom, Inc.
Price: $2,980.00

BAER 1911 NATIONAL MATCH HARDBALL PISTOL

Caliber: 45 ACP, 7-shot magazine. **Barrel:** 5". **Weight:** 37 oz. **Length:** 8.5" overall. **Stocks:** Checkered walnut. **Sights:** Baer dovetail front with undercut post, low-mount Bo-Mar rear with hidden leaf. **Features:** Baer NM forged steel frame, double serrated slide and barrel with stainless bushing; slide fitted to frame; Baer match trigger with 4-lb. pull; polished feed ramp, throated barrel; checkered front strap, arched mainspring housing; Baer beveled magazine well; lowered, flared ejection port; tuned extractor; Baer extended ejector, checkered slide stop; recoil buff. Made in U.S. by Les Baer Custom, Inc.
Price: $1,335.00

Baer 1911 Bullseye Wadcutter Pistol

Similar to the National Match Hardball except designed for wadcutter loads only. Has polished feed ramp and barrel throat; Bo-Mar rib on slide;

full-length recoil rod; Baer speed trigger with 3-1/2-lb. pull; Baer deluxe hammer and sear; Baer beavertail grip safety with pad; flat mainspring housing checkered 20 lpi. Blue finish; checkered walnut grips. Made in U.S. by Les Baer Custom, Inc.
Price: From. $1,495.00
Price: With 6" barrel, from $1,690.00

BENELLI MP90S WORLD CUP PISTOL

Caliber: 22 Long Rifle, 6- or 9-shot magazine. **Barrel:** 4.4" **Weight:** 2.5 lbs. **Length:** 11.75". **Grip:** Walnut. **Sights:** Blade front, fully adjustable rear. **Features:** Single-action target pistol with fully adjustable trigger and adjustable heel rest; integral scope rail mount; attachment system for optional external weights.
Price: $1,190.00

Benelli MP95E Atlanta Pistol

Similar to MP90S World Cup Pistol, but available in blue finish with walnut grip or chrome finish with laminate grip. Overall length 11.25". Trigger overtravel adjustment only.
Price: (blue finish, walnut grip) $740.00
Price: (chrome finish, laminate grip) $810.00

BERETTA MODEL 89 GOLD STANDARD PISTOL

Caliber: 22 LR, 8-shot magazine. **Barrel:** 6". **Weight:** 41 oz. **Length:** 9.5" overall. **Stocks:** Target-type walnut with thumbrest. **Sights:** Interchangeable blade front, fully adjustable rear. **Features:** Single action target pistol. Matte black, Bruniton finish. Imported from Italy by Beretta U.S.A.
Price: $802.00

BERETTA MODEL 96 COMBAT PISTOL

Caliber: 40 S&W, 10-shot magazine. **Barrel:** 4.9" (5.9" with weight). **Weight:** 34.4 oz. **Length:** 8.5" overall. **Stocks:** Checkered black plastic. **Sights:** Blade front, fully adjustable target rear. **Features:** Uses heavier Brigadier slide with front and rear serrations; extended frame-mounted safety; extended, reversible magazine release; single-action-only with competition-tuned trigger with extra-short let-off and over-travel adjust-

BF Ultimate

Browning Buck Mark Bullseye

Browning Buck Mark Target 5.5

Colt Gold Cup Trophy

ment. Comes with tool kit. Introduced 1997. Imported from Italy by Beretta U.S.A.

Price: **$1,593.00**
Price: 4.9" barrel.. **$1,341.00**
Price: 5.9" barrel.. **$1,634.00**
Price: Combo **$1,599.00**

Beretta Model 96 Stock Pistol

Similar to the Model 96 Combat except is single/double action, with half-cock notch. Has front and rear slide serrations, rubber magazine bumper, replaceable accurizing barrel bushing, ultra-thin fine-checkered grips (aluminum optional), checkered front and back straps, radiused back strap, fitted case. Weighs 35 oz., 8.5" overall. Introduced 1997. Imported from Italy by Beretta U.S.A.

Price: **$1,700.00**

BF ULTIMATE SINGLE SHOT PISTOL

Caliber: 7mm U.S., 22 LR Match and 100 other chamberings. **Barrel:** 10.75" Heavy Match Grade with 11"target crown. **Weight:** 3 lbs., 15 oz. **Length:** 16" overall. **Stocks:** Thumbrest target style. **Sights:** Bo-Mar/Bond ScopeRib I Combo with hooded post front adjustable for height and width, rear notch available in .032", .062", .080" and .100" widths; 1/2-MOA clicks. **Features:** Designed to meet maximum rules for IHMSA Production Gun. Falling block action gives rigid barrel-receiver mating. Hand fitted and headspaced. Etched receiver; gold-colored trigger. Introduced 1988. Made in U.S. by E.A. Brown Mfg.

Price: **$895.00**

BROWNING BUCK MARK SILHOUETTE

Caliber: 22 LR, 10-shot magazine. **Barrel:** 9-7/8". **Weight:** 53 oz. **Length:** 14" overall. **Stocks:** Smooth walnut stocks and forend, or finger-groove walnut. **Sights:** Post-type hooded front adjustable for blade width and height; Pro Target rear fully adjustable for windage and elevation. **Features:** Heavy barrel with .900" diameter; 12-1/2" sight radius. Special sighting plane forms scope base. Introduced 1987. Made in U.S. From Browning.

Price: **$448.00**

Browning Buck Mark Target 5.5

Same as the Buck Mark Silhouette except has a 5-1/2" barrel with .900" diameter. Has hooded sights mounted on a scope base that accepts an optical or reflex sight. Rear sight is a Browning fully adjustable Pro Target, front sight is an adjustable post that customizes to different widths, and can be adjusted for height. Contoured walnut grips with thumbrest, or finger-groove walnut. Matte blue finish. Overall length is 9-5/8", weighs 35-1/2 oz. Has 10-shot magazine. Introduced 1990. From Browning.

Price: **$425.00**
Price: Target 5.5 Gold (as above with gold anodized frame and top rib) **$477.00**
Price: Target 5.5 Nickel (as above with nickel frame and top rib) **$477.00**

Browning Buck Mark Field 5.5

Same as the Target 5.5 except has hoodless ramp-style front sight and low profile rear sight. Matte blue finish, contoured or finger-groove walnut stocks. Introduced 1991.

Price: **$425.00**

Browning Buck Mark Bullseye

Similar to the Buck Mark Silhouette except has 7-1/4" heavy barrel with three flutes per side; trigger is adjustable from 2-1/2 to 5 lbs.; specially designed rosewood target or three-finger-groove stocks with competition-style heel rest, or with contoured rubber grip. Overall length is 11-5/16", weighs 36 oz. Introduced 1996. Made in U.S.A. From Browning.

Price: With ambidextrous moulded composite stocks **$389.00**
Price: With rosewood stocks, or wrap-around finger groove **$500.00**

COLT GOLD CUP TROPHY MK IV/SERIES 80

Caliber: 45 ACP, 8-shot magazine. **Barrel:** 5", with new design bushing. **Weight:** 39 oz. **Length:** 8-1/2". **Stocks:** Checkered rubber composite with silver-plated medallion. **Sights:** Patridge-style front, Colt-Elliason rear adjustable for windage and elevation, sight radius 6-3/4". **Features:** Arched or flat housing; wide, grooved trigger with adjustable stop; ribbed-top slide, hand fitted, with improved ejection port.

Price: Blue **$1,224.00**
Price: Stainless....................................... **$1,300.00**

COLT NATIONAL MATCH PISTOL

Caliber: 45 ACP, 8-shot magazine. **Barrel:** 5". **Weight:** 39 oz. **Length:** 8-1/2" overall. **Stocks:** Double-diamond checkered rosewood. **Sights:** Dovetailed Patridge front, fully adjustable rear; three-dot system. **Features:** Adjustable two-cut aluminum trigger; Defender grip safety; ambidextrous manual safety. Introduced 1999. Made in U.S. by Colt's Mfg., Inc.

Price: .... **NA**

Colt National Match

E.A.A. Witness Gold Team

Competitor Single Shot

Freedom Arms 252 Silhouette

COMPETITOR SINGLE SHOT PISTOL

Caliber: 22 LR through 50 Action Express, including belted magnums. **Barrel:** 14" standard; 10.5" silhouette; 16" optional. **Weight:** About 59 oz. (14" bbl.). **Length:** 15.12" overall. **Stocks:** Ambidextrous; synthetic (standard) or laminated or natural wood. **Sights:** Ramp front, adjustable rear. **Features:** Rotary canon-type action cocks on opening; cammed ejector; interchangeable barrels, ejectors. Adjustable single stage trigger, sliding thumb safety and trigger safety. Matte blue finish. Introduced 1988. From Competitor Corp., Inc.
Price: 14", standard calibers, synthetic grip **$414.95**
Price: Extra barrels, from **$159.95**

CZ 75 CHAMPION COMPETITION PISTOL

Caliber: 9mm Para., 9x21, 40 S&W, 10-shot magazine. **Barrel:** 4.49". **Weight:** 35 oz. **Length:** 9.44" overall. **Stocks:** Black rubber. **Sights:** Blade front, fully adjustable rear. **Features:** Single-action trigger mechanism; three-port compensator (40 S&W, 9mm have two port) full-length guide rod; extended magazine release; ambidextrous safety; flared magazine well; fully adjustable match trigger. Introduced 1999. Imported from the Czech Republic by CZ USA.
Price: 9mm Para., 9x21, 40 S&W, dual-tone finish **$1,484.00**

CZ 75 ST IPSC AUTO PISTOL

Caliber: 40 S&W, 10-shot magazine. **Barrel:** 5.12". **Weight:** 2.9 lbs. **Length:** 8.86" overall. **Stocks:** Checkered walnut. **Sights:** Fully adjustable rear. **Features:** Single-action mechanism; extended slide release and ambidextrous safety; full-length slide rail; double slide serrations. Introduced 1999. Imported from the Czech Republic by CZ-USA.
Price: Dual-tone finish **$1,038.00**

EAA/BAIKAL IZH35 AUTO PISTOL

Caliber: 22 LR, 5-shot magazine. **Barrel:** 6". **Weight:** NA. **Length:** NA. **Grips:** Walnut; fully adjustable right-hand target-style. **Sights:** Fully adjustable rear, blade front; detachable scope mount. **Features:** Hammer-forged target barrel; machined steel receiver; adjustable trigger; manual slide hold back, grip and manual trigger-bar disconnect safeties; cocking indicator. Introduced 2000. Imported from Russia by European American Armory.
Price: Blued finish. **$519.00**

E.A.A. WITNESS GOLD TEAM AUTO

Caliber: 9mm Para., 9x21, 38 Super, 40 S&W, 45 ACP. **Barrel:** 5.1". **Weight:** 41.6 oz. **Length:** 9.6" overall. **Stocks:** Checkered walnut, competition style. **Sights:** Square post front, fully adjustable rear. **Features:** Triple-chamber cone compensator; competition SA trigger; extended safety and magazine release; competition hammer; beveled magazine well; beavertail grip. Hand-fitted major components. Hard chrome finish. Match-grade barrel. From E.A.A. Custom Shop. Introduced 1992. From European American Armory.
Price: **$2,150.00**

E.A.A. Witness Silver Team Auto

Similar to the Witness Gold Team except has double-chamber compensator, oval magazine release, black rubber grips, double-dip blue finish. Comes with Super Sight and drilled and tapped for scope mount. Built for the intermediate competition shooter. Introduced 1992. From European American Armory Custom Shop.
Price: 9mm Para., 9x21, 38 Super, 40 S&W, 45 ACP **$968.00**

ENTRÉPRISE TOURNAMENT SHOOTER MODEL I

Caliber: 45 ACP, 10-shot magazine. **Barrel:** 6". **Weight:** 40 oz. **Length:** 8.5" overall. **Stocks:** Black ultra-slim double diamond checkered synthetic. **Sights:** Dovetailed Patridge front, adjustable Competizione "melded" rear. **Features:** Oversized magazine release button; flared magazine well; fully machined parallel slide rails; front and rear slide serrations; serrated top of slide; stainless ramped bull barrel with fully supported chamber; full-length guide rod with plug; stainless firing pin; match extractor; polished ramp; tuned match extractor; black oxide. Introduced 1998. Made in U.S. by Entréprise Arms.
Price: **$2,300.00**
Price: TSMIII (Satin chrome finish, two-piece guide rod) **$2,700.00**

FREEDOM ARMS CASULL MODEL 252 SILHOUETTE

Caliber: 22 LR, 5-shot cylinder. **Barrel:** 10". **Weight:** 63 oz. **Length:** 15.5" overall. **Stocks:** Black micarta, western style. **Sights:** Adjustable front with bead, Iron Sight Gun Works silhouette rear, click adjustable for windage and elevation. **Features:** Stainless steel. Built on the Model 83. Two-point firing pin, lightened hammer for fast lock time. Trigger pull is 3 to 5 lbs. with pre-set overtravel screw. Introduced 1991. From Freedom Arms.
Price: Silhouette Class **$1,578.00**
Price: Extra fitted 22 WMR cylinder **$264.00**

GAUCHER GP SILHOUETTE PISTOL

Caliber: 22 LR, single shot. **Barrel:** 10". **Weight:** 42.3 oz. **Length:** 15.5" overall. **Stocks:** Stained hardwood. **Sights:** Hooded post on ramp front, open rear adjustable for windage and elevation. **Features:** Matte chrome barrel, blued bolt and sights. Other barrel lengths available on special order. Introduced 1991. Imported by Mandall Shooting Supplies.
Price: **$425.00**

HANDGUNS

NEW!

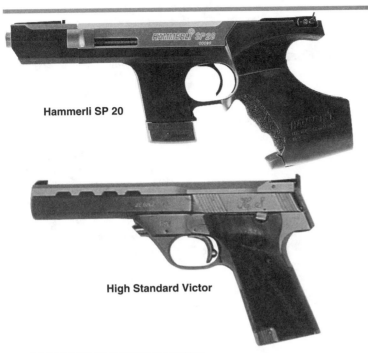

Hammerli SP 20

High Standard Victor

High Standard Trophy

HAMMERLI SP 20 TARGET PISTOL

Caliber: 22 LR, 32 S&W. **Barrel:** 4.6". **Weight:** 34.6-41.8 oz. **Length:** 11.8" overall. **Stocks:** Anatomically shaped synthetic Hi-Grip available in five sizes. **Sights:** Integral front in three widths, adjustable rear with changeable notch widths. **Features:** Extremely low-level sight line; anatomically shaped trigger; adjustable JPS buffer system for different recoil characteristics. Receiver available in red, blue, gold, violet or black. Introduced 1998. Imported from Switzerland by SIGARMS, Inc and Hammerli Pistols USA.
Price: . . . . **NA**

HARRIS GUNWORKS SIGNATURE JR. LONG RANGE PISTOL

Caliber: Any suitable caliber. **Barrel:** To customer specs. **Weight:** 5 lbs. **Stock:** Gunworks fiberglass. **Sights:** None furnished; comes with scope rings. **Features:** Right- or left-hand benchrest action of titanium or stainless steel; single shot or repeater. Comes with bipod. Introduced 1992. Made in U.S. by Harris Gunworks, Inc.
Price: **$2,700.00**

HIGH STANDARD TROPHY TARGET PISTOL

Caliber: 22 LR, 10-shot magazine. **Barrel:** 5-1/2" bull or 7-1/4" fluted. **Weight:** 44 oz. **Length:** 9.5" overall. **Stock:** Checkered hardwood with thumbrest. **Sights:** Undercut ramp front, frame-mounted micro-click rear adjustable for windage and elevation; drilled and tapped for scope mounting. **Features:** Gold-plated trigger, slide lock, safety-lever and magazine release; stippled front grip and backstrap; adjustable trigger and sear. Barrel weights optional. From High Standard Manufacturing Co., Inc.
Price: 5-1/2", scope base **$510.00**
Price: 7.25" **$650.00**
Price: 7.25", scope base **$591.00**

HIGH STANDARD VICTOR TARGET PISTOL

Caliber: 22 LR, 10-shot magazine. **Barrel:** 4-1/2" or 5-1/2"; push-button takedown. **Weight:** 46 oz. **Length:** 9.5" overall. **Stock:** Checkered hardwood with thumbrest. **Sights:** Undercut ramp front, micro-click rear adjustable for windage and elevation. Also available with scope mount, rings, no sights. **Features:** Stainless steel construction. Full-length vent rib. Gold-plated trigger, slide lock, safety-lever and magazine release; stippled front grip and backstrap; polished slide; adjustable trigger and sear. Comes with barrel weight. From High Standard Manufacturing Co., Inc.
Price: **$591.00**
Price: With Weaver rib **$532.00**

KIMBER SUPER MATCH AUTO PISTOL

Caliber: 45 ACP, 7-shot magazine. **Barrel:** 5". **Weight:** 38 oz. **Length:** 18.7" overall. **Sights:** Blade front, Kimber fully adjustable rear. **Features:**

Guaranteed to have shot 3" group at 50 yards. Stainless steel frame, black KimPro slide; two-piece magazine well; premium aluminum match-grade trigger; 30 lpi front strap checkering; stainless match-grade barrel; ambidextrous safety; special Custom Shop markings. Introduced 1999. Made in U.S. by Kimber Mfg., Inc.
Price: **$1,871.00**

MORINI MODEL 84E FREE PISTOL

Caliber: 22 LR, single shot. **Barrel:** 11.4". **Weight:** 43.7 oz. **Length:** 19.4" overall. **Stocks:** Adjustable match type with stippled surfaces. **Sights:** Interchangeable blade front, match-type fully adjustable rear. **Features:** Fully adjustable electronic trigger. Introduced 1995. Imported from Switzerland by Nygord Precision Products.
Price: **$1,450.00**

PARDINI MODEL SP, HP TARGET PISTOLS

Caliber: 22 LR, 32 S&W, 5-shot magazine. **Barrel:** 4.7". **Weight:** 38.9 oz. **Length:** 11.6" overall. **Stocks:** Adjustable; stippled walnut; match type. **Sights:** Interchangeable blade front, interchangeable, fully adjustable rear. **Features:** Fully adjustable match trigger. Introduced 1995. Imported from Italy by Nygord Precision Products.
Price: Model SP (22 LR) **$950.00**
Price: Model HP (32 S&W) **$1,050.00**

PARDINI GP RAPID FIRE MATCH PISTOL

Caliber: 22 Short, 5-shot magazine. **Barrel:** 4.6". **Weight:** 43.3 oz. **Length:** 11.6" overall. **Stocks:** Wrap-around stippled walnut. **Sights:** Interchangeable post front, fully adjustable match rear. **Features:** Model GP Schuman has extended rear sight for longer sight radius. Introduced 1995. Imported from Italy by Nygord Precision Products.
Price: Model GP **$1,095.00**
Price: Model GP Schuman **$1,595.00**

PARDINI K22 FREE PISTOL

Caliber: 22 LR, single shot. **Barrel:** 9.8". **Weight:** 34.6 oz. **Length:** 18.7" overall. **Stocks:** Wrap-around walnut; adjustable match type. **Sights:** Interchangeable post front, fully adjustable match open rear. **Features:** Removable, adjustable match trigger. Barrel weights mount above the barrel. New model introduced in 1999. Imported from Italy by Nygord Precision Products.
Price: **$1,295.00**

RUGER MARK II TARGET MODEL AUTOLOADING PISTOL

Caliber: 22 LR, 10-shot magazine. **Barrel:** 6-7/8". **Weight:** 42 oz. **Length:** 11-1/8" overall. **Stocks:** Checkered hard plastic. **Sights:** .125" blade front, micro-click rear, adjustable for windage and elevation. Sight radius 9-3/8". Comes with lockable plastic case with lock.
Features: Introduced 1982.
Price: Blued (MK-678) **$326.00**
Price: Stainless (KMK-678) **$408.00**

Ruger Mark II Government Target Model

Same gun as the Mark II Target Model except has 6-7/8" barrel, higher sights and is roll marked "Government Target Model" on the right side of the receiver below the rear sight. Identical in all aspects to the military model used for training U.S. Armed Forces except for markings. Comes with factory test target. Comes with lockable plastic case with lock. Introduced 1987.
Price: Blued (MK-678G) **$393.00**
Price: Stainless (KMK-678G) **$470.00**

HANDGUNS

Ruger Mark II Bull Barrel

Safari Arms Big Deuce

Smith & Wesson Model 41

Springfield 1911A1 Trophy Match

Ruger Stainless Competition Model Pistol

Similar to the Mark II Government Target Model stainless pistol except has 6-7/8" slab-sided barrel; the receiver top is fitted with a Ruger scope base of blued, chrome moly steel; comes with Ruger 1" stainless scope rings for mounting a variety of optical sights; has checkered laminated grip panels with right-hand thumbrest. Has blued open sights with 9-1/4" radius. Overall length is 11-1/8", weight 45 oz. Comes with lockable plastic case with lock. Introduced 1991.
Price: KMK-678GC **$486.00**

Ruger Mark II Bull Barrel

Same gun as the Target Model except has 5-1/2" or 10" heavy barrel (10" meets all IHMSA regulations). Weight with 5-1/2" barrel is 42 oz., with 10" barrel, 51 oz. Comes with lockable plastic case with lock.
Price: Blued (MK-512) **$326.00**
Price: Blued (MK-10) **$330.00**
Price: Stainless (KMK-10) **$413.00**
Price: Stainless (KMK-512) **$408.00**

SAFARI ARMS BIG DEUCE PISTOL

Caliber: 45 ACP, 7-shot magazine. **Barrel:** 6", 416 stainless steel. **Weight:** 40.3 oz. **Length:** 9.5" overall. **Stocks:** Smooth walnut. **Sights:** Ramped blade front, LPA adjustable rear. **Features:** Beavertail grip safety; extended thumb safety and slide release; Commander-style hammer. Throated, polished and tuned. Parkerized matte black slide with satin stainless steel frame. Introduced 1995. Made in U.S. by Safari Arms, Inc.
Price: **$714.00**

SMITH & WESSON MODEL 41 TARGET

Caliber: 22 LR, 10-shot clip. **Barrel:** 5-1/2", 7". **Weight:** 44 oz. (5-1/2" barrel). **Length:** 9" overall (5-1/2" barrel). **Stocks:** Checkered walnut with modified thumbrest, usable with either hand. **Sights:** 1/8" Patridge on ramp base; micro-click rear adjustable for windage and elevation. **Features:** 3/8" wide, grooved trigger; adjustable trigger stop.
Price: S&W Bright Blue, either barrel **$801.00**

SMITH & WESSON MODEL 22A TARGET PISTOL

Caliber: 22 LR, 10-shot magazine. **Barrel:** 5-1/2" bull. **Weight:** 38.5 oz. **Length:** 9-1/2" overall. **Stocks:** Dymondwood with ambidextrous thumbrests and flared bottom or rubber soft touch with thumbrest. **Sights:** Patridge front, fully adjustable rear. **Features:** Sight bridge with Weaver-style integral optics mount; alloy frame, stainless barrel and slide; matte black finish. Introduced 1997. Made in U.S. by Smith & Wesson.
Price: **$320.00**

Smith & Wesson Model 22S Target Pistol

Similar to the Model 22A except has stainless steel frame. Introduced 1997. Made in U.S. by Smith & Wesson.
Price: **$379.00**

Springfield, Inc. 1911A1 Trophy Match Pistol

Similar to the 1911A1 except factory accurized, Videki speed trigger, skeletonized hammer; has 4- to 5-1/2-lb. trigger pull, click adjustable rear sight, match-grade barrel and bushing. Comes with cocobolo grips. Introduced 1994. From Springfield, Inc.
Price: Blue **$1,089.00**
Price: Stainless steel **$1,149.00**
Price: High Capacity (stainless steel, 10-shot magazine, front slide serrations, checkered slide serrations) **$1,118.00**

Springfield, Inc. Expert Pistol

Similar to the Competition Pistol except has triple-chamber tapered cone compensator on match barrel with dovetailed front sight; lowered and flared ejection port; fully tuned for reliability; fitted slide to frame; extended ambidextrous thumb safety, extended magazine release button; beavertail grip safety; Pachmayr wrap-around grips. Comes with two magazines, plastic carrying case. Introduced 1992. From Springfield, Inc.
Price: 45 ACP, Duotone finish **$1,724.00**
Price: Expert Ltd. (non-compensated) **$1,624.00**

Springfield, Inc. Distinguished Pistol

Has all the features of the 1911A1 Expert except is full-house pistol with deluxe Bo-Mar low-mounted adjustable rear sight; full-length recoil spring guide rod and recoil spring retainer; checkered frontstrap; S&A magazine well; walnut grips. Hard chrome finish. Comes with two magazines with slam pads, plastic carrying case. From Springfield, Inc.
Price: 45 ACP **$2,445.00**
Price: Distinguished Limited (non-compensated) **$2,345.00**

SPRINGFIELD, INC. 1911A1 BULLSEYE WADCUTTER PISTOL

Caliber: 38 Super, 45 ACP. **Barrel:** 5". **Weight:** 45 oz. **Length:** 8.59" overall (5" barrel). **Stocks:** Checkered walnut. **Sights:** Bo-Mar rib with undercut blade front, fully adjustable rear. **Features:** Built for wadcutter loads only. Has full-length recoil spring guide rod, fitted Videki speed trigger with 3.5-lb. pull; match Commander hammer and sear; beavertail grip safety; lowered and flared ejection port; tuned extractor; fitted slide to frame; recoil buffer system; beveled and polished magazine well; checkered front strap and steel mainspring housing (flat housing standard); polished and throated National Match barrel and bushing. Comes with two magazines with slam pads, plastic carrying case, test target. Introduced 1992. From Springfield, Inc.
Price: **$1,499.00**

Wichita Silhouette

Thompson/Center Super 14 Contender

Unique D.E.S. 69U

Springfield, Inc. Basic Competition Pistol

Has low-mounted Bo-Mar adjustable rear sight, undercut blade front; match throated barrel and bushing; polished feed ramp; lowered and flared ejection port; fitted Videki speed trigger with tuned 3.5-lb. pull; fitted slide to frame; recoil buffer system; checkered walnut grips; serrated, arched mainspring housing. Comes with two magazines with slam pads, plastic carrying case. Introduced 1992. From Springfield, Inc.

Price: 45 ACP, blue, 5" only **$1,295.00**

Springfield, Inc. 1911A1 N.M. Hardball Pistol

Has Bo-Mar adjustable rear sight with undercut front blade; fitted match Videki trigger with 4-lb. pull; fitted slide to frame; throated National Match barrel and bushing, polished feed ramp; recoil buffer system; tuned extractor; Herrett walnut grips. Comes with two magazines, plastic carrying case, test target. Introduced 1992. From Springfield, Inc.

Price: 45 ACP, blue **$1,336.00**

STI EAGLE 5.1 PISTOL

Caliber: 9mm Para., 38 Super, 40 S&W, 45 ACP, 10-ACP, 10-shot magazine. **Barrel:** 5", bull. **Weight:** 34 oz. **Length:** 8.62" overall. **Stocks:** Checkered polymer. **Sights:** Bo-Mar blade front, Bo-Mar fully adjustable rear. **Features:** Modular frame design; adjustable match trigger; skeletonized hammer; extended grip safety with locator pad; match-grade fit of all parts. Many options available. Introduced 1994. Made in U.S. by STI International.

Price: **$1,792.00**

THOMPSON/CENTER SUPER 14 CONTENDER

Caliber: 22 LR, 222 Rem., 223 Rem., 7-30 Waters, 30-30 Win., 357 Rem. Maximum, 44 Mag., single shot. **Barrel:** 14". **Weight:** 45 oz. **Length:** 17-1/4" overall. **Stocks:** T/C "Competitor Grip" (walnut and rubber). **Sights:** Fully adjustable target-type. **Features:** Break-open action with auto safety. Interchangeable barrels for both rimfire and centerfire calibers. Introduced 1978.

Price: Blued $520.24
Price: Stainless steel $578.40
Price: Extra barrels, blued $251.06
Price: Extra barrels, stainless steel $278.68

Thompson/Center Super 16 Contender

Same as the T/C Super 14 Contender except has 16-1/4" barrel. Rear sight can be mounted at mid-barrel position (10-3/4" radius) or moved to the rear (using scope mount position) for 14-3/4" radius. Overall length is 20-1/4". Comes with T/C Competitor Grip of walnut and rubber. Available in, 223 Rem., 45-70 Gov't. Also available with 16" vent rib barrel with internal choke, caliber 45 Colt/410 shotshell.

Price: Blue $525.95
Price: 45-70 Gov't., blue $531.52
Price: Super 16 Vent Rib, blued $559.70

Price: Extra 16" barrel, blued $245.61
Price: Extra 45-70 barrel, blued $251.08
Price: Extra Super 16 vent rib barrel, blue $278.73

UNIQUE D.E.S. 32U TARGET PISTOL

Caliber: 32 S&W Long wadcutter. **Barrel:** 5.9". **Weight:** 40.2 oz. **Stocks:** Anatomically shaped, adjustable stippled French walnut. **Sights:** Blade front, micrometer click rear. **Features:** Trigger adjustable for weight and position; dry firing mechanism; slide stop catch. Optional sleeve weights. Introduced 1990. Imported from France by Nygord Precision Products.

Price: Right-hand, about **$1,350.00**
Price: Left-hand, about **$1,380.00**

UNIQUE D.E.S. 69U TARGET PISTOL

Caliber: 22 LR, 5-shot magazine. **Barrel:** 5.91". **Weight:** 35.3 oz. **Length:** 10.5" overall. **Stocks:** French walnut target-style with thumbrest and adjustable shelf; hand-checkered panels. **Sights:** Ramp front, micro. adjustable rear mounted on frame; 8.66" sight radius. **Features:** Meets U.I.T. standards. Comes with 260-gram barrel weight; 100, 150, 350-gram weights available. Fully adjustable match trigger; dry-firing safety device. Imported from France by Nygord Precision Products.

Price: Right-hand, about $1,250.00
Price: Left-hand, about $1,290.00

UNIQUE MODEL 96U TARGET PISTOL

Caliber: 22 LR, 5- or 6-shot magazine. **Barrel:** 5.9". **Weight:** 40.2 oz. **Length:** 11.2" overall. **Stocks:** French walnut. Target style with thumbrest and adjustable shelf. **Sights:** Blade front, micrometer rear mounted on frame. **Features:** Designed for Sport Pistol and Standard U.I.T. shooting. External hammer; fully adjustable and movable trigger; dry-firing device. Introduced 1997. Imported from France by Nygord Precision Products.

Price: $1,350.00

WALTHER GSP MATCH PISTOL

Caliber: 22 LR, 32 S&W Long (GSP-C), 5-shot magazine. **Barrel:** 4.22". **Weight:** 44.8 oz. (22 LR), 49.4 oz. (32). **Length:** 11.8" overall. **Stocks:** Walnut. **Sights:** Post front, match rear adjustable for windage and elevation. **Features:** Available with either 2.2-lb. (1000 gm) or 3-lb. (1360 gm) trigger. Spare magazine, barrel weight, tools supplied. Imported from Germany by Nygord Precision Products.

Price: GSP, with case $1,495.00
Price: GSP-C, with case $1,595.00

WICHITA SILHOUETTE PISTOL

Caliber: 308 Win. F.L., 7mm IHMSA, 7mm-308. **Barrel:** 14-15/16". **Weight:** 4-1/2 lbs. **Length:** 21-3/8" overall. **Stock:** American walnut with oil finish. Glass bedded. **Sights:** Wichita Multi-Range sight system. **Features:** Comes with left-hand action with right-hand grip. Round receiver and barrel. Fluted bolt, flat bolt handle. Wichita adjustable trigger. Introduced 1979. From Wichita Arms.

Price: Center grip stock $1,800.00
Price: As above except with Rear Position Stock and target-type
Lightpull trigger $1,800.00

WICHITA CLASSIC SILHOUETTE PISTOL

Caliber: All standard calibers with maximum overall length of 2.800". **Barrel:** 11-1/4". **Weight:** 3 lbs., 15 oz. **Stocks:** AAA American walnut with oil finish, checkered grip. **Sights:** Hooded post front, open adjustable rear. **Features:** Three locking lug bolt, three gas ports; completely adjustable Wichita trigger. Introduced 1981. From Wichita Arms.

Price: $3,450.00

HANDGUNS

Includes models suitable for hunting and competitive courses of fire, both police and international.

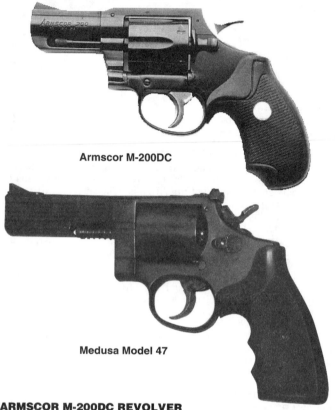

Armscor M-200DC

Ruger GP161

Medusa Model 47

Ruger KSP-931

ARMSCOR M-200DC REVOLVER

Caliber: 38 Spec., 6-shot cylinder. **Barrel:** 2-1/2", 4". **Weight:** 22 oz. (2-1/2" barrel). **Length:** 7-3/8" overall (2-1/2" barrel). **Stocks:** Checkered rubber. **Sights:** Blade front, fixed notch rear. **Features:** All-steel construction; floating firing pin, transfer bar ignition; shrouded ejector rod; blue finish. Reintroduced 1996. Imported from the Philippines by K.B.I., Inc.
Price: 2-1/2" $199.99
Price: 4" $205.00

ARMSPORT MODEL 4540 REVOLVER

Caliber: 38 Special. **Barrel:** 4". **Weight:** 32 oz **Length:** 9" overall. **Sights:** Fixed rear, blade front. **Features:** Ventilated rib; blued finish. Imported from Argentina by Armsport Inc.
Price: $140.00

E.A.A. STANDARD GRADE REVOLVERS

Caliber: 38 Spec., 6-shot; 357 magnum, 6-shot. **Barrel:** 2", 4". **Weight:** 38 oz. (22 rimfire, 4"). **Length:** 8.8" overall (4" bbl.). **Stocks:** Rubber with finger grooves. **Sights:** Blade front, fixed or adjustable on rimfires; fixed only on 32, 38. **Features:** Swing-out cylinder; hammer block safety; blue finish. Introduced 1991. Imported from Germany by European American Armory.
Price: 38 Special 2" $180.00
Price: 38 Special, 4" $199.00
Price: 357 Magnum, 2" $199.00
Price: 357 Magnum, 4" $233.00

MEDUSA MODEL 47 REVOLVER

Caliber: Most 9mm, 38 and 357 caliber cartridges; 6-shot cylinder. **Barrel:** 2-1/2", 3", 4", 5", 6"; fluted. **Weight:** 39 oz. **Length:** 10" overall (4" barrel). **Stocks:** Gripper-style rubber. **Sights:** Changeable front blades, fully adjustable rear. **Features:** Patented extractor allows gun to chamber, fire and extract over 25 different cartridges in the .355- to .357 range, without half-moon clips. Steel frame and cylinder; match quality barrel. Matte blue finish. Introduced 1996. Made in U.S. by Phillips & Rogers, Inc.
Price: $899.00

RUGER GP-100 REVOLVERS

Caliber: 38 Spec., 357 Mag., 6-shot. **Barrel:** 3", 3" full shroud, 4", 4" full shroud, 6", 6" full shroud. **Weight:** 3" barrel—35 oz., 3" full shroud—36 oz., 4" barrel—37 oz., 4" full shroud—38 oz. **Sights:** Fixed; adjustable on 4" full shroud and all 6" barrels. **Stocks:** Ruger Santoprene Cushioned Grip with Goncalo Alves inserts. **Features:** Uses action and frame incorporating improvements and features of both the Security-Six and Redhawk revolvers. Full length and short ejector shroud. Satin blue and stainless steel.
Price: GP-141 (357, 4" full shroud, adj. sights, blue) $462.00
Price: GP-160 (357, 6", adj. sights, blue) $462.00
Price: GP-161 (357, 6" full shroud, adj. sights, blue), 46 oz. $462.00
Price: GPF-331 (357, 3" full shroud) $445.00
Price: GPF-340 (357, 4") $445.00
Price: GPF-341 (357, 4" full shroud) $445.00
Price: KGP-141 (357, 4" full shroud, adj. sights, stainless) $498.00
Price: KGP-160 (357, 6", adj. sights, stainless), 43 oz. $498.00
Price: KGP-161 (357, 6" full shroud, adj. sights, stainless) 46 oz. $498.00
Price: KGPF-330 (357, 3", stainless) $480.00
Price: KGPF-331 (357, 3" full shroud, stainless) $480.00
Price: KGPF-340 (357, 4", stainless), KGPF-840 (38 Spec.) $480.00
Price: KGPF-341 (357, 4" full shroud, stainless) $480.00

Ruger SP101 Double-Action-Only Revolver

Similar to the standard SP101 except is double-action-only with no single-action sear notch. Has spurless hammer for snag-free handling, floating firing pin and Ruger's patented transfer bar safety system. Available with 2-1/4" barrel in 357 Magnum. Weighs 25-1/2 oz., overall length 7.06". Natural brushed satin or high-polish stainless steel. Introduced 1993.
Price: KSP321XL (357 Mag.) $458.00

RUGER SP101 REVOLVERS

Caliber: 22 LR, 32 H&R Mag., 6-shot; 9mm Para., 38 Spec. +P, 357 Mag., 5-shot. **Barrel:** 2-1/4", 3-1/16", 4". **Weight:** (38 & 357 mag models) 2-1/4"—25 oz.; 3-1/16"—27 oz. **Sights:** Adjustable on 22, 32, fixed on others. **Stocks:** Ruger Santoprene Cushioned Grip with Xenoy inserts. **Features:** Incorporates improvements and features found in the GP-100

Ruger KSRH-7

Smith & Wesson Model 10

Smith & Wesson Model 14

Smith & Wesson Model 19

revolvers into a compact, small frame, double-action revolver. Full-length ejector shroud. Stainless steel only. Introduced 1988.

Price: KSP-821 (2-1/2", 38 Spec.) **$458.00**
Price: KSP-831 (3-1/16", 38 Spec.) **$458.00**
Price: KSP-221 (2-1/4", 22 LR, 32 oz. **$458.00**
Price: KSP-240 (4", 22 LR), 33 oz. **$458.00**
Price: KSP-241 (4" heavy bbl., 22 LR), 34 oz. **$458.00**
Price: KSP-3231 (3-1/16", 32 H&R), 30 oz. **$458.00**
Price: KSP-921 (2-1/4", 9mm Para.) **$458.00**
Price: KSP-931 (3-1/16", 9mm Para.) **$458.00**
Price: KSP-321 (2-1/4", 357 Mag.) **$458.00**
Price: KSP331X (3-1/16", 357 Mag.) **$458.00**

RUGER REDHAWK

Caliber: 44 Rem. Mag., 45 Colt, 6-shot. **Barrel:** 5-1/2", 7-1/2". **Weight:** About 54 oz. (7-1/2" bbl.). **Length:** 13" overall (7-1/2" barrel). **Stocks:** Square butt Goncalo Alves. **Sights:** Interchangeable Patridge-type front, rear adjustable for windage and elevation. **Features:** Stainless steel, brushed satin finish, or blued ordnance steel. Has a 9-1/2" sight radius. Introduced 1979.
Price: Blued, 44 Mag., 5-1/2" RH-445, 7-1/2" RH-44 . . . . **$545.00**
Price: Blued, 44 Mag., 7-1/2" RH44R, with scope mount, rings . . **$578.00**
Price: Stainless, 44 Mag., 5-1/2", 7-1/2" KRH-445 . . . . **$603.00**
Price: Stainless, 44 Mag., 7-1/2", with scope mount, rings
KRH-44 . . . . **$629.00**
Price: Stainless, 45 Colt, 5-1/2", 7-1/2" KRH-455 . . . . **$603.00**
Price: Stainless, 45 Colt, 7-1/2", with scope mount KRH-45 . . . . **$629.00**

Ruger Super Redhawk Revolver

Similar to the standard Redhawk except has a heavy extended frame with the Ruger Integral Scope Mounting System on the wide topstrap. Also available in 454 Casull. The wide hammer spur has been lowered for better scope clearance. Incorporates the mechanical design features and improvements of the GP-100. Choice of 7-1/2" or 9-1/2" barrel, both with ramp front sight base with Redhawk-style Interchangeable Insert sight blades, adjustable rear sight. Comes with Ruger "Cushioned Grip" panels of Santoprene with Goncalo Alves wood panels. Satin stainless steel. Introduced 1987.
Price: KSRH-7 (7-1/2"), KSRH-9 (9-1/2") **$629.00**
Price: KSRH-7454 (7-1/2") 454 Casull **$745.00**

Ruger Super Redhawk 454 Casull Revolver

Similar to the Ruger Super Redhawk except chambered for 454 Casull (also accepts 45 Colt cartridges). Unfluted cylinder, 7" barrel, weighs 53 ounces. Comes with 1" stainless scope rings. Introduced 2000.
Price: (satin or target gray stainless steel finishes) **$745.00**

SMITH & WESSON MODEL 10 M&P HB REVOLVER

Caliber: 38 Spec., 6-shot. **Barrel:** 4". **Weight:** 33.5 oz. **Length:** 9-5/16" overall. **Stocks:** Uncle Mike's Combat soft rubber; square butt. **Sights:** Fixed; ramp front, square notch rear.
Price: Blue **$458.00**

SMITH & WESSON MODEL 14 FULL LUG REVOLVER

Caliber: 38 Spec., 6-shot. **Barrel:** 6", full lug. **Weight:** 47 oz. **Length:** 11-1/8" overall. **Stocks:** Hogue soft rubber. **Sights:** Pinned Patridge front,

adjustable micrometer click rear. **Features:** Has .500" target hammer, .312" smooth combat trigger. Polished blue finish. Reintroduced 1991. Limited production.
Price: **$498.00**

SMITH & WESSON MODEL 15 COMBAT MASTERPIECE

Caliber: 38 Spec., 6-shot. **Barrel:** 4". **Weight:** 32 oz. **Length:** 9-5/16" (4" bbl.). **Stocks:** Uncle Mike's Combat soft rubber. **Sights:** Serrated ramp front, micro-click rear adjustable for windage and elevation.
Price: Blued **$450.00**

SMITH & WESSON MODEL 19 COMBAT MAGNUM

Caliber: 357 Mag. and 38 Spec., 6-shot. **Barrel:** 4". **Weight:** 36 oz. **Length:** 9-9/16" (4" bbl.). **Stocks:** Uncle Mike's Combat soft rubber; wood optional. **Sights:** Red ramp front, micro-click rear adjustable for windage and elevation.
Price: 4" **$457.00**

SMITH & WESSON MODEL 629 REVOLVERS

Caliber: 44 Magnum, 6-shot. **Barrel:** 5", 6", 8-3/8". **Weight:** 47 oz. (6" bbl.). **Length:** 11-3/8" overall (6" bbl.). **Stocks:** Soft rubber; wood optional. **Sights:** 1/8" red ramp front, micro-click rear, adjustable for windage and elevation.
Price: Model 629 (stainless steel), 5" **$625.00**
Price: Model 629, 6" **$631.00**
Price: Model 629, 8-3/8" barrel **$646.00**

Smith & Wesson Model 65LS

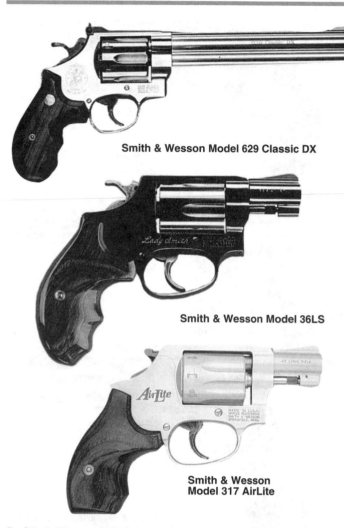

Smith & Wesson Model 629 Classic DX

Smith & Wesson Model 36LS

Smith & Wesson
Model 317 AirLite

Smith & Wesson Model 629 Classic Revolver

Similar to the standard Model 629 except has full-lug 5", 6-1/2" or 8-3/8" barrel; chamfered front of cylinder; interchangeable red ramp front sight with adjustable white outline rear; Hogue grips with S&W monogram; the frame is drilled and tapped for scope mounting. Factory accurizing and endurance packages. Overall length with 5" barrel is 10-1/2"; weighs 51 oz. Introduced 1990.
Price: Model 629 Classic (stainless), 5", 6-1/2" **$670.00**
Price: As above, 8-3/8". **$691.00**

Smith & Wesson Model 629 Classic DX Revolver

Similar to the Model 629 Classic except offered only with 6-1/2" or 8-3/8" full-lug barrel; comes with five front sights: red ramp; black Patridge; black Patridge with gold bead; black ramp; and black Patridge with white dot. Comes with Hogue combat-style and wood round butt grip. Introduced 1991.
Price: Model 629 Classic DX, 6-1/2" **$860.00**
Price: As above, 8-3/8". **$888.00**

SMITH & WESSON
MODEL 36, 37 CHIEFS SPECIAL & AIRWEIGHT

Caliber: 38 Spec.+P, 5-shot. **Barrel:** 1-7/8". **Weight:** 19-1/2 oz. (2" bbl.); 13-1/2 oz. (Airweight). **Length:** 6-1/2" (round butt). **Stocks:** Round butt soft rubber. **Sights:** Fixed, serrated ramp front, square notch rear.
Price: Blue, standard Model 36 . . . . **$406.00**
Price: Blue, Airweight Model 37 . . . . **$483.00**

Smith & Wesson Model 36LS, 60LS LadySmith

Similar to the standard Model 36. Available with 1-7/8" barrel, 38 Special. Comes with smooth, contoured rosewood grips with the S&W monogram.

Has a speedloader cutout. Comes in a fitted carry/storage case. Introduced 1989.
Price: Model 36LS **$478.00**
Price: Model 60LS, as above except in stainless, 357 Magnum . **$539.00**

SMITH & WESSON MODEL 60 357 MAGNUM

Caliber: 357 Magnum, 5-shot. **Barrel:** 2-1/8" or 3". **Weight:** 24 oz. **Length:** 7-1/2 overall (3" barrel). **Stocks:** Uncle Mike's Combat. **Sights:** Fixed, serrated ramp front, square notch rear. **Features:** Stainless steel construction. Made in U.S. by Smith & Wesson.
Price: 2-1/8" barrel **$505.00**
Price: 3" barrel **$536.00**

SMITH & WESSON MODEL 65

Caliber: 357 Mag. and 38 Spec., 6-shot. **Barrel:** 3", 4". **Weight:** 34 oz. **Length:** 9-5/16" overall (4" bbl.). **Stocks:** Uncle Mike's Combat. **Sights:** 1/8" serrated ramp front, fixed square notch rear. **Features:** Heavy barrel. Stainless steel construction.
Price: **$501.00**

SMITH & WESSON
MODEL 317 AIRLITE, 317 LADYSMITH REVOLVERS

Caliber: 22 LR, 8-shot. **Barrel:** 1-7/8" 3". **Weight:** 9.9 oz. **Length:** 6-3/16" overall. **Stocks:** Dymondwood Boot or Uncle Mike's Boot. **Sights:** Serrated ramp front, fixed notch rear. **Features:** Aluminum alloy, carbon and stainless steels, and titanium construction. Short spur hammer, smooth combat trigger. Clear Cote finish. Introduced 1997. Made in U.S. by Smith & Wesson.
Price: With Uncle Mike's Boot grip **$508.00**
Price: With DymondWood Boot grip, 3" barrel **$537.00**
Price: Model 317 LadySmith (DymondWood only, comes
with display case) **$568.00**

Smith & Wesson Model 637 Airweight Revolver

Similar to the Model 37 Airweight except has alloy frame, stainless steel barrel, cylinder and yoke; rated for 38 Spec. +P; Uncle Mike's Boot Grip. Weighs 15 oz. Introduced 1996. Made in U.S. by Smith & Wesson.
Price: **$459.00**

SMITH & WESSON MODEL 64 STAINLESS M&P

Caliber: 38 Spec., 6-shot. **Barrel:** 2", 3", 4". **Weight:** 34 oz. **Length:** 9-5/16" overall. **Stocks:** Soft rubber. **Sights:** Fixed, 1/8" serrated ramp front, square notch rear. **Features:** Satin finished stainless steel, square butt.
Price: 2" **$487.00**
Price: 3", 4". **$496.00**

SMITH & WESSON MODEL 65LS LADYSMITH

Caliber: 357 Magnum, 6-shot. **Barrel:** 3". **Weight:** 31 oz. **Length:** 7.94" overall. **Stocks:** Rosewood, round butt. **Sights:** Serrated ramp front, fixed notch rear. **Features:** Stainless steel with frosted finish. Smooth combat trigger, service hammer, shrouded ejector rod. Comes with case. Introduced 1992.
Price: **$539.00**

Smith & Wesson Model 586,
686 Distinguished Combat

Smith & Wesson Model 625

SMITH & WESSON MODEL 66 STAINLESS COMBAT MAGNUM

Caliber: 357 Mag. and 38 Spec., 6-shot. **Barrel:** 2-1/2", 4", 6". **Weight:** 36 oz. (4" barrel). **Length:** 9-9/16" overall. **Stocks:** Soft rubber. **Sights:** Red ramp front, micro-click rear adjustable for windage and elevation. **Features:** Satin finish stainless steel.

Price: 2-1/2"	$545.00
Price: 4", 6"	$551.00

SMITH & WESSON MODEL 67 COMBAT MASTERPIECE

Caliber: 38 Special, 6-shot. **Barrel:** 4". **Weight:** 32 oz. **Length:** 9-5/16" overall. **Stocks:** Soft rubber. **Sights:** Red ramp front, micro-click rear adjustable for windage and elevation. **Features:** Stainless steel with satin finish. Smooth combat trigger, semi-target hammer. Introduced 1994.

Price:	$546.00

SMITH & WESSON MODEL 242 AIRLITE Ti REVOLVER

Caliber: 38 Special, 7-shot. **Barrel:** 2-1/2". **Weight:** 18.9 oz. **Length:** 7-3/8" overall. **Stocks:** Uncle Mike's Boot grip. **Sights:** Serrated ramp front, fixed notch rear. **Features:** Alloy frame, yoke and barrel shroud; titanium cylinder; stainless barrel insert. Medium L-frame size. Introduced 1999. Made in U.S. by Smith & Wesson.

Price:	$658.00

SMITH & WESSON MODEL 296 AIRLITE Ti REVOLVER

Caliber: 44 Spec. **Barrel:** 2-1/2". **Weight:** 18.9 oz. **Length:** 7-3/8" overall. **Stocks:** Uncle Mike's Boot grip. **Sights:** Serrated ramp front, fixed notch rear. **Features:** Alloy frame, yoke and barrel shroud; titanium cylinder; stainless steel barrel insert. Medium, L-frame size. Introduced 1999. Made in U.S. by Smith & Wesson.

Price:	$718.00

SMITH & WESSON MODEL 586, 686 DISTINGUISHED COMBAT MAGNUMS

Caliber: 357 Magnum. **Barrel:** 4", 6" (M 586); 2-1/2", 4", 6", 8-3/8" (M 686). **Weight:** 46 oz. (6"), 41 oz. (4"). **Stocks:** Soft rubber. **Sights:** Red ramp front, S&W micrometer click rear. Drilled and tapped for scope mount. **Features:** Uses L-frame, but takes all K-frame grips. Full-length ejector rod shroud. Smooth combat-type trigger, semi-target type hammer. Also available in stainless as Model 686. Introduced 1981.

Price: Model 586, blue, 4", from	$494.00
Price: Model 586, blue, 6"	$499.00
Price: Model 686, 6", ported barrel	$564.00
Price: Model 686, 8-3/8"	$550.00
Price: Model 686, 2-1/2"	$514.00

Smith & Wesson Model 686 Magnum PLUS Revolver

Similar to the Model 686 except has 7-shot cylinder, 2-1/2", 4" or 6" barrel. Weighs 34-1/2 oz., overall length 7-1/2" (2-1/2" barrel). Hogue rubber grips. Introduced 1996. Made in U.S. by Smith & Wesson.

Price: 2-1/2" barrel	$534.00
Price: 4" barrel	$542.00
Price: 6" barrel	$550.00

SMITH & WESSON MODEL 625 REVOLVER

Caliber: 45 ACP, 6-shot. **Barrel:** 5". **Weight:** 46 oz. **Length:** 11.375" overall. **Stocks:** Soft rubber; wood optional. **Sights:** Patridge front on ramp, S&W micrometer click rear adjustable for windage and elevation. **Features:** Stainless steel construction with .400" semi-target hammer, .312" smooth combat trigger; full lug barrel. Introduced 1989.

Price:	$636.00

SMITH & WESSON MODEL 640 CENTENNIAL

Caliber: 357 Mag., 5-shot. **Barrel:** 2-1/8". **Weight:** 25 oz. **Length:** 6-3/4" overall. **Stocks:** Uncle Mike's Boot Grip. **Sights:** Serrated ramp front, fixed notch rear. **Features:** Stainless steel. Fully concealed hammer, snag-proof smooth edges. Introduced 1995 in 357 Magnum.

Price:	$502.00

SMITH & WESSON MODEL 617 FULL LUG REVOLVER

Caliber: 22 LR, 6- or 10-shot. **Barrel:** 4", 6", 8-3/8". **Weight:** 42 oz. (4" barrel). **Length:** NA. **Stocks:** Soft rubber. **Sights:** Patridge front, adjustable rear. Drilled and tapped for scope mount. **Features:** Stainless steel with satin finish; 4" has .312" smooth trigger, .375" semi-target hammer; 6" has either .312" combat or .400" serrated trigger, .375" semi-target or .500" target hammer; 8-3/8" with .400" serrated trigger, .500" target hammer. Introduced 1990.

Price: 4"	$534.00
Price: 6", target hammer, target trigger	$524.00
Price: 6", 10-shot	$566.00
Price: 8-3/8", 10 shot	$578.00

SMITH & WESSON MODEL 610 CLASSIC HUNTER REVOLVER

Caliber: 10mm, 6-shot cylinder. **Barrel:** 6-1/2" full lug. **Weight:** 52 oz. **Length:** 12" overall. **Stocks:** Hogue rubber combat. **Sights:** Interchangeable blade front, micro-click rear adjustable for windage and elevation. **Features:** Stainless steel construction; target hammer, target trigger; un-fluted cylinder; drilled and tapped for scope mounting. Introduced 1998.

Price:	$684.00

SMITH & WESSON MODEL 331, 332 AIRLITE Ti REVOLVERS

Caliber: 32 H&R Mag., 6-shot. **Barrel:** 1-7/8". **Weight:** 11.2 oz. (with wood grip). **Length:** 6-15/16" overall. **Stocks:** Uncle Mike's Boot or Dymondwood Boot. **Sights:** Black serrated ramp front, fixed notch rear. **Features:** Aluminum alloy frame, barrel shroud and yoke; titanium cylinder; stainless steel barrel liner. Matte finish. Introduced 1999. Made in U.S. by Smith & Wesson.

Price: Model 331 Chiefs	$682.00
Price: Model 332	$699.00

SMITH & WESSON MODEL 337 CHIEFS SPECIAL AIRLITE Ti

Caliber: 38 Spec., 5-shot. **Barrel:** 1-7/8". **Weight:** 11.2 oz. (Dymondwood grips). **Length:** 6-5/16" overall. **Stocks:** Uncle Mike's Boot or Dymondwood Boot. **Sights:** Black serrated front, fixed notch rear. **Features:** Aluminum alloy frame, barrel shroud and yoke; titanium cylinder; stainless steel barrel liner. Matte finish. Introduced 1999. Made in U.S. by Smith & Wesson.

Price:	$682.00

SMITH & WESSON MODEL 342 CENTENNIAL AIRLITE Ti

Caliber: 38 Spec., 5-shot. **Barrel:** 1-7/8". **Weight:** 11.3 oz. (Dymondwood stocks). **Length:** 6-15/16" overall. **Stocks:** Uncle Mike's Boot or Dymondwood Boot. **Sights:** Black serrated ramp front, fixed notch rear. **Features:**

Smith & Wesson Model 442

Smith & Wesson Model 649

Smith & Wesson Model 696

Taurus Model 82

Aluminum alloy frame, barrel shroud and yoke; titanium cylinder; stainless steel barrel liner. Shrouded hammer. Matte finish. Introduced 1999. Made in U.S. by Smith & Wesson.
Price: **$699.00**

Smith & Wesson Model 442 Centennial Airweight
Similar to the Model 640 Centennial except has alloy frame giving weight of 15.8 oz. Chambered for 38 Special, 1-7/8" carbon steel barrel; carbon steel cylinder; concealed hammer; Uncle Mike's Boot grip. Fixed square notch rear sight, serrated ramp front. Introduced 1993.
Price: Blue **$459.00**

SMITH & WESSON MODEL 638 AIRWEIGHT BODYGUARD
Caliber: 38 Spec., 5-shot. **Barrel:** 1-7/8". **Weight:** 15 oz. **Length:** 6-15/16" overall. **Stocks:** Uncle Mike's Boot grip. **Sights:** Serrated ramp front, fixed notch rear. **Features:** Alloy frame, stainless cylinder and barrel; shrouded hammer. Introduced 1997. Made in U.S. by Smith & Wesson.
Price: With Uncle Mike's Boot grip **$492.00**

Smith & Wesson Model 642 Airweight Revolver
Similar to the Model 442 Centennial Airweight except has stainless steel barrel, cylinder and yoke with matte finish; Uncle Mike's Boot Grip; weighs 15.8 oz. Introduced 1996. Made in U.S. by Smith & Wesson.
Price: **$474.00**

Smith & Wesson Model 642LS LadySmith Revolver
Same as the Model 642 except has smooth combat wood grips, and comes with case; aluminum alloy frame, stainless cylinder, barrel and yoke; frosted matte finish. Weighs 15.8 oz. Introduced 1996. Made in U.S. by Smith & Wesson.
Price: **$505.00**

SMITH & WESSON MODEL 649 BODYGUARD REVOLVER
Caliber: 357 Mag., 5-shot. **Barrel:** 2-1/8". **Weight:** 20 oz. **Length:** 6-5/16" overall. **Stocks:** Uncle Mike's Combat. **Sights:** Black pinned ramp front, fixed notch rear. **Features:** Stainless steel construction; shrouded hammer; smooth combat trigger. Made in U.S. by Smith & Wesson.
Price: **$502.00**

SMITH & WESSON MODEL 657 REVOLVER
Caliber: 41 Mag., 6-shot. **Barrel:** 6". **Weight:** 48 oz. **Length:** 11-3/8" overall. **Stocks:** Soft rubber. **Sights:** Pinned 1/8" red ramp front, micro-click rear adjustable for windage and elevation. **Features:** Stainless steel construction.
Price: **$564.00**

SMITH & WESSON MODEL 696 REVOLVER
Caliber: 44 Spec., 5-shot. **Barrel:** 3". **Weight:** 35.5 oz. **Length:** 8-1/4" overall. **Stocks:** Uncle Mike's Combat. **Sights:** Red ramp front, click adjustable white outline rear. **Features:** Stainless steel construction; round butt frame; satin finish. Introduced 1997. Made in U.S. by Smith & Wesson.
Price: **$525.00**

TAURUS MODEL 65 REVOLVER
Caliber: 357 Mag., 6-shot. **Barrel:** 4". **Weight:** 38 oz. **Length:** 10-1/2" overall. **Stocks:** Soft rubber. **Sights:** Serrated front, notch rear. **Features:** Solid rib barrel; +P rated. Imported by Taurus International.
Price: Blue **$313.00**
Price: Stainless....................................... **$359.00**

Taurus Model 66 Revolver
Same to the Model 65 except with 4" or 6" barrel, 7-shot cylinder, adjustable rear sight. Imported by Taurus International.
Price: Blue **$359.00**
Price: Stainless....................................... **$406.00**

TAURUS MODEL 82 HEAVY BARREL REVOLVER
Caliber: 38 Spec., 6-shot. **Barrel:** 4", heavy. **Weight:** 34 oz. (4" bbl.). **Length:** 9-1/4" overall (4" bbl.). **Stocks:** Soft black rubber. **Sights:** Serrated ramp front, square notch rear. **Features:** Imported by Taurus International.
Price: Blue **$297.00**
Price: Polished, stainless **$344.00**

TAURUS MODEL 85 REVOLVER
Caliber: 38 Spec., 5-shot. **Barrel:** 2", 3". **Weight:** 21 oz. **Stocks:** Black rubber, boot grip. **Sights:** Ramp front, square notch rear. **Features:** Blue finish or stainless steel. Introduced 1980. Imported by Taurus International.

Taurus Model 85 **Taurus Model 85Ti/731Ti** **Taurus Model 85CH** **Taurus Model 94UL**

Price: Blue, 2", 3"	**$286.00**
Price: Stainless steel	**$327.00**
Price: Blue, 2", ported barrel	**$305.00**
Price: Stainless, 2", ported barrel	**$345.00**
Price: Blue, Ultra-Lite (17 oz.), 2"	**$311.00**
Price: Stainless, Ultra-Lite (17 oz.), 2", ported barrel	**$342.00**
Price: Blue with gold trim, ported	**$350.00**

Taurus Model 85UL/Ti Revolver

Similar to the Model 85 except has titanium cylinder, aluminum alloy frame, and ported aluminum barrel with stainless steel sleeve. Weight is 13.5 oz. International.
Price: **$515.00**

Taurus Model 85Ti, Model 731Ti Revolvers

Similar to the 2" Model 85 except has titanium frame, cylinder and ported barrel with stainless steel liner; yoke detent and extended ejector rod. Weight is 15.4 oz. Comes with soft, ridged Ribber grips. Available in Bright and Matte Spectrum blue, Matte Spectrum gold, and Steel Gray colors. Introduced 1999. Imported by Taurus International.
Price: Model 85Ti **$529.00**
Price: Model 731Ti (32 H&R mag., 6-shot). **$529.00**

Taurus Model 85CH Revolver

Same as the Model 85 except has 2" barrel only and concealed hammer. Double aciton only. Soft rubber boot grip. Introduced 1991. Imported by Taurus International.
Price: Blue **$286.00**
Price: Stainless................................... **$327.00**
Price: Blue, ported barrel **$305.00**
Price: Stainless, ported barrel **$345.00**

TAURUS MODEL 94 REVOLVER

Caliber: 22 LR, 9-shot cylinder. **Barrel:** 2", 4", 5". **Weight:** 25 oz. **Stocks:** Soft black rubber. **Sights:** Serrated ramp front, click-adjustable rear for windage and elevation. **Features:** Floating firing pin, color case-hardened hammer and trigger. Introduced 1989. Imported by Taurus International.
Price: Blue **$308.00**
Price: Stainless................................... **$356.00**

Taurus Model 22H Raging Hornet

Price: Model 94 UL, blue, 2", fixed sight, weighs 14 oz. **$342.00**
Price: As above, stainless **$391.00**

TAURUS MODEL 22H RAGING HORNET REVOLVER

Caliber: 22 Hornet, 8-shot cylinder. **Barrel:** 10". **Weight:** 50 oz. **Length:** 6.5" overall. **Stocks:** Soft black rubber. **Sights:** Patridge front, micrometer click adjustable rear. **Features:** Ventilated rib; 1:10: twist rifling; comes with scope base; stainless steel construction with matte finish. Introduced 1999. Imported by Taurus International.
Price: **$898.00**

TAURUS MODEL 44 REVOLVER

Caliber: 44 Mag., 6-shot. **Barrel:** 4", 6-1/2", 8-3/8". **Weight:** 44-3/4 oz. (4" barrel). **Length:** NA. **Stocks:** Soft black rubber. **Sights:** Serrated ramp front, micro-click rear adjustable for windage and elevation. **Features:** Heavy solid rib on 4", vent rib on 6-1/2", 8-3/8". Compensated barrel. Blued model has color case-hardened hammer and trigger. Introduced 1994. Imported by Taurus International.
Price: Blue, 4".................................... **$447.00**
Price: Blue, 6-1/2", 8-3/8" **$466.00**
Price: Stainless, 4" **$508.00**
Price: Stainless, 6-1/2", 8-3/8" **$530.00**

Taurus Model 44

Taurus Model 415

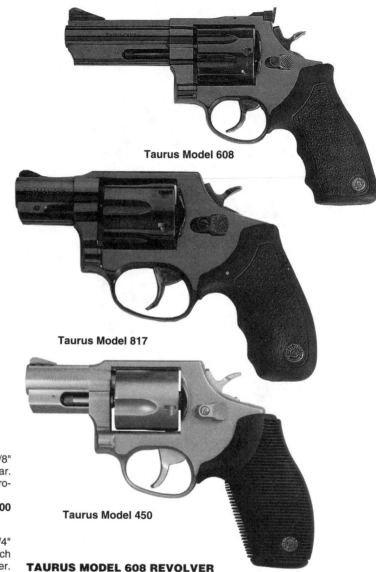

Taurus Model 608

Taurus Model 817

Taurus Model 450

TAURUS MODEL 415 REVOLVER

Caliber: 41 Mag., 5-shot. **Barrel:** 2-1/2". **Weight:** 30 oz. **Length:** 7-1/8" overall. **Stocks:** Soft, ridged Ribber. **Sights:** Serrated front, notch rear. **Features:** Stainless steel construction; matte finish; ported barrel. Introduced 1999. Imported by Taurus International.
Price: $452.00

TAURUS MODEL 445, 445CH REVOLVERS

Caliber: 44 Special, 5-shot. **Barrel:** 2". **Weight:** 28.25 oz. **Length:** 6-3/4" overall. **Stocks:** Soft black rubber. **Sights:** Serrated ramp front, notch rear. **Features:** Blue or stainless steel. Standard or concealed hammer. Introduced 1997. Imported by Taurus International.
Price: Blue $323.00
Price: Blue, ported $342.00
Price: Stainless $370.00
Price: Stainless, ported $389.00
Price: M445CH, concealed hammer, blue, DAO $323.00
Price: M445CH, blue, ported $342.00
Price: M445CH, stainless $370.00
Price: M445CH, stainless, ported $389.00
Price: M445CH, Ultra-Lite, stainless, ported $483.00

TAURUS MODEL 605 REVOLVER

Caliber: 357 Mag., 5-shot. **Barrel:** 2-1/4", 3". **Weight:** 24.5 oz. **Length:** NA. **Stocks:** Soft black rubber. **Sights:** Serrated ramp front, fixed notch rear. **Features:** Heavy, solid rib barrel; floating firing pin. Blue or stainless. Introduced 1995. Imported by Taurus International.
Price: Blue $303.00
Price: Stainless $344.00
Price: Model 605CH (concealed hammer) 2-1/4", blue, DAO . . . $303.00
Price: Model 605CH, stainless, 2-1/4" $344.00
Price: Blue, 2-1/4", ported barrel $322.00
Price: Stainless, 2-1/4", ported barrel $363.00
Price: Blue, 2-1/4", ported barrel, concealed hammer, DAO $322.00
Price: Stainless, 2-1/4", ported barrel, concealed hammer, DAO $363.00

TAURUS MODEL 608 REVOLVER

Caliber: 357 Mag., 8-shot. **Barrel:** 4", 6-1/2", 8-3/8". **Weight:** 44 oz. **Length:** 9-3/8" overall. **Stocks:** Soft black rubber. **Sights:** Serrated ramp front, fully adjustable rear. **Features:** Built-in compensator. Available in blue or stainless. Introduced 1995. Imported by Taurus international.
Price: Blue, 4", solid rib **$447.00**
Price: Blue, 6-1/2", 8-3/8", vent rib **$466.00**
Price: Stainless, 4", solid rib **$508.00**
Price: Stainless, 6-1/2", 8-3/8", vent rib **$530.00**

TAURUS MODEL 817 REVOLVER

Caliber: 38 Spec., 7-shot. **Barrel:** 2". **Weight:** 21 oz. **Length:** 6-1/2" overall. **Stocks:** Soft rubber. **Sights:** Serrated front, notch rear. **Features:** Compact alloy frame. Introduced 1999. Imported by Taurus International.
Price: Blue **$350.00**
Price: Blue, ported **$369.00**
Price: Matte, stainless **$389.00**
Price: Matte, stainless, ported **$408.00**

TAURUS MODEL 450 REVOLVER

Caliber: 45 Colt, 5-shot cylinder. **Barrel:** 2". **Weight:** 28 oz. **Length:** 6-5/8" overall. **Stocks:** Soft, ridged rubber. **Sights:** Serrated front, notch rear. **Features:** Stainless steel construction; ported barrel. Introduced 1999. Imported by Taurus International.
Price: **$452.00**
Price: Ultra-Lite (alloy frame) **$483.00**

Taurus Model 454 Raging Bull

Taurus Model 941

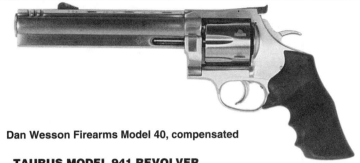

Dan Wesson Firearms Model 40, compensated

TAURUS MODEL 45, 444, 454 RAGING BULL REVOLVER

Caliber: 454 Casull, 5-shot. **Barrel:** 5", 6-1/2", 8-3/8". **Weight:** 53 oz. (6-1/2" barrel). **Length:** 12" overall (6-1/2" barrel). **Stocks:** Soft black rubber. **Sights:** Patridge front, micrometer click adjustable rear. **Features:** Ventilated rib; integral compensating system. Introduced 1997. Imported by Taurus International.

Price: 6-1/2", 8-3/8", blue $750.00
Price: 6-1/2", polished, stainless $820.00
Price: 5", 6-1/2", 8-3/8", matte stainless $820.00
Price: 5", 6-1/2", 8-3/8", color case-hardened frame $845.00
Price: Model 45 (45 Colt), blue, 6-1/2", 8-3/8" $545.00
Price: Model 45, stainless, 6-1/2", 8-3/8" $608.00
Price: Model 444 (44 Mag.), blue, 6-1/2", 8-3/8" $545.00
Price: Model 444, matte, stainless, 6-1/2", 8-3/8" $608.00

TAURUS MODEL 617, 606CH REVOLVER

Caliber: 357 Magnum, 7-shot. **Barrel:** 2". **Weight:** 29 oz. **Length:** 6-3/4" overall. **Stocks:** Soft black rubber. **Sights:** Serrated ramp front, notch rear. **Features:** Heavy, solid barrel rib, ejector shroud. Available with porting, concealed hammer. Introduced 1998. Imported by Taurus International.

Price: Blue, regular or concealed hammer $355.00
Price: Stainless, regular or concealed hammer $402.00
Price: Blue, ported $373.00
Price: Stainless, ported. $420.00
Price: Blue, concealed hammer, ported $373.00
Price: Stainless, concealed hammer, ported $420.00

Taurus Model 415Ti, 445Ti, 450Ti, 617Ti Revolvers

Similar to the Model 617 except has titanium frame, cylinder, and ported barrel with stainless steel liner; yoke detent and extended ejector rod; +P rated; ridged Ribber grips. Available in Bright and Matte Spectrum Blue, Matte Spectrum Gold, and Stealth Gray. Introduced 1999. Imported by Taurus International.

Price: Model 617Ti, (357 Mag., 7-shot, 19.9 oz.) $599.00
Price: Model 415Ti (41 Mag., 5-shot, 20.9 oz.) $599.00
Price: Model 450Ti (45 Colt, 5-shot, 19.2 oz.) $599.00
Price: Model 445Ti (44 Spec., 5-shot, 19.8 oz.) $599.00

TAURUS MODEL 941 REVOLVER

Caliber: 22 WMR, 8-shot. **Barrel:** 2", 4", 5". **Weight:** 27.5 oz. (4" barrel). **Length:** NA. **Stocks:** Soft black rubber. **Sights:** Serrated ramp front, rear adjustable for windage and elevation. **Features:** Solid rib heavy barrel with full-length ejector rod shroud. Blue or stainless steel. Introduced 1992. Imported by Taurus International.

Price: Blue $331.00
Price: Stainless. $384.00
Price: Model 941 Ultra Lite, blue, 2", fixed sight, weighs 8.5 oz. . . $366.00
Price: As above, stainless $419.00

DAN WESSON FIREARMS MODEL 22 SILHOUETTE REVOLVER

Caliber: 22 LR, 6-shot. **Barrel:** 10", regular vent or vent heavy. **Weight:** 53 oz. **Stocks:** Combat style. **Sights:** Patridge-style front, .080" narrow notch rear. **Features:** Single action only. Available in blue or stainless. Reintroduced 1997. Made in U.S. by Dan Wesson Firearms.

Price: Blue, regular vent $474.00
Price: Blue, vent heavy. $492.00
Price: Stainless, regular vent $504.00
Price: Stainless, vent heavy $532.00

DAN WESSON FIREARMS
MODEL 322/7322 TARGET REVOLVER

Caliber: 32-20, 6-shot. **Barrel:** 2.5", 4", 6", 8", standard vent, vent heavy. **Weight:** 43 oz. (6" VH). **Length:** 11.25" overall. **Stocks:** Checkered walnut. **Sights:** Red ramp interchangeable front, fully adjustable rear. **Features:** Bright blue or stainless. Reintroduced 1997. Made in U.S. by Dan Wesson Firearms.

Price: 6", vent heavy, blue $619.00
Price: 6", vent heavy, stainless. $659.00
Price: 8", vent heavy, blue $649.00
Price: 8", vent heavy, stainless. $699.00

DAN WESSON FIREARMS MODEL 40 SILHOUETTE

Caliber: 357 Maximum, 6-shot. **Barrel:** 4", 6", 8", 10". **Weight:** 64 oz. (8" bbl.). **Length:** 14.3" overall (8" bbl.). **Stocks:** Smooth walnut, target-style. **Sights:** 1/8" serrated front, fully adjustable rear. **Features:** Meets criteria for IHMSA competition with 8" slotted barrel. Blue or stainless steel. Made in U.S. by Dan Wesson Firearms.

Price: Blue, 4". $702.00
Price: Blue, 6". $749.00
Price: Blue, 8". $795.00
Price: Blue, 10". $858.00
Price: Stainless, 4" $834.00
Price: Stainless, 6" $892.00
Price: Stainless, 8" slotted $1,024.00
Price: Stainless, 10" $998.00
Price: 4", 6", 8" Compensated, blue . . . . $749.00 to $885.00
Price: As above, stainless . . . . $893.00 to $1,061.00

DAN WESSON FIREARMS MODEL 22 REVOLVER

Caliber: 22 LR, 22 WMR, 6-shot. **Barrel:** 2-1/2", 4", 6", 8"; interchangeable. **Weight:** 36 oz. (2-1/2"), 44 oz. (6"). **Length:** 9-1/4" overall (4" barrel). **Stocks:** Checkered; undercover, service or over-size target. **Sights:** 1/8" serrated, interchangeable front, white outline rear adjustable for windage and elevation. **Features:** Built on the same frame as the Wesson 357; smooth, wide trigger with over-travel adjustment, wide spur hammer, with short double-action travel. Available in Brite blue or stainless steel. Reintroduced 1997. Contact Dan Wesson Firearms for complete price list.

**Dan Wesson Firearms
Model 445 Supermag**

Price: 2-1/2" bbl., blue **$489.00**
Price: As above, stainless **$509.00**
Price: With 4", vent heavy, blue **$509.00**
Price: As above, stainless **$539.00**
Price: Blue Pistol Pac, 22 LR **$1,199.00**

Dan Wesson Firearms Model 414, 445 SuperMag Revolvers

Similar size and weight as the Model 40 revolvers. Chambered for the 445 SuperMag cartridge, a longer version of the 44 Magnum and 414 Super-Mag. Barrel lengths of 4", 6", 8", 10". Contact maker for complete price list. Reintroduced 1997. Made in the U.S. by Dan Wesson Firearms.

Price: 4", vent heavy, blue **$797.00**
Price: As above, stainless **$829.00**
Price: 8", vent heavy, blue **$899.00**
Price: As above, stainless **$929.00**
Price: 10", vent heavy, blue **$959.00**
Price: As above, stainless **$995.00**
Price: 8", vent slotted, blue......................... **$987.00**
Price: As above, stainless **$1,134.00**
Price: 10", vent slotted, blue......................... **$1,195.00**
Price: As above, stainless **$1,285.00**
Price: 4", 6", 8" Compensated, blue .... **$859.00 to $979.00**
Price: As above, stainless .... **$899.00 to $995.00**

DAN WESSON FIREARMS MODEL 15 & 32 REVOLVERS

Caliber: 32-20, 32 H&R Mag. (Model 32), 357 Mag. (Model 15). **Barrel:** 2-1/2", 4", 6", 8" (M32), 2-1/2", 4", 6", 8", 10" (M15); vent heavy. **Weight:** 36 oz. (2-1/2" barrel). **Length:** 9-1/4" overall (4" barrel). **Stocks:** Checkered, interchangeable. **Sights:** 1/8" serrated front, fully adjustable rear. **Features:** New Generation Series. Interchangeable barrels; wide, smooth trigger, wide hammer spur; short double-action travel. Available in blue or stainless. Reintroduced 1997. Made in U.S. by Dan Wesson Firearms. Contact maker for full list of models.

Price: Model 15, blue, 2-1/2" **$489.00**
Price: Model 15, blue, 8" **$569.00**
Price: Model 15, stainless, 4" **$539.00**
Price: Model 15, stainless, 6" **$569.00**
Price: Model 15, blue, compensated .... **$579.00 to $699.00**
Price: Model 15, stainless, compensated........... **$619.00 to $759.00**
Price: Model 32, blue, 4" **$589.00**
Price: Model 32, blue, 8" **$649.00**
Price: Model 32, stainless, 2-1/2" **$589.00**
Price: Model 32, stainless, 6" **$659.00**

DAN WESSON FIREARMS MODEL 41V, 44V, 45V REVOLVERS

Caliber: 41 Mag., 44 Mag., 45 Colt, 6-shot. **Barrel:** 4", 6", 8", 10"; interchangeable; 4", 6", 8" Compensated. **Weight:** 48 oz. (4"). **Length:** 12" overall (6" bbl.) **Stocks:** Smooth. **Sights:** 1/8" serrated front, white outline rear adjustable for windage and elevation. **Features:** Available in blue or stainless steel. Smooth, wide trigger with adjustable over-travel; wide hammer spur. Available in Pistol Pac set also. Reintroduced 1997. Contact Dan Wesson Firearms for complete price list.

Price: 41 Mag., 4", vent heavy **$579.00**
Price: As above except in stainless **$599.00**
Price: 44 Mag., 4", blue **$579.00**
Price: As above except in stainless **$599.00**
Price: 45 Colt, 4", vent heavy........................... **$599.00**

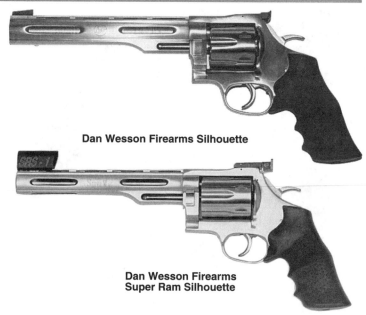

Dan Wesson Firearms Silhouette

**Dan Wesson Firearms
Super Ram Silhouette**

Price: As above except in stainless **$619.00**
Price: Model 41, 44, 45, blue, 4", 6", 8" compensated . **$633.00 to $727.00**
Price: As above in stainless .... **$752.00 to $868.00**

DAN WESSON FIREARMS MODEL 360 REVOLVER

Caliber: 357 Mag. **Barrel:** 4", 6", 8", 10"; vent heavy. **Weight:** 64 oz. (8" barrel). **Length:** NA. **Stocks:** Hogue rubber finger groove. **Sights:** Interchangeable ramp or Patridge front, fully adjustable rear. **Features:** New Generation Large Frame Series. Interchangeable barrels and grips; smooth trigger, wide hammer spur. Blue or stainless. Introduced 1999. Made in U.S. by Dan Wesson Firearms.

Price: Blue, from... **$639.00**
Price: Stainless, from **$669.00**

DAN WESSON FIREARMS MODEL 460 REVOLVER

Caliber: 45 ACP and 460 Rowland. **Barrel:** 4", 6", 8", 10"; vent heavy. **Weight:** 49 oz. (4" barrel). **Length:** NA. **Stocks:** Hogue rubber finger groove; interchangeable. **Sights:** Interchangeable ramp or Patridge front, fully adjustable rear. **Features:** New Generation Large Frame Series. Shoots 45 ACP and 460 Rowland. Interchangeable barrels and grips. Available with non-fluted cylinder and Slotted Lightweight barrel shroud. Introduced 1999. Made in U.S. by Dan Wesson Firearms.

Price: .... **NA**

DAN WESSON FIREARMS STANDARD SILHOUETTE REVOLVER

Caliber: 357 SuperMag/Maxi, 41 Mag., 414 SuperMag, 445 SuperMag. **Barrel:** 8", 10" **Weight:** 64 oz. (8" barrel). **Length:** 14.3" overall (8" barrel). **Stocks:** Hogue rubber finger groove; interchangeable. **Sights:** Patridge front, fully adjustable rear. **Features:** Interchangeable barrels and grips; fluted or non-fluted cylinder; blue or stainless. Introduced 1999. Made in U.S. by Dan Wesson Firearms.

Price: 357 SuperMag/Maxi, 8", blue or stainless **$949.00**
Price: 41 Mag., 10", blue or stainless...................... **$929.00**
Price: 414 SuperMag., 8", blue or stainless **$949.00**
Price: 445 SuperMag., 8", blue or stainless **$949.00**

Dan Wesson Firearms Super Ram Silhouette Revolver

Similar to the Standard Silhouette except has 10 land and groove Laser Coat barrel, Bo-Mar target sights with hooded front, and special laser engraving. Fluted or non-fluted cylinder. Introduced 1999. Made in U.S. by Dan Wesson Firearms.

Price: 357 SuperMag/Maxi, 414 SuperMag., 445 SuperMag., 8", blue or stainless **$1,195.00**
Price: 41 Magnum, 44 Magnum, 8", blue or stainless **$1,099.00**
Price: 41 Magnum, 44 Magnum, 10", blue or stainless **$1,139.00**

Both classic six-shooters and modern adaptations for hunting and sport.

American Frontier 1871-1872 Open-Top

American Frontier 1851 Mason

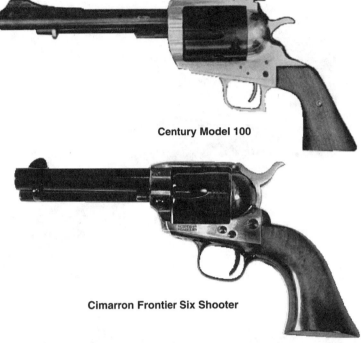

Century Model 100

Cimarron Frontier Six Shooter

AMERICAN FRONTIER 1851 NAVY CONVERSION

Caliber: 38, 44. **Barrel:** 5-1/2", 7-1/2", octagon. **Weight:** NA. **Length:** NA. **Stocks:** Varnished walnut, Navy size. **Sights:** Blade front, fixed rear. **Features:** Shoots metallic cartridge ammunition. Non-rebated cylinder; blued steel backstrap and trigger guard; color case-hardened hammer, trigger, ramrod, plunger; no ejector rod assembly. Introduced 1996.
Price: **$795.00**

AMERICAN FRONTIER 1871-1872 OPEN-TOP REVOLVERS

Caliber: 38, 44. **Barrel:** 5-1/2", 7-1/2", 8" round. **Weight:** NA. **Length:** NA. **Stocks:** Varnished walnut. **Sights:** Blade front, fixed rear. **Features:** Reproduction of the early cartridge conversions from percussion. Made for metallic cartridges. High polish blued steel, silver-plated brass backstrap and trigger guard, color case-hardened hammer; straight non-rebated cylinder with naval engagement engraving; stamped with original patent dates. Does not have conversion breechplate.
Price: **$795.00**

AMERICAN FRONTIER RICHARDS 1860 ARMY

Caliber: 38, 44. **Barrel:** 5-1/2", 7-1/2", round. **Weight:** NA. **Length:** NA. **Stocks:** Varnished walnut, Army size. **Sights:** Blade front, fixed rear. **Features:** Shoots metallic cartridge ammunition. Rebated cylinder; available with or without ejector assembly; high-polish blue including backstrap; silver-plated trigger guard; color case-hardened hammer and trigger. Introduced 1996.
Price: **$795.00**

American Frontier 1851 Navy Richards & Mason Conversion

Similar to the 1851 Navy Conversion except has Mason ejector assembly. Introduced 1996. Imported from Italy by American Frontier Firearms Mfg.
Price: **$695.00**

CENTURY GUN DIST. MODEL 100 SINGLE-ACTION

Caliber: 30-30, 375 Win., 444 Marlin, 45-70, 50-70. **Barrel:** 6-1/2" (standard), 8", 10". **Weight:** 6 lbs. (loaded). **Length:** 15" overall (8" bbl.). **Stocks:** Smooth walnut. **Sights:** Ramp front, Millett adjustable square notch rear. **Features:** Highly polished high tensile strength manganese bronze frame, blue cylinder and barrel; coil spring trigger mechanism. Contact maker for full price information. Introduced 1975. Made in U.S. From Century Gun Dist., Inc.
Price: 6-1/2" barrel, 45-70 . . . . **$2,000.00**

CIMARRON U.S. CAVALRY MODEL SINGLE-ACTION

Caliber: 45 Colt. **Barrel:** 7-1/2". **Weight:** 42 oz. **Length:** 13-1/2" overall. **Stocks:** Walnut. **Sights:** Fixed. **Features:** Has "A.P. Casey" markings; "U.S." plus patent dates on frame, serial number on backstrap, trigger guard, frame and cylinder, "APC" cartouche on left grip; color case-hardened frame and hammer, rest charcoal blue. Exact copy of the original. Imported by Cimarron F.A. Co.
Price: **$499.00**

Cimarron Rough Rider Artillery Model Single-Action

Similar to the U.S. Cavalry model except has 5-1/2" barrel, weighs 39 oz., and is 11-1/2" overall. U.S. markings and cartouche, case-hardened frame and hammer; 45 Colt only.
Price: **$499.00**

CIMARRON 1873 FRONTIER SIX SHOOTER

Caliber: 38 WCF, 357 Mag., 44 WCF, 44 Spec., 45 Colt. **Barrel:** 4-3/4", 5-1/2", 7-1/2". **Weight:** 39 oz. **Length:** 10" overall (4" barrel). **Stocks:** Walnut. **Sights:** Blade front, fixed or adjustable rear. **Features:** Uses "old model" blackpowder frame with "Bullseye" ejector or New Model frame. Imported by Cimarron F.A. Co.
Price: 4-3/4" barrel **$469.00**
Price: 5-1/2" barrel **$469.00**
Price: 7-1/2" barrel **$469.00**

Cimarron Bisley Model Single-Action Revolvers

Similar to the 1873 Frontier Six Shooter except has special grip frame and trigger guard, knurled wide-spur hammer, curved trigger. Available in 357 Mag., 44 WCF, 45 Schofield, 45 Colt. Introduced 1999. Imported by Cimarron F.A. Co.
Price: **$499.00**

Cimarron Flat Top Single-Action Revolvers

Similar to the 1873 Frontier Six Shooter except has flat top strap with windage-adjustable rear sight, elevation-adjustable front sight. Available in 357 Mag., 44 WCF, 45 Schofield, 45 Colt; 4-3/4", 5-1/2", 7-1/2" barrel. Introduced 1999. Imported by Cimarron F.A. Co.
Price: **$479.00**

Cimarron Bisley Flat Top Revolver

Similar to the Flat Top revolver except has special grip frame and trigger guard, wide spur hammer, curved trigger. Introduced 1999. Imported by Cimarron F.A. Co.
Price: **$509.00**

CIMARRON THUNDERER REVOLVER

Caliber: 357 Mag., 44 WCF, 44 Spec., 45 Colt, 6-shot. **Barrel:** 3-1/2", 4-3/4", 5-1/2", 7-1/2", with ejector. **Weight:** 38 oz. (3-1/2" barrel). **Length:** NA. **Stocks:** Smooth walnut. **Sights:** Blade front, notch rear. **Features:**

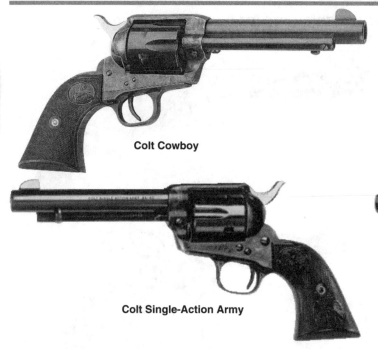

Colt Cowboy

Colt Single-Action Army

E.A.A. Bounty Hunter

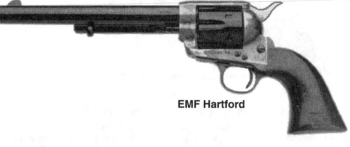

EMF Hartford

EMF 1894 Bisley

Thunderer grip; color case-hardened frame with balance blued. Introduced 1993. Imported by Cimarron F.A. Co.

Price: 3-1/2", 4-3/4", smooth grips $489.00
Price: As above, checkered grips $524.00
Price: 5-1/2", 7-1/2", smooth grips $529.00
Price: As above, checkered grips $564.00

CIMARRON 1872 OPEN-TOP REVOLVER

Caliber: 38 Spec., 38 Colt, 44 Spec., 44 Colt, 44 Russian, 45 Schofield. **Barrel:** 7-1/2". **Weight:** NA. **Length:** NA. **Stocks:** Smooth walnut. **Sights:** Blade front, fixed rear. **Features:** Replica of the original production. Color case-hardened frame, rest blued, including grip frame. Introduced 1999. Imported from Italy by Cimarron F.A. Co.
Price: $579.00

COLT COWBOY SINGLE-ACTION REVOLVER

Caliber: 45 Colt, 6-shot. **Barrel:** 5-1/2". **Weight:** 42 oz. **Stocks:** Black composition, first generation style. **Sights:** Blade front, notch rear. **Features:** Dimensional replica of Colt's original Peacemaker with medium-size color case-hardened frame; transfer bar safety system; half-cock loading. Introduced 1998. Made in U.S. by Colt's Mfg. Co.
Price: About $599.00

COLT SINGLE-ACTION ARMY REVOLVER

Caliber: 44-40, 45 Colt, 6-shot. **Barrel:** 4-3/4", 5-1/2", 7-1/2". **Weight:** 40 oz. (4-3/4" barrel). **Length:** 10-1/4" overall (4-3/4" barrel). **Stocks:** Black Eagle composite. **Sights:** Blade front, notch rear. **Features:** Available in full nickel finish with nickel grip medallions, or Royal Blue with color case-hardened frame, gold grip medallions. Reintroduced 1992.
Price: $1,900.00

E.A.A. BOUNTY HUNTER SA REVOLVERS

Caliber: 22 LR/22 WMR, 357 Mag., 44 Mag., 45 Colt, 6-shot. **Barrel:** 4-1/2", 7-1/2". **Weight:** 2.5 lbs. **Length:** 11" overall (4-5/8" barrel). **Stocks:** Smooth walnut. **Sights:** Blade front, grooved topstrap rear. **Features:** Transfer bar safety; three position hammer; hammer forged barrel. Introduced 1992. Imported by European American Armory.
Price: Blue or case-hardened $280.00
Price: Nickel $298.00
Price: 22LR/22WMR, blue $187.20
Price: As above, nickel $204.36

EMF HARTFORD SINGLE-ACTION REVOLVERS

Caliber: 22 LR, 357 Mag., 32-20, 38-40, 44-40, 44 Spec., 45 Colt. **Barrel:** 4-3/4", 5-1/2", 7-1/2". **Weight:** 45 oz. **Length:** 13" overall (7-1/2" barrel).

Stocks: Smooth walnut. **Sights:** Blade front, fixed rear. **Features:** Identical to the original Colts with inspector cartouche on left grip, original patent dates and U.S. markings. All major parts serial numbered using original Colt-style lettering, numbering. Bullseye ejector head and color case-hardening on frame and hammer. Introduced 1990. From E.M.F.
Price: $600.00
Price: Cavalry or Artillery $655.00
Price: Nickel plated $725.00
Price: Engraved, nickel plated $840.00

EMF 1894 Bisley Revolver

Similar to the Hartford single-action revolver except has special grip frame and trigger guard, wide spur hammer; available in 45 Colt only, 5-1/2" or 7-1/2" barrel. Introduced 1995. Imported by E.M.F.
Price: Blue $680.00
Price: Nickel $805.00

EMF Hartford Pinkerton Single-Action Revolver

Same as the regular Hartford except has 4" barrel with ejector tube and birds head grip. Calibers 32-20, 38-40, 44-40, 44 Special, 45 Colt. Introduced 1997. Imported by E.M.F.
Price: $475.00

EMF Hartford Express Single-Action Revolver

Same as the regular Hartford model except uses grip of the Colt Lightning revolver. Barrel lengths of 4", 4-3/4", 5-1/2". Introduced 1997. Imported by E.M.F.
Price: $475.00

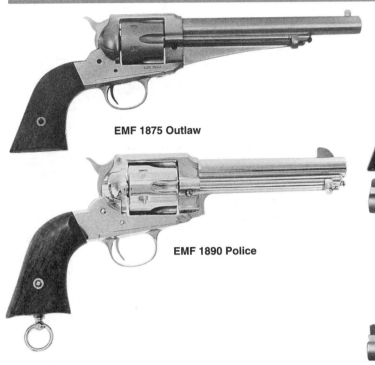

EMF 1875 Outlaw

EMF 1890 Police

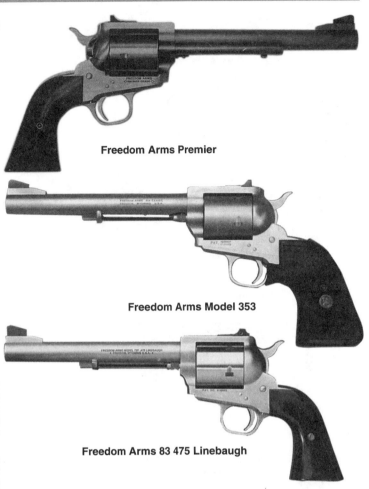

Freedom Arms Premier

Freedom Arms Model 353

Freedom Arms 83 475 Linebaugh

EMF 1875 OUTLAW REVOLVER
Caliber: 357 Mag., 44-40, 45 Colt. **Barrel:** 7-1/2". **Weight:** 46 oz. **Length:** 13-1/2" overall. **Stocks:** Smooth walnut. **Sights:** Blade front, fixed groove rear. **Features:** Authentic copy of 1875 Remington with firing pin in hammer; color case-hardened frame, blue cylinder, barrel, steel backstrap and brass trigger guard. Also available in nickel, factory engraved. Imported by E.M.F.
Price: All calibers **$465.00**
Price: Nickel **$550.00**
Price: Engraved **$600.00**
Price: Engraved nickel **$710.00**

EMF 1890 Police Revolver
Similar to the 1875 Outlaw except has 5-1/2" barrel, weighs 40 oz., with 12-1/2" overall length. Has lanyard ring in butt. No web under barrel. Calibers 357, 44-40, 45 Colt. Imported by E.M.F.
Price: All calibers **$470.00**
Price: Nickel **$560.00**
Price: Engraved **$620.00**
Price: Engraved nickel **$725.00**

FREEDOM ARMS MODEL 83 454 SINGLE-ACTION REVOLVER
Caliber: 357 Mag., 41 Rem. Mag., 44 Rem. Mag., 454 Casull, 50 AE, 5-shot. **Barrel:** 4-3/4", 6", 7-1/2", 10". **Weight:** 50 oz. **Length:** 14" overall (7-1/2" bbl.). **Stocks:** Impregnated hardwood (Premier grade), or Pachmayr (Field Grade). **Sights:** Blade front, notch or adjustable rear. **Features:** All stainless steel construction; sliding bar safety system. Lifetime warranty. Made in U.S. by Freedom Arms, Inc.
Price: Premier Grade, 454 Casull, 50 AE, adj. sight **$1,958.00**
Price: Premier Grade, 454 Casull, fixed sight. **$1,894.00**
Price: Field Grade, 454 Casull, 50 AE, adj. sight **$1,519.00**
Price: Field Grade, 454 Casull, fixed sight **$1,484.00**
Price: Premier Grade, 357 Mag., 41 Rem. Mag., 44 Rem. Mag.,
adj. sight **$1,882.00**
Price: Premier Grade, 44 Rem. Mag., fixed sight **$1,816.00**
Price: Field Grade, 357 Mag., 41 Rem. Mag., 44 Rem. Mag.,
adj. sight **$1,442.00**

Freedom Arms Model 83 353 Revolver
Made on the Model 83 frame. Chambered for 357 Magnum with 5-shot cylinder; 4-3/4", 6", 7-1/2" or 9" barrel. Weighs 59 oz. with 7-1/2" barrel. Field grade model has adjustable sights, matte finish, Pachmayr grips.

Silhouette has 9" barrel, adjustable front sight blade with hood, Iron Sight Gun Works Silhouette adjustable rear, Pachmayr grips, trigger over-travel adjustment screw. All stainless steel. Introduced 1992.
Price: Field Grade **$1,340.00**
Price: Premier Grade (brushed finish, impregnated hardwood grips, Premier Grade sights) **$1,760.00**
Price: Silhouette (9", 357 Mag., 10", 44 Mag.) **$1,448.00**

Freedom Arms Model 83 654 Revolver
Made on the Model 83 frame. Chambered for 41 Magnum with 5-shot cylinder. Introduced 1998. Made in U.S. by Freedom Arms.
Price: Field Grade, adjustable sights **$1,400.00**
Price: Premier Grade, adjustable sights **$1,820.00**
Price: Silhouette **$1,448.00**

FREEDOM ARMS MODEL 83 475 LINEBAUGH REVOLVER
Caliber: 475 Linebaugh, 5-shot. **Barrel:** 4.75", 6", 7.5". **Weight:** NA. **Length:** NA. **Stocks:** Impregnated hardwood (Premier Grade) or Pachmayr (Field Grade). **Sights:** Removable ramp front, fully adjustable notch rear. **Features:** All stainless steel construction with brushed finish (Premier Grade) or matte finish (Field Grade); patented slide bar safety. Introduced 1999. Made in U.S. by Freedom Arms.
Price: Premier Grade **$1,958.00**
Price: Field Grade **$1,519.00**

Freedom Arms Model 83 555 Revolver
Made on the Model 83 frame. Chambered for the 50 A.E. (Action Express) cartridge. Offered in Premier and Field Grades with adjustable sights, 4-3/4", 6", 7-1/2" or 10" barrel. Introduced 1994. Made in U.S. by Freedom Arms, Inc.
Price: Premier Grade **$1,820.00**
Price: Field Grade **$1,400.00**

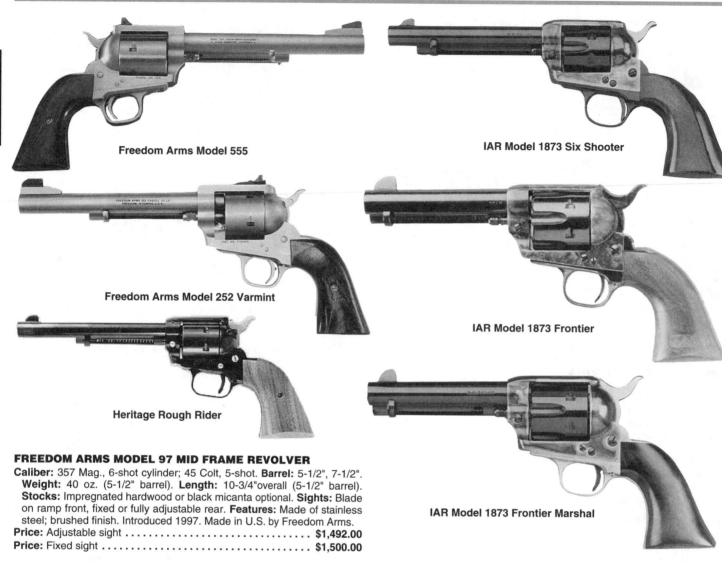

Freedom Arms Model 555

IAR Model 1873 Six Shooter

Freedom Arms Model 252 Varmint

IAR Model 1873 Frontier

Heritage Rough Rider

IAR Model 1873 Frontier Marshal

FREEDOM ARMS MODEL 97 MID FRAME REVOLVER

Caliber: 357 Mag., 6-shot cylinder; 45 Colt, 5-shot. **Barrel:** 5-1/2", 7-1/2". **Weight:** 40 oz. (5-1/2" barrel). **Length:** 10-3/4"overall (5-1/2" barrel). **Stocks:** Impregnated hardwood or black micanta optional. **Sights:** Blade on ramp front, fixed or fully adjustable rear. **Features:** Made of stainless steel; brushed finish. Introduced 1997. Made in U.S. by Freedom Arms.
Price: Adjustable sight **$1,492.00**
Price: Fixed sight **$1,500.00**

FREEDOM ARMS MODEL 252 VARMINT CLASS REVOLVER

Caliber: 22 LR, 5-shot. **Barrel:** 5.125", 7.5". **Weight:** 58 oz. (7.5" barrel). **Length:** NA. **Stocks:** Black and green laminated hardwood. **Sights:** Brass bead express front, express rear with shallow V-notch. **Features:** All stainless steel construction. Dual firing pins; lightened hammer; pre-set trigger stop. Built on Model 83 frame and accepts Model 83 Freedom Arms sights and/or scope mounts. Introduced 1991. Made in U.S. by Freedom Arms.
Price: **$1,527.00**
Price: Extra fitted 22 WMR cylinder **$264.00**

HERITAGE ROUGH RIDER REVOLVER

Caliber: 22 LR, 22 LR/22 WMR combo, 6-shot. **Barrel:** 2-3/4", 3-1/2", 4-3/4", 6-1/2", 9". **Weight:** 31 to 38 oz. **Length:** NA. **Stocks:** Exotic hardwood. **Sights:** Blade front, fixed rear. Adjustable sight on 6-1/2" only. **Features:** Hammer block safety. High polish blue or nickel finish. Introduced 1993. Made in U.S. by Heritage Mfg., Inc.
Price: .... **$119.95 to $174.95**
Price: 2-3/4", 3-1/2", 4-3/4" bird's-head grip .... **$139.95 to $174.95**

IAR MODEL 1873 SIX SHOOTER

Caliber: 22 LR/22 WMR combo. **Barrel:** 5-1/2". **Weight:** 36-1/2" oz. **Length:** 11-3/8" overall. **Stocks:** One-piece walnut. **Sights:** Blade front, notch rear. **Features:** A 3/4-scale reproduction. Color case-hardened frame, blued barrel. All-steel construction. Made by Uberti. Imported from Italy by IAR, Inc.
Price: **$360.00**

IAR MODEL 1873 FRONTIER REVOLVER

Caliber: 22 RL, 22 LR/22 WMR. **Barrel:** 4-3/4". **Weight:** 45 oz. **Length:** 10-1/2" overall. **Stocks:** One-piece walnut with inspector's cartouche. **Sights:** Blade front, notch rear. **Features:** Color case-hardened frame, blued barrel, black nickel-plated brass trigger guard and backstrap. Bright nickel and engraved versions available. Introduced 1997. Imported from Italy by IAR, Inc.
Price: **$395.00**
Price: Nickel-plated **$485.00**
Price: 22 LR/22WMR combo **$425.00**

IAR MODEL 1873 FRONTIER MARSHAL

Caliber: 357 Mag., 45 Colt. **Barrel:** 4-3/4", 5-1/2, 7-1/2". **Weight:** 39 oz. **Length:** 10-1/2" overall. **Stocks:** One-piece walnut. **Sights:** Blade front, notch rear. **Features:** Bright brass trigger guard and backstrap, color case-hardened frame, blued barrel and cylinder. Introduced 1998. Imported from Italy by IAR, Inc.
Price: **$395.00**

MAGNUM RESEARCH BFR SINGLE-ACTION REVOLVER

Caliber: 22 Hornet, 45 Colt +P, 454 Casull, 50 A.E. (Little Max, standard cylinder). **Barrel:** 7-1/2", 10". **Weight:** 4 lbs. **Length:** 11" overall with 7-1/2" barrel. **Stocks:** Uncle Mike's checkered rubber. **Sights:** Orange blade on ramp front, fully adjustable rear. **Features:** Stainless steel construction. Optional pearl and finger-groove grips available. Introduced 1997. Made in U.S. From Magnum Research, Inc.
Price: **$999.00**

Navy Arms Flat Top Navy Arms Pinched Frame Navy Arms Bisley Navy Arms 1873 Navy Arms Schofield

MAGNUM RESEARCH LITTLE MAX REVOLVER

Caliber: 22 Hornet, 45 Colt, 454 Casull, 50 A.E. **Barrel:** 6-1/2", 7-1/2", 10". **Weight:** 45 oz. **Length:** 13" overall (7-1/2" barrel). **Stocks:** Rubber. **Sights:** Ramp front, adjustable rear. **Features:** Single action; stainless steel construction. Announced 1998. Made in U.S. From Magnum Research.

Price: **$999.00**
Price: Maxline model (7-1/2", 10", 45 Colt, 45-70, 444 Marlin). . . **$999.00**

NAVY ARMS FLAT TOP TARGET MODEL REVOLVER

Caliber: 45 Colt, 6-shot cylinder. **Barrel:** 7-1/2". **Weight:** 40 oz. **Length:** 13-1/4" overall. **Stocks:** Smooth walnut. **Sights:** Spring-loaded German silver front, rear adjustable for windage. **Features:** Replica of Colt's Flat Top Frontier target revolver made from 1888 to 1896. Blue with color case-hardened frame. Introduced 1997. Imported by Navy Arms.

Price: $425.00

NAVY ARMS "PINCHED FRAME" SINGLE-ACTION REVOLVER

Caliber: 45 Colt, 6-shot. **Barrel:** 7-1/2". **Weight:** 37 oz. **Length:** 13" overall. **Stocks:** Smooth walnut **Sights:** German silver blade, notch rear. **Features:** Replica of Colt's original Peacemaker. Color case-hardened frame, hammer, rest charcoal blued. Introduced 1997. Imported by Navy Arms.

Price: **$415.00**

NAVY ARMS BISLEY MODEL SINGLE-ACTION REVOLVER

Caliber: 44-40 or 45 Colt, 6-shot cylinder. **Barrel:** 4-3/4", 5-1/2", 7-1/2". **Weight:** 40 oz. **Length:** 12-1/2" overall (7-1/2" barrel). **Stocks:** Smooth walnut. **Sights:** Blade front, notch rear. **Features:** Replica of Colt's Bisley Model. Polished blue finish, color case-hardened frame. Introduced 1997. Imported by Navy Arms.

Price: **$405.00**

Navy Arms Bisley Model Flat Top Target Revolver

Similar to the standard Bisley model except with flat top strap, 7-1/2" barrel only, and a spring-loaded German silver front sight blade, standing leaf rear sight adjustable for windage. Polished blue finish, color case-hardened frame. Introduced 1998. Imported by Navy Arms.

Price: **$435.00**

NAVY ARMS 1872 OPEN TOP REVOLVER

Caliber: 38 Spec., 6-shot. **Barrel:** 5-1/2" or 7-1/2". **Weight:** 2 lbs., 12 oz. **Length:** 11" or 13". **Stocks:** Smooth walnut. **Sights:** Blade front, notch rear. **Features:** Replica of Colt's first production cartridge "six shooter." Polished blue finish with color case hardened frame, silver plated trigger guard and backstrap Introduced 2000. Imported by Navy Arms.

Price: **$390.00**

NAVY ARMS 1873 SINGLE-ACTION REVOLVER

Caliber: 357 Mag., 44-40, 45 Colt, 6-shot cylinder. **Barrel:** 4-3/4", 5-1/2", 7-1/2". **Weight:** 36 oz. **Length:** 10-3/4" overall (5-1/2" barrel). **Stocks:** Smooth walnut. **Sights:** Blade front, notch rear. **Features:** Blue with color case-hardened frame. Introduced 1991. Imported by Navy Arms.

Price: $385.00
Price: 1873 U.S. Cavalry Model (7-1/2", 45 Colt, arsenal
markings) **$455.00**
Price: 1895 U.S. Artillery Model (as above, 5-1/2" barrel) **$455.00**

NAVY ARMS SHOOTIST MODEL SINGLE-ACTION REVOLVER

Caliber: 357 Mag., 44-40, 45 Colt, 6-shot cylinder. **Barrel:** 4-3/4", 5-1/2", 7-1/2". **Weight:** 36 oz. **Length:** 11-1/4" overall (5-1/2" barrel). **Stocks:** Smooth walnut. **Sights:** Blade front, notch rear. **Features:** Replica of Colt's Single Action Army. Parts interchange with first and second generation Colts. Polished blue, color case-hardened frame. Introduced 1999. Imported by Navy Arms.

Price: **$385.00**

NAVY ARMS 1875 SCHOFIELD REVOLVER

Caliber: 44-40, 45 Colt, 6-shot cylinder. **Barrel:** 3-1/2", 5", 7". **Weight:** 39 oz. **Length:** 10-3/4" overall (5" barrel). **Stocks:** Smooth walnut. **Sights:** Blade front, notch rear. **Features:** Replica of Smith & Wesson Model 3 Schofield. Single-action, top-break with automatic ejection. Polished blue finish. Introduced 1994. Imported by Navy Arms.

Price: Hideout Model, 3-1/2" barrel **$695.00**
Price: Wells Fargo, 5" barrel. **$695.00**
Price: U.S. Cavalry model, 7" barrel, military markings **$695.00**

Navy Arms New Model Russian

North American Mini

North American Mini-Master

North American Black Widow

Ruger Blackhawk

Navy Arms Deluxe 1875 Schofield Revolver

Similar to standard Schofield except has hand-cut "A" engraving and gold inlays, charcoal blue finish. Available in either Wells Fargo (5" barrel) or Cavalry (7" barrel) model. Introduced 1999. Imported by Navy Arms.
Price: **$1,875.00**

NAVY ARMS NEW MODEL RUSSIAN REVOLVER

Caliber: 44 Russian, 6-shot cylinder. **Barrel:** 6-1/2". **Weight:** 40 oz. **Length:** 12" overall. **Stocks:** Smooth walnut. **Sights:** Blade front, notch rear. **Features:** Replica of the S&W Model 3 Russian Third Model revolver. Spur trigger guard, polished blue finish. Introduced 1999. Imported by Navy Arms.
Price: **$745.00**

NAVY ARMS 1851 NAVY CONVERSION REVOLVER

Caliber: 38 Spec., 38 Long Colt. **Barrel:** 5-1/2", 7-1/2". **Weight:** 44 oz. **Length:** 14" overall (7-1/2" barrel). **Stocks:** Smooth walnut. **Sights:** Bead front, notch rear. **Features:** Replica of Colt's cartridge conversion revolver. Polished blue finish with color case-hardened frame, silver plated trigger guard and backstrap. Introduced 1999. Imported by Navy Arms.
Price: **$365.00**

NAVY ARMS 1860 ARMY CONVERSION REVOLVER

Caliber: 38 Spec., 38 Long Colt. **Barrel:** 5-1/2", 7-1/2". **Weight:** 44 oz. **Length:** 13-1/2" overall (7-1/2" barrel). **Stocks:** Smooth walnut. **Sights:** Blade front, notch rear. **Features:** Replica of Colt's conversion revolver. Polished blue finish with color case-hardened frame, full-size 1860 Army grip with blued steel backstrap. Introduced 1999. Imported by Navy Arms.
Price: **$365.00**

NAVY ARMS 1861 NAVY CONVERSION REVOLVER

Caliber: 38 Spec., 38 Long Colt. **Barrel:** 5-1/2", 7-1/2". **Weight:** 44 oz. **Length:** 13-1/2" overall (7-1/2" barrel). **Stocks:** Smooth walnut. **Sights:** Blade front, notch rear. **Features:** Replica of Colt's cartridge conversion. Polished blue finish with color case-hardened frame, silver plated trigger guard and backstrap. Introduced 1999. Imported by Navy Arms.
Price: **$365.00**

NORTH AMERICAN MINI-REVOLVERS

Caliber: 22 Short, 22 LR, 22 WMR, 5-shot. **Barrel:** 1-1/8", 1-5/8". **Weight:** 4 to 6.6 oz. **Length:** 3-5/8" to 6-1/8" overall. **Stocks:** Laminated wood. **Sights:** Blade front, notch fixed rear. **Features:** All stainless steel construction. Polished satin and matte finish. Engraved models available. From North American Arms.
Price: 22 Short, 22 LR **$176.00**
Price: 22 WMR, 1-5/8" bbl. **$194.00**
Price: 22 WMR, 1-1/8" or 1-5/8" bbl. with extra 22 LR cylinder . . **$231.00**

NORTH AMERICAN MINI-MASTER

Caliber: 22 LR, 22 WMR, 5-shot cylinder. **Barrel:** 4". **Weight:** 10.7 oz. **Length:** 7.75" overall. **Stocks:** Checkered hard black rubber. **Sights:** Blade front, white outline rear adjustable for elevation, or fixed. **Features:** Heavy vent barrel; full-size grips. Non-fluted cylinder. Introduced 1989.
Price: Adjustable sight, 22 WMR or 22 LR **$299.00**
Price: As above with extra WMR/LR cylinder **$336.00**
Price: Fixed sight, 22 WMR or 22 LR **$281.00**
Price: As above with extra WMR/LR cylinder **$318.00**

North American Black Widow Revolver

Similar to the Mini-Master except has 2" heavy vent barrel. Built on the 22 WMR frame. Non-fluted cylinder, black rubber grips. Available with either Millett Low Profile fixed sights or Millett sight adjustable for elevation only. Overall length 5-7/8", weighs 8.8 oz. From North American Arms.
Price: Adjustable sight, 22 LR or 22 WMR **$269.00**
Price: As above with extra WMR/LR cylinder **$306.00**
Price: Fixed sight, 22 LR or 22 WMR **$251.00**
Price: As above with extra WMR/LR cylinder **$288.00**

RUGER NEW MODEL BLACKHAWK REVOLVER

Caliber: 30 Carbine, 357 Mag./38 Spec., 41 Mag., 45 Colt, 6-shot. **Barrel:** 4-5/8" or 5-1/2", either caliber; 7-1/2" (30 Carbine and 45 Colt). **Weight:** 42 oz. (6-1/2" bbl.). **Length:** 12-1/4" overall (5-1/2" bbl.). **Stocks:** American walnut. **Sights:** 1/8" ramp front, micro-click rear adjustable for windage and elevation. **Features:** Ruger transfer bar safety system, independent firing pin, hardened chrome-moly steel frame, music wire springs throughout. Comes with plastic lockable case and lock.
Price: Blue 30 Carbine, 7-1/2" (BN31) **$399.00**
Price: Blue, 357 Mag., 4-5/8", 6-1/2" (BN34, BN36) **$399.00**
Price: As above, stainless (KBN34, KBN36) **$489.00**

HANDGUNS

Ruger Super Blackhawk

Ruger New Bearcat

Ruger Vaquero

Ruger Super Single-Six

Ruger Bisley Single-Action

Price: 357 Mag. KBNV34 (4-5/8"), KBNV35 (5-1/2") stainless . . . **$498.00**
Price: BNV44 (4-5/8"), BNV445 (5-1/2"), BNV45 (7-1/2"), blue . . **$498.00**
Price: KBNV44 (4-5/8"), KBNV455 (5-1/2"), KBNV45 (7-1/2"),
   stainless **$498.00**
Price: 45 Colt BNV455, all blue finish, 4-5/8" or 5-1/2" **$498.00**
Price: 45 Colt KBNV455, stainless, 5-1/2" **$498.00**

Ruger Bisley-Vaquero Single-Action Revolver

Similar to the Vaquero except has Bisley-style hammer, grip and trigger and is available in 357 Magnum, 44 Magnum and 45 Colt only, with 4-5/8" or 5-1/2" barrel. Has smooth rosewood grips with Ruger medallion. Roll-engraved, unfluted cylinder. Introduced 1997. From Sturm, Ruger & Co.
Price: Color case-hardened frame, blue grip frame, barrel and cylinder,
   RBNV-475, RBNV-455 . . . . **$498.00**
Price: High-gloss stainless steel, KRBNV-475, KRBNV-455 . . . . . **$529.00**
Price: For simulated ivory grips add **$36.00**
Price: 44-40 BNV40 (4-5/8"), BNV405 (5-1/2"), BNV407 (7-1/2") . **$498.00**
Price: 44-40 KBNV40 (4-5/8"), KBNV405 (5-1/2"), KBNV407 (7-1/2")
   stainless **$498.00**

Price: Blue, 357 Mag./9mm Convertible, 4-5/8", 6-1/2" (BN34X,
   BN36X) **$449.00**
Price: Blue, 41 Mag., 4-5/8", 6-1/2" (BN41, BN42) **$399.00**
Price: Blue, 45 Colt, 4-5/8", 5-1/2", 7-1/2" (BN44, BN455, BN45) **$399.00**
Price: Stainless, 45 Colt, 4-5/8", 7-1/2" (KBN44, KBN45) **$489.00**
Price: Blue, 45 Colt/45 ACP Convertible, 4-5/8", 5-1/2" (BN44X, BN455X)
    . . . . **$449.00**

RUGER NEW MODEL SUPER BLACKHAWK

Caliber: 44 Mag., 6-shot. Also fires 44 Spec. **Barrel:** 4-5/8", 5-1/2", 7-1/2", 10-1/2" bull. **Weight:** 48 oz. (7-1/2" bbl.), 51 oz. (10-1/2" bbl.). **Length:** 13-3/8" overall (7-1/2" bbl.). **Stocks:** American walnut. **Sights:** 1/8" ramp front, micro-click rear adjustable for windage and elevation. **Features:** Ruger transfer bar safety system, fluted or un-fluted cylinder, steel grip and cylinder frame, round or square back trigger guard, wide serrated trigger and wide spur hammer. Comes with plastic lockable case and lock.
Price: Blue, 4-5/8", 5-1/2", 7-1/2" (S458N, S45N, S47N) **$478.00**
Price: Blue, 10-1/2" bull barrel (S411N) **$485.00**
Price: Stainless, 4-5/8", 5-1/2", 7-1/2" (KS458N, KS45N, KS47N). **$499.00**
Price: Stainless, 10-1/2" bull barrel (KS411N) **$505.00**

RUGER VAQUERO SINGLE-ACTION REVOLVER

Caliber: 357 Mag., 44-40, 44 Mag., 45 Colt, 6-shot. **Barrel:** 4-5/8", 5-1/2", 7-1/2". **Weight:** 41 oz. **Length:** 13-1/8" overall (7-1/2" barrel). **Sights:** Blade front, fixed notch rear. **Features:** Uses Ruger's patented transfer bar safety system and loading gate interlock with classic styling. Blued model has color case-hardened finish on the frame, the rest polished and blued. Stainless model has high-gloss polish. Introduced 1993. From Sturm, Ruger & Co.
Price: 357 Mag. BNV34 (4-5/8"), BNV35 (5-1/2") **$498.00**

RUGER NEW BEARCAT SINGLE-ACTION

Caliber: 22 LR, 6-shot. **Barrel:** 4". **Weight:** 24 oz. **Length:** 8-7/8" overall. **Stocks:** Smooth rosewood with Ruger medallion. **Sights:** Blade front, fixed notch rear. **Features:** Reintroduction of the Ruger Bearcat with slightly lengthened frame, Ruger patented transfer bar safety system. Available in blue only. Introduced 1993. Comes with plastic lockable case and lock. From Sturm, Ruger & Co.
Price: SBC4, blue **$347.00**

RUGER SINGLE-SIX AND SUPER SINGLE-SIX CONVERTIBLE

Caliber: 22 LR, 6-shot; 22 WMR in extra cylinder. **Barrel:** 4-5/8", 5-1/2", 6-1/2", 9-1/2" (6-groove). **Weight:** 35 oz. (6-1/2" bbl.). **Length:** 11-13/16" overall (6-1/2" bbl.). **Stocks:** Smooth American walnut. **Sights:** Improved Patridge front on ramp, fully adjustable rear protected by integral frame ribs (super single-six); or fixed sight 9single six). **Features:** Ruger transfer bar safety system, loading gate interlock, hardened chrome-moly steel frame, wide trigger, music wire springs throughout, independent firing pin.
Price: 4-5/8", 5-1/2", 6-1/2", 9-1/2" barrel, blue, adjustable sight NR4, NR6,
   NR9, NR5 . . . . **$352.00**
Price: 5-1/2", 6-1/2" bbl. only, stainless steel, adjustable sight
   KNR5, KNR6 . . . . **$436.00**
Price: 5-1/2", 6-1/2" barrel, blue fixed sights **$347.00**

Traditions 1851 Navy

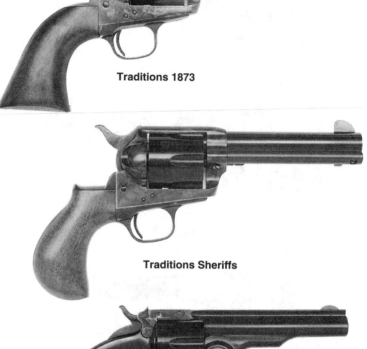

Traditions 1873

Traditions 1861 Navy

Traditions Sheriffs

Traditions 1875 Schofield

Ruger Bisley Small Frame Revolver

Similar to the Single-Six except frame is styled after the classic Bisley "flat-top." Most mechanical parts are unchanged. Hammer is lower and smoothly curved with a deeply checkered spur. Trigger is strongly curved with a wide smooth surface. Longer grip frame designed with a hand-filling shape, and the trigger guard is a large oval. Adjustable dovetail rear sight; front sight base accepts interchangeable square blades of various heights and styles. Has an unfluted cylinder and roll engraving. Weighs 41 oz. Chambered for 22 LR, 6-1/2" barrel only. Comes with plastic lockable case and lock. Introduced 1985.
Price: RB-22AW $402.00

Ruger Bisley Single-Action Revolver

Similar to standard Blackhawk except the hammer is lower with a smoothly curved, deeply checkered wide spur. The trigger is strongly curved with a wide smooth surface. Longer grip frame has a hand-filling shape. Adjustable rear sight, ramp-style front. Has an unfluted cylinder and roll engraving, adjustable sights. Chambered for 357, 44 Mags. and 45 Colt; 7-1/2" barrel; overall length of 13"; weighs 48 oz. Comes with plastic lockable case and lock. Introduced 1985.
Price: RB-35W, 357Mag, R3-44W, 44Mag, RB-45W, 45 Colt . . . $498.00

TRADITIONS 1851 NAVY CONVERSION REVOLVER

Caliber: 38 Spec. Barrel: 7-1/2". Weight: 40 oz. Length: 14-1/2" overall. Stocks: Smooth walnut. Sights: Post front, hammer-notch rear. Features: Steel frame, brass trigger guard. Introduced 1998. From Traditions.
Price: $395.00

TRADITIONS 1858 REMINGTON CONVERSION REVOLVER

Caliber: 38 Spec. Barrel: 7-1/2". Weight: 2 lbs., 8 oz. Length: 14-1/2" overall. Stocks: Smooth walnut. Sights: Post front, notch rear. Features: Replica of converted Remington. Blued steel grip frame and trigger guard. Introduced 1999. Imported by Traditions.
Price: $425.00

TRADITIONS 1860 ARMY CONVERSION REVOLVER

Caliber: 38 Spec. Barrel: 7-1/2". Weight: 44 oz. Length: 14-1/2" overall. Stocks: Smooth walnut. Sights: Blade front, notch rear. Features: Replica of Colt's conversion revolver. Polished blue finish with color case-hardened frame, full-size 1860 Army grip with blued steel backstrap. Introduced 1999. Imported by Traditions.
Price: $410.00

TRADITIONS 1861 NAVY CONVERSION REVOLVER

Caliber: 38 Spec. Barrel: 7-1/2". Weight: 44 oz. Length: 14-1/2" overall. Stocks: Smooth walnut. Sights: Blade front, notch rear. Features: Replica of Colt's cartridge conversion. Polished blue finish with color case-hardened frame, brass trigger guard and backstrap. Introduced 1999. Imported by Traditions.
Price: $410.00

TRADITIONS 1872 OPEN-TOP CONVERSION REVOLVER

Caliber: 38 Spec. Barrel: 8". Weight: 2 lbs. 8 oz. Length: 14-1/2" overall. Stocks: Smooth walnut. Sights: Blade front, fixed rear. Features: Replica of the original production. Color case-hardened frame, rest blued, including grip frame. Introduced 1999. Imported from Italy by Traditions.
Price: $410.00

TRADITIONS 1873 SINGLE-ACTION REVOLVER

Caliber: 22 LR, 357 Mag., 44-40, 45 Colt, 6-shot cylinder. Barrel: 4-3/4", 5-1/2", 7-1/2". Weight: 44 oz. Length: 10-3/4" overall (5-1/2" barrel). Stocks: Walnut. Sights: Blade front, groove in topstrap rear. Features: Blued barrel, cylinder, color case-hardened frame, blue or brass trigger guard. Nickel-plated frame with polished brass trigger guard available in 357 Mag., 44-40, 45 Colt. Introduced 1998. From Traditions.
Price: . . . . $300.00 to $395.00

Traditions Sheriffs Revolver

Similar to the 1873 single-action revolver except has special birds-head grip with spur, and smooth or checkered walnut grips. Introduced 1998. From Traditions.
Price: With smooth walnut grips $370.00

TRADITIONS 1875 SCHOFIELD REVOLVER

Caliber: 44-40, 45 Schofield, 45 Colt, 6-shot cylinder. Barrel: 5-1/2". Weight: 40 oz. Length: 11-1/4" overall. Stocks: Walnut. Sights: Blade front, notch rear. Features: Blue finish, case-hardened frame, hammer, trigger. Introduced 1998. From Traditions.
Price: $659.00

Uberti Cattleman

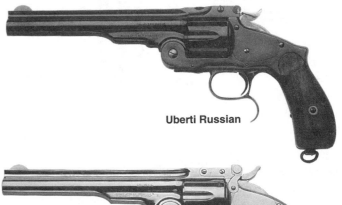

Uberti Russian

Uberti 1875 Army

Uberti Schofield

Uberti 1890 Army

Uberti Bisley

UBERTI 1873 CATTLEMAN SINGLE-ACTION

Caliber: 22 LR/22 WMR, 38 Spec., 357 Mag., 44 Spec., 44-40, 45 Colt/45 ACP, 6-shot. **Barrel:** 4-3/4", 5-1/2", 7-1/2"; 44-40, 45 Colt also with 3", 3-1/2", 4". **Weight:** 38 oz. (5-1/2" bbl.). **Length:** 10-3/4" overall (5-1/2" bbl.). **Stocks:** One-piece smooth walnut. **Sights:** Blade front, groove rear; fully adjustable rear available. **Features:** Steel or brass backstrap, trigger guard; color case-hardened frame, blued barrel, cylinder. Imported from Italy by Uberti U.S.A.
Price: Steel backstrap, trigger guard, fixed sights $435.00
Price: Brass backstrap, trigger guard, fixed sights $365.00
Price: Bisley model $435.00

Uberti 1873 Buckhorn Single-Action

A slightly larger version of the Cattleman revolver. Available in 44 Magnum or 44 Magnum/44-40 convertible, otherwise has same specs.
Price: Steel backstrap, trigger guard, fixed sights $410.00
Price: Convertible (two cylinders) $475.00

UBERTI 1875 SA ARMY OUTLAW REVOLVER

Caliber: 357 Mag., 44-40, 45 Colt, 45 Colt/45 ACP convertible, 6-shot. **Barrel:** 5-1/2", 7-1/2". **Weight:** 44 oz. **Length:** 13-3/4" overall. **Stocks:** Smooth walnut. **Sights:** Blade front, notch rear. **Features:** Replica of the 1875 Remington S.A. Army revolver. Brass trigger guard, color case-hardened frame, rest blued. Imported by Uberti U.S.A.
Price: $435.00
Price: 45 Colt/45 ACP convertible $475.00

UBERTI 1890 ARMY OUTLAW REVOLVER

Caliber: 357 Mag., 44-40, 45 Colt, 45 Colt/45 ACP convertible, 6-shot. **Barrel:** 5-1/2", 7-1/2". **Weight:** 37 oz. **Length:** 12-1/2" overall. **Stocks:** American walnut. **Sights:** Blade front, groove rear. **Features:** Replica of the 1890 Remington single-action. Brass trigger guard, rest is blued. Imported by Uberti U.S.A.
Price: $435.00
Price: 45 Colt/45 ACP convertible $475.00

UBERTI NEW MODEL RUSSIAN REVOLVER

Caliber: 44 Russian, 6-shot cylinder. **Barrel:** 6-1/2". **Weight:** 40 oz. **Length:** 12" overall. **Stocks:** Smooth walnut. **Sights:** Blade front, notch rear. **Features:** Repica of the S&W Model 3 Russian Third Model revolver. Spur trigger guard, polished blue finish. Introduced 1999. Imported by Uberti USA.
Price: $775.00

UBERTI 1875 SCHOFIELD REVOLVER

Caliber: 44-40, 45 Colt, 6-shot cylinder. **Barrel:** 5", 7". **Weight:** 39 oz. **Length:** 10-3/4" overall (5" barrel). **Stocks:** Smooth walnut. **Sights:** Blade front, notch rear. **Features:** Replica of Smith & Wesson Model 3 Schofield. Single-action, top-break with automatic ejection. Polished blue finish. Introduced 1994. Imported by Uberti USA.
Price: $700.00

UBERTI BISLEY MODEL SINGLE-ACTION REVOLVER

Caliber: 38-40, 357 Mag., 44 Spec., 44-40 or 45 Colt, 6-shot cylinder. **Barrel:** 4-3/4", 5-1/2", 7-1/2". **Weight:** 40 oz. **Length:** 12-1/2" overall (7-1/2" barrel). **Stocks:** Smooth walnut. **Sights:** Blade front, notch rear. **Features:** Replica of Colt's Bisley Model. Polished blue finish, color case-hardened frame. Introduced 1997. Imported by Uberti USA.
Price: 435.00

Uberti Bisley Flat Top

Uberti Bisley Model Flat Top Target Revolver

Similar to the standard Bisley model except with flat top strap, 7-1/2" barrel only, and a spring-loaded German silver front sight blade, standing leaf rear sight adjustable for windage. Polished blue finish, color case-hardened frame. Introduced 1998. Imported by Uberti USA.

Price: **$455.00**

U.S. PATENT FIRE-ARMS SINGLE ACTION ARMY REVOLVER

Caliber: 22 LR, 22 WMR, 357 Mag., 44 Russian, 38-40, 44-40, 45 Colt, 6-shot cylinder. **Barrel:** 3", 4", 4-3/4", 5-1/2", 7-1/2", 10". **Weight:** 37 oz. **Length:** NA. **Stocks:** Smooth walnut. **Sights:** Blade front, notch rear. **Features:** Recreation of original guns; 3" and 4" have no ejector. Available with all-blue, blue with color case-hardening, or full nickel-plate finish. Made in Italy; available from United States Patent Fire-Arms Mfg. Co.

Price: 3" blue **$600.00**
Price: 4-3/4", blue/cased-colors **$732.00**
Price: 7-1/2", blue/case-colors **$739.00**
Price: 10", nickel. **$847.50**

U.S. Patent Fire-Arms Nettleton Cavalry Revolver

Similar to the Single Action Army, except in 45 Colt only, with 7-1/2" barrel, color case-hardened/blue finish, and has old-style hand numbering, exact cartouche branding and correct inspector hand-stamp markings. Made in Italy; available from United States Patent Fire-Arms Mfg. Co.

Price: **$950.00**
Price: Artillery Model, 5-1/2" barrel. **$950.00**

U.S. Patent Fire-Arms Bird Head Model Revolver

Similar to the Single Action Army except has bird's-head grip and comes with 3-1/2", 4" or 4-1/2" barrel. Made in Italy; available from United States Patent Fire-Arms Mfg. Co.

Price: 3-1/2", blue. **$635.50**
Price: 4", blue with color case-hardening. **$735.00**
Price: 4-1/2", nickel-plated **$795.50**

U.S. Patent Fire-Arms Flattop Target Revolver

Similar to the Single Action Army except 4-3/4", 5-1/2" or 7-1/2" barrel, two-piece hard rubber stocks, flat top frame, adjustable rear sight. Made in Italy; available from United States Patent Fire-Arms Mfg. Co.

Price: 4-3/4", blue, polished hammer **$690.00**
Price: 4-3/4", blue, case-colored hammer **$813.00**
Price: 5-1/2", blue, case-colored hammer **$816.00**
Price: 5-1/2", nickel-plated **$765.00**
Price: 7-1/2", blue, polished hammer **$717.00**
Price: 7-1/2", blue, case-colored hammer **$822.00**

U.S. PATENT FIRE-ARMS BISLEY MODEL REVOLVER

Caliber: 4 Colt, 6-shot cylinder. **Barrel:** 4-3/4", 5-1/2", 7-1/2", 10". **Weight:** 38 oz. (5-1/2" barrel). **Length:** NA. **Stocks:** Smooth walnut. **Sights:** Blade front, notch rear. **Features:** Available in all-blue, blue with color case-hardening, or full nickel plate finish. Made in Italy; available from United States Patent Fire-Arms Mfg. Co.

Price: 4-3/4", blue. **$652.00**
Price: 5-1/2", blue/case-colors **$750.50**
Price: 7-1/2", blue/case-colors **$756.00**
Price: 10", nickel. **$862.50**

HANDGUNS

Specially adapted single-shot and multi-barrel arms.

American Derringer Model 1

Bond Arms C2K Defender

AMERICAN DERRINGER MODEL 1

Caliber: 22 LR, 22 WMR, 30 Carbine, 30 Luger, 30-30 Win., 32 H&R Mag., 32-20, 380 ACP, 38 Super, 38 Spec., 38 Spec. shotshell, 38 Spec. +P, 9mm Para., 357 Mag., 357 Mag./45/410, 357 Maximum, 10mm, 40 S&W, 41 Mag., 38-40, 44-40 Win., 44 Spec., 44 Mag., 45 Colt, 45 Win. Mag., 45 ACP, 45 Colt/410, 45-70 single shot. **Barrel:** 3". **Weight:** 15-1/2 oz. (38 Spec.). **Length:** 4.82" overall. **Stocks:** Rosewood, Zebra wood. **Sights:** Blade front. **Features:** Made of stainless steel with high-polish or satin finish. Two-shot capacity. Manual hammer block safety. Introduced 1980. Available in almost any pistol caliber. Contact the factory for complete list of available calibers and prices. From American Derringer Corp.

Price: 22 LR	$260.00
Price: 38 Spec.	$285.00
Price: 357 Maximum	$310.00
Price: 357 Mag.	$300.00
Price: 9mm, 380	$285.00
Price: 40 S&W	$300.00
Price: 44 Spec.	$363.00
Price: 44-40 Win.	$363.00
Price: 45 Colt	$350.00
Price: 30-30, 45 Win. Mag.	$425.00
Price: 41, 44 Mags.	$400.00
Price: 45-70, single shot	$352.00
Price: 45 Colt, 410, 2-1/2"	$363.00
Price: 45 ACP, 10mm Auto	$300.00

American Derringer Model 4

Similar to the Model 1 except has 4.1" barrel, overall length of 6", and weighs 16-1/2 oz.; chambered for 357 Mag., 357 Maximum, 45-70, 3" 410-bore shotshells or 45 Colt or 44 Mag. Made of stainless steel. Manual hammer block safety. Introduced 1985.

Price: 3" 410/45 Colt	$390.00
Price: 45-70 (Alaskan Survival model)	$440.00
Price: 44 Mag. with oversize grips	$480.00
Price: Alaskan Survival model (45-70 upper barrel, 410 or 45 Colt lower)	$400.00

American Derringer Model 6

Similar to the Model 1 except has 6" barrel chambered for 3" 410 shotshells or 22 WMR, 357 Mag., 45 ACP, 45 Colt; rosewood stocks; 8.2" o.a.l. and weighs 21 oz. Shoots either round for each barrel. Manual hammer block safety. Introduced 1986.

Price: 22 WMR	$405.00
Price: 357 Mag.	$405.00
Price: 45 Colt/410	$415.00
Price: 45 ACP	$405.00

American Derringer Model 7 Ultra Lightweight

Similar to Model 1 except made of high strength aircraft aluminum. Weighs 7-1/2 oz., 4.82" o.a.l., rosewood stocks. Available in 22 LR, 22 WMR, 32 H&R Mag., 380 ACP, 38 Spec., 44 Spec. Introduced 1986.

Price: 22 LR, WMR	$290.00

Price: 38 Spec.	$290.00
Price: 380 ACP	$290.00
Price: 32 H&R Mag/32 S&W Long	$290.00
Price: 44 Spec.	$530.00

American Derringer Model 10 Lightweight

Similar to the Model 1 except frame is of aluminum, giving weight of 10 oz. Stainless barrels. Available in 38 Spec., 45 Colt or 45 ACP only. Matte gray finish. Introduced 1989.

Price: 45 Colt	$350.00
Price: 45 ACP	$295.00
Price: 38 Spec.	$270.00

American Derringer Lady Derringer

Same as the Model 1 except has tuned action, is fitted with scrimshawed synthetic ivory grips; chambered for 32 H&R Mag. and 38 Spec.; 357 Mag., 45 Colt, 45/410. Deluxe Grade is highly polished; Deluxe Engraved is engraved in a pattern similar to that used on 1880s derringers. All come in a French fitted jewelry box. Introduced 1991.

Price: 32 H&R Mag.	$340.00
Price: 357 Mag.	$370.00
Price: 38 Spec.	$325.00
Price: 45 Colt, 45/410	$400.00

American Derringer Texas Commemorative

A Model 1 Derringer with solid brass frame, stainless steel barrel and rosewood grips. Available in 38 Spec., 44-40 Win., or 45 Colt. Introduced 1987.

Price: 38 Spec.	$330.00
Price: 44-40	$385.00
Price: Brass frame, 45 Colt	$415.00

AMERICAN DERRINGER DA 38 MODEL

Caliber: 22 LR, 9mm Para., 38 Spec., 357 Mag., 40 S&W. **Barrel:** 3". **Weight:** 14.5 oz. **Length:** 4.8" overall. **Stocks:** Rosewood, walnut or other hardwoods. **Sights:** Fixed. **Features:** Double-action only; two-shots. Manual safety. Made of satin-finished stainless steel and aluminum. Introduced 1989. From American Derringer Corp.

Price: 22 LR, 38 Spec.	$400.00
Price: 9mm Para.	$410.00
Price: 357 Mag.	$415.00
Price: 40 S&W	$440.00

ANSCHUTZ MODEL 64P SPORT/TARGET PISTOL

Caliber: 22 LR, 22 WMR, 5-shot magazine. **Barrel:** 10". **Weight:** 3 lbs., 8 oz. **Length:** 18-1/2" overall. **Stock:** Choate Rynite. **Sights:** None furnished; grooved for scope mounting. **Features:** Right-hand bolt; polished blue finish. Introduced 1998. Imported from Germany by AcuSport.

Price: 22 LR	$455.95
Price: 22 WMR	$479.95

BOND ARMS TEXAS DEFENDER DERRINGER

Caliber: 9mm Para, 38 Spec./357 Mag., 40 S&W, 44 Spec./44 Mag., 45 Colt/410 shotshell. **Barrel:** 3", 3-1/2". **Weight:** 21 oz. **Length:** 5" overall.

Davis Big Bore

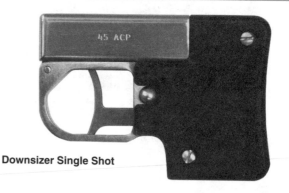

Downsizer Single Shot

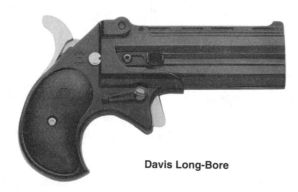

Davis Long-Bore

Gaucher GN1 Silhouette

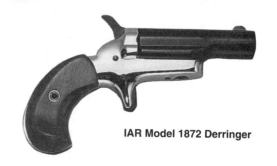

IAR Model 1872 Derringer

Stocks: Laminated black ash or rosewood. **Sights:** Blade front, fixed rear. **Features:** Interchangeable barrels; retracting firing pins; rebounding firing pins; cross-bolt safety; removable trigger guard; automatic extractor for rimmed calibers. Stainless steel construction with blasted/polished and ground combination finish. Introduced 1997. Made in U.S. by Bond Arms, Inc.
Price: **$349.00**
Price: Century 2000 Defender (410-bore, 3-1/2" barrels) **$369.00**

BROWN CLASSIC SINGLE SHOT PISTOL

Caliber: 17 Ackley Hornet through 45-70 Govt. **Barrel:** 15" airgauged match grade. **Weight:** About 3 lbs., 7 oz. **Stocks:** Walnut; thumbrest target style. **Sights:** None furnished; drilled and tapped for scope mounting. **Features:** Falling block action gives rigid barrel-receiver mating; hand-fitted and headspaced. Introduced 1998. Made in U.S. by E.A. Brown Mfg.
Price: **$499.00**

DAVIS BIG BORE DERRINGERS

Caliber: 22 WMR, 38 Spec., 9mm Para. **Barrel:** 2.75". **Weight:** 11.5 oz. **Length:** 4.65" overall. **Stocks:** Textured black synthetic. **Sights:** Blade front, fixed notch rear. **Features:** Alloy frame, steel-lined barrels, steel breech block. Plunger-type safety with integral hammer block. Chrome or black Teflon finish. Introduced 1992. Made in U.S. by Davis Industries.
Price: **$98.00**
Price: 9mm Para. **$104.00**

DAVIS LONG-BORE DERRINGERS

Caliber: 22 WMR, 38 Spec., 9mm Para. **Barrel:** 3.5". **Weight:** 13 oz. **Length:** 5.65" overall. **Stocks:** Textured black synthetic. **Sights:** Fixed. **Features:** Chrome or black Teflon finish. Larger than Davis D-Series models. Introduced 1995. Made in U.S. by Davis Industries.
Price: **$104.00**
Price: 9mm Para. **$110.00**
Price: Big-Bore models (same calibers, 3/4" shorter barrels) **$98.00**

DAVIS D-SERIES DERRINGERS

Caliber: 22 LR, 22 WMR, 25 ACP, 32 ACP. **Barrel:** 2.4". **Weight:** 9.5 oz. **Length:** 4" overall. **Stocks:** Laminated wood or pearl. **Sights:** Blade front,

fixed notch rear. **Features:** Choice of black Teflon or chrome finish; spur trigger. Introduced 1986. Made in U.S. by Davis Industries.
Price: **$99.50**

DOWNSIZER WSP SINGLE SHOT PISTOL

Caliber: 9mm Para, 357 Magnum, 40 S&W, 45 ACP. **Barrel:** 2.10". **Weight:** 11 oz. **Length:** 3.25" overall. **Stocks:** Black polymer. **Sights:** None. **Features:** Single shot, tip-up barrel. Double action only. Stainless steel construction. Measures .900" thick. Introduced 1997. From Downsizer Corp.
Price: **$354.00**

GAUCHER GN1 SILHOUETTE PISTOL

Caliber: 22 LR, single shot. **Barrel:** 10". **Weight:** 2.4 lbs. **Length:** 15.5" overall. **Stocks:** European hardwood. **Sights:** Blade front, open adjustable rear. **Features:** Bolt action, adjustable trigger. Introduced 1990. Imported from France by Mandall Shooting Supplies.
Price: About **$525.00**
Price: Model GP Silhouette **$425.00**

IAR MODEL 1872 DERRINGER

Caliber: 22 Short. **Barrel:** 2-3/8". **Weight:** 7 oz. **Length:** 5-1/8" overall. **Stocks:** Smooth walnut. **Sights:** Blade front, notch rear. **Features:** Gold or nickel frame with blue barrel. Reintroduced 1996 using original Colt designs and tooling for the Colt Model 4 Derringer. Made in U.S. by IAR, Inc.
Price: **$99.00**
Price: Single cased gun **$125.00**
Price: Double cased set **$215.00**

IAR MODEL 1888 DOUBLE DERRINGER

Caliber: 38 Special. **Barrel:** 2-3/4". **Weight:** 16 oz. **Length:** NA. **Stocks:** Smooth walnut. **Sights:** Blade front, notch rear. **Features:** All steel con-

IAR Model 1888 Derringer

Maximum Single Shot

RPM XL Pistol

Magnum Research Lone Eagle

Savage 510F Striker

struction. Blue barrel, color case-hardened frame. Uses original designs and tooling for the Uberti New Maverick Derringer. Introduced 1999. Made in U.S. by IAR, Inc.
Price: **$395.00**

MAGNUM RESEARCH LONE EAGLE SINGLE SHOT PISTOL
Caliber: 22 Hornet, 223, 22-250, 243, 260 Rem., 7mm BR, 7mm-08, 30-30, 7.62x39, 308, 30-06, 357 Max., 35 Rem., 358 Win., 44 Mag., 444 Marlin, 440 Cor-Bon. **Barrel:** 14", interchangeable. **Weight:** 4 lbs., 3 oz. to 4 lbs., 7 oz. **Length:** 15" overall. **Stocks:** Ambidextrous. **Sights:** None furnished; drilled and tapped for scope mounting and open sights. Open sights optional. **Features:** Cannon-type rotating breech with spring-activated ejector. Ordnance steel with matte blue finish. Cross-bolt safety. External cocking lever on left side of gun. Muzzle brake optional. Introduced 1991. Available from Magnum Research, Inc.
Price: Complete pistol, black **$438.00**
Price: Barreled action only, black **$319.00**
Price: Complete pistol, chrome **$478.00**
Price: Barreled action, chrome **$359.00**
Price: Scope base **$14.00**
Price: Adjustable open sights **$35.00**

MAXIMUM SINGLE SHOT PISTOL
Caliber: 22 LR, 22 Hornet, 22 BR, 22 PPC, 223 Rem., 22-250, 6mm BR, 6mm PPC, 243, 250 Savage, 6.5mm-35M, 270 MAX, 270 Win., 7mm TCU, 7mm BR, 7mm-35, 7mm INT-R, 7mm-08, 7mm Rocket, 7mm Super-Mag., 30 Herrett, 30 Carbine, 30-30, 308 Win., 30x39, 32-20, 350 Rem. Mag., 357 Mag., 357 Maximum, 358 Win., 375 H&H, 44 Mag., 454 Casull. **Barrel:** 8-3/4", 10-1/2", 14". **Weight:** 61 oz. (10-1/2" bbl.); 78 oz. (14" bbl.). **Length:** 15", 18-1/2" overall (with 10-1/2" and 14" bbl., respectively). **Stocks:** Smooth walnut stocks and forend. Also available with 17" finger groove grip. **Sights:** Ramp front, fully adjustable open rear. **Features:** Falling block action; drilled and tapped for M.O.A. scope mounts; integral grip frame/receiver; adjustable trigger; Douglas barrel (interchangeable). Introduced 1983. Made in U.S. by M.O.A. Corp.
Price: Stainless receiver, blue barrel **$799.00**
Price: Stainless receiver, stainless barrel **$883.00**
Price: Extra blued barrel **$254.00**

Price: Extra stainless barrel **$317.00**
Price: Scope mount **$60.00**

RPM XL SINGLE SHOT PISTOL
Caliber: 22 LR through 45-70. **Barrel:** 8", 10-3/4", 12", 14". **Weight:** About 60 oz. **Length:** NA. **Stocks:** Smooth Goncalo Alves with thumb and heel rests. **Sights:** Hooded front with interchangeable post, or Patridge; ISGW rear adjustable for windage and elevation. **Features:** Barrel drilled and tapped for scope mount. Visible cocking indicator. Spring-loaded barrel lock, positive hammer-block safety. Trigger adjustable for weight of pull and over-travel. Contact maker for complete price list. Made in U.S. by RPM.
Price: Hunter model (stainless frame, 5/16" underlug, latch lever and positive extractor) **$1,295.00**
Price: Extra barrel, 8" through 10-3/4" **$387.50**
Price: Extra barrel with positive extractor, add **$100.00**
Price: Muzzle brake **$100.00**

SAVAGE STRIKER BOLT-ACTION HUNTING HANDGUN
Caliber: 223, 22-250, 243, 206, 7mm-08, 308, 2-shot magazine. **Barrel:** 14". **Weight:** About 5 lbs. **Length:** 22-1/2" overall. **Stock:** Black composite ambidextrous mid-grip; grooved forend; "Dual Pillar" bedding. **Sights:** None furnished; drilled and tapped for scope mounting. **Features:** Short left-hand bolt with right-hand ejection; free-floated barrel; uses Savage Model 110 rifle scope rings/bases. Introduced 1998. Made in U.S. by Savage Arms, Inc.
Price: Model 510F (blued barrel and action) **$425.00**
Price: Model 516FSS (stainless barrel and action) **$462.00**
Price: Model 516FSAK (stainless, adjustable muzzle brake) **$512.00**
Super Striker **$512.00**

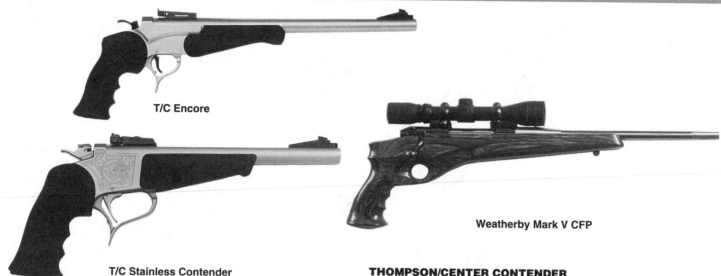

T/C Encore

T/C Stainless Contender

Weatherby Mark V CFP

Savage Sport Striker Bolt-Action Hunting Handgun

Similar to the Striker, but chambered in 22 LR and 22 WMR. Detachable, 10-shot magazine (5-shot magazine for 22 WMR). Overall length 19", weighs 4 lbs. Ambidextrous fiberglass/graphite composite rear grip. Drilled and tapped, scope mount installed. Introduced 2000. Made in U.S. by Savage Arms Inc.

Price: Model 501F (blue finish, 22LR) **$201.00**
Price: Model 502F (blue finish, 22 WMR) **$221.00**

THOMPSON/CENTER ENCORE PISTOL

Caliber: 22-250, 223, 260 Rem., 7mm-08, 243, 308, 270, 30-06, 44 Mag., 454 Casull, 444 Marlin single shot. **Barrel:** 12", 15", tapered round. **Weight:** NA. **Length:** 21" overall with 12" barrel. **Stocks:** American walnut with finger grooves, walnut forend. **Sights:** Blade on ramp front, adjustable rear, or none. **Features:** Interchangeable barrels; action opens by squeezing the trigger guard; drilled and tapped for scope mounting; blue finish. Announced 1996. Made in U.S. by Thompson/Center Arms.

Price: **$554.06**
Price: Extra 12" barrels **$240.68**
Price: Extra 15" barrels **$248.14**
Price: 45 Colt/410 barrel, 12" **$263.24**
Price: 45 Colt/410 barrel, 15" **$280.39**

Thompson/Center Stainless Encore Pistol

Similar to the blued Encore except made of stainless steel and available wtih 15" barrel in 223, 22-250 7mm-08, 308. Comes with black rubber grip and forend. Made in U.S. by Thompson/Center Arms.

Price: **$620.99**

Thompson/Center Stainless Super 14

Same as the standard Super 14 and Super 16 except they are made of stainless steel with blued sights. Both models have black Rynite forend and finger-groove, ambidextrous grip with a built-in rubber recoil cushion that has a sealed-in air pocket. Receiver has a different cougar etching. Available in 22 LR Match, .223 Rem., 30-30 Win., 35 Rem. (Super 14) 45 Colt/410. Introduced 1993.

Price: **$578.40**
Price: 45 Colt/410, 14" **$613.94**

Thompson/Center Contender Shooter's Package

Package contains a 14" barrel without iron sights (10" for the 22 LR Match); Weaver-style base and rings; 2.5x-7x Recoil Proof pistol scope; and a soft carrying case. Calibers 22 LR, 223, 7-30 Waters, 30-30. Frame and barrel are blued; grip and forend are black composite. Introduced 1998. Made in U.S. by Thompson/Center Arms.

Price **$735.00**

THOMPSON/CENTER CONTENDER

Caliber: 7mm TCU, 30-30 Win., 22 LR, 22 WMR, 22 Hornet, 223 Rem., 270 Rem., 7-30 Waters, 32-20 Win., 357 Mag., 357 Rem. Max., 44 Mag., 10mm Auto, 445 SuperMag., 45/410, single shot. **Barrel:** 10", bull barrel and vent. rib. **Weight:** 43 oz. (10" bbl.). **Length:** 13-1/4" (10" bbl.). **Stock:** T/C "Competitor Grip." Right or left hand. **Sights:** Under-cut blade ramp front, rear adjustable for windage and elevation. **Features:** Break-open action with automatic safety. Single-action only. Interchangeable bbls., both caliber (rim & centerfire), and length. Drilled and tapped for scope. Engraved frame. See T/C catalog for exact barrel/caliber availability.

Price: Blued (rimfire cals.) **$509.03**
Price: Blued (centerfire cals.) **$509.03**
Price: Extra bbls. **$229.02**
Price: 45/410, internal choke bbl. **$235.11**

Thompson/Center Stainless Contender

Same as the standard Contender except made of stainless steel with blued sights, black Rynite forend and ambidextrous finger-groove grip with a built-in rubber recoil cushion that has a sealed-in air pocket. Receiver has a different cougar etching. Available with 10" bull barrel in 22 LR, 22 LR Match, 22 Hornet, 223 Rem., 30-30 Win., 357 Mag., 44 Mag., 45 Colt/410. Introduced 1993.

Price: **$566.59**
Price: 45 Colt/410 . . . . **$590.44**
Price: With 22 LR match chamber **$578.40**

UBERTI ROLLING BLOCK TARGET PISTOL

Caliber: 22 LR, 22 WMR, 22 Hornet, 357 Mag., 45 Colt, single shot. **Barrel:** 9-7/8", half-round, half-octagon. **Weight:** 44 oz. **Length:** 14" overall. **Stock:** Walnut grip and forend. **Sights:** Blade front, fully adjustable rear. **Features:** Replica of the 1871 rolling block target pistol. Brass trigger guard, color case-hardened frame, blue barrel. Imported by Uberti U.S.A.

Price: **$410.00**

WEATHERBY MARK V CFP PISTOL

Caliber: 22-250, 243, 7mm-08, 308. **Barrel:** 15" fluted stainless. **Weight:** NA. **Length:** NA. **Stock:** Brown laminate with ambidextrous rear grip. **Sights:** None furnished; drilled and tapped for scope mounting. **Features:** Uses Mark V lightweight receiver of chrome-moly steel, matte blue finish. Introduced 1998. Made in U.S. From Weatherby.

Price: **$1,049.00**

WEATHERBY MARK V ACCUMARK CFP PISTOL

Caliber: 223, 22-250, 243, 7mm-08, 308; 3-shot magazine. **Barrel:** 15"; 1:12" twist (223). **Weight:** 5 lbs. **Length:** 26-1/2" overall. **Stock:** Kevlar-fiberglass composite. **Sights:** None; drilled and tapped for scope mounting. **Features:** Molded-in aluminum bedding plate; fluted stainless steel barrel; fully adjustable trigger. Introduced 2000. From Weatherby.

Price: . . . . **NA**

CENTERFIRE RIFLES — AUTOLOADERS

Both classic arms and recent designs in American-style repeaters for sport and field shooting.

Armalite M15A2

Armalite AR-10A4

Auto-Ordnance 1927 A-1 Thompson

Barrett Model 82A-1

AA ARMS AR9 SEMI-AUTOMATIC RIFLE
Caliber: 9mm Para., 10-shot magazine. **Barrel:** 16". **Weight:** 6 lbs. **Length:** 31" overall. **Stock:** Fixed **Sights:** Post front adjustable for elevation, open rear for windage. **Features:** Blue or electroless nickel finish. Made in U.S. by AA Arms, Inc.
Price: Blue $695.00

ARMALITE M15A2 CARBINE
Caliber: 223, 7-shot magazine. **Barrel:** 16" heavy chrome lined; 1:9" twist. **Weight:** 7 lbs. **Length:** 35-11/16" overall. **Stock:** Green or black composition. **Sights:** Standard A2. **Features:** Upper and lower receivers have push-type pivot pin; hard coat anodized; A2-style forward assist; M16A2-type raised fence around magazine release button. Made in U.S. by ArmaLite, Inc.
Price: Green $930.00
Price: Black $945.00

ARMALITE AR-10A4 SPECIAL PURPOSE RIFLE
Caliber: 308 Win., 10-shot magazine. **Barrel:** 20" chrome-lined, 1:12" twist. **Weight:** 9.6 lbs. **Length:** 41" overall **Stock:** Green or black composition. **Sights:** Detachable handle, front sight, or scope mount available; comes with international style flattop receiver with Picatinny rail. **Features:** Proprietary recoil check. Forged upper receiver with case deflector. Receivers are hard-coat anodized. Introduced 1995. Made in U.S. by ArmaLite, Inc.
Price: Green $1,378.00
Price: Black $1,393.00

AUTO-ORDNANCE 1927 A-1 THOMPSON
Caliber: 45 ACP. **Barrel:** 16-1/2". **Weight:** 13 lbs. **Length:** About 41" overall (Deluxe). **Stock:** Walnut stock and vertical forend. **Sights:** Blade front, open rear adjustable for windage. **Features:** Recreation of Thompson Model 1927. Semi-auto only. Deluxe model has finned barrel, adjustable rear sight and compensator; Standard model has plain barrel and military sight. From Auto-Ordnance Corp.
Price: Deluxe $950.00
Price: 1927A1C Lightweight model (9-1/2 lbs.) $950.00

Auto-Ordnance Thompson M1
Similar to the 1927 A-1 except is in the M-1 configuration with side cocking knob, horizontal forend, smooth unfinned barrel, sling swivels on butt and forend. Matte black finish. Introduced 1985.
Price: $950.00

Auto-Ordnance 1927A1 Commando
Similar to the 1927A1 except has Parkerized finish, black-finish wood butt, pistol grip, horizontal forend. Comes with black nylon sling. Introduced 1998. Made in U.S. by Auto-Ordnance Corp.
Price: $950.00

BARRETT MODEL 82A-1 SEMI-AUTOMATIC RIFLE
Caliber: 50 BMG, 10-shot detachable box magazine. **Barrel:** 29". **Weight:** 28.5 lbs. **Length:** 57" overall. **Stock:** Composition with energy-absorbing recoil pad. **Sights:** Scope optional. **Features:** Semi-automatic, recoil op-

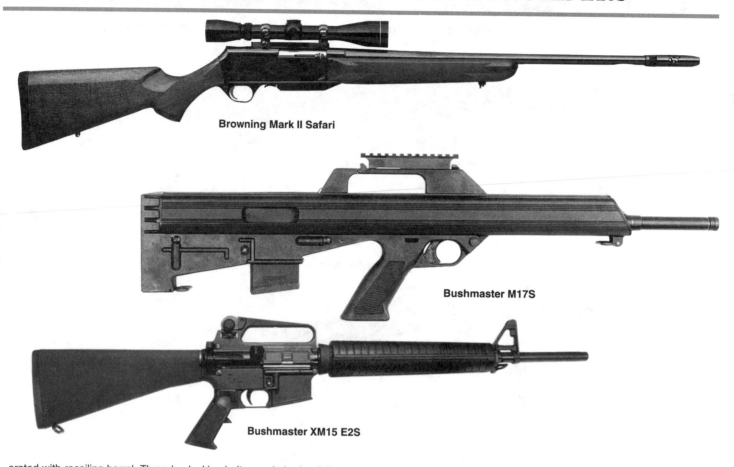

Browning Mark II Safari

Bushmaster M17S

Bushmaster XM15 E2S

erated with recoiling barrel. Three-lug locking bolt; muzzle brake. Adjustable bipod. Introduced 1985. Made in U.S. by Barrett Firearms.
Price: From **$7,200.00**

BROWNING BAR MARK II SAFARI SEMI-AUTO RIFLE

Caliber: 22-250, 243, 25-06, 270, 30-06, 308. **Barrel:** 22" round tapered. **Weight:** 7-3/8 lbs. **Length:** 43" overall. **Stock:** French walnut pistol grip stock and forend, hand checkered. **Sights:** Gold bead on hooded ramp front, click adjustable rear, or no sights. **Features:** Has new bolt release lever; removable trigger assembly with larger trigger guard; redesigned gas and buffer systems. Detachable 4-round box magazine. Scroll-engraved receiver is tapped for scope mounting. BOSS barrel vibration modulator and muzzle brake system available only on models without sights. Mark II Safari introduced 1993. Imported from Belgium by Browning.
Price: Safari, with sights **$760.00**
Price: Safari, no sights **$743.00**
Price: Safari, no sights, 270 Wea. Mag. **$797.00**
Price: Safari, no sights, BOSS **$803.00**

Browning BAR MARK II Lightweight Semi-Auto

Similar to the Mark II Safari except has lighter alloy receiver and 20" barrel. Available in 243, 308, 270, 30-06, 7mm Rem. Mag., 300 Win. Mag., 338 Win. Mag. Weighs 7 lbs., 2 oz.; overall length 41". Has dovetailed, gold bead front sight on hooded ramp, open rear click adjustable for windage and elevation. BOSS system optional. Introduced 1997. Imported from Belgium by Browning.
Price: 243, 308, 30-06 . . . . **$760.00**
Price: 7mm Rem. Mag., 300 Win. Mag., 338 Win. Mag **$814.00**
Price: As above with BOSS **$857.00**

Browning BAR Mark II Safari Magnum Rifle

Same as the standard caliber model, except weighs 8-3/8 lbs., 45" overall, 24" bbl., 3-round mag. Cals. 7mm Mag., 300 Win. Mag., 338 Win. Mag. BOSS barrel vibration modulator and muzzle brake system available only on models without sights. Introduced 1993.

Price: Safari, with sights **$814.00**
Price: Safari, no sights **$797.00**
Price: Safari, no sights, BOSS **$857.00**

BUSHMASTER M17S BULLPUP RIFLE

Caliber: 223, 10-shot magazine. **Barrel:** 21.5", chrome lined; 1:9" twist. **Weight:** 8.2 lbs. **Length:** 30" overall. **Stock:** Fiberglass-filled nylon. **Sights:** Designed for optics—carrying handle incorporates scope mount rail for Weaver-type rings; also includes 25-meter open iron sights. **Features:** Gas-operated, short-stroke piston system; ambidextrous magazine release. Introduced 1993. Made in U.S. by Bushmaster Firearms, Inc./Quality Parts Co.
Price: **$625.00**

BUSHMASTER SHORTY XM15 E2S CARBINE

Caliber: 223, 10-shot magazine. **Barrel:** 16", heavy; 1:9" twist. **Weight:** 7.2 lbs. **Length:** 34.75" overall. **Stock:** A2 type; fixed black composition. **Sights:** Fully adjustable M16A2 sight system. **Features:** Patterned after Colt M-16A2. Chrome-lined barrel with manganese phosphate finish. "Shorty" handguards. Has forged aluminum receivers with push-pin. Made in U.S. by Bushmaster Firearms Inc.
Price: **$780.00**

Bushmaster XM15 E2S Dissipator Carbine

Similar to the XM15 E2S Shorty carbine except has full-length "Dissipator" handguards. Weighs 7.6 lbs.; 34.75" overall; forged aluminum receivers with push-pin style takedown. Made in U.S. by Bushmaster Firearms, Inc.
Price **$790.00**

Bushmaster XM15 E25 AK Shorty Carbine

Similar to the XM15 E2S Shorty except has 14.5" barrel with an AK muzzle brake permanently attached giving 16" barrel length. Weighs 7.3 lbs. Introduced 1999. Made in U.S. by Bushmaster Firearms, Inc.
Price: **$800.00**

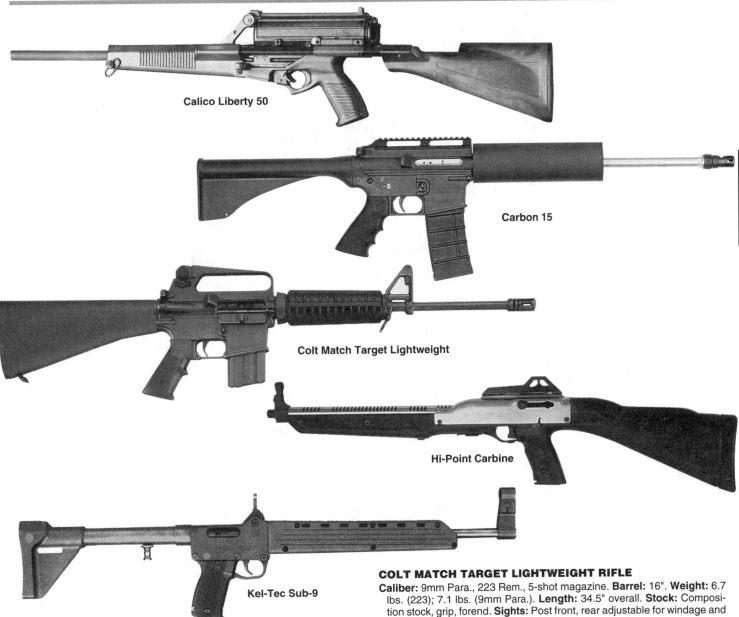

Calico Liberty 50

Carbon 15

Colt Match Target Lightweight

Hi-Point Carbine

Kel-Tec Sub-9

CALICO LIBERTY 50, 100 CARBINES

Caliber: 9mm Para. **Barrel:** 16.1". **Weight:** 7 lbs. **Length:** 34.5" overall. **Stock:** Glass-filled, impact resistant polymer. **Sights:** Adjustable front post, fixed notch and aperture flip rear. **Features:** Helical feed magazine; ambidextrous, rotating sear/striker block safety; static cocking handle; retarded blowback action; aluminum alloy receiver. Introduced 1995. Made in U.S. by Calico.

Price: Liberty 50 .... **$860.00**
Price: Liberty 100 .... **$925.00**

CARBON 15 (TYPE 97) AUTO RIFLE

Caliber: 223. **Barrel:** 16". **Weight:** 3.9 lbs. **Length:** 35" overall. **Stock:** Carbon fiber butt and forend, rubberized pistol grip. **Sights:** None furnished; optics base. **Features:** Carbon fiber upper and lower receivers; stainless steel match-grade barrel; hard-chromed bolt and carrier; quick-detachable compensator. Made in U.S. by Professional Ordnance Inc.

Price: **$1,700.00**
Price: Type 20 (light-profile stainless barrel, compensator
optional) **$1,550.00**

COLT MATCH TARGET LIGHTWEIGHT RIFLE

Caliber: 9mm Para., 223 Rem., 5-shot magazine. **Barrel:** 16". **Weight:** 6.7 lbs. (223); 7.1 lbs. (9mm Para.). **Length:** 34.5" overall. **Stock:** Composition stock, grip, forend. **Sights:** Post front, rear adjustable for windage and elevation. **Features:** 5-round detachable box magazine, flash suppressor, sling swivels. Forward bolt assist included. Introduced 1991.

Price: **$1,111.00**

HI-POINT 9MM CARBINE

Caliber: 9mm Para., 40 S&W, 10-shot magazine. **Barrel:** 16-1/2" (17-1/2" for 40 S&W). **Weight:** 4-1/2 lbs. **Length:** 31-1/2" overall. **Stock:** Black polymer. **Sights:** Protected post front, aperture rear. Integral scope mount. **Features:** Grip-mounted magazine release. Black or chrome finish. Sling swivels. Introduced 1996. Made in U.S. by MKS Supply, Inc.

Price: Black or chrome, 9mm **$199.00**
Price: 40 S&W **$225.00**

KEL-TEC SUB-9 AUTO RIFLE

Caliber: 9mm Para or 40 S&W. **Barrel:** 16.1". **Weight:** 4.6 lbs. **Length:** 30" overall (extended), 15.9" (closed). **Stock:** Metal tube; grooved rubber butt pad. **Sights:** Hooded post front, flip-up rear. Interchangeable grip assemblies allow use of most double-column high capacity pistol magazines. **Features:** Barrel folds back over the butt for transport and storage. Introduced 1997. Made in U.S. by Kel-Tec CNC Industries, Inc.

Price: 9mm **$700.00**
Price: 40 S&W **$725.00**

RIFLES

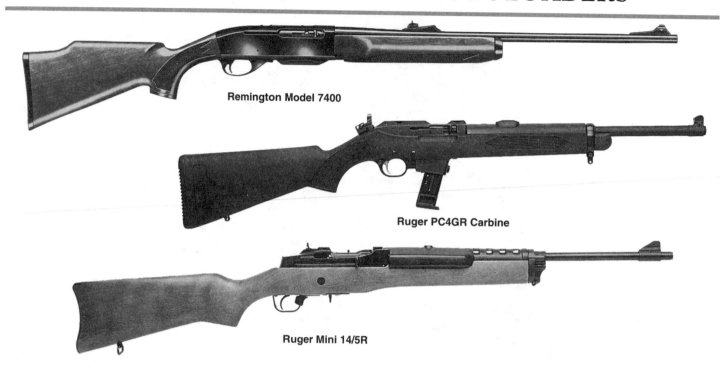

Remington Model 7400

Ruger PC4GR Carbine

Ruger Mini 14/5R

LR 300 SR LIGHT SPORT RIFLE

Caliber: 223. **Barrel:** 16-1/4"; 1:9" twist. **Weight:** 7.2 lbs. **Length:** 36" overall (extended stock), 26-1/4" (stock folded). **Stock:** Folding, tubular steel, with thumbhold-type grip. **Sights:** Trijicon post front, Trijicon rear. **Features:** Uses AR-15 type upper and lower receivers; flattop receiver with weaver base. Accepts all AR-15/M-16 magazines. Introduced 1996. Made in U.S. from Z-M Weapons.
Price: $2,550.00

OLYMPIC ARMS CAR-97 RIFLES

Caliber: 223, 7-shot; 9mm Para., 45 ACP, 40 S&W, 10mm, 10-shot. **Barrel:** 16". **Weight:** 7 lbs. **Length:** 34.75" overall. **Stock:** A2 stowaway grip, telescoping-look butt. **Sights:** Post front, fully adjustable aperature rear. **Features:** Based on AR-15 rifle. Post-ban version of the CAR-15. Made in U.S. by Olympic Arms, Inc.
Price: 223 .... $780.00
Price: 9mm Para., 45 ACP, 40 S&W, 10mm $840.00
Price: PCR Eliminator (223, full-length handguards) $803.00

OLYMPIC ARMS PCR-4 RIFLE

Caliber: 223, 10-shot magazine. **Barrel:** 20". **Weight:** 8 lbs., 5 oz. **Length:** 38.25" overall. **Stock:** A2 stowaway grip, trapdoor buttstock. **Sights:** Post front, A1 rear adjustable for windage. **Features:** Based on the AR-15 rifle. Barrel is button rifled with 1:9" twist. No bayonet lug. Introduced 1994. Made in U.S. by Olympic Arms, Inc.
Price: $792.00

OLYMPIC ARMS PCR-6 RIFLE

Caliber: 7.62x39mm (PCR-6), 10-shot magazine. **Barrel:** 16". **Weight:** 7 lbs. **Length:** 34" overall. **Stock:** A2 stowaway grip, trapdoor buttstock. **Sights:** Post front, A1 rear adjustable for windage. **Features:** Based on the CAR-15. No bayonet lug. Button-cut rifling. Introduced 1994. Made in U.S. by Olympic Arms, Inc.
Price: $845.00

REMINGTON MODEL 7400 AUTO RIFLE

Caliber: 243 Win., 270 Win., 280 Rem., 308 Win., 30-06, 4-shot magazine. **Barrel:** 22" round tapered. **Weight:** 7-1/2 lbs. **Length:** 42-5/8" overall. **Stock:** Walnut, deluxe cut checkered pistol grip and forend. Satin or high-gloss finish. **Sights:** Gold bead front sight on ramp; step rear sight with windage adjustable. **Features:** Redesigned and improved version of the Model 742. Positive cross-bolt safety. Receiver tapped for scope mount. Introduced 1981.

Price: About $612.00
Price: Carbine (18-1/2" bbl., 30-06 only) $612.00
Price: With black synthetic stock, matte black metal, rifle or carbine $509.00

ROCK RIVER ARMS STANDARD A2 RIFLE

Caliber: 45 ACP. **Barrel:** N/A. **Weight:** 8.2 lbs. **Length:** N/A. **Stock:** Thermoplastic. **Sights:** Standard AR-15 style sights. **Features:** Two-stage, national match trigger; optional muzzle brake. Made in U.S. From River Rock Arms.
Price: $925.00

RUGER PC4, PC9 CARBINES

Caliber: 9mm Para., 40 cal., 10-shot magazine. **Barrel:** 16.25". **Weight:** 6 lbs., 4 oz. **Length:** 34.75" overall. **Stock:** Black DuPont (Zytel) with checkered grip and forend. **Sights:** Blade front, open adjustable rear; integral Ruger scope mounts. **Features:** Delayed blowback action; manual push-button cross bolt safety and internal firing pin block safety automatic slide lock. Introduced 1997. Made in U.S. by Sturm, Ruger & Co.
Price: PC9, PC4, (9mm, 40 cal.) $575.00
Price: PC9G4, PC4GR (ghost ring sight) $598.00

RUGER MINI-14/5 AUTOLOADING RIFLE

Caliber: 223 Rem., 5-shot detachable box magazine. **Barrel:** 18-1/2". Rifling twist 1:9". **Weight:** 6.4 lbs. **Length:** 37-1/4" overall. **Stock:** American hardwood, steel reinforced. **Sights:** Ramp front, fully adjustable rear. **Features:** Fixed piston gas-operated, positive primary extraction. New buffer system, redesigned ejector system. Ruger S100RH scope rings included.
Price: Mini-14/5R, Ranch Rifle, blued, scope rings $649.00
Price: K-Mini-14/5R, Ranch Rifle, stainless, scope rings $710.00
Price: Mini-14/5, blued, no scope rings $606.00
Price: K-Mini-14/5, stainless, no scope rings $664.00
Price: K-Mini-14/5P, stainless, synthetic stock.............. $664.00
Price: K-Mini-14/5RP, Ranch Rifle, stainless, synthetic stock $710.00

Ruger Mini Thirty Rifle

Similar to the Mini-14 Ranch Rifle except modified to chamber the 7.62x39 Russian service round. Weight is about 6-7/8 lbs. Has 6-groove barrel with 1:10" twist, Ruger Integral Scope Mount bases and folding peep rear sight. Detachable 5-shot staggered box magazine. Blued finish. Introduced 1987.
Price: Blue, scope rings $649.00
Price: Stainless, scope rings $710.00

Springfield M1A

Springfield National Match M1A

Springfield Super Match with Camo M1A

RIFLES

SPRINGFIELD, INC. M1A RIFLE
Caliber: 7.62mm NATO (308), 5- or 10-shot box magazine. **Barrel:** 25-1/16" with flash suppressor, 22" without suppressor. **Weight:** 8-3/4 lbs. **Length:** 44-1/4" overall. **Stock:** American walnut with walnut-colored heat-resistant fiberglass handguard. Matching walnut handguard available. Also available with fiberglass stock. **Sights:** Military, square blade front, full click-adjustable aperture rear. **Features:** Commercial equivalent of the U.S. M-14 service rifle with no provision for automatic firing. From Springfield, Inc.
Price: M1A-A1, black fiberglass stock **$1,319.00**
Price: Standard M1A rifle, about. **$1,448.00**
Price: National Match, about **$1,995.00**
Price: Super Match (heavy premium barrel), about **$2,479.00**

STONER SR-15 M-5 RIFLE
Caliber: 223. **Barrel:** 20". **Weight:** 7.6 lbs. **Length:** 38" overall. **Stock:** Black synthetic. **Sights:** Post front, fully adjustable rear. **Features:** Modular weapon system. Black finish. Introduced 1998. Made in U.S. by Knight's Mfg.
Price: **$1,295.00**
Price: M-4 Carbine (16" barrel, 6.8 lbs) **$1,295.00**

STONER SR-25 CARBINE
Caliber: 7.62 NATO, 10-shot steel magazine. **Barrel:** 16" free-floating **Weight:** 7-3/4 lbs. **Length:** 35.75" overall. **Stock:** Black synthetic. **Sights:** Integral Weaver-style rail. Scope rings, iron sights optional. **Features:** Shortened, non-slip handguard; removable carrying handle. Matte black finish. Introduced 1995. Made in U.S. by Knight's Mfg. Co.
Price: **$2,995.00**

STONER SR-50 LONG RANGE PRECISION RIFLE
Caliber: 50 BMG, 10-shot magazine. **Barrel:** 35.5". **Weight:** 31.5 lbs. **Length:** 58.37" overall. **Stock:** Tubular steel. **Sights:** Scope mount. **Features:** Gas-operated semi-automatic action; two-stage target-type trigger; M-16-type safety lever; easily removable barrel. Introduced 1996. Made in U.S. by Knight's Mfg. Co.
Price: **$6,995.00**

Both classic arms and recent designs in American-style repeaters for sport and field shooting.

American Arms/Uberti 1873 Sporting

American Arms/Uberti 1866 Sporting

Browning BPR

Browning Lightning BLR

AMERICAN ARMS/UBERTI 1873 SPORTING RIFLE
Caliber: 44-40, 45 Colt. **Barrel:** 24-1/4", 30", octagonal. **Weight:** 8.1 lbs. **Length:** 43-1/4" overall. **Stock:** Walnut. **Sights:** Blade front adjustable for windage, open rear adjustable for elevation. **Features:** Color case-hardened frame, blued barrel, hammer, lever, buttplate, brass elevator. Imported from Italy by American Arms, Inc.
Price: 24-1/4" barrel $860.00
Price: 30" barrel $940.00

AMERICAN ARMS/UBERTI 1866 SPORTING RIFLE, CARBINE
Caliber: 22 LR, 22 WMR, 38 Spec., 44-40, 45 Colt. **Barrel:** 24-1/4", octagonal. **Weight:** 8.1 lbs. **Length:** 43-1/4" overall. **Stock:** Walnut. **Sights:** Blade front adjustable for windage, rear adjustable for elevation. **Features:** Frame, buttplate, forend cap of polished brass, balance charcoal blued. Imported by American Arms, Inc.
Price: $730.00
Price: Yellowboy Carbine (19" round bbl.) $710.00

AMERICAN ARMS/UBERTI 1860 HENRY RIFLE
Caliber: 44-40, 45 Colt. **Barrel:** 24-1/4", half-octagon. **Weight:** 9.2 lbs. **Length:** 43-3/4" overall. **Stock:** American walnut. **Sights:** Blade front, rear adjustable for elevation. **Features:** Frame, elevator, magazine follower, buttplate are brass, balance blue. Imported by American Arms, Inc.
Price: $940.00
Price: 1860 Henry White (polished steel finish) $990.00

AMERICAN ARMS/UBERTI 1860 HENRY TRAPPER CARBINE
Similar to the 1860 Henry Rifle except has 18-1/2" barrel, measures 37-3/4" overall, and weighs 8 lbs. Introduced 1999. Imported from Italy by American Arms.
Price: Brass frame, blued barrel......................... $940.00
Price: Henry Trapper White (brass frame, polished steel barrel) .. $990.00

BROWNING BPR PUMP RIFLE
Caliber: 243, 308 (short action); 270, 30-06, 7mm Rem. Mag., 300 Win. Mag., 4-shot magazine (3 for magnums). **Barrel:** 22"; 24" for magnum calibers. **Weight:** 7 lbs., 3 oz. **Length:** 43" overall (22" barrel). **Stock:** Select walnut with full pistol grip, high gloss finish. **Sights:** Gold bead on hooded ramp front, open click adjustable rear. **Features:** Slide-action mechanism cams forend down away from the barrel. Seven-lug rotary bolt; cross-bolt safety behind trigger; removable magazine; alloy receiver. Introduced 1997. Imported from Belgium by Browning.
Price: Standard calibers.................................. $718.00
Price: Magnum calibers $772.00

BROWNING LIGHTNING BLR LEVER-ACTION RIFLE
Caliber: 223, 22-250, 243, 7mm-08, 308 Win., 4-shot detachable magazine. **Barrel:** 20" round tapered. **Weight:** 6 lbs., 8 oz. **Length:** 39-1/2" overall. **Stock:** Walnut. Checkered grip and forend, high-gloss finish. **Sights:** Gold bead on ramp front; low profile square notch adjustable rear. **Features:** Wide, grooved trigger; half-cock hammer safety; fold-down hammer. Receiver tapped for scope mount. Recoil pad installed. Introduced 1996. Imported from Japan by Browning.
Price: $600.00

Browning Lightning BLR Long Action
Similar to the standard Lightning BLR except has long action to accept 30-06, 270, 7mm Rem. Mag. and 300 Win. Mag. Barrel lengths are 22" for 30-06 and 270, 24" for 7mm Rem. Mag. Has six-lug rotary bolt; bolt and receiver are full-length fluted. Fold-down hammer at half-cock. Weighs about 7 lbs., overall length 42-7/8" (22" barrel). Introduced 1996.
Price: $634.00

Cabela's Henry Replica

Cimarron 1866 Winchester Replica

Cabela's 1873 Winchester

Cimarron Long Range 30"

CIMARRON 1860 HENRY REPLICA
Caliber: 44 WCF, 13-shot magazine. **Barrel:** 24-1/4" (rifle), 22" (carbine). **Weight:** 9-1/2 lbs. **Length:** 43" overall (rifle). **Stock:** European walnut. **Sights:** Bead front, open adjustable rear. **Features:** Brass receiver and buttplate. Uses original Henry loading system. Faithful to the original rifle. Introduced 1991. Imported by Cimarron F.A. Co.
Price: **$1,029.00**

CIMARRON 1866 WINCHESTER REPLICAS
Caliber: 22 LR, 22 WMR, 38 Spec., 44 WCF. **Barrel:** 24-1/4" (rifle), 19" (carbine). **Weight:** 9 lbs. **Length:** 43" overall (rifle). **Stock:** European walnut. **Sights:** Bead front, open adjustable rear. **Features:** Solid brass receiver, buttplate, forend cap. Octagonal barrel. Faithful to the original Winchester '66 rifle. Introduced 1991. Imported by Cimarron F.A. Co.
Price: Rifle **$839.00**
Price: Carbine. **$829.00**

CABELA'S 1858 HENRY REPLICA
Caliber: 44-40, 45 Colt. **Barrel:** 24-1/4". **Weight:** 9.5 lbs. **Length:** 43" overall. **Stock:** European walnut. **Sights:** Bead front, open adjustable rear. **Features:** Brass receiver and buttplate. Uses original Henry loading system. Faithful to the original rifle. Introduced 1994. Imported by Cabela's.
Price: **$749.99**

CABELA'S 1866 WINCHESTER REPLICA
Caliber: 44-40, 45 Colt. **Barrel:** 24-1/4". **Weight:** 9 lbs. **Length:** 43" overall. **Stock:** European walnut. **Sights:** Bead front, open adjustable rear. **Features:** Solid brass receiver, buttplate, forend cap. Octagonal barrel. Faithful to the original Winchester '66 rifle. Introduced 1994. Imported by Cabela's.
Price: **$619.99**

CABELA'S 1873 WINCHESTER REPLICA
Caliber: 44-40, 45 Colt. **Barrel:** 24-1/4", 30". **Weight:** 8.5 lbs. **Length:** 43-1/4" overall. **Stock:** European walnut. **Sights:** Bead front, open adjustable rear; globe front, tang rear. **Features:** Color case-hardened steel receiver. Faithful to the original Model 1873 rifle. Introduced 1994. Imported by Cabela's.
Price: Sporting model, 30" barrel, 44-40, 45 Colt............ **$749.99**
Price: Sporting model, 24" or 25" barrel.................... **$729.99**

CIMARRON 1873 SHORT RIFLE
Caliber: 22 LR, 22 WMR, 357 Mag., 44-40, 45 Colt. **Barrel:** 20" tapered octagon. **Weight:** 7.5 lbs. **Length:** 39" overall. **Stock:** Walnut. **Sights:** Bead front, adjustable semi-buckhorn rear. **Features:** Has half "button" magazine. Original-type markings, including caliber, on barrel and elevator and "Kings" patent. From Cimarron F.A. Co.
Price: **$799.00**

CIMARRON 1873 LONG RANGE RIFLE
Caliber: 22 LR, 22 WMR, 357 Mag., 38-40, 44-40, 45 Colt. **Barrel:** 30", octagonal. **Weight:** 8-1/2 lbs. **Length:** 48" overall. **Stock:** Walnut. **Sights:** Blade front, semi-buckhorn ramp rear. Tang sight optional. **Features:** Color case-hardened frame; choice of modern blue-black or charcoal blue for other parts. Barrel marked "Kings Improvement." From Cimarron F.A. Co.
Price: **$999.00**

Dixie 1873

IAR 1873 Revolver Carbine

Marlin 1894S Lever-Action

Marlin 1894CS

Cimarron 1873 Sporting Rifle

Similar to the 1873 Long Range except has 24" barrel with half-magazine.
Price: **$949.00**
Price: 1873 Saddle Ring Carbine, 19" barrel **$949.00**

DIXIE ENGRAVED 1873 RIFLE

Caliber: 44-40, 11-shot magazine. **Barrel:** 20", round. **Weight:** 7-3/4 lbs. **Length:** 39" overall. **Stock:** Walnut. **Sights:** Blade front, adjustable rear. **Features:** Engraved and case-hardened frame. Duplicate of Winchester 1873. Made in Italy. From 21 Gun Works.
Price: **$1,295.00**
Price: Plain, blued carbine **$850.00**

E.M.F. 1860 HENRY RIFLE

Caliber: 44-40 or 44 rimfire. **Barrel:** 24.25". **Weight:** About 9 lbs. **Length:** About 43.75" overall. **Stock:** Oil-stained American walnut. **Sights:** Blade front, rear adjustable for elevation. **Features:** Reproduction of the original Henry rifle with brass frame and buttplate, rest blued. From E.M.F.
Price: Standard .... **$,850.00**

E.M.F. 1866 YELLOWBOY LEVER ACTIONS

Caliber: 38 Spec., 44-40. **Barrel:** 19" (carbine), 24" (rifle). **Weight:** 9 lbs. **Length:** 43" overall (rifle). **Stock:** European walnut. **Sights:** Bead front, open adjustable rear. **Features:** Solid brass frame, blued barrel, lever, hammer, buttplate. Imported from Italy by E.M.F.
Price: Rifle **$690.00**
Price: Carbine **$675.00**

E.M.F. HARTFORD MODEL 1892 LEVER-ACTION RIFLE

Caliber: 45 Colt. **Barrel:** 24", octagonal. **Weight:** 7-1/2 lbs. **Length:** 43" overall. **Stock:** European walnut. **Sights:** Blade front, open adjustable rear. **Features:** Color case-hardened frame, lever, trigger and hammer with blued barrel, or overall blue finish. Introduced 1998. Imported by E.M.F.
Price: Standard **$1,000.00**
Price: Deluxe **$1,085.00**
Price: Premier **$1,250.00**

E.M.F. MODEL 73 LEVER-ACTION RIFLE

Caliber: 357 Mag., 44-40, 45 Colt. **Barrel:** 24". **Weight:** 8 lbs. **Length:** 43-1/4" overall. **Stock:** European walnut. **Sights:** Bead front, rear adjustable for windage and elevation. **Features:** Color case-hardened frame (blue on carbine). Imported by E.M.F.
Price: Rifle **$865.00**
Price: Carbine, 19" barrel **$865.00**

IAR MODEL 1873 REVOLVER CARBINE

Caliber: 357 Mag., 45 Colt. **Barrel:** 18". **Weight:** 4 lbs., 8 oz. **Length:** 34" overall. **Stock:** One-piece walnut. **Sights:** Blade front, notch rear. **Features:** Color case-hardened frame, blue barrel, backstrap and trigger-guard. Introduced 1998. Imported from Italy by IAR, Inc.
Price: Standard **$490.00**

MARLIN MODEL 1894S LEVER-ACTION CARBINE

Caliber: 44 Spec./44 Mag., 10-shot tubular magazine. **Barrel:** 20" Ballard-type rifling. **Weight:** 6 lbs. **Length:** 37-1/2" overall. **Stock:** Checkered American black walnut, straight grip and forend. Mar-Shield® finish. Rubber rifle butt pad; swivel studs. **Sights:** Wide-Scan hooded ramp front, semi-buckhorn folding rear adjustable for windage and elevation. **Features:** Hammer-block safety. Receiver tapped for scope mount, offset hammer spur, solid top receiver sand blasted to prevent glare.
Price: **$510.00**

Marlin Model 1894CS Carbine

Similar to the standard Model 1894S except chambered for 38 Spec./357 Mag. with full-length 9-shot magazine, 18-1/2" barrel, hammer-block safety, hooded front sight. Introduced 1983.
Price: **$510.00**

MARLIN MODEL 1894 COWBOY, COWBOY II

Caliber: 357 Mag., 44 Mag., 44-40, 45 Colt, 10-shot magazine. **Barrel:** 24" tapered octagon, deep cut rifling. **Weight:** 7-1/2 lbs. **Length:** 41-1/2" overall. **Stock:** Straight grip American black walnut with cut checkering, hard rubber buttplate, Mar-Shield® finish. **Sights:** Marble carbine front, adjustable Marble semi-buckhorn rear. **Features:** Squared finger lever; straight grip stock; blued steel forend tip. Designed for Cowboy Shooting events. Introduced 1996. Made in U.S. by Marlin.
Price: Cowboy I, 45 Colt **$752.00**
Price: Cowboy II, 357 Mag., 44 Mag., 44-40 .... **$752.00**

RIFLES

Marlin 1894 Cowboy II

Marlin 444P Outfitter

Marlin 1895SS

Marlin 336CS

Marlin 336CB Cowboy

RIFLES

MARLIN MODEL 444SS LEVER-ACTION SPORTER

Caliber: 444 Marlin, 5-shot tubular magazine. **Barrel:** 22" deep cut Ballard rifling. **Weight:** 7-1/2 lbs. **Length:** 40-1/2" overall. **Stock:** Checkered American black walnut, capped pistol grip with white line spacers, rubber rifle butt pad. Mar-Shield® finish; swivel studs. **Sights:** Hooded ramp front, folding semi-buckhorn rear adjustable for windage and elevation. **Features:** Hammer-block safety. Receiver tapped for scope mount; offset hammer spur.
Price: **$582.00**

Marlin Model 444P Outfitter Lever-Action

Similar to the 444SS except has a ported 18-1/2" barrel with deep-cut Ballard-type rifling; weighs 6-3/4 lbs.; overall length 37". Available only in 444 Marlin. Introduced 1999. Made in U.S. by Marlin.
Price: **$595.00**

MARLIN MODEL 1895SS LEVER-ACTION RIFLE

Caliber: 45-70, 4-shot tubular magazine. **Barrel:** 22" round. **Weight:** 7-1/2 lbs. **Length:** 40-1/2" overall. **Stock:** Checkered American black walnut, full pistol grip. Mar-Shield® finish; rubber butt pad; quick detachable swivel studs. **Sights:** Bead front with Wide-Scan hood, semi-buckhorn folding rear adjustable for windage and elevation. **Features:** Hammer-block safety. Solid receiver tapped for scope mounts or receiver sights; offset hammer spur.
Price: **$582.00**

Marlin Model 1895G Guide Gun Lever Action

Similar to the Model 1895SS except has 18-1/2" ported barrel with deep-cut Ballard-type rifling; straight-grip walnut stock. Overall length is 37", weighs 6-3/4 lbs. Introduced 1998. Made in U.S. by Marlin.
Price: **$595.00**

MARLIN MODEL 336CS LEVER-ACTION CARBINE

Caliber: 30-30 or 35 Rem., 6-shot tubular magazine. **Barrel:** 20" Micro-Groove®. **Weight:** 7 lbs. **Length:** 38-1/2" overall. **Stock:** Checkered American black walnut, capped pistol grip with white line spacers. Mar-Shield® finish; rubber butt pad; swivel studs. **Sights:** Ramp front with Wide-Scan hood, semi-buckhorn folding rear adjustable for windage and elevation. **Features:** Hammer-block safety. Receiver tapped for scope mount, offset hammer spur; top of receiver sand blasted to prevent glare.
Price: **$493.00**

Marlin Model 336CB Cowboy

Similar to the Model 336CS except chambered for 30-30 and 38-55 Win., 24" tapered octagon barrel with deep-cut Ballard-type rifling; straight-grip walnut stock with hard rubber buttplate; blued steel forend cap; weighs 7-1/2 lbs.; 42-1/2" overall. Introduced 1999. Made in U.S. by Marlin.
Price: **$677.00**

Marlin Model 336AS Lever-Action Carbine

Same as the Marlin 336CS except has cut-checkered, walnut-finished Maine birch pistol grip stock with swivel studs, 30-30 only, 6-shot. Hammer-block safety. Adjustable rear sight, brass bead front.
Price: **$418.00**
Price: With 4x scope and mount **$462.00**

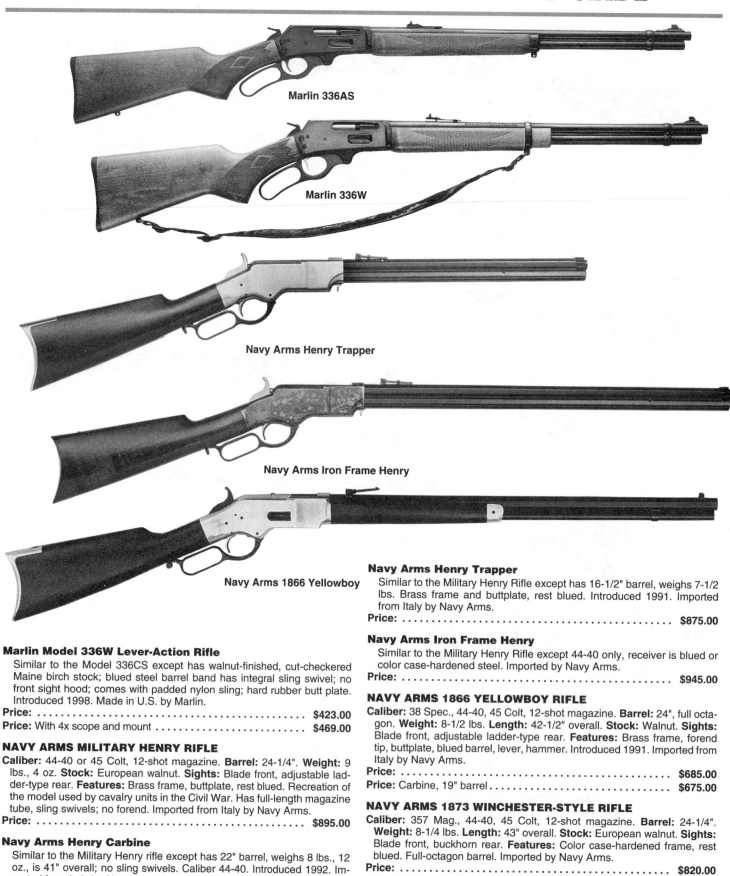

Marlin 336AS

Marlin 336W

Navy Arms Henry Trapper

Navy Arms Iron Frame Henry

Navy Arms 1866 Yellowboy

Marlin Model 336W Lever-Action Rifle

Similar to the Model 336CS except has walnut-finished, cut-checkered Maine birch stock; blued steel barrel band has integral sling swivel; no front sight hood; comes with padded nylon sling; hard rubber butt plate. Introduced 1998. Made in U.S. by Marlin.

Price: $423.00
Price: With 4x scope and mount $469.00

NAVY ARMS MILITARY HENRY RIFLE

Caliber: 44-40 or 45 Colt, 12-shot magazine. **Barrel:** 24-1/4". **Weight:** 9 lbs., 4 oz. **Stock:** European walnut. **Sights:** Blade front, adjustable ladder-type rear. **Features:** Brass frame, buttplate, rest blued. Recreation of the model used by cavalry units in the Civil War. Has full-length magazine tube, sling swivels; no forend. Imported from Italy by Navy Arms.

Price: $895.00

Navy Arms Henry Carbine

Similar to the Military Henry rifle except has 22" barrel, weighs 8 lbs., 12 oz., is 41" overall; no sling swivels. Caliber 44-40. Introduced 1992. Imported from Italy by Navy Arms.

Price: $875.00

Navy Arms Henry Trapper

Similar to the Military Henry Rifle except has 16-1/2" barrel, weighs 7-1/2 lbs. Brass frame and buttplate, rest blued. Introduced 1991. Imported from Italy by Navy Arms.

Price: $875.00

Navy Arms Iron Frame Henry

Similar to the Military Henry Rifle except 44-40 only, receiver is blued or color case-hardened steel. Imported by Navy Arms.

Price: $945.00

NAVY ARMS 1866 YELLOWBOY RIFLE

Caliber: 38 Spec., 44-40, 45 Colt, 12-shot magazine. **Barrel:** 24", full octagon. **Weight:** 8-1/2 lbs. **Length:** 42-1/2" overall. **Stock:** Walnut. **Sights:** Blade front, adjustable ladder-type rear. **Features:** Brass frame, forend tip, buttplate, blued barrel, lever, hammer. Introduced 1991. Imported from Italy by Navy Arms.

Price: $685.00
Price: Carbine, 19" barrel.................................. $675.00

NAVY ARMS 1873 WINCHESTER-STYLE RIFLE

Caliber: 357 Mag., 44-40, 45 Colt, 12-shot magazine. **Barrel:** 24-1/4". **Weight:** 8-1/4 lbs. **Length:** 43" overall. **Stock:** European walnut. **Sights:** Blade front, buckhorn rear. **Features:** Color case-hardened frame, rest blued. Full-octagon barrel. Imported by Navy Arms.

Price: $820.00
Price: Carbine, 19" barrel................................. $800.00
Price: Border model, 20" octagon barrel $820.00

Navy Arms 1873 Winchester Style

Navy Arms 1892 Rifle

Navy Arms 1892 Short Rifle

Remington 7600 Rifle

Ruger Model 96/44

RIFLES

Navy Arms 1873 Sporting Rifle

Similar to the 1873 Winchester-Style rifle except has checkered pistol grip stock, 30" octagonal barrel (24-1/4" available). Introduced 1992. Imported by Navy Arms.
Price: 30" barrel **$960.00**
Price: 24-1/4" barrel **$930.00**

NAVY ARMS 1892 RIFLE

Caliber: 357 Mag., 44-40, 45 Colt. **Barrel:** 24-1/4" octagonal. **Weight:** 7 lbs. **Length:** 42" overall. **Stock:** American walnut. **Sights:** Blade front, semi-buckhorn rear. **Features:** Replica of Winchester's early Model 1892 with octagonal barrel, forend cap and crescent buttplate. Blued or color case-hardened receiver. Introduced 1998. Imported by Navy Arms.
Price: **$495.00**

Navy Arms 1892 Carbine

Similar to the 1892 Rifle except has 20" round barrel, weighs 5-3/4 lbs., and is 37-1/2" overall. Introduced 1998. Imported by Navy Arms.
Price: **$465.00**

Navy Arms 1892 Short Rifle

Similar to the 1892 Rifle except has 20" octagonal barrel, weighs 6-1/4 lbs., and is 37-3/4" overall. Replica of the rare, special order 1892 Winchester nicknamed the "Texas Special." Blued or color case-hardened receiver and furniture. Introduced 1998. Imported by Navy Arms.
Price: **$495.00**
Price: (stainless steel, 20" octagon barrel) **$535.00**
Price: Stainless carbine (20"round barrel, saddle ring) **$470.00**

NAVY ARMS 1892 STAINLESS RIFLE

Caliber: 357 Mag., 44-40, 45 Colt. **Barrel:** 24-1/4" octagonal. **Weight:** 7 lbs. **Length:** 42". **Stock:** American walnut. **Sights:** Brass bead front, semi-buckhorn rear. **Features:** Designed for the Cowboy Action Shooter. Stainless steel barrel, receiver and furniture. Introduced 2000. Imported by Navy Arms.
Price: **$535.00**

REMINGTON MODEL 7600 PUMP ACTION

Caliber: 243, 270, 280, 30-06, 308. **Barrel:** 22" round tapered. **Weight:** 7-1/2 lbs. **Length:** 42-5/8" overall. **Stock:** Cut-checkered walnut pistol grip and forend, Monte Carlo with full cheekpiece. Satin or high-gloss finish. **Sights:** Gold bead front sight on matted ramp, open step adjustable sporting rear. **Features:** Redesigned and improved version of the Model 760. Detachable 4-shot clip. Cross-bolt safety. Receiver tapped for scope mount. Introduced 1981.
Price: **$576.00**
Price: Carbine (18-1/2" bbl., 30-06 only) **$576.00**
Price: With black synthetic stock, matte black metal, rifle or
carbine **$473.00**

RUGER MODEL 96/44 LEVER-ACTION RIFLE

Caliber: 44 Mag., 4-shot rotary magazine. **Barrel:** 18-1/2". **Weight:** 5-7/8 lbs. **Length:** 37-5/16" overall. **Stock:** American hardwood. **Sights:** Gold bead front, folding leaf rear. **Features:** Solid chrome-moly steel receiver. Manual cross-bolt safety, visible cocking indicator; short-throw lever action; integral scope mount; blued finish; color case-hardened lever. Introduced 1996. Made In U.S. by Sturm, Ruger & Co.
Price: 96/44M, 44 Mag **$470.00**

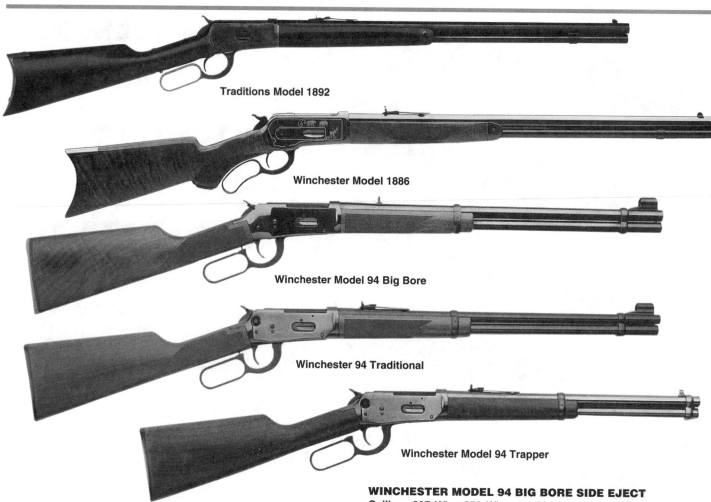

Traditions Model 1892

Winchester Model 1886

Winchester Model 94 Big Bore

Winchester 94 Traditional

Winchester Model 94 Trapper

TRADITIONS MODEL 1892 LEVER-ACTION RIFLE

Caliber: 357 Mag., 44-40, 45 Colt. **Barrel:** 24" octagonal. **Weight:** 7 lbs. **Length:** 42" overall. **Stock:** Walnut. **Sights:** Blade front, semi-buckhorn rear. **Features:** Replica of Winchester's Model 1892 with octagonal barrel, forend cap, crescent buttplate. Antique silver, brass frame, or color case-hardened receiver. Introduced 1999. Imported by Traditions.
Price: Color case-hardened $615.00
Price: Antique silver $660.00
Price: Brass $630.00

Traditions Model 1892 Carbine
Similar to the 1892 Rifle except has 20" round barrel, saddle ring, weighs 6 lbs., and is 38" overall. Introduced 1999. Imported by Traditions.
Price: $615.00

VEKTOR H5 SLIDE-ACTION RIFLE

Caliber: 223 Rem., 5-shot magazine. **Barrel:** 18", 22". **Weight:** 9 lbs., 15 oz. **Length:** 42-1/2" overall (22" barrel). **Stock:** Walnut thumbhole. **Sights:** Comes with 1" 4x32 scope with low-light reticle. **Features:** Rotating bolt mechanism. Matte black finish. Introduced 1999. Imported from South Africa by Vektor USA.
Price: $849.95

WINCHESTER MODEL 1886
EXTRA LIGHT LEVER-ACTION RIFLE

Caliber: 45-70, 8-shot magazine. **Barrel:** 26", full octagon. **Weight:** 9-1/4 lbs. **Length:** 45" overall. **Stock:** Smooth walnut. **Sights:** Bead front, ramp-adjustable buckhorn-style rear. **Features:** Recreation of the Model 1886. Polished blue finish; crescent metal butt plate; metal forend cap; pistol grip stock. Reintroduced 1998. From U.S. Repeating Arms Co., Inc.
Price: Grade I $1,156.00
Price: High Grade $1,447.00

WINCHESTER MODEL 94 BIG BORE SIDE EJECT

Caliber: 307 Win., 356 Win., 444 Marlin, 6-shot magazine. **Barrel:** 20". **Weight:** 7 lbs. **Length:** 38-5/8" overall. **Stock:** American walnut. Satin finish. **Sights:** Hooded ramp front, semi-buckhorn rear adjustable for windage and elevation. **Features:** All external metal parts have Winchester's deep blue finish. Rifling twist 1:12". Rubber recoil pad fitted to buttstock. Introduced 1983. From U.S. Repeating Arms Co., Inc.
Price: $446.00

Winchester Timber Carbine
Similar to the Model 94 Big Bore. Chambered only for 444 Marlin; 17-3/4" barrel is ported; half-pistol grip stock with butt pad; checkered grip and forend. Introduced 1999. Made in U.S. by U.S. Repeating Arms Co., Inc.
Price: $548.00

WINCHESTER MODEL 94 TRADITIONAL

Caliber: 30-30 Win., 44 Mag., 6-shot tubular magazine. **Barrel:** 20". **Weight:** 6-1/2 lbs. **Length:** 37-3/4" overall. **Stock:** Straight grip walnut stock and forend. **Sights:** Hooded blade front, semi-buckhorn rear. Drilled and tapped for scope mount. Post front sight on Trapper model. **Features:** Solid frame, forged steel receiver; side ejection, exposed rebounding hammer with automatic trigger-activated transfer bar. Introduced 1984.
Price: 30-30 . . . . $430.00
Price: 44 Mag. $452.00
Price: Checkered walnut $404.00
Price: No checkering, walnut, 30-30 only $398.00

Winchester Model 94 Trapper Side Eject
Same as the Model 94 Walnut Side Eject except has 16" barrel, 5-shot magazine in 30-30, 9-shot in 357 Mag., 44 Magnum/44 Special, 45 Colt. Has stainless steel claw extractor, saddle ring, hammer spur extension, walnut wood.
Price: 30-30 . . . . $337.00
Price: 44 Mag., 357 Mag., 45 Colt $355.00

RIFLES

Winchester Model 94 Trails End

Winchester Model 94 Black Shadow

Winchester Model 94 Legacy

Winchester Model 1895

Winchester Model 94 Trails End

Similar to the Model 94 Walnut except chambered only for 357 Mag., 44-40, 44 Mag., 45 Colt; 11-shot magazine. Available with standard lever loop. Introduced 1997. From U.S. Repeating Arms Co., Inc.
Price: With standard lever loop. **$434.00**

Winchester Model 94 Black Shadow Lever-Action Rifle

Similar to the Model 94 Walnut except has black synthetic stock with higher comb for easier scope use, and fuller forend. Non-glare finish; recoil pad. Available in 30-30 with 20" or 24" barrel, 44 Mag. or as Big Bore model in 444 Marlin. Introduced 1998. Made in U.S. by U.S. Repeating Arms Co., Inc.
Price: Black Shadow, 30-30, 44 Mag. . . . . **$381.00 to $394.00**
Price: Black Shadow Big Bore, 444 Marlin. **$395.00**

Winchester Model 94 Legacy

Similar to the Model 94 Side Eject except has half-pistol grip walnut stock, checkered grip and forend. Chambered for 30-30, 357 Mag., 44 Mag., 45 Colt; 24" barrel. Introduced 1995. Made in U.S. by U.S. Repeating Arms Co., Inc.
Price: With 24" barrel **$446.00**

Winchester Model 94 Ranger Compact

Similar to the Model 94 Ranger except has 16" barrel and 12-1/2" length of pull, rubber recoil pad, post front sight. Introduced 1998. Made in U.S. by U.S. Repeating Arms Co., Inc.
Price: 357 Mag. **$368.00**
Price: 30-30 . . . . **$347.00**

WINCHESTER MODEL 1895 LEVER-ACTION RIFLE

Caliber: 405 Win, 4-shot magazine. **Barrel:** 24", round. **Weight:** 8 lbs. **Length:** 42" overall. **Stock:** American walnut. **Sights:** Gold bead front, buckhorn rear adjustable for elevation. **Features:** Recreation of the original Model 1895. Polished blue finish with Nimschke-style scroll engraving on receiver. Scalloped receiver, two-piece cocking lever, Schnabel forend, straight-grip stock. Introduced 1995. From U.S. Repeating Arms Co., Inc.
Price: Grade I. **$1,050.00**
Price: High Grade **$1,540.00**

CENTERFIRE RIFLES — BOLT ACTION

Includes models for a wide variety of sporting and competitive purposes and uses.

Anschutz 1733D

Arnold Arms Alaskan

Arnold Arms Safari

ANSCHUTZ 1743D BOLT-ACTION RIFLE

Caliber: 222 Rem., 3-shot magazine. **Barrel:** 19.7". **Weight:** 6.4 lbs. **Length:** 39" overall. **Stock:** European walnut. **Sights:** Hooded blade front, folding leaf rear. **Features:** Receiver grooved for scope mounting; single stage trigger; claw extractor; sling safety; sling swivels. Imported from Germany by AcuSport Corp.
Price: $1,588.95

ANSCHUTZ 1740 MONTE CARLO RIFLE

Caliber: 22 Hornet, 5-shot clip; 222 Rem., 3-shot clip. **Barrel:** 24". **Weight:** 6-1/2 lbs. **Length:** 43.25" overall. **Stock:** Select European walnut. **Sights:** Hooded ramp front, folding leaf rear; drilled and tapped for scope mounting. **Features:** Uses match 54 action. Adjustable single stage trigger. Stock has roll-over Monte Carlo cheekpiece, slim forend with Schnabel tip, Wundhammer palm swell on grip, rosewood gripcap with white diamond insert. Skip-line checkering on grip and forend. Introduced 1997. Imported from Germany by AcuSport Corp.
Price: From $1,439.00
Price: Model 1730 Monte Carlo, as above except in 22 Hornet $1,439.00

Anschutz 1733D Rifle

Similar to the 1740 Monte Carlo except has full-length, walnut, Mannlicher-style stock with skip-line checkering, rosewood Schnabel tip, and is chambered for 22 Hornet. Weighs 6.4 lbs., overall length 39", barrel length 19.7". Imported from Germany by AcuSport Corp.
Price: $1,588.95

ARNOLD ARMS ALASKAN RIFLE

Caliber: 243 to 338 Magnum. **Barrel:** 22" to 26". **Weight:** NA. **Length:** NA. **Stock:** Synthetic; black, woodland or arctic camouflage. **Sights:** Optional; drilled and tapped for scope mounting. **Features:** Uses Apollo, Remington or Winchester action with controlled round feed or push feed; chrome-moly steel or stainless; one-piece bolt, handle, knob; cone head bolt and breech; three-position safety; fully adjustable trigger. Introduced 1996. Made in U.S. by Arnold Arms Co.
Price: From $2,695.00

Arnold Arms Alaskan Guide Rifle

Similar to the Alaskan rifle except chambered for 257 to 338 Magnum; choice of A-grade English walnut or synthetic stock; three-position safety; scope mount only. Introduced 1996. Made in U.S. by Arnold Arms Co.
Price: From $3,249.00

Arnold Arms Grand Alaskan Rifle

Similar to the Alaskan rifle except has AAA fancy select or exhibition-grade English walnut; barrel band swivel; comes with iron sights and scope mount; 24" to 26" barrel; 300 Magnum to 458 Win. Mag. Introduced 1996. Made in U.S. by Arnold Arms Co.
Price: From $7,570.00

Arnold Arms Alaskan Trophy Rifle

Similar to the Alaskan rifle except chambered for 300 Magnum to 458 Win. Mag.; 24" to 26" barrel; black synthetic or laminated stock; comes with barrel band on 375 H&H and larger; scope mount; iron sights. Introduced 1996. Made in U.S. by Arnold Arms Co.
Price: From $3,249.00

ARNOLD ARMS SAFARI RIFLE

Caliber: 243 to 458 Win. Mag. **Barrel:** 22" to 26". **Weight:** NA. **Length:** NA. **Stock:** Grade A and AA Fancy English walnut. **Sights:** Optional; drilled and tapped for scope mounting. **Features:** Uses Apollo, Remington or Winchester action with controlled or push round feed; one-piece bolt, handle, knob; cone head bolt and breech; three-position safety; fully adjustable trigger; chrome-moly steel in matte blue, polished, or bead blasted stainless. Introduced 1996. Made in U.S. by Arnold Arms Co.
Price: From $6,495.00

Arnold Arms African Trophy Rifle

Similar to the Safari rifle except has AAA Extra Fancy English walnut stock with wrap-around checkering; matte blue chrome-moly or polished or bead blasted stainless steel; scope mount standard or optional Express sights. Introduced 1996. Made in U.S. by Arnold Arms Co.
Price: Blued chrome-moly steel $6,921.00
Price: Stainless steel $6,971.00

Arnold Arms Grand African Rifle

Similar to the Safari rifle except has Exhibition Grade stock; polished blue chrome-moly steel or bead-blasted or Teflon-coated stainless; barrel band; scope mount, express sights; calibers 338 Magnum to 458 Win. Mag.; 24" to 26" barrel. Introduced 1996. Made in U.S. by Arnold Arms Co.
Price: Chrome-moly steel $8,172.00
Price: Stainless steel $8,022.00

Beretta Mato Deluxe

Barrett Model 95

Beretta Mato Synthetic

Blaser R93 Classic

BARRETT MODEL 95 BOLT-ACTION RIFLE

Caliber: 50 BMG, 5-shot magazine. **Barrel:** 29". **Weight:** 22 lbs. **Length:** 45" overall. **Stock:** Energy-absorbing recoil pad. **Sights:** Scope optional. **Features:** Bolt-action, bullpup design. Disassembles without tools; extendable bipod legs; match-grade barrel; high efficiency muzzle brake. Introduced 1995. Made in U.S. by Barrett Firearms Mfg., Inc.
Price: From **$4,950.00**

BERETTA MATO DELUXE BOLT-ACTION RIFLE

Caliber: 270, 280 Rem., 30-06, 7mm Rem. Mag., 300 Win. Mag., 338 Win. Mag., 375 H&H. **Barrel:** 23.6". **Weight:** 7.9 lbs. **Length:** 44.5" overall. **Stock:** XXX claro walnut with ebony forend tip, hand-rubbed oil finish. **Sights:** Bead on ramp front, open fully adjustable rear; drilled and tapped for scope mounting. **Features:** Mauser-style action with claw extractor; three-position safety; removable box magazine; 375 H&H has muzzle brake. Introduced 1998. From Beretta U.S.A.
Price: **$2,470.00**
Price: 375 H&H. **$2,795.00**

Beretta Mato Synthetic Bolt-Action Rifle

Similar to the Mato except has fiberglass/Kevlar/carbon fiber stock in classic American style with shadow line cheekpiece, aluminum bedding block and checkering. Introduced 1998. From Beretta U.S.A.
Price: **$1,660.00**
Price: 375 H&H. **$2,015.00**

BLASER R93 BOLT-ACTION RIFLE

Caliber: 22-250, 243, 6.5x55, 270, 7x57, 7mm-08, 308, 30-06, 257 Wea. Mag., 7mm Rem. Mag., 300 Win. Mag., 300 Wea. Mag., 338 Win Mag., 375 H&H, 416 Rem. Mag. **Barrel:** 22" (standard calibers), 26" (magnum). **Weight:** 7 lbs. **Length:** 40" overall (22" barrel). **Stock:** Two-piece European walnut. **Sights:** None furnished; drilled and tapped for scope mounting. **Features:** Straight pull-back bolt action with thumb-activated safety slide/cocking mechanism; interchangeable barrels and bolt heads. Introduced 1994. Imported from Germany by SIGARMS.
Price: R93 Classic **$3,680.00**
Price: R93 LX **$1,895.00**
Price: R93 Synthetic (black synthetic stock) **$1,595.00**
Price: R93 Safari Synthetic (416 Rem. Mag. only) **$1,855.00**
Price: R93 Grand Lux. **$4,915.00**
Price: R93 Attaché **$5,390.00**

BRNO 98 BOLT-ACTION RIFLE

Caliber: 7x64, 243, 270, 308, 30-06, 300 Win. Mag., 9.3x62. **Barrrel:** 23.6". **Weight:** 7.2 lbs. **Length:** 40.9" overall. **Stock:** European walnut. **Sights:** Blade on ramp front, open adjustable rear. **Features:** Uses Mauser 98-type action; polished blue. Announced 1998. Imported from the Czech Republic by Euro-Imports.
Price: Standard calibers **$507.00**
Price: Magnum calibers **$547.00**
Price: With set trigger, standard calibers **$615.00**
Price: As above, magnum calibers. **$655.00**
Price: With full stock, set trigger, standard calibers **$703.00**
Price: As above, magnum calibers. **$743.00**

Browning A-Bolt II Medallion

Browning A-Bolt II Eclipse M-1000

Browning A-Bolt II Micro

BROWNING ACERA STRAIGHT-PULL RIFLE

Caliber: 30-06, 300 Win. Mag. **Barrel:** 22"; 24" for magnums. **Weight:** 6 lbs., 9 oz. **Length:** 41-1/4" overall. **Stock:** American walnut with high gloss finish. **Sights:** Blade on ramp front, open adjustable rear. **Features:** Straight-pull action; detachable box magazine; Teflon coated breechblock; drilled and tapped for scope mounting. Introduced 1999. Imported by Browning.
Price: 30-06, no sights $845.00
Price: 300 Win. Mag., no sights $877.00
Price: 30-06 with sights $869.00
Price: 300 Win. Mag., with sights $901.00
Price: 30-06, with BOSS................................. $901.00
Price: 300 Win. Mag., with BOSS........................ $933.00

BROWNING A-BOLT II RIFLE

Caliber: 25-06, 270, 30-06, 260 Rem., 280, 7mm Rem. Mag., 300 Win. Mag., 338 Win. Mag., 375 H&H Mag. **Barrel:** 22" medium sporter weight with recessed muzzle; 26" on mag. cals. **Weight:** 6-1/2 to 7-1/2 lbs. **Length:** 44-3/4" overall (magnum and standard); 41-3/4" (short action). **Stock:** Classic style American walnut; recoil pad standard on magnum calibers. **Features:** Short-throw (60") fluted bolt, three locking lugs, plunger-type ejector; adjustable trigger is grooved and gold-plated. Hinged floorplate, detachable box magazine (4 rounds std. cals., 3 for magnums). Slide tang safety. Medallion has glossy stock finish, rosewood grip and forend caps, high polish blue. BOSS barrel vibration modulator and muzzle brake system not available in 375 H&H. Introduced 1985. Imported from Japan by Browning.
Price: Medallion, no sights $662.00
Price: Hunter, no sights $557.00
Price: Medallion, 375 H&H Mag., no sights $767.00
Price: For BOSS add $60.00

Browning A-Bolt II Short Action

Similar to the standard A-Bolt except has short action for 223, 22-250, 243, 257 Roberts, 260 Rem., 7mm-08, 284 Win., 308 chamberings. Available in Hunter or Medallion grades. Weighs 6-1/2 lbs. Other specs essentially the same. BOSS barrel vibration modulator and muzzle brake system optional. Introduced 1985.
Price: Medallion, no sights $662.00
Price: Hunter, no sights $557.00
Price: Composite stalker, no sights $580.00
Price: For BOSS, add................................... $60.00

Browning A-Bolt II Medallion Left-Hand

Same as the Medallion model A-Bolt except has left-hand action and is available in 25-06, 270, 280, 30-06, 7mm Rem. Mag., 300 Win. Mag., 338 Win. Mag., 375 H&H. Introduced 1987.

Price: $688.00
Price: With BOSS...................................... $748.00

Browning A-Bolt II White Gold Medallion

Similar to the standard A-Bolt except has select walnut stock with brass spacers between rubber recoil pad and between the rosewood gripcap and forend tip; gold-filled barrel inscription; palm-swell pistol grip, Monte Carlo comb, 22 lpi checkering with double borders; engraved receiver flats. In 270, 30-06, 7mm Rem. Mag. only. Introduced 1988.
Price: $949.00
Price: For BOSS, add................................. $60.00

Browning A-Bolt II Custom Trophy Rifle

Similar to the A-Bolt Medallion except has select American walnut stock with recessed swivel studs, octagon barrel, skeleton pistol gripcap, gold highlights, shadowline cheekpiece. Calibers 270, 30-06, 7mm Rem. Mag., 300 Win. Mag. Introduced 1998. Imported from Japan by Browning.
Price: $1,360.00

Browning A-Bolt II Eclipse

Similar to the A-Bolt II except has gray/black laminated, thumbhole stock, BOSS barrel vibration modulator and muzzle brake. Available in long and short action with standard weight barrel, or short-action Varmint with heavy barrel. Introduced 1996. Imported from Japan by Browning.
Price: Standard barrel, Hunter, with BOSS $941.00
Price: Varmint with BOSS $969.00

Browning A-Bolt II Eclipse M-1000

Similar to the A-Bolt II Eclipse except has long action and heavy target barrel. Chambered only for 300 Win. Mag. Adjustable trigger, bench-style forend, 3-shot magazine; laminated thumbhold stock; BOSS system standard. Introduced 1997. Imported for Japan by Browning.
Price: $969.00

Browning A-Bolt II Varmint Rifle

Same as the A-Bolt II Hunter except has heavy varmint/target barrel, laminated wood stock with special dimensions, flat forend and palm swell grip. Chambered only for 223, 22-250, 308. Comes with BOSS barrel vibration modulator and muzzle brake system. Introduced 1994.
Price: With BOSS, gloss or matte finish.................... $853.00

Browning A-Bolt II Micro Hunter

Similar to the A-Bolt II Hunter except has 13-5/16" length of pull, 20" barrel, and comes in 260 Rem., 243, 308, 7mm-08, 22-250, 22 Hornet. Weighs 6 lbs., 1 oz. Introduced 1999. Imported by Browning.
Price: $557.00

Browning A-Bolt II Classic Series

Similar to the A-Bolt II Hunter except has low-luster bluing and walnut stock with Monte Carlo comb, pistol grip palm swell, double-border checkering. Available in 270, 30-06, 7mm Rem. Mag., 300 Win. Mag. Introduced 1999. Imported by Browning.
Price: $633.00

RIFLES

Charles Daly Superior

CZ 527

Browning A-Bolt II Stainless Stalker

Similar to the Hunter model A-Bolt except receiver and barrel are made of stainless steel; the rest of the exposed metal surfaces are finished with a durable matte silver-gray. Graphite-fiberglass composite textured stock. No sights are furnished. Available in 223, 22-250, 243, 308, 7mm-08, 270, 30-06, 7mm Rem. Mag., 375 H&H. Introduced 1987.

Price: **$737.00**
Price: With BOSS **$797.00**
Price: Left-hand, no sights **$760.00**
Price: With BOSS **$820.00**
Price: 375 H&H, with sights **$899.00**
Price: 375 H&H, left-hand, no sights **$865.00**
Price: Carbon-fiber barrel, 22-250, 300 Win. Mag. .... **NA**

Browning A-Bolt II Composite Stalker

Similar to the A-Bolt II Hunter except has black graphite-fiberglass stock with textured finish. Matte blue finish on all exposed metal surfaces. Available in 223, 22-250, 243, 7mm-08, 308, 30-06, 270, 280, 25-06, 7mm Rem. Mag., 300 Win. Mag., 338 Win. Mag. BOSS barrel vibration modulator and muzzle brake system offered in all calibers. Introduced 1994.

Price: No sights **$580.00**
Price: No sights, BOSS **$640.00**

CHARLES DALY SUPERIOR BOLT-ACTION RIFLE

Caliber: 22 Hornet, 5-shot magazine. **Barrel:** 22.6". **Weight:** 6.6 lbs. **Length:** 41.25" overall. **Stock:** Walnut-finished hardwood with Monte Carlo comb and cheekpiece. **Sights:** Ramped blade front, fully adjustable open rear. **Features:** Receiver dovetailed for tip-off scope mount. Introduced 1996. Imported by K.B.I., Inc.

Price: **$364.95**

Charles Daly Empire Grade Rifle

Similar to the Superior except has oil-finished American walnut stock with 18 lpi hand checkering; black hardwood gripcap and forend tip; highly polished barreled action; jewelled bolt; recoil pad; swivel studs. Imported by K.B.I., Inc.

Price: **$469.95**

COLT LIGHT RIFLE BOLT ACTION

Caliber: 243, 7x57, 7mm-08, 308 (short action); 25-06, 270, 280, 7mm Rem., Mag., 30-06, 300 Win. Mag. **Barrel:** 24" **Weight:** 5.4 to 6 lbs. **Length:** NA. **Stock:** Black synthetic. **Sights:** None furnished; low, medium, high scope mounts. **Features:** Matte black finish; three-position safety. Introduced 1999. Made in U.S. From Colt's Mfg., Inc.

Price: **$779.00**

COOPER MODEL 22 BOLT-ACTION RIFLE

Caliber: 22 BR, 22-250 Rem., 22-250 Ackley Imp., 243, 25-06, 25-06 Ackley Imp., 220 Swift, 257 Roberts, 257 Roberts Ackley Imp., 6mm Rem., 6mm PPC, 6mm BR, 7mm-08, single shot. **Barrel:** 24" stainless match grade. **Weight:** 7-3/4 to 8 lbs. **Stock:** AA Claro walnut, 20 lpi checkering.

Sights: None furnished. **Features:** Uses three front locking lug system. Fully adjustable trigger. Many options available. Made in U.S. by Cooper Firearms.

Price: Classic **$1,295.00**
Price: Varminter **$1,199.00**
Price: Varmint Extreme **$1,895.00**
Price: Custom Classic **$2,195.00**
Price: Western Classic **$2,495.00**

COOPER MODEL 21, 38 BOLT-ACTION RIFLES

Caliber: 17 Rem., 17 Mach IV, 17 Javelina, 19-223 Calhoon, 20 VarTag, 22 PPC, Model 21, 6mm PPC, 221 Fireball, 222 Rem., 222 Rem. Mag., 223 Rem., 223 Ackley Imp., 6x45, 6x47, single shot; Model 38—17 Squirrel, 17 HeBee, 17 Ackley Hornet, 22 Hornet, 22 K Hornet, 218 Mashburn Bee, 218 Bee, 22 Squirrel, single shot. **Barrel:** 24" stainless match grade. **Weight:** 6-1/2 to 7-1/4 lbs. **Stock:** AA Claro walnut; 20 l.p.i. checkering. **Sights:** None furnished. **Features:** Uses three front locking lug system. Fully adjustable trigger. Many options available. Contact maker for details. Made in U.S. by Cooper Firearms.

Price: Classic **$1,050.00**
Price: Varminter **$995.00**
Price: Varmint Extreme **$1,795.00**
Price: Custom Classic **$1,995.00**
Price: Western Classic **$2,295.00**

COOPER ARMS MODEL 22 PRO VARMINT EXTREME

Caliber: 22-250, 220 Swift, 243, 25-06, 6mm PPC, 308, single shot. **Barrel:** 26"; stainless steel match grade, straight taper; free-floated. **Weight:** NA. **Length:** NA. **Stock:** AAA Claro walnut, oil finish, 22 lpi wrap-around borderless ribbon checkering, beaded cheekpiece, steel gripcap, flared varminter forend, Pachmayr pad. **Sights:** None furnished; drilled and tapped for scope mounting. **Features:** Uses a three front locking lug system. Available with sterling silver inlaid medallion, skeleton gripcap, and French walnut. Introduced 1995. Made in U.S. by Cooper Arms.

Price: **$1,795.00**
Price: Benchrest model with Jewell trigger. **$2,195.00**
Price: Black Jack model (McMillan synthetic stock) **$1,795.00**

CZ 527 LUX BOLT-ACTION RIFLE

Caliber: 22 Hornet, 222 Rem., 223 Rem., detachable 5-shot magazine. **Barrel:** 23-1/2"; standard or heavy barrel. **Weight:** 6 lbs., 1 oz. **Length:** 42-1/2" overall. **Stock:** European walnut with Monte Carlo. **Sights:** Hooded front, open adjustable rear. **Features:** Improved mini-Mauser action with non-rotating claw extractor; single set trigger; grooved receiver. Imported from the Czech Republic by CZ-USA.

Price: **$540.00**
Price: Model FS, full-length stock, cheekpiece. **$607.00**

CZ 527 American Classic Bolt-Action Rifle

Similar to the CZ 527 Lux except has classic-style stock with 18 l.p.i. checkering; free-floating barrel; recessed target crown on barrel. No sights furnished. Introduced 1999. Imported from the Czech Republic by CZ-USA.

Price: 22 Hornet, 222 Rem., 223 Rem. **$540.00**

CZ 550 Lux

CZ 550
American Classic

CZ 550
Magnum

Dakota 76
Classic

CZ 550 LUX BOLT-ACTION RIFLE

Caliber: 22-250, 243, 6.5x55, 7x57, 7x64, 308 Win., 9.3x62, 270 Win., 30-06. **Barrel:** 20.47". **Weight:** 7.5 lbs. **Length:** 44.68" overall. **Stock:** Turkish walnut in Bavarian style or FS (Mannlicher). **Sights:** Hooded front, adjustable rear. **Features:** Improved Mauser-style action with claw extractor, fixed ejector, square bridge dovetailed receiver; single set trigger. Imported from the Czech Republic by CZ-USA.

Price: Lux . . . . $561.00 to $609.00
Price: FS (full stock) $645.00

CZ 550 American Classic Bolt-Action Rifle

Similar to the CZ 550 Lux except has American classic-style stock with 18 l.p.i. checkering; free-floating barrel; recessed target crown. Has 25.6" barrel; weighs 7.48 lbs. No sights furnished. Introduced 1999. Imported from the Czech Republic by CZ-USA.

Price: . . . . $576.00 to $609.00

CZ 550 Magnum Bolt-Action Rifle

Similar to the CZ 550 Lux except has long action for 300 Win. Mag., 375 H&H, 416 Rigby, 458 Win. Mag. Overall length is 46.45"; barrel length 25"; weighs 9.24 lbs. Comes with hooded front sight, express rear with one standing, two folding leaves. Imported from the Czech Republic by CZ-USA.

Price: 300 Win. Mag. $717.00
Price: 375 H&H. $756.00
Price: 416 Rigby $796.00
Price: 458 Win. Mag. $744.00

DAKOTA 76 TRAVELER TAKEDOWN RIFLE

Caliber: 257 Roberts, 25-06, 7x57, 270, 280, 30-06, 338-06, 35 Whelen (standard length); 7mm Rem. Mag., 300 Win. Mag., 338 Win. Mag., 416 Taylor, 458 Win. Mag. (short magnums); 7mm, 300, 330, 375 Dakota Magnums. **Barrel:** 23". **Weight:** 7-1/2 lbs. **Length:** 43-1/2" overall. **Stock:** Medium fancy-grade walnut in classic style. Checkered grip and forend; solid butt pad. **Sights:** None furnished; drilled and tapped for scope mounts. **Features:** Threadless disassembly—no threads to wear or

stretch, no interrupted cuts, and headspace remains constant. Uses modified Model 76 design with many features of the Model 70 Winchester. Left-hand model also available. Introduced 1989. Made in U.S. by Dakota Arms, Inc.

Price: Classic $4,295.00
Price: Safari $5,295.00
Price: Extra barrels. $1,650.00 to $1,950.00

DAKOTA 76 CLASSIC BOLT-ACTION RIFLE

Caliber: 257 Roberts, 270, 280, 30-06, 7mm Rem. Mag., 338 Win. Mag., 300 Win. Mag., 375 H&H, 458 Win. Mag. **Barrel:** 23". **Weight:** 7-1/2 lbs. **Length:** 43-1/2" overall. **Stock:** Medium fancy grade walnut in classic style. Checkered pistol grip and forend; solid butt pad. **Sights:** None furnished; drilled and tapped for scope mounts. **Features:** Has many features of the original Model 70 Winchester. One-piece rail trigger guard assembly; steel gripcap. Model 70-style trigger. Many options available. Left-hand rifle available at same price. Introduced 1988. From Dakota Arms, Inc.

Price: $3,495.00

Dakota 76 Classic Rifles

A scaled-down version of the standard Model 76. Standard chamberings are 22-250, 243, 6mm Rem., 250-3000, 7mm-08, 308, others on special order. Short Classic Grade has 21" barrel; Alpine Grade is lighter (6-1/2 lbs.), has a blind magazine and slimmer stock. Introduced 1989.

Price: Short Classic $3,195.00

DAKOTA 76 SAFARI BOLT-ACTION RIFLE

Caliber: 270 Win., 7x57, 280, 30-06, 7mm Dakota, 7mm Rem. Mag., 300 Dakota, 300 Win. Mag., 330 Dakota, 338 Win. Mag., 375 Dakota, 458 Win. Mag., 300 H&H, 375 H&H, 416 Rem. **Barrel:** 23". **Weight:** 8-1/2 lbs. **Length:** 43-1/2" overall. **Stock:** XXX fancy walnut with ebony forend tip; point-pattern with wrap-around forend checkering. **Sights:** Ramp front, standing leaf rear. **Features:** Has many features of the original Model 70 Winchester. Barrel band front swivel, inletted rear. Cheekpiece with shadow line. Steel gripcap. Introduced 1988. From Dakota Arms, Inc.

Price: Wood stock $4,495.00

Dakota 76 Safari

Dakota Longbow

Dakota 97 Lightweight Hunter

Dakota Hunter

Dakota 416 Rigby African

Similar to the 76 Safari except chambered for 404 Jeffery, 416 Rigby, 416 Dakota, 450 Dakota, 4-round magazine, select wood, two stock cross-bolts. Has 24" barrel, weight of 9-10 lbs. Ramp front sight, standing leaf rear. Introduced 1989.

Price: **$4,995.00**

DAKOTA LONGBOW TACTICAL E.R. RIFLE

Caliber: 300 Dakota Magnum, 330 Dakota Magnum, 338 Lapua Magnum. **Barrel:** 28", .950" at muzzle **Weight:** 13.7 lbs. **Length:** 50" to 52" overall. **Stock:** Ambidextrous McMillan A-2 fiberglass, black or olive green color; adjustable cheekpiece and buttplate. **Sights:** None furnished. Comes with Picatinny one-piece optical rail. **Features:** Uses the Dakota 76 action with controlled-round feed; three-position firing pin block safety, claw extractor; Model 70-style trigger. Comes with bipod, case tool kit. Introduced 1997. Made in U.S. by Dakota Arms, Inc.

Price: **$4,250.00**

DAKOTA 97 VARMINT HUNTER

Caliber: 17 Rem., 222 Rem., 223 Rem., 220 Swift, 22-250, 22 BR, 22 PPC, 6mm BR. **Barrel:** 24". **Weight:** 8 lbs. **Length:** NA. **Stock:** X walnut; 13-5/8" length of pull. **Sights:** Optional. **Features:** Round short action; solid-bottom single shot; chrome-moly #4 barrel; adjustable trigger. Introduced 1998. Made in U.S. by Dakota Arms.

Price: **$1,795.00**

DAKOTA 97 LIGHTWEIGHT HUNTER

Caliber: 22-250 to 308. **Barrel:** 22"-24". **Weight:** 6.1-6.5 lbs. **Length:** 43" overall. **Stock:** Fiberglass. **Sights:** Optional. **Features:** Matte blue finish, black stock. Right-hand action only. Introduced 1998. Made in U.S. by Dakota Arms, Inc.

Price: **$1,795.00**

DAKOTA LONG RANGE HUNTER RIFLE

Caliber: 25-06, 257 Roberts, 270 Win., 280 Rem., 7mm Rem. Mag., 7mm Dakota Mag., 30-06, 300 Win. Mag., 300 Dakota Mag., 338 Win. Mag., 330 Dakota Mag., 375 H&H Mag., 375 Dakota Mag. **Barrel:** 24", 26", match-quality; free-floating. **Weight:** 7.7 lbs. **Length:** 45" to 47" overall. **Stock:** H-S Precision black synthetic, with one-piece bedding block system. **Sights:** None furnished. Drilled and tapped for scope mounting. **Features:** Cylindrical machined receiver controlled round feed; Mauser-style extractor; three-position striker blocking safety; fully adjustable match trigger. Right-hand action only. Introduced 1997. Made in U.S. by Dakota Arms, Inc.

Price: **$1,795.00**

HARRIS GUNWORKS SIGNATURE CLASSIC SPORTER

Caliber: 22-250, 243, 6mm Rem., 7mm-08, 284, 308 (short action); 25-06, 270, 280 Rem., 30-06, 7mm Rem. Mag., 300 Win. Mag., 300 Wea. (long action); 338 Win. Mag., 340 Wea., 375 H&H (magnum action). **Barrel:** 22", 24", 26". **Weight:** 7 lbs. (short action). **Stock:** Fiberglass in green, beige, brown or black. Recoil pad and 1" swivels installed. Length of pull up to 14-1/4". **Sights:** None furnished. Comes with 1" rings and bases. **Features:** Uses right- or left-hand action with matte black finish. Trigger pull set at 3 lbs. Four-round magazine for standard calibers; three for magnums. Aluminum floorplate. Wood stock optional. Introduced 1987. From Harris Gunworks, Inc.

Price: **$2,700.00**

RIFLES

Harris Gunworks Alaskan

Harris Gunworks Signature Titanium Mountain

Harris Gunworks Signature Super Varminter

Harris Gunworks Talon Safari

Harris Gunworks Signature Classic Stainless Sporter

Similar to the Signature Classic Sporter except action is made of stainless steel. Same calibers, in addition to 416 Rem. Mag. Comes with fiberglass stock, right- or left-hand action in natural stainless, glass bead or black chrome sulfide finishes. Introduced 1990. From Harris Gunworks, Inc.

Price: **$2,900.00**

Harris Gunworks Signature Alaskan

Similar to the Classic Sporter except has match-grade barrel with single leaf rear sight, barrel band front, 1" detachable rings and mounts, steel floorplate, electroless nickel finish. Has wood Monte Carlo stock with cheekpiece, palm-swell grip, solid butt pad. Chambered for 270, 280 Rem., 30-06, 7mm Rem. Mag., 300 Win. Mag., 300 Wea., 358 Win., 340 Wea., 375 H&H. Introduced 1989.

Price: **$3,800.00**

Harris Gunworks Signature Titanium Mountain Rifle

Similar to the Classic Sporter except action made of titanium alloy, barrel of chrome-moly steel. Stock is of graphite reinforced fiberglass. Weight is 5-1/2 lbs. Chambered for 270, 280 Rem., 30-06, 7mm Rem. Mag., 300 Win. Mag. Fiberglass stock optional. Introduced 1989.

Price: **$3,300.00**
Price: With graphite-steel composite light weight barrel. **$3,700.00**

Harris Gunworks Signature Varminter

Similar to the Signature Classic Sporter except has heavy contoured barrel, adjustable trigger, field bipod and special hand-bedded fiberglass stock. Chambered for 223, 22-250, 220 Swift, 243, 6mm Rem., 25-06, 7mm-08, 7mm BR, 308, 350 Rem. Mag. Comes with 1" rings and bases. Introduced 1989.

Price: **$2,700.00**

HARRIS GUNWORKS TALON SAFARI RIFLE

Caliber: 300 Win. Mag., 300 Wea. Mag., 300 Phoenix, 338 Win. Mag., 30/378, 338 Lapua, 300 H&H, 340 Wea. Mag., 375 H&H, 404 Jeffery, 416 Rem. Mag., 458 Win. Mag. (Safari Magnum); 378 Wea. Mag., 416 Rigby, 416 Wea. Mag., 460 Wea. Mag. (Safari Super Magnum). **Barrel:** 24". **Weight:** About 9-10 lbs. **Length:** 43" overall. **Stock:** Gunworks fiberglass Safari. **Sights:** Barrel band front ramp, multi-leaf express rear. **Features:** Uses Harris Gunworks Safari action. Has quick detachable 1" scope mounts, positive locking steel floorplate, barrel band sling swivel. Match-grade barrel. Matte black finish standard. Introduced 1989. From Harris Gunworks, Inc.

Price: Talon Safari Magnum. **$3,900.00**
Price: Talon Safari Super Magnum **$4,200.00**

HARRIS GUNWORKS TALON SPORTER RIFLE

Caliber: 22-250, 243, 6mm Rem., 6mm BR, 7mm BR, 7mm-08, 25-06, 270, 280 Rem., 284, 308, 30-06, 350 Rem. Mag. (long action); 7mm Rem. Mag., 7mm STW, 300 Win. Mag., 300 Wea. Mag., 300 H&H, 338 Win. Mag., 340 Wea. Mag., 375 H&H, 416 Rem. Mag. **Barrel:** 24" (standard). **Weight:** About 7-1/2 lbs. **Length:** NA. **Stock:** Choice of walnut or fiberglass. **Sights:** None furnished; comes with rings and bases. Open sights optional. **Features:** Uses pre-'64 Model 70-type action with cone breech, controlled feed, claw extractor and three-position safety. Barrel and action are of stainless steel; chrome-moly optional. Introduced 1991. From Harris Gunworks, Inc.

Price: **$2,900.00**

HOWA LIGHTNING BOLT-ACTION RIFLE

Caliber: 223, 22-250, 243, 270, 308, 30-06, 7mm Rem. Mag., 300 Win. Mag., 338 Win. Mag. **Barrel:** 22", 24" magnum calibers. **Weight:** 7-1/2 lbs.

Howa Lightning

Howa M-1500 Hunter

Howa M-1500 PCS Police Counter Sniper

Howa M-1500 Varmint

L.A.R. Grizzly

Length: 42" overall (22" barrel). **Stock:** Black Bell & Carlson Carbelite composite with Monte Carlo comb; checkered grip and forend. **Sights:** None furnished. Drilled and tapped for scope mounting. **Features:** Sliding thumb safety; hinged floorplate; polished blue/black finish. Introduced 1993. From Legacy Sports International.

Price: Blue, standard calibers..$435.00
Price: Blue, magnum calibers......................................$455.00
Price: Stainless, standard calibers $485.00
Price: Stainless, magnum calibers $505.00

Howa M-1500 Hunter Bolt-Action Rifle
Similar to the Lightning model except has walnut-finished hardwood stock. Polished blue finish or stainless steel. Introduced 1999. From Legacy Sports International.

Price: Blue, standard calibers..$455.00
Price: Stainless, standard calibers $505.00
Price: Blue, magnum calibers......................................$475.00
Price: Stainless, magnum calibers $525.00

Howa M-1500 PCS Police Counter Sniper Rifle
Similar to the M-1500 Lightning except chambered only for 308 Win., 24" hammer-forged heavy barrel. Trigger is factory set at 4 lbs. Available in blue or stainless steel, polymer or hardwood stock. Introduced 1999. Imported from Japan by Legacy Sports International.

Price: Blue, polymer stock $465.00
Price: Stainless, polymer stock.............................$525.00
Price: Blue, wood stock $485.00
Price: Stainless, wood stock...........................$545.00

Howa M-1500 Varmint Rifle
Similar to the M-1500 Lightning except has heavy 24" hammer-forged barrel. Chambered for 223 and 22-250. Weighs 9.3 lbs.; overall length 44.5". Introduced 1999. Imported from Japan by Interarms/Howa.

Price: Blue, polymer stock $465.00
Price: Stainless, polymer stock $525.00
Price: Blue, wood stock $485.00
Price: Stainless, wood stock.............................$545.00

L.A.R. GRIZZLY 50 BIG BOAR RIFLE
Caliber: 50 BMG, single shot. **Barrel:** 36". **Weight:** 28.4 lbs. **Length:** 45.5" overall. **Stock:** Integral. Ventilated rubber recoil pad. **Sights:** None furnished; scope mount. **Features:** Bolt-action bullpup design; thumb safety. All-steel construction. Introduced 1994. Made in U.S. by L.A.R. Mfg., Inc.
Price: $2,570.00

MOUNTAIN EAGLE RIFLE
Caliber: 222 Rem., 223 Rem. (Varmint); 270, 280, 30-06 (long action); 7mm Rem. Mag., 7mm STW, 300 Win. Mag., 338 Win. Mag., 300 Wea. Mag., 375 H&H, 416 Rem. Mag. (magnum action). **Barrel:** 24", 26" (Varmint); match-grade; fluted stainless on Varmint. Free floating. **Weight:** 7 lbs., 13 oz. **Length:** 44" overall (24" barrel). **Stock:** Kevlar-graphite with aluminum bedding block, high comb, recoil pad, swivel studs; made by H-S Precision. **Sights:** None furnished; accepts any Remington 700-type base. **Features:** Special Sako action with one-piece forged bolt, hinged steel floorplate, lengthened receiver ring; adjustable trigger. Krieger cut-rifled benchrest barrel. Introduced 1996. From Magnum Research, Inc.
Price: Right-hand $1,499.00

Mountain Eagle Varmint

Raptor Bolt-Action

Remington 700 ADL Synthetic

Remington 700 BDL

Remington 700 BDL Left Hand

Price: Left-hand $1,549.00
Price: Varmint Edition. $1,629.00
Price: 375 H&H, 416 Rem., add. $300.00
Price: Magnum Lite (graphite barrel) $2,295.00

RAPTOR BOLT-ACTION RIFLE

Caliber: 270, 30-06, 243, 25-06, 308; 4-shot magazine. **Barrel:** 22".
Weight: 7 lbs., 6 oz. **Length:** 42.5" overall. **Stock:** Black synthetic, fiberglass reinforced; checkered grip and forend; vented recoil pad; Monte Carlo cheekpiece. **Sights:** None furnished; drilled and tapped for scope mounts. **Features:** Rust-resistant "Taloncote" treated barreled action; pillar bedded; stainless bolt with three locking lugs; adjustable trigger. Announced 1997. Made in U.S. by Raptor Arms Co., Inc.
Price: $249.00

REMINGTON MODEL 700 CLASSIC RIFLE

Caliber: 223 Rem. **Barrel:** 24". **Weight:** About 7-1/4 lbs. **Length:** 44-1/2" overall. **Stock:** American walnut, 20 lpi checkering on pistol grip and forend. Classic styling. Satin finish. **Sights:** None furnished. Receiver drilled and tapped for scope mounting. **Features:** A "classic" version of the BDL with straight comb stock. Fitted with rubber recoil pad. Sling swivel studs installed. Hinged floorplate. Limited production in 2000 only.
Price: $633.00

REMINGTON MODEL 700 ADL DELUXE RIFLE

Caliber: 270, 308, 30-06 and 7mm Rem. Mag. **Barrel:** 22" or 24" round tapered. **Weight:** 7-1/4 to 7-1/2 lbs. **Length:** 41-5/8" to 44-1/2" overall. **Stock:** Walnut. Satin-finished pistol grip stock with fine-line cut checkering, Monte Carlo. **Sights:** Gold bead ramp front; removable, step-adjustable rear with windage screw. **Features:** Side safety, receiver tapped for scope mounts.
Price: From. $531.00

Remington Model 700 ADL Synthetic

Similar to the 700 ADL except has a fiberglass-reinforced synthetic stock with straight comb, raised cheekpiece, positive checkering, and black rubber butt pad. Metal has matte finish. Available in 22-250, 223, 243, 270, 308, 30-06 with 22" barrel, 300 Win. Mag., 7mm Rem. Mag. with 24" barrel. Introduced 1996.
Price: From. $457.00

Remington Model 700 ADL Synthetic Youth

Similar to the Model 700 ADL Synthetic except has 1" shorter stock, 20" barrel. Chambered for 243, 308. Introduced 1998.
Price: $484.00

Remington Model 700 BDL Custom Deluxe Rifle

Same as the 700 ADL except chambered for 222, 223 (short action, 24" barrel), 22-250, 25-06. (short action, 22" barrel), 243, 270, 30-06; skip-line checkering; black forend tip and gripcap with white line spacers. Matted receiver top, fine-line engraving, quick-release floorplate. Hooded ramp front sight; quick detachable swivels. 7mm-08, .280.
Price: $633.00
Also available in 17 Rem., 7mm Rem. Mag., 7mm-08, 280, 300 Win. Mag. (long action, 24" barrel); 338 Win. Mag., (long action, 22" barrel); 300 Rem. Ultra Mag. 338 Rem. Ultra Mag. (26" barrel). Overall length 44-1/2", weight about 7-1/2 lbs. 338 Rem Ultra Mag.
Price: $660.00

Remington 700 BDL SS DM

Remington 700 BDL SS DM-B

Remington 700 Safari KS

Remington 700 APR African Plains

Remington Model 700 BDL Left Hand Custom Deluxe

Same as 700 BDL except mirror-image left-hand action, stock. Available in 270, 30-06, 7mm Rem. Mag., 300 Rem. Ultra Mag.
Price: **$660.00**
Price: 7mm Rem. Mag., 300 Rem. Ultra Mag. **$687.00**

Remington Model 700 BDL DM Rifle

Same as the 700 BDL except has detachable box magazine (4-shot, standard calibers, 3-shot for magnums). Has glossy stock finish, fine-line engraving, open sights, recoil pad, sling swivels. Available in 270, 30-06, 7mm Rem. Mag., 300 Win. Mag. Introduced 1995.
Price: From **$681.00**

Remington Model 700 BDL SS Rifle

Similar to the 700 BDL rifle except has hinged floorplate, 24" standard weight barrel in all calibers; magnum calibers have magnum-contour barrel. No sights supplied, but comes drilled and tapped. Has corrosion-resistant follower and fire control, stainless BDL-style barreled action with fine matte finish. Synthetic stock has straight comb and cheekpiece, textured finish, positive checkering, plated swivel studs. Calibers—270, 30-06; magnums—7mm Rem. Mag., 300 Rem. Ultra Mag. (26" barrel) 300 Win. Mag., 338 Win. Mag., 338 Rem. Ultra Mag., 375 H&H. Weighs 7-3/8 - 7-1/2 lbs. Introduced 1993.
Price: From **$681.00**

Remington Model 700 BDL SS DM Rifle

Same as the 700 BDL SS except has detachable box magazine. Barrel, receiver and bolt made of #416 stainless steel; black synthetic stock, fine-line engraving. Available in 25-06, 260 Rem., 270, 280, 30-06, 7mm Rem. Mag., 7mm-08, 300 Win. Mag., 300 Wea. Mag. Introduced 1995.
Price: From **$756.00**

Remington Model 700 BDL SS DM-B

Same as the 700 BDL SS DM except has muzzle brake, fine-line engraving. Available only in 7mm STW, 300 Win. Mag. Introduced 1996.
Price: **$845.00**

Remington Model 700 Custom KS Mountain Rifle

Similar to the 700 BDL except custom finished with Kevlar reinforced resin synthetic stock. Available in both left- and right-hand versions. Chambered for 270 Win., 280 Rem., 30-06, 7mm Rem. Mag., 7mm STW, 300 Rem. Ultra Mag., 338 Rem. Ultra Mag., 300 Win. Mag., 300 Wea. Mag., 35 Whelen, 338 Win. Mag., 8mm Rem. Mag., 375 H&H, with 24" barrel (except 300 Rem. Ultra Mag., 26"). Weighs 6 lbs., 6 oz. Introduced 1986.
Price: .338 Ultra **$1,221.00**

Remington Model 700 LSS Mountain Rifle

Similar to Model 700 Custom KS Mountain Rifle except has stainless steel 22" barrel and two-tone laminated stock. Chambered in 260 Rem., 7mm-08, 270 Winchester and 30-06. Overall length 42-1/2", weighs 6-5/8 oz. Introduced 1999. From Remington Arms Co.
Price: **$744.00**

Remington Model 700 Safari Grade

Similar to the 700 BDL except custom finished and tuned. In 8mm Rem. Mag., 375 H&H, 416 Rem. Mag. or 458 Win. Mag. calibers only with heavy barrel. Hand checkered, oil-finished stock in classic or Monte Carlo style with recoil pad installed. Classic available in right- and left-hand versions.
Price: From **$1,225.00**
Price: Safari KS (Kevlar stock), from **$1,410.00**

Remington Model 700 AWR Alaskan Wilderness Rifle

Similar to the Model 700 BDL except has stainless barreled action with satin blue finish; special 24" Custom Shop barrel profile; matte gray stock of fiberglass and graphite, reinforced with DuPont Kevlar, straight comb with raised cheekpiece, magnum-grade black rubber recoil pad. Chambered for 7mm Rem. Mag., 7mm STW, 300 Rem. Ultra Mag., 300 Win. Mag., 300 Wea. Mag., 338 Rem. Ultra Mag., 338 Win. Mag., 375 H&H. Introduced 1994.
Price: From **$1,480.00**

Remington Model 700 APR African Plains Rifle

Similar to the Model 700 BDL except has magnum receiver and specially contoured 26" Custom Shop barrel with satin finish, laminated wood stock with raised cheekpiece, satin finish, black butt pad, 20 lpi cut checkering. Chambered for 7mm Rem. Mag., 300 Rem. Ultra Mag., 300 Win. Mag., 300 Wea. Mag., 338 Win. Mag., 338 Rem. Ultra Mag., 375 H&H. Introduced 1994.
Price: **$1,593.00**

Remington 700 VLS

Remington 700 Varmint Synthetic

Remington 700 VS Composite

Remington 700 VF SF

Remington 700 Sendero SF

Remington Model 700 EtronX Electronic Ignition Rifle

NEW! Similar to Model 700 VS SF except features battery-powered ignition system for near-zero lock time and electronic trigger mechanism. Requires ammunition with EtronX electrically fired primers. Aluminum-bedded 26" heavy, stainless steel, fluted barrel; overall length 45-7/8"; weight 8 lbs., 14 oz. Black, Kevlar-reinforced composite stock. Light-emitting diode display on grip top indicates fire or safe mode, loaded or unloaded chamber, battery condition. Introduced 2000. From Remington Arms Co.
Price: 220 Swift, 22-250 or 243 Win. $1,999.00

Remington Model 700 LSS Rifle

Similar to the 700 BDL except has stainless steel barreled action, gray laminated wood stock with Monte Carlo comb and cheekpiece. No sights furnished. Available in 7mm Rem. Mag., 300 Rem. Ultra Mag., 300 Win. Mag., and 338 Rem. Ultra Mag. in right-hand, and 270, 7mm Rem. Mag., 30-06, 300 Rem. Ultra Mag., 300 Win. Mag., 338 Rem. Ultra Mag. in left-hand model. Introduced 1996.
Price: From $771.00

Remington Model 700 MTN DM Rifle

Similar to the 700 BDL except weighs 6-1/2 to 6-5/8 lbs., has a 22" tapered barrel. Redesigned pistol grip, straight comb, contoured cheekpiece, hand-rubbed oil stock finish, deep cut checkering, hinged floorplate and magazine follower, two-position thumb safety. Chambered for 260 Rem., 270 Win., 7mm-08, 25-06, 280 Rem., 30-06, 4-shot detachable box magazine. Overall length is 41-5/8"-42-1/2". Introduced 1995.
Price: About $681.00

Remington Model 700 VLS Varmint Laminated Stock

Similar to the 700 BDL except has 26" heavy barrel without sights, brown laminated stock with beavertail forend, gripcap, rubber butt pad. Available in 223 Rem., 22-250, 6mm, 243, 308. Polished blue finish. Introduced 1995.
Price: From $675.00

Remington Model 700 VS Varmint Synthetic Rifles

Similar to the 700 BDL Varmint Laminated except has composite stock reinforced with DuPont Kevlar, fiberglass and graphite. Has aluminum bedding block that runs the full length of the receiver. Free-floating 26" barrel. Metal has black matte finish; stock has textured black and gray finish and swivel studs. Available in 223, 22-250, 308. Right- and left-hand. Introduced 1992.
Price: From $759.00

Remington Model 700 VS Composite Rifle

Similar to the Model 700 VS Varmint Synthetic except has a composite varmint-weight barrel, weighs 7-1/8 lbs., and is available in right-hand in 22-250, 223, 308 Win. Introduced 1999.
Price: $1,912.00

Remington Model 700 VS SF Rifle

Similar to the Model 700 Varmint Synthetic except has satin-finish stainless barreled action with 26" fluted barrel, spherical concave muzzle crown. Chambered for 223, 220 Swift, 22-250. Introduced 1994.
Price: From $916.00

Remington Model 700 Sendero Rifle

Similar to the Model 700 Varmint Synthetic except has long action for magnum calibers. Has 26" heavy varmint barrel with spherical concave crown. Chambered for 25-06, 270, 7mm Rem. Mag., 300 Win. Mag. Introduced 1994.
Price: From $759.00

RIFLES

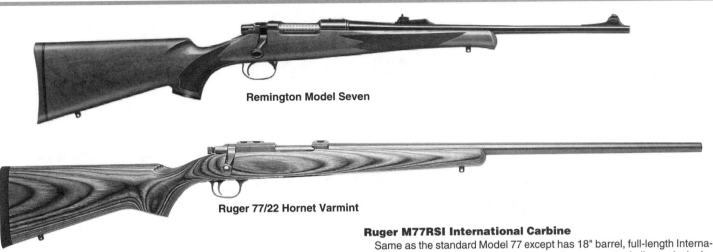

Remington Model Seven

Ruger 77/22 Hornet Varmint

Remington Model 700 Sendero SF Rifle

Similar to the 700 Sendero except has stainless steel action and 26" fluted stainless barrel. Weighs 8-1/2 lbs. Chambered for 25-06, 7mm Rem. Mag., 300 Wea. Mag., 7mm STW, 300 Rem. Ultra Mag., 338 Rem. Ultra Mag., 300 Win. Mag. Introduced 1996.
Price: From **$943.00**

REMINGTON MODEL SEVEN LSS BOLT-ACTION RIFLE

Caliber: 22-250, 243, 7mm-08. **Barrel:** 20". **Weight:** 6-1/2 lbs. **Length:** 39-1/4" overall. **Stock:** Brown laminated. Cut checkering. **Sights:** Ramp front, adjustable open rear. **Features:** Short-action design; silent side safety; free-floated barrel except for single pressure point at forend tip. Introduced 1983.
Price: **$727.00**

Remington Model Seven Custom KS

Similar to the Model Seven except has gray Kevlar reinforced stock with 1" black rubber recoil pad and swivel studs. Metal has black matte finish. No sights on 223, 260 Rem., 7mm-08, 308; 35 Rem. and 350 Rem. have iron sights.
Price: **$1,221.00**

Remington Model Seven LSS

Similar to Model Seven except has satin-finished, brown laminated stock, stainless steel 20" barrel and receiver. Overall length, 39-1/4", weighs 6-1/2 lbs. Chambered for 22-250, 243, 7mm-08 Rem. Introduced 2000.
Price: **$633.00**

Remington Model Seven LS

Similar to Model Seven except has satin-finished, brown laminated stock with 20" carbon steel barrel. Introduced 2000.
Price: **$633.00**

Remington Model Seven SS

Similar to the Model Seven except has stainless steel barreled action and black synthetic stock, 20" barrel. Chambered for 223, 243, 260 Rem., 7mm-08, 308. Introduced 1994.
Price: **$681.00**

Remington Model Seven Custom MS Rifle

Similar to the Model Seven except has full-length Mannlicher-style stock of laminated wood with straight comb, solid black recoil pad, black steel forend tip, cut checkering, gloss finish. Barrel length 20", weighs 6-3/4 lbs. Available in 222 Rem., 223, 22-250, 243, 6mm Rem., 260 Rem., 7mm-08 Rem., 308, 350 Rem. Mag. Calibers 250 Savage, 257 Roberts, 35 Rem. Polished blue finish. Introduced 1993. From Remington Custom Shop.
Price: From **$1,236.00**

Remington Model Seven Youth Rifle

Similar to the Model Seven except has hardwood stock with 12-3/16" length of pull and chambered for 223, 243, 260 Rem., 7mm-08. Introduced 1993.
Price: **$519.00**

Ruger M77RSI International Carbine

Same as the standard Model 77 except has 18" barrel, full-length International-style stock, with steel forend cap, loop-type steel sling swivels. Integral-base receiver, open sights, Ruger 1" steel rings. Improved front sight. Available in 243, 270, 308, 30-06. Weighs 7 lbs. Length overall is 38-3/8".
Price: M77RSIMKII **$713.00**

RUGER M77 MARK II EXPRESS RIFLE

Caliber: 270, 30-06, 7mm Rem. Mag., 300 Win. Mag., 338 Win. Mag., 4-shot magazine (3-shot Magnum calibers). **Barrel:** 22" (std. calibers) or 24" (Magnum calibers), with integral steel rib; barrel-mounted front swivel stud; hammer forged. **Weight:** 7.5 lbs. **Length:** 42.125" overall. **Stock:** Hand-checkered circassian walnut with steel gripcap, black rubber butt pad, swivel studs. **Sights:** Ramp front, V-notch two-leaf express rear adjustable for windage mounted on rib. **Features:** Mark II action with three-position safety, stainless steel bolt, steel trigger guard, hinged steel floorplate. Introduced 1991.
Price: M77RSEXPMKII **$1,695.00**

RUGER 77/22 HORNET BOLT-ACTION RIFLE

Caliber: 22 Hornet, 6-shot rotary magazine. **Barrel:** 20". **Weight:** About 6 lbs. **Length:** 39-3/4" overall. **Stock:** Checkered American walnut, black rubber butt pad. **Sights:** Brass bead front, open adjustable rear; also available without sights. **Features:** Same basic features as the rimfire model except has slightly lengthened receiver. Uses Ruger rotary magazine. Three-position safety. Comes with 1" Ruger scope rings. Introduced 1994.
Price: 77/22RH (rings only) **$525.00**
Price: 77/22RSH (with sights) **$550.00**
Price: K77/22VHZ Varmint, laminated stock, no sights **$575.00**

RUGER M77 MARK II RIFLE

Caliber: 223, 220 Swift, 22-250, 243, 6mm Rem., 257 Roberts, 25-06, 6.5x55 Swedish, 270, 7x57mm, 260 Rem., 280 Rem., 308, 30-06, 7mm Rem. Mag., 300 Win. Mag., 338 Win. Mag., 4-shot magazine. **Barrel:** 20", 22"; 24" (magnums). **Weight:** About 7 lbs. **Length:** 39-3/4" overall. **Stock:** Hand-checkered American walnut; swivel studs, rubber butt pad. **Sights:** None furnished. Receiver has Ruger integral scope mount base, comes with Ruger 1" rings. Some models have iron sights. **Features:** Short action with new trigger and three-position safety. New trigger guard with re-designed floorplate latch. Left-hand model available. Introduced 1989.
Price: M77RMKII (no sights) **$634.00**
Price: M77RSMKII (open sights) **$713.00**
Price: M77LRMKII (left-hand, 270, 30-06, 7mm Rem. Mag.,300 Win. Mag.)
. . . . **$634.00**

Ruger M77 Mark II All-Weather Stainless Rifle

Similar to the wood-stock M77 Mark II except all metal parts are of stainless steel, and has an injection-moulded, glass-fiber-reinforced Du Pont Zytel stock. Also offered with laminated wood stock. Chambered for 223, 243, 270, 308, 30-06, 7mm Rem. Mag., 300 Win. Mag., 338 Win. Mag. Has the fixed-blade-type ejector, three-position safety, and new trigger guard with patented floorplate latch. Comes with integral Scope Base Receiver and 1" Ruger scope rings, built-in sling swivel loops. Introduced 1990.

Ruger M77 Mark II All-Weather

Ruger 77/44

Ruger M77VT Target

Sako TRG-S

Price: K77RPMKII. **$604.00**
Price: K77RLPMKII Ultra-Light, synthetic stock, rings, no sights . . **$604.00**
Price: K77LRBBZMKII, left-hand bolt, rings, no sights, laminated
stock **$673.00**
Price: K77RSPMKII, synthetic stock, open sights **$672.00**
Price: K77RBZMKII, no sights, laminated wood stock, 223, 22/250, 243,
270, 280 Rem., 7mm Rem. Mag., 30-06, 308, 300 Win. Mag., 338
Win. Mag. **$673.00**
Price: K77RSBZMKII, open sights, laminated wood stock, 243, 270,
7mm Rem. Mag., 30-06, 300 Win. Mag., 338 Win. Mag. **$740.00**

Ruger M77RL Ultra Light

Similar to the standard M77 except weighs only 6 lbs., chambered for
223, 243, 308, 270, 30-06, 257 Roberts; barrel tapped for target scope
blocks; has 20" Ultra Light barrel. Overall length 40". Ruger's steel 1"
scope rings supplied. Introduced 1983.
Price: M77RLMKII **$677.00**

RUGER M77 MARK II MAGNUM RIFLE

Caliber: 375 H&H, 4-shot magazine; 416 Rigby, 3-shot magazine. **Barrel:**
23", with integral steel rib; hammer forged. **Weight:** 9.25 lbs. (375); 9-3/4
lbs. (416, Rigby). **Length:** 40.5" overall. **Stock:** Circassian walnut with
hand-cut checkering, swivel studs, steel gripcap, rubber butt pad. **Sights:**
Ramp front, two leaf express on serrated integral steel rib. Rib also serves
as base for front scope ring. **Features:** Uses an enlarged Mark II action
with three-position safety, stainless bolt, steel trigger guard and hinged
steel floorplate. Controlled feed. Introduced 1989.
Price: M77RSMMKII. **$1,695.00**

RUGER 77/44 BOLT-ACTION RIFLE

Caliber: 44 Magnum, 4-shot magazine. **Barrel:** 18-1/2". **Weight:** 6 lbs.
Length: 38-1/4" overall. **Stock:** American walnut with rubber butt pad and

swivel studs or black polymer (stainless only). **Sights:** Gold bead front,
folding leaf rear. Comes with Ruger 1" scope rings. **Features:** Uses same
action as the Ruger 77/22. Short bolt stroke; rotary magazine; three-position safety. Introduced 1997. Made in U.S. by Sturm, Ruger & Co.
Price: Blue, walnut, 77/44RS **$580.00**
Price: Stainless, polymer, stock, K77/44RS **$580.00**

RUGER M77VT TARGET RIFLE

Caliber: 22-250, 220 Swift, 223, 243, 25-06, 308. **Barrel:** 26" heavy stainless steel with target gray finish. **Weight:** 9-3/4 lbs. **Length:** Approx. 44"
overall. **Stock:** Laminated American hardwood with beavertail forend,
steel swivel studs; no checkering or gripcap. **Sights:** Integral scope mount
bases in receiver. **Features:** Ruger diagonal bedding system. Ruger steel
1" scope rings supplied. Fully adjustable trigger. Steel floorplate and trigger guard. New version introduced 1992.
Price: K77VTMKII. **$759.00**

SAKO TRG-S BOLT-ACTION RIFLE

Caliber: 243, 7mm-08, 270, 6.5x55, 30-06, 7mm Rem. Mag., 300 Win.
Mag., 338 Win. Mag., 270 Wea. Mag., 7mm Wea. Mag., 340 Wea. Mag.,
375 H&H, 416 Rem. Mag., 5-shot magazine (4-shot for 375 H&H). **Barrel:**
22", 24" (magnum calibers). **Weight:** 7.75 lbs. **Length:** 45.5" overall.
Stock: Reinforced polyurethane with Monte Carlo comb. **Sights:** None
furnished. **Features:** Resistance-free bolt with 60-degree lift. Recoil pad
adjustable for length. Free-floating barrel, detachable magazine, fully adjustable trigger. Matte blue metal. Introduced 1993. Imported from Finland
by Stoeger.
Price: 243, 7mm-08, 270, 30-06 . . . . **$854.00**
Price: Magnum calibers **$894.00**

SAKO 75 HUNTER BOLT-ACTION RIFLE

Caliber: 22-250, 243, 7MM-08, 308 Win., 25-06, 270, 280, 30-06; 270 Wea.
Mag., 7mm Rem. Mag., 7mm STW, 7mm Wea. Mag., 300 Win. Mag., 300
Wea. Mag., 338 Win. Mag., 340 Wea. Mag., 375 H&H, 416 Rem. Mag.
Barrel: 22", standard calibers; 24", 26" magnum calibers. **Weight:** About
6 lbs. **Length:** NA. **Stock:** European walnut with matte lacquer finish.
Sights: None furnished; dovetail scope mount rails. **Features:** New de-
sign with three locking lugs and a mechanical ejector; key locks firing pin
and bolt; cold hammer-forged barrel is free-floating; two-position safety;

Sako 75 Hunter

Sako 75 Deluxe

Sako 75 Stainless Hunter

Sako 75 Varmint

hinged floorplate or detachable magazine that can be loaded from the top; short 70 degree bolt lift. Available in five action lengths. Introduced 1997. Imported from Finland by Stoeger Industries.
Price: Standard calibers **$1,184.00**
Price: Magnum Calibers **$1,219.00**

Sako 75 Stainless Synthetic Rifle
Similar to the 75 Hunter except all metal is of stainless steel, and the synthetic stock has soft composite panels moulded into the forend and pistol grip. Available in 22-250, 243, 308 Win., 25-06, 270, 30-06 with 22" barrel, 7mm Rem. Mag., 300 Win. Mag. with 24" barrel. Introduced 1997. Imported from Finland by Stoeger Industries.
Price: Standard calibers **$1,284.00**
Price: Magnum calibers **$1,314.00**

Sako 75 Deluxe Rifle
Similar to the 75 Hunter except has select wood rosewood gripcap and forend tip. Available in 25-06, 270, 280, 30-06; 270 Wea. Mag., 7mm Rem. Mag., 7mm STW, 7mm Wea. Mag., 300 Win. Mag., 300 Wea. Mag., 338 Win. Mag., 340 Wea. Mag., 375 H&H, 416 Rem. Mag. Introduced 1997. Imported from Finland by Stoeger Industries.
Price: Standard calibers **$1,724.00**
Price: Magnum calibers **$1,754.00**

Sako 75 Stainless Hunter Rifle
Similar to the Sako 75 Hunter except all metal is of stainless steel. Comes with walnut stock with matte lacquer finish, rubber butt pad. Introduced 1999. Imported from Finland by Stoeger Industries.
Price: 270, 30-06 . . . . **$1,284.00**
Price: 7mm Rem. Mag., 7mm STW, 300 Win. Mag., 300 Wea. Mag., 338 Win. Mag. **$1,314.00**

Sako 75 Varmint Stainless Laminated Rifle
Similar to the Sako 75 Hunter except chambered only for 222, 223, 22-250, 22 PPC USA, 6 PPC USA; has heavy 24" barrel with recessed crown; all metal is of stainless steel; has laminated wood stock with beavertail forend. Introduced 1999. Imported from Finland by Stoeger Industries.
Price: **$1,459.00**

Sako 75 Varmint Rifle
Similar to the Model 75 Hunter except chambered only for 17 Rem., 222 Rem., 223 Rem., 22-250 Rem.; 24" heavy barrel with recessed crown; beavertail forend. Introduced 1998. Imported from Finland by Stoeger Industries.
Price: **$1,364.00**

SAUER 202 BOLT-ACTION RIFLE
Caliber: Standard—243, 6.5x55, 270 Win., 308 Win., 30-06; magnum— 7mm Rem. Mag., 300 Win. Mag., 300 Wea. Mag., 375 H&H. **Barrel:** 23.6" (standard), 26" (magnum). **Weight:** 7.7 lbs. (standard). **Length:** 44.3" overall (23.6" barrel). **Stock:** Select American Claro walnut with high-gloss epoxy finish, rosewood grip and forend caps; 22 lpi checkering. Synthetic also available. **Sights:** None furnished; drilled and tapped for scope mounting. **Features:** Short 60" bolt throw; detachable box magazine; six-lug bolt; quick-change barrel; tapered bore; adjustable two-stage trigger; firing pin cocking indicator. Introduced 1994. Imported from Germany by Sigarms, Inc.
Price: Standard calibers, right-hand **$1,035.00**
Price: Magnum calibers, right-hand **$1,106.00**
Price: Standard calibers, synthetic stock **$985.00**
Price: Magnum calibers, synthetic stock **$1,056.00**

SAVAGE MODEL 110GXP3, 110GCXP3 PACKAGE GUNS
Caliber: 223, 22-250, 243, 25-06, 270, 300 Sav., 30-06, 308, 7mm Rem. Mag., 7mm-08, 300 Win. Mag. (Model 110GXP3); 270, 30-06, 7mm Rem. Mag., 300 Win. Mag. (Model 110GCXP3). **Barrel:** 22" (standard calibers), 24" (magnum calibers). **Weight:** 7.25-7.5 lbs. **Length:** 43.5" overall (22" barrel). **Stock:** Monte Carlo-style hardwood with walnut finish, rubber butt pad, swivel studs. **Sights:** None furnished. **Features:** Model 110GXP3 has fixed, top-loading magazine, Model 110GCXP3 has detachable box magazine. Rifles come with a factory-mounted and bore-sighted 3-9x32 scope, rings and bases, quick-detachable swivels, sling. Left-hand models available in all calibers. Introduced 1991 (GXP3); 1994 (GCXP3). Made in U.S. by Savage Arms, Inc.
Price: Model 110GXP3, right- or left-hand **$513.00**
Price: Model 110GCXP3, right- or left-hand **$513.00**

Savage Model 111FXP3, 111FCXP3 Package Guns
Similar to the Model 110 Series Package Guns except with lightweight, black graphite/fiberglass composite stock with non-glare finish, positive

RIFLES

Savage Model 10FM

Savage Model 10FP

Savage Model 11F

Savage Model 11G

checkering. Same calibers as Model 110 rifles, plus 338 Win. Mag. Model 111FXP3 has fixed top-loading magazine; Model 111FCXP3 has detachable box. Both come with mounted 3-9x32 scope, quick-detachable swivels, sling. Introduced 1994. Made in U.S. by Savage Arms, Inc.

Price: Model 111FXP3, right- or left-hand **$476.00**
Price: Model 111FCXP3, right- or left-hand **$525.00**

SAVAGE MODEL 110FM SIERRA ULTRA LIGHT WEIGHT RIFLE

Caliber: 243, 270, 308, 30-06. **Barrel:** 20". **Weight:** 6-1/4 lbs. **Length:** 41-1/2" overall. **Stock:** Graphite/fiberglass-filled composite. **Sights:** None furnished; drilled and tapped for scope mounting. **Features:** Comes with black nylon sling and quick-detachable swivels. Introduced 1996. Made in U.S. by Savage Arms, Inc.

Price: **$449.00**

Savage Model 10FM Sierra Ultra Light Rifle

Similar to the Model 110FM Sierra except has a true short action, chambered for 223, 243, 308; weighs 6 lbs. "Dual Pillar" bedding in black synthetic stock with silver medallion in gripcap. Comes with sling and quick-detachable swivels. Introduced 1998. Made in U.S. by Savage Arms, Inc.

Price: **$449.00**

SAVAGE MODEL 110FP TACTICAL RIFLE

Caliber: 223, 25-06, 308, 30-06, 300 Win. Mag., 7mm Rem. Mag., 4-shot magazine. **Barrel:** 24", heavy; recessed target muzzle. **Weight:** 8-1/2 lbs. **Length:** 45.5" overall. **Stock:** Black graphite/fiberglass composition; positive checkering. **Sights:** None furnished. Receiver drilled and tapped for scope mounting. **Features:** Pillar-bedded stock. Black matte finish on all metal parts. Double swivel studs on the forend for sling and/or bipod mount. Right or left-hand. Introduced 1990. From Savage Arms, Inc.

Price: Right- or left-hand. **$476.00**

Savage Model 10FP Tactical Rifle

Similar to the Model 110FP except has true short action, chambered for 223, 308; black synthetic stock with "Dual Pillar" bedding. Introduced 1998. Made in U.S. by Savage Arms, Inc.

Price: **$476.00**
Price: Model 10FLP (left-hand) **$476.00**

SAVAGE MODEL 111 CLASSIC HUNTER RIFLES

Caliber: 223, 22-250, 243, 250 Sav., 25-06, 270, 300 Sav., 30-06, 308, 7mm Rem. Mag., 7mm-08, 300 Win. Mag., 338 Win. Mag. (Models 111G, GL, GNS, F, FL, FNS); 270, 30-06, 7mm Rem. Mag., 300 Win. Mag. (Models 111GC, GLC, FAK, FC, FLC). **Barrel:** 22", 24" (magnum calibers). **Weight:** 6.3 to 7 lbs. **Length:** 43.5" overall (22" barrel). **Stock:** Walnut-finished hardwood (M111G, GC); graphite/fiberglass filled composite. **Sights:** Ramp front, open fully adjustable rear; drilled and tapped for scope mounting. **Features:** Three-position top tang safety, double front locking lugs, free-floated button-rifled barrel. Comes with trigger lock, target, ear puffs. Introduced 1994. Made in U.S. by Savage Arms, Inc.

Price: Model 111FC (detachable magazine, composite stock, right- or left-hand) **$445.00**
Price: Model 111F (top-loading magazine, composite stock, right- or left-hand) **$419.00**
Price: Model 111FNS (as above, no sights, right-hand only).... **$411.00**
Price: Model 111G (wood stock, top-loading magazine, right- or left-hand) **$395.00**
Price: Model 111GC (as above, detachable magazine), right- or left-hand **$433.00**
Price: Model 111GNS (wood stock, top-loading magzine, no sights, right-hand only) **$389.00**
Price: Model 111FAK Express (blued, composite stock, top loading magazine, Adjustable muzzle brake) .... **NA**

Savage Model 11 Hunter Rifles

Similar to the Model 111F except has true short action, chambered for 223, 22-250, 243, 308; black synthetic stock with "Dual Pillar" bedding, positive checkering. Introduced 1998. Made in U.S. by Savage Arms, Inc.

Price: Model 11F **$419.00**
Price: Model 11FL (left-hand)............................. **$419.00**
Price: Model 11FNS (right-hand, no sights) **$411.00**
Price: Model 11G (wood stock) **$395.00**
Price: Model 11GL (as above, left-hand) **$395.00**
Price: Model 11GNS (wood stock, no sights)................ **$389.00**

Savage Model 10GY

Savage Model 114CE

Savage Model 12FV

Savage Model 10GY, 110GY Rifle

Similar to the Model 111G except weighs 6.3 lbs., is 42-1/2" overall, and the stock is scaled for ladies, small-framed adults and youths. Chambered for 223, 243, 270, 308. Ramp front sight, open adjustable rear; drilled and tapped for scope mounts. Made in U.S. by Savage Arms, Inc.

Price: Model 110GY **$395.00**
Price: Model 10GY (short action, calibers 223, 243, 308) **$395.00**

SAVAGE MODEL 114C CLASSIC RIFLE

Caliber: 270, 30-06, 7mm Rem. Mag., 300 Win. Mag.; 4-shot detachable box magazine in standard calibers, 3-shot for magnums. **Barrel:** 22" for standard calibers, 24" for magnums. **Weight:** 7-1/8 lbs. **Length:** 45-1/2" overall. **Stock:** Oil-finished American walnut; checkered grip and forend. **Sights:** None furnished; drilled and tapped for scope mounting. **Features:** High polish blue on barrel, receiver and bolt handle; Savage logo laser-etched on bolt body; push-button magazine release. Introduced 1996. Made in U.S. by Savage Arms, Inc.

Price: **$556.00**

Savage Model 114CE Classic European

Similar to the Model 114C except the oil-finished walnut stock has a Schnabel forend tip, cheekpiece and skip-line checkering; bead on blade front sight, fully adjustable open rear; solid red butt pad. Chambered for 270, 30-06, 7mm Rem. Mag., 300 Win. Mag. Introduced 1996. Made in U.S. by Savage Arms, Inc.

Price: **$635.00**

Savage Model 114U Ultra Rifle

Similar to the Model 114C except has high-luster blued finish, high-gloss walnut stock with custom cut checkering, ebony tip. No sights; drilled and tapped for scope. Chambered for 270, 30-06, 7mm Rem. Mag., 7mm STW and 300 Win.

Price: **$504.00**

SAVAGE MODEL 112 LONG RANGE RIFLES

Caliber: 22-250, 223, 5-shot magazine. **Barrel:** 26" heavy. **Weight:** 8.8 lbs. **Length:** 47.5" overall. **Stock:** Black graphite/fiberglass filled composite with positive checkering. **Sights:** None furnished; drilled and tapped for scope mounting. **Features:** Pillar-bedded stock. Blued barrel with recessed target-style muzzle. Double front swivel studs for attaching bipod. Introduced 1991. Made in U.S. by Savage Arms, Inc.

Price: Model 112FVSS (cals. 223, 22-250, 25-06, 7mm Rem. Mag., 300 Win. Mag., stainless barrel, bolt handle, trigger guard), right- or left-hand **$549.00**
Price: Model 112FVSS-S (as above, single shot) **$549.00**

Price: Model 112BVSS (heavy-prone laminated stock with high comb, Wundhammer swell, fluted stainless barrel, bolt handle, trigger guard) **$575.00**
Price: Model 112BVSS-S (as above, single shot) **$575.00**

Savage Model 12 Long Range Rifles

Similar to the Model 112 Long Range except with true short action, chambered for 223, 22-250, 308. Models 12FV, 12FVSS have black synthetic stocks with "Dual Pillar" bedding, positive checkering, swivel studs; model 12BVSS has brown laminated stock with beavertail forend, fluted stainless barrel. Introduced 1998. Made in U.S. by Savage Arms, Inc.

Price: Model 12FV (223, 22-250 only, blue) **$455.00**
Price: Model 12FVSS (blue action, fluted stainless barrel) **$549.00**
Price: Model 12FLVSS (as above, left-hand) **$549.00**
Price: Model 12FVSS-S (blue action, fluted stainless barrel, single shot) **$549.00**
Price: Model 12BVSS (laminated stock) **$575.00**
Price: Model 12BVSS-S (as above, single shot) **$575.00**

Savage Model 12VSS Varminter Rifle

Similar to other Model 12s except has blue/stainless steel action, fluted stainless barrel, Choate full pistol-grip, adjustable synthetic stock and Sharp Shooter trigger. Overall length 47-1/2 inches, weighs about 15 pounds. No sights; drilled and tapped for scope mounts. Chambered in 223 and 22-250. Made in U.S. by Savage Arms Inc.

Price: **$852.00**

SAVAGE MODEL 116SE SAFARI EXPRESS RIFLE

Caliber: 300 Win. Mag., 338 Win. Mag., 375 H&H, 458 Win. Mag. **Barrel:** 24". **Weight:** 8.5 lbs. **Length:** 45.5" overall. **Stock:** Classic-style select walnut with ebony forend tip, deluxe cut checkering. Two cross bolts; internally vented recoil pad. **Sights:** Bead on ramp front, three-leaf express rear. **Features:** Controlled-round feed design; adjustable muzzle brake; one-piece barrel band stud. Satin-finished stainless steel barreled action. Introduced 1994. Made in U.S. by Savage Arms, Inc.

Price: **$925.00**

SAVAGE MODEL 116 WEATHER WARRIORS

Caliber: 223, 243, 270, 30-06, 7mm Rem. Mag., 300 Win. Mag., 338 Win. Mag. (Model 116FSS); 270, 30-06, 7mm Rem. Mag., 300 Win. Mag. (Models 116FCSAK, 116FCS); 270, 30-06, 7mm Rem. Mag., 300 Win. Mag., 338 Win. Mag. (Models 116FSAK, 116FSK). **Barrel:** 22", 24" for 7mm Rem. Mag., 300 Win. Mag., 338 Win. Mag. (M116FSS only). **Weight:** 6.25 to 6.5 lbs. **Length:** 43.5" overall (22" barrel). **Stock:** Graphite/fiberglass filled composite. **Sights:** None furnished; drilled and tapped for scope mounting. **Features:** Stainless steel with matte finish; free-floated barrel; quick-detachable swivel studs; laser-etched bolt; scope bases and rings. Left-hand models available in all models, calibers at same price. Models

Savage Model 16FSS

Savage Model 116FCSAK

Sigarms SHR 970

Steyr Mannlicher SBS

Steyr SBS Forester

116FCS, 116FSS introduced 1991; Model 116FSK introduced 1993; Model 116FCSAK, 116FSAK introduced 1994. Made in U.S. by Savage Arms, Inc.
Price: Model 116FSS (top-loading magazine) **$528.00**
Price: Model 116FCS (detachable box magazine). . . . . **NA**
Price: Model 116FCSAK (as above with Savage Adjustable Muzzle Brake system). **$668.00**
Price: Model 116FSAK (top-loading magazine, Savage Adjustable Muzzle Brake system). **$602.00**
Price: Model 116FSK Kodiak (as above with 22" Shock-Suppressor barrel). **$569.00**

Savage Model 16FSS Rifle
Similar to the Model 116FSS except has true short action, chambered for 223, 243, 308; 22" free-floated barrel; black graphite/fiberglass stock with "Dual Pillar" bedding. Introduced 1998. Made in U.S. by Savage Arms, Inc.
Price: **$528.00**
Price: Model 16FLSS (left-hand) **$528.00**

SIGARMS SHR 970 SYNTHETIC RIFLE
Caliber: 270, 30-06. **Barrel:** 22". **Weight:** 7.2 lbs. **Length:** 41.9" overall. **Stock:** Textured black fiberglass or walnut. **Sights:** None furnished; drilled and tapped for scope mounting. **Features:** Quick takedown; interchangeable barrels; removable box magazine; cocking indicator; three-position safety. Introduced 1998. Imported by Sigarms, Inc.
Price: Synthetic stock. **$499.00**
Price: Walnut stock. **$550.00**

STEYR MANNLICHER SBS RIFLE
Caliber: 243, 25-06, 308, 6.5x55, 6.5x57, 270, 7x64 Brenneke, 7mm-08, 7.5x55, 30-06, 9.3x62, 6.5x68, 7mm Rem. Mag., 300 Win. Mag., 8x685, 4-shot magazine. **Barrel:** 23.6" standard; 26" magnum; 20" full stock standard calibers. **Weight:** 7 lbs. **Length:** 40.1" overall. **Stock:** Hand-checkered fancy European oiled walnut with standard forend. **Sights:** Ramp front adjustable for elevation, V-notch rear adjustable for windage. **Features:** Single adjustable trigger; 3-position roller safety with "safe-bolt" setting; drilled and tapped for Steyr factory scope mounts. Introduced 1997. Imported from Austria by GSI, Inc.
Price: Half-stock, standard calibers **$2,795.00**
Price: Half-stock, magnum calibers **$2,995.00**
Price: Full-stock, standard calibers **$2,995.00**

STEYR SBS FORESTER RIFLE
Caliber: 243, 25-06, 270, 7mm-08, 308 Win., 30-06, 7mm Rem. Mag., 300 Win. Mag. Detachable 4-shot magazine. **Barrel:** 23.6", standard calibers; 25.6", magnum calibers. **Weight:** 7.5 lbs. **Length:** 44.5" overall (23.6" barrel). **Stock:** Oil-finished American walnut with Monte Carlo cheekpiece. Pachmayr 1" swivels. **Sights:** None furnished. Drilled and tapped for Browning A-Bolt mounts. **Features:** Steyr Safe Bolt systems, three-position ambidextrous roller tang safety, for Safe, Loading Fire. Matte finish on barrel and receiver; adjustable trigger. Rotary cold-hammer forged barrel. Introduced 1997. Imported by GSI, Inc.
Price: Standard calibers. **$899.00**
Price: Magnum calibers **$1,045.00**

Steyr SBS Prohunter Rifle
Similar to the SBS Forester except has ABS synthetic stock with adjustable butt spacers, straight comb without cheekpiece, palm swell, Pachmayr 1" swivels. Special 10-round magazine conversion kit available. Introduced 1997. Imported by GSI.
Price Standard calibers **$799.00**
Price Magnum calibers. **$899.00**

Steyr SBS Prohunter

Steyr Scout Rifle

Tikka Whitetail Hunter

Tikka Whitetail Hunter Stainless Synthetic

Tikka Varmint

RIFLES

STEYR SCOUT BOLT-ACTION RIFLE

Caliber: 308 Win., 5-shot magazine. **Barrel:** 19", fluted. **Weight:** NA. **Length:** NA. **Stock:** Gray Zytel. **Sights:** None furnished; comes with Leupold M8 2.5x28 IER scope on Picatinny optic rail with Steyr mounts. **Features:** Comes with luggage case, scout sling, two stock spacers, two magazines. Introduced 1998. From GSI.
Price: From **$2,699.00**

STEYR SSG BOLT-ACTION RIFLE

Caliber: 308 Win., detachable 5-shot rotary magazine. **Barrel:** 26" **Weight:** 8.5 lbs. **Length:** 44.5" overall. **Stock:** Black ABS Cycolac with spacers for length of pull adjustment. **Sights:** Hooded ramp front adjustable for elevation, V-notch rear adjustable for windage. **Features:** Sliding safety; NATO rail for bipod; 1" swivels; Parkerized finish; single or double-set triggers. Imported from Austria by GSI, Inc.
Price: SSG-PI, iron sights. **$1,699.00**
Price: SSG-PII, heavy barrel, no sights **$1,699.00**
Price: SSG-PIIK, 20" heavy barrel, no sights **$1,699.00**
Price: SSG-PIV, 16.75" threaded heavy barrel with flash hider . **$2,659.00**

TIKKA WHITETAIL HUNTER BOLT-ACTION RIFLE

Caliber: 22-250, 223, 243, 7mm-08, 25-06, 270, 308, 30-06, 7mm Rem. Mag., 300 Win. Mag., 338 Win. Mag. **Barrel:** 22-1/2" (std. cals.), 24-1/2" (magnum cals.). **Weight:** 7-1/8 lbs. **Length:** 43" overall (std. cals.). **Stock:** European walnut with Monte Carlo comb, rubber butt pad, checkered grip and forend. **Sights:** None furnished. **Features:** Detachable four-shot magazine (standard calibers), three-shot in magnums. Receiver dovetailed for scope mounting. Reintroduced 1996. Imported from Finland by Stoeger Industries.
Price: Standard calibers **$609.00**
Price: Magnum calibers **$639.00**

Tikka Continental Varmint Rifle

Similar to the standard Tikka rifle except has 26" heavy barrel, extra-wide forend. Chambered for 22-250, 223, 308. Reintroduced 1996. Made in Finland by Sako. Imported by Stoeger.
Price: **$709.00**

Tikka Whitetail Hunter Deluxe Rifle

Similar to the Whitetail Hunter except has select walnut stock with rollover Monte Carlo comb, rosewood grip cap and forend tip. Has adjustable trigger, detachable magazine, free-floating barrel. Same calibers as the Hunter. Introduced 1999. Imported from Finland by Stoeger Industries.
Price: Standard calibers **$734.00**
Price: Magnum calibers **$764.00**

Tikka Whitetail Hunter Synthetic Rifle

Similar to the Whitetail Hunter except has black synthetic stock; calibers 223, 308, 25-06, 270 Win., 30-06, 7mm Rem. Mag., 300 Win. Mag., 338 Win. Mag. Introduced 1996. Imported from Finland by Stoeger.
Price: Standard calibers **$609.00**
Price: Magnum calibers **$639.00**

Weatherby Mark V Lazermark

Weatherby Mark V Euromark

Weatherby Mark V Stainless

Tikka Continental Long Range Hunting Rifle

Similar to the Whitetail Hunter except has 26" heavy barrel. Available in 25-06, 270 Win., 7mm Rem. Mag., 300 Win. Mag. Introduced 1996. Imported from Finland by Stoeger.

Price: 25-06, 270 Win. **$709.00**
Price: 7 Rem. Mag., 300 Win. Mag. **$739.00**

Tikka Whitetail Hunter Stainless Synthetic

Similar to the Whitetail Hunter except all metal is of stainless steel, and it has a black synthetic stock. Available in 22-250, 243, 25-06, 308, 30-06, 7mm Rem. Mag., 300 Win. Mag., 338 Win. Mag. Introduced 1997. Imported from Finland by Stoeger.

Price: Standard calibers **$669.00**
Price: Magnum calibers **$699.00**

VEKTOR BUSHVELD BOLT-ACTION RIFLE

Caliber: 243, 308, 7x57, 7x64 Brenneke, 270 Win., 30-06, 300 Win. Mag., 300 H&H, 9.3x62. **Barrel:** 22"-26". **Weight:** NA. **Length:** NA. **Stock:** Turkish walnut with wrap-around hand checkering. **Sights:** Blade on ramp front, fixed standing leaf rear. **Features:** Combines the best features of the Mauser 98 and Winchester 70 actions. Controlled-round feed; Mauser-type extractor; no cut-away through the bolt locking lug; M70-type three-position safety; Timney-type adjustable trigger. Introduced 1999. Imported from South Africa by Vektor USA.

Price: .... **$1,595.00 to $1,695.00**

VEKTOR MODEL 98 BOLT-ACTION RIFLE

Caliber: 243, 308, 7x57, 7x64 Brenneke, 270 Win., 30-06, 300 Win. Mag., 300 H&H, 375 H&H, 9.3x62. **Barrel:** 22"-26". **Weight:** NA. **Length:** NA. **Stock:** Turkish walnut with hand-checkered grip and forend. **Sights:** None furnished; drilled and tapped for scope mounting. **Features:** Bolt has guide rib; non-rotating, long extractor enhances positive feeding; polished blue finish. Updated Mauser 98 action. Introduced 1999. Imported from South Africa by Vektor USA.

Price: .... **$1,149.00 to $1,249.00**

WEATHERBY MARK V DELUXE BOLT-ACTION RIFLE

Caliber: All Weatherby calibers plus 22-250, 243, 25-06, 270 Win., 280 Rem., 7mm-08, 308 Win. **Barrel:** 26" round tapered. **Weight:** 8-1/2 to 10-1/2 lbs. **Length:** 46-5/8" to 46-3/4" overall. **Stock:** Walnut, Monte Carlo with cheekpiece; high luster finish; checkered pistol grip and

forend; recoil pad. **Sights:** None furnished. **Features:** Cocking indicator; adjustable trigger; hinged floorplate, thumb safety; quick detachable sling swivels. Made in U.S. From Weatherby.

Price: 257, 270, 7mm. 300, 340 Wea. Mags., 26" barrel **$1,649.00**
Price: 416 Wea. Mag. with Accubrake, 26" barrel **$1,931.00**
Price: 460 Wea. Mag. with Accubrake, 26" barrel **$2,259.00**

Weatherby Mark V Lazermark Rifle

Same as Mark V Deluxe except stock has extensive oak leaf pattern laser carving on pistol grip and forend. Introduced 1981.

Price: 257, 270, 7mm Wea. Mag., 300, 340, 26" **$1,799.00**
Price: 378 Wea. Mag., 26" **$2,097.00**
Price: 416 Wea. Mag., 26", Accubrake.................... **$2,097.00**
Price: 460 Wea. Mag., 26", Accubrake.................... **$2,464.00**

Weatherby Mark V Sporter Rifle

Same as the Mark V Deluxe without the embellishments. Metal has low-luster blue, stock is Claro walnut with high-gloss epoxy finish, Monte Carlo comb, recoil pad. Introduced 1993.

Price: 257, 270, 7mm, 300, 340 Wea. Mags., 26" **$1,049.00**
Price: 375 H&H, 24" **$1,049.00**
Price: 7mm Rem. Mag., 300 Win. Mag., 338 Win. Mag., 24", .. **$1,049.00**

Weatherby Mark V Euromark Rifle

Similar to the Mark V Deluxe except has raised-comb Monte Carlo stock with hand-rubbed oil finish, fine-line hand-cut checkering, ebony grip and forend tips. All metal has low-luster blue. Right-hand only. Uses Mark V action. Introduced 1995. Made in U.S. From Weatherby.

Price: 257, 270, 7mm, 300, 340 Wea. Mags., 26" barrel **$1,049.00**
Price: 7mm Rem. Mag., 300 Win. Mag., 338 Win. Mag.,
375 H&H, 24" barrel **$1,049.00**

Weatherby Mark V Stainless Rifle

Similar to the Mark V Deluxe except made of 400-series stainless steel. Also available in 30-378 Wea. Mag. Has lightweight injection-moulded synthetic stock with raised Monte Carlo comb, checkered grip and forend, custom floorplate release. Right-hand only. Introduced 1995. Made in U.S. From Weatherby.

Price: 257, 270, 7mm, 300, 340 Wea. Mags., 26" barrel **$999.00**
Price: 7mm Rem. Mag., 300, 338 Win. Mags., 24" barrel **$999.00**
Price: 375 H&H, 24" barrel **$999.00**
Price: 30-378 Wea. Mag. **$1,149.00**

RIFLES

Weatherby Mark V Synthetic

Weatherby Accumark

Weatherby Accumark Lightweight

Weatherby Mark V SLS Stainless Laminate Sporter

Similar to the Mark V Stainless except all metalwork is 400 series stainless with a corrosion-resistant black oxide bead-blast matte finish. Action is hand-bedded in a laminated stock with a 1" recoil pad. Weighs 8-1/2 lbs. Introduced 1997. Made in U.S. From Weatherby.

Price: 257, 270, 7mm, 300, 340 Wea. Mag., 26" barrel **$1,299.00**
Price: 7mm Rem. Mag., 300 Win. Mag., 338 Win. Mag., 24" barrel
.... **$1,299.00**

Weatherby Mark V Eurosport Rifle

Similar to the Mark V Deluxe except has raised-comb Monte Carlo stock with hand-rubbed satin oil finish, low-luster blue metal. No gripcap or forend tip. Right-hand only. Introduced 1995. Made in U.S. From Weatherby.

Price: 257, 270, 7mm, 300, 340 Wea. Mags., 26" barrel **$1,049.00**
Price: 7mm Rem. Mag., 300, 338 Win. Mags., 24" barrel **$1,049.00**
Price: 375 H&H, 24" barrel **$1,049.00**

WEATHERBY MARK V SPORTER BOLT ACTION RIFLE

Caliber: 22-250, 243, 25-06, 270, 7MM-08, 280, 30-06, 308, 240 Wea. Mag. **Barrel:** 24". **Weight:** 6-3/4 lbs. **Length:** 44" overall. **Stock:** Claro walnut. Monte Carlo with cheekpiece; high luster finish, checkered pistol grip and forend, recoil pad. **Sights:** None furnished. Drilled and tapped for scope mounting. **Features:** Cocking indicator; adjustable trigger; hinged floorplate; thumb safety; six locking lugs; quick detachable swivels. Introduced 1997. Made in U.S. from Weatherby.

Price: **$999.00**

Weatherby Mark V Stainless

Similar to the Sporter except made of 400 series stainless steel; injection moulded synthetic stock with Monte Carlo comb, checkered grip and forend. Weighs 6-1/2 lbs. Introduced 1997. Made in U.S. From Weatherby.

Price: **$899.00**
Price: Stainless Carbine (as above with 20" barrel, 243 Win., 7mm-08 Rem., 308 Win.), weighs 6 lbs. **$899.00**

Weatherby Mark V Synthetic

Similar to the Mark V Stainless except made of matte finished blued steel. Injection moulded synthetic stock. Weighs 6-1/2 lbs., 24" barrel. Available in 22-250, 240 Wea. Mag., 243, 25-06, 270, 7mm-08, 280, 30-06, 308. Introduced 1997. Made in U.S. From Weatherby.

Price: **$699.00**

Weatherby Mark V Synthetic Rifle

Similar to the Mark V except has synthetic stock with raised Monte Carlo comb, dual-taper checkered forend. Low-luster blued metal. Weighs 8 lbs. Uses Mark V action. Right-hand only. Also available in 30-378 Wea. Mag. Introduced 1995. Made in U.S. From Weatherby.

Price: 257, 270, 7mm, 300, 340 Wea. Mags., 26" barrel **$799.00**
Price: 7mm Rem. Mag., 300, 338 Win. Mags., 24" barrel **$799.00**
Price: 375 H&H, 24" barrel **$799.00**

Weatherby Mark V Carbine

Similar to the Mark V Synthetic except has 20" barrel; injection moulded synthetic stock. Available in 243, 7mm-08, 308. Weighs 6 lbs.; overall length 40". Introduced 1997. Made in U.S. From Weatherby.

Price: **$699.00**

WEATHERBY MARK V SVM RIFLE

Caliber: 223, 22-250, 220 Swift, 243, 7mm-08, 308. **Barrel:** 26" fluted stainless steel. **Weight:** 8 1/2 lbs. **Length:** 46" overall. **Stock:** Free-floated barrel; aluminum bedding block; fully adjustable trigger. Introduced 2000. From Weatherby.

Price: .... **NA**

WEATHERBY MARK V ACCUMARK RIFLE

Caliber: 257, 270, 7mm, 300, 340 Wea. Mags., 338-378 Wea. Mag., 30-378 Wea. Mag., 7mm STW, 7mm Rem. Mag., 300 Win. Mag. **Barrel:** 26". **Weight:** 8-1/2 lbs. **Length:** 46-5/8" overall. **Stock:** H-S Precision Pro-Series synthetic with aluminum bedding plate. **Sights:** None furnished. Drilled and tapped for scope mounting. **Features:** Uses Mark V action with heavy-contour stainless barrel with black oxidized flutes, muzzle diameter of .705". Introduced 1996. Made in U.S. From Weatherby.

Price: **$1,549.00**
Price: 30-378 Wea. Mag., 338-378 Wea. Mag., 26",
Accubrake. **$1,649.00**
Price: Accumark Left-Hand 257, 270, 7mm, 300, 340 Wea.
Mag., 7mm Rem. Mag., 7mm STW, 300 Win. Mag. **$1,449.00**
Price: Accumark Left-Hand 30-378, 333-378 Wea. Mags. **$1,649.00**

Weatherby Mark V Accumark Ultra Light Weight Rifle

Similar to the Mark V Accumark except weighs 5-3/4 lbs.; free-floated 24" fluted barrel with recessed target crown; hand-laminated stock with CNC-machined aluminum bedding plate and faint gray "spider web" finish. Available in 257, 270, 7mm, 300 Wea. Mags., 243, 240 Wea. Mag., 25-06, 270 Win., 280 Rem., 7mm-08, 7mm Rem. Mag., 30-06, 308, 300 Win. Mag. Introduced 1998. Made in U.S. from Weatherby.

Price: **$1,299.00**

Wilderness Explorer

Winchester Model 70 Classic

Winchester Model 70 Classic Stainless

Winchester Model 70 Classic Laminated

Weatherby Mark V Accumark Rifle

Similar to the Mark V Accumark except chambered for 22-250, 243, 240 Wea. Mag., 25-06, 270, 280 Rem., 7mm-08, 30-06, 308; fluted 24" heavy-contour stainless barrel; hand-laminated Monte Carlo-style stock with aluminum bedding plate. Weighs 7 lbs.; 44" overall. Introduced 1998. Made in U.S. from Weatherby.
Price: **$1,349.00**

WICHITA VARMINT RIFLE

Caliber: 222 Rem., 222 Rem. Mag., 223 Rem., 22 PPC, 6mm PPC, 22-250, 243, 6mm Rem., 308 Win.; other calibers on special order. **Barrel:** 20-1/8". **Weight:** 9 lbs. **Length:** 40-1/8" overall. **Stock:** AAA Fancy American walnut. Hand-rubbed finish, hand checkered, 20 lpi pattern. Hand-inletted, glass bedded, steel gripcap. Pachmayr rubber recoil pad. **Sights:** None. Drilled and tapped for scope mounts. **Features:** Right- or left-hand Wichita action with three locking lugs. Available as a single shot only. Checkered bolt handle. Bolt is hand fitted, lapped and jeweled. Side thumb safety. Firing pin fall is 3/16". Non-glare blue finish. From Wichita Arms.
Price: Single shot **$3,000.00**

WICHITA CLASSIC RIFLE

Caliber: 17-222, 17-222 Mag., 222 Rem., 222 Rem. Mag., 223 Rem., 6x47; other calibers on special order. **Barrel:** 21-1/8". **Weight:** 8 lbs. **Length:** 41" overall. **Stock:** AAA Fancy American walnut. Hand-rubbed and checkered (20 lpi). Hand-inletted, glass bedded, steel gripcap. Pachmayr rubber recoil pad. **Sights:** None. Drilled and tapped for scope mounting. **Features:** Available as single shot only. Octagonal barrel and Wichita action, right- or left-hand. Checkered bolt handle. Bolt is hand-fitted, lapped and jeweled. Adjustable trigger is set at 2 lbs. Side thumb safety. Firing pin fall is 3/16". Non-glare blue finish. From Wichita Arms.
Price: Single shot **$3,495.00**

WILDERNESS EXPLORER MULTI-CALIBER CARBINE

Caliber: 22 Hornet, 218 Bee, 44 Magnum, 50 A.E. (interchangeable). **Barrel:** 18", match grade. **Weight:** 5.5 lbs **Length:** 38-1/2" overall. **Stock:**
Synthetic or wood. **Sights:** None furnished; comes with Weaver-style mount on barrel. **Features:** Quick-change barrel and bolt face for caliber switch. Removable box magazine; adjustable trigger with side safety; detachable swivel studs. Introduced 1997. Made in U.S. by Phillips & Rogers, Inc.
Price: **$995.00**

WINCHESTER MODEL 70 CLASSIC SPORTER LT

Caliber: 25-06, 270 Win., 270 Wea., 30-06, 264 Win. Mag., 7mm STW, 7mm Rem. Mag., 300 Win. Mag., 338 Win. Mag., 3-shot magazine; 5-shot for 25-06, 270 Win., 30-06. **Barrel:** 24", 26" for magnums. **Weight:** 7-3/4 lbs. **Length:** 44-3/4" overall. **Stock:** American walnut with cut checkering and satin finish. Classic style with straight comb. **Sights:** Optional hooded ramp front, adjustable folding leaf rear. Drilled and tapped for scope mounting. **Features:** Uses pre-64-type action with controlled round feeding. Three-position safety, stainless steel magazine follower; rubber butt pad; epoxy bedded receiver recoil lug. From U.S. Repeating Arms Co.
Price: Without sights. **$669.00**
Price: Left-hand, 270, 30-06, 7mm Rem. Mag., 7mm STW, 300 Win. Mag., 338 Win. Mag. **$669.00**

Winchester Model 70 Classic Stainless Rifle

Same as the Model 70 Classic Sporter except has stainless steel barrel and pre-64-style action with controlled round feeding and matte gray finish, black composite stock impregnated with fiberglass and graphite, contoured rubber recoil pad. Available in 22-250, 243, 308, 270 Win., 270 Wea. Mag., 30-06, 7mm Rem. Mag., 300 Win. Mag., 300 Wea. Mag., 338 Win. Mag., 375 H&H Mag. (24" barrel), 3- or 5-shot magazine. Weighs 6.75 lbs. Introduced 1994.
Price: Without sights. **$737.00**
Price: 375 H&H Mag., with sights. **$823.00**
Price: Classic Laminated Stainless (gray laminated stock, 270, 30-06, 7mm Rem. Mag., 300 Win. Mag., 338 Win. Mag.) . . **$737.00**

Winchester Model 70 Classic Featherweight

Winchester Model 70 Classic Compact

Winchester Model 70 Ranger

Winchester Model 70 Classic Super Grade

Winchester Model 70 Classic Featherweight

Same as the Model 70 Classic except has claw controlled-round feeding system; action is bedded in a standard-grade walnut stock. Available in 22-250, 243, 6.5x55, 308, 7mm-08, 270 Win., 280 Rem., 30-06. Drilled and tapped for scope mounts. Weighs 7.25 lbs. Introduced 1992.
Price: **$680.00**

Winchester Model 70 Classic Compact

Similar to the Classic Featherweight except scaled down for smaller shooters. Has 20" barrel, 12-1/2" length of pull. Pre-'64-type action. Available in 243, 308 or 7mm-08. Introduced 1998. Made in U.S. by U. S. Repeating Arms Co.
Price: **$680.00**

WINCHESTER RANGER RIFLE

Caliber: 223, 22-250, 243, 270, 30-06, 7mm Rem. Mag. **Barrel:** 22". **Weight:** 7-3/4 lbs. **Length:** 42" overall. **Stock:** Stained hardwood. **Sights:** Hooded blade front, adjustable open rear. **Features:** Three-position safety; push feed bolt with recessed-style bolt face; polished blue finish; drilled and tapped for scope mounting. Introduced 1985. From U.S. Repeating Arms Co.
Price: **$528.00**
Price: Ranger Compact, 22-250, 243, 7mm-08, 308 only, scaled-down stock **$528.00**

Winchester Model 70 Black Shadow

Similar to the Ranger except has black composite stock, matte blue barrel and action. Push-feed bolt design; hinged floorplate. Available in 270, 30-06, 7mm Rem. Mag., 300 Win. Mag. Made in U.S. by U.S. Repeating Arms Co.
Price: **$491.00**

WINCHESTER MODEL 70 STEALTH RIFLE

Caliber: 223, 22-250, 308 Win. **Barrel:** 26". **Weight:** 10-3/4 lbs. **Length:** 46" overall. **Stock:** Kevlar/fiberglass/graphite Pillar Plus Accu-Block with full-length aluminum bedding block. **Sights:** None furnished. **Features:** Push-feed bolt design; matte finish. Introduced 1999. Made in U. S. by U.S. Repeating Arms Co.
Price: 223 . . . . **$737.00**
Price: 22-250, 308 Win. **$737.00**

WINCHESTER MODEL 70 CLASSIC SUPER GRADE

Caliber: 270, 30-06, 5-shot magazine; 7mm Rem. Mag., 7mm STW, 300 Win. Mag., 338 Win. Mag., 3-shot magazine. **Barrel:** 24", 26" for magnums. **Weight:** About 7-3/4 lbs. to 8 lbs. **Length:** 44-1/2" overall (24" bbl.) **Stock:** Walnut with straight comb, sculptured cheekpiece, wrap-around cut checkering, tapered forend, solid rubber butt pad. **Sights:** None furnished; comes with scope bases and rings. **Features:** Controlled round feeding with stainless steel claw extractor, bolt guide rail, three-position safety; all steel bottom metal, hinged floorplate, stainless magazine follower. Introduced 1994. From U.S. Repeating Arms Co.
Price: **$702.00**

WINCHESTER MODEL 70 CLASSIC SAFARI EXPRESS MAGNUM

Caliber: 375 H&H Mag., 416 Rem. Mag., 458 Win. Mag., 3-shot magazine. **Barrel:** 24". **Weight:** 8-1/4 to 8-1/2 lbs. **Stock:** American walnut with Monte Carlo cheekpiece. Wrap-around checkering and finish. **Sights:** Hooded ramp front, open rear. **Features:** Controlled round feeding. Two steel cross bolts in stock for added strength. Front sling swivel stud mounted on barrel. Contoured rubber butt pad. From U.S. Repeating Arms Co.
Price: **$1,007.00**
Price: Left-hand, 375 H&H only **$1,042.00**

Ballard No. 5 Pacific

Ballard No. 7

Brown Model 97D

AMERICAN ARMS SHARPS 1874 DELUXE SPORTING RIFLE

Caliber: 45-70. **Barrel:** 28". **Weight:** 9 lbs., 3 oz. **Length:** 45-3/4" overall. **Stock:** European walnut; checkered grip and forend. **Sights:** Brass blade front, ladder-type adjustable rear. **Features:** Double-set triggers. Color case-hardened receiver, hammer, lever, browned barrel. Introduced 1999. Imported by American Arms, Inc.

Price: $705.00
Price: With blued barrel $685.00

American Arms Sharps Cavalry, Frontier Carbines

Similar to the 1874 Sporting RIfle except with 22" barrel. The Cavalry Carbine has double-set triggers; single trigger on Frontier, which also has a barrel band. Introduced 1999. Imported by American Arms, Inc.

Price: Cavalry carbine $660.00
Price: Frontier carbine $675.00

AMERICAN ARMS/UBERTI 1885 SINGLE SHOT

Caliber: 45-70. **Barrel:** 28". **Weight:** 8.75 lbs. **Length:** 44.5" overall. **Stock:** European walnut. **Sights:** Bead on blade front, open step-adjustable rear. **Features:** Recreation of the 1885 Winchester. Color case-hardened receiver and lever, blued barrel. Introduced 1998. Imported from Italy by American Arms. Inc.

Price: $810.00

ARMSPORT 1866 SHARPS RIFLE, CARBINE

Caliber: 45-70. **Barrel:** 28", round or octagonal. **Weight:** 8.10 lbs. **Length:** 46" overall. **Stock:** Walnut. **Sights:** Blade front, folding adjustable rear. Tang sight set optionally available. **Features:** Replica of the 1866 Sharps. Color case-hardened frame, rest blued. Imported by Armsport.

Price:. $865.00
Price: With octagonal barrel $900.00
Price: Carbine, 22" round barrel $850.00

BALLARD NO. 5 PACIFIC SINGLE-SHOT RIFLE

Caliber: 32-40, 38-55, 40-65, 40-90, 40-70 SS, 45-70 Govt., 45-110 SS, 50-70 Govt., 50-90 SS. **Barrel:** 30", or 32" octagonal. **Weight:** 10-1/2 lbs. **Length:** NA. **Stock:** High-grade walnut; rifle or shotgun style. **Sights:** Blade front, Rocky Mountain rear. **Features:** Standard or heavy barrel;

double-set triggers; under-barrel wiping rod; ring lever. Introduced 1999. Made in U.S. by Ballard Rifle & Cartridge Co.

Price: $2,575.00

BALLARD NO. 7 LONG RANGE RIFLE

Caliber: 32-40, 38-55, 40-65, 40-70 SS, 45-70 Govt., 45-90, 45-110. **Barrel:** 32", 34" half-octagon. **Weight:** 11-3/4 lbs. **Length:** NA. **Stock:** Fancy walnut; checkered pistol grip shotgun butt, ebony forend cap. **Sights:** Globe front. **Features:** Designed for shooting up to 1000 yards. Standard or heavy barrel; single or double-set trigger; hard rubber or steel buttplate. Introduced 1999. Made in U.S. by Ballard Rifle & Cartridge Co.

Price: From. $2,950.00

BALLARD NO. 8 UNION HILL RIFLE

Caliber: 22 LR, 32-40, 38-55, 40-65 Win., 40-70 SS. **Barrel:** 30" half-octagon. **Weight:** About 10-1/2 lbs. **Length:** NA. **Stock:** Fancy walnut; pistol grip butt with cheekpiece. **Sights:** Globe front. **Features:** Designed for 200-yard offhand shooting. Standard or heavy barrel; double-set triggers; full loop lever; hook Schuetzen buttplate. Introduced 1999. Made in U.S. by Ballard Rifle & Cartridge Co.

Price: From. $2,850.00

BALLARD MODEL 1885 HIGH WALL SINGLE SHOT RIFLE

Caliber: 17 Bee, 22 Hornet, 218 Bee, 219 Don Wasp, 219 Zipper, 22 Hi-Power, 225 Win., 25-20 WCF, 25-35 WCF, 25 Krag, 7mmx57R, 30-30, 30-40 Krag, 303 British, 33 WCF, 348 WCF, 35 WCF, 35-30/30, 9.3x74R, 405 WCF, 50-110 WCF, 500 Express, 577 Express. **Barrel:** Lengths to 34". **Weight:** N/A. **Length:** N/A. **Stock:** Straight-grain American walnut. **Sights:** buckhorn or flat top rear, blade front. **Features:** Faithful copy of original Model 1885 High Wall; parts interchange with original rifles; variety of options available. Introduced 2000. Made in U.S. by Ballard Rifle & Cartridge LLC.

Price: From $1,850.00
Price: With single set trigger from $2,050.00

CENTERFIRE RIFLES — SINGLE SHOT

Browning Model 1885 Traditional Hunter

Browning Model 1885 Low Wall

Cabela's Sharps

BARRETT MODEL 99 SINGLE SHOT RIFLE
Caliber: 50 BMG. **Barrel:** 33". **Weight:** 25 lbs. **Length:** 50.4" overall. **Stock:** Anodized aluminum with energy-absorbing recoil pad. **Sights:** None furnished; integral M1913 scope rail. **Features:** Bolt action; detachable bipod; match-grade barrel with high-efficiency muzzle brake. Introduced 1999. Made in U.S. by Barrett Firearms.
Price: From.. **$3,000.00**

BROWN MODEL 97D SINGLE SHOT RIFLE
Caliber: 17 Ackley Hornet through 45-70 Govt. **Barrel:** Up to 26", air gauged match grade. **Weight:** About 5 lbs., 11 oz. **Stock:** Sporter style with pistol grip, cheekpiece and Schnabel forend. **Sights:** None furnished; drilled and tapped for scope mounting. **Features:** Falling block action gives rigid barrel-receiver matting; polished blue/black finish. Hand-fitted action. Made in U.S. by E. A. Brown Mfg.
Price: **$599.00**

BROWNING MODEL 1885 HIGH WALL SINGLE SHOT RIFLE
Caliber: 22-250, 30-06, 270, 7mm Rem. Mag., 454 Casull, 45-70. **Barrel:** 28". **Weight:** About 8-1/2 lbs. **Length:** 43-1/2" overall. **Stock:** Walnut with straight grip, Schnabel forend. **Sights:** None furnished; drilled and tapped for scope mounting. **Features:** Replica of J.M. Browning's high-wall falling block rifle. Octagon barrel with recessed muzzle. Imported from Japan by Browning. Introduced 1985.
Price: **$987.00**

Browning Model 1885 BPCR Rifle
Similar to the 1885 High Wall rifle except the ejector system and shell deflector have been removed; chambered only for 40-65 and 45-70; color case-hardened full-tang receiver, lever, buttplate and gripcap; matte blue 30" part octagon, part round barrel. The Vernier tang sight has indexed elevation, is screw adjustable windage, and has three peep diameters. The hooded front sight has a built-in spirit level and comes with sight interchangeable inserts. Adjustable trigger. Overall length 46-1/8", weighs about 11 lbs. Introduced 1996. Imported from Japan by Browning.
Price: **$1,749.00**
Price: BPCR Creedmoor (45-90, 34" barrel with wind gauge sight) **$1,764.00**

Browning Model 1885 Traditional Hunter
Similar to the Model 1885 High Wall except chambered for 357 Mag., 44 Mag., 45 Colt, 30-30, 38-55 and 45-70 only; steel crescent buttplate; 1/16" gold bead front sight, adjustable buckhorn rear, and tang-mounted peep sight with barrel-type elevation adjuster and knob-type windage adjustments. Barrel is drilled and tapped for a Browning scope base. Oil-finished select walnut stock with swivel studs. Introduced 1997. Imported for Japan by Browning.
Price: High Wall **$1,208.95**
Price: Low Wall.. **$1,276.00**

Browning Model 1885 Low Wall Rifle
Similar to the Model 1885 High Wall except has trimmer receiver, thinner 24" octagonal barrel. Forend is mounted to the receiver. Adjustable trigger. Walnut pistol grip stock, trim Schnabel forend with high-gloss finish. Available in 22 Hornet, 223 Rem., 243 Win., 260 Rem. Overall length 39-1/2", weighs 6 lbs., 4 oz. Rifling twist rates: 1:16" (22 Hornet); 1:12" (223); 1:10" (243). Polished blue finish. Introduced 1995. Imported from Japan by Browning.
Price: **$987.00**

BRNO ZBK 110 SINGLE SHOT RIFLE
Caliber: 222 Rem., 5.6x52R, 22 Hornet, 5.6x50 Mag., 6.5x57R, 7x57R, 8x57JRS. **Barrel:** 23.6". **Weight:** 5.9 lbs. **Length:** 40.1" overall. **Stock:** European walnut. **Sights:** None furnished; drilled and tapped for scope mounting. **Features:** Top tang opening lever; cross-bolt safety; polished blue finish. Announced 1998. Imported from The Czech Republic by Euro-Imports.
Price: Standard calibers.................................. **$223.00**
Price: 7x57R, 8x57JRS **$245.00**
Price: Lux model, standard calibers...................... **$311.00**
Price: Lux model, 7x57R, 8x57JRS **$333.00**

CABELA'S SHARPS SPORTING RIFLE
Caliber: 45-70. **Barrel:** 32", tapered octagon. **Weight:** 9 lbs. **Length:** 47-1/4" overall. **Stock:** Checkered walnut. **Sights:** Blade front, open adjustable rear. **Features:** Color case-hardened receiver and hammer, rest blued. Introduced 1995. Imported by Cabela's.
Price: **$849.99**

CIMARRON BILLY DIXON 1874 SHARPS SPORTING RIFLE
Caliber: 40-65, 45-70. **Barrel:** 32" tapered octagon. **Weight:** NA. **Length:** NA. **Stock:** European walnut. **Sights:** Blade front, Creedmoor rear. **Features:** Color case-hardened frame, blued barrel. Hand-checkered grip and forend; hand-rubbed oil finish. Introduced 1999. Imported by Cimarron F.A. Co.
Price: **$1,495.00**

CIMARRON MODEL 1885 HIGH WALL RIFLE
Caliber: 38-55, 40-65, 45-70, 45-90. **Barrel:** 30" octagonal. **Weight:** NA. **Length:** NA. **Stock:** European walnut. **Sights:** Bead front, semi-buckhorn rear. **Features:** Replica of the Winchester 1885 High Wall rifle. Color case-hardened receiver and lever, blued barrel. Curved buttplate. Introduced 1999. Imported by Cimarron F.A. Co.
Price: **$995.00**

CIMARRON CREEDMOOR ROLLING BLOCK RIFLE
Caliber: 40-65, 45-70. **Barrel:** 30" tapered octagon. **Weight:** NA. **Length:** NA. **Stock:** European walnut. **Sights:** Globe front, fully adjustable rear. **Features:** Color case-hardened receiver, blued barrel. Hand-checkered pistol grip and forend; hand-rubbed oil finish. Introduced 1999. Imported by Cimarron F.A. Co.
Price: **$1,295.00**

Cumberland Mountain Plateau

Dakota Single Shot

Dixie 1874 Sharps Silhouette

H&R Ultra Hunter

CUMBERLAND MOUNTAIN PLATEAU RIFLE

Caliber: 40-65, 45-70. **Barrel:** Up to 32"; round. **Weight:** About 10-1/2 lbs. (32" barrel). **Length:** 48" overall (32" barrel). **Stock:** American walnut. **Sights:** Marble's bead front, Marble's open rear. **Features:** Falling block action with underlever. Blued barrel and receiver. Stock has lacquer finish, crescent buttplate. Introduced 1995. Made in U.S. by Cumberland Mountain Arms, Inc.

Price: $1,085.00

DAKOTA SINGLE SHOT RIFLE

Caliber: Most rimmed and rimless commercial calibers. **Barrel:** 23". **Weight:** 6 lbs. **Length:** 39-1/2" overall. **Stock:** Medium fancy grade walnut in classic style. Checkered grip and forend. **Sights:** None furnished. Drilled and tapped for scope mounting. **Features:** Falling block action with under-lever. Top tang safety. Removable trigger plate for conversion to single set trigger. Introduced 1990. Made in U.S. by Dakota Arms.

Price: $3,495.00
Price: Barreled action $2,050.00
Price: Action only $1,675.00
Price: Magnum calibers $3,595.00
Price: Magnum barreled action $2,050.00
Price: Magnum action only $1,775.00

DIXIE 1874 SHARPS BLACKPOWDER SILHOUETTE RIFLE

Caliber: 45-70. **Barrel:** 30"; tapered octagon; blued; 1:18" twist. **Weight:** 10 lbs., 3 oz. **Length:** 47-1/2" overall. **Stock:** Oiled walnut. **Sights:** Blade front, ladder-type hunting rear. **Features:** Replica of the Sharps #1 Sporter. Shotgun-style butt with checkered metal buttplate; color case-hardened receiver, hammer, lever and buttplate. Tang is drilled and tapped for tang sight. Double-set triggers. Meets standards for NRA blackpowder cartridge matches. Introduced 1995. Imported from Italy by Dixie Gun Works.

Price: $995.00

Dixie 1874 Sharps Lightweight Hunter/Target Rifle

Same as the Dixie 1874 Sharps Blackpowder Silhouette model except has a straight-grip buttstock with military-style buttplate. Based on the 1874 military model. Introduced 1995. Imported from Italy by Dixie Gun Works.

Price: $995.00

E.M.F. SHARPS RIFLE

Caliber: 45-70. **Barrel:** 28", octagon. **Weight:** 10-3/4 lbs. **Length:** NA. **Stock:** Oiled walnut. **Sights:** Blade front, flip-up open rear. **Features:** Replica of the 1874 Sharps Sporting rifle. Color case-hardened lock; double-set trigger; blue finish. Imported by E.M.F.

Price: $950.00
Price: With browned finish $1,000.00
Price: Carbine (round 22" barrel, barrel band) $860.00

HARRINGTON & RICHARDSON ULTRA VARMINT RIFLE

Caliber: 223, 243. **Barrel:** 24", heavy. **Weight:** About 7.5 lbs. **Length:** NA. **Stock:** Hand-checkered laminated birch with Monte Carlo comb. **Sights:** None furnished. Drilled and tapped for scope mounting. **Features:** Break-open action with side-lever release, positive ejection. Comes with scope mount. Blued receiver and barrel. Swivel studs. Introduced 1993. From H&R 1871, Inc.

Price: $254.95

Harrington & Richardson Ultra Hunter Rifle

Similar to the Ultra Varmint rifle except chambered for 25-06 with 26" barrel, or 308 Win., 357 Rem. Max. with 22" barrel. Stock and forend are of cinnamon-colored laminate; hand-checkered grip and forend. Introduced 1995. Made in U.S. by H&R 1871, Inc.

Price: $249.95

Harrington & Richardson Ultra Comp Rifle

Similar to the Ultra Varmint except chambered for 270 or 30-06; has compensator to reduce recoil; camo-laminate stock and forend; blued, highly polished frame; scope mount. Made in U.S. by H&R 1871, Inc.

Price: $289.95

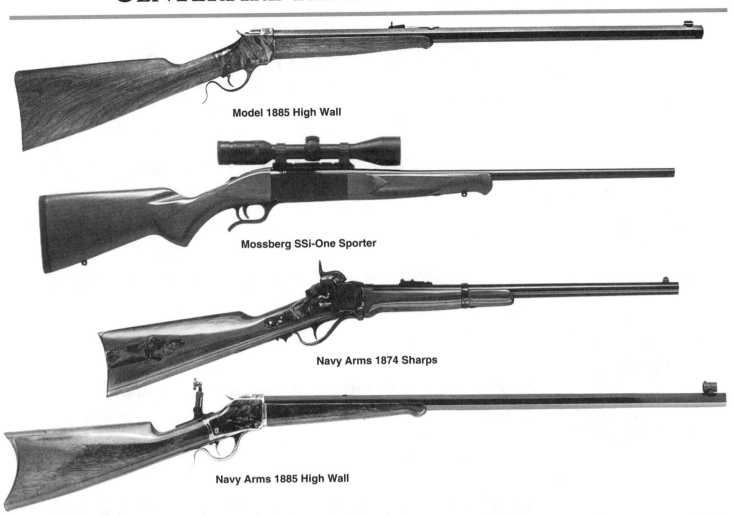

Model 1885 High Wall

Mossberg SSi-One Sporter

Navy Arms 1874 Sharps

Navy Arms 1885 High Wall

HARRIS GUNWORKS ANTIETAM SHARPS RIFLE

Caliber: 40-65, 45-75. **Barrel:** 30", 32", octagon or round, hand-lapped stainless or chrome-moly. **Weight:** 11.25 lbs. **Length:** 47" overall. **Stock:** Choice of straight grip, pistol grip or Creedmoor with Schnabel forend; pewter tip optional. Standard wood is A Fancy; higher grades available. **Sights:** Montana Vintage Arms #111 Low Profile Spirit Level front, #108 mid-range tang rear with windage adjustments. **Features:** Recreation of the 1874 Sharps sidehammer. Action is color case-hardened, barrel satin black. Chrome-moly barrel optionally blued. Optional sights include #112 Spirit Level Globe front with windage, #107 Long Range rear with windage. Introduced 1994. Made in U.S. by Harris Gunworks.
Price: **$2,400.00**

MODEL 1885 HIGH WALL RIFLE

Caliber: 30-40 Krag, 32-40, 38-55, 40-65 WCF, 45-70. **Barrel:** 26" (30-40), 28" all others. Douglas Premium #3 tapered octagon. **Weight:** NA. **Length:** NA. **Stock:** Premium American black walnut. **Sights:** Marble's standard ivory bead front, #66 long blade top rear with reversible notch and elevator. **Features:** Recreation of early octagon top, thick-wall High Wall with Coil spring action. Tang drilled, tapped for High Wall tang sight. Receiver, lever, hammer and breechblock color case-hardened. Introduced 1991. Available from Montana Armory, Inc.
Price: **$1,095.00**

MOSSBERG SSi-ONE SINGLE SHOT RIFLE

Caliber: 223 Rem., 22-250 Rem., 243 Win., 270 Win., 308 Rem., 30-06. **Barrel:** 24". **Weight:** 8 lbs. **Length:** 40". **Stock:** Satin-finished walnut, fluted and checkered; sling-swivel studs. **Sights:** None (scope base furnished). **Features:** Frame accepts interchangeable barrels, including 12-gauge, fully rifled slug barrel. Lever-opening, break-action design; single-stage trigger; ambidextrous, top-tang safety; internal eject/extract selector. Introduced 2000. From Mossberg.

Price: SSi-One Sporter (standard barrel) **$400.00**
Price: SSi-One Varmint (bull barrel, 22-250 Rem. only; weighs 10 lbs.) **$400.00**
Price: SSi-One 12-gauge Slug (fully rifled barrel, no sights, scope base) **$400.00**

NAVY ARMS 1874 SHARPS CAVALRY CARBINE

Caliber: 45-70. **Barrel:** 22". **Weight:** 7 lbs., 12 oz. **Length:** 39" overall. **Stock:** Walnut. **Sights:** Blade front, military ladder-type rear. **Features:** Replica of the 1874 Sharps military carbine. Color case-hardened receiver and furniture. Imported by Navy Arms.
Price: **$935.00**

Navy Arms 1874 Sharps Sniper Rifle

Similar to the Navy Arms Sharps Carbine except has 30" barrel, double-set triggers; weighs 8 lbs., 8 oz., overall length 46-3/4". Introduced 1984. Imported by Navy Arms.
Price: **$1,115.00**
Price: 1874 Sharps Infantry Rifle (three-band) **$1,060.00**

NAVY ARMS 1885 HIGH WALL RIFLE

Caliber: 45-70; others available on special order. **Barrel:** 28" round, 30" octagonal. **Weight:** 9.5 lbs. **Length:** 45-1/2" overall (30" barrel). **Stock:** Walnut. **Sights:** Blade front, buckhorn rear; globe front, Vernier tang-mounted peep rear. **Features:** Replica of Winchester's High Wall designed by Browning. Color case-hardened receiver, blued barrel. Introduced 1998. Imported by Navy Arms.
Price: 28", round barrel, buckhorn sights **$745.00**
Price: As above, target sights. **$845.00**
Price: 30" octagonal barrel, buckhorn sight **$815.00**
Price: As above, target sights. **$915.00**

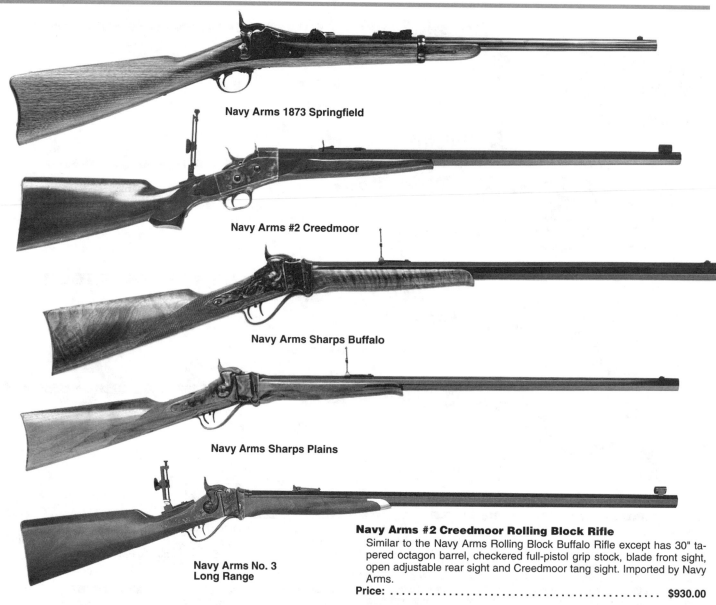

Navy Arms 1873 Springfield

Navy Arms #2 Creedmoor

Navy Arms Sharps Buffalo

Navy Arms Sharps Plains

Navy Arms No. 3
Long Range

NAVY ARMS 1873 SPRINGFIELD CAVALRY CARBINE

Caliber: 45-70. **Barrel:** 22". **Weight:** 7 lbs. **Length:** 40-1/2" overall. **Stock:** Walnut. **Sights:** Blade front, military ladder rear. **Features:** Blued lockplate and barrel; color case-hardened breechblock; saddle ring with bar. Replica of 7th Cavalry gun. Imported by Navy Arms.
Price: $870.00

Navy Arms 1873 Springfield Infantry Rifle

Same action as the 1873 Springfield Cavalry Carbine except in rifle configuration with 32-1/2" barrel, three-band full-length stock. Introduced 1997. Imported by Navy Arms.
Price: $995.00

NAVY ARMS ROLLING BLOCK BUFFALO RIFLE

Caliber: 45-70. **Barrel:** 26", 30". **Stock:** Walnut. **Sights:** Blade front, adjustable rear. **Features:** Reproduction of classic rolling block action. Available with full-octagon or half-octagon-half-round barrel. Color case-hardened action, steel fittings. From Navy Arms.
Price: $765.00

Navy Arms #2 Creedmoor Rolling Block Rifle

Similar to the Navy Arms Rolling Block Buffalo Rifle except has 30" tapered octagon barrel, checkered full-pistol grip stock, blade front sight, open adjustable rear sight and Creedmoor tang sight. Imported by Navy Arms.
Price: $930.00

NAVY ARMS 1874 SHARPS BUFFALO RIFLE

Caliber: 45-70, 45-90. **Barrel:** 28" heavy octagon. **Weight:** 10 lbs., 10 oz. **Length:** 46" overall. **Stock:** Walnut; checkered grip and forend. **Sights:** Blade front, ladder rear; tang sight optional. **Features:** Color case-hardened receiver, blued barrel; double-set triggers. Imported by Navy Arms.
Price: $1,090.00

Navy Arms Sharps Plains Rifle

Similar to the Sharps Buffalo rifle except 45-70 only, has 32" medium-weight barrel, weighs 9 lbs., 8 oz., and is 49" overall. Imported by Navy Arms.
Price: $1,055.00

Navy Arms Sharps Sporting Rifle

Same as the Navy Arms Sharps Plains Rifle except has pistol grip stock. Introduced 1997. Imported by Navy Arms.
Price: 45-70 only $1,090.00

NAVY ARMS SHARPS NO. 3 LONG RANGE RIFLE

Caliber: 45-70, 45-90. **Barrel:** 34" octagon. **Weight:** 10 lbs., 12 oz. **Length:** 51-1/2". **Stock:** Deluxe walnut. **Sights:** Globe target front and match grade rear tang. **Features:** Shotgun buttplate, German silver forend cap, color case hardenend receiver. Imported by Navy Arms.
Price: $1,745.00

New England Firearms Handi-Rifle

New England Firearms Super Light

New England Firearms Survivor

Remington No. 1 Mid-Range

NEW ENGLAND FIREARMS HANDI-RIFLE

Caliber: 22 Hornet, 223, 243, 7x57, 7x64 Brenneke, 30-30, 270, 280 Rem., 308, 30-06, 44 Mag., 45-70. **Barrel:** 22", 24"; 26" for 280 Rem. **Weight:** 7 lbs. **Stock:** Walnut-finished hardwood; black rubber recoil pad. **Sights:** Ramp front, folding rear (22 Hornet, 30-30, 45-70). Drilled and tapped for scope mount; 223, 243, 270, 280, 30-06 have no open sights, come with scope mounts. **Features:** Break-open action with side-lever release. The 223, 243, 270 and 30-06 have recoil pad and Monte Carlo stock for shooting with scope. Swivel studs on all models. Blue finish. Introduced 1989. From New England Firearms.

Price: $209.95
Price: 7x57, 7x64 Brenneke, 24" barrel $211.95
Price: 280 Rem., 26" barrel $214.95
Price: Synthetic Handi-Rifle (black polymer stock and forend, swivels, recoil pad). $219.95
Price: Handi-Rifle Youth (223, 243) $209.95

New England Firearms Super Light Rifle

Similar to the Handi-Rifle except has new barrel taper, shorter 20" barrel with recessed muzzle and special lightweight synthetic stock and forend. No sights are furnished on the 223 and 243 versions, but have a factory-mounted scope base and offset hammer spur; Monte Carlo stock; 22 Hornet has ramp front, fully adjustable open rear. Overall length is 36", weight is 5.5 lbs. Introduced 1997. Made in U.S. by New England Firearms.
Price: 22 Hornet, 223 Rem. or 243 Win. $219.95

NEW ENGLAND FIREARMS SURVIVOR RIFLE

Caliber: 223, 357 Mag., single shot. **Barrel:** 22". **Weight:** 6 lbs. **Length:** 36" overall. **Stock:** Black polymer, thumbhole design. **Sights:** Blade front, fully adjustable open rear. **Features:** Receiver drilled and tapped for scope mounting. Stock and forend have storage compartments for ammo, etc.; comes with integral swivels and black nylon sling. Introduced 1996. Made in U.S. by New England Firearms.
Price: Blue $219.95
Price: Electroless nickel $234.95

REMINGTON NO. 1 ROLLING BLOCK MID-RANGE SPORTER

Caliber: 45-70. **Barrel:** 30" round. **Weight:** 8-3/4 lbs. **Length:** 46-1/2" overall. **Stock:** American walnut with checkered pistol grip and forend. **Sights:** Beaded blade front, adjustable center-notch buckhorn rear. **Features:** Recreation of the original. Polished blue metal finish. Many options available. Introduced 1998. Made in U.S. by Remington.
Price: $1,348.00

Ruger No. 1B

Ruger K1-B-BBZ

Ruger No. 1V Varminter

Ruger No. 1 RSI

Ruger No. 1H Tropical

RUGER NO. 1B SINGLE SHOT

NEW! **Caliber:** 218 Bee, 22 Hornet, 220 Swift, 22-250, 223, 243, 6mm Rem., 25-06, 257 Roberts, 270, 280, 30-06, 7mm Rem. Mag., 300 Win. Mag., 338 Win. Mag., 270 Wea., 300 Wea. **Barrel:** 26" round tapered with quarter-rib; with Ruger 1" rings. **Weight:** 8 lbs. **Length:** 43-3/8" overall. **Stock:** Walnut, two-piece, checkered pistol grip and semi-beavertail forend. **Sights:** None, 1" scope rings supplied for integral mounts. **Features:** Under-lever, hammerless falling block design has auto ejector, top tang safety.
Price: 1B **$774.00**
Price: Barreled action **$555.00**
Price: K1-B-BBZ Stainless steel, laminated stock 25-06, 7MM mag, 7MM STW, 300 Win Mag. **$820.00**

Ruger No. 1A Light Sporter

Similar to the No. 1B Standard Rifle except has lightweight 22" barrel, Alexander Henry-style forend, adjustable folding leaf rear sight on quarter-rib, dovetailed ramp front with gold bead. Calibers 243, 30-06, 270 and 7x57. Weighs about 7-1/4 lbs.
Price: No. 1A **$774.00**
Price: Barreled action **$555.00**

Ruger No. 1V Varminter

Similar to the No. 1B Standard Rifle except has 24" heavy barrel. Semi-beavertail forend, barrel ribbed for target scope block, with 1" Ruger scope rings. Calibers 22-250, 220 Swift, 223, 25-06. Weight about 9 lbs.

Price: No. 1V **$774.00**
Price: Barreled action **$555.00**
Price: K1-U-BBZ stainless steel, laminated stock 22-250 . . . . . . **$820.00**

Ruger No. 1 RSI International

Similar to the No. 1B Standard Rifle except has lightweight 20" barrel, full-length International-style forend with loop sling swivel, adjustable folding leaf rear sight on quarter-rib, ramp front with gold bead. Calibers 243, 30-06, 270 and 7x57. Weight is about 7-1/4 lbs.
Price: No. 1 RSI **$794.00**
Price: Barreled action **$555.00**

Ruger No. 1H Tropical Rifle

Similar to the No. 1B Standard Rifle except has Alexander Henry forend, adjustable folding leaf rear sight on quarter-rib, ramp front with dovetail gold bead, 24" heavy barrel. Calibers 375 H&H, 416 Rem. Mag. (weighs about 8-1/4 lbs.), 416 Rigby, and 458 Win. Mag. (weighs about 9 lbs.).
Price: No. 1H **$774.00**
Price: Barreled action **$555.00**

Ruger No. 1S Medium Sporter

Similar to the No. 1B Standard Rifle except has Alexander Henry-style forend, adjustable folding leaf rear sight on quarter-rib, ramp front sight base and dovetail-type gold bead front sight. Calibers 218 Bee, 7mm Rem. Mag., 338 Win. Mag., 300 Win. Mag. with 26" barrel, 45-70 with 22" barrel. Weighs about 7-1/2 lbs. In 45-70.
Price: No. 1S **$774.00**
Price: Barreled action **$555.00**

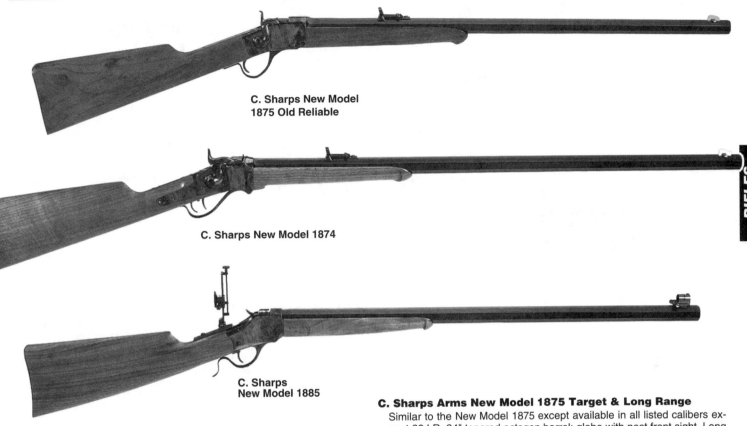

C. Sharps New Model 1875 Old Reliable

C. Sharps New Model 1874

C. Sharps New Model 1885

Ruger No. 1 Stainless Steel Rifles

Similar to No. 1 Standard except has stainless steel receiver and barrel, laminated hardwood stock. Calibers 25-06, 7mm Rem. Mag., 7mm STW, 300 Win. Mag. (Standard) or 22-250 (Varminter). Introduced 2000.

Price: No. 1 Stainless Standard (26" barrel, 8 lbs.) **$820.00**
Price: No. 1 Stainless Varminter (24" heavy barrel,
9 lbs.) **$820.00**

C. SHARPS ARMS NEW MODEL 1875 OLD RELIABLE RIFLE

Caliber: 22LR, 32-40 & 38-55 Ballard, 38-56 WCF, 40-65 WCF, 40-90 3-1/4", 40-90 2-5/8", 40-70 2-1/10", 40-70 2-1/4", 40-70 2-1/2", 40-50 1-11/16", 40-50 1-7/8", 45-90, 45-70, 45-100, 45-110, 45-120. Also available on special order only in 50-70, 50-90, 50-140. **Barrel:** 24", 26", 30" (standard), 32", 34" optional. **Weight:** 8-12 lbs. **Stock:** Walnut, straight grip, shotgun butt with checkered steel buttplate. **Sights:** Silver blade front, Rocky Mountain buckhorn rear. **Features:** Recreation of the 1875 Sharps rifle. Production guns will have case colored receiver. Available in Custom Sporting and Target versions upon request. Announced 1986. From C. Sharps Arms Co. and Montana Armory, Inc.

Price: 1875 Carbine (24" tapered round bbl.) **$810.00**
Price: 1875 Saddle Rifle (26" tapered oct. bbl.) **$910.00**
Price: 1875 Sporting Rifle (30" tapered oct. bbl.) **$975.00**
Price: 1875 Business Rifle (28" tapered round bbl.) **$860.00**

C. Sharps Arms 1875 Classic Sharps

Similar to the New Model 1875 Sporting Rifle except has 26", 28" or 30" full octagon barrel, crescent buttplate with toe plate, Hartford-style forend with cast German silver nose cap. Blade front sight, Rocky Mountain buckhorn rear. Weighs 10 lbs. Introduced 1987. From C. Sharps Arms Co. and Montana Armory, Inc.

Price: **$1,185.00**

C. Sharps Arms New Model 1875 Target & Long Range

Similar to the New Model 1875 except available in all listed calibers except 22 LR; 34" tapered octagon barrel; globe with post front sight, Long Range Vernier tang sight with windage adjustments. Pistol grip stock with cheek rest; checkered steel buttplate. Introduced 1991. From C. Sharps Arms Co. and Montana Armory, Inc.

Price: **$1,535.00**

C. SHARPS ARMS NEW MODEL 1874 OLD RELIABLE

Caliber: 40-50, 40-70, 40-90, 45-70, 45-90, 45-100, 45-110, 45-120, 50-70, 50-90, 50-140. **Barrel:** 26", 28", 30" tapered octagon. **Weight:** About 10 lbs. **Length:** NA. **Stock:** American black walnut; shotgun butt with checkered steel buttplate; straight grip, heavy forend with Schnabel tip. **Sights:** Blade front, buckhorn rear. Drilled and tapped for tang sight. **Features:** Recreation of the Model 1874 Old Reliable Sharps Sporting Rifle. Double set triggers. Reintroduced 1991. Made in U.S. by C. Sharps Arms. Available from Montana Armory, Inc.

Price: **$1,175.00**

C. SHARPS ARMS NEW MODEL 1885 HIGHWALL RIFLE

Caliber: 22 LR, 22 Hornet, 219 Zipper, 25-35 WCF, 32-40 WCF, 38-55 WCF, 40-65, 30-40-Krag, 40-50 ST or BN, 40-70 ST or BN, 40-90 ST or BN, 45-70 2-1/10" ST, 45-90 2-4/10" ST, 45-100 2-6/10" ST, 45-110 2-7/8" ST, 45-120 3-1/4" ST. **Barrel:** 26", 28", 30", tapered full octagon. **Weight:** About 9 lbs. **Length:** 47" overall. **Stock:** Oil-finished American walnut; Schnabel-style forend. **Sights:** Blade front, buckhorn rear. Drilled and tapped for optional tang sight. **Features:** Single trigger; octagonal receiver top; checkered steel buttplate; color case-hardened receiver and buttplate, blued barrel. Many options available. Made in U.S. by C. Sharps Arms Co. Available from Montana Armory, Inc.

Price: From **$1,195.00**

SHARPS 1874 RIFLE

Caliber: 45-70. **Barrel:** 28", octagonal. **Weight:** 9-1/4 lbs. **Length:** 46" overall. **Stock:** Checkered walnut. **Sights:** Blade front, adjustable rear. **Features:** Double set triggers on rifle. Color case-hardened receiver and buttplate, blued barrel. Imported from Italy by E.M.F.

Price: Rifle or carbine **$950.00**
Price: Military rifle, carbine **$860.00**
Price: Sporting rifle **$860.00**

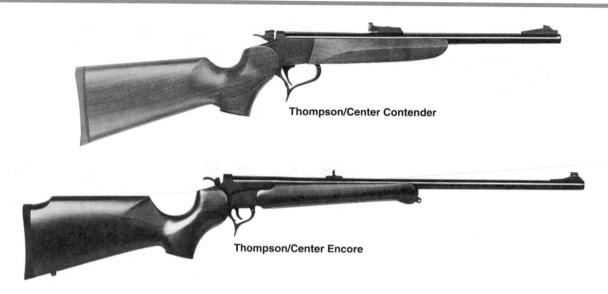

Thompson/Center Contender

Thompson/Center Encore

SHILOH SHARPS 1874 LONG RANGE EXPRESS

Caliber: 40-50 BN, 40-70 BN, 40-90 BN, 45-70 ST, 45-90 ST, 45-110 ST, 50-70 ST, 50-90 ST, 50-110 ST, 32-40, 38-55, 40-70 ST, 40-90 ST. **Barrel:** 34" tapered octagon. **Weight:** 10-1/2 lbs. **Length:** 51" overall. **Stock:** Oil-finished semi-fancy walnut with pistol grip, shotgun-style butt, traditional cheek rest, Schnabel forend. **Sights:** Globe front, sporting tang rear. **Features:** Recreation of the Model 1874 Sharps rifle. Double set triggers. Made in U.S. by Shiloh Rifle Mfg. Co.

Price: **$1,796.00**
Price: Sporting Rifle No. 1 (similar to above except with 30" bbl., blade front, buckhorn rear sight) **$1,706.00**
Price: Sporting Rifle No. 3 (similar to No. 1 except straight-grip stock, standard wood) **$1,504.00**
Price: 1874 Hartford model. **$1,702.00**

Shiloh Sharps 1874 Montana Roughrider

Similar to the No. 1 Sporting Rifle except available with half-octagon or full-octagon barrel in 24", 26", 28", 30", 34" lengths; standard supreme or semi-fancy wood, shotgun, pistol grip or military-style butt. Weight about 8-1/2 lbs. Calibers 30-40, 30-30, 40-50x1-11/16"BN, 40-70x2-1/10" BN, 45-70x2-1/10"ST. Globe front and tang sight optional.
Price: Standard supreme **$1,504.00**
Price: Semi-fancy **$1,704.00**

Shiloh Sharps 1874 Business Rifle

Similar to No. 3 Rifle except has 28" heavy round barrel, military-style buttstock and steel buttplate. Weight about 9-1/2 lbs. Calibers 40-50 BN, 40-70 BN, 40-90 BN, 45-70 ST, 45-90 ST, 50-70 ST, 50-100 ST, 32-40, 38-55, 40-70 ST, 40-90 ST.
Price: **$1,604.00**
Price: 1874 Saddle Rifle (similar to Carbine except has 26" octagon barrel, semi-fancy shotgun butt) **$1,706.00**

THOMPSON/CENTER CONTENDER CARBINE

Caliber: 22 LR, 22 Hornet, 223 Rem., 7x30 Waters, 30-30 Win. **Barrel:** 21". **Weight:** 5 lbs., 2 oz. **Length:** 35" overall. **Stock:** Checkered American walnut with rubber butt pad. Also with Rynite stock and forend. **Sights:** Blade front, open adjustable rear. **Features:** Uses the T/C Contender action. Eleven interchangeable barrels available, all with sights, drilled and tapped for scope mounting. Introduced 1985. Offered as a complete Carbine only.
Price: Rifle calibers. **$571.38**
Price: Extra barrels, rifle calibers, each **$251.08**

THOMPSON/CENTER ENCORE RIFLE

Caliber: 22-250, 223, 243, 25-06, 270, 7mm-08, 308, 30-06, 7mm Rem. Mag., 300 Win. Mag. **Barrel:** 24", 26". **Weight:** 6 lbs., 12 oz. (24" barrel). **Length:** 38-1/2" (24" barrel). **Stock:** American walnut. Monte Carlo style; Schnabel forend or black composite. **Sights:** Ramp-style white bead front, fully adjustable leaf-type rear. **Features:** Interchangeable barrels; action opens by squeezing trigger guard; drilled and tapped for T/C scope mounts; polished blue finish. Introduced 1996. Made in U.S. by Thompson/Center Arms.
Price: **$582.29**
Price: Extra barrels. **$249.10**
Price: With black composite stock and forend **$582.29**

Thompson/Center Stainless Encore Rifle

Similar to the blued Encore except made of stainless steel with blued sights, and has black composite stock and forend. Available in 22-250, 223, 7mm-08, 30-06, 308. Introduced 1999. Made in U.S. by Thompson/Center Arms.
Price: **$650.42**

UBERTI ROLLING BLOCK BABY CARBINE

Caliber: 22 LR, 22 WMR, 22 Hornet, 357 Mag., single shot. **Barrel:** 22". **Weight:** 4.8 lbs. **Length:** 35-1/2" overall. **Stock:** Walnut stock and forend. **Sights:** Blade front, fully adjustable open rear. **Features:** Resembles Remington New Model No. 4 carbine. Brass trigger guard and buttplate; color case-hardened frame, blued barrel. Imported by Uberti USA Inc.
Price: **$490.00**

WESSON & HARRINGTON BUFFALO CLASSIC RIFLE

Caliber: 45-70. **Barrel:** 32" heavy. **Weight:** 9 lbs. **Length:** 52" overall. **Stock:** American black walnut. **Sights:** None furnished; drilled and tapped for peep sight; barrel dovetailed for front sight. **Features:** Color case-hardened Handi-Rifle action with exposed hammer; color case-hardened crescent buttplate; 19th century checkering pattern. Introduced 1995. Made in U.S. by H&R 1871, Inc.
Price: About **$349.95**

Wesson & Harrington 38-55 Target Rifle

Similar to the Buffalo Classic rifle except chambered for 38-55 Win., has 28" barrel. The barrel and steel furniture, including steel trigger guard and forend spacer, are highly polished and blued. Color case-hardened receiver and buttplate. Barrel is dovetailed for a front sight, and drilled and tapped for receiver sight or scope mount. Introduced 1998. Made in U.S. by H&R 1871, Inc.
Price: **$389.95**

RIFLES

DRILLINGS, COMBINATION GUNS, DOUBLE GUNS

Designs for sporting and utility purposes worldwide.

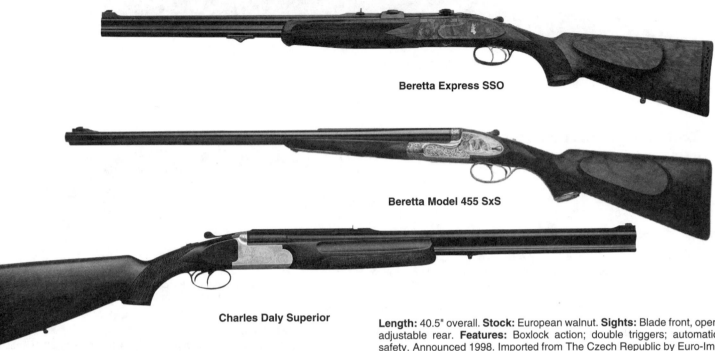

Beretta Express SSO

Beretta Model 455 SxS

Charles Daly Superior

AMERICAN ARMS SILVER EXPRESS O/U DOUBLE RIFLE
Caliber: 8x57 JRS, 9.3x74R. **Barrel:** 24". **Weight:** 7 lbs., 14 oz. **Length:** 41-1/4" overall. **Stock:** European walnut. **Sights:** Ramped high-visibility front, standing leaf rear on rib. **Features:** Boxlock action with single trigger, extractors; engraved, silvered receiver; blued barrels; no barrel center rib. Introduced 1999. Imported by American Arms, Inc.
Price: **$1,949.00**

BERETTA EXPRESS SSO O/U DOUBLE RIFLES
Caliber: 375 H&H, 458 Win. Mag., 9.3x74R. **Barrel:** 25.5". **Weight:** 11 lbs. **Stock:** European walnut with hand-checkered grip and forend. **Sights:** Blade front on ramp, open V-notch rear. **Features:** Sidelock action with color case-hardened receiver (gold inlays on SSO6 Gold). Ejectors, double triggers, recoil pad. Introduced 1990. Imported from Italy by Beretta U.S.A.
Price: SSO6 . . . . **$21,000.00**
Price: SSO6 Gold **$23,500.00**

BERETTA MODEL 455 SxS EXPRESS RIFLE
Caliber: 375 H&H, 458 Win. Mag., 470 NE, 500 NE 3", 416 Rigby. **Barrel:** 23-1/2" or 25-1/2". **Weight:** 11 lbs. **Stock:** European walnut with hand-checkered grip and forend. **Sights:** Blade front, folding leaf V-notch rear. **Features:** Sidelock action with easily removable sideplates; color case-hardened finish (455), custom big game or floral motif engraving (455EELL). Double triggers, recoil pad. Introduced 1990. Imported from Italy by Beretta U.S.A.
Price: Model 455. . . . . **$36,000.00**
Price: Model 455EELL **$47,000.00**

BRNO 500 COMBINATION GUNS
Caliber/Gauge: 12 (2-3/4" chamber) over 5.6x52R, 5.6x50R, 222 Rem., 243, 6.x55, 308, 7x57R, 7x65R, 30-06. **Barrel:** 23.6". **Weight:** 7.6 lbs. **Length:** 40.5" overall. **Stock:** European walnut. **Sights:** Bead front, V-notch rear; grooved for scope mounting. **Features:** Boxlock action; double set trigger; blue finish with etched engraving. Announced 1998. Imported from The Czech Republic by Euro-Imports.
Price: **$1,023.00**
Price: O/U double rifle, 7x57R, 7x65R, 8x57JRS **$1,125.00**

BRNO ZH 300 COMBINATION GUN
Caliber/Gauge: 22 Hornet, 5.6x50R Mag., 5.6x52R, 7x57R, 7x65R, 8x57JRS over 12, 16 (2-3/4" chamber). **Barrel:** 23.6". **Weight:** 7.9 lbs.

Length: 40.5" overall. **Stock:** European walnut. **Sights:** Blade front, open adjustable rear. **Features:** Boxlock action; double triggers; automatic safety. Announced 1998. Imported from The Czech Republic by Euro-Imports.
Price: **$724.00**

BRNO ZH Double Rifles
Similar to the ZH 300 combination guns except with double rifle barrels. Available in 7x65R, 7x57R and 8x57JRS. Announced 1998. Imported from The Czech Republic by Euro-Imports.
Price: **$1,125.00**

CHARLES DALY SUPERIOR COMBINATION GUN
Caliber/Gauge: 12 ga. over 22 Hornet, 223 Rem., 22-250, 243 Win., 270 Win., 308 Win., 30-06. **Barrel:** 23.5", shotgun choked Imp. Cyl. **Weight:** About 7.5 lbs. **Stock:** Checkered walnut pistol grip buttstock and semi-beavertail forend. **Features:** Silvered, engraved receiver; chrome-moly steel barrels; double triggers; extractors; sling swivels; gold bead front sight. Introduced 1997. Imported from Italy by K.B.I. Inc.
Price: **$1,249.95**

Charles Daly Empire Combination Gun
Same as the Superior grade except has deluxe wood with European-style comb and cheekpiece; slim forend. Introduced 1997. Imported from Italy by K.B.I., Inc.
Price: **$1,789.95**

CZ 584 SOLO COMBINATION GUN
Caliber/Gauge: 7x57R; 12, 2-3/4" chamber. **Barrel:** 24.4". **Weight:** 7.37 lbs. **Length:** 45.25" overall. **Stock:** Circassian walnut. **Sights:** Blade front, open rear adjustable for windage. **Features:** Kersten-style double lump locking system; double-trigger Blitz-type mechanism with drop safety and adjustable set trigger for the rifle barrel; auto safety, dual extractors; receiver dovetailed for scope mounting. Imported from the Czech Republic by CZ-USA.
Price: **$850.00**

EAA/BAIKAL IZH-94 COMBINATION GUN

Caliber/Gauge: 12, 3" chamber; 222 Rem., 223, 5.6x50R, 5.6x55E, 7x57R, 7x65R, 7.62x39, 7.62x51, 308, 7.62x53R, 7.62x54R, 30-06. **Barrel:** 24", 26"; imp., mod. and full choke tubes. **Weight:** 7.28 lbs. **Stock:** Walnut; rubber butt pad. **Sights:** Express style. **Features:** Hammer-forged barrels with chrome-lined bores; machined receiver; single-selective or double triggers. Imported by European American Armory.
Price: Blued finish. **$499.00**

DRILLINGS, COMBINATION GUNS, DOUBLE GUNS

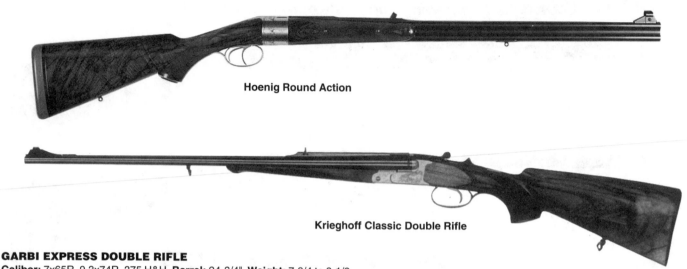

Hoenig Round Action

Krieghoff Classic Double Rifle

GARBI EXPRESS DOUBLE RIFLE

Caliber: 7x65R, 9.3x74R, 375 H&H. **Barrel:** 24-3/4". **Weight:** 7-3/4 to 8-1/2 lbs. **Length:** 41-1/2" overall. **Stock:** Turkish walnut. **Sights:** Quarter-rib with express sight. **Features:** Side-by-side double; H&H-pattern sidelock ejector with reinforced action, chopper lump barrels of Boehler steel; double triggers; fine scroll and rosette engraving, or full coverage ornamental; coin-finished action. Introduced 1997. Imported from Spain by Wm. Larkin Moore.

Price: **$21,800.00**

HOENIG ROTARY ROUND ACTION DOUBLE RIFLE

Caliber: Most popular calibers from 225 Win. to 9.3x74R. **Barrel:** 22"-26". **Weight:** NA. **Length:** NA. **Stock:** English Walnut; to customer specs. **Sights:** Swivel hood front with button release (extra bead stored in trap door gripcap), express-style rear on quarter-rib adjustable for windage and elevation; scope mount. **Features:** Round action opens by rotating barrels, pulling forward. Has inertia extractor system; rotary safety blocks the strikers; single lever quick-detachable scope mount. Simple takedown without removing forend. Introduced 1997. Made in U.S. by George Hoenig.

Price: **$19,980.00**

KRIEGHOFF CLASSIC DOUBLE RIFLE

Caliber: 7x65R, 308 Win., 30-06, 30R Blaser, 8x57 JRS, 8x75RS, 9.3x74R. **Barrel:** 23.5". **Weight:** 7.3 to 8 lbs. **Length:** NA. **Stock:** High grade European walnut. Standard has conventional rounded cheekpiece, Bavaria has Bavarian-style cheekpiece. **Sights:** Bead front with removable, adjustable wedge (375 H&H and below), standing leaf rear on quarter-rib. **Features:** Boxlock action; double triggers; short opening angle for fast loading; quiet extractors; sliding, self-adjusting wedge for secure bolting; Purdey-style barrel extension; horizontal firing pin placement. Many options available. Introduced 1997. Imported from Germany by Krieghoff International.

Price: With small Arabesque engraving **$7,850.00**
Price: With engraved sideplates. **$9,800.00**
Price: For extra barrels. **$4,500.00**
Price: Extra 20-ga., 28" shotshell barrels **$3,200.00**

Krieghoff Classic Big Five Double Rifle

Similar to the standard Classic excpet available in 375 Flanged Mag. N.E., 500/416 N.E., 470 N.E., 500 N.E. 3". Has hinged front trigger, non-removable muzzle wedge (larger than 375-caliber), Universal Trigger System, Combi Cocking Device, steel trigger guard, specially weighted stock bolt for weight and balance. Many options available. Introduced 1997. Imported from Germany by Krieghoff International.

Price: **$9,450.00**
Price: With engraved sideplates. **$11,400.00**

LEBEAU - COURALLY EXPRESS RIFLE SxS

Caliber: 7x65R, 8x57JRS, 9.3x74R, 375 H&H, 470 N.E. **Barrel:** 24" to 26". **Weight:** 7-3/4 to 10-1/2 lbs. **Stock:** Fancy French walnut with cheekpiece. **Sights:** Bead on ramp front, standing left express rear on quarter-rib. **Fea-**tures: Holland & Holland-type sidelock with automatic ejectors; double triggers. Imported from Belgium by Wm. Larkin Moore.

Price: **$51,000.00**

MERKEL DRILLINGS

Caliber/Gauge: 12, 20, 3" chambers, 16, 2-3/4" chambers; 22 Hornet, 5.6x50R Mag., 5.6x52R, 222 Rem., 243 Win., 6.5x55, 6.5x57R, 7x57R, 7x65R, 308, 30-06, 8x57JRS, 9.3x74R, 375 H&H. **Barrel:** 25.6". **Weight:** 7.9 to 8.4 lbs. depending upon caliber. **Length:** NA. **Stock:** Oil-finished walnut with pistol grip; cheekpiece on 12-, 16-gauge. **Sights:** Blade front, fixed rear. **Features:** Double barrel locking lug with Greener cross-bolt; scroll-engraved, case-hardened receiver; automatic trigger safety; Blitz action; double triggers. Imported from Germany by GSI.

Price: Model 96K (manually cocked rifle system), from **$6,495.00**
Price: Model 96K Engraved (hunting series on receiver) **$7,995.00**

MERKEL OVER/UNDER DOUBLE RIFLES

Caliber: 22 Hornet, 5.6x50R Mag., 5.6x52R, 222 Rem., 243 Win., 6.5x55, 6.5x57R, 7x57R, 7x65R, 308, 30-06, 8x57JRS, 9.3x74R. **Barrel:** 25.6". **Weight:** About 7.7 lbs, depending upon caliber. **Length:** NA. **Stock:** Oil-finished walnut with pistol grip, cheekpiece. **Sights:** Blade front, fixed rear. **Features:** Kersten double cross-bolt lock; scroll-engraved, case-hardened receiver; Blitz action with double triggers. Imported from Germany by GSI.

Price: Model 221 E (silver-grayed receiver finish, hunting scene engraving). **$10,895.00**

MERKEL MODEL 160 SIDE-BY-SIDE DOUBLE RIFLE

Caliber: 22 Hornet, 5.6x50R Mag., 5.6x52R, 222 Rem., 243 Win., 6.5x55, 6.5x57R, 7x57R, 7x65R, 308, 30-06, 8x57JRS, 9.3x74R, 375 H&H. **Barrel:** 25.6". **Weight:** About 7.7 lbs, depending upon caliber. **Length:** NA. **Stock:** Oil-finished walnut with pistol grip, cheekpiece. **Sights:** Blade front on ramp, fixed rear. **Features:** Sidelock action. Double barrel locking lug with Greener cross-bolt; fine engraved hunting scenes on sideplates; Holland & Holland ejectors; double triggers. Imported from Germany by GSI.

Price: From. **$13,295.00**

Merkel Boxlock Double Rifles

Similar to the Model 160 double rifle except with Anson & Deely boxlock action with cocking indicators, double triggers, engraved color case-hardened receiver. Introduced 1995. Imported from Germany by GSI.

Price: Model 140-1, from **$5,995.00**
Price: Model 140-1.1 (engraved silver-gray receiver), from **$6,995.00**
Price: Model 150-1 (false sideplates, silver-gray receiver, Arabesque engraving), from **$7,495.00**
Price: Model 150-1.1 (as above with English Arabesque engraving), from **$8,995.00**

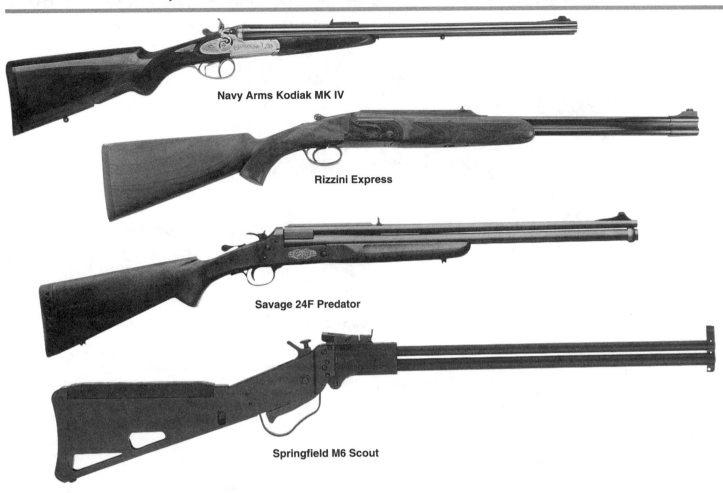

Navy Arms Kodiak MK IV

Rizzini Express

Savage 24F Predator

Springfield M6 Scout

NAVY ARMS KODIAK MK IV DOUBLE RIFLE

Caliber: 45-70. **Barrel:** 24". **Weight:** 10 lbs., 3 oz. **Length:** 39-3/4" overall. **Stock:** Checkered European walnut. **Sights:** Bead front, folding leaf express rear. **Features:** Blued, semi-regulated barrels; color case-hardened receiver and hammers; double triggers. Replica of Colt double rifle 1879-1885. Introduced 1996. Imported by Navy Arms.

Price: **$2,815.00**
Price: Engraved satin-finished receiver, browned barrels **$3,690.00**

RIZZINI EXPRESS 90L DOUBLE RIFLE

Caliber: 30-06, 7x65R, 9.3x74R. **Barrel:** 24". **Weight:** 7-1/2 lbs. **Length:** 40" overall. **Stock:** Select European walnut with satin oil finish; English-style cheekpiece. **Sights:** Ramp front, quarter-rib with express sight. **Features:** Color case-hardened boxlock action; automatic ejectors; single selective trigger; polished blue barrels. Extra 20-gauge shotshell barrels available. Imported for Italy by Wm. Larkin Moore.

Price: With case **$4,500.00**

SAVAGE 24F PREDATOR O/U COMBINATION GUN

Caliber/Gauge: 22 Hornet, 223, 30-30 over 12 (24F-12) or 22 LR, 22 Hornet, 223, 30-30 over 20-ga. (24F-20); 3" chambers. **Action:** Takedown, low rebounding visible hammer. Single trigger, barrel selector spur on hammer. **Barrel:** 24" separated barrels; 12-ga. has Full, Mod., Imp. Cyl. choke tubes, 20-ga. has fixed Mod. choke. **Weight:** 8 lbs. **Length:** 40-1/2" overall. **Stock:** Black Rynite composition. **Sights:** Ramp front, rear open adjustable for elevation. Grooved for tip-off scope mount. **Features:** Removable butt cap for storage and accessories. Introduced 1989.

Price: 24F-12 .... **$476.00**
Price: 24F-20 .... **$449.00**

Savage 24F-12/410 Combination Gun

Similar to the 24F-12 except comes with "Four-Tenner" adaptor for shooting 410-bore shotshells. Rifle barrel chambered for 22 Hornet, 223 Rem., 30-30 Win. Introduced 1998. Made in U.S. by Savage Arms, Inc.

Price: **$504.00**

SPRINGFIELD, INC. M6 SCOUT RIFLE/SHOTGUN

Caliber/Gauge: 22 LR or 22 Hornet over 410-bore. **Barrel:** 18.25". **Weight:** 4 lbs. **Length:** 32" overall. **Stock:** Folding detachable with storage for 15 22 LR, four 410 shells. **Sights:** Blade front, military aperture for 22; V-notch for 410. **Features:** All-metal construction. Designed for quick disassembly and minimum maintenance. Folds for compact storage. Introduced 1982; reintroduced 1996. Imported from the Czech Republic by Springfield, Inc.

Price: Parkerized **$185.00**
Price: Stainless steel **$219.00**

Designs for hunting, utility and sporting purposes, including training for competition

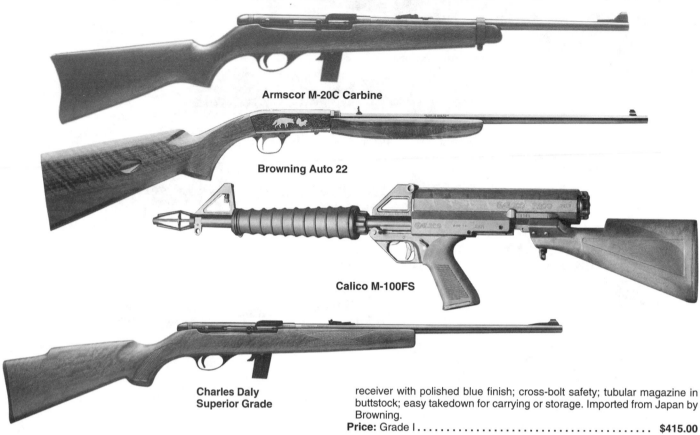

Armscor M-20C Carbine

Browning Auto 22

Calico M-100FS

Charles Daly
Superior Grade

AR-7 EXPLORER CARBINE

Caliber: 22 LR, 8-shot magazine. **Barrel:** 16". **Weight:** 2-1/2 lbs. **Length:** 34-1/2" / 16-1/2" stowed. **Stock:** Moulded Cycolac; snap-on rubber butt pad. **Sights:** Square blade front, aperture rear. **Features:** Takedown design stores barrel and action in hollow stock. Light enough to float. Reintroduced 1999. From AR-7 Industries, LLC.

Price: $150.00
Price: AR-20 Explorer (tubular stock, barrel shroud) $200.00

ARMSCOR MODEL AK22 AUTO RIFLE

Caliber: 22 LR, 10-shot magazine. **Barrel:** 18.5". **Weight:** 7.5 lbs. **Length:** 38" overall. **Stock:** Plain mahogany. **Sights:** Adjustable post front, leaf rear adjustable for elevation. **Features:** Resembles the AK-47. Matte black finish. Introduced 1987. Imported from the Philippines by K.B.I., Inc.

Price: About $219.95

ARMSCOR M-1600 AUTO RIFLE

Caliber: 22 LR, 10-shot magazine. **Barrel:** 18.25". **Weight:** 6.2 lbs. **Length:** 38.5" overall. **Stock:** Black finished mahogany. **Sights:** Post front, aperture rear. **Features:** Resembles Colt AR-15. Matte black finish. Introduced 1987. Imported from the Philippines by K.B.I., Inc.

Price: About $199.95

ARMSCOR M-20C AUTO CARBINE

Caliber: 22 LR, 10-shot magazine. **Barrel:** 18.25". **Weight:** 6.5 lbs. **Length:** 38" overall. **Stock:** Walnut-finished mahogany. **Sights:** Hooded front, rear adjustable for elevation. **Features:** Receiver grooved for scope mounting. Blued finish. Introduced 1990. Imported from the Philippines by K.B.I., Inc.

Price: $154.95

BROWNING AUTO-22 RIFLE

Caliber: 22 LR, 11-shot. **Barrel:** 19-1/4". **Weight:** 4-3/4 lbs. **Length:** 37" overall. **Stock:** Checkered select walnut with pistol grip and semi-beavertail forend. **Sights:** Gold bead front, folding leaf rear. **Features:** Engraved receiver with polished blue finish; cross-bolt safety; tubular magazine in buttstock; easy takedown for carrying or storage. Imported from Japan by Browning.

Price: Grade I $415.00

Browning Auto-22 Grade VI

Same as the Grade I Auto-22 except available with either grayed or blued receiver with extensive engraving with gold-plated animals: right side pictures a fox and squirrel in a woodland scene; left side shows a beagle chasing a rabbit. On top is a portrait of the beagle. Stock and forend are of high-grade walnut with a double-bordered cut checkering design. Introduced 1987.

Price: Grade VI, blue or gray receiver $860.00

BRNO ZKM 611 AUTO RIFLE

Caliber: 22 WMR, 6- or 10-shot magazine. **Barrel:** 20.4". **Weight:** 5.9 lbs. **Length:** 38.9" overall. **Stock:** European walnut. **Sights:** Hooded blade front, open adjustable rear. **Features:** Removable box magazine; polished blue finish; cross-bolt safety; grooved receiver for scope mounting; easy takedown for storage. Imported from The Czech Republic by Euro-Imports.

Price: $475.00

CALICO M-100FS CARBINE

Caliber: 22 LR. **Barrel:** 16.25". **Weight:** 5 lbs. **Length:** 36" overall. **Stock:** Glass-filled, impact-resistant polymer. **Sights:** Adjustable post front, notch rear. **Features:** Has helical-feed magazine; aluminum receiver; ambidextrous safety. Made in U.S. by Calico.

Price: $650.00

CHARLES DALY FIELD GRADE AUTO RIFLE

Caliber: 22 LR, 10-shot magazine. **Barrel:** 20-3/4". **Weight:** 6.5 lbs. **Length:** 40-1/2" overall. **Stock:** Walnut-finished hardwood with Monte Carlo. **Sights:** Hooded front, adjustable open rear. **Features:** Receiver grooved for scope mounting; blue finish; shell deflector. Introduced 1998. Imported by K.B.I.

Price: $124.00
Price: Superior Grade (cut checkered stock, fully adjustable sight) $199.00

RIFLES

CZ 511 Auto

Henry U.S. Survival

Marlin Model 60

Marlin Model 60 SSK

Marlin Model 70PSS

Charles Daly Empire Grade Auto Rifle

Similar to the Field Grade except has select California walnut stock with 24 l.p.i. hand checkering, contrasting forend and gripcaps, damascened bolt, high-polish blue. Introduced 1998. Imported by K.B.I.

Price: **$369.00**

CZ 511 AUTO RIFLE

Caliber: 22 LR, 8-shot magazine. **Barrel:** 22.2". **Weight:** 5.39 lbs. **Length:** 38.6" overall. **Stock:** Walnut with checkered pistol grip. **Sights:** Hooded front, adjustable rear. **Features:** Polished blue finish; detachable magazine; sling swivel studs. Imported from the Czech Republic by CZ-USA.

Price: **$351.00**

HENRY U.S. SURVIVAL RIFLE .22

Caliber: 22 LR, 8-shot magazine. **Barrel:** 16" steel lined. **Weight:** 2.5 lbs. **Stock:** ABS plastic. **Sights:** Blade front on ramp, aperture rear. **Features:** Takedown design stores barrel and action in hollow stock. Light enough to float. Silver, black or camo finish. Comes with two magazines. Introduced 1998. From Henry Repeating Arms Co.

Price: **$165.00**

MAGTECH MT 7022 AUTO RIFLE

Caliber: 22 LR, 10-shot magazine. **Barrel:** 18". **Weight:** 4.8 lbs. **Length:** 37" overall. **Stock:** Brazilian hardwood. **Sights:** Hooded blade front, fully adjustable open rear. **Features:** Cross-bolt safety; last-shot bolt hold-open; alloy receiver is drilled and tapped for scope mounting. Introduced 1998. Imported from Brazil by Magtech Ammunition Co.

Price: **$100.00**

MARLIN MODEL 60 SELF-LOADING RIFLE

Caliber: 22 LR, 14-shot tubular magazine. **Barrel:** 22" round tapered. **Weight:** About 5-1/2 lbs. **Length:** 40-1/2" overall. **Stock:** Press-checkered, walnut-finished Maine birch with Monte Carlo, full pistol grip; Mar-Shield® finish. **Sights:** Ramp front, open adjustable rear. **Features:** Matted receiver is grooved for scope mount. Manual bolt hold-open; automatic last-shot bolt hold-open.

Price: **$172.00**
Price: With 4x scope. **$179.00**

Marlin Model 60SS Self-Loading Rifle

Same as the Model 60 except breech bolt, barrel and outer magazine tube are made of stainless steel; most other parts are either nickel-plated or coated to match the stainless finish. Monte Carlo stock is of black/gray Maine birch laminate, and has nickel-plated swivel studs, rubber butt pad. Introduced 1993.

Price: **$273.00**
Price: Model 60SSK (black fiberglass-filled stock) **$236.00**
Price: Model 60SSK with 4x scope **$251.00**
Price: Model 60SB (walnut-finished birch stock) **$219.00**
Price: Model 60SB with 4x scope. **$232.00**

MARLIN 70PSS STAINLESS RIFLE

Caliber: 22 LR, 7-shot magazine. **Barrel:** 16-1/4" stainless steel, Micro-Groove® rifling. **Weight:** 3-1/4 lbs. **Length:** 35-1/4" overall. **Stock:** Black fiberglass-filled synthetic with abbreviated forend, nickel-plated swivel studs, moulded-in checkering. **Sights:** Ramp front with orange post, cut-away Wide Scan® hood; adjustable open rear. Receiver grooved for scope mounting. **Features:** Takedown barrel; cross-bolt safety; manual bolt hold-open; last shot bolt hold-open; comes with padded carrying case. Introduced 1986. Made in U.S. by Marlin.

Price: **$278.00**

RIFLES

Marlin
Model 922

Marlin 7000

Marlin 795

Remington 597

MARLIN MODEL 922 MAGNUM SELF-LOADING RIFLE

Caliber: 22 WMR, 5-shot magazine. **Barrel:** 20.5". **Weight:** 6.5 lbs. **Length:** 39.75" overall. **Stock:** Now walnut finished hardwood, swivel studs, rubber butt pad. **Sights:** Ramp front with bead and removable Wide-Scan® hood, adjustable folding semi-buckhorn rear. **Features:** Action based on the centerfire Model 9 Carbine. Receiver drilled and tapped for scope mounting. Automatic last-shot bolt hold-open; magazine safety. Introduced 1993.
Price: $441.00

MARLIN MODEL 7000 SELF-LOADING RIFLE

Caliber: 22 LR, 10-shot magazine **Barrel:** 18" heavy target with 12-groove Micro-Groove® rifling, recessed muzzle. **Weight:** 5-1/2 lbs. **Length:** 37" overall. **Stock:** Black fiberglass-filled synthetic with Monte Carlo combo, swivel studs, moulded-in checkering. **Sights:** None furnished; comes with ring mounts. **Features:** Automatic last-shot bolt hold-open; manual bolt hold-open; cross-bolt safety; steel charging handle; blue finish, nickel-plated magazine. Introduced 1997. Made in U.S. by Marlin Firearms Co.
Price: $232.00

Marlin Model 795 Self-Loading Rifle

Similar to the Model 7000 except has standard-weight 18" barrel with 16-groove Micro-Groove rifling. Comes with ramp front sight with brass bead, screw adjustable open rear. Receiver grooved for scope mount. Introduced 1997. Made in U.S. by Marlin Firearms Co.
Price: $164.00
Price: With 4x scope........................... $171.00

REMINGTON MODEL 552 BDL DELUXE SPEEDMASTER RIFLE

Caliber: 22 S (20), L (17) or LR (15) tubular mag. **Barrel:** 21" round tapered. **Weight:** 5-3/4 lbs. **Length:** 40" overall. **Stock:** Walnut. Checkered grip and forend. **Sights:** Bead front, step open rear adjustable for windage and elevation. **Features:** Positive cross-bolt safety, receiver grooved for tip-off mount.
Price: $365.00

REMINGTON 597 AUTO RIFLE

Caliber: 22 LR, 10-shot clip. **Barrel:** 20". **Weight:** 5-1/2 lbs. **Length:** 40" overall. **Stock:** Gray synthetic. **Sights:** Bead front, fully adjustable rear. **Features:** Matte black finish, nickel-plated bolt. Receiver is grooved and drilled and tapped for scope mounts. Introduced 1997. Made in U.S. by Remington.
Price: $163.00
Price: Model 597 Magnum, 22 WMR, 8-shot clip............. $321.00
Price: Model 597 Magnum LS (laminated stock) $377.00
Price: Model 597 Sporter (22 LR, wood stock)............... $199.00
Price: Model 597 SS (22 LR, stainless steel, black synthetic stock) $217.00
Price: Model 597 Stainless Sporter / wood stock, SS barrel, 10-shot clip.. $239.00

Remington 597 LSS Auto Rifle

Similar to the Model 597 except has satin-finish stainless barrel, gray-toned alloy receiver with nickel-plated bolt, and laminated wood stock. Receiver is grooved and drilled and tapped for scope mounting. Introduced 1997. Made in U.S. by Remington.
Price: $272.00

Ruger 10/22 International

Savage Model 64FV

RUGER 10/22 AUTOLOADING CARBINE

Caliber: 22 LR, 10-shot rotary magazine. **Barrel:** 18-1/2" round tapered. **Weight:** 5 lbs. **Length:** 37-1/4" overall. **Stock:** American hardwood with pistol grip and barrel. band. **Sights:** Brass bead front, folding leaf rear adjustable for elevation. **Features:** Detachable rotary magazine fits flush into stock, cross-bolt safety, receiver tapped and grooved for scope blocks or tip-off mount. Scope base adaptor furnished with each rifle.

Price: Model 10/22 RB (blue) **$235.00**
Price: Model K10/22RB (bright finish stainless barrel) **$273.00**
Price: Model 10/22RP (blue, synthetic stock)................ **$230.00**

Ruger 10/22 International Carbine

Similar to the Ruger 10/22 Carbine except has full-length International stock of American hardwood, checkered grip and forend; comes with rubber butt pad, sling swivels. Reintroduced 1994.

Price: Blue (10/22RBI) **$267.00**
Price: Stainless (K10/22RBI) **$267.00**

Ruger 10/22 Deluxe Sporter

Same as 10/22 Carbine except walnut stock with hand checkered pistol grip and forend; straight buttplate, no barrel band, has sling swivels.
Price: Model 10/22 DSP................................ **$279.00**

Ruger 10/22T Target Rifle

Similar to the 10/22 except has 20" heavy, hammer-forged barrel with tight chamber dimensions, improved trigger pull, laminated hardwood stock dimensioned for optical sights. No iron sights supplied. Introduced 1996. Made in U.S. by Sturm, Ruger & Co.
Price: 10/22T **$397.50**
Price: K10/22T, stainless steel........................... **$445.00**

Ruger K10/22RP All-Weather Rifle

Similar to the stainless K10/22/RP except has black composite stock of thermoplastic polyester resin reinforced with fiberglass; checkered grip and forend. Brushed satin, natural metal finish with clear hardcoat finish. Weighs 5 lbs., measures 36-3/4" overall. Introduced 1997. From Sturm, Ruger & Co.
Price: **$273.00**

RUGER 10/22 MAGNUM AUTOLOADING CARBINE

Caliber: 22 WMR, 10-shot rotary magazine. **Barrel:** 18-1/2". **Weight:** 6 lbs. **Length:** 37-1/4" overall. **Stock:** Birch. **Sights:** Gold bead front, folding rear. **Features:** All-steel receiver has integral Ruger scope bases for the included 1" rings. Introduced 1999. Made in U.S. by Sturm, Ruger & Co.
Price: **$430.00**

SAVAGE MODEL 64G AUTO RIFLE

Caliber: 22 LR, 10-shot magazine. **Barrel:** 20". **Weight:** 5-1/2 lbs. **Length:** 40" overall. **Stock:** Walnut-finished hardwood with Monte Carlo-type comb, checkered grip and forend. **Sights:** Bead front, open adjustable rear. Receiver grooved for scope mounting. **Features:** Thumb-operated rotating safety. Blue finish. Side ejection, bolt hold-open device. Introduced 1990. Made in Canada, from Savage Arms.
Price: **$134.00**
Price: Model 64F, black synthetic stock **$124.00**
Price: Model 64GXP Package Gun includes 4x15 scope and
  mounts **$140.00**
Price: Model 64FXP (black stock, 4x15 scope) **$128.00**

Savage Model 64FV Auto Rifle

Similar to the Model 64F except has heavy 21" barrel with recessed crown; no sights provided—comes with Weaver-style bases. Introduced 1998. Imported from Canada by Savage Arms, Inc.
Price: **$164.00**

THOMPSON/CENTER 22 LR CLASSIC RIFLE

Caliber: 22 LR, 8-shot magazine. **Barrel:** 22" match-grade. **Weight:** 5-1/2 pounds. **Length:** 39-1/2" overall. **Stock:** Satin-finished American walnut with Monte Carlo-type comb and pistol grip cap, swivel studs. **Sights:** Ramp-style front and fully adjustable rear, both with fiber optics. **Features:** All-steel receiver drilled and tapped for scope mounting; barrel threaded to receiver; thumb-operated safety; trigger-guard safety lock included.
Price: T/C 22 LR Classic (blue) **$335.55**

WINCHESTER MODEL 63 AUTO RIFLE

Caliber: 22 LR, 10-shot magazine. **Barrel:** 23". **Weight:** 6-1/4 lbs. **Length:** 39" overall. **Stock:** Walnut. **Sights:** Bead front, open adjustable rear. **Features:** Recreation of the original Model 63. Magazine tube loads through a port in the buttstock; forward cocking knob at front of forend; easy takedown for cleaning, storage; engraved receiver. Reintroduced 1997. From U.S. Repeating Arms Co.
Price: Grade I.. **$678.00**
Price: High grade, select walnut, cut checkering, engraved scenes
  with gold accents on receiver (made in 1997 only) **$1,083.00**

Classic and modern models for sport and utility, including training.

Browning BL-22

Henry Lever-Action 22

Henry Goldenboy 22

Henry Pump-Action 22

Marlin Model 39AS

BROWNING BL-22 LEVER-ACTION RIFLE

Caliber: 22 S (22), L (17) or LR (15), tubular magazine. **Barrel:** 20" round tapered. **Weight:** 5 lbs. **Length:** 36-3/4" overall. **Stock:** Walnut, two-piece straight grip Western style. **Sights:** Bead post front, folding-leaf rear. **Features:** Short throw lever, half-cock safety, receiver grooved for tip-off scope mounts. Imported from Japan by Browning.
Price: Grade I $360.00
Price: Grade II (engraved receiver, checkered grip and forend) . $412.00

HENRY LEVER-ACTION 22

Caliber: 22 Long Rifle (15-shot). **Barrel:** 18-1/4" round. **Weight:** 5-1/2 lbs. **Length:** 34" overall. **Stock:** Walnut. **Sights:** Hooded blade front, open adjustable rear. **Features:** Polished blue finish; full-length tubular magazine; side ejection; receiver grooved for scope mounting. Introduced 1997. Made in U.S. by Henry Repeating Arms Co.
Price: $239.95
Price: Youth model (33" overall, 11-rounds 22 LR) $229.95

HENRY GOLDENBOY 22 LEVER-ACTION RIFLE

Caliber: 22 LR, 16-shot. **Barrel:** 20" octagonal. **Weight:** 6.25 lbs. **Length:** 38" overall. **Stock:** American walnut. **Sights:** Blade front, open rear. **Features:** Brasslite receiver, brass buttplate, blued barrel and lever. Introduced 1998. Made in U.S. from Henry Repeating Arms Co.
Price: $329.95

HENRY PUMP-ACTION 22 PUMP RIFLE

Caliber: 22 LR, 15-shot. **Barrel:** 18.25". **Weight:** 5.5 lbs. **Length:** NA. **Stock:** American walnut. **Sights:** Bead on ramp front, open adjustable rear. **Features:** Polished blue finish; receiver groved for scope mount; grooved slide handle; two barrel bands. Introduced 1998. Made in U.S. from Henry Repeating Arms Co.
Price: $249.95

MARLIN MODEL 39AS GOLDEN LEVER-ACTION RIFLE

Caliber: 22 S (26), L (21), LR (19), tubular magazine. **Barrel:** 24" Micro-Groove®. **Weight:** 6-1/2 lbs. **Length:** 40" overall. **Stock:** Checkered American black walnut with white line spacers at pistol gripcap and buttplate; Mar-Shield® finish. Swivel studs; rubber butt pad. **Sights:** Bead ramp front with detachable Wide-Scan™ hood, folding rear semi-buckhorn adjustable for windage and elevation. **Features:** Hammer-block safety; rebounding hammer. Takedown action, receiver tapped for scope mount (supplied), offset hammer spur; gold-plated steel trigger.
Price: $509.00

Marlin Model 1897CB Cowboy Lever Action Rifle

Similar to the Model 39AS except it has straight-grip stock with hard rubber buttplate; blued steel forend cap; 24" tapered octagon barrel with Micro-Groove® rifling; adjustable Marble semi-buckhorn rear sight, Marble carbine front with brass bead; overall length 40". Introduced 1999. Made in U.S. by Marlin.
Price: $687.00

Remington Model 572

Ruger Model 96/22

Winchester 9422 Large Loop

Winchester Model 9422 Trapper

REMINGTON 572 BDL DELUXE FIELDMASTER PUMP RIFLE
Caliber: 22 S (20), L (17) or LR (14), tubular magazine. **Barrel:** 21" round tapered. **Weight:** 5-1/2 lbs. **Length:** 40" overall. **Stock:** Walnut with checkered pistol grip and slide handle. **Sights:** Blade ramp front; sliding ramp rear adjustable for windage and elevation. **Features:** Cross-bolt safety; removing inner magazine tube converts rifle to single shot; receiver grooved for tip-off scope mount.
Price: **$379.00**

RUGER MODEL 96/22 LEVER-ACTION RIFLE
Caliber: 22 LR, 10-shot rotary magazine; 22 WMR, 9-shot rotary magazine. **Barrel:** 18-1/2". **Weight:** 5-1/4 lbs. **Length:** 37-1/4" overall. **Stock:** American hardwood. **Sights:** Gold bead front, folding leaf rear. **Features:** Cross-bolt safety, visible cocking indicator; short-throw lever action. Screw-on dovetail scope base. Introduced 1996. Made in U.S. by Sturm, Ruger & Co.
Price: 96/22 (22 LR) **$332.50**
Price: 96/22M (22 WMR) **$350.00**

TAURUS MODEL 62R PUMP RIFLE
Caliber: 22 LR, 13-shot. **Barrel:** 23" round. **Weight:** 5-3/4 lbs. **Length:** 39" overall. **Stock:** Walnut-finished hardwood, straight grip, grooved forend. **Sights:** Fixed front, adjustable rear. **Features:** Blue finish; bolt-mounted safety; quick takedown. Imported from Brazil by Interarms.
Price: **$279.00**

Taurus Model 62C Pump Carbine
Same as standard model except 22 LR, has 16-1/2" barrel. Magazine holds 12 cartridges.
Price: **$279.00**

WINCHESTER MODEL 9422 LEVER-ACTION RIFLE
Caliber: 22 LR, 22 WMR, tubular magazine. **Barrel:** 20-1/2". **Weight:** 6-1/4 lbs. **Length:** 37-1/8" overall. **Stock:** American walnut, two-piece, straight grip (no pistol grip). **Sights:** Hooded ramp front, adjustable semi-buckhorn rear. **Features:** Side ejection, receiver grooved for scope mounting, take-down action. From U.S. Repeating Arms Co.
Price: Traditional **$437.00**
Price: Model 9422 Legacy (semi-pistol grip stock, 22 LR and 22 WMR)
.... **$467.00**

Winchester Model 9422 Magnum Lever-Action Rifle
Same as the 9422 except chambered for 22 WMR cartridge, has 11-round mag. capacity.
Price: Traditional **$457.00**
Price: Legacy 22 WMR **$488.00**

Winchester Model 9422 Trapper
Similar to the Model 9422 with walnut stock except has 16-1/2" barrel, overall length of 33-1/8", weighs 5-1/2 lbs. Magazine holds 15 Shorts, 12 Longs, 11 Long Rifles. Introduced 1996.
Price: **$437.00**
Price: 22 WMR, 8-shot **$457.00**

WINCHESTER MODEL 1892 SHORT LEVER-ACTION RIFLE
Caliber: 44 Mag.; 11-shot magazine. **Barrel:** 20". **Weight:** 6-1/4 lbs. **Length:** 37-3/4" overall. **Stock:** Smooth walnut. **Sights:** Blade front, buckhorn-style, ramp-adjustable rear. **Features:** Dual, vertical locking lugs; compact design with shorter forearm resembles original design. From U.S. Repeating Co., Inc.
Price: **$752.00**

WINCHESTER MODEL 1886 EXTRA LIGHT GRADE I

Caliber: 45-70, 4-shot magazine. **Barrel:** 22". **Weight:** 7-1.4 lbs. **Length:** 40-1/2" overall. **Sights:** Blade front, buckhorn-style ramp-adjustable rear. **Features:** Round, tapered barrel; shotgun-style steel buttplate; half-magazine. Limited production. Introduced 2000. From U.S. Repeating Arms Co., Inc.
Price: **$1,156.00**
Price: High Grade (extra-fancy, checkered walnut stock,
engraved elk and deer scenes) **$1,447.00**

Anschutz 1518D Luxus

Anschutz 1710D

Charles Daly Field Grade

ANSCHUTZ 1416D/1516D CLASSIC RIFLES

Caliber: 22 LR (1416D), 5-shot clip; 22 WMR (1516D), 4-shot clip. **Barrel:** 22-1/2". **Weight:** 6 lbs. **Length:** 41" overall. **Stock:** European hardwood with walnut finish; classic style with straight comb, checkered pistol grip and forend. **Sights:** Hooded ramp front, folding leaf rear. **Features:** Uses Match 64 action. Adjustable single stage trigger. Receiver grooved for scope mounting. Imported from Germany by AcuSport Corp.

Price: 1416D, 22 LR $755.95
Price: 1516D, 22 WMR.................................. $779.95
Price: 1416D Classic left-hand........................ $679.95

Anschutz 1416D/1516D Walnut Luxus Rifles

Similar to the Classic models except have European walnut stocks with Monte Carlo cheekpiece, slim forend with Schnabel tip, cut checkering on grip and forend. Introduced 1997. Imported from Germany by AcuSport Corp.

Price: 1416D (22 LR) $755.95
Price: 1516D (22 WMR) $779.95

ANSCHUTZ 1518D LUXUS BOLT-ACTION RIFLE

Caliber: 22 WMR, 4-shot magazine. **Barrel:** 19-3/4". **Weight:** 5-1/2 lbs. **Length:** 37-1/2" overall. **Stock:** European walnut. **Sights:** Blade on ramp front, folding leaf rear. **Features:** Receiver grooved for scope mounting; single stage trigger; skip-line checkering; rosewood forend tip; sling swivels. Imported from Germany by AcuSport Corp.

Price: $1,186.95

ANSCHUTZ 1710D CUSTOM RIFLE

Caliber: 22 LR, 5-shot clip. **Barrel:** 24-1/4". **Weight:** 7-3/8 lbs. **Length:** 42-1/2" overall. **Stock:** Select European walnut. **Sights:** Hooded ramp front, folding leaf rear; drilled and tapped for scope mounting. **Features:** Match 54 action with adjustable single-stage trigger; roll-over Monte Carlo cheekpiece, slim forend with Schnabel tip, Wundhammer palm swell on pistol grip, rosewood gripcap with white diamond insert; skip-line checkering on grip and forend. Introduced 1988. Imported from Germany by AcuSport Corp.

Price: $1,289.95

CABANAS MASTER BOLT-ACTION RIFLE

Caliber: 177, round ball or pellet; single shot. **Barrel:** 19-1/2". **Weight:** 8 lbs. **Length:** 45-1/2" overall. **Stocks:** Walnut target-type with Monte Carlo. **Sights:** Blade front, fully adjustable rear. **Features:** Fires round ball or pellet with 22-cal. blank cartridge. Bolt action. Imported from Mexico by Mandall Shooting Supplies. Introduced 1984.

Price: $189.95
Price: Varmint model (has 21-1/2" barrel, 4-1/2 lbs., 41" overall length, varmint-type stock)................................... $119.95

Cabanas Leyre Bolt-Action Rifle

Similar to Master model except 44" overall, has sport/target stock.
Price: $149.95
Price: Model R83 (17" barrel, hardwood stock, 40" o.a.l.) $79.95
Price: Mini 82 Youth (16-1/2" barrel, 33" overall length, 3-1/2 lbs.) . $69.95
Price: Pony Youth (16" barrel, 34" overall length, 3.2 lbs.) $69.95

Cabanas Espronceda IV Bolt-Action Rifle

Similar to the Leyre model except has full sporter stock, 18-3/4" barrel, 40" overall length, weighs 5-1/2 lbs.
Price: $134.95

CABANAS LASER RIFLE

Caliber: 177. **Barrel:** 19". **Weight:** 6 lbs., 12 oz. **Length:** 42" overall. **Stock:** Target-type thumbhole. **Sights:** Blade front, open fully adjustable rear. **Features:** Fires round ball or pellets with 22 blank cartridge. Imported from Mexico by Mandall Shooting Supplies.

Price: $159.95

CHARLES DALY SUPERIOR BOLT-ACTION RIFLE

Caliber: 22 LR, 10-shot magazine. **Barrel:** 22-5/8". **Weight:** 6.7 lbs. **Length:** 41.25" overall. **Stock:** Walnut-finished mahogany. **Sights:** Bead front, rear adjustable for elevation. **Features:** Receiver grooved for scope mounting. Blued finish. Introduced 1998. Imported by K.B.I., Inc.

Price: $189.95

Charles Daly Field Grade Rifle

Similar to the Superior except has short walnut-finished hardwood stock for small shooters. Introduced 1998. Imported by K.B.I., Inc.

Price: $134.95
Price: Field Youth (17.5" barrel) $144.95

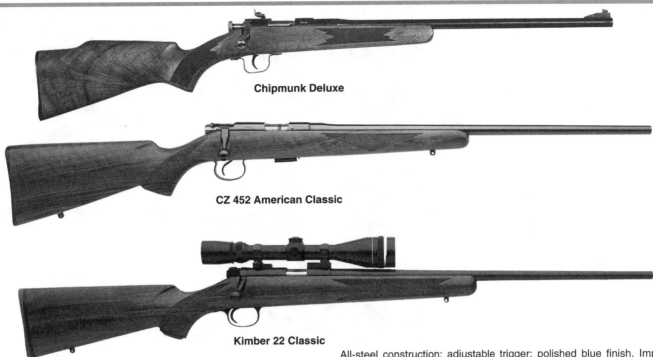

Chipmunk Deluxe

CZ 452 American Classic

Kimber 22 Classic

Charles Daly Superior Magnum Grade Rifle

Similar to the Superior except chambered for 22 WMR. Has 22.6" barrel, double lug bolt, checkered stock, weighs 6.5 lbs. Introduced 1987.
Price: About **$204.95**

Charles Daly Empire Magnum Grade Rifle

Similar to the Superior Magnum except has oil-finished American walnut stock with 18 lpi hand checkering; black hardwood gripcap and forend tip; highly polished barreled action; jewelled bolt; recoil pad; swivel studs. Imported from the Philippines by K.B.I., Inc.
Price: **$364.95**

Charles Daly Empire Grade Rifle

Similar to the Superior except has oil-finished American walnut stock with 18 lpi hand checkering; black hardwood gripcap and forend tip; highly polished barreled action; jewelled bolt; recoil pad; swivel studs. Imported by K.B.I., Inc.
Price: **$329.00**

CHARLES DALY TRUE YOUTH BOLT-ACTION RIFLE

Caliber: 22 LR, single shot. **Barrel:** 16-1/4". **Weight:** About 3 lbs. **Length:** 32" overall. **Stock:** Walnut-finished hardwood. **Sights:** Blade front, adjustable rear. **Features:** Scaled-down stock for small shooters. Blue finish. Introduced 1998. Imported by K.B.I., Inc.
Price: **$154.95**

CHIPMUNK SINGLE SHOT RIFLE

Caliber: 22, S, L, LR, single shot. **Barrel:** 16-1/8". **Weight:** About 2-1/2 lbs. **Length:** 30" overall. **Stocks:** American walnut. **Sights:** Post on ramp front, peep rear adjustable for windage and elevation. **Features:** Drilled and tapped for scope mounting using special Chipmunk base ($13.95). Made in U.S. Introduced 1982. From Rogue Rifle Co., Inc.
Price: Standard. **$194.25**
Price: Deluxe (better wood, checkering). **$246.95**
Price: With black, brown or camouflage laminate stock **$209.95**
Price: With black polyurethane-coated wood stock **$183.95**
Price: Bull barrel models of above, add **$16.00**

CZ 452 M 2E LUX BOLT-ACTION RIFLE

Caliber: 22 LR, 22 WMR, 5-shot detachable magazine. **Barrel:** 24.8". **Weight:** 6.6 lbs. **Length:** 42.63" overall. **Stock:** Walnut with checkered pistol grip. **Sights:** Hooded front, fully adjustable tangent rear. **Features:**

All-steel construction; adjustable trigger; polished blue finish. Imported from the Czech Republic by CZ-USA.
Price: 22 LR **$351.00**
Price: 22 WMR **$378.00**
Price: Synthetic stock, nickel finish, 22 LR. **$344.00**

CZ 452 M 2E Varmint Rifle

Similar to the Lux model except has heavy 20.8" barrel; stock has beavertail forend; weighs 7 lbs.; no sights furnished. Available only in 22 LR. Imported from the Czech Republic by CZ-USA.
Price: **$369.00**

CZ 452 American Classic Bolt-Action Rifle

Similar to the CZ 452 M 2E Lux except has classic-style stock of Circassian walnut; 22.5" free-floating barrel with recessed target crown; receiver dovetail for scope mounting. No open sights furnished. Introduced 1999. Imported from the Czech Republic by CZ-USA.
Price: 22 LR **$351.00**
Price: 22 WMR **$378.00**

KIMBER 22 CLASSIC BOLT-ACTION RIFLE

Caliber: 22 LR, 5-shot magazine. **Barrel:** 22" Kimber match grade; 11-degree target crown. **Weight:** About 6.5 lbs. **Length:** 40.5" overall. **Stock:** Classic style in Claro walnut with 18 l.p.i. hand-cut checkering; satin finish; steel gripcap; swivel studs. **Sights:** None furnished; Kimber sculpted bases available that accept all rotary dovetail rings. **Features:** All-new action with Mauser-style full-length claw extractor; two-position in M70-type safety; fully adjustable trigger set at 2 lbs.; pillar-bedded action with recoil lug, free-floated barrel. Introduced 1999. Made in U.S. by Kimber Mfg., Inc.
Price: **$919.00**

Kimber 22 SuperAmerica Bolt-Action Rifle

Similar to the 22 Classic except has AAA Claro walnut stock with wraparound 22 l.p.i. hand-cut checkering, ebony forened tip, beaded cheekpiece. Introduced 1999. Made in U.S. by Kimber Mfg., Inc.
Price: **$1,493.00**

Kimber 22 SVT Bolt-Action Rilfe

Similar to the 22 Classic except has 18" stainless steel, fluted bull barrel, gray laminated, high-comb target-style stock with deep pistol grip, high comb, and beavertail forend with bipod stud. Weighs 7.5 lbs., overall length 36.5". Matte finish on action. Introduced 1999. Made in U.S. by Kimber Mfg., Inc.
Price: **$915.00**

Kimber 22 SVT

Kimber 22 HS

Marlin Model 15YN

Marlin Model 880SS

Marlin 880SQ Squirrel

Kimber 22 HS (Hunter Silhouette) Bolt-Action Rifle

Similar to the 22 Classic except has 24" medium sporter match-grade barrel with half-fluting; high comb, walnut, Monte Carlo target stock with 18 l.p.i. checkering; matte blue metal finish. Introduced 1999. Made in U.S. by Kimber Mfg., Inc.

Price: $748.00

MARLIN MODEL 15YN "LITTLE BUCKAROO"

Caliber: 22 S, L, LR, single shot. **Barrel:** 16-1/4" Micro-Groove®. **Weight:** 4-1/4 lbs. **Length:** 33-1/4" overall. **Stock:** One-piece walnut-finished, press-checkered Maine birch with Monte Carlo; Mar-Shield® finish. **Sights:** Ramp front, adjustable open rear. **Features:** Beginner's rifle with thumb safety, easy-load feed throat, red cocking indicator. Receiver grooved for scope mounting. Introduced 1989.

Price: $193.00

MARLIN MODEL 880SS BOLT-ACTION RIFLE

Caliber: 22 LR, 7-shot clip magazine. **Barrel:** 22" Micro-Groove®. **Weight:** 6 lbs. **Length:** 41" overall. **Stock:** Black fiberglass-filled synthetic with nickel-plated swivel studs and moulded-in checkering. **Sights:** Ramp front with orange post and cutaway Wide-Scan™ hood, adjustable semi-buck-

horn folding rear. **Features:** Stainless steel barrel, receiver, front breech bolt and striker; receiver grooved for scope mounting. Introduced 1994. Made in U.S. by Marlin.

Price: $289.00

Marlin Model 81TS Bolt-Action Rifle

Same as the Marlin 880SS except blued steel, tubular magazine, holds 17 Long Rifle cartridges. Weighs 6 lbs.

Price: $196.00
Price: With 4x scope. $203.00

Marlin Model 880SQ Squirrel Rifle

Similar to the Model 880SS except uses the heavy target barrel of Marlin's Model 2000L target rifle. Black synthetic stock with moulded-in checkering; double bedding screws; matte blue finish. Comes without sights, no dovetail or filler screws; receiver grooved for scope mount. Weighs 7 lbs. Introduced 1996. Made in U.S. by Marlin.

Price: $302.00

Marlin Model 25N Bolt-Action Repeater

Similar to Marlin 880, except walnut-finished p.g. stock, adjustable open rear sight, ramp front.

Price: $195.00
Price: With 4x scope. $201.00

Marlin 883SS

Ruger K77/22 Varmint

Ruger 77/22R

Sako Finnfire

Marlin Model 25MN Bolt-Action Rifle

Similar to the Model 25N except chambered for 22 WMR. Has 7-shot clip magazine, 22" Micro-Groove® barrel, checkered walnut-finished Maine birch stock. Introduced 1989.

Price: $223.00
Price: With 4x scope................................... $229.00

Marlin Model 882 Bolt-Action Rifle

Same as the Marlin 880 except 22 WMR cal. only with 7-shot clip magazine; weight about 6 lbs. Comes with swivel studs.

Price: $296.00
Price: Model 882L (laminated hardwood stock) $313.00

Marlin Model 883 Bolt-Action Rifle

Same as Marlin 882 except tubular magazine holds 12 rounds of 22 WMR ammunition.

Price: $308.00

Marlin Model 882SS Bolt-Action Rifle

Same as the Marlin Model 882 except has stainless steel front breech bolt, barrel, receiver and bolt knob. All other parts are either stainless steel or nickel-plated. Has black Monte Carlo stock of fiberglass-filled polycarbonate with moulded-in checkering, nickel-plated swivel studs. Introduced 1995. Made in U.S. by Marlin Firearms Co.

Price: $314.00

Marlin Model 882SSV Bolt-Action Rifle

Similar to the Model 882SS except has selected heavy 22" stainless steel barrel with recessed muzzle, and comes without sights; receiver is grooved for scope mount and 1" ring mounts are included. Weighs 7 lbs. Introduced 1997. Made in U.S. by Marlin Firearms Co.

Price: $309.00

Marlin Model 883SS Bolt-Action Rifle

Same as the Model 883 except front breech bolt, striker knob, trigger stud, cartridge lifter stud and outer magazine tube are of stainless steel; other parts are nickel-plated. Has two-tone brown laminated Monte Carlo stock with swivel studs, rubber butt pad. Introduced 1993.

Price: $326.00

RUGER K77/22 VARMINT RIFLE

Caliber: 22 LR, 10-shot, 22 WMR, 9-shot detachable rotary magazine. **Barrel:** 24", heavy. **Weight:** 7.25 lbs. **Length:** 43.25" overall. **Stock:** Laminated hardwood with rubber butt pad, quick-detachable swivel studs. No checkering or gripcap. **Sights:** None furnished. Comes with Ruger 1" scope rings. **Features:** Made of stainless steel with target gray finish. Three-position safety, dual extractors. Stock has wide, flat forend. Introduced 1993.

Price: K77/22VBZ, 22 LR $539.00
Price: K77/22VMBZ, 22 WMR $539.00

RUGER 77/22 RIMFIRE BOLT-ACTION RIFLE

Caliber: 22 LR, 10-shot rotary magazine; 22 WMR, 9-shot rotary magazine. **Barrel:** 20". **Weight:** About 5-3/4 lbs. **Length:** 39-3/4" overall. **Stock:** Checkered American walnut or injection-moulded fiberglass-reinforced DuPont Zytel with Xenoy inserts in forend and grip, stainless sling swivels. **Sights:** Brass bead front, adjustable folding leaf rear or plain barrel with 1" Ruger rings. **Features:** Mauser-type action uses Ruger's 10-shot rotary magazine. Three-position safety, simplified bolt stop, patented bolt locking system. Uses the dual-screw barrel attachment system of the 10/22 rifle. Integral scope mounting system with 1" Ruger rings. Blued model introduced in 1983. Stainless steel model and blued model with the synthetic stock introduced in 1989.

Price: 77/22R (no sights, rings, walnut stock) $498.00
Price: 77/22RS (open sights, rings, walnut stock) $506.00
Price: K77/22RP (stainless, no sights, rings, synthetic stock) ... $498.00
Price: K77/22RSP (stainless, open sights, rings, synthetic stock) . $491.00
Price: 77/22RM (22 WMR, blue, walnut stock)............... $483.00
Price: K77/22RSMP (22 WMR, stainless, open sights, rings, synthetic stock) $491.00
Price: K77/22RMP (22 WMR, stainless, synthetic stock)....... $483.00
Price: 77/22RSM (22 WMR, blue, open sights, rings, walnut stock)... $491.00

SAKO FINNFIRE HUNTER BOLT-ACTION RIFLE

Caliber: 22 LR, 5-shot magazine. **Barrel:** 22". **Weight:** 5.75 lbs. **Length:** 39-1/2" overall. **Stock:** European walnut with checkered grip and forend. **Sights:** Hooded blade front, open adjustable rear. **Features:** Adjustable single-stage trigger; has 50-degree bolt lift. Introduced 1994. Imported from Finland by Stoeger Industries.

Price: $874.00
Price: Varmint (heavy barrel) $924.00

RIFLES

Savage Mark II-FXP

Savage Model 93G

Winchester Model 52B

SAKO FINNFIRE SPORTER RIFLE

Caliber: 22 LR. **Barrel:** 22"; heavy, free-floating. **Weight:** NA. **Length:** NA. **Stock:** Match style of European walnut; adjustable cheekpiece and buttplate; stippled pistol grip and forend. **Sights:** None furnished; has 11mm integral dovetail scope mount. **Features:** Based on the Sako P94S action with two bolt locking lugs, 50-degree bolt lift and 30mm throw; adjustable trigger. Introduced 1999. Imported from Finland by Stoeger Industries.

Price: $984.00

SAVAGE MARK I-G BOLT-ACTION RIFLE

Caliber: 22 LR, single shot. **Barrel:** 20-3/4". **Weight:** 5-1/2 lbs. **Length:** 39-1/2" overall. **Stock:** Walnut-finished hardwood with Monte Carlo-type comb, checkered grip and forend. **Sights:** Bead front, open adjustable rear. Receiver grooved for scope mounting. **Features:** Thumb-operated rotating safety. Blue finish. Rifled or smooth bore. Introduced 1990. Made in Canada, from Savage Arms Inc.

Price: Mark I, rifled or smooth bore, right- or left-handed $119.00
Price: Mark I-GY (Youth), 19" barrel, 37" overall, 5 lbs. $127.00

SAVAGE MARK II-G BOLT-ACTION RIFLE

Caliber: 22 LR, 10-shot magazine. **Barrel:** 20-1/2". **Weight:** 5-1/2 lbs. **Length:** 39-1/2" overall. **Stock:** Walnut-finished hardwood with Monte Carlo-type comb, checkered grip and forend. **Sights:** Bead front, open adjustable rear. Receiver grooved for scope mounting. **Features:** Thumb-operated rotating safety. Blue finish. Introduced 1990. Made in Canada, from Savage Arms, Inc.

Price: $140.00
Price: Mark II-GY (youth), 19" barrel, 37" overall, 5 lbs. $140.00
Price: Mark II-GL, left-hand $140.00
Price: Mark II-GLY (youth) left-hand. $140.00
Price: Mark II-GXP Package Gun (comes with 4x15 scope),
right- or left-handed $147.00
Price: Mark II-FXP (as above except with black synthetic
stock) $133.00
Price: Mark II-F (as above, no scope) $127.00

Savage Mark II-LV Heavy Barrel Rifle

Similar to the Mark II-G except has heavy 21" barrel with recessed target-style crown; gray, laminated hardwood stock with cut checkering. No sights furnished, but has dovetailed receiver for scope mounting. Overall length is 39-3/4", weight is 6-1/2 lbs. Comes with 10-shot clip magazine. Introduced 1997. Imported from Canada by Savage Arms, Inc.

Price: $222.00
Price: Mark II-FV, with black graphite/polymer stock $194.00

Savage Mark II-FSS Stainless Rifle

Similar to the Mark II-G except has stainless steel barreled action and graphite/polymer filled stock; free-floated barrel. Weighs 5 lbs. Introduced 1997. Imported from Canada by Savage Arms, Inc.

Price: $169.00

Savage Model 93FVSS Magnum Rifle

Similar to the Model 93FSS Magnum except has 21" heavy barrel with recessed target-style crown; satin-finished stainless barreled action; black graphite/fiberglass stock. Drilled and tapped for scope mounting; comes with Weaver-style bases. Introduced 1998. Imported from Canada by Savage Arms, Inc.

Price: $222.00

SAVAGE MODEL 93G MAGNUM BOLT-ACTION RIFLE

Caliber: 22 WMR, 5-shot magazine. **Barrel:** 20-3/4". **Weight:** 5-3/4 lbs. **Length:** 39-1/2" overall. **Stock:** Walnut-finished hardwood with Monte Carlo-type comb, checkered grip and forend. **Sights:** Bead front, adjustable open rear. Receiver grooved for scope mount. **Features:** Thumb-operated rotary safety. Blue finish. Introduced 1994. Made in Canada, from Savage Arms.

Price: About $160.00
Price: Model 93F (as above with black graphite/fiberglass
stock) $154.00

Savage Model 93FSS Magnum Rifle

Similar to the Model 93G except has stainless steel barreled action and black synthetic stock with positive checkering. Weighs 5-1/2 lbs. Introduced 1997. Imported from Canada by Savage Arms, Inc.

Price: $194.00

WINCHESTER MODEL 52B BOLT-ACTION RIFLE

Caliber: 22 Long Rifle, 5-shot magazine. **Barrel:** 24". **Weight:** 7 lbs. **Length:** 41-3/4" overall. **Stock:** Walnut with checkered grip and forend. **Sights:** None furnished; grooved receiver and drilled and tapped for scope mounting. **Features:** Has Micro Motion trigger adjustable for pull and over-travel; match chamber; detachable magazine. Reintroduced 1997. From U.S. Repeating Arms Co.

Price: $654.00

RIFLES

Includes models for classic American and ISU target competition and other sporting and competitive shooting.

Anschutz 1451 Target

Anschutz 2013

ANSCHUTZ 1451R SPORTER TARGET RIFLE

Caliber: 22 LR, 5-shot magazine. **Barrel:** 22" heavy match. **Weight:** 6.4 lbs. **Length:** 39.75" overall. **Stock:** European hardwood with walnut finish. **Sights:** None furnished. Grooved receiver for scope mounting or Anschutz micrometer rear sight. **Features:** Sliding safety, two-stage trigger. Adjustable buttplate; forend slide rail to accept Anschutz accessories. Imported from Germany by AcuSport Corp.
Price: $549.00

ANSCHUTZ 1451 TARGET RIFLE

Caliber: 22 LR. **Barrel:** 22". **Weight:** About 6.5 lbs. **Length:** 40". **Sights:** Optional. Receiver grooved for scope mounting. **Features:** Designed for the beginning junior shooter with adjustable length of pull from 13.25" to 14.25" via removable butt spacers. Two-stage trigger factory set at 2.6 lbs. Introduced 1999. Imported from Germany by Gunsmithing, Inc.
Price: $347.00
Price: #6834 Match Sight Set $227.10

ANSCHUTZ 1808D-RT SUPER RUNNING TARGET RIFLE

Caliber: 22 LR, single shot. **Barrel:** 32-1/2". **Weight:** 9 lbs. **Length:** 50" overall. **Stock:** European walnut. Heavy beavertail forend; adjustable cheekpiece and buttplate. Stippled grip and forend. **Sights:** None furnished. Grooved for scope mounting. **Features:** Designed for Running Target competition. Nine-way adjustable single-stage trigger, slide safety. Introduced 1991. Imported from Germany by Accuracy International, Gunsmithing, Inc.
Price: Right-hand $1,364.10

ANSCHUTZ 1903 MATCH RIFLE

Caliber: 22 LR, single shot. **Barrel:** 25.5", .75" diameter. **Weight:** 10.1 lbs. **Length:** 43.75" overall. **Stock:** Walnut-finished hardwood with adjustable cheekpiece; stippled grip and forend. **Sights:** None furnished. **Features:** Uses Anschutz Match 64 action and #5098 two-stage trigger. A medium weight rifle for intermediate and advanced Junior Match competition. Introduced 1987. Imported from Germany by Accuracy International, Gunsmithing, Inc.
Price: Right-hand $720.40
Price: Left-hand $757.90

ANSCHUTZ 64-MSR SILHOUETTE RIFLE

Caliber: 22 LR, 5-shot magazine. **Barrel:** 21-1/2", medium heavy; 7/8" diameter. **Weight:** 8 lbs. **Length:** 39.5" overall. **Stock:** Walnut-finished hardwood, silhouette-type. **Sights:** None furnished. **Features:** Uses Match 64 action. Designed for metallic silhouette competition. Stock has stippled checkering, contoured thumb groove with Wundhammer swell.

Two-stage #5098 trigger. Slide safety locks sear and bolt. Introduced 1980. Imported from Germany by AcuSport Corp., Accuracy International, Gunsmithing, Inc.
Price: 64-MSR $704.30

ANSCHUTZ 2013 BENCHREST RIFLE

Caliber: 22 LR, single shot. **Barrel:** 19.6". **Weight:** About 10.3 lbs. **Length:** 37.75" to 42.5" overall. **Stock:** Benchrest style of European hardwood. Stock length adjustable via spacers and buttplate. **Sights:** None furnished. Receiver grooved for mounts. **Features:** Uses the Anschutz 2013 target action, #5018 two-stage adjustable target trigger factory set at 3.9 oz. Introduced 1994. Imported from Germany by Accuracy International, Gunsmithing, Inc.
Price: $1,757.20

Anschutz 2007 Match Rifle

Uses same action as the Model 2013, but has a lighter barrel. European walnut stock in right-hand, true left-hand or extra-short models. Sights optional. Available with 19.6" barrel with extension tube, or 26", both in stainless or blue. Introduced 1998. Imported from Germany by Gunsmithing, Inc., Accuracy International.
Price: Right-hand, blue, no sights $1,766.60
Price: Right-hand, blue, no sights, extra-short stock $1,756.60
Price: Left-hand, blue, no sights $1,856.80

ANSCHUTZ 1827 BIATHLON RIFLE

Caliber: 22 LR, 5-shot magazine. **Barrel:** 21-1/2". **Weight:** 8-1/2 lbs. with sights. **Length:** 42-1/2" overall. **Stock:** European walnut with cheekpiece, stippled pistol grip and forend. **Sights:** Optional globe front specially designed for Biathlon shooting, micrometer rear with hinged snow cap. **Features:** Uses Super Match 54 action and nine-way adjustable trigger; adjustable wooden buttplate, Biathlon butthook, adjustable hand-stop rail. Introduced 1982. Imported from Germany by Accuracy International, Gunsmithing, Inc.
Price: Right-hand, with sights, about .... $1,500.50 to $1,555.00

Anschutz 1827BT Fortner Biathlon Rifle

Similar to the Anschutz 1827 Biathlon rifle except uses Anschutz/Fortner system straight-pull bolt action, blued or stainless steel barrel. Introduced 1982. Imported from Germany by Accuracy International, Gunsmithing, Inc.
Price: Right-hand, with sights .... $1,908.00 to $2,210.00
Price: Left-hand, with sights .... $2,099.20 to $2,395.00
Price: Right-hand, sights, stainless barrel (Gunsmithing, Inc.) $2,045.20

Anschutz 54.18MS REP

Armalite AR-10 (T)

ANSCHUTZ SUPER MATCH SPECIAL MODEL 2013 RIFLE

Caliber: 22 LR, single shot. **Barrel:** 25.9". **Weight:** 13 lbs. **Length:** 41.7-42.9". **Stock:** A thumbhole version made of European walnut, both the cheekpiece and buttplate are highly adjustable. **Sights:** None furnished. **Features:** Developed by Anschütz for women to shoot in the sport rifle category. Stainless or blue. This top of the line rifle was introduced in 1997.

Price: Right-hand, blue, no sights, walnut **$2,219.30**
Price: Right-hand, stainless, no sights, walnut **$2,345.30**
Price: Left-hand, blue, no sights, walnut **$2,319.50**

ANSCHUTZ 2012 SPORT RIFLE

Caliber: 22 LR, 5-shot magazine. **Barrel:** 22.4" match; detachable muzzle tube. **Weight:** 7.9 lbs. **Length:** 40.9" overall. **Stock:** European walnut, thumbhole design. **Sights:** None furnished. **Features:** Uses Anschutz 54.18 barreled action with two-stage match trigger. Introduced 1997. Imported from Germany by Accuracy International, AcuSport Corp.

Price: .... $1,425.00 to **$2,219.95**

ANSCHUTZ 1911 PRONE MATCH RIFLE

Caliber: 22 LR, single shot. **Barrel:** 27-1/4". **Weight:** 11 lbs. **Length:** 46" overall. **Stock:** Walnut-finished European hardwood; American prone-style with adjustable cheekpiece, textured pistol grip, forend with swivel rail and adjustable rubber buttplate. **Sights:** None furnished. Receiver grooved for Anschutz sights (extra). **Features:** Two-stage #5018 trigger adjustable from 2.1 to 8.6 oz. Extremely fast lock time. Stainless or blue barrel. Imported from Germany by Accuracy International, Gunsmithing, Inc.

Price: Right-hand, no sights........................... **$1,714.20**

ANSCHUTZ 1912 SPORT RIFLE

Caliber: 22 LR, single shot. **Barrel:** 25.9". **Weight:** About 11.4 lbs. **Length:** 41.7-42.9". **Stock:** European walnut or aluminum. **Sights:** None furnished. **Features:** Light weight sport rifle version. Still uses the 54 match action like the 1913 but weighs 1.5 pounds less. Stainless or blue barrel. Introduced 1997.

Price: Right-hand, blue, no sights, walnut **$1,789.50**
Price: Right-hand, blue, no sights, aluminum **$2,129.80**
Price: Right-hand, stainless, no sights, walnut **$1,910.30**
Price: Left-hand, blue, no sights, walnut **$1,879.00**

ANSCHUTZ 1913 SUPER MATCH RIFLE

Caliber: 22 LR, single shot. **Barrel:** 27.1". **Weight:** About 14.3 lbs. **Length:** 44.8-46". **Stock:** European walnut, color laminate, or aluminum. **Sights:** None furnished. **Features:** Two-stage #5018 trigger. Extremely fast lock time. Stainless or blue barrel.

Price: Right-hand, blue, no sights, walnut stock **$2,262.90**
Price: Right-hand, blue, no sights, color laminate stock **$2,275.10**
Price: Right-hand, blue, no sights, aluminum stock **$2,262.90**
Price: Left-hand, blue, no sights, walnut stock **$2,382.20**

Anschutz 1913 Super Match Rifle

Same as the Model 1911 except European walnut International-type stock with adjustable cheekpiece, or color laminate, both available with straight or lowered forend, adjustable aluminum hook buttplate, adjustable hand stop, weighs 15.5 lbs., 46" overall. Stainless or blue barrel. Imported from Germany by Accuracy International, Gunsmithing, Inc.

Price: Right-hand, blue, no sights, walnut stock. . . **$2,139.00 to $2,175.00**
Price: Right-hand, blue, no sights, color laminate stock....... **$2,199.40**
Price: Right-hand, blue, no sights, walnut, lowered forend **$2,181.80**
Price: Right-hand, blue, no sights, color laminate, lowered forend.. **$2,242.20**
Price: Left-hand, blue, no sights, walnut stock... **$2,233.10 to $2,275.00**

Anschutz 54.18MS REP Deluxe Silhouette Rifle

Same basic action and trigger specifications as the Anschutz 1913 Super Match but with removable 5-shot clip magazine, 22.4" barrel extendable to 30" using optional extension and weight set. Weight id 8.1 lbs. Receiver drilled and tapped for scope mounting. Stock is Thumbhole silhouette version or standard silhouette version, both are European walnut. Introduced 1990. Imported from Germany by Accuracy International, Gunsmithing, Inc.

Price: Thumbhole stock **$1,461.40**
Price: Standard stock **$1,212.00**

Anschutz 1907 Standard Match Rifle

Same action as Model 1913 but with 7/8" diameter 26" barrel (stainless or blue). Length is 44.5" overall, weighs 10.5 lbs. Choice of stock configurations. Vented forend. Designed for prone and position shooting ISU requirements; suitable for NRA matches. Also available with walnut flat-forend stock for benchrest shooting. Imported from Germany by Accuracy International, Gunsmithing, Inc.

Price: Right-hand, blue, no sights, hardwood stock . **$1,253.40 to $1,299.00**
Price: Right-hand, blue, no sights, colored laminated stock .... **$1,316.10 to $1,375.00**
Price: Right-hand, blue, no sights, walnut stock............. **$1,521.10**
Price: Left-hand, blue barrel, no sights, walnut stock......... **$1,584.60**

ARMALITE AR-10 (T) RIFLE

Caliber: 308, 10-shot magazine. **Barrel:** 24" target-weight Rock 5R custom. **Weight:** 10.4 lbs. **Length:** 43.5" overall. **Stock:** Green or black compostion; N.M. fiberglass handguard tube. **Sights:** Detachable handle, front sight, or scope mount available. Comes with international-style flat-top receiver with Picatinny rail. **Features:** National Match two-stage trigger. Forged upper receiver. Receivers hard-coat anodized. Introduced 1995. Made in U.S. by ArmaLite, Inc.

Price: Green **$2,075.00**
Price: Black **$2,090.00**

RIFLES

Bushmaster XM15 E2S Target

Bushmaster DCM

Colt Match Target HBAR

Price: AR-10 (T) Carbine, lighter 16" barrel, single stage trigger, weighs 8.8 lbs. Green **$1,970.00**
Price: Black **$1,985.00**

ARMALITE M15A4 (T) EAGLE EYE RIFLE

Caliber: 223, 7-shot magazine. **Barrel:** 24" heavy stainless; 1:8" twist. **Weight:** 9.2 lbs. **Length:** 42-3/8" overall. **Stock:** Green or black butt, N.M. fiberglass handguard tube. **Sights:** One-piece international-style flattop receiver with Weaver-type rail, including case deflector. **Features:** Detachable carry handle, front sight and scope mount (30mm or 1") available. Upper and lower receivers have push-type pivot pin, hard coat anodized. Made in U.S. by ArmaLite, Inc.
Price: Green **$1,378.00**
Price: Black **$1,393.00**

ARMALITE M15A4 ACTION MASTER RIFLE

Caliber: 223, 7-shot magazine. **Barrel:** 20" heavy stainless; 1:9" twist. **Weight:** 9 lbs. **Length:** 40-1/2" overall. **Stock:** Green or black plastic; N.M. fiberglass handguard tube. **Sights:** One-piece international-style flattop receiver with Weaver-type rail. **Features:** Detachable carry handle, front sight and scope mount available. National Match two-stage trigger group; Picatinny rail; upper and lower receivers have push-type pivot pin; hard coat anodized finish. Made in U.S. by ArmaLite, Inc.
Price: **$1,175.00**

BLASER R93 LONG RANGE RIFLE

Caliber: 308 Win., 10-shot detachable box magazine. **Barrel:** 24". **Weight:** 10.4 lbs. **Length:** 44" overall. **Stock:** Aluminum with synthetic lining. **Sights:** None furnished; accepts detachable scope mount.**Features:** Straight-pull bolt action with adjustable trigger; fully adjustable stock; quick takedown; corrosion resistant finish. Introduced 1998. Imported from Germany by Sigarms.
Price: **$2,360.00**

BUSHMASTER XM15 E2S TARGET MODEL RIFLE

Caliber: 223. **Barrel:** 20", 24", 26"; 1:9" twist; heavy. **Weight:** 8.3 lbs. **Length:** 38.25" overall (20" barrel). **Stock:** Black composition; A2 type. **Sights:** Adjustable post front, adjustable aperture rear. **Features:** Patterned after Colt M-16A2. Chrome-lined barrel with manganese phos-

phate exterior. Forged aluminum receivers with push-pin takedown. Made in U.S. by Bushmaster Firearms Co./Quality Parts Co.
Price: 20" match heavy barrel **$960.00**

Bushmaster DCM Competition Rifle

Similar to the XM15 E2S Target Model except has 20" extra-heavy (1" diameter) barrel with 1.8" twist for heavier competition bullets. Weighs about 12 lbs. with balance weights. Has special competition rear sight with interchangeable apertures, extra-fine 1/2- or 1/4-MOA windage and elevation adjustments; specially ground front sight post in choice of three widths. Full-length handguards over free-floater barrel tube. Introduced 1998. Made in U.S. by Bushmaster Firearms, Inc.
Price: **$1,525.00**

BUSHMASTER XM15 E2S V-MATCH RIFLE

Caliber: 223. **Barrel:** 20", 24", 26"; 1:9" twist; heavy. **Weight:** 8.1 lbs. **Length:** 38.25" overall (20" barrel). **Stock:** Black composition. A2 type. **Sights:** None furnished; upper receiver has integral scope mount base. **Features:** Chrome-lined .950" heavy barrel with counterbored crown, manganese phosphate finish; free-floating aluminum handguard; forged aluminum receivers with push-pin takedown, hard anodized mil-spec finish. Competition trigger optional. Made in U.S. by Bushmaster Firearms, Inc.
Price: 20" Match heavy barrel **$1,025.00**
Price: 24" Match heavy barrel **$1,040.00**
Price: V-Match Carbine (16" barrel) **$1,015.00**

COLT MATCH TARGET MODEL RIFLE

Caliber: 223 Rem., 8-shot magazine. **Barrel:** 20". **Weight:** 7.5 lbs. **Length:** 39" overall. **Stock:** Composition stock, grip, forend. **Sights:** Post front, aperture rear adjustable for windage and elevation. **Features:** Five-round detachable box magazine, standard-weight barrel, sling swivels. Has forward bolt assist. Military matte black finish. Model introduced 1991.
Price: **$1,144.00**
Price: With compensator **$1,150.00**

Colt Accurized Rifle

Similar to the Colt Match Target Model except has 24" stainless steel heavy barrel with 1.9" rifling, flattop receiver with scope mount and 1" rings, weighs 9.25 lbs. Introduced 1998. Made in U.S. by Colt's Mfg. Co., Inc.
Price: **$1,424.00**

Colt Match Target HBAR Rifle

Similar to the Target Model except has heavy barrel, 800-meter rear sight adjustable for windage and elevation. Introduced 1991.
Price: **$1,194.00**

Harris Gunworks Long Range

Harris Gunworks M-86

Marlin Model 2000L

Colt Match Target Competition HBAR Rifle

Similar to the Sporter Target except has flat-top receiver with integral Weaver-type base for scope mounting. Counter-bored muzzle, 1:9" rifling twist. Introduced 1991.
Price: Model R6700 .... $1,199.00

Colt Match Target Competition HBAR II Rifle

Similar to the Match Target Competition HBAR except has 16:1" barrel, weighs 7.1 lbs., overall length 34.5"; 1:9" twist barrel. Introduced 1995.
Price: $1,172.00

E.A.A./HW 660 MATCH RIFLE

Caliber: 22 LR. **Barrel:** 26". **Weight:** 10.7 lbs. **Length:** 45.3" overall. **Stock:** Match-type walnut with adjustable cheekpiece and buttplate. **Sights:** Globe front, match aperture rear. **Features:** Adjustable match trigger; stippled pistol grip and forend; forend accessory rail. Introduced 1991. Imported from Germany by European American Armory.
Price: About $999.00
Price: With laminate stock $1,159.00

HARRIS GUNWORKS NATIONAL MATCH RIFLE

Caliber: 7mm-08, 308, 5-shot magazine. **Barrel:** 24", stainless steel. **Weight:** About 11 lbs. (std. bbl.). **Length:** 43" overall. **Stock:** Fiberglass with adjustable buttplate. **Sights:** Barrel band and Tompkins front; no rear sight furnished. **Features:** Gunworks repeating action with clip slot, Canjar trigger. Match-grade barrel. Available in right-hand only. Fiberglass stock, sight installation, special machining and triggers optional. Introduced 1989. From Harris Gunworks, Inc.
Price: $3,500.00

HARRIS GUNWORKS LONG RANGE RIFLE

Caliber: 300 Win. Mag., 7mm Rem. Mag., 300 Phoenix, 338 Lapua, single shot. **Barrel:** 26", stainless steel, match-grade. **Weight:** 14 lbs. **Length:** 46-1/2" overall. **Stock:** Fiberglass with adjustable buttplate and cheekpiece. Adjustable for length of pull, drop, cant and cast-off. **Sights:** Barrel band and Tompkins front; no rear sight furnished. **Features:** Uses Gunworks solid bottom single shot action and Canjar trigger. Barrel twist 1:12". Introduced 1989. From Harris Gunworks, Inc.
Price: $3,620.00

HARRIS GUNWORKS M-86 SNIPER RIFLE

Caliber: 308, 30-06, 4-shot magazine; 300 Win. Mag., 3-shot magazine. **Barrel:** 24", Gunworks match-grade in heavy contour. **Weight:** 11-1/4 lbs. (308), 11-1/2 lbs. (30-06, 300). **Length:** 43-1/2" overall. **Stock:** Specially designed McHale fiberglass stock with textured grip and forend, recoil pad. **Sights:** None furnished. **Features:** Uses Gunworks repeating action. Comes with bipod. Matte black finish. Sling swivels. Introduced 1989. From Harris Gunworks, Inc.
Price: $2,700.00

HARRIS GUNWORKS M-89 SNIPER RIFLE

Caliber: 308 Win., 5-shot magazine. **Barrel:** 28" (with suppressor). **Weight:** 15 lbs., 4 oz. **Stock:** Fiberglass; adjustable for length; recoil pad. **Sights:** None furnished. Drilled and tapped for scope mounting. **Features:** Uses Gunworks repeating action. Comes with bipod. Introduced 1990. From Harris Gunworks, Inc.
Price: Standard (non-suppressed) $3,200.00

HARRIS GUNWORKS
COMBO M-87 SERIES 50-CALIBER RIFLES

Caliber: 50 BMG, single shot. **Barrel:** 29, with muzzle brake. **Weight:** About 21-1/2 lbs. **Length:** 53" overall. **Stock:** Gunworks fiberglass. **Sights:** None furnished. **Features:** Right-handed Gunworks stainless steel receiver, chrome-moly barrel with 1:15" twist. Introduced 1987. From Harris Gunworks, Inc.
Price: $3,885.00
Price: M87R 5-shot repeater $4,000.00
Price: M-87 (5-shot repeater) "Combo" $4,300.00
Price: M-92 Bullpup (shortened M-87 single shot with bullpup stock) $4,770.00
Price: M-93 (10-shot repeater with folding stock, detachable magazine).. $4,150.00

MARLIN MODEL 2000L TARGET RIFLE

Caliber: 22 LR, single shot. **Barrel:** 22" heavy, Micro-Groove® rifling, match chamber, recessed muzzle. **Weight:** 8 lbs. **Length:** 41" overall. **Stock:** Laminated black/gray with ambidextrous pistol grip. **Sights:** Hooded front with ten aperture inserts, fully adjustable target rear peep. **Features:** Buttplate adjustable for length of pull, height and angle. Aluminum forend rail with stop and quick-detachable swivel. Two-stage target trigger; red cocking indicator. Five-shot adaptor kit available. Introduced 1991. From Marlin.
Price: $689.00

Marlin Model 7000T

Savage Model 900TR

Savage Model 112BT

MARLIN MODEL 7000T SELF-LOADING RIFLE

Caliber: 22 LR, 10-shot magazine. **Barrel:** 18" heavy target with Micro-Groove® rifling. **Weight:** 7-1/2 lbs. **Length:** 37" overall. **Stock:** Laminated red, white and blue hardwood with ambidextrous pistol grip, adjustable buttplate, aluminum forend rail. **Sights:** None furnished; grooved receiver for scope mounting. **Features:** Trigger stop; last-shot bolt hold-open; blue finish; scope mounts included. Introduced 1999. Made in U.S. by Marlin.
Price: $465.00

OLYMPIC ARMS PCR-SERVICEMATCH RIFLE

Caliber: 223, 10-shot magazine. **Barrel:** 20", broach-cut 416 stainless steel. **Weight:** About 10 lbs. **Length:** 39.5" overall. **Stock:** A2 stowaway grip and trapdoor buttstock. **Sights:** Post front, E2-NM fully adjustable aperture rear. **Features:** Based on the AR-15. Conforms to all DCM standards. Free-floating 1:8.5" or 1:10" barrel; crowned barrel; no bayonet lug. Introduced 1996. Made in U.S. by Olympic Arms, Inc.
Price: $1,062.00

OLYMPIC ARMS PCR-1 RIFLE

Caliber: 223, 10-shot magazine. **Barrel:** 20", 24"; 416 stainless steel. **Weight:** 10 lbs., 3 oz. **Length:** 38.25" overall with 20" barrel. **Stock:** A2 stowaway grip and trapdoor butt. **Sights:** None supplied; flattop upper receiver, cut-down front sight base. **Features:** Based on the AR-15 rifle. Broach-cut, free-floating barrel with 1:8.5" or 1:10" twist. No bayonet lug. Crowned barrel; fluting available. Introduced 1994. Made in U.S. by Olympic Arms, Inc.
Price: $1,038.00

Olympic Arms PCR-2, PCR-3 Rifles

Similar to the PCR-1 except has 16" barrel, weighs 8 lbs., 2 oz.; has post front sight, fully adjustable aperture rear. Model PCR-3 has flattop upper receiver, cut-down front sight base. Introduced 1994. Made in U.S. by Olympic Arms, Inc.
Price: $958.00

REMINGTON 40-XB RANGEMASTER TARGET CENTERFIRE

Caliber: 15 calibers from 220 Swift to 300 Win. Mag. **Barrel:** 27-1/4". **Weight:** 11-1/4 lbs. **Length:** 47" overall. **Stock:** American walnut, laminated thumbhole or Kevlar with high comb and beavertail forend stop. Rubber non-slip buttplate. **Sights:** None. Scope blocks installed. **Features:** Adjustable trigger. Stainless barrel and action. Receiver drilled and tapped for sights.
Price: Standard single shot $1,565.00
Price: Repeater $1,684.00

REMINGTON 40-XBBR KS

Caliber: Five calibers from 22 BR to 308 Win. **Barrel:** 20" (light varmint class), 24" (heavy varmint class). **Weight:** 7-1/4 lbs. (light varmint class); 12 lbs. (heavy varmint class). **Length:** 38" (20" bbl.), 42" (24" bbl.). **Stock:** Kevlar. **Sights:** None. Supplied with scope blocks. **Features:** Unblued stainless steel barrel, trigger adjustable from 1-1/2 lbs. to 3-1/2 lbs. Special 2-oz. trigger at extra cost. Scope and mounts extra.
Price: With Kevlar stock $1,742.00

REMINGTON 40-XC TARGET RIFLE

Caliber: 7.62 NATO, 5-shot. **Barrel:** 24", stainless steel. **Weight:** 11 lbs. without sights. **Length:** 43-1/2" overall. **Stock:** Kevlar, with palm rail. **Sights:** None furnished. **Features:** Designed to meet the needs of competitive shooters. Stainless steel barrel and action.
Price: $1,742.00

SAKO TRG-22 BOLT-ACTION RIFLE

Caliber: 308 Win., 10-shot magazine. **Barrel:** 26". **Weight:** 10-1/4 lbs. **Length:** 45-1/4" overall. **Stock:** Reinforced polyurethane with fully adjustable cheekpiece and buttplate. **Sights:** None furnished. Optional quick-detachable, one-piece scope mount base, 1" or 30mm rings. **Features:** Resistance-free bolt, free-floating heavy stainless barrel, 60-degree bolt lift. Two-stage trigger is adjustable for length, pull, horizontal or vertical pitch. Introduced 2000. Imported from Finland by Stoeger Industries.
Price: $2,699.00
Price: Model TRG-42, as above except in 338 Lapua Mag or 300 Win. Mag. $3,099.00

SAVAGE MODEL 900TR TARGET RIFLE

Caliber: 22 LR, 5-shot magazine. **Barrel:** 25". **Weight:** 8 lbs. **Length:** 43-5/8" overall. **Stock:** Target-type, walnut-finished hardwood. **Sights:** Target front with inserts, peep rear with 1/4-minute click adjustments. **Features:** Comes with shooting rail and hand stop. Introduced 1991. Made in Canada, from Savage Arms Inc.
Price: Right- or left-hand $440.00

Springfield, Inc. M1A Super Match

Springfield, Inc. M1A/M-21

SAVAGE MODEL 112BT COMPETITION GRADE RIFLE

Caliber: 223, 308, 5-shot magazine, 300 Win. Mag., single shot. **Barrel:** 26", heavy contour stainless with black finish; 1:9" twist (223), 1:10" (308). **Weight:** 10.8 lbs. **Length:** 47.5" overall. **Stock:** Laminated wood with straight comb, adjustable cheek rest, Wundhammer palm swell, ventilated forend. Recoil pad is adjustable for length of pull. **Sights:** None furnished; drilled and tapped for scope mounting and aperture target-style sights. Recessed target-style muzzle has .812" diameter section for universal target sight base. **Features:** Pillar-bedded stock, matte black alloy receiver. Bolt has black titanium nitride coating, large handle ball. Has alloy accessory rail on forend. Comes with safety gun lock, target and ear puffs. Introduced 1994. Made in U.S. by Savage Arms, Inc.

Price: **$1,028.00**
Price: 300 Win. Mag. (single shot 112BT-S) **$1,028.00**

SPRINGFIELD, INC. M1A SUPER MATCH

Caliber: 308 Win. **Barrel:** 22", heavy Douglas Premium. **Weight:** About 10 lbs. **Length:** 44.31" overall. **Stock:** Heavy walnut competition stock with longer pistol grip, contoured area behind the rear sight, thicker butt and forend, glass bedded. **Sights:** National Match front and rear. **Features:** Has figure-eight-style operating rod guide. Introduced 1987. From Springfield, Inc.

Price: About **$2,479.00**

Springfield, Inc. M1A/M-21 Tactical Model Rifle

Similar to the M1A Super Match except has special sniper stock with adjustable cheekpiece and rubber recoil pad. Weighs 11.2 lbs. From Springfield, Inc.

Price: **$2,975.00**

STONER SR-15 MATCH RIFLE

Caliber: 223. **Barrel:** 20". **Weight:** 7.9 lbs. **Length:** 38" overall. **Stock:** Black synthetic. **Sights:** None furnished; flat-top upper receiver for scope mounting. **Features:** Short Picatinny rail; two-stage match trigger. Introduced 1998. Made in U.S. by Knight's Mfg.Co.

Price: **$1,595.00**

STONER SR-25 MATCH RIFLE

Caliber: 7.62 NATO, 10-shot steel magazine, 5-shot optional. **Barrel:** 24" heavy match; 1:11.25" twist. **Weight:** 10.75 lbs. **Length:** 44" overall. **Stock:** Black synthetic AR-15A2 design. Full floating forend of Mil-spec synthetic attaches to upper receiver at a single point. **Sights:** None furnished. Has integral Weaver-style rail. Rings and iron sights optional. **Features:** Improved AR-15 trigger; AR-15-style seven-lug rotating bolt. Gas block rail mounts detachable front sight. Introduced 1993. Made in U.S. by Knight's Mfg. Co.

Price: **$2,995.00**
Price: SR-25 Lightweight Match (20" medium match target contour barrel, 9.5 lbs., 40" overall) **$2,995.00**

TANNER 50 METER FREE RIFLE

Caliber: 22 LR, single shot. **Barrel:** 27.7". **Weight:** 13.9 lbs. **Length:** 44.4" overall. **Stock:** Seasoned walnut with palm rest, accessory rail, adjustable hook buttplate. **Sights:** Globe front with interchangeable inserts, Tanner micrometer-diopter rear with adjustable aperture. **Features:** Bolt action with externally adjustable set trigger. Supplied with 50-meter test target. Imported from Switzerland by Mandall Shooting Supplies. Introduced 1984.

Price: About **$3,900.00**

TANNER STANDARD UIT RIFLE

Caliber: 308, 7.5mm Swiss, 10-shot. **Barrel:** 25.9". **Weight:** 10.5 lbs. **Length:** 40.6" overall. **Stock:** Match style of seasoned nutwood with accessory rail; coarsely stippled pistol grip; high cheekpiece; vented forend. **Sights:** Globe front with interchangeable inserts, Tanner micrometer-diopter rear with adjustable aperture. **Features:** Two locking lug revolving bolt encloses case head. Trigger adjustable from 1/2 to 6-1/2 lbs.; match trigger optional. Comes with 300-meter test target. Imported from Switzerland by Mandall Shooting Supplies. Introduced 1984.

Price: About **$4,700.00**

TANNER 300 METER FREE RIFLE

Caliber: 308 Win., 7.5 Swiss, single shot. **Barrel:** 27.58". **Weight:** 15 lbs. **Length:** 45.3" overall. **Stock:** Seasoned walnut, thumbhole style, with accessory rail, palm rest, adjustable hook butt. **Sights:** Globe front with interchangeable inserts, Tanner-design micrometer-diopter rear with adjustable aperture. **Features:** Three-lug revolving-lock bolt design; adjustable set trigger; short firing pin travel; supplied with 300-meter test target. Imported from Switzerland by Mandall Shooting Supplies. Introduced 1984.

Price: About **$4,900.00**

TIKKA SPORTER RIFLE

Caliber: 223, 22-250, 308, detachable 5-shot magazine. **Barrel:** 23-1/2" heavy. **Weight:** 9 lbs. **Length:** 43-5/8" overall. **Stock:** European walnut with adjustable comb, adjustable buttplate; stippled grip and forend. **Sights:** None furnished; drilled and tapped for scope mounting. **Features:** Buttplate is adjustable for distance, angle, height and pitch; adjustable trigger; free-floating barrel. Introduced 1998. Imported from Finland by Stoeger Industries.

Price: **$939.00**

RIFLES

Includes a wide variety of sporting guns and guns suitable for various competitions.

Benelli Legacy

Benelli Limited Edition Legacy 12 gauge

Benelli M1 Super 90 Camouflage

Benelli Super Black Eagle

AMERICAN ARMS PHANTOM AUTO SHOTGUNS

Gauge: 12, 3" chamber. **Barrel:** 24", 26", 28" (Imp. Cyl., Mod., Full choke tubes). **Stock:** European walnut or black synthetic. **Features:** Gas-operated action; blued barrel; checkered pistol grip and forend; vent rib barrel. Introduced 1999. Imported by American Arms, Inc.

Price: .... NA

BENELLI LEGACY SHOTGUN

Gauge: 12, 20, 3" chamber. **Barrel:** 26", 28" (Full, Mod., Imp. Cyl., Imp. Mod., Skeet choke tubes). Mid-bead sight. **Weight:** 7.1 to 7.6 lbs. **Length:** 49-5/8" overall (26" barrel). **Stock:** European walnut with high-gloss finish. Special competition stock comes with drop adjustment kit. **Features:** Uses the rotating bolt inertia recoil operating system with a two-piece steel/aluminum etched receiver (bright on lower, blue upper). Drop adjustment kit allows the stock to be custom fitted without modifying the stock. Black lower receiver finish, blued upper. Introduced 1998. Imported from Italy by Heckler & Koch, Inc.

Price: $1,350.00

Benelli Limited Edition Legacy

Similar to the Legacy model except receiver has gold-filled, etched game scenes and limited to 250 12 gauge (28" barrel) and 250 20 gauge (26" barrel) guns to commemorate the year 2000.

Price $1,600.00

Benelli Sport Shotgun

Similar to the Legacy model except has matte blue receiver, two carbon fiber interchangeable ventilated ribs, adjustable butt pad, adjustable buttstock, and functions with ultra-light target loads. Walnut stock with satin finish. Introduced 1997. Imported from Italy by Benelli U.S.A.

Price: $1,340.00

BENELLI M1 FIELD AUTO SHOTGUN

Gauge: 12, 3" chamber. **Barrel:** 21", 24", 26", 28" (choke tubes). **Weight:** 7 lbs., 4 oz. **Stock:** High impact polymer; wood on 26", 28". **Sights:** Metal bead front. **Features:** Sporting version of the military & police gun. Uses the rotating Montefeltro bolt system. Ventilated rib; blue finish. Comes with set of five choke tubes. Imported from Italy by Benelli U.S.A.

Price: $920.00
Price: Wood stock version $935.00
Price: 24" rifled barrel, polymer stock. $1,000.00
Price: 24" rifled barrel, camo stock $1,100.00
Price: Synthetic stock, left-hand version (24", 26", 28" brls) $935.00
Price: Camo Stock, left-hand version (24", 26", 28" brls.) $1,025.00

Benelli Montefeltro 90 Shotgun

Similar to the M1 Super 90 except has checkered walnut stock with high-gloss finish. Uses the Montefeltro rotating bolt system with a simple inertia recoil design. Full, Imp. Mod, Mod., Imp. Cyl. choke tubes. Weighs 6.8-7.1 lbs. Finish is matte black. Introduced 1987.

Price: 24", 26", 28" $940.00
Price: Left-hand, 26", 28" $960.00

Benelli Montefeltro 20 gauge Shotgun

Similar to the 12 gauge Montefeltro except chambered for 3" 20 gauge, 24" or 26" barrel (choke tubes), weighs 5-1/2 lbs., has drop-adjustable walnut stock with satin or camo finish, blued receiver. Overall length 47.5". Introduced 1993. Imported from Italy by Benelli U.S.A.

Price: 26" barrels $940.00
Price: 26", camouflage finish $1,040.00
Price: Montefeltro Short Stock, 24" and 26" brls. $975.00

BENELLI SUPER BLACK EAGLE SHOTGUN

Gauge: 12, 3-1/2" chamber. **Barrel:** 24", 26", 28" (Cyl. Imp. Cyl., Mod., Imp. Mod., Full choke tubes). **Weight:** 7 lbs., 5 oz. **Length:** 49-5/8" overall (28" barrel). **Stock:** European walnut with satin finish, or polymer. Adjustable for drop. **Sights:** Bead front. **Features:** Uses Montefeltro inertia recoil bolt system. Fires all 12 gauge shells from 2-3/4" to 3-1/2" magnums. Introduced 1991. Imported from Italy by Benelli U.S.A.

Price: With 26" and 28" barrel, wood stock $1,240.00
Price: With 24", 26" and 28" barrel, polymer stock. $1,220.00
Price: Left-hand, 24", 26", 28", polymer stock $1,250.00
Price: Left-hand, 24", 26", 28", camo stock $1,330.00

SHOTGUNS

Beretta Urika Gold Sporting

Beretta Urika Sporting

Beretta Urika Gold Trap

Benelli Super Black Eagle Slug Gun

Similar to the Benelli Super Black Eagle except has 24" rifled barrel with 3" chamber, and drilled and tapped for scope. Uses the inertia recoil bolt system. Matte-finish receiver. Weight is 7.5 lbs., overall length 45.5". Wood or polymer stocks available. Introduced 1992. Imported from Italy by Benelli U.S.A.

Price: With wood stock.................................. $1,280.00
Price: With polymer stock.............................. $1,270.00
Price: 26" barrels $1,390.00

Benelli Executive Series Shotguns

Similar to the Super Black Eagle except has grayed steel lower receiver, hand-engraved and gold inlaid (Grade III), and has highest grade of walnut stock with drop adjustment kit. Barrel lengths 26" or 28"; 3" chamber. **Special order only.** Introduced 1995. Imported from Italy by Benelli U.S.A.

Price: Grade I (engraved game scenes)................... $5,035.00
Price: Grade II (game scenes with scroll engraving) $5,720.00
Price: Grade III (full coverage, gold inlays)............... $6,670.00

NEW! BERETTA AL391 URIKA AUTO SHOTGUNS

Gauge: 12, 20 gauge; 3" chamber. **Barrel:** 22", 24", 26", 28", 30"; five Mobilchoke choke tubes. **Weight:** 5.95 to 7.28 lbs. **Length:** Varies by model. **Stock:** Walnut, black or camo synthetic; shims, spacers and interchangeable recoil pads allow custom fit. **Features:** Self-compensating gas operation handles full range of loads; recoil reducer in receiver; enlarged trigger guard; reduced-weight receiver, barrel and forend; hard-chromed bore. Introduced 2000. Imported from Italy by Beretta USA.

Price: AL391 Urika (12 ga., 26", 28", 30" barrels) $960.00
Price: AL391 Urika (20 ga., 24", 26", 28" barrels) $960.00
Price: AL391 Urika Synthetic (12 ga., 24", 26", 28", 30" barrels) $960.00
Price: AL391 Urika Camo. (12 ga., Realtree Hardwoods
or Advantage Wetlands) $1,055.00

NEW! Beretta AL391 Urika Gold and Gold Sporting Auto Shotguns

Similar to AL391 Urika except features deluxe wood, jeweled bolt and carrier, gold-inlaid receiver with black or silver finish. Introduced 2000. Imported from Italy by Beretta USA.

Price: AL391 Urika Gold (12 or 20 ga., black receiver) $1,150.00
Price: AL391 Urika Gold (silver, lightweight receiver). $1,185.00
Price: AL391 Urika Gold Sporting (12 or 20, black or silver
receiver, scroll engraving). $1,195.00

Beretta AL391 Urika Sporting Auto Shotguns

Similar to AL391 Urika except has competition sporting stock with rounded rubber recoil pad, wide ventilated rib with white front and mid-rib beads, satin-black receiver with silver markings. Available in 12 and 20 gauge. Introduced 2000. Imported from Italy by Beretta USA.

Price: AL391 Urika Sporting. $1,000.00

Beretta AL391 Urika Trap and Gold Trap Auto Shotguns

Similar to AL391 Urika except in 12 ga. only, has wide ventilated rib with white front and mid-rib beads, Monte Carlo stock and special trap recoil pad. Gold Trap features highly figured walnut stock and forend, gold-filled Beretta logo and signature on receiver. Introduced 2000. Imported from Italy by Beretta USA.

Price: AL391 Urika Trap $1,000.00
Price: AL391 Urika Gold Trap. $1,195.00

Beretta AL391 Urika Parallel Target RL and SL Auto Shotguns

Similar to AL391 Urika except has parallel-comb, Monte Carlo stock with tighter grip radius to reduce trigger reach and stepped ventilated rib. SL model has same features but with 13.5" length of pull stock. Introduced 2000. Imported from Italy by Beretta USA.

Price: AL391 Urika Parallel Target RL $1,000.00
Price: AL391 Urika Parallel Target SL $1,000.00

Beretta AL391 Urika Slug Shotgun

Similar to AL391 except has a 22" barrel with V-shaped rear sight, hooded blade front sight, special rib, receiver designed to accept Weaver scope bases. Introduced 2000. From Beretta USA.

Price: .... NA

Beretta AL391 Urika Youth Shotgun

Similar to AL391 except has a 24" or 26" barrel with 13.5" stock for youth and smaller shooters. Introduced 2000. From Beretta USA.

Price: $960.00

BERETTA ES100 NWTF SPECIAL AUTO SHOTGUN

Gauge: 12, 3" chamber. **Barrel:** 24", MC3 tubes and Briley extended Extra-Full Turkey. **Weight:** 7.3 lbs. **Stock:** Synthetic, checkered. **Sights:** Truglo fiber optic front and rear three-dot system. **Features:** Short recoil inertia operation. Mossy Oak Break-Up camouflage finish on stock and forend, black matte finish on all metal. Comes with camouflage sling. Introduced 1999. Imported from Italy by Beretta U.S.A.

Price: $945.00

Browning Gold Deer Hunter

Browning Gold Sporting Golden Clays

Browning Gold Waterfowl

BROWNING GOLD HUNTER AUTO SHOTGUN

Gauge: 12, 20, 3" chamber. **Barrel:** 12 ga.—26", 28", 30", Invector Plus choke tubes; 20 ga.—26", 30", Invector choke tubes. **Weight:** 7 lbs., 9 oz. (12 ga.), 6 lbs., 12 oz. (20 ga.). **Length:** 46-1/4" overall (20 ga., 26" barrel). **Stock:** 14"x1-1/2"x2-1/3"; select walnut with gloss finish; palm swell grip. **Features:** Self-regulating, self-cleaning gas system shoots all loads; lightweight receiver with special non-glare deep black finish; large reversible safety button; large rounded trigger guard, gold trigger. The 20 gauge has slightly smaller dimensions; 12 gauge have back-bored barrels, Invector Plus tube system. Introduced 1994. Imported by Browning.

Price: 12 or 20 gauge **$772.00**
Price: Extra barrels **$290.00**

Browning Gold Deer Hunter Auto Shotgun

Similar to the Gold Hunter except 12 gauge only, 22" rifled or smooth Standard Invector barrel with 5" rifled choke tube, cantilever scope mount, extra-thick recoil pad. Weighs 7 lbs., 12 oz., overall length 42-1/2". Sling swivel studs fitted on the magazine cap and butt. Introduced 1997. Imported by Browning.

Price: **$839.00**
Price: With Mossy Oak Break-up camouflage **$909.00**

Browning Gold Deer Stalker

Similar to the Gold Deer Hunter except has black composite stock and forend, fully rifled barrel, cantilever scope mount. Introduced 1999. Imported by Browning.

Price: **$839.00**

Browning Gold Sporting Clays Auto

Similar to the Gold Hunter except 12 gauge only with 28" or 30" barrel; front and center beads on tapered ventilated rib; ported and back-bored Invector Plus barrel; 2-3/4" chamber; satin-finished stock with solid, radiused recoil pad with hard heel insert; non-glare black alloy receiver has "Sporting Clays" inscribed in gold. Introduced 1996. Imported from Japan by Browning.

Price: **$798.00**

Browning Gold Sporting Golden Clays

Similar to the Sporting Clays except has silvered receiver with gold engraving, high grade wood. Introduced 1999. Imported by Browning.

Price: **$1,267.00**

Browning Gold Ladies/Youth Sporting Clays Auto

Similar to the Gold Sporting Clays except has stock dimensions of 14-1/4"x1-3/4"x2" for women and younger shooters. Introduced 1999. Imported by Browning.

Price: **$798.00**

Browning Gold Stalker Auto Shotgun

Similar to the Gold Hunter except has black composite stock and forend. Choice of 3" or 3-1/2" chamber.

Price: With 3" chamber. **$772.00**
Price: With 3-1/2" chamber. **$929.00**

Browning Gold Waterfowl Shotgun

Similar to the Gold Hunter except 12 gauge only, completely covered with Mossy Oak Shadow Grass comouflage. Choice of 3" or 3-1/2" chamber. Introduced 1999. Imported by Browning.

Price: 26", 28". **$999.00**

Browning Gold Classic Hunter Auto Shotgun

Similar to the Gold Hunter 3" except has semi-hump back receiver, magazine cut-off, adjustable comb, and satin-finish wood. Introduced 1999. Imported by Browning.

Price: 12 gauge **$772.00**
Price: 20 gauge **$772.00**
Price: High Grade (silvered, gold engraved receiver, high grade wood) **$1,427.00**

Browning Gold Classic Stalker

Similar to the Gold Classic Hunter except has adjustable composite stock and forend. Introduced 1999. Imported by Browning.

Price: **$772.00**

Browning Gold Turkey/Waterfowl Hunter Auto

Similar to the Gold Hunter except available with 3" or 3-1/2" chamber; has 24" barrel with Hi-Viz front sight. Introduced 1999. Imported by Browning.

Price: **$929.00**

Browning Gold Turkey/Waterfowl Camo Shotgun

Similar to the Gold Turkey/Waterfowl Hunter except 12 gauge only, 3" or 3-1/2" chamber, 24" barrel with Extra-Full Turkey choke tube, Hi-Viz front sight. Completely covered with Mossy Oak Breakup camouflage. Introduced 1999. Imported by Browning.

Price: **$929.00**
Price: Turkey/Waterfowl Stalker (black stock and metal) **$949.00**

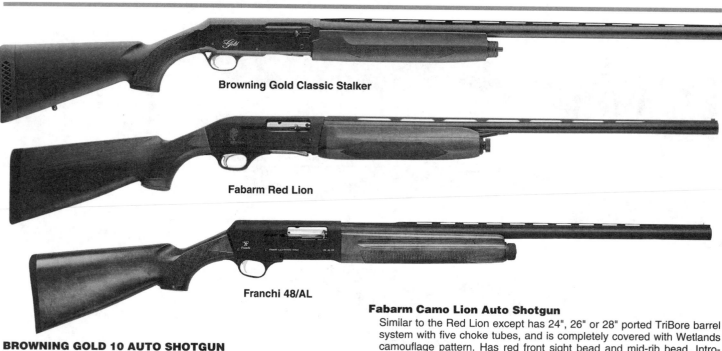

Browning Gold Classic Stalker

Fabarm Red Lion

Franchi 48/AL

BROWNING GOLD 10 AUTO SHOTGUN

Gauge: 10, 3-1/2" chamber, 5-shot magazine. **Barrel:** 26", 28", 30" (Imp. Cyl., Mod., Full standard Invector). **Weight:** 10 lbs. 7 oz. (28" barrel). **Stock:** 14-3/8"x1-1/2"x2-3/8". Select walnut with gloss finish, cut checkering, recoil pad. **Features:** Short-stroke, gas-operated action, cross-bolt safety. Forged steel receiver with polished blue finish. Introduced 1993. Imported by Browning.

Price: **$1,007.95**
Price: Extra barrel...................................... **$276.00**

Browning Gold 10 gauge Auto Combo

Similar to the Gold 10 except comes with 24" and 26" barrels with Imp. Cyl., Mod., Full Invector choke tubes. Introduced 1999. Imported by Browning.

Price: **$1,059.00**

EAA/BAIKAL MP-153 AUTO SHOTGUN

NEW! **Gauge:** 12, 3-1/2" chamber. **Barrel:** 18-1/2", 20", 24", 26", 28"; imp., mod. and full choke tubes. **Weight:** 7.8 lbs. **Stock:** Walnut. **Features:** Gas-operated action with automatic gas-adjustment valve allows use of light and heavy loads interchangeably; 4-round magazine; rubber recoil pad. Introduced 2000. Imported by European American Armory.

Price: MP-153 (blued finish, walnut stock and forend).......... **$459.00**

FABARM RED LION AUTO SHOTGUN

Gauge: 12, 3" chamber. **Barrel:** 24", 26", 28", choke tubes. **Weight:** 7 lbs. **Length:** 45.5" overall. **Stock:** European walnut with gloss finish. **Features:** TriBore barrel, reversible safety; nickel-plated trigger and carrier release button; leather-covered rubber recoil pad. Introduced 1998. Imported from Italy by Heckler & Koch, Inc.

Price: **$820.00**
Price: Gold Lion (as above except gold-plated trigger, carrier release button, olive wood gripcap).................................. **$915.00**

Fabarm Sporting Clays Lion Auto Shotgun

Similar to the Red Lion except has 28" TriBore ported barrel with interchangeable colored front-sight beads, mid-rib bead, 10mm channeled vent rib, oil-finished walnut stock and forend with olive wood grip-cap. Stock dimensions are 14.58"x1.58"x2.44". Has distinctive gold-colored receiver logo. Available in 12 gauge only, 3" chamber. Introduced 1999. Imported from Italy by Heckler & Koch, Inc.

Price: **$959.00**

Fabarm Sporting Clays Extra

Same as Sporting Clays Lion Auto but has carbon fiber finish.
Price: **$1,249.00**

Fabarm Camo Lion Auto Shotgun

Similar to the Red Lion except has 24", 26" or 28" ported TriBore barrel system with five choke tubes, and is completely covered with Wetlands camouflage pattern. Has red front sight bead and mid-rib bead. Introduced 1999. Imported from Italy by Heckler & Koch, Inc.

Price: **$1,019.00**

FRANCHI AL 48 SHOTGUN

Gauge: 12, 20 or 28, 2-3/4" chamber. **Barrel:** 24", 26", 28" (Franchoke cyl. imp. cyl., mod., choke tubes). **Weight:** 5.5 lbs. (20 gauge). **Length:** NA **Stock:** 14-1/4"x1-5/8"x2-1/2". Walnut with checkered grip and forend. **Features:** Recoil-operated action. Chrome-lined bore; cross-bolt safety. Imported from Italy by Benelli U.S.A.

Price: 12 ga. **$630.00**
Price: 20 ga. **$613.00**
Price: 28 ga. **$680.00**

Franchi AL 48 Deluxe Shotgun

Similar to AL 48 but with select walnut stock and forend and high-polish blue finish. Introduced 2000.
Price: (20 gauge, 26" barrel) **$710.00**
Price: (28 gauge, 26" barrel) **$680.00**

Franchi AL 48 Short Stock Shotgun

Similar to AL 48 but with stock shortened to 12 1/2 " length of pull.
Price: (20 gauge, 26" barrel) **$594.00**

FRANCHI VARIOPRESS 612 SHOTGUN

Gauge: 12, 3" chamber. **Barrel:** 24", 26", 28", Franchoke tubes. **Weight:** 7 lbs., 2 oz. **Length:** 47-1/2" overall. **Stock:** 14-1/4"x1-1/2"x2-1/2". European walnut. **Features:** Alloy frame with matte black finish; gas-operated with Variopress System; four-lug rotating bolt; loaded chamber indicator. Introduced 1996. Imported from Italy by Benelli U.S.A.

Price: **$595.00**
Price: Camo (Advantage camo) **$657.00**
Price: Synthetic (black synthetic stock, forend) **$579.00**
Price: (20 gauge, 24", 26", 28") **$595.00**
Price: Variopress 620 (Advantage camo)................... **$657.00**

Franchi Variopress 612 Defense Shotgun

Similar to Variopress 612 except has 18 1/2 ", cylinder-bore barrel with black, synthetic stock. Available in 12 gauge, 3" chamber only. Weighs 6-1/2 pounds. Introduced 2000.
Price: **$520.00**

Franchi Variopress 612 Sporting Shotgun

Similar to Variopress 612 except has 30" ported barrel to reduce muzzle jump. Available in 12 gauge, 3" chamber only. Introduced 2000.
Price: **$900.00**

Mossberg Model 9200 Trophy

Mossberg 9200 Viking

Remington Model 11-87 Premier

Franchi Variopress 620 Short Stock Shotgun

Similar to Variopress 620 but with stock shortened to 12 1/2 "length of pull for smaller shooters. Introduced 2000.
Price: (20 gauge, 26" barrel) **$605.00**

LUGER ULTRA LIGHT SEMI-AUTOMATIC SHOTGUNS

Gauge: 12, 3" and 3-1/2" chambers. **Barrel:** 26", 28"; imp. cyl., mod. and full choke tubes. **Weight:** 6-1/2 lbs. **Length:** 48" overall (28" barrel) **Stock:** Gloss-finish European walnut, checkered grip and forend. **Features:** Gas-operated action handles 2-3/4" and 3" loads; chrome-line barrel handles steel shot; blued finish. Introduced 2000. From Stoeger Industries.
Price: **$479.00**

MOSSBERG MODEL 9200 CROWN GRADE AUTO SHOTGUN

Gauge: 12, 3" chamber. **Barrel:** 24" (rifled bore), 24", 28" (Accu-Choke tubes); vent. rib. **Weight:** About 7.5 lbs. **Length:** 48" overall (28" bbl.). **Stock:** Walnut with high-gloss finish, cut checkering. **Features:** Shoots all 2-3/4" or 3" loads without adjustment. Alloy receiver, ambidextrous top safety. Introduced 1992.
Price: 28", vent. rib **$574.00**
Price: Trophy, 24" with scope base, rifled bore, Dual-Comb stock **$552.00**
Price: 24", Fiber Optic or standard rifle sights, rifled bore **$517.00**

Mossberg Model 9200 Viking

Similar to the Model 9200 Crown Grade except has black matte metal finish, moss-green synthetic stock and forend; 28" Accu-Choke vent. rib barrel with Imp. Cyl., Full and Mod. tubes. Made in U.S. by Mossberg. Introduced 1996.
Price: **$556.00**

Mossberg Model 9200 Camo Shotgun

Same as the Model 9200 Crown Grade except completely covered with Mossy Oak Tree Stand, Mossy Oak Shadowbranch, Realtree AP gray or OFM camouflage finish. Available with 24" barrel with Accu-Choke tubes. Has synthetic stock and forend. Introduced 1993.
Price: Turkey, 24" vent. rib, Mossy Oak or Realtree finish **$538.00**
Price: 28" vent. rib, Accu-Chokes, Woodlands camo finish **$556.00**

Mossberg Model 9200 Special Hunter

Similar to the Model 9200 Crown Grade except with 28" vent rib barrel with Accu choke set, Parkerized finish, black synthetic stock and forend, and sling and swivels. Introduced 1998. Made in U.S. by Mossberg.
Price: **$491.00**

Mossberg Model 9200 Custom Grade Sporting Shotgun

Same as the Model 9200 Crown Grade except has custom engraved receiver. Comes with 28" vent. rib barrel with Accu-Choke tubes (including Skeet), cut-checkered walnut stock and forend. Introduced 1993.
Price: **$590.00**

Mossberg Model 9200 Bantam

Same as the Model 9200 Crown Grade except has 1" shorter stock, 22" vent. rib barrel with three Accu-Choke tubes. Made in U.S. by Mossberg. Introduced 1996.
Price: **$574.00**

REMINGTON MODEL 11-87 PREMIER SHOTGUN

Gauge: 12, 20, 3" chamber. **Barrel:** 26", 28", 30" Rem Choke tubes. Light Contour barrel. **Weight:** About 7-3/4 lbs. **Length:** 46" overall (26" bbl.). **Stock:** Walnut with satin or high-gloss finish; cut checkering; solid brown buttpad; no white spacers. **Sights:** Bradley-type white-faced front, metal bead middle. **Features:** Pressure compensating gas system allows shooting 2-3/4" or 3" loads interchangeably with no adjustments. Stainless magazine tube; redesigned feed latch, barrel support ring on operating bars; pinned forend. Introduced 1987.
Price: **$756.00**
Price: Left-hand **$809.00**
Price: Premier Cantilever Deer Barrel, sling, swivels, Monte Carlo
   stock **$836.00**

Remington Model 11-87 Special Purpose Magnum

Similar to the 11-87 Premier except has dull stock finish, Parkerized exposed metal surfaces. Bolt and carrier have dull blackened coloring. Comes with 26" or 28" barrel with Rem Chokes, padded Cordura nylon sling and quick detachable swivels. Introduced 1987.
Price: **$756.00**
Price: With synthetic stock and forend (SPS) **$756.00**

Remington Model 11-87 SPS Special Purpose Synthetic Camo

Similar to the 11-87 Special Purpose Magnum except has synthetic stock and all metal (except bolt and trigger guard) and stock covered with Mossy Oak Break-Up camo finish. In 12 gauge only, 26", Rem Choke. Comes with camo sling, swivels. Introduced 1992.
Price: **$869.00**

Remington Model 11-87 SPS Camo

Remington Model 11-87 SPS-T Turkey Camo

Remington Model 11-87 SC NP

Remington Model 1100 Youth Turkey Camo

Remington Model 11-87 SPS-T Turkey Camo

Similar to the 11-87 Special Purpose Magnum except with synthetic stock, 21" vent. rib barrel with Rem choke tube. Completely covered with Mossy Oak Break-Up Brown camouflage. Bolt body, trigger guard and recoil pad are non-reflective black.
Price: **$869.00**
Price: Model 11-87 SPS-T RS/TG (TruGlo fiber optics sights). ... **$808.00**
Price: Model 11-87 SPS-T Camo CL/RD (Leupold/Gilmore
red dot sight) **$1,193.00**

Remington Model 11-87 SPS-Deer Shotgun

Similar to the 11-87 Special Purpose Camo except has fully-rifled 21" barrel with rifle sights, black non-reflective, synthetic stock and forend, black carrying sling. Introduced 1993.
Price: **$789.00**
Price: With wood stock (Model 11-87 SP Deer gun) Rem choke, 21" barrel w/rifle sights **$736.00**

Remington Model 11-87 SPS Cantilever Shotgun

Similar to the 11-87 SPS except has fully rifled barrel; synthetic stock with Monte Carlo comb; cantilever scope mount deer barrel. Comes with sling and swivels. Introduced 1994.
Price: **$836.00**

Remington Model 11-87 SC NP Shotgun

Similar to the Model 11-87 Sporting Clays except has low-luster nickel-plated receiver with fine-line engraving, and ported 28" or 30" Rem choke barrel with matte finish. Tournament-grade American walnut stock measures 14-3/16"x2-1/4"x1-1/2". Sporting Clays choke tubes have knurled extensions. Introduced 1997. Made in U.S. by Remington.
Price: **$948.00**

Remington Model 11-87 SP and SPS Super Magnum Shotguns

Similar to Model 11-87 Special Purpose Magnum except has 3-1/2" chamber. Available in flat-finish American walnut or black synthetic stock, 26" or 28" black-matte finished barrel and receiver; imp. cyl., modified and full Rem Choke tubes. Overall length 45-3/4", weighs 8 lbs., 2 oz. Introduced 2000. From Remington Arms Co.
Price: 11-87 SP Super Magnum (walnut stock) **$852.00**
Price: 11-87 SPS Super Magnum (synthetic stock) **$852.00**

Remington Model 11-87 Upland Special Shotgun

Similar to 11-87 Premier except has 23" ventilated rib barrel with straight-grip, English-style walnut stock. Available in 12 or 20 gauge. Overall length 43-1/2", weighs 7-1/4 lbs. (6-1/2 lbs. in 20 ga.). Comes with imp. cyl., modified and full choke tubes. Introduced 2000. From Remington Arms Co.
Price: 12 or 20 gauge **$756.00**

REMINGTON MODEL 1100 SYNTHETIC LT-20

Gauge: 20. **Barrel:** 26" Rem Chokes. **Weight:** 6-3/4 lbs. **Stock:** 14"x1-1/2"x2-1/2". Black synthetic, checkered pistol grip and forend. **Features:** Matted receiver top with scroll work on both sides of receiver.
Price: **$540.00**
Price: Youth Gun LT-20 (21" Rem Choke) **$540.00**

Remington Model 1100 Synthetic

12 gauge, and has black synthetic stock; vent. rib 28" barrel on 12 gauge, both with Mod. Rem Choke tube. Weighs about 7-1/2 lbs. Introduced 1996.
Price: **$540.00**

Remington Model 1100 Youth Synthetic Turkey Camo

Similar to the Model 1100 LT-20 except has 1" shorter stock, 21" vent rib barrel with Full Rem Choke tube; 3" chamber; synthetic stock and forend are covered with RealTree Advantage camo, and barrel and receiver have non-reflective, black matte finish. Introduced 1999.
Price: **$603.00**

Remington Model 1100 Sporting 28

Remington SP-10 NWTF

Weatherby SAS

Remington Model 1100 LT-20 Synthetic FR RS Shotgun

Similar to the Model 1100 LT-20 except has 21" fully rifled barrel with rifle sights, 2-3/4" chamber, and fiberglass-reinforced synthetic stock. Introduced 1997. Made in U.S. by Remington.
Price: **$573.00**

Remington Model 1100 Sporting 28

Similar to the 1100 LT-20 except in 28 gauge with 25" barrel; comes with Skeet, Imp. Cyl., Light Mod., Mod. Rem Choke tube. Semi-Fancy walnut with gloss finish, Sporting rubber butt pad. Made in U.S. by Remington. Introduced 1996.
Price: **$859.00**

Remington Model 1100 Sporting 20 Shotgun

Similar to the Model 1100 LT-20 except has tournament-grade American walnut stock with gloss finish and sporting-style recoil pad, 28" Rem-Choke barrel for Skeet, Imp. Cyl., Light Modified and Modified. Introduced 1998.
Price: **$859.00**

Remington Model 1100 Classic Trap Shotgun

Similar to Standard Model 1100 except 12 gauge with 30", low-profile barrel, semi-fancy American walnut stock and high-polish blued receiver with engraving and gold eagle inlay. Comes with singles, mid handicap and long handicap choke tubes. Overall length 50-1/2", weighs 8 lbs., 4 oz. Introduced 2000. From Remington Arms Co.
Price: **$885.00**

Remington Model 1100 Sporting 12 Shotgun

Similar to Model 1100 Sporting 20 Shotgun except in 12 gauge, has 28" ventilated barrel with semi-fancy American walnut stock, gold-plated trigger. Overall length 49", weighs 8 lbs. Introduced 2000. From Remington Arms Co.
Price: **$859.00**

Remington Model 1100 Synthetic FR CL Shotgun

Similar to the Model 1100 LT-20 except 12 gauge, has 21" fully rifled barrel with cantilever scope mount and fiberglass-reinforced synthetic stock with Monte Carlo comb. Introduced 1997. Made in U.S. by Remington.
Price: **$620.00**

REMINGTON MODEL SP-10 MAGNUM SHOTGUN

Gauge: 10, 3-1/2" chamber, 2-shot magazine. **Barrel:** 26", 30" (Full and Mod. Rem Chokes). **Weight:** 10-3/4 to 11 lbs. **Length:** 47-1/2" overall (26" barrel). **Stock:** Walnut with satin finish or black synthetic. Checkered grip and forend. **Sights:** Twin bead. **Features:** Stainless steel gas system with moving cylinder; 3/8" ventilated rib. Receiver and barrel have matte finish. Brown recoil pad. Comes with padded Cordura nylon sling. Introduced 1989.
Price: **$1,199.00**
Price: SP-10 Magnum Turkey Camo (23" vent rib barrel, Turkey Extra-Full Rem Choke tube) Mossy Oak Break-up. **$1,319.00**

Remington Model SP-10 Magnum Camo Shotgun

Similar to the SP-10 Magnum except buttstock, forend, receiver, barrel and magazine cap are covered with Mossy Oak Break-Up camo finish; bolt body and trigger guard have matte black finish. Rem Choke tube, 26" vent. rib barrel with mid-rib bead and Bradley-style front sight, swivel studs and quick-detachable swivels, and a non-slip Cordura carrying sling in the same camo pattern. Introduced 1993.
Price: **$1,319.00**
Price: SP-10 Magnum Synthetic **$1,199.00**

SARSILMAZ SEMI-AUTOMATIC SHOTGUN

Gauge: 12, 3" chamber. **Barrel:** 26" or 28"; fixed chokes. **Weight:** N/A. **Length:** N/A. **Stock:** Walnut or synthetic. **Features:** Handles 2-3/4" or 3" magnum loads. Introduced 2000. Imported from Turkey by Armsport Inc.
Price: With walnut stock **$969.95**
Price: With synthetic stock **$919.95**

WEATHERBY SAS AUTO SHOTGUN

Gauge: 12, 20, 2-3/4" or 3" chamber. **Barrel:** 26", 28" (20 ga.); 26", 28", 30" (12 ga.); Briley Multi-Choke tubes. **Weight:** 6-3/4 to 7-3/4 lbs. **Stock:** 14-1/4"x2-1/4"x1-1/2". Claro walnut. **Features:** Alloy receiver with matte finish; gold-plated trigger; magazine cut-off. Introduced 1999. Imported by Weatherby.
Price: 12 or 20 ga. **$899.00**

WINCHESTER SUPER X2 AUTO SHOTGUN

Gauge: 12, 3", 3-1/2" chamber. **Barrel:** 24", 26", 28"; Invector Plus choke tubes. **Weight:** 7-1/4 to 7-1/2 lbs. **Stock:** 14-1/4"x1-3/4"x2". Walnut or black synthetic. **Features:** Gas-operated action shoots all loads without adjustment; vent. rib barrels. Introduced 1999. Made in U.S. by U.S. Repeating Arms Co.
Price: Field, walnut or synthetic stock, 3". **$799.00**
Price: Camo Waterfowl, 3-1/2", Mossy Oak Shadow Grass. **$1,033.00**
Price: Turkey, 3-1/2", synthetic stock, 24" **$955.00**
Price: Magnum, 3-1/2", synthetic stock **$941.00**

Includes a wide variety of sporting guns and guns suitable for competitive shooting.

Armscor M-30F Field

Benelli Nova Pump

Benelli Nova Pump Rifled Slug

Browning BPS 10 gauge

ARMSCOR M-30F FIELD PUMP SHOTGUN

Gauge: 12, 3" chamber. **Barrel:** 28" fixed Mod., or with Mod. and Full choke tubes. **Weight:** 7.6 lbs. **Stock:** Walnut-finished hardwood. **Features:** Double action slide bars; blued steel receiver; damascened bolt. Introduced 1996. Imported from the Philippines by K.B.I., Inc.
Price: With fixed choke.................................. $239.00
Price: With choke tubes $269.00

BENELLI NOVA PUMP SHOTGUN

Gauge: 12, 3-1/2" chamber. **Barrel:** 24", 26", 28"; chrome lined, vent rib; choke tubes. **Weight:** 8 lbs. **Length:** 47.5" overall. **Stock:** Black polymer. **Features:** Montefeltro rotating bolt design with dual action bars; magazine cut-0ff; synthetic trigger assembly. Four-shot magazine Introduced 1999. Imported from Italy by Benelli USA.
Price: With black stock................................... $390.00
Price: With Camo finish $456.00

Benelli Nova Pump Slug Gun

Similar to the Nova except has 18.5" barrel with adjustable rifle-type or ghost ring sights; weighs 7.2 lbs.; black synthetic stock. Introduced 1999. Imported from Italy by Benelli USA.
Price: With rifle sights.................................. $320.00
Price: With ghost-ring sights $355.00

Benelli Nova Pump Rifled Slug Gun

NEW!

Similar to Nova Pump Slug Gun except has 24" barrel and rifled bore; open rifle sights; synthetic stock; weighs 8.1 pounds.
Price: $544.00

BROWNING BPS PUMP SHOTGUN

Gauge: 10, 12, 3-1/2" chamber; 12 or 20, 3" chamber (2-3/4" in target guns), 28, 2-3/4" chamber, 5-shot magazine, 410 ga., 3" chamber. **Barrel:** 10 ga.—24" Buck Special, 28", 30", 32" Invector; 12, 20 ga.—22", 24", 26", 28", 30", 32" (Imp. Cyl., mod. or full). 410 ga.—26" barrel. (Imp. Cyl., mod. and full choke tubes.) Also available with Invector choke tubes, 12 or 20 ga.; Upland Special has 22" barrel with Invector tubes. BPS 3" and 3-1/2" have back-bored barrel. **Weight:** 7 lbs., 8 oz. (28" barrel). **Length:** 48-3/4" overall (28" barrel). **Stock:** 14-1/4"x1-1/2"x2-1/2". Select walnut, semi-beavertail forend, full pistol grip stock. **Features:** All 12 gauge 3" guns except Buck Special and game guns have back-bored barrels with Invector Plus choke tubes. Bottom feeding and ejection, receiver top safety, high post vent. rib. Double action bars eliminate binding. Vent. rib barrels only. All 12 and 20 gauge guns with 3" chamber available with fully engraved receiver flats at no extra cost. Each gauge has its own unique game scene. Introduced 1977. Imported from Japan by Browning.
Price: 10 ga., Hunting, Invector $532.00
Price: 12 ga., 3-1/2" Mag., Hunting, Invector Plus $532.00
Price: 12, 20 ga., Hunting, Invector Plus $444.00
Price: 12 ga. Buck Special $408.00
Price: 28 ga., Hunting, Invector $444.00
Price: 410 ga., Hunting, Invector .... NA

Browning BPS 10 gauge Turkey

Similar to the BPS Hunter except has 24" barrel with Hi-Viz front sight for turkey hunting. Available with either walnut or black composite stock and forend. Introduced 1999. Imported by Browning.
Price: Hunter (walnut)................................... $532.00
Price: Stalker (composite) $532.00

Browning BPS 10 gauge Camo Pump

Similar to the BPS 10 gauge Hunter except completely covered with Mossy Oak Shadow Grass camouflage. Available with 24", 26", 28" barrel. Introduced 1999. Imported by Browning.
Price: $602.00

SHOTGUNS

Browning BPS Stalker

Ithaca Model 37 Turkeyslayer

Browning BPS Waterfowl Camo Pump Shotgun

Similar to the BPS Hunter except completely covered with Mossy Oak Shadow Grass camouflage. Available in 12 gauge, with 24", 26" or 28" barrel, 3" chamber. Introduced 1999. Imported by Browning.
Price: $514.00

Browning BPS Game Gun Deer Special

Similar to the standard BPS except has newly designed receiver/magazine tube/barrel mounting system to eliminate play, heavy 20.5" barrel with rifle-type sights with adjustable rear, solid receiver scope mount, "rifle" stock dimensions for scope or open sights, sling swivel studs. Gloss or matte finished wood with checkering, polished blue metal. Introduced 1992.
Price: $516.00

Browning BPS Game Gun Turkey Special

Similar to the standard BPS except has satin-finished walnut stock and dull-finished barrel and receiver. Receiver is drilled and tapped for scope mounting. Rifle-style stock dimensions and swivel studs. Has Extra-Full Turkey choke tube. Introduced 1992.
Price: $482.00

Browning BPS Stalker Pump Shotgun

Same gun as the standard BPS except all exposed metal parts have a matte blued finish and the stock has a durable black finish with a black recoil pad. Available in 10 ga. (3-1/2") and 12 ga. with 3" or 3-1/2" chamber, 22", 28", 30" barrel with Invector choke system. Introduced 1987.
Price: 12 ga., 3" chamber, Invector Plus $444.00
Price: 10, 12 ga., 3-1/2" chamber........................$532.00

Browning BPS Micro Pump Shotgun

Same as BPS Upland Special except 20 ga. only, 22" Invector barrel, stock has pistol grip with recoil pad. Length of pull is 13-1/4". Introduced 1986.
Price: $444.00

EAA/BAIKAL IZH-81 PUMP SHOTGUN

Gauge: 12, 3" chamber. **Barrel:** 18-1/2", 20", 22", 24", 26", 28"; imp., mod. and full choke tubes. **Weight:** N/A. **Stock:** Hardwood. **Features:** Hammer-forged barrel; machined receiver; push-button, trigger-block safety; 5-round, detachable steel magazine; two, opposing extractors for sure ejection. Introduced 2000. Imported by European American Armory.
Price: IZH-81 (blued finish, hardwood stock) $269.00

EAA/BAIKAL MP-133 PUMP SHOTGUN

Gauge: 12, 3-1/2" chamber. **Barrel:** 18-1/2", 20", 24", 26", 28"; imp., mod. and full choke tubes. **Weight:** N/A. **Stock:** Walnut; checkered grip and grooved forearm. **Features:** Hammer-forged, chrome-lined barrel with ventilated rib; machined steel parts; dual action bars; trigger-block safety; 4-shot magazine tube; handles 2-3/4" through 3-1/2" shells. Introduced 2000. Imported by European American Armory.
Price: MP-133 (blued finish, walnut stock and forend) $299.00

ITHACA MODEL 37 DELUXE PUMP SHOTGUN

Gauge: 12, 16, 20, 3" chamber. **Barrel:** 26", 28", 30" (12 gauge), 26", 28" (16 and 20 gauge), choke tubes. **Weight:** 7 lbs. **Stock:** Walnut with cut-checkered grip and forend. **Features:** Steel receiver; bottom ejection; brushed blue finish, vent rib barrels. Reintroduced 1996. Made in U.S. by Ithaca Gun Co.
Price: $545.95
Price: With straight English-style stock $545.95
Price: Model 37 New Classic (ringtail forend, sunburst recoil pad, hand-finished walnut stock, 26" or 28" barrel)....................$695.95

Ithaca Model 37 Waterfowler

Similar to the Model 37 Deluxe except in 12 gauge only with 28" barrel, special extended steel shot choke tube system. Complete coverage of Advantage Wetlands couflage. Introduced 1999. Made in U.S. by Ithaca Gun Co.
Price: $595.00

Ithaca Model 37 Turkeyslayer Pump Shotgun

Similar to the Model 37 Deluxe except has 22" barrel with rifle sights, extended ported choke tube and full-coverage, Realtree Advantage, Realtree All-Purpose Brown, All-Purpose Grey, or Xtra Brown camouflage finish. Introduced 1996. Made in U.S. by Ithaca Gun Co.
Price: 12 ga. only $569.95
Price: Youth Turkeyslayer (20 gauge, 6.5 lbs., shorter stock) $569.95

ITHACA MODEL 37 DEERSLAYER II PUMP SHOTGUN

Gauge: 12, 20, 3" chamber. **Barrel:** 20", 25", fully rifled. **Weight:** 7 lbs. **Stock:** Cut-checkered American walnut with Monte Carlo comb. **Sights:** Rifle-type. **Features:** Integral barrel and receiver. Bottom ejection. Brushed blue finish. Reintroduced 1997. Made in U.S. by Ithaca Gun Co.
Price: $565.95
Price: Smooth Bore Deluxe $515.95
Price: Rifled Deluxe $515.95

Ithaca Model 37 Hardwoods 20/2000 Deerslayer

Similar to the Model 37 Deerslayer II except has synthetic stock and forend, and has the Truglo Fibre Optic sight system. Drilled and tapped for scope mounting. Complete coverage of RealTree 20/2000 Hardwoods camouflage. Introduced 1999. Made in U.S. by Ithaca Gun Co.
Price: $565.95

Ithaca Model 37 Hardwoods 20/2000 Turkeyslayer

Similar to the Model 37 Turkeyslayer except has synthetic stock and forend, Extra-Full extended and ported choke tube, long forcing cone, and Truglo Fibre Optic sight system. Complete coverage of RealTree Hardwoods 20/2000 camouflage. Introduced 1999. Made in U.S. by Ithaca Gun Co.
Price: $565.95

MOSSBERG MODEL 835 CROWN GRADE ULTI-MAG PUMP

Gauge: 12, 3-1/2" chamber. **Barrel:** Ported 24" rifled bore, 24", 28", Accu-Mag choke tubes for steel or lead shot. **Weight:** 7-3/4 lbs. **Length:** 48-1/2"

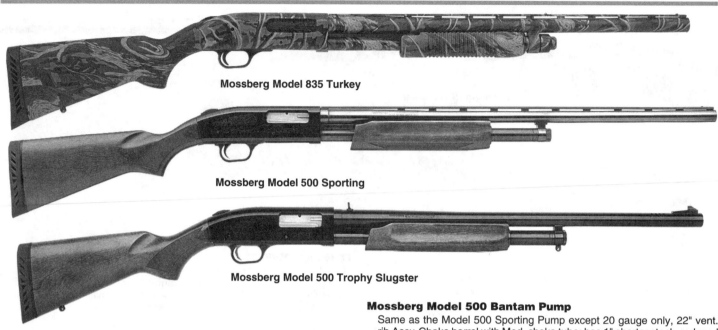

Mossberg Model 835 Turkey

Mossberg Model 500 Sporting

Mossberg Model 500 Trophy Slugster

overall. **Stock:** 14"x1-1/2"x2-1/2". Dual Comb. Cut-checkered hardwood or camo synthetic; both have recoil pad. **Sights:** White bead front, brass mid-bead; Fiber Optic. **Features:** Shoots 2-3/4", 3" or 3-1/2" shells. Back-bored and ported barrel to reduce recoil, improve patterns. Ambidextrous thumb safety, twin extractors, dual slide bars. Mossberg Cablelock included. Introduced 1988.

Price: 28" vent. rib, hardwood stock **$361.00**
Price: Combo, 24" rifled bore, rifle sights, 28" vent. rib, Accu-Mag choke tubes Woodlands camo finish . . . . **NA**
Price: RealTree or Mossy Oak Camo Turkey, 24" vent. rib, Accu-Mag Extra-Full tube, synthetic stock. . . . . **NA**
Price: RealTree Camo, 28" vent. rib, Accu-Mag tubes, synthetic stock **$571.00**
Price: RealTree Camo Combo, 24" rifled bore, rifle sights, 24" vent. rib, Accu-Mag choke tubes, synthetic stock, hard case **$561.00**
Price: OFM Camo, 28" vent. rib, Accu-Mag tubes, synthetic stock . . . . **NA**
Price: OFM Camo Combo, 24" rifled bore, rifle sights, 28" vent. rib, Accu-Mag tubes, synthetic stock . . . . **NA**

Mossberg American Field Model 835 Pump Shotgun
Same as the Model 835 Crown Grade except has walnut-stained hardwood stock and comes only with Modified choke tube, 28" barrel. Introduced 1992.
Price: **$331.00**

Mossberg Model 835 Special Hunter
Similar to the Model 835 Crown Grade except with 24" or 28" ported barrel with Accu-Mag Mod. choke tube, Parkerized finish, black synthetic stock and forend; comes with sling and swivels. Introduced 1998. Made in U.S. by Mossberg.
Price: **$363.00**

MOSSBERG MODEL 500 SPORTING PUMP
Gauge: 12, 20, 410, 3" chamber. **Barrel:** 18-1/2" to 28" with fixed or Accu-Choke, plain or vent. rib. **Weight:** 6-1/4 lbs. (410), 7-1/4 lbs. (12). **Length:** 48" overall (28" barrel). **Stock:** 14"x1-1/2"x2-1/2". Walnut-stained hardwood. Cut-checkered grip and forend. **Sights:** White bead front, brass mid-bead; Fiber Optic. **Features:** Ambidextrous thumb safety, twin extractors, disconnecting safety, dual action bars. Quiet Carry forend. Many barrels are ported. Mossberg Cablelock included. From Mossberg.
Price: From about. **$322.00**
Price: Sporting Combos (field barrel and Slugster barrel), from . . **$382.00**

Mossberg Model 500 Bantam Pump
Same as the Model 500 Sporting Pump except 20 gauge only, 22" vent. rib Accu-Choke barrel with Mod. choke tube; has 1" shorter stock, reduced length from pistol grip to trigger, reduced forend reach. Introduced 1992.
Price: **$336.00**
Price: With full Woodlands camouflage finish **$376.00**

Mossberg Model 500 Camo Pump
Same as the Model 500 Sporting Pump except 12 gauge only and entire gun is covered with special camouflage finish. Receiver drilled and tapped for scope mounting. Comes with quick detachable swivel studs, swivels, camouflage sling, Mossberg Cablelock.
Price: From about. **$346.00**
Price: Camo Combo (as above with extra Slugster barrel), from about. **$422.00**

Mossberg Model 500 Persuader/Cruiser Shotguns
Similar to Mossberg Model 500 except has 18-1/2" or 20" barrel with cylinder bore choke, synthetic stock and blue or parkerized finish. Available in 12, 20 and 410 gauge with bead or ghost ring sights, 6- or 8-shot magazines. From Mossberg.
Price: 12 gauge, 20" barrel, bead sight. **$294.00**
Price: 20 or 410 gauge, 18-1/2" barrel, bead sight **$305.00**
Price: 12 gauge, parkerized finish, 18-1/2" barrel, ghost ring sights **$416.00**
Price: Home Security 410 (410 gauge, 18-1/2" barrel with spreader choke) **$319.00**

Mossberg Model 590 Special Purpose Shotguns
Similar to Model 500 except has parkerized or Marinecote finish, 9-shot magazine and black synthetic stock (some models feature Speed Feed. Available in 12 gauge only with 20", cylinder bore barrel. Weighs 7-1/4 lbs. From Mossberg.
Price: Bead sight, heat shield over barrel **$370.00**
Price: Ghost ring sight, Speed Feed stock. **$519.00**

MOSSBERG MODEL 500 SLUGSTER
Gauge: 12, 20, 3" chamber. **Barrel:** 24", ported rifled bore. Integral scope mount. **Weight:** 7-1/4 lbs. **Length:** 44" overall. **Stock:** 14" pull, 1-3/8" drop at heel. Walnut; Dual Comb design for proper eye positioning with or without scoped barrels. Recoil pad and swivel studs. **Features:** Ambidextrous thumb safety, twin extractors, dual slide bars. Comes with scope mount. Mossberg Cablelock included. Introduced 1988.
Price: Rifled bore, with integral scope mount, Dual-Comb stock, 12 or 20 . . . . **$367.00**
Price: Fiber Optic, rifle sights **$398.00**
Price: Rifled bore, rifle sights **$398.00**
Price: 20 ga., Standard or Bantam, from **$367.00**

Remington 870 Wingmaster

Remington Model 870 Express Super Magnum

Remington Model 870 Express Rifle-Sighted Deer Gun

REMINGTON MODEL 870 WINGMASTER
Gauge: 12, 3" chamber. **Barrel:** 26", 28", 30" (Rem Chokes). Light Contour barrel. **Weight:** 7-1/4 lbs. **Length:** 46-1/2" overall (26" bbl.). **Stock:** 14"x2-1/2"x1". American walnut with satin or high-gloss finish, cut-checkered pistol grip and forend. Rubber butt pad. **Sights:** Ivory bead front, metal mid-bead. **Features:** Double action bars; cross-bolt safety; blue finish. Introduced 1986.
Price: **$569.00**
Price: 870 Wingmaster Super Magnum **$649.00**

Remington Model 870 50th Anniversary Classic Trap Shotgun
Similar to Model 870 TC Wingmaster except has 30" ventilated rib with singles, mid handicap and long handicap choke tubes, semi-fancy American walnut stock and high-polish blued receiver with engraving and gold shield inlay. From Remington Arms Co.
Price: **$775.00**

Remington Model 870 Marine Magnum
Similar to the 870 Wingmaster except all metal is plated with electroless nickel and has black synthetic stock and forend. Has 18" plain barrel (Cyl.), bead front sight, 7-shot magazine. Introduced 1992.
Price: **$545.00**

Remington Model 870 Wingmaster LW 20 ga.
Similar to the Model 870 Wingmaster except in 28 gauge and 410-bore only, 25" vent rib barrel with Rem Choke tubes, high-gloss wood finish. 26" & 28" barrels-20 ga.
Price: 20 gauge **$569.00**
Price: 410-bore.. **$596.00**
Price: 28 gauge **$649.00**

Remington Model 870 Express
Similar to the 870 Wingmaster except has a walnut-toned hardwood stock with solid, black recoil pad and pressed checkering on grip and forend. Outside metal surfaces have a black oxide finish. Comes with 26" or 28" vent. rib barrel with a Mod. Rem Choke tube. Introduced 1987.
Price: 12 or 20 .... **$329.00**
Price: Express Combo, 12 ga., 26" vent rib with Mod. Rem Choke and 20" fully rifled barrel with rifle sights **$436.00**
Price: Express 20 ga., 26" or 28" with Mod. Rem Choke tubes .. **$329.00**
Price: Express L-H (left-hand), 12 ga., 28" vent rib with Mod. Rem Choke tube.. **$356.00**
Price: Express Synthetic, 12-ga, 26" or 28" **$329.00**
Price: Express Combo (20 ga.) with extra Deer rifled barrel **$436.00**

Remington Model 870 Express Super Magnum
Similar to the 870 Express except has 28" vent. rib barrel with 3-1/2" chamber, vented recoil pad. Introduced 1998.
Price: **$369.00**
Price: Super Magnum Synthetic........................... **$376.00**
Price: Super Magnum Turkey Camo (Turkey Extra Full Rem Choke, full-coverage RealTree Advantage camo) **$500.00**
Price: Super Magnum Combo (26" with Mod. Rem Choke and 20" fully rifled deer barrel with 3" chamber and rifle sights; wood stock) **$516.00**
Price: Super Magnum Synthetic Turkey (black) **$389.00**

Remington Model 870 Wingmaster Super Magnum Shotgun
Similar to Model 870 Express Super Magnum except has high-polish blued finish, 28" ventilated barrel with imp. cyl., modified and full choke tubes, checkered high-gloss walnut stock. Overall length 48", weighs 7-1/2 lbs. Introduced 2000.
Price: **$649.00**

NEW!

Remington Model 870 Express Youth Gun
Same as the Model 870 Express except comes with 13" length of pull, 21" barrel with Mod. Rem Choke tube. Hardwood stock with low-luster finish. Introduced 1991.
Price: 20 ga. Express Youth (1" shorter stock), from **$329.00**
Price: 20 ga. Youth Deer 20" FR/RS **$363.00**

Remington Model 870 Express Rifle-Sighted Deer Gun
Same as the Model 870 Express except comes with 20" barrel with fixed Imp. Cyl. choke, open iron sights, Monte Carlo stock. Introduced 1991.
Price: **$329.00**
Price: With fully rifled barrel **$363.00**
Price: Express Synthetic Deer (black synthetic stock, black matte metal) **$369.00**

Remington Model 870 Express Turkey
Same as the Model 870 Express except comes with 3" chamber, 21" vent. rib turkey barrel and Extra-Full Rem Choke Turkey tube; 12 ga. only. Introduced 1991.
Price: **$343.00**
Price: Express Turkey Camo stock has RealTree Advantage camo, matte black metal **$396.00**
Price: Express Youth Turkey camo (as above with 1" shorter length of pull).. **$396.00**

Remington Model 870 Express Synthetic HD Home Defense
Similar to the 870 Express with 18" barrel except has synthetic stock and forend. Introduced 1994.
Price: **$316.00**

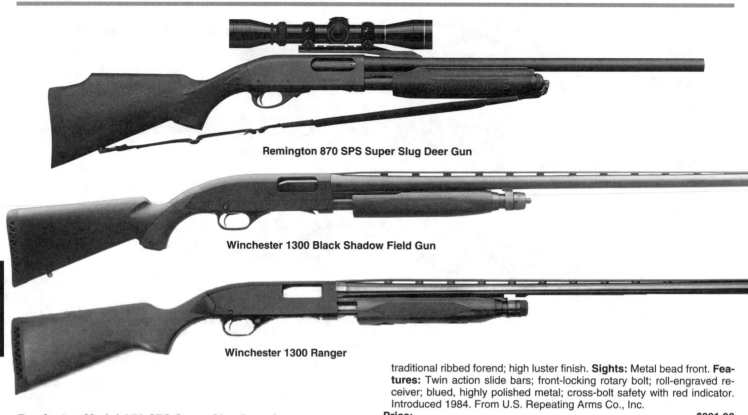

Remington 870 SPS Super Slug Deer Gun

Winchester 1300 Black Shadow Field Gun

Winchester 1300 Ranger

Remington Model 870 SPS Super Slug Deer Gun

Similar to the Model 870 Express Synthetic except has 23" rifled, modified contour barrel with cantilever scope mount. Comes with black synthetic stock and forend with swivel studs, black Cordura nylon sling. Introduced 1999. Fully rifled centilever barrel.

Price: $555.00

Remington Model 870 SPS Super Magnum Camo

Has synthetic stock and all metal (except bolt and trigger guard) and stock covered with Mossy Oak Break-Up camo finish In 12 gauge 3-1/2", 26" vent. rib, Rem Choke. Comes with camo sling, swivels.

Price: $569.00
Price: Model 870 SPS-T Super Magnum Camo (3-1/2" chamber). $569.00
Price: Model 870 SPS-T RS/TG (TruGlo fiber optics sights) $544.00
Price: Model 870 SPS-T Super Mag Camo CL/RD (Leupold/Gilmore dot sight). $889.00

SARSILMAZ PUMP SHOTGUN

NEW! **Gauge:** 12, 3" chamber. **Barrel:** 26" or 28". **Weight:** N/A. **Length:** N/A. **Stocks:** Oil-finished hardwood. **Features:** Includes extra pistol-grip stock. Introduced 2000. Imported from Turkey by Armsport Inc.

Price: With pistol-grip stock $299.95
Price: With metal stock................................. $349.95

TRISTAR MODEL 1887 LEVER-ACTION SHOTGUN

Gauge: 12, 2-3/4" chamber, 5-shot magazine. **Barrel:** 30" (Full). **Weight:** 8 lbs. **Length:** 48" overall. **Stocks:** 12-3/4" pull. Rounded-knob pistol grip; walnut with oil finish; blued, checkered steel buttplate. Dimensions duplicate original WRA Co. specifications. **Sights:** Brass, bead front. **Features:** Recreation of Browning's original 1885 patents and design as made by Winchester Repeating Arms. External hammer with half- and full-cock positions; has original-type WRA Co. logo on left side of receiver; two-piece walnut forend. Announced 1997. Imported by Tristar Sporting Arms.

Price: .... NA

WINCHESTER MODEL 1300 WALNUT PUMP

Gauge: 12, 20, 3" chamber, 5-shot capacity. **Barrel:** 26", 28", vent. rib, with Full, Mod., Imp. Cyl. Winchoke tubes. **Weight:** 6-3/8 lbs. **Length:** 42-5/8" overall. **Stock:** American walnut, with deep cut checkering on pistol grip, traditional ribbed forend; high luster finish. **Sights:** Metal bead front. **Features:** Twin action slide bars; front-locking rotary bolt; roll-engraved receiver; blued, highly polished metal; cross-bolt safety with red indicator. Introduced 1984. From U.S. Repeating Arms Co., Inc.

Price: $391.00

Winchester Model 1300 Upland Special Pump Gun

Similar to the Model 1300 Walnut except has straight-grip stock, 24" barrel. Introduced 1999. Made in U.S. by U.S. Repeating Arms Co.

Price: $391.00

Winchester Model 1300 Black Shadow Field Gun

Similar to the Model 1300 Walnut except has black composite stock and forend, matte black finish. Has vent. rib 26" or 28" barrel, 3" chamber, comes with Mod. Winchoke tube. Introduced 1995. From U.S. Repeating Arms Co., Inc.

Price: 12 or 20 gauge................................. $330.00

Winchester Model 1300 Black Shadow Deer Gun

Similar to the Model 1300 Black Shadow Turkey Gun except has ramp-type front sight, fully adjustable rear, drilled and tapped for scope mounting. Black composite stock and forend, matte black metal. Smoothbore 22" barrel with one Imp. Cyl. WinChoke tube; 12 gauge only, 3" chamber. Weighs 7-1/4 lbs. Introduced 1994. From U.S. Repeating Arms Co., Inc.

Price: $329.00
Price: With rifled barrel.............................. $353.00

WINCHESTER MODEL 1300 RANGER PUMP GUN

Gauge: 12, 20, 3" chamber, 5-shot magazine. **Barrel:** 26", 28" vent. rib with Full, Mod., Imp. Cyl. Winchoke tubes. **Weight:** 7 to 7-1/4 lbs. **Length:** 48-5/8" to 50-5/8" overall. **Stock:** Walnut-finished hardwood with ribbed forend. **Sights:** Metal bead front. **Features:** Cross-bolt safety, black rubber recoil pad, twin action slide bars, front-locking rotating bolt. From U.S. Repeating Arms Co., Inc.

Price: Vent. rib barrel, Winchoke $344.00
Price: Model 1300 Compact, 20 ga., 22" vent. rib $343.00

Winchester Model 1300 Black Shadow Turkey Gun

Similar to the Model 1300 RealTree® Turkey except synthetic stock and forend are matte black, and all metal surfaces finished matte black. Drilled and tapped for scope mounting. In 12 or 20 gauge, 3" chamber, 22" vent. rib barrel; comes with one Extra-Full Winchoke tube (20 gauge has Full). Introduced 1994. From U.S. Repeating Arms Co., Inc.

Price: $329.00

Includes a variety of game guns and guns for competitive shooting.

American Arms Silver Sporting

Beretta 682 Gold Skeet

AMERICAN ARMS SILVER I O/U

Gauge: 12, 20, 28, 410, 3" chamber (28 has 2-3/4"). **Barrel:** 26" (Imp. Cyl. & Mod., all gauges), 28" (Mod. & Full, 12, 20). **Weight:** About 6-3/4 lbs. **Stock:** 14-1/8"x1-3/8"x2-3/8". Checkered walnut. **Sights:** Metal bead front. **Features:** Boxlock action with scroll engraving, silver finish. Single selective trigger, extractors. Chrome-lined barrels. Manual safety. Rubber recoil pad. Introduced 1987. Imported from Italy by American Arms, Inc.
Price: 12 or 20 gauge **$649.00**
Price: 28 or 410 . . . . **$679.00**

American Arms Silver II Shotgun

Similar to the Silver I except 26" barrel (Imp. Cyl., Mod., Full choke tubes, 12 and 20 ga.), 28" (Imp. Cyl., Mod., Full choke tubes, 12 ga. only), 26" (Imp. Cyl. & Mod. fixed chokes, 28 and 410), automatic selective ejectors. Weight is about 6 lbs., 15 oz. (12 ga., 26").
Price: **$765.00**
Price: 28, 410 . . . . **$815.00**
Price: Two-barrel sets. **$1,239.00**

AMERICAN ARMS SILVER SPORTING O/U

Gauge: 12, 2-3/4" chambers, 20 3" chambers. **Barrel:** 28", 30" (Skeet, Imp. Cyl., Mod., Full choke tubes). **Weight:** 7-3/8 lbs. **Length:** 45-1/2" overall. **Stock:** 14-3/8"x1-1/2"x2-3/8". Figured walnut, cut checkering; Sporting Clays quick-mount buttpad. **Sights:** Target bead front. **Features:** Boxlock action with single selective mechanical trigger, automatic selective ejectors; special broadway channeled rib; vented barrel rib; chrome bores. Chrome-nickel finish on frame, with engraving. Introduced 1990. Imported from Italy by American Arms, Inc.
Price: **$965.00**

AMERICAN ARMS WS/OU 12, TS/OU 12 SHOTGUNS

Gauge: 12, 3-1/2" chambers. **Barrel:** WS/OU—28" (Imp. Cyl., Mod., Full choke tubes); TS/OU—24" (Imp. Cyl., Mod., Full choke tubes). **Weight:** 6 lbs., 15 oz. **Length:** 46" overall. **Stock:** 14-1/8"x1-1/8"x2-3/8". European walnut with cut checkering, black vented recoil pad, matte finish. **Features:** Boxlock action with single selective trigger, automatic selective ejectors; chrome bores. Matte metal finish. Imported by American Arms, Inc.
Price: **$799.00**
Price: With Mossy Oak Break-Up camo **$885.00**

American Arms WT/OU 10 Shotgun

Similar to the WS/OU 12 except chambered for 10 gauge 3-1/2" shell, 26" (Full & Full, choke tubes) barrel. Single selective trigger, extractors. Non-reflective finish on wood and metal. Imported by American Arms, Inc.
Price: **$995.00**

APOLLO TR AND TT SHOTGUNS

 Gauge: 12, 20, 410, 3" chambers; 28 2-3/4" chambers. **Barrel:** 26", 28", 30", 32". **Weight:** 6 to 7-1/4 lbs. **Length:** N/A. **Stock:** Oil-finished European wal-

nut. **Features:** Boxlock action; hard-chromed bores; automatic ejectors; single selective trigger; choke tubes (12 and 20 ga. only). Introduced 2000. From Sigarms.
Price: Apollo TR 30 Field (color casehardened side plates) . . . **$2,240.00**
Price: Apollo TR 40 Gold (gold overlays on game scenes) **$2,675.00**
Price: Apollo TT 25 Competition (wide vent. rib with mid-bead). **$1,995.00**

BERETTA DT 10 TRIDENT SHOTGUNS

Gauge: 12, 2-3/4", 3" chambers. **Barrel:** 28", 30", 32", 34"; competition-style vent rib; fixed or Optima Choke tubes. **Weight:** 7.9 to 9 lbs. **Length:** N/A. **Stock:** High-grade walnut stock with oil finish; hand-checkered grip and forend; adjustable stocks available. **Features:** Detachable, adjustable trigger group; raised and thickened receiver; forend iron has replaceable nut to guarantee wood-to-metal fit; Optima Bore to improve shot pattern and reduce felt recoil. Introduced 2000. Imported from Italy by Beretta USA.
Price: DT 10 Trident Trap (selective, lockable single trigger; adjustable stock) **$9,450.00**
Price: DT 10 Trident Trap Combo (single and o/u barrels) . . . **$11,995.00**
Price: DT 10 Trident Skeet (skeet stock with rounded recoil pad, tapered rib).. . . . . **$9,450.00**
Price: DT 10 Trident Sporting (sporting clays stock with rounded recoil pad).. . . . . **$9,240.00**

BERETTA SERIES S682 GOLD SKEET, TRAP OVER/UNDERS

Gauge: 12, 2-3/4" chambers. **Barrel:** Skeet—28"; trap—30" and 32", Imp. Mod. & Full and Mobilchoke; trap mono shotguns—32" and 34" Mobilchoke; trap top single guns—32" and 34" Full and Mobilchoke; trap combo sets—from 30" O/U, to 32" O/U, 34" top single. **Stock:** Close-grained walnut, hand checkered. **Sights:** White Bradley bead front sight and center bead. **Features:** Receiver has Greystone gunmetal gray finish with gold accents. Trap Monte Carlo stock has deluxe trap recoil pad. Various grades available; contact Beretta USA for details. Imported from Italy by Beretta USA
Price: S682 Gold Skeet **$2,850.00**
Price: S682 Gold Skeet, adjustable stock **$3,515.00**
Price: S682 Gold Trap **$3,100.00**
Price: S682 Gold Trap Top Combo **$4,085.00**
Price: S682 Gold Trap with adjustable stock **$3,625.00**
Price: S686 Silver Pigeon Trap **$1,850.00**
Price: S686 Silver Pigeon Trap Top Mono **$1,850.00**
Price: S686 Silver Pigeon Skeet (28") **$1,760.00**
Price: S687 EELL Diamond Pigeon Trap **$4,815.00**
Price: S687 EELL Diamond Pigeon Skeet **$4,790.00**
Price: S687 EELL Diamond Pigeon Skeet, adjustable stock . . . **$5,810.00**
Price: S687 EELL Diamond Pigeon Trap Top Mono. . . . . **$5,055.00 to $5,105.00**
Price: ASE Gold Skeet **$12,060.00**
Price: ASE Gold Trap **$12,145.00**
Price: ASE Gold Trap Combo **$16,055.00**

Beretta 682 Gold Sporting

Beretta Over/Under Field Shotgun

BERETTA MODEL S686 WHITEWING O/U

Gauge: 12, 3" chambers. **Barrel:** 26", 28", Mobilchoke tubes (Imp. Cyl., Mod., Full). **Weight:** 6.7 lbs. **Length:** 45.7" overall (28" barrels). **Stock:** 14.5"x2.2"x1.4". American walnut; radiused black buttplate. **Features:** Matte chrome finish on receiver, matte blue barrels; hard-chrome bores; low-profile receiver with dual conical locking lugs; single selective trigger, ejectors. Introduced 1999. Imported from Italy by Beretta U.S.A.
Price: $1,295.00

BERETTA S686 ONYX SPORTING O/U SHOTGUN

Gauge: 12, 3" chambers. **Barrel:** 28", 30" (Mobilchoke tubes). **Weight:** 7.7 lbs. **Stock:** Checkered American walnut. **Features:** Intended for the beginning Sporting Clays shooter. Has wide, vented 12.5mm target rib, radiused recoil pad. Polished black finish on receiver and barrels. Introduced 1993. Imported from Italy by Beretta U.S.A.
Price: $1,575.00

BERETTA ULTRALIGHT OVER/UNDER

Gauge: 12, 2-3/4" chambers. **Barrel:** 26", 28", Mobilchoke choke tubes. **Weight:** About 5 lbs., 13 oz. **Stock:** Select American walnut with checkered grip and forend. **Features:** Low-profile aluminum alloy receiver with titanium breech face insert. Electroless nickel receiver with game scene engraving. Single selective trigger; automatic safety. Introduced 1992. Imported from Italy by Beretta U.S.A.
Price: $1,795.00

Beretta Ultralight Deluxe Over/Under Shotgun

Similar to the Ultralight except has matte electroless nickel finish receiver with gold game scene engraving; matte oil-finished, select walnut stock and forend. Introduced 1999. Imported from Italy by Beretta U.S.A.
Price: $1,985.00

BERETTA OVER/UNDER FIELD SHOTGUNS

Gauge: 12, 20, 28, and 410 bore, 2-3/4", 3" and 3-1/2" chambers. **Barrel:** 26" and 28" (Mobilchoke tubes). **Stock:** Close-grained walnut. **Features:** Highly-figured, American walnut stocks and forends, and a unique, weather-resistant finish on barrels. The S686 Onyx bears a gold P. Beretta signature on each side of the receiver. Silver designates standard 686, 687 models with silver receivers; 686 Silver Pigeon has enhanced engraving pattern, Schnabel forend; 686 Silver Essential has matte chrome finish; Gold indicates higher grade 686EL, 687EL models with full sideplates; Diamond is for 687EELL models with highest grade wood, engraving. Case provided with Gold and Diamond grades. Silver Gold, Diamond grades introduced 1994. Imported from Italy by Beretta U.S.A.
Price: S686 Onyx $1,565.00
Price: S686 Silver Pigeon two-bbl. set $2,560.00
Price: S686 Silver Pigeon. $1,850.00
Price: S687 Silver Pigeon. $2,255.00
Price: S687 Silver Pigeon II (deep relief game scene engraving, oil finish wood, 12 ga. only) $2,110.00
Price: S687EL Gold Pigeon (gold inlays, sideplates) $3,935.00
Price: S687EL Gold Pigeon, 410, 26"; 28 ga., 28" $4,230.00

Price: S687EELL Diamond Pigeon (engraved sideplates) $5,540.00
Price: S687EELL Diamond Pigeon Combo, 20 and 28 ga., 26". $6,180.00

BERETTA MODEL SO5, SO6, SO9 SHOTGUNS

Gauge: 12, 2-3/4" chambers. **Barrel:** To customer specs. **Stock:** To customer specs. **Features:** SO5—Trap, Skeet and Sporting Clays models SO5; SO6—SO6 and SO6 EELL are field models. SO6 has a case-hardened or silver receiver with contour hand engraving. SO6 EELL has hand-engraved receiver in a fine floral or "fine English" pattern or game scene, with bas-relief chisel work and gold inlays. SO6 and SO6 EELL are available with sidelocks removable by hand. Imported from Italy by Beretta U.S.A.
Price: SO5 Trap, Skeet, Sporting $13,000.00
Price: SO6 Trap, Skeet, Sporting $17,500.00
Price: SO6 EELL Field, custom specs $28,000.00
Price: SO9 (12, 20, 28, 410, 26", 28", 30", any choke) $31,000.00

BERETTA SPORTING CLAYS SHOTGUNS

Gauge: 12 and 20, 2-3/4" and 3" chambers. **Barrel:** 28", 30", 32" Mobilchoke. **Stock:** Close-grained walnut. **Features:** Equipped with Beretta Mobilchoke flush-mounted screw-in choke tube system. Dual-purpose O/U for hunting and Sporting Clays.12 or 20 gauge, 28", 30" Mobilchoke tubes (four, Skeet, Imp. Cyl., Mod., Full). Wide 12.5mm top rib with 2.5mm center groove; 686 Silver Pigeon has silver receiver with scroll engraving; 687 Silver Pigeon Sporting has silver receiver, highly figured walnut; 687 EL Pigeon Sporting has game scene engraving with gold inlaid animals on full sideplate. Introduced 1994. Imported from Italy by Beretta USA.
Price: 682 Gold Sporting, 28", 30", 31" (with case) $3,100.00
Price: 682 Gold Sporting, 28", 30", ported, adj. l.o.p. $3,230.00
Price: 686 Silver Pigeon Sporting. $1,915.00
Price: 686 Silver Pigeon Sporting (20 gauge) $1,915.00
Price: 687 Silver Pigeon Sporting. $2,270.00
Price: 687 Silver Pigeon Sporting (20 gauge) $2,270.00
Price: 687 Diamond Pigeon EELL Sporter (hand engraved sideplates, deluxe wood) $5,515.00
Price: ASE Gold Sporting Clay $12,145.00

Beretta S687EL Gold Pigeon Sporting O/U

Similar to the S687 Silver Pigeon Sporting except has sideplates with gold inlay game scene, vent. side and top ribs, bright orange front sight. Stock and forend are of high grade walnut with fine-line checkering. Available in 12 gauge only with 28" or 30" barrels and Mobilchoke tubes. Weight is 6 lbs., 13 oz. Introduced 1993. Imported from Italy by Beretta USA.
Price: $4,015.00

BRNO ZH 300 OVER/UNDER SHOTGUN

Gauge: 12, 2-3/4" chambers. **Barrel:** 26", 27-1/2", 29" (Skeet, Imp. Cyl., Mod., Full). **Weight:** 7 lbs. **Length:** 44.4" overall. **Stock:** European walnut. **Features:** Double triggers; automatic safety; polished blue finish engraved receiver. Announced 1998. Imported from the Czech Republic by Euro-Imports.
Price: ZH 301, field. $594.00
Price: ZH 302, Skeet $608.00
Price: ZH 303, 12 ga. trap $608.00
Price: ZH 321, 16 ga. $595.00

SHOTGUNS

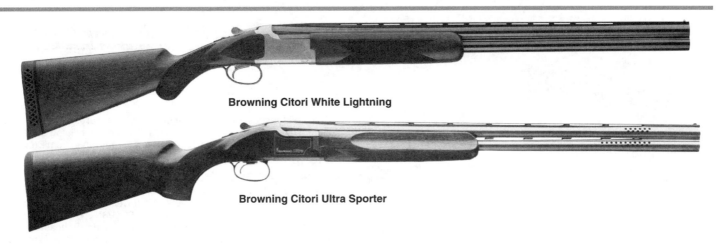

Browning Citori White Lightning

Browning Citori Ultra Sporter

BRNO 501.2 OVER/UNDER SHOTGUN

Gauge: 12, 2-3/4" chambers. **Barrel:** 27.5" (Full & Mod.). **Weight:** 7 lbs. **Length:** 44" overall. **Stock:** European walnut. **Features:** Boxlock action with double triggers, ejectors; automatic safety; hand-cut checkering. Announced 1998. Imported from The Czech Republic by Euro-Imports.
Price: $850.00

BROWNING CITORI O/U SHOTGUN

Gauge: 12, 20, 28 and 410. **Barrel:** 26", 28" in 28 and 410. Offered with Invector choke tubes. All 12 and 20 gauge models have back-bored barrels and Invector Plus choke system. **Weight:** 6 lbs., 8 oz. (26" 410) to 7 lbs., 13 oz. (30" 12 ga.). **Length:** 43" overall (26" bbl.). **Stock:** Dense walnut, hand checkered, full pistol grip, beavertail forend. Field-type recoil pad on 12 ga. field guns and trap and Skeet models. **Sights:** Medium raised beads, German nickel silver. **Features:** Barrel selector integral with safety, automatic ejectors, three-piece takedown. Imported from Japan by Browning. Contact Browning for complete list of models and prices.
Price: Grade I, Hunting, Invector, 12 and 20 .... $1,388.00
Price: Grade I, Lightning, 28 and 410, Invector $1,489.00
Price: Grade III, Lightning, 28 and 410, Invector $2,377.00
Price: Grade VI, 28 and 410 Lightning, Invector............. $3,344.00
Price: Grade I, Lightning, Invector Plus, 12, 20 .... $1,432.00
Price: Grade I, Hunting, 28", 30" only, 3-1/2", Invector Plus.... $1,489.00
Price: Grade III, Lightning, Invector, 12, 20 .... $2,127.00
Price: Grade VI, Lightning, Invector, 12, 20 .... $3,095.00
Price: Gran Lightning, 26", 28", Invector, 12, 20 .... $1,963.00
Price: Gran Lightning, 28, 410 .... $2,068.00
Price: White Lightning (silver nitride receiver with engraved scroll and rosette, 12 ga., 26", 28") $1,478.00
Price: Citori Satin Hunter (12 ga., satin-finished wood, matte-finished barrels and receiver) 3" chambers $1,318.00
Price: As above, 3-1/2" chambers $1,420.00

Browning Superlight Citori Over/Under

Similar to the standard Citori except available in 12, 20 with 24", 26" or 28" Invector barrels, 28 or 410 with 26" barrels choked Imp. Cyl. & Mod. or 28" choked Mod. & Full. Has straight grip stock, Schnabel forend tip. Superlight 12 weighs 6 lbs., 9 oz. (26" barrels); Superlight 20, 5 lbs., 12 oz. (26" barrels). Introduced 1982.
Price: Grade I only, 28 or 410, Invector $1,511.00
Price: Grade III, Invector, 12............................ $2,127.00
Price: Grade VI, Invector, 12 or 20, gray or blue $3,095.00
Price: Grade VI, 28 or 410, Invector, gray or blue $3,334.00
Price: Grade I Invector, 12 or 20 .... $1,442.00
Price: Grade I Invector, Upland Special (24" bbls.), 12 or 20... $1,442.00
Price: Citori Superlight Feather (12 ga., alloy receiver, 6 lbs. 6 oz.) $1,592.00

Browning Citori O/U Special Skeet

Similar to standard Citori except 26", 28" barrels, ventilated side ribs, Invector choke tubes; stock dimensions of 14-3/8"x1-1/2"x2", fitted with

Skeet-style recoil pad; conventional target rib and high post target rib.
Price: Grade I Invector, 12, 20 ga., Invector Plus (high post rib) $1,658.00
Price: Grade I, 28 and 410 (high post rib) $1,627.00
Price: Grade III, 28, 410 (high post rib) $2,316.00
Price: Golden Clays,12, 20............................... $3,434.00
Price: Golden Clays, 28, 410 .... $3,356.00
Price: Grade III, 12, 20, Invector Plus $2,310.00
Price: Adjustable comb stock, add........................ $210.00

Browning Citori Special Trap Models

Similar to standard Citori except 12 gauge only; 30", 32" ported or non-ported (Invector Plus); Monte Carlo cheekpiece (14-3/8"x1-3/8"x1-3/8"x2"); fitted with trap-style recoil pad; high post target rib, ventilated side ribs.
Price: Grade I, Invector Plus, ported bbls. $1,658.00
Price: Grade III, Invector Plus Ported...................... $2,310.00
Price: Golden Clays $3,434.00
Price: Grade I, adjustable stock $1,878.00
Price: Grade III, adjustable stock $2,530.00
Price: Golden Clays, adjustable stock $3,654.00

Browning Citori XT Trap Over/Under

Similar to the Citori Special Trap except has engraved silver nitride receiver with gold highlights, vented side barrel rib. Available in 12 gauge with 30" or 32" barrels, Invector-Plus choke tubes. Introduced 1999. Imported by Browning.
Price: $1,834.00
Price: With adjustable-comb stock...................... $2,054.00

Browning Micro Citori Lightning

Similar to the standard Citori 20 ga. Lightning except scaled down for smaller shooter. Comes with 24" Invector Plus back-bored barrels, 13-3/4" length of pull. Weighs about 6 lbs., 3 oz. Introduced 1991.
Price: Grade I....................................... $1,486.00

Browning Citori Lightning Feather O/U

Similar to the 12 gauge Citori Grade I except has 2-3/4" chambers, rounded pistol grip, Lightning-style forend, and lighweight alloy receiver. Weighs 7 lbs. 9 oz. with 26" barrels. Silvered, engraved receiver. Introduced 1999. Imported by Browning.
Price: $1,582.00

Browning Citori Ultra Sporter

Similar to the Citori Hunting except has slightly grooved, semi-beavertail forend, satin-finish stock, radiused rubber butt pad. Has three interchangeable trigger shoes, trigger has three length of pull adjustments. Ventilated rib tapers from 13mm to 10mm, 28" or 30" barrels (ported or non-ported) with Invector Plus choke tubes. Ventilated side ribs. Introduced 1989.
Price: With ported barrels, gray or blue receiver $1,800.00
Price: Golden Clays $3,396.00

Browning 425
Sporting Clays

Browning Citori Sporting Hunter

Similar to the Citori Hunting I except has Sporting Clays stock dimensions, a Superposed-style forend, and Sporting Clays butt pad. Available in 12 gauge with 3" chambers, back-bored 26", 28", all with Invector Plus choke tube system. Introduced 1998. Imported from Japan by Browning.
Price: 12 gauge, 3-1/2"................................. $1,595.00
Price: 12, 20 gauge, 3"................................ $1,500.00

Browning Citori Ultra XS Skeet

NEW! Similar to other Citori Ultra models except features a semi-beavertail forearm with deep finger grooves, ported barrels and triple system. Adjustable comb is optional. Introduced 2000.
Price: 28" or 30" barrel................................ $2,059.00

Browning Citori Feather XS Shotguns

NEW! Similar to the standard Citori except has lightweight alloy receiver, silver nitrade Nitex receiver, Schnabel forearm, ventilated side rib and Hi-Viz Comp fiber optics sight. Available in 12, 20, 28 and 410 gauges. Introduced 2000.
Price: 28" or 30" barrel.................... $2,200.00 to $2,270.00

Browning Citori High Grade Shotguns

NEW! Similar to standard Citori except has full sideplates with engraved hunting scenes and gold inlays, highgrade, hand-oiled walnut stock and forearm. Introduced 2000. From Browning.
Price: Citori Privilege (fully embellished sideplates)......... $5,120.00
Price: Citori BG VI Lightning (gold inlays of ducks and pheasants)
.... from $3,340.00
Price: Citori BG III Superlight (scroll engraving on grayed receiver, gold inlays).. $2,190.00

Browning Nitra Citori XS Sporting Clays

Similar to the Citori Grade I except has silver nitride receiver with gold accents, stock dimensions of 14-3/4"x1-1/2"x2-1/4" with satin finish, right-hand palm swell, Schnabel forend. Comes with Modified, Imp. Cyl. and Skeet Invector-Plus choke tubes. Back-bored barrels; vented side ribs. Introduced 1999. Imported by Browning.
Price: 12, 20 ga.. $2,011.00
Price: 28 ga., 410-bore................................ $2,077.00

Browning Special Sporting Clays

Similar to the Citori Ultra Sporter except has full pistol grip stock with palm swell, gloss finish, 28", 30" or 32" barrels with back-bored Invector Plus chokes (ported or non-ported); high post tapered rib. Also available as 28" and 30" two-barrel set. Introduced 1989.
Price: With ported barrels.............................. $1,636.00
Price: As above, adjustable comb $1,856.00

Browning Lightning Sporting Clays

Similar to the Citori Lightning with rounded pistol grip and classic forend. Has high post tapered rib or lower hunting-style rib with 30" back-bored Invector Plus barrels, ported or non-ported, 3" chambers. Gloss stock finish, radiused recoil pad. Has "Lightning Sporting Clays Edition" engraved and gold filled on receiver. Introduced 1989.
Price: Low-rib, ported................................. $1,564.00
Price: High-rib, ported................................ $1,636.00

BROWNING LIGHT SPORTING 802 ES O/U

Gauge: 12, 2-3/4" chambers. Barrel: 28", back-bored Invector Plus. Comes with flush-mounted Imp. Cyl. and Skeet; 2" extended Imp. Cyl. and Mod.; and 4" extended Imp. Cyl. and Mod. tubes. Weight: 7 lbs., 5 oz. Length: 45" overall. Stock: 14-3/8" x 1/8" x 1-9/16" x 1-3/4". Select walnut with ra-

diused solid recoil pad, Schnabel-type forend. Features: Trigger adjustable for length of pull; narrow 6.2mm ventilated rib; ventilated barrel side rib; blued receiver. Introduced 1996. Imported from Japan from Browning.
Price: $1,965.00

BROWNING 425 SPORTING CLAYS

Gauge: 12, 20, 2-3/4" chambers. Barrel: 12 ga.—28", 30", 32" (Invector Plus tubes), back-bored; 20 ga.—28", 30" (Invector Plus tubes). Weight: 7 lbs., 13 oz. (12 ga., 28"). Stock: 14-13/16" (1/8")x1-7/16"x2-3/16" (12 ga.). Select walnut with gloss finish, cut checkering, Schnabel forend. Features: Grayed receiver with engraving, blued barrels. Barrels are ported on 12 gauge guns. Has low 10mm wide vent rib. Comes with three interchangeable trigger shoes to adjust length of pull. Introduced in U.S. 1993. Imported by Browning.
Price: Grade I, 12, 20 ga., Invector Plus $1,855.00
Price: Golden Clays, 12, 20 ga., Invector Plus.............. $3,507.00
Price: With adjustable comb stock, add $2,075.00

Browning 425 WSSF Shotgun

Similar to the 425 Sporting Clays except in 12 gauge only, 28" barrels, has stock dimensions specifically tailored to women shooters (14-1/4"x1-1/2"x1-1/2"); top lever and takedown lever are easier to operate. Stock and forend have teal-colored finish or natural walnut with Women's Shooting Sports Foundation logo. Weighs 7 lbs., 4 oz. Introduced 1995. Imported by Browning.
Price: $1,855.00

CHARLES DALY SUPERIOR TRAP AE MC

Gauge: 12, 2-3/4" chambers. Barrel: 30" choke tubes. Weight: About 7 lbs. Stock: Checkered walnut; pistol grip, semi-beavertail forend. Features: Silver engraved receiver, chrome moly steel barrels; gold single selective trigger; automatic safety, automatic ejectors; red bead front sight, metal bead center; recoil pad. Introduced 1997. Imported from Italy by K.B.I., Inc.
Price: $1,219.00

CHARLES DALY FIELD HUNTER OVER/UNDER SHOTGUN

Gauge: 12, 20, 28 and 410 bore (3" chambers, 28 ga. has 2-3/4"). Barrel: 28" Mod & Full, 26" Imp. Cyl. & Mod (410 is Full & Full). Weight: About 7 lbs. Length: NA. Stock: Checkered walnut pistol grip and forend. Features: Blued engraved receiver, chrome moly steel barrels; gold single selective trigger; automatic safety; extractors; gold bead front sight. Introduced 1997. Imported from Italy by K.B.I., Inc.
Price: 12 or 20 ga. $749.00
Price: 28 ga. $809.00
Price: 410 bore $849.00

Charles Daly Field Hunter AE Shotgun

Similar to the Field Hunter except 28 gauge and 410-bore only; 26" (Imp. Cyl. & Mod., 28 gauge), 26" (Full & Full, 410); automatic; ejectors. Introduced 1997. Imported from Italy by K.B.I., Inc.
Price: 28 .... $889.00
Price: 410 .... $929.00

Charles Daly Superior Hunter AE Shotgun

Similar to the Field Hunter AE except has silvered, engraved receiver. Introduced 1997. Imported from Italy by F.B.I., Inc.
Price: 28 ga. $1,059.00
Price: 410 bore $1,099.00

Charles Daly Field Hunter AE-MC

Similar to the Field Hunter except in 12 or 20 only, 26" or 28" barrels with five multichoke tubes; automatic ejectors. Introduced 1997. Imported from Italy by K.B.I., Inc.
Price: 12 or 20 .... $979.95

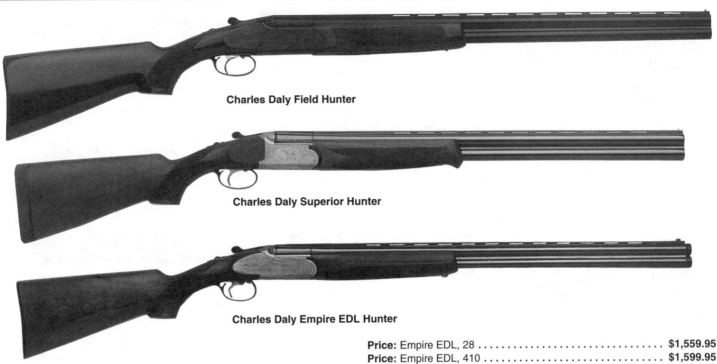

Charles Daly Field Hunter

Charles Daly Superior Hunter

Charles Daly Empire EDL Hunter

Charles Daly Superior Sporting O/U

Similar to the Field Hunter AE-MC except 28" or 30" barrels; silvered, engraved receiver; five choke tubes; ported barrels; red bead front sight. Introduced 1997. Imported from Italy by K.B.I., Inc.

Price: **$1,259.95**

CHARLES DALY EMPIRE TRAP AE MC

Gauge: 12, 2-3/4" chambers. **Barrel:** 30" choke tubes. **Weight:** About 7 lbs. **Stock:** Checkered walnut; pistol grip, semi-beavertail forend. **Features:** Silvered, engraved, reinforced receiver; chrome moly steel barrels; gold single selective trigger; automatic safety, automatic ejector; red bead front sight, metal bead center; recoil pad. Introduced 1997. Imported from Italy by K.B.I., Inc.

Price: **$1,539.95**

CHARLES DALY DIAMOND REGENT GTX DL HUNTER O/U

Gauge: 12, 20, 410, 3" chambers, 28, 2-3/4" chambers. **Barrel:** 26", 28", 30" (choke tubes), 26" (Imp. Cyl. & Mod. in 28, 26" (Full & Full) in 410. **Weight:** About 7 lbs. **Stock:** Extra select fancy European walnut with 24" hand checkering, hand rubbed oil finish. **Features:** Boss-type action with internal side lumps. Deep cut hand-engraved scrollwork and game scene set in full sideplates. GTX detachable single selective trigger system with coil springs; chrome moly steel barrels; automatic safety; automatic ejectors, white bead front sight, metal bead center sight. Introduced 1997. Imported from Italy by K.B.I., Inc.

Price: 12 or 20 .... **$22,299.00**
Price: 28 .... **$22,369.00**
Price: 410 .... **$22,419.00**
Price: Diamond Regent GTX EDL Hunter (as above with engraved scroll and birds, 10 gold inlays), 12 or 20 .... **$26,249.00**
Price: As above, 28 .... **$26,499.00**
Price: As above, 410 .... **$26,549.00**

CHARLES DALY EMPIRE EDL HUNTER O/U

Gauge: 12, 20, 410, 3" chambers, 28 ga., 2-3/4". **Barrel:** 26", 28" (12, 20, choke tubes), 26" (Imp. Cyl. & Mod., 28 ga.), 26" (Full & Full, 410). **Weight:** About 7 lbs. **Stocks:** Checkered walnut pistol grip buttstock, semi-beavertail forend; recoil pad. **Features:** Silvered, engraved receiver; chrome moly barrels; gold single selective trigger; automatic safety; automatic ejectors; red bead front sight, metal bead middle sight. Introduced 1997. Imported from Italy by K.B.I., Inc.

Price: Empire EDL (dummy sideplates) 12 or 20 .... **$1,559.95**

Price: Empire EDL, 28 .... **$1,559.95**
Price: Empire EDL, 410 .... **$1,599.95**

Charles Daly Empire Sporting O/U

Similar to the Empire EDL Hunter except 12 or 20 gauge only, 28", 30" barrels with choke tubes; ported barrels; special stock dimensions. Introduced 1997. Imported from Italy by K.B.I., Inc.

Price: **$1,499.95**

CHARLES DALY DIAMOND GTX SPORTING O/U SHOTGUN

Gauge: 12, 20, 3" chambers. **Barrel:** 28", 30" with choke tubes. **Weight:** About 8.5 lbs. **Stock:** Checkered deluxe walnut; Sporting clays dimensions. Pistol grip; semi-beavertail forend; hand rubbed oil finish. **Features:** Chromed, hand-engraved receiver; chrome moly steel barrels; GTX detachable single selective trigger system with coil springs, automatic safety; automatic ejectors; red bead front sight; ported barrels. Introduced 1997. Imported from Italy by K.B.I., Inc.

Price: **$5,804.95**

CHARLES DALY DIAMOND GTX TRAP AE-MC O/U SHOTGUN

Gauge: 12, 2-3/4" chambers. **Barrel:** 30" (Full & Full). **Weight:** About 8.5 lbs. **Stock:** Checkered deluxe walnut; pistol grip; trap dimensions; semi-beavertail forend; hand-rubbed oil finish. **Features:** Silvered, hand-engraved receiver; chrome moly steel barrels; GTX detachable single selective trigger system with coil springs, automatic safety, automatic-ejectors, red bead front sight, metal bead middle; recoil pad. Introduced 1997. Imported from Italy by K.B.I., Inc.

Price: **$5,804.95**

CHARLES DALY DIAMOND GTX DL HUNTER O/U

Gauge: 12, 20, 410, 3" chambers, 28, 2-3/4" chambers. **Barrel:** 26, 28", choke tubes in 12 and 20 ga., 26" (Imp. Cyl. & Mod.), 26" (Full & Full) in 410-bore. **Weight:** About 8.5 lbs. **Stock:** Select fancy European walnut stock, with 24 lpi hand checkering; hand-rubbed oil finish. **Features:** Boss-type action with internal side lugs, hand-engraved scrollwork and game scene. GTX detachable single selective trigger system with coil springs; chrome moly steel barrels, automatic safety, automatic ejectors, red bead front sight, recoil pad. Introduced 1997. Imported from Italy by K.B.I., Inc.

Price: 12 or 20 .... **$12,399.00**
Price: 28 .... **$12,489.00**
Price: 410 .... **$12,529.00**
Price: GTX EDL Hunter (with gold inlays), 12, 20 .... **$15,999.00**
Price: As above, 28 .... **$16,179.00**
Price: As above, 410 .... **$16,219.00**

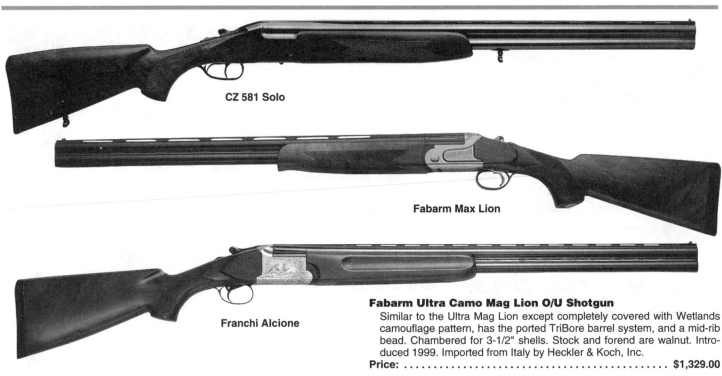

CZ 581 Solo

Fabarm Max Lion

Franchi Alcione

CZ 581 SOLO OVER/UNDER SHOTGUN

Gauge: 12, 2-3/4" chambers. **Barrel:** 27.6" (Mod. & Full). **Weight:** 7.37 lbs. **Length:** 44.5" overall. **Stock:** Circassian walnut. **Features:** Automatic ejectors; double triggers; Kersten-style double lump locking system. Imported from the Czech Republic by CZ-USA.
Price: **$799.00**

EAA/BAIKAL MP-233 OVER/UNDER SHOTGUN

NEW! **Gauge:** 12, 3" chambers. **Barrel:** 26", 28", 30"; imp., mod. and full choke tubes. **Weight:** 7.28 lbs. **Stock:** Walnut; checkered forearm and grip. **Features:** Hammer-forged barrels; chrome-lined bores; removable trigger assembly (optional single selective trigger or double trigger); ejectors. Introduced 2000. Imported by European American Armory.
Price: MP-233. . . . . **$879.00**

EAA/BAIKAL IZH-27 OVER/UNDER SHOTGUN

Gauge: 12 (3" chambers), 16 (2-3/4" chambers), 20 (3" chambers), 28 (2-3/4" chambers), 410 (3"). **Barrel:** 26-1/2", 28-1/2" (imp., mod. and full choke tubes for 12 and 20 gauges; improved cylinder and modified for 16 and 28 gauges; improved modified and full for 410; 16 also offered in mod. and full). **Weight:** N/A. **Stock:** Walnut, checkered forearm and grip. Imported by European American Armory.
Price: IZH-27 (12, 16 and 20 gauge) **$459.00**
Price: IZH-27 (28 and 410 gauge) **$499.00**

FABARM MAX LION OVER/UNDER SHOTGUNS

Gauge: 12, 3" chambers, 20, 3" chambers. **Barrel:** 26", 28", 30" (12 ga.); 26", 28" (20 ga.), choke tubes. **Weight:** 7.4 lbs. **Length:** 47.5" overall (26" barrel). **Stock:** European walnut; leather-covered recoil pad. **Features:** TriBore barrel, boxlock action with single selective trigger, manual safety, automatic ejectors; chrome-lined barrels; adjustable trigger. Silvered, engraved receiver. Comes with locking, fitted luggage case. Introduced 1998. Imported from Italy by Heckler & Koch, Inc.
Price: 12 or 20 . . . . **$1,939.00**

FABARM ULTRA MAG LION O/U SHOTGUN

Gauge: 12, 3-1/2" chambers. **Barrel:** 28" (Cyl., Imp. Cyl., Mod., Imp. Mod., Full, SS-Mod., SS-Full choke tubes). **Weight:** 7.9 lbs. **Length:** 50" overall. **Stock:** Black-colored walnut. **Features:** TriBore barrel, matte finished metal surfaces; single selective trigger; non-auto ejectors; leather-covered recoil pad. Comes with locking hard plastic case. Introduced 1998. Imported from Italy by Heckler & Koch, Inc.
Price: **$1,229.00**

Fabarm Ultra Camo Mag Lion O/U Shotgun

Similar to the Ultra Mag Lion except completely covered with Wetlands camouflage pattern, has the ported TriBore barrel system, and a mid-rib bead. Chambered for 3-1/2" shells. Stock and forend are walnut. Introduced 1999. Imported from Italy by Heckler & Koch, Inc.
Price: **$1,329.00**

FABARM SILVER LION OVER/UNDER SHOTGUNS

Gauge: 12, 3" chambers, 20, 3" chambers. **Barrel:** 26", 28", 30" (12 ga.); 26", 28" (20 ga.), choke tubes. **Weight:** 7.2 lbs. **Length:** 47.5" overall (26" barrels). **Stock:** Walnut; leather-covered recoil pad. **Features:** TriBore barrel, boxlock action with single selective trigger; silvered receiver with engraving; automatic ejectors. Comes with locking hard plastic case. Introduced 1998. Imported from Italy by Heckler & Koch, Inc.
Price: 12 or 20 . . . . **$1,299.00**
Price: Super Light Lion (12 ga. only, 24" barrels, weighs 6.5 lbs.). **$1,159.00**

Fabarm Silver Lion Cub Model O/U

Similar to the Silver Lion except has 12.5" length of pull, is in 20 gauge only (3-1/2" chambers), and comes with 24" TriBore barrel system. Weight is 6 lbs. Introduced 1999. Imported from Italy by Heckler & Koch, Inc.
Price: **$1,379.00**
Price: Super Light Lion Cub (12 ga. only, 6 lbs., blued receiver) **$1,099.00**

FABARM CAMO TURKEY MAG O/U SHOTGUN

Gauge: 12, 3-1/2" chambers. **Barrel:** 20" TriBore (Ultra-Full ported tubes). **Weight:** 7.5 lbs. **Length:** 46" overall. **Stock:** 14.5"x1.5"x2.29". Walnut. **Sights:** Front bar, Picatinny rail scope base. **Features:** Completely covered with Xtra Brown camouflage finish. Unported barrels. Introduced 1999. Imported from Italy by Heckler & Koch, Inc.
Price: **$1,339.00**

FABARM SPORTING CLAYS COMPETITION LION O/U

Gauge: 12, 20, 3" chambers. **Barrel:** 12 ga. has 30", 20 ga. has 28"; ported TriBore barrel system with five tubes. **Weight:** 7 to 7.8 lbs. **Length:** 49.6" overall (20 ga.). **Stock:** 14.50"x1.38"x2.17" (20 ga.); deluxe walnut; leather-covered recoil pad. **Features:** Single selective trigger, auto ejectors; recoil reducer installed in buttstock; 10mm channeled rib; silvered, engraved receiver. Introduced 1999. Imported from Italy by Heckler & Koch, Inc.
Price: **$1,419.00**

Fabarm Sporting Clays Competition Extra

Same as Sporting Clays Competition Lion O/U but has carbon fiber finish.
Price: **$1,750.00**

FRANCHI ALCIONE FIELD OVER/UNDER SHOTGUN

Gauge: 12, 3" chambers. **Barrel:** 26", 28"; Franchoke tubes. **Weight:** 7.5 lbs. **Length:** 43" overall with 26" barrels. **Stock:** European walnut. **Features:**

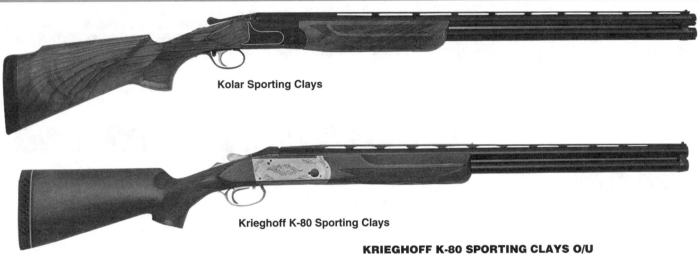

Kolar Sporting Clays

Krieghoff K-80 Sporting Clays

Boxlock action with ejectors; barrel selector is mounted on the trigger; silvered, engraved receiver; vent center rib; automatic safety. Imported from Italy by Benelli USA. Hard case included.

Price: $993.00
Price: (20 gauge barrel set) $336.00

Franchi Alcione Sport O/U Shotgun

Similar to the Alcione except has 2-3/4" chambers, elongated forcing cones and porting for Sporting Clays shooting. 10mm vent rib, tightly curved pistol grip, manual safety, removeable sideplates. Imported from Italy by Benelli USA.

Price: $1,300.00

Franchi Alcione Light Field (LF) Shotgun

Similar to Alcione Field except features alloy frame, weighs 6.8 pounds (12 gauge) or 6.7 pounds (20 gauge). Both frames accept either the 2 3/4 "-chamber 12 gauge or 3"-chamber 20 gauge barrel sets.

Price: $1,100.00

KOLAR SPORTING CLAYS O/U SHOTGUN

Gauge: 12, 2-3/4" chambers. **Barrel:** 28", 30", 32"; extended choke tubes. **Stock:** 14-5/8"x2-1/2"x1-7/8"x1-3/8". French walnut. **Features:** Single selective trigger, detachable, adjustable for length; overbored barrels with long forcing cones; flat tramline rib; matte blue finish. Made in U.S. by Kolar.

Price: Standard. $7,250.00
Price: Elite $10,050.00
Price: Elite Gold $11,545.00
Price: Legend $13,045.00
Price: Custom Gold $24,750.00

Kolar AAA Competition Trap Over/Under Shotgun

Similar to the Sporting Clays gun except has 32" O/U / 34" Unsingle or 30" O/U / 34" Unsingle barrels as an over/under, unsingle, or combination set. Stock dimensions are 14-1/2"x2-1/2"x1-1/2"; American or French walnut; step parallel rib standard. Contact maker for full listings. Made in U.S. by Kolar.

Price: Over/under, choke tubes, Standard $7,025.00
Price: Unsingle, choke tubes, Standard $7,775.00
Price: Combo (30"/34", 32"/34"), Standard. $10,170.00

Kolar AAA Competition Skeet Over/Under Shotgun

Similar to the Sporting Clays gun except has 28" or 30" barrels with Kolarite AAA sub gauge tubes; stock of American or French walnut with matte finish; flat tramline rib; under barrel adjustable for point of impact. Many options available. Contact maker for complete listing. Made in U.S. by Kolar.

Price: Standard, choke tubes $8,645.00
Price: Standard, choke tubes, two-barrel set $10,710.00

KRIEGHOFF K-80 SPORTING CLAYS O/U

Gauge: 12. **Barrel:** 28", 30" or 32" with choke tubes. **Weight:** About 8 lbs. **Stock:** #3 Sporting stock designed for gun-down shooting. **Features:** Choice of standard or lightweight receiver with satin nickel finish and classic scroll engraving. Selective mechanical trigger adjustable for position. Choice of tapered flat or 8mm parallel flat barrel rib. Free-floating barrels. Aluminum case. Imported from Germany by Krieghoff International, Inc.
Price: Standard grade with five choke tubes, from $8,150.00

KRIEGHOFF K-80 SKEET SHOTGUN

Gauge: 12, 2-3/4" chambers. **Barrel:** 28" (Skeet & Skeet, optional Tula or choke tubes). **Weight:** About 7-3/4 lbs. **Stock:** American Skeet or straight Skeet stocks, with palm-swell grips. Walnut. **Features:** Satin gray receiver finish. Selective mechanical trigger adjustable for position. Choice of ventilated 8mm parallel flat rib or ventilated 8-12mm tapered flat rib. Introduced 1980. Imported from Germany by Krieghoff International, Inc.

Price: Standard, Skeet chokes......................... $6,900.00
Price: As above, Tula chokes........................ $7,825.00
Price: Lightweight model (weighs 7 lbs.), Standard $6,900.00
Price: Two-Barrel Set (tube concept), 12 ga., Standard...... $11,840.00
Price: Skeet Special (28", tapered flat rib, Skeet & Skeet choke
tubes) $7,575.00

Krieghoff K-80 Four-Barrel Skeet Set

Similar to the Standard Skeet except comes with barrels for 12, 20, 28, 410. Comes with fitted aluminum case.
Price: Standard grade $16,950.00

Krieghoff K-80 International Skeet

Similar to the Standard Skeet except has 1/2" ventilated Broadway-style rib, special Tula chokes with gas release holes at muzzle. International Skeet stock. Comes in fitted aluminum case.
Price: Standard grade $7,825.00

KRIEGHOFF K-80 O/U TRAP SHOTGUN

Gauge: 12, 2-3/4" chambers. **Barrel:** 30", 32" (Imp. Mod. & Full or choke tubes). **Weight:** About 8-1/2 lbs. **Stock:** Four stock dimensions or adjustable stock available; all have palm swell grips. Checkered European walnut. **Features:** Satin nickel receiver. Selective mechanical trigger, adjustable for position. Ventilated step rib. Introduced 1980. Imported from Germany by Krieghoff International, Inc.

Price: K-80 O/U (30", 32", Imp. Mod. & Full), from.......... $7,375.00
Price: K-80 Unsingle (32", 34", Full), Standard, from $7,950.00
Price: K-80 Combo (two-barrel set), Standard, from $9,975.00
Price: $1,310.00

LEBEAU - COURALLY BOSS-VEREES O/U

Gauge: 12, 20, 2-3/4" chambers. **Barrel:** 25" to 32". **Weight:** To customer specifications. **Stock:** Exhibition-quality French walnut. **Features:** Boss-type sidelock with automatic ejectors; single or double triggers; chopper lump barrels. A custom gun built to customer specifications. Imported from Belgium by Wm. Larkin Moore.
Price: From....................................... $81,000.00

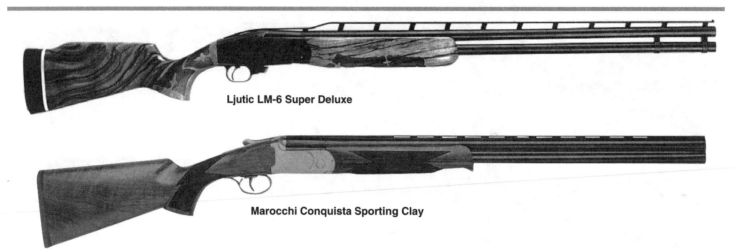

Ljutic LM-6 Super Deluxe

Marocchi Conquista Sporting Clay

LJUTIC LM-6 SUPER DELUXE O/U SHOTGUN

Gauge: 12. **Barrel:** 28" to 34", choked to customer specs for live birds, trap, International Trap. **Weight:** To customer specs. **Stock:** To customer specs. Oil finish, hand checkered. **Features:** Custom-made gun. Hollow-milled rib, pull or release trigger, pushbutton opener in front of trigger guard. From Ljutic Industries.

Price: Super Deluxe LM-6 O/U **$17,995.00**
Price: Over/under Combo (interchangeable single barrel, two trigger
guards, one for single trigger, one for doubles) **$24,995.00**
Price: Extra over/under barrel sets, 29"-32" **$5,995.00**

LUGER CLASSIC O/U SHOTGUNS

NEW! **Gauge:** 12, 3" and 3-1/2" chambers. **Barrel:** 26", 28", 30"; imp. cyl. mod. and full choke tubes. **Weight:** 7-1/2 lbs. **Length:** 45" overall (28" barrel) **Stock:** Select-grade European walnut, hand-checkered grip and forend. **Features:** Gold, single selective trigger; automatic ejectors. Introduced 2000. From Stoeger Industries.

Price: Classic (26", 28" or 30" barrel; 3-1/2" chambers) **$919.00**
Price: Classic Sporting (30" barrel; 3" chambers) **$964.00**

MAROCCHI CONQUISTA SPORTING CLAYS O/U SHOTGUNS

Gauge: 12, 2-3/4" chambers. **Barrel:** 28", 30", 32" (ContreChoke tubes); 10mm concave vent. rib. **Weight:** About 8 lbs. **Stock:** 14-1/2"-14-7/8"x2-3/16"x1-7/16"; American walnut with checkered grip and forend; Sporting Clays butt pad. **Sights:** 16mm luminescent front. **Features:** Has lower monoblock and frame profile. Fast lock time. Ergonomically-shaped trigger is adjustable for pull length. Automatic selective ejectors. Coin-finished receiver, blued barrels. Comes with five choke tubes, hard case. Also available as true left-hand model—opening lever operates from left to right; stock has left-hand cast. Introduced 1994. Imported from Italy by Precision Sales International.

Price: Grade I, right-hand **$1,995.00**
Price: Grade I, left-hand **$2,120.00**
Price: Grade II, right-hand **$2,330.00**
Price: Grade II, left-hand **$2,685.00**
Price: Grade III, right-hand, from **$3,599.00**
Price: Grade III, left-hand, from **$3,995.00**

Marocchi Lady Sport O/U Shotgun

Ergonomically designed specifically for women shooters. Similar to the Conquista Sporting Clays model except has 28" or 30" barrels with five Contrechoke tubes, stock dimensions of 13-7/8"-14-1/4"x1-11/32"x2-9/32"; weighs about 7-1/2 lbs. Also available as left-hand model—opening lever operates from left to right; stock has left-hand cast. Also available with colored graphics finish on frame and opening lever. Introduced 1995. Imported from Italy by Precision Sales International.

Price: Grade I, right-hand **$2,120.00**
Price: Left-hand, add (all grades) **$101.00**
Price: Lady Sport Spectrum (colored receiver panel) **$2,199.00**
Price: Lady Sport Spectrum, left-hand **$2,300.00**

Marocchi Conquista Trap Over/Under Shotgun

Similar to the Conquista Sporting Clays model except has 30" or 32" barrels choked Full & Full, stock dimensions of 14-1/2"- 14-7/8"x1-11/16"x1-9/32"; weighs about 8-1/4 lbs. Introduced 1994. Imported from Italy by Precision Sales International.

Price: Grade I, right-hand **$1,995.00**
Price: Grade II, right-hand **$2,330.00**
Price: Grade III, right-hand, from **$3,599.00**

Marocchi Conquista Skeet Over/Under Shotgun

Similar to the Conquista Sporting Clays except has 28" (Skeet & Skeet) barrels, stock dimensions of 14-3/8"- 14-3/4"x2-3/16"x1-1/2". Weighs about 7-3/4 lbs. Introduced 1994. Imported from Italy by Precision Sales International.

Price: Grade I, right-hand **$1,995.00**
Price: Grade II, right-hand **$2,330.00**
Price: Grade III, right-hand, from **$3,599.00**

MAROCCHI CLASSIC DOUBLES
MODEL 92 SPORTING CLAYS O/U SHOTGUN

Gauge: 12, 3" chambers. **Barrel:** 30"; back-bored, ported (ContreChoke Plus tubes); 10 mm concave ventilated top rib, ventilated middle rib. **Weight:** 8 lbs. 2 oz. **Stock:** 14-1/4"- 14-5/8"x 2-1/8"x1-3/8"; American walnut with checkered grip and forend; Sporting Clays butt pad. **Features:** Low profile frame; fast lock time; automatic selective ejectors; blued receiver and barrels. Comes with three choke tubes. Ergonomically shaped trigger adjustable for pull length without tools. Barrels are back-bored and ported. Introduced 1996. Imported from Italy by Precision Sales International.

Price: **$1,598.00**

MERKEL MODEL 2001EL O/U SHOTGUN

Gauge: 12, 20, 3" chambers, 28, 2-3/4" chambers. **Barrel:** 12—28"; 20, 28 ga.—26-3/4". **Weight:** About 7 lbs. (12 ga.). **Stock:** Oil-finished walnut; English or pistol grip. **Features:** Self-cocking Blitz boxlock action with cocking indicators; Kersten double cross-bolt lock; silver-grayed receiver with engraved hunting scenes; coil spring ejectors; single selective or double triggers. Imported from Germany by GSI, Inc.

Price: 12, 20 . . . . **$6,495.00**
Price: 28 ga. **$6,495.00**
Price: Model 2000EL (scroll engraving, 12 or 20) **$5,195.00**

Merkel Model 303EL O/U Shotgun

Similar to the Model 2001 EL except has Holland & Holland-style sidelock action with cocking indicators; English-style Arabesque engraving. Available in 12, 20 gauge. Imported from Germany by GSI, Inc.

Price: **$19,995.00**

Merkel Model 2002 EL O/U Shotgun

Similar to the Model 2001 EL except has dummy sideplates, Arabesque engraving with hunting scenes; 12, 20 gauge. Imported from Germany by GSI, Inc.

Price: **$9,995.00**

Perazzi MX8

Perazzi Sporting Classic

Perazzi MX8 Special Combo Single Barrel

Perazzi MX28

PERAZZI MX8 SPECIAL SPORTING O/U

Gauge: 12, 2-3/4" chambers. **Barrel:** 28-3/8" (Imp. Mod. & Extra Full), 29-1/2" (choke tubes). **Weight:** 7 lbs., 12 oz. **Stock:** Special specifications. **Features:** Has single selective trigger; flat 7/16"x5/16" vent. rib. Many options available. Imported from Italy by Perazzi U.S.A., Inc.
Price: $9,790.00

Perazzi Sporting Classic O/U

Same as the Special Sporting except is deluxe version with select wood and engraving, Available with flush mount choke tubes, 29.5" barrels. Introduced 1993.
Price: From $11,160.00

PERAZZI MX12 HUNTING OVER/UNDER

Gauge: 12, 2-3/4" chambers. **Barrel:** 26", 27-5/8", 28-3/8", 29-1/2" (Mod. & Full); choke tubes available in 27-5/8", 29-1/2" only (MX12C). **Weight:** 7 lbs., 4 oz. **Stock:** To customer specs; Interchangeable. **Features:** Single selective trigger; coil springs used in action; Schnabel forend tip. Imported from Italy by Perazzi U.S.A., Inc.
Price: From $8,840.00
Price: MX12C (with choke tubes), from $9,460.00

Perazzi MX20 Hunting Over/Under

Similar to the MX12 except 20 ga. frame size. Available in 20, 28, 410 with 2-3/4" or 3" chambers. 26" standard, and choked Mod. & Full. Weight is 6 lbs.
Price: From $8,840.00
Price: MX20C (as above, 20 ga. only, choke tubes), from $9,460.00

PERAZZI MX8/MX8 SPECIAL TRAP, SKEET

Gauge: 12, 2-3/4" chambers. **Barrel:** Trap—29-1/2" (Imp. Mod. & Extra Full), 31-1/2" (Full & Extra Full). Choke tubes optional. Skeet—27-5/8" (Skeet & Skeet). **Weight:** About 8-1/2 lbs. (Trap); 7 lbs., 15 oz. (Skeet). **Stock:** Interchangeable and custom made to customer specs. **Features:** Has detachable and interchangeable trigger group with flat V springs. Flat

7/16" ventilated rib. Many options available. Imported from Italy by Perazzi U.S.A., Inc.
Price: From $8,840.00
Price: MX8 Special (adj. four-position trigger), from $9,350.00
Price: MX8 Special Combo (o/u and single barrel sets), from . $12,340.00

Perazzi MX8 Special Skeet Over/Under

Similar to the MX8 Skeet except has adjustable four-position trigger, Skeet stock dimensions.
Price: From $9,350.00

Perazzi MX8/20 Over/Under Shotgun

Similar to the MX8 except has smaller frame and has a removable trigger mechanism. Available in trap, Skeet, sporting or game models with fixed chokes or choke tubes. Stock is made to customer specifications. Introduced 1993.
Price: From $9,790.00

PERAZZI MX10 OVER/UNDER SHOTGUN

Gauge: 12, 2-3/4" chambers. **Barrel:** 29.5", 31.5" (fixed chokes). **Weight:** NA. **Stock:** Walnut; cheekpiece adjustable for elevation and cast. **Features:** Adjustable rib; vent. side rib. Externally selective trigger. Available in single barrel, combo, over/under trap, Skeet, pigeon and sporting models. Introduced 1993. Imported from Italy by Perazzi U.S.A., Inc.
Price: From $11,030.00

PERAZZI MX28, MX410 GAME O/U SHOTGUNS

Gauge: 28, 2-3/4" chambers, 410, 3" chambers. **Barrel:** 26" (Imp. Cyl. & Full). **Weight:** NA. **Stock:** To customer specifications. **Features:** Made on scaled-down frames proportioned to the gauge. Introduced 1993. Imported from Italy by Perazzi U.S.A., Inc.
Price: From $17,670.00

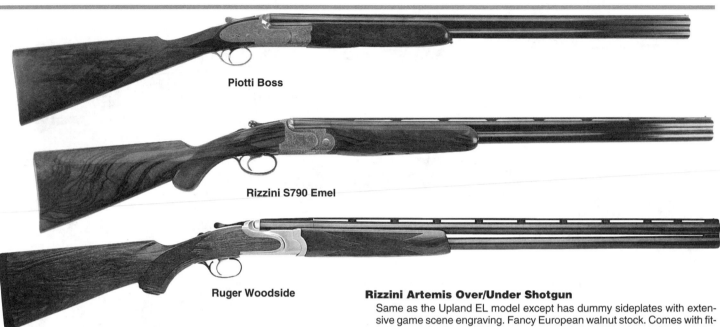

Piotti Boss

Rizzini S790 Emel

Ruger Woodside

PIOTTI BOSS OVER/UNDER SHOTGUN

Gauge: 12, 20. **Barrel:** 26" to 32", chokes as specified. **Weight:** 6.5 to 8 lbs. **Stock:** Dimensions to customer specs. Best quality figured walnut. **Features:** Essentially a custom-made gun with many options. Introduced 1993. Imported from Italy by Wm. Larkin Moore.
Price: From. **$39,200.00**

REMINGTON MODEL 300 IDEAL O/U SHOTGUN

NEW! **Gauge:** 12, 3" chambers. **Barrel:** 26", 28", 30" (imp. cyl., mod. and full Rem Choke tubes). **Weight:** 7 lbs. 6 oz. to 7 lbs. 14 oz. **Length:** 42-3/4" overall (26" brl.) **Stock:** Satin-finished American walnut; checkered forearm and grip; rubber recoil pad. **Features:** Low-profile rib; mid-bead and ivory front bead; fine-line engraved receiver with high-polish blued finish; automatic ejectors. Introduced 2000. From Remington Arms Co.
Price: **$1,999.00**

RIZZINI S790 EMEL OVER/UNDER SHOTGUN

Gauge: 20, 28, 410. **Barrel:** 26", 27.5" (Imp. Cyl. & Imp. Mod.). **Weight:** About 6 lbs. **Stock:** 14"x1-1/2"x2-1/8". Extra-fancy select walnut. **Features:** Boxlock action with profuse engraving; automatic ejectors; single selective trigger; silvered receiver. Comes with Nizzoli leather case. Introduced 1996. Imported from Italy by Wm. Larkin Moore.
Price: From. **$9,600.00**

Rizzini S792 EMEL Over/Under Shotgun

Similar to the S790 EMEL except has dummy sideplates with extensive engraving coverage. Comes with Nizzoli leather case. Introduced 1996. Imported from Italy by Wm. Larkin Moore & Co.
Price: From. **$9,400.00**

RIZZINI S790 SPORTING EL OVER/UNDER

Gauge: 12, 2-3/4" chambers. **Barrel:** 28", 29.5", Imp. Mod., Mod., Full choke tubes. **Weight:** 8.1 lbs. **Stock:** 14-1/2"x1-1/2"x2-1/4". Extra-fancy select walnut. **Features:** Boxlock action; automatic ejectors; single selective trigger; 10mm top rib. Comes with case. Introduced 1996. Imported from Italy by Wm. Larkin Moore & Co.
Price: **$6,250.00**

RIZZINI UPLAND EL OVER/UNDER SHOTGUN

Gauge: 12, 16, 20, 28, 410. **Barrel:** 26", 27-1/2", Mod. & Full, Imp. Cyl. & Imp. Mod. choke tubes. **Weight:** About 6.6 lbs. **Stock:** 14-1/2"x1-1/2"x2-1/4". **Features:** Boxlock action; single selective trigger; ejectors; profuse engraving on silvered receiver. Comes with fitted case. Introduced 1996. Imported from Italy by Wm. Larkin Moore & Co.
Price: From. **$3,500.00**

Rizzini Artemis Over/Under Shotgun

Same as the Upland EL model except has dummy sideplates with extensive game scene engraving. Fancy European walnut stock. Comes with fitted case. Introduced 1996. Imported from Italy by Wm. Larkin Moore & Co.
Price: From. **$2,375.00**

RIZZINI S782 EMEL OVER/UNDER SHOTGUN

Gauge: 12, 2-3/4" chambers. **Barrel:** 26", 27.5" (Imp. Cyl. & Imp. Mod.). **Weight:** About 6.75 lbs. **Stock:** 14-1/2"x1-1/2"x2-1/4". Extra fancy select walnut. **Features:** Boxlock action with dummy sideplates; extensive engraving with gold inlaid game birds; silvered receiver; automatic ejectors; single selective trigger. Comes with Nizzoli leather case. Introduced 1996. Imported from Italy by Wm. Larkin Moore & Co.
Price: From. **$12,250.00**

ROTTWEIL PARAGON OVER/UNDER

Gauge: 12, 2-3/4" chambers. **Barrel:** 28", 30", five choke tubes. **Weight:** 7 lbs. **Stock:** 14-1/2"x1-1/2"x2-1/2"; European walnut. **Features:** Boxlock action. Detachable trigger assembly; ejectors can be deactivated; convertible top lever for right- or left-hand use; trigger adjustable for position. Imported from Germany by Dynamit Nobel-RWS, Inc.
Price: **$5,995.00**

RUGER WOODSIDE OVER/UNDER SHOTGUN

Gauge: 12, 3" chambers. **Barrel:** 26", 28", 30" (Full, Mod., Imp. Cyl. and two Skeet tubes). **Weight:** 7-1/2 to 8 lbs. **Stock:** 14-1/8"x1-1/2"x2-1/2". Select Circassian walnut; pistol grip or straight English grip. **Features:** Has a newly patented Ruger cocking mechanism for easier, smoother opening. Buttstock extends forward into action as two side panels. Single selective mechanical trigger, selective automatic ejectors; serrated free-floating rib; back-bored barrels with stainless steel choke tubes. Blued barrels, stainless steel receiver. Engraved action available. Introduced 1995. Made in U.S. by Sturm, Ruger & Co.
Price: **$1,849.00**
Price: Woodside Sporting Clays (30" barrels) **$1,849.00**

RUGER RED LABEL O/U SHOTGUN

Gauge: 12, 20, 3" chambers; 28 2-3/4" chambers. **Barrel:** 26", 28" (Skeet [two], Imp. Cyl., Full, Mod. screw-in choke tubes). Proved for steel shot. **Weight:** About 7 lbs. (20 ga.); 7-1/2 lbs. (12 ga.). **Length:** 43" overall (26" barrels). **Stock:** 14"x1-1/2"x2-1/2". Straight grain American walnut or black synthetic. Checkered pistol grip and forend, rubber butt pad. **Features:** Stainless steel receiver. Single selective mechanical trigger, selective automatic ejectors; serrated free-floating vent. rib. Comes with two Skeet, one Imp. Cyl., one Mod., one Full choke tube and wrench. Made in U.S. by Sturm, Ruger & Co.
Price: Red Label with pistol grip stock **$1,369.00**
Price: English Field with straight-grip stock **$1,369.00**
Price: All-Weather Red Label with black synthetic stock **$1,369.00**
Price: Factory engraved All-Weather models . . . . **$1,575.00** to **$1,650.00**

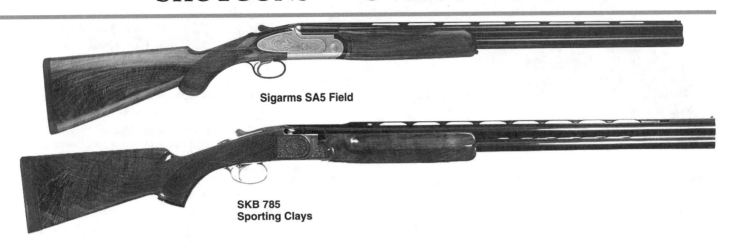

Sigarms SA5 Field

SKB 785 Sporting Clays

Ruger Engraved Red Label O/U Shotguns

Similar to Red Label except has scroll engraved receiver with 24-carat gold game bird (pheasant in 12 gauge, grouse in 20 gauge, woodcock in 28 gauge, duck on All-Weather 12 gauge). Introduced 2000.

Price: Engraved Red Label (12 gauge, 30" barrel)........... $1,650.00
Price: Engraved Red Label (12, 20 and 28 gauge in 26" and 28" barrels) $1,575.00
Price: Engraved Red Label, All-Weather (synthetic stock, 12 gauge only; 26" and 28" brls.) $1,575.00
Price: Engraved Red Label, All-Weather (synthetic stock, 12 gauge only, 30" barrel) $1,650.00

Ruger Sporting Clays O/U Shotgun

Similar to the Red Label except 30" back-bored barrels, stainless steel choke tubes. Weighs 7.75 lbs., overall length 47". Stock dimensions of 14-1/8"x1-1/2"x2-1/2". Free-floating serrated vent. rib with brass front and mid-rib beads. No barrel side spacers. Comes with two Skeet, one Imp. Cyl., one Mod. + Full choke tubes. 12 ga. introduced 1992, 20 ga. introduced 1994.

Price: 12 or 20 .... $1,443.00
Price: All-Weather with black synthetic stock............... $1,443.00

SARSILMAZ OVER/UNDER SHOTGUN

Gauge: 12, 3" chambers. **Barrel:** 26", 28"; fixed chokes or choke tubes. **Weight:** N/A. **Length:** N/A. **Stock:** Oil-finished hardwood. **Features:** Double or single selective trigger; wide ventilated rib; chrome-plated parts; blued finish. Introduced 2000. Imported from Turkey by Armsport Inc.

Price: Double triggers; mod. and full or imp. cyl. and mod. fixed chokes $499.95
Price: Single selective trigger; imp. cyl. and mod. or mod. and full fixed chokes.................................. $575.00
Price: Single selective trigger; five choke tubes and wrench $695.00

SIGARMS SA5 OVER/UNDER SHOTGUN

Gauge: 12, 20, 3" chamber. **Barrel:** 26-1/2", 27" (Full, Imp. Mod., Mod., Imp. Cyl., Cyl. choke tubes). **Weight:** 6.9 lbs. (12 gauge), 5.9 lbs. (20 gauge). **Stock:** 14-1/2" x 1-1/2" x 2-1/2". Select grade walnut; checkered 20 l.p.i. at grip and forend. **Features:** Single selective trigger, automatic ejectors; hand-engraved detachable sideplated; matte nickel receiver, rest blued; tapered bolt lock-up. Introduced 1997. Imported by Sigarms, Inc.

Price: Field, 12 gauge................................. $2,670.00
Price: Sporting Clays $2,800.00
Price: Field 20 gauge $2,670.00

SKB Model 505 Shotguns

Similar to the Model 585 except blued receiver, standard bore diameter, standard Inter-Choke system on 12, 20, 28, different receiver engraving. Imported from Japan by G.U. Inc.

Price: Field, 12 (26", 28"), 20 (26", 28") $1,049.00
Price: Sporting Clays, 12 (28", 30") $1,149.00

SKB Model 585 Gold Package

Similar to the Model 585 Field except has gold-plated trigger, two gold-plated game inlays, and Schnabel forend. Silver or blue receiver. Introduced 1998. Imported from Japan by G.U. Inc.

Price: 12, 20 ga. $1,489.00
Price: 28, 410.. $1,539.00

SKB MODEL 785 OVER/UNDER SHOTGUN

Gauge: 12, 20, 3"; 28, 2-3/4"; 410, 3". **Barrel:** 26", 28", 30", 32" (Inter-Choke tubes). **Weight:** 6 lbs., 10 oz. to 8 lbs. **Stock:** 14-1/8"x1-1/2"x2-3/16" (Field). Hand-checkered American black walnut with high-gloss finish; semi-beavertail forend. Target stocks available in standard or Monte Carlo styles. **Sights:** Metal bead front (Field), target style on Skeet, trap, Sporting Clays models. **Features:** Boxlock action with Greener-style cross bolt; single selective chrome-plated trigger, chrome-plated selective ejectors; manual safety. Chrome-plated, over-size, back-bored barrels with lengthened forcing cones. Introduced 1995. Imported from Japan by G.U. Inc.

Price: Field, 12 or 20 .... $1,949.00
Price: Field, 28 or 410 .... $2,029.00
Price: Field set, 12 and 20 .... $2,829.00
Price: Field set, 20 and 28 or 28 and 410 .... $2,929.00
Price: Sporting Clays, 12 or 20........................ $2,099.00
Price: Sporting Clays, 28 .... $2,169.00
Price: Sporting Clays set, 12 and 20 .... $2,999.00
Price: Skeet, 12 or 20................................ $2,029.00
Price: Skeet, 28 or 410............................... $2,069.00
Price: Skeet, three-barrel set, 20, 28, 410 .... $4,089.00
Price: Trap, standard or Monte Carlo.................... $2,029.00
Price: Trap combo, standard or Monte Carlo.............. $2,829.00

SKB MODEL 585 OVER/UNDER SHOTGUN

Gauge: 12 or 20, 3"; 28, 2-3/4"; 410, 3". **Barrel:** 12 ga.—26", 28", 30", 32", 34" (Inter-Choke tube); 20 ga.—26", 28" (Inter-Choke tube); 28—26", 28" (Inter-Choke tube); 410—26", 28" (Imp. Cyl. & Mod., Mod. & Full). Ventilated side ribs. **Weight:** 6.6 to 8.5 lbs. **Length:** 43" to 51-3/8" overall. **Stock:** 14-1/8"x1-1/2"x2-3/16". Hand checkered walnut with high-gloss finish. Target stocks available in standard and Monte Carlo. **Sights:** Metal bead front (field), target style on Skeet, trap, Sporting Clays. **Features:** Boxlock action; silver nitride finish with Field or Target pattern engraving; manual safety, automatic ejectors, single selective trigger. All 12 gauge barrels are back-bored, have lengthened forcing cones and longer choke tube system. Sporting Clays models in 12 gauge with 28" or 30" barrels available with optional 3/8" step-up target-style rib, matte finish, nickel center bead, white front bead. Introduced 1992. Imported from Japan by G.U., Inc.

Price: Field $1,329.00
Price: Two-barrel Field Set, 12 & 20 .... $2,129.00
Price: Two-barrel Field Set, 20 & 28 or 28 & 410........... $2,179.00
Price: Trap, Skeet.................................... $1,429.00
Price: Two-barrel trap combo........................... $2,129.00
Price: Sporting Clays model.............. $1,149.00 to $1,529.00
Price: Skeet Set (20, 28, 410) $3,329.00

Tristar-TR-SC

STOEGER/IGA CONDOR I OVER/UNDER SHOTGUN

Gauge: 12, 20, 3" chambers. **Barrel:** 26" (Imp. Cyl. & Mod. choke tubes), 28" (Mod. & Full choke tubes). **Weight:** 6-3/4 to 7 lbs. **Stock:** 14-1/2"x1-1/2"x2-1/2". Oil-finished hardwood with checkered pistol grip and forend. **Features:** Manual safety, single trigger, extractors only, ventilated top rib. Introduced 1983. Imported from Brazil by Stoeger Industries.
Price: With choke tubes **$559.00**
Price: Condor Supreme (same as Condor I with single trigger, choke tubes, but with auto. ejectors), 12 or 20 ga., 26", 28" . . . **$674.00**

Stoeger/IGA Condor Waterfowl O/U

Similar to the Condor I except has Advantage camouflage on the barrels, stock and forend; all other metal has matte black finish. Comes only with 30" choke tube barrels, 3" chambers, automatic ejectors, single trigger and manual safety. Designed for steel shot. Introduced 1997. Imported from Brazil by Stoeger.
Price: **$729.00**

Stoeger/IGA Turkey Model O/U

Similar to the Condor I model except has Advantage camouflage on the barrels stock and forend. All exposed metal and recoil pad are matte black. Has 26" (Full & Full) barrels, single trigger, manual safety, 3" chambers. Introduced 1997. Imported from Brazil by Stoeger.
Price: **$729.00**

TRISTAR-TR-SC "EMILLIO RIZZINI" OVER/UNDER

Gauge: 12, 20, 2-3/4" chambers. **Barrel:** 28", 30" (Imp. Cyl., Mod., Full choke tubes). **Weight:** 7-1/2 lbs. **Length:** 46" overall (28" barrel). **Stock:** 1-1/2"x2-3/8"x14-3/8". Semi-fancy walnut; pistol grip with palm swell; semi-beavertail forend; black Sporting Clays recoil pad. **Features:** Silvered boxlock action with Four Locks locking system, auto ejectors, single selective (inertia) trigger, auto safety. Hard chrome bores. Vent. 10mm rib with target-style front and mid-rib beads, vent. spacer rib. Introduced 1998. Imported from Italy by Tristar Sporting Arms, Ltd.
Price: **$949.00**
Price: 20 ga. **$1,022.00**

Tristar TR-Royal Emillio Rizzini Over/Under

Similar to the TR-SC except has special parallel stock dimensions (1-1/2"x1-5/8"x14-3/8") to give low felt recoil; Rhino ported, extended choke tubes; solid barrel spacer; has "TR-Royal" gold engraved on the silvered receiver. Available in 12 gauge (28", 30") 20 and 28 gauge (28" only). Introduced 1999. Imported from Italy by Tristar Sporting Arms, Ltd.
Price: 12 ga. **$1,277.00**
Price: 20, 28 ga. **$1,345.00**

Tristar-TR-L "Emillio Rizzinni" Over/Under

Similar to the TR-SC except has stock dimensions designed for female shooters (1-1/2" x 3" x 13-1/2"). Standard grade walnut. Introduced 1998. Imported from Italy by Tristar Sporting Arms, Ltd.
Price: **$966.00**

TRISTAR-TR-I, II "EMILLIO RIZZINI" OVER/UNDERS

Gauge: 12, 20, 3" chambers (TR-I); 12, 16, 20, 28, 410 3" chambers (except 28, 2-3/4"). **Barrel:** 12 ga., 26" (Imp. Cyl. & Mod.), 28" (Mod. & Full); 20 ga., 26" (Imp. Cyl. & Mod.), fixed chokes. **Weight:** 7-1/2 lbs. **Stock:** 1-1/2"x2-3/8"x14-3/8". Walnut with palm swell pistol grip, hand checkering, semi-beavertail forend, black recoil pad. **Features:** Boxlock action with blued finish, Four Locks® locking system, gold single selective (inertia) trigger system, automatic safety, extractors. Introduced 1998. Imported from Italy by Tristar Sporting Arms, Ltd.

Price: TR-I **$654.00**
Price: TR-II (automatic ejectors, choke tubes) 12, 16 ga. **$852.00**
Price: 20, 28 ga., 410. . . . . **$880.00**

Tristar-TR-MAG "Emillio Rizzini" Over/Under

Similar to the TR-I except 12 gauge, 3-1/2" chambers; choke tubes; 24" or 28" barrels with three choke tubes; extractors; auto safety. Matte blue finish on all metal, non-reflective wood finish. Introduced 1998. Imported from Italy by Tristar Sporting Arms, Ltd.
Price: **$728.00**

TRISTAR TR-CLASS SL EMILLIO RIZZINI O/U

Gauge: 12, 2-3/4" chambers. **Barrel:** 28", 30", (Imp. Cyl., Mod., Full choke tubes). **Weight:** 7-1/2-7-3/4 lbs. **Stock:** 1-1/2"x1-3/8"x14-1/4". Fancy walnut with palm swell, hand checkering, semi-beavertail forend, black recoil pad, gloss finish. **Features:** Boxlock action with silvered, engraved sideplates; Four Lock locking system; automatic ejectors; hard chrome bores; vent tapered 7mm rib with target-style front bead. hand-fitted gun. Introduced 1999. Imported from Italy by Tristar Sporting Arms, Ltd.
Price: **$1,690.00**

VERONA LX501 HUNTING O/U SHOTGUNS

Gauge: 12, 20, (3" chambers), 28, 410 (2-3/4"). **Barrel:** 28"; 12, 20 ga. have Interchoke tubes, 28 ga. and 410 have fixed Full & Mod. **Weight:** 6-7 lbs. **Stock:** Matte-finished walnut with machine-cut checkering. **Features:** Gold-plated single-selective trigger; ejectors; engraved, blued receiver, non-automatic safety; coil spring-operated firing pins. Introduced 1999. Imported from Italy by B.C. Outdoors.
Price: 12 and 20 ga. **$720.00**
Price: 28 ga. and 410 . . . . **$755.00**

Verona LX692 Gold Hunting Over/Under Shotguns

Similar to tthe Verona LX501 except has engraved, silvered receiver with false sideplates showing gold-inlaid bird hunting scenes on three sides; Schnabel forend tip; hand-cut checkering; black rubber butt pad. Available in 12 and 20 gauge only, with five InterChoke tubes. Introduced 1999. Imported from Italy by B.C. Outdoors.
Price: **$1,295.00**

Verona LX680 Sporting Over/Under Shotguns

Similar to the Verona LX501 except has engraved, silvered receiver; ventilated middle rib; beavertail forend; hand-cut checkering; available in 12 or 20 gauge only with 2-3/4" chambers. Introduced 1999. Imported from Italy by B.C. Outdoors.
Price: **$1,020.00**

Verona LX680 Skeet/Sporting, Trap O/U Shotguns

Similar to the Verona LX501 except with Skeet or trap stock dimensions; beavertail forend, palm swell on pistol grip; ventilated center barrel rib. Introduced 1999. Imported from Italy by B.C. Outdoors.
Price: **$1,130.00**
Price: Gold Competition (false sideplates with gold-inlaid hunting scenes) **$1,500.00**

Verona LX692 Gold Sporting Over/Under Shotguns

Similar to the Verona LX680 except with false sideplates that have gold-inlaid bird hunting scenes on three sides; red high-visibility front sight. Introduced 1999. Imported from Italy by B.C. Outdoors.
Price: **$1,365.00**

WEATHERBY ATHENA GRADE IV O/U SHOTGUNS

Gauge: 12, 20, 3" chambers. **Action:** Boxlock (simulated sidelock) top lever break-open. Selective auto ejectors, single selective trigger (selector inside trigger guard). **Barrel:** 26", 28", IMC Multi-Choke tubes. **Weight:** 12 ga., 7-3/8 lbs.; 20 ga. 6-7/8 lbs. **Stock:** American walnut, checkered pistol grip and forend (14-1/4"x1-1/2"x2-1/2"). **Features:** Mechanically operated trigger. Top tang safety, Greener cross bolt, fully engraved receiver, recoil pad installed. IMC models furnished with three interchangeable flush-fitting choke tubes. Imported from Japan by Weatherby. Introduced 1982.

SHOTGUNS

SHOTGUNS — OVER/UNDERS

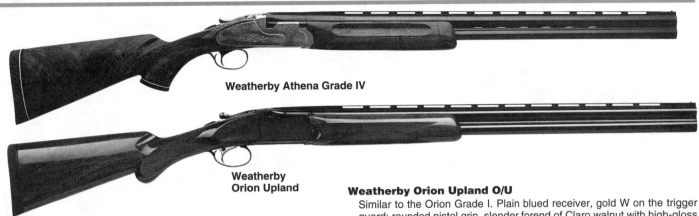

Weatherby Athena Grade IV

Weatherby
Orion Upland

Price: 12 ga., IMC, 26", 28" $2,399.00
Price: 20 ga., IMC, 26", 28" $2,399.00

Weatherby Athena Grade V Classic Field O/U

Similar to the Athena Grade IV except has rounded pistol grip, slender forend, oil-finished Claro walnut stock with fine-line checkering, Old English recoil pad. Sideplate receiver has rose and scroll engraving. Available in 12 gauge, 26", 28", 20 gauge, 26", 28", all with 3" chambers. Introduced 1993.
Price: $2,799.00

WEATHERBY ORION GRADE III FIELD O/U SHOTGUNS

Gauge: 12, 20, 3" chambers. **Barrel:** 26", 28", IMC Multi-Choke tubes. **Weight:** 6-1/2 to 9 lbs. **Stock:** 14-1/4"x1-1/2"x2-1/2". American walnut, checkered grip and forend. Rubber recoil pad. **Features:** Selective automatic ejectors, single selective inertia trigger. Top tang safety, Greener cross bolt. Has silver-gray receiver with engraving and gold duck/pheasant. Imported from Japan by Weatherby.
Price: Orion III, Field, 12, IMC, 26", 28" $1,799.00
Price: Orion III, Field, 20, IMC, 26", 28" $1,799.00

Weatherby Orion Grade III Classic Field O/U

Similar to the Orion III Field except the stock has a rounded pistol grip, satin oil finish, slender forend, Old English recoil pad. Introduced 1993. Imported from Japan by Weatherby.
Price: $1,799.00

Weatherby Orion Grade II Classic Field O/U

Similar to the Orion III Classic Field except stock has high-gloss finish, and the bird on the receiver is not gold. Available in 12 gauge, 26", 28", 30" barrels, 20 gauge, 26" 28", both with 3" chambers, 28 gauge, 26", 2-3/4" chambers. All have IMC choke tubes. Imported from Japan by Weatherby.
Price: $1,499.00

Weatherby Athena III Classic Field O/U

Has Grade III Claro walnut with oil finish, rounded pistol grip, slender forend; silver nitride/gray receiver has rose and scroll engraving with gold-overlay upland game scenes. Introduced 1999. Imported from Japan by Weatherby.
Price: $1,999.00

Weatherby Orion Grade I Field O/U

Similar to the Orion Grade III Field except has blued receiver with engraving, and the bird is not gold. Available in 12 gauge, 26", 28", 30", 20 gauge, 20", 28", both with 3" chambers and IMC choke tubes. Imported from Japan by Weatherby.
Price: $1,449.00

Weatherby Orion Upland O/U

Similar to the Orion Grade I. Plain blued receiver, gold W on the trigger guard; rounded pistol grip, slender forend of Claro walnut with high-gloss finish; black butt pad. Available in 12 and 20 gauge with 26" and 28" barrels. Introduced 1999. Imported from Japan by Weatherby.
Price: $1,199.00

WEATHERBY ORION SSC OVER/UNDER SHOTGUN

Gauge: 12, 3" chambers. **Barrel:** 28", 30", 32" (Skeet, SC1, Imp. Cyl., SC2, Mod. IMC choke tubes). **Weight:** About 8 lbs. **Stock:** 14-3/4"x2-1/4"x1-1/2". Claro walnut with satin oil finish; Schnabel forend tip; Sporter-style pistol grip; Pachmayr Decelerator recoil pad. **Features:** Designed for Sporting Clays competition. Has lengthened forcing cones and back-boring; ported barrels with 12mm grooved rib with mid-bead sight; mechanical trigger is adjustable for length of pull. Introduced 1998. Imported from Japan by Weatherby.
Price: $1,899.00

Weatherby Orion III English Field O/U

Similar to the Orion III Classic Field except has straight grip English-style stock. Available in 12 gauge (28"), 20 gauge (26", 28") with IMC Multi-Choke tubes. Silver/gray nitride receiver is engraved and has gold-plate overlay. Introduced 1997. Imported from Japan by Weatherby.
Price: $1,879.00

Weatherby Orion Grade II Classic Sporting O/U

Similar to the Orion II Classic Field except in 12 gauge only with (3" chambers), 28", 30" barrels with Skeet, SC1, SC2 Imp. Cyl., Mod. chokes. Weighs 7.5-8 lbs. Competition center vent rib; middle barrel and enlarged front beads. Rounded grip; high gloss stock. Radiused heel recoil pad. Receiver finished in silver nitride with acid-etched, gold-plate clay pigeon monogram. Barrels have lengthened forcing cones. Introduced 1993. Imported by Weatherby.
Price: $1,649.00

Weatherby Orion Grade II Sporting Clays

Similar to the Orion II Classic Sporting except has traditional pistol grip with diamond inlay, and standard full-size forend. Available in 12 gauge only, 28", 30" barrels with Skeet, Imp. Cyl., SC2, Mod. Has lengthened forcing cones, back-boring, stepped competition rib, radius heel recoil pad, hand-engraved, silver/nitride receiver. Introduced 1992. Imported by Weatherby.
Price: $1,649.00

WINCHESTER SUPREME O/U SHOTGUNS

Gauge: 12, 2-3/4", 3" chambers. **Barrel:** 28", 30", Invector Plus choke tubes. **Weight:** 7 lbs. 6 oz. to 7 lbs. 12. oz. **Length:** 45" overall (28" barrel). **Stock:** Checkered walnut stock. **Features:** Chrome-plated chambers; back-bored barrels; tang barrel selector/safety; deep-blued finish. Introduced 2000. From U.S. Repeating Arms. Co.
Price: Supreme Field (28" barrel, 6mm ventilated rib) $1,324.00
Price: Supreme Sporting (28" or 30" barrel, 10mm rib,
adj. trigger) $1,485.00

Variety of models for utility and sporting use, including some competitive shooting.

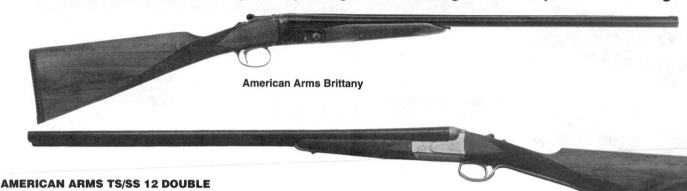

American Arms Brittany

**Beretta Model 470
Silver Hawk**

AMERICAN ARMS TS/SS 12 DOUBLE

Gauge: 12, 3-1/2" chambers. **Barrel:** 26", choke tubes; solid raised rib. **Weight:** 7 lbs., 6 oz. **Stock:** Walnut; cut-checked grip and forend. **Features:** Non-reflective metal and wood finishes; boxlock action; single trigger; extractors. Imported by American Arms, Inc.
Price: **$799.00**

AMERICAN ARMS WT/SS 10 DOUBLE

Gauge: 10, 3-1/2" chambers. **Barrel:** 28", choke tubes. **Weight:** 10 lbs., 3 oz. **Length:** 45" overall. **Stock:** 14-1/4"x1-1/8"x2-3/8"; walnut. **Features:** Boxlock action with extractors; single selective trigger; non-reflective wood and metal finishes. Imported by American Arms, Inc.
Price: **$860.00**

AMERICAN ARMS GENTRY DOUBLE SHOTGUN

Gauge: 12, 20, 410, 3" chambers; 28 ga. 2-3/4" chambers. **Barrel:** 26" (Imp. Cyl. & Mod., all gauges), 28" (Mod., & Full, 12 and 20 gauges). **Weight:** 6-1/4 to 6-3/4 lbs. **Stock:** 14-1/8"x1-3/8"x2-3/8". Hand-checkered walnut with semi-gloss finish. **Sights:** Metal bead front. **Features:** Boxlock action with English-style scroll engraving, color case-hardened finish. Single trigger, extractors. Independent floating firing pins. Manual safety. Five-year warranty. Introduced 1987. Imported from Spain by American Arms, Inc.
Price: 12 or 20 . . . . **$750.00**
Price: 28 or 410 . . . . **$795.00**

AMERICAN ARMS BRITTANY SHOTGUN

Gauge: 12, 20, 3" chambers. **Barrel:** 12 ga.—27"; 20 ga.—25" (Imp. Cyl., Mod., Full choke tubes). **Weight:** 6 lbs., 7 oz. (20 ga.). **Stock:** 14-1/8"x1-3/8"x2-3/8". Hand-checkered walnut with oil finish, straight English-style with semi-beavertail forend. **Features:** Boxlock action with case-color finish, engraving; single selective trigger, automatic selective ejectors; rubber recoil pad. Introduced 1989. Imported from Spain by American Arms, Inc.
Price: **$885.00**

ARRIETA SIDELOCK DOUBLE SHOTGUNS

Gauge: 12, 16, 20, 28, 410. **Barrel:** Length and chokes to customer specs. **Weight:** To customer specs. **Stock:** 14-1/2"x1-1/2"x2-1/2 (standard dimensions), or to customer specs. Straight English with checkered butt (standard), or pistol grip. Select European walnut with oil finish. **Features:** Essentially a custom gun with myriad options. Holland & Holland-pattern hand-detachable sidelocks, selective automatic ejectors, double triggers (hinged front) standard. Some have self-opening action. Finish and engraving to customer specs. Imported from Spain by Wingshooting Adventures.
Price: Model 557, auto ejectors, from. **$2,750.00**
Price: Model 570, auto ejectors, from. **$3,380.00**
Price: Model 578, auto ejectors, from. **$3,740.00**
Price: Model 600 Imperial, self-opening, from **$4,990.00**
Price: Model 601 Imperial Tiro, self-opening, from. **$5,750.00**
Price: Model 801, from **$7,950.00**
Price: Model 802, from **$7,950.00**
Price: Model 803, from **$5,850.00**
Price: Model 871, auto ejectors, from. **$4,290.00**
Price: Model 872, self-opening, from **$9,790.00**
Price: Model 873, self-opening, from **$6,850.00**

Price: Model 874, self-opening, from **$7,950.00**
Price: Model 875, self-opening, from **$12,950.00**

BERETTA MODEL 470 SILVER HAWK SHOTGUN

Gauge: 12, 20, 3" chambers. **Barrel:** 26" (Imp. Cyl. & Imp. Mod.), 28" (Mod. & Full). **Weight:** 5.9 lbs. (20 gauge). **Stock:** Select European walnut, straight English grip. **Features:** Boxlock action with single selective trigger; selector provides automatic ejection or extraction; silver-chrome action and forend iron with fine engraving; top lever highlighted with gold inlaid hawk's head. Comes with ABS case. Introduced 1997. Imported from Italy by Beretta U.S.A.
Price: 12 ga. **$3,630.00**
Price: 20 ga. **$3,755.00**

CHARLES DALY SUPERIOR HUNTER DOUBLE SHOTGUN

Gauge: 12, 20, 3" chambers, 28, 2-3/4" chambers. **Barrel:** 28" (Mod. & Full) 26" (Imp. Cyl. & Mod.). **Weight:** About 7 lbs. **Stock:** Checkered walnut pistol grip buttstock, splinter forend. **Features:** Silvered, engraved receiver; chrome-lined barrels; gold single trigger; automatic safety; extractors; gold bead front sight. Introduced 1997. Imported from Italy by K.B.I. , Inc.
Price: **$1,179.95**
Price: 28 ga., 26" **$1,094.95**

Charles Daly Empire Hunter Double Shotgun

Similar to the Superior Hunter except has deluxe wood, game scene engraving, automatic ejectors. Introduced 1997. Imported from Italy by K.B.I., Inc.
Price: 12 or 20 . . . . **$1,595.95**

CHARLES DALY DIAMOND REGENT DL DOUBLE SHOTGUN

Gauge: 12, 20, 410, 3" chambers, 28, 2-3/4" chambers. **Barrel:** 28" (Mod. & Full), 26" (Imp. Cyl. & Mod.), 26" (Full & Full, 410). **Weight:** About 5-7 lbs. **Stock:** Special select fancy European walnut, English-style butt, splinter forend; hand-checkered; hand-rubbed oil finish. **Features:** Drop-forged action with gas escape valves; demiblock barrels of chrome-nickel steel with concave rib; selective automatic-ejectors; hand-detachable, double-safety H&H sidelocks with demi-relief hand engraving; H&H pattern easy-opening feature; hinged trigger; coin finished action. Introduced 1997. Imported from Spain by K.B.I., Inc.
Price: 12 or 20 . . . . **$19,999.00**
Price: 28 . . . . **$20,499.00**
Price: 410 . . . . **$20,499.00**

CHARLES DALY FIELD HUNTER DOUBLE SHOTGUN

Gauge: 10, 12, 20, 28, 410 (3" chambers; 28 has 2-3/4"). **Barrel:** 32" (Mod. & Mod.), 28, 30" (Mod. & Full), 26" (Imp. Cyl. & Mod.) 410 (Full & Full). **Weight:** 6 lbs. to 11.4 lbs. **Stock:** Checkered walnut pistol grip and forend. **Features:** Silvered, engraved receiver; gold single selective trigger in 10-, 12, and 20 ga.; double triggers in 28 and 410; automatic safety; extractors; gold bead front sight. Introduced 1997. Imported from Spain by K.B.I., Inc.

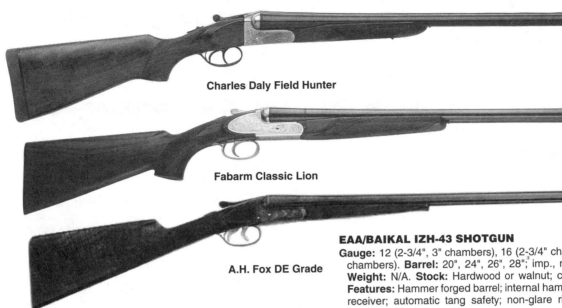

Charles Daly Field Hunter

Fabarm Classic Lion

A.H. Fox DE Grade

Price: 10 ga. **$984.95**
Price: 12 or 20 ga. **$809.95**
Price: 28 ga. **$854.95**
Price: 410-bore. **$854.95**
Price: As above, 12 or 20 AE. MC **$939.95**

CHARLES DALY DIAMOND DL DOUBLE SHOTGUN

Gauge: 12, 20, 410, 3" chambers, 28, 2-3/4" chambers. **Barrel:** 28" (Mod. & Full), 26" (Imp. Cyl. & Mod.), 26" (Full & Full, 410). **Weight:** About 5-7 lbs. **Stock:** Select fancy European walnut, English-style butt, beavertail forend; hand-checkered, hand-rubbed oil finish. **Features:** Drop-forged action with gas escape valves; demiblock barrels with concave rib; selective automatic ejectors; hand-detachable double safety sidelocks with hand-engraved rose and scrollwork. Hinged front trigger. Color case-hardened receiver. Introduced 1997. Imported from Spain by K.B.I., Inc.
Price: 12 or 20 . . . . **$6,959.95**
Price: 28 . . . . **$7,274.95**
Price: 410 . . . . **$7,274.95**

DAKOTA PREMIER GRADE SHOTGUNS

Gauge: 12, 16, 20, 28, 410. **Barrel:** 27". **Weight:** N/A. **Length:** N/A. **Stock:** Exhibition-grade English walnut, hand-rubbed oil finish with straight grip and splinter forend. **Features:** French grey finish; 50 percent coverage engraving; double triggers; selective ejectors. Finished to customer specifications. Made in U.S. by Dakota Arms.
Price: 12, 16, 20 gauge **$12,950.00**
Price: 28 and 410 gauge. **$14,245.00**

Dakota The Dakota Legend Shotguns

Similar to Premier Grade except has special selection English walnut, full-coverage scroll engraving, oak and leather case. Made in U.S. by Dakota Arms.
Price: 12, 16, 20 gauge **$18,000.00**
Price: 28 and 410 gauge 19,800.00

EAA/BAIKAL BOUNTY HUNTER IZH-43K SHOTGUN

Gauge: 12 (2-3/4", 3" chambers), 20 (3" chambers), 28 (2-3/4" chambers), 410 (3" chambers). **Barrel:** 18-1/2", 20", 24", 26", 28", three choke tubes. **Weight:** 7.28 lbs. **Overall length:** N/A. **Stock:** Walnut, checkered forearm and grip. **Features:** Machined receiver; hammer-forged barrels with chrome-line bores; external hammers; double triggers (single, selective trigger available); rifle barrel inserts optional. Imported by European American Armory.
Price: IZH-43K (12 gauge) **$439.00**
Price: IZH-43K (20, 28 and 410 gauge) **$469.00**

EAA/BAIKAL IZH-43 SHOTGUN

Gauge: 12 (2-3/4", 3" chambers), 16 (2-3/4" chambers), 20 (2-3/4" and 3" chambers). **Barrel:** 20", 24", 26", 28"; imp., mod. and full choke tubes. **Weight:** N/A. **Stock:** Hardwood or walnut; checkered forend and grip. **Features:** Hammer forged barrel; internal hammers; extractors; engraved receiver; automatic tang safety; non-glare rib. Imported by European American Armory.
Price: IZH-43 Bounty Hunter (12 gauge, 2-3/4" chambers, 20" brl., dbl. triggers) **$269.00**
Price: IZH-43 Bounty Hunter (12 or 20 gauge, 2-3/4" chambers, 20" brl., dbl. triggers) **$309.00**
Price: IZH-43 (12 gauge, single selective trigger, walnut stock) . . **$339.00**
Price: IZH-43 (16 or 20 gauge). **$399.00**
Price: IZH-43 (20/28 gauge two-barrel set) **$579.00**

EAA/BAIKAL MP-213 SHOTGUN

Gauge: 12, 3" chambers. **Barrel:** 24", 26", 28"; imp., mod. and full choke tubes. **Weight:** 7.28 lbs. **Stock:** Walnut, checkered forearm and grip; rubber butt pad. **Features:** Hammer-forged barrels; chrome-lined bores; machined receiver; double trigger (each trigger fires both barrels independently); ejectors. Introduced 2000. Imported by European American Armory.
Price: IZH-213 . . . . **$879.00**

EAA/BAIKAL BOUNTY HUNTER MP-213 COACH GUN

Gauge: 12, 3" chamber. **Barrel:** 18.5", 20", 24", 26", 28", imp., mod. and full choke tubes. **Weight:** 7 lbs. **Stock:** Walnut, checkered forend and grip. **Features:** Selective double trigger with removable assembly (single trigger and varied pull weights available); ejectors; engraved receiver. Imported by European American Armory.
Price: MP-213. . . . . **$879.00**

FABARM CLASSIC LION DOUBLE SHOTGUN

Gauge: 12, 3" chambers. **Barrel:** 26" (Cyl., Imp. Cyl., Mod., Imp. Mod., Full choke tubes). **Weight:** 7.2 lbs. **Length:** 47.6" overall. **Stock:** Oil-finished European walnut. **Features:** Boxlock action with single selective trigger, automatic ejectors, automatic safety. Introduced 1998. Imported from Italy by Heckler & Koch, Inc.
Price: Grade I **$1,488.00**
Price: Grade II (sidelock action) **$2,110.00**

A.H. FOX SIDE-BY-SIDE SHOTGUNS

Gauge: 16, 20, 28, 410. **Barrel:** Length and chokes to customer specifications. Rust-blued Chromox or Krupp steel. **Weight:** 5-1/2 to 6-3/4 lbs. **Stock:** Dimensions to customer specifications. Hand-checkered Turkish Circassian walnut with hand-rubbed oil finish. Straight, semi- or full pistol grip; splinter, Schnabel or beavertail forend; traditional pad, hard rubber buttplate or skeleton butt. **Features:** Boxlock action with automatic ejectors; double or Fox single selective trigger. Scalloped, rebated and color case-hardened receiver; hand finished and hand-engraved. Grades differ in engraving, inlays, grade of wood, amount of hand finishing. Add $1,000 for 28 or 410-bore. Introduced 1993. Made in U.S. by Connecticut Shotgun Mfg.

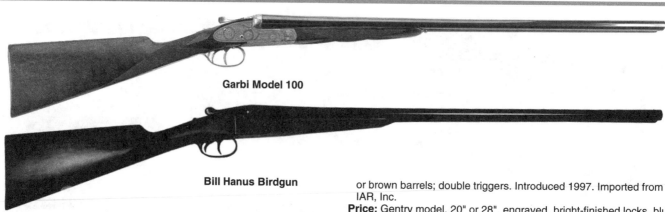

Garbi Model 100

Bill Hanus Birdgun

Price: CE Grade **$9,500.00**
Price: XE Grade **$11,000.00**
Price: DE Grade **$13,500.00**
Price: FE Grade **$18,500.00**
Price: Exhibition Grade. **$26,000.00**
Price: 28/410 CE Grade **$8,200.00**
Price: 28/410 XE Grade **$9,700.00**
Price: 28/410 DE Grade **$13,800.00**
Price: 28/410 FE Grade **$14,700.00**
Price: 28/410 Exhibition Grade. **$26,000.00**

GARBI MODEL 100 DOUBLE

Gauge: 12, 16, 20, 28. **Barrel:** 26", 28", choked to customer specs. **Weight:** 5-1/2 to 7-1/2 lbs. **Stock:** 14-1/2"x2-1/4"x1-1/2". European walnut. Straight grip, checkered butt, classic forend. **Features:** Sidelock action, automatic ejectors, double triggers standard. Color case-hardened action, coin finish optional. Single trigger; beavertail forend, etc. optional. Five other models are available. Imported from Spain by Wm. Larkin Moore.
Price: From. **$4,600.00**

Garbi Model 200 Side-by-Side

Similar to the Garbi Model 100 except has heavy-duty locks, magnum proofed. Very fine Continental-style floral and scroll engraving, well figured walnut stock. Other mechanical features remain the same. Imported from Spain by Wm. Larkin Moore.
Price: **$10,000.00**

Garbi Model 101 Side-by-Side

Similar to the Garbi Model 100 except is hand engraved with scroll engraving, select walnut stock. Better overall quality than the Model 100. Imported from Spain by Wm. Larkin Moore.
Price: From. **$5,950.00**

Garbi Model 103A, B Side-by-Side

Similar to the Garbi Model 100 except has Purdey-type fine scroll and rosette engraving. Better overall quality than the Model 101. Model 103B has nickel-chrome steel barrels, H&H-type easy opening mechanism; other mechanical details remain the same. Imported from Spain by Wm. Larkin Moore.
Price: Model 103A, from. **$7,400.00**
Price: Model 103B, from. **$10,400.00**

BILL HANUS BIRDGUN

Gauge: 16, 20, 28. **Barrel:** 27", 20 and 28 ga.; 28", 16 ga. (Skeet 1 & Skeet 2). **Weight:** 5 lbs., 4 oz. to 6 lbs., 4 oz. **Stock:** 14-3/8"x1-1/2"x2-3/8", with 1/4" cast-off. Select walnut. **Features:** Boxlock action with ejectors; splinter forend, straight English grip; checkered butt; English leather-covered handguard included. Made by AYA. Introduced 1998. Imported from Spain by Bill Hanus Birdguns.
Price: **$1,895.00**

IAR COWBOY SHOTGUNS

Gauge: 12. **Barrel:** 20", 28". **Weight:** 7 lbs. (20" barrel). **Length:** 36-7/8" overall (20" barrel). **Stock:** Walnut. **Features:** Exposed hammers; blued or brown barrels; double triggers. Introduced 1997. Imported from Italy by IAR, Inc.
Price: Gentry model, 20" or 28", engraved, bright-finished locks, blue barrels **$1,895.00**
Price: Cowboy model, 20" or 28", no engraving on color case-hardened locks, brown patina barrels. **$1,895.00**

ITHACA CLASSIC DOUBLES SPECIAL FIELD GRADE SxS

Gauge: 20, 28, 2-3/4" chambers, 410, 3". **Barrel:** 26", 28", 30", fixed chokes. **Weight:** 5 lbs., 14 oz. (20 gauge). **Stock:** 14-1/2"x2-1/4"x1-3/8". High-grade American black walnut, hand-rubbed oil finish; splinter or beavertail forend, straight or pistol grip. **Features:** Double triggers, ejectors; color case-hardened, engraved action body with matted top surfaces. Introduced 1999. Made in U.S. by Ithaca Clasic Doubles.
Price: From **$3,150.00**

Ithaca Classic Doubles Grade 4E SxS Shotgun

Similar to the Special Field Grade except has gold-plated triggers, jeweled barrel flats and hand-turned locks. Feather crotch and flame-grained black walnut is hand-checkered 28 lpi with fleur de lis pattern. Action body is engraved with three game scenes and bank note scroll, and color case-hardened. Introduced 1999. Made in U.S. by Ithaca Classic Doubles.
Price: From **$4,199.00**

Ithaca Classic Doubles Grade 7E SxS Shotgun

Similar to the Special Field Grade except engraved with bank note scroll and flat 24k gold game scenes: gold setter and gold pointer on opposite action sides, and an American bald eagle is inlaid on the bottom plate. Hand-timed, polished, jeweled ejectors and locks. Exhibition grade American black walnut stock and forend with eight-panel fleur de lis borders. Introduced 1999. Made in U.S. by Itaca Classic Doubles.
Price: From. **$8,399.00**

LEBEAU - COURALLY BOXLOCK SxS SHOTGUN

Gauge: 12, 16, 20, 28, 410-bore. **Barrel:** 25" to 32". **Weight:** To customer specifications. **Stock:** French walnut. **Features:** Anson & Deely-type action with automatic ejectors; single or double triggers. Essentially a custom gun built to customer specifications. Imported from Belgium by Wm. Larkin Moore.
Price: From. **$23,000.00**

LEBEAU - COURALLY SIDELOCK SxS SHOTGUN

Gauge: 12, 16, 20, 28, 410-bore. **Barrel:** 25" to 32". **Weight:** To customer specifications. **Stock:** Fancy French walnut. **Features:** Holland & Holland-type action with automatic ejectors; single or double triggers. Essentially a custom gun built to customer specifications. Imported from Belgium by Wm. Larkin Moore.
Price: From. **$47,000.00**

MERKEL MODEL 47E, 147E SIDE-BY-SIDE SHOTGUNS

Gauge: 12, 3" chambers, 16, 2-3/4" chambers, 20, 3" chambers. **Barrel:** 12, 16 ga.—28"; 20 ga.—26-3/4" (Imp. Cyl. & Mod., Mod. & Full). **Weight:** About 6-3/4 lbs. (12 ga.). **Stock:** Oil-finished walnut; straight English or pistol grip. **Features:** Anson & Deeley-type boxlock action with single selective or double triggers, automatic safety, cocking indicators. Color case-hardened receiver with standard Arabesque engraving. Imported from Germany by GSI.
Price: Model 47E (H&H ejectors) **$2,795.00**
Price: Model 147E (as above with ejectors). **$3,395.00**

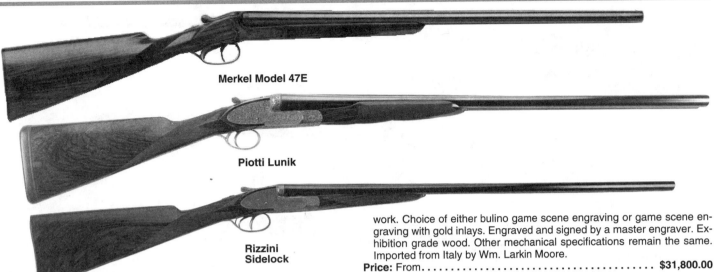

Merkel Model 47E

Piotti Lunik

Rizzini Sidelock

Merkel Model 47SL, 147SL Side-by-Sides

Similar to the Model 122 except with Holland & Holland-style sidelock action with cocking indicators, ejectors. Silver-grayed receiver and sideplates have Arabesque engraving, engraved border and screws (Model 47S), or fine hunting scene engraving (Model 147S). Imported from Germany by GSI.

Price: Model 47SL **$5,395.00**
Price: Model 147SL **$6,995.00**
Price: Model 247SL (English-style engraving, large scrolls) . . . **$6,995.00**
Price: Model 447SL (English-style engraving, small scrolls) . . . **$8,995.00**

Merkel Model 280EL and 360EL Shotguns

Similar to Model 47E except has smaller frame. Greener cross bolt with double under-barrel locking lugs, fine engraved hunting scenes on silver-grayed receiver, luxury-grade wood, Anson and Deely box-lock action. Holland & Holland ejectors, single-selective or double triggers. Introduced 2000. From Merkel.

Price: Model 280EL (28 gauge, 28" barrel, imp. cyl. and
mod. chokes) 4 mod. chokes).. . . . . **$4,995.00**
Price: Model 360EL (410 gauge, 28" barrel, mod. and
full chokes). **$4,995.00**
Price: Model 280/360EL two-barrel set (28 and 410 gauge
as above) **$7,495.00**

Merkel Model 280SL and 360SL Shotguns

Similar to Model 280EL and 360EL except has sidelock action, double triggers, English-style Arabesque engraving. Introduced 2000. From Merkel.

Price: Model 280SL (28 gauge, 28" barrel, imp. cyl. and
mod. chokes) **$7,495.00**
Price: Model 360SL (410 gauge, 28" barrel, mod. and
full chokes) **$7,495.00**
Price: Model 280/360SL two-barrel set **$10,995.00**

PIOTTI KING NO. 1 SIDE-BY-SIDE

Gauge: 12, 16, 20, 28, 410. **Barrel:** 25" to 30" (12 ga.), 25" to 28" (16, 20, 28, 410). To customer specs. Chokes as specified. **Weight:** 6-1/2 lbs. to 8 lbs. (12 ga. to customer specs.). **Stock:** Dimensions to customer specs. Finely figured walnut; straight grip with checkered butt with classic splinter forend and hand-rubbed oil finish standard. Pistol grip, beavertail forend, satin luster finish optional. **Features:** Holland & Holland pattern sidelock action, automatic ejectors. Double trigger with front trigger hinged standard; non-selective single trigger optional. Coin finish standard; color case-hardened optional. Top rib; level, file-cut standard; concave, ventilated optional. Very fine, full coverage scroll engraving with small floral bouquets, gold crown in top lever, name in gold, and gold crest in forend. Imported from Italy by Wm. Larkin Moore.

Price: From. **$25,600.00**

Piotti King Extra Side-by-Side

Similar to the Piotti King No. 1 except highest quality wood and metal work. Choice of either bulino game scene engraving or game scene engraving with gold inlays. Engraved and signed by a master engraver. Exhibition grade wood. Other mechanical specifications remain the same. Imported from Italy by Wm. Larkin Moore.

Price: From **$31,800.00**

Piotti Lunik Side-by-Side

Similar to the Piotti King No. 1 in overall quality. Has Renaissance-style large scroll engraving in relief, gold crown in top lever. Best quality Holland & Holland-pattern sidelock ejector double with chopper lump (demi-bloc) barrels. Other mechanical specifications remain the same. Imported from Italy by Wm. Larkin Moore.

Price: From. **$27,500.00**

PIOTTI PIUMA SIDE-BY-SIDE

Gauge: 12, 16, 20, 28, 410. **Barrel:** 25" to 30" (12 ga.), 25" to 28" (16, 20, 28, 410). **Weight:** 5-1/2 to 6-1/4 lbs. (20 ga.). **Stock:** Dimensions to customer specs. Straight grip stock with walnut checkered butt, classic splinter forend, hand-rubbed oil finish are standard; pistol grip, beavertail forend, satin luster finish optional. **Features:** Anson & Deeley boxlock ejector double with chopper lump barrels. Level, file-cut rib, light scroll and rosette engraving, scalloped frame. Double triggers with hinged front standard, single non-selective optional. Coin finish standard, color case-hardened optional. Imported from Italy by Wm. Larkin Moore.

Price: From. **$13,400.00**

RIZZINI SIDELOCK SIDE-BY-SIDE

Gauge: 12, 16, 20, 28, 410. **Barrel:** 25" to 30" (12, 16, 20 ga.), 25" to 28" (28, 410). To customer specs. Chokes as specified. **Weight:** 6-1/2 lbs. to 8 lbs. (12 ga. to customer specs.). **Stock:** Dimensions to customer specs. Finely figured walnut; straight grip with checkered butt with classic splinter forend and hand-rubbed oil finish standard. Pistol grip, beavertail forend, satin luster finish optional. **Features:** Holland & Holland pattern sidelock action, auto ejectors. Double triggers with front trigger hinged optional; non-selective single trigger standard. Coin finish standard. Top rib level, file cut standard; concave optional. Imported from Italy by Wm. Larkin Moore.

Price: 12, 20 ga., from **$45,000.00**
Price: 28, 410 bore, from **$50,000.00**

SKB Model 385 Sporting Clays

Similar to the Field Model 385 except 12 gauge only; 28" barrel with choke tubes; raised ventilated rib with metal middle bead and white front. Stock dimensions 14-1/4"x1-7/16"x1-7/8". Introduced 1998. Imported from Japan by G.U. Inc.

Price: **$1,899.00**
Price: Sporting Clays set, 20, 28 ga. **$2,699.00**

SKB MODEL 385 SIDE-BY-SIDE

Gauge: 12, 20, 3" chambers; 28, 2-3/4" chambers. **Barrel:** 26" (Imp. Cyl., Mod., Skeet choke tubes). **Weight:** 6-3/4 lbs. **Length:** 42-1/2" overall. **Stock:** 14-1/8"x1-1/2"x2-1/2" American walnut with straight or pistol grip stock, semi-beavertail forend. **Features:** Boxlock action. Silver nitrided receiver with engraving; solid barrel rib; single selective trigger, selective automatic ejectors, automatic safety. Introduced 1996. Imported from Japan by G.U. Inc.

Price: **$1,799.00**
Price: Field Set, 20, 28 ga., 26" or 28", English or pistol grip. . . **$2,579.00**

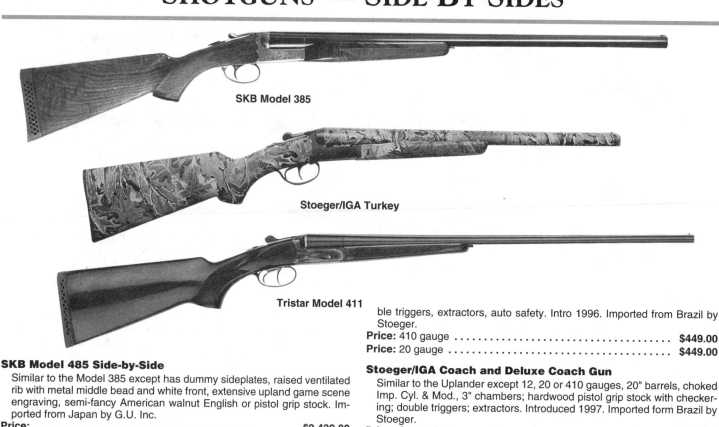

SKB Model 385

Stoeger/IGA Turkey

Tristar Model 411

SKB Model 485 Side-by-Side

Similar to the Model 385 except has dummy sideplates, raised ventilated rib with metal middle bead and white front, extensive upland game scene engraving, semi-fancy American walnut English or pistol grip stock. Imported from Japan by G.U. Inc.

Price: **$2,439.00**
Price: Field set, 20, 28 ga., 26" **$3,479.00**

STOEGER/IGA UPLANDER SIDE-BY-SIDE SHOTGUN

Gauge: 12, 20, 28, 2-3/4" chambers; 410, 3" chambers. **Barrel:** 26" (Full & Full, 410 only, Imp. Cyl. & Mod.), 28" (Mod. & Full). **Weight:** 6-3/4 to 7 lbs. **Stock:** 14-1/2"x1-1/2"x2-1/2". Oil-finished hardwood. Checkered pistol grip and forend. **Features:** Automatic safety, extractors only, solid matted barrel rib. Double triggers only. Introduced 1983. Imported from Brazil by Stoeger Industries.

Price: **$437.00**
Price: With choke tubes **$477.00**
Price: Coach Gun, 12, 20, 410, 20" bbls. **$415.00**
Price: Coach Gun, nickel finish, black stock. **$464.00**
Price: Coach Gun, engraved stock. **$479.00**

Stoeger/IGA Ladies Side-by-Side

Similar to the Uplander except in 20 ga. only with 24" barrels (Imp. Cyl. & Mod. choke tubes), 13" length of pull, ventilated rubber recoil pad. Has extractors, double triggers, automatic safety. Introduced 1996. Imported from Brazil by Stoeger.

Price: **$489.00**

Stoeger/IGA Turkey Side-by-Side

Similar to the Uplander Model except has Advantage camouflage on stock, forend and barrels; 12 gauge only with 3" chambers, and has 24" choke tube barrels. Overall length 40". Introduced 1997. Imported from Brazil by Stoeger.

Price: **$559.00**

Stoeger/IGA English Stock Side-by-Side

Similar to the Uplander except in 410 or 20 ga. only with 24" barrels, straight English stock and beavertail forend. Has automatic safety, extractors, double triggers. Intro 1996. Imported from Brazil by Stoeger.

Price: 410 ga (mod. and mod. chokes). **$437.00**
Price: 20 ga (imp. cyl and mod. choke tubes) **$477.00**

Stoeger/IGA Youth Side-by-Side

Similar to the Uplander except in 410-bore with 24" barrels (Mod.), or 20 ga. (imp. cyl. and mod.), 13" length of pull, ventilated recoil pad. Has dou-

ble triggers, extractors, auto safety. Intro 1996. Imported from Brazil by Stoeger.

Price: 410 gauge **$449.00**
Price: 20 gauge **$449.00**

Stoeger/IGA Coach and Deluxe Coach Gun

Similar to the Uplander except 12, 20 or 410 gauges, 20" barrels, choked Imp. Cyl. & Mod., 3" chambers; hardwood pistol grip stock with checkering; double triggers; extractors. Introduced 1997. Imported form Brazil by Stoeger.

Price: Coach Gun. **$415.00**
Price: Deluxe Coach Gun (engraved stagecoach on stock). . . . **$415.00**

Stoeger/IGA Uplander Shotgun

Gauge: 12, 20, 410 (3" chambers); 28 (2-3/4" chambers). **Barrel:** 24", 26", 28". **Weight:** 6-3/4 lbs. **Length:** 40" to 44" overall. **Stock:** Brazilian hardwood; checkered grip and forearm. **Feautures:** Automatic safety; extractors; handles steel shot. Introduced 1997. Imported from Brazil by Stoeger.

Price: With chokes tubes **$477.00**

Stoeger/IGA Deluxe Uplander Supreme Shotgun

Similar to the Uplander except with semi-fancy American walnut with thin black Pachmayr rubber recoil pad, matte lacquer finish. Choke tubes and 3" chambers standard 12 and 20 gauge; 28 gauge has 26", 3" chokes, fixed Mod. & Full. Double gold plated triggers; extractors. Introduced 1997. Imported from Brazil by Stoeger.

Price: 12, 20 . . . . **$599.00**

TRISTAR MODEL 411 SIDE-BY-SIDE

Gauge: 12, 16, 20, 410, 3" chambers; 28, 2-3/4". **Barrel:** 12 ga., 26", 28"; 16, 20, 28 ga., 410-bore, 26"; 12 and 20 ga. have three choke tubes, 16, 28 (Imp. Cyl. & Mod.), 410 (Mod. & Full) fixed chokes. **Weight:** 6-6-3/4 lbs. **Stock:** 14-3/8" l.o.p. Standard walnut with pistol grip, splinter-style forend; hand checkered. **Features:** Engraved, color case-hardened boxlock action; double triggers, extractors; solid barrel rib. Introduced 1998. Imported from Italy by Tristar Sporting Arms, Ltd.

Price: **$808.00**

Tristar Model 411D Side-by-Side

Similar to the model 411 except has automatic ejectors, straight English-style stock, single trigger. Solid barrel rib with matted surface; chrome bores; color case-hardened frame; splinter forend. Introduced 1999. Imported from Italy by Tristar Sporting Arms, Ltd.

Price: **$1,057.00**

Tristar Model 411R Coach Gun Side-by-Side

Similar to the Model 411 except in 12 or 20 gauge only with 20" barrels and fixed chokes (Cyl. & Cyl.). Has double triggers, extractors, choke tubes. Introduced 1999. Imported from Italy by Tristar Sporting Arms, Ltd.

Price: **$705.00**

Variety of designs for utility and sporting purposes, as well as for competitive shooting.

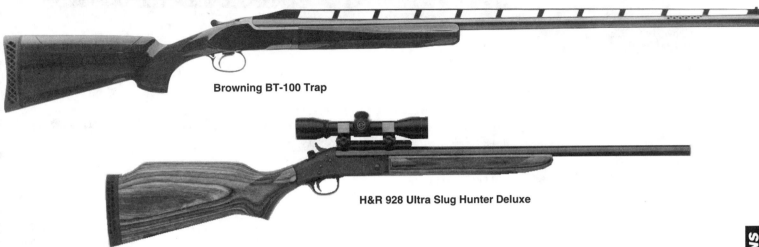

Browning BT-100 Trap

H&R 928 Ultra Slug Hunter Deluxe

BERETTA DT 10 TRIDENT TRAP TOP SINGLE SHOTGUN
Gauge: 12, 3" chamber. **Barrel:** 34"; five Optima Choke tubes (full, full, imp. modified, mod. and imp. cyl.). **Weight:** 8.8 lbs. **Length:** N/A. **Stock:** High-grade walnut; adjustable. **Features:** Detachable, adjustable trigger group; Optima Bore for improved shot pattern and reduced recoil; slim Optima Choke tubes; raised and thickened receiver for long life. Introduced 2000. Imported from Italy by Beretta USA.
Price: **$9,450.00**

BRNO ZBK 100 SINGLE BARREL SHOTGUN
Gauge: 12 or 20. **Barrel:** 27.5". **Weight:** 5.5 lbs. **Length:** 44" overall. **Stock:** Beech. **Features:** Polished blue finish; sling swivels. Announced 1998. Imported from The Czech Republic by Euro-Imports.
Price: **$185.00**

BROWNING BT-100 TRAP SHOTGUN
Gauge: 12, 2-3/4" chamber. **Barrel:** 32", 34" (Invector Plus); back-bored; also with fixed Full choke. **Weight:** 8 lbs., 9 oz. **Length:** 48-1/2" overall (32" barrel). **Stock:** 14-3/8"x1-9/16"x1-7/16x2" (Monte Carlo); 14-3/8"x1-3/4"x1-1/4"x2-1/8" (thumbhole). Walnut with high gloss finish; cut checkering. Wedge-shaped forend with finger groove. **Features:** Available in stainless steel or blue. Has drop-out trigger adjustable for weight of pull from 3-1/2 to 5-1/2 lbs., and for three length positions; Ejector-Selector allows ejection or extraction of shells. Available with adjustable comb stock and thumbhole style. Introduced 1995. Imported from Japan by Browning.
Price: Grade I, blue, Monte Carlo, Invector Plus **$2,095.00**
Price: As above, fixed Full choke **$2,046.00**
Price: With low-luster wood **$1,667.00**
Price: Stainless steel, Monte Carlo, Invector Plus **$2,536.00**
Price: As above, fixed Full choke **$2,487.00**
Price: Thumbhole stock, blue, Invector Plus **$2,384.00**
Price: Thumbhole stock, stainless, Invector Plus **$2,825.00**
Price: Thumbhole stock, blue, fixed choke **$2,337.00**
Price: Thumbhole stock, stainless, fixed choke **$2,778.00**
Price: BT-100 Satin (no ejector-selector, satin finish wood, metal) **$1,667.00**

EAA/BAIKAL IZH-18 SINGLE BARREL SHOTGUN
Gauge: 12 (2-3/4" and 3" chambers), 20 (2-3/4" and 3"), 16 (2-3/4"), 410 (3"). **Barrel:** 26-1/2", 28-1/2"; modified or full choke (12 and 20 gauge); full only (16 gauge), improved cylinder (20 gauge) and full or improved modified (410). **Weight:** N/A. **Stock:** Walnut-stained hardwood; rubber recoil pad. **Features:** Hammer-forged steel barrel; machined receiver; cross-block safety; cocking lever with external cocking indicator; optional automatic ejector; screw-in chokes and rifle barrel. Imported by European American Armory.
Price: IZH-18 (12, 16, 20 or 410) **$95.00**
Price: IZH-18 (20 gauge with imp. cyl. or 410 with imp. mod.) **$109.00**

HARRINGTON & RICHARDSON SB2-980 ULTRA SLUG
Gauge: 12, 20, 3" chamber. **Barrel:** 22" (20 ga. Youth) 24", fully rifled. **Weight:** 9 lbs. **Length:** NA. **Stock:** Walnut-stained hardwood. **Sights:** None furnished; comes with scope mount. **Features:** Uses the H&R 10 gauge action with heavy-wall barrel. Monte Carlo stock has sling swivels; comes with black nylon sling. Introduced 1995. Made in U.S. by H&R 1871, Inc.
Price: **$209.95**

Harrington & Richardson Model 928 Ultra Slug Hunter Deluxe
Similar to the SB2-980 Ultra Slug except uses 12 gauge action and 12 gauge barrel blank bored to 20 gauge, then fully rifled with 1:35" twist. Has hand-checkered camo laminate Monte Carlo stock and forend. Comes with Weaver-style scope base, offset hammer extension, ventilated recoil pad, sling swivels and camo nylon sling. Introduced 1997. Made in U.S. by H&R 1871 Inc.
Price: **$239.95**

HARRINGTON & RICHARDSON TAMER SHOTGUN
Gauge: 410, 3" chamber. **Barrel:** 19-1/2" (Full). **Weight:** 5-6 lbs. **Length:** 33" overall. **Stock:** Thumbhole grip of high density black polymer. **Features:** Uses H&R Topper action with matte electroless nickel finish. Stock holds four spare shotshells. Introduced 1994. From H&R 1871, Inc.
Price: **$124.95**

HARRINGTON & RICHARDSON TOPPER MODEL 098
Gauge: 12, 16, 20, 28 (2-3/4"), 410, 3" chamber. **Barrel:** 12 ga.—28" (Mod., Full); 16 ga.— 28" (Mod.); 20 ga.—26" (Mod.); 28 ga.—26" (Mod.); 410 bore—26" (Full). **Weight:** 5-6 lbs. **Stock:** Black-finish hardwood with full pistol grip; semi-beavertail forend. **Sights:** Gold bead front. **Features:** Break-open action with side-lever release, automatic ejector. Satin nickel frame, blued barrel. Reintroduced 1992. From H&R 1871, Inc.
Price: **$114.95**
Price: Topper Junior 098 (as above except 22" barrel, 20 ga. (Mod.), 410-bore (Full), 12-1/2" length of pull) **$119.95**

Harrington & Richardson Topper Deluxe Model 098
Similar to the standard Topper 098 except 12 gauge only with 3-1/2" chamber, 28" barrel with choke tube (comes with Mod. tube, others optional). Satin nickel frame, blued barrel, black-finished wood. Introduced 1992. From H&R 1871, Inc.
Price: **$134.95**

Harrington & Richardson Topper Junior Classic Shotgun
Similar to the Topper Junior 098 except available in 20 gauge (3", Mod.), 410-bore (Full) with 3" chamber; 28 gauge, 2-3/4" chamber (Mod.); all have 22" barrel. Stock is American black walnut with cut-checkered pistol grip and forend. Ventilated rubber recoil pad with white line spacers. Blued barrel, blued frame. Introduced 1992. From H&R 1871, Inc.
Price: **$144.95**

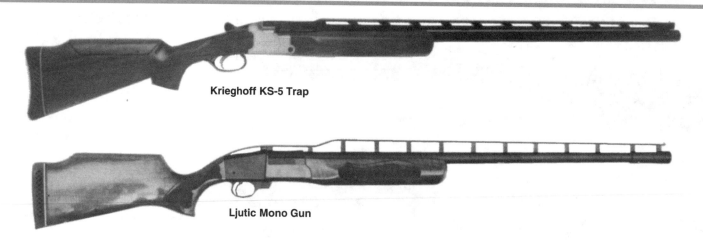

Krieghoff KS-5 Trap

Ljutic Mono Gun

Harrington & Richardson Topper Deluxe Rifled Slug Gun
Similar to the 12 gauge Topper Model 098 except has fully rifled and ported barrel, ramp front sight and fully adjustable rear. Barrel twist is 1:35". Nickel-plated frame, blued barrel, black-finished stock and forend. Introduced 1995. Made in U.S. by H&R 1871, Inc.
Price: **$169.95**

KRIEGHOFF K-80 SINGLE BARREL TRAP GUN
Gauge: 12, 2-3/4" chamber. **Barrel:** 32" or 34" Unsingle; 34" Top Single. Fixed Full or choke tubes. **Weight:** About 8-3/4 lbs. **Stock:** Four stock dimensions or adjustable stock available. All hand-checkered European walnut. **Features:** Satin nickel finish with K-80 logo. Selective mechanical trigger adjustable for finger position. Tapered step vent. rib. Adjustable point of impact on Unsingle.
Price: Standard grade full Unsingle, from.................. **$7,950.00**
Price: Standard grade full Top Single combo (special order), from **$9,975.00**
Price: RT (removable trigger) option, add **$1,000.00**

KRIEGHOFF KS-5 TRAP GUN
Gauge: 12, 2-3/4" chamber. **Barrel:** 32", 34"; Full choke or choke tubes. **Weight:** About 8-1/2 lbs. **Stock:** Choice of high Monte Carlo (1-1/2"), low Monte Carlo (1-3/8") or factory adjustable stock. European walnut. **Features:** Ventilated tapered step rib. Adjustable trigger or optional release trigger. Satin gray electroless nickel receiver. Comes with fitted aluminum case. Introduced 1988. Imported from Germany by Krieghoff International, Inc.
Price: Fixed choke, cased **$3,695.00**
Price: With choke tubes **$4,120.00**

Krieghoff KS-5 Special
Same as the KS-5 except the barrel has a fully adjustable rib and adjustable stock. Rib allows shooter to adjust point of impact from 50%/50% to nearly 90%/10%. Introduced 1990.
Price: **$4,695.00**

LJUTIC MONO GUN SINGLE BARREL
Gauge: 12 only. **Barrel:** 34", choked to customer specs; hollow-milled rib, 35-1/2" sight plane. **Weight:** Approx. 9 lbs. **Stock:** To customer specs. Oil finish, hand checkered. **Features:** Totally custom made. Pull or release trigger; removable trigger guard contains trigger and hammer mechanism; Ljutic pushbutton opener on front of trigger guard. From Ljutic Industries.
Price: With standard, medium or Olympic rib, custom 32"-34" bbls., and fixed choke. **$5,795.00**
Price: As above with screw-in choke barrel **$6,095.00**
Price: Stainless steel mono gun........................ **$6,795.00**

Ljutic LTX PRO 3 Deluxe Mono Gun
Deluxe light weight version of the Mono Gun with high quality wood, upgrade checkering, special rib height, screw in chokes, ported and cased.

Price: **$8,995.00**
Price: Stainless steel model **$9,995.00**

MARLIN MODEL 55GDL GOOSE GUN BOLT-ACTION SHOTGUN
Gauge: 12 only, 2-3/4" or 3" chamber. **Action:** Bolt action, thumb safety, detachable two-shot clip. Red cocking indicator. **Barrel:** 36" (Full) with burnished bore for lead or steel shot. **Weight:** 8 lbs. **Length:** 56-3/4" overall. **Stock:** Black fiberglass-filled synthetic with moulded-in checkering and swivel studs; ventilated recoil pad. **Sights:** Brass bead front, U-groove rear. **Features:** Brushed blue finish; thumb safety; red cocking indicator; 2-shot detachable box magazine. Introduced 1997. Made in U.S. by Marlin Firearms Co.
Price: **$396.00**

MARLIN MODEL 25MG GARDEN GUN SHOTGUN
Gauge: 22 WMR shotshell, 7-shot magazine. **Barrel:** 22" smoothbore. **Weight:** 6 lbs. **Length:** 41" overall. **Stock:** Press-checkered hardwood. **Sights:** High-visibility bead front. **Features:** Bolt action; thumb safety; red cocking indicator. Introduced 1999. Made in U.S. by Marlin.
Price: **$231.00**

MARLIN MODEL 512P SLUGMASTER SHOTGUN
Gauge: 12, 3" chamber; 2-shot detachable box magazine. **Barrel:** 21", rifled (1:28" twist). **Weight:** 8 lbs. **Length:** 41-3/4" overall. **Stock:** Black fiberglass-filled synthetic stock with moulded-in checkering, swivel studs; ventilated recoil pad; padded black nylon sling. **Sights:** Ramp front with brass bead and removable Wide-Scan hood and fiber-optic inserts, adjustable fiber-optic rear. Drilled and tapped for scope mounting. **Features:** Uses Model 55 action with thumb safety. Designed for shooting saboted slugs. Comes with special Weaver scope mount. Introduced 1997. Made in U.S. by Marlin Firearms Co.
Price: **$377.00**

Marlin Model 512P Slugmaster Shotgun
Similar to the Model 512 except has black fiberglass-filled synthetic stock with moulded-in checkering, swivel studs; ventilated recoil pad; padded black nylon sling. Has 21" fully rifled and ported barrel with 1:28" rifling twist. Introduced 1997. Made in U.S. by Marlin Firearms Co.
Price: **$377.00**

MOSSBERG MODEL 695 SLUGSTER
Gauge: 12, 3" chamber. **Barrel:** 22"; fully rifled, ported. **Weight:** 7-1/2 lbs. **Stock:** Black synthetic, with swivel studs and rubber recoil pad. **Sights:** Blade front, folding rifle-style leaf rear; Fiber Optic. Comes with Weaver-style scope bases. **Features:** Matte metal finish; rotating thumb safety; detachable 2-shot magazine. Mossberg Cablelock. Made in U.S. by Mossberg. Introduced 1996.
Price: **$345.00**
Price: With Fiber Optic rifle sights **$367.00**
Price: Scope Combo Model includes Protecto case and Bushnell 1.5-4.5x scope .... **NA**
Price: With woodlands camo stock, Fiber Optic sights.......... **$397.00**

Mossberg 695

New England Firearms Camo Turkey

Ruger KTS-1234-BRE

MOSSBERG SSi-ONE 12 GAUGE SLUG SHOTGUN

Gauge: 12, 3" chamber. **Barrel:** 24", fully rifled. **Weight:** 8 pounds. **Length:** 40" overall. **Stock:** Walnut, fluted and cut checkered; sling-swivel studs; drilled and tapped for scope base. **Sights:** None (scope base supplied). **Features:** Frame accepts interchangeable rifle barrels (see Mossberg SSi-One rifle listing); lever-opening, break-action design; ambidextrous, top-tang safety; internal eject/extract selector. Introduced 2000. From Mossberg.

Price: **$400.00**

NEW ENGLAND FIREARMS CAMO TURKEY SHOTGUN

Gauge: 10, 3 1/2 "chamber. **Barrel:** 24"; extra-full, screw-in choke tube. **Weight:** N/A. **Stock:** American hardwood, green and black camouflage finish with sling swivels and ventilated recoil pad. **Sights:** Bead front. **Features:** Matte metal finish; stock counterweight to reduce recoil; patented transfer bar system for hammer-down safety; includes camo sling and trigger lock. Accepts other factory-fitted barrels. Introduced 2000. From New England Firearms.

Price: **$205.95**

NEW ENGLAND FIREARMS TRACKER SLUG GUN

Gauge: 12, 20, 3" chamber. **Barrel:** 24" (Cyl.). **Weight:** 5-1/4 lbs. **Length:** 40" overall. **Stock:** Walnut-finished hardwood with full pistol grip, recoil pad. **Sights:** Blade front, fully adjustable rifle-type rear. **Features:** Break-open action with side-lever release; blued barrel, color case-hardened frame. Introduced 1992. From New England Firearms.

Price: Tracker... **$129.95**
Price: Tracker II (as above except fully rifled bore) **$139.95**

NEW ENGLAND FIREARMS SPECIAL PURPOSE SHOTGUNS

Gauge: 10, 3-1/2" chamber. **Barrel:** 28" (Full), 32" (Mod.). **Weight:** 9.5 lbs. **Length:** 44" overall (28" barrel). **Stock:** American hardwood with walnut or matte camo finish; ventilated rubber recoil pad. **Sights:** Bead front. **Features:** Break-open action with side-lever release; ejector. Matte finish on metal. Introduced 1992. From New England Firearms.

Price: Walnut-finish wood sling and swivels................. **$149.95**
Price: Camo finish, sling and swivels **$159.95**
Price: Camo finish, 32", sling and swivels **$179.95**
Price: Black matte finish, 24", Turkey Full choke tube, sling and swivels
.... **$184.95**

NEW ENGLAND FIREARMS SURVIVOR

Gauge: 12, 20, 410/45 Colt, 3" chamber. **Barrel:** 22" (Mod.); 20" (410/45 Colt, rifled barrel, choke tube). **Weight:** 6 lbs. **Length:** 36 overall. **Stock:** Black polymer with thumbhole/pistol grip, sling swivels; beavertail forend. **Sights:** Bead front. **Features:** Buttplate removes to expose storage for extra ammunition; forend also holds extra ammunition. Black or nickel finish. Introduced 1993. From New England Firearms.

Price: Black **$129.95**
Price: Nickel.. **$145.95**
Price: 410/45 Colt, black **$145.95**
Price: 410/45 Colt, nickel **$164.95**

NEW ENGLAND FIREARMS STANDARD PARDNER

Gauge: 12, 20, 410, 3" chamber; 16, 28, 2-3/4" chamber. **Barrel:** 12 ga.— 28" (Full, Mod.), 32" (Full); 16 ga.—28" (Full), 32" (Full); 20 ga.—26" (Full, Mod.); 28 ga.—26" (Mod.); 410-bore—26" (Full). **Weight:** 5-6 lbs. **Length:** 43" overall (28" barrel). **Stock:** Walnut-finished hardwood with full pistol grip. **Sights:** Bead front. **Features:** Transfer bar ignition; break-open action with side-lever release. Introduced 1987. From New England Firearms.

Price: **$99.95**
Price: Youth model (12, 20, 28 ga., 410, 22" barrel, recoil pad).. **$109.95**
Price: 12 ga., 32" (Full)................................. **$104.95**

RUGER KTS-1234-BRE TRAP MODEL
SINGLE-BARREL SHOTGUN

Gauge: 12, 2 3/4" chamber. **Barrel:** 34". **Weight:** 9 lbs. **Length:** 50 1/2" overall. **Stock:** Select walnut checkered; adjustable pull length 13 -15". **Features:** Fully adjustable rib for pattern position; adjustable stock comb cast for right- or left-handed shooters; straight grooves the length of barrel to keep wad from rotating for pattern improvement. Full and modified choke tubes supplied. Gold inlaid eagle and Ruger name on receiver. Introduced 2000. From Sturm Ruger & Co.

Price: **$2,850.00**

ROSSI MODEL 12-G SHOTGUN

Gauge: 12, 20, 2-3/4" chamber; 410, 3" chamber. **Barrel:** 28". **Weight:** 5 lbs. **Length:** NA. **Stock:** Stained hardwood. **Features:** Spur hammer; intregral safety; ejector; spur hammer. Imported from Brazil by BrazTech.

Price: **$119.00**
Price: Youth (shorter stock, 22" barrel) **$119.00**

Tar-Hunt Mountaineer

SAVAGE MODEL 210F MASTER SHOT SLUG GUN

Gauge: 12, 3" chamber; 2-shot magazine. **Barrel:** 24" 1:35" rifling twist. **Weight:** 7-1/2 lbs. **Length:** 43.5" overall. **Stock:** Glass-filled polymer with positive checkering. **Features:** Based on the Savage Model 110 action; 60 bolt lift; controlled round feed; comes with scope mount. Introduced 1996. Made in U.S. by Savage Arms.
Price: $402.00

Savage Model 210FT Master Shot Shotgun

Similar to the Model 210F except has smoothbore barrel threaded for Winchoke-style choke tubes (comes with one Full tube); Advantage camo pattern covers the stock; pillar-bedded synthetic stock; bead front sight, U-notch rear. Introduced 1997. Made in U.S. by Savage Arms, Inc.
Price: $466.00

SNAKE CHARMER II SHOTGUN

Gauge: 410, 3" chamber. **Barrel:** 18-1/4". **Weight:** About 3-1/2 lbs. **Length:** 28-5/8" overall. **Stock:** ABS grade impact resistant plastic. **Features:** Thumbhole-type stock holds four extra rounds. Stainless steel barrel and frame. Reintroduced 1989. From Sporting Arms Mfg., Inc.
Price: $149.00
Price: Snake Charmer II Field Gun (as above except has conventional wood buttstock with 14" length of pull, 24" barrel 410 or 28 ga.) $160.00
Price: New Generation Snake Charmer (as above except with black carbon steel bbl.) $139.00

TAR-HUNT RSG-12 PROFESSIONAL RIFLED SLUG GUN

Gauge: 12, 2-3/4" chamber, 1-shot magazine. **Barrel:** 21-1/2"; fully rifled, with muzzle brake. **Weight:** 7-3/4 lbs. **Length:** 41-1/2" overall. **Stock:** Matte black McMillan fiberglass with Pachmayr Decelerator pad. **Sights:** None furnished; comes with Leupold windage bases only. **Features:** Uses rifle-style action with two locking lugs; two-position safety; Shaw barrel; single-stage, trigger; muzzle brake. Many options available. Right- and left-hand models at same prices. Introduced 1991. Made in U.S. by Tar-Hunt Custom Rifles, Inc.
Price: Professional model, right- or left hand $1,395.00
Price: Matchless model (400-grit gloss metal finish, McMillan Fibergrain stock), right- or left-hand $1,873.00
Price: Peerless model NP-3 nickel/Teflon metal finish, McMillan Fibergrain stock, right- or left-hand. $2,072.00

Tar-Hunt RSG-20 Mountaineer Slug Gun

Similar to the RSG-12 Professional except chambered for 20 gauge (2-3/4") shells; 21" Shaw rifled barrel, with muzzle brake; two-lug bolt; one-shot blind magazine; matte black finish; McMillan fiberglass stock with Pachmayr Decelerator pad; receiver drilled and tapped for Rem. 700 bases. Weighs 6-1/2 lbs. Introduced 1997. Made in U.S. by Tar-Hunt Custom Rifles, Inc.
Price: $1,295.00

THOMPSON/CENTER ENCORE RIFLED SLUG GUN

Gauge: 20, 3" chamber. **Barrel:** 26", fully rifled. **Weight:** About 7 pounds. **Length:** 40-1/2" overall. **Stock:** Walnut with walnut forearm. **Sights:** Steel, click-adjustable rear and ramp-style front, both with fiber optics. **Features:** Encore system features a variety of rifle, shotgun and muzzle-loading rifle barrels interchangeable with the same frame. Break-open design operates by pulling up and back on trigger guard spur. Composite stock and forearm available. Introduced 2000.
Price: $612.48

WESSON & HARRINGTON LONG TOM CLASSIC SHOTGUN

Gauge: 12, 3" chamber. **Barrel:** 32", (Full). **Weight:** 7-1/2 lbs. **Length:** 46" overall. **Stock:** 14"x1-3/4"x2-5/8". American black walnut with hand-checkered grip and forend. **Features:** Color case-hardened receiver and crescent steel buttplate, blued barrel. Receiver engraved with the National Wild Turkey Federation logo. Introduced 1998. Made in U.S. by H&R 1871, Inc.
Price: $349.95

Designs for utility, suitable for and adaptable to competitions and other sporting purposes.

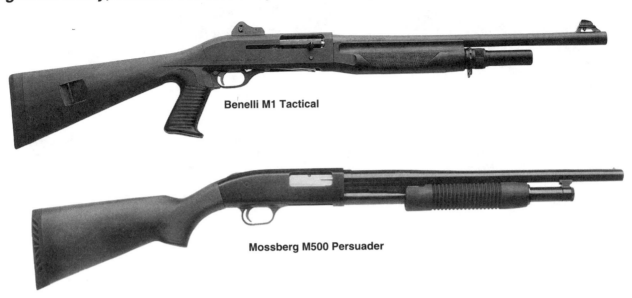

Benelli M1 Tactical

Mossberg M500 Persuader

AMERICAN ARMS PHANTOM HP AUTO SHOTGUN
Gauge: 12, 3" chamber. **Barrel:** 19"; threaded for external choke tubes. **Stock:** Black synthetic. **Sights:** Bead front. **Features:** Gas-operated action; blue/black finish; five-shot extended magazine tube. Imported by American Arms, Inc.
Price: .... **NA**

BENELLI M3 CONVERTIBLE SHOTGUN
Gauge: 12, 3" chamber, 5-shot magazine. **Barrel:** 19-3/4" (Cyl.). **Weight:** 7 lbs., 8 oz. **Length:** 41" overall. **Stock:** High-impact polymer with sling loop in side of butt; rubberized pistol grip on stock. **Sights:** Post front, buckhorn rear adjustable for windage. Ghost ring system available. **Features:** Combination pump/auto action. Alloy receiver with inertia recoil rotating locking lug bolt; matte finish; automatic shell release lever. Introduced 1989. Imported by Benelli USA.
Price: With standard stock, open rifle sights.............. **$1,060.00**
Price: With ghost ring sight system, standard stock......... **$1,100.00**
Price: With ghost ring sights, pistol grip stock **$1,120.00**

BENELLI M1 TACTICAL SHOTGUN
Gauge: 12, 3", 5-shot magazine. **Barrel:** 18.5", choke tubes. **Weight:** 6.5 lbs. **Length:** 39.75" overall. **Stock:** Black polymer. **Sights:** Rifle type with Ghost Ring system, tritium night sights optional. **Features:** Semi-auto intertia recoil action. Cross-bolt safety; bolt release button; matte-finish metal. Introduced 1993. Imported from Italy by Benelli USA.
Price: With rifle sights, standard stock **$890.00**
Price: With ghost ring rifle sights, standard stock............. **$960.00**
Price: With ghost ring sights, pistol grip stock **$970.00**
Price: With rifle sights, pistol grip stock **$910.00**

Benelli M1 Practical
Similar to M1 Field Shotgun, but with Picatinny receiver rail for scope mounting, nine-round magazine, 26" compensated barrel and ghost-ring sights. Designed for IPSC competition.
Price: **$1,200.00**

BENELLI M4 SUPER 90 JOINT SERVICE COMBAT SHOTGUN
Gauge: 12, 3" chamber. **Barrel:** 18.5". **Weight:** 8.4 pounds. **Length:** 39.8 inches. **Stock:** Synthetic, modular. **Sights:** Ghost-ring style, rear adjustable for windage and elevation using cartridge rim. **Features:** Auto-regulating, gas-operated (ARGO) action. Integral, Picatinny rail on receiver for sight mounting. Black matte finish. Improved cylinder. Can be reconfigured without tools with three buttstocks and two barrels. Introduced 2000. Imported from Italy by Benelli USA.
Price: .... **NA**

BERETTA MODEL 1201FP GHOST RING AUTO SHOTGUN
Gauge: 12, 3" chamber. **Barrel:** 18" (Cyl.). **Weight:** 6.3 lbs. **Stock:** Special strengthened technopolymer, matte black finish. **Stock:** Fixed rifle type. **Features:** Has 5-shot magazine. Adjustable Ghost Ring rear sight, tritium front. Introduced 1988. Imported from Italy by Beretta U.S.A.
Price: **$860.00**

CROSSFIRE SHOTGUN/RIFLE
Gauge/Caliber: 12, 2-3/4" chamber 4-shot/223 Rem. (5-shot). **Barrel:** 20" (shotgun), 18" (rifle). **Weight:** About 8.6 lbs. **Length:** 40" overall. **Stock:** Composite. **Sights:** Meprolight night sights. Integral Weaver-style scope rail. **Features:** Combination pump-action shotgun, rifle; single selector, single trigger; dual action bars for both upper and lower actions; ambidextrous selector and safety. Introduced 1997. Made in U.S. From Hesco.
Price: About **$1,895.00**
Price: With camo finish................................... **$1,995.00**

FABARM FP6 PUMP SHOTGUN
Gauge: 12, 3" chamber. **Barrel:** 20" (Cyl.); accepts choke tubes. **Weight:** 6.6 lbs. **Length:** 41.25" overall. **Stock:** Black polymer with textured grip, grooved slide handle. **Sights:** Blade front. **Features:** Twin action bars; anodized finish; free carrier for smooth reloading. Introduced 1998. Imported from Italy by Heckler & Koch, Inc.
Price: **$499.00**
Price: With flip-up front sight, Picatinny rail with rear sight, oversize safety button **$499.00**

MOSSBERG MODEL 500 PERSUADER SECURITY SHOTGUNS
Gauge: 12, 20, 410, 3" chamber. **Barrel:** 18-1/2", 20" (Cyl.). **Weight:** 7 lbs. **Stock:** Walnut-finished hardwood or black synthetic. **Sights:** Metal bead front. **Features:** Available in 6- or 8-shot models. Top-mounted safety, double action slide bars, swivel studs, rubber recoil pad. Blue, Parkerized, Marinecote finishes. Mossberg Cablelock included. From Mossberg.
Price: 12 or 20 ga., 18-1/2", blue, wood or synthetic stock, 6-shot **$307.00**
Price: Cruiser, 12 or 20 ga., 18-1/2", blue, pistol grip, heat shield .... **$298.00** to **$307.00**
Price: As above, 410-bore **$305.00**

Mossberg Model 500, 590 Mariner Pump
Similar to the Model 500 or 590 Security except all metal parts finished with Marinecote metal finish to resist rust and corrosion. Synthetic field stock; pistol grip kit included. Mossberg Cablelock included.
Price: 6-shot, 18-1/2" barrel **$416.00**
Price: 9-shot, 20" barrel **$370.00**

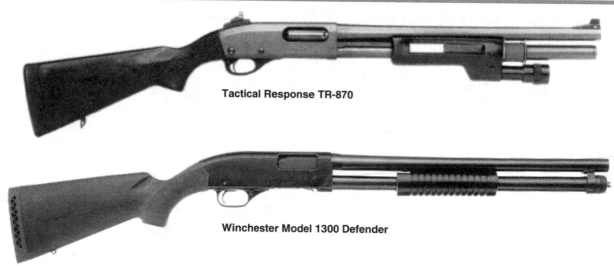

Tactical Response TR-870

Winchester Model 1300 Defender

Mossberg Model HS410 Shotgun

Similar to the Model 500 Security pump except chambered for 20 gauge or 410 with 3" chamber; has pistol grip forend, thick recoil pad, muzzle brake and has special spreader choke on the 18.5" barrel. Overall length is 37.5", weight is 6.25 lbs. Blue finish; synthetic field stock. Mossberg Cablelock and video included. Introduced 1990.

Price: HS 410 . . . . **$319.00**

Mossberg Model 500, 590 Ghost-Ring Shotguns

Similar to the Model 500 Security except has adjustable blade front, adjustable Ghost-Ring rear sight with protective "ears." Model 500 has 18.5" (Cyl.) barrel, 6-shot capacity; Model 590 has 20" (Cyl.) barrel, 9-shot capacity. Both have synthetic field stock. Mossberg Cablelock included. Introduced 1990. From Mossberg.

Price: Model 500, blue **$307.00**
Price: As above, Parkerized. **$416.00**
Price: Model 590, blue **$370.00**
Price: As above, Parkerized. **$425.00**
Price: Parkerized Speedfeed stock . . . . **$462.00 to $519.00**

MOSSBERG MODEL 9200A1 JUNGLE GUN

Gauge: 12, 2-3/4" chamber; 5-shot magazine. **Barrel:** 18" (Cyl.). **Weight:** About 7 lbs. **Length:** 38-1/2" overall. **Stock:** Black synthetic. **Sights:** Bead front. **Features:** Designed to function only with 2-3/4" 00 Buck loads; Parkerized finish; mil-spec heavy wall barrel; military metal trigger housing; ambidextrous metal tang safety. Introduced 1998. Made in U.S. by Mossberg.

Price: **$704.00**

MOSSBERG MODEL 590 SHOTGUN

Gauge: 12, 3" chamber. **Barrel:** 20" (Cyl.). **Weight:** 7-1/4 lbs. **Stock:** Synthetic field or Speedfeed. **Sights:** Metal bead front. **Features:** Top-mounted safety, double slide action bars. Comes with heat shield, bayonet lug, swivel studs, rubber recoil pad. Blue, Parkerized or Marinecote finish. Mossberg Cablelock included. From Mossberg.

Price: Blue, synthetic stock. **$370.00**
Price: Parkerized, synthetic stock. **$425.00**
Price: Parkerized, Speedfeed stock **$450.00**

Mossberg 590DA Double-Action Pump Shotgun

NEW!

Similar to Model 590 except trigger requires a long stroke for each shot, duplicating the trigger pull of double-action-only pistols and revolvers. Available in 12 gauge only with black synthetic stock and parkerized finish with 14" (law enforcement only), 18 1/2 "and 20" barrels. Six-shot magazine tube (nine-shot for 20" barrel). Front bead or ghost ring sights. Weighs 7 pounds (18 1/2" barrel). Introduced 2000. From Mossberg.

Price: Bead sight, 6-shot magazine **$510.00**
Price: Ghost ring sights, 6-shot magazine **$558.00**
Price: Bead sight, 9-shot magazine **$541.00**
Price: Ghost ring sights, 9-shot magazine **$597.00**

TACTICAL RESPONSE TR-870 STANDARD MODEL SHOTGUN

Gauge: 12, 3" chamber, 7-shot magazine. **Barrel:** 18" (Cyl.). **Weight:** 9 lbs. **Length:** 38" overall. **Stock:** Fiberglass-filled polypropolene with non-snag recoil absorbing butt pad. Nylon tactical forend houses flashlight. **Sights:** Trak-Lock ghost ring sight system. Front sight has tritium insert. **Features:** Highly modified Remington 870P with Parkerized finish. Comes with nylon three-way adjustable sling, high visibility non-binding follower, high performance magazine spring, Jumbo Head safety, and Side Saddle extended 6-shot shell carrier on left side of receiver. Introduced 1991. From Scattergun Technologies, Inc.

Price: Standard model **$815.00**
Price: FBI model. **$770.00**
Price: Patrol model. **$595.00**
Price: Border Patrol model **$605.00**
Price: K-9 model (Rem. 11-87 action) **$995.00**
Price: Urban Sniper, Rem. 11-87 action. **$1,290.00**
Price: Louis Awerbuck model. **$705.00**
Price: Practical Turkey model. **$725.00**
Price: Expert model **$1,350.00**
Price: Professional model. **$815.00**
Price: Entry model **$840.00**
Price: Compact model **$635.00**
Price: SWAT model **$1,195.00**

WINCHESTER MODEL 1300 DEFENDER PUMP GUN

Gauge: 12, 20, 3" chamber, 5- or 8-shot capacity. **Barrel:** 18" (Cyl.). **Weight:** 6-3/4 lbs. **Length:** 38-5/8" overall. **Stock:** Walnut-finished hardwood stock and ribbed forend, or synthetic; or pistol grip. **Sights:** Metal bead front. **Features:** Cross-bolt safety, front-locking rotary bolt, twin action slide bars. Black rubber butt pad. From U.S. Repeating Arms Co.

Price: 8-shot, wood or synthetic stock **$321.00**

Winchester 8-Shot Pistol Grip Pump Security Shotgun

Same as regular Defender Pump but with pistol grip and forend of high-impact resistant ABS plastic with non-glare black finish. Introduced 1984.

Price: Pistol Grip Defender. **$321.00**

Winchester Model 1300 Stainless Marine Pump Gun

Same as the Defender except has bright chrome finish, stainless steel barrel, rifle-type sights only. Phosphate coated receiver for corrosion resistance. Pistol grip optional.

Price: **$511.00**

SHOTGUNS

CVA Hawken   Dixie Pennsylvania   Harper's Ferry   Kentucky   Le Page

BLACKPOWDER

CVA HAWKEN PISTOL

Caliber: 50. **Barrel:** 9-3/4"; 15/16" flats. **Weight:** 50 oz. **Length:** 16-1/2" overall. **Stocks:** Select hardwood. **Sights:** Beaded blade front, fully adjustable open rear. **Features:** Color case-hardened lock, polished brass wedge plate, instep, ramrod thimble, trigger guard, grip cap. Imported by CVA.
Price: **$149.95**
Price: Kit **$119.95**

DIXIE PENNSYLVANIA PISTOL

Caliber: 44 (.430" round ball). **Barrel:** 10", (7/8" octagon). **Weight:** 2-1/2 labs. **Stocks:** Walnut-stained hardwood. **Sights:** Blade front, open rear drift-adjustable for windage; brass. **Features:** Available in flint only. Brass trigger guard, thimbles, instep, wedge plates; high-luster blue barrel. Imported from Italy by Dixie Gun Works.
Price: Finished **$195.00**
Price: Kit **$185.00**

FRENCH-STYLE DUELING PISTOL

Caliber: 44. **Barrel:** 10". **Weight:** 35 oz. **Length:** 15-3/4" overall. **Stocks:** Carved walnut. **Sights:** Fixed. **Features:** Comes with velvet-lined case and accessories. Imported by Mandall Shooting Supplies.
Price: **$295.00**

HARPER'S FERRY 1806 PISTOL

Caliber: 58 (.570" round ball). **Barrel:** 10". **Weight:** 40 oz. **Length:** 16" overall. **Stocks:** Walnut. **Sights:** Fixed. **Features:** Case-hardened lock, brass-mounted browned barrel. Replica of the first U.S. Gov't.-made flintlock pistol. Imported by Navy Arms, Dixie Gun Works.
Price: .... **$275.00** to **$405.00**
Price: Kit (Dixie) **$249.00**

KENTUCKY FLINTLOCK PISTOL

Caliber: 44, 45. **Barrel:** 10-1/8". **Weight:** 32 oz. **Length:** 15-1/2" overall. **Stocks:** Walnut. **Sights:** Fixed. **Features:** Specifications, including caliber, weight and length may vary with importer. Case-hardened lock, blued barrel; available also as brass barrel flint Model 1821. Imported by Navy Arms, The Armoury.
Price: .... **$145.00** to **$235.00**
Price: In kit form, from .... **$90.00** to **$112.00**
Price: Single cased set (Navy Arms) **$360.00**
Price: Double cased set (Navy Arms) **$590.00**

Kentucky Percussion Pistol

Similar to flint version but percussion lock. Imported by The Armoury, Navy Arms, CVA (50-cal.).
Price: .... **$129.95** to **$225.00**
Price: Steel barrel (Armoury) **$179.00**
Price: Single cased set (Navy Arms) **$355.00**
Price: Double cased set (Navy Arms) **$600.00**

LE PAGE PERCUSSION DUELING PISTOL

Caliber: 44. **Barrel:** 10", rifled. **Weight:** 40 oz. **Length:** 16" overall. **Stocks:** Walnut, fluted butt. **Sights:** Blade front, notch rear. **Features:** Double-set triggers. Blued barrel; trigger guard and buttcap are polished silver. Imported by Dixie Gun Works.
Price: **$259.95**

LYMAN PLAINS PISTOL

Caliber: 50 or 54. **Barrel:** 8"; 1:30" twist, both calibers. **Weight:** 50 oz. **Length:** 15" overall. **Stocks:** Walnut half-stock. **Sights:** Blade front, square notch rear adjustable for windage. **Features:** Polished brass trigger guard and ramrod tip, color case-hardened coil spring lock, spring-loaded trigger, stainless steel nipple, blackened iron furniture. Hooked patent breech, detachable belt hook. Introduced 1981. From Lyman Products.
Price: Finished **$229.95**
Price: Kit **$184.95**

Lyman Plains Pistol   **Pedersoli Mang**   **Queen Anne**   **Traditions Pioneer**   **Traditions William Parker**

Traditions Buckhunter Pro

PEDERSOLI MANG TARGET PISTOL

Caliber: 38. **Barrel:** 10.5", octagonal; 1:15" twist, **Weight:** 2.5 lbs. **Length:** 17.25" overall. **Stocks:** Walnut with fluted grip. **Sights:** Blade front, open rear adjustable for windage.
Features: Browned barrel, polished breech plug, rest color case-hardened. Imported from Italy by Dixie Gun Works.
Price: **$786.00**

QUEEN ANNE FLINTLOCK PISTOL

Caliber: 50 (.490" round ball). **Barrel:** 7-1/2", smoothbore. **Stocks:** Walnut.
Sights: None. **Features:** Browned steel barrel, fluted brass trigger guard, brass mask on butt. Lockplate left in the white. Made by Pedersoli in Italy. Introduced 1983. Imported by Dixie Gun Works.
Price: **$225.00**
Price: Kit **$175.00**

THOMPSON/CENTER ENCORE 209x50 MAGNUM PISTOL

NEW!

Caliber: 50. **Barrel:** 15"; 1:20" twist. **Weight:** About 4 lbs. **Grips:** American walnut grip and forend. **Sights:** Click-adjustable, steel rear, ramp front.
Features: Uses 209 shotgun primer for closed-breech ignition; accepts charges up to 110 grains of FFg black powder or two, 50-grain Pyrodex pellets. Introduced 2000.
Price: **$569.47**

TRADITIONS BUCKHUNTER PRO IN-LINE PISTOL

Caliber: 50, 54. **Barrel:** 9-1/2", round. **Weight:** 48 oz. **Length:** 14" overall. **Stocks:** Smooth walnut or black epoxy coated grip and forend. **Sights:** Beaded blade front, folding adjustable rear. **Features:** Thumb safety; removable stainless steel breech plug; adjustable trigger, barrel drilled and tapped for scope mounting. From Traditions.
Price: With walnut grip **$219.00**
Price: Nickel with black grip **$234.00**
Price: With walnut grip and 12-1/2" barrel **$234.00**

TRADITIONS KENTUCKY PISTOL

Caliber: 50. **Barrel:** 10"; octagon with 7/8" flats; 1:20" twist. **Weight:** 40 oz. **Length:** 15" overall. **Stocks:** Stained beech. **Sights:** Blade front, fixed rear. **Features:** Birds-head grip; brass thimbles; color case-hardened lock. Percussion only. Introduced 1995. From Traditions.
Price: Finished **$138.00**
Price: Kit **$109.00**

TRADITIONS PIONEER PISTOL

Caliber: 45. **Barrel:** 9-5/8"; 13/16" flats, 1:16" twist. **Weight:** 31 oz. **Length:** 15" overall. **Stocks:** Beech. **Sights:** Blade front, fixed rear. **Features:** V-type mainspring. Single trigger. German silver furniture, blackened hardware. From Traditions.
Price: **$140.00**
Price: Kit **$116.00**

TRADITIONS TRAPPER PISTOL

Caliber: 50. **Barrel:** 9-3/4"; 7/8" flats; 1:20" twist. **Weight:** 2-3/4 lbs. **Length:** 16" overall. **Stocks:** Beech. **Sights:** Blade front, adjustable rear. **Features:** Double-set triggers; brass buttcap, trigger guard, wedge plate, forend tip, thimble. From Traditions.
Price: Percussion **$189.00**
Price: Flintlock **$204.00**
Price: Kit **$145.00**

TRADITIONS WILLIAM PARKER PISTOL

Caliber: 50. **Barrel:** 10-3/8"; 15/16" flats; polished steel. **Weight:** 37 oz. **Length:** 17-1/2" overall. **Stocks:** Walnut with checkered grip. **Sights:** Brass blade front, fixed rear. **Features:** Replica dueling pistol with 1:20" twist, hooked breech. Brass wedge plate, trigger guard, cap guard; separate ramrod. Double-set triggers. Polished steel barrel, lock. Imported by Traditions.
Price: **$262.00**

BLACKPOWDER REVOLVERS

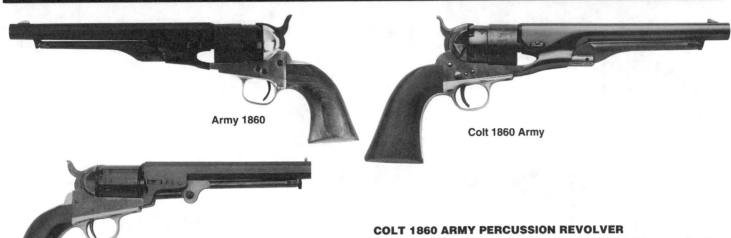

Army 1860

Colt 1860 Army

Baby Dragoon 1848

ARMY 1851 PERCUSSION REVOLVER

Caliber: 44, 6-shot. **Barrel:** 7-1/2". **Weight:** 45 oz. **Length:** 13" overall. **Stocks:** Walnut finish. **Sights:** Fixed. **Features:** 44-caliber version of the 1851 Navy. Imported by The Armoury, Armsport.
Price: **$129.00**

ARMY 1860 PERCUSSION REVOLVER

Caliber: 44, 6-shot. **Barrel:** 8". **Weight:** 40 oz. **Length:** 13-5/8" overall. **Stocks:** Walnut. **Sights:** Fixed. **Features:** Engraved Navy scene on cylinder; brass trigger guard; case-hardened frame, loading lever and hammer. Some importers supply pistol cut for detachable shoulder stock, have accessory stock available. Imported by Cabela's (1860 Lawman), E.M.F., Navy Arms, The Armoury, Cimarron, Dixie Gun Works (half-fluted cylinder, not roll engraved), Euroarms of America (brass or steel model), Armsport, Traditions (brass or steel), Uberti U.S.A. Inc., United States Patent Fire-Arms.
Price: About .... **$92.95 to $395.00**
Price: Hartford model, steel frame, German silver trim,
   cartouches (E.M.F.) **$215.00**
Price: Single cased set (Navy Arms) **$300.00**
Price: Double cased set (Navy Arms). **$490.00**
Price: 1861 Navy: Same as Army except 36-cal., 7-1/2" bbl., weighs 41 oz., cut for shoulder stock; round cylinder (fluted available), from Cabela's, CVA (brass frame, 44-cal.), United States Patent Fire-Arms
   .... **$99.95 to $385.00**
Price: Steel frame kit (E.M.F., Euroarms). .... **$125.00 to $216.25**
Price: Colt Army Police, fluted cyl., 5-1/2", 36-cal. (Cabela's) ... **$124.95**
Price: With nickeled frame, barrel and backstrap, gold-tone fluted cylinder, trigger and hammer, simulated ivory grips (Traditions) **$199.00**

BABY DRAGOON 1848, 1849 POCKET, WELLS FARGO

Caliber: 31. **Barrel:** 3", 4", 5", 6"; seven-groove; RH twist. **Weight:** About 21 oz. **Stocks:** Varnished walnut. **Sights:** Brass pin front, hammer notch rear. **Features:** No loading lever on Baby Dragoon or Wells Fargo models. Unfluted cylinder with stagecoach holdup scene; cupped cylinder pin; no grease grooves; one safety pin on cylinder and slot in hammer face; straight (flat) mainspring. From Armsport, Cimarron F.A. Co., Dixie Gun Works, Uberti U.S.A. Inc.
Price: 6" barrel, with loading lever (Dixie Gun Works) **$254.95**
Price: 4" (Uberti USA Inc.) **$335.00**

CABELA'S STARR PERCUSSION REVOLVERS

Caliber: 44. **Barrel:** 6", 8". **Weight:** N/A. **Length:** N/A. **Grips:** Walnut. **Sights:** Blade front. **Features:** Replicas of government-contract revolvers made by Ebenezer T. Starr. Knurled knob allows quick removal and replacement of cylinder. Introduced 2000. From Cabela's.
Price: Starr 1858 Army double action, 6" barrel. **$349.99**
Price: Starr 1863 Army single action, 8" barrel **$349.99**

COLT 1860 ARMY PERCUSSION REVOLVER

Caliber: 44. **Barrel:** 8", 7-groove, left-hand twist. **Weight:** 42 oz. **Stocks:** One-piece walnut. **Sights:** German silver front sight, hammer notch rear. **Features:** Steel backstrap cut for shoulder stock; brass trigger guard. Cylinder has Navy scene. Color case-hardened frame, hammer, loading lever. Reproduction of original gun with all original markings. From Colt Blackpowder Arms Co.
Price: **$449.95**

COLT 1848 BABY DRAGOON REVOLVER

Caliber: 31, 5-shot. **Barrel:** 4". **Weight:** About 21 oz. **Stocks:** Smooth walnut. **Sights:** Brass pin front, hammer notch rear. **Features:** Color case-hardened frame; no loading lever; square-back trigger guard; round bolt cuts; octagonal barrel; engraved cylinder scene. Imported by Colt Blackpowder Arms Co.
Price: **$429.95**

Colt 1860 "Cavalry Model" Percussion Revolver

Similar to the 1860 Army except has fluted cylinder. Color case-hardened frame, hammer, loading lever and plunger; blued barrel, backstrap and cylinder, brass trigger guard. Has four-screw frame cut for optional shoulder stock. From Colt Blackpowder Arms Co.
Price: **$399.95**

COLT 1851 NAVY PERCUSSION REVOLVER

Caliber: 36. **Barrel:** 7-1/2", octagonal; 7-groove left-hand twist. **Weight:** 40-1/2 oz. **Stocks:** One-piece oiled American walnut. **Sights:** Brass pin front, hammer notch rear. **Features:** Faithful reproduction of the original gun. Color case-hardened frame, loading lever, plunger, hammer and latch. Blue cylinder, trigger, barrel, screws, wedge. Silver-plated brass backstrap and square-back trigger guard. From Colt Blackpowder Arms Co.
Price: **$449.95**

COLT 1861 NAVY PERCUSSION REVOLVER

Caliber: 36. **Barrel:** 7-1/2". **Weight:** 42 oz. **Length:** 13-1/8" overall. **Stocks:** One-piece walnut. **Sights:** Blade front, hammer notch rear. **Features:** Color case-hardened frame, loading lever, plunger; blued barrel, backstrap, trigger guard; roll-engraved cylinder and barrel. From Colt Blackpowder Arms Co.
Price: **$449.95**

COLT 1849 POCKET DRAGOON REVOLVER

Caliber: 31. **Barrel:** 4". **Weight:** 24 oz. **Length:** 9-1/2" overall. **Stocks:** One-piece walnut. **Sights:** Fixed. Brass pin front, hammer notch rear. **Features:** Color case-hardened frame. No loading lever. Unfluted cylinder with engraved scene. Exact reproduction of original. From Colt Blackpowder Arms Co.
Price: **$429.95**

COLT 1862 POCKET POLICE "TRAPPER MODEL" REVOLVER

Caliber: 36. **Barrel:** 3-1/2". **Weight:** 20 oz. **Length:** 8-1/2" overall. **Stocks:** One-piece walnut. **Sights:** Blade front, hammer notch rear. **Features:** Has separate 4-5/8" brass ramrod. Color case-hardened frame and hammer; silver-plated backstrap and trigger guard; blued semi-fluted cylinder, blued barrel. From Colt Blackpowder Arms Co.
Price: **$429.95**

BLACKPOWDER REVOLVERS

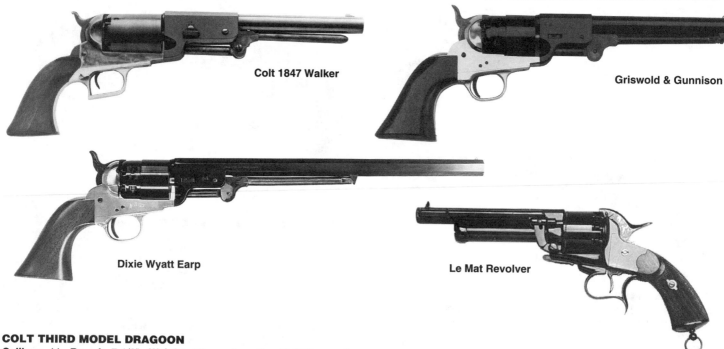

Colt 1847 Walker

Griswold & Gunnison

Dixie Wyatt Earp

Le Mat Revolver

COLT THIRD MODEL DRAGOON

Caliber: 44. **Barrel:** 7-1/2". **Weight:** 66 oz. **Length:** 13-3/4" overall. **Stocks:** One-piece walnut. **Sights:** Blade front, hammer notch rear. **Features:** Color case-hardened frame, hammer, lever and plunger; round trigger guard; flat mainspring; hammer roller; rectangular bolt cuts. From Colt Blackpowder Arms Co.
Price: Three-screw frame with brass grip straps $499.95
Price: First Dragoon (oval bolt cuts in cylinder, square-back
trigger guard) $499.95
Price: Second Dragoon (rectangular bolt cuts in cylinder,
square-back trigger guard) $499.95

Colt Walker 150th Anniversary Revolver

Similar to the standard Walker except has original-type "A Company No. 1" markings embellished in gold. Serial numbers begin with 221, a continuation of A Company numbers. Imported by Colt Blackpowder Arms Co.
Price: $699.95

COLT 1847 WALKER PERCUSSION REVOLVER

Caliber: 44. **Barrel:** 9", 7-groove; right-hand twist. **Weight:** 73 oz. **Stocks:** One-piece walnut. **Sights:** German silver front sight, hammer notch rear. **Features:** Made in U.S. Faithful reproduction of the original gun, including markings. Color case-hardened frame, hammer, loading lever and plunger. Blue steel backstrap, brass square-back trigger guard. Blue barrel, cylinder, trigger and wedge. From Colt Blackpowder Arms Co.
Price: $499.95

DIXIE WYATT EARP REVOLVER

Caliber: 44. **Barrel:** 12", octagon. **Weight:** 46 oz. **Length:** 18" overall. **Stocks:** Two-piece walnut. **Sights:** Fixed. **Features:** Highly polished brass frame, backstrap and trigger guard; blued barrel and cylinder; case-hardened hammer, trigger and loading lever. Navy-size shoulder stock ($45) will fit with minor fitting. From Dixie Gun Works.
Price: $150.00

GRISWOLD & GUNNISON PERCUSSION REVOLVER

Caliber: 36 or 44, 6-shot. **Barrel:** 7-1/2". **Weight:** 44 oz. (36-cal.). **Length:** 13" overall. **Stocks:** Walnut. **Sights:** Fixed. **Features:** Replica of famous Confederate pistol. Brass frame, backstrap and trigger guard; case-hardened loading lever; rebated cylinder (44-cal. only). Rounded Dragoon-type barrel. Imported by Navy Arms as Reb Model 1860.
Price: $115.00
Price: Kit $90.00
Price: Single cased set $235.00
Price: Double cased set $365.00

LE MAT REVOLVER

Caliber: 44/65. **Barrel:** 6-3/4" (revolver); 4-7/8" (single shot). **Weight:** 3 lbs., 7 oz. **Stocks:** Hand-checkered walnut. **Sights:** Post front, hammer notch rear. **Features:** Exact reproduction with all-steel construction; 44-cal. 9-shot cylinder, 65-cal. single barrel; color case-hardened hammer with selector; spur trigger guard; ring at butt; lever-type barrel release. From Navy Arms.
Price: Cavalry model (lanyard ring, spur trigger guard) $595.00
Price: Army model (round trigger guard, pin-type barrel release) $595.00
Price: Naval-style (thumb selector on hammer) $595.00
Price: Engraved 18th Georgia cased set $795.00
Price: Engraved Beauregard cased set $1,000.00

NAVY ARMS NEW MODEL POCKET REVOLVER

Caliber: 31, 5-shot. **Barrel:** 3-1/2", octagon. **Weight:** 15 oz. **Length:** 7-3/4". **Stocks:** Two-piece walnut. **Sights:** Fixed. **Features:** Replica of the Remington New Model Pocket. Available with polishehd brass frame or nickel plated finish. Introduced 2000. Imported by Navy Arms.
Price: Brass frame $165.00
Price: Nickel plated $175.00

NAVY ARMS DELUXE 1858 REMINGTON-STYLE REVOLVER

Caliber: 44. **Barrel:** 6". **Weight:** 3 lbs. **Length:** 11-3/4". **Stocks:** Smooth walnut. **Sights:** Blade front, notch rear. **Features:** Replica of the famous percussion double action revolver. Polished blue finish. Introduced 1999. Imported by Navy Arms.
Price: $355.00

NAVY ARMS STARR SINGLE ACTION MODEL 1863 ARMY REVOLVER

Caliber: 44. **Barrel:** 8". **Weight:** 3 lbs. **Length:** 13-3/4". **Stocks:** Smooth walnut. **Sights:** Blade front, notch rear. **Features:** Replica of the third most popular revolver used by Union forces during the Civil War. Polished blue finish. Introduced 1999. Imported by Navy Arms.
Price: $355.00

NAVY ARMS STARR DOUBLE ACTION MODEL 1858 ARMY REVOLVER

Caliber: 44. **Barrel:** 8". **Weight:** 2 lbs., 13 oz. **Stocks:** Smooth walnut. **Sights:** Dovetailed blade front. **Features:** First exact reproduction—correct in size and weight to the original, with progressive rifling; highly polished with blue finish. From Navy Arms.
Price: Deluxe model $415.00

BLACKPOWDER REVOLVERS

Uberti 1858

Rogers & Spencer

North American Companion

Ruger Old Army

Pocket Police 1862

NAVY MODEL 1851 PERCUSSION REVOLVER

Caliber: 36, 44, 6-shot. **Barrel:** 7-1/2". **Weight:** 44 oz. **Length:** 13" overall. **Stocks:** Walnut finish. **Sights:** Post front, hammer notch rear. **Features:** Brass backstrap and trigger guard; some have 1st Model squareback trigger guard, engraved cylinder with navy battle scene; case-hardened frame, hammer, loading lever. Imported by The Armoury, Cabela's, Cimarron F.A. Co., Navy Arms, E.M.F., Dixie Gun Works, Euroarms of America, Armsport, CVA (44-cal. only), Traditions (44 only), Uberti U.S.A. Inc., United States Patent Fire-Arms.

Price: Brass frame	$99.95 to $385.00
Price: Steel frame	$130.00 to $285.00
Price: Kit form	$110.00 to $123.95
Price: Engraved model (Dixie Gun Works)	$159.95
Price: Single cased set, steel frame (Navy Arms)	$280.00
Price: Double cased set, steel frame (Navy Arms)	$455.00
Price: Confederate Navy (Cabela's)	$89.99
Price: Hartford model, steel frame, German silver trim, cartouche (E.M.F.)	$190.00

NEW MODEL 1858 ARMY PERCUSSION REVOLVER

Caliber: 36 or 44, 6-shot. **Barrel:** 6-1/2" or 8". **Weight:** 38 oz. **Length:** 13-1/2" overall. **Stocks:** Walnut. **Sights:** Blade front, groove-in-frame rear. **Features:** Replica of Remington Model 1858. Also available from some importers as Army Model Belt Revolver in 36-cal., a shortened and lightened version of the 44. Target Model (Uberti U.S.A. Inc., Navy Arms) has fully adjustable target rear sight, target front, 36 or 44. Imported by Cabela's, Cimarron F.A. Co., CVA (as 1858 Army, brass frame, 44 only), Dixie Gun Works, Navy Arms, The Armoury, E.M.F., Euroarms of America (engraved, stainless and plain), Armsport, Traditions (44 only), Uberti U.S.A. Inc.

Price: Steel frame, about	$99.95 to $280.00
Price: Steel frame kit (Euroarms, Navy Arms)	$115.95 to $150.00
Price: Single cased set (Navy Arms)	$290.00
Price: Double cased set (Navy Arms)	$480.00
Price: Stainless steel Model 1858 (Euroarms, Uberti U.S.A. Inc., Cabela's, Navy Arms, Armsport, Traditions)	$169.95 to $380.00
Price: Target Model, adjustable rear sight (Cabela's, Euroarms, Uberti U.S.A. Inc., Stone Mountain Arms)	$95.95 to $399.00
Price: Brass frame (CVA, Cabela's, Traditions, Navy Arms)	$79.95 to $144.95
Price: As above, kit (Dixie Gun Works, Navy Arms)	$145.00 to $188.95

Price: Buffalo model, 44-cal. (Cabela's)	$119.99
Price: Hartford model, steel frame, German silver trim, cartouche (E.M.F.)	$215.00

NORTH AMERICAN COMPANION PERCUSSION REVOLVER

Caliber: 22. **Barrel:** 1-1/8". **Weight:** 5.1 oz. **Length:** 4-5/10" overall. **Stocks:** Laminated wood. **Sights:** Blade front, notch fixed rear. **Features:** All stainless steel construction. Uses standard #11 percussion caps. Comes with bullets, powder measure, bullet seater, leather clip holster, gun rug. Long Rifle or Magnum frame size. Introduced 1996. Made in U.S. by North American Arms.

Price: Long Rifle frame	$191.00

North American Magnum Companion Percussion Revolver

Similar to the Companion except has larger frame. Weighs 7.2 oz., has 1-5/8" barrel, measures 5-7/16" overall. Comes with bullets, powder measure, bullet seater, leather clip holster, gun rag. Introduced 1996. Made in U.S. by North American Arms.

Price:	$209.00

POCKET POLICE 1862 PERCUSSION REVOLVER

Caliber: 36, 5-shot. **Barrel:** 4-1/2", 5-1/2", 6-1/2", 7-1/2". **Weight:** 26 oz. **Length:** 12" overall (6-1/2" bbl.). **Stocks:** Walnut. **Sights:** Fixed. **Features:** Round tapered barrel; half-fluted and rebated cylinder; case-hardened frame, loading lever and hammer; silver or brass trigger guard and backstrap. Imported by Dixie Gun Works, Navy Arms (5-1/2" only), Uberti U.S.A. Inc. (5-1/2", 6-1/2" only), United States Patent Fire-Arms and Cimarron F.A. Co.

Price: About	$139.95 to $335.00
Price: Single cased set with accessories (Navy Arms)	$365.00
Price: Hartford model, steel frame, German silver trim, cartouche (E.M.F.)	$215.00

ROGERS & SPENCER PERCUSSION REVOLVER

Caliber: 44. **Barrel:** 7-1/2". **Weight:** 47 oz. **Length:** 13-3/4" overall. **Stocks:** Walnut. **Sights:** Cone front, integral groove in frame for rear. **Features:** Accurate reproduction of a Civil War design. Solid frame; extra large nipple cut-out on rear of cylinder; loading lever and cylinder easily removed for cleaning. From Dixie Gun Works, Euroarms of America (standard blue, engraved, burnished, target models), Navy Arms.

Price:	$160.00 to $299.95
Price: Nickel-plated	$215.00

BLACKPOWDER REVOLVERS

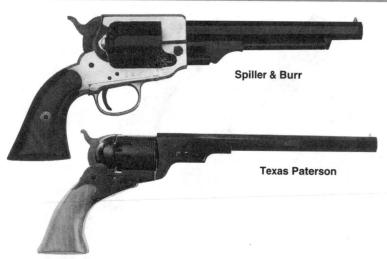

Spiller & Burr

Texas Paterson

Walker

Price: Engraved (Euroarms) $287.00
Price: Kit version . . . . $245.00 to $252.00
Price: Target version (Euroarms) . . . . $239.00 to $270.00
Price: Burnished London Gray (Euroarms) . . . . $245.00 to $270.00

RUGER OLD ARMY PERCUSSION REVOLVER

Caliber: 45, 6-shot. Uses .457" dia. lead bullets. **Barrel:** 7-1/2" (6-groove; 16" twist). **Weight:** 46 oz. **Length:** 13-3/4" overall. **Stocks:** Smooth walnut. **Sights:** Ramp front, rear adjustable for windage and elevation; or fixed (groove). **Features:** Stainless steel; standard size nipples, chrome-moly steel cylinder and frame, same lockwork as in original Super Blackhawk. Also available in stainless steel. Made in USA. From Sturm, Ruger & Co.
Price: Stainless steel (Model KBP-7) $499.00
Price: Blued steel (Model BP-7) $478.00
Price: Blued steel, fixed sight (BP-7F) $478.00
Price: Stainless steel, fixed sight (KBP-7F) $499.00

SHERIFF MODEL 1851 PERCUSSION REVOLVER

Caliber: 36, 44, 6-shot. **Barrel:** 5". **Weight:** 40 oz. **Length:** 10-1/2" overall. **Stocks:** Walnut. **Sights:** Fixed. **Features:** Brass backstrap and trigger guard; engraved navy scene; case-hardened frame, hammer, loading lever. Imported by E.M.F.
Price: Steel frame $172.00
Price: Brass frame $140.00

SPILLER & BURR REVOLVER

Caliber: 36 (.375" round ball). **Barrel:** 7", octagon. **Weight:** 2-1/2 lbs. **Length:** 12-1/2" overall. **Stocks:** Two-piece walnut. **Sights:** Fixed. **Features:** Reproduction of the C.S.A. revolver. Brass frame and trigger guard. Also available as a kit. From Dixie Gun Works, Navy Arms.
Price: $145.00
Price: Kit form (Dixie) $149.95
Price: Single cased set (Navy Arms) $270.00
Price: Double cased set (Navy Arms) $430.00

TEXAS PATERSON 1836 REVOLVER

Caliber: 36 (.375" round ball). **Barrel:** 7-1/2". **Weight:** 42 oz. **Stocks:** One-piece walnut. **Sights:** Fixed. **Features:** Copy of Sam Colt's first commercially-made revolving pistol. Has no loading lever but comes with loading tool. From Cimarron F.A. Co., Dixie Gun Works, Navy Arms, Uberti U.S.A. Inc.
Price: About . . . . $310.00 to $395.00
Price: With loading lever (Uberti U.S.A. Inc.) $450.00
Price: Engraved (Navy Arms) $485.00

Uberti 1861 Navy Percussion Revolver

Similar to Colt 1851 Navy except has round 7-1/2" barrel, rounded trigger guard, German silver blade front sight, "creeping" loading lever. Available with fluted or round cylinder. Imported by Uberti U.S.A. Inc.
Price: Steel backstrap, trigger guard, cut for stock $300.00

1ST U.S. MODEL DRAGOON

Caliber: 44. **Barrel:** 7-1/2", part round, part octagon. **Weight:** 64 oz. **Stocks:** One-piece walnut. **Sights:** German silver blade front, hammer notch rear. **Features:** First model has oval bolt cuts in cylinder, square-back flared trigger guard, V-type mainspring, short trigger. Ranger and Indian scene roll-case-engraved on cylinder. Color case-hardened frame, loading lever, plunger and hammer; blue barrel, cylinder, trigger and wedge. Available with old-time charcoal blue or standard blue-black finish. Polished brass backstrap and trigger guard. From Cimarron F.A. Co., Uberti U.S.A. Inc., United States Patent Fire-Arms, Navy Arms.
Price: . . . . $325.00 to $435.00

2nd U.S. Model Dragoon Revolver

Similar to the 1st Model except distinguished by rectangular bolt cuts in the cylinder. From Cimarron F.A. Co., Uberti U.S.A. Inc., United States Patent Fire-Arms, Navy Arms.
Price: . . . . $325.00 to $435.00

3rd U.S. Model Dragoon Revolver

Similar to the 2nd Model except for oval trigger guard, long trigger, modifications to the loading lever and latch. Imported by Cimarron F.A. Co., Uberti U.S.A. Inc., United States Patent Fire-Arms.
Price: Military model (frame cut for shoulder stock,
steel backstrap) . . . . $330.00 to $435.00
Price: Civilian (brass backstrap, trigger guard) $325.00

1862 POCKET NAVY PERCUSSION REVOLVER

Caliber: 36, 5-shot. **Barrel:** 5-1/2", 6-1/2", octagonal, 7-groove, LH twist. **Weight:** 27 oz. (5-1/2" barrel). **Length:** 10-1/2" overall (5-1/2" bbl.). **Stocks:** One-piece varnished walnut. **Sights:** Brass pin front, hammer notch rear. **Features:** Rebated cylinder, hinged loading lever, brass or silver-plated backstrap and trigger guard, color-cased frame, hammer, loading lever, plunger and latch, rest blued. Has original-type markings. From Cimarron F.A. Co. and Uberti U.S.A. Inc.
Price: With brass backstrap, trigger guard $310.00

1861 Navy Percussion Revolver

Similar to Colt 1851 Navy except has round 7-1/2" barrel, rounded trigger guard, German silver blade front sight, "creeping" loading lever. Fluted or round cylinder. Imported by Cimarron F.A. Co., Uberti U.S.A. Inc.
Price: Steel backstrap, trigger guard, cut for stock $300.00

U.S. PATENT FIRE-ARMS 1862 POCKET NAVY

Caliber: 36. **Barrel:** 4-1/2", 5-1/2", 6-1/2". **Weight:** 27 oz. (5-1/2" barrel). **Length:** 10-1/2" overall (5-1/2" barrel). **Stocks:** Smooth walnut. **Sights:** Brass pin front, hammer notch rear. **Features:** Blued barrel and cylinder, color case-hardened frame, hammer, lever; silver-plated backstrap and trigger guard. Imported from Italy; available from United States Patent Fire-Arms Mfg. Co.
Price: $335.00

WALKER 1847 PERCUSSION REVOLVER

Caliber: 44, 6-shot. **Barrel:** 9". **Weight:** 84 oz. **Length:** 15-1/2" overall. **Stocks:** Walnut. **Sights:** Fixed. **Features:** Case-hardened frame, loading lever and hammer; iron backstrap; brass trigger guard; engraved cylinder. Imported by Cabela's, Cimarron F.A. Co., Navy Arms, Dixie Gun Works, Uberti U.S.A. Inc., E.M.F., Cimarron, Traditions, United States Patent Fire-Arms.
Price: About . . . . $225.00 to $445.00
Price: Single cased set (Navy Arms) $405.00
Price: Deluxe Walker with French fitted case (Navy Arms) $540.00
Price: Hartford model, steel frame, German silver trim,
cartouche (E.M.F.) $295.00

BLACKPOWDER

Armoury R140 Hawken

Cabela's Blue Ridge

Cabela's Traditional Hawken

Cabela's Lightning Fire Fluted

ARMOURY R140 HAWKEN RIFLE

Caliber: 45, 50 or 54. **Barrel:** 29". **Weight:** 8-3/4 to 9 lbs. **Length:** 45-3/4" overall. **Stock:** Walnut, with cheekpiece. **Sights:** Dovetail front, fully adjustable rear. **Features:** Octagon barrel, removable breech plug; double set triggers; blued barrel, brass stock fittings, color case-hardened percussion lock. From Armsport, The Armoury.
Price: .... **$225.00 to $245.00**

AUSTIN & HALLECK MODEL 420 LR IN-LINE RIFLE

Caliber: 50. **Barrel:** 26", 1" octagon to 3/4" round; 1:28" twist. **Weight:** 7-7/8 lbs. **Length:** 47-1/2" overall. **Stock:** Lightly figured maple in Classic or Monte Carlo style. **Sights:** Ramp front, fully adjustable rear. **Features:** Blue or electroless nickel finish; in-line percussion action with removable weather shroud; Timney adjustable target trigger with sear block safety. Introduced 1998. Made in U.S. by Austin & Halleck.
Price: Blue **$459.00**
Price: Stainless steel **$520.00**
Price: Blue, hand-select highly figured wood **$737.00**

Austin & Halleck Model 320 LR In-Line Rifle

Similar to the Model 420 LR except has black resin synthetic stock with checkered grip and forend. Introduced 1998. Made in U.S. by Austin & Halleck.
Price: Blue **$380.00**
Price: Stainless steel **$446.00**

AUSTIN & HALLECK MOUNTAIN RIFLE

Caliber: 50. **Barrel:** 32"; 1:66" twist; 1" flats. **Weight:** 7-1/2 lbs. **Length:** 49" overall. **Stock:** Curly maple. **Sights:** Silver blade front, buckhorn rear. **Features:** Available in percussion or flintlock; double throw adjustable set triggers; rust brown finish. Made in U.S. by Austin & Halleck.
Price: Flintlock **$539.00**
Price: Percussion **$578.00**
Price: Fancy wood **$592.00**

BOSTONIAN PERCUSSION RIFLE

Caliber: 45. **Barrel:** 30", octagonal. **Weight:** 7-1/4 lbs. **Length:** 46" overall. **Stock:** Walnut. **Sights:** Blade front, fixed notch rear. **Features:** Color case-hardened lock, brass trigger guard, buttplate, patchbox. Imported from Italy by E.M.F.
Price: **$285.00**

CABELA'S TRADITIONAL HAWKEN

Caliber: 50, 54. **Barrel:** 29". **Weight:** About 9 lbs. **Stock:** Walnut. **Sights:** Blade front, open adjustable rear. **Features:** Flintlock or percussion. Adjustable double-set triggers. Polished brass furniture, color case-hardened lock. Imported by Cabela's.
Price: Percussion, right-hand **$189.99**
Price: Percussion, left-hand **$199.99**
Price: Flintlock, right-hand **$224.99**

CABELA'S BLUE RIDGE RIFLE

Caliber: 32, 36, 45, 50. **Barrel:** 39", octagonal. **Weight:** About 7-3/4 lbs. **Length:** 55" overall. **Stock:** American black walnut. **Sights:** Blade front, rear drift adjustable for windage. **Features:** Color case-hardened lockplate and cock/hammer, brass trigger guard and buttplate, double set, double-phased triggers. From Cabela's.
Price: Percussion **$379.99**
Price: Flintlock **$399.99**

CABELA'S LIGHTNING FIRE FLUTED RIFLE

Caliber: 50. **Barrel:** 24", fluted; 1:32" twist; muzzle brake. **Weight:** 7 lbs. **Length:** NA. **Stock:** Black synthetic or laminated wood. **Sights:** Blade front, open fully adjustable rear. **Features:** Bolt-action in-line ignition uses musket caps. Introduced 1999. From Cabela's.
Price: Stainless, laminated stock **$299.99**
Price: Nickel barrel with muzzle brake, black stock **$279.99**

BLACKPOWDER MUSKETS & RIFLES

Cabela's Timber Ridge

Cabela's Lightning Fire Sidelock

Cook & Brother

CABELA'S KODIAK EXPRESS DOUBLE RIFLE

Caliber: 50, 54, 58, 72. **Barrel:** Length n/a; 1:48" twist. **Weight:** 9.3 lbs. **Length:** 45-1/4" overall. **Stock:** European walnut, oil finish. **Sights:** Fully adjustable double folding-leaf rear, ramp front. **Features:** Percussion. Barrels regulated to point of aim at 75 yards; polished and engraved lock, top tang and trigger guard. From Cabela's.
Price: 50, 54, 58 calibers $649.99
Price: 72 caliber $679.99

CABELA'S LEGACY IN-LINE RIFLE

Caliber: 50. **Barrel:** 22"; 1:28" twist. **Weight:** 9-2/3 lbs. **Length:** 40-1/2" overall. **Stock:** Walnut-stained hardwood with rubber recoil pad. **Sights:** Adjustable rear, ramp front. **Features:** In-line ignition; double safety system; removable breech plug; drilled and tapped for scope mount. Introduced 2000. From Cabela's.
Price: $99.99

CABELA'S LIGHTNING FIRE SIDELOCK RIFLE

Caliber: 50. **Barrel:** 28-3/4"; 1:32" twist. **Weight:** 7.85 lbs. **Length:** NA. **Stock:** Walnut-stained hardwood. **Sights:** Fiber optic front and rear. **Features:** Uses musket cap ignition. Comes with sling swivels, rubber recoil pad, color case-hardened lock. Introduced 1999. From Cabela's.
Price: $219.99

CABELA'S TIMBER RIDGE RIFLE

Caliber: 50, 54. **Barrel:** 24"; 1:32" twist (50-cal.), 1:48" twist (54-cal.). **Weight:** 7-1/2 lbs. **Length:** 42" overall. **Stock:** Composite; black or Advantage camo. **Sights:** Bead on ramp front, open adjustable rear. **Features:** In-line ignition system; sling swivel studs; synthetic ramrod; stainless steel breech plug. Introduced 1999. From Cabela's.
Price: Black stock....................................$129.99
Price: Advantage camo stock...........................$159.99

Cabela's Sporterized Hawken Hunter Rifle

Similar to the Traditional Hawken's except has more modern stock style with rubber recoil pad, blued furniture, sling swivels. Percussion only, in 50- or 54-caliber.
Price: Carbine or rifle, right-hand $219.99

COLT MODEL 1861 MUSKET

Caliber: 58. **Barrel:** 40". **Weight:** 9 lbs., 3 oz. **Length:** 56" overall. **Stock:** Oil-finished walnut. **Sight:** Blade front, adjustable folding leaf rear. **Features:** Made to original specifications and has authentic Civil War Colt markings. Bright-finished metal, blued nipple and rear sight. Bayonet and accessories available. From Colt Blackpowder Arms Co.
Price: $799.95

COOK & BROTHER CONFEDERATE CARBINE

Caliber: 58. **Barrel:** 24". **Weight:** 7-1/2 lbs. **Length:** 40-1/2" overall. **Stock:** Select walnut. **Features:** Recreation of the 1861 New Orleans-made artillery carbine. Color case-hardened lock, browned barrel. Buttplate, trigger guard, barrel bands, sling swivels and nosecap of polished brass. From Euroarms of America.
Price: $447.00
Price: Cook & Brother rifle (33" barrel)................... $480.00

CUMBERLAND MOUNTAIN BLACKPOWDER RIFLE

Caliber: 50. **Barrel:** 26", round. **Weight:** 9-1/2 lbs. **Length:** 43" overall. **Stock:** American walnut. **Sights:** Bead front, open rear adjustable for windage. **Features:** Falling block action fires with shotshell primer. Blued receiver and barrel. Introduced 1993. Made in U.S. by Cumberland Mountain Arms, Inc.
Price: $931.50

CVA COLORADO MUSKET MAG 100 RIFLE

Caliber: 50, 54 **Barrel:** 26"; 1:32" twist. **Weight:** 7-1/2 lbs. **Length:** 42" overall. **Stock:** Synthetic; black, Hardwoods or X-Tra Brown camo. **Sights:** Illuminator front and rear. **Features:** Sidelock action uses musket caps for ignition. Introduced 1999. From CVA.
Price: With black stock....................................$184.95
Price: With camo stock....................................$219.95

CVA YOUTH HUNTER RIFLE

Caliber: 50. **Barrel:** 24"; 1:48" twist, octagonal. **Weight:** 5-1/2 lbs. **Length:** 38" overall. **Stock:** Stained hardwood. **Sights:** Bead front, Williams adjustable rear. **Features:** Oversize trigger guard; wooden ramrod. Introduced 1999. From CVA.
Price: $129.95

CVA Firebolt

CVA St. Louis Hawken

CVA Accubolt Pro

Dixie English Matchlock

CVA BOBCAT RIFLE

Caliber: 50 and 54. **Barrel:** 26"; 1:48" twist. **Weight:** 6-1/2 lbs. **Length:** 40" overall. **Stock:** Dura-Grip synthetic. **Sights:** Blade front, open rear. **Features:** Oversize trigger guard; wood ramrod; matte black finish. Introduced 1995. From CVA.
Price: **$125.95**

CVA ECLIPSE IN-LINE RIFLE

Caliber: 50, 54. **Barrel:** 24" round; 1:32" rifling. **Weight:** 7 lbs. **Length:** 42" overall. **Stock:** Black Advantage camo synthetic. **Sights:** Illuminator Fiber Optic Sight System; drilled and tapped for scope mounting. **Features:** In-line action uses modern trigger with automatic safety; stainless percussion bolt; swivel studs. Three-way ignition system (No. 11, musket or No. 209 shotgun primers). From CVA.
Price: 50 or 54, blue, black stock **$159.95**
Price: 50 or 54, blue, Advantage Brown camo stock **$199.95**
Price: 50 or 54, Hardwoods camo **$199.95**

CVA Staghorn Rifle

Similar to the Eclipse except has standard open sights, manual safety, black DuraGrip stock and ramrod. From CVA.
Price: 50 or 54 .... **$134.95**

CVA MOUNTAIN RIFLE

Caliber: 50. **Barrel:** 32"; 1:66" rifling. **Weight:** 8-1/2 lbs. **Length:** NA **Stock:** American hard maple. **Sights:** Blade front, buckhorn rear. **Features:** Browned steel furniture; German silver wedge plates; patchbox. Made in U.S. From CVA.
Price: **$379.95**

CVA ST. LOUIS HAWKEN RIFLE

Caliber: 50, 54. **Barrel:** 28", octagon; 15/16" across flats; 1:48" twist. **Weight:** 8 lbs. **Length:** 44" overall. **Stock:** Select hardwood. **Sights:**

Beaded blade front, fully adjustable open rear. **Features:** Fully adjustable double-set triggers; synthetic ramrod (kits have wood); brass patchbox, wedge plates, nosecap, thimbles, trigger guard and buttplate; blued barrel; color case-hardened, engraved lockplate. V-type mainspring. Button breech. Introduced 1981. From CVA.
Price: St. Louis Hawken, finished (50-, 54-cal.) **$194.95**
Price: Left-hand, percussion.......................... **$234.95**
Price: Flintlock, 50-cal. only **$234.95**
Price: Percussion kit (50-cal., blued, wood ramrod).......... **$169.95**

CVA HunterBolt MusketMag Rifle

Similar to the Firebolt except has standard open sights, black DuraGrip synthetic stock. Available in camo X-Tra Brown and Hardwoods camo. Three-way ignition system. From CVA.
Price: 50 or 54 .... **$184.95 to $239.95**

CVA FIREBOLT MUSKETMAG BOLT-ACTION IN-LINE RIFLES

Caliber: 50, 54. **Barrel:** 24". **Weight:** 7 lbs. **Length:** NA. **Stock:** DuraGrip synthetic; thumbhole, traditional, camo. **Sights:** CVA Illuminator Fiber Optic Sight System. **Features:** Bolt-action, in-line ignition system. Stainless steel or matte blue barrel; removable breech plug; trigger-block safety. Introduced 1997. Three-way ignition system. From CVA.
Price: Stainless barrel, traditional stock **$299.95**
Price: Matte blue barrel, camo stock **$279.95**
Price: Matte blue barrel, traditional stock **$239.95**
Price: With Teflon finish, black stock **$279.95**
Price: As above, synthetic Sniper stock **$299.95**
Price: As above, synthetic Advantage camo stock............. **$299.95**

DIXIE ENGLISH MATCHLOCK MUSKET

Caliber: 72. **Barrel:** 44". **Weight:** 8 lbs. **Length:** 57.75" overall. **Stock:** Walnut with satin oil finish. **Sights:** Blade front, open rear adjustable for windage. **Features:** Replica of circa 1600-1680 English matchlock. Getz barrel with 11" octagonal area at rear, rest is round with cannon-type muzzle. All steel finished in the white. Imported by Dixie Gun Works.
Price: **$895.00**

Dixie Inline Carbine

Dixie 1859 Sharps

Dixie Model 1816

Dixie U.S. Model 1861

DIXIE EARLY AMERICAN JAEGER RIFLE

NEW! **Caliber:** 54. **Barrel:** 27-1/2" octagonal; 1:24" twist. **Weight:** 8-1/4 lbs. **Length:** 43-1/2" overall. **Stock:** American walnut; sliding wooden patchbox on on butt. **Sights:** Notch rear, blade front. **Features:** Flintlock or percussion. Browned steel furniture. Introduced 2000. Imported from Italy by Dixie Gun Works.
Price: Flintlock or percussion **$695.00**

DIXIE DELUXE CUB RIFLE

Caliber: 40. **Barrel:** 28". **Weight:** 6-1/2 lbs. **Stock:** Walnut. **Sights:** Fixed.**Features:** Short rifle for small game and beginning shooters. Brass patchbox and furniture. Flint or percussion. From Dixie Gun Works.
Price: Finished **$415.00**
Price: Kit **$375.00**
Price: Super Cub (50-caliber) **$367.00**

DIXIE 1863 SPRINGFIELD MUSKET

Caliber: 58 (.570" patched ball or .575" Minie). **Barrel:** 50", rifled. **Stock:** Walnut stained. **Sights:** Blade front, adjustable ladder-type rear. **Features:** Bright-finish lock, barrel, furniture. Reproduction of the last of the regulation muzzleloaders. Imported from Japan by Dixie Gun Works.
Price: Finished **$595.00**
Price: Kit **$525.00**

DIXIE INLINE CARBINE

Caliber: 50, 54. **Barrel:** 24"; 1:32" twist. **Weight:** 6.5 lbs. **Length:** 41" overall. **Stock:** Walnut-finished hardwood with Monte Carlo comb. **Sights:** Ramp front with red insert, open fully adjustable rear. **Features:** Sliding "bolt" fully encloses cap and nipple. Fully adjustable trigger, automatic safety. Aluminum ramrod. Imported from Italy by Dixie Gun Works.
Price: **$349.95**

DIXIE PEDERSOLI 1857 MAUSER RIFLE

NEW! **Caliber:** 54. **Barrel:** 39-3/8". **Weight:** N/A. **Length:** 52" overall. **Stock:** European walnut with oil finish, sling swivels. **Sights:** Fully adjustable rear, lug front. **Features:** Percussion (musket caps). Armory bright finish with color case-hardened lock and barrel tang, engraved lockplate, steel ramrod. Introduced 2000. Imported from Italy by Dixie Gun Works.
Price: **$895.00**

DIXIE PEDERSOLI 1766 CHARLEVILLE MUSKET

Caliber: 69. **Barrel:** 44-3/4". **Weight:** 10-1/2 lbs. **Length:** 57-1/2" overall. **Stock:** European walnut with oil finish. **Sights:** Fixed rear, lug front. **Features:** Smoothbore flintlock. Armory bright finish with steel furniture and ramrod. Introduced 2000. Imported from Italy by Dixie Gun Works.
Price: **$795.00**

DIXIE SHARPS NEW MODEL 1859 MILITARY RIFLE

Caliber: 54. **Barrel:** 30", 6-groove; 1:48" twist. **Weight:** 9 lbs. **Length:** 45-1/2" overall. **Stock:** Oiled walnut. **Sights:** Blade front, ladder-style rear. **Features:** Blued barrel, color case-hardened barrel bands, receiver, hammer, nosecap, lever, patchbox cover and buttplate. Introduced 1995. Imported from Italy by Dixie Gun Works.
Price: **$895.00**

DIXIE U.S. MODEL 1816 FLINTLOCK MUSKET

Caliber: 69. **Barrel:** 42", smoothbore. **Weight:** 9.75 lbs. **Length:** 56.5" overall. **Stock:** Walnut with oil finish. **Sights:** Blade front. **Features:** All metal finished "National Armory Bright"; three barrel bands with springs; steel ramrod with button-shaped head. Imported by Dixie Gun Works.
Price: **$725.00**

DIXIE U.S. MODEL 1861 SPRINGFIELD

Caliber: 58. **Barrel:** 40". **Weight:** About 8 lbs. **Length:** 55-13/16" overall. **Stock:** Oil-finished walnut. **Sights:** Blade front, step adjustable rear. **Features:** Exact recreation of original rifle. Sling swivels attached to trigger guard bow and middle barrel band. Lockplate marked "1861" with eagle motif and "U.S. Springfield" in front of hammer; "U.S." stamped on top of buttplate. From Dixie Gun Works.
Price: **$595.00**
Price: From Stone Mountain Arms **$599.00**
Price: Kit **$525.00**

Euroarms Volunteer

Euroarms 1861

Gonic Model 93 Thumbhole

Great American Sporting

E.M.F. 1863 SHARPS MILITARY CARBINE
Caliber: 54. **Barrel:** 22", round. **Weight:** 8 lbs. **Length:** 39" overall. **Stock:** Oiled walnut. **Sights:** Blade front, military ladder-type rear. **Features:** Color case-hardened lock, rest blued. Imported by E.M.F.
Price: $600.00

EUROARMS VOLUNTEER TARGET RIFLE
Caliber: .451. **Barrel:** 33" (two-band), 36" (three-band). **Weight:** 11 lbs. (two-band). **Length:** 48.75" overall (two-band). **Stock:** European walnut with checkered wrist and forend. **Sights:** Hooded bead front, adjustable rear with interchangeable leaves. **Features:** Alexander Henry-type rifling with 1:20" twist. Color case-hardened hammer and lockplate, brass trigger guard and nosecap, rest blued. Imported by Euroarms of America.
Price: Two-band $720.00
Price: Three-band $773.00

EUROARMS 1861 SPRINGFIELD RIFLE
Caliber: 58. **Barrel:** 40". **Weight:** About 10 lbs. **Length:** 55.5" overall. **Stock:** European walnut. **Sights:** Blade front, three-leaf military rear. **Features:** Reproduction of the original three-band rifle. Lockplate marked "1861" with eagle and "U.S. Springfield." Metal left in the white. Imported by Euroarms of America.
Price: $530.00

GONIC MODEL 93 M/L RIFLE
Caliber: 45, 50. **Barrel:** 26"; 1:24" twist. **Weight:** 6-1/2 to 7 lbs. **Length:** 43" overall. **Stock:** American hardwood with black finish. **Sights:** Adjustable or aperture rear, hooded post front. **Features:** Adjustable trigger with side safety; unbreakable ram rod; comes with A. Z. scope bases installed. Introduced 1993. Made in U.S. by Gonic Arms, Inc.
Price: Model 93 Standard (blued barrel). $686.00
Price: Model 93 Standard (stainless brl., 50 cal. only) $745.00

Gonic Model 93 Deluxe M/L Rifle
Similar to the Model 93 except has classic-style walnut or gray laminated wood stock. Introduced 1998. Made in U.S. by Gonic Arms, Inc.
Price: Blue barrel, sights, scope base, choice of stock $859.00
Price: Stainless barrel, sights, scope base, choice of stock
(50 cal. only)....................................... $918.00
Price: Blue barrel, peep sight, scope bases, choice of stock..... $869.00
Price: Stainless barrel, peep sight, scope base, choice of stock
(50 cal. only)....................................... $928.00

Gonic Model 93 Mountain Thumbhole M/L Rifles
Similar to the Model 93 except has high-grade walnut or gray laminate stock with extensive hand-checkered panels, Monte Carlo cheekpiece and beavertail forend; integral muzzle brake. Introduced 1998. Made in U.S. by Gonic Arms, Inc.
Price: Blue or stainless............................... $2,500.00

Gonic Model 93 Deluxe Rifle
Price: Blue or stainless barrel, walnut or gray laminate stock .. $1,612.00

GREAT AMERICAN SPORTING RIFLE
Caliber: 69. **Barrel:** 28", 1-1/4" octagon to 1-1/8" round. **Weight:** 10 lbs. **Length:** NA **Stock:** Walnut. **Sights:** Silver blade front, adjustable semi-buckhorn rear. **Features:** Hooked, patent Manton-style breech plug; iron furniture; bedded barrel; brown finish. Made in U.S. by October Country Muzzleloading, Inc.
Price: $1,495.00

HARPER'S FERRY 1803 FLINTLOCK RIFLE
Caliber: 54 or 58. **Barrel:** 35". **Weight:** 9 lbs. **Length:** 59-1/2" overall. **Stock:** Walnut with cheekpiece. **Sights:** Brass blade front, fixed steel rear. **Features:** Brass trigger guard, sideplate, buttplate; steel patchbox. Imported by Euroarms of America, Navy Arms (54-cal. only), Cabela's.
Price: .... $495.95 to $729.00
Price: 54-cal. (Navy Arms) $625.00
Price: 54-caliber (Cabela's) $599.99

BLACKPOWDER MUSKETS & RIFLES

Harper's Ferry 1803

J.P. Murray

Kentucky Flintlock

Knight T-Bolt M/L

HAWKEN RIFLE

Caliber: 45, 50, 54 or 58. **Barrel:** 28", blued, 6-groove rifling. **Weight:** 8-3/4 lbs. **Length:** 44" overall. **Stock:** Walnut with cheekpiece. **Sights:** Blade front, fully adjustable rear. **Features:** Coil mainspring, double-set triggers, polished brass furniture. From Armsport, Navy Arms, E.M.F.
Price: . . . . $220.00 to $345.00

J.P. MURRAY 1862-1864 CAVALRY CARBINE

Caliber: 58 (.577" Minie). **Barrel:** 23". **Weight:** 7 lbs., 9 oz. **Length:** 39" overall. **Stock:** Walnut. **Sights:** Blade front, rear drift adjustable for windage. **Features:** Browned barrel, color case-hardened lock, blued swivel and band springs, polished brass buttplate, trigger guard, barrel bands. From Navy Arms, Euroarms of America.
Price: . . . . $405.00 to $453.00

J.P. HENRY TRADE RIFLE

Caliber: 54. **Barrel:** 34"; 1" flats. **Weight:** 8-1/2 lbs. **Length:** 45" overall. **Stock:** Premium curly maple. **Sights:** Silver blade front, fixed buckhorn rear. **Features:** Brass buttplate, side plate, trigger guard and nosecap; browned barrel and lock; L&R Large English percussion lock; single trigger. Made in U.S. by J.P. Gunstocks, Inc.
Price: $965.50

KENTUCKIAN RIFLE

Caliber: 44. **Barrel:** 35". **Weight:** 7 lbs. (Rifle), 5-1/2 lbs. (Carbine). **Length:** 51" overall (Rifle), 43" (Carbine). **Stock:** Walnut stain. **Sights:** Brass blade front, steel V-ramp rear. **Features:** Octagon barrel, case-hardened and engraved lockplates. Brass furniture. Imported by Dixie Gun Works.
Price: Flintlock $269.95
Price: Percussion $259.95

KENTUCKY FLINTLOCK RIFLE

Caliber: 44, 45, or 50. **Barrel:** 35". **Weight:** 7 lbs. **Length:** 50" overall. **Stock:** Walnut stained, brass fittings. **Sights:** Fixed. **Features:** Available in carbine model also, 28" bbl. Some variations in detail, finish. Kits also available from some importers. Imported by Navy Arms, The Armoury.
Price: About . . . . $217.95 to $345.00
Price: Flintlock, 45 or 50-cal. (Navy Arms) $435.00

Kentucky Percussion Rifle

Similar to flintlock except percussion lock. Finish and features vary with importer. Imported by Navy Arms, The Armoury, CVA.
Price: About $259.95
Price: 45- or 50-cal. (Navy Arms) $425.00
Price: Kit, 50-cal. (CVA) $189.95

KNIGHT T-BOLT IN-LINE RIFLE

Caliber: 50. **Barrel:** 22", 26"; 1:28" twist. **Weight:** 6 lbs. **Length:** 41" overall. **Stock:** Composite black, Mossy Oak Break-Up or Advantage camo. **Sights:** Bead on ramp front, fully adjustable rear; drilled and tapped for scope mounts. **Features:** Straight-pull T-Bolt action with double-safety system, removable hammer, removable stainless steel breech plug; adjustable trigger. Introduced 1998. Made in U.S. by Knight Rifles.
Price: Blue or stainless . . . . $399.95 to $519.95

KNIGHT DISC IN-LINE RIFLE

Caliber: 50. **Barrel:** 24", 26". **Weight:** 7 lbs., 14 oz. **Length:** 43" overall (24" barrel). **Stock:** Checkered synthetic with palm swell grip, rubber recoil pad, swivel studs; black, Advantage or Mossy Oak Break-Up camouflage. **Sights:** Bead on ramp front, fully adjustable open rear. **Features:** Bolt-action in-line system uses #209 shotshell primer for ignition; primer is held in plastic drop-in Primer Disc. Available in blued or stainless steel. Made in U.S. by Knight Rifles.
Price: . . . . $449.95 to $569.95

BLACKPOWDER

Knight Disc M/L

Knight Bighorn In/Line

Knight LK-93 Wolverine

Knight Wolverine II

Knight Master Hunter Disc In-Line Rifle

Similar to Knight Disc rifle except features premier, wood laminated two-tone stock, gold-plated trigger and engraved trigger guard, jeweled bolt and fluted, air-gauged Green Mountain 26" barrel. Length 45" overall, weighs 7 lbs., 7 oz. Includes black composite thumbhole stock. Introduced 2000. Made in U.S. by Knight Rifles.
Price: **$999.95**

KNIGHT BIGHORN IN-LINE RIFLE

Caliber: 50. **Barrel:** 22", 26"; 1:28" twist. **Weight:** 7 lbs. **Length:** 41" overall (22" barrel). **Stock:** Synthetic; black Advantage or Mossy Oak Break-Up camouflage. Black rubber recoil pad. **Sights:** Bead on ramp front, full adjustable open rear. **Features:** Patented double safety system; adjustable trigger; comes with #11 Red Hot Nipple. Available in blue or stainless steel. Made in U.S. by Knight Rifles.
Price: .... **$329.95 to $439.95**

KNIGHT AMERICAN KNIGHT M/L RIFLE

Caliber: 50. **Barrel:** 22"; 1:28" twist. **Weight:** 6 lbs. **Length:** 41" overall. **Stock:** Black composite. **Sights:** Bead on ramp front, open fully adjustable rear. **Features:** Double safety system; one-piece removable hammer assembly; drilled and tapped for scope mounting. Introduced 1998. Made in U.S. by Knight Rifles.
Price: **$199.95**

KNIGHT MK-85 RIFLE

Caliber: 50, 54. **Barrel:** 24". **Weight:** 6-3/4 lbs. **Stock:** Walnut, laminated or composite. **Sights:** Hooded blade front on ramp, open adjustable rear.

Features: Patented double safety; Sure-Fire in-line percussion ignition; Timney Featherweight adjustable trigger; aluminum ramrod; receiver drilled and tapped for scope bases. Made in U.S. by Knight Rifles.
Price: Hunter, walnut stock. **$549.95**
Price: Stalker, laminated or composite stock **$569.95**
Price: Predator (stainless steel), laminated or composite stock. . **$649.95**
Price: Knight Hawk, stainless, composite thumbhole stock **$769.95**

KNIGHT LK-93 WOLVERINE RIFLE

Caliber: 50, 54. **Barrel:** 22", blued. **Weight:** 6 lbs. **Stock:** Black Advantage; Mossy Oak Break-Up camo. **Sights:** Bead front on ramp, open adjustable rear. **Features:** Patented double safety system; removable breech plug; Sure-Fire in-line percussion ignition system. Made in U.S. by Knight Rifles.
Price: From. **$269.95**
Price: LK-93 Stainless, from. **$339.95**
Price: LK-93 Thumbhole, from **$309.95**
Price: Youth model, blued, 50-cal. only **$279.95**

Knight Wolverine II In-Line Rifle

Similar to Wolverine except features solid composite stock in black, Advantage Timber, Mossy Oak Break-Up or Realtree Hardwoods camo patterns; adjustable trigger; blued or stainless steel; 50 or 54 caliber. Length 41" overall, weighs 6 lbs., 11 oz. Introduced 2000. Made in U.S. by Knight Rifles.
Price: Blued finish, black composite stock **$269.95**

LONDON ARMORY 2-BAND 1858 ENFIELD

Caliber: .577" Minie, .575" round ball. **Barrel:** 33". **Weight:** 10 lbs. **Length:** 49" overall. **Stock:** Walnut. **Sights:** Folding leaf rear adjustable for elevation. **Features:** Blued barrel, color case-hardened lock and hammer, polished brass buttplate, trigger guard, nosecap. From Navy Arms, Euroarms of America, Dixie Gun Works.
Price: .... **$385.00 to $531.00**

London Armory 1861

Lyman Cougar In/Line

Lyman Trade

Lyman Deerstalker

LONDON ARMORY 1861 ENFIELD MUSKETOON

Caliber: 58, Minie ball. **Barrel:** 24", round. **Weight:** 7 - 7-1/2 lbs. **Length:** 40-1/2" overall. **Stock:** Walnut, with sling swivels. **Sights:** Blade front, graduated military-leaf rear. **Features:** Brass trigger guard, nosecap, buttplate; blued barrel, bands, lockplate, swivels. Imported by Euroarms of America, Navy Arms.

Price: .... $300.00 to $427.00
Price: Kit .... $365.00 to $373.00

LONDON ARMORY 3-BAND 1853 ENFIELD

Caliber: 58 (.577" Minie, .575" round ball, .580" maxi ball). **Barrel:** 39". **Weight:** 9-1/2 lbs. **Length:** 54" overall. **Stock:** European walnut. **Sights:** Inverted "V" front, traditional Enfield folding ladder rear. **Features:** Recreation of the famed London Armory Company Pattern 1853 Enfield Musket. One-piece walnut stock, brass buttplate, trigger guard and nosecap. Lockplate marked "London Armoury Co." and with a British crown. Blued Baddeley barrel bands. From Dixie Gun Works, Euroarms of America, Navy Arms.

Price: About .... $350.00 to $495.00
Price: Assembled kit (Dixie, Euroarms of America) .. $425.00 to $431.00

LYMAN COUGAR IN-LINE RIFLE

Caliber: 50 or 54. **Barrel:** 22"; 1:24" twist. **Weight:** NA. **Length:** NA. **Stock:** Smooth walnut; swivel studs. **Sights:** Bead on ramp front, folding adjustable rear. Drilled and tapped for Lyman 57WTR receiver sight and Weaver scope bases. **Features:** Blued barrel and receiver. Has bolt safety notch and trigger safety. Rubber recoil pad. Delrin ramrod. Introduced 1996. From Lyman.

Price: $249.95
Price: Stainless steel $299.95

LYMAN TRADE RIFLE

Caliber: 50, 54. **Barrel:** 28" octagon;1:48" twist. **Weight:** 8-3/4 lbs. **Length:** 45" overall. **Stock:** European walnut. **Sights:** Blade front, open rear adjustable for windage or optional fixed sights. **Features:** Fast twist rifling for conical bullets. Polished brass furniture with blue steel parts, stainless steel nipple. Hook breech, single trigger, coil spring percussion lock. Steel barrel rib and ramrod ferrules. Introduced 1980. From Lyman.

Price: Percussion $299.95
Price: Flintlock $324.95

LYMAN DEERSTALKER RIFLE

Caliber: 50, 54. **Barrel:** 24", octagonal; 1:48" rifling. **Weight:** 7-1/2 lbs. **Stock:** Walnut with black rubber buttpad. **Sights:** Lyman #37MA beaded front, fully adjustable fold-down Lyman #16A rear. **Features:** Stock has less drop for quick sighting. All metal parts are blackened, with color casehardened lock; single trigger. Comes with sling and swivels. Available in flint or percussion. Introduced 1990. From Lyman.

Price: 50- or 54-cal., percussion........................... $304.95
Price: 50- or 54-cal., flintlock $334.95
Price: 50- or 54-cal., percussion, left-hand.................. $319.95
Price: 50-cal., flintlock, left-hand $349.95
Price: Stainless steel $384.95

LYMAN GREAT PLAINS RIFLE

Caliber: 50- or 54-cal. **Barrel:** 32"; 1:60" twist. **Weight:** 9 lbs. **Stock:** Walnut. **Sights:** Steel blade front, buckhorn rear adjustable for windage and elevation and fixed notch primitive sight included. **Features:** Blued steel furniture. Stainless steel nipple. Coil spring lock, Hawken-style trigger guard and double-set triggers. Round thimbles recessed and sweated into rib. Steel wedge plates and toe plate. Introduced 1979. From Lyman.

Price: Percussion $434.95
Price: Flintlock $459.95
Price: Percussion kit.................................... $349.95
Price: Flintlock kit $374.95
Price: Left-hand percussion $444.95
Price: Left-hand flintlock................................ $469.95

Lyman Great Plains

Markesbery Black Bear

Markesbery KM Colorado

Markesbery KM Grizzly Bear

Lyman Great Plains Hunter Rifle

Similar to the Great Plains model except has 1:32" twist shallow-groove barrel and comes drilled and tapped for the Lyman 57GPR peep sight.
Price: .... **$434.95 to $459.95**

MARKESBERY KM BLACK BEAR M/L RIFLE

Caliber: 36, 45, 50, 54. **Barrel:** 24"; 1:26" twist. **Weight:** 6-1/2 lbs. **Length:** 38-1/2" overall. **Stock:** Two-piece American hardwood, walnut, black laminate, green laminate, black composition, X-Tra or Mossy Oak Break-Up camouflage. **Sights:** Bead front, open fully adjustable rear. **Features:** Interchangeable barrels; exposed hammer; Outer-Line Magnum ignition system uses small rifle primer or standard No. 11 cap and nipple. Blue, black matte, or stainless. Made in U.S. by Markesbery Muzzle Loaders.
Price: American hardwood walnut, blue finish **$536.63**
Price: American hardwood walnut, stainless **$553.09**
Price: Black laminate, blue finish **$539.67**
Price: Camouflage stock, blue finish **$556.46**
Price: Black composite, blue finish........................ **$532.65**

MARKESBERY KM COLORADO ROCKY MOUNTAIN M/L RIFLE

Caliber: 36, 45, 50, 54. **Barrel:** 24"; 1:26" twist. **Weight:** 6-1/2 lbs. **Length:** 38-1/2" overall. **Stock:** American hardwood walnut, green or black laminate. **Sights:** Firesight bead on ramp front, fully adjustable open rear. **Features:** Replicates Reed/Watson rifle of 1851. Straight grip stock with or without two barrel bands, rubber recoil pad, large-spur hammer. Made in U.S. by Markesbery Muzzle Loaders, Inc.
Price: American hardwood walnut, blue finish **$545.92**
Price: Black or green laminate, blue finish **$548.30**
Price: American hardwood walnut, stainless **$563.17**
Price: Black or green laminate, stainless **$566.34**

Markesbery KM Brown Bear M/L Rifle

Similar to the KM Black Bear except has one-piece thumbhole stock with Monte Carlo comb. Stock available in Crotch Walnut composite, green or black laminate, black composite or X-Tra or Mossy Oak Break-Up camouflage. Contact maker for complete price listing. Made in U.S. by Markesbery Muzzle Loaders, Inc.
Price: Black composite, blue finish......................... **$658.83**
Price: Crotch Walnut composite, stainless **$676.11**
Price: Green laminate, stainless............................ **$680.07**

Markesbery KM Grizzly Bear M/L Rifle

Similar to the KM Black Bear except has thumbhole buttstock with Monte Carlo comb. Stock available in Crotch Walnut composite, green or black laminate, black composite or X-Tra or Mossy Oak Break-Up camouflage. Contact maker for complete price listing. Made in U.S. by Markesbery Muzzle Loaders, Inc.
Price: Black composite, blue finish......................... **$642.96**
Price: Crotch Walnut composite, stainless **$660.98**
Price: Camouflage composite, blue finish **$666.67**

Markesbery KM Polar Bear M/L Rifle

Similar to the KM Black Bear except has one-piece stock with Monte Carlo comb. Stock available in American Hardwood walnut, green or black laminate, black composite, or X-Tra or Mossy Oak Break-Up camouflage. Has interchangeable barrel system, Outer-Line ignition system, cross-bolt double safety. Available in 36, 45, 50, 54 caliber. Contact maker for full price listing. Made in U.S. by Markesbery Muzzle Loaders, Inc.
Price: American Hardwood walnut , blue finish **$539.01**
Price: Black composite, blue finish......................... **$536.63**
Price: Black laminate, blue finish **$541.17**
Price: Camouflage, stainless **$573.94**

Markesbery KM Brown Bear

Mississippi 1841

Navy Arms 1763

Navy Arms 1859 Sharps

Navy Arms Berdan

Mississippi 1841 Percussion Rifle

Similar to Zouave rifle but patterned after U.S. Model 1841. Imported by Dixie Gun Works, Euroarms of America, Navy Arms.
Price: About . . . . **$430.00** to **$500.00**

NAVY ARMS HAWKEN HUNTER RIFLE/CARBINE

Caliber: 50, 54, 58. **Barrel:** 22-1/2" or 28"; 1:48" twist. **Weight:** 6 lbs., 12 oz. **Length:** 39" overall. **Stock:** Walnut with cheekpiece. **Sights:** Blade front, fully adjustable rear. **Features:** Double-set triggers; all metal has matte black finish; rubber recoil pad; detachable sling swivels. Imported by Navy Arms.
Price: Rifle or Carbine **$240.00**

NAVY ARMS 1763 CHARLEVILLE

Caliber: 69. **Barrel:** 44-5/8". **Weight:** 8 lbs., 12 oz. **Length:** 59-3/8" overall. **Stock:** Walnut. **Sights:** Brass blade front. **Features:** Replica of the French musket used by American troops during the Revolution. Imported by Navy Arms.
Price: **$925.00**

NAVY ARMS PARKER-HALE VOLUNTEER RIFLE

Caliber: .451. **Barrel:** 32". **Weight:** 9-1/2 lbs. **Length:** 49" overall. **Stock:** Walnut, checkered wrist and forend. **Sights:** Globe front, adjustable lad-

der-type rear. **Features:** Recreation of the type of gun issued to volunteer regiments during the 1860s. Rigby-pattern rifling, patent breech, detented lock. Stock is glass bedded for accuracy. Imported by Navy Arms.
Price: **$850.00**

NAVY ARMS 1859 SHARPS CAVALRY CARBINE

Caliber: 54. **Barrel:** 22". **Weight:** 7-3/4 lbs. **Length:** 39" overall. **Stock:** Walnut. **Sights:** Blade front, military ladder-type rear. **Features:** Color case-hardened action, blued barrel. Has saddle ring. Introduced 1991. Imported from Navy Arms.
Price: **$940.00**

NAVY ARMS BERDAN 1859 SHARPS RIFLE

Caliber: 54. **Barrel:** 30". **Weight:** 8 lbs., 8 oz. **Length:** 46-3/4" overall. **Stock:** Walnut. **Sights:** Blade front, folding military ladder-type rear. **Features:** Replica of the Union sniper rifle used by Berdan's 1st and 2nd Sharpshooter regiments. Color case-hardened receiver, patchbox, furniture. Double-set triggers. Imported by Navy Arms.
Price: **$1,095.00**
Price: 1859 Sharps Infantry Rifle (three-band) **$1,030.00**

NAVY ARMS PENNSYLVANIA LONG RIFLE

Caliber: 32, 45. **Barrel:** 40-1/2". **Weight:** 7-1/2 lbs. **Length:** 56-1/2" overall. **Stock:** Walnut. **Sights:** Blade front, fully adjustable rear. **Features:** Browned barrel, brass furniture, polished lock with double-set triggers. Imported by Navy Arms.
Price: Percussion **$490.00**
Price: Flintlock **$505.00**

BLACKPOWDER MUSKETS & RIFLES

Navy Arms Whitworth

Navy Arms Smith Carbine

Navy Arms 1863

Pacific Model 1837 Zephyr

NAVY ARMS PARKER-HALE WHITWORTH MILITARY TARGET RIFLE

Caliber: 45. **Barrel:** 36". **Weight:** 9-1/4 lbs. **Length:** 52-1/2" overall. **Stock:** Walnut. Checkered at wrist and forend. **Sights:** Hooded post front, open step-adjustable rear. **Features:** Faithful reproduction of the Whitworth rifle, only bored for 45-cal. Trigger has a detented lock, capable of being adjusted very finely without risk of the sear nose catching on the half-cock bent and damaging both parts. Introduced 1978. Imported by Navy Arms.
Price: $875.00

NAVY ARMS SMITH CARBINE

Caliber: 50. **Barrel:** 21-1/2". **Weight:** 7-3/4 lbs. **Length:** 39" overall. **Stock:** American walnut. **Sights:** Brass blade front, folding ladder-type rear. **Features:** Replica of the breech-loading Civil War carbine. Color case-hardened receiver, rest blued. Cavalry model has saddle ring and bar, Artillery model has sling swivels. Imported by Navy Arms.
Price: Cavalry model $600.00
Price: Artillery model. $600.00

NAVY ARMS 1863 C.S. RICHMOND RIFLE

Caliber: 58. **Barrel:** 40". **Weight:** 10 lbs. **Length:** NA. **Stocks:** Walnut. **Sights:** Blade front, adjustable rear. **Features:** Copy of the three-band rifle musket made at Richmond Armory for the Confederacy. All steel polished bright. Imported by Navy Arms.
Price: $550.00

NAVY ARMS 1863 SPRINGFIELD

Caliber: 58, uses .575 Minie. **Barrel:** 40", rifled. **Weight:** 9-1/2 lbs. **Length:** 56" overall. **Stock:** Walnut. **Sights:** Open rear adjustable for elevation. **Features:** Full-size, three-band musket. Polished bright metal, including lock. From Navy Arms.
Price: Finished rifle. $550.00

NAVY ARMS 1861 SPRINGFIELD RIFLE

Caliber: 58. **Barrel:** 40" **Weight:** 10 lbs., 4 oz. **Length:** 56" overall. **Stock:** Walnut. **Sights:** Blade front, military leaf rear. **Features:** Steel barrel, lock and all furniture have polished bright finish. Has 1855-style hammer. Imported by Navy Arms.
Price: $550.00

PACIFIC RIFLE MODEL 1837 ZEPHYR

Caliber: 62. **Barrel:** 30", tapered octagon. **Weight:** 7-3/4 lbs. **Length:** NA. **Stock:** Oil-finished fancy walnut. **Sights:** German silver blade front, semi-buckhorn rear. Options available. **Features:** Improved underhammer action. First production rifle to offer Forsyth rifle, with narrow lands and shallow rifling with 1:144" pitch for high-velocity round balls. Metal finish is slow rust brown with nitre blue accents. Optional sights, finishes and integral muzzle brake available. Introduced 1995. Made in U.S. by Pacific Rifle Co.
Price: From. $995.00

Pacific Rifle Big Bore, African Rifles

Similar to the 1837 Zephyr except in 72-caliber and 8-bore. The 72-caliber is available in standard form with 28" barrel, or as the African with flat buttplate, checkered upgraded wood; weight is 9 lbs. The 8-bore African has dual-cap ignition, 24" barrel, weighs 12 lbs., checkered English walnut, engraving, gold inlays. Introduced 1998. Made in U.S. by Pacific Rifle Co.
Price: 72-caliber, from $1,150.00
Price: 8-bore from. $2,500.00

PEIFER MODEL TS-93 RIFLE

Caliber: 45, 50. **Barrel:** 24" Douglas premium; 1:20" twist in 45; 1:28" in 50. **Weight:** 7 lbs. **Length:** 43-1/4" overall. **Stock:** Bell & Carlson solid composite, with recoil pad, swivel studs. **Sights:** Williams bead front on ramp, fully adjustable open rear. Drilled and tapped for Weaver scope mounts with dovetail for rear peep. **Features:** In-line ignition uses #209 shotshell primer; extremely fast lock time; fully enclosed breech; adjustable trigger; automatic safety; removable primer holder. Blue or stainless. Made in U.S. by Peifer Rifle Co. Introduced 1996.

Peifer TS-93

Remington Model 700 ML

C.S. Richmond 1863

Ruger K77/50RSBBZ

Price: Blue, black stock **$730.00**
Price: Blue, wood or camouflage composite stock, or stainless
with black composite stock **$803.00**
Price: Stainless, wood or camouflage composite stock **$876.00**

PRAIRIE RIVER ARMS PRA CLASSIC RIFLE

Caliber: 50, 54. **Barrel:** 26"; 1:28" twist. **Weight:** 7-1/2 lbs. **Length:** 40-1/2" overall. **Stock:** Hardwood or black all-weather. **Sights:** Blade front, open adjustable rear. **Features:** Patented internal percussion ignition system. Drilled and tapped for scope mount. Introduced 1995. Made in U.S. by Prairie River Arms, Ltd.
Price: 4140 alloy barrel, hardwood stock **$375.00**
Price: As above, stainless barrel **$425.00**
Price: 4140 alloy barrel, black all-weather stock **$390.00**
Price: As above, stainless barrel **$440.00**

PRAIRIE RIVER ARMS PRA BULLPUP RIFLE

Caliber: 50, 54. **Barrel:** 28"; 1:28" twist. **Weight:** 7-1/2 lbs. **Length:** 31-1/2" overall. **Stock:** Hardwood or black all-weather. **Sights:** Blade front, open adjustable rear. **Features:** Bullpup design thumbhole stock. Patented internal percussion ignition system. Left-hand model available. Dovetailed for scope mount. Introduced 1995. Made in U.S. by Prairie River Arms, Ltd.
Price: 4140 alloy barrel, hardwood stock **$375.00**
Price: As above, black stock. **$390.00**
Price: Stainless barrel, hardwood stock **$425.00**
Price: As above, black stock. **$440.00**

REMINGTON MODEL 700 ML, MLS RIFLES

Caliber: 50, 54. **Barrel:** 24"; 1:28" twist. **Weight:** 7-3/4 lbs. **Length:** 44-1/2" overall. **Stock:** Black fiberglass-reinforced synthetic with checkered grip and forend; magnum-style buttpad. **Sights:** Ramped bead front, open fully adjustable rear. Drilled and tapped for scope mounts. **Features:** Uses the Remington 700 bolt action, stock design, safety and trigger mechanisms; removable stainelss steel breech plug, No. 11 nipple; solid aluminum ramrod. Comes with cleaning tools and accessories.
Price: ML, blued, 50-caliber only **$396.00**
Price: MLS, stainless, 50- or 54-caliber **$496.00**
Price: ML, blued, Mossy Oak Break-Up camo stock **$439.00**
Price: MLS, stainless, Mossy Oak Break-Up camo stock **$532.00**
Price: ML Youth (12-3/8" length of pull, 21" barrel) **$396.00**

C.S. RICHMOND 1863 MUSKET

Caliber: 58. **Barrel:** 40". **Weight:** 11 lbs. **Length:** 56-1/4" overall. **Stock:** European walnut with oil finish. **Sights:** Blade front, adjustable folding leaf rear. **Features:** Reproduction of the three-band Civil War musket. Sling swivels attached to trigger guard and middle barrel band. Lockplate marked "1863" and "C.S. Richmond." All metal left in the white. Brass buttplate and forend cap. Imported by Euroarms of America, Navy Arms.
Price: . . . . **NA**

RUGER 77/50 IN-LINE PERCUSSION RIFLE

Caliber: 50. **Barrel:** 22"; 1:28" twist. **Weight:** 6-1/2 lbs. **Length:** 41-1/2" overall. **Stock:** Birch with rubber buttpad and swivel studs. **Sights:** Gold bead front, folding leaf rear. Comes with Ruger scope mounts. **Features:** Shares design features with the Ruger 77/22 rifle. Stainless steel bolt and nipple/breech plug; uses #11 caps; three-position safety; blued steel ramrod. Introduced 1997. Made in U.S. by Sturm, Ruger & Co.
Price: 77/50RS **$434.00**
Price: 77/50RSO Officer's (straight-grip checkered walnut stock,
blued) **$555.00**
Price: K77/50RSBBZ (stainless steel, black laminated stock) **$601.00**
Price: K77/50RSP All-Weather (stainless steel,
synthetic stock). **$580.00**

BLACKPOWDER MUSKETS & RIFLES

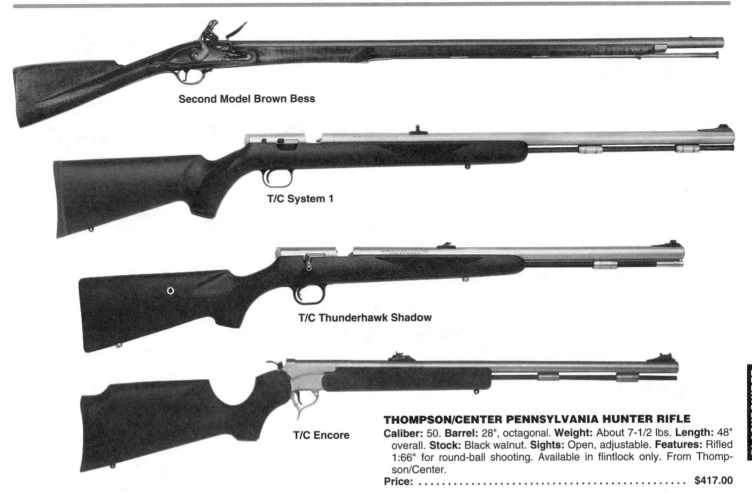

Second Model Brown Bess

T/C System 1

T/C Thunderhawk Shadow

T/C Encore

SECOND MODEL BROWN BESS MUSKET

Caliber: 75, uses .735" round ball. **Barrel:** 42", smoothbore. **Weight:** 9-1/2 lbs. **Length:** 59" overall. **Stock:** Walnut (Navy); walnut-stained hardwood (Dixie). **Sights:** Fixed. **Features:** Polished barrel and lock with brass trigger guard and buttplate. Bayonet and scabbard available. From Navy Arms, Dixie Gun Works, Cabela's.
Price: Finished .... $475.00 to $850.00
Price: Kit (Dixie Gun Works, Navy Arms) .... $575.00 to $625.00
Price: Carbine (Navy Arms) $835.00

THOMPSON/CENTER BLACK MOUNTAIN MAGNUM RIFLE

Caliber: 50, 54. **Barrel:** 26"; 1:28" twist. **Weight:** 7 lbs. **Length:** 4-3/4" overall. **Stock:** American Walnut or black composite. **Sights:** Ramp front with Tru-Glo fiber optic inseat, click adjustable open rear with Tru-Glo fiber optic inserts. **Features:** Side lock percussion with breeech designed for Pyrodex Pellets, loose blackpowder and Pyrodex. blued steel. Uses QLA muzzle system. Introduced 1999. Made in U.S. by Thompson/Center Arms.
Price: Blue, composite stock, 50-cal. $353.52
Price: Blue, walnut stock, 50- or 54-cal. (westraner) $387.16

THOMPSON/CENTER FIRE STORM RIFLE

Caliber: 50. **Barrel:** 26"; 1:28" twist. **Weight:** 7 lbs. **Length:** 41-3/4" overall. **Stock:** Black synthetic with rubber recoil pad, swivel studs. **Sights:** Click-adjustable steel rear and ramp-style front, both with fiber optic inserts. **Features:** Side hammer lock is the first designed for up to three 50-grain Pyrodex pellets; patented Pyrodex Pyramid breech directs ignition fire 360 degrees around base of pellet; uses 209 shotgun primers; Quick Load Accurizor Muzzle System; aluminum ramrod. Introduced 2000. Made in U.S. by Thomson/Center Arms.
Price: Blue finish, percussion model. $391.00
Price: Blue finish, flintlock model with 1:48" twist for round balls, conicals. $391.00

THOMPSON/CENTER PENNSYLVANIA HUNTER RIFLE

Caliber: 50. **Barrel:** 28", octagonal. **Weight:** About 7-1/2 lbs. **Length:** 48" overall. **Stock:** Black walnut. **Sights:** Open, adjustable. **Features:** Rifled 1:66" for round-ball shooting. Available in flintlock only. From Thompson/Center.
Price: $417.00

Thompson/Center Pennsylvania Hunter Carbine

Similar to the Pennsylvania Hunter except has 21" barrel, weighs 6.5 lbs., and has an overall length of 38". Designed for shooting patched round balls. Available in flintlock only. Introduced 1992. From Thompson/Center.
Price: $438.00

THOMPSON/CENTER SYSTEM 1 IN-LINE RIFLE

Caliber: 32, 50, 54, 58; 12-gauge. **Barrel:** 26" round; 1:38" twist. **Weight:** About 7-1/2lbs. **Length:** 44" overall. **Stock:** American black walnut or composite. **Sights:** Ramp front with white bead, adjustable leaf rear. **Features:** In-line ignition. Interchangeable barrels; removable breech plug allows cleaning from the breech; fully adjustable trigger; sliding thumb safety; QLA muzzle system; rubber recoil pad; sling swivel studs. Introduced 1997. Made in U.S. by Thompson/Center Arms.
Price: Blue, walnut stock $396.00
Price: Stainless, composite stock, 50-, 54-caliber $440.00
Price: Stainless, camo composite stock, 50-caliber $479.00
Price: Extra barrels, blue $176.00
Price: Extra barrels, stainless, 50-, 54-caliber $220.00

THOMPSON/CENTER ENCORE 209x50 MAGNUM

Caliber: 50. **Barrel:** 26"; interchangeable with centerfire calibers. **Weight:** 7 lbs. **Length:** 40-1/2" overall. **Stock:** American walnut butt and forend, or black composite. **Sights:** Tru-Glo Fiber Optic front, Tru-Glo Fiber Optic rear. **Features:** Blue or stainless steel. Uses the stock, frame and forend of the Encore centerfire pistol; break-open design using trigger guard spur; stainless steel universal breech plug; uses #209 shotshell primers. Introduced 1998. Made in U.S. by Thompson/Center Arms.
Price: $590.03
Price: Blue, walnut stock and forend $590.03
Price: Blue, composite stock and forend $590.03
Price: Stainless, composite stock and forend. $665.91

T/C Black Diamond

T/C Hawken

Traditions Buckhunter Pro In-Line

Traditions Buckhunter

THOMPSON/CENTER THUNDERHAWK SHADOW

Caliber: 50, 54. **Barrel:** 24"; 1:38" twist. **Weight:** 7 lbs. **Length:** 41-3/4" overall. **Stock:** American walnut or black composite with rubber recoil pad. **Sights:** Bead on ramp front, adjustable leaf rear. **Features:** Uses modern in-line ignition system, adjustable trigger. Knurled striker handle indicators for Safe and Fire. Black wood ramrod, Drilled and tapped for T/C scope mounts. Introduced 1996. From Thompson/Center Arms.
Price: Blued $294.00

THOMPSON/CENTER BLACK DIAMOND RIFLE

Caliber: 50. **Barrel:** 22-1/2" with QLA; 1:28" twist. **Weight:** 6 lbs., 9 oz. **Length:** 41-1/2" overall. **Stock:** Black Rynite with moulded-in checkering and grip cap, or walnut. **Sights:** Tru-Glo Fiber Optic ramp-style front, Tru-Glo Fiber Optic open rear. **Features:** In-line ignition system for musket cap, No. 11 cap, or 209 shotshell primer; removable universal breech plug; stainless steel construction. Introduced 1998. Made in U.S. by Thompson/Center Arms.
Price: $312.87
Price: With walnut stock $353.32

THOMPSON/CENTER HAWKEN RIFLE

Caliber: 45, 50 or 54. **Barrel:** 28" octagon, hooked breech. **Stock:** American walnut. **Sights:** Blade front, rear adjustable for windage and elevation. **Features:** Solid brass furniture, double-set triggers, button rifled barrel, coil-type mainspring. From Thompson/Center Arms.
Price: Percussion model (45-, 50- or 54-cal.) $489.35
Price: Flintlock model (50-cal.) $501.14

TRADITIONS BUCKHUNTER PRO IN-LINE RIFLES

Caliber: 50 (1:32" twist); 54 (1:48" twist). **Barrel:** 24" tapered round. **Weight:** 7-1/2 lbs. **Length:** 42" overall. **Stock:** Composite or thumbhole available in black, Break-Up or camouflage. **Sights:** Beaded blade front, fully adjustable open rear. Drilled and tapped for scope mounting. **Features:** In-line percussion ignition system; adjustable trigger; manual thumb safety; removable stainless steel breech plug. Eleven models available. Introduced 1996. From Traditions.
Price: . . . . $169.00 to $219.00

TRADITIONS BUCKSKINNER CARBINE

Caliber: 50. **Barrel:** 21"; 15/16" flats, half octagon, half round; 1:20" or 1:66" twist. **Weight:** 6 lbs. **Length:** 37" overall. **Stock:** Beech or black laminated. **Sights:** Beaded blade front, fiber optic open rear click adjustable for windage and elevation or fiber optics. **Features:** Uses V-type mainspring, single trigger. Non-glare hardware. From Traditions.
Price: Flintlock $218.00
Price: Flintlock, laminated stock $292.00

TRADITIONS IN-LINE BUCKHUNTER SERIES RIFLES

Caliber: 50, 54. **Barrel:** 24", round; 1:32" (50); 1:48" (54) twist. **Weight:** 7 lbs., 6 oz. to 8 lbs. **Length:** 41" overall. **Stock:** All-Weather black or camo composite. **Sights:** Fiber Optic blade front, click adjustable rear. Drilled and tapped for scope mounting. **Features:** Removable breech plug; PVC ramrod; sling swivels. Introduced 1995. From Traditions.
Price: $175.00
Price: With RS Redi-Pak (powder measure, powder flask, two fast loaders, 5-in-1 loader, capper, ball starter, ball puller, cleaning jag, nipple wrench, bullets) 50- and 54-caliber. $199.00
Price: Pro Model (fiber optics front & rear sights) . . . . $169.00 to $219.00

TRADITIONS DEERHUNTER RIFLE SERIES

Caliber: 32, 50 or 54. **Barrel:** 24", octagonal; 15/16" flats; 1:48" or 1:66" twist. **Weight:** 6 lbs. **Length:** 40" overall. **Stock:** Stained hardwood or All-Weather composite with rubber buttpad, sling swivels. **Sights:** Blade front, fixed rear or adjustable fiber optics. **Features:** Flint or percussion with color case-hardened lock. Hooked breech, oversized trigger guard, blackened furniture, PVC ramrod. All-Weather has composite stock and C-Nickel barrel. Drilled and tapped for scope mounting. Imported by Traditions, Inc.
Price: Percussion, 50 or 54; 1:48" twist $161.00
Price: Flintlock, 50-caliber only; 1:66" twist $183.00
Price: Flintlock, All-Weather, 50-cal. $161.00
Price: Percussion, All-Weather, 50 or 54 . . . . $152.00

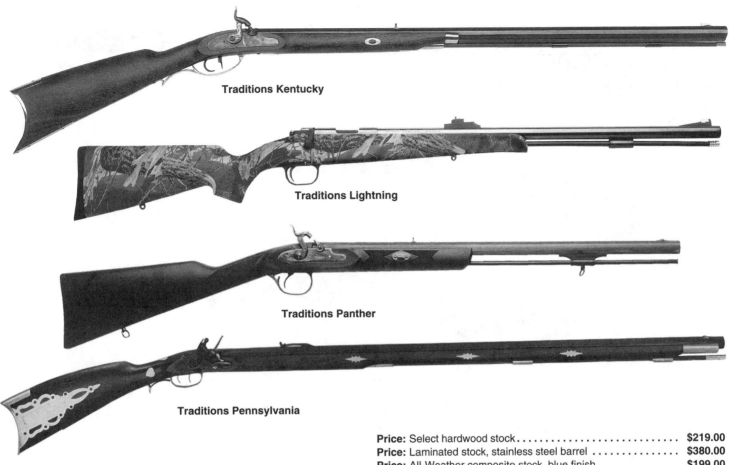

Traditions Kentucky

Traditions Lightning

Traditions Panther

Traditions Pennsylvania

Traditions Deerhunter All-Weather Composite Stock Rifle

Black composite stock with checkered grip and forend. Blued barrel, C-Nickel or Advantage camouflage finish, 50-caliber flintlock. Introduced 1996. Imported by Traditions.
Price: Blued, flintlock, 50-cal. **$160.00**
Price: Blued or Hardwoods, 50-cal. **$175.00**

TRADITIONS HAWKEN WOODSMAN RIFLE

Caliber: 50 and 54. **Barrel:** 28"; 15/16" flats. **Weight:** 7 lbs., 11 oz. **Length:** 44-1/2" overall. **Stock:** Walnut-stained hardwood. **Sights:** Beaded blade front, hunting-style open rear adjustable for windage and elevation. **Features:** Percussion only. Brass patchbox and furniture. Double triggers. From Traditions.
Price: 50 or 54 . . . . **$219.00**
Price: 50-cal., left-hand. **$233.00**
Price: 50-caliber, flintlock **$248.00**

TRADITIONS KENTUCKY RIFLE

Caliber: 50. **Barrel:** 33-1/2"; 7/8" flats; 1:66" twist. **Weight:** 7 lbs. **Length:** 49" overall. **Stock:** Beech; inletted toe plate. **Sights:** Blade front, fixed rear. **Features:** Full-length, two-piece stock; brass furniture; color case-hardened lock. Introduced 1995. From Traditions.
Price: Finished **$226.00**
Price: Kit. **$175.00**

TRADITIONS LIGHTNING BOLT-ACTION MUZZLELOADER

Caliber: 50, 54. **Barrel:** 24" round; blued, stainless, C-Nickel or Ultra Coat. **Weight:** 7 lbs. **Length:** 43" overall. **Stock:** Brown laminated, All-Weather composite, Advantage, or Break-Up camouflage. **Sights:** Fiber Optic blade front, fully adjustable open rear. **Features:** Twenty-one variations available. Field-removable stainless steel bolt; silent thumb safety; adjustable trigger; drilled and tapped for scope mounting. Lightning Fire System allows use of No. 11 or musket caps. Introduced 1997. Imported by Traditions.

Price: Select hardwood stock. **$219.00**
Price: Laminated stock, stainless steel barrel **$380.00**
Price: All-Weather composite stock, blue finish **$199.00**
Price: All-Weather composite, stainless steel **$279.00**
Price: Camouflage composite **$307.00**
Price: All-Weather composite **$307.00**
Price: Camouflage composite **$351.00**
Price: Composite, with muzzle brake. **$249.00**
Price: Composite, with muzzle brake, stainless, fluted barrel **$376.00**

Traditions Lightning Lightweight Bolt-Action Rifles

Similar to Lightning except features 22" lightweight, fluted barrel and Spider Web-pattern black composite stock. Overall length 41", weighs 6 lb., 5 oz. Introduced 2000. From Traditions.
Price: Blued finish. **$239.00**
Price: C-Nickel finish. **$249.00**
Price: Stainless **$289.00**

TRADITIONS PANTHER RIFLE

Caliber: 50. **Barrel:** 24" octagon (1:48" twist); 15/16" flats. **Weight:** 6 lbs. **Length:** 40" overall. **Stock:** All-Weather composite. **Sights:** Brass blade front, fixed rear. **Features:** Percussion only; color case-hardened lock; blackened furniture; sling swivels; PVC ramrod. Introduced 1996. Imported by Traditions.
Price: **$116.00**
Price: With RS Redi-Pak (powder measure, flask, fast loaders, 5-in-1 loader, capper, ball starter, ball puller, cleaning jag, nipple wrench). **$169.00**

TRADITIONS PENNSYLVANIA RIFLE

Caliber: 50. **Barrel:** 40-1/4"; 7/8" flats; 1:66" twist, octagon. **Weight:** 9 lbs. **Length:** 57-1/2" overall. **Stock:** Walnut. **Sights:** Blade front, adjustable rear. **Features:** Brass patchbox and ornamentation. Double-set triggers. From Traditions.
Price: Flintlock **$474.00**
Price: Percussion **$467.00**

Traditions Shenandoah

Traditions Tennessee

Traditions Thunder

Zouave Percussion

TRADITIONS SHENANDOAH RIFLE

Caliber: 50. **Barrel:** 33-1/2" octagon; 1:66" twist. **Weight:** 7 lbs., 3 oz. **Length:** 49-1/2" overall. **Stock:** Walnut. **Sights:** Blade front, buckhorn rear. **Features:** V-type mainspring; double-set trigger; solid brass buttplate, patchbox, nosecap, thimbles, trigger guard. Introduced 1996. From Traditions.
Price: Flintlock $365.00
Price: Percussion $350.00

TRADITIONS TENNESSEE RIFLE

Caliber: 50. **Barrel:** 24", octagon; 15/16" flats; 1:66" twist. **Weight:** 6 lbs. **Length:** 40-1/2" overall. **Stock:** Stained beech. **Sights:** Blade front, fixed rear. **Features:** One-piece stock has inletted brass furniture, cheekpiece; double-set trigger; V-type mainspring. Flint or percussion. Introduced 1995. From Traditions.
Price: Percussion $270.00
Price: Flintlock $284.00

TRADITIONS THUNDER MAGNUM RIFLE

Caliber: 50. **Barrel:** 24"; 1:32" twist. **Weight:** 7 lbs., 9 oz. **Length:** 42-1/2" overall. **Stock:** Hardwood or composite. **Sights:** Fiber optic front, adjustable rear. **Features:** Sidelock action with thumb-activated safety. Introduced 1999. From Traditions.
Price: Hardwood... $349.00
Price: Composite $339.00
Price: Composite, C-Nickel.............................. $359.00

TRYON TRAILBLAZER RIFLE

Caliber: 50, 54. **Barrel:** 28", 30". **Weight:** 9 lbs. **Length:** 48" overall. **Stock:** European walnut with cheekpiece. **Sights:** Blade front, semi-buckhorn rear. **Features:** Reproduction of a rifle made by George Tryon about 1820. Double-set triggers, back action lock, hooked breech with long tang. From Armsport.
Price: About $825.00

WHITE MODEL 97 WHITETAIL HUNTER RIFLE

Caliber: 45, 50. **Barrel:** 22", 1:24" twist (50 cal.). **Weight:** 7.6 lbs. **Length:** 39-7/8" overall. **Stock:** Black laminated wood or black composite with swivel studs. **Sights:** Marble fully adjustable, steel rear with white diamond; red-bead front with high-visibility inserts. **Features:** In-line ignition with FlashFire one-piece nipple and breech plug that uses standard or magnum No. 11 caps; fully adjustable trigger; double safety system; aluminum ramrod; drilled and tapped for scope. Includes hard gun case. Introduced 2000. Made in U.S. by Muzzleloading Technologies Inc.
Price: Laminated wood stock $549.95
Price: Black composite stock $549.95

White Model 98 Elite Hunter Rifle

Similar to Model 97 but features 24" barrel with longer action for extended sight radius. Overall length 43-5/16", weighs 8.2 lbs. Choice of black laminated or black hardwood stock. From Muzzleloading Technologies Inc.
Price: Black laminated stock (45 or 50 cal.) $699.95
Price: Black hardwood stock (45 or 50 cal.).................. $699.95

ZOUAVE PERCUSSION RIFLE

Caliber: 58, 59. **Barrel:** 32-1/2". **Weight:** 9-1/2 lbs. **Length:** 48-1/2" overall. **Stock:** Walnut finish, brass patchbox and buttplate. **Sights:** Fixed front, rear adjustable for elevation. **Features:** Color case-hardened lockplate, blued barrel. From Navy Arms, Dixie Gun Works, E.M.F., Cabela's.
Price: About .... **$325.00** to **$465.00**

Cabela's 12-Gauge

Dixie Magnum

Knight TK2000

Traditions Buckhunter Pro

CABELA'S BLACKPOWDER SHOTGUNS

Gauge: 10, 12, 20. **Barrel:** 10-ga., 30"; 12-ga., 28-1/2" (Extra-Full, Mod., Imp. Cyl. choke tubes); 20-ga., 27-1/2" (Imp. Cyl. & Mod. fixed chokes). **Weight:** 6-1/2 to 7 lbs. **Length:** 45" overall (28-1/2" barrel). **Stock:** American walnut with checkered grip; 12- and 20-gauge have straight stock, 10-gauge has pistol grip. **Features:** Blued barrels, engraved, color case-hardened locks and hammers, brass ramrod tip. From Cabela's.
Price: 10-gauge $499.99
Price: 12-gauge $449.99
Price: 20-gauge $429.99

CVA TRAPPER PERCUSSION

Gauge: 12. **Barrel:** 28". **Weight:** 6 lbs. **Length:** 46" overall. **Stock:** English-style checkered straight grip of walnut-finished hardwood. **Sights:** Brass bead front. **Features:** Single-blued barrel; color case-hardened lockplate and hammer; screw adjustable sear engagements, V-type mainspring; brass wedge plates; color case-hardened and engraved trigger guard and tang. From CVA.
Price: Finished $239.95

DIXIE MAGNUM PERCUSSION SHOTGUN

Gauge: 10, 12, 20. **Barrel:** 30" (Imp. Cyl. & Mod.) in 10-gauge; 28" in 12-gauge. **Weight:** 6-1/4 lbs. **Length:** 45" overall. **Stock:** Hand-checkered walnut, 14" pull. **Features:** Double triggers; light hand engraving; case-hardened locks in 12-gauge, polished steel in 10-gauge; sling swivels. From Dixie Gun Works.
Price: Upland $449.00
Price: 12-ga. kit $375.00
Price: 20-ga. $495.00
Price: 10-ga. $495.00
Price: 10-ga. kit $395.00

KNIGHT TK2000 MUZZLELOADING SHOTGUN

Gauge: 12. **Barrel:** 26", extra-full choke tube. **Weight:** 7 lbs., 9 oz. **Length:** 45" overall. **Stock:** Synthetic black or Realtree X-tra Brown; recoil pad; swivel studs. **Sights:** Fully adjustable rear, blade front with fiber optics. **Features:** Receiver drilled and tapped for scope mount; in-line ignition; adjustable trigger; removable breech plug; double safety system; imp. cyl. choke tube available. Introduced 2000. Made in U.S. by Knight Rifles.
Price: $349.95

NAVY ARMS STEEL SHOT MAGNUM SHOTGUN

Gauge: 10. **Barrel:** 28" (Cyl. & Cyl.). **Weight:** 7 lbs., 9 oz. **Length:** 45-1/2" overall. **Stock:** Walnut, with cheekpiece. **Features:** Designed specifically for steel shot. Engraved, polished locks; sling swivels; blued barrels. Imported by Navy Arms.
Price: $605.00

NAVY ARMS T&T SHOTGUN

Gauge: 12. **Barrel:** 28" (Full & Full). **Weight:** 7-1/2 lbs. **Stock:** Walnut. **Sights:** Bead front. **Features:** Color case-hardened locks, double triggers, blued steel furniture. From Navy Arms.
Price: $580.00

TRADITIONS BUCKHUNTER PRO SHOTGUN

Gauge: 12. **Barrel:** 24", choke tube. **Weight:** 6 lbs., 4 oz. **Length:** 43" overall. **Stock:** Composite matte black, Break-Up or Advantage camouflage. **Features:** In-line action with removable stainless steel breech plug; thumb safety; adjustable trigger; rubber buttpad. Introduced 1996. From Traditions.
Price: $248.00
Price: With Advantage, Shadow Branch, or Break-Up camouflage stock $292.00

THOMPSON/CENTER
BLACK MOUNTAIN MAGNUM SHOTGUN

Gauge: 12. **Barrel:** 27" screw-in Turkey choke tube. **Weight:** 7 lbs. **Length:** 41-3/4" overall. **Stock:** Black composite. **Sights:** Bead front. **Features:** Sidelock percussion action. Polished blue finish. Introduced in 1999. Made in U.S. by Thompson/Center Arms.
Price: $387.16

BEEMAN P1 MAGNUM AIR PISTOL

Caliber: 177, 5mm, single shot. **Barrel:** 8.4". **Weight:** 2.5 lbs. **Length:** 11" overall. **Power:** Top lever cocking; spring-piston. **Stocks:** Checkered walnut. **Sights:** Blade front, square notch rear with click micrometer adjustments for windage and elevation. Grooved for scope mounting. **Features:** Dual power for 177 and 20-cal.: low setting gives 350-400 fps; high setting 500-600 fps. Rearward expanding mainspring simulates firearm recoil. All Colt 45 auto grips fit gun. Dry-firing feature for practice. Optional wooden shoulder stock. Introduced 1985. Imported by Beeman.
Price: 177, 5mm **$415.00**

Beeman P2 Match Air Pistol

Similar to the Beeman P1 Magnum except shoots only 177 pellets; completely recoilless single-stroke pnuematic action. Weighs 2.2 lbs. Choice of thumbrest match grips or standard style. Introduced 1990.
Price: 177, 5mm, standard grip **$385.00**
Price: 177, match grip **$455.00**

BEEMAN P3 AIR PISTOL

NEW!

Caliber: 177 pellet, single shot. **Barrel:** N/A. **Weight:** 1.7 lbs. **Length:** 9.6" overall. **Power:** Single-stroke pneumatic; overlever barrel cocking. **Grips:** Reinforced polymer. **Sights:** Adjustable rear, blade front. **Features:** Velocity 410 fps. Polymer frame; automatic safety; two-stage trigger; built-in muzzle brake. Introduced 1999 by Beeman.
Price: **$159.00**

BEEMAN/FEINWERKBAU 65 MKII AIR PISTOL

Caliber: 177, single shot. **Barrel:** 6.1", removable bbl. wgt. available. **Weight:** 42 oz. **Length:** 13.3" overall. **Power:** Spring, sidelever cocking. **Stocks:** Walnut, stippled thumbrest; adjustable or fixed. **Sights:** Front, interchangeable post element system, open rear, click adjustable for windage and elevation and for sighting notch width. Scope mount available. **Features:** New shorter barrel for better balance and control. Cocking effort 9 lbs. Two-stage trigger, four adjustments. Quiet firing, 525 fps. Programs instantly for recoil or recoilless operation. Permanently lubricated. Steel piston ring. Imported by Beeman.
Price: Right-hand **$1,070.00**

BEEMAN/FEINWERKBAU 103 PISTOL

Caliber: 177, single shot. **Barrel:** 10.1", 12-groove rifling. **Weight:** 2.5 lbs. **Length:** 16.5" overall. **Power:** Single-stroke pneumatic, underlever cocking. **Stocks:** Stippled walnut with adjustable palm shelf. **Sights:** Blade front, open rear adjustable for windage and elevation. Notch size adjustable for width. Interchangeable front blades. **Features:** Velocity 510 fps. Fully adjustable trigger. Cocking effort of 2 lbs. Imported by Beeman.
Price: Right-hand **$1,195.00**
Price: Left-hand **$1,235.00**

BEEMAN/FWB P30 MATCH AIR PISTOL

Caliber: 177, single shot. **Barrel:** 10-5/16", with muzzlebrake. **Weight:** 2.4 lbs. **Length:** 16.5" overall. **Power:** Pre-charged pneumatic. **Stocks:** Stippled walnut; adjustable match type. **Sights:** Undercut blade front, fully adjustable match rear. **Features:** Velocity to 525 fps; up to 200 shots per CO_2 cartridge. Fully adjustable trigger; built-in muzzlebrake. Introduced 1995. Imported from Germany by Beeman.
Price: Right-hand **$1,275.00**
Price: Left-hand **$1,350.00**

BEEMAN/FWB C55 CO_2 RAPID FIRE PISTOL

Caliber: 177, single shot or 5-shot magazine. **Barrel:** 7.3". **Weight:** 2.5 lbs. **Length:** 15" overall. **Power:** Special CO_2 cylinder. **Stocks:** Anatomical, adjustable. **Sights:** Interchangeable front, fully adjustable open micro-click rear with adjustable notch size. **Features:** Velocity 510 fps. Has 11.75" sight radius. Built-in muzzlebrake. Introduced 1993. Imported by Beeman Precision Airguns.
Price: Right-hand **$1,460.00**
Price: Left-hand **$1,520.00**

BEEMAN HW70A AIR PISTOL

Caliber: 177, single shot. **Barrel:** 6-1/4", rifled. **Weight:** 38 oz. **Length:** 12-3/4" overall. **Power:** Spring, barrel cocking. **Stocks:** Plastic, with thumbrest. **Sights:** Hooded post front, square notch rear adjustable for windage and elevation. Comes with scope base. **Features:** Adjustable trigger, 31-lb. cocking effort, 440 fps MV; automatic barrel safety. Imported by Beeman.
Price: **$185.00**
Price: HW70S, black grip, silver finish **$210.00**

BEEMAN/WEBLEY TEMPEST AIR PISTOL

Caliber: 177, 22, single shot. **Barrel:** 6-7/8". **Weight:** 32 oz. **Length:** 8.9" overall. **Power:** Spring-piston, break barrel. **Stocks:** Checkered black plastic with thumbrest. **Sights:** Blade front, adjustable rear. **Features:** Velocity 500 fps (177), 400 fps (22). Aluminum frame; black epoxy finish; manual safety. Imported from England by Beeman.
Price: **$180.00**

BRNO-Tau-CO_2 Match

Beeman/Webley Hurricane Air Pistol

Similar to the Tempest except has extended frame in the rear for a click-adjustable rear sight; hooded front sight; comes with scope mount. Imported from England by Beeman.
Price: **$225.00**

BENJAMIN SHERIDAN CO_2 PELLET PISTOLS

Caliber: 177, 20, 22, single shot. **Barrel:** 6-3/8", rifled brass. **Weight:** 29 oz. **Length:** 9.8" overall. **Power:** 12-gram CO_2 cylinder. **Stocks:** Walnut. **Sights:** High ramp front, fully adjustable notch rear. **Features:** Velocity to 500 fps. Turn-bolt action with cross-bolt safety. Gives about 40 shots per CO_2 cylinder. Black or nickel finish. Made in U.S. by Benjamin Sheridan Co.
Price: Black finish, EB17 (177), EB20 (20), about **$115.23**

BENJAMIN SHERIDAN PNEUMATIC PELLET PISTOLS

Caliber: 177, 20, 22, single shot. **Barrel:** 9-3/8", rifled brass. **Weight:** 38 oz. **Length:** 13-1/8" overall. **Power:** Underlever pnuematic, hand pumped. **Stocks:** Walnut stocks and pump handle. **Sights:** High ramp front, fully adjustable notch rear. **Features:** Velocity to 525 fps (variable). Bolt action with cross-bolt safety. Choice of black or nickel finish. Made in U.S. by Benjamin Sheridan Co.
Price: Black finish, HB17 (177), HB20 (20), HB22 (22), about **$129.50**

BERETTA 92 FS/CO_2 AIR PISTOLS

Caliber: 177 pellet, 8-shot magazine. **Barrel:** 4.9". **Weight:** 44.4 oz. **Length:** 8.2" (10.2" with compensator). **Power:** CO_2 cartridge. **Grips:** plastic or wood. **Sights:** Adjustable rear, blade front. **Features:** Velocity 375 fps. Replica of Beretta 92 FS pistol. Single- and double-action trigger; ambidextrous safety; black or nickel-plated finish. Made by Umarex for Beretta USA.
Price: Starting at **$200.00**

BRNO TAU-7 CO_2 MATCH PISTOL

Caliber: 177. **Barrel:** 10.24". **Weight:** 37 oz. **Length:** 15.75" overall. **Power:** 12.5-gram CO_2 cartridge. **Stocks:** Stippled hardwood with adjustable palm rest. **Sights:** Blade front, open fully adjustable rear. **Features:** Comes with extra seals and counterweight. Blue finish. Imported by Great Lakes Airguns.
Price: About **$299.50**

BSA 240 MAGNUM AIR PISTOL

Caliber: 177, 22, single shot. **Barrel:** 6". **Weight:** 2 lbs. **Length:** 9" overall. **Power:** Spring-air, top-lever cocking. **Stocks:** Walnut. **Sights:** Blade front, micrometer adjustable rear. **Features:** Velocity 510 fps (177), 420 fps (22); crossbolt safety. Combat autoloader styling. Imported from U.K. by Precision Sales International, Inc.
Price: **$259.99**

COLT GOVERNMENT 1911 A1 AIR PISTOL

Caliber: 177, 8-shot cylinder magazine. **Barrel:** 5", rifled. **Weight:** 38 oz. **Length:** 8-1/2" overall. **Power:** CO_2 cylinder. **Stocks:** Checkered black plastic or smooth wood. **Sights:** Post front, adjustable rear. **Features:** Velocity to 393 fps. Quick-loading cylinder magazine; single and double action; black or silver finish. Introduced 1998. Imported by Colt's Mfg. Co., Inc.
Price: Black finish **$199.00**
Price: Silver finish **$209.00**

CROSMAN BLACK VENOM PISTOL

Caliber: 177 pellets, BB, 17-shot magazine; darts, single shot. **Barrel:** 4.75" smoothbore. **Weight:** 16 oz. **Length:** 10.8" overall. **Power:** Spring. **Stocks:** Checkered. **Sights:** Blade front, adjustable rear. **Features:** Velocity to 270 fps (BBs), 250 fps (pellets). Spring-fed magazine; cross-bolt safety. Introduced 1996. Made in U.S. by Crosman Corp.
Price: About **$20.00**

CROSMAN BLACK FANG PISTOL

Caliber: 177 BB, 17-shot magazine. **Barrel:** 4.75" smoothbore. **Weight:** 10 oz. **Length:** 10.8" overall. **Power:** Spring. **Stocks:** Checkered. **Sights:** Blade front, fixed notch rear. **Features:** Velocity to 250 fps. Spring-fed magazine; cross-bolt safety. Introduced 1996. Made in U.S. by Crosman Corp.
Price: About **$16.00**

Daisy/Power Line 717

CROSMAN MODEL 1322, 1377 AIR PISTOLS
Caliber: 177 (M1377), 22 (M1322), single shot. **Barrel:** 8", rifled steel. **Weight:** 39 oz. **Length:** 13-5/8". **Power:** Hand pumped. **Sights:** Blade front, rear adjustable for windage and elevation. **Features:** Bolt action moulded plastic grip, hand size pump forearm. Cross-bolt safety. From Crosman.
Price: About $60.00

CROSMAN AUTO AIR II PISTOL
Caliber: BB, 17-shot magazine, 177 pellet, single shot. **Barrel:** 8-5/8" steel, smoothbore. **Weight:** 13 oz. **Length:** 10-3/4" overall. **Power:** CO2 Powerlet. **Stocks:** Grooved plastic. **Sights:** Blade front, adjustable rear; highlighted system. **Features:** Velocity to 480 fps (BBs), 430 fps (pellets). Semi-automatic action with BBs, single shot with pellets. Silvered finish. Introduced 1991. From Crosman.
Price: About $38.00

CROSMAN MODEL 357 SERIES AIR PISTOL
Caliber: 177 10-shot pellet clips. **Barrel:** 4" (Model 3574GT), 6" (Model 3576GT). **Weight:** 32 oz. (6"). **Length:** 11-3/8" overall (357-6). **Power:** CO2 Powerlet. **Stocks:** Grip, wrap-around style. **Sights:** Ramp front, fully adjustable rear. **Features:** Average 430 fps (Model 3574GT). Break-open barrel for easy loading. Single or double action. Vent. rib barrel. Wide, smooth trigger. Two cylinders come with each gun. Black finish. From Crosman.
Price: 4" or 6", about $65.00

CROSMAN MODEL 1008 REPEAT AIR
Caliber: 177, 8-shot pellet clip. **Barrel:** 4.25", rifled steel. **Weight:** 17 oz. **Length:** 8.625" overall. **Power:** CO2 Powerlet. **Stocks:** Checkered black plastic. **Sights:** Post front, adjustable rear. **Features:** Velocity about 430 fps. Break-open barrel for easy loading; single or double semi-automatic action; two 8-shot clips included. Optional carrying case available. Introduced 1992. From Crosman.
Price: About $60.00
Price: With case, about $70.00
Price: Model 1008SB (silver and black finish), about. $60.00

DAISY MODEL 2003 PELLET PISTOL
Caliber: 177 pellet, 35-shot clip. **Barrel:** Rifled steel. **Weight:** 2.2 lbs. **Length:** 11.7" overall. **Power:** CO2. **Stocks:** Checkered plastic. **Sights:** Blade front, open rear. **Features:** Velocity to 400 fps. Crossbolt trigger-block safety. Made in U.S. by Daisy Mfg. Co.
Price: About $67.95

DAISY MODEL 454 AIR PISTOL
Caliber: 177 BB, 20-shot clip. **Barrel:** Smoothbore steel. **Weight:** 1.6 lbs. **Length:** 10.4" overall. **Power:** CO2. **Stocks:** Moulded black, ribbed composition. **Sights:** Blade front, fixed rear. **Features:** Velocity to 420 fps. Semi-automatic action; crossbolt safety; black finish. Introduced 1998. Made in U.S. by Dairy Mfg. Co.
Price: $61.95

DAISY/POWERLINE 717 PELLET PISTOL
Caliber: 177, single shot. **Barrel:** 9.61". **Weight:** 2.25 lbs. **Length:** 13-1/2" overall. **Stocks:** Moulded wood-grain plastic, with thumbrest. **Sights:** Blade and ramp front, micro-adjustable notch rear. **Features:** Single pump pneumatic pistol. Rifled steel barrel. Cross-bolt trigger block. Muzzle velocity 385 fps. From Daisy Mfg. Co. Introduced 1979.
Price: About $71.95

Daisy/PowerLine 747 Pistol
Similar to the 717 pistol except has a 12-groove rifled steel barrel by Lothar Walther, and adjustable trigger pull weight. Velocity of 360 fps. Manual cross-bolt safety.
Price: About $140.00

DAISY/POWERLINE 1140 PELLET PISTOL
Caliber: 177, single shot. **Barrel:** Rifled steel. **Weight:** 1.3 lbs. **Length:** 11.7" overall. **Power:** Single-stroke barrel cocking. **Stocks:** Checkered resin. **Sights:** Hooded

post front, open adjustable rear. **Features:** Velocity to 325 fps. Made of black lightweight engineering resin. Introduced 1995. From Daisy.
Price: About $38.95

DAISY/POWERLINE 44 REVOLVER
Caliber: 177 pellets, 6-shot. **Barrel:** 6", rifled steel; interchangeable 4" and 8". **Weight:** 2.7 lbs. **Length:** 13.1" overall. **Power:** CO2. **Stocks:** Moulded plastic with checkering. **Sights:** Blade on ramp front, fully adjustable notch rear. **Features:** Velocity up to 400 fps. Replica of 44 Magnum revolver. Has swingout cylinder and interchangeable barrels. Introduced 1987. From Daisy Mfg. Co.
Price: $59.95

DAISY/POWERLINE 1270 CO2 AIR PISTOL
Caliber: BB, 60-shot magazine. **Barrel:** Smoothbore steel. **Weight:** 17 oz. **Length:** 11.1" overall. **Power:** CO2 pump action. **Stocks:** Moulded black polymer. **Sights:** Blade on ramp front, adjustable rear. **Features:** Velocity to 420 fps. Crossbolt trigger block safety; plated finish. Introduced 1997. Made in U.S. by Daisy Mfg. Co.
Price: About $39.95

EAA/BAIKAL IZH-46 TARGET AIR PISTOL
Caliber: 177, single shot. **Barrel:** 11.02". **Weight:** 2.87 lbs. **Length:** 16.54" overall. **Power:** Underlever single-stroke pneumatic. **Grips:** Adjustable wooden target. **Sights:** Micrometer fully adjustable rear, blade front. **Features:** Velocity about 420 fps. Hammer-forged, rifled barrel. Imported from Russia by European American Armory.
Price: $275.00

EAA/BAIKAL MP-654K AIR PISTOL
Caliber: 177 BB, detachable 13-shot magazine. **Barrel:** 3.75". **Weight:** 1.6 lbs. **Length:** 6.34". **Power:** CO2 cartridge. **Grips:** Black checkered plastic. **Sights:** Notch rear, blade front. **Features:** Velocity about 380 fps. Double-action trigger; slide safety; metal slide and frame. Replica of Makarov pistol. Imported from Russia by European American Armory.
Price: $110.00

EAA/BAIKAL MP-651K AIR PISTOL/RIFLE
Caliber: 177 pellet (8-shot magazine); 177 BB (23-shot). **Barrel:** 5.9" (17.25" with rifle attachment). **Weight:** 1.54 lbs. (3.3 lbs. with rifle attachment). **Length:** 9.4" (31.3" with rifle attachment) **Power:** CO2 cartridge, semi-automatic. **Stock:** Plastic. **Sights:** Notch rear/blade front (pistol); periscopic sighting system (rifle). **Features:** Velocity 328 fps. Unique pistol/rifle combination allows the pistol to be inserted into the rifle shell. Imported from Russia by European American Armory.
Price: $95.00

"GAT" AIR PISTOL
Caliber: 177, single shot. **Barrel:** 7-1/2" cocked, 9-1/2" extended. **Weight:** 22 oz. **Power:** Spring-piston. **Stocks:** Cast checkered metal. **Sights:** Fixed. **Features:** Shoots pellets, corks or darts. Matte black finish. Imported from England by Stone Enterprises, Inc.
Price: $24.95

HAMMERLI 480 MATCH AIR PISTOL
Caliber: 177, single shot. **Barrel:** 9.8". **Weight:** 37 oz. **Length:** 16.5" overall. **Power:** Air or CO2. **Stocks:** Walnut with 7-degree rake adjustment. Stippled grip area. **Sights:** Undercut blade front, fully adjustable open match rear. **Features:** Underbarrel cannister charges with air or CO2 for power supply; gives 320 shots per filling. Trigger adjustable for position. Introduced 1994. Imported from Switzerland by Hammerli Pistols U.S.A.
Price: $1,325.00

Hammerli 480K2 Match Air Pistol
Similar to the 480 except has a short, detachable aluminum air cylinder for use only with compressed air; can be filled while on the gun or off; special adjustable barrel weights. Muzzle velocity of 470 fps, gives about 180 shots. Has stippled black composition grip with adjustable palm shelf and rake angle. Comes with air pressure gauge. Introduced 1996. Imported from Switzerland by SIGARMS, Inc.
Price: $1,112.50

MARKSMAN 1010 REPEATER PISTOL
Caliber: 177, 18-shot BB repeater. **Barrel:** 2-1/2", smoothbore. **Weight:** 24 oz. **Length:** 8-1/4" overall. **Power:** Spring. **Features:** Velocity to 200 fps. Thumb safety. Black finish. Uses BBs, darts, bolts or pellets. Repeats with BBs only. From Marksman Products.
Price: Matte black finish $26.00
Price: Model 2000 (as above except silver-chrome finish). $27.00

MARKSMAN 2005 LASERHAWK SPECIAL EDITION AIR PISTOL
Caliber: 177, 24-shot magazine. **Barrel:** 3.8", smoothbore. **Weight:** 22 oz. **Length:** 10.3" overall. **Power:** Spring-air. **Stocks:** Checkered. **Sights:** Fixed fiber optic front sight. **Features:** Velocity to 300 fps with Hyper-Velocity pellets. Square trigger guard with skeletonized trigger; extended barrel for greater velocity and accuracy. Shoots BBs, pellets, darts or bolts. Made in the U.S. From Marksman Products.
Price: $32.00

AIRGUNS

MORINI 162E MATCH AIR PISTOL

Caliber: 177, single shot. **Barrel:** 9.4". **Weight:** 32 oz. **Length:** 16.1" overall. **Power:** Scuba air. **Stocks:** Adjustable match type. **Sights:** Interchangeable blade front, fully adjustable match-type rear. **Features:** Power mechanism shuts down when pressure drops to a pre-set level. Adjustable electronic trigger. Introduced 1995. Imported from Switzerland by Nygord Precision Products.
Price: $995.00

PARDINI K58 MATCH AIR PISTOL

Caliber: 177, single shot. **Barrel:** 9.0". **Weight:** 37.7 oz. **Length:** 15.5" overall. **Power:** Pre-charged compressed air; single-stroke cocking. **Stocks:** Adjustable match type; stippled walnut. **Sights:** Interchangeable post front, fully adjustable match rear. **Features:** Fully adjustable trigger. Introduced 1995. Imported from Italy by Nygord Precision Products.
Price: $750.00
Price: K2 model, precharged air pistol, introduced in 1998 .... $895.00

RWS/DIANA MODEL 5G AIR PISTOL

Caliber: 177, single shot. **Barrel:** 7". **Weight:** 2-3/4 lbs. **Length:** 15" overall. **Power:** Spring-air, barrel cocking. **Stocks:** Plastic, thumbrest design. **Sights:** Tunnel front, micro-click open rear. **Features:** Velocity of 450 fps. Adjustable two-stage trigger with automatic safety. Imported from Germany by Dynamit Nobel-RWS, Inc.
Price: $260.00

RWS C-225 AIR PISTOLS

Caliber: 177, 8-shot rotary magazine. **Barrel:** 4", 6". **Weight:** NA. **Length:** NA. **Power:** CO_2. **Stocks:** Checkered black plastic. **Sights:** Post front, rear adjustable for windage. **Features:** Velocity to 385 fps. Semi-automatic fire; decocking lever. Imported from Germany by Dynamit Nobel-RWS.
Price: 4", blue $210.00
Price: 4", nickel $220.00
Price: 6", blue $220.00
Price: 6", nickel $245.00

STEYR LP 5CP MATCH AIR PISTOL

Caliber: 177, 5-shot magazine. **Barrel:** NA. **Weight:** 40.7 oz. **Length:** 15.2" overall. **Power:** Pre-charged air cylinder. **Stocks:** Adjustable match type. **Sights:** Interchangeable blade front, fully adjustable match rear. **Features:** Adjustable sight radius; fully adjustable trigger. Has barrel compensator. Introduced 1995. Imported from Austria by Nygord Precision Products.
Price: $1,150.00

STEYR LP10P MATCH PISTOL

Caliber: 177, single shot. **Barrel:** 9". **Weight:** 38.7 oz. **Length:** 15.3" overall. **Power:** Scuba air. **Stocks:** Fully adjustable Morini match with palm shelf; stippled walnut. **Sights:** Interchangeable blade in 4mm, 4.5mm or 5mm widths, fully adjustable open rear with interchangeable 3.5mm or 4mm leaves. **Features:** Velocity about 500 fps. Adjustable trigger, adjustable sight radius from 12.4" to 13.2". With compensator. Imported from Austria by Nygord Precision Products.
Price: $1,195.00

TECH FORCE SS2 OLYMPIC COMPETITION AIR PISTOL

Caliber: 177 pellet, single shot. **Barrel:** 7.4". **Weight:** 2.8 lbs. **Length:** 16.5" overall. **Power:** Spring piston, sidelever. **Grips:** Hardwood. **Sights:** Extended adjustable rear, blade front accepts inserts. **Features:** Velocity 520 fps. Recoilless design; adjustments allow duplication of a firearm's feel. Match-grade, adjustable trigger; includes carrying case. Imported from China by Compasseco Inc.
Price: $295.00

TECH FORCE 35 AIR PISTOL

Caliber: 177 pellet, single shot. **Barrel:** N/A. **Weight:** 2.86 lbs. **Length:** 14.9" overall. **Power:** Spring piston, underlever. **Grips:** Hardwood. **Sights:** Micrometer adjustable rear, blade front. **Features:** Velocity 400 fps. Grooved for scope mount; trigger safety. Imported from China by Compasseco Inc.
Price: $49.95

Tech Force 8 Air Pistol

Similar to Tech Force 35, but with break-barrel action, ambidextrous polymer grips. From Compasseco Inc.
Price: $59.95

Tech Force S2-1 Air Pistol

Similar to Tech Force 8, but more basic grips and sights for plinking. From Compasseco Inc.
Price: $29.95

WALTHER CP88 PELLET PISTOL

Caliber: 177, 8-shot rotary magazine. **Barrel:** 4", 6". **Weight:** 37 oz. (4" barrel) **Length:** 7" (4" barrel). **Power:** CO_2. **Stocks:** Checkered plastic. **Sights:** Blade front, fully adjustable rear. **Features:** Faithfully replicates size, weight and trigger pull of the 9mm Walther P88 compact pistol. Has SA/DA trigger mechanism; ambidextrous safety, levers. Comes with two magazines, 500 pellets, one CO2 cartridge. Introduced 1997. Imported from Germany by Interarms.
Price: Blue $179.00
Price: Nickel $189.00

WALTHER LP20I MATCH PISTOL

Caliber: 177, single shot. **Barrel:** 8.66". **Weight:** NA. **Length:** 15.1" overall. **Power:** Scuba air. **Stocks:** Orthopaedic target type. **Sights:** Undercut blade front, open match rear fully adjustable for windage and elevation. **Features:** Adjustable velocity; matte finish. Introduced 1995. Imported from Germany by Nygord Precision Products.
Price: $1,095.00

Walther CP88 Competition Pellet Pistol

Similar to the standard CP88 except has 6" match-grade barrel, muzzle weight, wood or plastic stocks. Weighs 41 oz., has overall length of 9". Introduced 1997. Imported from Germany by Interarms.
Price: Blue, plastic grips $170.00
Price: Nickel, plastic grips $195.00
Price: Blue, wood grips $205.00
Price: Nickel, wood grips $232.00

WALTHER CP99 AIR PISTOL

Caliber: 177 pellet, 8-shot rotary magazine. **Barrel:** 3". **Weight:** 26 oz. **Length:** 7.1" overall. **Power:** CO2 cartridge. **Grip:** Polymer. **Sights:** Drift-adjustable rear, blade front. **Features:** Velocity 320 fps. Replica of Walther P99 pistol. Trigger allows single and double action; ambidextrous magazine release; interchangeable backstraps to fit variety of hand sizes. Introduced 2000. From Walther USA.
Price: .... NA

WALTHER PPK/S AIR PISTOL

Caliber: 177 BB. **Barrel:** N/A. **Weight:** 20 oz. **Length:** 6.3" overall. **Power:** CO2 cartridge. **Grip:** Plastic. **Sights:** Fixed rear, blade front. **Features:** Replica of Walther PPK pistol. Blow back system moves slide when fired; trigger allows single and double action. Introduced 2000. From Walther USA.
Price: .... NA

Anschutz 2002

AIRROW MODEL A-8SRB STEALTH AIR GUN
Caliber: 177, 22, 25, 38, 9-shot. **Barrel:** 19.7"; rifled. **Weight:** 6 lbs. **Length:** 34" overall. **Power:** CO₂ or compressed air; variable power. **Stock:** Telescoping CAR-15-type. **Sights:** Variable 3.5-10x scope. **Features:** Velocity 1100 fps in all calibers. Pneumatic air trigger. All aircraft aluminum and stainless steel construction. Mil-spec materials and finishes. Introduced 1992. From Swivel Machine Works, Inc.
Price: About $2,599.00

AIRROW MODEL A-8S1P STEALTH AIR GUN
Caliber: #2512 16" arrow. **Barrel:** 16". **Weight:** 4.4 lbs. **Length:** 30.1" overall. **Power:** CO₂ or compressed air; variable power. **Stock:** Telescoping CAR-15-type. **Sights:** Scope rings only. **Features:** Velocity to 650 fps with 260-grain arrow. Pneumatic air trigger. All aircraft aluminum and stainless steel construction. Mil-spec materials and finishes. Waterproof case. Introduced 1991. From Swivel Machine Works, Inc.
Price: About $1,699.00

ARS/KING HUNTING MASTER AIR RIFLE
Caliber: 22, 5-shot repeater. **Barrel:** 22-3/4". **Weight:** 7-3/4 lbs. **Length:** 42" overall. **Power:** Pre-compressed air from 3000 psi diving tank. **Stock:** Indonesian walnut with checkered grip and forend; rubber buttpad. **Sights:** Blade front, fully adjustable open rear. Receiver grooved for scope mounting. **Features:** Velocity over 1000 fps with 32-grain pellet. High and low power switch for hunting or target velocities. Side lever cocks action and inserts pellet. Rotary magazine. Imported from Korea by Air Rifle Specialists.
Price: $580.00
Price: Hunting Master 900 (9mm, limited production) $1,000.00

ARS/Magnum 6 Air Rifle
Similar to the King Hunting Master except is 6-shot repeater with 23-3/4" barrel, weighs 8-1/4 lbs. Stock is walnut-stained hardwood with checkered grip and forend; rubber buttpad. Velocity of 1000+ fps with 32-grain pellet. Imported from Korea by Air Rifle Specialists.
Price: $500.00

ARS HUNTING MASTER AR6 AIR RIFLE
Caliber: 22, 6-shot repeater. **Barrel:** 25-1/4". **Weight:** 7 lbs. **Length:** 41-1/4" overall. **Power:** Pre-compressed air from 3000 psi diving tank. **Stock:** Indonesian walnut with checkered grip; rubber buttpad. **Sights:** Blade front, adjustable peep rear. **Features:** Velocity over 1000 fps with 32-grain pellet. Receiver grooved for scope mounting. Has 6-shot rotary magazine. Imported by Air Rifle Specialists.
Price: $580.00

ARS/CAREER 707 AIR RIFLE
Caliber: 22, 6-shot repeater. **Barrel:** 23". **Weight:** 7.75 lbs. **Length:** 40.5" overall. **Power:** Pre-compressed air; variable power. **Stock:** Indonesian walnut with checkered grip, gloss finish. **Sights:** Hooded post front with interchangeable inserts, fully adjustable diopter rear. **Features:** Velocity to 1000 fps. Lever-action with straight feed magazine; pressure gauge in lower front air reservoir; scope mounting rail included. Introduced 1996. Imported from the Philippines by Air Rifle Specialists.
Price: $580.00

ARS/FARCO FP SURVIVAL AIR RIFLE
Caliber: 22, 25, single shot. **Barrel:** 22-3/4". **Weight:** 5-3/4 lbs. **Length:** 42-3/4" overall. **Power:** Multi-pump foot pump. **Stock:** Philippine hardwood. **Sights:** Blade front, fixed rear. **Features:** Velocity to 850 fps (22 or 25). Receiver grooved for scope mounting. Imported from the Philippines by Air Rifle Specialists.
Price: $295.00

ARS/FARCO CO₂ AIR SHOTGUN
Caliber: 51 (28-gauge). **Barrel:** 30". **Weight:** 7 lbs. **Length:** 48-1/2" overall. **Power:** 10-oz. refillable CO₂ tank. **Stock:** Hardwood. **Sights:** Blade front, fixed rear. **Features:** Gives over 100 ft. lbs. energy for taking small game. Imported from the Philippines by Air Rifle Specialists.
Price: $460.00

ARS/Farco CO₂ Stainless Steel Air Rifle
Similar to the ARS/Farco CO₂ shotgun except in 22- or 25-caliber with 21-1/2" barrel; weighs 6-3/4 lbs., 42-1/2" overall; Philippine hardwood stock with stippled grip and forend; blade front sight, adjustable rear, grooved for scope mount. Uses 10-oz. refillable CO₂ cylinder. Made of stainless steel. Imported from the Philippines by Air Rifle Specialists.
Price: Including CO₂ cylinder $460.00

ARS/QB77 DELUXE AIR RIFLE
Caliber: 177, 22, single shot. **Barrel:** 21-1/2". **Weight:** 5-1/2 lbs. **Length:** 40" overall. **Power:** Two 12-oz. CO₂ cylinders. **Stock:** Walnut-stained hardwood. **Sights:** Blade front, adjustable rear. **Features:** Velocity to 625 fps (22), 725 fps (177). Receiver grooved for scope mounting. Comes with bulk-fill valve. Imported by Air Rifle Specialists.
Price: $195.00

ANSCHUTZ 2002 MATCH AIR RIFLE
Caliber: 177, single shot. **Barrel:** 25.2". **Weight:** 10.4 lbs. **Length:** 44.5" overall. **Stock:** European walnut, blonde hardwood or colored laminated hardwood; stippled grip and forend. Also available with flat-forend walnut stock for benchrest shooting and aluminum. **Sights:** Optional sight set #6834. **Features:** Muzzle velocity 575 fps. Balance, weight match the 1907 ISU smallbore rifle. Uses #5021 match trigger. Recoil and vibration free. Fully adjustable cheekpiece and buttplate; accessory rail under forend. Available in Pneumatic and Compressed Air versions. Introduced 1988. Imported from Germany by Gunsmithing, Inc., Accuracy International, Champion's Choice.
Price: Right-hand, blonde hardwood stock, with sights $1,275.00
Price: Right-hand, walnut stock $1,275.00
Price: Right-hand, color laminate stock $1,300.00
Price: Right-hand, aluminum stock, butt plate $1,495.00
Price: Left-hand, color laminate stock $1,595.00
Price: Model 2002D-RT Running Target, right-hand, no sights $1,248.90
Price: #6834 Sight Set $227.10

BEEMAN BEARCUB AIR RIFLE
Caliber: 177, single shot. **Barrel:** 13". **Weight:** 7.2 lbs. **Length:** 37.8" overall. **Power:** Spring-piston, barrel cocking. **Stock:** Stained hardwood. **Sights:** Hooded post front, open fully adjustable rear. **Features:** Velocity to 915 fps. Polished blue finish; receiver dovetailed for scope mounting. Imported from England by Beeman Precision Airguns.
Price: $325.00

BEEMAN CROW MAGNUM AIR RIFLE
Caliber: 20, 22, 25, single shot. **Barrel:** 16"; 10-groove rifling. **Weight:** 8.5 lbs. **Length:** 46" overall. **Power:** Gas-spring; adjustable power to 32 foot pounds muzzle energy. **Stock:** Classic-style hardwood; hand checkered. **Sights:** For scope use only; built-in base and 1" rings included. **Features:** Adjustable two-stage trigger. Automatic safety. Also available in 22-caliber on special order. Introduced 1992. Imported by Beeman.
Price: $1,220.00

BEEMAN KODIAK AIR RIFLE
Caliber: 25, single shot. **Barrel:** 17.6". **Weight:** 9 lbs. **Length:** 45.6" overall. **Power:** Spring-piston, barrel cocking. **Stock:** Stained hardwood. **Sights:** Blade front, open fully adjustable rear. **Features:** Velocity to 820 fps. Up to 30 foot pounds muzzle energy. Introduced 1993. Imported by Beeman.
Price: $625.00

BEEMAN MAKO AIR RIFLE
Caliber: 177, single shot. **Barrel:** 20", with compensator. **Weight:** 7.3 lbs. **Length:** 38.5" overall. **Power:** Pre-charged pneumatic. **Stock:** Stained beech; Monte Carlo cheekpiece; checkered grip. **Sights:** None furnished. **Features:** Velocity to 930 fps. Gives over 50 shots per charge. Manual safety; brass trigger blade; vented rubber butt pad. Requires scuba tank for air. Introduced 1994. Imported from England by Beeman.
Price: $1,000.00
Price: Mako FT (thumbhole stock) $1,350.00

BEEMAN R1 AIR RIFLE
Caliber: 177, 20 or 22, single shot. **Barrel:** 19.6", 12-groove rifling. **Weight:** 8.5 lbs. **Length:** 45.2" overall. **Power:** Spring-piston, barrel cocking. **Stock:** Walnut-stained beech; cut-checkered pistol grip; Monte Carlo comb and cheekpiece; rubber buttpad. **Sights:** Tunnel front with interchangeable inserts, open rear click-adjustable for windage and elevation. Grooved for scope mounting. **Features:** Velocity of 940-1000 fps (177), 860 fps (20), 800 fps (22). Non-drying nylon piston and breech seals.

Adjustable metal trigger. Milled steel safety. Right- or left-hand stock. Available with adjustable cheekpiece and buttplate at extra cost. Custom and Super Laser versions available. Imported by Beeman.

Price: Right-hand, 177, 20, 22 .... **$540.00**
Price: Left-hand, 177, 20, 22 .... **$575.00**

BEEMAN R6 AIR RIFLE

Caliber: 177, single shot. **Barrel:** NA. **Weight:** 7.1 lbs. **Length:** 41.8" overall. **Power:** Spring-piston, barrel cocking. **Stock:** Stained hardwood. **Sights:** Tunnel post front, open fully adjustable rear. **Features:** Velocity to 815 fps. Two-stage Rekord adjustable trigger; receiver dovetailed for scope mounting; automatic safety. Introduced 1996. Imported from Germany by Beeman Precision Airguns.

Price: **$285.00**

BEEMAN R1 LASER MK II AIR RIFLE

Caliber: 177, 20, 22, 25, single shot. **Barrel:** 16.1" or 19.6". **Weight:** 8.4 lbs. **Length:** 41.7" overall. **Power:** Spring-piston, barrel cocking. **Stock:** Laminated wood with high cheekpiece, ventilated recoil pad. **Sights:** Tunnel front with interchangeable inserts, open adjustable rear; receiver grooved for scope mounting. **Features:** Velocity to 1150 fps (177). Special powerplant components. Built from the Beeman R1 rifle by Beeman.

Price: **$895.00**

BEEMAN R7 AIR RIFLE

Caliber: 177, 20, single shot. **Barrel:** 17". **Weight:** 6.1 lbs. **Length:** 40.2" overall. **Power:** Spring piston. **Stock:** Stained beech. **Sights:** Hooded front, fully adjustable micrometer click open rear. **Features:** Velocity to 700 fps (177), 620 fps (20). Receiver grooved for scope mounting; double-jointed cocking lever; fully adjustable trigger; checkered grip. Imported by Beeman.

Price: **$280.00**

BEEMAN R9 AIR RIFLE

Caliber: 177, 20, single shot. **Barrel:** NA. **Weight:** 7.3 lbs. **Length:** 43" overall. **Power:** Spring-piston, barrel cocking. **Stock:** Stained hardwood. **Sights:** Tunnel post front, fully adjustable open rear. **Features:** Velocity to 1000 fps (177), 800 fps (20). Adjustable Rekord trigger; automatic safety; receiver dovetailed for scope mounting. Introduced 1996. Imported from Germany by Beeman Precision Airguns.

Price: **$320.00**

Beeman R9 Deluxe Air Rifle

Same as the R9 except has an extended forend stock, checkered pistol grip, grip cap, carved Monte Carlo cheekpiece. Globe front sight with inserts. Introduced 1997. Imported by Beeman.

Price: **$370.00**

BEEMAN R11 AIR RIFLE

Caliber: 177, single shot. **Barrel:** 19.6". **Weight:** 8.8 lbs. **Length:** 47" overall. **Power:** Spring-piston, barrel cocking. **Stock:** Walnut-stained beech; adjustable buttplate and cheekpiece. **Sights:** None furnished. Has dovetail for scope mounting. **Features:** Velocity 910-940 fps. All-steel barrel sleeve. Imported by Beeman.

Price: **$530.00**

BEEMAN SUPER 12 AIR RIFLE

Caliber: 22, 25, 12-shot magazine. **Barrel:** 19", 12-groove rifling. **Weight:** 7.8 lbs. **Length:** 41.7" overall. **Power:** Pre-charged pneumatic; external air reservoir. **Stock:** European walnut. **Sights:** None furnished; drilled and tapped for scope mounting; scope mount included. **Features:** Velocity to 850 fps (25-caliber). Adjustable power setting gives 30-70 shots per 400 cc air bottle. Requires scuba tank for air. Introduced 1995. Imported by Beeman.

Price: **$1,675.00**

BEEMAN S1 MAGNUM AIR RIFLE

Caliber: 177, single shot. **Barrel:** 19". **Weight:** 7.1 lbs. **Length:** 45.5" overall. **Power:** Spring-piston, barrel cocking. **Stock:** Stained beech with Monte Carlo cheekpiece; checkered grip. **Sights:** Hooded post front, fully adjustable micrometer click rear. **Features:** Velocity to 900 fps. Automatic safety; receiver grooved for scope mounting; two-stage adjustable trigger; curved rubber buttpad. Introduced 1995. Imported by Beeman.

Price: **$210.00**

BEEMAN RX-1 GAS-SPRING MAGNUM AIR RIFLE

Caliber: 177, 20, 22, 25, single shot. **Barrel:** 19.6", 12-groove rifling. **Weight:** 8.8 lbs. **Power:** Gas-spring piston air; single stroke barrel cocking. **Stock:** Walnut-finished hardwood, hand checkered, with cheekpiece. Adjustable cheekpiece and buttplate. **Sights:** Tunnel front, click-adjustable rear. **Features:** Velocity adjustable to about 1200 fps. Uses special sealed chamber of air as a mainspring. Gas-spring cannot take a set. Introduced 1990. Imported by Beeman.

Price: 177, 20, 22 or 25 regular, right-hand **$590.00**
Price: 177, 20, 22, 25, left-hand.... **$625.00**

BEEMAN R1 CARBINE

Caliber: 177, 20, 22, 25, single shot. **Barrel:** 16.1". **Weight:** 8.6 lbs. **Length:** 41.7" overall. **Power:** Spring-piston, barrel cocking. **Stock:** Stained beech; Monte Carlo comb and checkpiece; cut checkered pistol grip; rubber buttpad. **Sights:** Tunnel front with interchangeable inserts, open adjustable rear; receiver grooved for scope mounting. **Features:** Velocity up to 1000 fps (177). Non-drying nylon piston and breech seals. Adjustable metal trigger. Machined steel receiver end cap and safety. Right- or left-hand stock. Imported by Beeman.

Price: 177, 20, 22, 25, right-hand.... **$540.00**
Price: As above, left-hand **$575.00**
Price: R1-AW (synthetic stock, nickel plating) **$650.00**

BEEMAN/FEINWERKBAU 300-S SERIES MATCH RIFLE

Caliber: 177, single shot. **Barrel:** 19.9", fixed solid with receiver. **Weight:** Approx. 10 lbs. with optional bbl. sleeve. **Length:** 42.8" overall. **Power:** Spring-piston, single stroke sidelever. **Stock:** Match model—walnut, deep forend, adjustable buttplate. **Sights:** Globe front with interchangeable inserts. Click micro. adjustable match aperture rear. Front and rear sights move as a single unit. **Features:** Recoilless, vibration free. Five-way adjustable match trigger. Grooved for scope mounts. Permanent lubrication, steel piston ring. Cocking effort 9 lbs. Optional 10-oz. barrel sleeve. Available from Beeman.

Price: Right-hand **$1,235.00**
Price: Left-hand **$1,370.00**

BEEMAN/FEINWERKBAU 603 AIR RIFLE

Caliber: 177, single shot. **Barrel:** 16.6". **Weight:** 10.8 lbs. **Length:** 43" overall. **Power:** Single stroke pneumatic. **Stock:** Special laminated hardwoods and hard rubber for stability. Multi-colored stock also available. **Sights:** Tunnel front with interchangeable inserts, click micrometer match aperture rear. **Features:** Velocity to 570 fps. Recoilless action; double supported barrel; special, short rifled area frees pellet form barrel faster so shooter's motion has minimum effect on accuracy. Fully adjustable match trigger with separately adjustable trigger and trigger slack weight. Trigger and sights blocked when loading latch is open. Introduced 1997. Imported by Beeman.

Price: Right-hand **$1,625.00**
Price: Left-hand **$1,775.00**

BEEMAN/FEINWERKBAU 300-S MINI-MATCH

Caliber: 177, single shot. **Barrel:** 17-1/8". **Weight:** 8.8 lbs. **Length:** 40" overall. **Power:** Spring-piston, single stroke sidelever cocking. **Stock:** Walnut. Stippled grip, adjustable buttplate. Scaled-down for youthful or slightly built shooters. **Sights:** Globe front with interchangeable inserts, micro. adjustable rear. Front and rear sights move as a single unit. **Features:** Recoilless, vibration free. Grooved for scope mounts. Steel piston ring. Cocking effort about 9-1/2 lbs. Barrel sleeve optional. Left-hand model available. Introduced 1978. Imported by Beeman.

Price: Right-hand **$1,270.00**
Price: Left-hand **$1,370.00**

BEEMAN/FEINWERKBAU P70 AIR RIFLE

Caliber: 177, single shot. **Barrel:** 16.6". **Weight:** 10.6 lbs. **Length:** 42.6" overall. **Power:** Precharged pneumatic. **Stock:** Laminated hardwoods and hard rubber for stability. Multi-colored stock also available. **Sights:** Tunnel front with interchangeable inserts, click micormeter match aperture rear. **Features:** Velocity to 570 fps. Recoilless action; double supported barrel; special short rifled area frees pellet from barrel faster so shooter's motion has minimum effect on accuracy. Fully adjustable match trigger with separately adjustable trigger and trigger slack weight. Trigger and sights blocked when loading latch is open. Introduced 1997. Imported by Beeman.

Price: P70, pre-charged, right-hand.... **$1,545.00**
Price: P70, pre-charged, left-hand.... **$1,640.00**
Price: P70, pre-charged, right-hand, multi **$1,645.00**
Price: P70, pre-charged, left-hand, multi **$1,745.00**

BEEMAN/HW 97 AIR RIFLE

Caliber: 177, 20, single shot. **Barrel:** 17.75". **Weight:** 9.2 lbs. **Length:** 44.1" overall. **Power:** Spring-piston, underlever cocking. **Stock:** Walnut-stained beech; rubber buttpad. **Sights:** None. Receiver grooved for scope mounting. **Features:** Velocity 830 fps (177). Fixed barrel with fully opening, direct loading breech. Adjustable trigger. Introduced 1994. Imported by Beeman Precision Airguns.

Price: Right-hand only **$530.00**

BENJAMIN SHERIDAN PNEUMATIC (PUMP-UP) AIR RIFLES

Caliber: 177 or 22, single shot. **Barrel:** 19-3/8", rifled brass. **Weight:** 5-1/2 lbs. **Length:** 36-1/4" overall. **Power:** Underlever pneumatic, hand pumped. **Stock:** American walnut stock and forend. **Sights:** High ramp front, fully adjustable notch rear. **Features:** Variable velocity to 800 fps. Bolt action with ambidextrous push-pull safety. Black or nickel finish. Introduced 1991. Made in the U.S. by Benjamin Sheridan Co.

Price: Black finish, Model 397 (177), Model 392 (22), about **$140.00**
Price: Nickel finish, Model S397 (177), Model S392 (22), about **$150.00**

BENJAMIN SHERIDAN W.F. AIR RIFLE

Caliber: 177 single-shot. **Barrel:** 19-3/8", rifled brass. **Weight:** 5 lbs. **Length:** 36-1/2" overall. Power 12-gram CO_2 cylinder. **Stocks:** American walnut with buttplate. **Sights:** High ramp front, fully adjustable notch rear. **Features:** Velocity to 680 fps (177). Bolt action with ambidextrous push-pull safety. Gives about 40 shots per cylinder. Black finish. Introduced 1991. Made in the U.S. by Benjamin Sheridan Co.

Price: Black finish, Model G397 (177) **$140.00**

BRNO TAU-200 Sporter

BRNO TAU-200 AIR RIFLE
Caliber: 177, single shot. **Barrel:** 19", rifled. **Weight:** 7-1/2 lbs. **Length:** 42" overall. **Power:** 6-oz. CO_2 cartridge. **Stock:** Wood match style with adjustable comb and buttplate. **Sights:** Globe front with interchangeable inserts, fully adjustable open rear. **Features:** Adjustable trigger. Comes with extra seals, large CO_2 bottle, counterweight. Introduced 1993. Imported by Century International Arms, Great Lakes Airguns. Available in Standard Universal, Deluxe Universal, International and Target Sporter versions.
Price: Standard Universal (ambidex. stock with buttstock extender, adj. cheekpiece).. .... $349.50
Price: Deluxe Universal (as above but with micro-adj. aperture sight) $449.50
Price: International (like Deluxe Universal but with right- or left-hand stock) $454.50
Price: Target Sporter (like Std. Universal but with 4X scope, no sights) $412.50

BSA MAGNUM SUPERSTAR™ MK2 MAGNUM AIR RIFLE, CARBINE
Caliber: 177, 22, 25, single shot. **Barrel:** 18". **Weight:** 8 lbs., 8 oz. **Length:** 43" overall. **Power:** Spring-air, underlever cocking. **Stock:** Oil-finished hardwood; Monte Carlo with cheekpiece, checkered at grip; recoil pad. **Sights:** Ramp front, micrometer adjustable rear. Maxi-Grip scope rail. **Features:** Velocity 1020 fps (177), 800 fps (22), 675 fps (25). Patented rotating breech design. Maxi-Grip scope rail protects optics from recoil; automatic anti-beartrap plus manual safety. Imported from U.K. by Precision Sales International, Inc.
Price: $479.99
Price: MKII Carbine (14" barrel, 39-1/2" overall) $479.99

BSA MAGNUM SUPERSPORT™ AIR RIFLE
Caliber: 177, 22, 25, single shot. **Barrel:** 18". **Weight:** 6 lbs., 8 oz. **Length:** 41" overall. **Power:** Spring-air, barrel cocking. **Stock:** Oil-finished hardwood; Monte Carlo with cheekpiece, recoil pad. **Sights:** Ramp front, micrometer adjustable rear. Maxi-Grip scope rail. **Features:** Velocity 1020 fps (177), 800 fps (22), 675 fps (25). Patented Maxi-Grip scope rail protects optics from recoil; automatic anti-beartrap plus manual tang safety. Muzzle brake standard. Imported for U.K. by Precision Sales International, Inc.
Price: $279.99
Price: Carbine, 14" barrel, muzzle brake $299.99

BSA MAGNUM GOLDSTAR MAGNUM AIR RIFLE
Caliber: 177, 22, 10-shot repeater. **Barrel:** 18". **Weight:** 8 lbs., 8 oz. **Length:** 42.5" overall. **Power:** Spring-air, underlever cocking. **Stock:** Oil-finished hardwood; Monte Carlo with cheekpiece, checkered at grip; recoil pad. **Sights:** Ramp front, micrometer adjustable rear; comes with Maxi-Grip scope rail. **Features:** Velocity 1020 fps (177), 800 fps (22). Patented 10-shot indexing magazine; Maxi-Grip scope rail protects optics from recoil; automatic anti-beartrap plus manual safety; muzzlebrake standard. Imported from U.K. by Precision Sales International, Inc.
Price: $699.99

BSA MAGNUM SUPERTEN AIR RIFLE
Caliber: 177, 22 10-shot repeater. **Barrel:** 17-1/2". **Weight:** 7 lbs., 8 oz. **Length:** 37" overall. **Power:** Precharged pneumatic via buddy bottle. **Stock:** Oil-finished hardwood; Monte Carlo with cheekpiece, cut checkering at grip; adjustable recoil pad. **Sights:** No sights; intended for scope use. **Features:** Velocity 1300+ fps (177), 1000+ fps (22). Patented 10-shot indexing magazine, bolt-action loading. Left-hand version also available. Imported from U.K. by Precision Sales International, Inc.
Price: $879.99
Price: Left-hand $1,069.00

BSA METEOR MK6 AIR RIFLE
Caliber: 177, 22, single shot. **Barrel:** 18". **Weight:** 6 lbs. **Length:** 41" overall. **Power:** Spring-air, barrel cocking. **Stock:** Oil-finished hardwood. **Sights:** Ramp front, micrometer adjustable rear. **Features:** Velocity 650 fps (177), 500 fps (22). Automatic anti-beartrap; manual tang safety. Receiver grooved for scope mounting. Imported from U.K. by Precision Sales International, Inc.
Price: Rifle $199.99
Price: Carbine $219.99

COPPERHEAD BLACK SERPENT RIFLE
Caliber: 177 pellets, 5-shot, on BB, 195-shot magazine. **Barrel:** 19-1/2" smoothbore steel. **Weight:** 2 lbs., 14 oz. **Length:** 35-7/8" overall. **Power:** Pneumatic, single pump. **Stock:** Textured plastic. **Sights:** Blade front, open adjustable rear. **Features:** Velocity to 405 fps. Introduced 1996. Made in U.S. by Crosman Corp.
Price: About $48.00

CROSMAN MODEL 66 POWERMASTER
Caliber: 177 (single shot pellet) or BB, 200-shot reservoir. **Barrel:** 20", rifled steel. **Weight:** 3 lbs. **Length:** 38-1/2" overall. **Power:** Pneumatic; hand pumped. **Stock:** Wood-grained ABS plastic; checkered pistol grip and forend. **Sights:** Ramp front, fully adjustable open rear. **Features:** Velocity about 645 fps. Bolt action, cross-bolt safety. Introduced 1983. From Crosman.
Price: About $60.00
Price: Model 664X (as above, with 4x scope) $70.00
Price: Model 664SB (as above with silver and black finish), about $75.00
Price: Model 664GT (black and gold finish, 4x scope) about $73.00

CROSMAN MODEL 760 PUMPMASTER
Caliber: 177 pellets (single shot) or BB (200-shot reservoir). **Barrel:** 19-1/2", rifled steel. **Weight:** 2 lbs., 12 oz. **Length:** 33.5" overall. **Power:** Pneumatic, hand pumped. **Stock:** Walnut-finished ABS plastic stock and forend. **Features:** Velocity to 590 fps (BBs, 10 pumps). Short stroke, power determined by number of strokes. Post front sight and adjustable rear sight. Cross-bolt safety. Introduced 1966. From Crosman.
Price: About $40.00
Price: Model 760SB (silver and black finish), about.................... $55.00

CROSMAN MODEL 782 BLACK DIAMOND AIR RIFLE
Caliber: 177 pellets (5-shot clip) or BB (195-shot reservoir). **Barrel:** 18", rifled steel. **Weight:** 3 lbs. **Power:** CO_2 Powerlet. **Stock:** Wood-grained ABS plastic; checkered grip and forend. **Sights:** Blade front, open adjustable rear. **Features:** Velocity up to 595 fps (pellets), 650 fps (BB). Black finish with white diamonds. Introduced 1990. From Crosman.
Price: About $63.00

CROSMAN MODEL 795 SPRING MASTER RIFLE
Caliber: 177, single shot. **Barrel:** Rifled steel. **Weight:** 4 lbs., 8 oz. **Length:** 42" overall. **Power:** Spring-piston. **Stock:** Black synthetic. **Sights:** Hooded front, fully adjustable rear. **Features:** Velocity about 550 fps. Introduced 1995. From Crosman.
Price: About $90.00

CROSMAN MODEL 1077 REPEATAIR RIFLE
Caliber: 177 pellets, 12-shot clip. **Barrel:** 20.3", rifled steel. **Weight:** 3 lbs., 11 oz. **Length:** 38.8" overall. **Power:** CO_2 Powerlet. **Stock:** Textured synthetic or American walnut. **Sights:** Blade front, fully adjustable rear. **Features:** Velocity 590 fps. Removable 12-shot clip. True semi-automatic action. Introduced 1993. From Crosman.
Price: About $75.00
Price: 1077W (walnut stock)............................... $110.00

CROSMAN MODEL 2289 RIFLE
Caliber: .22, single shot. **Barrel:** 14.625", rifled steel. **Weight:** 3 lbs. 3 oz. **Length:** 31" overall. **Power:** Hand pumped, pneumatic. **Stock:** Composition, skeletal type. **Sights:** Blade front, rear adjustable for windage and elevation. **Features:** Velocity to 575 fps. Detachable stock. Metal parts blued. From Crosman.
Price: About $73.00

CROSMAN MODEL 2100 CLASSIC AIR RIFLE
Caliber: 177 pellets (single shot), or BB (200-shot BB reservoir). **Barrel:** 21", rifled. **Weight:** 4 lbs., 13 oz. **Length:** 39-3/4" overall. **Power:** Pump-up, pneumatic. **Stock:** Wood-grained checkered ABS plastic. **Features:** Three pumps give about 450 fps, 10 pumps about 755 fps (BBs). Cross-bolt safety; concealed reservoir holds over 200 BBs. From Crosman.
Price: About $75.00
Price: Model 2104GT (black and gold finish, 4x scope), about $95.00
Price: Model 2100W (walnut stock, pellets only), about................. $120.00

AIRGUNS

CROSMAN MODEL 2200 MAGNUM AIR RIFLE

Caliber: 22, single shot. **Barrel:** 19", rifled steel. **Weight:** 4 lbs., 12 oz. **Length:** 39" overall. **Stock:** Full-size, wood-grained ABS plastic with checkered grip and forend or American walnut. **Sights:** Ramp front, open step-adjustable rear. **Features:** Variable pump power—three pumps give 395 fps, six pumps 530 fps, 10 pumps 595 fps (average). Full-size adult air rifle. Has white line spacers at pistol grip and buttplate. Introduced 1978. From Crosman.

Price: About **$75.00**
Price: 2200W, about **$120.00**

DAISY MODEL 840

Caliber: 177 pellet single shot; or BB 350-shot. **Barrel:** 19", smoothbore, steel. **Weight:** 2.7 lbs. **Length:** 36.8" overall. **Power:** Pneumatic, single pump. **Stock:** Moulded wood-grain stock and forend. **Sights:** Ramp front, open, adjustable rear. **Features:** Muzzle velocity 335 fps (BB), 300 fps (pellet). Steel buttplate; straight pull bolt action; cross-bolt safety. Forend forms pump lever. Introduced 1978. From Daisy Mfg. Co.

Price: About **$32.95**

DAISY/POWERLINE 853

Caliber: 177 pellets. **Barrel:** 20.9"; 12-groove rifling, high-grade solid steel by Lothar Waltherô, precision crowned; bore size for precision match pellets. **Weight:** 5.08 lbs. **Length:** 38.9" overall. **Power:** Single-pump pneumatic. **Stock:** Full-length, select American hardwood, stained and finished; black buttplate with white spacers. **Sights:** Globe front with four aperture inserts; precision micrometer adjustable rear peep sight mounted on a standard 3/8" dovetail receiver mount. **Features:** Single shot. From Daisy Mfg. Co.

Price: About **$225.00**

DAISY/POWERLINE 856 PUMP-UP AIRGUN

Caliber: 177 pellets (single shot) or BB (100-shot reservoir). **Barrel:** Rifled steel with shroud. **Weight:** 2.7 lbs. **Length:** 37.4" overall. **Power:** Pneumatic pump-up. **Stock:** Moulded wood-grain with Monte Carlo cheekpiece. **Sights:** Ramp and blade front, open rear adjustable for elevation. **Features:** Velocity from 315 fps (two pumps) to 650 fps (10 pumps). Shoots BBs or pellets. Heavy die-cast metal receiver. Cross-bolt trigger-block safety. Introduced 1984. From Daisy Mfg. Co.

Price: About **$39.95**

DAISY MODEL 990 DUAL-POWER AIR RIFLE

Caliber: 177 pellets (single shot) or BB (100-shot magazine). **Barrel:** Rifled steel. **Weight:** 4.1 lbs. **Length:** 37.4" overall. **Power:** Pneumatic pump-up and 12-gram CO_2. **Stock:** Moulded woodgrain. **Sights:** Ramp and blade front, adjustable open rear. **Features:** Velocity to 650 fps (BB), 630 fps (pellet). Choice of pump or CO_2 power. Shoots BBs or pellets. Heavy die-cast receiver dovetailed for scope mount. Cross-bolt trigger block safety. Introduced 1993. From Daisy Mfg. Co.

Price: About **$58.95**

DAISY 1938 RED RYDER 60th ANNIVERSARY CLASSIC

Caliber: BB, 650-shot repeating action. **Barrel:** Smoothbore steel with shroud. **Weight:** 2.2 lbs. **Length:** 35.4" overall. **Stock:** Walnut stock burned with Red Ryder lariat signature. **Sights:** Post front, adjustable V-slot rear. **Features:** Walnut forend. Saddle ring with leather thong. Lever cocking. Gravity feed. Controlled velocity. One of Daisy's most popular guns. From Daisy Mfg. Co.

Price: About **$39.95**

DAISY/POWERLINE 1170 PELLET RIFLE

Caliber: 177, single shot. **Barrel:** Rifled steel. **Weight:** 5.5 lbs. **Length:** 42.5" overall. **Power:** Spring-air, barrel cocking. **Stock:** Hardwood. **Sights:** Hooded post front, micrometer adjustable open rear. **Features:** Velocity to 800 fps. Monte Carlo comb. Introduced 1995. From Daisy Mfg. Co.

Price: About **$129.95**
Price: Model 131 (velocity to 600 fps) **$117.95**
Price: Model 1150 (black copolymer stock, velocity to 600 fps) **$77.95**

DAISY/POWERLINE EAGLE 7856 PUMP-UP AIRGUN

Caliber: 177 (pellets), BB, 100-shot BB magazine. **Barrel:** Rifled steel with shroud. **Weight:** 3.3 lbs. **Length:** 37.4" overall. **Power:** Pneumatic pump-up. **Stock:** Moulded wood-grain plastic. **Sights:** Ramp and blade front, open rear adjustable for elevation. **Features:** Velocity from 315 fps (two pumps) to 650 fps (10 pumps). Finger grooved forend. Cross-bolt trigger-block safety. Introduced 1985. From Daisy Mfg. Co.

Price: With 4x scope, about **$49.95**

DAISY/POWERLINE 880

Caliber: 177 pellet or BB, 50-shot BB magazine, single shot for pellets. **Barrel:** Rifled steel. **Weight:** 3.7 lbs. **Length:** 37.6" overall. **Power:** Multi-pump pneumatic. **Stock:** Moulded wood grain; Monte Carlo comb. **Sights:** Hooded front, adjustable rear. **Features:** Velocity to 685 fps. (BB). Variable power (velocity and range) increase with pump strokes; resin receiver with dovetail scope mount. Introduced 1997. Made in U.S. by Daisy Mfg. Co.

Price: About **$50.95**
Price: Model 4880 with Glo-Point fiber optic sight **$57.95**

DAISY/POWERLINE 1000 AIR RIFLE

Caliber: 177, single shot. **Barrel:** NA. **Weight:** 6.15 lbs. **Length:** 43" overall. **Power:** Spring-air, barrel cocking. **Stock:** Stained hardwood. **Sights:** Hooded blade front on ramp, fully adjustable micrometer rear. **Features:** Velocity to 1000 fps. Blued finish; trigger block safety. Introduced 1997. From Daisy Mfg. Co.

Price: About **$208.95**

DAISY/YOUTHLINE MODEL 105 AIR RIFLE

Caliber: BB, 400-shot magazine. **Barrel:** 13-1/2". **Weight:** 1.6 lbs. **Length:** 29.8" overall. **Power:** Spring. **Stock:** Moulded woodgrain. **Sights:** Blade on ramp front, fixed rear. **Features:** Velocity to 275 fps. Blue finish. Cross-bolt trigger block safety. Made in U.S. by Daisy Mfg. Co.

Price: **$28.95**

DAISY/YOUTHLINE MODEL 95 AIR RIFLE

Caliber: BB, 700-shot magazine. **Barrel:** 18". **Weight:** 2.4 lbs. **Length:** 35.2" overall. **Power:** Spring. **Stock:** Stained hardwood. **Sights:** Blade on ramp front, open adjustable rear. **Features:** Velocity to 325 fps. Cross-bolt trigger block safety. Made in U.S. by Daisy Mfg. Co.

Price: **$38.95**

EAA/BAIKAL IZH-32BK AIR RIFLE

Caliber: 177 pellet, single shot. **Barrel:** 11.68". **Weight:** 12.13 lbs. **Length:** 47.24" overall. **Power:** Single-stroke pneumatic. **Stock:** Walnut with full pistol grip, adjustable cheek piece and butt stock. **Sights:** None; integral rail for scope mount. **Features:** Velocity 541 fps. Side-cocking mechanism; hammer-forged, rifled barrel; five-way adjustable trigger. Designed for 10-meter running target competition. Introduced 2000. Imported from Russia by European American Armory.

Price: **$1,105.00**

EAA/BAIKAL IZH-61 AIR RIFLE

Caliber: 177 pellet, 5-shot magazine. **Barrel:** 17.75". **Weight:** 6.39 lbs. **Length:** 30.98" overall. **Power:** Spring piston, side-cocking lever. **Stock:** Black plastic. **Sights:** Adjustable rear, fully hooded front. **Features:** Velocity 490 fps. Futuristic design with adjustable stock. Imported from Russia by European American Armory.

Price: **$85.00**

EAA/BAIKAL MP-512 AIR RIFLE

Caliber: 177 or 22 pellet, single shot. **Barrel:** 17.7". **Weight:** 6.17 lbs. **Length:** 41.34" overall. **Power:** Spring-piston, single stroke. **Stock:** Black synthetic. **Sights:** Adjustable rear, hooded front. **Features:** Velocity 490 fps. Hammer-forged, rifled barrel; automatic safety; scope mount rail. Introduced 2000. Imported from Russia by European American Armory.

Price: 177 caliber **$50.00**
Price: 22 caliber **$63.00**

EAA/BAIKAL MP-532 AIR RIFLE

Caliber: 177 pellet, single shot. **Barrel:** 15.75". **Weight:** 9.26 lbs. **Length:** 46.06" overall. **Power:** Single-stroke pneumatic. **Stock:** One- or two-piece competition-style stock with adjustable butt pad, pistol grip. **Sights:** Fully adjustable rear, hooded front. **Features:** Velocity 460 fps. Five-way adjustable trigger. Introduced 2000. Imported from Russia by European American Armory.

Price: **$595.00**

HAMMERLI AR 50 AIR RIFLE

Caliber: 177. **Barrel:** 19.8". **Weight:** 10 lbs. **Length:** 43.2" overall. **Power:** Compressed air. **Stock:** Anatomically-shaped universal and right-hand; match style; multi-colored laminated wood. **Sights:** Interchangeable element tunnel front, fully adjustable Hammerli peep rear. **Features:** Vibration-free firing release; fully adjustable match trigger and trigger stop; stainless air tank, built-in pressure gauge. Gives 270 shots per filling. Introduced 1998. Imported from Switzerland by Sigarms, Inc.

Price: . . . . **$1,062.50 to $1,400.00**

HAMMERLI MODEL 450 MATCH AIR RIFLE

Caliber: 177, single shot. **Barrel:** 19.5". **Weight:** 9.8 lbs. **Length:** 43.3" overall. **Power:** Pneumatic. **Stock:** Match style with stippled grip, rubber buttpad. Beach or walnut. **Sights:** Match tunnel front, Hammerli diopter rear. **Features:** Velocity about 560 fps. Removable sights; forend sling rail; adjustable trigger; adjustable comb. Introduced 1994. Imported from Switzerland by Sigarms, Inc.

Price: Beech stock **$1,355.00**
Price: Walnut stock. **$1,395.00**

MARKSMAN BB BUDDY AIR RIFLE

Caliber: 177, 20-shot magazine. **Barrel:** 10.5" smoothbore. **Weight:** 1.6 lbs. **Length:** 33" overall. **Power:** Spring-air. **Stock:** Moulded composition. **Sights:** Blade on ramp front, adjustable V-slot rear. **Features:** Velocity 275 fps. Positive feed; automatic safety. Youth-sized lightweight design. Introduced 1998. Made in U.S. From Marksman Products.

Price: **$27.95**

MARKSMAN 1798 COMPETITION TRAINER AIR RIFLE

Caliber: 177, single shot. **Barrel:** 15", rifled. **Weight:** 4.7 lbs. **Power:** Spring-air, barrel cocking. **Stock:** Synthetic. **Sights:** Laserhawk fiber optic front, match-style diopter rear. **Features:** Velocity about 495 fps. Automatic safety. Introduced 1998. Made in U.S. From Marksman Products.

Price: **$70.00**

MARKSMAN 1745 BB REPEATER AIR RIFLE

Caliber: 177 BB or pellet, 18-shot BB reservoir. **Barrel:** 15-1/2", rifled. **Weight:** 4.75 lbs. **Length:** 36" overall. **Power:** Spring-air. **Stock:** Moulded composition with ambidextrous Monte Carlo cheekpiece and rubber recoil pad. **Sights:** Hooded front, adjustable rear. **Features:** Velocity about 450 fps. Break-barrel action; automatic safety. Uses BBs, pellets, darts or bolts. Introduced 1997. Made in the U.S. From Marksman Products.

Price: **$58.00**
Price: Model 1745S (same as above except comes with #1804 4x20 scope). **$73.00**

MARKSMAN 1790 BIATHLON TRAINER

Caliber: 177, single shot. **Barrel:** 15", rifled. **Weight:** 4.7 lbs. **Power:** Spring-air, barrel cocking. **Stock:** Synthetic. **Sights:** Hooded front, match-style diopter rear. **Features:** Velocity of 450 fps. Endorsed by the U.S. Shooting Team. Introduced 1989. From Marksman Products.

Price: **$70.00**

MARKSMAN 2015 LASERHAWK™ BB REPEATER AIR RIFLE

Caliber: 177 BB, 20-shot magazine. **Barrel:** 10.5" smoothbore. **Weight:** 1.6 lbs. **Length:** Adjustable to 33", 34" or 35" overall. **Power:** Spring-air. **Stock:** Moulded composition. **Sights:** Fixed fiber optic front sight, adjustable elevation V-slot rear. **Features:** Velocity about 275 fps. Positive feed; automatic safety. Adjustable stock. Introduced 1997. Made in the U.S. From Marksman Products.

Price: **$33.00**

RWS/DIANA MODEL 24 AIR RIFLE

Caliber: 177, 22, single shot. **Barrel:** 17", rifled. **Weight:** 6 lbs. **Length:** 42" overall. **Power:** Spring-air, barrel cocking. **Stock:** Beech. **Sights:** Hooded front, adjustable rear. **Features:** Velocity of 700 fps (177). Easy cocking effort; blue finish. Imported from Germany by Dynamit Nobel-RWS, Inc.

Price: **$215.00**
Price: Model 24C **$215.00**

RWS/Diana Model 34 Air Rifle

Similar to the Model 24 except has 19" barrel, weighs 7.5 lbs. Gives velocity of 1000 fps (177), 800 fps (22). Adjustable trigger, synthetic seals. Comes with scope rail.

Price: 177 or 22 .... **$290.00**
Price: Model 34N (nickel-plated metal, black epoxy-coated wood stock) ... **$350.00**
Price: Model 34BC (matte black metal, black stock, 4x32 scope, mounts) .. **$510.00**

RWS/DIANA MODEL 36 AIR RIFLE

Caliber: 177, 22, single shot. **Barrel:** 19", rifled. **Weight:** 8 lbs. **Length:** 45" overall. **Power:** Spring-air, barrel cocking. **Stock:** Beech. **Sights:** Hooded front (interchangeable inserts available), adjustable rear. **Features:** Velocity of 1000 fps (177-cal.). Comes with scope mount; two-stage adjustable trigger. Imported from Germany by Dynamit Nobel-RWS, Inc.

Price: **$435.00**
Price: Model 36 Carbine (same as Model 36 rifle except has 15" barrel) ... **$435.00**

RWS/DIANA MODEL 52 AIR RIFLE

Caliber: 177, 22, single shot. **Barrel:** 17", rifled. **Weight:** 8-1/2 lbs. **Length:** 43" overall. **Power:** Spring-air, sidelever cocking. **Stock:** Beech, with Monte Carlo, cheekpiece, checkered grip and forend. **Sights:** Ramp front, adjustable rear. **Features:** Velocity of 1100 fps (177). Blue finish. Solid rubber buttpad. Imported from Germany by Dynamit Nobel-RWS, Inc.

Price: **$565.00**
Price: Model 52 Deluxe (select walnut stock, rosewood grip and forend caps, palm swell grip) **$810.00**
Price: Model 48B (as above except matte black metal, black stock) **$535.00**
Price: Model 48 (same as Model 52 except no Monte Carlo, cheekpiece or checkering) **$510.00**

RWS/DIANA MODEL 45 AIR RIFLE

Caliber: 177, single shot. **Weight:** 8 lbs. **Length:** 45" overall. **Power:** Spring-air, barrel cocking. **Stock:** Walnut-finished hardwood with rubber recoil pad. **Sights:** Globe front with interchangeable inserts, micro. click open rear with four-way blade. **Features:** Velocity of 820 fps. Dovetail base for either micrometer peep sight or scope mounting. Automatic safety. Imported from Germany by Dynamit Nobel-RWS, Inc.

Price: **$350.00**

RWS/DIANA MODEL 54 AIR KING RIFLE

Caliber: 177, 22, single shot. **Barrel:** 17". **Weight:** 9 lbs. **Length:** 43" overall.**Power:** Spring-air, sidelever cocking. **Stock:** Walnut with Monte Carlo cheekpiece, checkered grip and forend. **Sights:** Ramp front, fully adjustable rear. **Features:** Velocity to 1000 fps (177), 900 fps (22). Totally recoilless system; floating action absorbs recoil. Imported from Germany by Dynamit Nobel-RWS, Inc.

Price: **$785.00**

SAVAGE MODEL 1000G AIR RIFLE NEW!

Caliber: 177 pellet, single shot. **Barrel:** 18". **Weight:** 7.25 lbs. **Length:** 45.3" overall. **Power:** Spring piston, break-barrel action. **Stock:** Walnut-finished hardwood with recoil pad. **Sights:** Adjustable rear notch, hooded front post. **Features:** Velocity 1,000 fps. Also available with 2.5-power scope. Introduced 2000. From Savage Arms.

Price: **$181.00**

SAVAGE MODEL 600F AIR RIFLE NEW!

Caliber: 177 pellet, 25-shot tubular magazine. **Barrel:** 18" polymer-coated steel. **Weight:** 6 lbs. **Length:** 40" overall. **Power:** spring piston, break-barrel action. **Stock:** Black polymer stock with lacquer finish. **Sights:** Adjustable rear notch, hooded front post. **Features:** Velocity 600 fps. Repeating action. Also available with 2.5-power scope. Introduced 2000. From Savage Arms.

Price: **$126.00**

SAVAGE MODEL 560F AIR RIFLE NEW!

Caliber: 177 pellet, single shot. **Barrel:** 18" polymer-coated steel. **Weight:** 5.5 lbs. **Length:** 39" overall. **Power:** Spring piston, break-barrel action. **Stock:** Metallic-black finished polymer stock. **Sights:** Adjustable notch rear, post front. **Features:** Velocity 560 fps. Introduced 2000. From Savage Arms.

Price: **$92.00**

STEYR LG1P AIR RIFLE

Caliber: 177, single shot. **Barrel:** 23.75", (13.75" rifled). **Weight:** 10.5 lbs. **Length:** 51.7" overall. **Power:** Precharged air. **Stock:** Match. Laminated wood. Adjustable buttplate and cheekpiece. **Sights:** Precision diopter. **Features:** Velocity 577 fps. Air cylinders are refillable; about 320 shots per cylinder. Designed for 10-meter shooting. Introduced 1996. Imported from Austria by Nygord Precision Products.

Price: About **$1,295.00**
Price: Left-hand, about.................... **$1,350.00**

TECH FORCE BS4 OLYMPIC COMPETITION AIR RIFLE

Caliber: 177 pellet, single shot. **Barrel:** N/A. **Weight:** 10.8 lbs. **Length:** 43.3" overall. **Power:** Spring piston, sidelever action. **Stock:** Wood with semi-pistol grip, adjustable butt plate. **Sights:** Micro-adjustable competition rear, hooded front. **Features:** Velocity 640 fps. Recoilless action; adjustable trigger. Includes carrying case. Imported from China by Compasseco Inc.

Price: **$595.00**
Price: Optional diopter rear sight.................... **$79.95**

TECH FORCE 6 AIR RIFLE

Caliber: 177 pellet, single shot. **Barrel:** 14". **Weight:** 6 lbs. **Length:** 35.5" overall. **Power:** Sspring piston, sidelever action. **Stock:** Paratrooper-style folding, full pistol grip. **Sights:** Adjustable rear, hooded front. **Features:** Velocity 800 fps. All-metal construction; grooved for scope mounting. Imported from China by Compasseco Inc.

Price: **$69.95**

Tech Force 51 Air Rifle

Similar to Tech Force 6, but with break-barrel cocking mechanism and folding stock fitted with recoil pad. Overall length, 36". Weighs 6 lbs. From Compasseco Inc.

Price: **$69.95**

TECH FORCE 25 AIR RIFLE

Caliber: 177, 22 pellet; single shot. **Barrel:** N/A. **Weight:** 7.5 lbs. **Length:** 46.2" overall. **Power:** Spring piston, break-action barrel. **Stock:** Oil-finished wood; Monte Carlo stock with recoil pad. **Sights:** Adjustable rear, hooded front with insert. **Features:** Velocity 1,000 fps (177); grooved receiver and scope stop for scope mounting; adjustable trigger; trigger safety. Imported from China by Compasseco Inc.

Price:177 or 22 caliber **$125.00**
Price: Includes rifle and Tech Force 96 red dot point sight **$164.95**

TECH FORCE 36 AIR RIFLE

Caliber: 177 pellet, single shot. **Barrel:** N/A. **Weight:** 7.4 lbs. **Length:** 43" overall. **Power:** Spring piston, underlever cocking. **Stock:** Monte Carlo hardwood stock; recoil pad. **Sights:** Adjustable rear, hooded front. **Features:** Velocity 900 fps; grooved receiver and scope stop for scope mounting; auto-reset safety. Imported from China by Compasseco Inc.

Price: **$89.95**

WHISCOMBE JW SERIES AIR RIFLES

Caliber: 177, 20, 22, 25, single shot. **Barrel:** 15", Lothar Walther. Polygonal rifling. **Weight:** 9 lbs., 8 oz. **Length:** 39" overall. **Power:** Dual spring-piston, multi-stroke; underlever cocking. **Stock:** Walnut with adjustable buttplate and cheekpiece. **Sights:** None furnished; grooved scope rail. **Features:** Velocity 660-1000 (JW80) fps (22-caliber, fixed barrel) depending upon model. Interchangeable barrels; automatic safety; muzzle weight; semi-floating action; twin opposed pistons with counter-wound springs; adjustable trigger. All models include H.O.T. System (Harmonic Optimization Tunable System). Introduced 1995. Imported from England by Pelaire Products.

Price: JW50, MKII fixed barrel only **$1,895.00**
Price: JW60, MKII fixed barrel only **$1,895.00**
Price: JW70, MKII fixed barrel only **$1,950.00**
Price: JW80, MKII.................... **$1,995.00**

AIRGUNS

CH4D Heavyweight Champion

Frame: Cast iron
Frame Type: O-frame
Die Thread: 7/8-14 or 1-14
Avg. Rounds Per Hour: NA
Ram Stroke: 3-1/4"
Weight: 26 lbs.
Features: 1.185" diameter ram with 16 square inches of bearing surface; ram drilled to allow passage of spent primers; solid steel handle; toggle that slightly breaks over the top dead center. Includes universal primer arm with large and small punches. From CH Tool & Die/4D Custom Die.
Price: $220.00

CH4D No. 444

Frame: Aluminum alloy
Frame Type: H-frame
Die Thread: 7/8-14
Avg. Rounds Per Hour: 200
Ram Stroke: 3-3/4"
Weight: 12 lbs.
Features: Two 7/8" solid steel shaft "H" supports; platen rides on permanently lubed bronze bushings; loads smallest pistol to largest magnum rifle cases and has strength to full-length resize. Includes four rams, large and small primer arm and primer catcher. From CH Tool & Die/4D Custom Die, Co.
Price: $195.00

CH4D No. 444-X Pistol Champ

Frame: Aluminum alloy
Frame Type: H-frame
Die Thread: 7/8-14
Avg. Rounds Per Hour: 200
Ram Stroke: 3-3/4"
Weight: 12 lbs.
Features: Tungsten carbide sizing die; Speed Seater seating die with tapered entrance to automatically align bullet on case mouth; automatic primer feed for large or small primers; push-button powder measure with easily changed bushings for 215 powder/load combinations; taper crimp die. Conversion kit for caliber changeover available. From CH Tool & Die/4D Custom Die, Co.
Price: .... $292.00-$316.50

FORSTER Co-Ax Press B-2

Frame: Cast iron
Frame Type: Modified O-frame
Die Thread: 7/8-14
Avg. Rounds Per Hour: 120
Ram Stroke: 4"
Weight: 18 lbs.
Features: Snap in/snap out die change; spent primer catcher with drop tube threaded into carrier below shellholder; automatic, handle-activated, cammed shellholder with opposing spring-loaded jaws to contact extractor groove; floating guide rods for alignment and reduced friction; no torque on the head due to design of linkage and pivots; shellholder jaws that float with die permitting case to center in the die; right- or left-hand operation; priming device for seating to factory specifications. "S" shellholder jaws included. From Forster Products.
Price: $298.00
Price: Extra shellholder jaws $26.00

HOLLYWOOD Senior Press

Frame: Ductile iron
Frame Type: O-frame
Die Thread: 7/8-14
Avg. Rounds Per Hour: 50-100
Ram Stroke: 6-1/2"
Weight: 50 lbs.
Features: Leverage and bearing surfaces ample for reloading cartridges or swaging bullets. Precision ground one-piece 2-1/2" pillar with base; operating

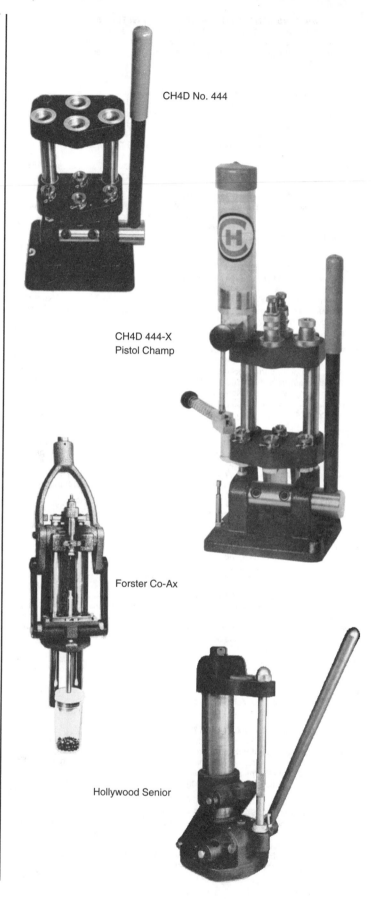

CH4D No. 444

CH4D 444-X
Pistol Champ

Forster Co-Ax

Hollywood Senior

METALLIC CARTRIDGE PRESSES

Hollywood Senior Turret

Lee Hand Press

Hornady Lock-N-Load Classic

Lee Challenger

handle of 3/4" steel and 15" long; 5/8" steel tie-down rod fro added strength when swaging; heavy steel toggle and camming arms held by 1/2" steel pins in reamed holes. The 1-1/2" steel die bushing takes standard threaded dies; removed, it allows use of Hollywood shotshell dies. From Hollywood Engineering.

Price: **$500.00**

HOLLYWOOD Senior Turret Press

Frame: Ductile iron
Frame Type: H-frame
Die Thread: 7/8-14
Avg. Rounds Per Hour: 50-100
Ram Stroke: 6-1/2"
Weight: 50 lbs.
Features: Same features as Senior press except has three-position turret head; holes in turret may be tapped 1-1/2" or 7/8" or four of each. Height, 15". Comes complete with one turret indexing handle; one 1-1/2" to 7/8" die hole bushing; one 5/8" tie down bar for swaging. From Hollywood Engineering.

Price: **$600.00**

HORNADY Lock-N-Load Classic

Frame: Die cast heat-treated aluminum alloy
Frame Type: O-frame
Die Thread: 7/8-14
Avg. Rounds Per Hour: NA
Ram Stroke: 3-5/8"
Weight: 14 lbs.
Features: Features Lock-N-Load bushing system that allows instant die changeovers. Solid steel linkage arms that rotate on steel pins; 30° angled frame design for improved visibility and accessibility; primer arm automatically moves in and out of ram for primer pickup and solid seating; two primer arms for large and small primers; long offset handle for increased leverage and unobstructed reloading; lifetime warranty. Comes as a package with primer catcher, PPS automatic primer feed and three Lock-N-Load die bushings. Dies and shellholder available separately or as a kit with primer catcher, positive priming system, automatic primer feed, three die bushings and reloading accessories. From Hornady Mfg. Co.

Price: Classic Reloading Package **$99.95**
Price: Classic Reloading Kit **$239.95**

LEE Hand Press

Frame: ASTM 380 aluminum
Frame Type: NA
Die Thread: 7/8-14
Avg. Rounds Per Hour: 100
Ram Stroke: 3-1/4"
Weight: 1 lb., 8 oz.
Features: Small and lightweight for portability; compound linkage for handling up to 375 H&H and case forming. Dies and shellholder not included. From Lee Precision, Inc.

Price: **$22.98**

LEE Challenger Press

Frame: ASTM 380 aluminum
Frame Type: O-frame
Die Thread: 7/8-14
Avg. Rounds Per Hour: 100
Ram Stroke: 3-1/2"
Weight: 4 lbs., 1 oz.
Features: Larger than average opening with 30° offset for maximum hand clearance; steel connecting pins; spent primer catcher; handle adjustable for start and stop positions; handle repositions for left- or right-hand use; shortened handle travel to prevent springing the frame from alignment. Dies and shellholders not included. From Lee Precision, Inc.

Price: **$39.98**

METALLIC CARTRIDGE PRESSES

LEE Loader
Kit consists of reloading dies to be used with mallet or soft hammer. Neck sizes only. Comes with powder charge cup. From Lee Precision, Inc.
Price: **$19.98**

LEE Reloader Press
Frame: ASTM 380 aluminum
Frame Type: C-frame
Die Thread: 7/8-14
Avg. Rounds Per Hour: 100
Ram Stroke: 3"
Weight: 1 lb., 12 oz.
Features: Balanced lever to prevent pinching fingers; unlimited hand clearance; left- or right-hand use. Dies and shellholders not included. From Lee Precision, Inc.
Price: **$22.98**

Lee Reloader

LEE Turret Press
Frame: ASTM 380 aluminum
Frame Type: O-frame
Die Thread: 7/8-14
Avg. Rounds Per Hour: 300
Ram Stroke: 3"
Weight: 7 lbs., 2 oz.
Features: Replaceable turret lifts out by rotating 30°; T-primer arm reverses for large or small primers; built-in primer catcher; adjustable handle for right- or left-hand use or changing angle of down stroke; accessory mounting hole for Lee Auto-Disk powder measure. Optional Auto-Index rotates die turret to next station for semi-progressive use. Safety override prevents overstressing should turret not turn. From Lee Precision, Inc.
Price: **$69.98**
Price: With Auto-Index **$83.98**
Price: Extra turret **$10.98**

Lee Turret

LYMAN 310 Tool
Frame: Stainless steel
Frame Type: NA
Die Thread: 7/8-14
Avg. Rounds Per Hour: NA
Ram Stroke: NA
Weight: 10 oz.
Features: Compact, portable reloading tool for pistol or rifle cartridges. Adapter allows loading rimmed or rimless cases. Die set includes neck resizing/decapping die; primer seating chamber; neck expanding die; bullet seating die; and case head adapter. From Lyman Products Corporation.
Price: Dies **$39.95**
Price: Press **$44.95**
Price: Carrying pouch **$9.95**

LYMAN AccuPress
Frame: Die cast
Frame Type: C-frame
Die Thread: 7/8-14
Avg. Rounds Per Hour: 75
Ram Stroke: 3.4"
Weight: 4 lbs.
Features: Reversible, contoured handle for bench mount or hand-held use; for rifle or pistol; compound leverage; Delta frame design. Accepts all standard powder measures. From Lyman Products Corporation.
Price: **$33.25**

Lyman 310

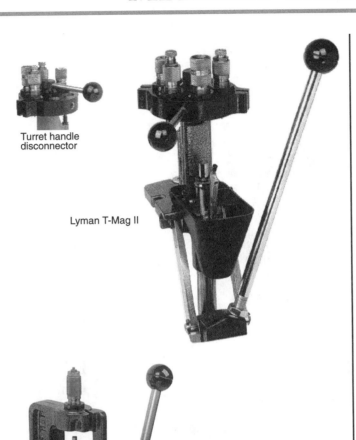

Turret handle disconnector

Lyman T-Mag II

Lyman Crusher II

Ponsness/Warren
Metal-Matic P-200

LYMAN Crusher II

Frame: Cast iron
Frame Type: O-frame
Die Thread: 7/8-14
Avg. Rounds Per Hour: 75
Ram Stroke: 3-7/8"
Weight: 19 lbs.
Features: Reloads both pistol and rifle cartridges; 1" diameter ram; 4-1/2" press opening for loading magnum cartridges; direct torque design; right- or left-hand use. New base design with 14 square inches of flat mounting surface with three bolt holes. Comes with priming arm and primer catcher. Dies and shellholders not included. From Lyman Products Corporation.
Price: **$112.50**

LYMAN T-Mag II

Frame: Cast iron with silver metalflake powder finish
Frame Type: Turret
Die Thread: 7/8-14
Avg. Rounds Per Hour: 125
Ram Stroke: 3-13/16"
Weight: 18 lbs.
Features: Reengineered and upgraded with new turret system for ease of indexing and tool-free turret removal for caliber changeover; new flat machined base for bench mounting; new nickel-plated non-rust handle and links; and new silver hammertone powder coat finish for durability. Right- or left-hand operation; handles all rifle or pistol dies. Comes with priming arm and primer catcher. Dies and shellholders not included. From Lyman Products Corporation.
Price: **$154.95**
Price: Extra turret **$36.00**

PONSNESS/WARREN Metal-Matic P-200

Frame: Die cast aluminum
Frame Type: Unconventional
Die Thread: 7/8-14
Avg. Rounds Per Hour: 200+
Weight: 18 lbs.
Features: Designed for straight-wall cartridges; die head with 10 tapped holes for holding dies and accessories for two calibers at one time; removable spent primer box; pivoting arm moves case from station to station. Comes with large and small primer tool. Optional accessories include primer feed, extra die head, primer speed feeder, powder measure extension and dust cover. Dies, powder measure and shellholder not included. From Ponsness/Warren.
Price: **$199.00**
Price: Extra die head **$44.95**
Price: Powder measure extension **$26.95**
Price: Primer feed **$42.95**
Price: Primer speed feed **$13.95**
Price: Dust cover **$20.95**

RCBS Partner

Frame: Aluminum
Frame Type: O-frame
Die Thread: 7/8-14
Avg. Rounds Per Hour: 50-60
Ram Stroke: 3-5/8"
Weight: 5 lbs.
Features: Designed for the beginning reloader. Comes with primer arm equipped with interchangeable primer plugs and sleeves for seating large and small primers. Shellholder and dies not included. Available in kit form (see Metallic Presses—Accessories). From RCBS.
Price: **$54.95**

ACCESSORIES

RCBS AmmoMaster Single

Frame: Aluminum base; cast iron top plate connected by three steel posts.
Frame Type: NA
Die Thread: 1-1/4"-12 bushing; 7/8-14 threads
Avg. Rounds Per Hour: 50-60
Ram Stroke: 5-1/4"
Weight: 19 lbs.
Features: Single-stage press convertible to progressive. Will form cases or swage bullets. Case detection system to disengage powder measure when no case is present in powder charging station; five-station shellplate; Uniflow Powder measure with clear powder measure adaptor to make bridged powders visible and correctable. 50-cal. conversion kit allows reloading 50 BMG. Kit includes top plate to accommodate either 1-3/8" x 12 or 1-1/2" x 12 reloading dies. Piggyback die plate for quick caliber change-overs available. Reloading dies not included. From RCBS.
Price: **$186.95**
Price: 50 conversion kit **$74.95**
Price: Piggyback/AmmoMaster die plate **$22.95**
Price: Piggyback/AmmoMaster shellplate **$27.95**
Price: Press cover **$10.95**

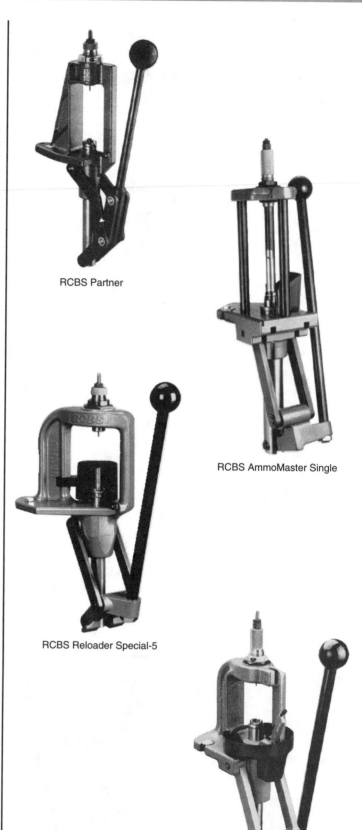

RCBS Partner

RCBS AmmoMaster Single

RCBS Reloader Special-5

Frame: Aluminum
Frame Type: 30° offset O-frame
Die Thread: 1-1/4"-12 bushing; 7/8-14 threads
Avg. Rounds Per Hour: 50-60
Ram Stroke: 3-1/16"
Weight: 7.5 lbs.
Features: Single-stage press convertible to progressive with RCBS Piggyback II. Primes cases during resizing operation. Will accept RCBS shotshell dies. From RCBS.
Price: **$103.95**

RCBS Rock Chucker

Frame: Cast iron
Frame Type: O-frame
Die Thread: 1-1/4"-12 bushing; 7/8-14 threads
Avg. Rounds Per Hour: 50-60
Ram Stroke: 3-1/16"
Weight: 17 lbs.
Features: Designed for heavy-duty reloading, case forming and bullet swaging. Provides 4" of ram-bearing surface to support 1" ram and ensure alignment; ductile iron toggle blocks; hardened steel pins. Comes standard with Universal Primer Arm and primer catcher. Can be converted from single-stage to progressive with Piggyback II conversion unit. From RCBS.
Price: **$130.95**

RCBS Reloader Special-5

REDDING Turret Press

Frame: Cast iron
Frame Type: Turret
Die Thread: 7/8-14
Avg. Rounds Per Hour: NA
Ram Stroke: 3.4"
Weight: 23 lbs., 2 oz.
Features: Strength to reload pistol and magnum rifle, case form and bullet swage; linkage pins heat-treated, precision ground and in double shear; hollow ram to collect spent primers; removable turret head for caliber changes; progressive linkage for increased power as ram nears die; slight frame tilt for comfortable operation; rear turret support for stability and precise alignment; six-station turret head; priming arm for both large and small primers. Also available in kit form with shellholder, primer catcher and one die set. From

RCBS Rock Chucker

METALLIC CARTRIDGE PRESSES

Redding Model 25

Redding Boss

Rock Crusher

Redding Ultramag

Redding Reloading Equipment.
Price: **$298.50**
Price: Kit **$334.50**

REDDING Boss

Frame: Cast iron
Frame Type: O-frame
Die Thread: 7/8-14
Avg. Rounds Per Hour: NA
Ram Stroke: 3.4"
Weight: 11 lbs., 8 oz.
Features: 36˚ frame offset for visibility and accessibility; primer arm positioned at bottom ram travel; positive ram travel stop machined to hit exactly top-dead-center. Also available in kit form with shellholder and set of Redding A dies. From Redding Reloading Equipment.
Price: **$129.00**
Price: Kit **$165.00**

REDDING Ultramag

Frame: Cast iron
Frame Type: Non-conventional
Die Thread: 7/8-14
Avg. Rounds Per Hour: NA
Ram Stroke: 4-1/8"
Weight: 23 lbs., 6 oz.
Features: Unique compound leverage system connected to top of press for tons of ram pressure; large 4-3/4" frame opening for loading outsized cartridges; hollow ram for spent primers. Kit available with shellholder and one set Redding A dies. From Redding Reloading Equipment.
Price: **$298.50**
Price: Kit **$334.50**

ROCK CRUSHER Press

Frame: Cast iron
Frame Type: O-frame
Die Thread: 2-3/4"-12 with bushing reduced to 1-1/2"-12
Avg. Rounds Per Hour: 50
Ram Stroke: 6"
Weight: 67 lbs.
Features: Designed to load and form ammunition from 50 BMG up to 23x115 Soviet. Frame opening of 8-1/2"x3-1/2"; 1-1/2"x12"; bushing can be removed and bushings of any size substituted; ram pressure can exceed 10,000 lbs. with normal body weight; 40mm diameter ram. Angle block for bench mounting and reduction bushing for RCBS dies available. Accessories for Rock Crusher include powder measure, dies, shellholder, bullet puller, priming tool, case gauge and other accessories found elsewhere in this catalog. From The Old Western Scrounger.
Price: **$785.00**
Price: Angle block **$57.95**
Price: Reduction bushing **$21.00**
Price: Shellholder, 50 BMG, 12.7, 55 Boyes **$36.75**
Price: Shellholder, 23 Soviet **$65.00**
Price: Shellholder, all others **$47.95**
Price: Priming tool, 50 BMG, 20 Lahti **$65.10**

PROGRESSIVE PRESSES

DILLON AT 500

Frame: Aluminum alloy
Frame Type: NA
Die Thread: 7/8-14
Avg. Rounds Per Hour: 200-300
Ram Stroke: 3-7/8"
Weight: NA
Features: Four stations; removable tool head to hold dies in alignment and allow caliber changes without die adjustment; manual indexing; capacity to be upgraded to progressive RL 550B. Comes with universal shellplate to accept

ACCESSORIES

METALLIC CARTRIDGE PRESSES

223, 22-250, 243, 30-06, 9mm, 38/357, 40 S&W, 45 ACP. Dies not included.
From Dillon Precision Products.
Price: **$193.95**

DILLON RL 550B

Frame: Aluminum alloy
Frame Type: NA
Die Thread: 7/8-14
Avg. Rounds Per Hour: 500-600
Ram Stroke: 3-7/8"
Weight: 25 lbs.
Features: Four stations; removable tool head to hold dies in alignment and allow caliber changes without die adjustment; auto priming system that emits audible warning when primer tube is low; a 100-primer capacity magazine contained in DOM steel tube for protection; new auto powder measure system with simple mechanical connection between measure and loading platform for positive powder bar return; a separate station for crimping with star-indexing system; 220 ejected-round capacity bin; 3/4-lb. capacity powder measure. Height above bench, 35"; requires 3/4" bench overhang. Will reload 120 different rifle and pistol calibers. Comes with one caliber conversion kit. Dies not included. From Dillon Precision Products, Inc.
Price: **$325.95**

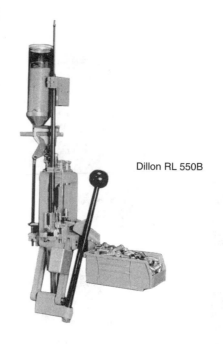

Dillon RL 550B

DILLON RL 1050

Frame: Ductile iron
Frame Type: Platform type
Die Thread: 7/8-14
Avg. Rounds Per Hour: 1000-1200
Ram Stroke: 2-5/16"
Weight: 62 lbs.
Features: Eight stations; auto case feed; primer pocket swager for military cartridge cases; auto indexing; removable tool head; auto prime system with 100-primer capacity; low primer supply alarm; positive powder bar return; auto powder measure; 515 ejected round bin capacity; 500-600 case feed capacity; 3/4-lb. capacity powder measure. Loads all pistol rounds as well as 30 M1 Carbine, 223, and 7.62x39 rifle rounds. Height above the bench, 43". Dies not included. From Dillon Precision Products, Inc.
Price: **$1,199.95**

Dillon RL 1050

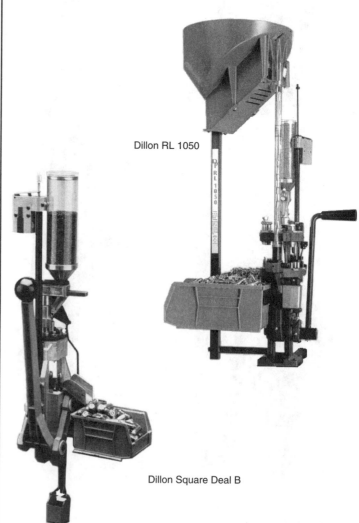

DILLON Square Deal B

Frame: Zinc alloy
Frame Type: NA
Die Thread: None (unique Dillon design)
Avg. Rounds Per Hour: 400-500
Ram Stroke: 2-5/16"
Weight: 17 lbs.
Features: Four stations; auto indexing; removable tool head; auto prime system with 100-primer capacity; low primer supply alarm; auto powder measure; positive powder bar return; 170 ejected round capacity bin; 3/4-lb. capacity powder measure. Height above the bench, 34". Comes complete with factory adjusted carbide die set. From Dillon Precision Products, Inc.
Price: **$252.95**

DILLON XL 650

Frame: Aluminum alloy
Frame Type: NA
Die Thread: 7/8-14
Avg. Rounds Per Hour: 800-1000
Ram Stroke: 4-9/16"
Weight: 46 lbs.
Features: Five stations; auto indexing; auto case feed; removable tool head; auto prime system with 100-primer capacity; low primer supply alarm; auto

Dillon Square Deal B

powder measure; positive powder bar return; 220 ejected round capacity bin; 3/4-lb. capacity powder measure. 500-600 case feed capacity with optional auto case feed. Loads all pistol/rifle calibers less than 3-1/2" in length. Height above the bench, 44"; 3/4" bench overhang required. From Dillon Precision Products, Inc.

Price: Less dies. **$443.95**

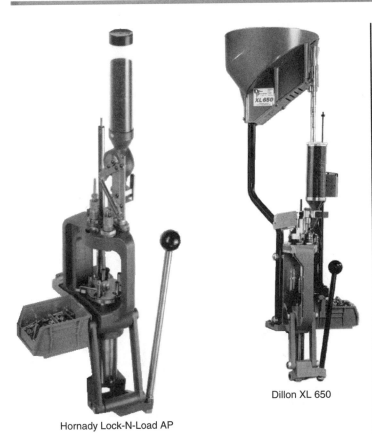

Hornady Lock-N-Load AP

Dillon XL 650

HORNADY Lock-N-Load AP

Frame: Die cast heat-treated aluminum alloy
Frame Type: O-frame
Die Thread: 7/8-14
Avg. Rounds Per Hour: NA
Ram Stroke: 3-3/4"
Weight: 26 lbs.
Features: Features Lock-N-Load bushing system that allows instant die changeovers; five-station die platform with option of seating and crimping separately or adding taper-crimp die; auto prime with large and small primer tubes with 100-primer capacity and protective housing; brass kicker to eject loaded rounds into 80-round capacity cartridge catcher; offset operating handle for leverage and unobstructed operation; 2" diameter ram driven by heavy-duty cast linkage arms rotating on steel pins. Comes with five Lock-N-Load die bushings, shellplate, deluxe powder measure, auto powder drop, and auto primer feed and shut-off, brass kicker and primer catcher. Lifetime warranty. From Hornady Mfg. Co.

Price: **$367.65**

LEE Load-Master

Frame: ASTM 380 aluminum
Frame Type: O-frame
Die Thread: 7/8-14
Avg. Rounds Per Hour: 600
Ram Stroke: 3-1/4"
Weight: 8 lbs., 4 oz.
Features: Available in kit form only. A 1-3/4" diameter hard chrome ram for handling largest magnum cases; loads rifle or pistol rounds; five station press to factory crimp and post size; auto indexing with wedge lock mechanism to hold one ton; auto priming; removable turrets; four-tube case feeder with optional case collator and bullet feeder (late 1995); loaded round ejector with chute to optional loaded round catcher; quick change shellplate; primer catcher. Dies and shellholder for one caliber included. From Lee Precision, Inc.

Price: Rifle. **$320.00**
Price: Pistol. **$330.00**
Price: Extra turret **$10.98**
Price: Adjustable charge bar. **$9.98**

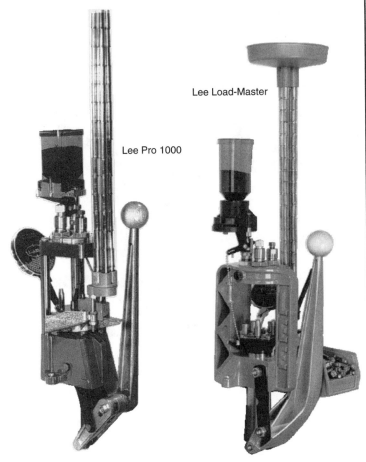

Lee Load-Master

Lee Pro 1000

LEE Pro 1000

Frame: ASTM 380 aluminum and steel
Frame Type: O-frame
Die Thread: 7/8-14
Avg. Rounds Per Hour: 600
Ram Stroke: 3-1/4"
Weight: 8 lbs., 7 oz.
Features: Optional transparent large/small or rifle case feeder; deluxe auto-disk case-activated powder measure; case sensor for primer feed. Comes complete with carbide die set (steel dies for rifle) for one caliber. Optional accessories include: case feeder for large/small pistol cases or rifle cases; shell plate carrier with auto prime, case ejector, auto-index and spare parts; case collator for case feeder. From Lee Precision, Inc.

Price: **$199.98**

ACCESSORIES

METALLIC CARTRIDGE PRESSES

PONSNESS/WARREN Metallic II

Frame: Die cast aluminum
Frame Type: H-frame
Die Thread: 7/8-14
Avg. Rounds Per Hour: 150+
Ram Stroke: NA
Weight: 32 lbs.
Features: Die head with five tapped 7/8-14 holes for dies, powder measure or other accessories; pivoting die arm moves case from station to station; depriming tube for removal of spent primers; auto primer feed; interchangeable die head. Optional accessories include additional die heads, powder measure extension tube to accommodate any standard powder measure, primer speed feeder to feed press primer tube without disassembly. Comes with small and large primer seating tools. Dies, powder measure and shellholder not included. From Ponsness/Warren.
Price: $359.00
Price: Extra die head $54.95
Price: Primer speed feeder.................................. $13.95
Price: Powder measure extension $26.95
Price: Dust cover $27.95

RCBS AmmoMaster

RCBS AmmoMaster-Auto

Frame: Aluminum base; cast iron top plate connected by three steel posts.
Frame Type: NA
Die Thread: 1-1/4-12 bushing; 7/8-14 threads
Avg. Rounds Per Hour: 400-500
Ram Stroke: 5-1/4"
Weight: 19 lbs.
Features: Progressive press convertible to single-stage. Features include: 1-1/2" solid ram; automatic indexing, priming, powder charging and loaded round ejection. Case detection system disengages powder measure when no case is present in powder charging station. Comes with five-station shellplate and Uniflow powder measure with clear powder measure adaptor to make bridged powders visible and correctable. Piggyback die plate for quick caliber change-over available. Reloading dies not included. From RCBS.
Price: $394.95
Price: Piggyback/AmmoMaster die plate $22.95
Price: Piggyback/AmmoMaster shellplate $27.95
Price: Press cover $10.95

STAR Universal Pistol Press

Frame: Cast iron with aluminum base
Frame Type: Unconventional
Die Thread: 11/16-24 or 7/8-14
Avg. Rounds Per Hour: 300
Ram Stroke: NA
Weight: 27 lbs.
Features: Four or five-station press depending on need to taper crimp; handles all popular handgun calibers from 32 Long to 45 Colt. Comes completely assembled and adjusted with carbide dies (except 30 Carbine) and shellholder to load one caliber. Prices slightly higher for 9mm and 30 Carbine. From Star Machine Works.
Price: With taper crimp...................................... $950.00
Price: Without taper crimp $925.00
Price: Extra tool head, taper crimp.......................... $381.00
Price: Extra tool head, w/o taper crimp...................... $356.00

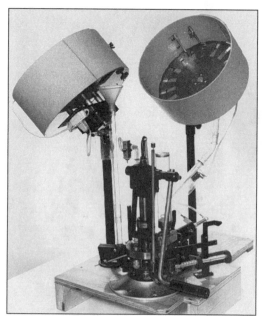

Fully-automated Star Universal

Dillon SL 900

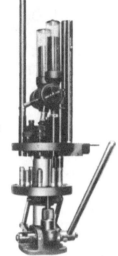

Hollywood Automatic

Hollywood Senior Turret Press

Hornady 366 Auto

Lee Load-All II

DILLON SL 900

Press Type: Progressive
Avg. Rounds Per Hour: 700-900
Weight: 51 lbs.
Features: 12-ga. only; factory adjusted to load AA hulls; extra large 25-pound capacity shot hopper; fully-adjustable case-activated shot system; hardened steel starter crimp die; dual-action final crimp and taper die; tilt-out wad guide; auto prime; auto index; strong mount machine stand. From Dillon Precision Products.
Price: **$819.95**

HOLLYWOOD Automatic Shotshell Press

Press Type: Progressive
Avg. Rounds Per Hour: 1,800
Weight: 100 lbs.
Features: Ductile iron frame; fully automated press with shell pickup and ejector; comes completely set up for one gauge; one starter crimp; one finish crimp; wad guide for plastic wads; decap and powder dispenser unit; one wrench for inside die lock screw; one medium and one large spanner wrench for spanner nuts; one shellholder; powder and shot measures. Available for 10, 12, 20, 28 or 410. From Hollywood Engineering.
Price: **$3,600.00**

HOLLYWOOD Senior Turret Press

Press Type: Turret
Avg. Rounds Per Hour: 200
Weight: 50 lbs.
Features: Multi-stage press constructed of ductile iron comes completely equipped to reload one gauge; one starter crimp; one finish crimp; wad guide for plastic wads; decap and powder dispenser unit; one wrench for inside die lock screw; one medium and one large spanner wrench for spanner nuts; one shellholder; powder and shot measures. Available for 10, 12, 16, 20, 28 or 410. From Hollywood Engineering.
Price: Press with die set. **$875.00**
Price: Press only **$600.00**
Price: Senior Single-Stage Press. **$500.00**

HORNADY 366 Auto

Press Type: Progressive
Avg. Rounds Per Hour: NA
Weight: 25 lbs.
Features: Heavy-duty die cast and machined steel body and components; auto primer feed system; large capacity shot and powder tubes; adjustable for right- or left-hand use; automatic charge bar with shutoff; swing-out wad guide; primer catcher at base of press; interchangeable shot and powder bushings; life-time warranty. Available for 12, 20, 28 2-3/4 and 410 2-1/2. From Hornady Mfg. Co.
Price: **$434.95**
Price: Die set, 12, 20, 28 . . . .**$196.86**
Price: Magnum conversion dies, 12, 20. . . . .**$43.25**

LEE Load-All II

Press Type: Single stage
Avg. Rounds Per Hour: 100
Weight: 3 lbs., 3 oz.
Features: Loads steel or lead shot; built-in primer catcher at base with door in front for emptying; recesses at each station for shell positioning; optional primer feed. Comes with safety charge bar with 24 shot and powder bushings. Available for 12-, 16- or 20-gauge. From Lee Precision, Inc.
Price: **$49.98**

ACCESSORIES

SHOTSHELL RELOADING PRESSES

MEC 600 Jr. Mark V

Press Type: Single stage
Avg. Rounds Per Hour: 200
Weight: 10 lbs.
Features: Spindex crimp starter for shell alignment during crimping; a cam-action crimp die; Pro-Check to keep charge bar properly positioned; adjustable for three shells. Available in 10, 12, 16, 20, 28 gauges and 410 bore. Die set not included. From Mayville Engineering Company, Inc.
Price: $79.95
Price: Die set $59.38

MEC 650

Press Type: Progressive
Avg. Rounds Per Hour: 400
Weight: NA
Features: Six-station press; does not resize except as separate operation; auto primer feed standard; three crimping stations for starting, closing and tapering crimp. Die sets not available. Available in 12, 16, 20, 28 and 410. From Mayville Engineering Company, Inc.
Price: $174.95

MEC 8567 Grabber

Press Type: Progressive
Avg. Rounds Per Hour: 400
Weight: 15 lbs.
Features: Ten-station press; auto primer feed; auto-cycle charging; three-stage crimp; power ring resizer returns base to factory specs; resizes high and low base shells; optional kits to reload three shells and steel shot. Available in 12, 16, 20, 28 gauge and 410 bore. From Mayville Engineering Company, Inc.
Price: $232.95
Price: 3" kit, 12-ga. $60.00
Price: 3" kit, 20-ga. $30.00
Price: Steel shot kit. $23.22

MEC 9000G

Press Type: Progressive
Avg. Rounds Per Hour: 400
Weight: 18 lbs.
Features: All same features as the MEC Grabber, but with auto-indexing and auto-eject. Finished shells automatically ejected from shell carrier to drop chute for boxing. Available in 12, 16, 20, 28 and 410. From Mayville Engineering Company, Inc.
Price: $266.95
Price: 3" kit, 12-ga. $60.00
Price: 3" kit, 20-ga. $30.00
Price: Steel shot kit. $23.22

MEC 9000H

Press Type: Progressive
Avg. Rounds Per Hour: 400
Weight: 23 lbs.
Features: Same features as 9000G with addition of foot pedal-operated hydraulic system for complete automation. Operates on standard 110V household current. Comes with bushing-type charge bar and three bushings. Available in 12, 16, 20, 28 gauge and 410 bore. From Mayville Engineering Company, Inc.
Price: $659.95
Price: Steel shot kit. $23.22

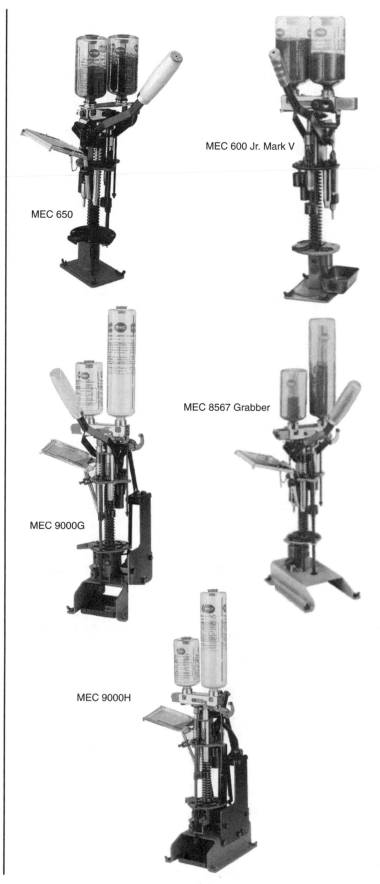

MEC 600 Jr. Mark V

MEC 650

MEC 8567 Grabber

MEC 9000G

MEC 9000H

SHOTSHELL RELOADING PRESSES

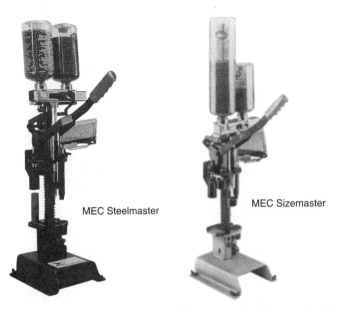

MEC Steelmaster

MEC Sizemaster

Ponsness/Warren
Hydro-Multispeed

Ponsness/Warren
Du-O-Matic 375C

Ponsness/Warren
L/S-1000

MEC Sizemaster

Press Type: Single stage
Avg. Rounds Per Hour: 150
Weight: 13 lbs.
Features: Power ring eight-fingered collet resizer returns base to factory specs; handles brass or steel, high or low base heads; auto primer feed; adjustable for three shells. Available in 10, 12, 16, 20, 28 gauges and 410 bore. From Mayville Engineering Company, Inc.
Price: $125.95
Price: Die set, 12, 16, 20, 28, 410 . . . .$88.67
Price: Die set, 10-ga. $104.06
Price: Steel shot kit $12.95
Price: Steel shot kit, 12-ga. 3-1/2" $70.27

MEC Steelmaster

Press Type: Single stage
Avg. Rounds Per Hour: 150
Weight: 13 lbs.
Features: Same features as Sizemaster except can load steel shot. Press is available for 3-1/2" 10-ga. and 12-ga. 2-3/4" ,3" or 3-1/2". For loading lead shot, die sets available in 10, 12, 16, 20, 28 and 410. From Mayville Engineering Company, Inc.
Price: $134.95
Price: 12 ga. 3-1/2" $144.95

PONSNESS/WARREN Du-O-Matic 375C

Press Type: Progressive
Avg. Rounds Per Hour: NA
Weight: 31 lbs.
Features: Steel or lead shot reloader; large shot and powder reservoirs; bushing access plug for dropping in shot buffer or buckshot; positive lock charging ring to prevent accidental flow of powder; double-post construction for greater leverage; removable spent primer box; spring-loaded ball check for centering size die at each station; tip-out wad guide; two-gauge capacity tool head. Available in 10 (extra charge), 12, 16, 20, 28 and 410 with case lengths of 2-1/2, 2-3/4, 3 and 3-1/2 inches. From Ponsness/ Warren.
Price: $269.00
Price: 12-ga. 3-1/2"; 3" 12, 20, 410 . . . .$285.00
Price: 12, 20 2-3/4 . . . .$373.95
Price: 10-ga. press $295.00

PONSNESS/WARREN Hydro-Multispeed

Hydraulic system developed for the Ponsness/Warren L/S-1000. Also usable for the 950, 900 and 800 series presses. Three reloading speed settings operated with variable foot pedal control. Features stop/reverse at any station; automatic shutdown with pedal control release; fully adjustable hydraulic cylinder rod to prevent racking or bending of machine; quick disconnect hoses for ease of installation. Comes preassembled with step-by-step instructions. From Ponsness/Warren.
Price: $849.00
Price: Cylinder kit $379.95

PONSNESS/WARREN L/S-1000

Frame: Die cast aluminum
Avg. Rounds Per Hour: NA
Weight: 55 lbs.
Features: Fully progressive press to reload steel, bismuth or lead shot. Equipped with new Uni-Drop shot measuring and dispensing system which

allows the use of all makes of shot in any size. Shells automatically resized and deprimed with new Auto-Size and De-Primer system. Loaded rounds drop out of shellholders when completed. Each shell pre-crimped and final crimped with Tru-Crimp system. Available in 10-gauge 3-1/2 or 12-gauge 2-3/4" and 3". 12-gauge 3-1/2" conversion kit also available. 20-gauge 2-3/4 and 3 special order only. From Ponsness/Warren.

Price: 12 ga. **$755.00**
Price: 10 ga. **$799.00**
Price: Conversion kit. **$189.00**

PONSNESS/WARREN Size-O-Matic 900 Elite

Press Type: Progressive
Avg. Rounds Per Hour: 500-800
Weight: 49 lbs.
Features: Progressive eight-station press; frame of die cast aluminum; center post design index system ensures positive indexing; timing factory set, drilled and pinned. Automatic features include index, deprime, reprime, powder and shot drop, crimp start, tapered final crimp, finished shell ejection. Available in 12, 20, 28 and 410. 16-ga. special order. Kit includes the new shellholders, seating port, resize/primer knockout assembly and new crimp assembly. From Ponsness/Warren.

Price: **$699.00**
Price: Conversion tooling, 12, 20, 28, 410 . . . . **$185.00**

PONSNESS/WARREN Platinum 2000

Press Type: Progressive
Avg. Rounds Per Hour: 500-800
Weight: 52 lbs.
Features: Progressive eight-station press is similar to the 900 and 950 except has die removal system that allows removal of any die component during the reloading cycle. Comes standard with 25-lb. shot tube, 19" powder tube, brass adjustable priming feed allows adjustment of primer seating depth. From Ponsness/Warren.

Price **$879.00**

Ponsness/Warren
Size-O-Matic 900 Elite

Ponsness/Warren
Platinum 2000

Maker and Model	Magn.	Field at 100 Yds. (feet)	Eye Relief (in.)	Length (in.)	Tube Dia. (in.)	W & E Adjustments	Weight (ozs.)	Price	Other Data
ADCO									[1]Multi-Color Dot system changes from red to green. [2]For airguns, paintball, rimfires. Uses common lithium water battery. [3]Comes with standard dovetail mount. [4].75" dovetail mount; poly body; adj. intensity diode. [5]10 MOA dot; black or nickel. [6]Square format; with mount battery. From ADCO Sales.
Magnum 45 mm[5]	0	—	—	4.1	45 mm	Int.	6.8	$279.00	
MIRAGE Ranger 1"	0	—	—	5.2	1	Int.	3.9	159.00	
MIRAGE Ranger 30mm	0	—	—	5.5	30mm	Int.	5	179.00	
MIRAGE Sportsman[1]	0	—	—	5.2	1	Int.	4.5	229.00	
MIRAGE Competitor	0	—	—	5.5	30mm	Int.	5.5	229.00	
IMP Sight[2]	0	—	—	4.5	—	Int.	1.3	17.95	
Square Shooter[3]	0	—	—	5	—	Int.	5	125.00	
MIRAGE Eclipse[1]	0	—	—	5.5	30mm	Int.	5.5	229.00	
MIRAGE Champ Red Dot	0	—	—	4.5	—	Int.	2	33.95	
Vantage 1"	0	—	—	3.9	1	Int.	3.9	129.00	
Vantage 30mm	0	—	—	4.2	30mm	Int.	4.9	132.00	
Vision 2000[6]	0	60	—	4.7	—	Int.	6.2	79.00	
AIMPOINT									Illuminates red dot in field of view. Noparallax (dot does not need to be centered). Unlimited field of view and eye relief. On/off, adj. intensity. Dot covers 3" @100 yds. [1]Comes with 30mm rings, battery, lense cloth. [2]Requires 1" rings. Black finish. AP Comp avail. in black, blue, SS, camo. [3]Black finish (AP 5000-B) ; avail. with regular 3-min. or 10-min. Mag Dot as B2 or S2. [4]Band pass reflection coating for compatibility with night vision equipment; U.S. Army contract model; with anti-reflex coated lenses (Comp ML), $359.00. From Aimpoint U.S.A.
Comp	0	—	—	4.6	30mm	Int.	4.3	331.00	
Comp M[4]	0	—	—	5	30mm	Int.	6.1	409.00	
Series 5000[3]	0	—	—	6	30mm	Int.	6	297.00	
Series 3000 Universal[2]	0	—	—	6.25	1	Int.	6	232.00	
Series 5000/2x[1]	2	—	—	7	30mm	Int.	9	388.00	
ARMSON O.E.G.									Shown red dot aiming point. No batteries needed. Standard model fits 1" ring mounts (not incl.). Other O.E.G. models for shotguns and rifles can be special ordered. [1]Daylight Only Sight with .375" dovetail mount for 22s. Does not contain tritium. From Trijicon, Inc.
Standard	0	—	—	5.125	1	Int.	4.3	202.00	
22 DOS[1]	0	—	—	3.75	—	Int.	3	127.00	
22 Day/Night	0	—	—	3.75	—	Int.	3	169.00	
M16/AR-15	0	—	—	5.125	—	Int.	5.5	226.00	
ARTEMIS 2000									Click-stop windage and elevation adjustments; constantly centered reticle; rubber eyepiece ring; nitrogen filled. Imported from the Czech Republic by CZ-USA.
4x32	4	34.4	3.15	10.7	1	Int.	17.5	215.00	
6x42	6	23	3.15	13.7	1	Int.	17.5	317.00	
7x50	7	18.7	3.15	13.9	1	Int.	17.5	329.00	
1.5-6x42	1.5-6	40-12.8	2.95	12.4	30mm	Int.	19.4	522.00	
2-8x42	2-8	31-9.5	2.95	13.1	30mm	Int.	21.1	525.00	
3-9x42	3-9	24.6-8.5	2.95	12.4	30mm	Int.	19.4	466.00	
3-12x50	3-12	20.6-6.2	2.95	14	30mm	Int.	22.9	574.00	
BEC									Black matte finish. Multi-coated lenses; 1/4-MOA click adjustments (1/2-MOA on EL4x25, AR4x22WA); fog and water-proof. [1]For AR-15;bullet drop compensator; q.d. mount. [2]Rubber armored. Imported by BEC Inc.
EuroLux									
EL2510x56	2.5-10	39.4-11.5	3.25-2	15.1	30mm	Int.	25.4	249.90	
EL39x42	3-9	34.1-13.2	3.5-3	12.3	30mm	Int.	17.7	99.80	
EL28x36	2-8	44.9-11.5	3.8-3	12.2	30mm	Int.	15.9	149.50	
ELA39x40RB[2]	3-9	39-13	3	12.7	30mm	Int.	14.3	95.95	
EL6x42	6	21	3	12.6	30mm	Int.	14.8	69.00	
EL4x42	.4	29	3	12.6	30mm	Int.	14.8	59.60	
EL4x36	4	29	3	12	30mm	Int.	14	49.90	
EL4x25	4	26	3	7	30mm	Int.	7.6	37.00	
AR4x22WA[1]	4	24	3	7	34mm	Int.	13.6	109.97	
BEEMAN									All scopes have 5 point reticle, all glass fully coated lenses. [1]Parallel adjustable. [2]Reticle lighted by ambient light. [3]Available with lighted Electro-Dot reticle. Imported by Beeman.
Rifle Scopes									
5045[1]	4-12	26.9-9	3	13.2	1	Int.	15	275.00	
5046[1]	6-24	18-4.5	3	16.9	1	Int.	20.2	395.00	
5050[1]	4	26	3.5	11.7	1	Int.	11	80.00	
5055[1]	3-9	38-13	3.5	10.75	1	Int.	11.2	90.00	
5060[1]	4-12	30-10	3	12.5	1	Int.	16.2	210.00	
5065[1]	6-18	17-6	3	14.7	1	Int.	17.3	265.00	
5066RL[2]	2-7	58-15	3	11.4	1	Int.	17	380.00	
5047L[2]	4	25	3.5	7	1	Int.	13.7	NA	
Pistol Scopes									
5021	2	19	10-24	9.1	1	Int.	7.4	85.50	
5020	1.5	14	11-16	8.3	.75	Int.	3.6	NA	
BSA									[1]Waterproof, fogproof; multi-coated lenses; finger-adjustable knobs. [2]Waterproof, fogproof; matte black finish. [3]With 4" sunshade; target knobs; 1/8-MOA click adjustments. [4]Adjustable for parallax; with sunshades; target knobs, 1/8-MOA adjustments. Imported by BSA. [5]Illuminated reticle model; also available in 3-10x and 3.5-10x. [6]Red dot sights also available in 42mm and 50mm versions.
Catseye[1]									
CE1545x32	1.5-4.5	78-23	4	11.25	1	Int.	12	89.95	
CE310x44	3-10	39-12	3.25	12.75	1	Int.	16	149.95	
CE3510x50	3.5-10	30-10.5	3.25	13.25	1	Int.	17.25	169.95	
CE416x50	4-16	25-6	3	15.25	1	Int.	22	189.95	
CE624x50	6-24	16-3	3	16	1	Int.	23	219.95	
CE1545x32IR	1.5-4.5	78-23	5	11.25	1	Int.	12	119.95	
Deer Hunter[2]									
DH25x20	2.5	72	6	7.5	1	Int.	7.5	59.95	
DH4x32	4	32	3	12	1	Int.	12.5	49.95	
DH39x32	3-9	39-13	3	12	1	Int.	11	69.95	
DH39x40	3-9	39-13	3	13	1	Int.	12.1	89.95	
DH39x50	3-9	41-15	3	12.75	1	Int.	13	109.95	
DH2510x44	2.5-10	42-12	3	13	1	Int.	12.5	99.95	
DH1545x32	1.5-4.5	78-23	5	11.25	1	Int.	12	79.95	

ACCESSORIES

Maker and Model	Magn.	Field at 100 Yds. (feet)	Eye Relief (in.)	Length (in.)	Tube Dia. (in.)	W & E Adjustments	Weight (ozs.)	Price	Other Data
BSA (cont'd.)									
Contender[3]									
CT24x40TS	24	6	3	15	1	Int.	18	129.95	
CT36x40TS	36	3	3	15.25	1	Int.	19	139.95	
CT312x40TS	3-12	28-7	3	13	1	Int.	17.5	119.95	
CT416x40TS	4-16	21-5	3	13.5	1	Int.	18	129.95	
CT624x40TS	6-24	16-4	3	15.5	1	Int.	20	144.95	
CT832x40TS	8-32	11-3	3	15.5	1	Int.	20	169.95	
CT24x50TS	24	6	3	15	1	Int.	22	149.95	
CT36x50TS	36	3	3	15.25	1	Int.	23	159.95	
CT312x50TS	3-12	28-7	3	13.75	1	Int.	21	129.95	
CT416x50TS	4-16	21-5	3	15.25	1	Int.	22	149.95	
CT624x50TS	6-24	16-4	3	16	1	Int.	23	169.95	
CT832x50TS	8-32	11-3	3	16.5	1	Int.	24	189.95	
Pistol									
P52x20	2	N/A	N/A	N/A	N/A	Int.	N/A	79.95	
P54x28	4	N/A	N/A	N/A	N/A	Int.	N/A	89.95	
Platinum[4]									
PT24x44TS	24	4.5	3	16.25	1	Int.	17.9	189.55	
PT36x44TS	36	3	3	14.9	1	Int.	17.9	199.95	
PT624x44TS	6-24	15-4.5	3	15.25	1	Int.	18.5	219.95	
PT832x44TS	8-32	11-3.5	3	17.25	1	Int.	19.5	239.95	
PT1050x60TS	10-50	7-2	3	18	1	Int.	22	399.95	
.22 Special									
S25x20WR	2.5	58	3	8	1	Int.	7	39.95	
S4x32WR	4	26	3	10.75	1	Int.	9	49.95	
Air Rifle									
AR4x32	4	33	3	13	1	Int.	14	69.95	
AR27x32	2-7	48	3	12.25	1	Int.	14	79.95	
AR312x44	3-12	36	3	12.25	1	Int.	15	109.95	
Red Dot									
RD30[6]	1	88	unlimited	3.8	30mm	Int.	5	59.95	
BURRIS									
Mr. T Black Diamond Titanium									
2.5-10x50[A]	2.5-10	4.25-4.75		13.6	30mm	Int.	29	2,129.00	
Black Diamond									
3-12x50[3,4,6]	3.2-11.9	34-12	3.5-4	13.8	30mm	Int.	25	880.00	
6-24x50	6-24	18-6	3.5-4	16.2	30mm	Int.	25	954.00	
Fullfield & Fullfield II									
2.5x[9]	2.5	55	3.5-3.75	10.25	1	Int.	9	308.00	
4x[1,2,3]	3.75	36	3.5-3.75	11.25	1	Int.	11.5	314.00	
6x[1,3]	5.8	23	3.5-3.75	13	1	Int.	12	343.00	
1.75-5x[1,2,9,10]	1.7-4.6	66-25	3.5-3.75	10.875	1	Int.	13	374.00	
2-7x[1,2,3]	2.5-6.8	47-18	3.5-3.75	12	1	Int.	14	399.00	
3-9x40[1,2,3,10]	3.3-8.7	38-15	3.5-3.75	12.625	1	Int.	15	356.00	
3-9x50	3-9	35-15	3.5-3.75	13	1	Int.	18	427.00	
3.5-10x50mm[3,5,10]	3.7-9.7	29.5-11	3.5-3.75	14	1	Int.	19	496.00	
4-12x1[1,4,8,11]	4.4-11.8	27-10	3.5-3.75	15	1	Int.	18	500.00	
6-18x[1,3,4,6,7,8]	6.5-17.6	16.7	3.5-3.75	15.8	1	Int.	18.5	527.00	
Compact Scopes									
1x XER[3]	1	51	4.5-20	8.8	1	Int.	7.9	290.00	
4x[4,5]	3.6	24	3.75-5	8.25	1	Int.	7.8	270.00	
6x[1,4]	5.5	17	3.75-5	9	1	Int.	8.2	287.00	
6x HBR[1,5,8]	6	13	4.5	11.25	1	Int.	13	451.00	
1-4x XER[3]	1-3.8	53-15	4.25-30	8.8	1	Int.	10.3	377.00	
3-9x[4,5]	3.6-8.8	25-11	3.75-5	12.625	1	Int.	11.5	368.00	
4-12x[1,4,6]	4.5-11.6	19-8	3.75-4	15	1	Int.	15	500.00	
Signature Series									
1.5-6x[2,3,5,9,10]	1.7-5.8	70-20	3.5-4	10.8	1	Int.	13	484.00	
6x[3]	6	20	3.5-4	12.125	1	Int.	14	413.00	
2-8x[3,5,11]	2.1-7.7	53-17	3.5-4	11.75	1	Int.	14	558.00	
3-9x[3,5,10,13]	3.3-8.8	36-14	3.5-4	12.875	1	Int.	15.5	571.00	
2.50-10x[3,5,10]	2.7-9.5	37-10.5	3.5-4	14	1	Int.	19	635.00	
3-12x[3,10]	3.3-11.7	34-9	3.5-4	14.25	1	Int.	21	691.00	
4-16x[1,3,5,6,8,10]	4.3-15.7	33-9	3.5-4	15.4	1	Int.	23.7	723.00	
6-24x[1,3,5,6,8,10,13]	6.6-23.8	17-6	3.5-4	16	1	Int.	22.7	742.00	
8-32x[8,10,12]	8.6-31.4	13-3.8	3.5-4	17	1	Int.	24	798.00	
Speeddot 135[13]									
Red Dot	1	—	—	4.85	35mm	Int.	5	291.00	
Handgun									
1.50-4x LER[1,5,10]	1.6-3.	16-11	11-25	10.25	1	Int.	11	363.00	
2-7x LER[3,4,5,10]	2-6.5	21-7	7-27	9.5	1	Int.	12.6	401.00	
3-9x LER[4,5,10]	3.4-8.4	12-5	22-14	11	1	Int.	14	453.00	
2x LER[4,5,6]	1.7	21	10-24	8.75	1	Int.	6.8	265.00	
4x LER[1,4,5,6,10]	3.7	11	10-22	9.625	1	Int.	9	296.00	
10x LER[1,4,6]	9.5	4	8-12	13.5	1	Int.	14	460.00	
Scout Scope									
1xXER[3,9]	1.5	32	4-24	9	1	Int.	7.0	290.00	
2.75x[3,9]	2.7	15	7-14	9.375	1	Int.	7.0	319.00	

[A]Available in Carbon Black, Titanium Gray and Autumn Gold finishes.
Black Diamond & Fullfield: All scopes avail. with Plex reticle. Steel-on-steel click adjustments. [1]Dot reticle on some models. [2]Post crosshair reticle extra. [3]Matte satin finish. [4]Available with parallax adjustment (standard on 10x, 12x, 4-12x, 6-12x, 6-18x, 6x HBR and 3-12x Signature). [5]Silver matte finish extra. [6]Target knobs extra, standard on silhouette models. LER and XER with P.A., 6x HBR. [7]Sunshade avail. [8]Avail. with Fine Plex reticle. [9]Available with Heavy Plex reticle. [10]Available with Posi-Lock. [11]Available with Peep Plex reticle. [12]Also avail. for rimfires, airguns. [13]Selected models available with camo finish.
Signature Series: LER=Long Eye Relief; IER=Intermediate Eye Relief; XER=Extra Eye Relief.
Speeddot 135: [13]Waterproof, fogproof, coated lenses, 11 brightness settings;3-MOA or 11-MOA dot size; includes Weaver-style rings and battery. **Partial listing shown.** Contact Burris for complete details.

Plex   **Fine Plex**

Heavy Plex & Electro-Dot Plex   **Peep Plex**   **Ballistic Mil-Dot**

Target Dot   **Mil-Dot**

Maker and Model	Magn.	Field at 100 Yds. (feet)	Eye Relief (in.)	Length (in.)	Tube Dia. (in.)	W & E Adjustments	Weight (ozs.)	Price	Other Data
BUSHNELL (Bausch & Lomb Elite rifle scopes now sold under Bushnell name)									
Elite 4200 RainGuard									
40-6244A[1]	6-24	18-6	3	16.9	1	Int.	20.2	729.95	
40-2104G[2]	2.5-10	41.5-10.8	3	13.5	1	Int.	16	642.95	
40-1636M[3]	1.5-6	61.8-16.1	3	12.8	1	Int.	15.4	608.95	
42-3640A	36	3	3	15	1	Int.	17.6	955.95	
42-4165M[5]	4-16	26-7	3	15.6	1	Int.	22	834.95	
Elite 3200 RainGuard									
32-5155M	5-15	21-7	3	15.9	1	Int.	24	528.95	
32-4124A[1]	4-12	26.9-9	3	13.2	1	Int.	15	469.95	
32-3940G[4]	3-9	33.8-11.5	3	12.6	1	Int.	13	351.95	
32-2732M[5]	2-7	44.6-12.7	3	11.6	1	Int.	12	342.95	
32-3950G[6]	3-9	31.5-10.5	3	15.7	1	Int.	19	428.95	
32-3955E	3-9	31.5-10.5	3	15.6	30mm	Int.	22	640.95	
Elite 3200 Handgun									
32-2632G[7]	2-6	10-4	20	9	1	Int.	10	444.95	
32-2632G	2-6	10-4	20	9	1	Int.	10	444.95	
Scopechief									
70-1563M[4]	1.5-6	74-20	3.5	10.7	1	Int.	14.4	337.95	
70-3104M[4]	3.5-10	43-15	3.5	13	1	Int.	17	294.95	
70-3940M[4]	3-9	42-14	3.5	11.5	1	Int.	16	255.95	
70-4145A[12]	4-14	31-9	3.5	14.1	1	Int.	23	408.95	
70-6204A[12]	6-20	21-6	3.5	15.75	1	Int.	21	583.95	
Trophy									
73-1500[1]	1.75-5	68-23	3.5	10.8	1	Int.	12.3	262.95	
73-4124[1]	4-12	32-11	3	12.5	1	Int.	16.1	285.95	
73-3940	3-9	42-14	3	11.7	1	Int.	13.2	159.95	
73-6184	6-18	17.3-6	3	14.8	1	Int.	17.9	360.95	
73-4154M	4-15	26-7.7	3	13.7	1	Int.	18.7	337.95	
73-3941[5]	3-9	37-12.5	3	13	1	Int.	16	410.95	
Turkey & Brush									
73-1420	1.75-4	73-30	3.5	10.8	32mm	Int.	10.9	255.95	
HOLOsight Model[8]	1	—	—	6	—	Int.	8.7	562.95	
Trophy Handgun									
73-0232[2]	2	20	9-26	8.7	1	Int.	7.7	218.95	
73-2632[3]	2-6	21-7	9-26	9.1	1	Int.	9.6	287.95	
Banner									
71-1545	1.5-4.5	67-23	3.5	10.5	1	Int.	10.5	116.95	
71-3944[9]	3-9	36-13	4	11.5	1	Int.	12.5	125.95	
71-3950[10]	3-9	31-10	3	16	1	Int.	19	186.95	
71-4124[7]	4-12	29-11	3	12	1	Int.	15	157.95	
71-4228	4	26.5	3	11.75	1	Int.	10	81.95	
71-6185[10]	6-18	17-6	3	16	1	Int.	18	209.95	
Sportview									
79-0004	4	31	4	11.7	1	Int.	11.2	98.95	
79-0039	3-9	38-13	3.5	10.75	1	Int.	11.2	116.95	
79-0412[7]	4-12	27-9	3.2	13.1	1	Int.	14.6	141.95	
79-1393[6]	3-9	35-12	3.5	11.75	1	Int.	10	68.95	
79-1545	1.5-4.5	69-24	3	10.7	1	Int.	8.6	86.95	
79-1548[11]	1.5-4.5	71-25	3.5	10.4	1	Int.	11.8	104.95	
79-2538[11]	2.5	45	3	11	1	Int.	10	76.95	
79-1403	4	29	4	11.75	1	Int.	9.2	57.95	
79-6184	6-18	19.1-6.8	3	14.5	1	Int.	15.9	170.95	
79-3940M	3-9	42-14	3	12.7	1	Int.	12.5	95.95	
C-MORE SYSTEMS									
Classic AR[1]	4	225	3	7.2	35mm	Int.	14.6	249.00	
SSE[2]	6	159	3.3	12.8	30mm	Int.	22.8	499.00	
Tactical Elite[3]	6	159	3.38	13	30mm	Int.	22.6	469.00	
Compact 1-5x20[4]	1-5	301-62	3.45	9.5	30mm	Int.	14.2	359.00	
Tactical[5]	6	157	3.35	12.2	30mm	Int.	13.8	449.00	
Handgun 1.5x20[6]	1.5	183	11-22	5.4	1	Int.	6.8	159.00	
Handgun 4x32	4	91	11-22	8.6	1	Int.	7.6	165.00	
Handgun 1.5-4.5x20	1.5-4.5	190-88	11-22	7.7	1	Int.	7.6	215.00	
Handgun 2.5-7x28	2.5-7	135-52	11-22	9.3	1	Int.	8.6	245.00	
Red Dots									
Railway[1]	1	—	—	4.8	—	Int.	5	299.00	
Colt Scout[2]	1	—	—	11	—	Int.	7.5	368.00	
Serendipity[4]	1	—	—	5.3	—	Int.	3.75	299.00	
Slide Ride[5]	1	—	—	4.8	—	Int.	3	249.00	
Colt Tactical[3]	1	—	—	8	—	Int.	12	444.00	
DOCTER OPTIC									
Fixed Power									
4x32	4	31	3	10.7	26mm	Int.	10	898.00	
6x42	6	20	3	12.8	26mm	Int.	12.7	1,004.00	
8x56[1]	8	15	3	14.7	26mm	Int.	15.6	1,240.00	
Variables									
1-4x24	1-4	79.7-31.3	3	10.8	30mm	Int.	13	1,300.00	
1.2-5x32	1.2-5	65-25	3	11.6	30mm	Int.	15.4	1,345.00	
1.5-6x42	1.5-6	41.3-20.6	3	12.7	30mm	Int.	16.8	1,378.00	
2.5-10x48	2.5-10	36.6-12.4	3	13.7	30mm	Int.	18.6	1,378.00	
2-12x56	3-12	44.2-13.8	3	14.8	30mm	Int.	20.3	1,425.00	
3-10x40	3-10	34.4-11.7	3	13	1	Int.	18	795.00	

(Bausch & Lomb Elite)
[1]Adj. objective, sunshade; also in matte and with 1/4-MOA dot reticle. [2]Also in matte and silver finish. [3]Only in matte finish. [4]Also in matte and silver finish. [5]Adjustable objective. [6]50mm objective; also in matte finish. [7]Also in silver finish. **Partial listings shown. Contact Bushnell Sports Optics for details.**

(Bushnell) [1]Wide Angle. [2]Also silver finish. [3]Also silver finish. [4]Matte finish. [5]Selective red L.E.D. dot for low light hunting. [6]Also silver finish. [7]Adj. obj. [8]Variable intensity; **$111.95**; fits Weaver-style base. Comp model 430 with diamond reticle and 1911 No-hole or 5-hole pattern mount, or STI mount, **$631.00**. (2x magnification adapter **$248.95**). [9]Blackpowder scope; extended eye relief, Circle-X reticle. [10]50mm objective. [11]With Circle-X reticle, matte finish. [12]Matte finish, adjustable objective.

HOLOSIGHT RETICLES

MOA Dot **Standard**

SCOPE RETICLES

CP2 **Multi** **Euro** **Circle-X**

[1]All Weaver and Picatinny-style rail mounts. [2]Carry handle mount for A1/A2-style receivers. [3]Flattop mount for A3-style receivers. [4]Most popular auto pistols. [5]Mounts to any flat surface, custom mounts, shotgun ribs; Glock adapter plate for direct slide mounting. From C-More Systems, Inc.

Matte black and matte silver finish available. All lenses multi-coated. Illuminated reticle avail., choice of reticles. [1]Rail mount, aspherical lenses avail. Aspherical lens model, **$1,375.00**. Imported from Germany by Docter Optic Technologies, Inc.

Maker and Model	Magn.	Field at 100 Yds. (feet)	Eye Relief (in.)	Length (in.)	Tube Dia. (in.)	W & E Adjustments	Weight (ozs.)	Price	Other Data
EUROPTIK SUPREME									
4x36K	4	39	3.5	11.6	26mm	Int.	14	795.00	[1]Military scope with adjustable parallax. Fixed powers have 26mm tubes, variables have 30mm tubes. Some models avail. with steel tubes. All lenses multi-coated. Dust and water tight. From Europtik.
6x42K	6	21	3.5	13	26mm	Int.	15	875.00	
8x56K	8	18	3.5	14.4	26mm	Int.	20	925.00	
1.5-6x42K	1.5-6	61.7-23	3.5	12.6	30mm	Int.	17	1,095.00	
2-8x42K	2-8	52-17	3.5	13.3	30mm	Int.	17	1,150.00	
2.5-10x56K	2.5-10	40-13.6	3.5	15	30mm	Int.	21	1,295.00	
3-12x56 Super	3-12	10.8-34.7	3.5-2.5	15.2	30mm	Int.	24	1,495.00	
4-16x56 Super	4-16	9.8-3.9	3.1	18	30mm	Int.	26	1,575.00	
3-9x40 Micro	3-9	3.2-12.1	2.7	13	1	Int.	14	1,450.00	
2.5-10x46 Micro	2.5-10	13.7-33.4	2.7	14	30mm	Int.	20	1,395.00	
4-16x56 EDP[1]	4-16	22.3-7.5	3.1	18	30mm	Int.	29	1,995.00	
7-12x50 Target	7-12	8.8-5.5	3.5	15	30mm	Int.	21	1,495.00	
KAHLES									
4x36	4	34.5	3.15	11.2	1	Int.	12.7	555.00	Aluminum tube. Multi-coated, waterproof. [1]Also available with illuminated reticle. Imported from Austria by Swarovski Optik.
6x42[1]	6	23	3.15	12.4	1	Int.	14.4	694.00	
8x50[1]	8	17.3	3.15	13	1	Int.	16.5	749.00	
1.1-4x24	1.1-4	108-31.8	3.5	10.8	30mm	Int.	12.7	722.00	
1.5-6x42[1]	1.5-6	72-21.3	3.5	12.0	30mm	Int.	15.8	832.00	
2.5-10x50[1]	2.5-10	43.5-12.9	3.5	12.8	30mm	Int.	15.8	1,353.00	
3-9x42	3-9	43-16	3.5	12	1	Int.	13	621.06	
3-9x42AH	3-9	43-15	3.5	12.36	1	Int.	12.7	665.00	
3-12x56[1]	3-12	30-11	3.5	15.4	30mm	Int.	18	1,377.72	

No. 4A	No. 7A	Plex	Illuminated No. 4N	Illuminated Plex N	TD Smith

Maker and Model	Magn.	Field at 100 Yds. (feet)	Eye Relief (in.)	Length (in.)	Tube Dia. (in.)	W & E Adjustments	Weight (ozs.)	Price	Other Data
KILHAM									
Hutson Handgunner II	1.7	8	—	5.5	.875	Int.	5.1	119.95	Unlimited eye relief; internal click adjustments; crosshair reticle. Fits Thompson/Center rail mounts, for S&W K, N, Ruger Blackhawk, Super, Super Single-Six, Contender.
Hutson Handgunner	3	8	10-12	6	.875	Int.	5.3	119.95	
LEICA									
Ultravid 1.75-6x32	1.75-6	47-18	4.8-3.7	11.25	30mm	Int.	14	749.00	Aluminum tube with hard anodized matte black finish with titanium accents; finger-adjustable windage and elevation with 1/4-MOA clicks. Made in U.S. From Leica.
Ultravid 3.5-10x42	3.5-10	29.5-10.7	4.6-3.6	12.62	30mm	Int.	16	849.00	
Ultravid 4.5-14x42	4.5-14	20.5-7.4	5-3.7	12.28	30mm	Int.	18	949.00	

Leicaplex Standard	Leica Dot	Standard Dot	Crosshair	Euro	Post & Plex

Maker and Model	Magn.	Field at 100 Yds. (feet)	Eye Relief (in.)	Length (in.)	Tube Dia. (in.)	W & E Adjustments	Weight (ozs.)	Price	Other Data
LEUPOLD									
Vari-X III 3.5x10 Tactical	3.5-10	29.5-10.7	3.6-4.6	12.5	1	Int.	13.5	801.80	Constantly centered reticles, choice of Duplex, tapered CPC, Leupold Dot, Crosshair and Dot. CPC and Dot reticles extra. [1]2x and 4x scopes have from 12"-24" of eye relief and are suitable for handguns, top ejection arms and muzzleloaders. [2]3x9 Compact, 6x Compact, 12x, 3x9, and 6.5x20 come with adjustable objective. Sunshade available for all adjustable objective scopes, **$23.20-$41.10**. [3]Silver finish about **$25.00** extra. [4]Long Range scopes have side focus parallax adjustment, additional windage and elevation travel. Partial listing shown. **Contact Leupold for complete details.**
M8-2X EER[1]	1.7	21.2	12-24	7.9	1	Int.	6	312.50	
M8-2X EER Silver[1]	1.7	21.2	12-24	7.9	1	Int.	6	337.50	
M8-2.5x28 IER Scout	2.3	22	9.3	10.1	1	Int.	7.5	408.90	
M8-4X EER[1]	3.7	9	12-24	8.4	1	Int.	7	425.00	
M8-4X EER Silver[1]	3.7	9	12-24	8.4	1	Int.	7	425.00	
Vari-X 2.5-8 EER	2.5-8	13-4.3	11.7-12	9.7	1	Int.	10.9	608.90	*Models available with illuminated reticle for additional cost.
M8-4X Compact	3.6	25.5	4.5	9.2	1	Int.	7.5	382.10	
Vari-X 2-7x Compact	2.5-6.6	41.7-16.5	5-3.7	9.9	1	Int.	8.5	478.60	
Vari-X 3-9x Compact	3.2-8.6	34-13.5	4-3	11-11.3	1	Int.	11	519.60	
M8-4X	4	24	4	10.7	1	Int.	9.3	385.70	
M8-6X36mm	5.9	17.7	4.3	11.4	1	Int.	10	410.70	
M8-6x 42mm	6	17	4.5	12	1	Int.	11.3	510.70	
*M8-6x42 A.O. Tactical	6	17	4.2	12.1	1	Int.	11.3	628.60	
M8-12x A.O. Varmint	11.6	9.1	4.2	13	1	Int.	13.5	571.40	
Vari-X 3-9x Compact EFR A.O.	3.8-8.6	34-13.5	4-3	11	1	Int.	11	550.00	
Vari-X-II 1x4	1.6-4.2	70.5-28.5	4.3-3.8	9.2	1	Int.	9	396.40	
Vari-X-II 2x7	2.5-6.6	42.5-17.8	4.9-3.8	11	1	Int.	10.5	428.60	
Vari-X-II 3x9[1,3]	3.3-8.6	32.3-14	4.1-3.7	12.3	1	Int.	13.5	432.10	
Vari-X-II 3-9x50mm	3.3-8.6	32.3-14	4.7-3.7	12	1	Int.	13.6	510.70	
Vari-X II 3-9x40 Tactical	3-9	32.3-14	4.7-3.7	12.2	1	Int.	13	535.70	
Vari-X-II 4-12 A.O. Matte	4.4-11.6	22.8-11	5-3.3	12.3	1	Int.	13.5	594.60	
*Vari-X-III 1.5-5x20	1.5-4.5	66-23	5.3-3.7	9.4	1	Int.	9.5	635.70	
Vari-X-III 1.75-6x32	1.9-5.6	47-18	4.8-3.7	9.8	1	Int.	11	683.90	
Vari-X-III 2.5x8	2.6-7.8	37-13.5	4.7-3.7	11.3	1	Int.	11.5	678.60	
Vari-X-III 3.5-10x40 Long Range M3[4]	3.9-9.7	29.8-11	4-3.5	13.5	30mm	Int.	19.5	1,157.10	
Vari-X-III 3.5-10x50	3.3-9.7	29.5-10.7	4.6-3.6	12.4	1	Int.	13	796.40	*Models available with illuminated reticle for additional cost.

Duplex	CPC	Post & Duplex

Leupold Dot	Dot

Maker and Model	Magn.	Field at 100 Yds. (feet)	Eye Relief (in.)	Length (in.)	Tube Dia. (in.)	W & E Adjustments	Weight (ozs.)	Price	Other Data
LEUPOLD (cont'd.)									
Vari-X-III 4.5-14x40 A.O.	4.7-13.7	20.8-7.4	5-3.7	12.4	1	Int.	14.5	780.40	
*Vari-X-III 4.5-14x50 A.O.	4.7-13.7	20.8-7.4	5-3.7	12.4	1	Int.	14.5	903.60	
Vari-X III 4.5-14x 50 Long Range Tactical[4]	4.9-14.3	19-6	5-3.7	12.1	30mm	Int.	17.5	1,082.10	
Vari-X-III 6.5-20 A.O.	6.5-19.2	14.2-5.5	5.3-3.6	14.2	1	Int.	17.5	823.20	
Vari-X-III 6.5x20xTarget EFR A.O.	6.5-19.2	—	5.3-3.6	14.2	1	Int.	16.5	919.60	
Vari-X III 6.5-20x 50 Long Range Target[4]	6.8-19.2	14.7-5.4	4.9-3.7	14.3	30mm	Int.	19	1,166.10	
Vari-X III 8.5-25x40 A.O. Target	8.5-25	10.86-4.2	5.3	14.3	1	Int.	17.5	900.00	
Vari-X III 8.5-25x 50 Long Range Target[4]	8.3-24.2	11.4-4.3	4.4-3.6	14.3	30mm	Int.	19	1,260.70	
Mark 4 M1-10x40	10	11.1	3.6	13.125	30mm	Int.	21	1,807.10	
Mark 4 M1-16x40	16	6.6	4.1	12.875	30mm	Int.	22	1,807.10	
Mark 4 M3-10x40	10	11.1	3.6	13.125	30mm	Int.	21	1,807.10	
Vari-X III 6.5x20[2] A.O.	6.5-19.2	14.2-5.5	5.3-3.6	14.2	1	Int.	16	823.20	
BR-D 24x40 A.O. Target	24	4.7	3.2	13.6	1	Int.	15.3	1,035.70	
BR-D 36x-40 A.O. Target	36	3.2	3.4	14.1	1	Int.	15.6	1,083.90	
LPS 1.5-6x42	1.5-6	58.7-15.7	4	11.2	30mm	Int.	16	1,476.80	
LPS 3.5-14x52 A.O.	3.5-14	28-7.2	4	13.1	30mm	Int.	22	1,569.60	
Rimfire									
Vari-X 2-7x RF Special	3.6	25.5	4.5	9.2	1	Int.	7.5	478.60	
Shotgun									
M8 4x33	3.7	9	12-24	8.4	1	Int.	6	410.70	
Vari-X II 1x4	1.6-4.2	70.5-28.5	4.3-3.8	9.2	1	Int.	9	421.40	
Vari-X-II 2x7	2.5-6.6	42.5-17.8	4.9-3.8	11	1	Int.	9	453.60	
LYMAN									
Super TargetSpot[1]	10, 12, 15, 20, 25, 30	5.5	2	24.3	.75	Int.	27.5	685.00	Made under license from Lyman to Lyman's orig. specs. Blue steel. Three-point suspension rear mount with .25-min. click adj. Data listed are for 20x model. [1]Price approximate. Made in U.S. by Parsons Optical Mfg. Co.
McMILLAN									
Vision Master 2.5-10x	2.5-10	14.2-4.4	4.3-3.3	13.3	30mm	Int.	17	1,250.00	42mm obj. lens; .25-MOA clicks; nitrogen filled, fogproof, waterproof; etched duplex-type reticle. [1]Tactical Scope with external adj. knobs, military reticle; 60+ min. adj.
Vision Master Model 1[1]	2.5-10	14.2-4.4	4.3-3.3	13.3	30mm	Int.	17	1,250.00	
MEPROLIGHT									
Meprolight Reflex Sights 14-21 5.5 MOA 1x30[1]	1	—	—	4.4	30mm	Int.	5.2	335.00	[1]Also available with 4.2 MOA dot. Uses tritium and fiber optics-no batteries required. From Hesco, Inc.
MILLETT									
Buck 3-9x44	3-9	38-14	3.25-4	13	1	Int.	16.2	549.00	[1]3-MOA dot. [2]5-MOA dot. [3]3-, 5-, 8-, 10-MOA dots. [4]10-MOA dot. All have click adjustments; waterproof, shockproof; 11 dot intensity settings. All avail. in matte/black or silver finish. From Millett Sights.
SP-1 Compact[1] Red Dot	1	36.65	—	4.1	1	Int.	3.2	149.95	
SP-2 Compact[2] Red Dot	1	58	—	4.5	30mm	Int.	4.3	149.95	
MultiDot SP[3]	1	50	—	4.8	30mm	Int.	5.3	289.95	
30mm Wide View[4]	1	60	—	5.5	30mm	Int.	5	289.95	
MIRADOR									
RXW 4x40[1]	4	37	3.8	12.4	1	Int.	12	179.95	[1]Wide angle scope. Multi-coated objective lens. Nitrogen filled; waterproof; shockproof. From Mirador Optical Corp.
RXW 1.5-5x20[1]	1.5-5	46-17.4	4.3	11.1	1	Int.	10	188.95	
RXW 3-9x40	3-9	43-14.5	3.1	12.9	1	Int.	13.4	251.95	
NIGHTFORCE									
2.5-10x50	2.5-10	31.4-9.4	3.3	13.9	30mm	Int.	28	847.87	Lighted reticles with eleven intensity levels. Most scopes have choice of reticles. From Lightforce U.S.A.
3.5-15x56	3.5-15	24.5-6.9	3	15.8	30mm	Int.	32	507.78	
5.5-22x56	5.5-22	15.7-4.4	3	19.4	30mm	Int.	38.5	965.53	
8-32x56	8-32	9.4-3.1	3	16.6	30mm	Int.	36	997.90	
12-42x56	12-42	6.7-2.3	3	17	30mm	Int.	36	1,053.64	
NIKON									
Monarch UCC									Super multi-coated lenses and blackening of all internal metal parts for maximum light gathering capability; positive .25-MOA; fogproof; waterproof; shockproof; luster and matte finish. [1]Also available in matte silver finish. [2]Available in silver matte finish. [3]Available with TurkeyPro or Nikoplex reticle. [4]Silver Shadow finish; black matte **$296.95**. Partial listing shown. From Nikon, Inc.
4x40[2]	4	26.7	3.5	11.7	1	Int.	11.7	330.95	
1.5-4.5x20[3]	1.5-4.5	67.8-22.5	3.7-3.2	10.1	1	Int.	9.5	364.95	
2-7x32	2-7	46.7-13.7	3.9-3.3	11.3	1	Int.	11.3	426.95	
3-9x40[1]	3-9	33.8-11.3	3.6-3.2	12.5	1	Int.	12.5	430.95	
3.5-10x50	3.5-10	25.5-8.9	3.9-3.8	13.7	1	Int.	15.5	644.95	
4-12x40 A.O.	4-12	25.7-8.6	3.6-3.2	14	1	Int.	16.6	552.95	
6.5-20x44	6.5-19.4	16.2-5.4	3.5-3.1	14.8	1	Int.	19.6	684.95	
2x20 EER	2	22	26.4	8.1	1	Int.	6.3	248.95	

German #1 German #2 Turkey Reticle

3/4-Mil. Dot Crosshair

ACCESSORIES

Maker and Model	Magn.	Field at 100 Yds. (feet)	Eye Relief (in.)	Length (in.)	Tube Dia. (in.)	W & E Adjustments	Weight (ozs.)	Price	Other Data
NIKON (cont'd.)									
Buckmasters									
4x40	4	30.4	3.3	12.7	1	Int.	11.8	244.95	
3-9x40[4]	3.3-8.6	33.8-11.3	3.5-3.4	12.7	1	Int.	13.4	324.95	
3-9x50	3.3-8.6	33.8-11.3	3.5-3.4	12.9	1	Int.	18.2	452.95	
NORINCO									
N2520	2.5	44.1	4	—	1	Int.	—	52.28	Partial listing shown. Some with Ruby Lens coating, blue/black and matte finish. Imported by Nic Max, Inc.
N420	4	29.3	3.7	—	1	Int.	—	52.70	
N640	6	20	3.1	—	1	Int.	—	67.88	
N154520	1.5-4.5	63.9-23.6	4.1-3.2	—	1	Int.	—	80.14	
N251042	2.5-10	27-11	3.5-2.8	—	1	Int.	—	206.60	
N3956	3-9	35.1-6.3	3.7-2.6	—	1	Int.	—	231.88	
N31256	3-12	26-10	3.5-2.8	—	1	Int.	—	290.92	
NC2836M	2-8	50.8-14.8	3.6-2.7	—	1	Int.	—	255.60	
PARSONS									
Parsons Long Scope	6	10	2	28-34+	.75	Ext.	13	475.00- 525.00	Adjustable for parallax, focus. Micrometer rear mount with .25-min. click adjustments. Price is approximate. Made in U.S. by Parsons Optical Mfg. Co.
PENTAX									
Lightseeker 1.75-6x[1]	1.75-6	71-20	3.5-4	10.8	1	Int.	13	526.00	[1]Glossy finish; Matte finish, Heavy Plex or Penta-Plex, $546.00 [2]Glossy finish; Matte finish, $594.00. [3]Glossy finish; Matte finish, $628.00; Heavy Plex, add $20.00. [4]Matte finish; Mil-Dot, $798.00. [5]Glossy finish; Matte finish, $652.00; Heavy Plex, add $10.00. [6]Glossy finish; Matte finish, $816.00; with Heavy Plex, $830.00; with Mil-Dot, $978.00. [7]Matte finish; with Mil-Dot, $1,018.00. [8]Matte finish, with Mil-Dot, $1098.00. [9]Lightseeker II, Matte finish, $844.00. [10]Lightseeker II, Glossy finish, $636.00. [11]Lightseeker II, Matte finish, $660.00. [12]Lightseeker II, Matte finish, $878.00. [13]Matte finish; Advantage finish, Break-up Mossy Oak finish, Treestand Mossy Oak finish, $364.00. From Pentax Corp.
Lightseeker 2-8x[2]	2-8	53-17	3.5-4	11.7	1	Int.	14	560.00	
Lightseeker 3-9x [3, 4, 10, 11]	3-9	36-14	3.5-4	12.7	1	Int.	15	594.00	
Lightseeker 3.5-10x[5]	3.5-10	29.5-11	3.5-4	14	1	Int.	19.5	630.00	
Lightseeker 4-16x[6, 9]	4-16	33-9	3.5-4	15.4	1	Int.	22.7	796.00	
Lightseeker 6-24x [7, 12]	6-24	18-5.5	3.5-4	16	1	Int.	23.7	856.00	
Lightseeker 8.5-32x[8]	8.5-32	13-3.8	3.5-4	17.2	1	Int.	24	944.00	
Shotgun									
Lightseeker 2.5x[13]	2.5	55	3.5-4	10	1	Int.	9	350.00	
Lightseeker Zero-X SG Plus	0	51	4.5-15	8.9	1	Int.	7.9	372.00	
Lightseeker Zero-X/V Still-Target	0-4	53.8-15	3.5-7	8.9	1	Int.	10.3	476.00	
Lightseeker Zero X/V	0-4	53.8-15	3.5-7	8.9	1	Int.	10.3	454.00	
RWS									
300	4	36	3.5	11.75	1	Int.	13.2	170.00	
400[1]	2-7	55-16	3.5	11.75	1	Int.	13.2	190.00	
450	3-9	43-14	3.5	12	1	Int.	14.3	215.00	
500	4	36	3.5	12.25	1	Int.	13.9	225.00	
550	2-7	55-16	3.5	12.75	1	Int.	14.3	235.00	
600	3-9	43-14	3.5	13	1	Int.	16.5	260.00	
SCHMIDT & BENDER									
Fixed									
4x36	4	30	3.25	11	1	Int.	14	760.00	All scopes have 30-yr. warranty, click adjustments, centered reticles, rotation indicators. [1]Glass reticle; aluminum. Available in aluminum with mounting rail. [2]Aluminum only. [3]Aluminum tube. Choice of two bullet drop compensators, choice of two sunshades, two range finding reticles. From Schmidt & Bender, Inc. [4]Parallax adjustment in third turret; extremely fine crosshairs. [5]Available with illuminated reticle that glows red; third turret houses on/off switch, dimmer and battery. 6[4-16x50/Long Range. [7]Also with Long Eye Relief. From Schmidt & Bender, Inc. Available with illuminated crosshairs and parallax adjustment.
6x42	6	21	3.25	13	1	Int.	17	835.00	
8x56	8	16.5	3.25	14	1	Int.	22	960.00	
10x42	10	10.5	3.25	13	1	Int.	18	955.00	
Variables									
1.25-4x20[5]	1.25-4	96-16	3.75	10	30mm	Int.	15.5	995.00	
1.5-6x42[1, 5]	1.5-6	60-19.5	3.70	12	30mm	Int.	19.7	1,125.00	
2.5-10x56[1, 5]	2.5-10	37.5-12	3.90	14	30mm	Int.	24.6	1,390.00	
3-12x42[2]	3-12	34.5-11.5	3.90	13.5	30mm	Int.	19	1,290.00	
3-12x50[1, 5]	3-12	33.3-12.6	3.90	13.5	30mm	Int.	22.9	1,360.00	
4-16x50 Varmint[4, 6]	4-16	22.5-7.5	3.90	14	30mm	Int.	26	1,525.00	
Police/Marksman II									
3-12x50[7]	3-12	33.3-12.6	3.74	13.9	34mm	Int.	18.5	1,555.00	
SHEPHERD									
310-P1[1]	3-10	41.5-15	3-3.5	12.8	1	Int.	17	549.00	[1]Also avail. as 310-P1, 310-P2, 310-P3, 310-PlA, 310-PE1, 310-P22, 310-P22 Mag., 310-PE, $549.00. All have patented Dual Reticle system with range finder bullet drop compensation; multi-coated lenses, waterproof, shock-proof, nitrogen filled, matte finish. From Shepherd Scope, Ltd.
6x18x40 Varminter	6-18	5.5 (16x)	3-3.5	16.25	40mm	Int.	20.8	625.00	
SIGHTRON									
Variables									
SII 1.56x42	1.5-6	50-15	3.8-4	11.69	1	Int.	15.35	259.95	[1]Adjustable objective. [2][3]MOA dot; also with 5 or 10 MOA dot. [3]Variable 3, 5, 10 MOA dot; black finish; also stainless. [4]Satin black; also stainless. Electronic Red Dot scopes come with ring mount, front and rear extension tubes, polarizing filter, battery, haze filter caps, wrench. Rifle, pistol, shotgun scopes have aluminum tubes, Exac Trak adjustments. Lifetime warranty. From Sightron, Inc. [5]3" sun shade. [6]Mil Dot or Plex reticle. [7]Dot or Plex reticle. [8]Double Diamond reticle.
SII 2.5-7x32SG[8]	2.5-7	26-7	4.3	10.9	1	Int.	8.46	199.95	
SII 2.58x42	2.5-8	36-12	3.6-4.2	11.89	1	Int.	12.82	233.95	
SII 39x42[2, 4, 6, 7]	3-9	34-12	3.6-4.2	12.00	1	Int.	13.22	246.95	
SII 312x42[6]	3-12	32-9	3.6-4.2	11.89	1	Int.	12.99	261.95	
SII 3.510x42	3.5-10	32-11	3.6	11.89	1	Int.	13.16	261.95	
SII 4.514x42[1]	4.5-14	22-7.9	3.6	13.88	1	Int.	16.07	340.95	
Target									
SII6x42HBR	6	20	4	12.48	1	Int.	12.3	259.95	
SII 24x44	24	4.1	4.33	13.30	1	Int.	15.87	279.95	
SII 416x42[1, 4, 5,6, 7]	4-16	26-7	3.6	13.62	1	Int.	16	317.95	
SII 624-42[1, 4, 5, 7]	6-24	16-5	3.6	14.6	1	Int.	18.7	334.95	
SII1040x42	10-40	8.9-4	3.6	16.1	1	Int.	19	399.95	

Heavy Plex   **Fine Plex**   **Penta-Plex**

Reticle No. 6   **Reticle No. 7**   **P3 Mil-Dot**

Maker and Model	Magn.	Field at 100 Yds. (feet)	Eye Relief (in.)	Length (in.)	Tube Dia. (in.)	W & E Adjustments	Weight (ozs.)	Price	Other Data
SIGHTRON (cont'd.)									
Compact									
SII 4x32	4	25	4.5	9.69	1	Int.	9.34	123.95	
SII2.5-10x32	2.5-10	41-10.5	3.75-3.5	10.9	1	Int.	10.39	233.95	
Shotgun									
SII 2.5x20SG	2.5	41	4.3	10.28	1	Int.	8.46	133.95	
Pistol									
SII 1x28P[4]	1	30	9-24	9.49	1	Int.	8.46	135.95	
SII 2x28P[4]	2	16-10	9-24	9.49	1	Int.	8.28	135.95	
SIMMONS									
AETEC									
2100[8]	2.8-10	44-14	5	11.9	1	Int.	15.5	234.99	
2104[16]	3.8-12	33-11	4	13.5	1	Int.	20	259.99	
44Mag									
M-1044[3]	3-10	34-10.5	3	12.75	1	Int.	15.5	179.99	
M-1045[3]	4-12	29.5-9.5	3	13.2	1	Int.	18.25	278.99	
M-1047[3]	6.5-20	14-9	2.6-3.4	12.8	1	Int.	19.5	224.99	
1048[3,20] (3)	6.5-20	16-5.5	2.6-3.4	14.5	1	Int.	20	259.99	
M-1050DM[3,19]	3.8-12	26-9	3	13.08	1	Int.	16.75	269.99	
8-Point									
4-12x40mmAO[3]	4-12	29-10	3-2 7/8	13.5	1	Int.	15.75	129.99	
4x32mm[3]	4	28.75	3	11.625	1	Int.	14.25	44.99	
3-9x32mm[3]	3-9	37.5-13	3-2 7/8	11.875	1	Int.	11.5	60.99	
3-9x40mm[18]	3-9	37-13	3-2 7/8	12.25	1	Int.	12.25	84.99-94.99	
3-9x50mm[3]	3-9	32-11.75	3-2 7/8	13	1	Int.	15.25	97.99	
Prohunter									
7700	2-7	53-16.25	3	11.5	1	Int.	12.5	124.99	
7710[2]	3-9	36-13	3	12.6	1	Int.	13.5	139.99	
7716	4-12	26-9	3	12.6	1	Int.	16.75	159.99	
7721	6-18	18.5-6	3	13.75	1	Int.	16	179.99	
7740[3]	6	21.75	3	12.5	1	Int.	12	120.99	
Prohunter Handgun									
7732[18]	2	22	9-17	8.75	1	Int.	7	139.99	
7738[18]	4	15	11.8-17.6	8.5	1	Int.	8	149.99	
Whitetail Classic									
WTC 11[4]	1.5-5	75-23	3.4-3.2	9.3	1	Int.	9.7	184.99	
WTC 12[4]	2.5-8	45-14	3.2-3	11.3	1	Int.	13	199.99	
WTC 13[4]	3.5-10	30-10.5	3.2-3	12.4	1	Int.	13.5	209.99	
WTC 15[4]	3.5-10	29.5-11.5	3.2	12.75	1	Int.	13.5	289.99	
WTC 45[4]	4.5-14	22.5-8.6	3.2	13.2	1	Int.	14	265.99	
Whitetail Expedition									
1.5-6x32mm[3]	1.5-6	72-19	3	11.16	1	Int.	15	289.99	
3-9x42mm[3]	3-9	40-13.5	3	13.2	1	Int.	17.5	309.99	
4-12x42mm[3]	4-12	29-9.6	3	13.46	1	Int.	21.25	334.99	
6-18x42mm[3]	6-18	18.3-6.5	3	15.35	1	Int.	22.5	364.99	
Pro50									
8800[10]	4-12	27-9	3.5	13.2	1	Int.	18.25	219.99	
8810[10]	6-18	17-5.8	3.6	13.2	1	Int.	18.25	239.99	
Shotgun									
21004	4	16	5.5	8.8	1	Int.	9.1	84.99	
21005	2.5	24	6	7.4	1	Int.	7	59.99	
7789D	2	31	5.5	8.8	1	Int.	8.75	99.99	
7790D	4	17	5.5	8.5	1	Int.	8.75	114.99	
7791D	1.5-5	76-23.5	3.4	9.5	1	Int.	10.75	138.99	
Rimfire									
1031[18]	4	23.5	3	7.25	1	Int.	8.25	79.99	
1022[7]	4	29.5	3	11.75	1	Int.	11	69.99	
1022T	3-9	42-14	3.5	11.5	1	Int.	12	166.99	
1039[18]	3-9	38-13	3.3-2.9	11.6	1	Int.	13	84.99	
Blackpowder									
BP0420M[17]	4	19.5	4	7.5	1	Int.	8.3	114.99	
BP2732M[12]	2-7	57.7-16.6	3	11.6	1	Int.	12.4	135.99	
Red Dot									
51004[21]	1	—	—	4.8	25mm	Int.	4.7	59.99	
51112[22]	1	—	—	5.25	30mm	Int.	6	99.99	
Pro Air Gun									
21608 A.O.	4	25	3.5	12	1	Int.	11.3	109.99	
21613 A.O.	4-12	25-9	3.1-2.9	13.1	1	Int.	15.8	199.99	
21619 A.O.	6-18	18-7	2.9-2.7	13.8	1	Int.	18.2	209.99	
SPRINGFIELD ARMORY									
6x40 Government Model 7.62mm[1]	6	—	3.5	13	1	Int.	14.7	379.00	
4-14x70 Tactical Government Model[2]	4-14	—	3.5	14.25	1	Int.	15.8	395.00	
4-14x56 1st Gen. Government Model[3]	4-14	—	3.5	14.75	30mm	Int.	23	480.00	
10x56 Mil Dot Government Model[4]	10	—	3.5	14.75	30mm	Int.	28	672.00	
6-20x56 Mil Dot Government Model	6-20	—	3.5	18.25	30mm	Int.	33	783.00	

[1]Matte; also polished finish. [2]Silver; also black matte or polished. [3]Black matte finish. [4]Granite finish. [5]Camouflage. [6]Black polish. [7]With ring mounts. [8]Silver; black polish avail. [10]50mm obj.; black matte. [11]Black or silver matte. [12]275-yd. parallax; black or silver matte. [13]TV view. [14]Adj. obj. [15]Silver matte. [16]Adj. objective; 4" sunshade; black matte. [17]Octagon body; rings included; black matte or silver finish. [18]Black matte finish; also available in silver. [19]Smart reticle. [20]Target turrets. [21]With dovetail rings. [23]With 3V lithium battery, extension tube, polarizing filter, Weaver rings. **Only selected models shown.** Contact Simmons Outdoor Corp. for complete details.

[1]Range finding reticle with automatic bullet drop compensator for 308 match ammo to 700 yds. [2]Range finding reticle with automatic bullet drop compensator for 223 match ammo to 700 yds. [3]Also avail. as 2nd Gen. with target knobs and adj. obj., **$549.00**; as 3rd Gen. with illuminated reticle, **$749.00**; as Mil Dot model with illuminated Target Tracking reticle, target knobs, adj. obj., **$698.00**. [4]Unlimited range finding, target knobs, adj. obj., illuminated Target Tracking green reticle. All scopes have matte black finish, internal bubble level, 1/4-MOA clicks. From Springfield, Inc.

ACCESSORIES

Maker and Model	Magn.	Field at 100 Yds. (feet)	Eye Relief (in.)	Length (in.)	Tube Dia. (in.)	W & E Adjustments	Weight (ozs.)	Price	Other Data
STEINER									
Hunting Z									Waterproof, fogproof, nitrogen filled. [1]Heavy-Duplex, Duplex or European
1.5-5x20[1]	1.5-5	32-12	4.3	9.6	30mm	Int.	11.7	1,399.00	#4 reticle. Aluminum tubes; matte black finish. From Pioneer Research.
2.5-8x36[1]	2.5-8	40-15	4	11.6	30mm	Int.	13.4	1,599.00	
3.5-10x50[1]	3.5-10	77-25	4	12.4	30mm	Int.	16.9	1,799.00	
SWAROVSKI OPTIK									
PF Series									[1]Aluminum tubes; special order for steel. [2]Also with 56mm obj.,
8x50[1, 3]	8	17	3.15	13.9	30mm	Int.	21.5	987.78	**$1,398.89.** [3]Also available with illuminated reticle. [4]Aluminum only.
8x56[1, 3]	8	17	3.15	14.29	30mm	Int.	24	1,032.22	Imported from Austria by Swarovski Optik.
PH Series									
1.25-4x24[1]	1.25-4	98.4-31.2	3.15	10.63	30mm	Int.	16.2	1,065.55	
1.5-6x42[1]	1.5-6	65.4-21	3.15	12.99	30mm	Int.	20.8	1,187.78	
2.5-10x42[1, 2]	2.5-10	39.6-12.6	3.15	13.23	30mm	Int.	19.8	1,354.44	
3-12x50[1]	3-12	33-10.5	3.15	14.33	30mm	Int.	22.4	1,387.78	
4-16x50	4-16	30-8.5	3.15	14.22	30mm	Int.	22.3	1,443.34	
6-24x50	6-24	18.6-5.4	3.15	15.4	30mm	Int.	23.6	1,587.78	
A-Line Series									
3-9x36AV[4]	3-9	39-13.5	3.35	11.8	1	Int.	11.7	754.44	
3-10x42AV[4]	3-10	33-11.7	3.35	12.44	1	Int.	12.7	798.89	
4-12x50AV[4]	4-12	29.1-9.9	3.35	13.5	1	Int.	13.9	821.11	

No. 1   No. 1A   No. 2

No. 4   No. 4A   No. 7A

Maker and Model	Magn.	Field at 100 Yds. (feet)	Eye Relief (in.)	Length (in.)	Tube Dia. (in.)	W & E Adjustments	Weight (ozs.)	Price	Other Data
SWIFT									
600 4x15	4	17	2.8	10.6	.75	Int.	3.5	20.00	All Swift scopes, with the exception of the 4x15, have Quadraplex reticles
601 3-7x20	3-7	25-12	3-2.9	11	.75	Int.	5.6	45.00	and are fogproof and waterproof. The 4x15 has crosshair reticle and is
650 4x32	4	26	4	12	1	Int.	9.1	88.00	non-waterproof. [1]Available in regular matte black or silver finish. [2]Comes
653 4x40WA[1]	4	35	4	12.2	1	Int.	12.6	116.00	with ring mounts, wrench, lens caps, extension tubes, filter, battery.
654 3-9x32	3-9	35-12	3.4-2.9	12	1	Int.	9.8	116.00	[3]Regular and matte black finish. [4]Speed Focus scopes. From Swift Instru-
656 3-9x40WA[1]	3-9	40-14	3.4-2.8	12.6	1	Int.	12.3	126.00	ments.
657 6x40	6	28	4	12.6	1	Int.	10.4	116.00	
658 2-7x40WA[3]	2-7	55-18	3.3-3	11.6	1	Int.	12.5	151.00	
659 3.5-10x44WA	3.5-10	34-12	3-2.8	12.8	1	Int.	13.5	226.00	
665 1.5-4.5x21	1.5-4.5	69-24.5	3.5-3	10.9	1	Int.	9.6	123.00	
665M 1.5-4.5x21	1.5-4.5	69-24.5	3.5-3	10.9	1	Int.	9.6	123.00	
666M Shotgun 1x20	1	113	3.2	7.5	1	Int.	9.6	126.00	
667 Fire-Fly[2]	1	40	—	5.4	30mm	Int.	5	220.00	
668M 4x32	4	25	4	10	1	Int.	8.9	116.00	
669M 6-18x44	6-18	18-6.5	2.8	14.5	1	Int.	17.6	216.00	
Premier[4]									
649R 4-12x50WA[3]	4-12	29.5-9.5	3.2-3	13.8	1	Int.	17.8	235.00	
671M 3-9x50WA	3-9	35-12	3.24-3.12	15.5	1	Int.	18.2	245.00	
672M 6-18x50WA	6-18	19.4-6.7	3.25-3	15.8	1	Int.	20.9	255.00	
673M 2.5-10x50WA	2.5-10	33-9	4-3.5	11.8	30mm	Int.	18.9	290.00	
674M 3-5x40WA	3-9	40-14.2	3.6-2.9	12	1	Int.	13.1	160.00	
676 4-12x40WA[1]	4-12	29.3-10.5	3.15-2.9	12.4	1	Int.	15.4	170.00	
Pistol									
679M 1.25-4x28	1.25-4	23-9	23-15	9.3	1	Int.	8.2	212.00	
Pistol Scopes									
661 4x32	4	90	10-22	9.2	1	Int.	9.5	126.00	
663 2x20[1]	2	18.3	9-21	7.2	1	Int.	8.4	126.00	
TASCO									
Mag IV									[1]Water, fog & shockproof; fully coated optics; .25-min. click stops; haze
W312x40[1, 2, 4]	3-12	35-9	3	12.25	1	Int.	12	89.99	filter caps; 30-day/limited lifetime warranty. [2]30/30 range finding reticle.
W416x40[1, 2, 4, 13, 14]	4-16	26-7	3	14.25	1	Int.	15.6	124.99	[3]Fits most popular auto pistols, MP5, AR-15/M16. [4]1/3 greater zoom
W416x50	4-16	31-8	4	13.5	1	Int.	16	124.99	range. [5]Trajectory compensating scopes, Opti-Centered® stadia reticle.
DW520x50[23]	5-20	24-6	4	13.5	1	Int.	16	189.99	[6]Black gloss or stainless. [7]True one-power scope. [8]Coated optics;
Golden Antler									crosshair reticle; ring mounts included to fit most 22, 10mm receivers.
DMGA4x32TV	4	32	3	13	1	Int.	12.7	34.99	[9]Red dot; also with switchable red/green dot (EZ02, **$42.05**). [10]Also matte
DMGA39x32TV[1]	3-9	39-13	3	—	1	Int.	12.2	49.99	aluminum finish. [11]11-position rheostat, 10-MOA dot; built-in dovetail-
DMGA39x40TV	3-9	39-13	3	12.5	1	Int.	13	69.99	style mount. Also with crosshair reticle. [12]Also 30/30 reticle. [13]Also in
Silver Antler									stainless finish. [14]Black matte or stainless finish. [15]Also with stainless
DMSA4x40	4	32	3	12	1	Int.	12.5	39.99	finish. [16]Also in matte black. [17]Available with 5-min., or 10-min. dot. [18]Red
DMSA39x32	3-9	39-13	3	13.25	1	Int.	12.2	49.99	dot device; can be used on rifles, shotguns, handguns; 3.5 or 7 MOA dot.
DMSA39x40WA[10]	3-9	41-15	3	12.75	1	Int.	13	69.99	Available with 10, 15, 20-min. dot. [19]20mm; black. [20]20mm; also 32mm. [21]Pro-Shot reticle. [22]Has 4, 8, 12,
Pronghorn									16MOA dots (switchable). [23]Available with BDC. **Contact Tasco for**
PH4x32	4	32	3	12	1	Int.	12.5	29.99	**details on complete line.**
PH39x32	3-9	39-13	3	12	1	Int.	11	34.99	
PH39x40	3-9	39-13	3	13	1	Int.	12.1	44.99	
Bantam									
S1.5-45x20A[19, 21]	1.5-4.5	69.5-23	4	10.25	1	Int.	10	54.99	
S1.54x32A[21]	1.5-4.5	69.5-23	4	11.25	1	Int.	12	54.99	
S2.5x20A[20, 21]	2.5	22	6	7.5	1	Int.	7.5	44.99	
SA2.5x32A	2.5	32	6	8.5	1	Int.	8.5	44.99	
Airgun									
AG4x32N	4	30	3	—	1	Int.	12.25	84.99	
Rimfire									
RF4x15[8]	4	22.5	2.5	11	.75	Int.	4	6.99	
RF4x20WA	4	23	2.5	10.5	.75	Int.	3.8	9.99	

Maker and Model	Magn.	Field at 100 Yds. (feet)	Eye Relief (in.)	Length (in.)	Tube Dia. (in.)	W & E Adjustments	Weight (ozs.)	Price	Other Data
TASCO (cont'd.)									
RF4x32[16]	4	31	3	12.25	1	Int.	12.6	29.99	
RF37x20	3-7	24-11	2.5	11.5	.75	Int.	5.7	19.99	
Propoint									
PDP2[10, 17]	1	40	Unltd.	5	30mm	Int.	5	109.99	
PDP3[10, 17]	1	52	Unltd.	5	30mm	Int.	5	129.99	
PDP3CMP	1	68	Unltd.	4.75	33mm	Int.	—	144.99	
PDP5CMP[22]	1	82	Unltd.	4	47mm	Int.	8	204.99	
Optima 2000									
OPP2000-3.5[3, 20]	1	—	—	1.5	—	Int.	1/2	249.99	
OPP2000-7[3, 20]	1	—	—	1.5	—	Int.	1.2	249.99	
Pistol Scopes									
PX20[10]	2	21	10-23	8	1	Int.	6.5	69.99	
P1.254x28[10]	1.25-4	23-9	15-23	9.25	1	Int.	8.2	109.99	
Tactical & Target									
TAC840x56M	8-40	11.5-2.6	3	16	30mm	Int.	31.5	734.99	
EZ01	1	35	—	4.75	1	Int.	2.5	19.99	
World Class Plus									
WCP4x44	4	32	3.25	12.75	1	Int.	13.5	249.55	
WCP3.510x50[18]	3.5-10	30-10.5	3.75	13	1	Int.	17.1	159.99	
WCP39x44[1,16]	3-9	39-14	3.5	12.75	1	Int.	15.8	154.99	
WCP416x40	4-16	26-7	3	14.25	1	Int.	16.8	244.99	
WCP624x40	6-24	17.4	3	15.5	1	Int.	17.5	254.99	
THOMPSON/CENTER RECOIL PROOF SERIES									
Pistol Scopes									[1]Black finish; silver optional. [2]Black; lighted reticle. From Thompson/Center Arms.
8315[2]	2.5-7	15-5	8-21, 8-11	9.25	1	Int.	9.2	308.99	
8326[4]	2.5-7	15-5	8-21, 8-11	9.25	1	Int.	10.5	360.49	
Muzzleloader Scopes									
8658	1	60	3.8	9.125	1	Int.	10.2	125.99	
8662	4	16	3	8.8	1	Int.	9.1	125.99	
TRIJICON									
ReflexII 1x24	1	—	—	4.25	1	Int.	4.6	379.00	[1]Advanced Combat Optical Gunsight for AR-15, M16, with intergral mount. Other mounts available. All models feature tritium and fiber optics dual lighting system that requires no batteries. From Trijicon, Inc.
TA44 1.5x16[1]	1.5	43.8	2.4	4.1	—	Int.	3.5	695.00	
TA45 1.5x24[1]	1.5	28.9	3.6	5.6	—	Int.	3.9	675.00	
TA47 2x20[1]	2	33.1	2.1	4.5	—	Int.	3.8	695.00	
TA50 3x24[1]	3	28.9	1.4	4.8	—	Int.	3.9	695.00	
TA11 3.5x35[1]	3.5	28.9	2.4	8	—	Int.	14	1,295.00	
TAO1 4x32[1]	4	36.8	1.5	5.8	—	Int.	9.9	895.00	
Variable AccuPoint									
3-9x40	3-9	—	3.2-3.6	12.2	1	Int.	12.8	699.00	
1.25-4x24	1.25-4	61.6-20.5	3.4-4.8	10.2	1	Int.	11.4	599.00	
ULTRA DOT									
Micro-Dot Scopes[1]									[1]Brightness-adjustable fiber optic red dot reticle. Waterproof, nitrogen-filled one-piece tube. Tinted see-through lens covers and battery included. [2]Parallax adjustable. [3]Ultra Dot sights include rings, battery, polarized filter, and 5-year warranty. All models available in black or satin finish. [4]Illuminated red dot has eleven brightness settings. Shock-proof aluminum tube. From Ultra Dot Distribution.
1.5-4.5x20 Rifle	1.5-4.5	80-26	3	9.8	1	Int.	10.5	297.00	
2-7x32	2-7	54-18	3	11	1	Int.	12.1	308.00	
3-9x40	3-9	40-14	3	12.2	1	Int.	13.3	327.00	
4x-12x56[2]	4-12	30-10	3	14.3	1	Int.	18.3	417.00	
Ultra-Dot Sights[3]									
Ultra-Dot 25[4]	1	—	—	5.1	1	Int.	3.9	159.00	
Ultra-Dot 30[4]	1	—	—	5.1	30mm	Int.	4	179.00	
UNERTL									
1" Target	6, 8, 10	16-10	2	21.5	.75	Ext.	21	358.00	[1]Dural .25-MOA click mounts. Hard coated lenses. Non-rotating objective lens focusing. [2].25-MOA click mounts. [3]With target mounts. [4]With calibrated head. [5]Same as 1" Target but without objective lens focusing. [6]With new Posa mounts. [7]Range focus unit near rear of tube. Price is with Posa or standard mounts. Magnum clamp. From Unertl.
1.25: Target[1]	8, 10, 12, 14	12-16	2	25	.75	Ext.	21	466.00	
1.5" Target	10, 12, 14, 16, 18, 20	11.5-3.2	2.25	25.5	.75	Ext.	31	487.00	
2" Target[2]	10, 12, 14, 16, 18, 24, 30, 32, 36,	8	2.25	26.25	1	Ext.	44	642.00	
Varmint, 1.25"[3]	6, 8, 10, 12 8, 10, 12,	1-7	2.50	19.50	.875	Ext.	26	466.00	
Ultra Varmint, 2"[4]	15	12.6-7	2.25	24	1	Ext.	34	630.00	
Small Game[5]	3, 4, 6	25-17	2.25	18	.75	Ext.	16	284.00	
Programmer 200[7]	10, 12, 14, 16, 18, 20, 24, 30, 36	11.3-4	—	26.5	1	Ext.	45	805.00	
BV-20[8]	2	8	4.4	17.875	1	Ext.	21.25	595.00	
Tube Sight	—	—	—	17	—	Ext.	—	262.50	
U.S. OPTICS									
SN-1/TAR Fixed Power System									Prices shown are estimates; scopes built to order; choice of reticles; choice of front or rear focal plane; extra-heavy MIL-SPEC construction; extra-long turrets; individual w&e rebound springs; up to 100MOA objectives; up to 50mm tubes; all lenses multi-coated. Other magnifications available. [1]Modular components allow a variety of fixed or variable magnifications, night vision, etc. Made in U.S. by U.S. Optics.
16.2x	15	8.6	4.3	16.5	30mm	Int.	27	1,700.00	
22.4x	20	5.8	3.8	18	30mm	Int.	29	1,800.00	
26x	24	5	3.4	18	30mm	Int.	31	1,900.00	
31x	30	4.6	3.5	18	30mm	Int.	32	2,100.00	
37x	36	4	3.6	18	30mm	Int.	32	2,300.00	
48x	50	3	3.8	18	30mm	Int.	32	2,500.00	

ACCESSORIES

Maker and Model	Magn.	Field at 100 Yds. (feet)	Eye Relief (in.)	Length (in.)	Tube Dia. (in.)	W & E Adjustments	Weight (ozs.)	Price	Other Data
U.S. OPTICS (cont'd.)									
Variables									
SN-2	4-22	26.8-5.8	5.4-3.8	18	30mm	Int.	24	1,762.00	
SN-3	1.6-8	—	4.4-4.8	18.4	30mm	Int.	36	1,435.00	
SN-4	1-4	116-31.2	4.6-4.9	18	30mm	Int.	35	1,065.00	
Fixed Power									
SN-6	8, 10, 17, 22	14-8.5	3.8-4.8	9.2	30mm	Int.	18	1,195.00	
SN-8 Modular[1]	4, 10, 20, 40	32	3.3	7.5	30mm	Int.	11.1	890.00-4,000.00	
WEAVER									
Riflescopes									
K2.5[1]	2.5	35	3.7	9.5	1	Int.	7.3	179.99	
K4[1-2]	3.7	26.5	3.3	11.3	1	Int.	10	194.99	
K6[1]	5.7	18.5	3.3	11.4	1	Int.	10	194.99	
KT15[1]	14.6	7.5	3.2	12.9	1	Int.	14.7	374.99	
V3[1-2]	1.1-2.8	88-32	3.9-3.7	9.2	1	Int.	8.5	299.99	
V9[1-2]	2.8-8.7	33-11	3.5-3.4	12.1	1	Int.	11.1	249.99-299.99	
V9x50[1-2]	3-9	29.4-9.9	3.6-3	13.1	1	Int.	14.5	319.99	
V10[1-2-3]	2.2-9.6	38.5-9.5	3.4-3.3	12.2	1	Int.	11.2	259.99-269.99	
V10-50[1-2-3]	2.3-9.7	40.2-9.2	2.9-2.8	13.75	1	Int.	15.2	365.99	
V16 MDX[2-3]	3.8-15.5	26.8-6.8	3.1	13.9	1	Int.	16.5	434.99	
V16 MFC[2-3]	3.8-15.5	26.8-6.8	3.1	13.9	1	Int.	16.5	434.99	
V16 MDT[2-3]	3.8-15.5	26.8-6.8	3.1	13.9	1	Int.	16.5	434.99	
V24 Varmint[2]	6-24	15.3-4	3.15	14.3	1	Int.	17.5	509.99	
Handgun									
H2[1-3]	2	21	4-29	8.5	1	Int.	6.7	212.99-224.99	
H4[1-3]	4	18	11.5-18	8.5	1	Int.	6.7	234.99	
VH4[1-3]	1.5-4	13.6-5.8	11-17	8.6	1	Int.	8.1	289.99	
VH8[1-2-3]	2.5-8	8.5-3.7	12.16	9.3	1	Int.	8.3	299.99	
Rimfire									
R4[2-3]	3.9	29	3.9	9.7	1	Int.	8.8	159.99	
RV7[2]	2.5-7	37-13	3.7-3.3	10.75	1	Int.	10.7	184.99-189.99	
Grand Slam									
6-20x40mm Varminter Reticle[2]	6-20X	16.5-5.25	2.75-3	14.48	1	Int.	17.75	499.99	
6-20x40mm Fine Crosshairs with a Dot[2]	6-20X	16.5-5.25	2.75-3	14.48	1	Int.	17.75	499.99	
1.5-5x32mm[2]	1.5-5X	71-21	3.25	10.5	1	Int.	10.5	429.99	
4.75x40mm[2]	4.75X	14.75	3.25	11	1	Int.	10.75	359.99	
3-10x40mm[2]	3-10X	35-11.33	3.5-3	12.08	1	Int.	12.08	379.99	
3.5-10x50mm[2]	3.5-10X	30.5-10.8	3.5-3	12.96	1	Int.	16.25	459.99	
4.5-14x40mm	4.5-14X	22.5-10.5	3.5-3	14.48	1	Int.	17.5	499.99	
T-Series									
T-6[4]	614	14	3.58	12.75	1	Int.	14.9	424.95	
T-36[3-4]	36	3	3	15.1	1	Int.	16.7	794.99	
ZEISS									
Z/ZM									
6x42MC	6	22.9	3.2	12.7	1	Int.	13.4	799.00	
8x56MC	8	18	3.2	13.8	1	Int.	17.6	899.00	
1.25-4x24MC	1.25-4	105-33	3.2	11.46	30mm	Int.	17.3	949.00	
1.5-6x42MC	1.5-6	65.5-22.9	3.2	12.4	30mm	Int.	18.5	1,049.00	
2.5-10x48MC[1]	2.5-10	33-11.7	3.2	14.5	30mm	Int.	24	1,249.00	
3-12x56MC[1]	3-12	27.6-9.9	3.2	15.3	30mm	Int.	25.8	1,399.00	
Diavari									
3-9x36MC	3-9	36-13	3.5	11.9	1	Int.	15	615.00	
VM/V									
1.1-4x24[2]	1.1-4	120-34	3.5	11.8	30mm	Int.	15.8	1,799.00	
1.5-6x42T*	1.5-6	65.5-22.9	3.2	12.4	30mm	Int.	18.5	1,349.00	
2.5-10x50T*[1]	2.5-10	47.1-13	3.5	12.5	30mm	Int.	16.25	1,549.00	
3-12x56T*	3-12	37.5-10.5	3.5	13.5	30mm	Int.	19.5	1,599.00	
3-9x42T*	3-9	42-15	3.74	13.3	1	Int.	15.3	1,249.00	
5-15x42T*	5-15	25.7-8.5	3.74	13.3	1	Int.	15.4	1,499.00	

[1]Gloss black, [2]Matte black, [3]Silver, [4]Satin, [5]Silver and black (slightly higher in price). [6]Field of view measured at 18" eye relief..25 MOA click adjustments, except T-Series which vary from .125 to .25 clicks. One-piece tubes with multi-coated lenses. All scopes are shock-proof, water-proof, and fogproof. Dual-X reticle available in all except V24 which has a fine X-hair and ot; T-Series in which certain models are available in fine X-hair and dots; Qwik-Point red dot scopes which are available in fixed 4 or 12 MOA, or variable 4-8-12 MOA. V16 also available with fine X-hair, dot or Dual-X reticle. T-Series scopes have Micro-Trac® adjustments. From Weaver Products.

[1]Also avail. with illuminated reticle. [2]Illuminated Vari-point reticle. Black matte finish. All scopes have .25-min. click-stop adjustments. Choice of Z-Plex or fine crosshair reticles. Rubber armored objective bell, rubber eyepiece ring. Lenses have T-Star coating for highest light transmission. VM/V scopes avail. with rail mount. From Carl Zeiss Optical, Inc.

Hunting scopes in general are furnished with a choice of reticle—crosshairs, post with crosshairs, tapered or blunt post, or dot crosshairs, etc. The great majority of target and varmint scopes have medium or fine crosshairs but post or dot reticles may be ordered. W—Windage E—Elevation MOA—Minute of Angle or 1" (approx.) at 100 yards, etc.

ACCESSORIES

LASER SIGHTS

Lasergrips LG-206

Alpec Mini Shot

Laser Devices ULS 2001 with TLS 8R light

Maker and Model	Wavelength (nm)	Beam Color	Lens	Operating Temp. (degrees F.)	Weight (ozs.)	Price	Other Data
ALPEC							[1]Range 1000 yards. [2]Range 300 yards. Mini Shot II range 500 yards, output 650mm, **$129.95**. [3]Range 300 yards; Laser Shot II 500 yards; Super Laser Shot 1000 yards. Black or stainless finish aluminum; removable pressure or push-button switch. Mounts for most handguns, many rifles and shotguns. From Alpec Team, Inc.
Power Shot[1]	635	Red	Glass	NA	2.5	$199.95	
Mini Shot[2]	670	Red	Glass	NA	2.5	99.95	
Laser Shot[3]	670	Red	Glass	NA	3.0	99.95	
BEAMSHOT							[1]Black or silver finish; adj. for windage and elevation; 300-yd. range; also M1000/S (500-yd. range), M1000/u (800-yd.). [2]Black finish; 300-, 500-, 800-yd. models. All come with removable touch pad switch, 5" cable. Mounts to fit virtually any firearm. From Quarton USA Co.
1000[1]	670	Red	Glass	—	3.8	NA	
3000[2]	635/670	Red	Glass	—	2	NA	
1001/u	635	Red	Glass	—	3.8	NA	
780	780	Red	Glass	—	3.8	NA	
BSA							[1]Comes with mounts for 22/air rifle and Weaver-style bases.
LS650[1]	N/A	Red	N/A	N/A	N/A	69.95	
LASERAIM							[1]Red dot/laser combo; 300-yd. range: LA3xHD Hotdot has 500-yd. range **$249.00**; 4 MOA dot size, laser gives 2" dot at 100 yds. [2]30mm obj. lens: 4 MOA dot at 100 yds: fits Weaver base. [3]300-yd range; 2" dot at 100 yds.; rechargeable Nicad battery [4]1.5-mile range; 1" dot at 100 yds.; 20+ hrs. batt. life. [5]1.5-mile range; 1" dot at 100 yds; rechargeable Nicad battery (comes with in-field charger); [6]Black or satin finish. With mount, **$169.00**. [7]Laser projects 2" dot at 100 yds.: with rotary switch; with Hotdot **$237.00**. [8]For Glock 17-27; G1 Hotdot **$299.00**; price installed. [10]Fits std. Weaver base, no rings required; 6-MOA dot; seven brightness settings. All have w&e adj.; black or satin silver finish. From Laseraim Technologies, Inc.
LA10 Hotdot[4]	—	—	—	—	NA	199.00	
Lasers							
MA-35RB Mini Aimer[7]	—	—	—	—	1.0	129.00	
G1 Laser[8]	—	—	—	—	2.0	229.00	
LASER DEVICES							[1]For S&W P99 semi-auto pistols; also BA-2, 5 oz., **$339.00**. [2]For revolvers. [3]For HK, Walther P99. [4]For semi-autos. [5]For rifles; also FA-4/ULS, 2.5 oz., **$325.00**. [6]For HK sub guns. [7]For military rifles. [8]For shotguns. [9]For SIG-Pro pistol. [10]Universal, semi-autos. [11]For AR-15 variants. All avail. with Magnum Power Point (650nM) or daytime-visible Super Power Point (632nM) diode. Infrared diodes avail. for law enforcement. From Laser Devices, Inc.
BA-1[1]	632	Red	Glass	—	2.4	372.00	
BA-3[2]	632	Red	Glass	—	3.3	332.50	
BA-5[3]	632	Red	Glass	—	3.2	372.00	
Duty-Grade[4]	632	Red	Glass	—	3.5	372.00	
FA-4[5]	632	Red	Glass	—	2.6	358.00	
LasTac[1]	632	Red	Glass	—	5.5	298.00 to 477.00	
MP-5[6]	632	Red	Glass	—	2.2	495.00	
MR-2[7]	632	Red	Glass	—	6.3	485.00	
SA-2[8]	632	Red	Glass	—	3.0	360.00	
SIG-Pro[9]	632	Red	Glass	—	2.6	372.00	
ULS-2001[10]	632	Red	Glass	—	4.5	210.95	
Universal AR-2A	632	Red	Glass	—	4.5	445.00	
LASERGRIPS							Replaces existing grips with built-in laser high in the right grip panel. Integrated pressure sensitive pad in grip activates the laser. Also has master on/off switch. [1]For Beretta 92, 96, Colt 1911/Commander, Ruger MkII, S&W J-frames, SIG Sauer P228, P229. [2]For all Glock models. Option on/off switch. Requires factory installation. [3]For S&W K, L, N frames, round or square butt (LG-207); [4]For Taurus small-frame revolvers. [5]For Ruger SP-101. [6]For SIG Sauer P226. From Crimson Trace Corp.
LG-201[1]	633	Red-Orange	Glass	NA	—	349.00	
LG-206[2]	633	Red-Orange	Glass	NA	—	289.00	
LG-085[4]	633	Red-Orange	Glass	NA	—	279.00	
LG-101[5]	633	Red-Orange	Glass	NA	—	289.00	
LG-226[6]	633	Red-Orange	Glass	NA	—	379.00	
GLS-630[2]	633	Red-Orange	Glass	NA	—	595.00	
LASERLYTE							[1]Dot/circle or dot/crosshair projection; black or stainless. [2]Also 635/645mm model. From TacStar Laserlyte.
LLX-0006-140/090[1]	635/645	Red	—	—	1.4	159.95	
WPL-0004-140/090[2]	670	Red	—	—	1.2	109.95	
TPL-0004-140/090[2]	670	Red	—	—	1.2	109.95	
T7S-0004-140[2]	670	Red	—	—	0.8	109.95	
LASERMAX							Replaces the recoil spring guide rod; includes a customized takedown lever that serves as the laser's instant on/off switch. For Glock, Smith & Wesson, Sigarms, Beretta and select Taurus models. Installs in most pistols without gunsmithing. Battery life 1/2 hour to 2 hours in continuous use. From LaserMax.
LMS-1000 Internal Guide Rod	635	Red-Orange	Glass	40-120	.25	From 394.95	
NIGHT STALKER							Waterproof; LCD panel displays power remaining; programmable blink rate; constant or memory on. From Wilcox Industries Corp.
S0 Smart	635	Red	NA	NA	2.46	515.00	

Maker, Model, Type	Adjust.	Scopes	Price
AIMTECH			
Handguns			
AMT Auto Mag II .22 Mag.	No	Weaver rail	$56.99
Astra .44 Mag Revolver	No	Weaver rail	63.25
Beretta/Taurus 92/99	No	Weaver rail	63.25
Browning Buckmark/Challenger II	No	Weaver rail	56.99
Browning Hi-Power	No	Weaver rail	63.25
Glock 17, 17L, 19, 23, 24 etc. no rail	No	Weaver rail	63.25
Glock 20, 21 no rail	No	Weaver rail	63.25
Glock 9mm and .40 with access. rail	No	Weaver rail	74.95
Govt. 45 Auto/.38 Super	No	Weaver rail	63.25
Hi-Standard (Mitchell version) 107	No	Weaver rail	63.25
H&K USP 9mm/40 rail mount	No	Weaver rail	74.95
Rossi 85/851/951 Revolvers	No	Weaver rail	63.25
Ruger Mk I, Mk II	No	Weaver rail	49.95
Ruger P85/P89	No	Weaver rail	63.25
S&W K, L, N frames	No	Weaver rail	63.25
S&W K. L, N with tapped top strap*	No	Weaver rail	69.95
S&W Model 41 Target 22	No	Weaver rail	63.25
S&W Model 52 Target 38	No	Weaver rail	63.25
S&W Model 99 Walther frame rail mount	No	Weaver rail	74.95
S&W 2nd Gen. 59/459/659 etc.	No	Weaver rail	56.99
S&W 3rd Gen. full size 5906 etc.	No	Weaver rail	69.95
S&W 422, 622, 2206	No	Weaver rail	56.99
S&W 645/745	No	Weaver rail	56.99
S&W Sigma	No	Weaver rail	64.95
Taurus PT908	No	Weaver rail	63.25
Taurus 44 6.5" bbl.	No	Weaver rail	69.95
Walther 99	No	Weaver rail	74.95
Shotguns			
Benelli M-1 Super 90**	No	Weaver rail	44.95
Benelli Montefeltro	No	Weaver rail	44.95
Benelli Nova**	No	Weaver rail	69.95
Benelli Super Black Eagle**	No	Weaver rail	49.95
Browning A-5 12-ga.	No	Weaver rail	40.95
Browning BPS 12-ga.	No	Weaver rail	40.95
Browning Gold Hunter 12-ga.	No	Weaver rail	44.95
Browning Gold Hunter 20-ga.	No	Weaver rail	49.95
Browning Gold Hunter 10-ga.	No	Weaver rail	49.95
Beretta 303 12-ga.	No	Weaver rail	44.95
Beretta 390 12-ga.**	No	Weaver rail	44.95
Beretta Pintail	No	Weaver rail	44.95
H&K Fabarms Gold/SilverLion	no	Weaver rail	49.95
Ithaca 37/87 12-ga.**	No	Weaver rail	40.95
Ithaca 37/87 20-ga.**	No	Weaver rail	40.95
Mossberg 500/Maverick 12-ga.**	No	Weaver rail	40.95
Mossberg 500/Maverick 20-ga.**	No	Weaver rail	40.95
Mossberg 835 3.5" Ulti-Mag**	No	Weaver rail	40.95
Mossberg 5500/9200	No	Weaver rail	40.95
Remington 1100/1187 12-ga.**	No	Weaver rail	40.95
Remington 1100/1187 12-ga. LH	No	Weaver rail	40.95
Remington 1100/1187 20-ga.**	No	Weaver rail	40.95
Remington 1100/1187 20-ga. LH	No	Weaver rail	40.95
Remington 870 12-ga.**	No	Weaver rail	40.95
Remington 870 12-ga. LH	No	Weaver rail	40.95
Remington 870 20-ga.**	No	Weaver rail	40.95
Remington 870 20-ga. LH	No	Weaver rail	40.95
Remington 870 Express Magnum**	No	Weaver rail	40.95
Remington SP-10 10-ga.**	No	Weaver rail	49.95
Winchester 1300 12-ga.**	No	Weaver rail	40.95
Winchester 1400 12-ga.**	No	Weaver rail	40.95
Winchester Super X2	No	Weaver rail	44.95
Rifles			
AR-15/M16	No	Weaver rail	21.95
Browning A-Bolt	No	Weaver rail	21.95
Browning BAR	No	Weaver rail	21.95
Browning BLR	No	Weaver rail	21.95
CVA Apollo	No	Weaver rail	21.95
Marlin 336	No	Weaver rail	21.95
Mauser Mark X	No	Weaver rail	21.95
Modern Muzzleloading	No	Weaver rail	21.95
Remington 700 Short Action	No	Weaver rail	21.95
Remington 700 Long Action	No	Weaver rail	21.95
Remington 7400/7600	No	Weaver rail	21.95
Ruger 10/22	No	Weaver rail	21.95
Ruger Mini 14 Scout Rail***	No	Weaver rail	89.50
Savage 110, 111, 113, 114, 115, 116	No	Weaver rail	21.95
Thompson Center Thunderhawk	No	Weaver rail	21.95
Traditions Buckhunter	No	Weaver rail	21.95
White W Series	No	Weaver rail	21.95
White G Series	No	Weaver rail	21.95
White WG Series	No	Weaver rail	21.95
Winchester Model 70	No	Weaver rail	21.95
Winchester 94 AE	No	Weaver rail	21.95

Maker, Model, Type	Adjust.	Scopes	Price
AIMTECH (cont.)			
All mounts no-gunsmithing, iron sight usable. Rifle mounts are solid see-through bases. All mounts accommodate standard Weaver-style rings of all makers. From Aimtech division, L&S Technologies, Inc. *3-blade sight mount combination. **These models available exclusively in Realtree or Advantage camo patterns. ***Replacement handguard and mounting rail.			
A.R.M.S.			
M16A1,A2,AR-15	No	Weaver rail	$59.95
Multibase	No	Weaver rail	59.95
#19 ACOG Throw Lever Mt.	No	Weaver rail	150.00
#19 Weaver/STANAG Throw Lever Rail	No	Weaver rail	140.00
STANAG Rings	No	30mm	75.00
Throw Lever Rings	No	Weaver rail	99.00
Ring Inserts	No	1", 30mm	29.00
#22M68 Aimpoint Comp	No	Weaver rail	89.00
Ring Throw Lever			
#38 Std. Swan Sleeve[1]	No	—	180.00
#39 A2 Plus Mod. Mt.	No	#39T rail	125.00
[1]Avail. in three lengths. From A.R.M.S., Inc.			
ARMSON			
AR-15[1]	No	1"	45.00
Mini-14[2]	No	1"	66.00
H&K[3]	No	1"	82.00
[1]Fastens with one nut. [2]Models 181, 182, 183, 184, etc. [3]Claw mount. From Trijicon, Inc.			
ARMSPORT			
100 Series [1]	No	1" rings, Low, med., high	10.75
104 22-cal.	No	1"	10.75
201 See-Thru	No	1"	13.00
1-Piece Base[2]	No	—	5.50
2-Piece Base[2]	No	—	2.75
[1]Weaver-type ring. [2]Weaver-type base; most popular rifles. Made in U.S. From Armsport.			
ASHLEY			
Ashley/Lever Scout Scope	No	Weaver rail	50.00
No gunsmithing required for lever-action rifles with 8" Weaver-style rails; surrounds barrel shank; 6" long; low profile. Ashley Outdoors, Inc.			
B-SQUARE			
Pistols (centerfire)			
Beretta 92/Taurus 99	No	Weaver rail	64.95
Colt M1911	E only	Weaver rail	64.95
Desert Eagle	No	Weaver rail	64.95
Glock	No	Weaver rail	64.95
H&K USP, 9mm and 40 S&W	No	Weaver rail	64.95
Ruger P85/89	E only	Weaver rail	64.95
SIG Sauer P226	E only	Weaver rail	64.95
Pistols (rimfire)			
Browning Buck Mark	No	Weaver rail	29.95
Colt 22	No	Weaver rail	33.95
Ruger Mk I/II, bull or taper	No	Weaver rail	29.95-49.95
Smith & Wesson 41, 2206	No	Weaver rail	36.95-49.95
Revolvers			
Colt Anaconda/Python	No	Weaver rail	29.95-64.95
Ruger Single-Six	No	Weaver rail	64.95
Ruger GP-100	No	Weaver rail	64.95
Ruger Blackhawk, Super	No	Weaver rail	64.95
Ruger Redhawk, Super	No	Weaver rail	64.95
Smith & Wesson K, L, N	No	Weaver rail	36.95-64.95
Taurus 66, 669, 607, 608	No	Weaver rail	64.95
Rifles (sporting)			
Browning BAR, A-Bolt	No	Weaver rail	49.90
Marlin MR7	No	Weaver rail	49.90
Mauser 98 Large Ring	No	Weaver rail	49.90
Mauser 91/93/95/96 Small Ring	No	Weaver rail	49.90
Remington 700, 740, 742, 760	No	Weaver rail	49.90
Remington 7400, 7600	No	Weaver rail	49.90
Remington Seven	No	Weaver rail	49.90
Rossi 22 Pump	No	Weaver rail	44.95
Ruger Mini-14	W&E	Weaver rail	64.95
Ruger 96/22	No	Weaver rail	49.90
Ruger M77 (short and long)	No	Weaver rail	69.96
Ruger 10/22 (reg. and See-Thru)	No	Weaver rail	49.90
Savage 110-116, 10-16	No	Weaver rail	49.90
Modern Military (rings incl.)			
AK-47/MAC 90	No	Weaver rail	64.95
Colt AR-15 (Flat Top)[1]	No	Weaver rail	74.95
FN/FAL/LAR (See-Thru rings)	No	Weaver rail	99.95

ACCESSORIES

SCOPE RINGS & BASES

Maker, Model, Type	Adjust.	Scopes	Price
B-SQUARE (cont.)			
Classic Military (rings incl.)			
FN 49	No	Weaver rail	69.95
Hakim	No	Weaver rail	69.95
B-SQUARE (cont.)			
Mauser 38, 94, 96, 98	E only	Weaver rail	64.95
Mosin-Nagant 91	E only	Weaver rail	64.95
Air Rifles			
RWS, Diana, BSA, Gamo	W&E	11mm rail	44.95
Weihrauch, Anschutz, Beeman, Webley	W&E	11mm rail	54.95
Shotguns/Slug Guns			
Benelli Super 90 (See-Thru)	No	Weaver rail	49.95
Browning BPS, A-5 9 (See-Thru)	No	Weaver rail	49.95
Browning Gold 10/12/20-ga. (See-Thru)	No	Weaver rail	49.95
Ithaca 37, 87	No	Weaver rail	49.95
Mossberg 500/Mav. 88	No	Weaver rail	49.95
Mossberg 835/Mav. 91	No	Weaver rail	49.95
Remington 870/1100/11-87	No	Weaver rail	49.95
Remington SP10	No	Weaver rail	49.95
Winchester 1200-1500	No	Weaver rail	49.95

[1]Handle mount (see-Through) $64.95. Prices shown for anodized black finish; add $10 for stainless finish. Partial listing of mounts shown here. Contact B-Square for complete listing and details.

BEEMAN			
Two-Piece, Med.	No	1"	31.50
Deluxe Two-Piece, High	No	1"	33.00
Deluxe Two-Piece	No	30mm	41.00
Deluxe One-Piece	No	1"	50.00
Dampa Mount	No	1"	120.00

All grooved receivers and scope bases on all known air rifles and 22-cal. rimfire rifles (1/2" to 5/8"—6mm to 15mm).

BOCK			
Swing ALK[1]	W&E	1", 26mm, 30mm	349.00
Safari KEMEL[2]	W&E	1", 26mm, 30mm	149.00
Claw KEMKA[3]	W&E	1", 26mm, 30mm	224.00
ProHunter Fixed[4]	No	1", 26mm, 30mm	95.00

[1]Q.D.: pivots right for removal. For Steyr-Mannlicher, Win. 70, Rem. 700, Mauser 98, Dakota, Sako, Sauer 80, 90. Magnum has extra-wide rings, same price. [2]Heavy-duty claw-type reversible for front or rear removal. For Steyr-Mannlicher rifles. [3]True claw mount for bolt-action rifles. Also in extended model. For Steyr-Mannlicher, Win. 70, Rem. 700. Also avail. as Gunsmith Bases—bases not drilled or contoured—same price. [4]Extra-wide rings. Imported from Germany by GSI, Inc.

BURRIS			
Supreme (SU) One-Piece (T)[1]	W only	1" split rings, 3 heights	1-piece base - 23.00-27.00
Trumount (TU) Two-Piece (T)	W only	1" split rings, 3 heights	2-piece base - 21.00-30.00
Trumount (TU) Two-Piece Ext.	W only	1" split rings	26.00
Browning 22-cal. Auto Mount[2]	No	1" split rings	20.00
1" 22-cal. Ring Mounts[3]	No	1" split rings	1" rings - 24.00-41.00
L.E.R. (LU) Mount Bases[4]	W only	1" split rings	24.00-52.00
L.E.R. No Drill-No Tap Bases[4,7,8]	W only	1" split rings	48.00-52.00
Extension Rings[5]	No	1" scopes	28.00-46.00
Ruger Ring Mount[6,9]	W only	1" split rings	50.00-68.00
Std. 1" Rings[9]	—	Low, medium, high heights	29.00-43.00
Zee Rings[9]	—	Fit Weaver bases; medium and high heights	29.00-44.00
Signature Rings	No	30mm split rings	68.00
Rimfire/Airgun Rings	W only	1" split rings, med. & high	24.00-41.00
Double Dovetail (DD) Bases	No	30mm Signature	23.00-26.00

[1]Most popular rifles. Universal rings, mounts fit Burris, Universal, Redfield, Leupold and Browning bases. Comparable prices. [2]Browning Standard 22 Auto rifle. [3]Grooved receivers. [4]Universal dovetail; accepts Burris, Universal, Redfield, Leupold rings. For Dan Wesson, S&W, Virginian, Ruger Blackhawk, Win. 94. [5]Medium standard front, extension rear, per pair. Low standard front, extension rear per pair. [6]Compact scopes, scopes with 2" bell for M77R. [7]Selected rings and bases available with matte Safari or silver finish. [8]For S&W K, L, N frames, Colt Python, Dan Wesson with 6" or longer barrels. [9]Also in 30mm.

CATCO			
Enfield Drop-In	No	1"	39.95

Uses Weaver-style rings (not incl.). No gunsmithing required. See-Thru design. From CATCO.

Maker, Model, Type	Adjust.	Scopes	Price
CLEAR VIEW			
Universal Rings, Mod. 101[1]	No	1" split rings	21.95
Standard Model[2]	No	1" split rings	21.95
Broad View[3]	No	1"	21.95
22 Model[4]	No	3/4", 7/8", 1"	13.95
SM-94 Winchester[5]	No	1" split rings	23.95
94 EJ[6]	No	1" split rings	21.95

[1]Most rifles by using Weaver-type base; allows use of iron sights. [2]Most popular rifles; allows use of iron sights. [3]Most popular rifles; low profile, wide field of view. [4]22 rifles with grooved receiver. [5]Side mount. [6]For Win. A.E. From Clear View Mfg.

CONETROL			
Huntur[1]	W only	1", split rings, 3 heights	99.96
Gunnur[2]	W only	1", split rings, 3 heights	119.88
Custom[3]	W only	1", split rings, 3 heights	149.88
One-Piece Side Mount Base[4]	W only	1", 26mm, 26.5mm solid or split rings, 3 heights	NA
DapTar Bases[5]	W only	1", 26mm, 26.5mm solid or split rings, 3 heights	NA
Pistol Bases, 2-or 3-ring[6]	W only	—	NA
Fluted Bases[7]	W only	Standard Conetrol rings	119.88
Metric Rings[8]	W only	26mm, 26.5mm, 30mm	99.96-149.88

[1]All popular rifles, including metric-drilled foreign guns. Price shown for base, two rings. Matte finish. [2]Gunnur grade has mirror-finished rings to match scopes. Satin-finish base to match guns. Price shown for base, two rings. [3]Custom grade has mirror-finished rings and mirror-finished, streamlined base. Price shown for base, two rings. [4]Win. 94, Krag, older split-bridge Mannlicher-Schoenauer, Mini-14, etc. Prices same as above. [5]For all popular guns with integral mounting provision, including Sako. BSA Ithacagun, Ruger, Tikka, H&K, BRNO—$39.96-$59.94—and many others. Also for grooved-receiver rimfires and air rifles. Prices same as above. [6]For XP-100, T/C Contender, Colt SAA, Ruger Blackhawk, S&W and others. [7]Sculptured two-piece bases as found on fine custom rifles. Price shown is for base alone. Also available unfinished—$79.92, or finished but unblued—$99.96. [8]26mm, 26.5mm, and 30mm rings made in projectionless style, in three heights. Three-ring mount for T/C Contender and other pistols in Conetrol's three grades. Any Conetrol mount available in stainless or Teflon for double regular cost of grade.

CUSTOM QUALITY			
Custom See-Thru	No	Up to 44mm	29.95
Dovetail 101-1 See-Thru	No	1"	29.95
Removable Rings	No	1"	29.95
Solid Dovetail	No	1", 30mm vertically split	29.95
Dovetail 22 See-Thru	No	1"	29.95

Mounts for many popular rifles. From Custom Quality Products, Inc.

EAW			
Quick-Loc Mount	W&E	1", 26mm	253.00
	W&E	30mm	271.00
Magnum Fixed Mount	W&E	1", 26mm	198.00
	W&E	30mm	215.00

Fit most popular rifles. Avail. in 4 heights, 4 extensions. Reliable return to zero. Stress-free mounting. Imported by New England Custom Gun Svc.

EXCEL INDUSTRIES, INC.			
Titanium Weaver-Style Rings	No	1" and 30mm, low and high	179.00
Steel Weaver-Style Rings	No	1" and 30mm, low and high	149.00
Flashlight Mounts - Titanium and Steel	No	1" and 30mm, low and high	89.50/75.00

GENTRY			
Feather-Light Rings and Bases	No	1", 30mm	90.00-125.00

Bases for Rem. Seven, 700, Mauser 98, Browning A-Bolt, Weatherby Mk. V, Win. 70, HVA, Dakota. Two-piece base for Rem. Seven, chrome moly or stainless. Rings in matte or regular blue, or stainless gray; four heights. From David Gentry.

GRIFFIN & HOWE			
Topmount[1]	No	1", 30mm	625.00
Sidemount[2]	No	1", 30mm	255.00
Garand Mount[3]	No	1"	255.00

[1]Quick-detachable, double-lever mount with 1" rings, installed; with 30mm rings $875.00. [2]Quick-detachable, double-lever mount with 1" rings; with 30mm rings $375.00; installed, 1" rings. $405.00; installed, 30mm rings $525.00. [3]Price installed, with 1" rings $405.00. From Griffin & Howe.

ACCESSORIES

G. G. & G.

Maker, Model, Type	Adjust.	Scopes	Price
Remington 700 Rail	No	Weaver base	135.00
Sniper Grade Rings	No	30mm	159.95
M16/AR15 F.I.R.E. Std.[1]	No	Weaver rail	75.00
M16/AR15 F.I.R.E. Scout	No	Weaver rail	82.95
Aimpoint Standard Ring	No	—	164.95
Aimpoint Cantilever Ring	No	Weaver rail	212.95

[1]For M16/A3, AR15 flat top receivers; also in extended length. [2]For Aimpoint 5000 and Comp; quick detachable; spare battery compartment. [3]Low profile; quick release. From G. G. & G.

IRONSIGHTER

Maker, Model, Type	Adjust.	Scopes	Price
Ironsighter See-Through Mounts[1]	No	1" split rings	29.40-64.20
Ironsighter S-94	No	1" split rings	45.28
Ironsighter AR-15/M-16[8]	No	1", 30mm	70.10
Ironsighter 22-Cal.Rimfire[2]	No	1"	18.45
Model #570[9]	No	1" split rings	29.40
Model #573[9]	No	30mm split rings	45.28
Model #727[3]	No	.875" split rings	18.45
Blackpowder Mount[7]	No	—	34.20-78.25

[1]Most popular rifles. Rings have oval holes to permit use of iron sights. [2]For 1" dia. scopes. [3]For .875 dia. scopes. [4]For 1" dia. extended eye relief scopes. [6]732—Ruger 77/22 R&RS, No. 1, Ranch Rifle; 778 fits Ruger 77R, RS. Both 733, 778 fit Ruger Integral bases. [7/8]Fits most popular blackpowder rifles; two-piece (CVA, Knight, Marlin and Austin & Halleck) and one-piece integral (T/C). [8]Model 716 with 1" #540 rings; Model 717 with 30mm #530 rings. [9]Fits Weaver-style bases. Some models in stainless finish. From Ironsighter Co.

K MOUNT By KENPATABLE

Maker, Model, Type	Adjust.	Scopes	Price
Shotgun Mount	No	1", laser or red dot device	49.95
SKS[1]	No	1"	39.95

Wrap-around design; no gunsmithing required. Models for Browning BPS, A-5 12-ga., Sweet 16, 20, Rem. 870/1100 (LTW, and L.H.), S&W 916, Mossberg 500, Ithaca 37 & 51 12-ga., S&W 1000/3000, Win. 1400. [1]Requires simple modification to gun. From KenPatable Ent.

KRIS MOUNTS

Maker, Model, Type	Adjust.	Scopes	Price
Side-Saddle[1]	No	1",26mm split rings	12.98
Two-Piece (T)[2]	No	1", 26mm split rings	8.98
One Piece (T)[3]	No	1", 26mm split rings	12.98

[1]One-piece mount for Win. 94. [2]Most popular rifles and Ruger. [3]Blackhawk revolver. Mounts have oval hole to permit use of iron sights.

KWIK-SITE

Maker, Model, Type	Adjust.	Scopes	Price
KS-See-Thru[1]	No	1"	27.95-57.95
AA-22 See-Thru[2]	No	1"	21.95
KS-W94[3]	No	1"	42.95
KS-WEV (Weaver-style rings)	No	1"	19.95
KS-WEV-HIGH	No	1"	19.95
KS-T22 1"[4]	No	1"	17.95
KS-FL Flashlite[5]	No	Mini or C cell flashlight	37.95
KS-T88[6]	No	1"	21.95
KS-T89	No	30mm	21.95
KSN 22 See-Thru	No	1", 7/8"	17.95
KSN-T22	No	1", 7/8"	17.95
KSN-M-16 See-Thru (for M16 + AR-15)	No	1"	49.95
KS-202[1]	No	1"	27.97
KS-203	No	30mm	42.95
KSBP[7]	No	Integral	76.95
KSB Base Set	—	—	5.95
Combo Bases & Rings	No	1"	21.95

Bases interchangeable with Weaver bases. [1]Most rifles. Allows use of iron sights. [2]22-cal. rifles with grooved receivers. Allows use of iron sights. [3]Model 94, 94 Big Bore. No drilling or tapping. Also in adjustable model $57.95. [4]Non-See-Thru model for grooved receivers. [5]Allows C-cell or, Mini Mag Lites to be mounted atop See-Thru mounts. [6]Fits any Redfield, Tasco, Weaver or Universal-style Kwik-Site dovetail base. [7]Blackpowder mount with integral rings and sights. [8]Shotgun side mount. Bright blue, black matte or satin finish. Standard, high heights.

LASER AIM

Maker, Model, Type	Adjust.	Scopes	Price
	No	Laser Aim	19.99-69.00

Mounts Laser Aim above or below barrel. Avail. for most popular handguns, rifles, shotguns, including militaries. From Laser Aim Technologies, Inc.

LEUPOLD

Maker, Model, Type	Adjust.	Scopes	Price
STD Bases[1]	W only	One- or two-piece bases	24.60
STD Rings[2]	—	1" super low, low, medium, high	32.40
DD RBH Handgun Mounts[2]	No	—	59.40
Dual Dovetail Bases[3]	No	—	24.60
Dual Dovetail Rings[8]	—	1", low, med, high	32.40
Ring Mounts[4,5,6]	No	7/8", 1"	81.00
22 Rimfire[8]	No	7/8", 1"	60.00

LEOPOLD (cont.)

Maker, Model, Type	Adjust.	Scopes	Price
Gunmaker Base[7]	W only	1"	16.50
Quick Release Rings	—	1", low, med., high	33.00-71.00
Quick Release Bases[9]	No	1", one- or two-piece	71.40

[1]Base and two rings; Casull, Ruger, S&W, T/C; add $5.00 for silver finish. [2]Rem. 700, Win. 70-type actions. For Ruger No. 1, 77, 77/22; interchangeable with Ruger units. For dovetailed rimfire rifles. Sako; high, medium, low. [7]Must be drilled, tapped for each action. [8]13mm dovetail receiver. [9]BSA Monarch, Rem. 40x, 700, 721, 725, Ruger M77, S&W 1500, Weatherby Mark V, Vanguard, Win. M70.

MARLIN

Maker, Model, Type	Adjust.	Scopes	Price
One-Piece QD (T)	No	1" split rings	10.10

Most Marlin lever actions.

MILLETT

Maker, Model, Type	Adjust.	Scopes	Price
Black Onyx Smooth	—	1", low, medium, high	31.15
Chaparral Engraved	—	engraved	46.15
One-Piece Bases[6]	Yes	1"	23.95
Universal Two-Piece Bases			
700 Series	W only	Two-piece bases	25.15
FN Series	W only	Two-piece bases	25.15
70 Series[1]	W only	1", two-piece bases	25.15
Angle-Loc Rings[2]	W only	1", low, medium, high	32.20-47.20
Ruger 77 Rings[3]	—	1"	47.20
Shotgun Rings[4]	—	1"	28.29
Handgun Bases, Rings[5]	—	1"	34.60-69.15
30mm Rings[7]	—	30mm	37.75-42.95
Extension Rings[8]	—	1"	35.65
See-Thru Mounts[9]	No	1"	27.95-32.95
Shotgun Mounts[10]	No	1"	49.95
Timber Mount	No	1"	78.00

BRNO, Rem. 40x, 700, 722, 725, 7400 Ruger 77 (round top), Marlin, Weatherby, FN Mauser, FN Brownings, Colt 57, Interarms Mark X, Parker-Hale, Savage 110, Sako (round receiver), many others. [1]Fits Win. M70 70XTR, 670, Browning BBR, BAR, BLR, A-Bolt, Rem. 7400/7600, Four, Six, Marlin 336, Win. 94 A. E., Sav. 110. [2]To fit Weaver-type bases. [3]Engraved. Smooth $34.60. [4]For Rem. 870, 1100; smooth. [5]Two- and three-ring sets for Colt Python, Trooper, Diamondback, Peacekeeper, Dan Wesson, Ruger Redhawk, Super Redhawk. [6]Turn-in bases and Weaver-style for most popular rifles and T/C Contender, XP-100 pistols. [7]Both Weaver and turn-in styles; three heights. [8]Med. or high; ext. front—std. rear, ext. rear—std. front, ext. front—ext. rear; $40.90 for double extension. [9]Many popular rifles, Knight MK-85, T/C Hawken, Renegade, Mossberg 500 Slugster, 835 slug. [10]For Rem. 879/1100, Win. 1200, 1300/1400, 1500, Mossberg 500. Some models available in nickel at extra cost. [11]For T/C Hawken and Renegade; See-Thru with adj. open sight inside. From Millett Sights.

MMC

Maker, Model, Type	Adjust.	Scopes	Price
AK[1]	No	—	39.95
FN FAL/LAR[2]	No	—	59.95

[1]Fits all AK derivative receivers; Weaver-style base; low-profile scope position. [2]Fits all FAL versions; Weaver-style base. From MMC.

RAM-LINE

Maker, Model, Type	Adjust.	Scopes	Price
Mini-14 Mount	Yes	1"	24.97

No drilling or tapping. Uses std. dovetail rings. Has built-in shell deflector. Made of solid black polymer. From Ram-Line, Inc.

REDFIELD

Maker, Model, Type	Adjust.	Scopes	Price
JR-SR (T)[1]. One/two-piece bases.	W only	3/4", 1", 26mm, 30mm	JR-15.99-46.99 SR-15.99-33.49
Ring (T)[2]	No	3/4" and 1"	27.95-29.95
Widefield See-Thru Mounts	No	1"	15.95
Ruger Rings[4]	No	1", med., high	30.49-36.49
Ruger 30mm[5]	No	1"	37.99-40.99
Midline Ext. Rings	No	1"	24.95

[1]Low, med. & high, split rings. Reversible extension front rings for 1". 2-piece bases for Sako. Colt Sauer bases $39.95. Med. Top Access JR rings nickel-plated, $28.95. SR two-piece ABN mount nickel-plated $22.95. [2]Split rings for grooved 22s; 30mm, black matte $42.95. [3]Used with MP scopes for; S&W K, L or N frame, XP-100, T/C Contender, Ruger receivers. [4]For Ruger Model 77 rifles, medium and high; medium only for M77/22. [5]For Model 77. Also in matte finish $45.95. [6]Aluminun 22 groove mount $14.95; base and medium rings $18.95. [7]Fits American or Weaver-style base. Non-Gunsmithing mount system. For many popular shotguns, rifles, handguns and blackpowder rifles. Uses existing screw holes.

S&K

Maker, Model, Type	Adjust.	Scopes	Price
Insta-Mount (T) Bases and Rings[1]	W only	Uses S&K rings only	47.00-117.00
Conventional Rings and Bases[2]	W only	1" split rings	From 65.00
Sculptured Bases, Rings[2]	W only	1", 26mm, 30mm	From 65.00
Smooth Contoured Rings[3]	Yes	1", 26mm, 30mm	90.00-120.00

[1]1903, A3, M1 Carbine, Lee Enfield #1. Mk.III, #4, #5, M1917, M98 Mauser, AR-15, AR-180, M-14, M-1, Ger. K-43, Mini-14, M1-A, Krag, AKM, Win. 94, SKS Type 56, Daewoo, H&K. [2]Most popular rifles already drilled and tapped and Sako, Tikka dovetails. [3]No projections; weigh 1/2-oz. each; matte or gloss finish. Horizontally and vertically split rings, matte or high gloss.

SCOPE RINGS & BASES

Maker, Model, Type	Adjust.	Scopes	Price
SAKO			
QD Dovetail	W only	1"	70.00-155.00
Sako, or any rifle using Sako action, 3 heights available. Stoeger, importer.			
SPRINGFIELD, INC.			
M1A Third Generation	No	1" or 30mm	123.00
M1A Standard	N0	1" or 30mm	77.00
M6 Scout Mount	No	—	29.00
Weaver-style bases. From Springfield, Inc.			
TALBOT			
QD Bases	No	—	180.00-190.00
Rings	No	1", 30mm	50.00-70.00
Blue or stainless steel; standard or extended bases; rings in three heights. For most popular rifles. From Talbot QD Mounts.			
TASCO			
World Class			
Aluminum Ringsets	Yes	1", 30mm	12.00-17.00
See-Thru	No	1"	19.00
Shotgun Bases	Yes		34.00
From Tasco.			
THOMPSON/CENTER			
Duo-Ring Mount[1]	No	1"	61.99-62.99
Weaver-Style Bases	No	—	10.28-33.36
Weaver-Style Rings[3]	No	1"	27.74-42.13
Weaver-Style See-Thru Rings[4]	No	1"	27.74
[1]Attaches directly to T/C Contender bbl., no drilling/tapping; also for T/C M/L rifles, needs base adapter; blue or stainless. [3]Medium and high; blue or silver finish. [4]For T.C FireHawk, ThunderHawk; blue; silver **$29.80**. From Thompson/Center.			
UNERTL			
1/4 Click[1]	Yes	3/4", 1" target scopes	Per set 186.00
[1]Unertl target or varmint scopes. Posa or standard mounts, less bases. From Unertl.			
WARNE			
Premier Series (all steel)			
T.P.A. (Permanently Attached)	No	1", 4 heights	87.75
		30mm, 2 heights	98.55
Sako	No	1", 4 heights	87.75
		30mm, 3 heights	98.55
Premier Series Rings fit Premier Series Bases			
Premier Series (all-steel Q.D. rings)			
Premier Series (all-steel)	No	1", 4 heights	125.00
Quick detachable lever		26mm, 2 heights	129.95
		30mm, 3 heights	136.70
BRNO 19mm	No	1", 3 heights	125.00
		30mm, 2 heights	136.70
BRNO 16mm	No	1", 2 heights	125.00
Ruger	No	1", 4 heights	125.00
		30mm, 3 heights	136.70
Ruger M77	No	1", 3 heights	125.00
		30mm, 2 heights	136.70
Sako Medium & Long Action	No	1", 4 heights	125.00
		30mm, 3 heights	136.70
Sako Short Action	No	1", 3 heights	125.00
All-Steel One-Piece Base, ea.			38.50
All-Steel Two-Piece Base, ea.			14.00
Maxima Series (fits all Weaver-style bases)			
Permanently Attached[1]	No	1", 3 heights	34.55
		30mm, 3 heights	50.00
Adjustable Double Lever[2]	No	1", 3 heights	72.60
		30mm, 3 heights	80.75
Thumb Knob	No	1", 3 heights	59.95
		30mm, 3 heights	68.25
Stainless-Steel Two-Piece Base, ea.			15.25
Vertically split rings with dovetail clamp, precise return to zero. Fit most popular rifles, handguns. Regular blue, matte blue, silver finish. [1]All-Steel, non-Q.D. rings. [2]All-steel, Q.D. rings. From Warne Mfg. Co.			
WEAVER			
Detachable Mounts			
Top Mount	No	7/8", 1", 30mm, 33mm	24.95-38.95
Side Mount	No	1", 1" long	14.95-34.95
Tip-Off Rings	No	7/8", 1"	24.95-32.95
Pivot Mounts	No	1"	38.95
Complete Mount Systems			
Pistol	No	1"	75.00-105.00

Maker, Model, Type	Adjust.	Scopes	Price
WEAVER (cont.)			
Rifle	No	1"	32.95
SKS Mount System	No	1"	49.95
Pro-View (no base required)	No	1"	13.95-15.95
Converta-Mount, 12-ga. (Rem. 870, Moss. 500)	No	1", 30mm	74.95
See-Thru Mounts			
Detachable	No	1"	27.00-32.00
System (no base required)	No	1"	15.00-35.00
Tip-Off	No	1"	15.00
Nearly all modern rifles, pistols, and shotguns. Detachable rings in standard, See-Thru, and extension styles, in Low, Medium, High or X-High heights; gloss (blued), silver and matte finishes to match scopes. Extension rings are only available in 1" High style and See-Thru X-tensions only in gloss finish. Tip-Off rings only for 3/8" grooved receivers or 3/8"grooved adaptor bases; no base required. See-Thru & Pro-View mounts for most modern big bore rifles, some in silver. No Drill & Tap Pistol systems in gloss or silver for: Colt Python, Trooper, 357, Officer's Model; Ruger Single-Six, Security-Six (gloss finish only), Blackhawk, Super Blackhawk, Blackhawk SRM 357, Redhawk, Mini-14 Series (not Ranch), Ruger 22 Auto Pistols, Mark II; Smith & Wesson I- and current K-frames with adj. rear sights. Converta-Mount Systems in Standard and See-Under for: Mossberg 500 (12- and 20-ga.); Remington 870, 11-87 (12- and 20-ga. lightweight); Winchester 1200, 1300, 1400, 1500. Converta Brackets, Bases, Rings also avail. for Beretta A303 and A390; Browning A-5, BPS Pump; Ithaca 37, 87. From Weaver.			
WEIGAND			
Browning Buck Mark[1]	No	—	29.95
Colt 22 Automatic[1]	No	—	19.95
Integra Mounts[2]	No	—	39.95-69.00
S&W Revolver[3]	No	—	29.95
Ruger 10/22[4]	No	—	14.95-39.95
Ruger Revolver[5]	No	—	29.95
Taurus Revolver[4]	No	—	29.95-65.00
T/C Encore Monster Mount	No	—	69.00
T/C Contender Monster Mount	No	—	69.00
Lightweight Rings	No	1", 30mm	29.95-39.95
1911, P-9 Scopemounts			
SM3[6]	No	Weaver rail	99.95
SRS 1911-2[7]	No	30mm	59.95
APCMNT[8]	No	—	69.95
[1]No gunsmithing. [2] S&W K, L, N frames; Taurus vent rib models; Colt Anaconda/Python; Ruger Redhawk; Ruger 10/22. [3]K, L, N frames. [4]Three models. [5] Redhawk, Blackhawk, GP-100. [6]3rd Gen.; drill and tap; without slots **$59.95**. [7]Ringless design, silver only. [8]For Aimpoint Comp. Red Dot scope, silver only. From Weigand Combat Handguns, Inc.			
WIDEVIEW			
Premium 94 Angle Eject and side mount	No	1"	18.70
Premium See-Thru	No	1"	18.70
22 Premium See-Thru	No	3/4", 1"	13.60
Universal Ring Angle Cut	No	1"	18.70
Universal Ring Straight Cut	No	1"	18.70
Solid Mounts			
Lo Ring Solid[1]	No	1"	13.60
Hi Ring Solid[1]	No	1"	13.60
SR Rings	—	1", 30mm	13.60
22 Grooved Receiver	No	1"	13.60
Blackpowder Mounts[2]	No	1"	18.70-37.40
High, extra-high ring mounts with base	No	up to 60mm	18.70
Desert Eagle Pistol Mount	No	1", 30mm	34.95-44.95
[1]For Weaver-type base. Models for many popular rifles. Low ring, high ring and grooved receiver types. [2]No drilling, tapping, for T/C Renegade, Hawken, CVA, Knight Traditions guns. From Wideview Scope Mount Corp.			
WILLIAMS			
Side Mount with HCO Rings[1]	No	1", split or extension rings	74.35
Side Mount, Offset Rings[2]	No	Same	61.45
Sight-Thru Mounts[3]	No	1", 7/8" sleeves	19.50
Streamline Mounts	No	1" (bases form rings)	26.50
[1]Most rifles, Br. S.M.L.E. (round rec.) **$14.41** extra. [2]Most rifles including Win. 94 Big Bore. [3]Many modern rifles, including CVA Apollo, others with 1" octagon barrels.			
YORK			
M-1 Garand	Yes	1"	39.95
Centers scope over the action. No drilling, tapping or gunsmithing. Uses standard dovetail rings. From York M-1 Conversions.			

NOTES

(S)—Side Mount; (T)—Top Mount; 22mm=.866"; 25.4mm=1.024"; 26.5mm=1.045"; 30mm=1.81".

ACCESSORIES

METALLIC SIGHTS

Sporting Leaf and Open Sights

ERA EXPRESS SIGHTS A wide variety of open sights and bases for custom installation. Partial listing shown. From New England Custom Gun Service.
Price: One-leaf express **$66.00**
Price: Two-leaf express **$71.50**
Price: Three-leaf express **$77.00**
Price: Bases for above **$27.50**
Price: Standing rear sight, straight **$13.25**
Price: Base for above **$16.50**
ERA PROFESSIONAL EXPRESS SIGHTS Standing or folding leaf sights are securely locked to the base with the ERA Magnum Clamp, but can be loosened for sighting in. Base can be attached with two socket-head cap screws or soldered. Finished and blued. Barrel diameters from .600" to .930".
Price: Standing leaf **$54.00**
Price: One-leaf express **$96.00**
Price: Two-leaf express **$101.00**
Price: Three-leaf express **$109.00**
ERA MASTERPIECE REAR SIGHT Adjustable for windage and elevation, adjusted and locked with a small screwdriver. Comes with 8-36 socket-head cap screw and wrench. Barrel diameters from .600" to .930".
Price: **$75.00**
G.G. & G. SAME PLANE APERTURE M-16/AR-15 A2-style dual aperture rear sight with both large and small apertures centered on the same plane.
Price: **$45.00**

Williams Ruger Fire Sight

LYMAN No.16 Middle sight for barrel dovetail slot mounting. Folds flat when scope or peep sight is used. Sight notch plate adjustable for elevation. White triangle for quick aiming. 3 heights: A-.400" to.500", B-.345" to .445", C-.500" to .600".
Price: **$12.25**
MARBLE FALSE BASE #76, #77, #78 New screw-on base for most rifles replaces factory base. 3/8" dovetail slot permits installation of any folding rear sight. Can be had in sweat-on models also.
Price: **$8.00**
MARBLE FOLDING LEAF Flat-top or semi-buckhorn style. Folds down when scope or peep sights are used. Reversible plate gives choice of "U" or "V" notch. Adjustable for elevation.
Price: **$16.00**
Price: Also available with both windage and elevation adjustment **$18.00**
MARBLE SPORTING REAR With white enamel diamond, gives choice of two "U" and two "V" notches or different sizes. Adjustment in height by means of double step elevator and sliding notch piece. For all rifles; screw or dovetail installation.
Price: . . . . **$16.00-$17.00**
MARBLE #20 UNIVERSAL New screw or sweat-on base. Both have .100" elevation adjustment. In five base sizes. Three styles of U-notch, square notch, peep. Adjustable for windage and elevation.
Price: Screw-on **$23.00**
Price: Sweat-on **$21.00**
MILLETT SPORTING & BLACKPOWDER RIFLE Open click adjustable rear fits 3/8" dovetail cut in barrel. Choice of white outline, target black or open express V rear blades. Also available is a replacement screw-on sight with express V, .562" hole centers. Dovetail fronts in white or blaze orange in seven heights (.157"-.540").
Price: Dovetail or screw-on rear **$55.60**
Price: Front sight **$12.34**
MILLETT SCOPE-SITE Open, adjustable or fixed rear sights dovetail into a base integral with the top scope-mounting ring. Blaze orange front ramp sight is integral with the front ring half. Rear sights have white outline aperture. Provides fast, short-radius, Patridge-type open sights on the top of the scope. Can be used with all Millett rings, Weaver-style bases, Ruger 77 (also fits Redhawk), Ruger Ranch Rifle, No. 1, No. 3, Rem. 870, 1100; Burris, Leupold and Redfield bases.
Price: Scope-Site top only, windage only **$31.15**
Price: As above, fully adjustable **$66.10**
Price: Scope-Site Hi-Turret, fully adjustable, low, medium, high **$66.10**
WICHITA MULTI RANGE SIGHT SYSTEM Designed for silhouette shooting. System allows you to adjust the rear sight to four repeatable range settings, once it is pre-set. Sight clicks to any of the settings by turning a serrated wheel. Front sight is adjustable for weather and light conditions with one adjustment. Specify gun when ordering.
Price: Rear sight **$120.00**
Price: Front sight **$90.00**
WILLIAMS DOVETAIL OPEN SIGHT (WDOS) Open rear sight with windage and elevation adjustment. Furnished with "U" notch or choice of blades. Slips into dovetail and locks with gib lock. Heights from .281" to .531".
Price: With blade **$15.86**
Price: Less Blade **$9.92**

WILLIAMS GUIDE OPEN SIGHT (WGOS) Open rear sight with windage and elevation adjustment. Bases to fit most military and commercial barrels. Choice of square "U" or "V" notch blade, 3/16", 1/4", 5/16", or 3/8" high.
Price: Less blade **$16.34**
Price: Extra blades, each **$6.37**
WILLIAMS WGOS OCTAGON Open rear sight for 1" octagon barrels. Installs with two 6-48 screws and uses same hole spacing as most T/C muzzleloading rifles. Four heights, choice of square, U, V, B blade.
Price: **$21.80**
WILLIAMS WSKS, WAK47 Replaces original military-type rear sight. Adjustable for windage and elevation. No drilling or tapping. Peep aperture or open. For SKS carbines, AK-47.
Price: Aperture **$24.67**
Price: Open **$22.61**
WILLIAMS WM-96 Fits Mauser 96-type military rifles, replaces original rear sight with open blade or aperture. Fully adjustable for windage and elevation. No drilling; tapping.
Price: Aperture **$24.67**
Price: Open **$22.61**
WILLIAMS FIRE RIFLE SETS Replacement front and rear fiber optic sights, red bead front, two green elements in the fully adjustable rear. Made of CNC-machined metal.
Price: For Ruger 10/22 . . . . **$34.95**
Price: For most Marlin and Win. (3/8" dovetail) **$29.95**
Price: For Remington (newer style sight base) **$24.95**

Aperture and Micrometer Receiver Sights

Ashley Ghost Ring

ASHLEY GHOST RING HUNTING SIGHT Fully adjustable for windage and elevation. Available for most rifles, including blackpowder guns. Minimum gunsmithing required for most installations; matches most mounting holes. From Ashley Outdoors, Inc.
Price: **$60.00**
Price: White Stripe front post **$30.00**
ASHLEY AR-15/M-16 APERTURE Drop-in replacement of factory sights. Both apertures are on the same plane. Large ghost ring has .230" inside diameter; small ghost ring has .100" inside diameter. From Ashley Outdoors, Inc.
Price: **$30.00**
BEEMAN/FEINWERKBAU 5454 MATCH APERTURE SIGHT Small size, new-design sight uses constant-pressure flat springs to eliminate point of impact shifts.
Price: **$350.00**
BEEMAN SPORT APERTURE SIGHT Positive click micrometer adjustments. Standard units with flush surface screwdriver adjustments. Deluxe version has target knobs. For air rifles with grooved receivers.
Price: Standard **$40.00**
Price: Deluxe **$50.00**

Williams Fire Sight Peep Set

EAW RECEIVER SIGHT A fully adjustable aperture sight that locks securely into the EAW quick-detachable scope mount rear base. Made by New England Custom Gun Service.
Price: **$95.00**
G.G.&G. MAD IRIS Multiple Aperture Device is a four sight, rotatins aperture disk with small and large apertures on the same plane. Mounts on M-16/AR-15 flat top receiver. Fully adjustable.
Price: **$129.00**
Price: A2 IRIS, two apertures, full windage adjustments **$120.00**

METALLIC SIGHTS

LYMAN NO. 2 TANG SIGHT Designed for the Winchester Model 94. Has high index marks on aperture post; comes with both .093″ quick sighting aperture, .040″ large disk aperture, and replacement mounting screws.
Price: $69.95
Price: For Marlin lever actions $71.56

Lyman No. 57 GPR

LYMAN No. 57 1/4-minute clicks. Stayset knobs. Quick release slide, adjustable zero scales. Made for almost all modern rifles.
Price:...$62.50
Price: No. 57SME, 57SMET (for White Systems Model 91 and Whitetail rifles) $62.50
LYMAN 57GPR Designed especially for the Lyman Great Plains Rifle. Mounts directly onto the tang of the rifle and has 1/4-minute micrometer click adjustments.
Price:...$62.50
LYMAN No. 66 Fits close to the rear of flat-sided receivers, furnished with Stayset knobs. Quick release slide, 1/4-min. adjustments. For most lever or slide action or flat-sided automatic rifles.
Price:...$62.50
Price: No. 66MK (for all current versions of the Knight MK-85 in-line rifle with flat-sided receiver) $62.50
Price: No. 66 SKS fits Russian and Chinese SKS rifles; large and small apertures $62.50
LYMAN No. 66U Light weight, designed for most modern shotguns with a flat-sided, round-top receiver. 1/4-minute clicks. Requires drilling, tapping. Not for Browning A-5, Rem. M11.
Price: $71.50
LYMAN 90MJT RECEIVER SIGHT Mounts on standard Lyman and Williams FP bases. Has 1/4-minute audible micrometer click adjustments, target knobs with direction indicators. Adjustable zero scales, quick release slide. Large 7/8″ diameter aperture disk.
Price: Right- or left-hand $72.50
MARBLE PEEP TANG SIGHT All-steel construction. Micrometer-like click adjustments for windage and elevation. For most popular old and new lever-action rifles.
Price: $125.00
MILLETT PEEP RIFLE SIGHTS Fully adjustable, heat-treated nickel steel peep aperture receiver sight for the Mini-14. Has fine windage and elevation adjustments; replaces original.
Price: Rear sight, Mini-14 ....$49.00
Price: Front sight, Mini-14 ....$18.75
Price: Front and rear combo with hood......................$64.00
WILLIAMS FIRE SIGHT PEEP SETS Combines the Fire Sight front bead with Williams fully adjustable metallic peep rear.
Price: For SKS $39.95
Price: For Ruger 10/22 ....$39.95
Price: For Marlin or Winchester lever actions $73.95
WILLIAMS FP Internal click adjustments. Positive locks. For virtually all rifles, T/C Contender, Heckler & Koch HK-91, Ruger Mini-14, plus Win., Rem. and Ithaca shotguns.
Price: From $59.95
Price: With Target Knobs $71.20
Price: With Square Notched Blade $63.03
Price: With Target Knobs & Square Notched Blade $74.45
Price: FP-GR (for dovetail-grooved receivers, 22s and air guns) $59.95
Price: FP-94BBSE (for Win. 94 Big Bore A.E.; uses top rear scope mount holes)..$59.95
WILLIAMS TARGET FP Similar to the FP series but developed for most bolt-action rimfire rifles. Target FP High adjustable from 1.250″ to 1.750″ above centerline of bore; Target FP Low adjustable from .750″ to 1.250″. Attaching bases for Rem. 540X, 541-S, 580, 581, 582 (#540); Rem. 510, 511, 512, 513-T, 521-T (#510); Win. 75 (#75); Savage/Anschutz 64 and Mark 12 (#64). Some rifles require drilling, tapping.
Price: High or Low..$77.15
Price: Base only $12.98
Price: FP-T/C Scout rifle, from $59.95
Price: FP-94BBSE (for Win. 94 Big Bore A.E.; uses top rear scope mount holes)..$59.95
WILLIAMS 5-D SIGHT Low cost sight for shotguns, 22s and the more popular big game rifles. Adjustment for windage and elevation. Fits most guns without drilling and tapping. Also for British SMLE, Winchester M94 Side Eject.
Price: From $31.47
Price: With Shotgun Aperture $31.47
WILLIAMS GUIDE (WGRS) Receiver sight for 30 M1 Carbine, M1903A3 Springfield, Savage 24s, Savage-Anschutz and Weatherby XXII. Utilizes military dovetail; no drilling. Double-dovetail windage adjustment, sliding dovetail adjustment for elevation.
Price:...$30.85
Price: WGRS-CVA (for rifles with octagon barrels, receivers) $30.85

Front Sights

ASHLEY AR-15/M-16 FRONT SIGHTS Drop-in replacement sight post. Double faced so it can be rotated 180 degrees for 2.5 MOA elevation adjustment. Available in .080″ width with .030″ white stripe, or .100″ with .040″ stripe. From Ashley Outdoors, Inc.
Price: $30.00
Price: Tritium Dot Express $60.00
ERA FRONT SIGHTS European-type front sights inserted from the front. Various heights available. From New England Custom Gun Service.
Price: 1/16″ silver bead...................................$11.50
Price: 3/32″ silver bead...................................$16.00
Price: Sourdough bead $14.50
Price: Tritium night sight $44.00
Price: Folding night sight with ivory bead $39.50
LYMAN HUNTING SIGHTS Made with gold or white beads 1/16″ to 3/32″ wide and in varying heights for most military and commercial rifles. Dovetail bases.
Price:..$8.75
MARBLE STANDARD Ivory, red, or gold bead. For all American-made rifles, 1/16″ wide bead with semi-flat face which does not reflect light. Specify type of rifle when ordering.
Price: $10.00
MARBLE CONTOURED Has 3/8″ dovetail base, .090″ deep, is 5/8″ long. Uses standard 1/16″ or 3/32″ bead, ivory, red, or gold. Specify rifle type.
Price: $11.50
WILLIAMS RISER BLOCKS For adding .250″ height to front sights when using a receiver sight. Two widths available: .250″ for Williams Streamlined Ramp or .340″ on all standard ramps having this base width. Uses standard 3/8″ dovetail.
Price: $5.46

Globe Target Front Sights

LYMAN 20 MJT TARGET FRONT Has 7/8″ diameter, one-piece steel globe with 3/8″ dovetail base. Height is .700″ from bottom of dovetail to center of aperture; height on 20 LJT is .750″. Comes with seven Anschutz-size steel inserts—two posts and five apertures .126″ through .177″.
Price: 20 MJT or 20 LJT $31.50
LYMAN No. 17A TARGET Includes seven interchangeable inserts: four apertures, one transparent amber and two posts .50″ and .100″ in width.
Price:...$26.00
Price: Insert set..$9.00

Lyman 17AEU

LYMAN 17AEU Similar to the Lyman 17A except has a special dovetail design to mount easily onto European muzzleloaders such as CVA, Traditions and Investarm. All steel, comes with eight inserts.
Price: $26.00
LYMAN No. 93 MATCH Has 7/8″ diameter, fits any rifle with a standard dovetail mounting block. Comes with seven target inserts and accepts most Anschutz accessories. Hooked locking bolt and nut allows quick removal, installation. Base available in .860″ (European) and .562″ (American) hole spacing.
Price:...$41.25
WILLIAMS TARGET GLOBE FRONT Adapts to many rifles. Mounts to the base with a knurled locking screw. Height is .545″ from center, not including base. Comes with inserts.
Price: $30.85
Price: Dovetail base (low) .220″ $17.00
Price: Dovetail base (high) .465″ $17.00
Price: Screw-on base, .300″ height, .300″ radius $15.45
Price: Screw-on base, .450″ height, .350″ radius $15.45
Price: Screw-on base, .215″ height, .400″ radius $15.45

Ramp Sights

ERA MASTERPIECE Banded ramps; 21 sizes; hand-detachable beads and hood; beads inserted from the front. Various heights available. From New England Custom Gun Service.
Price: Banded ramp $54.00
Price: Hood $10.50

Price: 1/16″ silver bead..$11.50
Price: 3/32″ silver bead..$16.00
Price: Sourdough bead...$14.50
Price: Tritium night sight.......................................$47.00
Price: Folding night sight with ivory bead.......................$39.50
LYMAN NO. 18 SCREW-ON RAMP Used with 8-40 screws but may also be brazed on. Heights from .10″ to .350″. Ramp without sight.
Price:...$13.75
MARBLE FRONT RAMPS Available in polished or dull matte finish or serrated style. Standard 3/8x.090″ dovetail slot. Made for MR-width (.340″) front sights. Can be used as screw-on or sweat-on. Heights: .100″, .150″, .300″.
Price: Polished or matte.......................................$14.00
Price: Serrated...$10.00
WILLIAMS SHORTY RAMP Companion to "Streamlined" ramp, about 1/2″ shorter. Screw-on or sweat-on. It is furnished in 1/8″, 3/16″, 9/32″, and 3/8″ heights without hood only. Also for shotguns.
Price:..$15.90
Price: With dovetail lock.......................................$18.55
WILLIAMS STREAMLINED RAMP Available in screw-on or sweat-on models. Furnished in 9/16″, 7/16″, 3/8″, 5/16″, 3/16″ heights.
Price:..$17.35
Price: Sight hood..$3.95
WILLIAMS STREAMLINED FRONT SIGHTS Narrow (.250″ width) for Williams Streamlined ramps and others with 1/4″ top width; medium (.340″ width) for all standard factory ramps. Available with white, gold or flourescent beads, 1/16″ or 3/32″.
Price:...$8.93 to $9.25

Handgun Sights

ASHLEY EXPRESS SIGHTS Low-profile, snag-free express-type sights. Shallow V rear with white vertical line, white dot front. All-steel, matte black finish. Rear is available in different heights. Made for most pistols, many with double set-screws. From Ashley Outdoors, Inc.
Price: Standard Set, front and rear.............................$60.00
Price: Big Dot Set, front and rear..............................$60.00
Price: Tritium Set, Standard or Big Dot.........................$90.00
BO-MAR DELUXE BMCS Gives 3/8″ windage and elevation adjustment at 50 yards on Colt Gov't 45; sight radius under 7″. For GM and Commander models only. Uses existing dovetail slot. Has shield-type rear blade.
Price:..$65.95
Price: BMCS-2 (for GM and 9mm)..............................$68.95
Price: Flat bottom..$65.95
Price: BMGC (for Colt Gold Cup), angled serrated blade, rear.....$68.95
Price: BMGC front sight.......................................$12.95
Price: BMCZ-75 (for CZ-75,TZ-75, P-9 and most clones). Works with factory front..................................$68.95
BO-MAR FRONT SIGHTS Dovetail style for S&W 4506, 4516, 1076; undercut style (.250″, .280″, 5/16″ high); Fast Draw style (.210″, .250″, .230″ high).
Price $12.95
BO-MAR BMU XP-100/T/C CONTENDER No gunsmithing required; has .080″ notch.
Price:..$77.00
BO-MAR BMML For muzzleloaders; has .062″ notch, flat bottom.
Price:..$65.95
Price: With 3/8″ dovetail.......................................$65.95
BO-MAR RUGER "P" ADJUSTABLE SIGHT Replaces factory front and rear sights.
Price: Rear sight...$65.95
Price: Front sight..$12.00
BO-MAR BMR Fully adjustable rear sight for Ruger MKI, MKII Bull barrel autos.
Price: Rear..$65.95
Price: Undercut front sight.....................................$12.00
BO-MAR GLOCK Fully adjustable, all-steel replacement sights. Sight fits factory dovetail. Longer sight radius. Uses Novak Glock .275″ high, .135″ wide front, or similar.
Price: Rear sight...$68.95
Price: Front sight..$20.95
BO-MAR LOW PROFILE RIB & ACCURACY TUNER Streamlined rib with front and rear sights; 7 1/8″ sight radius. Brings sight line closer to the bore than standard or extended sight and ramp. Weight 5 oz. Made for Colt Gov't 45, Super 38, and Gold Cup 45 and 38.
Price:...$140.00
BO-MAR COMBAT RIB For S&W Model 19 revolver with 4″ barrel. Sight radius 5 3/4″, weight 5 1/2 oz.
Price:...$127.00

Williams Fire Sight Set

BO-MAR WINGED RIB For S&W 4″ and 6″ length barrels—K-38, M10, HB 14 and 19. Weight for the 6″ model is about 7 1/4 oz.
Price:...$140.00
BO-MAR COVER-UP RIB Adjustable rear sight, winged front guards. Fits right over revolver's original front sight. For S&W 4″ M-10HB, M-13, M-58, M-64 & 65, Ruger 4″ models SDA-34, SDA-84, SS-34, SS-84, GF-34, GF-84.
Price:...$130.00
C-MORE SIGHTS Replacement front sight blades offered in two types and five styles. Made of Du Pont Acetal, they come in a set of five high-contrast colors: blue, green, pink, red and yellow. Easy to install. Patridge style for Colt Python (all barrels), Ruger Super Blackhawk (7 1/2″), Ruger Blackhawk (4 5/8″); ramp style for Python (all barrels), Blackhawk (4 5/8″), Super Blackhawk (7 1/2″ and 10 1/2″). From C-More Systems.
Price: Per set..$19.95
G.G. & G. GHOST RINGS Replaces the factory rear sight without gunsmithing. Black phosphate finish. Available for Colt M1911 and Commander, Beretta M92F, Glock, S&W, SIG Sauer.
Price:..$65.00
JP GHOST RING Replacement bead front, ghost rear for Glock and M1911 pistols. From JP Enterprises.
Price:..$79.95
Price: Bo-Mar replacement leaf with JP dovetail front bead.......$99.95
MMC TACTICAL ADJUSTABLE SIGHTS Low-profile, snag free design. Twenty-two click positions for elevation, drift adjustable for windage. Machined from 4140 steel and heat treated to 40 RC. Tritium and non-tritium. Ten different configurations and colors. Three different finishes. For 1911s, all Glock, HK USP, S&W, Browning Hi-Power.
Price: Sight set, tritium......................................$144.92
Price: Sight set, white outline or white dot.....................$99.90
Price: Sight set, black..$93.90
MEPROLIGHT TRITIUM NIGHT SIGHTS Replacement sight assemblies for use in low-light conditions. Available for rifles, shotguns, handguns and bows. **TRU-DOT** models carry a 12-year warranty on the useable illumination, while non-**TRU-DOT** have a 5-year warranty. Contact Hesco, Inc. for complete list of available models.
Price: Kahr K9, K40, fixed, **TRU-DOT**.......................$100.00
Price: Ruger P85, P89, P94, adjustable, **TRU-DOT**...........$156.00
Price: Ruger Mini-14R sights.................................$140.00
Price: SIG Sauer P220, P225, P226, P228, adjustable, **TRU-DOT**....$156.00
Price: Smith&Wesson autos, fixed or adjustable, **TRU-DOT**....$100.00
Price: Taurus PT92, PT100, adjustable, **TRU-DOT**............$156.00
Price: Walther P-99, fixed, **TRU-DOT**.......................$100.00
Price: Shotgun bead...$32.00
Price: Beretta M92, Cougar, Brigadier, fixed, **TRU-DOT**.......$100.00
Price: Browning Hi-Power, adjustable, **TRU-DOT**.............$156.00
Price: Colt M1911 Govt., adjustable, **TRU-DOT**...............$156.00
MILLETT SERIES 100 REAR SIGHTS All-steel highly visible, click adjustable. Blades in white outline, target black, silhouette, 3-dot, and tritium bars. Fit most popular revolvers and autos.
Price:...$49.30 to $80.00
MILLETT BAR-DOT-BAR TRITIUM NIGHT SIGHTS Replacement front and rear combos fit most automatics. Horizontal tritium bars on rear, dot front sight.
Price:...$145.00
MILLETT 3-DOT SYSTEM SIGHTS The 3-Dot System sights use a single white dot on the front blade and two dots flanking the rear notch. Fronts available in Dual-Crimp and Wide Stake-On styles, as well as special applications. Adjustable rear sight available for most popular auto pistols and revolvers.
Price: Front, from...$16.00
Price: Adjustable rear...$55.60
MILLETT REVOLVER FRONT SIGHTS All-steel replacement front sights with either white or orange bar. Easy to install. For Ruger GP-100, Redhawk, Security-Six, Police-Six, Speed-Six, Colt Trooper, Diamondback, King Cobra, Peacemaker, Python, Dan Wesson 22 and 15-2.
Price:...$13.60 to $16.00
MILLETT DUAL-CRIMP FRONT SIGHT Replacement front sight for automatic pistols. Dual-Crimp uses an all-steel two-point hollow rivet system. Available in eight heights and four styles. Has a skirted base that covers the front sight pad. Easily installed with the Millett Installation Tool Set. Available in Blaze Orange Bar, White Bar, Serrated Ramp, Plain Post.
Price:..$16.00
MILLETT STAKE-ON FRONT SIGHT Replacement front sight for automatic pistols. Stake-On sights have skirted base that covers the front sight pad. Easily installed with the Millet Installation Tool Set. Available in seven heights and four styles—Blaze Orange Bar, White Bar, Serrated Ramp, Plain Post.
Price:..$16.00
OMEGA OUTLINE SIGHT BLADES Replacement rear sight blades for Colt and Ruger single action guns and the Interarms Virginian Dragoon. Standard Outline available in gold or white notch outline on blue metal. From Omega Sales, Inc.
Price:...$8.95
OMEGA MAVERICK SIGHT BLADES Replacement "peep-sight" blades for Colt, Ruger SAs, Virginian Dragoon. Three models available—No. 1, Plain; No. 2, Single Bar; No. 3, Double Bar Rangefinder. From Omega Sales, Inc.
Price: Each..$6.95
PACHMAYR ACCU-SET Low-profile, fully adjustable rear sight to be used with existing front sight. Available with target, white outline or 3-dot blade. Blue finish. Uses factory dovetail and locking screw. For Browning, Colt, Glock, SIG Sauer, S&W and Ruger autos. From Pachmayr.
Price:...NA

ACCESSORIES

METALLIC SIGHTS

P-T TRITIUM NIGHT SIGHTS Self-luminous tritium sights for most popular handguns, Colt AR-15, H&K rifles and shotguns. Replacement handgun sight sets available in 3-Dot style (green/green, green/yellow, green/orange) with bold outlines around inserts; Bar-Dot available in green/green with or without white outline rear sight. Functional life exceeds 15 years. From Innovative Weaponry, Inc.
Price: Handgun sight sets..**$99.95**
Price: Rifle sight sets..**$99.95**
Price: Rifle, front only...**$49.95**
Price: Shotgun, front only..**$49.95**
TRIJICON NIGHT SIGHTS Three-dot night sight system uses tritium lamps in the front and rear sights. Tritium "lamps" are mounted in silicone rubber inside a metal cylinder. A polished crystal sapphire provides protection and clarity. Inlaid white outlines provide 3-dot aiming in daylight also. Available for most popular handguns. From Trijicon, Inc.
Price:..**$50.00 to $175.00**

Wichita Series 70/80

WICHITA SERIES 70/80 SIGHT Provides click windage and elevation adjustments with precise repeatability of settings. Sight blade is grooved and angled back at the top to reduce glare. Available in Low Mount Combat or Low Mount Target styles for Colt 45s and their copies, S&W 645, Hi-Power, CZ 75 and others.
Price: Rear sight, target or combat...............................**$75.00**
Price: Front sight, Patridge or ramp..............................**$15.00**
WICHITA GRAND MASTER DELUXE RIBS Ventilated rib has wings machined into it for better sight acquisition and is relieved for Mag-Na-Porting. Milled to accept Weaver see-thru-style rings. Made of stainless or blued steel; front and rear sights blued. Has Wichita Multi-Range rear sight system, adjustable front sight. Made for revolvers with 6″ barrel.
Price: Model 301S, 301B (adj. sight K frames with custom bbl. of 1″ to 1.032″ dia. L and N frame with 1.062″ to 1.100″ dia. bbl.)......................**$189.00**
Price: Model 303S, 303B (adj. sight K, L, N frames with factory barrel).....**$189.00**
WILLIAMS FIRE SIGHT SETS Red fiber optic metallic sight replaces the original. Rear sight has two green fiber optic elements. Made of CNC-machined aluminum. Fits all Glocks, Ruger P-Series (except P-85), S&W 910, Colt Gov't. Model Series 80, Ruger GP 100 and Redhawk, and SIG Sauer (front only).
Price: Front and rear set...**$39.95**
Price: SIG Sauer front..**$19.95**

Shotgun Sights

ACCURA-SITE For shooting shotgun slugs. Three models to fit most shotguns—"A" for vent. rib barrels, "B" for solid ribs, "C" for plain barrels. Rear sight has windage and elevation provisions. Easily removed and replaced. Includes front and rear sights. From All's, The Jim Tembeils Co.
Price:..**$27.95 to $34.95**
FIRE FLY EM-109 SL SHOTGUN SIGHT Made of aircraft-grade aluminum, this 1/4-oz. "channel" sight has a thick, sturdy hollowed post between the side rails to give a Patridge sight picture. All shooting is done with both eyes open, allowing the shooter to concentrate on the target, not the sights. The hole in the sight post gives reduced-light shooting capability and allows for fast, precise aiming. For sport or combat shooting. Model EM-109 fits all vent. rib and double barrel shotguns and muzzleloaders with octagon barrel. Model MOC-110 fits all plain barrel shotguns without screw-in chokes. From JAS, Inc.
Price:..**$35.00**
LYMAN Three sights of over-sized ivory beads. No. 10 Front (press fit) for double barrel or ribbed single barrel guns..**$4.50**; No. 10D Front (screw fit) for non-ribbed single barrel guns (comes with wrench)...**$5.50**; No. 11 Middle (press fit) for double and ribbed single barrel guns...**$4.75**.
MMC M&P COMBAT SHOTGUN SIGHT SET A durable, protected ghost ring aperture, combat sight made of steel. Fully adjustable for windage and elevation.
Price: M&P Sight Set (front and rear).............................**$73.45**
Price: As above, installed..**$83.95**
MMC TACTICAL GHOST RING SIGHT Click adjustable for elevation with 30 MOA total adjustment in 3 MOA increments. Click windage adjustment. Machined from 4140 steel, heat treated to 40 RC. Front sight available in banded tactical or serrated ramp. Front and rear sights available with or without tritium. Available in three different finishes.

Price: Rear Ghost Ring with tritium...............................**$119.95**
Price: Rear Ghost Ring without tritium.............................**$99.95**
Price: Front Banded Tactical with tritium..........................**$59.95**
Price: Front Banded Tactical without tritium.......................**$39.95**
Price: Front serrated ramp..**$24.95**
MARBLE SHOTGUN BEAD SIGHTS No. 214—Ivory front bead, 11/64″, tapered shank...**$4.40**; No. 223—Ivory rear bead, .080″, tapered shank...**$4.40**; No. 217—Ivory front bead, 11/64″, threaded shank...**$4.75**; No. 223-T—Ivory rear bead, .080″, threaded shank...**$5.95**. Reamers, taps and wrenches available from Marble Arms.
MILLETT SHURSHOT SHOTGUN SIGHT A sight system for shotguns with ventilated rib. Rear sight attaches to the rib, front sight replaces the front bead. Front has an orange face, rear has two orange bars. For 870, 1100 or other models.
Price: Rear...**$13.15**
Price: Adjustable front and rear set..............................**$31.00**
Price: Front..**$12.95**
POLY-CHOKE Replacement front shotgun sights in four styles—Xpert, Poly Bead, Xpert Mid Rib sights, and Bev-L-Block. Xpert Front available in 3x56, 6x48 thread, 3/32″ or 5/32″ shank length, gold, ivory...**$4.70**; or Sun Spot orange bead...**$5.95**; Poly Bead is standard replacement 1/8″ bead, 6x48...**$2.95**; Xpert Mid Rib in tapered carrier (ivory only) ...**$5.95**, or 3x56 threaded shank (gold only)...**$2.95**; Hi and Lo Blok sights with 6x48 thread, gold or ivory...**$5.25**. From Marble Arms.
SLUG SIGHTS Made of non-marring black nylon, front and rear sights stretch over and lock onto the barrel. Sights are low profile with blaze orange front blade. Adjustable for windage and elevation. For plain-barrel (non-ribbed) guns in 12-, 16- and 20-gauge, and for shotguns with 5/16″ and 3/8″ ventilated ribs. From Innovision Ent.
Price:..**$11.95**
WILLIAMS GUIDE BEAD SIGHT Fits all shotguns, 1/8″ ivory, red or gold bead. Screws into existing sight hole. Various thread sizes and shank lengths.
Price:..**$4.77**
WILLIAMS SLUGGER SIGHTS Removable aluminum sights attach to the shotgun rib. High profile front, fully adjustable rear. Fits 1/4″, 5/16″ or 3/8″ (special) ribs.
Price:..**$34.95**
WILLIAMS FIRE SIGHTS Fiber optic light gathering front sights in red or yellow, glow with natural light. Fit 1/4″, 5/16″ or 3/8″ vent. ribs, most popular shotguns.
Price:..**$13.95**

Sight Attachments

MERIT ADJUSTABLE APERTURES Eleven clicks give 12 different apertures. No. 3 Disc and Master, primarily target types, 0.22″ to .125″; No. 4, 1/2″ dia. hunting type, .025″ to .155″. Available for all popular sights. The Master, with flexible rubber light shield, is particularly adapted to extension, scope height, and tang sights. All models have internal click springs; are hand fitted to minimum tolerance.
Price: No. 3 Master Disk..**$66.00**
Price: No. 3 Target Disc (Plain Face)..............................**$56.00**
Price: No. 4 Hunting Disc...**$48.00**
MERIT LENS DISC Similar to Merit Iris Shutter (Model 3 or Master) but incorporates provision for mounting prescription lens integrally. Lens may be obtained locally from your optician. Sight disc is 7/16″ wide (Model 3), or 3/4″ wide (Master).
Price: No. 3 Target Lens Disk.....................................**$68.00**
Price: No. 3 Master Lens Disk.....................................**$78.00**

Merit Optical Attachment

MERIT OPTICAL ATTACHMENT For iron sight shooting with handgun or rifle. Instantly attached by rubber suction cup to prescription or shooting glasses. Swings aside. Aperture adjustable from .020″ to .156″.
Price:..**$65.00**
WILLIAMS APERTURES Standard thread, fits most sights. Regular series 3/8″ to 1/2″ O.D., .050″ to .125″ hole. "Twilight" series with white reflector ring.
Price: Regular series...**$4.97**
Price: Twilight series...**$6.79**
Price: Wide open 5/16″ aperture for shotguns fits 5-D or Foolproof sights (specify model)...**$8.77**

Nikon
Fieldscope 78mm

Swift M700T Scout

BAUSCH & LOMB PREMIER HDR 60mm objective, 15x-45x zoom. Straight or 45° eyepiece. Field at 1000 yds. 125 ft. (15x), 68 ft. (45x). Length 13.0"; weight 38 oz. Interchangeable bayonet-style eyepieces.
Price: Straight, 15-45x **$590.95**
Price: Angled, 15-45x with 45° eyepiece **$638.95**
Price: 22x wide angle eyepiece **$86.95**
Price: 30x long eye relief eyepiece **$136.95**

BAUSCH & LOMB DISCOVERER 15x to 60x zoom, 60mm objective. Constant focus throughout range. Field at 1000 yds. 38 ft (60x), 150 ft. (15x). Comes with lens caps. Length 17 1/2"; weight 48.5 oz.
Price: **$391.95**

BAUSCH & LOMB ELITE 15x to 45x zoom, 60mm objective. Field at 1000 yds., 125-65 ft. Length is 12.2". weight, 26.5 oz. Waterproof, armored. Tripod mount. Comes with black case.
Price: **$766.95**

BAUSCH & LOMB ELITE ZOOM 20x-60x, 70mm objective. Roof prism. Field at 1000 yds. 90-50 ft. Length is 16"; weight 40 oz. Waterproof, armored. Tripod mount. Comes with black case.
Price: **$921.95**

BAUSCH & LOMB 80MM ELITE 20x-60x zoom, 80mm objective. Field of view at 1000 yds. 108-62 ft. (zoom). Weight 51 oz. (20x, 30x), 54 oz. (zoom); length 16.8". Interchangeable bayonet-style eyepieces. Built-in peep sight.
Price: With EDPrime Glass **$1,212.95**

BURRIS 18-45x SIGNATURE SPOTTER 60mm objective, 18x-45x, constant focus, Field at 1000 yds. 112-63 ft.; weighs 29oz.; length 12.6". Camera adapters available.
Price: **$819.00**

BURRIS LANDMARK SPOTTER 15x-45x, 60mm objective. Straight type. Field at 100 yds. 146-72 ft. Length 12.7"; weight 24 oz. Rubber armor coating, multi-coated lenses, 22mm eye relief. Recessed focus adjustment. Nitrogen filled. .
Price: 30x 60mm **$644.00**

BUSHNELL TROPHY 63mm objective, 20x-60x zoom. Field at 1000 yds. 90ft. (20x), 45 ft. (60x). Length 12.7"; weight 20 oz. Black rubber armored, waterproof. Case included.
Price: **$421.95**

BUSHNELL COMPACT TROPHY 50mm objective, 20x-50x zoom. Field at 1000 yds. 92 ft. (20x), 52 ft. (50x). Length 12.2"; weight 17 oz. Black rubber armored, waterproof. Case included.
Price: **$337.95**

BUSHNELL BANNER SENTRY 18x-36x zoom, 50mm objective. Field at 1000 yds. 115-78 ft. Length 14.5", weight 27 oz. Black rubber armored. Built-in peep sight. Comes with tripod and hardcase.
Price: **$180.95**
Price: With 45 field eyepiece, includes tripod **$202.95**

BUSHNELL SPACEMASTER 20x-45x zoom. Long eye relief. Rubber armored, prismatic. 60mm objective. Field at 1000 yds. 98-58 ft. Minimum focus 20 ft. Length 12.7"; weight 43 oz.
Price: With tripod, carrying case and 20x-45x LER eyepiece. **$560.95**

BUSHNELL SPORTVIEW 12x-36x 200m, 50mm objective. Field at 100 yds. 160 ft. (12x), 90 ft. (36x). Length 14.6"; weight 25 oz.
Price: With tripod and carrying case **$159.95**

HERMES 1 70mm objective, 16x, 25x, 40x. Field at 1000 meters 160 ft. (16x), 75ft. (40x). Length 12.2"; weight 33 oz. From CZ-USA.
Price: Body **$359.00**
Price: 25x eyepiece **$86.00**
Price: 40x eyepiece **$128.00**

KOWA TSN SERIES Offset 45 or straight body. 77mm objective, 20x WA, 25x, 25x LER, 30x WA, 40x, 60x, 77x and 20-60x zoom. Field at 1000 yds. 179 ft. (20xWA), 52 ft. (60x). Available with flourite lens.
Price: TSN-1 (without eyepiece) 45 offset scope **$696.00**

Price: TSN-2 (without eyepiece) Straight scope **$660.00**
Price: 20x W.A. (wide angle) eyepiece **$230.00**
Price: 25x eyepiece **$143.00**
Price: 25x LER (long eye relief) eyepiece **$214.00**
Price: 30x W.A. (wide angle) eyepiece **$266.00**
Price: 40x eyepiece **$159.00**
Price: 60x W.A. (wide angle) eyepiece **$230.00**
Price: 77x eyepiece **$235.00**
Price: 20-60x zoom eyepiece **$302.00**

KOWA TS-610 SERIES Offset 45 or straight body. 60mm objective, 20x WA, 25x, 25x LER, 27x WA, 40x and 20x-60x zoom. Field at 1000 yds. 162 ft. (20x WA), 51 ft. (60x). Available with ED lens.
Price: TS-611 (without eyepiece) 45 offset scope **$510.00**
Price: TS-612 (without eyepiece) Straight scope **$462.00**
Price: 20x W.A. (wide angle) eyepiece **$111.00**
Price: 25x eyepiece **$95.00**
Price: 25x LER (long eye relief) eyepiece **$214.00**
Price: 27x W.A. (wide angle) eyepiece **$166.00**
Price: 40x eyepiece **$98.00**
Price: 20-60x zoom eyepiece **$207.00**

KOWA TS-9 SERIES Offset 45 , straight or rubber armored (straight only). 50mm objective, 15x, 20x and 11-33x zoom. Field at 1000 yds. 188 ft. (15x), 99 ft. (33x).
Price: TS-9B (without eyepiece) 45 offset scope **$223.00**
Price: TS-9C (without eyepiece) straight scope **$176.00**
Price: TS-9R (without eyepiece) straight rubber armored scope/black **$197.00**
Price: 15x eyepiece **$38.00**
Price: 20x eyepiece **$36.00**
Price: 11-33x zoom eyepiece **$122.00**

LEUPOLD 12-40x60 VARIABLE 60mm objective, 12-40x. Field at 100 yds. 17.5-5.3 ft.; eye relief 1.2" (20x). Overall length 11.5", weight 32 oz. Rubber armored.
Price: **$1,217.90**

LEUPOLD 25x50 COMPACT 50mm objective, 25x. Field at 100 yds. 8.3 ft.; eye relief 1"; length overall 9.4"; weight 20.5 oz.
Price: Armored model **$848.20**
Price: Packer Tripod **$96.40**

MIRADOR TTB SERIES Draw tube armored spotting scopes. Available with 75mm or 80mm objective. Zoom model (28x-62x, 80mm) is 11 7/8" (closed), weighs 50 oz. Field at 1000 yds. 70-42 ft. Comes with lens covers.
Price: 28-62x80mm **$1,133.95**
Price: 32x80mm **$971.95**
Price: 26-58x75mm **$989.95**
Price: 30x75mm **$827.95**

MIRADOR SSD SPOTTING SCOPES 60mm objective, 15x, 20x, 22x, 25x, 40x, 60x, 20-60x; field at 1000 yds. 37 ft.; length 10 1/4"; weight 33 oz.
Price: 25x **$575.95**
Price: 22x Wide Angle **$593.95**
Price: 20-60x Zoom **$746.95**
Price: As above, with tripod, case. **$944.95**

MIRADOR SIA SPOTTING SCOPES Similar to the SSD scopes except with 45° eyepiece. Length 12 1/4"; weight 39 oz.
Price: 25x **$809.95**
Price: 22x Wide Angle **$827.95**
Price: 20-60x Zoom **$980.95**

MIRADOR SSR SPOTTING SCOPES 50mm or 60mm objective. Similar to SSD except rubber armored in black or camouflage. Length 11 1/8"; weight 31 oz.
Price: Black, 20x **$521.95**
Price: Black, 18x Wide Angle **$539.95**
Price: Black, 16-48x Zoom **$692.95**
Price: Black, 20x, 60mm, EER **$692.95**
Price: Black, 22x Wide Angle, 60mm **$701.95**
Price: Black, 20-60x Zoom **$854.95**

MIRADOR SSF FIELD SCOPES Fixed or variable power, choice of 50mm, 60mm, 75mm objective lens. Length 9 3/4"; weight 20 oz. (15-32x50).
Price: 20x50mm **$359.95**
Price: 25x60mm **$440.95**
Price: 30x75mm **$584.95**
Price: 15-32x50mm Zoom **$548.95**
Price: 18-40x60mm Zoom **$629.95**
Price: 22-47x75mm Zoom **$773.95**

Spotting Scopes

MIRADOR SRA MULTI ANGLE SCOPES Similar to SSF Series except eyepiece head rotates for viewing from any angle.
Price: 20x50mm $503.95
Price: 25x60mm $647.95
Price: 30x75mm $764.95
Price: 15-32x50mm Zoom $692.95
Price: 18-40x60mm Zoom $836.95
Price: 22-47x75mm Zoom $953.95

MIRADOR SIB FIELD SCOPES Short-tube, 45° scopes with porro prism design. 50mm and 60mm objective. Length 10 1/4″; weight 18.5 oz. (15-32x50mm); field at 1000 yds. 129-81 ft.
Price: 20x50mm $386.95
Price: 25x60mm $449.95
Price: 15-32x50mm Zoom $575.95
Price: 18-40x60mm Zoom $638.95

NIKON FIELDSCOPES 60mm and 78mm lens. Field at 1000 yds. 105 ft. (60mm, 20x), 126 ft. (78mm, 25x). Length 12.8″ (straight 60mm), 12.6″ (straight 78mm); weight 34.5-47.5 oz. Eyepieces available separately.
Price: 60mm straight body $690.95
Price: 60mm angled body $796.95
Price: 60mm straight ED body $1,200.95
Price: 60mm angled ED body $1,314.95
Price: 78mm straight ED body $2,038.95
Price: 78mm angled ED body $2,170.95
Price: Eyepieces (15x to 60x) .... $146.95 to $324.95
Price: 20-45x eyepiece (25-56x for 78mm) $318.95

NIKON SPOTTING SCOPE 60mm objective, 20x fixed power or 15-45x zoom. Field at 1000 yds. 145 ft. (20x). Gray rubber armored. Straight or angled eyepiece. Weighs 44.2 oz., length 12.1″ (20x).
Price: 20x60 fixed (with eyepiece) $368.95
Price: 15-45x zoom (with case, tripod, eyepiece) $578.95

PENTAX PF-80ED spotting scope 80mm objective lens available in 18x, 24x, 36x, 48x, 72x and 20-60x. Length 15.6″, weight 11.9 to 19.2 oz.
Price: $1,320.00

SIGHTRON SII 2050X63 63mm objective lens, 20x-50x zoom. Field at 1000 yds 91.9 ft. (20x), 52.5 ft. (50x). Length 14″; weight 30.8 oz. Black rubber finish. Also available with 80mm objective lens.
Price: 63mm or 80mm $339.95

SIMMONS 1280 50mm objective, 15-45x zoom. Black matte finish. Ocular focus. Peep finder sight. Waterproof. FOV 95-51 ft. @ 1000 yards. Wgt. 33.5 oz., length 12″.
Price: With tripod $267.99

SIMMONS 1281 60mm objective, 20-60x zoom. Black matte finish. Ocular focus. Peep finder sight. Waterproof. FOV 78-43 ft. @ 1000 yards. Wgt. 34.5 oz. Length 12″.
Price: With tripod $295.99

SIMMONS 77206 PROHUNTER 50mm objectives, 25x fixed power. Field at 1000 yds. 113 ft.; length 10.25″; weighs 33.25 oz. Black rubber armored.
Price: With tripod case $160.60

SIMMONS 41200 REDLINE 50mm objective, 15x-45x zoom. Field at 1000 yds. 104-41 ft.; length 16.75″; weighs 32.75 oz.
Price: With hard case and tripod $99.99
Price: 20-60x, Model 41201 .... $129.99

STEINER FIELD TELESCOPE 24x, 80mm objective. Field at 1000 yds. 105 ft. Weight 44 oz. Tripod mounts. Rubber armored.
Price: $1,299.00

SWAROVSKI CT EXTENDIBLE SCOPES 75mm or 85mm objective, 20-60x zoom, or fixed 15x, 22x, 30x, 32x eyepieces. Field at 1000 yds. 135 ft. (15x), 99 ft. (32x); 99 ft. (20x), 5.2 ft. (60x) for zoom. Length 12.4″ (closed), 17.2″ (open) for the CT75; 9.7″/17.2″ for CT85. Weight 40.6 oz. (CT75), 49.4 oz. (CT85). Green rubber armored.
Price: CT75 body $765.56
Price: CT85 body $1,094.44
Price: 20-60x eyepiece $343.33
Price: 15x, 22x eyepiece $232.22
Price: 30x eyepiece $265.55

SWAROVSKI AT-80/ST-80 SPOTTING SCOPES 80mm objective, 20-60x zoom, or fixed 15x, 22x, 30x, 32x eyepieces. Field at 1000 yds. 135 ft. (15x), 99 ft. (32x); 99 ft. (20x), 52.5 ft. (60x) for zoom. Length 16″ (AT-80), 15.6″ (ST-80); weight 51.8 oz. Available with HD (high density) glass.
Price: AT-80 (angled) body $1,094.44
Price: ST-80 (straight) body $1,094.44
Price: With HD glass $1,555.00
Price: 20-60x eyepiece $343.33
Price: 15x, 22x eyepiece $232.22
Price: 30x eyepiece $265.55

SWIFT LYNX M836 15x-45x zoom, 60mm objective. Weight 7 lbs., length 14″. Has 45° eyepiece, sunshade.
Price: $315.00

SWIFT NIGHTHAWK M849U 80mm objective, 20x-60x zoom, or fixed 19, 25x, 31x, 50x, 75x eyepieces. Has rubber armored body, 1.8x optical finder, retractable lens hood, 45° eyepiece. Field at 1000 yds. 60 ft. (28x), 41 ft. (75x). Length 13.4 oz.; weight 39 oz.
Price: Body only $870.00
Price: 20-68x eyepiece $370.00
Price: Fixed eyepieces .... $130.00 to $240.00
Price: Model 849 (straight) body $795.00

SWIFT NIGHTHAWK M850U 65mm objective, 16x-48x zoom, or fixed 19x, 20x, 25x, 40x, 60x eyepieces. Rubber armored with a 1.8x optical finder, retractable lens hood. Field at 1000 yds. 83 ft. (22x), 52 ft. (60x). Length 12.3″; weight 30 oz. Has 45° eyepiece.
Price: Body only $650.00
Price: 16x-48x eyepiece $370.00
Price: Fixed eyepieces .... $130.00 to $240.00
Price: Model 850 (straight) body $575.00

SWIFT LEOPARD M837 50mm objective, 25x. Length 9 11/16″ to 10 1/2″. Weight with tripod 28 oz. Rubber armored. Comes with tripod.
Price: $160.00

SWIFT TELEMASTER M841 60mm objective. 15x to 60x variable power. Field at 1000 yds. 160 feet (15x) to 40 feet (60x). Weight 3.25 lbs.; length 18″ overall.
Price: $399.50

SWIFT PANTHER M844 15x-45x zoom or 22x WA, 15x, 20x, 40x. 60mm objective. Field at 1000 yds. 141 ft. (15x), 68 ft. (40x), 95-58 ft. (20x-45x).
Price: Body only $380.00
Price: 15x-45x zoom eyepiece $120.00
Price: 20x-45x zoom (long eye relief) eyepiece $140.00
Price: 15x, 20x, 40x eyepiece $65.00
Price: 22x WA eyepiece $80.00

SWIFT M700T 12x-36x, 50mm objective. Field of view at 100 yds. 16 ft. (12x), 9 ft. (36x). Length 14″; weight with tripod 3.22 lbs.
Price: $225.00

SWIFT SEARCHER M839 60mm objective, 20x, 40x. Field at 1000 yds. 118 ft. (30x), 59 ft. (40x). Length 12.6″; weight 3 lbs. Rotating eyepiece head for straight or 45° viewing.
Price: $580.00
Price: 30x, 50x eyepieces, each $67.00

TASCO 29TZBWP WATERPROOF SPOTTER 60mm objective lens, 20x-60x zoom. Field at 100 yds. 7 ft., 4 in. to 3 ft., 8 in. Black rubber armored. Comes with tripod, hard case.
Price: $356.50

TASCO WC28TZ WORLD CLASS SPOTTING SCOPE 50mm objective, 12-36x zoom. Field at 100 yds. World Class. 13-3.8 ft. Comes with tripod and case.
Price: $220.00

TASCO CW5001 COMPACT ZOOM 50mm objective, 12x-36x zoom. Field at 100 yds. 16 ft., 9 in. Includes photo adapter tube, tripod with panhead lever, case.
Price: $280.00

TASCO 3700WP WATERPROOF SPOTTER 50mm objective, 18x-36x zoom. Field at 100 yds. 12ft., 6 in. to 7 ft., 9 in. Black rubber armored. Comes with tripod, hard case.
Price: $288.60

TASCO 3700, 3701 SPOTTING SCOPE 50mm objective. 18x-36x zoom. Field at 100 yds. 12 ft., 6 in. to 7 ft., 9 in. Black rubber armored.
Price: Model 3700 (black, with tripod, case) $237.00
Price: Model 3701 (as above, brown camo) $237.00

TASCO 21EB ZOOM 50mm objective lens, 15x-45x zoom. Field at 100 yds. 11 ft. (15x). Weight 22 oz.; length 18.3″ overall. Comes with panhead lever tripod.
Price: $119.00

TASCO 22EB ZOOM 60mm objective lens, 20x-60x zoom. Field at 100 yds. 7 ft., 2 in. (20x). Weight 28 oz.; length 21.5″ overall. Comes with micro-adjustable tripod.
Price: $183.00

UNERTL "FORTY-FIVE" 54mm objective. 20x (single fixed power). Field at 100 yds. 10′,10″; eye relief 1″; focusing range infinity to 33 ft. Weight about 32 oz.; overall length 153/4″. With lens covers.
Price: With multi-layer lens coating $662.00
Price: With mono-layer magnesium coating $572.00

UNERTL STRAIGHT PRISMATIC 63.5mm objective, 24x. Field at 100 yds., 7 ft. Relative brightness, 6.96. Eye relief 1/2″. Weight 40 oz.; length closed 19″. Push-pull and screw-focus eyepiece. 16x and 32x eyepieces **$125.00** each.
Price: $515.00

UNERTL 20x STRAIGHT PRISMATIC 54mm objective, 20x. Field at 100 yds. 8.5 ft. Relative brightness 6.1. Eye relief 1/2″. Weight 36 oz.; length closed 13 1/2″. Complete with lens covers.
Price: $477.00

UNERTL TEAM SCOPE 100mm objective. 15x, 24x, 32x eyepieces. Field at 100 yds. 13 to 7.5 ft. Relative brightness, 39.06 to 9.79. Eye relief 2″ to 11/2″. Weight 13 lbs.; length 29 7/8″ overall. Metal tripod, yoke and wood carrying case furnished (total weight 80 lbs.).
Price: $2,810.00

WEAVER 20x50 50mm objective. Field of view 124 ft. at 100 yds. Eye relief .85″; weighs 21 oz.; overall length 10″. Waterproof, armored.
Price: $368.99

WEAVER 15-40x60 ZOOM 60mm objective. 15x-40x zoom. Field at 100 yds. 119 ft. (15x), 66 ft. (60x). Overall length 12.5″, weighs 26 oz. Waterproof, armored.
Price: $551.99

ACCESSORIES

CHOKES & BRAKES

Briley Screw-In Chokes

Installation of these choke tubes requires that all traces of the original choking be removed, the barrel threaded internally with square threads and then the tubes are custom fitted to the specific barrel diameter. The tubes are thin and, therefore, made of stainless steel. Cost of installation for single-barrel guns (pumps, autos), lead shot, 12-gauge, **$149.00**, 20-gauge **$159.00**; steel shot **$179.00** and **$189.00**, all with three chokes; un-single target guns run **$219.00**; over/unders and side-by-sides, lead shot, 12-gauge, **$369.00**, 20-gauge **$389.00**; steel shot **$469.00** and **$489.00**, all with five chokes. For 10-gauge auto or pump with two steel shot chokes, **$189.00**; over/unders, side-by-sides with three steel shot chokes, **$349.00**. For 16-gauge auto or pump, three lead shot chokes, **$179.00**; over/unders, side-by-sides with five lead shot chokes, **$449.00**. The 28 and 410-bore run **$179.00** for autos and pumps with three lead shot chokes, **$449.00** for over/unders and side-by-sides with five lead shot chokes.

Cutts Compensator

The Cutts Compensator is one of the oldest variable choke devices available. Manufactured by Lyman Gunsight Corporation, it is available with a steel body. A series of vents allows gas to escape upward and downward. For the 12-ga. Comp body, six fixed-choke tubes are available: the Spreader—popular with Skeet shooters; Improved Cylinder; Modified; Full; Superfull, and Magnum Full. Full, Modified and Spreader tubes are available for 12 or 20. Cutts Compensator, complete with wrench, adaptor and any single tube **$87.50**. All single choke tubes **$26.00** each. No factory installation available.

Dayson Automatic Brake System

This system fits most single barrel shotguns threaded for choke tubes, and cuts away 30 grooves on the exterior of a standard one-piece wad as it exits the muzzle. This slows the wad, allowing shot and wad to separate faster, reducing shot distortion and tightening patterns. The A.B.S. Choke Tube is claimed to reduce recoil by about 25 percent, and with the Muzzle Brake up to 60 percent. Ventilated Choke Tubes available from .685″ to .725″, in .005″ increments. Model I Ventilated Choke Tube for use with A.B.S. Muzzle Brake, **$49.95**; for use without Muzzle Brake, **$52.95**; A.B.S. Muzzle Brake, from **$69.95**. Contact Dayson Arms for more data.

Gentry Quiet Muzzle Brake

Developed by gunmaker David Gentry, the "Quiet Muzzle Brake" is said to reduce recoil by up to 85 percent with no loss of accuracy or velocity. There is no increase in noise level because the noise and gases are directed away from the shooter. The barrel is threaded for installation and the unit is blued to match the barrel finish. Price, installed, is **$150.00**. Add **$15.00** for stainless steel, **$45.00** for knurled cap to protect threads. Shipping extra.

JP Muzzle Brake

JP Muzzle Brake

Designed for single shot handguns, AR-15, Ruger Mini-14, Ruger Mini Thirty and other sporting rifles, the JP Muzzle Brake redirects high pressure gases against a large frontal surface which applies forward thrust to the gun. All gases are directed up, rearward and to the sides. Priced at **$79.95** (AR-15 or sporting rifles), **$89.95** (bull barrel and SKS, AK models), **$89.95** (Ruger Minis), Dual Chamber model **$79.95**. From JP Enterprises, Inc.

KDF Slim Line Muzzle Brake

This threaded muzzle brake has 30 pressure ports that direct combustion gases in all directions to reduce felt recoil up to a claimed 80 percent without affecting accuracy or ballistics. It is said to reduce felt recoil of a 30-06 to that of a 243. Price, installed, is **$179.00**. From KDF, Inc.

Laseraim

Simple, no-gunsmithing compensator reduces felt recoil and muzzle flip by up to 30 percent. Machined from single piece of Stainless Steel (Beretta/Taurus model made of aircract aluminum). In black and polished finish. For Colt Government/Commander and Beretta/Taurus full-size pistols. Weighs 1 ounce. **$49.00**. From Laseraim Arms Inc.

Mag-Na-Port

Electrical Discharge Machining works on any firearm except those having non-conductive shrouded barrels. EDM is a metal erosion technique using carbon electrodes that control the area to be processed. The Mag-Na-Port venting process utilizes small trapezoidal openings to direct powder gases upward and outward to reduce recoil. No effect is had on bluing or nickeling outside the Mag-Na-Port area so no refinishing is needed. Rifle-style porting on single shot or large caliber handguns with barrels 7 1/2″ or longer is **$110.00**; Dual Trapezoidal porting on most handguns with minimum barrel length of 3″, **$100.00**; standard revolver porting, **$78.50**; porting through the slide and barrel for semi-autos, **$115.00**; traditional rifle porting, **$125.00**. Prices do not include shipping, handling and insurance. From Mag-Na-Port International.

Mag-Na-Brake

A screw-on brake under 2″ long with progressive integrated exhaust chambers to neutralize expanding gases. Gases dissipate with an opposite twist to prevent the brake from unscrewing, and with a 5-degree forward angle to minimize sound pressure level. Available in blue, satin blue, bright or satin stainless. Standard and Light Contour installation cost **$179.00** for bolt-action rifles, many single action and single shot handguns. A knurled thread protector supplied at extra cost. Also available in Varmint style with exhaust chambers covering 220 degrees for prone-position shooters. From Mag-Na-Port International.

Poly-Choke

Marble Arms Corp., manufacturer of the Poly-Choke adjustable shotgun choke, now offers two models in 12-, 16-, 20-, and 28-gauge—the Ventilated and Standard style chokes. Each provides nine choke settings including Xtra-Full and Slug. The Ventilated model reduces 20 percent of a shotgun's recoil, the company claims, and is priced at **$135.00**. The Standard Model is **$125.00**. Postage not included. Contact Marble Arms for more data.

Pro-port

A compound ellipsoid muzzle venting process similar to Mag-Na-Porting, only exclusively applied to shotguns. Like Mag-Na-Porting, this system reduces felt recoil, muzzle jump, and shooter fatigue. Very helpful for trap doubles shooters. Pro-Port is a patented process and installation is available in both the U.S. and Canada. Cost for the Pro-Port process is **$129.50** for over/unders (both barrels); **$99.50** for only the top or bottom barrel; and **$78.50** for single-barrel shotguns. Optional pigeon porting costs **$25.00** extra per barrel. Prices do not include shipping and handling. From Pro-port Ltd.

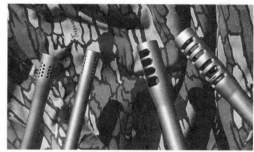

SSK Arrestor muzzle brakes.

SSK Arrestor Brake

This is a true muzzle brake with an expansion chamber. It takes up about 1″ of barrel and reduces velocity accordingly. Some Arrestors are added to a barrel, increasing its length. Said to reduce the felt recoil of a 458 to that approaching a 30-06. Can be set up to give zero muzzle rise in any caliber, and can be added to most guns. For handgun or rifle. Prices start at **$95.00**. Contact SSK Industries for full data.

Periodical Publications

AAFTA News (M)
5911 Cherokee Ave., Tampa, FL 33604. Official newsletter of the American Airgun Field Target Assn.

Action Pursuit Games Magazine (M)
CFW Enterprises, Inc., 4201 W. Vanowen Pl., Burbank, CA 91505 818-845-2656. $4.99 single copy U.S., $5.50 Canada. Editor: Dan Reeves. World's leading magazine of paintball sports.

Air Gunner Magazine
4 The Courtyard, Denmark St., Wokingham, Berkshire RG11 2AZ, England/011-44-734-771677. $U.S. $44 for 1 yr. Leading monthly airgun magazine in U.K.

Airgun Ads
Box 33, Hamilton, MT 59840/406-363-3805; Fax: 406-363-4117. $35 1 yr. (for first mailing; $20 for second mailing; $35 for Canada and foreign orders.) Monthly tabloid with extensive For Sale and Wanted airgun listings.

The Airgun Letter
Gapp, Inc., 4614 Woodland Rd., Ellicott City, MD 21042-6329/410-730-5496; Fax: 410-730-9544; e-mail: staff@airgnltr.net; http://www.airgunletter.com. $21 U.S., $24 Canada, $27 Mexico and $33 other foreign orders, 1 yr. Monthly newsletter for airgun users and collectors.

Airgun World
4 The Courtyard, Denmark St., Wokingham, Berkshire RG40 2AZ, England/011-44-734-771677. Call for subscription rates. Oldest monthly airgun magazine in the U.K., now a sister publication to *Air Gunner*.

Alaska Magazine
Morris Communications, 735 Broad Street, Augusta, GA 30901/706-722-6060. Hunting, Fishing and Life on the Last Frontier articles of Alaska and western Canada.

American Firearms Industry
Nat'l. Assn. of Federally Licensed Firearms Dealers, 2455 E. Sunrise Blvd., Suite 916, Ft. Lauderdale, FL 33304. $35.00 yr. For firearms retailers, distributors and manufacturers.

American Guardian
NRA, 11250 Waples Mill Rd., Fairfax, VA 22030. Publications division. $15.00 1 yr. Magazine features personal protection; home-self-defense; family recreation shooting; women's issues; etc.

American Gunsmith
Belvoir Publications, Inc., 75 Holly Hill Lane, Greenwich, CT 06836-2626/203-661-6111. $49.00 (12 issues). Technical journal of firearms repair and maintenance.

American Handgunner*
Publisher's Development Corp., 591 Camino de la Reina, Suite 200, San Diego, CA 92108/800-537-3006 $16.95 yr. Articles for handgun enthusiasts, competitors, police and hunters.

American Hunter (M)
National Rifle Assn., 11250 Waples Mill Rd., Fairfax, VA 22030 (Same address for both.) Publications Div. $35.00 yr. Wide scope of hunting articles.

American Rifleman (M)
National Rifle Assn., 11250 Waples Mill Rd., Fairfax, VA 22030 (Same address for both). Publications Div. $35.00 yr. Firearms articles of all kinds.

American Single Shot Rifle News* (M)
Membership Secy. Tim Mather, 1180 Easthill SE, N. Canton, Ohio. Annual dues $20 for 6 issues. Official journal of the American Single Shot Rifle Assn.

American Survival Guide
McMullen Angus Publishing, Inc., 774 S. Placentia Ave., Placentia, CA 92670-6846. 12 issues $19.95/714-572-2255; FAX: 714-572-1864.

Arms Collecting (Q)
Museum Restoration Service, P.O. Box 70, Alexandria Bay, NY 13607-0070. $22.00 yr.; $62.00 3 yrs.; $112.00 5 yrs.

Australian Shooters Journal
Sporting Shooters' Assn. of Australia, Inc., P.O. Box 2066, Kent Town SA 5071, Australia. $45.00 yr. locally; $55.00 yr. overseas surface mail only. Hunting and shooting articles.

The Backwoodsman Magazine
P.O. Box 627, Westcliffe, CO 81252. $16.00 for 6 issues per yr.; $30.00 for 2 yrs.; sample copy $2.75. Subjects include muzzle-loading, woodslore, primitive survival, trapping, homesteading, blackpowder cartridge guns, 19th century how-to.

Black Powder Cartridge News (Q)
SPG, Inc., P.O. Box 761, Livingston, MT 59047/Phone/Fax: 406-222-8416. $17 yr. (4 issues) ($6 extra 1st class mailing). For the blackpowder cartridge enthusiast.

Blackpowder Hunting (M)
Intl. Blackpowder Hunting Assn., P.O. Box 1180Z, Glenrock, WY 82637/307-436-9817. $20.00 1 yr., $36.00 2 yrs. How-to and where-to features by experts on hunting; shooting; ballistics; traditional and modern blackpowder rifles, shotguns, pistols and cartridges.

Black Powder Times
P.O. Box 234, Lake Stevens, WA 98258. $20.00 yr.; add $5 per year for Canada, $10 per year other foreign. Tabloid newspaper for blackpowder activities; test reports.

Blade Magazine
Krause Publications, 700 East State St., Iola, WI 54990-0001. $25.98 for 12 issues. Foreign price (including Canada-Mexico) $50.00. A magazine for all enthusiasts of handmade, factory and antique knives.

Caliber
GFI-Verlag, Theodor-Heuss Ring 62, 50668 K"ln, Germany. For hunters, target shooters and reloaders.

The Caller (Q) (M)
National Wild Turkey Federation, P.O. Box 530, Edgefield, SC 29824. Tabloid newspaper for members; 4 issues per yr. (membership fee $25.00)

Cartridge Journal (M)
Robert Mellichamp, 907 Shirkmere, Houston, TX 77008/713-869-0558. Dues $12 for U.S. and Canadian members (includes the newsletter); 6 issues.

The Cast Bullet*(M)
Official journal of The Cast Bullet Assn. Director of Membership, 203 E. 2nd St., Muscatine, IA 52761. Annual membership dues $14, includes 6 issues.

COLTELLI, che Passione (Q)
Casella postale N.519, 20101 Milano, Italy/Fax:02-48402857. $15 1 yr., $27 2 yrs. Covers all types of knives—collecting, combat, historical. Italian text.

Combat Handguns*
Harris Publications, Inc., 1115 Broadway, New York, NY 10010.

Deer & Deer Hunting Magazine
Krause Publications, 700 E. State St., Iola, WI 54990-0001. $19.95 yr. (9 issues). For the serious deer hunter. Website: www.krause.com

The Derringer Peanut (M)
The National Association of Derringer Collectors, P.O. Box 20572, San Jose, CA 95160. A newsletter dedicated to developing the best derringer information. Write for details.

Deutsches Waffen Journal
Journal-Verlag Schwend GmbH, Postfach 100340, D-74503 Schwäbisch Hall, Germany/0791-404-500; FAX:0791-404-505 and 404-424. DM102 p. yr. (interior); DM125.30 (abroad), postage included. Antique and modern arms and equipment. German text.

Double Gun Journal
P.O. Box 550, East Jordan, MI 49727/800-447-1658. $35 for 4 issues.

Ducks Unlimited, Inc. (M)
1 Waterfowl Way, Memphis, TN 38120

The Engraver (M) (Q)
P.O. Box 4365, Estes Park, CO 80517/970-586-2388; Fax: 970-586-0394. Mike Dubber, editor. The journal of firearms engraving.

The Field
King's Reach Tower, Stamford St., London SE1 9LS England. £36.40 U.K. 1 yr.; 49.90 (overseas, surface mail) yr.; £82.00 (overseas, air mail) yr. Hunting and shooting articles, and all country sports.

Field & Stream
Times Mirror Magazines, Two Park Ave., New York, NY 10016/212-779-5000. Monthly shooting column. Articles on hunting and fishing. Website: www.timesmirror.com

Field Tests
Belvoir Publications, Inc., 75 Holly Hill Lane; P.O. Box 2626, Greenwich, CT 06836-2626/203-661-6111; 800-829-3361 (subscription line). U.S. & Canada $29 1 yr., $58 2 yrs.; all other countries $45 1 yr., $90 2 yrs. (air).

Fur-Fish-Game
A.R. Harding Pub. Co., 2878 E. Main St., Columbus, OH 43209. $15.95 yr. Practical guidance regarding trapping, fishing and hunting.

The Gottlieb-Tartaro Report
Second Amendment Foundation, James Madison Bldg., 12500 NE 10th Pl., Bellevue, WA 98005/206-454-7012;Fax:206-451-3959. $30 for 12 issues. An insiders guide for gun owners.

Gray's Sporting Journal
Gray's Sporting Journal, P.O. Box 1207, Augusta, GA 30903. $36.95 per yr. for 6 issues. Hunting and fishing journals. Expeditions and Guides Book (Annual Travel Guide).

Gun List†
700 E. State St., Iola, WI 54990. $36.98 yr. (26 issues); $65.98 2 yrs. (52 issues). Indexed market publication for firearms collectors and active shooters; guns, supplies and services. Website: www.krause.com

Gun News Digest (Q)
Second Amendment Fdn., P.O. Box 488, Station C, Buffalo, NY 14209/716-885-6408;Fax:716-884-4471. $10 U.S.; $20 foreign.

The Gun Report
World Wide Gun Report, Inc., Box 38, Aledo, IL 61231-0038. $33.00 yr. For the antique and collectable gun dealer and collector.

Gunmaker (M) (Q)
ACGG, P.O. Box 812, Burlington, IA 52601-0812. The journal of custom gunmaking.

The Gunrunner
Div. of Kexco Publ. Co. Ltd., Box 565G, Lethbridge, Alb., Canada T1J 3Z4. $23.00 yr., sample $2.00. Monthly newspaper, listing everything from antiques to artillery.

Gun Show Calendar (Q)
700 E. State St., Iola, WI 54990. $14.95 yr. (4 issues). Gun shows listed; chronologically and by state. Website: www.krause.com

Gun Tests
11 Commerce Blvd., Palm Coast, FL 32142. The consumer resource for the serious shooter. Write for information.

Gun Trade News
Bruce Publishing Ltd., P.O. Box 82, Wantage, Ozon OX12 7A8, England/44-1-235-771770; Fax: 44-1-235-771848. Britain's only "trade only" magazine exclusive to the gun trade.

Gun Week†
Second Amendment Foundation, P.O. Box 488, Station C, Buffalo, NY 14209. $35.00 yr. U.S. and possessions; $45.00 yr. other countries. Tabloid paper on guns, hunting, shooting and collecting (36 issues).

Gun World
Y-Visionary Publishing, LP 265 South Anita Drive, Ste. 120, Orange, CA 92868. $21.97 yr.; $34.97 2 yrs. For the hunting, reloading and shooting enthusiast.

Guns & Ammo
EMAP USA, 6420 Wilshire Blvd., Los Angeles, CA 90048/213-782-2780. $23.94 yr. Guns, shooting, and technical articles.

Guns
Publishers Development Corporation, P.O. Box 85201, San Diego, CA 92138/800-537-3006. $19.95 yr. In-depth articles on a wide range of guns, shooting equipment and related accessories for gun collectors, hunters and shooters.

Guns Review
Ravenhill Publishing Co. Ltd., Box 35, Standard House, Bonhill St., London EC 2A 4DA, England. £20.00 sterling (approx. U.S. $38 USA & Canada) yr. For collectors and shooters.

H.A.C.S. Newsletter (M)
Harry Moon, Pres., P.O. Box 50117, South Slope RPO, Burnaby BC, V5J 5G3, Canada/604-438-0950;Fax:604-277-3646. $25 p. yr. U.S. and Canada. Official newsletter of The Historical Arms Collectors of B.C. (Canada).

Handgunner*
Richard A.J. Munday, Seychelles house, Brightlingsen, Essex CO7 ONN, England/012063-305201. £ 18.00 (sterling).

Handguns
EMAP USA, 6420 Wilshire Blvd., Los Angeles, CA 90048/323-782-2868. $23/94 yr. For the handgunning and shooting enthusiast. Website: www.petersenco.com

Handloader*
Wolfe Publishing Co., 6471 Airpark Dr., Prescott, AZ 86301/520-445-7810;Fax:520-778-5124. $22.00 yr. The journal of ammunition reloading.

INSIGHTS*
NRA, 11250 Waples Mill Rd., Fairfax, VA 22030. Editor, John E. Robbins. $15.00 yr., which includes NRA junior membership; $10.00 for adult subscriptions (12 issues). Plenty of details for the young hunter and target shooter; emphasizes gun safety, marksmanship training, hunting skills.

International Arms & Militaria Collector (Q)
Arms & Militaria Press, P.O. Box 80, Labrador, Qld. 4215, Australia. A$39.50 yr. (U.S. & Canada), 2 yrs. A$77.50; A$37.50 (others), 1 yr., 2 yrs. $73.50 all air express mail; surface mail is less. Editor: Ian D. Skennerton.

International Shooting Sport*/UIT Journal
International Shooting Union (UIT), Bavariaring 21, D-80336 Munich, Germany. Europe: (Deutsche Mark) DM44.00 yr., 2 yrs. DM83.00; outside Europe: DM50.00 yr., 2 yrs. DM95.00 (air mail postage included.) For international sport shooting.

Internationales Waffen-Magazin
Habegger-Verlag Zürich, Postfach 9230, CH-8036 Zürich, Switzerland. SF 105.00 (approx. U.S. $73.00) surface mail for 10 issues. Modern and antique arms, self-defense. German text; English summary of contents.

The Journal of the Arms & Armour Society (M)
A. Dove, P.O. Box 10232, London, SW19 2ZD England. £15.00 surface mail; £20.00 airmail sterling only yr. Articles for the historian and collector.

Journal of the Historical Breechloading Smallarms Assn.
Published annually. P.O. Box 12778, London, SE1 6XB, England. $21.00 yr. Articles for the collector plus mailings of short articles on specific arms, reprints, newsletters, etc.

Knife World
Knife World Publications, P.O. Box 3395, Knoxville, TN 37927. $15.00 yr.; $25.00 2 yrs. Published monthly for knife enthusiasts and collectors. Articles on custom and factory knives; other knife-related interests, monthly column on knife identification, military knives.

Man At Arms*
P.O. Box 460, Lincoln, RI 02865. $27.00 yr., $52.00 2 yrs. plus $8.00 for foreign subscribers. The N.R.A. magazine of arms collecting-investing, with excellent articles for the collector of antique arms and militaria.

---

*Published bi-monthly
† Published weekly
‡Published three times per month. All others are published monthly.

M=Membership requirements; write for details.
Q=Published Quarterly.

REFERENCE

PERIODICAL PUBLICATIONS

The Mannlicher Collector (Q)(M)
Mannlicher Collectors Assn., Inc., P.O. Box 7144, Salem Oregon 97303. $20/ yr. subscription included in membership.

MAN/MAGNUM
S.A. Man (Pty) Ltd., P.O. Box 35204, Northway, Durban 4065, Republic of South Africa. SA Rand 200.00 for 12 issues. Africa's only publication on hunting, shooting, firearms, bushcraft, knives, etc.

The Marlin Collector (M)
R.W. Paterson, 407 Lincoln Bldg., 44 Main St., Champaign, IL 61820.

Muzzle Blasts (M)
National Muzzle Loading Rifle Assn., P.O. Box 67, Friendship, IN 47021/812-667-5131. $35.00 yr. annual membership. For the blackpowder shooter.

Muzzleloader Magazine*
Scurlock Publishing Co., Inc., Dept. Gun, Route 5, Box 347-M, Texarkana, TX 75501. $18.00 U.S.; $22.50 U.S./yr. for foreign subscribers. The publication for blackpowder shooters.

National Defense (M)*
American Defense Preparedness Assn., Two Colonial Place, Suite 400, 2101 Wilson Blvd., Arlington, VA 22201-3061/703-522-1820; FAX: 703-522-1885. $35.00 yr. Articles on both military and civil defense field, including weapons, materials technology, management.

National Knife Magazine (M)
Natl. Knife Coll. Assn., 7201 Shallowford Rd., P.O. Box 21070, Chattanooga, TN 37424-0070. Membership $35 yr.; $65.00 International yr.

National Rifle Assn. Journal (British) (Q)
Natl. Rifle Assn. (BR.), Bisley Camp, Brookwood, Woking, Surrey, England. GU24, OPB. £24.00 Sterling including postage.

National Wildlife*
Natl. Wildlife Fed., 1400 16th St. NW, Washington, DC 20036, $16.00 yr. (6 issues); *International Wildlife*, 6 issues, $16.00 yr. Both, $22.00 yr., includes all membership benefits. Write attn.: Membership Services Dept., for more information.

New Zealand GUNS*
Waitekauri Publishing, P.O. 45, Waikino 3060, New Zealand. $NZ90.00 (6 issues) yr. Covers the hunting and firearms scene in New Zealand.

New Zealand Wildlife (Q)
New Zealand Deerstalkers Assoc., Inc., P.O. Box 6514, Wellington, N.Z. $30.00 (N.Z.). Hunting, shooting and firearms/game research articles.

North American Hunter* (M)
P.O. Box 3401, Minnetonka, MN 55343/612-936-9333; e-mail: huntingclub@pclink.com. $18.00 yr. (7 issues). Articles on all types of North American hunting.

Outdoor Life
Times Mirror Magazines, Two Park Ave., New York, NY 10016. $16.95/yr. Extensive coverage of hunting and shooting. Shooting column by Jim Carmichel. Website: www.timesmirror.com

La Passion des Courteaux (Q)
Phenix Editions, 25 rue Mademoiselle, 75015 Paris, France. French text.

Paintball Games International Magazine
Aceville Publications, Castle House, 97 High St., Colchester, Essex, England CO1 1TH/011-44-206-564840. Write for subscription rates. Leading magazine in the U.K. covering competitive paintball activities.

Paintball News
PBN Publishing, P.O. Box 1608, 24 Henniker St., Hillsboro, NH 03244/603-464-6080. $35 U.S. 1 yr. Bi-weekly. Newspaper covering the sport of paintball, new product reviews and industry features.

Paintball Sports (Q)
Paintball Publications, Inc., 540 Main St., Mount Kisco, NY 10549/941-241-7400. $24.75 U.S. 1 yr., $32.75 foreign. Covering the competitive paintball scene.

Performance Shooter
Belvoir Publications, Inc., 75 Holly Hill Lane, Greenwich, CT 06836-2626/203-661-6111. $45.00 yr. (12 issues). Techniques and technology for improved rifle and pistol accuracy.

Petersen's HUNTING Magazine
EMAP USA, 6420 Wilshire Blvd., Los Angeles, CA 90048. $19.94 yr.; Canada $29.34 yr.; foreign countries $29.94 yr. Hunting articles for all game; test reports.

P.I. Magazine
America's Private Investigation Journal, 755 Bronx Dr., Toledo, OH 43609. Chuck Klein, firearms editor with column about handguns.

Pirsch
BLV Verlagsgesellschaft mbH, Postfach 400320, 80703 Munich, Germany/089-12704-0;Fax:089-12705-354. German text.

Point Blank
Citizens Committee for the Right to Keep and Bear Arms (sent to contributors), Liberty Park, 12500 NE 10th Pl., Bellevue, WA 98005

POINTBLANK (M)
Natl. Firearms Assn., Box 4384 Stn. C, Calgary, AB T2T 5N2, Canada. Official publication of the NFA.

The Police Marksman*
6000 E. Shirley Lane, Montgomery, AL 36117. $17.95 yr. For law enforcement personnel.

Police Times (M)
3801 Biscayne Blvd., Miami, FL 33137/305-573-0070.

Popular Mechanics
Hearst Corp., 224 W. 57th St., New York, NY 10019. Firearms, camping, outdoor oriented articles.

Precision Shooting
Precision Shooting, Inc., 222 McKee St., Manchester, CT 06040. $32.00 yr. U.S. Journal of the International Benchrest Shooters, and target shooting in general. Also considerable coverage of varmint shooting, as well as big bore, small bore, schuetzen, lead bullet, wildcats and precision reloading.

Rifle*
Wolfe Publishing Co., 6471 Airpark Dr., Prescott, AZ 86301/520-445-7810; Fax: 520-778-5124. $19.00 yr. The sporting firearms journal.

Rifle's Hunting Annual
Wolfe Publishing Co., 6471 Airpark Dr., Prescott, AZ 86301/520-445-7810; Fax: 520-778-5124. $4.99 Annual. Dedicated to the finest pursuit of the hunt.

Rod & Rifle Magazine
Lithographic Serv. Ltd., P.O. Box 38-138, Wellington, New Zealand. $50.00 yr. (6 issues). Hunting, shooting and fishing articles.

Safari* (M)
Safari Magazine, 4800 W. Gates Pass Rd., Tucson, AZ 85745/602-620-1220. $55.00 (6 times). The journal of big game hunting, published by Safari Club International. Also publish *Safari Times*, a monthly newspaper, included in price of $55.00 national membership.

Second Amendment Reporter
Second Amendment Foundation, James Madison Bldg., 12500 NE 10th Pl., Bellevue, WA 98005. $15.00 yr. (non-contributors).

Shooter's News
23146 Lorain Rd., Box 349, North Olmsted, OH 44070/216-979-5258;Fax:216-979-5259. $29 U.S. 1 yr., $54 2 yrs.; $52 foreign surface. A journal dedicated to precision riflery.

Shooting Industry
Publisher's Dev. Corp., 591 Camino de la Reina, Suite 200, San Diego, CA 92108. $50.00 yr. To the trade. $25.00.

Shooting Sports USA
National Rifle Assn. of America, 11250 Waples Mill Road, Fairfax, VA 22030. Annual subscriptions for NRA members are $5 for classified shooters and $10 for non-classified shooters. Non-NRA member subscriptions are $15. Covering events, techniques and personalities in competitive shooting.

Shooting Sportsman*
P.O. Box 11282, Des Moines, IA 50340/800-666-4955 (for subscriptions). Editorial: P.O. Box 1357, Camden, ME 04843. $19.95 for six issues. The magazine of wingshooting and fine guns.

The Shooting Times & Country Magazine (England)†
IPC Magazines Ltd., King's Reach Tower, Stamford St, 1 London SE1 9LS, England/0171-261-6180;Fax:0171-261-7179. £65 (approx. $98.00) yr.; £79 yr. overseas (52 issues). Game shooting, wild fowling, hunting, game fishing and firearms articles. Britain's best selling field sports magazine.

Shooting Times
Primedia, News Plaza, P.O. Box 1790, Peoria, IL 61656/309-682-6626. $16.97 yr. Guns, shooting, reloading; articles on every gun activity.

The Shotgun News‡
Primedia, News Plaza, P.O. Box 1790, Peoria, IL 61656/800-495-8362. $28.95 yr.; foreign subscription call for rates. Sample copy $4.00. Gun ads of all kinds.

SHOT Business
Flintlock Ridge Office Center, 11 Mile Hill Rd., Newtown, CT 06470-2359/203-426-1320; FAX: 203-426-1087. For the shooting, hunting and outdoor trade retailer.

Shotgun Sports
P.O. Box 6810, Auburn, CA 95604/916-889-2220; FAX:916-889-9106. $31.00 yr. Trapshooting how-to's, shotshell reloading, shotgun patterning, shotgun tests and evaluations, Sporting Clays action, waterfowl/upland hunting. Call 1-800-676-8920 for a free sample copy.

The Sixgunner (M)
Handgun Hunters International, P.O. Box 357, MAG, Bloomingdale, OH 43910

The Skeet Shooting Review
National Skeet Shooting Assn., 5931 Roft Rd., San Antonio, TX 78253. $20.00 yr. (Assn. membership includes mag.) Competition results, personality profiles of top Skeet shooters, how-to articles, technical, reloading information.

Soldier of Fortune
Subscription Dept., P.O. Box 348, Mt. Morris, IL 61054. $29.95 yr.; $39.95 Canada; $50.95 foreign.

Sporting Clays Magazine
Patch Communications, 5211 South Washington Ave., Titusville, FL 32780/407-268-5010; FAX: 407-267-7216. $29.95 yr. (12 issues). Official publication of the National Sporting Clays Association.

Sporting Goods Business
Miller Freeman, Inc., One Penn Plaza, 10th Fl., New York, NY 10119-0004. Trade journal.

Sporting Goods Dealer
Two Park Ave., New York, NY 10016. $100.00 yr. Sporting goods trade journal.

Sporting Gun
Bretton Court, Bretton, Peterborough PE3 8DZ, England. £27.00 (approx. U.S. $36.00), airmail £35.50 yr. For the game and clay enthusiasts.

Sports Afield
11650 Riverside Drive, North Hollywood, CA 91602-1066/818-904-9981.

The Squirrel Hunter
P.O. Box 368, Chireno, TX 75937. $14.00 yr. Articles about squirrel hunting.

Stott's Creek Calendar
Stott's Creek Printers, 2526 S 475 W, Morgantown, IN 46160/317-878-5489. 1 yr (3 issues) $11.50; 2 yrs. (6 issues) $20.00. Lists all gun shows everywhere in convenient calendar form; call for information.

Super Outdoors
2695 Aiken Road, Shelbyville, KY 40065/502-722-9463; 800-404-6064; Fax: 502-722-8093. Mark Edwards, publisher. Contact for details.

TACARMI
Via E. De Amicis, 25; 20123 Milano, Italy. $100.00 yr. approx. Antique and modern guns. (Italian text.)

Territorial Dispatch—1800s Historical Publication (M)
National Assn. of Buckskinners, 4701 Marion St., Suite 324, Livestock Exchange Bldg., Denver, CO 80216. Michael A. Nester & Barbara Wyckoff, editors. 303-297-9671.

Trap & Field
1000 Waterway Blvd., Indianapolis, IN 46202. $25.00 yr. Official publ. Amateur Trapshooting Assn. Scores, averages, trapshooting articles.

Turkey Call* (M)
Natl. Wild Turkey Federation, Inc., P.O. Box 530, Edgefield, SC 29824. $25.00 with membership (6 issues per yr.)

Turkey & Turkey Hunting*
Krause Publications, 700 E. State St., Iola, WI 54990-0001. $13.95 (6 issue p. yr.). Magazine with leading-edge articles on all aspects of wild turkey behavior, biology and the successful ways to hunt better with that info. Learn the proper techniques to calling, the right equipment, and more.

The U.S. Handgunner* (M)
U.S. Revolver Assn., 40 Larchmont Ave., Taunton, MA 02780. $10.00 yr. General handgun and competition articles. Bi-monthly sent to members.

U.S. Airgun Magazine
P.O. Box 2021, Benton, AR 72018/800-247-4867; Fax: 501-316-8549. 10 issues a yr. Cover the sport from hunting, 10-meter, field target and collecting. Write for details.

The Varmint Hunter Magazine (Q)
The Varmint Hunters Assn., Box 759, Pierre, SD 57501/800-528-4868. $24.00 yr.

Waffenmarkt-Intern
GFI-Verlag, Theodor-Heuss Ring 62, 50668 K"ln, Germany. Only for gunsmiths, licensed firearms dealers and their suppliers in Germany, Austria and Switzerland.

Wild Sheep (M) (Q)
Foundation for North American Wild Sheep, 720 Allen Ave., Cody, WY 82414. Website: http://iigi.com/os/non/fnaws/fnaws.htm; e-mail: fnaws@wyoming.com. Official journal of the foundation.

Wisconsin Outdoor Journal
Krause Publications, 700 E. State St., Iola, WI 54990-0001. $17.97 yr. (8 issues). For Wisconsin's avid hunters and fishermen, with features from all over that state with regional reports, legislative updates, etc. Website: www.krause.com

Women & Guns
P.O. Box 488, Sta. C, Buffalo, NY 14209. $24.00 yr. U.S.; $72.00 foreign (12 issues). Only magazine edited by and for women gun owners.

World War II*
Cowles History Group, 741 Miller Dr. SE, Suite D-2, Leesburg, VA 20175-8920. Annual subscriptions $19.95 U.S.; $25.95 Canada; 43.95 foreign. The title says it—WWII; good articles, ads, etc.

---

*Published bi-monthly
† Published weekly
‡Published three times per month. All others are published monthly.

M=Membership requirements; write for details.
Q=Published Quarterly.

THE ARMS LIBRARY

FOR COLLECTOR ◆ HUNTER ◆ SHOOTER ◆ OUTDOORSMAN

IMPORTANT NOTICE TO BOOK BUYERS

Books listed here may be bought from Ray Riling Arms Books Co., 6844 Gorsten St., P.O. Box 18925, Philadelphia, PA 19119, Phone 215/438-2456; FAX: 215-438-5395. E-Mail: sales@rayrilingarms-books.com. - Joe Riling is the researcher and compiler of "The Arms Library" and a seller of gun books for over 30 years. The Riling stock includes books classic and modern, many hard-to-find items, and many not obtainable elsewhere. These pages list a portion of the current stock. They offer prompt, complete service, with delayed shipments occurring only on out-of-print or out-of-stock books.

Visit our web site at **www.rayrilingarmsbooks.com** and order all of your favorite titles on line from our secure site.

NOTICE FOR ALL CUSTOMERS: Remittance in U.S. funds must accompany all orders. For your convenience we now accept Visa, Mastercard & American Express. For Shipments in the U.S. add $5.00 for the 1st book and

$2.00 for each additional book for postage and insurance. Minimum order $10.00. International Orders add $8.00 for the 1st book and $5.00 for each additional book. All International orders are shipped at the buyer's risk unless an additional $5 for insurance is included. USPS does not offer insurance to all countries unless shipped Air-Mail please e-mail or call for pricing.

Payments in excess of order or for "Backorders" are credited or fully refunded at request. Books "As-Ordered" are not returnable except by permission and a handling charge on these of $2.00 per book is deducted from refund or credit. Only Pennsylvania customers must include current sales tax.

A full variety of arms books also available from Rutgers Book Center, 127 Raritan Ave., Highland Park, NJ 08904/908-545-4344; FAX: 908-545-6686 or I.D.S.A. Books, 1324 Stratford Drive, Piqua, OH 45356/937-773-4203; FAX: 937-778-1922.

* denotes new edition

BALLISTICS AND HANDLOADING

ABC's of Reloading, 6th Edition, by C. Rodney James and the editors of Handloader's Digest, DBI Books, a division of Krause Publications, Iola, WI, 1997. 288 pp., illus. Paper covers. $21.95.
The definitive guide to every facet of cartridge and shotshell reloading.

Ammo and Ballistics, by Robert W. Forker, Safari Press, Inc., Huntington Beach, CA., 1999. 252 pp., illustrated. Paper covers. $18.95.
Ballistic data on 125 calibers and 1,400 loads out to 500 yards.

Ammunition Making, by George E. Frost, National Rifle Association of America, Washington, D.C., 1990. 160 pp., illus. Paper covers. $17.95.
Reflects the perspective of "an insider" with half a century's experience in successful management of ammunition manufacturing operations.

Barnes Reloading Manual #2, Barnes Bullets, American Fork, UT, 1999. 668 pp., illus. $24.95.
Features data and trajectories on the new weight X, XBT and Solids in calibers from .22 to .50 BMG.

Basic Handloading, by George C. Nonte, Jr., Outdoor Life Books, New York, NY, 1982. 192 pp., illus. Paper covers. $6.95.
How to produce high-quality ammunition using the safest, most efficient methods.

Big Bore Rifles And Cartridges, Wolfe Publishing Co., Prescott, AZ, 1991. Paper covers. $26.00.
This book covers cartridges from 8mm to .600 Nitro with loading tables.

Black Powder Guide, 2nd Edition, by George C. Nonte, Jr., Stoeger Publishing Co., So. Hackensack, NJ, 1991. 288 pp., illus. Paper covers. $14.95.
How-to instructions for selection, repair and maintenance of muzzleloaders, making your own bullets, restoring and refinishing, shooting techniques.

Blackpowder Loading Manual, 3rd Edition, by Sam Fadala, DBI Books, a division of Krause Publications, Iola, WI, 1995. 368 pp., illus. Paper covers. $20.95.
Revised and expanded edition of this landmark blackpowder loading book. Covers hundreds of loads for most of the popular blackpowder rifles, handguns and shotguns.

*Cartridges of the World, 9th Edition, by Frank Barnes, edited by M. L. McPherson, DBI Books, a division of Krause Publications, Iola, WI, 1997. 512 pp., illus. Paper covers. $24.95.
Completely revised edition of the general purpose reference work for which collectors, police, scientists and laymen reach first for answers to cartridge identification questions.

Cartridge Reloading Tools of the Past, by R.H. Chamberlain and Tom Quigley, Tom Quigley, Castle Rock, WA, 1998. 167 pp., illustrated. Paper covers. $25.00.
A detailed treatment of the extensive Winchester and Ideal line of handloading tools and bullet molds, plus Remington, Marlin, Ballard, Browning, Maynard, and many others.

Cast Bullets for the Black Powder Rifle, by Paul A. Matthews, Wolfe Publishing Co., Prescott, AZ, 1996. 133 pp., illus. Paper covers. $22.50.
The tools and techniques used to make your cast bullet shooting a success.

Complete Blackpowder Handbook, 3rd Edition, by Sam Fadala, DBI Books, a division of Krause Publications, Iola, WI, 1997. 400 pp., illus. Paper covers. $21.95.
Expanded and completely rewritten edition of the definitive book on the subject of blackpowder.

Complete Reloading Guide, by Robert & John Traister, Stoeger Publishing Co., Wayne, NJ, 1997. 608 pp., illus. Paper covers. $34.95.
Perhaps the finest, most comprehensive work ever published on the subject of reloading.

Game Loads and Practical Ballistics for the American Hunter, by Bob Hagel, Wolfe Publishing Co., Prescott, AZ, 1992. 310 pp., illus. $27.90.
Hagel's knowledge gained as a hunter, guide and gun enthusiast is gathered in this informative text.

Handbook for Shooters and Reloaders, by P.O. Ackley, Salt Lake City, UT, 1970, (Vol. I), 567 pp., illus. (Vol. II), a new printing with specific new material. 495 pp., illus. $18.95 each.

Handloader's Digest, 17th Edition, edited by Bob Bell. DBI Books, a division of Krause Publications, Iola, WI, 1997. 480 pp., illustrated. Paper covers. $27.95.
Top writers in the field contribute helpful information on techniques and components. Greatly expanded and fully indexed catalog of all currently available tools, accessories and components for metallic, blackpowder cartridge, shotgun reloading and swaging.

Handloader's Guide, by Stanley W. Trzoniec, Stoeger Publishing Co., So. Hackensack, NJ, 1985. 256 pp., illus. Paper covers. $14.95.
The complete step-by-step fully illustrated guide to handloading ammunition.

Handloader's Manual of Cartridge Conversions, by John J. Donnelly, Stoeger Publishing Co., So. Hackensack, NJ, 1986. Unpaginated. $34.95.
From 14 Jones to 70-150 Winchester in English and American cartridges, and from 4.85 U.K. to 15.2x28R Gevelot in metric cartridges. Over 900 cartridges described in detail.

Handloading for Hunters, by Don Zutz, Winchester Press, Piscataway, NJ, 1977. 288 pp., illus. $30.00.
Precise mixes and loads for different types of game and for various hunting situations with rifle and shotgun.

Hatcher's Notebook, by S. Julian Hatcher, Stackpole Books, Harrisburg, PA, 1992. 488 pp., illus. $39.95.
A reference work for shooters, gunsmiths, ballisticians, historians, hunters and collectors.

Hodgdon Powder Data Manual #27, Hodgdon Powder Co., Shawnee Mission, KS, 1999. 800 pp. $27.95
Reloading data for rifle and pistol loads.

Hodgdon Shotshell Data Manual, Hodgdon Powder Co., Shawnee Mission, KS, 1999. 208 pp. $19.95
Contains hundreds of loads for lead shot, buck shot, slugs, bismuth shot and steel shot plus articles on ballistics, patterning, special reloads and much more.

The Home Guide to Cartridge Conversions, by Maj. George C. Nonte Jr., The Gun Room Press, Highland Park, NJ, 1976. 404 pp., illus. $24.95.
Revised and updated version of Nonte's definitive work on the alteration of cartridge cases for use in guns for which they were not intended.

Hornady Handbook of Cartridge Reloading, 5th Edition, Vol. I and II, Edited by Larry Steadman, Hornady Mfg. Co., Grand Island, NE, 2000., illus. $40.00.
2 Volumes; Volume 1, 773 pp.; Volume 2, 717 pp. New edition of this famous reloading handbook covers rifle and handgun reloading data and ballistic tables. Latest loads, ballistic information, etc.

Hornady Handbook of Cartridge Reloading, Abridged Edition, Hornady Mfg. Co., Grand Island, NE, 1991. $19.95.
Ballistic data for 25 of the most popular cartridges.

Hornady Load Notes, Hornady Mfg. Co., Grand Island, NE, 1991. $4.95.
Complete load data and ballistics for a single caliber. Eight pistol 9mm-45ACP; 16 rifle, 222-45-70.

How-To's for the Black Powder Cartridge Rifle Shooter, by Paul A. Matthews, Wolfe Publishing Co., Prescott, AZ, 1995. 45 pp. Paper covers. $22.50.
Covers lube recipes, good bore cleaners and over-powder wads. Tips include compressing powder charges, combating wind resistance, improving ignition and much more.

REFERENCE

THE ARMS LIBRARY

The Illustrated Reference of Cartridge Dimensions, edited by Dave Scovill, Wolfe Publishing Co., Prescott, AZ, 1994. 343 pp., illus. Paper covers. $19.00.
A comprehensive volume with over 300 cartridges. Standard and metric dimensions have been taken from SAAMI drawings and/or fired cartridges.

Lee Modern Reloading, by Richard Lee, 350 pp. of charts and data and 85 illustrations. 512 pp. $24.95.
Bullet casting, lubricating and author's formula for calculating proper charges for cast bullets. Includes virtually all current load data published by the powder suppliers. Exclusive source of volume measured loads.

Loading the Black Powder Rifle Cartridge, by Paul A Matthews, Wolfe Publishing Co., Prescott, AZ, 1993. 121 pp., illus. Paper covers. $22.50.
Author Matthews brings the blackpowder cartridge shooter valuable information on the basics, including cartridge care, lubes and moulds, powder charges and developing and testing loads in his usual authoritative style.

Loading the Peacemaker—Colt's Model P, by Dave Scovill, Wolfe Publishing Co., Prescott, AZ, 1996. 227 pp., illus. $24.95.
A comprehensive work about the history, maintenance and repair of the most famous revolver ever made, including the most extensive load data ever published.

Lyman Cast Bullet Handbook, 3rd Edition, edited by C. Kenneth Ramage, Lyman Publications, Middlefield, CT, 1980. 416 pp., illus. Paper covers. $19.95.
Information on more than 5000 tested cast bullet loads and 19 pages of trajectory and wind drift tables for cast bullets.

Lyman Black Powder Handbook, edited by C. Kenneth Ramage, Lyman Products for Shooters, Middlefield, CT, 1975. 239 pp., illus. Paper covers. $14.95.
Comprehensive load information for the modern blackpowder shooter.

Lyman Pistol & Revolver Handbook, 2nd Edition, edited by Thomas J. Griffin, Lyman Products Co., Middlefield, CT, 1996. 287 pp., illus. Paper covers. $18.95.
The most up-to-date loading data available including the hottest new calibers, like 40 S&W, 9x21, 9mm Makarov, 9x25 Dillon and 454 Casull.

Lyman Reloading Handbook No. 47, edited by Edward A. Matunas, Lyman Publications, Middlefield, CT, 1992. 480 pp., illus. Paper covers. $24.95.
A comprehensive reloading manual complete with "How to Reload" information. Expanded data section with all the newest rifle and pistol calibers.

Lyman Shotshell Handbook, 4th Edition, edited by Edward A. Matunas, Lyman Products Co., Middlefield, CT, 1996. 330 pp., illus. Paper covers. $24.95.
Has 9000 loads, including slugs and buckshot, plus feature articles and a full color I.D. section.

Lyman's Guide to Big Game Cartridges & Rifles, by Edward Matunas, Lyman Publishing Corporation, Middlefield, CT, 1994. 287 pp., illus. Paper covers. $17.95.
A selection guide to cartridges and rifles for big game—antelope to elephant.

Making Loading Dies and Bullet Molds, by Harold Hoffman, H & P Publishing, San Angelo, TX, 1993. 230 pp., illus. Paper covers. $24.95.
A good book for learning tool and die making.

Metallic Cartridge Reloading, 3rd Edition, by M.L. McPherson, DBI Books, a division of Krause Publications, Iola, WI., 1996. 352 pp., illus. Paper covers. $21.95.
A true reloading manual with over 10,000 loads for all popular metallic cartridges and a wealth of invaluable technical data provided by a recognized expert.

Modern Combat Ammunition, by Duncan Long, Paladin Press, Boulder, CO, 1997, 8 1/2 x 11, soft cover, photos, illus., 216 pp. $34.00.
Now, Paladin's leading weapons author presents his exhaustive evaluation of the stopping power of modern rifle, pistol, shotgun and machine gun rounds based on actual case studies of shooting incidents.

Modern Exterior Ballistics, by Robert L. McCoy, Schiffer Publishing Co., Atglen, PA, 1999. 128 pp. $95.00
Advanced students of exterior ballistics and flight dynamics will find this comprehensive textbook on the subject a useful addition to their libraries.

Modern Handloading, by Maj. Geo. C. Nonte, Winchester Press, Piscataway, NJ, 1972. 416 pp., illus. $15.00.
Covers all aspects of metallic and shotshell ammunition loading, plus more loads than any book in print.

Modern Reloading, by Richard Lee, Inland Press, 1996. 510 pp., illus. $24.98.
The how-to's of rifle, pistol and shotgun reloading plus load data for rifle and pistol calibers.

Modern Sporting Rifle Cartridges, by Wayne van Zwoll, Stoeger Publishing Co., Wayne, NJ, 1998. 310 pp., illustrated. Paper covers. $21.95.
Illustrated with hundreds of photos and backed up by dozens of tables and schematic drawings, this four-part book tells the story of how rifle bullets and cartridges were developed and, in some cases, discarded.

Modern Practical Ballistics, by Art Pejsa, Pejsa Ballistics, Minneapolis, MN, 1990. 150 pp., illus. $24.95.
Covers all aspects of ballistics and new, simplified methods. Clear examples illustrate new, easy but very accurate formulas.

Mr. Single Shot's Cartridge Handbook, by Frank de Haas, Mark de Haas, Orange City, IA, 1996. 116 pp., illus. Paper covers. $21.50.
This book covers most of the cartridges, both commercial and wildcat, that the author has known and used.

Nick Harvey's Practical Reloading Manual, by Nick Harvey, Australian Print Group, Maryborough, Victoria, Australia, 1995. 235 pp., illus. Paper covers. $24.95.
Contains data for rifle and handgun including many popular wildcat and improved cartridges. Tools, powders, components and techniques for assembling optimum reloads with particular application to North America.

Nosler Reloading Manual #4, edited by Gail Root, Nosler Bullets, Inc., Bend, OR, 1996. 516 pp., illus. $24.99.
Combines information on their Ballistic Tip, Partition and Handgun bullets with traditional powders and new powders never before used, plus trajectory information from 100 to 500 yards.

The Paper Jacket, by Paul Matthews, Wolfe Publishing Co., Prescott, AZ, 1991. Paper covers. $13.50.
Up-to-date and accurate information about paper-patched bullets.

Propellant Profiles New and Expanded, 3rd Edition, Wolfe Publishing Co., Prescott, AZ, 1991. Paper covers. $16.95.

Reloading for Shotgunners, 4th Edition, by Kurt D. Fackler and M.L. McPherson, DBI Books, a division of Krause Publications, Iola, WI, 1997. 320 pp., illus. Paper covers. $19.95.
Expanded reloading tables with over 11,000 loads. Bushing charts for every major press and component maker. All new presentation on all aspects of shotshell reloading by two of the top experts in the field.

Sierra 50th Anniversary, 4th Edition Rifle Manual, edited by Ken Ramage, Sierra Bullets, Santa Fe Springs, CA, 1997. 800 pp., illus. $26.99.
New cartridge introductions, etc.

Sierra 50th Anniversary, 4th Edition Handgun Manual, edited by Ken Ramage, Sierra Bullets, Santa Fe, CA, 1997. 700 pp., illus. $21.99.
Histories, reloading recommendations, bullets, powders and sections on the reloading process, etc.

Sixgun Cartridges and Loads, by Elmer Keith, The Gun Room Press, Highland Park, NJ, 1986. 151 pp., illus. $24.95.
A manual covering the selection, uses and loading of the most suitable and popular revolver cartridges. Originally published in 1936. Reprint.

Speer Reloading Manual No. 13, edited by members of the Speer research staff, Omark Industries, Lewiston, ID, 1999. 621 pp., illustrated. $19.95.
With thirteen new sections containing the latest technical information and reloading trends for both novice and expert in this latest edition. More than 9,300 loads are listed, including new propellant powders from Accurate Arms, Alliant, Hodgdon and Vihtavuori.

Understanding Ballistics, by Robert A. Rinker, Mulberry House Publishing Co., Corydon, IN, 1997. 373 pp., illus Paper covers. $19.95.
Explains basic to advanced firearm ballistics in understandable terms.

Why Not Load Your Own?, by Col. T. Whelen, A. S. Barnes, New York, 1957, 4th ed., rev. 237 pp., illus. $20.00.
A basic reference on handloading, describing each step, materials and equipment. Includes loads for popular cartridges.

Wildcat Cartridges Volumes 1 & 2 Combination, by the editors of Handloaders magazine, Wolfe Publishing Co., Prescott, AZ, 1997. 350 pp., illus. Paper covers. $39.95.
A profile of the most popular information on wildcat cartridges that appeared in the Handloader magazine.

The Winchester Lever Legacy, by Clyde "Snooky" Williamson, Buffalo Press, Zachary, LA, 1988. 664 pp., illustrated. $39.95.
A book on reloading for the different calibers of the Winchester lever action rifle.

COLLECTORS

Age of the Gunfighter; Men and Weapons on the Frontier 1840-1900, by Joseph G. Rosa, University of Oklahoma Press, Norman, OK, 1999. 192 pp., illustrated. Paper covers. $21.95.
Stories of gunfighters and their encounters and detailed descriptions of virtually every firearm used in the old West.

Air Guns, by Eldon G. Wolff, Duckett's Publishing Co., Tempe, AZ, 1997. 204 pp., illus Paper covers. $35.00.
Historical reference covering many makers, European and American guns, canes and more.

American Beauty; The Prewar Colt National Match Government Model Pistol, by Timothy J. Mullin, Collector Grade Publications, Cobourg, Ontario, Canada. 72 pp., illustrated. $34.95.
Includes over 150 serial numbers, and 20 spectacular color photos of factory engraved guns and other authenticated upgrades, including rare "double-carved" ivory grips.

The American Cartridge, by Charles R. Suydam, Borden Publishing Co., Alhambra, CA, 1986. 184 pp., illus. $24.95.
An illustrated study of the rimfire cartridge in the United States.

The American Military Saddle, 1776-1945, by R. Stephen Dorsey & Kenneth L. McPheeters, Collector's Library, Eugene, OR, 1999. 400 pp., illustrated. $59.95.
The most complete coverage of the subject ever written on the American Military Saddle. Nearly 1000 actual photos and official drawings, from the major public and private collections in the U.S. and Great Britain.

American Police Collectibles; Dark Lanterns and Other Curious Devices, by Matthew G. Forte, Turn of the Century Publishers, Upper Montclair, NJ, 1999. 248 pp., illustrated. $24.95.
For collectors of police memorabilia (handcuffs, police dark lanterns, mechanical and chain nippers, rattles, billy clubs and nightsticks) and police historians.

Ammunition: Grenades and Projectile Munitions, by Ian V. Hogg, Stackpole Books, Mechanicsburg, PA, 1998. 144 pp., illus. $22.95.
Concise guide to modern ammunition. International coverage with detailed specifications and illustrations.

Antique Guns, the Collector's Guide, 2nd Edition, edited by John Traister, Stoeger Publishing Co., So. Hackensack, NJ, 1994. 320 pp., illus. Paper covers. $19.95.
Covers a vast spectrum of pre-1900 firearms: those manufactured by U.S. gunmakers as well as Canadian, French, German, Belgian, Spanish and other foreign firms.

THE ARMS LIBRARY

Arming the Glorious Cause; Weapons of the Second War for Independence, by James B. Whisker, Daniel D. Hartzler and Larry W. Tantz, Old Bedford Village Press, Bedford, PA., 1998. 175 pp., illustrated. $45.00.

A photographic study of Confederate weapons.

Arms & Accoutrements of the Mounted Police 1873-1973, by Roger F. Phillips and Donald J. Klancher, Museum Restoration Service, Ont., Canada, 1982. 224 pp., illus. $49.95.

A definitive history of the revolvers, rifles, machine guns, cannons, ammunition, swords, etc. used by the NWMP, the RNWMP and the RCMP during the first 100 years of the Force.

Arms and Equipment of the Civil War, by Jack Coggins, Barnes & Noble, Rockleight, N.J., 1999. 160 pp., illustrated. $12.98.

This unique encyclopedia provides a new perspective on the war. It provides lively explanations of how ingenious new weapons spelled victory or defeat for both sides. Aided by more than 500 illustrations and on-the-scene comments by Union and Confederate soldiers.

Arms Makers of Maryland, by Daniel D. Hartzler, George Shumway, York, PA, 1975. 200 pp., illus. $50.00.

A thorough study of the gunsmiths of Maryland who worked during the late 18th and early 19th centuries.

Arming the Dragon, Mauser Rifle Production in China 1895-1950, by Dolf L. Goldsmith, Dolf L. Goldsmith, San Antonio, TX, 1998. 47 pp., illustrated. Spiral bound Paper covers. $15.00.

Details the manufacture and history of the Mauser rifle China.

The Art of Gun Engraving, by Claude Gaier and Pietro Sabatti, Knickerbocker Press, N.Y., 1999. 160 pp., illustrated. $34.95.

The richness and detail lavished on early firearms represents a craftmanship nearly vanished. Beginning with crossbows in the 100's, hunting scenes, portraits, or mythological themes are intricately depicted within a few square inches of etched metal. The full-color photos contained herein recaptures this lost art with exquisite detail.

Artistry in Arms: The Guns of Smith & Wesson, by Roy G. Jinks, Smith & Wesson, Springfield, MA, 1991. 85 pp., illus. Paper covers. $19.95.

Catalog of the Smith & Wesson International Museum Tour 1991-1995 organized by the Connecticut Valley Historical Museum and Springfield Library and Museum Association.

Astra Automatic Pistols, by Leonardo M. Antaris, FIRAC Publishing Co., Sterling, CO, 1989. 248 pp., illus. $55.00.

Charts, tables, serial ranges, etc. The definitive work on Astra pistols.

Basic Documents on U.S. Martial Arms, commentary by Col. B. R. Lewis, reissue by Ray Riling, Phila., PA, 1956 and 1960. *Rifle Musket Model 1855.*

The first issue rifle of musket caliber, a muzzle loader equipped with the Maynard Primer, 32 pp. *Rifle Musket Model 1863.* The typical Union muzzle-loader of the Civil War, 26 pp. *Breech-Loading Rifle Musket Model 1866.* The first of our 50-caliber breechloading rifles, 12 pp. *Remington Navy Rifle Model 1870.* A commercial type breech-loader made at Springfield, 16 pp. *Lee Straight Pull Navy Rifle Model 1895.* A magazine cartridge arm of 6mm caliber. 23 pp. *Breech-Loading Arms* (five models) 27 pp. *Ward-Burton Rifle Musket 1871-*16 pp. Each $10.00.

Battle Weapons of the American Revolution, by George C. Neuman, Scurlock Publishing Co., Texarkana, TX, 1998. 400 pp. Illus. $65.00.

The most extensive photographic collection of Revolutionary War weapons ever in one volume. More than 1,600 photos of over 500 muskets, rifles, swords, bayonets, knives and other arms used by both sides in America's War for Independence.

Behold, the Longrifle Again, by James B. Whisker, Old Bedford Village Press, Bedford, PA, 1997. 176 pp., illus. $45.00.

Excellent reference work for the ocllector profusely illustrated with photographs of some of the finest Kentucky rifles showing front and back profiles and overall view.

The Belgian Rattlesnake; The Lewis Automatic Machine Gun, by William M. Easterly, Collector Grade Publications, Cobourg, Ontario, Canada, 1998. 584 pp., illustrated. $79.95.

The most complete account ever published on the life and times of Colonel Isaac Newton Lewis and his crowning invention, the Lewis Automatic machine gun.

Beretta Automatic Pistols, by J.B. Wood, Stackpole Books, Harrisburg, PA, 1985. 192 pp., illus. $24.95.

Only English-language book devoted to the Beretta line. Includes all important models.

The Big Guns, Civil War Siege, Seacoast, and Naval Cannon, by Edwin Olmstead, Wayne E. Stark, and Spencer C. Tucker, Museum Restoration Service, Bloomfield, Ontario, Canada, 1997. 360 pp., illustrated. $80.00.

This book is designed to identify and record the heavy guns available to both sides by the end of the Civil War.

Birmingham Gunmakers, by Douglas Tate, Safari Press, Inc., Huntington Beach, CA, 1997. 300 pp., illus. $50.00.

An invaluable work for anybody interested in the fine sporting arms crafted in this famous Birmingham gunmakers' city.

Blue Book of Gun Values, 21st Edition, edited by S.P. Fjestad, Blue Book Publications, Inc. Minniapolis, MN 2000. 1301 pp., illustrated Paper Covers. $34.95.

Covers all new 2000 firearms prices. Gives technical data on both new and discontinued domestic and foreign commercial and military guns.

Blacksmith Guide to Ruger Flat-Top & Super Blackhawks, by H.W. Ross, Jr., Blacksmith Corp., Chino Valley, AZ, 1990. 96 pp., illus. Paper covers. $9.95.

A key source on the extensively collected Ruger Blackhawk revolvers.

The Blunderbuss 1500-1900, by James D. Forman, Museum Restoration Service, Bloomfield, Ont., Canada, 1995. 40 pp., illus. Paper covers. $4.95.

The guns that had no peer as an anti-personal weapon throughout the flintlock era.

Boarders Away, Volume II: Firearms of the Age of Fighting Sail, by William Gilkerson, Andrew Mowbray, Inc. Publishers, Lincoln, RI, 1993. 331 pp., illus. $65.00.

Covers the pistols, muskets, combustibles and small cannon used aboard American and European fighting ships, 1626-1826.

Boothroyd's Revised Directory of British Gunmakers, by Geoffrey and Susan Boothroyd, Sand Lake Press, Amity, OR, 1997. 412 pp., illus. $34.95.

A new revised and enlarged edition. Lists all makers in alphabetical order.

Breech-Loading Carbines of the United States Civil War Period, by Brig. Gen. John Pitman, Armory Publications, Tacoma, WA, 1987. 94 pp., illus. $29.95.

The first in a series of previously unpublished manuscripts originated by the late Brigadier General John Putnam. Exploded drawings showing parts actual size follow each sectioned illustration.

The Breech-Loading Single-Shot Rifle, by Major Ned H. Roberts and Kenneth L. Waters, Wolfe Publishing Co., Prescott, AZ, 1995. 333 pp., illus. $28.50.

A comprehensive and complete history of the evolution of the Schutzen and single-shot rifle.

The Bren Gun Saga, by Thomas B. Dugelby, Collector Grade Publications, Cobourg, Ontario, Canada, 1999, revised and expanded edition. 406 pp., illustrated. $65.95.

A modern, definitive book on the Bren in this revised expanded edition, which in terms of numbers of pages and illustrations is nearly twice the size of the original.

The British Enfield Rifles, Volume 1, The SMLE Mk I and Mk III Rifles, by Charles R. Stratton, North Cape Pub. Tustin, CA, 1997. 150 pp., illus. Paper covers. $16.95.

A systematic and thorough examination on a part-by-part basis of the famous British battle rifle that endured for nearly 70 years as the British Army's number one battle rifle.

British Enfield Rifles, Volume 2, No.4 and No.5 Rifles, by Charles R. Stratton, North Cape Publications, Tustin, CA, 1999. 150 pp., illustrated. Paper covers. $16.95.

The historical background for the development of both rifles describing each variation and an explanation of all the "marks", "numbers" and codes found on most parts.

The British Falling Block Breechloading Rifle from 1865, by Jonathan Kirton, Tom Rowe Books, Maynardsville, TN, 2nd edition, 1997. 380 pp., illus. $70.00.

Expanded 2nd edition of a comprehensive work on the British falling block rifle.

British Gun Engraving, by Douglas Tate, Safari Press, Inc., Huntington Beach, CA, 1999. 240 pp., illustrated. Limited, signed and numbered edition, in a slipcase. $80.00

A historic and photographic record of the last two centuries.

British Military Firearms 1650-1850, by Howard L. Blackmore, Stackpole Books, Mechanicsburg, PA, 1994. 224 pp., illus. $65.00.

The definitive work on British military firearms.

British Service Rifles and Carbines 1888-1900, by Alan M. Petrillo, Excaliber Publications, Latham, NY, 1994. 72 pp., illus, Paper covers. $11.95.

A complete review of the Lee-Metford and Lee-Enfield rifles and carbines.

British Single Shot Rifles, Volume 1, Alexander Henry, by Wal Einfer, Tom Rowe, Manardville, TN, 1998, 200 pp., illus. $50.00.

Detailed Study of the single shot rifles made by Henry. Illustrated with hundreds of photographs and drawings.

British Single Shot Rifles Volume 2, George Gibbs, by Wal Winfer, Tom Rowe, Maynardville, TN, 1998. 177 pp., illus. $50.00.

Detailed study of the Farquharson as made by Gibbs. Hundreds of photos.

British Single Shot Rifles, Volume 3, Jeffery, by Wal Winfer, Rowe Publications, Rochester, N.Y., 1999. 260 pp., illustrated. $60.00.

The Farquharsen as made by Jeffery and his competitors, Holland & Holland, Bland, Westley, Manton, etc. Large section on the development of nitro cartridges including the .600.

The British Soldier's Firearms from Smoothbore to Rifled Arms, 1850-1864, by Dr. C.H. Roads, R&R Books, Livonia, NY, 1994. 332 pp., illus. $49.00.

A reprint of the classic text covering the development of British military hand and shoulder firearms in the crucial years between 1850 and 1864.

British Sporting Guns & Rifles, compiled by George Hoyem, Armory Publications, Coeur d'Alene, ID, 1997. 1024 pp., illus. In two volumes. $240.00.

Eighteen old sporting firearms trade catalogs and a rare book reproduced with their color covers in a limited, signed and numbered edition.

Browning Dates of Manufacture, compiled by George Madis, Art and Reference House, Brownsboro, TX, 1989. 48 pp. $10.00.

Gives the date codes and product codes for all models from 1824 to the present.

Browning Sporting Arms of Distinction 1903-1992, by Matt Eastman, Matt Eastman Publications, Fitzgerald, GA, 1995. 450 pp., illus. $49.95.

The most recognized publication on Browning sporting arms; covers all models.

Buffalo Bill's Wild West: An American Legend, by R.L. Wilson and Greg Martine, Random House, N.Y., 1999. 3,167 pp., illustrated. $60.00.

Over 225 color plates and 160 black-and-white illustrations, with in-depth text and captions, the colorful arms, posters, photos, costumes, saddles, accoutrement are brought to life.

Bullard Arms, by G. Scott Jamieson, The Boston Mills Press, Ontario, Canada, 1989. 244 pp., illus. $35.00.

The story of a mechanical genius whose rifles and cartridges were the equal to any made in America in the 1880s.

Burning Powder, compiled by Major D.B. Wesson, Wolfe Publishing Company, Prescott, AZ, 1992. 110 pp. Soft cover. $10.95.

A rare booklet from 1932 for Smith & Wesson collectors.

THE ARMS LIBRARY

The Burnside Breech Loading Carbines, by Edward A. Hull, Andrew Mowbray, Inc., Lincoln, RI, 1986. 95 pp., illus. $16.00.

No. 1 in the "Man at Arms Monograph Series." A model-by-model historical/technical examination of one of the most widely used cavalry weapons of the American Civil War based upon important and previously unpublished research.

Canadian Military Handguns 1855-1985, by Clive M. Law, Museum Restoration Service, Bloomfield, Ont. Canada, 1994. 130pp., illus. $40.00.

A long-awaited and important history for arms historians and pistol collectors.

Cap Guns, by James Dundas, Schiffer Publishing, Atglen, PA, 1996. 160 pp., illus. Paper covers. $29.95.

Over 600 full-color photos of cap guns and gun accessories with a current value guide.

Carbines of the Civil War, by John D. McAulay, Pioneer Press, Union City, TN, 1981. 123 pp., illus. Paper covers. $12.95.

A guide for the student and collector of the colorful arms used by the Federal cavalry.

Carbines of the U.S. Cavalry 1861-1905, by John D. McAulay, Andrew Mowbray Publishers, Lincoln, RI, 1996. $35.00.

Covers the crucial use of carbines from the beginning of the Civil War to the end of the cavalry carbine era in 1905.

Cartridge Carbines of the British Army, by Alan M. Petrillo, Excalibur Publications, Latham, NY, 1998. 72 pp., illustrated. Paper covers. $11.95.

Begins with the Snider-Enfield which was the first regulation cartridge carbine introduced in 1866 and ends with the .303 caliber No.5, Mark 1 Enfield.

Cartridge Catalogues, compiled by George Hoyem, Armory Publications, Coeur d'Alene, ID., 1997. 504 pp., illus. $125.00.

Fourteen old ammunition makers' and designers' catalogs reproduced with their color covers in a limited, signed and numbered edition.

*Cartridges of the World, 9th Edition, by Frank Barnes, edited by M. L. McPherson, DBI Books, a division of Krause Publications, Iola, WI, 2000. 512 pp., illus. Paper covers. $24.95.

Completely revised edition of the general purpose reference work for which collectors, police, scientists and laymen reach first for answers to cartridge identification questions. Available October, 1996.

Cartridge Reloading Tools of the Past, by R.H. Chamberlain and Tom Quigley, Tom Quigley, Castle Rock, WA, 1998. 167 pp., illustrated. Paper covers. $25.00.

A detailed treatment of the extensive Winchester and Ideal lines of handloading tools and bulletmolds plus Remington, Marlin, Ballard, Browning and many others.

Cartridges for Collectors, by Fred Datig, Pioneer Press, Union City, TN, 1999. In three volumes of 176 pp. each. Vol.1 (Centerfire); Vol.2 (Rimfire and Misc.) types; Vol.3 (Additional Rimfire, Centerfire, and Plastic). All illustrations are shown in full-scale drawings. Each volume $19.95.

Civil War Arms Makers and Their Contracts, edited by Stuart C. Mowbray and Jennifer Heroux, Andrew Mowbray Publishing, Lincoln, RI, 1998. 595 pp. $39.50.

A facsimile reprint of the Report by the Commissioner of Ordnance and Ordnance Stores, 1862.

Civil War Breech Loading Rifles, by John D. McAulay, Andrew Mowbray, Inc., Lincoln, RI, 1991. 144 pp., illus. Paper covers. $15.00.

All the major breech-loading rifles of the Civil War and most, if not all, of the obscure types are detailed, illustrated and set in their historical context.

Civil War Cartridge Boxes of the Union Infantryman, by Paul Johnson, Andrew Mowbray, Inc., Lincoln, RI, 1998. 352 pp., illustrated. $45.00.

There were four patterns of infantry cartridge boxes used by Union forces during the Civil War. The author describes the development and subsequent pattern changes to these cartridge boxes.

Civil War Firearms, by Joseph G. Bilby, Combined Books, Conshohocken, PA, 1996. 252 pp., illus. $34.95.

A unique work combining background data on each firearm including its battlefield use, and a guide to collecting and firing surviving relics and modern reproductions.

Civil War Guns, by William B. Edwards, Thomas Publications, Gerrysburg, PA, 1997. 444 pp., illus. $40.00.

The complete story of Federal and Confederate small arms; design, manufacture, identifications, procurement issue, employment, effectiveness, and postwar disposal by the recognized expert.

Civil War Pistols, by John D. McAulay, Andrew Mowbray Inc., Lincoln, RI, 1992. 166 pp., illus. $38.50.

A survey of the handguns used during the American Civil War.

Civil War Sharps Carbines and Rifles, by Earl J. Coates and John D. McAulay, Thomas Publications, Gettysburg, PA, 1996. 108 pp., illus. Paper covers. $12.95.

Traces the history and development of the firearms including short histories of specific serial numbers and the soldiers who received them.

Civil War Small Arms of the U.S. Navy and Marine Corps, by John D. McAulay, Mowbray Publishing, Lincoln, RI, 1999. 186 pp., illustrated. $39.00.

The first reliable and comprehensive guide to the firearms and edged weapons of the Civil War Navy and Marine Corps.

The W.F. Cody Buffalo Bill Collector's Guide with Values, by James W. Wojtowicz, Collector Books, Paducah, KY, 1998. 271 pp., illustrated. $24.95.

A profusion of colorful collectibles including lithographs, programs, photographs, books, medals, sheet music, guns, etc. and today's values.

Col. Burton's Spiller & Burr Revolver, by Matthew W. Norman, Mercer University Press, Macon, GA, 1997. 152 pp., illus. $22.95.

A remarkable archival research project on the arm together with a comprehensive story of the establishment and running of the factory.

Collector's Guide to Colt .45 Service Pistols Models of 1911 and 1911A1, Enlarged and revised edition. Clawson Publications, Fort Wayne, IN, 1998. 130 pp., illustrated. $45.00.

From 1911 to the end of production in 1945 with complete military identification including all contractors.

A Collector's Guide to United States Combat Shotguns, by Bruce N. Canfield, Andrew Mowbray Inc., Lincoln, RI, 1992. 184 pp., illus. Paper covers. $24.00.

This book provides full coverage of combat shotguns, from the earliest examples right up to the Gulf War and beyond.

A Collector's Guide to Winchester in the Service, by Bruce N. Canfield, Andrew Mowbray, Inc., Lincoln, RI, 1991. 192 pp., illus. Paper covers. $22.00.

The firearms produced by Winchester for the national defense. From Hotchkiss to the M14, each firearm is examined and illustrated.

A Collector's Guide to the '03 Springfield, by Bruce N. Canfield, Andrew Mowbray Inc., Lincoln, RI, 1989. 160 pp., illus. Paper covers. $22.00.

A comprehensive guide follows the '03 through its unparalleled tenure of service. Covers all of the interesting variations, modifications and accessories of this highly collectible military rifle.

Collector's Illustrated Encyclopedia of the American Revolution, by George C. Neumann and Frank J. Kravic, Rebel Publishing Co., Inc., Texarkana, TX, 1989. 286 pp., illus. $36.95.

A showcase of more than 2,300 artifacts made, worn, and used by those who fought in the War for Independence.

Colonial Frontier Guns, by T.M. Hamilton, Pioneer Press, Union City, TN, 1988. 176 pp., illus. Paper covers. $17.50.

A complete study of early flint muskets of this country.

The Colt Armory, by Ellsworth Grant, Man-at-Arms Bookshelf, Lincoln, RI, 1996. 232 pp., illus. $35.00.

A history of Colt's Manufacturing Company.

Colt Blackpowder Reproductions & Replica: A Collector's and Shooter's Guide, by Dennis Miller, Blue Book Publications, Minneapolis, MN, 1999. 288 pp., illustrated. Paper covers. $29.95.

The first book on this important subject, and a must for the investor, collector, and shooter.

Colt Heritage, by R.L. Wilson, Simon & Schuster, 1979. 358 pp., illus. $75.00.

The official history of Colt firearms 1836 to the present.

Colt Memorabilia Price Guide, by John Ogle, Krause Publications, Iola, WI, 1998. 256 pp., illus. Paper covers. $29.95.

The first book ever compiled about the vast array of non-gun merchandise produced by Sam Colt's companies, and other companies using the Colt name.

The Colt Model 1905 Automatic Pistol, by John Potocki, Andrew Mowbray Publishing, Lincoln, RI, 1998. 191 pp., illus. $28.00.

Covers all aspects of the Colt Model 1905 Automatic Pistol, from its invention by the legendary John Browning to its numerous production variations.

Colt Peacemaker British Model, by Keith Cochran, Cochran Publishing Co., Rapid City, SD, 1989. 160 pp., illus. $35.00.

Covers those revolvers Colt squeezed in while completing a large order of revolvers for the U.S. Cavalry in early 1874, to those magnificent cased target revolvers used in the pistol competitions at Bisley Commons in the 1890s.

Colt Peacemaker Encyclopedia, by Keith Cochran, Keith Cochran, Rapid City, SD, 1986. 434 pp., illus. $65.00.

A must book for the Peacemaker collector.

Colt Peacemaker Encyclopedia, Volume 2, by Keith Cochran, Cochran Publishing Co., SD, 1992. 416 pp., illus. $60.00.

Included in this volume are extensive notes on engraved, inscribed, historical and noted revolvers, as well as those revolvers used by outlaws, lawmen, movie and television stars.

Colt Percussion Accoutrements 1834-1873, by Robin Rapley, Robin Rapley, Newport Beach, CA, 1994. 432 pp., illus. Paper covers. $39.95.

The complete collector's guide to the identification of Colt percussion accoutrements; including Colt conversions and their values.

Colt Pocket Hammerless Pistols, by Dr. John W. Brunner, Phillips Publications, Williamstown, NJ, 1998. 212 pp., illustrated. $59.95.

You will never again have to question a .25, .32 or .380 with this well illustrated, definitive reference guide at hand.

Colt Revolvers and the Tower of London, by Joseph G. Rosa, Royal Armouries of the Tower of London, London, England, 1988. 72 pp., illus. Soft covers. $15.00.

Details the story of Colt in London through the early cartridge period.

Colt Rifles and Muskets from 1847-1870, by Herbert Houze, Krause Publications, Iola, WI, 1996. 192 pp., illus. $34.95.

Discover previously unknown Colt models along with an extensive list of production figures for all models.

Colt's SAA Post War Models, by George Garton, The Gun Room Press, Highland Park, NJ, 1995. 166 pp., illus. $39.95.

Complete facts on the post-war Single Action Army revolvers. Information on calibers, production numbers and variations taken from factory records.

Colt Single Action Army Revolvers: The Legend, the Romance and the Rivals, by "Doc" O'Meara, Krause Publications, Iola, WI, 2000. 160 pp., illustrated with 250 photos in b&w and a 16 page color section. $34.95.

Production figures, serial numbers by year, and rarities.

Colt Single Action Army Revolvers and Alterations, by C. Kenneth Moore, Mowbray Publishers, Lincoln, RI, 1999. 112 pp., illustrated. $35.00.

A comprehensive history of the revolvers that collectors call "Artillery Models." These are the most historical of all S.A.A. Colts, and this new book covers all the details.

Colt Single Action Army Revolvers and the London Agency, by C. Kenneth Moore, Andrew Mowbray Publishers, Lincoln, RI, 1990. 144 pp., illus. $35.00.
Drawing on vast documentary sources, this work chronicles the relationship between the London Agency and the Hartford home office.

The Colt U.S. General Officers' Pistols, by Horace Greeley IV, Andrew Mowbray Inc., Lincoln, RI, 1990. 199 pp., illus. $38.00.
These unique weapons, issued as a badge of rank to General Officers in the U.S. Army from WWII onward, remain highly personal artifacts of the military leaders who carried them. Includes serial numbers and dates of issue.

Colts from the William M. Locke Collection, by Frank Sellers, Andrew Mowbray Publishers, Lincoln, RI, 1996. 192 pp., illus. $55.00.
This important book illustrates all of the famous Locke Colts, with captions by arms authority Frank Sellers.

Colt's Dates of Manufacture 1837-1978, by R.L. Wilson, published by Maurie Albert, Coburg, Australia; N.A. distributor I.D.S.A. Books, Hamilton, OH, 1983. 61 pp. $6.00.
An invaluable pocket guide to the dates of manufacture of Colt firearms up to 1978.

Colt's 100th Anniversary Firearms Manual 1836-1936: A Century of Achievement, Wolfe Publishing Co., Prescott, AZ, 1992. 100 pp., illus. Paper covers. $12.95.
Originally published by the Colt Patent Firearms Co., this booklet covers the history, manufacturing procedures and the guns of the first 100 years of the genius of Samuel Colt.

Complete Guide to the M1 Garand and the M1 Carbine, by Bruce N. Canfield, 2nd printing, Andrew Mowbray Inc., Lincoln, RI, 1999. 296 pp., illus. $39.50.
Expanded and updated coverage of both the M1 Garand and the M1 Carbine, with more than twice as much information as the author's previous book on this topic.

The Complete Guide to U.S. Infantry Weapons of World War Two, by Bruce Canfield, Andrew Mowbray, Publisher, Lincoln, RI, 1995. 303 pp., illus. $35.00.
A definitive work on the weapons used by the United States Armed Forces in WWII.

Compliments of Col. Ruger: A Study of Factory Engraved Single Action Revolvers, by John C. Dougan, Taylor Publishing Co., El Paso, TX, 1992. 238 pp., illus. $46.50.
Clearly detailed black and white photographs and a precise text present an accurate history of the Sturm, Ruger & Co. single-action revolver engraving project.

Confederate Handguns, by William A. Albaugh, Hugh Benet, Jr. and Edward N. Simmons, Broadfoot Publishing Co., Wilmington, N.C., 1993. 250 pp., illustrated. $35.00.
Concerning the guns, the men who made them and the time of their use.

Cowboy Collectibles and Western Memorabilia, by Bob Bell and Edward Vebell, Schiffer Publishing, Atglen, PA, 1992. 160 pp., illus. Paper covers. $29.95.
The exciting era of the cowboy and the wild west collectibles including rifles, pistols, gun rigs, etc.

Cowboy Culture: The Last Frontier of American Antiques, by Michael Friedman, Schiffer Publishing, Ltd., West Chester, PA, 1992. 300 pp., illustrated.
Covers the artful aspects of the old west, the antiques and collectibles. Illustrated with clear color plates of over 1,000 items such as spurs, boots, guns, saddles etc.

Cowboy and Gunfighter Collectible, by Bill Mackin, Mountain Press Publishing Co., Missoula, MT, 1995. 178 pp., illus. Paper covers. $25.00.
A photographic encyclopedia with price guide and makers' index.

Cowboys and the Trappings of the Old West, by William Manns and Elizabeth Clair Flood, Zon International Publishing Co., Santa Fe, NM, 1997, 1st edition. 224 pp., illustrated. $45.00.
A pictorial celebration of the cowboy's dress and trappings.

Cowboy Hero Cap Pistols, by Rudy D'Angelo, Antique Trader Books, Dubuque, IA, 1998. 196 pp., illus. Paper covers. $34.95.
Aimed at collectors of cap pistols created and named for famous film and television cowboy heros, this in-depth guide hits all the marks. Current values are given.

Custom Firearms Engraving, by Tom Turpin, Krause Publications, Iola, WI, 1999. 208 pp., illustrated. $49.95.
Over 200 four-color photos with more than 75 master engravers profiled. Engravers Directory with addresses in the U.S. and abroad.

Czech Firearms and Ammunition Past and Present, 1919-1995, by Vladimir Dolinek & V. Karlicky, 190 pp., illus. in black & white and color. $49.95.
Covers Czech firearms from the earliest to the present day.

The Deringer in America, Volume 1, The Percussion Period, by R.L. Wilson and L.D. Eberhart, Andrew Mowbray Inc., Lincoln, RI, 1985. 271 pp., illus. $48.00.
A long awaited book on the American percussion deringer.

The Deringer in America, Volume 2, The Cartridge Period, by L.D. Eberhart and R.L. Wilson, Andrew Mowbray Inc., Publishers, Lincoln, RI, 1993. 284 pp., illus. $65.00.
Comprehensive coverage of cartridge deringers organized alphabetically by maker. Includes all types of deringers known by the authors to have been offered to the American market.

The Devil's Paintbrush: Sir Hiram Maxim's Gun, by Dolf Goldsmith, 3rd Edition, expanded and revised, Collector Grade Publications, Toronto, Canada, 2000. 384 pp., illus. $79.95
The classic work on the world's first true automatic machine gun.

Dr. Josephus Requa Civil War Dentist and the Billinghurst-Requa Volley Gun, by John M. Hyson, Jr., & Margaret Requa DeFrancisco, Museum Restoration Service, Bloomfield, Ont., Canada, 1999. 36 pp., illus. Paper covers. $6.95.
The story of the inventor of the first practical rapid-fire gun to be used during the American Civil War.

The Duck Stamp Story, by Eric Jay Dolin and Bob Dumaine, Krause Publications, Iola, WI, 2000. 208 pp., illustrated with color throughout. Paper covers. $29.95; Hardbound. $49.95.
Detailed information on the value and rarity of every federal duck stamp. Outstanding art and illustrations.

The Dutch Luger (Parabellum) A Complete History, by Bas J. Martens and Guus de Vries, Ironside International Publishers, Inc., Alexandria, VA, 1995. 268 pp., illus. $49.95.
The history of the Luger in the Netherlands. An extensive description of the Dutch pistol and trials and the different models of the Luger in the Dutch service.

The Eagle on U.S. Firearms, by John W. Jordan, Pioneer Press, Union City, TN, 1992. 140 pp., illus. Paper covers. $17.50.
Stylized eagles have been stamped on government owned or manufactured firearms in the U.S. since the beginning of our country. This book lists and illustrates these various eagles in an informative and refreshing manner.

Early Indian Trade Guns: 1625-1775, by T.M. Hamilton, Museum of the Great Plains, Lawton, OK, 1968. 34 pp., illus. Paper covers. $12.95.
Detailed descriptions of subject arms, compiled from early records and from the study of remnants found in Indian country.

Encyclopedia of Rifles & Handguns; A Comprehensive Guide to Firearms, edited by Sean Connolly, Chartwell Books, Inc., Edison, NJ., 1996. 160 pp., illustrated. $21.00.
A lavishly illustrated book providing a comprehensive history of military and civilian personal firepower.

Encyclopedia of Ruger Rimfire Semi-Automatic Pistols: 1949-1992, by Chad Hiddleson, Krause Publications, Iola, WI, 1993. 250 pp., illus. $29.95.
Covers all physical aspects of Ruger 22-caliber pistols including important features such as boxes, grips, muzzlebrakes, instruction manuals, serial numbers, etc.

Eprouvettes: A Comprehensive Study of Early Devices for the Testing of Gunpowder, by R.T.W. Kempers, Royal Armouries Museum, Leeds, England, 1999. 352 pp., illustrated with 240 black & white and 28 color plates. $125.00.
The first comprehensive study of eprouvettes ever attempted in a single volume.

European Firearms in Swedish Castles, by Kaa Wennberg, Bohuslaningens Boktryckeri AB, Uddevalla, Sweden, 1986. 156 pp., illus. $50.00.
The famous collection of Count Keller, the Ettersburg Castle collection, and others. English text.

European Sporting Cartridges, Part 1, by W.B. Dixon, Armory Publications, Inc., Coeur d'Alene, ID, 1997. 250 pp., illus. $63.00.
Photographs and drawings of over 550 centerfire cartridge case types in 1,300 illustrations produced in German and Austria from 1875 to 1995.

Fifteen Years in the Hawken Lode, by John D. Baird, The Gun Room Press, Highland Park, NJ, 1976. 120 pp., illus. $24.95.
A collection of thoughts and observations gained from many years of intensive study of the guns from the shop of the Hawken brothers.

'51 Colt Navies, by Nathan L. Swayze, The Gun Room Press, Highland Park, NJ, 1993. 243 pp., illus. $59.95.
The Model 1851 Colt Navy, its variations and markings.

Fighting Iron, by Art Gogan, Andrew Mowbray, Inc., Lincoln, R.I., 1999. 176 pp., illustrated. $28.00.
It doesn't matter whether you collect guns, swords, bayonets or accountrement—sooner or later you realize that it all comes down to the metal. If you don't understand the metal you don't understand your collection.

Fine Colts, The Dr. Joseph A. Murphy Collection, by R.L. Wilson, Sheffield Marketing Associates, Inc., Doylestown, PA, 1999. 258 pp., illustrated. Limited edition signed and numbered. $99.00.
This lavish new work covers exquisite, deluxe and rare Colt arms from Paterson and other percussion revolvers to the cartridge period and up through modern times.

Firearms, by Derek Avery, Desert Publications, El Dorado, AR, 1999. 95 pp., illustrated. $9.95.
The firearms included in this book are by necessity only a selection, but nevertheless one that represents the best and most famous weapons seen since the Second World War.

Firearms and Tackle Memorabilia, by John Delph, Schiffer Publishing, Ltd., West Chester, PA, 1991. 124 pp., illus. $39.95.
A collector's guide to signs and posters, calendars, trade cards, boxes, envelopes, and other highly sought after memorabilia. With a value guide.

Firearms of the American West 1803-1865, Volume 1, by Louis A. Garavaglia and Charles Worman, University of Colorado Press, Niwot, CO, 1998. 402 pp., illustrated. $59.95.
Traces the development and uses of firearms on the frontier during this period.

Firearms of the American West 1866-1894, by Louis A. Garavaglia and Charles G. Worman, University of Colorado Press, Niwot, CO, 1998. 416 pp., illus. $59.95.
A monumental work that offers both technical information on all of the important firearms used in the West during this period and a highly entertaining history of how they were used, who used them, and why.

Firearms from Europe, by David Noe, Larry W. Yantz, Dr. James B. Whisker, Rowe Publications, Rochester, N.Y., 1999. 192 pp., illustrated. $45.00.
A history and description of firearms imported during the American Civil War by the United States of America and the Confederate States of America.

Firepower from Abroad, by Wiley Sword, Andrew Mowbray Publishing, Lincoln, R.I., 2000. 120 pp., illustrated. $23.00.
The Confederate Enfield and the LeMat revolver and how they reached the Confederate market.

THE ARMS LIBRARY

Flayderman's Guide to Antique American Firearms and Their Values, 7th Edition, edited by Norm Flayderman, DBI books, a division of Krause Publications, Iola, WI, 1998. 656 pp., illus. Paper covers. $32.95.

A completely updated and new edition with more than 3,600 models and variants extensively described with all marks and specifications necessary for quick identification.

The FN-FAL Rifle, etal, by Duncan Long, Paladin Press, Boulder, CO, 1999. 144 pp., illustrated. Paper covers. $18.95.

Detailed descriptions of the basic models produced by Fabrique Nationale and the myriad variants that evolved as a result of the firearms universal acceptance.

The .45-70 Springfield, by Joe Poyer and Craig Riesch, North Cape Publications, Tustin, CA, 1996. 150 pp., illus. Paper covers. $16.95.

A revised and expanded second edition of a best-selling reference work organized by serial number and date of production to aid the collector in identifying popular "Trapdoor" rifles and carbines.

The French 1935 Pistols, by Eugene Medlin and Colin Doane, Eugene Medlin, El Paso, TX, 1995. 172 pp., illus. Paper covers. $25.95.

The development and identification of successive models, fakes and variants, holsters and accessories, and serial numbers by dates of production.

Freund & Bro. Pioneer Gunmakers to the West, by F.J. Pablo Balentine, Graphic Publishers, Newport Beach, CA, 1997. 380 pp., illustrated $69.95.

The story of Frank W. and George Freund, skilled German gunsmiths who plied their trade on the Western American frontier during the final three decades of the nineteenth century.

From the Kingdom of Lilliput: The Miniature Firearms of David Kucer, by K. Corey Keeble and **The Making of Miniatures,** by David Kucer, Museum Restoration Service, Ontario, Canada, 1994. 51 pp., illus, $25.00.

An overview of the subject of miniatures in general combined with an outline by the artist himself on the way he makes a miniature firearm.

Frontier Pistols and Revolvers, by Dominique Venner, Book Sales Inc., Edison, N.J., 1998. 144 pp., illus. $19.95.

Colt, Smith & Wesson, Remington and other early-brand revolvers which tamed the American frontier are shown amid vintage photographs, etchings and paintings to evoke the wild West.

The Fusil de Tulole in New France, 1691-1741, by Russel Bouchard, Museum Restorations Service, Bloomfield, Ontario, Canada, 1997. 36 pp., illus. Paper covers. $6.95

The development of the company and the identification of their arms.

Game Guns & Rifles: Percussion to Hammerless Ejector in Britain, by Richard Akehurst, Trafalgar Square, N. Pomfret, VT, 1993. 192 pp., illus. $39.95.

Long considered a classic this important reprint covers the period of British gunmaking between 1830-1900.

The Gas Trap Garand, by Billy Pyle, Collector Grade Publications, Cobourg, Ontario, Canada, 1999 316 pp., illustrated. $59.95.

The in-depth story of the rarest Garands of them all, the initial 80 Model Shop rifles made under the personal supervision of John Garand himself in 1934 and 1935, and the first 50,000 plus production "gas trap" M1's manufactured at Springfield Armory between August, 1937 and August, 1940.

George Schreyer, Sr. and Jr., Gunmakers of Hanover, Pennsylvania, by George Shumway, George Shumway Publishers, York, PA, 1990. 160pp., illus. $50.00.

This monograph is a detailed photographic study of almost all known surviving long rifles and smoothbore guns made by highly regarded gunsmiths George Schreyer, Sr. and Jr.

The German Assault Rifle 1935-1945, by Peter R. Senich, Paladin Press, Boulder, CO, 1987. 328 pp., illus. $60.00.

A complete review of machine carbines, machine pistols and assault rifles employed by Hitler's Wehrmacht during WWII.

The German K98k Rifle, 1934-1945: The Backbone of the Wehrmacht, by Richard D. Law, Collector Grade Publications, Toronto, Canada, 1993. 336 pp., illus. $69.95.

The most comprehensive study ever published on the 14,000,000 bolt-action K98k rifles produced in Germany between 1934 and 1945.

German Machineguns, by Daniel D. Musgrave, Revised edition, Ironside International Publishers, Inc. Alexandria, VA, 1992. 586 pp., 650 illus. $49.95.

The most definitive book ever written on German machineguns. Covers the introduction and development of machineguns in Germany from 1899 to the rearmament period after WWII.

German Military Rifles and Machine Pistols, 1871-1945, by Hans Dieter Gotz, Schiffer Publishing Co., West Chester, PA, 1990. 245 pp., illus. $35.00.

This book portrays in words and pictures the development of the modern German weapons and their ammunition including the scarcely known experimental types.

The German MP40 Maschinenpistole, by Frank Iannamico, Moose Lake Publishing, Harmony, ME, 1999. 185 pp., illustrated. Paper covers. $19.95.

The history, development and use of this famous gun of World War 2.

German 7.9mm Military Ammunition, by Daniel W. Kent, Daniel W. Kent, Ann Arbor, MI, 1991. 244 pp., illus. $35.00.

The long-awaited revised edition of a classic among books devoted to ammunition.

German Pistols and Holsters, 1934-1945, Volume 1, by Lt. Col. Robert D. Whittington, 3rd, U.S.A.R., Brownlee Books, Hooks, TX, 1991. 208 pp. $30.00.

Pistols and holsters issued in 412 selected armed forces, army and Waffen-SS units including information on personnel, other weapons and transportation.

The Golden Age of Remington, by Robert W.D. Ball, Krause Publications, Iola, WI, 1995. 194 pp., illus. $29.95.

For Remington collectors or firearms historians, this book provides a pictorial history of Remington through World War I. Includes value guide.

The Government Models, by William H.D. Goddard, Andrew Mowbray Publishing, Lincoln, RI, 1998. 296 pp., illustrated. $58.50.

The most authoritative source on the development of the Colt model of 1911.

Grasshoppers and Butterflies, by Adrian B. Caruana, Museum Restoration Service, Alexandria, Bay, N.Y., 1999. 32 pp., illustrated. Paper covers. $6.95.

No.39 in the Historical Arms Series. The light 3 pounders of Pattison and Townsend.

The Greener Story, by Graham Greener, Z-Hat Custom Dies, Casper, WY, 2000. 256 pp., illustrated with 32 pages of color photos. $64.50.

W.W. Greener, his family history, inventions, guns, patents, and more.

A Guide to Ballard Breechloaders, by George J. Layman, Pioneer Press, Union City, TN, 1997. 261 pp., illus. Paper covers. $19.95.

Documents the saga of this fine rifle from the first models made by Ball & Williams of Worchester, to its production by the Marlin Firearms Co, to the cessation of 19th century manufacture in 1891, and finally to the modern reproductions made in the 1990's.

A Guide to the Maynard Breechloader, by George J. Layman, George J. Layman, Ayer, MA, 1993. 125 pp., illus. Paper covers. $11.95.

The first book dedicated entirely to the Maynard family of breech-loading firearms. Coverage of the arms is given from the 1850s through the 1880s.

Guide to Ruger Single Action Revolvers Production Dates, 1953-73, by John C. Dougan, Blacksmith Corp., Chino Valley, AZ, 1991. 22 pp., illus. Paper covers. $9.95.

A unique pocket-sized handbook providing production information for the popular Ruger single-action revolvers manufactured during the first 20 years.

Gun Collecting, by Geoffrey Boothroyd, Sportsman's Press, London, 1989. 208 pp., illus. $29.95.

The most comprehensive list of 19th century British gunmakers and gunsmiths ever published.

Gun Collector's Digest, 5th Edition, edited by Joseph J. Schroeder, DBI Books, a division of Krause Publications, Iola, WI, 1989. 224 pp., illus. Paper covers. $17.95.

The latest edition of this sought-after series.

Gunmakers of London 1350-1850, by Howard L. Blackmore, George Shumway Publisher, York, PA, 1986. 222 pp., illus. $35.00.

A listing of all the known workmen of gun making in the first 500 years, plus a history of the guilds, cutlers, armourers, founders, blacksmiths, etc. 260 gunmarks are illustrated.

Gunmakers of London Supplement 1350-1850, by Howard L. Blackmore, Museum Restoration Service, Alexandria Bay, NY, 1999. 156 pp., illustrated. $60.00.

Begins with an introductory chapter on "foreighn" gunmakers followed by records of all the new information found about previously unidentified armourers, gunmakers and gunsmiths.

The Guns that Won the West: Firearms of the American Frontier, 1865-1898, by John Walter, Stackpole Books, Inc., Mechanicsburg, PA.,1999. 256 pp., illustrated. $34.95.

Here is the story of the wide range of firearms from pistols to rifles used by plainsmen and settlers, gamblers, native Americans and the U.S. Army.

Gunsmiths of Illinois, by Curtis L. Johnson, George Shumway Publishers, York, PA, 1995. 160 pp., illus. $50.00.

Genealogical information is provided for nearly one thousand gunsmiths. Contains hundreds of illustrations of rifles and other guns, of handmade origin, from Illinois.

The Gunsmiths of Manhattan, 1625-1900: A Checklist of Tradesmen, by Michael H. Lewis, Museum Restoration Service, Bloomfield, Ont., Canada, 1991. 40 pp., illus. Paper covers. $4.95.

This listing of more than 700 men in the arms trade in New York City prior to about the end of the 19th century will provide a guide for identification and further research.

The Guns of Dagenham: Lanchester, Patchett, Sterling, by Peter Laidler and David Howroyd, Collector Grade Publications, Inc., Cobourg, Ont., Canada, 1995. 310 pp., illus. $39.95.

An in-depth history of the small arms made by the Sterling Company of Dagenham, Essex, England, from 1940 until Sterling was purchased by British Aerospace in 1989 and closed.

Guns of the Western Indian War, by R. Stephen Dorsey, Collector's Library, Eugene, OR, 1997. 220 pp., illus. Paper covers. $30.00.

The full story of the guns and ammunition that made western history in the turbulent period of 1865-1890.

Gun Powder Cans & Kegs, by Ted & David Bacyk and Tom Rowe, Rowe Publications, Rochester, NY, 1999. 150 pp., illus. $65.00.

The first book devoted to powder tins and kegs. All cans and kegs in full color. With a price guide and rarity scale.

The Guns of Remington: Historic Firearms Spanning Two Centuries, compiled by Howard M. Madaus, Biplane Productions, Publisher, in cooperation with Buffalo Bill Historical Center, Cody, WY, 1998. 352 pp., illustrated with over 800 color photos. $79.95.

A complete catalog of the firearms in the exhibition, "It Never Failed Me: The Arms & Art of Remington Arms Company" at the Buffalo Bill Historical Center, Cody, Wyoming.

Gun Tools, Their History and Identification by James B. Shaffer, Lee A. Rutledge and R. Stephen Dorsey, Collector's Library, Eugene, OR, 1992. 375 pp., illus. $30.00.

Written history of foreign and domestic gun tools from the flintlock period to WWII.

Gun Tools, Their History and Identifications, Volume 2, by Stephen Dorsey and James B. Shaffer, Collectors' Library, Eugene, OR, 1997. 396 pp., illus. Paper covers. $30.00.

Gun tools from the Royal Armouries Museum in England, Pattern Room, Royal Ordnance Reference Collection in Nottingham and from major private collections.

THE ARMS LIBRARY

Gunsmiths of Maryland, by Daniel D. Hartzler and James B. Whisker, Old Bedford Village Press, Bedford, PA, 1998. 208 pp., illustrated. $45.00.
Covers firelock Colonial period through the breech-loading patent models. Featuring longrifles.

Hall's Military Breechloaders, by Peter A. Schmidt, Andrew Mowbray Publishers, Lincoln, RI, 1996. 232 pp., illus. $55.00.
The whole story behind these bold and innovative firearms.

The Handgun, by Geoffrey Boothroyd, David and Charles, North Pomfret, VT, 1989. 566 pp., illus. $60.00.
Every chapter deals with an important period in handgun history from the 14th century to the present.

Handgun of Military Rifle Marks 1866-1950, by Richard A. Hoffman and Noel P. Schott, Mapleleaf Militaria Publishing, St. Louis, MO, 1999, second edition. 60 pp., illustrated. Paper covers. $20.00.
An illustrated guide to identifying military rifle and marks.

Handguns & Rifles: The Finest Weapons from Around the World, by Ian Hogg, Random House Value Publishing, Inc., N.Y., 1999. 128 pp., illustrated. $18.98.
The serious gun collector will welcome this fully illustrated examination of international handguns and rifles. Each entry covers the history of the weapon, what purpose it serves, and its advantages and disadvantages.

The Hawken Rifle: Its Place in History, by Charles E. Hanson, Jr., The Fur Press, Chadron, NE, 1979. 104 pp., illus. Paper covers. $15.00.
A definitive work on this famous rifle.

Hawken Rifles, The Mountain Man's Choice, by John D. Baird, The Gun Room Press, Highland Park, NJ, 1976. 95 pp., illus. $29.95.
Covers the rifles developed for the Western fur trade. Numerous specimens are described and shown in photographs.

High Standard: A Collector's Guide to the Hamden & Hartford Target Pistols, by Tom Dance, Andrew Mowbray, Inc., Lincoln, RI, 1991. 192 pp., illus. Paper covers. $24.00.
From Citation to Supermatic, all of the production models and specials made from 1951 to 1984 are covered according to model number or series.

Historic Pistols: The American Martial Flintlock 1760-1845, by Samuel E. Smith & Edwin W. Bitter, The Gun Room Press, Highland Park, NJ, 1986. 353 pp., illus. $45.00.
Covers over 70 makers and 163 models of American martial arms.

Historical Hartford Hardware, by William W. Dalrymple, Colt Collector Press, Rapid City, SD, 1976. 42 pp., illus. Paper covers. $10.00.
Historically associated Colt revolvers.

The History and Development of Small Arms Ammunition, Volume 1, by George A. Hoyem, Armory Publications, Oceanside, CA, 1991. 230 pp., illus. $75.00.
Military musket, rifle, carbine and primitive machine gun cartridges of the 18th and 19th centuries, together with the firearms that chambered them.

The History and Development of Small Arms Ammunition, Volume 2, by George A. Hoyem, Armory Publications, Oceanside, CA, 1991. 303 pp., illus. $65.00.
Covers the blackpowder military centerfire rifle, carbine, machine gun and volley gun ammunition used in 28 nations and dominions, together with the firearms that chambered them.

The History and Development of Small Arms Ammunition, Volume 4, by George A. Hoyem, Armory Publications, Seattle, WA, 1998. 200 pp., illustrated $65.00.
A comprehensive book on American black powder and early smokeless rifle cartridges.

History of Modern U.S. Military Small Arms Ammunition. Volume 1, 1880-1939, revised by F.W. Hackley, W.H. Woodin and E.L. Scranton, Thomas Publications, Gettysburg, PA, 1998. 328 pp., illus. $49.95.
This revised edition incorporates all publicly available information concerning military small arms ammunition for the period 1880 through 1939 in a single volume.

The History of Smith and Wesson, by Roy G. Jinks, Willowbrook Enterprises, Springfield, MA, 1988. 290 pp., illus. $27.95.
Revised 10th Anniversary edition of the definite book on S&W firearms.

The History of Winchester Firearms 1866-1992, sixth edition, updated, expanded, and revised by Thomas Henshaw, New Win Publishing, Clinton, NJ, 1993. 280 pp., illus. $27.95.
This classic is the standard reference for all collectors and others seeking the facts about any Winchester firearm, old or new.

History of Winchester Repeating Arms Company, by Herbert G. Houze, Krause Publications, Iola, WI, 1994. 800 pp., illus. $50.00.
The complete Winchester history from 1856-1981.

Honour Bound: The Chauchat Machine Rifle, by Gerard Demaison and Yves Buffetaut, Collector Grade Publications, Inc., Cobourg, Ont., Canada, 1995. $39.95.
The story of the CSRG (Chauchat) machine rifle, the most manufactured automatic weapon of World War One.

Hopkins & Allen Revolvers & Pistols, by Charles E. Carder, Avil Onze Publishing, Delphos, OH, 1998, illustrated. Paper covers. $24.95.
Covers over 165 photos, graphics and patent drawings.

How to Buy and Sell Used Guns, by John Traister, Stoeger Publishing Co., So. Hackensack, NJ, 1984. 192 pp., illus. Paper covers. $10.95.
A new guide to buying and selling guns.

Hunting Weapons From the Middle Ages to the Twentieth Century, by Howard L. Blackmore, Dover Publications, Meneola, NY, 2000. 480 pp., illustrated. Paper covers. $18.95.
Dealing mainly with the different classes of weapons used in sport—swords, spears, crossbows, guns, and rifles—from the Middle Ages until the present day.

Identification Manual on the .303 British Service Cartridge, No. 1-Ball Ammunition, by B.A. Temple, I.D.S.A. Books, Piqua, OH, 1986. 84 pp., 57 illus. $12.50.

Identification Manual on the .303 British Service Cartridge, No. 2-Blank Ammunition, by B.A. Temple, I.D.S.A. Books, Piqua, OH, 1986. 95 pp., 59 illus. $12.50.

Identification Manual on the .303 British Service Cartridge, No. 3-Special Purpose Ammunition, by B.A. Temple, I.D.S.A. Books, Piqua, OH, 1987. 82 pp., 49 illus. $12.50.

Identification Manual on the .303 British Service Cartridge, No. 4-Dummy Cartridges Henry 1869-c.1900, by B.A. Temple, I.D.S.A. Books, Piqua, OH, 1988. 84 pp., 70 illus. $12.50.

Identification Manual on the .303 British Service Cartridge, No. 5-Dummy Cartridges (2), by B.A. Temple, I.D.S.A. Books, Piqua, OH, 1994. 78 pp. $12.50

The Illustrated Book of Guns, by David Miller, Salamander Books, N.Y., N.Y., 2000. 304 pp., illustrated in color. $34.95.
An illustrated directory of over 1,000 military and sporting firearms.

The Illustrated Encyclopedia of Civil War Collectibles, by Chuck Lawliss, Henry Holt and Co., New York, NY, 1997. 316 pp., illus. Paper covers. $22.95.
A comprehensive guide to Union and Confederate arms, equipment, uniforms, and other memorabilia.

Illustrations of United States Military Arms 1776-1903 and Their Inspector's Marks, compiled by Turner Kirkland, Pioneer Press, Union City, TN, 1988. 37 pp., illus. Paper covers. $7.00.
Reprinted from the 1949 Bannerman catalog. Valuable information for both the advanced and beginning collector.

Indian War Cartridge Pouches, Boxes and Carbine Boots, by R. Stephen Dorsey, Collector's Library, Eugene, OR, 1993. 156 pp., illus. Paper Covers. $20.00.
The key reference work to the cartridge pouches, boxes, carbine sockets and boots of the Indian War period 1865-1890.

An Introduction to the Civil War Small Arms, by Earl J. Coates and Dean S. Thomas, Thomas Publishing Co., Gettysburg, PA, 1990. 96 pp., illus. Paper covers. $10.00.
The small arms carried by the individual soldier during the Civil War.

Japanese Rifles of World War Two, by Duncan O. McCollum, Excalibur Publications, Latham, NY, 1996. 64 pp., illus. Paper covers. $18.95.
A sweeping view of the rifles and carbines that made up Japan's arsenal during the conflict.

Kalashnikov Arms, compiled by Alexei Nedelin, Design Military Parade, Ltd., Moscow, Russia, 1997. 240 pp., illus. $49.95.
Weapons versions stored in the St. Petersburg Military Historical Museum of Artillery, Engineer Troops and Communications and in the Izhmash JSC.

Kalashnikov "Machine Pistols, Assault Rifles, and Machine Guns, 1945 to the Present", by John Walter, Paladin Press, Boulder, CO, 1999, hardcover, photos, illus., 146 pp. $22.95
This exhaustive work published by Greenhill Military Manuals features a gun-by-gun directory of Kalashnikov variants. Technical specifications and illustrations are provided throughout, along with details of sights, bayonets, markings and ammunition. A must for the serious collector and historian.

The Kentucky Pistol, by Roy Chandler and James Whisker, Old Bedford Village Press, Bedford, PA, 1997. 225 pp., illus. $45.00.
A photographic study of Kentucky pistols from famous collections.

The Kentucky Rifle, by Captain John G.W. Dillin, George Shumway Publisher, York, PA, 1993. 221 pp., illus. $50.00.
This well-known book was the first attempt to tell the story of the American longrifle. This edition retains the original text and illustrations with supplemental footnotes provided by Dr. George Shumway.

The Kentucky Rifle, a True American Heritage in Picture, by the Kentucky Rifle Associations, Washington, D.C., 1997. Published by the Forte Group, Alexandria, VA. 109 pp., illus. $35.00.
This photographic essay reveals both the beauty and the decorative nature of the Kentucky by providing detailed photos of some of the most significant examples of American rifles, pistols and accoutrements.

Know Your Broomhandle Mausers, by R.J. Berger, Blacksmith Corp., Southport, CT, 1985. 96 pp., illus. Paper covers. $9.95.
An interesting story on the big Mauser pistol and its variations.

Krag Rifles, by William S. Brophy, The Gun Room Press, Highland Park, NJ, 1980. 200 pp., illus. $35.00.
The first comprehensive work detailing the evolution and various models, both military and civilian.

The Krieghoff Parabellum, by Randall Gibson, Midland, TX, 1988. 279 pp., illus. $40.00.
A comprehensive text pertaining to the Lugers manufactured by H. Krieghoff Waffenfabrik.

Las Pistolas Espanolas Tipo "Mauser," by Artemio Mortera Perez, Quiron Ediciones, Valladolid, Spain, 1998. 71 pp., illustrated. Paper covers. $34.95.
This book covers in detail Spanish machine pistols and C96 copies made in Spain. Covers all Astra "Mauser" pistol series and the complete line of Beistegui C96 type pistols. Spanish text.

Law Enforcement Memorabilia Price and Identification Guide, by Monty McCord, DBI Books, a division of Krause Publications, Inc. Iola, WI, 1999. 208 pp., illustrated. Paper covers. $19.95.
An invaluable reference to the growing wave of law enforcement collectors. Hundreds of items are covered from miniature vehicles to clothes, patches, and restraints.

Legendary Sporting Guns, by Eric Joly, Abbeville Press, New York, N.Y., 1999. 228 pp., illustrated. $65.00.
A survey of hunting through the ages and relates how many different types of firearms were created and refined for use afield.

REFERENCE

Legends and Reality of the AK, by Val Shilin and Charlie Cutshaw, Paladen Press, Boulder, CO, 2000. 192 pp., illustrated. Paper covers. $35.00.

A behind-the-scenes look at history, design and impact of the Kalashnikov family of weapons.

LeMat, the Man, the Gun, by Valmore J. Forgett and Alain F. and Marie-Antoinette Serpette, Navy Arms Co., Ridgefield, NJ, 1996. 218 pp., illus. $49.95.

The first definitive study of the Confederate revolvers invention, development and delivery by Francois Alexandre LeMat.

Les Pistolets Automatiques Francaise 1890-1990, by Jean Huon, Combined Books, Inc., Conshohocken, PA, 1997. 160 pp., illus. French text. $34.95.

French automatic pistols from the earliest experiments through the World Wars and Indo-China to modern security forces.

*Levine's Guide to Knives And Their Values, 5th Edition, by Bernard Levine, DBI Books, a division of Krause Publications, Iola, WI, 2000. 544 pp., illus. Paper covers. $27.95.

All the basic tools for identifying, valuing and collecting folding and fixed blade knives.

The London Gunmakers and the English Duelling Pistol, 1770-1830, by Keith R. Dill, Museum Restoration Service, Bloomfield, Ontario, Canada, 1997. 36 pp., illus. Paper covers. $6.95.

Ten gunmakers made London one of the major gunmaking centers of the world. This book examines how the design and construction of their pistols contributed to that reputation and how these characteristics may be used to date flintlock arms.

Longrifles of North Carolina, by John Bivens, George Shumway Publisher, York, PA, 1988. 256 pp., illus. $50.00.

Covers art and evolution of the rifle, immigration and trade movements. Committee of Safety gunsmiths, characteristics of the North Carolina rifle.

Longrifles of Pennsylvania, Volume 1, Jefferson, Clarion & Elk Counties, by Russel H. Harringer, George Shumway Publisher, York, PA, 1984. 200 pp., illus. $50.00.

First in series that will treat in great detail the longrifles and gunsmiths of Pennsylvania.

The Luger Handbook, by Aarron Davis, Krause Publications, Iola, WI, 1997. 112 pp., illus. Paper covers. $9.95.

Quick reference to classify Luger models and variations with complete details including proofmarks.

Lugers at Random, by Charles Kenyon, Jr., Handgun Press, Glenview, IL, 1990. 420 pp., illus. $59.95.

A new printing of this classic, comprehensive reference for all Luger collectors.

The Luger Story, by John Walter, Stackpole Books, Mechanicsburg, PA, 1995. 256 pp., illus. $39.95.

The standard history of the world's most famous handgun.

The M1 Garand Serial Numbers and Data Sheets, by Scott A. Duff, Export, PA, 1995. 101 pp., illus. Paper covers. $9.95.

Provides the reader with serial numbers related to dates of manufacture and a large sampling of data sheets to aid in identification or restoration.

The M1 Garand: Owner's Guide, by Scott A. Duff, Scott A. Duff, Export, PA, 1997. 126 pp., illus. Paper covers. $16.95.

This book answers the questions M1 owners most often ask concerning maintenance activities not encounted by military users.

Machine Guns of World War 1, by Robert Bruce, Combined Publishing, Conshohocken, PA, 1998. 128 pp., illus. $39.95.

Live firing classic military weapons in color photographs.

Maine Made Guns and Their Makers, by Dwight B. Demeritt Jr., Maine State Museum, Augusta, ME, 1998. 209 pp., illustrated. $55.00.

An authoritative, biographical study of Maine gunsmiths.

Marlin Firearms: A History of the Guns and the Company That Made Them, by Lt. Col. William S. Brophy, USAR, Ret., Stackpole Books, Harrisburg, PA, 1989. 672 pp., illus. $75.00.

The definitive book on the Marlin Firearms Co. and their products.

Martini-Henry .450 Rifles & Carbines, by Dennis Lewis, Excalibur Publications, Latham, NY, 1996. 72 pp., illus. Paper covers. $11.95.

The stories of the rifles and carbines that were the mainstay of the British soldier through the Victorian years.

Mauser Bolt Rifles, by Ludwig Olson, F. Brownell & Son, Inc., Montezuma, IA, 1999. 364 pp., illus. $51.95.

The most complete, detailed, authoritative and comprehensive work ever done on Mauser bolt rifles. Completely revised deluxe 3rd edition.

Mauser Military Rifles of the World, 2nd Edition, by Robert Ball, Krause Publications, Iola, WI, 2000. 304 pp., illustrated with 1,000 b&w photos and a 48 page color section. $44.95.

This 2nd edition brings more than 100 new photos of these historic rifles and the wars in which they were carried.

Mauser Smallbores Sporting, Target and Training Rifles, by Jon Speed, Collector Grade Publications, Cobourg, Ontario, Canada 1998. 349 pp., illustrated. $67.50.

A history of all the smallbore sporting, target and training rifles produced by the legendary Mauser-Werke of Obendorf Am Neckar.

Military Handguns of France 1858-1958, by Eugene Medlin and Jean Huon, Excalibur Publications, Latham, NY, 1994. 124 pp., illus. Paper covers. $35.00.

The first book written in English that provides students of arms with a thorough history of French military handguns.

Military Holsters of World War 2, by Eugene J. Bender, Rowe Publications, Rochester, NY, 1998. 200 pp., illustrated. $45.00.

A revised edition with a new price guide of the most definitive book on this subject.

Military Pistols of Japan, by Fred L. Honeycutt, Jr., Julin Books, Palm Beach Gardens, FL, 1991. 168 pp., illus. $42.00.

Covers every aspect of military pistol production in Japan through WWII.

The Military Remington Rolling Block Rifle, by George Layman, George Layman, Ayer, MA, 1996. 146 pp., illus. Paper covers. $24.95.

A standard reference for those with an interest in the Remington rolling block family of firearms.

Military Rifles of Japan, 4th Edition, by F.L. Honeycutt, Julin Books, Lake Park, FL, 1989. 208 pp., illus. $42.00.

A new revised and updated edition. Includes the early Murata-period markings, etc.

Military Small Arms Data Book, by Ian V. Hogg, Stackpole Books, Mechanicsburg, PA, 1999. $44.95. 336 pp., illustrated.

Data on more than 1,500 weapons. Covers a vast range of weapons from pistols to anti-tank rifles. Essential data, 1870-2000, in one volume.

M1 Carbine, by Larry Ruth, Gun room Press, Highland Park, NJ, 1987. 291 pp., illus. Paper $19.95.

The origin, development, manufacture and use of this famous carbine of World War II.

The M1 Garand 1936 to 1957, by Joe Poyer and Craig Riesch, North Cape Publications, Tustin, CA, 1996. 216 pp., illus. Paper covers. $19.95.

Describes the entire range of M1 Garand production in text and quick-scan charts.

The M1 Garand: Post World War, by Scott A. Duff, Scott A. Duff, Export, PA, 1990. 139 pp., illus. Soft covers. $19.95.

A detailed account of the activities at Springfield Armory through this period. International Harvester, H&R, Korean War production and quantities delivered. Serial numbers.

The M1 Garand: World War 2, by Scott A. Duff, Scott A. Duff, Export, PA, 1993. 210 pp., illus. Paper covers. $39.95.

The most comprehensive study available to the collector and historian on the M1 Garand of World War II.

Modern Beretta Firearms, by Gene Gangarosa, Jr., Stoeger Publishing Co., So. Hackensack, NJ, 1994. 288 pp., illus. Paper covers. $16.95.

Traces all models of modern Beretta pistols, rifles, machine guns and combat shotguns.

Modern Gun Values, The Gun Digest Book of, 10th Edition, by the Editors of Gun Digest, DBI Books, a division of Krause Publications, Iola, WI., 1996. 560 pp. illus. Paper covers. $21.95.

Greatly updated and expanded edition describing and valuing over 7,000 firearms manufactured from 1900 to 1996. The standard for valuing modern firearms.

Modern Gun Identification & Value Guide, Twelfth Edition, by Russell and Steve Quertermous, Collector Books, Paducah, KY, 1998. 504 pp., illus. Paper covers. $12.95.

Features current values for over 2,500 models of rifles, shotguns and handguns, with over 1,800 illustrations.

More Single Shot Rifles, by James C. Grant, The Gun Room Press, Highland Park, NJ, 1976. 324 pp., illus. $35.00.

Details the guns made by Frank Wesson, Milt Farrow, Holden, Borchardt, Stevens, Remington, Winchester, Ballard and Peabody-Martini.

Mortimer, the Gunmakers, 1753-1923, by H. Lee Munson, Andrew Mowbray Inc., Lincoln, RI, 1992. 320 pp., illus. $65.00.

Seen through a single, dominant, English gunmaking dynasty this fascinating study provides a window into the classical era of firearms artistry.

The Mosin-Nagant Rifle, by Terence W. Lapin, North Cape Publications, Tustin, CA, 1998. 30 pp., illustrated. Paper covers. $19.95.

The first ever complete book on the Mosin-Nagant rifle written in English. Covers every variation.

The Navy Luger, by Joachim Gortz and John Walter, Handgun Press, Glenview, IL, 1988. 128 pp., illus. $24.95.

The 9mm Pistole 1904 and the Imperial German Navy. A concise illustrated history.

The New World of Russian Small Arms and Ammunition, by Charlie Cutshaw, Paladin Press, Boulder, CO, 1998. 160 pp., illustrated. $42.95.

Detailed descriptions, specifications and first-class illustrations of the AN-94, PSS silent pistol, Bizon SMG, Saifa-12 tactical shotgun, the GP-25 grenade launcher and more cutting edge Russian weapons.

The Number 5 Jungle Carbine, by Alan M. Petrillo, Excalibur Publications, Latham, NY, 1994. 32 pp., illus. Paper covers. $7.95.

A comprehensive treatment of the rifle that collectors have come to call the "Jungle Carbine"—the Lee-Enfield Number 5, Mark 1.

The '03 Era: When Smokeless Revolutionized U.S. Riflery, by Clark S. Campbell, Collector Grade Publications, Inc., Ontario, Canada, 1994. 334 pp., illus. $44.50.

A much-expanded version of Campbell's The '03 Springfields, representing forty years of in-depth research into "all things '03."

Observations on Colt's Second Contract, November 2, 1847, by G. Maxwell Longfield and David T. Basnett, Museum Restoration Service, Bloomfield, Ontario, Canada, 1997. 36 pp., illus. Paper covers. $6.95.

This study traces the history and the construction of the Second Model Colt Dragoon supplied in 1848 to the U.S. Cavalry.

Official Guide to Gunmarks, 3rd Edition, by Robert H. Balderson, House of Collectibles, New York, NY, 1996. 367 pp., illus. Paper covers. $15.00.

Identifies manufacturers' marks that appear on American and foreign pistols, rifles and shotguns.

THE ARMS LIBRARY

Official Price Guide to Gun Collecting, by R.L. Wilson, Ballantine/House of Collectibles, New York, NY, 1998. 450 pp., illus. Paper covers. $21.50.
Covers more than 30,000 prices from Colt revolvers to Winchester rifles and shotguns to German Lugers and British sporting rifles and game guns.

Official Price Guide to Military Collectibles, 6th Edition, by Richard J. Austin, Random House, Inc., New York, NY, 1998. 200 pp., illus. Paper cover. $20.00.
Covers weapons and other collectibles from wars of the distant and recent past. More than 4,000 prices are listed. Illustrated with 400 black & white photos plus a full-color insert.

The Official Soviet SVD Manual, by Major James F. Gebhardt (Ret.) Paladin Press, Boulder, CO, 1999. 112 pp., illustrated. Paper covers. $15.00.
Operating instructions for the 7.62mm Dragunov, the first Russian rifle developed from scratch specifically for sniping.

Old Gunsights: A Collector's Guide, 1850 to 2000, by Nicholas Stroebel, Krause Publications, Iola, WI, 1998. 320 pp., illus. Paper covers. $29.95
An in-depth and comprehensive examination of old gunsights and the rifles on which they were used to get accurate feel for prices in this expanding market.

*Old Rifle Scopes, by Nicholas Stroebel, Krause Publications, Iola, WI, 2000. 400 pp., illustrated. Paper covers. $31.95.
This comprehensive collector's guide takes aim at more than 120 scope makers and 60 mount makers and features photos and current market values for 300 scopes and mounts manufactured from 1950-1985.

The P-08 Parabellum Luger Automatic Pistol, edited by J. David McFarland, Desert Publications, Cornville, AZ, 1982. 20 pp., illus. Paper covers. $11.95.
Covers every facet of the Luger, plus a listing of all known Luger models.

Packing Iron, by Richard C. Rattenbury, Zon International Publishing, Millwood, NY, 1993. 216 pp., illus. $45.00.
The best book yet produced on pistol holsters and rifle scabbards. Over 300 variations of holster and scabbards are illustrated in large, clear plates.

Parabellum: A Technical History of Swiss Lugers, by Vittorio Bobba, Priuli & Verlucca, Editori, Torino, Italy, 1996. Italian and English text. Illustrated. $100.00.

Patents for Inventions, Class 119 (Small Arms), 1855-1930. British Patent Office, Armory Publications, Oceanside, CA, 1993. 7 volume set. $250.00.
Contains 7980 abridged patent descriptions and their sectioned line drawings, plus a 37-page alphabetical index of the patentees.

Pattern Dates for British Ordnance Small Arms, 1718-1783, by DeWitt Bailey, Thomas Publications, Gettysburg, PA, 1997. 116 pp., illus. Paper covers. $20.00
The weapons discussed in this work are those carried by troops sent to North America between 1737 and 1783, or shipped to them as replacement arms while in America.

Pistols of the World, 3rd Edition, by Ian Hogg and John Weeks, DBI Books, a division of Krause Publications, Iola, WI, 1992. 320 pp., illus. Paper covers. $20.95.
A totally revised edition of one of the leading studies of small arms.

The Pitman Notes on U.S. Martial Small Arms and Ammunition, 1776-1933, Volume 2, Revolvers and Automatic Pistols, by Brig. Gen. John Pitman, Thomas Publications, Gettysburg, PA, 1990. 192 pp., illus. $29.95.
A most important primary source of information on United States military small arms and ammunition.

The Plains Rifle, by Charles Hanson, Gun Room Press, Highland Park, NJ, 1989. 169 pp., illus. $35.00.
All rifles that were made with the plainsman in mind, including pistols.

Powder and Ball Small Arms, by Martin Pegler, Windrow & Green, London, 1998. 128 pp., illus. $39.95.
Part of the new "Live Firing Classic Weapons" series featuring full color photos of experienced shooters dressed in authentic costumes handling, loading and firing historic weapons.

The Powder Flask Book, by Ray Riling, R&R Books, Livonia, NY, 1993. 514 pp., illus. $70.00.
The complete book on flasks of the 19th century. Exactly scaled pictures of 1,600 flasks are illustrated.

Proud Promise: French Autoloading Rifles, 1898-1979, by Jean Huon, Collector Grade Publications, Inc., Cobourg, Ont., Canada, 1995. 216 pp., illus. $39.95.
The author has finally set the record straight about the importance of French contributions to modern arms design.

E. C. Prudhomme's Gun Engraving Review, by E. C. Prudhomme, R&R Books, Livonia, NY, 1994. 164 pp., illus. $60.00.
As a source for engravers and collectors, this book is an indispensable guide to styles and techniques of the world's foremost engravers.

Reloading Tools, Sights and Telescopes for Single Shot Rifles, by Gerald O. Kelver, Brighton, CO, 1982. 163 pp., illus. Paper covers. $13.95.
A listing of most of the famous makers of reloading tools, sights and telescopes with a brief description of the products they manufactured.

The Remington-Lee Rifle, by Eugene F. Myszkowski, Excalibur Publications, Latham, NY, 1995. 100 pp., illus. Paper covers. $22.50.
Features detailed descriptions, including serial number ranges, of each model from the first Lee Magazine Rifle produced for the U.S. Navy to the last Remington-Lee Small Bores shipped to the Cuban Rural Guard.

Revolvers of the British Services 1854-1954, by W.H.J. Chamberlain and A.W.F. Taylerson, Museum Restoration Service, Ottawa, Canada, 1989. 80 pp., illus. $27.50.
Covers the types issued among many of the United Kingdom's naval, land or air services.

Rhode Island Arms Makers & Gunsmiths, by William O. Archibald, Andrew Mowbray, Inc., Lincoln, RI, 1990. 108 pp., illus. $16.50.
A serious and informative study of an important area of American arms making.

Rifles of the World, by Oliver Achard, Chartwell Books, Inc., Edison, NJ, 141 pp., illus. $24.95.
A unique insight into the world of long guns, not just rifles, but also shotguns, carbines and all the usual multi-barreled guns that once were so popular with European hunters, especially in Germany and Austria.

The Rock Island '03, by C.S. Ferris, C.S. Ferris, Arvada, CO, 1993. 58 pp., illus. Paper covers. $12.50.
A monograph of interest to the collector or historian concentrating on the U.S. M1903 rifle made by the less publicized of our two producing facilities.

Round Ball to Rimfire, Vol. 1, by Dean Thomas, Thomas Publications, Gerrysburg, PA, 1997. 144 pp., illus. $40.00.
The first of a two-volume set of the most complete history and guide for all small arms ammunition used in the Civil War. The information includes data from research and development to the arsenals that created it.

Ruger and his Guns, by R.L. Wilson, Simon & Schuster, New York, NY, 1996. 358 pp., illus. $65.00.
A history of the man, the company and their firearms.

Russell M. Catron and His Pistols, by Warren H. Buxton, Ucross Books, Los Alamos, NM, 1998. 224 pp., illustrated. Paper covers. $49.50.
An unknown American firearms inventor and manufacturer of the mid twentieth century. Military, commerical, ammunition.

The SAFN-49 and The FAL, by Joe Poyer and Dr. Richard Feirman, North Cape Publications, Tustin, CA, 1998. 160 pp., illus. Paper covers. $14.95.
The first complete overview of the SAFN-49 battle rifle, from its pre-World War 2 beginnings to its military service in countries as diverse as the Belgian Congo and Argentina. The FAL was "light" version of the SAFN-49 and it became the Free World's most adopted battle rifle.

Sam Colt's Own Record 1847, by John Parsons, Wolfe Publishing Co., Prescott, AZ, 1992. 167 pp., illus. $24.50.
Chronologically presented, the correspondence published here completes the account of the manufacture, in 1847, of the Walker Model Colt revolver.

J.P. Sauer & Sohn, Suhl, by Jim Cate & Nico Van Gun, CBC Book Co., Chattanooga, TN, 1998. 406 pp., illus. $65.00.
A historical study of Sauer automatic pistols. Over 500 photos showing the different variations of pistols, grips, magazines and holsters.

Scottish Firearms, by Claude Blair and Robert Woosnam-Savage, Museum Restoration Service, Bloomfield, Ont., Canada, 1995. 52 pp., illus. Paper covers. $4.95.
This revision of the first book devoted entirely to Scottish firearms is supplemented by a register of surviving Scottish long guns.

The Scottish Pistol, by Martin Kelvin. Fairleigh Dickinson University Press, Dist. By Associated University Presses, Cranbury, NJ, 1997. 256 pp., illus. $49.50.
The Scottish pistol, its history, manufacture and design.

Sharps Firearms, by Frank Seller, Frank M. Seller, Denver, CO, 1982. 358 pp., illus. $50.00.
Traces the development of Sharps firearms with full range of guns made including all martial variations.

Simeon North: First Official Pistol Maker of the United States, by S. North and R. North, The Gun Room Press, Highland Park, NJ, 1972. 207 pp., illus. $15.95.
Reprint of the rare first edition.

The SKS Carbine, by Steve Kehaya and Joe Poyer, North Cape Publications, Tustin, CA, 1997. 150 pp., illus. Paper covers. $16.95.
The first comprehensive examination of a major historical firearm used through the Vietnam conflict to the diamond fields of Angola.

The SKS Type 45 Carbines, by Duncan Long, Desert Publications, El Dorado, AZ, 1992. 110 pp., illus. Paper covers. $19.95
Covers the history and practical aspects of operating, maintaining and modifying this abundantly available rifle.

Smith & Wesson 1857-1945, by Robert J. Neal and Roy G. Jinks, R&R Books, Livonia, NY, 1996. 434 pp., illus. $50.00.
The bible for all existing and aspiring Smith & Wesson collectors.

Sniper Variations of the German K98k Rifle, by Richard D. Law, Collector Grade Publications, Ontario, Canada, 1997. 240 pp., illus. $47.50.
Volume 2 of "Backbone of the Wehrmacht" the author's in-depth study of the German K98k rifle. This volume concentrates on the telescopic-sighted rifle of choice for most German snipers during World War 2.

Southern Derringers of the Mississippi Valley, by Turner Kirkland, Pioneer Press, Tenn., 1971. 80 pp., illus., paper covers. $4.00.
A guide for the collector, and a much-needed study.

Soviet Russian Postwar Military Pistols and Cartridges, by Fred A. Datig, Handgun Press, Glenview, IL, 1988. 152 pp., illus. $29.95.
Thoroughly researched, this definitive sourcebook covers the development and adoption of the Makarov, Stechkin and the new PSM pistols. Also included in this source book is coverage on Russian clandestine weapons and pistol cartridges.

Soviet Russian Tokarev "TT" Pistols and Cartridges 1929-1953, by Fred Datig, Graphic Publishers, Santa Ana, CA, 1993. 168 pp., illus. $39.95.
Details of rare arms and their accessories are shown in hundreds of photos. It also contains a complete bibliography and index.

Soviet Small-Arms and Ammunition, by David Bolotin, Handgun Press, Glenview, IL, 1996. 264 pp., illus. $49.95.
An authoritative and complete book on Soviet small arms.

Sporting Collectibles, by Jim and Vivian Karsnitz, Schiffer Publishing Ltd., West Chester, PA, 1992. 160 pp., illus. Paper covers. $29.95.
The fascinating world of hunting related collectibles presented in an informative text.

THE ARMS LIBRARY

The Springfield 1903 Rifles, by Lt. Col. William S. Brophy, USAR, Ret., Stackpole Books Inc., Harrisburg, PA, 1985. 608 pp., illus. $75.00.

The illustrated, documented story of the design, development, and production of all the models, appendages, and accessories.

Springfield Armory Shoulder Weapons 1795-1968, by Robert W.D. Ball, Antique Trader Books, Dubuque, IA, 1998. 264 pp., illus. $34.95.

This book documents the 255 basic models of rifles, including test and trial rifles, produced by the Springfield Armory. It features the entire history of rifles and carbines manufactured at the Armory, the development of each weapon with specific operating characteristics and procedures.

Springfield Model 1903 Service Rifle Production and Alteration, 1905-1910, by C.S. Ferris and John Beard, Arvada, CO, 1995. 66 pp., illus. Paper covers. $12.50.

A highly recommended work for any serious student of the Springfield Model 1903 rifle.

Springfield Shoulder Arms 1795-1865, by Claud E. Fuller, S. & S. Firearms, Glendale, NY, 1986. 76 pp., illus. Paper covers. $17.95.

Exact reprint of the scarce 1930 edition of one of the most definitive works on Springfield flintlock and percussion muskets ever published.

Standard Catalog of Firearms, 10th Edition, by Ned Schwing, Krause Publications, Iola, WI, 2000. 1,312 pp., illustrated. Paper covers. $32.95.

Packed with more than 80,000 real-world prices and over 5,000 photos.

Standard Catalog of Smith and Wesson, by Jim Supica and Richard Nahas, Krause Publications, Iola, WI, 1996. 240 pp., illus. $29.95.

Clearly details hundreds of products by the legendary manufacturer. How to identify, evaluate the condition and assess the value of 752 Smith & Wesson models and variations.

Standard Catalog of Winchester, 1st Edition, edited by David D. Kowalski, Krause Publications, Iola, WI, 2000. 704 pp., illustrated with 2,000 B&W photos and 75 color photos. Paper covers. $39.95.

This book identifies and values more than 5,000 collectibles, including firearms, cartridges shotshells, fishing tackle, sporting goods and tools manufactured by Winchester Repeating Arms Co.

Steel Canvas: The Art of American Arms, by R.L. Wilson, Random House, NY, 1995, 384 pp., illus. $65.00.

Presented here for the first time is the breathtaking panorama of America's extraordinary engravers and embellishers of arms, from the 1700s to modern times.

Stevens Pistols & Pocket Rifles, by K.L. Cope, Museum Restoration Service, Alexandria Bay, NY, 1992. 114 pp., illus. $24.50.

This is the story of the guns and the man who designed them and the company which he founded to make them.

A Study of Colt Conversions and Other Percussion Revolvers, by R. Bruce McDowell, Krause Publications, Iola, WI, 1997. 464 pp., illus. $39.95.

The ultimate reference detailing Colt revolvers that have been converted from percussion to cartridge.

The Sumptuous Flaske, by Herbert G. Houze, Andrew Mowbray, Inc., Lincoln, RI, 1989. 158 pp., illus. Soft covers. $35.00.

Catalog of a recent show at the Buffalo Bill Historical Center bringing together some of the finest European and American powder flasks of the 16th to 19th centuries.

The Swedish Mauser Rifles, by Steve Kehaya and Joe Poyer, North Cape Publications, Tustin, CA, 1999. 267 pp., illustrated. Paper covers. $19.95.

Every known variation of the Swedish Mauser carbine and rifle is described including all match and target rifles and all sniper fersions. Includes serial number and production data.

Televisions Cowboys, Gunfighters & Cap Pistols, by Rudy A. D'Angelo, Antique Trader Books, Norfolk, VA, 1999. 287 pp., illustrated in color and black and white. Paper covers. $31.95.

Over 850 beautifully photographed color and black and white images of cap guns, actors, and the characters they portrayed in the "Golden Age of TV Westerns." With accurate descriptions and current values.

Thompson: The American Legend, by Tracie L. Hill, Collector Grade Publications, Ontario, Canada, 1996. 584 pp., illus. $85.00.

The story of the first American submachine gun. All models are featured and discussed.

Toys That Shoot and Other Neat Stuff, by James Dundas, Schiffer Books, Atglen, PA, 1999. 112 pp., illustrated. Paper covers. $24.95.

Shooting toys from the twentieth century, especially 1920's to 1960's, in over 420 color photographs of BB guns, cap shooters, marble shooters, squirt guns and more. Complete with a price guide.

The Trapdoor Springfield, by M.D. Waite and B.D. Ernst, The Gun Room Press, Highland Park, NJ, 1983. 250 pp., illus. $39.95.

The first comprehensive book on the famous standard military rifle of the 1873-92 period.

Treasures of the Moscow Kremlin: Arsenal of the Russian Tsars, A Royal Armories and the Moscow Kremlin exhibition. HM Tower of London 13, June 1998 to 11 September, 1998. BAS Printers, Over Wallop, Hampshire, England. xxii plus 192 pp. over 180 color illustrations.

For this exhibition catalog each of the 94 objects on display are photographed and described in detail to provide a most informative record of this important exhibition. Text in English and Russian. $65.00.

U.S. Breech-Loading Rifles and Carbines, Cal. 45, by Gen. John Pitman, Thomas Publications, Gettysburg, PA, 1992. 192 pp., illus. $29.95.

The third volume in the Pitman Notes on U.S. Martial Small Arms and Ammunition, 1776-1933. This book centers on the "Trapdoor Springfield" models.

U.S. Handguns of World War 2: The Secondary Pistols and Revolvers, by Charles W. Pate, Andrew Mowbray, Inc., Lincoln, RI, 1998. 515 pp., illus. $39.00.

This indispensable new book covers all of the American military handguns of World War 2 except for the M1911A1 Colt automatic.

United States Martial Flintlocks, by Robert M. Reilly, Mowbray Publishing Co., Lincoln, RI, 1997. 264 pp., illus. $40.00.

A comprehensive history of American flintlock longarms and handguns (mostly military) c. 1775 to c. 1840.

U.S. Martial Single Shot Pistols, by Daniel D. Hartzler and James B. Whisker, Old Bedford Village Pess, Bedford, PA, 1998. 128 pp., illus. $45.00.

A photographic chronicle of military and semi-martial pistols supplied to the U.S. Government and the several States.

U.S. Military Arms Dates of Manufacture from 1795, by George Madis, David Madis, Dallas, TX, 1989. 64 pp. Soft covers. $6.00.

Lists all U.S. military arms of collector interest alphabetically, covering about 250 models.

U.S. Military Small Arms 1816-1865, by Robert M. Reilly, The Gun Room Press, Highland Park, NJ, 1983. 270 pp., illus. $39.95.

Covers every known type of primary and secondary martial firearms used by Federal forces.

U.S. M1 Carbines: Wartime Production, by Craig Riesch, North Cape Publications, Tustin, CA, 1994. 72 pp., illus. Paper covers. $16.95.

Presents only verifiable and accurate information. Each part of the M1 Carbine is discussed fully in its own section; including markings and finishes.

U.S. Naval Handguns, 1808-1911, by Fredrick R. Winter, Andrew Mowbray Publishers, Lincoln, RI, 1990. 128 pp., illus. $26.00.

The story of U.S. Naval Handguns spans an entire century—included are sections on each of the important naval handguns within the period.

Walther: A German Legend, by Manfred Kersten, Safari Press, Inc., Huntington Beach, CA, 2000. 400 pp., illustrated. $85.00.

This comprehensive book covers, in rich detail, all aspects of the company and its guns, including an illustrious and rich history, the WW2 years, all the pistols (models 1 through 9), the P-38, P-88, the long guns, .22 rifles, centerfires, Wehrmacht guns, and even a gun that could shoot around a corner.

The Walther Handgun Story: A Collector's and Shooter's Guide, by Gene Gangarosa, Steiger Publications, 1999. 300., illustrated. Paper covers. $21.95.

Covers the entire history of the Walther empire. Illustrated with over 250 photos.

Walther Models PP and PPK, 1929-1945, by James L. Rankin, assisted by Gary Green, James L. Rankin, Coral Gables, FL, 1974. 142 pp., illus. $35.00.

Complete coverage on the subject as to finish, proofmarks and Nazi Party inscriptions.

Walther P-38 Pistol, by Maj. George Nonte, Desert Publications, Cornville, AZ, 1982. 100 pp., illus. Paper covers. $11.95.

Complete volume on one of the most famous handguns to come out of WWII. All models covered.

Walther Volume II, Engraved, Presentation and Standard Models, by James L. Rankin, J.L. Rankin, Coral Gables, FL, 1977. 112 pp., illus. $35.00.

The new Walther book on embellished versions and standard models. Has 88 photographs, including many color plates.

Walther, Volume III, 1908-1980, by James L. Rankin, Coral Gables, FL, 1981. 226 pp., illus. $35.00.

Covers all models of Walther handguns from 1908 to date, includes holsters, grips and magazines.

The Whitney Firearms, by Claud Fuller, Standard Publications, Huntington, WV, 1946, 334 pp., many plates and drawings. $50.00.

An authoritative history of all Whitney arms and their maker. Highly recommended. An exclusive with Ray Riling Arms Books Co.

Winchester: An American Legend, by R.L. Wilson, Random House, New York, NY, 1991. 403 pp., illus. $65.00.

The official history of Winchester firearms from 1849 to the present.

Winchester Bolt Action Military & Sporting Rifles 1877 to 1937, by Herbert G. Houze, Andrew Mowbray Publishing, Lincoln, RI, 1998. 295 pp., illus. $45.00.

Winchester was the first American arms maker to commercially manufacture a bolt action repeating rifle, and this book tells the exciting story of these Winchester bolt actions.

The Winchester Book, by George Madis, David Madis Gun Book Distributor, Dallas, TX, 1986. 650 pp., illus. $54.50.

A new, revised 25th anniversary edition of this classic book on Winchester firearms. Complete serial ranges have been added.

Winchester Dates of Manufacture 1849-1984, by George Madis, Art & Reference House, Brownsboro, TX, 1984. 59 pp. $6.00.

A most useful work, compiled from records of the Winchester factory.

Winchester Engraving, by R.L. Wilson, Beinfeld Books, Springs, CA, 1989. 500 pp., illus. $135.00.

A classic reference work of value to all arms collectors.

The Winchester Handbook, by George Madis, Art & Reference House, Lancaster, TX, 1982. 287 pp., illus. $24.95.

The complete line of Winchester guns, with dates of manufacture, serial numbers, etc.

The Winchester-Lee Rifle, by Eugene Myszkowski, Excalibur Publications, Tucson, AZ 2000. 96 pp., illustrated. Paper Covers. $22.95.

The development of the Lee Straight Pull, the cartridge and the approval for military use. Covers details of the inventor and memorabilia of Winchester-Lee related material.

THE ARMS LIBRARY

Winchester Lever Action Repeating Firearms, Vol. 1, The Models of 1866, 1873 and 1876, by Arthur Pirkie, North Cape Publications, Tustin, CA, 1995. 112 pp., illus. Paper covers. $19.95.
    Complete, part-by-part description, including dimensions, finishes, markings and variations throughout the production run of these fine, collectible guns.

Winchester Lever Action Repeating Rifles, Vol. 2, The Models of 1886 and 1892, by Arthur Pirkle, North Cape Publications, Tustin, CA, 1996. 150 pp., illus. Paper covers. $19.95.
    Describes each model on a part-by-part basis by serial number range complete with finishes, markings and changes.

Winchester Lever Action Repeating Rifles, Volume 3, The Model of 1894, by Arthur Pirkle, North Cape Publications, Tustin, CA, 1998. 150 pp., illus. Paper covers. $19.95.
    The first book ever to provide a detailed description of the Model 1894 rifle and carbine.

The Winchester Model 94: The First 100 Years, by Robert C. Renneberg, Krause Publications, Iola, WI, 1991. 208 pp., illus. $34.95.
    Covers the design and evolution from the early years up to the many different editions that exist today.

Winchester Shotguns and Shotshells, by Ronald W. Stadt, Krause Publications, Iola, WI, 1995. 256 pp., illus. $34.95.
    The definitive book on collectible Winchester shotguns and shotshells manufactured through 1961.

The Winchester Single-Shot, by John Cambell, Andrew Mowbray, Inc., Lincoln RI, 1995. 272 pp., illus. $55.00.
    Covers every important aspect of this highly-collectible firearm.

Winchester Slide-Action Rifles, Volume 1: Model 1890 & 1906, by Ned Schwing, Krause Publications, Iola, WI, 1992. 352 pp., illus. $39.95.
    First book length treatment of models 1890 & 1906 with over 50 charts and tables showing significant new information about caliber style and rarity.

Winchester Slide-Action Rifles, Volume 2: Model 61 & Model 62, by Ned Schwing, Krause Publications, Iola, WI, 1993. 256 pp., illus. $34.95.
    A complete historic look into the Model 61 and the Model 62. These favorite slide-action guns receive a thorough presentation which takes you to the factory to explore receivers, barrels, markings, stocks, stampings and engraving in complete detail.

Winchester's North West Mounted Police Carbines and other Model 1876 Data, by Lewis E. Yearout, The author, Great Falls, MT, 1999. 224 pp., illustrated. Paper covers. $38.00
    An impressive accumulation of the facts on the Model 1876, with particular empasis on those purchased for the North West Mounted Police.

Worldwide Webley and the Harrington and Richardson Connection, by Stephen Cuthbertson, Ballista Publishing and Distributing Ltd., Gabriola Island, Canada, 1999. 259 pp., illus. $50.00.
    A masterpiece of scholarship. Over 350 photographs plus 75 original documents, patent drawings, and advertisements accompany the text.

EDGED WEAPONS

The American Eagle Pommel Sword: The Early Years 1794-1830, by Andrew Mowbray, Manrat Arms Publications, Lincoln, RI, 1997. 244 pp., illus. $65.00.
    The standard guide to the most popular style of American sword.

American Indian Tomahawks, by Harold L. Peterson, The Gun Room Press, Highland Park, NJ, 1993. 142 pp., illus. $49.95.
    The tomahawk of the American Indian, in all its forms, as a weapon and as a tool.

American Knives; The First History and Collector's Guide, by Harold L. Peterson, The Gun Room Press, Highland Park, NJ, 1980. 178 pp., illus. $24.95.
    A reprint of this 1958 classic. Covers all types of American knives.

American Military Bayonets of the 20th Century, by Gary M. Cunningham, Scott A. Duff Publications, Export, PA, 1997. 116 pp., illus. Paper covers. $19.95.
    A guide for collectors, including notes on makers, markings, finishes, variations, scabbards, and production data.

American Premium Guide to Knives and Razors, 5th edition, by Jim Sargent, Krause Publications, Iola, WI, 1999. 496 pp., illustrated. Paper covers. $24.95.
    Updates current values for thousands of the most popular and collectible pocket knives and razors.

American Primitive Knives 1770-1870, by G.B. Minnes, Museum Restoration Service, Ottawa, Canada, 1983. 112 pp., illus. $24.95.
    Origins of the knives, outstanding specimens, structural details, etc.

American Socket Bayonets and Scabbards, by Robert M. Reilly, 2nd printing, Andrew Mowbray, Inc., Lincoln, RI, 1998. 208 pp., illustrated. $45.00.
    Full coverage of the socket bayonet in America, from Colonial times through the post-Civil War.

The American Sword, 1775-1945, by Harold L. Peterson, Ray Riling Arms Books, Co., Phila., PA, 1980. 286 pp. plus 60 pp. of illus. $45.00.
    1977 reprint of a survey of swords worn by U.S. uniformed forces, plus the rare "American Silver Mounted Swords, (1700-1815)."

American Swords and Sword Makers, by Richard H. Bezdek, Paladin Press, Boulder, CO, 1994. 648 pp., illus. $79.95.
    The long-awaited definitive reference volume to American swords, sword makers and sword dealers from Colonial times to the present.

American Swords & Sword Makers Volume 2, by Richard H. Bezdek, Paladin Press, Boulder, CO, 1999. 376 pp., illus. $69.95.
    More than 400 stunning photographs of rare, unusual and one-of-a-kind swords from the top collections in the country

American Swords from the Philip Medicus Collection, edited by Stuart C. Mowbray, with photographs and an introduction by Norm Flayderman, Andrew Mowbray Publishers, Lincoln, RI, 1998. 272 pp., with 604 swords illustrated. $55.00.
    Covers all areas of American sword collecting.

The Ames Sword Company, 1829-1935, by John D. Hamilton, Andrew Mowbray Publisher, Linclon, RI, 1995. 255 pp., illus. $45.00.
    An exhaustively researched and comprehensive history of America's foremost sword manufacturer and arms supplier during the Civil War.

Battle Blades: A Professional's Guide to Combat/Fighting Knives, by Greg Walker; Foreword by Al Mar, Paladin Press, Boulder, CO, 1993. 168 pp., illus. $40.95.
    The author evaluates daggers, Bowies, switchblades and utility blades according to their design, performance, reliability and cost.

The Bayonet in New France, 1665-1760, by Erik Goldstein, Museum Restoration Service, Bloomfield, Ontario, Canada, 1997. 36 pp., illus. Paper covers. $6.95.
    Traces bayonets from the recently developed plug bayonet, through the regulation socket bayonets which saw service in North America.

Bayonets, Knives & Scabbards; United States Army Weapons Report 1917 Thru 1945, edited by Frank Trzaska, Knife Books, Deptford, NJ, 1999. 80 pp., illustrated. Paper covers. $15.95.
    Follows the United States edged weapons from the close of World War I through the end of World War 2. Manufacturers involved, dates, numbers produced, problems encountered, and production data.

The Book of the Sword, by Richard F. Burton, Dover Publications, New York, NY, 1987. 199 pp., illus. Paper covers. $12.95.
    Traces the swords origin from its birth as a charged and sharpened stick through diverse stages of development.

Borders Away, Volume 1: With Steel, by William Gilkerson, Andrew Mowbray, Inc., Lincoln, RI, 1991. 184 pp., illus. $48.00.
    A comprehensive study of naval armament under fighting sail. This first voume covers axes, pikes and fighting blades in use between 1626-1826.

The Bowie Knife, by Raymond Thorp, Phillips Publications, Williamstown, NJ, 1992. 167 pp., illus. $9.95.
    After forty-five years, the classic work on the Bowie knife is once again available.

British & Commonwealth Bayonets, by Ian D. Skennerton and Robert Richardson, I.D.S.A. Books, Piqua, OH, 1986. 404 pp., 1300 illus. $40.00.

Civil War Knives, by Marc Newman, Paladin Press, Boulder, CO, 1999. 120 pp., illustrated. $44.95.
    The author delves into the blade designs used at Gettysburg, Vicksburg, Antitam, Chancellorsville, and Bull Run. Photos of rare and common examples of cut-down swords, poignards, ornate clip-point knives, exquisite presentation knives and more.

Collecting the Edged Weapons of Imperial Germany, by Thomas M. Johnson and Thomas T. Wittmann, Johnson Reference Books, Fredricksburg, VA, 1989. 363 pp., illus. $39.50
    An in-depth study of the many ornate military, civilian, and government daggers and swords of the Imperial era.

Collecting Indian Knives, 2nd Edition, by Lar Hothem, Krause Publications, Iola, WI, 2000. 176 pp., illustrated. Paper covers. $19.95.
    A must for anyone who collects or wants to learn about chipped Indian artifacts in the knife family.

Collector's Guide to Ames U.S. Contract Military Edged Weapons: 1832-1906, by Ron G. Hickox, Pioneer Press, Union City, IN, 1993. 70 pp., illus. Paper covers. $17.50.
    While this book deals primarily with edged weapons made by the Ames Manufacturing Company, this guide refers to other manufactureres of United States swords.

Collector's Handbook of World War 2 German Daggers, by LTC. Thomas M. Johnson, Johnson Reference Books, Fredericksburg, VA, 2nd edition, 1991. 252 pp., illus. Paper covers. $25.00.
    Concise pocket reference guide to Third Reich daggers and accoutrements in a convenient format. With value guide.

Collins Machetes and Bowies 1845-1965, by Danial E. Henry, Krause Publications, Iola, WI, 1996. 232 pp., illus. Paper covers. $19.95.
    A comprehensive history of Collins machetes and bowies including more than 1200 blade instruments and accessories.

Commando Daggers, "The Complete Illustrated History of the Fairbairn-Sykes Fighting Knife", by Leroy Thompson, Paladin Press, Boulder, CO, 2000. Softcover, photos, illus., 176 pp. $35.00
    The Fairbairn-Sykes dagger is recognized as the world's most important fighting knife. This book compiles photos of the F-S knife and its descendants, providing detailed info on markings, sheaths, crossguards, length and special characteristics. A foreword by Col. Rex Applegate and an extensive commando dagger ID section are included.

The Complete Bladesmith: Forging Your Way to Perfection, by Jim Hrisoulas, Paladin Press, Boulder, CO, 1987. 192 pp., illus. $42.95.
    Novice as well as experienced bladesmith will benefit from this definitive guide to smithing world-class blades.

The Complete Book of Pocketknife Repair, by Ben Kelly, Jr., Krause Publications, Iola, WI, 1995. 130 pp., illus. Paper covers. $10.95.
    Everything you need to know about repairing knives can be found in this step-by-step guide to knife repair.

Confederate Edged Weapons, by W.A. Albaugh, R&R Books, Lavonia, NY, 1994. 198 pp., illus. $30.00.
    The master reference to edged weapons of the Confederate forces. Features precise line drawings and an extensive text.

THE ARMS LIBRARY

The Craft of the Japanese Sword, by Leon and Hiroko Kapp, Yoshindo Yoshihara, Kodanska International, Tokyo, Japan, 1990. 167 pp., illus. $39.00.
The first book in English devoted to contemporary sword manufacturing in Japan.

Daggers and Bayonets a History, by Logan Thompson, Paladin Press, Boulder, CO, 1999. 128 pp., illustrated. $40.00.
This authoritative history of military daggers and bayonets examines all patterns of daggers in detail, from the utilitarian Saxon scamasax used at Hastings to lavishly decorated Cinquedas, Landsknecht and Holbein daggers of the late high Renaissance.

Eickhorn Edged Weapons Exports, Vol. 1: Latin America, by A.M. de Quesada, Jr. And Ron G. Hicock, Pioneer Press, Union City, TN, 1996. 120 pp., illus. Paper covers. $15.00.
This research studies the various Eickhorn edged weapons and accessories manufactured for various countries outside of Germany.

Encyclopedia of Native American Bows, Arrows & Quivers, Volume 1, by Steve Allely and Jim Hamm, The Lyons Press, N.Y., 1999. 137 pp., illustrated. $29.95.
Beautifully detailed full-page pen-and-ink drawings give dimensions, decorations, and construction details on more than a hundred historic bows, scores of arrows, and more than a dozen quivers from over thirty tribes.

Exploring the Dress Daggers of the German Army, by Thomas T. Wittmann, Johnson Reference Books, Fredericksburg, VA, 1995. 350 pp., illus. $59.95.
The first in-depth analysis of the dress daggers worn by the German Army.

The First Commando Knives, by Prof. Kelly Yeaton and Col. Rex Applegate, Phillips Publications, Williamstown, NJ, 1996. 115 pp., illus. Paper covers. $12.95.
Here is the full story of the Shanghai origins of the world's best known dagger.

German Clamshells and Other Bayonets, by G. Walker and R.J. Weinard, Johnson Reference Books, Fredericksburg, VA, 1994. 157 pp., illus. $22.95.
Includes unusual bayonets, many of which are shown for the first time. Current market values are listed.

German Military Fighting Knives 1914-1945, by Gordon A. Hughes, Johnson Reference Books, Fredericksburg, VA, 1994. 64 pp., illus. Paper covers. $24.50.
Documents the different types of German military fighting knives used during WWI and WWII. Makers' proofmarks are shown as well as details of blade inscriptions, etc.

German Swords and Sword Makers: Edged Weapons Makers from the 14ᵗʰ to the 20ᵗʰ Centuries, by Richard H. Bezdek, Paladin Press, Boulder, CO, 2000. 248 pp., illustrated. $59.95.
This book contains the most informations ever published on German swords and edged weapons makers from the Middle Ages to the present.

A Glossary of the Construction, Decoration and Use of Arms and Armor in all Countries and in all times, by George Cameron Stone, Dover Publications, Mineola, N.Y., 1999. 704 pp., illustrated. Paper covers. $49.95.
Unabridged republication of the work originally published in 1934. With a new introduction by Donald LaRocca, Associate Curator, Arms & Armor, The Metropolitan Museum of Art.

The Halberd and other European Polearms 1300-1650, by George Snook, Museum Restoration Service, Bloomfield, Ontario, Canada, 1998. 40 pp., illus. Paper covers. $6.95
A comprehensive introduction to the history, use, and identification of the staff weapons of Europe.

The Handbook of British Bayonets, by Ian D. Skennerton, I.D.S.A. Books, Piqua, OH. 64 pp. $4.95

The Hand Forged Knife, Krause Publications, Iola, WI. 136 pp., illus., $12.95.
Explains the techniques for forging, hardening and tempering knives and other stainless steel tools.

How to Make Folding Knives, by Ron Lake, Frank Centofante and Wayne Clay, Krause Publications, Iola, WI, 1995. 193 pp., illus. Paper covers. $13.95.
With step-by-step instructions, learn how to make your own folding knife from three top custom makers.

How to Make Knives, by Richard W. Barney and Robert W. Loveless, Krause Publications, Iola, WI, 1995. 182 pp., illus. Paper covers. $13.95.
Complete instructions from two premier knife makers on making high-quality, handmade knives.

How to Make Multi-Blade Folding Knives, by Eugene Shadley & Terry Davis, Krause Publications, Iola, WI, 1997. 192 pp., illus. Paper covers. $19.95.
This step-by-step instructional guide teaches knifemakers how to craft these complex folding knives.

How to Make a Tactical Folder, by Bob Tetzuola, Krause Publications, Iola, WI, 2000. 160 pp., illustrated. Paper covers. $16.95.
Step-by-step instructions and outstanding photography guide the knifemaker from start to finish.

The Modern Swordsman, by Fred Hutchinson, Paladin Press, Boulder, CO, 1999. 80 pp., illustrated. Paper covers. $22.00
Realistic training for serious self-defense.

The Wonder of Knifemaking, by Wayne Goddard, Krause Publications, Iola, WI, 2000. 160 pp., illustrated with 150 b&w photos and a 16 page color section. Paper covers. $19.95.
Tips for Knifemakers of all skill levels. Heat treating and steel selection.

Kentucky Knife Traders Manual No. 6, by R.B. Ritchie, Hindman, KY, 1980. 217 pp., illus. Paper covers. $10.00.
Guide for dealers, collectors and traders listing pocket knives and razor values.

Knife and Tomahawk Throwing: The Art of the Experts, by Harry K. McEvoy, Charles E. Tuttle, Rutland, VT, 1989. 150 pp., illus. Soft covers. $8.95.
The first book to employ side-by-side the fascinating art and science of knives and tomahawks.

Knife Talk, the Art and Science of Knifemaking, by Ed. Fowler, Krause Publications, Iola, WI, 1998. 158 pp., illus. Paper covers. $14.95.
Valuable how-to advice on knife design and construction plus 20 years of memorable articles from the pages of "Blade" Magazine.

Knifemakers of Old San Francisco, by Bernard Levine, 2nd edition, Paladin Press, Boulder, CO, 1998. 150 pp., illus. $39.95.
The definitive history of the knives and knife-makers of 19th century San Francisco.

Knifemaking, The Gun Digest Book of, by Jack Lewis and Roger Combs, DBI Books, a division of Krause Publications, Iola, WI, 1989. 256 pp., illus. Paper covers. $16.95.
All the ins and outs from the world of knifemaking in a brand new book.

Knives, 5th Edition, The Gun Digest Book of, edited by Jack Lewis and Roger Combs, DBI Books, a division of Krause Publications, Iola, WI, 1997. 256 pp., illus. Paper covers. $19.95.
Covers practically every aspect of the knife world.

*Knives 2001, 21st Annual Edition, edited by Joe Kertzman, DBI Books, a division of Krause Publications, Iola, WI, 1999. 304 pp., illustrated. Paper covers. $21.95.
More than 1,000 photos and listings of new knives plus articles from top writers in the field.

*Levine's Guide to Knives And Their Values, 5th Edition, by Bernard Levine, DBI Books, a division of Krause Publications, Iola, WI, 2000. Illus. Paper covers. $27.95.
All the basic tools for identifying, valuing and collecting folding and fixed blade knives.

The Master Bladesmith: Advanced Studies in Steel, by Jim Hrisoulas, Paladin Press, Boulder, CO, 1990. 296 pp., illus. $49.95.
The author reveals the forging secrets that for centuries have been protected by guilds.

Medieval Swordsmanship, Illustrated Methods and Techniques, by John Clements, Paladin Press, Boulder, CO, 1998. 344 pp., illustrated. $40.00.
The most comprehensive and historically accurate view ever written of the lost fighting arts of Medieval knights.

Military Swords of Japan 1868-1945, by Richard Fuller and Ron Gregory, Arms and Armour Press, London, England, 1986. 127 pp., illus. Paper covers. $18.95.
A wide-ranging survey of the swords and dirks worn by the armed forces of Japan until the end of World War II.

Modern Combat Blades, by Duncan Long, Paladin Press, Boulder, CO, 1993. 128 pp., illus. $30.00.
Long discusses the pros and cons of bowies, bayonets, commando daggers, kukris, switchblades, butterfly knives, belt-buckle blades and many more.

On Damascus Steel, by Dr. Leo S. Figiel, Atlantis Arts Press, Atlantis, FL, 1991. 145 pp., illus. $65.00.
The historic, technical and artistic aspects of Oriental and mechanical Damascus. Persian and Indian sword blades, from 1600-1800, which have never been published, are illustrated.

The Pattern-Welded Blade: Artistry in Iron, by Jim Hrisoulas, Paladin Press, Boulder, CO, 1994. 120 pp., illus. $44.95.
Reveals the secrets of this craft—from the welding of the starting billet to the final assembly of the complete blade.

Randall Made Knives, Krause Publications, Iola, WI. 292 pp., illus. $59.95.
Plots the designs of all 24 of Randall's unique knives.

Renaissance Swordsmanship, by John Clements, Paladin Press, Boulder, CO, 1997. 152 pp., illus. Paper covers. $25.00.
The illustrated use of rapiers and cut-and-thrust swords.

Rice's Trowel Bayonet, reprinted by Ray Riling Arms Books, Co., Phila., PA, 1968. 8 pp., illus. Paper covers. $3.00.
A facsimile reprint of a rare circular originally published by the U.S. government in 1875 for the information of U.S. troops.

The Samurai Sword, by John M. Yumoto, Charles E. Tuttle Co., Rutland, VT, 1958. 191 pp., illus. $23.95.
A must for anyone interested in Japanese blades, and the first book on this subject written in English.

The Scottish Dirk, by James D. Forman, Museum Restoration Service, Bloomfield, Ont., Canada, 1991. 60 pp., illus. Paper covers. $5.95.
More than 100 dirks are illustrated with a text that sets the dirk and Sgian Dubh in their socio-historic content following design changes through more than 300 years of evolution.

Scottish Swords from the Battlefield at Culloden, by Lord Archibald Campbell, The Mowbray Co., Providence, RI, 1973. 63 pp., illus. $15.00.
A modern reprint of an exceedingly rare 1894 privately printed edition.

The Sheffield Knife Book, by Geoffrey Tweedale, Krause Publications, Iola, WI. 320 pp., illus., $50.00.

Small Arms Identification Series, No. 6-British Service Sword & Lance Patterns, by Ian Skennerton, I.D.S.A. Books, Piqua, OH, 1994. 48 pp. $9.50.

Small Arms Series, No. 2. The British Spike Bayonet, by Ian Skennerton, I.D.S.A. Books, Piqua, OH, 1982. 32 pp., 30 illus. $9.00.

Socket Bayonets of the Great Powers, by Robert W. Shuey, Excalibur Publications, Tucson, AZ, 2000 96 pp., illus. Paper covers $22.95.
With 175 illustrations the author brings together in one place, many of the standard socket arrnagements used by some of the " Great Powers". With an illustrated glossary of blade shape and socket design.

Sure Defence, The Bowie Knife Book, by Kenneth J. Burton, I.D.S.A. Books, Piqua, OH, 1988. 100 pp., 115 illus. $37.50.

Swords and Sword Makers of the War of 1812, by Richard Bezdek, Paladin Press, Boulder, CO, 1997. 104 pp., illus. $49.95.
The complete history of the men and companies that made swords during and before the war. Includes examples of cavalry and artillery sabers.

REFERENCE

Sword of the Samurai, by George R. Parulski, Jr., Paladin Press, Boulder, CO, 1985. 144 pp., illus. $39.95.
The classical art of Japanese swordsmanship.

Swords from Public Collections in the Commonwealth of Pennsylvania, edited by Bruce S. Bazelon, Andrew Mowbray Inc., Lincoln, RI, 1987. 127 pp., illus. Paper covers. $12.00.
Contains new information regarding swordmakers of the Philadelphia area.

Swords and Blades of the American Revolution, by George C. Neumann, Rebel Publishing Co., Inc., Texarkana, TX, 1991. 288 pp., illus. $36.95.
The encyclopedia of bladed weapons—swords, bayonets, spontoons, halberds, pikes, knives, daggers, axes—used by both sides, on land and sea, in America's struggle for independence.

The Working Folding Knife, by Steven Dick, Stoeger Publishing Co., Wayne, NJ, 1998. 280 pp., illus. Paper covers. $21.95.
From the classic American Barlow to exotic folders like the spanish Navaja this book has it all.

GENERAL

Action Shooting: Cowboy Style, by John Taffin, Krause Publications, Iola, WI, 1999. 320 pp., illustrated. $39.95.
Details on the guns and ammunition. Explanations of the rules used for many events. The essential cowboy wardrobe.

Advanced Muzzleloader's Guide, by Toby Bridges, Stoeger Publishing Co., So. Hackensack, NJ, 1985. 256 pp., illus. Paper covers. $14.95.
The complete guide to muzzle-loading rifles, pistols and shotguns—flintlock and percussion.

Aids to Musketry for Officers & NCOs, by Capt. B.J. Friend, Excalibur Publications, Latham, NY, 1996. 40 pp., illus. Paper covers. $7.95.
A facsimile edition of a pre-WWI British manual filled with useful information for training the common soldier.

Air Gun Digest, 3rd Edition, by J.I. Galan, DBI Books, a division of Krause Publications, Iola, WI, 1995. 258 pp., illus. Paper covers. $19.95.
Everything from A to Z on air gun history, trends and technology.

American and Imported Arms, Ammunition and Shooting Accessories, Catalog No. 18 of the Shooter's Bible, Stoeger, Inc., reprinted by Fayette Arsenal, Fayetteville, NC, 1988. 142 pp., illus. Paper covers. $10.95.
A facsimile reprint of the 1932 Stoeger's Shooter's Bible.

America's Great Gunmakers, by Wayne van Zwoll, Stoeger Publishing Co., So. Hackensack, NJ, 1992. 288 pp., illus. Paper covers. $16.95.
This book traces in great detail the evolution of guns and ammunition in America and the men who formed the companies that produced them.

Ammunition: Small Arms, Grenades and Projected Munitions, by Ian V. Hogg, Greenhill Books, London, England, 1998. 144 pp., illustrated. $22.95.
The best concise guide to modern ammunition. Wide-ranging and international coverage. Detailed specifications and illustrations.

Armed and Female, by Paxton Quigley, E.P. Dutton, New York, NY, 1989. 237 pp., illus. $16.95.
The first complete book on one of the hottest subjects in the media today, the arming of the American woman.

Arming the Glorious Cause: Weapons of the Second War for Independence, by James B. Whisker, Daniel D. Hartzler and Larry W. Yantz, R & R Books, Livonia, NY, 1998. 175 pp., illustrated. $45.00.
A photographic study of Confederate weapons.

Arms and Armour in Antiquity and the Middle Ages, by Charles Boutell, Stackpole Books, Mechanicsburg, PA, 1996. 352 pp., illus. $22.95.
Detailed descriptions of arms and armor, the development of tactics and the outcome of specific battles.

Arms & Armor in the Art Institute of Chicago, by Walter J. Karcheski, Jr., Bulfinch Press, Boston, MA, 1995. 128 pp., illus. $35.00.
Now, for the first time, the Art Institute of Chicago's arms and armor collection is presented in the visual delight of 103 color illustrations.

Arms for the Nation: Springfield Longarms, edited by David C. Clark, Scott A. Duff, Export, PA, 1994. 73 pp., illus. Paper covers. $9.95.
A brief history of the Springfield Armory and the arms made there.

Arsenal of Freedom, The Springfield Armory, 1890-1948: A Year-by-Year Account Drawn from Official Records, compiled and edited by Lt. Col. William S. Brophy, USAR Ret., Andrew Mowbray, Inc., Lincoln, RI, 1991. 400 pp., illus. Soft covers. $29.95.
A "must buy" for all students of American military weapons, equipment and accoutrements.

Assault Pistols, Rifles and Submachine Guns, by Duncan Long, Paladin Press, Boulder, CO, 1997, 8 1/2 x 11, soft cover, photos, illus. 152 pp. $21.95.
This book offers up-to-date, practical information on how to operate and field-strip modern military, police and civilian combat weapons. Covers new developments and trends such as the use of fiber optics, liquid-recoil systems and lessening of barrel length are covered. Troubleshooting procedures, ballistic tables and a list of manufacturers and distributors are also included.

Assault Weapons, 5th Edition, The Gun Digest Book of, edited by Jack Lewis and David E. Steele, DBI Books, a division of Krause Publications, Iola, WI, 2000. 256 pp., illustrated. Paper covers. $21.95.
This is the latest word on true assault weaponry in use today by international military and law enforcement organizations.

The Belgian Rattlesnake: The Lewis Automatic Machine Gun, by William M. Easterly, Collector Grade Publications, Inc., Cobourg, Ont. Canada, 1998. 542 pp., illus. $79.95.
A social and technical biography of the Lewis automatic machine gun and its inventors.

The Big Guns: Civil War Siege, Seacoast, and Naval Cannon, by Edwin Olmstead, Wayne E. Stark and Spencer C. Tucker, Museum Restoration Service, Bloomfield, Ontario, Canada, 1997. 360 pp., illus. $80.00.
This book is designed to identify and record the heavy guns available to both sides during the Civil War.

Blackpowder Loading Manual, 3rd Edition, by Sam Fadala, DBI Books, a division of Krause Publications, Iola, WI, 1995. 368 pp., illus. Paper covers. $20.95.
Revised and expanded edition of this landmark blackpowder loading book. Covers hundreds of loads for most of the popular blackpowder rifles, handguns and shotguns.

Bolt Action Rifles, 3rd Edition, by Frank de Haas, DBI Books, a division of Krause Publications, Iola, WI, 1995. 528 pp., illus. Paper covers. $24.95.
A revised edition of the most definitive work on all major bolt-action rifle designs.

The Book of the Crossbow, by Sir Ralph Payne-Gallwey, Dover Publications, Mineola, NY, 1996. 416 pp., illus. Paper covers. $14.95.
Unabridged republication of the scarce 1907 London edition of the book on one of the most devastating hand weapons of the Middle Ages.

Bows and Arrows of the Native Americans, by Jim Hamm, Lyons & Burford Publishers, New York, NY, 1991. 156 pp., illus. $19.95.
A complete step-by-step guide to wooden bows, sinew-backed bows, composite bows, strings, arrows and quivers.

British Small Arms of World War 2, by Ian D. Skennerton, I.D.S.A. Books, Piqua, OH, 1988. 110 pp., 37 illus. $25.00.

"Carbine," the Story of David Marshall Williams, by Ross E. Beard, Jr. Phillips Publications, Williamstown, NJ, 1999. 225 pp., illus. $29.95.
The story of the firearms genius, David Marshall "Carbine" Williams. From prison to the pinnacles of fame, the tale of this North Carolinian is inspiring. The author details many of Williams' firearms inventions and developments.

*Cartridges of the World, 9th Edition, by Frank Barnes, edited by M. L. McPherson, DBI Books, a division of Krause Publications, Iola, WI, 2000. 512 pp., illus. Paper covers.
Completely revised edition of the general purpose reference work for which collectors, police, scientists and laymen reach first for answers to cartridge identification questions.

Combat Handgunnery, 4th Edition, The Gun Digest Book of, by Chuck Taylor, DBI Books, a division of Krause Publications, Iola, WI, 1997. 256 pp., illus. Paper covers. $18.95.
This edition looks at real world combat handgunnery from three different perspectives—military, police and civilian.

The Complete Blackpowder Handbook, 3rd Edition, by Sam Fadala, DBI Books, a division of Krause Publications, Iola, WI, 1997. 400 pp., illus. Paper covers. $21.95.
Expanded and completely rewritten edition of the definitive book on the subject of blackpowder.

The Complete Guide to Game Care and Cookery, 3rd Edition, by Sam Fadala, DBI Books, a division of Krause Publications, Iola, WI, 1994. 320 pp., illus. Paper covers. $18.95.
Over 500 photos illustrating the care of wild game in the field and at home with a separate recipe section providing over 400 tested recipes.

The Complete .50-caliber Sniper Course, by Dean Michaelis, Paladin Press, Boulder, CO, 2000. 576 pp, illustrated, $60.00.
The history from German Mauser T-Gewehr of World War 1 to the Soviet PTRD and beyond. Includes the author's Program of Instruction for Special Operations Hard-Target Interdiction Course.

Complete Guide to Guns & Shooting, by John Malloy, DBI Books, a division of Krause Publications, Iola, WI, 1995. 256 pp., illus. Paper covers. $18.95.
What every shooter and gun owner should know about firearms, ammunition, shooting techniques, safety, collecting and much more.

Cowboy Action Shooting, by Charly Gullett, Wolfe Publishing Co., Prescott, AZ, 1995. 400 pp., illus. Paper covers. $24.50.
The fast growing of the shooting sports is comprehensively covered in this text— the guns, loads, tactics and the fun and flavor of this Old West era competition.

Crossbows, edited by Roger Combs, DBI Books, a division of Krause Publications, Iola, WI, 1986. 192 pp., illus. Paper covers. $15.95.
Complete, up-to-date coverage of the hottest bow going—and the most controversial.

Custom Firearms Engraving, by Tom Turpin, Krause Publications, Iola, WI, 1999. 208 pp., illustrated. $49.95.
Provides a broad and comprehensive look at the world of firearms engraving. The exquisite styles of more than 75 master engravers are shown on beautiful examples of handguns, rifles, shotguns, and other firearms, as well as knives.

Dead On, by Tony Noblitt and Warren Gabrilska, Paladin Press, Boulder, CO, 1998. 176 pp., illustrated. Paper covers. $22.00
The long-range marksman's guide to extreme accuracy.

Death from Above: The German FG42 Paratrooper Rifle, by Thomas B. Dugelby and R. Blake Stevens, Collector Grade Publications, Toronto, Canada, 1990. 147 pp., illus. $39.95.
The first comprehensive study of all seven models of the FG42.

Early American Flintlocks, by Daniel D. Hartzler and James B. Whisker, Bedford Valley Press, Bedford, PA 2000. 192 pp., Illustrated.
Covers early Colonial Guns, New England Guns, Pennsylvania Guns and Souther Guns.

REFERENCE

THE ARMS LIBRARY

Encyclopedia of Modern Firearms, Vol. 1, compiled and publ. by Bob Brownell, Montezuma, IA, 1959. 1057 pp. plus index, illus. $70.00. Dist. By Bob Brownell, Montezuma, IA 50171.

Massive accumulation of basic information of nearly all modern arms pertaining to "parts and assembly." Replete with arms photographs, exploded drawings, manufacturers' lists of parts, etc.

Encyclopedia of Native American Bows, Arrows and Quivers, by Steve Allely and Jim Hamm, The Lyons Press, N.Y., 1999. 160 pp., illustrated. $29.95.

A landmark book for anyone interested in archery history, or Native Americans.

The Exercise of Armes, by Jacob de Gheyn, edited and with an introduction by Bas Kist, Dover Publications, Inc., Mineola, NY, 1999. 144 pp., illustrated. Paper covers. $12.95.

Republications of all 117 engravings from the 1607 classic military manual. A meticulously accurate portrait of uniforms and weapons of the 17th century Netherlands.

Exploded Handgun Drawings, The Gun Digest Book of, edited by Harold A. Murtz, DBI Books, a division of Krause Publications, Iola, WI, 1992. 512 pp., illus. Paper covers. $20.95.

Exploded or isometric drawings for 494 of the most popular handguns.

Exploded Long Gun Drawings, The Gun Digest Book of, edited by Harold A. Murtz, DBI Books, a division of Krause Publications, Iola, WI, 512 pp., illus. Paper covers. $20.95.

Containing almost 500 rifle and shotgun exploded drawings.

Fighting Iron; A Metals Handbook for Arms Collectors, by Art Gogan, Mowbray Publishers, Inc., Lincoln, RI, 1999. 176 pp., illustrated. $28.00.

A guide that is easy to use, explains things in simple English and covers all of the different historical periods that we are interested in.

The Fighting Submachine Gun, Machine Pistol, and Shotgun, a Hands-On Evaluation, by Timothy J. Mullin, Paladin Press, Boulder, CO, 1999. 224 pp., illustrated. Paper covers. $35.00.

An invaluable reference for military, police and civilian shooters who may someday need to know how a specific weapon actually performs when the targets are shooting back and the margin of errors is measured in lives lost.

Fireworks: A Gunsight Anthology, by Jeff Cooper, Paladin Press, Boulder, CO, 1998. 192 pp., illus. Paper cover. $27.00

A collection of wild, hilarious, shocking and always meaningful tales from the remarkable life of an American firearms legend.

Frank Pachmayr: The Story of America's Master Gunsmith and his Guns, by John Lachuk, Safari Press, Huntington Beach, CA, 1996. 254 pp., illus. First edition, limited, signed and slipcased. $85.00; Second printing trade edition. $50.00.

The colorful and historically significant biography of Frank A. Pachmayr, America's own gunsmith emeritus.

From a Stranger's Doorstep to the Kremlin Gate, by Mikhail Kalashnikov, Ironside International Publishers, Inc., Alexandria, VA, 1999. 460 pp., illustrated. $34.95.

A biography of the most influential rifle designer of the 20th century. His AK-47 assault rifle has become the most widely used (and copied) assault rifle of this century.

The Frontier Rifleman, by H.B. LaCrosse Jr., Pioneer Press, Union City, TN, 1989. 183 pp., illus. Soft covers. $17.50.

The Frontier rifleman's clothing and equipment during the era of the American Revolution, 1760-1800.

The Gatling Gun: 19th Century Machine Gun to 21st Century Vulcan, by Joseph Berk, Paladin Press, Boulder, CO, 1991. 136 pp., illus. $34.95.

Here is the fascinating on-going story of a truly timeless weapon, from its beginnings during the Civil War to its current role as a state-of-the-art modern combat system.

German Artillery of World War Two, by Ian V. Hogg, Stackpole Books, Mechanicsburg, PA, 1997. 304 pp., illus. $44.95.

Complete details of German artillery use in WWII.

Grand Old Lady of No Man's Land: The Vickers Machine Gun, by Dolf L. Goldsmith, Collector Grade Publications, Cobourg, Canada, 1994. 600 pp., illus. $79.95.

Goldsmith brings his years of experience as a U.S. Army armourer, machine gun collector and shooter to bear on the Vickers, in a book sure to become a classic in its field.

Great Shooters of the World, by Sam Fadala, Stoeger Publishing Co., So. Hackensack, NJ, 1991. 288 pp., illus. Paper covers. $18.95.

This book offers gun enthusiasts an overview of the men and women who have forged the history of firearms over the past 150 years.

The Grenade Recognition Manual, Volume 1, U.S. Grenades & Accessories, by Darryl W. Lynn, Service Publications, Ottawa, Canada, 1998. 112 pp., illus. Paper covers. $29.95.

This new book examines the hand grenades of the United States beginning with the hand grenades of the U.S. Civil War and continues through to the present.

Gun Digest Treasury, 7th Edition, edited by Harold A. Murtz, DBI Books, a division of Krause Publications, Iola, WI, 1994. 320 pp., illus. Paper covers. $17.95.

A collection of some of the most interesting articles which have appeared in Gun Digest over its first 45 years.

*Gun Digest 2001, 55th Edition, edited by Ken Ramage, DBI Books, a division of Krause Publications, Iola, WI, 2000. 544 pp., illustrated. Paper covers. $24.95.

This all new 55th edition continues the editorial excellence, quality, content and comprehensive cataloguing that firearms enthusiasts have come to know and expect. The most read gun book in the world for the last half century.

Gun Engraving, by C. Austyn, Safari Press Publication, Huntington Beach, CA, 1998. 128 pp., plus 24 pages of color photos. $50.00.

A well-illustrated book on fine English and European gun engravers. Includes a fantastic pictorial section that lists types of engravings and prices.

Gun Notes, Volume 1, by Elmer Keith, Safari Press, Huntington Beach, CA, 1995. 219 pp., illustrated Limited Edition, Slipcased. $75.00

A collection of Elmer Keith's most interesting columns and feature stories that appeared in "Guns & Ammo" magazine from 1961 to the late 1970's.

Gun Notes, Volume 2, by Elmer Keith, Safari Press, Huntington Beach, CA, 1997. 292 pp., illus. Limited 1st edition, numbered and signed by Keith's son. Slipcased. $75.00. Second edition. $35.00.

Covers articles from Keith's monthly column in "Guns & Ammo" magazine during the period from 1971 through Keith's passing in 1982.

Gun Talk, edited by Dave Moreton, Winchester Press, Piscataway, NJ, 1973. 256 pp., illus. $9.95.

A treasury of original writing by the top gun writers and editors in America. Practical advice about every aspect of the shooting sports.

The Gun That Made the Twenties Roar, by Wm. J. Helmer, rev. and enlarged by George C. Nonte, Jr., The Gun Room Press, Highland Park, NJ, 1977. Over 300 pp., illus. $24.95.

Historical account of John T. Thompson and his invention, the infamous "Tommy Gun."

Gun Trader's Guide, 22nd Edition, published by Stoeger Publishing Co., Wayne, NJ, 1999. 592 pp., illus. Paper covers. $23.95.

Complete specifications and current prices for used guns. Prices of over 5,000 handguns, rifles and shotguns both foreign and domestic.

Gun Writers of Yesteryear, compiled by James Foral, Wolfe Publishing Co., Prescott, AZ, 1993. 449 pp. $35.00.

Here, from the pre-American rifleman days of 1898-1920, are collected some 80 articles by 34 writers from eight magazines.

The Gunfighter, Man or Myth? by Joseph G. Rosa, Oklahoma Press, Norman, OK, 1969. 229 pp., illus. (including weapons). Paper covers. $14.95.

A well-documented work on gunfights and gunfighters of the West and elsewhere. Great treat for all gunfighter buffs.

Gunfitting: The Quest for Perfection, by Michael Yardley, Safari Press, Huntington Beach, CA, 1995. 128 pp., illus. $24.95.

The author, a very experienced shooting instructor, examines gun stocks and gunfitting in depth.

*Guns Illustrated 2001, 33rd Edition, edited by Ken Ramage, DBI Books, a division of Krause Publications, Iola, WI, 2000. 352 pp., illustrated. Paper covers. $22.95.

Highly informative, technical articles on a wide range of shooting topics by some of the top writers in the industry. A catalog section lists more than 3,000 firearms currently manufactured in or imported to the U.S.

Guns of the Wild West, by George Markham, Sterling Publishing Co., New York, NY, 1993. 160 pp., illus. Paper covers. $19.95.

Firearms of the American Frontier, 1849-1917.

Guns & Shooting: A Selected Bibliography, by Ray Riling, Ray Riling Arms Books Co., Phila., PA, 1982. 434 pp., illus. Limited, numbered edition. $75.00.

A limited edition of this superb bibliographical work, the only modern listing of books devoted to guns and shooting.

Guns, Bullets, and Gunfighters, by Jim Cirillo, Paladin Press, Boulder, CO, 1996. 119 pp., illus. Paper covers. $16.00.

Lessons and tales from a modern-day gunfighter.

Guns, Loads, and Hunting Tips, by Bob Hagel, Wolfe Publishing Co., Prescott, AZ, 1986. 509 pp., illus. $19.95.

A large hardcover book packed with shooting, hunting and handloading wisdom.

Handgun Digest, 3rd Edition, edited by Chris Christian, DBI Books, a division of Krause Publications, Iola, WI, 1995. 256 pp., illus. Paper covers. $18.95.

Full coverage of all aspects of handguns and handgunning from a highly readable and knowledgeable author.

Hidden in Plain Sight, "A Practical Guide to Concealed Handgun Carry" (Revised 2nd Edition), by Trey Bloodworth and Mike Raley, Paladin Press, Boulder, CO, 1997, 5 1/2 x 8 1/2, softcover, photos, 176 pp. $20.00

Concerned with how to comfortably, discreetly and safely exercise the privileges granted by a CCW permit? This invaluable guide offers the latest advice on what to look for when choosing a CCW, how to dress for comfortable, effective concealed carry, traditional and more unconventional carry modes, accessory holsters, customized clothing and accessories, accessibility data based on draw-time comparisons and new holsters on the market. Includes 40 new manufacturer listings.

HK Assault Rifle Systems, by Duncan Long, Paladin Press, Boulder, CO, 1995. 110 pp., illus. Paper covers. $27.95.

The little known history behind this fascinating family of weapons tracing its beginnings from the ashes of World War Two to the present time.

The Hunter's Table, by Terry Libby/Recipes of Chef Richard Blondin, Countrysport Press, Selma, AL, 1999. 230 pp. $30.00.

The Countrysport book of wild game guisine.

I Remember Skeeter, compiled by Sally Jim Skelton, Wolfe Publishing Co., Prescott, AZ, 1998. 401 pp., illus. Paper covers. $19.95.

A collection of some of the beloved storyteller's famous works interspersed with anecdotes and tales from the people who knew best.

In The Line of Fire, "A Working Cop's Guide to Pistol Craft", by Michael E. Conti, Paladin Press, Boulder, CO, 1997, 8 1/2 x 11, soft cover, photos, illus., 184 pp. $30.00

As a working cop, you want to end your patrol in the same condition you began: alive and uninjured. Improve your odds by reading and mastering the information in this book on pistol selection, stopping power, combat reloading, stoppages, carrying devices, stances, grips and Conti's "secrets" to accurate shooting.

Joe Rychertnik Reflects on Guns, Hunting, and Days Gone By, by Joe Rychetnik, Precision Shooting, Inc., Manchester, CT, 1999. 281 pp., illustrated. Paper covers. $16.95.

Thirty articles by a master story-teller.

THE ARMS LIBRARY

Kill or Get Killed, by Col. Rex Applegate, Paladin Press, Boulder, CO, 1996. 400 pp., illus. $39.95.
The best and longest-selling book on close combat in history.

The Long-Range War: Sniping in Vietnam, by Peter R. Senich, Paladin Press, Boulder, CO, 1994. 280 pp., illus. $49.95.
The most complete report on Vietnam-era sniping ever documented.

Machine Guns of World War I, by Robert Bruce, Windrow & Greene, London, 1997. 128 pp., illustrated. $39.95.
Seven classic automatic weapons of W.W.I. are illustrated in some 250 color photographs. Detailed sequences show them in close-up during field stripping and handling.

Manual for H&R Reising Submachine Gun and Semi-Auto Rifle, edited by George P. Dillman, Desert Publications, El Dorado, AZ, 1994. 81 pp., illus. Paper covers. $12.95.
A reprint of the Harrington & Richardson 1943 factory manual and the rare military manual on the H&R submachine gun and semi-auto rifle.

The Manufacture of Gunflints, by Sydney B.J. Skertchly, facsimile reprint with new introduction by Seymour de Lotbiniere, Museum Restoration Service, Ontario, Canada, 1984. 90 pp., illus. $24.50.
Limited edition reprinting of the very scarce London edition of 1879.

Master Tips, by J. Winokur, Potshot Press, Pacific Palisades, CA, 1985. 96 pp., illus. Paper covers. $11.95.
Basics of practical shooting.

The Military and Police Sniper, by Mike R. Lau, Precision Shooting, Inc., Manchester, CT, 1998. 352 pp., illustrated. Paper covers. $44.95.
Advanced precision shooting for combat and law enforcement.

Military Rifle & Machine Gun Cartridges, by Jean Huon, Paladin Press, Boulder, CO, 1990. 392 pp., illus. $34.95.
Describes the primary types of military cartridges and their principal loadings, as well as their characteristics, origin and use.

Military Small Arms of the 20th Century, 7th Edition, by Ian V. Hogg and John Weeks, DBI Books, a division of Krause Publications, Iola, WI, 2000. 416 pp., illustrated. Paper covers. $24.95.
Cover small arms of 46 countries. Over 800 photographs and illustrations.

Modern Custom Guns, Walnut, Steel, and Uncommon Artistry, by Tom Turpin, Krause Publications, Iola, WI, 1997. 206 pp., illus. $49.95.
From exquisite engraving to breathtaking exotic woods, the mystique of today's custom guns is expertly detailed in word and awe-inspiring color photos of rifles, shotguns and handguns.

Modern Guns Identification & Values, 13th Edition, by Russell & Steve Quertermous, Collector Books, Paducah, KY, 1999. 516 pp., illus. Paper covers. $12.95.
A standard reference for over 20 years. Over 1,800 illustrations of over 2,500 models with their current values.

Modern Law Enforcement Weapons & Tactics, 2nd Edition, by Tom Ferguson, DBI Books, a division of Krause Publications, Iola, WI, 1991. 256 pp., illus. Paper covers. $18.95.
An in-depth look at the weapons and equipment used by law enforcement agencies of today.

Modern Machine Guns, by John Walter, Stackpole Books, Inc. Mechanicsburg, PA, 2000. 144 pp., with 146 illustrations. $22.95.
A compact and authoritative guide to post-war machine-guns. A gun-by-gun directory identifying individual variants and types including detailed evaluations and technical data.

Modern Sporting Guns, by Christopher Austyn, Safari Press, Huntington Beach, CA, 1994. 128 pp., illus. $40.00.
A discussion of the "best" English guns; round action, over-and-under, boxlocks, hammer guns, bolt action and double rifles as well as accessories.

The More Complete Cannoneer, by M.C. Switlik, Museum & Collectors Specialties Co., Monroe, MI, 1990. 199 pp., illus. $19.95.
Compiled agreeably to the regulations for the U.S. War Department, 1861, and containing current observations on the use of antique cannons.

The MP-40 Machine Gun, Desert Publications, El Dorado, AZ, 1995. 32 pp., illus. Paper covers. $11.95.
A reprint of the hard-to-find operating and maintenance manual for one of the most famous machine guns of World War II.

Naval Percussion Locks and Primers, by Lt. J. A. Dahlgren, Museum Restoration Service, Bloomfield, Canada, 1996. 140 pp., illus. $35.00.
First published as an Ordnance Memoranda in 1853, this is the finest existing study of percussion locks and primers origin and development.

The Official Soviet AKM Manual, translated by Maj. James F. Gebhardt (Ret.), Paladin Press, Boulder, CO, 1999. 120 pp., illustrated. Paper covers. $18.00.
This official military manual, available in English for the first time, was originally published by the Soviet Ministry of Defence. Covers the history, function, maintenance, assembly and disassembly, etc. of the 7.62mm AKM assault rifle.

The One-Round War: U.S.M.C. Scout-Snipers in Vietnam, by Peter Senich, Paladin Press, Boulder, CO, 1996. 384 pp., illus. Paper covers $59.95.
Sniping in Vietnam focusing specifically on the Marine Corps program.

OSS Weapons, by Dr. John W. Brunner, Phillips Publications, Williamstown, NJ, 1996. 224 pp., illus. $44.95.
The most definitive book ever written on the weapons and equipment used by the supersecret warriors of the Office of Strategic Services.

Pin Shooting: A Complete Guide, by Mitchell A. Ota, Wolfe Publishing Co., Prescott, AZ, 1992. 145 pp., illus. Paper covers. $14.95.
Traces the sport from its humble origins to today's thoroughly enjoyable social event, including the mammoth eight-day Second Chance Pin Shoot in Michigan.

Powder and Ball Small Arms, by Martin Pegler, Windrow & Greene Publishing, London, 1998. 128 pp., illustrated with 200 color photos. $39.95.
Part of the new "Live Firing Classic Weapons" series. Full-color photos of experienced shooters dressed in authentic costumes handling, loading and firing historic weapons.

Principles of Personal Defense, by Jeff Cooper, Paladin Press, Boulder, CO, 1999. 56 pp., illustrated. Paper covers. $14.00.
This revised edition of Jeff Cooper's classic on personal defense offers great new illustrations and a new preface while retaining the timeliness theory of individual defense behavior presented in the original book.

E.C. Prudhomme, Master Gun Engraver, A Retrospective Exhibition: 1946-1973, intro. by John T. Amber, The R. W. Norton Art Gallery, Shreveport, LA, 1973. 32 pp., illus. Paper covers. $9.95.
Examples of master gun engravings by Jack Prudhomme.

The Quotable Hunter, edited by Jay Cassell and Peter Fiduccia, The lyons Press, N.Y., 1999. 224 pp., illustrated. $20.00.
This collection of more than three hundred memorable quotes from hunters through the ages captures the essence of the sport, with all its joys idiosyncrasies, and challenges.

A Rifleman Went to War, by H. W. McBride, Lancer Militaria, Mt. Ida, AR, 1987. 398 pp., illus. $29.95.
The classic account of practical marksmanship on the battlefields of World War I.

Sharpshooting for Sport and War, by W.W. Greener, Wolfe Publishing Co., Prescott, AZ, 1995. 192 pp., illus. $30.00.
This classic reprint explores the *first* expanding bullet; service rifles; shooting positions; trajectories; recoil; external ballistics; and other valuable information.

The Shooter's Bible 2000, No. 91, edited by William S. Jarrett, Stoeger Publishing Co., Wayne, NJ, 1999. 576 pp., illustrated. Paper covers. $23.95.
Over 3,000 firearms currently offered by major American and foreign gunmakers. Represented are handguns, rifles, shotguns and black powder arms with complete specifications and retail prices.

Shooting, by J.H. FitzGerald, Wolfe Publishing Co., Prescott, AZ, 1993. 421 pp., illus. $35.00.
A classic book and reference for anyone interested in pistol and revolver shooting.

Shooting To Live, by Capt. W. E. Fairbairn & Capt. E. A. Sykes, Paladin Press, Boulder, CO, 1997, 4 1/2 x 7, soft cover, illus., 112 pp. $14.00.
Shooting to Live is the product of Fairbairn's and Sykes' practical experience with the handgun. Hundreds of incidents provided the basis for the first true book on life-or-death shootouts with the pistol. Shooting to Live teaches all concepts, considerations and applications of combat pistol craft.

Shooting Sixguns of the Old West, by Mike Venturino, MLV Enterprises, Livingston, MT, 1997. 221 pp., illus. Paper covers. $26.50.
A comprehensive look at the guns of the early West: Colts, Smith & Wesson and Remingtons, plus blackpowder and reloading specs.

Sniper Training, FM 23-10, Reprint of the U.S. Army field manual of August, 1994, Paladin Press, Boulder, CO, 1995. 352pp., illus. Paper covers. $30.00.
The most up-to-date U.S. military sniping information and doctrine.

Sniping in France, by Major H. Hesketh-Prichard, Lancer Militaria, Mt. Ida, AR, 1993. 224 pp., illus. $24.95.
The author was a well-known British adventurer and big game hunter. He was called upon in the early days of "The Great War" to develop a program to offset an initial German advantage in sniping. How the British forces came to overcome this advantage.

Special Warfare: Special Weapons, by Kevin Dockery, Emperor's Press, Chicago, IL, 1997. 192 pp., illus. $29.95.
The arms and equipment of the UDT and SEALS from 1943 to the present.

Sporting Collectibles, by Dr. Stephen R. Irwin, Stoeger Publishing Co., Wayne, NJ, 1997. 256 pp., illus. Paper covers. $19.95.
A must book for serious collectors and admirers of sporting collectibles.

The Sporting Craftsmen: A Complete Guide to Contemporary Makers of Custom-Built Sporting Equipment, by Art Carter, Countrysport Press, Traverse City, MI, 1994. 240 pp., illus. $35.00.
Profiles leading makers of centerfire rifles; muzzleloading rifles; bamboo fly rods; fly reels; flies; waterfowl calls; decoys; handmade knives; and traditional longbows and recurves.

Sporting Rifle Takedown & Reassembly Guide, 2nd Edition, by J.B. Wood, DBI Books, a division of Krause Publications, Iola, WI, 1997. 480 pp., illus. $19.95.
An updated edition of the reference guide for anyone who wants to properly care for their sporting rifle. (Available September 1997)

2000 Standard Catalog of Firearms, the Collector's Price & Reference Guide, 10th Edition, by Ned Schwing, Krause Publications, Iola, WI, 2000. 1,248 pp., illus. Paper covers. $32.95.
Packed with more than 80,000 real world prices with more than 5,000 photos. Easy to use master index listing every firearm model.

The Street Smart Gun Book, by John Farnam, Police Bookshelf, Concord, NH, 1986. 45 pp., illus. Paper covers. $11.95.
Weapon selection, defensive shooting techniques, and gunfight-winning tactics from one of the world's leading authorities.

Stress Fire, Vol. 1: Stress Fighting for Police, by Massad Ayoob, Police Bookshelf, Concord, NH, 1984. 149 pp., illus. Paper covers. $9.95.
Gunfighting for police, advanced tactics and techniques.

Survival Guns, by Mel Tappan, Desert Publications, El Dorado, AZ, 1993. 456 pp., illus. Paper covers. $21.95.
Discusses in a frank and forthright manner which handguns, rifles and shotguns to buy for personal defense and securing food, and the ones to avoid.

The Tactical Advantage, by Gabriel Suarez, Paladin Press, Boulder, CO, 1998. 216 pp., illustrated. Paper covers. $22.00.
Learn combat tactics that have been tested in the world's toughest schools.

Tactical Marksman, by Dave M. Lauch, Paladin Press, Boulder, CO, 1996. 165 pp., illus. Paper covers. $35.00.
A complete training manual for police and practical shooters.

Thompson Guns 1921-1945, Anubis Press, Houston, TX, 1980. 215 pp., illus. Paper covers. $15.95.
Facsimile reprinting of five complete manuals on the Thompson submachine gun.

To Ride, Shoot Straight, and Speak the Truth, by Jeff Cooper, Paladin Press, Boulder, CO, 1997, 5 1/2 x 8 1/2, soft-cover, illus., 384 pp. $32.00.
Combat mind-set, proper sighting, tactical residential architecture, nuclear war - these are some of the many subjects explored by Jeff Cooper in this illustrated anthology. The author discusses various arms, fighting skills and the importance of knowing how to defend oneself, and one's honor, in our rapidly changing world.

Trailriders Guide to Cowboy Action Shooting, by James W. Barnard, Pioneer Press, Union City, TN, 1998. 134 pp., plus 91 photos, drawings and charts. Paper covers. $24.95.
Covers the complete spectrum of this shooting discipline, from how to dress to authentic leather goods, which guns are legal, calibers, loads and ballistics.

The Ultimate Sniper, by Major John L. Plaster, Paladin Press, Boulder, CO, 1994. 464 pp., illus. Paper covers. $42.95.
An advanced training manual for military and police snipers.

Unrepentant Sinner, by Col. Charles Askins, Paladin Press, Boulder, CO, 2000. 322 pp., illustrated. $29.95.
The autobiography of Colonel Charles Askins.

U.S. Marine Corp Rifle and Pistol Marksmanship, 1935, reprinting of a government publication, Lancer Militaria, Mt. Ida, AR, 1991. 99 pp., illus. Paper covers. $11.95.
The old corps method of precision shooting.

U.S. Marine Corps Scout/Sniper Training Manual, Lancer Militaria, Mt. Ida, AR, 1989. Soft covers. $19.95.
Reprint of the original sniper training manual used by the Marksmanship Training Unit of the Marine Corps Development and Education Command in Quantico, Virginia.

U.S. Marine Corps Scout-Sniper, World War II and Korea, by Peter R. Senich, Paladin Press, Boulder, CO, 1994. 236 pp., illus. $44.95.
The most thorough and accurate account ever printed on the training, equipment and combat experiences of the U.S. Marine Corps Scout-Snipers.

U.S. Marine Corps Sniping, Lancer Militaria, Mt. Ida, AR, 1989. Irregular pagination. Soft covers. $17.95.
A reprint of the official Marine Corps FMFM1-3B.

Weapons of the Waffen-SS, by Bruce Quarrie, Sterling Publishing Co., Inc., 1991. 168 pp., illus. $24.95.
An in-depth look at the weapons that made Hitler's Waffen-SS the fearsome fighting machine it was.

Weatherby: The Man, The Gun, The Legend, by Grits and Tom Gresham, Cane River Publishing Co., Natchitoches, LA, 1992. 290 pp., illus. $24.95.
A fascinating look at the life of the man who changed the course of firearms development in America.

The Winchester Era, by David Madis, Art & Reference House, Brownsville, TX, 1984. 100 pp., illus. $14.95.
Story of the Winchester company, management, employees, etc.

Winchester Repeating Arms Company by Herbert Houze, Krause Publications, Iola, WI. 512 pp., illus. $50.00.

With British Snipers to the Reich, by Capt. C. Shore, Lander Militaria, Mt. Ida, AR, 1988. 420 pp., illus. $29.95.
One of the greatest books ever written on the art of combat sniping.

The World's Sniping Rifles, by Ian V. Hogg, Paladin Press, Boulder, CO, 1998. 144 pp., illustrated. $22.95.
A detailed manual with descriptions and illustrations of more than 50 high-precision rifles from 14 countries and a complete analysis of sights and systems.

GUNSMITHING

Accurizing the Factory Rifle, by M.L. McPherson, Precision Shooting, Inc., Manchester, CT, 1999. 335 pp., illustrated. Paper covers. $44.95.
A long-awaited book, which bridges the gap between the rudimentary (mounting sling swivels, scope blocks and that general level of accomplishment) and the advanced (precision chambering, barrel fluting, and that general level of accomplishment) books that are currently available today.

Advanced Rebarreling of the Sporting Rifle, by Willis H. Fowler, Jr., Willis H. Fowler, Jr., Anchorage, AK, 1994. 127 pp., illus. Paper covers. $32.50.
A manual outlining a superior method of fitting barrels and doing chamber work on the sporting rifle.

The Art of Engraving, by James B. Meek, F. Brownell & Son, Montezuma, IA, 1973. 196 pp., illus. $38.95.
A complete, authoritative, imaginative and detailed study in training for gun engraving. The first book of its kind—and a great one.

Artistry in Arms, The R. W. Norton Gallery, Shreveport, LA, 1970. 42 pp., illus. Paper covers. $9.95.
The art of gunsmithing and engraving.

Barrels & Actions, by Harold Hoffman, H&P Publishers, San Angelo, TX, 1990. 309 pp., illus. Sprial bound. $29.95.
A manual on barrel making.

Black Powder Hobby Gunsmithing, by Sam Fadala and Dale Storey, DBI Books, a division of Krause Publications, Iola, WI., 1994. 256 pp., illus. Paper covers. $18.95.
A how-to guide for gunsmithing blackpowder pistols, rifles and shotguns from two men at the top of their respective fields.

Checkering and Carving of Gun Stocks, by Monte Kennedy, Stackpole Books, Harrisburg, PA, 1962. 175 pp., illus. $39.95.
Revised, enlarged cloth-bound edition of a much sought-after, dependable work.

The Complete Metal Finishing Book, by Harold Hoffman, H&P Publishers, San Angelo, TX, 1992. 364 pp., illus. Paper covers. $29.95.
Instructions for the different metal finishing operations that the normal craftsman or shop will use. Primarily firearm related.

Exploded Handgun Drawings, The Gun Digest Book of, edited by Harold A. Murtz, DBI Books, a division of Krause Publications, Iola, WI. 1992. 512 pp., illus. Paper covers. $20.95.
Exploded or isometric drawings for 494 of the most popular handguns.

Exploded Long Gun Drawings, The Gun Digest Book of, edited by Harold A. Murtz, DBI Books, a division of Krause Publications, Iola, WI. 512 pp., illus. Paper covers. $20.95.
Containing almost 500 rifle and shotgun exploded drawings. An invaluable aid to both professionals and hobbyists.

The Finishing of Gun Stocks, by Harold Hoffman, H&P Publishers, San Angelo, TX, 1994. 98 pp., illus. Paper covers. $17.95.
Covers different types of finishing methods and finishes.

*Firearms Assembly/Disassembly, Part I: Automatic Pistols, 2nd Edition, The Gun Digest Book of, by J.B. Wood, DBI Books, a division of Krause Publications, Iola, WI, 1999. 592 pp., illus. Paper covers. $24.95.
Covers 72 popular autoloading pistols plus 250 variants of those models integrated into the text and completely cross-referenced in the index.

*Firearms Assembly/Disassembly Part II: Revolvers, 2nd Edition, The Gun Digest Book of, by J.B. Wood, DBI Books, a division of Krause Publications, Iola, WI, 1990. 592 pp., illus. Paper covers. $24.95.
Covers 62 popular revolvers plus 140 variants. The most comprehensive and professional presentation available to either hobbyist or gunsmith.

Firearms Assembly/Disassembly Part III: Rimfire Rifles, Revised Edition, The Gun Digest Book of, by J. B. Wood, DBI Books, a division of Krause Publications, Iola, WI., 1994. 480 pp., illus. Paper covers. $19.95.
Greatly expanded edition covering 65 popular rimfire rifles plus over 100 variants all completely cross-referenced in the index.

Firearms Assembly/Disassembly Part IV: Centerfire Rifles, Revised Edition, The Gun Digest Book of, by J.B. Wood, DBI Books, a division of Krause Publications, Iola, WI, 1991. 480 pp., illus. Paper covers. $19.95.
Covers 54 popular centerfire rifles plus 300 variants. The most comprehensive and professional presentation available to either hobbyist or gunsmith.

Firearms Assembly/Disassembly, Part V: Shotguns, Revised Edition, The Gun Digest Book of, by J.B. Wood, DBI Books, a division of Krause Publications, Iola, WI, 1992. 480 pp., illus. Paper covers. $19.95.
Covers 46 popular shotguns plus over 250 variants with step-by-step instructions on how to dismantle and reassemble each. The most comprehensive and professional presentation available to either hobbyist or gunsmith.

Firearms Assembly/Disassembly Part VI: Law Enforcement Weapons, The Gun Digest Book of, by J.B. Wood, DBI Books, a division of Krause Publications, Iola, WI, 1981. 288 pp., illus. Paper covers. $16.95.
Step-by-step instructions on how to completely dismantle and reassemble the most commonly used firearms found in law enforcement arsenals.

Firearms Assembly 3: The NRA Guide to Rifle and Shotguns, NRA Books, Wash., DC, 1980. 264 pp., illus. Paper covers. $13.95.
Text and illustrations explaining the takedown of 125 rifles and shotguns, domestic and foreign.

Firearms Assembly 4: The NRA Guide to Pistols and Revolvers, NRA Books, Wash., DC, 1980. 253 pp., illus. Paper covers. $13.95.
Text and illustrations explaining the takedown of 124 pistol and revolver models, domestic and foreign.

Firearms Bluing and Browning, By R.H. Angier, Stackpole Books, Harrisburg, PA. 151 pp., illus. $19.95.
A world master gunsmith reveals his secrets of building, repairing and renewing a gun, quite literally, lock, stock and barrel. A useful, concise text on chemical coloring methods for the gunsmith and mechanic.

Firearms Disassembly—With Exploded Views, by John A. Karns & John E. Traister, Stoeger Publishing Co., S. Hackensack, NJ, 1995. 320 pp., illus. Paper covers. $19.95.
Provides the do's and don'ts of firearms disassembly. Enables owners and gunsmiths to disassemble firearms in a professional manner.

Guns and Gunmaking Tools of Southern Appalachia, by John Rice Irwin, Schiffer Publishing Ltd., 1983. 118 pp., illus. Paper covers. $9.95.
The story of the Kentucky rifle.

Gunsmithing: Rifles, by Patrick Sweeney, Krause Publications, Iola, WI, 1999. 352 pp., illustrated. Paper covers. $24.95.
Tips for lever-action rifles. Building a custom Ruger 10/22. Building a better hunting rifle.

Gunsmithing Tips and Projects, a collection of the best articles from the *Handloader* and *Rifle* magazines, by various authors, Wolfe Publishing Co., Prescott, AZ, 1992. 443 pp., illus. Paper covers. $25.00.
Includes such subjects as shop, stocks, actions, tuning, triggers, barrels, customizing, etc.

REFERENCE

THE ARMS LIBRARY

Gunsmith Kinks, by F.R. (Bob) Brownell, F. Brownell & Son, Montezuma, IA, 1st ed., 1969. 496 pp., well illus. $22.98.
A widely useful accumulation of shop kinks, short cuts, techniques and pertinent comments by practicing gunsmiths from all over the world.

Gunsmith Kinks 2, by Bob Brownell, F. Brownell & Son, Publishers, Montezuma, IA, 1983. 496 pp., illus. $22.95.
A collection of gunsmithing knowledge, shop kinks, new and old techniques, shortcuts and general know-how straight from those who do them best—the gunsmiths.

Gunsmith Kinks 3, edited by Frank Brownell, Brownells Inc., Montezuma, IA, 1993. 504 pp., illus. $24.95.
Tricks, knacks and "kinks" by professional gunsmiths and gun tinkerers. Hundreds of valuable ideas are given in this volume.

Gunsmithing, by Roy F. Dunlap, Stackpole Books, Harrisburg, PA, 1990. 742 pp., illus. $34.95.
A manual of firearm design, construction, alteration and remodeling. For amateur and professional gunsmiths and users of modern firearms.

Gunsmithing at Home: Lock, Stock and Barrel, by John Traister, Stoeger Publishing Co., Wayne, NJ, 1997. 320 pp., illus. Paper covers. $19.95.
A Complete step-by-step fully illustrated guide to the art of gunsmithing.

Gunsmithing: Pistols & Revolvers, by Patrick Sweeney, DBI Books, a division of Krause Publications, Iola, WI, 1998. 352 pp., illus. Paper covers. $24.95.
Do-it-Yourself projects, diagnosis and repair for pistols and revolvers.

The Gunsmith's Manual, by J.P. Stelle and Wm. B. Harrison, The Gun Room Press, Highland Park, NJ, 1982. 376 pp., illus. $19.95.
For the gunsmith in all branches of the trade.

Home Gunsmithing the Colt Single Action Revolvers, by Loren W. Smith, Ray Riling Arms Books, Co., Phila., PA, 1995. 119 pp., illus. $24.95.
Affords the Colt Single Action owner detailed, pertinent information on the operating and servicing of this famous and historic handgun.

How to Convert Military Rifles, Williams Gun Sight Co., Davision, MI, new and enlarged seventh edition, 1997. 76 pp., illus. Paper covers. $13.95.
This latest edition updated the changes that have occured over the past thirty years. Tips, instructions and illustraton on how to convert popular military rifles as the Enfield, Mauser 96 nad SKS just to name a few are presented.

Mauser M98 & M96, by R.A. Walsh, Wolfe Publishing Co., Prescott, AR, 1998. 123 pp., illustrated. Paper covers. $32.50.
How to build your own favorite custom Mauser rifle from two of the best bolt action rifle designs ever produced—the military Mauser Model 1898 and Model 1896 bolt rifles.

Mr. Single Shot's Gunsmithing-Idea-Book, by Frank de Haas, Mark de Haas, Orange City, IA, 1996. 168 pp., illus. Paper covers. $21.50.
Offers easy to follow, step-by-step instructions for a wide variety of gunsmithing procedures all reinforced by plenty of photos.

Pistolsmithing, by George C. Nonte, Jr., Stackpole Books, Harrisburg, PA, 1974. 560 pp., illus. $34.95.
A single source reference to handgun maintenance, repair, and modification at home, unequaled in value.

Practical Gunsmithing, by the editors of American Gunsmith, DBI Books, a division of Krause Publications, Iola, WI, 1996. 256 pp., illus. Paper covers. $19.95.
A book intended primarily for home gunsmithing, but one that will be extremely helpful to professionals as well.

Professional Stockmaking, by D. Wesbrook, Wolfe Publishing Co., Prescott AZ, 1995. 308 pp., illus. $54.00.
A step-by-step how-to with complete photographic support for every detail of the art of working wood into riflestocks.

Recreating the American Longrifle, by William Bu chele, et al, George Shumway Publisher, York, Pa, 5th edition, 1999. 175 pp., illustrated. $40.00.
Includes full size plans for building a Kentucky rifle.

Riflesmithing, The Gun Digest Book of, by Jack Mitchell, DBI Books, a division of Krause Publications, Iola, WI, 1982. 256 pp., illus. Paper covers. $16.95.
The art and science of rifle gunsmithing. Covers tools, techniques, designs, finishing wood and metal, custom alterations.

Shotgun Gunsmithing, The Gun Digest Book of, by Ralph Walker, DBI Books, a division of Krause Publications, Iola, WI, 1983. 256 pp., illus. Paper covers. $16.95.
The principles and practices of repairing, individualizing and accurizing modern shotguns by one of the world's premier shotgun gunsmiths.

Sporting Rifle Take Down & Reassembly Guide, 2nd Edition, by J.B. Wood, Krause Publications, Iola, WI, 1997. 480 pp., illus. Paper covers. $19.95.
Hunters and shooting enthusiasts must have this reference featuring 52 of the most popular and widely used sporting centerfire and rimfire rifles.

The Story of Pope's Barrels, by Ray M. Smith, R&R Books, Livonia, NY, 1993. 203 pp., illus. $39.00.
A reissue of a 1960 book whose author knew Pope personally. It will be of special interest to Schuetzen rifle fans, since Pope's greatest days were at the height of the Schuetzen-era before WWI.

Survival Gunsmithing, by J.B. Wood, Desert Publications, Cornville, AZ, 1986. 92 pp., illus. Paper covers. $11.95.
A guide to repair and maintenance of the most popular rifles, shotguns and handguns.

The Tactical 1911, by Dave Lauck, Paladin Press, Boulder, CO, 1998. 137 pp., illus. Paper covers. $20.00.
Here is the only book you will ever need to teach you how to select, modify, employ and maintain your Colt.

HANDGUNS

Advanced Master Handgunning, by Charles Stephens, Paladin Press, Boulder, CO., 1994. 72 pp., illus. Paper covers. $14.00.
Secrets and surefire techniques for winning handgun competitions.

The Ayoob Files: The Book, by Massad Ayoob, Police Bookshelf, Concord, NH, 1995. 223 pp., illus. Paper covers. $14.95.
The best of Massad Ayoob's acclaimed series in American Handgunner magazine.

Big Bore Sixguns, by John Taffin, Krause Publications, Iola, WI, 1997. 336 pp., illus. $39.95.
The author takes aim on the entire range of big bores from .357 Magnums to .500 Maximums, single actions and cap-and-ball sixguns to custom touches for big bores.

Black Powder Hobby Gunsmithing, by Sam Fadala and Dale Storey, DBI Books, a division of Krause Publications, Iola, WI., 1994. 256 pp., illus. Paper covers. $18.95.
A how-to guide for gunsmithing blackpowder pistols, rifles and shotguns from two men at the top of their respective fields.

Browning Hi-Power Pistols, Desert Publications, Cornville, AZ, 1982. 20 pp., illus. Paper covers. $9.95.
Covers all facets of the various military and civilian models of the Browning Hi-Power pistol.

The Colt .45 Auto Pistol, compiled from U.S. War Dept. Technical Manuals, and reprinted by Desert Publications, Cornville, AZ, 1978. 80 pp., illus. Paper covers. $9.95.
Covers every facet of this famous pistol from mechanical training, manual of arms, disassembly, repair and replacement of parts.

Colt Automatic Pistols, by Donald B. Brady, Pioneer Press, Union City, TN, 1999. 368 pp., illustrated. Soft. $19.95.
A revised and enlarged edition of a key work on a fascinating subject. Complete information on every Colt automatic pistol.

Combat Handgunnery, 4th Edition, by Chuck Taylor, DBI Books, a division of Krause Publications, Iola, WI, 1997. 256 pp., illus. Paper covers. $18.95.
This all-new edition looks at real world combat handgunnery from three different perspectives—military, police and civilian. Available, October, 1996.

Combat Revolvers, by Duncan Long, Paladin Press, Boulder, CO, 1999, 8 1/2 x 11, soft covers, 152 pp. $21.95.
This is an uncompromising look at modern combat revolvers. All the major foreign and domestic guns are covered: the Colt Python, S&W Model 29, Ruger GP 100 and hundreds more. Know the gun that you may one day stake your life on.

The Complete Book of Combat Handgunning, by Chuck Taylor, Desert Publications, Cornville, AZ, 1982. 168 pp., illus. Paper covers. $20.00.
Covers virtually every aspect of combat handgunning.

Complete Guide to Compact Handguns, by Gene Gangarosa, Jr., Stoeger Publishing Co., Wayne, NJ, 1997. 228 pp., illus. Paper covers. $22.95.
Includes hundreds of compact firearms, along with text results conducted by the author.

Complete Guide to Service Handguns, by Gene Gangarosa, Jr., Stoeger Publishing Co., Wayne, NJ, 1998. 320 pp., illus. Paper covers. $22.95.
The author explores the revolvers and pistols that are used around the globe by military, law enforcement and civilians.

The Custom Government Model Pistol, by Layne Simpson, Wolfe Publishing Co., Prescott, AZ, 1994. 639 pp., illus. Paper covers. $24.50.
The book about one of the world's greatest firearms and the things pistolsmiths do to make it even greater.

The CZ-75 Family: The Ultimate Combat Handgun, by J.M. Ramos, Paladin Press, Boulder, CO, 1990. 100 pp., illus. Soft covers. $25.00.
An in-depth discussion of the early-and-late model CZ-75s, as well as the many newest additions to the Czech pistol family.

Encyclopedia of Pistols & Revolvers, by A.E. Hartnik, Knickerbocker Press, New York, NY, 1997. 272 pp., illus. $19.95.
A comprehensive encyclopedia specially written for collectors and owners of pistols and revolvers.

Experiments of a Handgunner, by Walter Roper, Wolfe Publishing Co., Prescott, AZ, 1989. 202 pp., illus. $37.00.
A limited edition reprint. A listing of experiments with functioning parts of handguns, with targets, stocks, rests, handloading, etc.

Exploded Handgun Drawings, The Gun Digest Book of, edited by Harold A. Murtz, DBI Books, a division of Krause Publications, Iola, WI. 1992. 512 pp., illus. Paper covers. $20.95.
Exploded or isometric drawings for 494 of the most popular handguns.

The Farnam Method of Defensive Handgunning, by John S. Farnam, DTI, Inc., Seattle, WA, 1994. 191 pp., illus. Paper covers. $13.95.
A book intended to not only educate the new shooter, but also to serve as a guide and textbook for his and his instructor's training courses.

Fast and Fancy Revolver Shooting, by Ed. McGivern, Anniversary Edition, Winchester Press, Piscataway, NJ, 1984. 484 pp., illus. $18.95.
A fascinating volume, packed with handgun lore and solid information by the acknowledged dean of revolver shooters.

.45 ACP Super Guns, by J.M. Ramos, Paladin Press, Boulder, CO, 1991. 144 pp., illus. Paper covers. $24.00.
Modified .45 automatic pistols for competition, hunting and personal defense.

The .45, The Gun Digest Book of, by Dean A. Grennell, DBI Books, a division of Krause Publications, Iola, WI, 1989. 256 pp., illus. Paper covers. $17.95.
Definitive work on one of America's favorite calibers.

Glock: The New Wave in Combat Handguns, by Peter Alan Kasler, Paladin Press, Boulder, CO, 1993. 304 pp., illus. $27.00.

Kasler debunks the myths that surround what is the most innovative handgun to be introduced in some time.

Glock's Handguns, by Duncan Long, Desert Publications, El Dorado, AR, 1996. 180 pp., illus. Paper covers. $18.95.

An outstanding volume on one of the world's newest and most successful firearms of the century.

Hand Cannons: The World's Most Powerful Handguns, by Duncan Long, Paladin Press, Boulder, CO, 1995. 208 pp., illus. Paper covers. $22.00.

Long describes and evaluates each powerful gun according to their features.

The Handgun, by Geoffrey Boothroyd, Safari Press, Inc., Huntington Beach, CA, 1999. 566 pp., illustrated. $50.00.

A very detailed history of the handgun. Now revised and a completely new chapter written to take account of developments since the 1970 edition.

*Handguns 2001, 13th Edition, edited by Ken Ramage, DBI Books, a division of Krause Publications, Iola, WI, 2000. 320 pp., illustrated. Paper covers. $22.95.

Top writers in the handgun industry give you a complete report on new handgun developments, testfire reports on the newest introductions and previews on what's ahead.

Handgun Digest, 3rd Edition, edited by Chris Christian, DBI Books, a division of Krause Publications, Iola, WI, 1995. 256 pp., illus. Paper covers. $18.95.

Full coverage of all aspects of handguns and handgunning from a highly readable and knowledgeable author.

Handgun Reloading, The Gun Digest Book of, by Dean A. Grennell and Wiley M. Clapp, DBI Books, a division of Krause Publications, Iola, WI, 1987. 256 pp., illus. Paper covers. $16.95.

Detailed discussions of all aspects of reloading for handguns, from basic to complex. New loading data.

Handgun Stopping Power "The Definitive Study", by Evan P. Marshall & Edwin J. Sanow, Paladin Press, Boulder, CO, 1997, soft cover, photos, 240 pp. $45.00

Dramatic first-hand accounts of the results of handgun rounds fired into criminals by cops, storeowners, cabbies and others are the heart and soul of this long-awaited book. This is the definitive methodology for predicting the stopping power of handgun loads, the first to take into account what really happens when a bullet meets a man.

Heckler & Koch's Handguns, by Duncan Long, Desert Publications, El Dorado, AR, 1996. 142 pp., illus. Paper covers. $19.95.

Traces the history and the evolution of H&K's pistols from the company's beginning at the end of WWII to the present.

Hidden in Plain Sight, by Trey Bloodworth & Mike Raley, Professional Press, Chapel Hill, NC, 1995. Paper covers. $19.95.

A practical guide to concealed handgun carry.

High Standard Automatic Pistols 1932-1950, by Charles E. Petty, The Gunroom Press, Highland Park, NJ, 1989. 124 pp., illus. $19.95.

A definitive source of information for the collector of High Standard arms.

Hi-Standard Pistols and Revolvers, 1951-1984, by James Spacek, James Spacek, Chesire, CT, 1998. 128 pp., illustrated. Paper covers. $12.50.

Technical details, marketing features and instruction/parts manual of every model High Standard pistol and revolver made between 1951 and 1984. Most accurate serial number information available.

The Hi-Standard Pistol Guide, by Burr Leyson, Duckett's Sporting Books, Tempe AZ, 1995. 128 pp., illus. Paper covers. $22.00.

Complete information on selection, care and repair, ammunition, parts, and accessories.

How to Become a Master Handgunner: The Mechanics of X-Count Shooting, by Charles Stephens, Paladin Press, Boulder, CO, 1993. 64 pp., illus. Paper covers. $14.00.

Offers a simple formula for success to the handgunner who strives to master the technique of shooting accurately.

Hunting for Handgunners, by Larry Kelly and J.D. Jones, DBI Books, a division of Krause Publications, Iola, WI, 1990. 256 pp., illus. Paper covers. $16.95.

Covers the entire spectrum of hunting with handguns in an amusing, easy-flowing manner that combines entertainment with solid information.

Illustrated Encyclopedia of Handguns, by A.B. Zhuk, Stackpole Books, Mechanicsburg, PA, 1994. 256 pp., illus. Cloth cover, $49.95; paper cover, $29.95.

Identifies more than 2,000 military and commercial pistols and revolvers with details of more than 100 popular handgun cartridges.

Instinct Combat Shooting, by Chuck Klein, Chuck Klein, The Goose Creek, IN, 1989. 49 pp., illus. Paper covers. $12.00.

Defensive handgunning for police.

Know Your Czechoslovakian Pistols, by R.J. Berger, Blacksmith Corp., Chino Valley, AZ, 1989. 96 pp., illus. Soft covers. $9.95.

A comprehensive reference which presents the fascinating story of Czech pistols.

Know Your 45 Auto Pistols—Models 1911 & A1, by E.J. Hoffschmidt, Blacksmith Corp., Southport, CT, 1974. 58 pp., illus. Paper covers. $9.95.

A concise history of the gun with a wide variety of types and copies.

Know Your Walther P38 Pistols, by E.J. Hoffschmidt, Blacksmith Corp., Southport, CT, 1974. 77 pp., illus. Paper covers. $9.95.

Covers the Walther models Armee, M.P., H.P., P.38—history and variations.

Know Your Walther PP & PPK Pistols, by E.J. Hoffschmidt, Blacksmith Corp., Southport, CT, 1975. 87 pp., illus. Paper covers. $9.95.

A concise history of the guns with a guide to the variety and types.

The Mauser Self-Loading Pistol, by Belford & Dunlap, Borden Publ. Co., Alhambra, CA. Over 200 pp., 300 illus., large format. $29.95.

The long-awaited book on the "Broom Handles," covering their inception in 1894 to the end of production. Complete and in detail: pocket pistols, Chinese and Spanish copies, etc.

9mm Handguns, 2nd Edition, The Gun Digest Book of, edited by Steve Comus, DBI Books, a division of Krause Publications, Iola, WI, 1993. 256 pp., illus. Paper covers. $18.95.

Covers the 9mm cartridge and the guns that have been made for it in greater depth than any other work available.

9mm Parabellum; The History & Developement of the World's 9mm Pistols & Ammunition, by Klaus-Peter Konig and Martin Hugo, Schiffer Publishing Ltd., Atglen, PA, 1993. 304 pp., illus. $39.95.

Detailed history of 9mm weapons from Belguim, Italy, Germany, Israel, France, USA, Czechoslovakia, Hungary, Poland, Brazil, Finland and Spain.

The Official 9mm Markarov Pistol Manual, translated into English by Major James Gebhardt, U.S. Army (Ret.), Desert Publications, El Dorado, AR, 1996. 84 pp., illus. Paper covers. $12.95.

The information found in this book will be of enormous benefit and interest to the owner or a prospective owner of one of these pistols.

The Official Soviet 7.62mm Handgun Manual, by Translation by Maj. James F. Gebhardt Ret.), Paladin Press, Boulder, CO, 1997, soft cover, illus., 104 pp. $20.00

This Soviet military manual, now available in English for the first time, covers instructions for use and maintenance of two side arms, the Nagant 7.62mm revolver, used by the Russian tsarist armed forces and later the Soviet armed forces, and the Tokarev 7.62mm semi-auto pistol, which replaced the Nagant.

P-38 Automatic Pistol, by Gene Gangarosa, Jr., Stoeger Publishing Co., S. Hackensack, NJ, 1993. 272 pp., illus. Paper covers. $16.95.

This book traces the origins and development of the P-38, including the momentous political forces of the World War II era that caused its near demise and, later, its rebirth.

The P-38 Pistol: The Walther Pistols, 1930-1945. Volume 1. by Warren Buxton, Warren Buxton Ucross Books, Los Alamos, MN 1999. $68.50.

A limited run reprint of this scarce and sought-after work on the P-38 Pistol. 328 pp. with 160 illustrations.

The P-38 Pistol: The Contract Pistols, 1940-1945. Volume 2. by Warren Buxton, Warren Buxton Ucross Books, Los Alamos, MN 1999. $68.50. 256 pp. with 237 illustrations.

The P-38 Pistol: Postwar Distributions, 1945-1990. Volume 3. by Warren Buxton, Warren Buxton Ucross Books, Los Alamos, MN 1999. $68.50

Plus an addendum to Volumes 1 & 2. 272 pp. with 342 illustrations.

Pistols and Revolvers, by Jean-Noel Mouret, Barns and Noble, Rockleigh, N.J., 1999. 141 pp., illustrated. $12.98.

Here in glorious display is the master guidebook to flintlocks, minatures, the Sig P-210 limited edition, the Springfield Trophy Master with Aimpoint 5000 telescopic sight, every major classic and contemporary handgun, complete with their technical data.

Pistols of the World, 3rd Edition, by Ian Hogg and John Weeks, DBI Books, a division of Krause Publications, Iola, WI, 1992. 352 pp., illus. Paper covers. $20.95.

A totally revised edtion of one of the leading studies of small arms.

Report of Board on Tests of Revolvers and Automatic Pistols, From the Annual Report of the Chief of Ordnance, 1907. Reprinted by J.C. Tillinghast, Marlow, NH, 1969. 34 pp., 7 plates, paper covers. $9.95.

A comparison of handguns, including Luger, Savage, Colt, Webley-Fosbery and other makes.

Ruger Automatic Pistols and Single Action Revolvers, by Hugo A. Lueders, edited by Don Findley, Blacksmith Corp., Chino Valley, AZ, 1993. 79 pp., illus. Paper covers. $14.95.

The definitive work on Ruger automatic pistols and single action revolvers.

The Ruger "P" Family of Handguns, by Duncan Long, Desert Publications, El Dorado, AZ, 1993. 128 pp., illus. Paper covers. $14.95.

A full-fledged documentary on a remarkable series of Sturm Ruger handguns.

The Ruger .22 Automatic Pistol, Standard/Mark I/Mark II Series, by Duncan Long, Paladin Press, Boulder, CO, 1989. 168 pp., illus. Paper covers. $16.00.

The definitive book about the pistol that has served more than 1 million owners so well.

The Semiautomatic Pistols in Police Service and Self Defense, by Massad Ayoob, Police Bookshelf, Concord, NH, 1990. 25 pp., illus. Soft covers. $9.95.

First quantitative, documented look at actual police experience with 9mm and 45 police service automatics.

The Sharpshooter—How to Stand and Shoot Handgun Metallic Silhouettes, by Charles Stephens, Yucca Tree Press, Las Cruces, NM, 1993. 86 pp., illus. Paper covers. $10.00.

A narration of some of the author's early experiences in silhouette shooting, plus how-to information.

Shooting Colt Single Actions, by Mike Venturino, Livingston, MT, 1995.

A definitive work on the famous Colt SAA and the ammunition it shoots.

Sig/Sauer Handguns, by Duncan Long, Desert Publications, El Dorado, AZ, 1995. 150 pp., illus. Paper covers. $16.95.

The history of Sig/Sauer handguns, including Sig, Sig-Hammerli and Sig/Sauer variants.

Sixgun Cartridges and Loads, by Elmer Keith, reprint edition by The Gun Room Press, Highland Park, NJ, 1984. 151 pp., illus. $24.95.

A manual covering the selection, use and loading of the most suitable and popular revolver cartridges.

Sixguns, by Elmer Keith, Wolfe Publishing Company, Prescott, AZ, 1992. 336 pp. Paper covers. $29.95.
The history, selection, repair, care, loading, and use of this historic frontiersman's friend—the one-hand firearm.

Smith & Wesson's Automatics, by Larry Combs, Desert Publications, El Dorado, AZ, 1994. 143 pp., illus. Paper covers. $19.95.
A must for every S&W auto owner or prospective owner.

Standard Catalog of Smith and Wesson by Jim Supica and Richard Nahas, Krause Publications, Inc. Iola, WI, 1996. 240 pp., illus. $29.95.
Clearly details hundreds of products by the legendary manufacturer. How to identify, evaluate the conditions and assesses the value of 752 Smith & Wesson models and variations.

Street Stoppers: The Latest Handgun Stopping Power Street Results, by Evan P. Marshall & Edwin J. Sandow, Paladin Press, Boulder, CO, 1997. 392 pp., illus. Paper covers. $42.95.
Compilation of the results of real-life shooting incidents involving every major handgun caliber.

The Tactical 1911, by Dave Lauck, Paladin Press, Boulder, CO, 1999. 152 pp., illustrated. Paper covers. $22.00.
The cop's and SWAT operator's guide to employment and maintenance.

The Tactical Pistol, by Gabriel Suarez with a foreword by Jeff Cooper, Paladin Press, Boulder, CO, 1996. 216 pp., illus. Paper covers. $25.00.
Advanced gunfighting concepts and techniques.

The Thompson/Center Contender Pistol, by Charles Tephens, Paladin Press, Boulder, CO, 1997. 58 pp., illus. Paper covers. $14.00.
How to tune and time, load and shoot accurately with the Contender pistol.

The .380 Enfield No. 2 Revolver, by Mark Stamps and Ian Skennerton, I.D.S.A. Books, Piqua, OH, 1993. 124 pp., 80 illus. Paper covers. $19.95.

The Truth AboUt Handguns, by Duane Thomas, Paladin Press, Boulder, CO, 1997. 136 pp., illus. Paper covers. $18.00.
Exploding the myths, hype, and misinformation about handguns.

U.S. Handguns of World War 2, The Secondary Pistols and Revolvers, by Charles W. Pate, Mowbray Publishers, Lincoln, RI, 1997. 368 pp., illus. $39.00.
This indispensable new book covers all of the American military handguns of W.W.2 except for the M1911A1.

HUNTING

NORTH AMERICA

Advanced Black Powder Hunting, by Toby Bridges, Stoeger Publishing Co., Wayne, NJ, 1998. 288 pp., illus. Paper covers. $21.95.
The first modern day publication to be filled from cover to cover with guns, loads, projectiles, accessories and the techniques to get the most from today's front loading guns.

Advanced Strategies for Trophy Whitetails, by David Morris, Safari Press, Inc., Huntington Beach, CA, 1999. 399 pp., illustrated. $29.95.
This book is a must-have for any serious trophy hunter.

After the Hunt With Lovett Williams, by Lovett Williams, Krause Publications, Iola, WI, 1996. 256 pp., illus. Paper covers. $15.95.
The author carefully instructs you on how to prepare your trophy turkey for a trip to the taxidermist. Plus help on planning a grand slam hunt.

Aggressive Whitetail Hunting, by Greg Miller, Krause Publications, Iola, WI, 1995. 208 pp., illus. Paper covers. $14.95.
Learn how to hunt trophy bucks in public forests, private farmlands and exclusive hunting grounds from one of America's foremost hunters.

All About Bears, by Duncan Gilchrist, Stoneydale Press Publishing Co., Stevensville, MT, 1989. 176 pp., illus. $19.95.
Covers all kinds of bears—black, grizzly, Alaskan brown, polar and leans on a lifetime of hunting and guiding experiences to explore proper hunting techniques.

American Duck Shooting, by George Bird Grinnell, Stackpole Books, Harrisburg, PA, 1991. 640 pp., illus. Paper covers. $19.95.
First published in 1901 at the height of the author's career. Describes 50 species of waterfowl, and discusses hunting methods common at the turn of the century.

American Hunting and Fishing Books, 1800-1970, Volume 1, by Morris Heller, Nimrod and Piscator Press, Mesilla, NM, 1997. 220 pp., illus. A limited, numbered edition. $125.00.
An up-to-date, profusely illustrated, annotated bibliography on American hunting and fishing books and booklets.

The American Wild Turkey, Hunting Tactics and Techniques, by John McDaniel, The Lyons Press, New York, NY, 2000. 240 pp., illustrated. $29.95.
Loaded with turkey hunting anectdotes gleaned from a lifetime of experience.

American Wingshooting: A Twentieth Century Pictorial Saga, by Ben O. Williams, Willow Creek Press, Minocqua, WI, 2000. 160 pp., illustrated with 180 color photographs. $35.00.
A beautifully photographed celebration of upland bird hunting now and how as it once existed.

The Art of Super-Accurate Hunting with Scoped Rifles, by Don Judd, Wolfe Publishing Co., Prescott, AZ, 1996. 99 pp., illus. Paper covers. $14.95.
The philosophy of super-accurate hunting and the rewards of making your shot a trophy.

As I Look Back; Musings of a Birdhunter, by Robert Branen, Safari Press, Inc., Huntington Beach, CA, 1999. Limited, signed and numbered edition. $60.00.
The author shares his recollections of bird hunting around the world.

Autumn Passages, Compiled by the editors of Ducks Unlimited Magazine, Willow Creek Press, Minocqua, WI, 1997. 320 pp. $27.50.
An exceptional collection of duck hunting stories.

Awesome Antlers of North America, by Odie Sudbeck, HTW Publications, Seneca, KS, 1993. 150 pp., illus. $35.00.
500 world-class bucks in color and black and white. This book starts up where the Boone & Crockett recordbook leaves off.

Backtracking, by I.T. Taylor, Safari Press, Inc., Huntington Beach, CA, 1998. 201 pp., illustrated. $24.95.
Reminiscences of a hunter's life in rural America.

Bare November Days, by George Bird Evans et al, Countrysport Press, Traverse City, MI, 1992. 136 pp., illus. $39.50.
A new, original anthology, a tribute to ruffed grouse, king of upland birds.

Bear Attacks, by K. Etling, Safari Press, Long Beach, CA, 1998. 574 pp., illus. In 2 volumes. $75.00.
Classic tales of dangerous North American bears.

The Bear Hunter's Century, by Paul Schullery, Stackpole Books, Harrisburg, PA, 1989. 240 pp., illus. $19.95.
Thrilling tales of the bygone days of wilderness hunting.

The Best of Babcock, by Havilah Babcock, selected and with an introduction by Hugh Grey, The Gunnerman Press, Auburn Hills, MI, 1985. 262 pp., illus. $19.95.
A treasury of memorable pieces, 21 of which have never before appeared in book form.

The Best of Nash Buckingham, by Nash Buckingham, selected, edited and annotated by George Bird Evans, Winchester Press, Piscataway, NJ, 1973. 320 pp., illus. $35.00.
Thirty pieces that represent the very cream of Nash's output on his whole range of outdoor interests—upland shooting, duck hunting, even fishing.

Better on a Rising Tide, by Tom Kelly, Lyons & Burford Publishers, New York, NY, 1995. 184 pp. $22.95.
Tales of wild turkeys, turkey hunting and Southern folk.

Big Bucks the Benoit Way, by Bryce Towsley, Krause Publications Iola, WI, 1998. 208 pp., illus. $24.95.
Secrets from America's first family of whitetail hunting.

Big December Canvasbacks, by Worth Mathewson, Sand Lake Press, Amity, OR, 1997. 171 pp., illus. By David Hagenbaumer. Limited, signed and numbered edition. $29.95.
Duck hunting stories.

Big Game Hunting, by Duncan Gilchrist, Outdoor Expeditions, books and videos, Corvallis, MT, 1999. 192 pp., illustrated. $14.95.
Designed to be a warehouse of hunting information covering the major North American big game species.

Big Woods, by William Faulkner, wilderness adventures, Gallatin Gateway, MT, 1998. 208 pp., illus. Slipcased. $60.00.
A collection of Faulkner's best hunting stories that belongs in the library of every sportsman.

Birdhunter, by Richard S. Grozik, Safari Press, Huntington Beach, CA, 1998. 180 pp., illus. Limited, numbered and signed edition. Slipcased. $60.00.
An entertaining salute to the closeness between man and his dog, man and his gun, and man and the great outdoors.

Bird Dog Days, Wingshooting Ways, by Archibald Rutledge, edited by Jim Casada, Wilderness Adventure Press, Gallatin Gateway, MT, 1998. 200 pp., illus. $35.00.
One of the most popular and enduring outdoor writers of this century, the poet laureate of South Carolina.

Birds on the Horizon, by Stuart Williams, Countrysport Press, Traverse City, MI, 1993. 288 pp., illus. $49.50.
Wingshooting adventures around the world.

Blacktail Trophy Tactics, by Boyd Iverson, Stoneydale Press, Stevensville, MI, 1992. 166 pp., illus. Paper covers. $14.95.
A comprehensive analysis of blacktail deer habits, describing a deer's and man's use of scents, still hunting, tree techniques, etc.

Boone & Crockett Club's 23rd Big Game Awards, 1995-1997, Boone & Crockett Club, Missoula, MT, 1999. 600 pp., illustrated with black & white photographs plus a 16 page color section. $39.95.
A complete listing of the 3,511 trophies accepted in the 23rd Awards Entry Period.

Bowhunter's Handbook, Expert Strategies and Techniques, by M.R. James with Fred Asbell, Dave Holt, Dwight Schuh & Dave Samuel, DBI Books, a division of Krause Publications, Iola, WI, 1997. 256 pp., illus. Paper covers. $19.95.
Tips from the top on taking your bowhunting skills to the next level.

The Buffalo Harvest, by Frank Mayer as told to Charles Roth, Pioneer Press, Union City, TN, 1995. 96 pp., illus. Paper covers. $8.50.
The story of a hide hunter during his buffalo hunting days on the plains.

Bugling for Elk, by Dwight Schuh, Stoneydale Press Publishing Co., Stevensville, MT, 1983. 162 pp., illus. $18.95.
A complete guide to early season elk hunting.

Call of the Quail: A Tribute to the Gentleman Game Bird, by Michael McIntosh, et al., Countrysport Press, Traverse City, MI, 1990. 175 pp., illus. $35.00.
A new anthology on quail hunting.

Calling All Elk, by Jim Zumbo, Cody, WY, 1989. 169 pp., illus. Paper covers. $14.95.
The only book on the subject of elk hunting that covers every aspect of elk vocalization.

Campfires and Game Trails: Hunting North American Big Game, by Craig Boddington, Winchester Press, Piscataway, NJ, 1985. 295 pp., illus. $23.95.
How to hunt North America's big game species.

Come October, by Gene Hill et al, Countrysport Press, Inc., Traverse City, MI, 1991. 176 pp., illus. $39.50.
A new and all-original anthology on the woodcock and woodcock hunting.

The Complete Book of Grouse Hunting, by Frank Woolner, The Lyons Press, New York, NY, 2000. 192 pp., illustrated Paper covers. $24.95.
The history, habits, and habitat of one of America's great game birds—and the methods used to hunt it.

The Complete Book of Mule Deer Hunting, by Walt Prothero, The Lyons Press, New York, NY, 2000. 192 pp., illustrated. Paper covers. $24.95.
Field-tested practical advice on how to bag the trophy buck of a lifetime.

The Complete Book of Wild Turkey Hunting, by John Trout Jr., The Lyons Press, New York, NY, 2000. 192 pp., illustrated. Paper covers. $24.95.
An illustrated guide to hunting for one of America's most popular game birds.

The Complete Book of Woodcock Hunting, by Frank Woolner, The Lyons Press, New York, NY, 2000. 192 pp., illustrated. Paper covers. $24.95.
A thorough, practical guide to the American woodcock and to woodcock hunting.

The Complete Guide to Bird Dog Training, by John R. Falk, Lyons & Burford, New York, NY, 1994. 288 pp., illus. $22.95.
The latest on live-game field training techniques using released quail and recall pens. A new chapter on the services available for entering field trials and other bird dog competitions.

The Complete Guide to Game Care & Cookery, 3rd Edition, by Sam Fadala, DBI Books, a division of Krause Publications, Iola, WI, 1994. 320 pp., illus. Paper covers. $18.95.
Over 500 photos illustrating the care of wild game in the field and at home with a separate recipe section providing over 400 tested recipes.

The Complete Smoothbore Hunter, by Brook Elliot, Winchester Press, Piscataway, NJ, 1986. 240 pp., illus. $16.95.
Advice and information on guns and gunning for all varieties of game.

The Complete Venison Cookbook from Field to Table, by Jim & Ann Casada, Krause Publications, Iola, WI, 1996. 208 pp., Comb-bound. $12.95.
More than 200 kitchen tested recipes make this book the answer to a table full of hungry hunters or guests.

Coveys and Singles: The Handbook of Quail Hunting, by Robert Gooch, A.S. Barnes, San Diego, CA, 1981. 196 pp., illus. $11.95.
The story of the quail in North America.

Coyote Hunting, by Phil Simonski, Stoneydale Press, Stevensville, MT, 1994. 126 pp., illus. Paper covers. $12.95.
Probably the most thorough "How-to-do-it" book on coyote hunting ever written.

Dabblers & Divers: A Duck Hunter's Book, compiled by the editors of Ducks Unlimited Magazine, Willow Creek Press, Minocqua, WI, 1997. 160 pp., illus. $39.95.
A word-and-photographic portrayal of waterfowl hunter's singular intimacy with, and passion for, watery haunts and wildfowl.

Dancers in the Sunset Sky, by Robert F. Jones, The Lyons Press, New York, NY, 1997. 192 pp., illus. $22.95.
The musings of a bird hunter.

Deer & Deer Hunting, by Al Hofacker, Krause Publications, Iola, WI, 1993. 208 pp., illus. $34.95.
Coffee-table volume packed full of how-to-information that will guide hunts for years to come.

Deer and Deer Hunting: The Serious Hunter's Guide, by Dr. Robert Wegner, Stackpole Books, Harrisburg, PA, 1984. 384 pp., illus. Paper covers. $18.95.
In-depth information from the editor of "Deer & Deer Hunting" magazine. Major bibliography of English language books on deer and deer hunting from 1838-1984.

Deer and Deer Hunting Book 2, by Dr. Robert Wegner, Stackpole Books, Harrisburg, PA, 1987. 400 pp., illus. Paper covers. $18.95.
Strategies and tactics for the advanced hunter.

Deer and Deer Hunting, Book 3, by Dr. Robert Wegner, Stackpole Books, Harrisburg, PA, 1990. 368 pp., illus. $18.95.
This comprehensive volume covers natural history, deer hunting lore, profiles of deer hunters, and discussion of important issues facing deer hunters today.

The Deer Hunters: The Tactics, Lore, Legacy and Allure of American Deer Hunting, Edited by Patrick Durkin, Krause Publications, Iola, WI, 1997. 208 pp., illus. $29.95.
More than twenty years of research from America's top whitetail hunters, researchers, and photographers have gone in to the making of this book.

Deer Hunting, by R. Smith, Stackpole Books, Harrisburg, PA, 1978. 224 pp., illus. Paper covers. $14.95.
A professional guide leads the hunt for North America's most popular big game animal.

Doves and Dove Shooting, by Byron W. Dalrymple, New Win Publishing, Inc., Hampton, NJ, 1992. 256 pp., illus. $17.95.
The author reveals in this classic book his penchant for observing, hunting, and photographing this elegantly fashioned bird.

Dove Hunting, by Charley Dickey, Galahad Books, NY, 1976. 112 pp., illus. $10.00.
This indispensable guide for hunters deals with equipment, techniques, types of dove shooting, hunting dogs, etc.

Dreaming the Lion, by Thomas McIntyre, Countrysport Press, Traverse City, MI, 1994. 309 pp., illus. $35.00.
Reflections on hunting, fishing and a search for the wild. Twenty-three stories by *Sports Afield* editor, Tom McIntyre.

Duck Decoys and How to Rig Them, by Ralf Coykendall, revised by Ralf Coykendall, Jr., Nick Lyons Books, New York, NY, 1990. 137 pp., illus. Paper covers. $14.95.
Sage and practical advice on the art of decoying ducks and geese.

The Duck Hunter's Handbook, by Bob Hinman, revised, expanded, updated edition, Winchester Press, Piscataway, NJ, 1985. 288 pp., illus. $15.95.
The duck hunting book that has it all.

Eastern Upland Shooting, by Dr. Charles C. Norris, Countrysport Press, Traverse City, MI, 1990. 424 pp., illus. $49.00.
A new printing of this 1946 classic with a new, original Foreword by the author's friend and hunting companion, renowned author George Bird Evans.

Elk and Elk Hunting, by Hart Wixom, Stackpole Books, Harrisburg, PA, 1986. 288 pp., illus. $34.95.
Your practical guide to fundamentals and fine points of elk hunting.

Elk Hunting in the Northern Rockies, by Ed. Wolff, Stoneydale Press, Stevensville, MT, 1984. 162 pp., illus. $18.95.
Helpful information about hunting the premier elk country of the northern Rocky Mountain states—Wyoming, Montana and Idaho.

Elk Hunting with the Experts, by Bob Robb, Stoneydale Press, Stevensville, MT, 1992. 176 pp., illus. Paper covers. $15.95.
A complete guide to elk hunting in North America by America's top elk hunting expert.

Elk Rifles, Cartridges and Hunting Tactics, by Wayne van Zwoll, Larsen's Outdoor Publishing, Lakeland, FL, 1992. 414 pp., illus. $24.95.
The definitive work on which rifles and cartridges are proper for hunting elk plus the tactics for hunting them.

Encyclopedia of Deer, by G. Kenneth Whitehead, Safari Press, Huntington, CA, 1993. 704 pp., illus. $130.00.
This massive tome will be the reference work on deer for well into the next century.

A Fall of Woodcock, by Tom Huggler, Countrysport Press, Selman, AL, 1997. 256 pp., illus. $39.00.
A book devoted to the woodcock and to those who await his return to their favorite converts each autumn.

Firelight, by Burton L. Spiller, Gunnerman Press, Auburn Hills, MI, 1990. 196 pp., illus. $19.95.
Enjoyable tales of the outdoors and stalwart companions.

Following the Flight, by Charles S. Potter, Countrysport Books, Selma, AL, 1999. 130 pp., illustrated. $25.00.
The great waterfowl passage and the experiences of a young man who has lived their migration come to life in the pages of this book.

Fresh Looks at Deer Hunting, by Byron W. Dalrymple, New Win Publishing, Inc., Hampton, NJ, 1993. 288 pp., illus. $24.95.
Tips and techniques abound throughout the pages of this latest work by Mr. Dalrymple whose name is synonymous with hunting proficiency.

From the Peace to the Fraser, by Prentis N. Gray, Boone and Crockett Club, Missoula, MT, 1995. 400 pp., illus. $49.95.
Newly discovered North American hunting and exploration journals from 1900 to 1930.

Fur Trapping In North America, by Steven Geary, Winchester Press, Piscataway, NJ, 1985. 160 pp., illus. Paper covers. $19.95.
A comprehensive guide to techniques and equipment, together with fascinating facts about fur bearers.

Getting the Most Out of Modern Waterfowling, by John O. Cartier, St. Martin's Press, NY, 1974. 396 pp., illus. $29.95.
The most comprehensive, up-to-date book on waterfowling imaginable.

Getting a Stand, by Miles Gilbert, Pioneer Press, Union City, TN, 1993. 204 pp., illus. Paper covers. $13.95.
An anthology of 18 short personal experiences by buffalo hunters of the late 1800s, specifically from 1870-1882.

The Gordon MacQuarrie Sporting Treasury. Introduction and commentary by Zack Taylor. Countrysport Press, Selman, AL, 1999. $29.50.
Hunting and fishing masterpieces you can read over and over.

Gordon MacQuarrie Trilogy: Stories of the Old Duck Hunters, by Gordon MacQuarrie, Willow Creek Press, Minocqua, WI, 1994. $49.00.
A slip-cased three volume set of masterpieces by one of America's finest outdoor writers.

The Grand Passage: A Chronicle of North American Waterfowling, by Gene Hill, et al., Countrysport Press, Traverse City, MI, 1990. 175 pp., illus. $35.00.
A new original anthology by renowned sporting authors on our world of waterfowling.

Grouse and Woodcock, A Gunner's Guide, by Don Johnson, Krause Publications, Iola, WI, 1995. 256 pp., illus. Paper covers. $14.95.
Find out what you need in guns, ammo, equipment, dogs and terrain.

Grouse of North America, by Tom Huggler, NorthWord Press, Inc., Minocqua, WI, 1990. 160 pp., illus. $29.95.
A cross-continental hunting guide.

Grouse Hunter's Guide, by Dennis Walrod, Stackpole Books, Harrisburg, PA, 1985. 192 pp., illus. $19.95.
Solid facts, observations, and insights on how to hunt the ruffed grouse.

Gunning for Sea Ducks, by George Howard Gillelan, Tidewater Publishers, Centreville, MD, 1988. 144 pp., illus. $14.95.
A book that introduces you to a practically untouched arena of waterfowling.

Heartland Trophy Whitetails, by Odie Sudbeck, HTW Publications, Seneca, KS, 1992. 130 pp., illus. $35.00.
A completely revised and expanded edition which includes over 500 photos of Boone & Crockett class whitetail, major mulies and unusual racks.

The Heck with Moose Hunting, by Jim Zumbo, Wapiti Valley Publishing Co., Cody, WY, 1996. 199 pp., illus. $17.95.
Jim's hunts around the continent including encounters with moose, caribou, sheep, antelope and mountain goats.

High Pressure Elk Hunting, by Mike Lapinski, Stoneydale Press Publishing Co., Stevensville, MT, 1996. 192 pp., illus. $19.95.
The secrets of hunting educated elk revealed.

REFERENCE

The Arms Library

Hill Country, by Gene Hill, Countrysport Press, Traverse City, MI, 1996. 180 pp., illus. $25.00.
Stories about hunting, fishing, dogs and guns.

Home from the Hill, by Fred Webb, Safari Press, Huntington Beach, CA, 1997. 283 pp., illus. Limited edition, signed and numbered. In a slipcase. $50.00.
The story of a big-game guide in the Canadian wilderness.

Horns in the High Country, by Andy Russell, Alfred A. Knopf, NY, 1973. 259 pp., illus. Paper covers. $12.95.
A many-sided view of wild sheep and their natural world.

How to Hunt, by Dave Bowring, Winchester Press, Piscataway, NJ, 1982. 208 pp., illus. Hardcover $15.00.
A basic guide to hunting big game, small game, upland birds, and waterfowl.

Hunt Alaska Now: Self-Guiding for Trophy Moose & Caribou, by Dennis W. Confer, Wily Ventures, Anchorage, AK, 1997. 309 pp., illus. Paper covers. $26.95.
How to plan affordable, successfull, safe hunts you can do yourself.

The Hunters and the Hunted, by George Laycock, Outdoor Life Books, New York, NY, 1990. 280 pp., illus. $34.95.
The pursuit of game in America from Indian times to the present.

A Hunter's Fireside Book, by Gene Hill, Winchester Press, Piscataway, NJ, 1972. 192 pp., illus. $17.95.
An outdoor book that will appeal to every person who spends time in the field—or who wishes he could.

A Hunter's Road, by Jim Fergus, Henry Holt & Co., NY, 1992. 290 pp. $22.50.
A journey with gun and dog across the American uplands.

Hunt High for Rocky Mountain Goats, Bighorn Sheep, Chamois & Tahr, by Duncan Gilchrist, Stoneydale Press, Stevensville, MT, 1992. 192 pp., illus. Paper covers. $19.95.
The source book for hunting mountain goats.

The Hunter's Shooting Guide, by Jack O'Connor, Outdoor Life Books, New York, NY, 1982. 176 pp., illus. Paper covers. $9.95.
A classic covering rifles, cartridges, shooting techniques for shotguns/rifles/handguns.

The Hunter's World, by Charles F. Waterman, Winchester Press, Piscataway, NJ, 1983. 250 pp., illus. $29.95.
A classic. One of the most beautiful hunting books that has ever been produced.

Hunting Adventure of Me and Joe, by Walt Prothero, Safari Press, Huntington Beach, CA, 1995. 220 pp., illus. $22.50.
A collection of the author's best and favorite stories.

Hunting America's Game Animals and Birds, by Robert Elman and George Peper, Winchester Press, Piscataway, NJ, 1975. 368 pp., illus. $16.95.
A how-to, where-to, when-to guide—by 40 top experts—covering the continent's big, small, upland game and waterfowl.

Hunting Ducks and Geese, by Steven Smith, Stackpole Books, Harrisburg, PA, 1984. 160 pp., illus. $19.95.
Hard facts, good bets, and serious advice from a duck hunter you can trust.

Hunting for Handgunners, by Larry Kelly and J.D. Jones, DBI Books, a division of Krause Publications, Iola, WI, 1990. 256 pp., illus. Soft covers. $16.95.
A definitive work on an increasingly popular sport.

Hunting in Many Lands, edited by Theodore Roosevelt and George Bird Grinnell, et al., Boone & Crockett Club, Dumphries, VA, 1990. 447 pp., illus. $40.00.
A limited edition reprinting of the original Boone & Crockett Club 1895 printing.

Hunting Mature Bucks, by Larry L. Weishuhn, Krause Publications, Iola, WI, 1995. 256 pp., illus. Paper covers. $14.95.
One of North America's top white-tailed deer authorities shares his expertise on hunting those big, smart and elusive bucks.

Hunting Open-Country Mule Deer, by Dwight Schuh, Sage Press, Nampa, ID, 1989. 180 pp., illus. $18.95.
A guide taking Western bucks with rifle and bow.

Hunting Predators for Hides and Profits, by Wilf E. Pyle, Stoeger Publishing Co., So. Hackensack, NJ, 1985. 224 pp., illus. Paper covers. $11.95.
The author takes the hunter through every step of the hunting/marketing process.

Hunting the American Wild Turkey, by Dave Harbour, Stackpole Books, Harrisburg, PA, 1975. 256 pp., illus. $24.95.
The techniques and tactics of hunting North America's largest, and most popular, woodland game bird.

Hunting the Rockies, Home of the Giants, by Kirk Darner, Marceline, MO, 1996. 291 pp., illus. $25.00.
Understand how and where to hunt Western game in the Rockies.

Hunting the Sun, by Ted Nelson Lundrigan, Countrysport Press, Selma, AL, 1997. 240 pp., illus. $30.00.
One of the best books on grouse and woodcock ever published.

Hunting Trips in North America, by F.C. Selous, Wolfe Publishing Co., Prescott, AZ, 1988. 395 pp., illus. $52.00.
A limited edition reprint. Coverage of caribou, moose and other big game hunting in virgin wilds.

Hunting Trophy Deer, by John Wootters, The Lyons Press, New York, NY, 1997. 272 pp., illus. $24.95.
A revised edition of the definitive manual for identifying, scouting, and successfully hunting a deer of a lifetime.

Hunting Trophy Whitetails, by David Morris, Stoneydale Press, Stevensville, MT, 1993. 483 pp., illus. $29.95.
This is one of the best whitetail books published in the last two decades. The author is the former editor of *North American Whitetail* magazine.

Hunting Upland Birds, by Charles F. Waterman, Countrysport Press, Selma, AL, 1997. 220 pp., illus. $30.00.
Originally published a quarter of a century ago, this classic has been newly updated with the latest information for today's wingshooter.

Hunting Western Deer, by Jim and Wes Brown, Stoneydale Press, Stevensville, MT, 1994. 174 pp., illus. Paper covers. $14.95.
A pair of expert Oregon hunters provide insight into hunting mule deer and blacktail deer in the western states.

Hunting Wild Turkeys in the West, by John Higley, Stoneydale Press, Stevensville, MT, 1992. 154 pp., illus. Paper covers. $12.95.
Covers the basics of calling, locating and hunting turkeys in the western states.

Hunting with the Twenty-two, by Charles Singer Landis, R&R Books, Livonia, NY, 1994. 429 pp., illus. $35.00.
A miscellany of articles touching on the hunting and shooting of small game.

I Don't Want to Shoot an Elephant, by Havilah Babcock, The Gunnerman Press, Auburn Hills, MI, 1985. 184 pp., illus. $19.95.
Eighteen delightful stories that will enthrall the upland gunner for many pleasureable hours.

In Search of the Buffalo, by Charles G. Anderson, Pioneer Press, Union City, TN, 1996. 144 pp., illus. Paper covers. $13.95.
The primary study of the life of J. Wright Mooar, one of the few hunters fortunate enough to kill a white buffalo.

In Search of the Wild Turkey, by Bob Gooch, Greatlakes Living Press, Ltd., Waukegan, IL, 1978. 182 pp., illus. $9.95.
A state-by-state guide to wild turkey hot spots, with tips on gear and methods for bagging your bird.

In the Turket Woods, by Jerome B. Robinson, The Lyons Press, N.Y., 1998. 207 pp., illustrated. $24.95.
Practical expert advice on all aspects of turkey hunting—from calls to decoys to guns.

Indian Hunts and Indian Hunters of the Old West, by Dr. Frank C. Hibben, Safari Press, Long Beach, CA, 1989. 228 pp., illus. $24.95.
Tales of some of the most famous American Indian hunters of the Old West as told to the author by an old Navajo hunter.

Jack O'Connor's Gun Book, by Jack O'Connor, Wolfe Publishing Company, Prescott, AZ, 1992. 208 pp. Hardcover. $26.00.
Jack O'Connor imparts a cross-section of his knowledge on guns and hunting. Brings back some of his writings that have here-to-fore been lost.

Jaybirds Go to Hell on Friday, by Havilah Babcock, The Gunnerman Press, Auburn Hills, MI, 1985. 149 pp., illus. $19.95.
Sixteen jewels that reestablish the lost art of good old-fashioned yarn telling.

Last Casts and Stolen Hunts, edited by Jim Casada and Chuck Wechsler, Countrysport Press, Traverse City, MI, 1994. 270 pp., illus. $29.95.
The world's best hunting and fishing stories by writers such as Zane Grey, Jim Corbett, Jack O'Connor, Archibald Rutledge and others.

A Listening Walk...and Other Stories, by Gene Hill, Winchester Press, Piscataway, NJ, 1985. 208 pp., illus. $17.95. Vintage Hill. Over 60 stories.

Longbows in the Far North, by E. Donnall Thomas, Jr. Stackpole Books, Mechanicsburg, PA, 1994. 200 pp., illus. $18.95.
An archer's adventures in Alaska and Siberia.

Mammoth Monarchs of North America, by Odie Sudbeck, HTW Publications, Seneca, KA, 1995. 288 pp., illus. $35.00.
This book reveals eye-opening big buck secrets.

Matching the Gun to the Game, by Clair Rees, Winchester Press, Piscataway, NJ, 1982. 272 pp., illus. $17.95.
Covers selection and use of handguns, blackpowder firearms for hunting, matching rifle type to the hunter, calibers for multiple use, tailoring factory loads to the game.

Measuring and Scoring North American Big Game Trophies, 2nd Edition, by Wm. H. Nesbitt and Philip L. Wright, The Boone & Crockett Club, Missoula, MT, 1999. 150 pp., illustrated. $34.95.
The definitive manual for anyone wanting to learn the Club's world-famous big game measuring system.

Meditation on Hunting, by Jose Ortego y Gasset, Wilderness Adventures Press, Bozeman, MT, 1996. 140 pp., illus. In a slipcase. $60.00.
The classic work on the philosophy of hunting.

Montana—Land of Giant Rams, by Duncan Gilchrist, Stoneydale Press Publishing Co., Stevensville, MT, 1990. 208 pp., illus. $19.95.
Latest information on Montana bighorn sheep and why so many Montana bighorn rams are growing to trophy size.

Montana—Land of Giant Rams, Volume 2, by Duncan Gilchrist, Outdoor Expeditions and Books, Corvallis, MT, 1992. 208 pp., illus. $34.95.
The reader will find stories of how many of the top-scoring trophies were taken.

Montana—Land of Giant Rams, Volume 3, by Duncan Gilchrist, Outdoor Expeditions, books and videos, Corvallis, MT, 1999. 224 pp., illus. Paper covers. $19.95.
All new sheep information including over 70 photos. Learn about how Montana became the "Land of Giant Rams" and what the prospects of the future as we enter a new millenium.

More Grouse Feathers, by Burton L. Spiller, Crown Publ., NY, 1972. 238 pp., illus. $25.00.
Facsimile of the original Derrydale Press issue of 1938. Guns and dogs, the habits and shooting of grouse, woodcock, ducks, etc. Illus. by Lynn Bogue Hunt.

More Tracks: 78 Years of Mountains, People & Happinesss, by Howard Copenhaver, Stoneydale Press, Stevensville, MT, 1992. 150 pp., illus. $18.95.
A collection of stories by one of the back country's best storytellers about the people who shared with Howard his great adventure in the high places and wild Montana country.

Moss, Mallards and Mules, by Robert Brister, Countrysport Books, Selma, AL, 1998. 216 pp., illustrated by David Maass. $30.00.
Twenty-seven short stories on hunting and fishing on the Gulf Coast.

Mostly Huntin', by Bill Jordan, Everett Publishing Co., Bossier City, LA, 1987. 254 pp., illus. $21.95.
Jordan's hunting adventures in North America, Africa, Australia, South America and Mexico.

Mostly Tailfeathers, by Gene Hill, Winchester Press, Piscataway, NJ, 1975. 192 pp., illus. $17.95.
An interesting, general book about bird hunting.

"Mr. Buck": The Autobiography of Nash Buckingham, by Nash Buckingham, Countrysport Press, Traverse City, MI, 1990. 288 pp., illus. $40.00.
A lifetime of shooting, hunting, dogs, guns, and Nash's reflections on the sporting life, along with previously unknown pictures and stories written especially for this book.

Mule Deer: Hunting Today's Trophies, by Tom Carpenter and Jim Van Norman, Krause Publications, Iola, WI, 1998. 256 pp., illustrated. Paper covers. $19.95.
A tribute to both the deer and the people who hunt them. Includes info on where to look for big deer, prime mule deer habitat and effective weapons for the hunt.

Murry Burnham's Hunting Secrets, by Murry Burnham with Russell Tinsley, Winchester Press, Piscataway, NJ, 1984. 244 pp., illus. $17.95.
One of the great hunters of our time gives the reasons for his success in the field.

My Health is Better in November, by Havilah Babcock, University of S. Carolina Press, Columbia, SC, 1985. 284 pp., illus. $19.95.
Adventures in the field set in the plantation country and backwater streams of SC.

North American Big Game Animals, by Byron W. Dalrymple and Erwin Bauer, Outdoor Life Books/Stackpole Books, Harrisburg, PA, 1985. 258 pp., illus. $29.95.
Complete illustrated natural histories. Habitat, movements, breeding, birth and development, signs, and hunting.

North American Elk: Ecology and Management, edited by Jack Ward Thomas and Dale E. Toweill, Stackpole Books, Harrisburg, PA, 1982. 576 pp., illus. $39.95.
The definitive, exhaustive, classic work on the North American elk.

The North American Waterfowler, by Paul S. Bernsen, Superior Publ. Co., Seattle, WA, 1972. 206 pp. Paper covers. $9.95.
The complete inside and outside story of duck and goose shooting. Big and colorful, illustrations by Les Kouba.

Of Bears and Man, by Mike Cramond, University of Oklahoma Press, Norman, OK, 1986. 433 pp., illus. $29.95.
The author's lifetime association with bears of North America. Interviews with survivors of bear attacks.

The Old Man and the Boy, by Robert Ruark, Henry Holt & Co., New York, NY, 303 pp., illus. $24.95.
A timeless classic, telling the story of a remarkable friendship between a young boy and his grandfather as they hunt and fish together.

The Old Man's Boy Grows Older, by Robert Ruark, Henry Holt & Co., Inc., New York, NY, 1993. 300 pp., illus. $24.95.
The heartwarming sequel to the best-selling *The Old Man and the Boy.*

Old Wildfowling Tales, Volume 2, edited by Worth Mathewson, Sand Lake Press, Amity, OR, 1996. 240 pp. $21.95.
A collection of duck and geese hunting stories based around accounts from the past.

One Man, One Rifle, One Lane, by J.Y. Jones, Safari Press, Huntington Beach, CA, 2000. 400 pp., illustrated. $59.95.
Journey with J.Y. Jones as he hunts each of the big-game animals of North America—from the polar bear of the high Artic to the jaguar of the low-lands of Mexico—with just one rifle.

161 Waterfowling Secrets, edited by Matt Young, Willow Creek Press, Minocqua, WI, 1997. 78 pp., Paper covers. $10.95.
Time-honored, field-tested waterfowling tips and advice.

The Only Good Bear is a Dead Bear, by Jeanette Hortick Prodgers, Falcon Press, Helena, MT, 1986. 204 pp. Paper covers. $12.50.
A collection of the West's best bear stories.

Outdoor Pastimes of an American Hunter, by Theodore Roosevelt, Stackpole Books, Mechanicsburg, PA, 1994. 480 pp., illus. Paper covers. $18.95.
Stories of hunting big game in the West and notes about animals pursued and observed.

Outdoor Yarns & Outright Lies, by Gene Hill and Steve Smith, Stackpole Books, Harrisburg, PA, 1984. 168 pp., illus. $18.95.
Fifty or so stories by two good sports.

The Outlaw Gunner, by Harry M. Walsh, Tidewater Publishers, Cambridge, MD, 1973. 178 pp., illus. $22.95.
A colorful story of market gunning in both its legal and illegal phases.

Passing a Good Time, by Gene Hill, Countrysport Press, Traverse City, MI, 1996. 200 pp., illus. $25.00.
Filled with insights and observations of guns, dogs and fly rods that make Gene Hill a master essayist.

Pear Flat Philosophies, by Larry Weishuhn, Safari Press, Huntington Beach, CA, 1995. 234 pp., illus. $24.95.
The author describes his more lighthearted adventures and funny anecdotes while out hunting.

Pheasant Days, by Chris Dorsey, Voyageur Press, Stillwater, MN, 1992. 233 pp., illus. $24.95.
The definitive resource on ringnecks. Includes everything from basic hunting techniques to the life cycle of the bird.

Pheasant Hunter's Harvest, by Steve Grooms, Lyons & Burford Publishers, New York, NY, 1990. 180 pp. $22.95.
A celebration of pheasant, pheasant dogs and pheasant hunting. Practical advice from a passionate hunter.

Pheasant Tales, by Gene Hill et al, Countrysport Press, Traverse City, MI, 1996. 202 pp., illus. $39.00.
Charley Waterman, Michael McIntosh and Phil Bourjaily join the author to tell some of the stories that illustrate why the pheasant is America's favorite game bird.

Pheasants of the Mind, by Datus Proper, Wilderness Adventures Press, Bozeman, MT, 1994. 154 pp., illus. $25.00.
No single title sums up the life of the solitary pheasant hunter like this masterful work.

Pinnell and Talifson: Last of the Great Brown Bear Men, by Marvin H. Clark, Jr., Great Northwest Publishing and Distributing Co., Spokane, WA, 1980. 224 pp., Illus. $39.95.
The story of these famous Alaskan guides and some of the record bears taken by both of them.

Predator Calling with Gerry Blair, by Gerry Blair, Krause Publications, Iola, WI, 1996. 208 pp., illus. Paper covers. $14.95.
Time-tested secrets to lure predators closer to your camera or gun.

Proven Whitetail Tactics, by Greg Miller, Krause Publications, Iola, WI, 1997. 224 pp., illus. Paper covers. $19.95.
Proven tactics for scouting, calling and still-hunting whitetail.

Quail Hunting in America, by Tom Huggler, Stackpole Books, Harrisburg, PA, 1987. 288 pp., illus. $22.95.
Tactics for finding and taking bobwhite, valleys, Gambel's Mountain, scaled-blue, and Mearn's quail by season and habitat.

Quest for Dall Rams, by Duncan Gilchrist, Duncan Gilchrist Outdoor Expeditions and Books, Corvallis, MT, 1997. 224 pp., illus. Limited numbered edition. $34.95.
The most complete book of Dall sheep ever written. Covers information on Alaska and provinces with Dall sheep and explains hunting techniques, equipment, etc.

Quest for Giant Bighorns, by Duncan Gilchrist, Outdoor Expeditions and Books, Corvallis, MT, 1994. 224 pp., illus. Paper covers. $19.95.
How some of the most successful sheep hunters hunt and how some of the best bighorns were taken.

Radical Elk Hunting Strategies, by Mike Lapinski, Stoneydale Press Publishing Co., Stevensville, MT, 1988. 161 pp., illus. $18.95.
Secrets of calling elk in close.

Rattling, Calling & Decoying Whitetails, by Gary Clancy, Edited by Patrick Durkin, Krause Publications, Iola, WI, 2000. 208 pp., illustrated. Paper covers. $19.95.
How to consistently coax big bucks into range.

Records of North American Big Game 11th Edition, with hunting chapters by Craig Boddington, Tom McIntyre and Jim Zumbo, The Boone and Crockett Club, Missoula, MT, 1999. 700 pp., featuring a 32 page color section. $39.95.
Listing over 17,150, of the top trophy big game animals ever recorded. Over 4,000 new listings are featured in this latest edition.

Records of North American Big Game 1932, by Prentis N. Grey, Boone and Crockett Club, Dumfries, VA, 1988. 178 pp., illus. $79.95.
A reprint of the book that started the Club's record keeping for native North American big game.

Records of North American Caribou and Moose, Craig Boddington et al, The Boone & Crockett Club, Missoula, MT, 1997. 250 pp., illus. $24.95.
More than 1,800 caribou listings and more than 1,500 moose listings, organized by the state or Canadian province where they were taken.

Records of North American Elk and Mule Deer, 2nd Edition, edited by Jack and Susan Reneau, Boone & Crockett Club, Missoula, MT, 1996. 360 pp., illus. Paper cover, $18.95; hardcover, $24.95.
Updated and expanded edition featuring more than 150 trophy, field and historical photos of the finest elk and mule deer trophies ever recorded.

Records of North American Sheep, Rocky Mountain Goats and Pronghorn edited by Jack and Susan Reneau, Boone & Crockett Club, Missoula, MT, 1996. 400 pp., illus. Paper cover, $18.95; hardcover, $24.95.
The first B&C Club records book featuring all 3941 accepted wild sheep, Rocky Mountain goats and pronghorn trophies.

Return of Royalty; Wild Sheep of North America, by Dr. Dale E. Toweill and Dr. Valerius Geist, Boone and Crockett Club, Missoula, MT, 1999. 224 pp., illustrated. $59.95.
A celebration of the return of the wild sheep to many of its historical ranges.

The Rifles, the Cartridges, and the Game, by Clay Harvey, Stackpole Books, Harrisburg, PA, 1991. 254 pp., illus. $32.95.
Engaging reading combines with exciting photos to present the hunt with an intense level of awareness and respect.

Ringneck; A Tribute to Pheasants and Pheasant Hunting, by Steve Grooms, Russ Sewell and Dave Nomsen, The Lyons Press, New York, NY, 2000. 120 pp., illustrated. $40.00.
A glorious full-color coffee-table tribute to the pheasant and those who hunt them.

Ringneck! Pheasants & Pheasant Hunting, by Ted Janes, Crown Publ., NY, 1975. 120 pp., illus. $15.95.
A thorough study of one of our more popular game birds.

Rub-Line Secrets, by Greg Miller, edited by Patrick Dirkin, Krause Publications, Iola, WI, 1999. 208 pp., illustrated. Paper covers. $19.95.
Based on nearly 30 years experience. Proven tactics for finding, analyzing and hunting big bucks' rub-lines.

Ruffed Grouse, edited by Sally Atwater and Judith Schnell, Stackpole Books, Harrisburg, PA, 1989. 370 pp., illus. $59.95.

Everything you ever wanted to know about the ruffed grouse. More than 25 wildlife professionals provided in-depth information on every aspect of this popular game bird's life. Lavishly illustrated with over 300 full-color photos.

The Russell Annabel Adventure Series, by Russell Anabel, Safari Press, Huntington Beach, CA: Vol. 1, Alaskan Adventure, The Early Years $35.00; Vol. 2, Adventure is My Business, 1951-1955 $35.00; Vol. 3, Adventure is in My Blood, 1957-1964 $35.00; Vol. 4, High Road to Adventure, 1964-1970 $35.00; Vol. 5, The Way We Were, 1970-1979 $35.00.

A complete collection of previously unpublished magazine articles in book form by this gifted outdoor writer.

The Season, by Tom Kelly, Lyons & Burford, New York, NY, 1997. 160 pp., illus. $22.95.

The delight and challenges of a turkey hunter's Spring season.

Secret Strategies from North America's Top Whitetail Hunters, compiled by Nick Sisley, Krause Publications, Iola, WI, 1995. 256 pp., illus. Paper covers. $14.95.

Bow and gun hunters share their success stories.

Secrets of the Turkey Pros, by Glenn Sapir, North American Hunting Club, Minnetonka, MN, 1999. 176 pp., illustrated. $19.95.

This work written by a seasoned turkey hunter draws on the collective knowledge and experience on some of the most renowned names in the world of wild turkey.

Sheep Hunting in Alaska—The Dall Sheep Hunter's Guide, by Tony Russ, Outdoor Expeditions and Books, Corvallis, MT, 1994. 160 pp., illus. Paper covers. $19.95.

A how-to guide for the Dall sheep hunter.

Shorebirds: The Birds, The Hunters, The Decoys, by John M. Levinson & Somers G. Headley, Tidewater Publishers, Centreville, MD, 1991. 160 pp., illus. $49.95.

A thorough study of shorebirds and the decoys used to hunt them. Photographs of more than 200 of the decoys created by prominent carvers are shown.

Shots at Big Game, by Craig Boddington, Stackpole Books, Harrisburg, PA, 1989. 198 pp., illus. $24.95.

How to shoot a rifle accurately under hunting conditions.

Some Bears Kill!: True-Life Tales of Terror, by Larry Kanuit, Safari Press, Huntington Beach, CA, 1997. 313 pp., illus. $24.95.

A collection of 38 stories as told by the victims, and in the case of fatality, recounted by the author from institutional records, episodes involve all three species of North American bears.

Southern Deer & Deer Hunting, by Larry Weishuhn and Bill Bynum, Krause Publications, Iola, WI, 1995. 256 pp., illus. Paper covers. $14.95.

Mount a trophy southern whitetail on your wall with this firsthand account of stalking big bucks below the Mason-Dixon line.

Spring Gobbler Fever, by Michael Hanback, Krause Publications, Iola, WI, 1996. 256 pp., illus. Paper covers. $15.95.

Your complete guide to spring turkey hunting.

Spirit of the Wilderness, Compiled by Theodore J. Holsten, Jr., Susan C. Reneau and Jack Reneau, the Boone & Crockett Club, Missoula, MT, 1997 300 pp., illus. $29.95.

Stalking wild sheep, tracking a trophy cougar, hiking the back country of British Columbia, fishing for striped bass and coming face-to-face with a grizzly bear are some of the adventures found in this book.

Stand Hunting for Whitetails, by Richard P. Smith, Krause Publications, Iola, WI, 1996. 256 pp., illus. Paper covers. $14.95.

The author explains the tricks and strategies for successful stand hunting.

The Sultan of Spring: A Hunter's Odyssey Through the World of the Wild Turkey, by Bob Saile, The Lyons Press, New York, NY, 1998. 176 pp., illus. $22.95.

A literary salute to the magic and mysticism of spring turkey hunting.

Taking Big Bucks, by Ed Wolff, Stoneydale Press, Stevensville, MT, 1987. 169 pp., illus. $18.95.

Solving the whitetail riddle.

Taking More Birds, by Dan Carlisle and Dolph Adams, Lyons & Burford Publishers, New York, NY, 1993. 160 pp., illus. Paper covers. $15.95.

A practical handbook for success at Sporting Clays and wing shooting.

Tales of Quails 'n Such, by Havilah Babcock, University of S. Carolina Press, Columbia, SC, 1985. 237 pp. $19.95.

A group of hunting stories, told in informal style, on field experiences in the South in quest of small game.

Tears and Laughter, by Gene Hill, Countrysport Press, Traverse City, MI, 1996. 176 pp., illus. $25.00.

In twenty-six stories, Gene Hill explores the ancient and honored bond between man and dog.

Tenth Legion, by Tom Kelly, the Lyons Press, New York, NY, 1998. 128 pp., illus. $21.95.

The classic work on that frustrating, yet wonderful sport of turkey hunting.

They Left Their Tracks, by Howard Coperhaver, Stoneydale Press Publishing Co., Stevensville, MT, 1990. 190 pp., illus. $18.95.

Recollections of 60 years as an outfitter in the Bob Marshall Wilderness.

Timberdoodle, by Frank Woolner, Nick Lyons Books, N. Y., NY, 1987. 168 pp., illus. $18.95.

The classic guide to woodcock and woodcock hunting.

Timberdoodle Tales: Adventures of a Minnesota Woodcock Hunter, by T. Waters, Safari Press, Huntington Beach, CA, 1997. 220 pp., illus. $35.00.

The life history and hunt of the American woodcock by the author. A fresh appreciation of this captivating bird and the ethics of its hunt.

To Heck with Moose Hunting, by Jim Zumbo, Wapiti Publishing Co., Cody, WY, 1996. 199 pp., illus. $17.95.

Jim's hunts around the continent and even an African adventure.

Trail and Campfire, edited by George Bird Grinnel and Theodore Roosevelt, The Boone and Crockett Club, Dumfries, VA, 1989. 357 pp., illus. $39.50.

Reprint of the Boone and Crockett Club's 3rd book published in 1897.

Trailing a Bear, by Robert S. Munger, The Munger Foundation, Albion, MI, 1997. 352 pp., illus. Paper covers. $19.95.

An exciting and humorous account of hunting with legendary archer Fred Bear.

The Trickiest Thing in Feathers, by Corey Ford; compiled and edited by Laurie Morrow and illustrated by Christopher Smith, Wilderness Adventures, Gallatin Gateway, MT, 1998. 208 pp., illus. $29.95.

Here is a collection of Corey Ford's best wing-shooting stories, many of them previously unpublished.

Trophy Mule Deer: Finding & Evaluating Your Trophy, by Lance Stapleton, Outdoor Experiences Unlimited, Salem, OR, 1993. 290 pp., illus. Paper covers. $24.95.

The most comprehensive reference book on mule deer.

Turkey Hunter's Digest, Revised Edition, by Dwain Bland, DBI Books, a division of Krause Publications, Iola, WI, 1994. 256 pp., illus. Paper covers. $17.95.

A no-nonsense approach to hunting all five sub-species of the North American wild turkey that make up the Royal Grand Slam.

The Upland Equation: A Modern Bird-Hunter's Code, by Charles Fergus, Lyons & Burford Publishers, New York, NY, 1996. 86 pp. $18.00.

A book that deserves space in every sportsman's library. Observations based on firsthand experience.

Upland Tales, by Worth Mathewson (Ed.), Sand Lake Press, Amity, OR, 1996. 271 pp., illus. $29.95.

A collection of articles on grouse, snipe and quail.

A Varmint Hunter's Odyssey, by Steve Hanson with a guest chapter by Mike Johnson, Precision Shooting, Inc. Manchester, CT, 1999. 279 pp., illustrated. Paper covers. $37.95.

A new classic by a writer who eats, drinks and sleeps varmint hunting and varmint rifles.

Varmint and Small Game Rifles and Cartridges, by various authors, Wolfe Publishing Co., Prescott, AZ, 1993. 228 pp., illus. Paper covers. $26.00.

This is a collection of reprints of articles originally appearing in Wolfe's *Rifle* and *Handloader* magazines from 1966 through 1990.

Waterfowler's World, by Bill Buckley, Ducks Unlimited, Inc., Menphis, TN, 1999. 192 pp., illustrated in color. $37.50.

An unprecedented pictorial book on waterfowl and waterfowlers.

Waterfowling Horizons: Shooting Ducks and Geese in the 21st Century, by Chris and Jason Smith, Wilderness Adventures, Gallatin Gateway, MT, 1998. 320 pp., illus. $49.95.

A compendium of the very latest in everything for the duck and goose hunter today.

Waterfowling These Past 50 Years, Especially Brant, by David Hagerbaumer, Sand Lake Press, Amity, OR, 1999. 182 pp., illustrated. $35.00.

This is the compilation of David Hagerbaumer's experiences as a waterfowler since the end of WW2.

Wegner's Bibliography on Dear and Deer Hunting, by Robert Wegner, St. Hubert's Press, Deforest, WI, 1993. 333 pp., 16 full-page illustrations. $45.00.

A comprehensive annotated compilation of books in English pertaining to deer and their hunting 1413-1991.

Western Hunting Guide, by Mike Lapinski, Stoneydale Press Publishing Co., Stevensville, MT, 1989. 168 pp., illus. $18.95.

A complete where-to-go and how-to-do-it guide to Western hunting.

When the Duck Were Plenty, by Ed Muderlak, Safari Press, Inc., Huntington Beach, CA, 2000. 300 pp., illustrated. Limited edition, numbered, signed, slipcased. $49.95.

The golden age of waterfowling and duck hunting from 1840 till 1920. An anthology.

Whispering Wings of Autumn, by Gene Hill and Steve Smith, Wilderness Adventures Press, Bozeman, MT, 1994. 150 pp., illus. $29.00.

Hill and Smith, masters of hunting literature, treat the reader to the best stories of grouse and woodcock hunting.

Whitetail: Behavior Through the Seasons, by Charles J. Alsheimer, Krause Publications, Iola, WI, 1996. 208 pp., illus. $34.95.

In-depth coverage of whitetail behavior presented through striking portraits of the whitetail in every season.

Whitetail: The Ultimate Challenge, by Charles J. Alsheimer, Krause Publications, Iola, WI, 1995. 228 pp., illus. Paper covers. $14.95.

Learn deer hunting's most intriguing secrets—fooling deer using decoys, scents and calls—from America's premier authority.

Whitetails by the Moon, by Charles J. Alsheimer, edited by Patrick Durkin, Krause Publications, Iola, WI, 1999. 208 pp., illustrated. Paper covers. $19.95.

Predict peak times to hunt whitetails. Learn what triggers the rut.

Wildfowlers Season, by Chris Dorsey, Lyons & Burford Publishers, New York, NY, 1998. 224 pp., illus. $37.95.

Modern methods for a classic sport.

Wildfowling Tales, by William C. Hazelton, Wilderness Adventures Press, Belgrade, MT, 1999. 117 pp., illustrated with etchings by Brett Smith. In a slipcase. $50.00.

Tales from the great ducking resorts of the Continent.

Wildfowling Tales 1888-1913, Volume One, edited by Worth Mathewson, Sand Lake Press, Amity, OR, 1998. 186 pp., illustrated by David Hagerbaumer. $22.50.

A collection of some of the best accounts from our literary heritage.

Windward Crossings: A Treasury of Original Waterfowling Tales, by Chuck Petrie et al, Willow Creek Press, Minocqua, WI, 1999. 144 pp., 48 color art and etching reproductions. $35.00.

An illustrated, modern anthology of previously unpublished waterfowl hunting (fiction and creative non fiction) stories by America's finest outdoor journalists.

REFERENCE

Wings of Thunder: New Grouse Hunting Revisited, by Steven Mulak, Countrysport Books, Selma, AL, 1998. 168 pp. illustrated. $30.00.
The author examines every aspect of New England grouse hunting as it is today - the bird and its habits, the hunter and his dog, guns and loads, shooting and hunting techniques, practice on clay targets, clothing and equipment.

Wings for the Heart, by Jerry A. Lewis, West River Press, Corvallis, MT, 1991. 324 pp., illus. Paper covers. $14.95.
A delightful book on hunting Montana's upland birds and waterfowl.

Wisconsin Hunting, by Brian Lovett, Krause Publications, Iola, WI, 1997. 208 pp., illus. Paper covers. $16.95.
A comprehensive guide to Wisconsin's public hunting lands.

The Woodchuck Hunter, by Paul C. Estey, R&R Books, Livonia, NY, 1994. 135 pp., illus. $25.00.
This book contains information on woodchuck equipment, the rifle, telescopic sights and includes interesting stories.

Woodcock Shooting, by Steve Smith, Stackpole Books, Inc., Harrisburg, PA, 1988. 142 pp., illus. $16.95.
A definitive book on woodcock hunting and the characteristics of a good woodcock dog.

World Record Whitetails, by Gordon Whittington, Safari Press, Inc., Huntington Beach, CA, 1998. 246 pp. with over 100 photos in color and black-and-white. $32.95.
The first and only complete chronicle of all the bucks that have ever held the title "World record whitetail."

The Working Retrievers, Tom Quinn, The Lyons Press, New York, NY, 1998. 257 pp., illus. $40.00.
The author covers every aspect of the training of dogs for hunting and field trials — from the beginning to the most advanced levels — for Labradors, Chesapeakes, Goldens and others.

World Record Whitetails, by Gordon Whittington, Safari Press Books, Inc., Huntington Beach, CA, 1998. 246 pp., illustrated. $39.95.
The first and only complete chronicle of all the bucks that have ever held the title "World Record Whitetail." Covers the greatest trophies ever recorded in their categories, typical, non-typical, gun, bow, and muzzleloader.

AFRICA/ASIA/ELSEWHERE

A Hunter's Wanderings in Africa, by Frederick Courteney Selous, Wolfe Publishing Co., Prescott, Arizona, 1986. 504 pp., illustrated plus folding map. $29.95.
A reprinting of the 1920 London edition. A narrative of nine years spent amongst the game of the far interior of South Africa.

The Adventurous Life of a Vagabond Hunter, by Sten Cedergren, Safari Press, Inc., Huntington Beach, CA, 2000. 300 pp., illustrated. Limited edition, numbered, signed, and slipcased. $70.00.
An unusual story in the safari business by a remarkable character.

Africa's Greatest Hunter; The Lost Writings of Frederick C. Selous, edited by Dr. james A. Casada, Safari Press, Huntington Beach, CA, 1999. Limited, signed and numbered copy in a slipcase. $35.00.
All the stories in this volume relate to the continent that fascinated Selous his entire life. With many previously unpublished photos.

African Adventures, by J.F. Burger, Safari Press, Huntington Beach, CA, 1993. 222 pp., illus. $35.00.
The reader shares adventures on the trail of the lion, the elephant and buffalo.

The African Adventures: A Return to the Silent Places, by Peter Hathaway Capstick, St. Martin's Press, New York, NY, 1992. 220 pp., illus. $22.95.
This book brings to life four turn-of-the-century adventurers and the savage frontier they braved. Frederick Selous, Constaine "Iodine" Ionides, Johnny Boyes and Jim Sutherland.

African Camp-fire Nights, by J.E. Burger, Safari Press, Huntington Beach, CA, 1993. 192 pp., illus. $32.50.
In this book the author writes of the men who made hunting their life's profession.

African Game Trails, by Theodore Roosevelt, Peter Capstick, Series Editor, St. Martin's Press, New York, NY 1988. 583 pp., illustrated. $24.95.
The famed safari of the noted sportsman, conservationist, and President.

African Hunter, by James Mellon, Safari Press, Huntington Beach, CA, 1996. 522 pp., illus. Clothbound, $125.00; paper covers, $75.00.
Regarded as the most comprehensive title ever published on African hunting.

African Hunting and Adventure, by William Charles Baldwin, Books of Zimbabwe, Bulawayo, 1981. 451 pp., illus. $75.00.
Facsimile reprint of the scarce 1863 London edition. African hunting and adventure from Natal to the Zambezi.

African Jungle Memories, by J.F. Burger, Safari Press, Huntington Beach, CA, 1993. 192 pp., illus. $32.50.
A book of reminiscences in which the reader is taken on many exciting adventures on the trail of the buffalo, lion, elephant and leopard.

African Rifles & Cartridges, by John Taylor, The Gun Room Press, Highland Park, NJ, 1977. 431 pp., illus. $35.00.
Experiences and opinions of a professional ivory hunter in Africa describing his knowledge of numerous arms and cartridges for big game. A reprint.

African Safaris, by Major G.H. Anderson, Safari Press, Long Beach, CA, 1997. 173 pp., illus. $35.00.
A reprinting of one of the rarest books on African hunting, with a foreword by Tony Sanchez.

African Twilight, by Robert F. Jones, Wilderness Adventure Press, Bozeman, MT, 1994. 208 pp., illus. $36.00.
Details the hunt, danger and changing face of Africa over a span of three decades.

A Man Called Lion: The Life and Times of John Howard "Pondoro" Taylor, by P.H. Capstick, Safari Press, Huntington Beach, CA, 1994. 240 pp., illus. $24.95.
With the help of Brian Marsh, an old Taylor acquaintance, Peter Capstick has accumulated over ten years of research into the life of this mysterious man.

An Annotated Bibliography of African Big Game Hunting Books, 1785 to 1950, by Kenneth P. Czech, Land's Edge Press, St. Cloud, MN 2000. $50.00.
This bibliography features over 600 big game hunting titles describing the regions the authors hunted, species of game bagged, and physical descriptions of the books (pages, maps, plates, bindings, etc.) It also features a suite of 16 colored plates depicting decorated bindings from some of the books. Limited to 700 numbered, signed copies.

Argali: High-Mountain Hunting, by Ricardo Medem, Safari Press, Huntington Beach, CA, 1995. 304 pp., illus. Limited, signed edition. $150.00.
Medem describes hunting seven different countries in the pursuit of sheep and other mountain game.

Big Game and Big Game Rifles, by John "Pondoro" Taylor, Safari Press, Huntington Beach, CA, 1999. 215 pp., illus. $24.95.
Covers rifles and calibers for elephant, rhino, hippo, buffalo, and lion.

Big Game Hunting Around the World, by Bert Klineburger and Vernon W. Hurst, Exposition Press, Jericho, NY, 1969. 376 pp., illus. $30.00.
The first book that takes you on a safari all over the world.

Big Game Hunting in Asia, Africa, and Elsewhere, by Jacques Vettier, Trophy Room Books, Agoura, CA, 1993. 400 pp., illus. Limited, numbered edition. $150.00.
The first English language edition of the book that set a new standard in big game hunting book literature.

Big Game Hunting in North-Eastern Rhodesia, by Owen Letcher, St. Martin's Press, New York, NY, 1986. 272 pp., illus. $24.95.
A classic reprint and one of the very few books to concentrate on this fascinating area, a region that today is still very much safari country.

Big Game Shooting in Cooch Behar, the Duars and Assam, by The Maharajah of Cooch Behar, Wolfe Publishing Co., Prescott, AZ, 1993. 461 pp., illus. $49.50.
A reprinting of the book that has become legendary. This is the Maharajah's personal diary of killing 365 tigers.

A Country Boy in Africa, by George Hoffman, Trophy Room Books, Agoura, CA, 1998. 267 pp., illustrated with over 100 photos. Limited, numbered edition signed by the author. $85.00.
In addition to the author's long and successful hunting career, he is known for developing a most effective big game cartridge, the .416 Hoffman.

Buffalo, Elephant, and Bongo, by Dr. Reinald von Meurers, Safari Press, Huntington Beach, CA, 1999. Limited edition signed and in a slipcase. $75.00.
Alone in the Savannas and Rain Forests of the Cameroon.

Campfire Lies of a Canadian Guide, by Fred Webb, Safari Press, Inc., Huntington Beach, CA, 2000. 250 pp., illustrated. Limited edition, numbered, signed and slipcased. $50.00.
Forty years in the life of a guide in the North Country.

Cottar: The Exception was the Rule, by Pat Cottar, Trophy Room Books, Agoura, CA, 1999. 350 pp., illustrated. Limited, numbered and signed edition. $135.00.
The remarkable big game hunting stories of one of Kenya's most remarkable pioneers.

Death in a Lonely Land, by Peter Capstick, St. Martin's Press, New York, NY, 1990. 284 pp., illus. $22.95.
Twenty-three stories of hunting as only the master can tell them.

Death in the Dark Continent, by Peter Capstick, St. Martin's Press, New York, NY, 1983. 238 pp., illus. $22.95.
A book that brings to life the suspense, fear and exhilaration of stalking ferocious killers under primitive, savage conditions, with the ever present threat of death.

Death in the Long Grass, by Peter Hathaway Capstick, St. Martin's Press, New York, NY, 1977. 297 pp., illus. $22.95.
A big game hunter's adventures in the African bush.

Death in the Silent Places, by Peter Capstick, St. Martin's Press, New York, NY, 1981. 243 pp., illus. $23.95.
The author recalls the extraordinary careers of legendary hunters such as Corbett, Karamojo Bell, Stigand and others.

Duck Hunting in Australia, by Dick Eussen, Australia Outdoor Publishers Pty Ltd., Victoria, Australia, 1994. 106 pp., illus. Paper covers. $17.95.
Covers the many aspects of duck hunting from hides to hunting methods.

East Africa and its Big Game, by Captain Sir John C. Willowghby, Wolfe Publishing Co., Prescott, AZ, 1990. 312 pp., illus. $52.00.
A deluxe limited edition reprint of the very scarce 1889 edition of a narrative of a sporting trip from Zanzibar to the borders of the Masai.

Elephant Hunting in East Equatorial Africa, by A. Neumann, St. Martin's Press, New York, NY, 1994. 455 pp., illus. $26.95.
This is a reprint of one of the rarest elephant hunting titles ever.

Elephants of Africa, by Dr. Anthony Hall-Martin, New Holland Publishers, London, England, 1987. 120 pp., illus. $45.00.
A superbly illustrated overview of the African elephant with reproductions of paintings by the internationally acclaimed wildlife artist Paul Bosman.

Encounters with Lions, by Jan Hemsing, Trophy Room books, Agoura, CA, 1995. 302 pp., illus. $75.00.
Some stories fierce, fatal, frightening and even humorous of when man and lion meet.

Fourteen Years in the African Bush, by A. Marsh, Safari Press Publication, Huntington Beach, CA, 1998. 312 pp., illus. Limited signed, numbered, slipcased. $70.00.
An account of a Kenyan game warden. A graphic and well-written story.

THE ARMS LIBRARY

From Sailor to Professional Hunter: The Autobigraphy of John Northcote, Trophy Room Books, Agoura, CA, 1997. 400 pp., illus. Limited edition, signed and numbered. $125.00.

Only a handfull of men can boast of having a fifty-year professional hunting career throughout Africa as John Northcote has had.

Glory Days of Baja, by Larry Stanton, John Culler and Sons, Camden, SC, 1996. 184 pp., illus. $21.95.

This book represents twenty-five years of hunting in Mexico's Baja.

Great Hunters: Their Trophy Rooms and Collections, Volume 1, compiled and published by Safari Press, Inc., Huntington Beach, CA, 1997. 172 pp., illustrated in color. $60.00.

A rare glimpse into the trophy rooms of top international hunters. A few of these trophy rooms are museums.

Great Hunters: Their Trophy Rooms & Collections, Volume 2, compiled and published by Safari Press, Inc., Huntington Beach, CA, 1998. 224 pp., illustrated with 260 full-color photographs. $60.00.

Volume two of the world's finest, best produced series of books on trophy rooms and game collections. 46 sportsmen sharing sights you'll never forget on this guided tour.

Heart of an African Hunter, by Peter F. Flack, Safari Press, Inc., Huntington Beach, CA, 1999. Limited, numbered, slipcased edition. $70.00.

Stories on the Big Five and Tiny Ten.

Horned Death, by John F. Burger, Safari Press, Huntington Beach, CA, 1992. 343 pp.illus. $35.00.

The classic work on hunting the African buffalo.

Horn of the Hunter, by Robert Ruark, Safari Press, Long Beach, CA, 1987. 315 pp., illus. $35.00.

Ruark's most sought-after title on African hunting, here in reprint.

Horned Giants, by Capt. John Brandt, Safari Press, Inc., Huntington Beach, CA, 1999. 288 pp., illustrated. Limited edition, numbered, signed and slipcased. $80.00.

Hunting Eurasian wild cattle.

Hunter, by J.A. Hunter, Safari Press Publications, Huntington Beach, CA, 1999. 263 pp., illus. $24.95.

Hunter's best known book on African big-game hunting. Internationally recognized as being one of the all-time African hunting classics.

A Hunter's Africa, by Gordon Cundill, Trophy Room Books, Agoura, CA, 1998. 298 pp., over 125 photographic illustrations. Limited numbered edition signed by the author. $125.00.

A good look by the author at the African safari experience - elephant, lion, spiral-horned antelope, firearms, people and events, as well as the clients that make it worthwhile.

A Hunter's Wanderings in Africa, by Frederick Courteney Selous, Wolfe Publishing Co., Prescott, Arizona, 1986. 504 pp., illustrated plus folding map. $29.95.

A reprinting of the 1920 London edition. A narrative of nine years spent amongst the game of the far interior of South Africa.

Hunter's Tracks, by J.A. Hunter, Safari Press Publications, Huntington Beach, CA, 1999. 240 pp., illustrated. $24.95.

This is the exciting story of John Hunter's efforts to capture the shady headman of a gang of ivory poachers and smugglers. The story is interwoven with the tale of one of East Africa's most grandiose safaris taken with an Indian maharaja.

Hunting Adventures Worldwide, by Jack Atcheson, Jack Atcheson & Sons, Butte, MT, 1995. 256 pp., illus. $29.95.

The author chronicles the richest adventures of a lifetime spent in quest of big game across the world – including Africa, North America and Asia.

Hunting in Ethiopia, An Anthology, by Tony Sanchez-Arino, Safari Press, Huntington Beach, CA, 1996. 350 pp., illus. Limited, signed and numbered edition. $135.00.

The finest selection of hunting stories ever compiled on hunting in this great game country.

The Hunting Instinct, by Phillip D. Rowter, Safari Press, Inc., Huntington Beach, CA, 1999. Limited edition signed and numbered and in a slipcase. $50.00.

Safari chronicles from the Republic of South Africa and Namibia 1990-1998.

Hunting in Kenya, by Tony Sanchez-Arino, Safari Press, Inc., Huntington Beach, CA, 2000. 350 pp., illustrated. Limited, signed and numbered edition in a slipcase. $135.00.

The finest selection of hunting stories ever compiled on hunting in this great game country make up this anthology.

Hunting in Many Lands, by Theodore Roosevelt and George Bird Grinnel, The Boone and Crockett Club, Dumfries, VA, 1987. 447 pp., illus. $40.00.

Limited edition reprint of this 1895 classic work on hunting in Africa, India, Mongolia, etc.

Hunting in the Sudan, An Anthology, compiled by Tony Sanchez-Arino, Safari Press, Huntington Beach, CA, 1992. 350 pp., illus. Limited, signed and numbered edition in a slipcase. $125.00.

The finest selection of hunting stories ever compiled on hunting in this great game country.

Hunting, Settling and Remembering, by Philip H. Percival, Trophy Room Books, Agoura, CA, 1997. 230 pp., illus. Limited, numbered and signed edition. $85.00.

If Philip Percival is to come alive again, it will be through this, the first edition of his easy, intricate and magical book illustrated with some of the best historical big game hunting photos ever taken.

Hunting the Dangerous Game of Africa, by John Kingsley-Heath, Sycamore Island Books, Boulder, CO, 1998. 477 pp., illustrated. $95.00.

Written by one of the most respected, successful, and ethical P.H.'s to trek the sunlit plains of Botswana, Kenya, Uganda, Tanganyika, Somaliland, Eritrea, Ethiopia, and Mozambique. Filled with some of the most gripping and terrifying tales ever to come out of Africa.

In the Salt, by Lou Hallamore, Trophy Room Books, Agoura, CA, 1999. 227 pp., illustrated in black & white and full color. Limited, numbered and signed edition. $125.00.

A book about people, animals and the big game hunt, about being outwitted and out maneuvered. It is about knowing that sooner or later your luck will change and your trophy will be "in the salt."

International Hunter 1945-1999, Hunting's Greatest Era, by Bert klineburger, Sportsmen on Film, Kerrville, TX, 1999. 400 pp., illustrated. A limited, numbered and signed edition. $125.00.

The most important book of the greatest hunting era by the world's preeminent International hunter.

Jaguar Hunting in the Mato Grosso and Bolivia, by T. Almedia, Safari Press, Long Beach, CA, 1989. 256 pp., illus. $35.00.

Not since Sacha Siemel has there been a book on jaguar hunting like this one.

Jim Corbett, Master of the Jungle, by Tim Werling, Safari Press, Huntington Beach, CA, 1998. 215 pp., illus. $30.00.

A biography of India's most famous hunter of man-eating tigers and leopards.

King of the Wa-Kikuyu, by John Boyes, St. Martin Press, New York, NY, 1993. 240 pp., illus. $19.95.

In the 19th and 20th centuries, Africa drew to it a large number of great hunters, explorers, adventurers and rogues. Many have become legendary, but John Boyes (1874-1951) was the most legendary of them all.

Lake Ngami, by Charles Anderson, New Holland Press, London, England, 1987. 576 pp., illus. $35.00.

Originally published in 1856. Describes two expeditions into what is now Botswana, depicting every detail of landscape and wildlife.

Last Horizons: Hunting, Fishing and Shooting on Five Continents, by Peter Capstick, St. Martin's Press, New York, NY, 1989. 288 pp., illus. $19.95.

The first in a two volume collection of hunting, fishing and shooting tales from the selected pages of The American Hunter, Guns & Ammo and Outdoor Life.

Last of the Few: Forty-Two Years of African Hunting, by Tony Sanchez-Arino, Safari Press, Huntington Beach, CA, 1996. 250 pp., illus. $39.95.

The story of the author's career with all the highlights that come from pursuing the unusual and dangerous animals that are native to Africa.

Last of the Ivory Hunters, by John Taylor, Safari Press, Long Beach, CA, 1990. 354 pp., illus. $29.95.

Reprint of the classic book "Pondoro" by one of the most famous elephant hunters of all time.

Legends of the Field: More Early Hunters in Africa, by W.R. Foran, Trophy Room Press, Agoura, CA, 1997. 319 pp., illus. Limited edition. $100.00.

This book contains the biographies of some very famous hunters: William Cotton Oswell, F.C. Selous, Sir Samuel Baker, Arthur Neumann, Jim Sutherland, W.D.M. Bell and others.

The Lost Classics, by Robert Ruark, Safari Press, Huntington Beach, CA, 1996. 260 pp., illus. $35.00.

The magazine stories that Ruark wrote in the 1950s and 1960s finally in print in book form.

The Magic of Big Games, by Terry Wieland, Countrysport Books, Selma, AL, 1998. 200 pp., illus. $39.00.

Original essays on hunting big game around the world.

Mahonhboh, by Ron Thomson, Hartbeespoort, South Africa, 1997. 312 pp., illustrated. Limited signed and numbered edition. $50.00.

Elephants and elephant hunting in South Central Africa.

Man-Eaters & Jungle Killers, by Kenneth Anderson, John Culler & Sons, Camden, S.C., 1999. 199 pp., illustrated. $40.00.

Rogue elephants, deadly leopards and man-eating tigers in India's jungle. True adventure stories match man's cunning against killer instinct.

The Man-Eaters of Tsavo, by Lt. Colonel J.H. Patterson, Peter Capstick, series editor, St. Martin's Press, New York, NY, 1986, 5th printing. 346 pp., illus. $22.95.

The classic man-eating story of the lions that halted construction of a railway line and reportedly killed one hundred people, told by the man who risked his life to successfully shoot them.

McElroy Hunts Asia, by C.J. McElroy, Safari Press, Inc., Huntington Beach, CA, 1989. 272 pp., illustrated. $50.00.

From the founder of SCI comes a book on hunting the great continent of Asia for big game: tiger, bear, sheep and ibex. Includes the story of the all-time record Altai Argali as well as several markhor hunts in Pakistan.

Memoirs of an African Hunter, by Terry Irwin, Safari Press Publications, Huntington Beach, CA, 1998. 421 pp., illustrated. Limited numbered, signed and slipcased. $125.00.

A narrative of a professional hunter's experiences in Africa.

Memoirs of a Sheep Hunter, by Rashid Jamsheed, Safari Press, Inc., Huntington Beach, CA, 1996. 330 pp., illustrated. $70.00.

The author reveals his exciting accounts of obtaining world-record heads from his native Iran, and his eventual move to the U.S. where he procured a grand-slam of North American sheep.

Months of the Sun; Forty Years of Elephant Hunting in the Zambezi Valley, by Ian Nyschens, Safari Press, Huntington Beach, CA, 1998. 420 pp., illus. Limited signed and numbered edition. Slipcased. $100.00.

The author has shot equally as many elephants as Walter Bell, and under much more difficult circumstances. His book will rank, or surpass, the best elephant-ivory hunting books published this century.

Mundjamba: The Life Story of an African Hunter, by Hugo Seia, Trophy Room Books, Agoura, CA, 1996. 400 pp., illus. Limited, numbered and signed by the author. $125.00.

An autobiography of one of the most respected and appreciated professional African hunters.

THE ARMS LIBRARY

My Last Kambaku, by Leo Kroger, Safari Press, Huntington Beach, CA, 1997. 272 pp., illus. Limited edition signed and numbered and slipcased. $60.00.
One of the most engaging hunting memoirs ever published.

The Nature of the Game, by Ben Hoskyns, Quiller Press, Ltd., London, England, 1994. 160 pp., illus. $37.50.
The first complete guide to British, European and North American game.

On Target, by Christian Le Noel, Trophy Room Books, Agoura, CA, 1999. 275 pp., illustrated. Limited, numbered and signed edition. $85.00.
History and hunting in Central Africa.

One Long Safari, by Peter Hay, Trophy Room Books, Agoura, CA, 1998. 350 pp., with over 200 photographic illustrations and 7 maps. Limited numbered edition signed by the author. $100.00.
Contains hunts for leopards, sitatunga, hippo, rhino, snakes and, of course, the general African big game bag.

Optics for the Hunter, by John Barsness, Safari Press, Inc., Huntington Beach, CA, 1999. 236 pp., illustrated. $24.95.
An evaluation of binoculars, scopes, range finders, spotting scopes for use in the field.

Out in the Midday Shade, by William York, Safari Press, Inc., Huntington Beach, CA, 1999. Limited, signed and numbered edition in a slipcase. $70.00.
Memoirs of an African Hunter 1949-1968.

The Path of a Hunter, by Gilles Tre-Hardy, Trophy Room Books, Agoura, CA, 1997. 318 pp., illus. Limited Edition, signed and numbered. $85.00.
A most unusual hunting autobiography with much about elephant hunting in Africa.

The Perfect Shot; Shot Placement for African Big Game, by Kevin "Doctari" Robertson, Safari Press, Inc., Huntington Beach, CA, 1999. 230 pp., illustrated. $65.00.
The most comprehensive work ever undertaken to show the anatomical features for all classes of African game. Includes caliber and bullet selection, rifle selection, trophy handling.

Peter Capstick's Africa: A Return to the Long Grass, by Peter Hathaway Capstick, St. Martin's Press, N. Y., NY, 1987. 213 pp., illus. $35.00.
A first-person adventure in which the author returns to the long grass for his own dangerous and very personal excursion.

Pondoro, by John Taylor, Safari Press, Inc., Huntington Beach, CA, 1999. 354 pp., illustrated. $29.95.
The author is considered one of the best storytellers in the hunting book world, and Pondoro is highly entertaining. A classic African big-game hunting title.

The Quotable Hunter, by Jay Cassell and Peter Fiduccia, The Lyons Press, N.Y., 1999. 288 pp., illustrated. $20.00.
This collection of more than three hundred quotes from hunters through the ages captures the essence of the sport, with all its joys, idiosyncrasies, and challenges.

The Recollections of an Elephant Hunter 1864-1875, by William Finaughty, Books of Zimbabwe, Bulawayo, Zimbabwe, 1980. 244 pp., illus. $85.00.
Reprint of the scarce 1916 privately published edition. The early game hunting exploits of William Finaughty in Matabeleland and Nashonaland.

Records of Big Game, XXV (25th) Edition, Rowland Ward, distributed by Safari Press, Inc., Huntington Beach, CA, 1999. 1,000 pp., illustrated. Limited edition. $150.00.
Covers big game records of Africa, Asia, Europe, and the America's.

Robert Ruark's Africa, by Robert Ruark, edited by Michael McIntosh, Countrysport Press, Selma, AL, 1999. 256 pp illustrated with 19 original etchings by Bruce Langton. $32.00.
These previously uncollected works of Robert Ruark make this a classic big-game hunting book.

Safari: A Chronicle of Adventure, by Bartle Bull, Viking/Penguin, London, England, 1989. 383 pp., illus. $40.00.
The thrilling history of the African safari, highlighting some of Africa's best-known personalities.

Safari: A Dangerous Affair, by Walt Prothero, Safari Press, Huntington Beach, CA, 2000. 275 pp., illustrated. Limited edition, numbered, signed and slipcased. $60.00.
True accounts of hunters and animals of Africa.

Safari Rifles: Double, Magazine Rifles and Cartridges for African Hunting, by Craig Boddington, Safari Press, Huntington Beach, CA, 1990. 416 pp., illus. $37.50.
A wealth of knowledge on the safari rifle. Historical and present double-rifle makers, ballistics for the large bores, and much, much more.

Safari: The Last Adventure, by Peter Capstick, St. Martin's Press, New York, NY, 1984. 291 pp., illus. $22.95.
A modern comprehensive guide to the African Safari.

Sands of Silence, by Peter H. Capstick, Saint Martin's Press, New York, NY, 1991. 224 pp., illus. $35.00.
Join the author on safari in Nambia for his latest big-game hunting adventures.

Solo Safari, by T. Cacek, Safari Press, Huntington Beach, CA, 1995. 270 pp., illus. $30.00.
Here is the story of Terry Cacek who hunted elephant, buffalo, leopard and plains game in Zimbabwe and Botswana on his own.

South Pacific Trophy Hunter, by Murray Thomas, Safari Press, Long Beach, CA, 1988. 181 pp., illus. $37.50.
A record of a hunter's search for a trophy of each of the 15 major game species in the South Pacific region.

Spiral-Horn Dreams, by Terry Wieland, Trophy Room Books, Agoura, CA, 1996. 362 pp., illus. Limited, numbered and signed by the author. $85.00.
Everyone who goes to hunt in Africa is looking for something; this is for those who go to hunt the spiral-horned antelope—the bongo, myala, mountain nyala, greater and lesser kudu, etc.

Sport Hunting on Six Continents, by Ken Wilson, Sportsmen of Film, Kerrville, TX, 1999. 300 pp., illustrated. $69.95.
Hunting around the world....from Alaska to Australia...from the Americas, to Africa, Asia, and Europe.

Tales of the African Frontier, by J.A. Hunter, Safari Press Publications, Huntington Beach, CA, 1999. 308 pp., illus. $24.95.
The early days of East Africa is the subject of this powerful John Hunter book.

Trophy Hunter in Africa, by Elgin Gates, Safari Press, Huntington Beach, CA, 1994. 315 pp., illus. $40.00.
This is the story of one man's adventure in Africa's wildlife paradise.

Uganda Safaris, by Brian Herne, Winchester Press, Piscataway, NJ, 1979. 236 pp., illus. $24.95.
The chronicle of a professional hunter's adventures in Africa.

Under the African Sun, by Dr. Frank Hibben, Safari Press, Inc., Huntington Beach, CA, 1999. Limited edition signed, numbered and in a slipcase. $85.00.
Forty-eight years of hunting the African continent.

Under the Shadow of Man Eaters, by Jerry Jaleel, The Jim Corbett Foundation, Edmonton, Alberta, Canada, 1997. 152 pp., illus. A limited, numbered and signed edition. Paper covers. $35.00.
The life and legend of Jim Corbett of Kumaon.

Use Enough Gun, by Robert Ruark, Safari Press, Huntington Beach, CA, 1997. 333 pp., illus. $35.00.
Robert Ruark on big game hunting.

Warrior: The Legend of Col. Richard Meinertzhagen, by Peter H. Capstick, St. Martins Press, New York, NY, 1998. 320 pp., illus. $23.95.
A stirring and vivid biography of the famous British colonial officer Richard Meinertzhagen, whose exploits earned him fame and notoriety as one of the most daring and ruthless men to serve during the glory days of the British Empire.

The Waterfowler's World, by Bill Buckley, Willow Creek Press, Minocqua, WI, 1999. 176 pp., 225 color photographs. $37.50.
Waterfowl hunting from Canadian prairies, across the U.S. heartland, to the wilds of Mexico, from the Atlantic to the Pacific coasts and the Gulf of Mexico.

Where Lions Roar: Ten More Years of African Hunting, by Craig Boddington, Safari Press, Huntington Beach, CA, 1997. 250 pp $35.00.
The story of Boddington's hunts in the Dark Continent during the last ten years.

White Hunter, by J.A. Hunter, Safari Press Publications, Huntington Beach, CA, 1999. 282 pp., illustrated. $24.95.
This book is a seldom-seen account of John Hunter's adventures in pre-WW2 Africa.

A White Hunters Life, by Angus MacLagan, an African Heritage Book, published by Amwell Press, Clinton, NJ, 1983. 283 pp., illus. Limited, signed, and numbered deluxe edition, in slipcase. $100.00.
True to life, a sometimes harsh yet intriguing story.

Wild Sports of Southern Africa, by William Cornwallis Harris, New Holland Press, London, England, 1987. 376 pp., illus. $36.00.
Originally published in 1863, describes the author's travels in Southern Africa.

Wind, Dust and Snow, by Robert M. Anderson, Safari Press, Inc., Huntington Beach, CA, 1997. 240 pp., illustrated. $65.00.
A complete chronology of modern exploratory and pioneering Asian sheep-hunting expeditions from 1960 until 1996, with wonderful background history and previously untold stories.

With a Gun in Good Country, by Ian Manning, Trophy Room Books, Agoura, CA, 1996. Limited, numbered and signed by the author. $85.00.
A book written about that splendid period before the poaching onslaught which almost closed Zambia and continues to the granting of her independence. It then goes on to recount Manning's experiences in Botswana, Congo, and briefly in South Africa.

RIFLES

The Accurate Varmint Rifle, by Boyd Mace, Precision Shooting, Inc., Whitehall, NY, 1991. 184 pp., illus. $15.00.
A long overdue and long needed work on what factors go into the selection of components for and the subsequent assembly of...the accurate varmint rifle.

The AK-47 Assault Rifle, Desert Publications, Cornville, AZ, 1981. 150 pp., illus. Paper covers. $13.95.
Complete and practical technical information on the only weapon in history to be produced in an estimated 30,000,000 units.

American Hunting Rifles: Their Application in the Field for Practical Shooting, by Craig Boddington, Safari Press, Huntington Beach, CA, 1996. 446 pp., illus. First edition, limited, signed and slipcased. $85.00. Second printing trade edition. $35.00.
Covers all the hunting rifles and calibers that are needed for North America's diverse game.

The AR-15/M16, A Practical Guide, by Duncan Long. Paladin Press, Boulder, CO, 1985. 168 pp., illus. Paper covers. $22.00.
The definitive book on the rifle that has been the inspiration for so many modern assault rifles.

The Art of Shooting With the Rifle, by Col. Sir H. St. John Halford, Excalibur Publications, Latham, NY, 1996. 96 pp., illus. Paper covers. $12.95.
A facsimile edition of the 1888 book by a respected rifleman providing a wealth of detailed information.

The Art of the Rifle, by Jeff Cooper, Paladin Press, Boulder, CO, 1997. 104 pp., illus. $29.95.
Everything you need to know about the rifle whether you use it for security, meat or target shooting.

Australian Military Rifles & Bayonets, 200 Years of, by Ian Skennerton, I.D.S.A. Books, Piqua, OH, 1988. 124 pp., 198 illus. Paper covers. $19.50.

Australian Service Machineguns, 100 Years of, by Ian Skennerton, I.D.S.A. Books, Piqua, OH, 1989. 122 pp., 150 illus. Paper covers. $19.50.

The Big Game Rifle, by Jack O'Connor, Safari Press, Huntington Beach, CA, 1994. 370 pp., illus. $37.50.
An outstanding description of every detail of construction, purpose and use of the big game rifle.

Big Game Rifles and Cartridges, by Elmer Keith, reprint edition by The Gun Room Press, Highland Park, NJ, 1984. 161 pp., illus. $17.95.
Reprint of Elmer Keith's first book, a most original and accurate work on big game rifles and cartridges.

Black Magic: The Ultra Accurate AR-15, by John Feamster, Precision Shooting, Manchester, CT, 1998. 300 pp., illustrated. $29.95.
The author has compiled his experiences pushing the accuracy envelope of the AR-15 to its maximum potential. A wealth of advice on AR-15 loads, modifications and accessories for everything from NRA Highpower and Service Rifle competitions to benchrest and varmint shooting.

The Black Rifle, M16 Retrospective, R. Blake Stevens and Edward C. Ezell, Collector Grade Publications, Toronto, Canada, 1987. 400 pp., illus. $59.95.
The complete story of the M16 rifle and its development.

Bolt Action Rifles, 3rd Edition, by Frank de Haas, DBI Books, a division of Krause Publications, Iola, WI, 1995. 528 pp., illus. Paper covers. $24.95.
A revised edition of the most definitive work on all major bolt-action rifle designs.

The Book of the Garand, by Maj. Gen. J.S. Hatcher, The Gun Room Press, Highland Park, NJ, 1977. 292 pp., illus. $26.95.
A new printing of the standard reference work on the U.S. Army M1 rifle.

The Book of the Twenty-Two: The All American Caliber, by Sam Fadala, Stoeger Publishing Co., So. Hackensack, NJ, 1989. 288 pp., illus. Soft covers. $16.95.
The All American Caliber from BB caps up to the powerful 226 Barnes. It's about ammo history, plinking, target shooting, and the quest for the one-hole group.

British Military Martini, Treatise on the, Vol. 1, by B.A. Temple and Ian Skennerton, I.D.S.A. Books, Piqua, OH, 1983. 256 pp., 114 illus. $40.00.

British Military Martini, Treatise on the, Vol. 2, by B.A. Temple and Ian Skennerton, I.D.S.A. Books, Piqua, OH, 1989. 213 pp., 135 illus. $40.00.

British .22RF Training Rifles, by Dennis Lewis and Robert Washburn, Excaliber Publications, Latham, NY, 1993. 64 pp., illus. Paper covers. $10.95.
The story of Britain's training rifles from the early Aiming Tube models to the post-WWII trainers.

Classic Sporting Rifles, by Christopher Austyn, Safari Press, Huntington Beach, CA, 1997. 128 pp., illus. $50.00.
As the head of the gun department at Christie's Auction House the author examines the "best" rifles built over the last 150 years.

The Complete AR15/M16 Sourcebook, by Duncan Long, Paladin Press, Boulder, CO, 1993. 232 pp., illus. Paper covers. $35.00.
The latest development of the AR15/M16 and the many spin-offs now available, selective-fire conversion systems for the 1990s, the vast selection of new accessories.

The Competitive AR15: The Mouse That Roared, by Glenn Zediker, Zediker Publishing, Oxford, MS, 1999. 286 pp., illustrated. Paper covers. $29.95.
A thorough and detailed study of the newest precision rifle sensation.

Complete Book of U.S. Sniping, by Peter R. Senich, Paladin Press, Boulder, CO, 1997, 8 1/2 x 11, hardcover, photos, 288 pp. $52.95
Trace American sniping materiel from its infancy to today's sophisticated systems with this volume, compiled from Senich's early books, Limited War Sniping and The Pictorial History of U.S. Sniping. Almost 400 photos, plus information gleaned from official documents and military archives, pack this informative work.

The Complete M1 Garand, by Jim Thompson, Paladin Press, Boulder, CO, 1998. 160 pp., illustrated. Paper cover. $25.00.
A guide for the shooter and collector, heavily illustrated.

Exploded Long Gun Drawings, The Gun Digest Book of, edited by Harold A. Murtz, DBI Books, a division of Krause Publications, Iola, WI, 512 pp., illus. Paper covers. $20.95.
Containing almost 500 rifle and shotgun exploded drawings. An invaluable aid to both professionals and hobbyists.

The FAL Rifle, by R. Blake Stevens and Jean van Rutten, Collector Grade Publications, Cobourg, Canada, 1993. 848 pp., illus. $129.95.
Originally published in three volumes, this classic edition covers North American, UK and Commonwealth and the metric FAL's.

The Fighting Rifle, by Chuck Taylor, Paladin Press, Boulder, CO, 1983. 184 pp., illus. Paper covers. $25.00.
The difference between assault and battle rifles and auto and light machine guns.

Firearms Assembly/Disassembly Part III: Rimfire Rifles, Revised Edition, The Gun Digest Book of, by J. B. Wood, DBI Books, a division of Krause Publications, Iola, WI, 1994. 480 pp., illus. $19.95.
Covers 65 popular rimfires plus over 100 variants, all cross-referenced in the index.

Firearms Assembly/Disassembly Part IV: Centerfire Rifles, Revised Edition, The Gun Digest Book of, by J.B. Wood, DBI Books, a division of Krause Publications, Iola, WI, 1991. 480 pp., illus. Paper covers. $19.95.
Covers 54 popular centerfire rifles plus 300 variants. The most comprehensive and professional presentation available to either hobbyist or gunsmith.

The FN-FAL Rifle, et al, by Duncan Long, Delta Press, El Dorado, AR, 1998. 148 pp., illustrated. Paper covers. $18.95.
A comprehensive study of one of the classic assault weapons of all times. Detailed descriptions of the basic models plus the myriad of variants that evolved as a result of its universal acceptance.

Forty Years with the .45-70, second edition, revised and expanded, by Paul A. Matthews, Wolfe Publishing Co., Prescott, AZ, 1997. 184 pp., illus. Paper covers. $14.95.
This book is pure gun lore-lore of the .45-70. It not only contains a history of the cartridge, but also years of the author's personal experiences.

F.N.-F.A.L. Auto Rifles, Desert Publications, Cornville, AZ, 1981. 130 pp., illus. Paper covers. $16.95.
A definitive study of one of the free world's finest combat rifles.

German Sniper 1914-1945, by Peter R. Senich, Paladin Press, Boulder, CO, 1997 8 1/2 x 11, hardcover, photos, 468 pp. $69.95.
The complete story of Germany's sniping arms development through both World Wars. Presents more than 600 photos of Mauser 98's, Selbstladegewehr 41s and 43s, optical sights by Goerz, Zeiss, etc., plus German snipers in action. An exceptional hardcover collector's edition for serious military historians everywhere.

The Hammerless Double Rifle, by Alexander Gray, Wolfe Publishing Co., Prescott, AZ, 1994. 154 pp., illus. $39.50.
The history, design, construction and maintenance are explored for a better understanding of these firearms.

Hints and Advice on Rifle-Shooting, by Private R. McVittie with new introductory material by W.S. Curtis, W.S. Curtis Publishers, Ltd., Clwyd, England, 1993. 32 pp. Paper covers. $10.00.
A reprint of the original 1886 London edition.

How-To's for the Black Powder Cartridge Rifle Shooter, by Paul A. Matthews, Wolfe Publishing Co., Prescott, AZ, 1996. 136 pp., illus. Paper covers. $22.50.
Practices and procedures used in the reloading and shooting of blackpowder cartridges.

Hunting with the .22, by C.S. Landis, R&R Books, Livonia, NY, 1995. 429 pp., illus. $35.00.
A reprinting of the classical work on .22 rifles.

The Hunting Rifle, by Townsend Whelen, Wolfe Publishing Co., Prescott, Arizona, 1984. 463 pp., illustrated. $24.95.
A thoroughly dependable coverage on the materiel and marksmanhip with relation to the sportsman's rifle for big game.

Illustrated Handbook of Rifle Shooting, by A.L. Russell, Museum Restoration Service, Alexandria Bay, NY, 1992. 194 pp., illus. $24.50.
A new printing of the 1869 edition by one of the leading military marksman of the day.

Know Your M1 Garand, by E. J. Hoffschmidt, Blacksmith Corp., Southport, CT, 1975, 84 pp., illus. Paper covers. $9.95.
Facts about America's most famous infantry weapon. Covers test and experimental models, Japanese and Italian copies, National Match models.

Know Your Ruger 10/22 Carbine, by William E. Workman, Blacksmith Corp., Chino Valley, AZ, 1991. 96 pp., illus. Paper covers. $9.95.
The story and facts about the most popular 22 autoloader ever made.

The Lee Enfield No. 1 Rifles, by Alan M. Petrillo, Excaliber Publications, Latham, NY, 1992. 64 pp., illus. Paper covers. $10.95.
Highlights the SMLE rifles from the Mark 1-VI.

The Lee Enfield Number 4 Rifles, by Alan M. Petrillo, Excalibur Publications, Latham, NY, 1992. 64 pp., illus. Paper covers. $10.95.
A pocket-sized, bare-bones reference devoted entirely to the .303 World War II and Korean War vintage service rifle.

The Lee Enfield Story, by Ian Skennerton, I.D.S.A. Books, Piqua, OH, 1993. 504 pp., nearly 1,000 illus. $59.95.

Legendary Sporting Rifles, by Sam Fadala, Stoeger Publishing Co., So. Hackensack, NJ, 1992. 288 pp., illus. Paper covers. $16.95.
Covers a vast span of time and technology beginning with the Kentucky Long-rifle.

The Li'l M1 .30 Cal. Carbine, by Duncan Long, Desert Publications, El Dorado, AZ, 1995. 203 pp., illus. Paper covers. $14.95.
Traces the history of this little giant from its original creation.

Make It Accurate: Get the Maximum Performance from Your Hunting Rifle, by Craig Boddington, Safari Press Publications, Huntington Beach, CA, 1999. 224 pp., illustrated. $24.95.
Tips on how to select the rifle, cartridge, and scope best suited to your needs. A must-have for any hunter who wants to improve his shot.

Mauser Smallbore Sporting, Target and Training Rifles, by Jon Speed, Collector Grade Publications, Inc., Cobourg, Ont., Canada, 1998. 372 pp., illustrated. $67.50.
The history of all the smallbore sporting, target and training rifles produced by the legendary Mauser-Werke of Obendorf am Neckar.

Mauser: Original-Oberndorf Sporting Rifles, by Jon Speed, Collector Grade Publications, Inc., Cobourg, Ont., Canada, 1997. 508 pp., illustrated. $89.95.
The most exhaustive study ever published of the design origins and manufacturing history of the original Oberndorf Mauser Sporter.

M14/M14A1 Rifles and Rifle Markmanship, Desert Publications, El Dorado, AZ, 1995. 236 pp., illus. Paper covers. $18.95.
Contains a detailed description of the M14 and M14A1 rifles and their general characteristics, procedures for disassembly and assembly, operating and functioning of the rifles, etc.

THE ARMS LIBRARY

The M14 Owner's Guide and Match Conditioning Instructions, by Scott A. Duff and John M. Miller, Scott A. Duff Publications, Export, PA, 1996. 180 pp., illus. Paper covers. $19.95.

Traces the history and development from the T44 through the adoption and production of the M14 rifle.

The M-14 Rifle, facsimile reprint of FM 23-8, Desert Publications, Cornville, AZ, 50 pp., illus. Paper $11.95.

Well illustrated and informative reprint covering the M-14 and M-14E2.

The M14-Type Rifle: A Shooter's and Collector's Guide, by Joe Poyer, North Cape Publications, Tustin, CA, 1997. 82 pp., illus. Paper covers. $18.95.

Covers the history and development, commercial copies, cleaning and maintenance instructions, and targeting and shooting.

The M16/AR15 Rifle, by Joe Poyer, North Cape Publications, Tustin, CA, 1998. 150 pp., illustrated. Paper covers. $19.95.

From its inception as the first American assault battle rifle to the firing lines of the National Matches, the M16/AR15 rifle in all its various models and guises has made a significant impact on the American rifleman.

Military Bolt Action Rifles, 1841-1918, by Donald B. Webster, Museum Restoration Service, Alexander Bay, NY, 1993. 150 pp., illus. $34.50.

A photographic survey of the principal rifles and carbines of the European and Asiatic powers of the last half of the 19th century and the first years of the 20th century.

The Mini-14, by Duncan Long, Paladin Press, Boulder, CO, 1987. 120 pp., illus. Paper covers. $17.00.

History of the Mini-14, the factory-produced models, specifications, accessories, suppliers, and much more.

Mr. Single Shot's Book of Rifle Plans, by Frank de Haas, Mark de Haas, Orange City, IA, 1996. 85 pp., illus. Paper covers. $22.50.

Contains complete and detailed drawings, plans and instructions on how to build four different and unique breech-loading single shot rifles of the author's own proven design.

M1 Carbine Owner's Manual, M1, M2 & M3 .30 Caliber Carbines, Firepower Publications, Cornville, AZ, 1984. 102 pp., illus. Paper covers. $16.95.

The complete book for the owner of an M1 Carbine.

The M1 Garand Serial Numbers & Data Sheets, by Scott A. Duff, Scott A. Duff, Export, PA, 1995. 101 pp. Paper covers. $9.95.

This pocket reference book includes serial number tables and data sheets on the Springfield Armory, Gas Trap Rifles, Gas Port Rifles, Winchester Repeating Arms, International Harvester and H&R Arms Co. and more.

Modern Sniper Rifles, by Duncan Long, Paladin Press, Boulder, CO, 1997, 8 1/2 x 11, soft cover, photos, illus., 120 pp. $20.00

Noted weapons expert Duncan Long describes the .22 LR, single-shot, bolt-action, semiautomatic and large-caliber rifles that can be used for sniping purposes, including the U.S. M21, Ruger Mini-14, AUG and HK-94SG1. These and other models are evaluated on the basis of their features, accuracy, reliability and handiness in the field. The author also looks at the best scopes, ammunition and accessories.

More Single Shot Rifles and Actions, by Frank de Haas, Mark de Haas, Orange City, IA, 1996. 146 pp., illus. Paper covers. $22.50.

Covers 45 different single shot rifles. Includes the history plus photos, drawings and personal comments.

The Muzzle-Loading Rifle...Then and Now, by Walter M. Cline, National Muzzle Loading Rifle Association, Friendship, IN, 1991. 161 pp., illus. $32.00.

This extensive compilation of the muzzleloading rifle exhibits accumulative preserved data concerning the development of the "hallowed old arms of the Southern highlands."

The No. 4 (T) Sniper Rifle: An Armourer's Perspective, by Peter Laidler with Ian Skennerton, I.D.S.A. Books, Piqua, OH, 1993. 125 pp., 75 illus. Paper covers. $19.95.

Notes on Rifle-Shooting, by Henry William Heaton, reprinted with a new introduction by W.S. Curtis, W.S. Curtis Publishers, Ltd., Clwyd, England, 1993. 89 pp. $19.95.

A reprint of the 1864 London edition. Captain Heaton was one of the great rifle shots from the earliest days of the Volunteer Movement.

The Official SKS Manual, Translation by Major James F. Gebhardt (Ret.), Paladin Press, Boulder, CO, 1997. 96 pp., illus. Paper covers. $16.00.

This Soviet military manual covering the widely distributed SKS is now available in English.

The Pennsylvania Rifle, by Samuel E. Dyke, Sutter House, Lititz, PA, 1975. 61 pp., illus. Paper covers. $10.00.

History and development, from the hunting rifle of the Germans who settled the area. Contains a full listing of all known Lancaster, PA, gunsmiths from 1729 through 1815.

Police Rifles, by Richard Fairburn, Paladin Press, Boulder, CO, 1994. 248 pp., illus. Paper covers. $35.00.

Selecting the right rifle for street patrol and special tactical situations.

The Poor Man's Sniper Rifle, by D. Boone, Paladin Press, Boulder, CO, 1995. 152 pp., illus. Paper covers. $18.95.

Here is a complete plan for converting readily available surplus military rifles to high-performance sniper weapons.

A Potpourri of Single Shot Rifles and Actions, by Frank de Haas, Mark de Haas, Ridgeway, MO, 1993. 153 pp., illus. Paper covers. $22.50.

The author's 6th book on non-bolt-action single shots. Covers more than 40 single-shot rifles in historical and technical detail.

Precision Shooting with the M1 Garand, by Roy Baumgardner, Precision Shooting, Inc., Manchester, CT, 1999. 142 pp., illustrated. Paper covers. $12.95.

Starts off with the ever popular ten-article series on accurizing the M1 that originally appeared in Precision Shooting in the 1993-95 era. There follows nine more Baumgardner authored articles on the M1 Garand and finally a 1999 updating chapter.

The Remington 700, by John F. Lacy, Taylor Publishing Co., Dallas, TX, 1990. 208 pp., illus. $44.95.

Covers the different models, limited editions, chamberings, proofmarks, serial numbers, military models, and much more.

The Revolving Rifles, by Edsall James, Pioneer Press, Union City, TN, 1975. 23 pp., illus. Paper covers. $5.00.

Valuable information on revolving cylinder rifles, from the earliest matchlock forms to the latest models of Colt and Remington.

Rifle Guide, by Sam Fadala, Stoeger Publishing Co., S. Hackensack, NJ, 1993. 288 pp., illus. Paper covers. $16.95.

This comprehensive, fact-filled book beckons to both the seasoned rifleman as well as the novice shooter.

The Rifle: Its Development for Big-Game Hunting, by S.R. Truesdell, Safari Press, Huntington Beach, CA, 1992. 274 pp., illus. $35.00.

The full story of the development of the big-game rifle from 1834-1946.

Riflesmithing, The Gun Digest Book of, by Jack Mitchell, DBI Books, a division of Krause Publications, Iola, WI, 1982. 256 pp., illus. Paper covers. $16.95.

Covers tools, techniques, designs, finishing wood and metal, custom alterations.

Rifles of the World, 2nd Edition, edited by John Walter, DBI Books, a division of Krause Publications, Iola, WI, 1998. 384 pp., illus. $24.95.

The definitive guide to the world's centerfire and rimfire rifles.

Ned H. Roberts and the Schuetzen Rifle, edited by Gerald O. Kelver, Brighton, CO, 1982. 99 pp., illus. $13.95.

A compilation of the writings of Major Ned H. Roberts which appeared in various gun magazines.

Schuetzen Rifles, History and Loading, by Gerald O. Kelver, Gerald O. Kelver, Publisher, Brighton, CO, 1972. Illus. $13.95.

Reference work on these rifles, their bullets, loading, telescopic sights, accuracy, etc. A limited, numbered ed.

Shooting the Blackpowder Cartridge Rifle, by Paul A. Matthews, Wolfe Publishing Co., Prescott, AZ, 1994. 129 pp., illus. Paper covers. $22.50.

A general discourse on shooting the blackpowder cartridge rifle and the procedure required to make a particular rifle perform.

Shooting Lever Guns of the Old West, by Mike Venturino, MLV Enterprises, Livingston, MT, 1999. 300 pp., illustrated. Paper covers. $27.95.

Shooting the lever action type repeating rifles of our American west.

Single Shot Rifles and Actions, by Frank de Haas, Orange City, IA, 1990. 352 pp., illus. Soft covers. $27.00.

The definitive book on over 60 single shot rifles and actions.

Sixty Years of Rifles, by Paul A. Matthews, Wolfe Publishing Co., Prescott, AZ, 1991. 224 pp., illus. $19.50.

About rifles and the author's experience and love affair with shooting and hunting.

S.L.R.—Australia's F.N. F.A.L. by Ian Skennerton and David Balmer, I.D.S.A. Books, Piqua, OH, 1989. 124 pp., 100 illus. Paper covers. $19.50.

Small Arms Identification Series, No. 2—.303 Rifle, No. 4 Marks I, & I*, Marks 1/2, 1/3 & 2, by Ian Skennerton, I.D.S.A. Books, Piqua, OH, 1994. 48 pp. $9.50.

Small Arms Identification Series, No. 3—9mm Austen Mk I & 9mm Owen Mk I Sub-Machine Guns, by Ian Skennerton, I.D.S.A. Books, Piqua, OH, 1994. 48 pp. $9.50.

Small Arms Identification Series, No. 4—.303 Rifle, No. 5 Mk I, by Ian Skennerton, I.D.S.A. Books, Piqua, OH, 1994. 48 pp. $9.50.

Small Arms Identification Series, No. 5—.303-in. Bren Light Machine Gun, by Ian Skennerton, I.D.S.A. Books, Piqua, OH, 1994. 48 pp. $9.50.

Small Arms Series, No. 1 DeLisle's Commando Carbine, by Ian Skennerton, I.D.S.A. Books, Piqua, OH, 1988. 32 pp., 24 illus. $9.00.

Small Arms Identification Series, No. 1—.303 Rifle, No. 1 S.M.L.E. Marks III and III*, by Ian Skennerton, I.D.S.A. Books, Piqua, OH, 1981. 48 pp. $9.50.

Sporting Rifle Takedown & Reassembly Guide, 2nd Edition, by J.B. Wood, DBI Books, a division of Krause Publications, Iola, WI, 1997. 480 pp., illus. $19.95.

An updated edition of the reference guide for anyone who wants to properly care for their sporting rifle. (Available September 1997)

The Springfield Rifle M1903, M1903A1, M1903A3, M1903A4, Desert Publications, Cornville, AZ, 1982. 100 pp., illus. Paper covers. $12.00.

Covers every aspect of disassembly and assembly, inspection, repair and maintenance.

Still More Single Shot Rifles, by James J. Grant, Pioneer Press, Union City, TN, 1995. 211 pp., illus. $29.95.

This is Volume Four in a series of Single-Shot Rifles by America's foremost authority. It gives more in-depth information on those single-shot rifles which were presented in the first three books.

The Sturm, Ruger 10/22 Rifle and .44 Magnum Carbine, by Duncan Long, Paladin Press, Boulder, CO, 1988. 108 pp., illus. Paper covers. $15.00.

An in-depth look at both weapons detailing the elegant simplicity of the Ruger design. Offers specifications, troubleshooting procedures and ammunition recommendations.

The Tactical Rifle, by Gabriel Suarez, Paladin Press, Boulder, CO, 1999. 264 pp., illustrated. Paper covers. $25.00.

The precision tool for urban police operations.

Target Rifle in Australia, by J.E. Corcoran, R&R, Livonia, NY, 1996. 160 pp., illus. $40.00.

A most interesting study of the evolution of these rifles from 1860 - 1900. British rifles from the percussion period through the early smokeless era are discussed.

REFERENCE

THE ARMS LIBRARY

To the Dreams of Youth: The .22 Caliber Single Shot Winchester Rifle, by Herbert Houze, Krause Publications, Iola, WI, 1993. 192 pp., illus. $34.95.
A thoroughly researched history of the 22-caliber Winchester single shot rifle, including interesting photographs.

The Ultimate in Rifle Accuracy, by Glenn Newick, Stoeger Publishing Co., Wayne, N.J., 1999. 205 pp., illustrated. Paper covers. $11.95.
This handbook contains the information you need to extract the best performance from your rifle.

U.S. Marine Corps AR15/M16 A2 Manual, reprinted by Desert Publications, El Dorado, AZ, 1993. 262 pp., illus. Paper covers. $16.95.
A reprint of TM05538C-23&P/2, August, 1987. The A-2 manual for the Colt AR15/M16.

U.S. Rifle M14—From John Garand to the M21, by R. Blake Stevens, Collector Grade Publications, Inc., Toronto, Canada, revised second edition, 1991. 350 pp., illus. $49.50.
A classic, in-depth examination of the development, manufacture and fielding of the last wood-and-metal ("lock, stock, and barrel") battle rifle to be issued to U.S. troops.

War Baby!: The U.S. Caliber 30 Carbine, Volume I, by Larry Ruth, Collector Grade Publications, Toronto, Canada, 1992. 512 pp., illus. $69.95.
Volume 1 of the in-depth story of the phenomenally popular U.S. caliber 30 carbine. Concentrates on design and production of the military 30 carbine during World War II.

War Baby Comes Home: The U.S. Caliber 30 Carbine, Volume 2, by Larry Ruth, Collector Grade Pulications, Toronto, Canada, 1993. 386 pp., illus. $49.95.
The triumphant competion of Larry Ruth's two-volume in-depth series on the most popular U.S. military small arm in history.

The Winchester Model 52, Perfection in Design, by Herbert G. Houze, Krause Publicaitons, Iola, WI, 1997. 192 pp., illus. $34.95.
This book covers the complete story of this technically superior gun.

The Winchester Model 94: The First 100 Years, by Robert C. Renneberg, Krause Publications, Iola, WI, 1991. 208 pp., illus. $34.95.
Covers the design and evolution from the early years up to today.

Winchester Slide-Action Rifles, Volume I: Model 1890 and Model 1906 by Ned Schwing, Krause Publications, Iola, WI. 352 pp., illus. $39.95
Traces the history through word and picture in this chronolgy of the Model 1890 and 1906.

Winchester Slide-Action Rifles, Volume II: Model 61 & Model 62 by Ned Schwing, Krause Publications, Iola, WI. 256 pp., illus. $34.95
Historical look complete with markings, stampings and engraving.

SHOTGUNS

Advanced Combat Shotgun: The Stress Fire Concept, by Massad Ayoob, Police Bookshelf, Concord, NH, 1993. 197 pp., illus. Paper covers. $9.95.
Advanced combat shotgun fighting for police.

Best Guns, by Michael McIntosh, Countrysport Press, Selma, AL, 1999, revised edition. 418 pp. $39.00.
Combines the best shotguns ever made in America with information on British and Continental makers.

The Better Shot, by Ken Davies, Quiller Press, London, England, 1992. 136 pp., illus. $39.95.
Step-by-step shotgun technique with Holland and Holland.

The British Shotgun, Volume 1, 1850-1870, by I.M. Crudington and D.J. Baker, Barrie & Jenkins, London, England, 1979. 256 pp., illus. $65.00.
An attempt to trace, as accurately as is now possible, the evolution of the shotgun during its formative years in Great Britain.

Boothroyd on British Shotguns, by Geoffrey Boothroyd, Sand Lake Press, Amity, OR, 1996. 221 pp., illus. plus a 32 page reproduction of the 1914 Webley & Scott catalog. A limited, numbered edition. $34.95.
Based on articles by the author that appeared in the British Publication *Shooting Times & Country Magazine.*

The British Over-and-Under Shotgun, by Geoffrey and Susan Boothroyd, Sand Lake Press, Amity, OR, 1996. 137 pp., illus. $34.95.
Historical outline of the development of the O/U shotgun with individual chapters devoted to the twenty-two British makers.

The Browning Superposed: John M. Browning's Last Legacy, by Ned Schwing, Krause Publications, Iola, WI, 1996. 496 pp., illus. $49.95.
An exclusive story of the man, the company and the best-selling over-and-under shotgun in North America.

Clay Target Handbook, by Jerry Meyer, Lyons & Buford, Publisher, New York, NY, 1993. 182 pp., illus. $22.95.
Contains in-depth, how-to-do-it information on trap, skeet, sporting clays, international trap, international skeet and clay target games played around the country.

Clay Target Shooting, by Paul Bentley, A&C Black, London, England, 1987. 144 pp., illus. $25.00.
Practical book on clay target shooting written by a very successful international competitor, providing valuable professional advice and instruction for shooters of all disciplines.

A Collector's Guide to United States Combat Shotguns, by Bruce N. Canfield, Andrew Mowbray Inc., Publishers, Lincoln, RI, 1993. 184 pp., illus. Paper covers. $24.00.
Full coverage of the combat shotgun, from the earliest examples to the Gulf War and beyond.

Combat Shotgun and Submachine Gun, "A Special Weapons Analysis" by Chuck Taylor, Paladin Press, Boulder, CO, 1997, soft cover, photos, 176 pp. $25.00.
From one of America's top shooting instructors comes an analysis of two controversial, misunderstood and misemployed small arms. Hundreds of photos detail field-testing of both, basic and advanced training drills, tactical rules, gun accessories and modifications. Loading procedures, carrying and fighting positions and malfunction clearance drills are included to promote weapon effectiveness.

Cradock on Shotguns, by Chris Cradock, Banford Press, London, England, 1989. 200 pp., illus. $45.00.
A definitive work on the shotgun by a British expert on shotguns.

The Defensive Shotgun, by Louis Awerbuck, S.W.A.T. Publications, Cornville, AZ, 1989. 77 pp., illus. Soft covers. $14.95.
Cuts through the myths concerning the shotgun and its attendant ballistic effects.

The Double Shotgun, by Don Zutz, Winchester Press, Piscataway, NJ, 1985. 304 pp., illus. $22.95.
Revised, updated, expanded edition of the history and development of the world's classic sporting firearms.

Finding the Extra Target, by Coach John R. Linn & Stephen A. Blumenthal, Shotgun Sports, Inc., Auburn, CA, 1989. 126 pp., illus. Paper covers. $14.95.
The ultimate training guide for all the clay target sports.

Fine Gunmaking: Double Shotguns, by Steven Dodd Hughes, Krause Publications Iola, WI, 1998. 167 pp., illustrated. $34.95.
An in-depth look at the creation of fine shotguns.

Firearms Assembly/Disassembly, Part V: Shotguns, Revised Edition, The Gun Digest Book of, by J.B. Wood, DBI Books, a division of Krause Publications, Iola, WI, 1992. 480 pp., illus. Paper covers. $19.95.
Covers 46 popular shotguns plus over 250 variants. The most comprehensive and professional presentation available to either hobbyist or gunsmith.

A.H. Fox "The Finest Gun in the World", revised and enlarged edition, by Michael McIntosh, Countrysport, Inc., New Albany, OH, 1995. 408 pp., illus. $49.00.
The first detailed history of one of America's finest shotguns.

Game Shooting, by Robert Churchill, Countrysport Press, Selma, AL, 1998. 258 pp., illus. $30.00.
The basis for every shotgun instructional technique devised and the foundation for all wingshooting and the game of sporting clays.

The Golden Age of Shotgunning, by Bob Hinman, Wolfe Publishing Co., Inc., Prescott, AZ, 1982. $22.50.
A valuable history of the late 1800s detailing that fabulous period of development in shotguns, shotshells and shotgunning.

Grand Old Shotguns, by Don Zutz, Shotgun Sports Magazine, Auburn, CA, 1995. 136 pp., illus. Paper covers. $19.95.
A study of the great smoothbores, their history and how and why they were discontinued. Find out the most sought-after and which were the best shooters.

Gun Digest Book of Sporting Clays, 2nd Edition, edited by Harold A. Murtz, Krause Publications, Iola, WI, 1999. 256 pp., illus. Paper covers. $21.95.
A concise Gun Digest book that covers guns, ammo, chokes, targets and course layouts so you'll stay a step ahead.

The Gun Review Book, by Michael McIntosh, Countrysport Press, Selman, AL, 1999. Paper covers. $19.95.
Compiled here for the first time are McIntosh's popular gun reviews from Shooting Sportsman; The Magazine of Wingshooting and Fine Shotguns. The author traces the history of gunmakes, then examines, analyzes, and critique the fine shotguns of England, Continental Europe and the United States.

Hartman on Skeet, by Barney Hartman, Stackpole Books, Harrisburg, PA, 1973. 143 pp., illus. $19.95.
A definitive book on Skeet shooting by a pro.

The Heyday of the Shotgun, by David Baker, Safari Press, Inc., Huntington Beach, CA, 2000. 160 pp., illustrated. $39.95.
The art of the gunmaker at the turn of the last century when British craftsmen brought forth the finest guns ever made.

The Italian Gun, by Steve Smith & Laurie Morrow, wilderness Adventures, Gallatin Gateway, MT, 1997. 325 pp., illus. $49.95.
The first book ever written entirely in English for American enthusiasts who own, aspire to own, or simply admire Italian guns.

The Ithaca Featherlight Repeater; the Best Gun Going, by Walter C. Snyder, Southern Pines, NC, 1998. 300 pp., illus. $89.95.
Describes the complete history of each model of the legendary Ithaca Model 37 and Model 87 Repeaters from their conception in 1930 throught 1997.

The Ithaca Gun Company from the Beginning, by Walter C. Snyder, Cook & Uline Publishing Co., Southern Pines, NC, 2nd Edition, 1999. 384 pp., illustrated in color and black and white. $90.00.
The entire family of Ithaca Gun Company products is described along with new historical information and the serial number/date of manufacturing listing has been improved.

L.C. Smith Shotguns, by Lt. Col. William S. Brophy, The Gun Room Press, Highland Park, NJ, 1979. 244 pp., illus. $35.00.
The first work on this very important American gun and manufacturing company.

The Little Trapshooting Book, by Frank Little, Shotgun Sports Magazine, Auburn, CA, 1994. 168 pp., illus. Paper covers. $19.95.
Packed with know-how from one of the greatest trapshooters of all time.

THE ARMS LIBRARY

Lock, Stock, and Barrel, by C. Adams & R. Braden, Safari Press, Huntington Beach, CA, 1996. 254 pp., illus. $24.95.

The process of making a best grade English gun from a lump of steel and a walnut tree trunk to the ultimate product plus practical advise on consistent field shooting with a double gun.

Mental Training for the Shotgun Sports, by Michael J. Keyes, Shotgun Sports, Auburn, CA, 1996. 160 pp., illus. Paper covers. $24.95.

The most comprehensive book ever published on what it takes to shoot winning scores at trap, Skeet and Sporting Clays.

The Winchester Model Twelve, by George Madis, David Madis, Dallas, TX, 1984. 176 pp., illus. $24.95.

A definitive work on this famous American shotgun.

The Model 12, 1912-1964, by Dave Riffle, Dave Riffle, Ft. Meyers, FL, 1995. 274 pp., illus. $49.95.

The story of the greatest hammerless repeating shotgun ever built.

More Shotguns and Shooting, by Michael McIntosh, Countrysport Books, Selma, AL, 1998. 256 pp., illustrated. $30.00.

From specifics of shotguns to shooting your way out of a slump, it's McIntosh at his best.

The Mysteries of Shotgun Patterns, by George G. Oberfell and Charles E. Thompson, Oklahoma State University Press, Stillwater, OK, 1982. 164 pp., illus. Paper covers. $25.00.

Shotgun ballistics for the hunter in non-technical language.

Parker Guns "The Old Reliable", by Ed Muderiak, Safari Press, Inc., Huntington Beach, CA, 1997. 325 pp., illus. $40.00.

A look at the small beginnings, the golden years, and the ultimate decline of the most famous of all American shotgun manufacturers.

Positive Shooting, by Michael Yardley, Safari Press, Huntington Beach, CA, 1995. 160 pp., illus. $30.00.

This book will provide the shooter with a sound foundation from which to develop an effective, personal technique that can dramatically improve shooting performance.

Reloading for Shotgunners, 4th Edition, by Kurt D. Fackler and M.L. McPherson, DBI Books, a division of Krause Publications, Iola, WI, 1997. 320 pp., illus. Paper covers. $19.95.

Expanded reloading tables with over 11,000 loads. Bushing charts for every major press and component maker. All new presentation on all aspects of shotshell reloading by two of the top experts in the field. (Available October 1997.)

Remington Double Shotguns, by Charles G. Semer, Denver, CO, 1997. 617 pp., illus. $60.00.

This book deals with the entire production and all grades of double shotguns made by Remington during the period of their production 1873-1910.

75 Years with the Shotgun, by C.T. (Buck) Buckman, Valley Publ., Fresno, CA, 1974. 141 pp., illus. $10.00.

An expert hunter and trapshooter shares experiences of a lifetime.

The Shooting Field with Holland & Holland, by Peter King, Quiller Press, London, England, new & enlarged edition, 1990. 184 pp., illus. $40.00.

The story of a company which has produced excellence in all aspects of gunmaking.

The Shotgun in Combat, by Tony Lesce, Desert Publications, Cornville, AZ, 1979. 148 pp., illus. Paper covers. $14.00.

A history of the shotgun and its use in combat.

Shotgun Digest, 4th Edition, edited by Jack Lewis, DBI Books, a division of Krause Publications, Iola, WI, 1993. 256 pp., illus. Paper covers. $17.95.

A look at what's happening with shotguns and shotgunning today.

The Shotgun Encyclopedia, by John Taylor, Safari Press, Inc., Huntington Beach, CA, 2000. 260 pp., illustrated. $34.95.

A comprehensive reference work on all aspects of shotguns and shotgun shooting.

Shotgun Gunsmithing, The Gun Digest Book of, by Ralph Walker, DBI Books, a division of Krause Publications, Iola, WI, 1983. 256 pp., illus. Paper covers. $16.95.

The principles and practices of repairing, individualizing and accurizing modern shotguns by one of the world's premier shotgun gunsmiths.

The Shotgun: History and Development, by Geoffrey Boothroyd, Safari Press, Huntington Beach, CA, 1995. 240 pp., illus. $35.00.

The first volume in a series that traces the development of the British shotgun from the 17th century onward.

The Shotgun Handbook, by Mike George, The Croswood Press, London, England, 1999. 128 pp., illus. $35.00.

For all shotgun enthusiasts, this detailed guide ranges from design and selection of a gun to adjustment, cleaning, and maintenance.

Shotgun Stuff, by Don Zutz, Shotgun Sports, Inc., Auburn, CA, 1991. 172 pp., illus. Paper covers. $19.95.

This book gives shotgunners all the "stuff" they need to achieve better performance and get more enjoyment from their favorite smoothbore.

Shotgunner's Notebook: The Advice and Reflections of a Wingshooter, by Gene Hill, Countrysport Press, Traverse City, MI, 1990. 192 pp., illus. $25.00.

Covers the shooting, the guns and the miscellany of the sport.

Shotgunning: The Art and the Science, by Bob Brister, Winchester Press, Piscataway, NJ, 1976. 321 pp., illus. $18.95.

Hundreds of specific tips and truly novel techniques to improve the field and target shooting of every shotgunner.

Shotgunning Trends in Transition, by Don Zutz, Wolfe Publishing Co., Prescott, AZ, 1990. 314 pp., illus. $29.50.

This book updates American shotgunning from post WWII to present.

Shotguns and Cartridges for Game and Clays, by Gough Thomas, edited by Nigel Brown, A & C Black, Ltd., Cambs, England, 1989. 256 pp., illus. Soft covers. $24.95.

Gough Thomas' well-known and respected book for game and clay pigeon shooters in a thoroughly up-dated edition.

Shotguns and Gunsmiths: The Vintage Years, by Geoffrey Boothroyd, Safari Press, Huntington Beach, CA, 1995. 240 pp., illus. $35.00.

A fascinating insight into the lives and skilled work of gunsmiths who helped develop the British shotgun during the Victorian and Edwardian eras.

Shotguns and Shooting, by Michael McIntosh, Countrysport Press, New Albany, OH, 1995. 258 pp., illus. $35.00.

The art of guns and gunmaking, this book is a celebration no lover of fine doubles should miss.

Shotguns for Wingshooting, by John Barsness, DBI Books, a division of Krause Publications, Inc., Iola, WI, 1999. 208 pp., illustrated. $49.95.

Detailed information on all styles of shotgun. How to select the correct ammunition for specific hunting applications.

Sidelocks & Boxlocks, by Geoffrey Boothroyd, Sand Lake Press, Amity, OR, 1991. 271 pp., illus. $24.95.

The story of the classic British shotgun.

Spanish Best: The Fine Shotguns of Spain, by Terry Wieland, Countrysport, Inc., Traverse City, MI, 1994. 264 pp., illus. $45.00.

A practical source of information for owners of Spanish shotguns and a guide for those considering buying a used shotgun.

The Sporting Clay Handbook, by Jerry Meyer, Lyons and Burford Publishers, New York, NY, 1990. 140 pp., illus. Soft covers. $17.95.

Introduction to the fastest growing, and most exciting, gun game in America.

Streetsweepers, "The Complete Book of Combat Shotguns", by Duncan Long, Paladin Press, Boulder, CO, 1997, soft cover, 63 photos, illus., appendices, 160 pp. $24.95.

Streetsweepers is the newest, most comprehensive book out on combat shotguns, covering single- and double-barreled, slide-action, semi-auto and rotary cylinder shotguns, plus a chapter on grenade launchers you can mount on your weapon and info about shotgun models not yet on the market. Noted gun writer Duncan Long also advises on which ammo to use, accessories and combat shotgun tactics.

The Tactical Shotgun, by Gabriel Suzrez, Paladin Press, Boulder, CO, 1996. 232 pp., illus. Paper covers. $25.00.

The best techniques and tactics for employing the shotgun in personal combat.

Taking More Birds, by Dan Carlisle & Dolph Adams, Lyons & Burford, New York, NY, 1993. 120 pp., illus. $19.95.

A practical guide to greater success at sporting clays and wing shooting.

Trap & Skeet Shooting, 3rd Edition, by Chris Christian, DBI Books, a division of Krause Publications, Iola, WI, 1994. 288 pp., illus. Paper covers. $17.95.

A detailed look at the contemporary world of Trap, Skeet and Sporting Clays.

Trapshooting is a Game of Opposites, by Dick Bennett, Shotgun Sports, Inc., Auburn, CA, 1996. 129 pp., illus. Paper covers. $19.95.

Discover everything you need to know about shooting trap like the pros.

Turkey Hunter's Digest, Revised Edition, by Dwain Bland, DBI Books, a division of Krause Publications, Iola, WI, 1994. 256 pp., illus. Paper covers. $17.95.

Presents no-nonsense approach to hunting all five sub-species of the North American wild turkey.

U.S. Shotguns, All Types, reprint of TM9-285, Desert Publications, Cornville, AZ, 1987. 257 pp., illus. Paper covers. $9.95.

Covers operation, assembly and disassembly of nine shotguns used by the U.S. armed forces.

U.S. Winchester Trench and Riot Guns and Other U.S. Military Combat Shotguns, by Joe Poyer, North Cape Publications, Tustin, CA, 1992. 124 pp., illus. Paper covers. $15.95.

A detailed history of the use of military shotguns, and the acquisition procedures used by the U.S. Army's Ordnance Department in both World Wars.

The Winchester Model 42, by Ned Schwing, Krause Pub., Iola, WI, 1990. 160 pp., illus. $34.95.

Behind-the-scenes story of the model 42's invention and its early development. Production totals and manufacturing dates; reference work.

Winchester Shotguns and Shotshells, by Ron Stadt, Krause Pub., Iola, WI. 288 pp., illus. $34.95.

Must-have for Winchester collectors of shotguns manufactured through 1961.

Winchester's Finest, the Model 21, by Ned Schwing, Krause Publicatons, Iola, WI, 1990. 360 pp., illus. $49.95.

The classic beauty and the interesting history of the Model 21 Winchester shotgun.

The World's Fighting Shotguns, by Thomas F. Swearengen, T.B.N. Enterprises, Alexandria, VA, 1979. 500 pp., illus. $39.95.

The complete military and police reference work from the shotgun's inception to date, with up-to-date developments.

REFERENCE

ARMS ASSOCIATIONS

UNITED STATES

ALABAMA

Alabama Gun Collectors Assn.
Secretary, P.O. Box 70965, Tuscaloosa, AL 35407

ALASKA

Alaska Gun Collectors Assn., Inc.
C.W. Floyd, Pres., 5240 Little Tree, Anchorage, AK 99507

ARIZONA

Arizona Arms Assn.
Don DeBusk, President, 4837 Bryce Ave., Glendale, AZ 85301

CALIFORNIA

California Cartridge Collectors Assn.
Rick Montgomery, 1729 Christina, Stockton, CA 95204/209-463-7216 evs.

California Waterfowl Assn.
4630 Northgate Blvd., #150, Sacramento, CA 95834

Greater Calif. Arms & Collectors Assn.
Donald L. Bullock, 8291 Carburton St., Long Beach, CA 90808-3302

Los Angeles Gun Ctg. Collectors Assn.
F.H. Ruffra, 20810 Amie Ave., Apt. #9, Torrance, CA 90503

Stock Gun Players Assn.
6038 Appian Way, Long Beach, CA, 90803

COLORADO

Colorado Gun Collectors Assn.
L.E.(Bud) Greenwald, 2553 S. Quitman St., Denver, CO 80219/303-935-3850

Rocky Mountain Cartridge Collectors Assn.
John Roth, P.O. Box 757, Conifer, CO 80433

CONNECTICUT

Ye Connecticut Gun Guild, Inc.
Dick Fraser, P.O. Box 425, Windsor, CT 06095

FLORIDA

Unified Sportsmen of Florida
P.O. Box 6565, Tallahassee, FL 32314

GEORGIA

Georgia Arms Collectors Assn., Inc.
Michael Kindberg, President, P.O. Box 277, Alpharetta, GA 30239-0277

ILLINOIS

Illinois State Rifle Assn.
P.O. Box 637, Chatsworth, IL 60921

Mississippi Valley Gun & Cartridge Coll. Assn.
Bob Filbert, P.O. Box 61, Port Byron, IL 61275/309-523-2593

Sauk Trail Gun Collectors
Gordell M. Matson, P.O. Box 1113, Milan, IL 61264

Wabash Valley Gun Collectors Assn., Inc.
Roger L. Dorsett, 2601 Willow Rd., Urbana, IL 61801/217-384-7302

INDIANA

Indiana State Rifle & Pistol Assn.
Thos. Glancy, P.O. Box 552, Chesterton, IN 46304

Southern Indiana Gun Collectors Assn., Inc.
Sheila McClary, 309 W. Monroe St., Boonville, IN 47601/812-897-3742

IOWA

Beaver Creek Plainsmen Inc.
Steve Murphy, Secy., P.O. Box 298, Bondurant, IA 50035

Central States Gun Collectors Assn.
Dennis Greischar, Box 841, Mason City, IA 50402-0841

KANSAS

Kansas Cartridge Collectors Assn.
Bob Linder, Box 84, Plainville, KS 67663

KENTUCKY

Kentuckiana Arms Collectors Assn.
Charles Billips, President, Box 1776, Louisville, KY 40201

Kentucky Gun Collectors Assn., Inc.
Ruth Johnson, Box 64, Owensboro, KY 42302/502-729-4197

LOUISIANA

Washitaw River Renegades
Sandra Rushing, P.O. Box 256, Main St., Grayson, LA 71435

MARYLAND

Baltimore Antique Arms Assn.
Mr. Cillo, 1034 Main St., Darlington, MD 21304

MASSACHUSETTS

Bay Colony Weapons Collectors, Inc.
John Brandt, Box 111, Hingham, MA 02043

Massachusetts Arms Collectors
Bruce E. Skinner, P.O. Box 31, No. Carver, MA 02355/508-866-5259

MICHIGAN

Association for the Study and Research of .22 Caliber Rimfire Cartridges
George Kass, 4512 Nakoma Dr., Okemos, MI 48864

MINNESOTA

Sioux Empire Cartridge Collectors Assn.
Bob Cameron, 14597 Glendale Ave. SE, Prior Lake, MN 55372

MISSISSIPPI

Mississippi Gun Collectors Assn.
Jack E. Swinney, P.O. Box 16323, Hattiesburg, MS 39402

MISSOURI

Greater St. Louis Cartridge Collectors Assn.
Don MacChesney, 634 Scottsdale Rd., Kirkwood, MO 63122-1109

Mineral Belt Gun Collectors Assn.
D.F. Saunders, 1110 Cleveland Ave., Monett, MO 65708

Missouri Valley Arms Collectors Assn., Inc.
L.P Brammer II, Membership Secy., P.O. Box 33033, Kansas City, MO 64114

MONTANA

Montana Arms Collectors Assn.
Dean E. Yearout, Sr., Exec. Secy., 1516 21st Ave. S., Great Falls, MT 59405

Weapons Collectors Society of Montana
R.G. Schipf, Ex. Secy., 3100 Bancroft St., Missoula, MT 59801/406-728-2995

NEBRASKA

Nebraska Cartridge Collectors Club
Gary Muckel, P.O. Box 84442, Lincoln, NE 68501

NEW HAMPSHIRE

New Hampshire Arms Collectors, Inc.
James Stamatelos, Secy., P.O. Box 5, Cambridge, MA 02139

NEW JERSEY

Englishtown Benchrest Shooters Assn.
Michael Toth, 64 Cooke Ave., Carteret, NJ 07008

Jersey Shore Antique Arms Collectors
Joe Sisia, P.O. Box 100, Bayville, NJ 08721-0100

New Jersey Arms Collectors Club, Inc.
Angus Laidlaw, Vice President, 230 Valley Rd., Montclair, NJ 07042/201-746-0939; e-mail: acclaidlaw@juno.com

NEW YORK

Iroquois Arms Collectors Assn.
Bonnie Robinson, Show Secy., P.O. Box 142, Ransomville, NY 14131/716-791-4096

Mid-State Arms Coll. & Shooters Club
Jack Ackerman, 24 S. Mountain Terr., Binghamton, NY 13903

NORTH CAROLINA

North Carolina Gun Collectors Assn.
Jerry Ledford, 3231-7th St. Dr. NE, Hickory, NC 28601

OHIO

Ohio Gun Collectors Assn.
P.O. Box 9007, Maumee, OH 43537-9007/419-897-0861; Fax:419-897-0860

Shotshell Historical and Collectors Society
Madeline Bruemmer, 3886 Dawley Rd., Ravenna, OH 44266

The Stark Gun Collectors, Inc.
William I. Gann, 5666 Waynesburg Dr., Waynesburg, OH 44688

OREGON

Oregon Arms Collectors Assn., Inc.
Phil Bailey, P.O. Box 13000-A, Portland, OR 97213-0017/503-281-6864; off.:503-281-0918

Oregon Cartridge Collectors Assn.
Boyd Northrup, P.O. Box 285, Rhododendron, OR 97049

PENNSYLVANIA

Presque Isle Gun Collectors Assn.
James Welch, 156 E. 37 St., Erie, PA 16504

SOUTH CAROLINA

Belton Gun Club, Inc.
J.K. Phillips, 195 Phillips Dr., Belton, SC 29627

Gun Owners of South Carolina
Membership Div.: William Strozier, Secretary, P.O. Box 70, Johns Island, SC 29457-0070/803-762-3240;

Fax:803-795-0711; e-mail:76053.222@compuserve.com

SOUTH DAKOTA

Dakota Territory Gun Coll. Assn., Inc.
Curt Carter, Castlewood, SD 57223

TENNESSEE

Smoky Mountain Gun Coll. Assn., Inc.
Hugh W. Yabro, President, P.O. Box 23225, Knoxville, TN 37933

Tennessee Gun Collectors Assn., Inc.
M.H. Parks, 3556 Pleasant Valley Rd., Nashville, TN 37204-3419

TEXAS

Houston Gun Collectors Assn., Inc.
P.O. Box 741429, Houston, TX 77274-1429

Texas Cartridge Collectors Assn., Inc.
Robert Mellichamp, Memb. Contact, 907 Shirkmere, Houston, TX 77008/713-869-0558

Texas Gun Collectors Assn.
Bob Eder, Pres., P.O. Box 12067, El Paso, TX 79913/915-584-8183

Texas State Rifle Assn.
1131 Rockingham Dr., Suite 101, Richardson, TX 75080-4326

VIRGINIA

Virginia Gun Collectors Assn., Inc.
Addison Hurst, Secy., 38802 Charlestown Height, Waterford, VA 20197/540-882-3543

WASHINGTON

Association of Cartridge Collectors on the Pacific Northwest
Robert Jardin, 14214 Meadowlark Drive KPN, Gig Harbor, WA 98329

Washington Arms Collectors, Inc.
Joyce Boss, P.O. Box 389, Renton, WA, 98057-0389/206-255-8410

WISCONSIN

Great Lakes Arms Collectors Assn., Inc.
Edward C. Warnke, 2913 Woodridge Lane, Waukesha, WI 53188

Wisconsin Gun Collectors Assn., Inc.
Lulita Zellmer, P.O. Box 181, Sussex, WI 53089

WYOMING

Wyoming Weapons Collectors
P.O. Box 284, Laramie, WY 82073/307-745-4652 or 745-9530

NATIONAL ORGANIZATIONS

Amateur Trapshooting Assn.
David D. Bopp, Exec. Director, 601 W. National Rd., Vandalia, OH 45377/937-898-4638; Fax:937-898-5472

American Airgun Field Target Assn.
5911 Cherokee Ave., Tampa, FL 33604

American Coon Hunters Assn.
Opal Johnston, P.O. Cadet, Route 1, Box 492, Old Mines, MO 63630

American Custom Gunmakers Guild
Jan Billeb, Exec. Director, P.O. Box 812, Burlington, IA 52601-0812/319-752-6114 (Phone or Fax)

American Defense Preparedness Assn.
Two Colonial Place, 2101 Wilson Blvd., Suite 400, Arlington, VA 22201-3061

American Paintball League
P.O. Box 3561, Johnson City, TN 37602/800-541-9169

American Pistolsmiths Guild
Alex B. Hamilton, Pres., 1449 Blue Crest Lane, San Antonio, TX 78232/210-494-3063

American Police Pistol & Rifle Assn.
3801 Biscayne Blvd., Miami, FL 33137

American Single Shot Rifle Assn.
Gary Staup, Secy., 709 Carolyn Dr., Delphos, OH 45833/419-692-3866. Website: www.assra.com

American Society of Arms Collectors
George E. Weatherly, P.O. Box 2567, Waxahachie, TX 75165

American Tactical Shooting Assn.(A.T.S.A.)
c/o Skip Gochenour, 2600 N. Third St., Harrisburg, PA 17110/717-233-0402; Fax:717-233-5340

Association of Firearm and Tool Mark Examiners
Lannie G. Emanuel, Secy., Southwest Institute of Forensic Sciences, P.O. Box 35728, Dallas, TX 75235/214-920-5979; Fax:214-920-5928; Membership Secy., Ann D. Jones, VA Div. of Forensic Science, P.O. Box 999, Richmond, VA 23208/804-786-4706; Fax:804-371-8328

Boone & Crockett Club
250 Station Dr., Missoula, MT 59801-2753

Browning Collectors Assn.
Secretary:Scherrie L. Brennac, 2749 Keith Dr., Villa Ridge, MO 63089/314-742-0571

The Cast Bullet Assn., Inc.
Ralland J. Fortier, Editor, 4103 Foxcraft Dr., Traverse City, MI 49684

Citizens Committee for the Right to Keep and Bear Arms
Natl. Hq., Liberty Park, 12500 NE Tenth Pl., Bellevue, WA 98005

Colt Collectors Assn.
25000 Highland Way, Los Gatos, CA 95030/408-353-2658.

Ducks Unlimited, Inc.
Natl. Headquarters, One Waterfowl Way, Memphis, TN 38120/901-758-3937

Fifty Caliber Shooters Assn.
PO Box 111, Monroe UT 84754-0111

Firearms Coalition/Neal Knox Associates
Box 6537, Silver Spring, MD 20906/301-871-3006

Firearms Engravers Guild of America
Rex C. Pedersen, Secy., 511 N. Rath Ave., Lundington, MI 49431/616-845-7695(Phone and Fax)

Foundation for North American Wild Sheep
720 Allen Ave., Cody, WY 82414-3402/web site: http://iigi.com/os/non/fnaws/fnaws.htm; e-mail: fnaws@wyoming.com

ARMS ASSOCIATIONS

Freedom Arms Collectors Assn.
P.O. Box 160302, Miami, FL 33116-0302

Garand Collectors Assn.
P.O. Box 181, Richmond, KY 40475

Golden Eagle Collectors Assn. (G.E.C.A.)
Chris Showler, 11144 Slate Creek Rd., Grass Valley, CA 95945

Gun Owners of America
8001 Forbes Place, Suite 102, Springfield, VA 22151/703-321-8585

Handgun Hunters International
J.D. Jones, Director, P.O. Box 357 MAG, Bloomingdale, OH 43910

Harrington & Richardson Gun Coll. Assn.
George L. Cardet, 330 S.W. 27th Ave., Suite 603, Miami, FL 33135

High Standard Collectors' Assn.
John J. Stimson, Jr., Pres., 540 W. 92nd St., Indianapolis, IN 46260

Hopkins & Allen Arms & Memorabilia Society (HAAMS)
P.O. Box 187, 1309 Pamela Circle, Delphos, OH 45833

International Ammunition Association, Inc.
C.R. Punnett, Secy., 8 Hillock Lane, Chadds Ford, PA 19317/610-358-1285;Fax:610-358-1560

International Benchrest Shooters
Joan Borden, RR1, Box 250BB, Springville, PA 18844/717-965-2366

International Blackpowder Hunting Assn.
P.O. Box 1180, Glenrock, WY 82637/307-436-9817

IHMSA (Intl. Handgun Metallic Silhouette Assn.)
PO Box 368, Burlington, IA 52601 Website: www.ihmsa.cor

International Society of Mauser Arms Collectors
Michael Kindberg, Pres., P.O. Box 277, Alpharetta, GA 30239-0277

Jews for the Preservation of Firearms Ownership (JPFO) 501(c)(3)
2872 S. Wentworth Ave., Milwaukee, WI 53207/414-769-0760; Fax:414-483-8435

The Mannlicher Collectors Assn.
Membership Office: P.O. Box1249, The Dalles, Oregon 97058

Marlin Firearms Collectors Assn., Ltd.
Dick Paterson, Secy., 407 Lincoln Bldg., 44 Main St., Champaign, IL 61820

Merwin Hulbert Association,
2503 Kentwood Ct., High Point, NC 27265

Miniature Arms Collectors/Makers Society, Ltd.
Ralph Koebbeman, Pres., 4910 Kilburn Ave., Rockford, IL 61101/815-964-2569

M1 Carbine Collectors Assn. (M1-CCA)
623 Apaloosa Ln., Gardnerville, NV 89410-7840

National Association of Buckskinners (NAB)
Territorial Dispatch—1800s Historical Publication, 4701 Marion St., Suite 324, Livestock Exchange Bldg., Denver, CO 80216/303-297-9671

The National Association of Derringer Collectors
P.O. Box 20572, San Jose, CA 95160

National Assn. of Federally Licensed Firearms Dealers
Andrew Molchan, 2455 E. Sunrise, Ft. Lauderdale, FL 33304

National Association to Keep and Bear Arms
P.O. Box 78336, Seattle, WA 98178

National Automatic Pistol Collectors Assn.
Tom Knox, P.O. Box 15738, Tower Grove Station, St. Louis, MO 63163

National Bench Rest Shooters Assn., Inc.
Pat Ferrell, 2835 Guilford Lane, Oklahoma City, OK 73120-4404/405-842-9585; Fax: 405-842-9575

National Muzzle Loading Rifle Assn.
Box 67, Friendship, IN 47021 / 812-667-5131. Website: www.nmlra@nmlra.org

National Professional Paintball League (NPPL)
540 Main St., Mount Kisco, NY 10549/914-241-7400

National Reloading Manufacturers Assn.
One Centerpointe Dr., Suite 300, Lake Oswego, OR 97035

National Rifle Assn. of America
11250 Waples Mill Rd., Fairfax, VA 22030 / 703-267-1000. Website: www.nra.org

National Shooting Sports Foundation, Inc.
Robert T. Delfay, President, Flintlock Ridge Office Center, 11 Mile Hill Rd., Newtown, CT 06470-2359/203-426-1320; FAX: 203-426-1087

National Skeet Shooting Assn.
Dan Snyuder, Director, 5931 Roft Road, San Antonio, TX 78253-9261/800-877-5338. Website: nssa-nsca.com

National Sporting Clays Association
Ann Myers, Director, 5931 Roft Road, San Antonio, TX 78253-9261/800-877-5338. Website: nssa-nsca.com

National Wild Turkey Federation, Inc.
P.O. Box 530, 770 Augusta Rd., Edgefield, SC 29824

North American Hunting Club
P.O. Box 3401, Minnetonka, MN 55343/612-936-9333; Fax: 612-936-9755

North American Paintball Referees Association (NAPRA)
584 Cestaric Dr., Milpitas, CA 95035

North-South Skirmish Assn., Inc.
Stevan F. Meserve, Exec. Secretary, 507 N. Brighton Court, Sterling, VA 20164-3919

Remington Society of America
Gordon Fosburg, Secretary, 11900 North Brinton Road, Lake, MI 48623

Rocky Mountain Elk Foundation
P.O. Box 8249, Missoula, MT 59807-8249/406-523-4500;Fax: 406-523-4581
Website: www.rmef.org

Ruger Collector's Assn., Inc.
P.O. Box 240, Greens Farms, CT 06436

Safari Club International
4800 W. Gates Pass Rd., Tucson, AZ 85745/520-620-1220

Sako Collectors Assn., Inc.
Jim Lutes, 202 N. Locust, Whitewater, KS 67154

Second Amendment Foundation
James Madison Building, 12500 NE 10th Pl., Bellevue, WA 98005

Single Action Shooting Society (SASS)
23255-A La Palma Avenue, Yorba Linda, CA 92887/714-6941800; FAX: 714-694-1815/email: sasseot@aol.com Website: www.sassnet.com

Smith & Wesson Collectors Assn.
Cally Pletl, Admin. Asst.,PO Box 444, Afton, NY 13730

The Society of American Bayonet Collectors
P.O. Box 234, East Islip, NY 11730-0234

Southern California Schuetzen Society
Dean Lillard, 34657 Ave. E., Yucaipa, CA 92399

Sporting Arms and Ammunition Manufacturers' Institute (SAAMI)
Flintlock Ridge Office Center, 11 Mile Hill Rd., Newtown, CT 06470-2359/203-426-4358; FAX: 203-426-1087

Sporting Clays of America (SCA)
Ron L. Blosser, Pres., 9257 Buckeye Rd., Sugar Grove, OH 43155-9632/614-746-8334; Fax: 614-746-8605

The Thompson/Center Assn.
Joe Wright, President, Box 792, Northboro, MA 01532/508-845-6960

U.S. Practical Shooting Assn./IPSC
Dave Thomas, P.O. Box 811, Sedro Woolley, WA 98284/360-855-2245

U.S. Revolver Assn.
Brian J. Barer, 40 Larchmont Ave., Taunton, MA 02780/508-824-4836

U.S. Shooting Team
U.S. Olympic Shooting Center, One Olympic Plaza, Colorado Springs, CO 80909/719-578-4670

The Varmint Hunters Assn., Inc.
Box 759, Pierre, SD 57501/Member Services 800-528-4868

Weatherby Collectors Assn., Inc.
P.O. Box 888, Ozark, MO 65721

The Wildcatters
P.O. Box 170, Greenville, WI 54942

Winchester Arms Collectors Assn.
P.O. Box 230, Brownsboro, TX 75756/903-852-4027

The Women's Shooting Sports Foundation (WSSF)
4620 Edison Avenue, Ste. C, Colorado Springs, CO 80915/719-638-1299; FAX: 719-638-1271/email: wssf@world-net.att.net

ARGENTINA

Asociacion Argentina de Coleccionistas de Armes y Municiones
Castilla de Correos No. 28, Sucursal I B, 1401 Buenos Aires, Republica Argentina

AUSTRALIA

Antique & Historical Arms Collectors of Australia
P.O. Box 5654, GCMC Queensland 9726, Australia

The Arms Collector's Guild of Queensland Inc.
Ian Skennerton, P.O. Box 433, Ashmore City 4214, Queensland, Australia

Australian Cartridge Collectors Assn., Inc.
Bob Bennett, 126 Landscape Dr., E. Doncaster 3109, Victoria, Australia

Sporting Shooters Assn. of Australia, Inc.
P.O. Box 2066, Kent Town, SA 5071, Australia

CANADA

ALBERTA

Canadian Historical Arms Society
P.O. Box 901, Edmonton, Alb., Canada T5J 2L8

National Firearms Assn.
Natl. Hq: P.O. Box 1779, Edmonton, Alb., Canada T5J 2P1

BRITISH COLUMBIA

The Historical Arms Collectors of B.C. (Canada)
Harry Moon, Pres., P.O. Box 50117, South Slope RPO, Burnaby, BC V5J 5G3, Canada/604-438-0950; Fax:604-277-3646

ONTARIO

Association of Canadian Cartridge Collectors
Monica Wright, RR 1, Millgrove, ON, L0R IVO, Canada

Tri-County Antique Arms Fair
P.O. Box 122, RR #1, North Lancaster, Ont., Canada K0C 1Z0

EUROPE

BELGIUM

European Catridge Research Assn.
Graham Irving, 21 Rue Schaltin, 4900 Spa, Belgium/32.87.77.43.40; Fax:32.87.77.27.51

CZECHOSLOVAKIA

Spolecnost Pro Studium Naboju (Czech Cartridge Research Assn.)
JUDr. Jaroslav Bubak, Pod Homolko 1439, 26601 Beroun 2, Czech Republic

DENMARK

Aquila Dansk Jagtpatron Historic Forening (Danish Historical Cartridge Collectors Club)
Steen Elgaard Møller, Ulriksdalsvej 7, 4840 Nr. Alslev, Denmark 10045-53846218;Fax:00455384 6209

ENGLAND

Arms and Armour Society
Hon. Secretary A. Dove, P.O. Box 10232, London, 5W19 2ZD, England

Dutch Paintball Federation
Aceville Publ., Castle House 97 High Street, Colchester, Essex C01 1TH, England/011-44-206-564840

European Paintball Sports Foundation
c/o Aceville Publ., Castle House 97 High St., Colchester, Essex, C01 1TH, England

Historical Breechloading Smallarms Assn.
D.J. Penn M.A., Secy., P.O. Box 12778, London SE1 6BX, England. Journal and newsletter are $23 a yr., including airmail.

National Rifle Assn.
(Great Britain) Bisley Camp, Brookwood, Woking Surrey GU24 OPB, England/01483.797777; Fax: 014730686275

United Kingdom Cartridge Club
Ian Southgate, 20 Millfield, Elmley Castle, Nr. Pershore, Worcestershire, WR10 3HR, England

FRANCE

STAC-Western Co.
3 Ave. Paul Doumer (N.311); 78360 Montesson, France/01.30.53-43-65; Fax: 01.30.53.19.10

GERMANY

Bund Deutscher Sportschützen e.v. (BDS)
Borsigallee 10, 53125 Bonn 1, Germany

Deutscher Schützenbund
Lahnstrasse 120, 65195 Wiesbaden, Germany

SPAIN

Asociacion Espanola de Coleccionistas de Cartuchos (A.E.C.C.)
Secretary: Apdo. Correos No. 1086, 2880-Alcala de Henares (Madrid), Spain. President: Apdo. Correos No. 682, 50080 Zaragoza, Spain

SWEDEN

Scandinavian Ammunition Research Assn.
Box 107, 77622 Hedemora, Sweden

NEW ZEALAND

New Zealand Cartridge Collectors Club
Terry Castle, 70 Tiraumea Dr., Pakuranga, Auckland, New Zealand

New Zealand Deerstalkers Assn.
P.O. Box 6514 TE ARO, Wellington, New Zealand

SOUTH AFRICA

Historical Firearms Soc. of South Africa
P.O. Box 145, 7725 Newlands, Republic of South Africa

Republic of South Africa Cartridge Collectors Assn.
Arno Klee, 20 Eugene St., Malanshof Randburg, Gauteng 2194, Republic of South Africa

S.A.A.C.A. (Southern Africa Arms and Ammunition Assn.)
Gauteng Office: P.O. Box 7597, Weltevreden Park, 1715, Republic of South Africa/011-679-1151; Fax: 011-679-1131; e-mail: saaaca@iafrica.com. Kwa-Zulu Natal office: P.O. Box 4065, Kwa-zulu-Natal 4065, Republic of South Africa

SAGA (S.A. Gunowners' Assn.)
P.O. Box 35203, Northway, Kwa-zulu-Natal 4065, Republic of South Africa

2001
GUN DIGEST
DIRECTORY OF THE
ARMS TRADE

The **Product Directory** contains 78 product categories. The **Arms Trade Directory** alphabetically lists the manufacturers with their addresses, phone numbers, FAX numbers and Internet addresses, if available.

DIRECTORY OF THE ARMS TRADE INDEX

DIRECTORY

PRODUCT & SERVICE DIRECTORY

AMMUNITION COMPONENTS, SHOTSHELL

Garcia National Gun Traders, Inc.
Precision Reloading, Inc.
Tar-Hunt Custom Rifles, Inc.
Vitt/Boos

AMMUNITION COMPONENTS-- BULLETS, POWDER, PRIMERS, CASES

3-D Ammunition & Bullets
A-Square Co.,Inc.
Acadian Ballistic Specialties
Accuracy Unlimited
Accurate Arms Co., Inc.
Action Bullets & Alloy Inc.
ADCO Sales, Inc.
Alaska Bullet Works, Inc.
Alliant Techsystems Smokeless Powder Group
Allred Bullet Co.
Alpha LaFranck Enterprises
American Bullet
American Products, Inc.
Arco Powder
Arizona Ammunition, Inc.
Armfield Custom Bullets
Atlantic Rose, Inc.
Baer's Hollows
Ballard Rifle & Cartridge Co., LLC
Ballistic Product, Inc.
Barnes
Barnes Bullets, Inc.
Beartooth Bullets
Beeline Custom Bullets Limited
Bell Reloading, Inc.
Berger Bullets Ltd.
Berry's Mfg., Inc.
Big Bore Bullets of Alaska
Big Bore Express
Bitterroot Bullet Co.
Black Belt Bullets (See Big Bore Express)
Black Hills Shooters Supply
Black Powder Products
Blount, Inc., Sporting Equipment Div.
Blue Mountain Bullets
Brenneke KG, Wilhelm
Briese Bullet Co., Inc.
Brown Co, E. Arthur
Brown Dog Ent.
BRP, Inc. High Performance Cast Bullets
Buck Stix--SOS Products Co.
Buckeye Custom Bullets
Buckskin Bullet Co.
Buffalo Arms Co.
Buffalo Rock Shooters Supply
Bull-X, Inc.
Bullet, Inc.
Bullseye Bullets
Butler Enterprises
Buzztail Brass (See Grayback Wildcats)
Cambos Outdoorsman
Canyon Cartridge Corp.
Carnahan Bullets
Cascade Bullet Co., Inc.
Cast Performance Bullet Company
Casull Arms Corp.
CCI Div. of Blount, Inc.
Champion's Choice, Inc.
Cheddite France S.A.
CheVron Bullets
Chuck's Gun Shop
Clean Shot Technologies

Colorado Sutlers Arsenal (See Cumberland States Ar
Competitor Corp. Inc.
Cook Engineering Service
Cor-Bon Bullet & Ammo Co.
Cumberland States Arsenal
Cummings Bullets
Curtis Cast Bullets
Curtis Gun Shop (See Curtis Cast Bullets)
Custom Bullets by Hoffman
D&J Bullet Co. & Custom Gun Shop, Inc.
Dakota Arms, Inc.
Dick Marple & Associates
Dixie Gun Works, Inc.
DKT, Inc.
Dohring Bullets
Double A Ltd.
Eichelberger Bullets, Wm
Eldorado Cartridge Corp (See PMC/Eldorado Cartridge Corp.)
Elkhorn Bullets
Epps, Ellwood (See "Gramps" Antique Cartridges)
Federal Cartridge Co.
Fiocchi of America Inc.
Fish Mfg. Gunsmith Sptg. Co., Marshall F
Forkin, Ben (See Belt MTN Arms)
Forkin Arms
Fowler Bullets
Fowler, Bob (See Black Powder Products)
Foy Custom Bullets
Freedom Arms, Inc.
Fusilier Bullets
Garcia National Gun Traders, Inc.
Gehmann, Walter (See Huntington Die Specialties)
GOEX Inc.
Golden Bear Bullets
Gotz Bullets
Grayback Wildcats
Green Mountain Rifle Barrel Co., Inc.
Grier's Hard Cast Bullets
GTB
Gun City
Hammets VLD Bullets
Hardin Specialty Dist.
Harris Enterprises
Harrison Bullets
Hart & Son, Inc.
Hawk Laboratories, Inc. (See Hawk, Inc.)
Hawk, Inc.
Haydon Shooters Supply, Russ
Heidenstrom Bullets
Hercules, Inc. (See Alliant Techsystems, Smokeless Powder Group)
Hi-Performance Ammunition Company
Hirtenberger Aktiengesellschaft
Hobson Precision Mfg. Co.
Hodgdon Powder Co.
Hornady Mfg. Co.
HT Bullets
Hunters Supply, Inc.
Huntington Die Specialties
IMI Services USA, Inc.
Impact Case Co.
Imperial Magnum Corp.
IMR Powder Co.
Intercontinental Distributors, Ltd.
J&D Components
J&L Superior Bullets (See Huntington Die Specialist)
J-4 Inc.
J.R. Williams Bullet Co.

James Calhoon Mfg.
Jensen Bullets
Jensen's Firearms Academy
Jericho Tool & Die Co., Inc.
Jester Bullets
JLK Bullets
JRP Custom Bullets
Ka Pu Kapili
Kasmarsik Bullets
Kaswer Custom, Inc.
Keith's Bullets
Ken's Kustom Kartridges
Keng's Firearms Specialty, Inc./US Tactical Systems
Kent Cartridge Mfg. Co. Ltd.
KLA Enterprises
Knight Rifles
Knight Rifles (See Modern Muzzle Loading, Inc.)
Lage Uniwad
Lapua Ltd.
Lawrence Brand Shot (See Precision Reloading, Inc.)
Legend Products Corp.
Liberty Shooting Supplies
Lightfield Ammunition Corp. (See Slug Group, Inc.)
Lightning Performance Innovations, Inc.
Lindsley Arms Cartridge Co.
Littleton, J. F.
Lomont Precision Bullets
Loweth, Richard H.R.
Lyman Products Corp.
Magnus Bullets
Magtech Ammunition Co. Inc.
Maine Custom Bullets
Maionchi-L.M.I.
Marchmon Bullets
Markesbery Muzzle Loaders, Inc.
MarMik, Inc.
MAST Technology
McMurdo, Lynn (See Specialty Gunsmithing)
Meister Bullets (See Gander Mountain)
Men-Metallwerk Elisenhuette GmbH
Merkuria Ltd.
MI-TE Bullets
Michael's Antiques
Mitchell Bullets, R.F.
Montana Armory, Inc (See C. Sharps Arms Co. Inc.)
Montana Precision Swaging
Mountain State Muzzleloading Supplies, Inc.
Mt. Baldy Bullet Co.
Mulhern, Rick
Murmur Corp.
Mushroom Express Bullet Co.
Nagel's Custom Bullets
National Bullet Co.
Naval Ordnance Works
Necromancer Industries, Inc.
North American Shooting Systems
North Devon Firearms Services
Northern Precision Custom Swaged Bullets
Nosler, Inc.
Oklahoma Ammunition Co.
Old Wagon Bullets
Old Western Scrounger,Inc.
Oregon Trail Bullet Company
Pacific Cartridge, Inc.
Pacific Rifle Co.
Page Custom Bullets
Patrick Bullets
Pease Accuracy
Penn Bullets
Petro-Explo Inc.
Phillippi Custom Bullets, Justin

Pinetree Bullets
PMC/Eldorado Cartridge Corp.
Polywad, Inc.
Pomeroy, Robert
Power Plus Enterprises, Inc.
Precision Components
Precision Components and Guns
Precision Delta Corp.
Precision Munitions, Inc.
Prescott Projectile Co.
Price Bullets, Patrick W.
PRL Bullets, c/o Blackburn Enterprises
Professional Hunter Supplies (See Star Custom Bullets)
Proofmark Corp.
R.I.S. Co., Inc.
R.M. Precision
Rainier Ballistics Corp.
Ramon B. Gonzalez Guns
Ranger Products
Redwood Bullet Works
Reloading Specialties, Inc.
Remington Arms Co., Inc.
Rhino
Robinson H.V. Bullets
Rubright Bullets
SAECO (See Redding Reloading Equipment)
Scharch Mfg., Inc.
Schmidtman Custom Ammunition
Schneider Bullets
Schroeder Bullets
Schumakers Gun Shop
Scot Powder
Seebeck Assoc., R.E.
Shappy Bullets
Sharps Arms Co., Inc., C.
Shilen, Inc.
Sierra Bullets
SOS Products Co. (See Buck Stix-SOS Products Co.)
Southern Ammunition Co., Inc.
Specialty Gunsmithing
Speer Products Div. of Blount Inc. Sporting Equipment
Spencer's Custom Guns
Stanley Bullets
Star Ammunition, Inc.
Star Custom Bullets
Stark's Bullet Mfg.
Starke Bullet Company
Starline, Inc.
Stewart's Gunsmithing
Swift Bullet Co.
T.F.C. S.P.A.
Talon Mfg. Co., Inc.
Taracorp Industries, Inc.
TCCI
TCSR
The Ordnance Works
Thompson Precision
TMI Products (See Haselbauer Products, Jerry)
Traditions Performance Firearms
Trico Plastics
Trophy Bonded Bullets, Inc.
True Flight Bullet Co.
Tucson Mold, Inc.
Unmussig Bullets, D. L.
USAC
Vann Custom Bullets
Vihtavuori Oy/Kaltron-Pettibone
Vincent's Shop
Viper Bullet and Brass Works
Vom Hoffe (See Old Western Scrounger, Inc., The)
Warren Muzzleloading Co., Inc.
Watson Trophy Match Bullets
Weatherby, Inc.
Western Nevada West Coast Bullets

Widener's Reloading & Shooting Supply, Inc.
Winchester Div. Olin Corp.
Windjammer Tournament Wads Inc.
Winkle Bullets
Woodleigh (See Huntington Die Specialties)
Worthy Products, Inc.
Wosenitz VHP, Inc.
Wyant Bullets
Wyoming Bonded Bullets
Wyoming Custom Bullets
Yukon Arms Classic Ammunition
Zero Ammunition Co., Inc.

AMMUNITION, COMMERCIAL

3-D Ammunition & Bullets
3-Ten Corp.
A-Square Co.,Inc.
Ace Custom 45's, Inc.
American Ammunition
Arizona Ammunition, Inc.
Arms Corporation of the Philippines
Arundel Arms & Ammunition, Inc., A.
Atlantic Rose, Inc.
Badger Shooters Supply, Inc.
Ballistic Product, Inc.
Ben William's Gun Shop
Big Bear Arms & Sporting Goods, Inc.
Black Hills Ammunition, Inc.
Blammo Ammo
Blount, Inc., Sporting Equipment Div.
Brown Dog Ent.
Buffalo Bullet Co., Inc..
Bull-X, Inc.
Cambos Outdoorsman
Casull Arms Corp.
CBC
Champion's Choice, Inc.
Cor-Bon Bullet & Ammo Co.
Creekside Gun Shop Inc.
Cubic Shot Shell Co., Inc.
Cumberland States Arsenal
Daisy Mfg. Co.
Dead Eye's Sport Center
Delta Arms Ltd.
Diana (See U.S. Importer - Dynamit Nobel-RWS, Inc.)
Dynamit Nobel-RWS, Inc.
Effebi SNC-Dr. Franco Beretta
Eley Ltd.
Elite Ammunition
Estate Cartridge, Inc.
Executive Protection Institute
Federal Cartridge Co.
Fiocchi of America Inc.
Fish Mfg. Gunsmith Sptg. Co., Marshall F
Garcia National Gun Traders, Inc.
Garrett Cartridges Inc.
Garthwaite Pistolsmith, Inc., Jim
Gibbs Rifle Co., Inc.
Gil Hebard Guns
Glaser Safety Slug, Inc.
Groenewold, John
Gun City
Gun Hunter Trading Co.
Hansen & Co. (See Hansen Cartridge Co.)
Hart & Son, Inc.
Hi-Performance Ammunition Company
Hirtenberger Aktiengesellschaft
Hornady Mfg. Co.
Hunters Supply, Inc.
IMI

Intercontinental Distributors, Ltd.
Ion Industries, Inc.
Israel Military Industries Ltd. (See IMI)
Jones, J.D./SSK Industries
Keng's Firearms Specialty, Inc./US Tactical Systems
Kent Cartridge America, Inc.
Kent Cartridge Mfg. Co. Ltd.
Knight Rifles
Lapua Ltd.
Lightfield Ammunition Corp. (See Slug Group, Inc.)
Lock's Philadelphia Gun Exchange
Magnum Research, Inc.
MagSafe Ammo Co.
Maionchi-L.M.I.
McBros Rifle Co.
Men-Metallwerk Elisenhuette GmbH
Mullins Ammunition
New England Ammunition Co.
Oklahoma Ammunition Co.
Omark Industries,Div. of Blount,Inc.
Outdoor Sports Headquarters,Inc.
Pacific Cartridge, Inc.
Paragon Sales & Services, Inc.
Parker & Sons Shooting Supply
PMC/Eldorado Cartridge Corp.
Polywad, Inc.
Pony Express Reloaders
Precision Delta Corp.
Pro Load Ammunition, Inc.
R.E.I.
Remington Arms Co., Inc.
Rucker Dist. Inc.
RWS (See US Importer-Dynamit Nobel-RWS, Inc.)
Sellier & Bellot, USA Inc.
Slug Group, Inc.
Southern Ammunition Co., Inc.
Talon Mfg. Co., Inc.
TCCI
The BulletMakers Workshop
The Gun Room Press
Thompson Bullet Lube Co.
USAC
Valor Corp.
VAM Distribution Co LLC
Victory USA
Vihtavuori Oy/Kaltron-Pettibone
Voere-KGH m.b.H.
Vom Hoffe (See Old Western Scrounger, Inc., The)
Weatherby, Inc.
Westley Richards & Co.
Widener's Reloading & Shooting Supply, Inc.
Winchester Div. Olin Corp.
Zero Ammunition Co., Inc.

AMMUNITION, CUSTOM

3-D Ammunition & Bullets
3-Ten Corp.
A-Square Co.,Inc.
Accuracy Unlimited
AFSCO Ammunition
Allred Bullet Co.
American Derringer Corp.
American Products, Inc.
Arizona Ammunition, Inc.
Arms Corporation of the Philippines
Atlantic Rose, Inc.
Ballard Rifle & Cartridge Co., LLC
Belding's Custom Gun Shop
Berger Bullets Ltd.

Big Bore Bullets of Alaska
Black Hills Ammunition, Inc.
Blue Mountain Bullets
Brynin, Milton
Buckskin Bullet Co.
CBC
Cubic Shot Shell Co., Inc.
Custom Tackle and Ammo
Dakota Arms, Inc.
Dead Eye's Sport Center
Delta Frangible Ammunition LLC
DKT, Inc.
Elite Ammunition
Estate Cartridge, Inc.
Freedom Arms, Inc.
GDL Enterprises
GOEX Inc.
Gonzalez Guns, Ramon B.
Grayback Wildcats
Gun Accessories (See Glaser Safety Slug, Inc.)
Hirtenberger Aktiengesellschaft
Hobson Precision Mfg. Co.
Hoelscher, Virgil
Horizons Unlimited
Hornady Mfg. Co.
Hunters Supply, Inc.
IMI
Israel Military Industries Ltd. (See IMI)
James Calhoon Mfg.
Jensen Bullets
Jensen's Custom Ammunition
Jensen's Firearms Academy
Kaswer Custom, Inc.
Keeler, R. H.
Kent Cartridge Mfg. Co. Ltd.
L.A.R. Mfg., Inc.
Lindsley Arms Cartridge Co.
Linebaugh Custom Sixguns
MagSafe Ammo Co.
MAST Technology
McBros Rifle Co.
McKillen & Heyer, Inc.
McMurdo, Lynn (See Specialty Gunsmithing)
Men-Metallwerk Elisenhuette GmbH
Milstor Corp.
Mountain Rifles, Inc.
Mullins Ammunition
Naval Ordnance Works
Nygord Precision Products
Oklahoma Ammunition Co.
Old Western Scrounger,Inc.
Phillippi Custom Bullets, Justin
Power Plus Enterprises, Inc.
Precision Delta Corp.
Precision Munitions, Inc.
Precision Reloading, Inc.
Professional Hunter Supplies (See Star Custom Bullets)
R.E.I.
Ramon B. Gonzalez Guns
Sanders Custom Gun Service
Sandia Die & Cartridge Co.
SOS Products Co. (See Buck Stix-SOS Products Co.)
Specialty Gunsmithing
Spencer's Custom Guns
Star Custom Bullets
State Arms Gun Co.
Stewart's Gunsmithing
Talon Mfg. Co., Inc.
The BulletMakers Workshop
The Country Armourer
Unmussig Bullets, D. L.
Vitt/Boos
Vom Hoffe (See Old Western Scrounger, Inc., The)
Vulpes Ventures, Inc. Fox Cartridge Division
Walters, John
Warren Muzzleloading Co., Inc.

Weaver Arms Corp. Gun Shop
Worthy Products, Inc.
Yukon Arms Classic Ammunition
Zero Ammunition Co., Inc.

AMMUNITION, FOREIGN

A-Square Co.,Inc.
AFSCO Ammunition
Armscorp USA, Inc.
Atlantic Rose, Inc.
B & P America
B-West Imports, Inc.
Beeman Precision Airguns
CBC
Cheddite France S.A.
Cubic Shot Shell Co., Inc.
Dead Eye's Sport Center
Diana (See U.S. Importer - Dynamit Nobel-RWS, Inc.)
DKT, Inc.
Dynamit Nobel-RWS, Inc.
E. Arthur Brown Co.
Fiocchi of America Inc.
First Inc, Jack
Fisher Enterprises, Inc.
Fisher, R. Kermit (See Fisher Enterprises, Inc)
FN Herstal
Forgett Jr., Valmore J.
Gamebore Division, Polywad Inc.
Gibbs Rifle Co., Inc.
GOEX Inc.
Gunsmithing, Inc.
Hansen & Co. (See Hansen Cartridge Co.)
Heidenstrom Bullets
Hirtenberger Aktiengesellschaft
Hornady Mfg. Co.
IMI
IMI Services USA, Inc.
Intrac Arms International
Israel Military Industries Ltd. (See IMI)
Johnson's Gunsmithing, Inc, Neal
K.B.I. Inc.
MagSafe Ammo Co.
Magtech Ammunition Co. Inc.
Maionchi-L.M.I.
Marksman Products
MAST Technology
Merkuria Ltd.
Mullins Ammunition
Naval Ordnance Works
Navy Arms Co.
Neal Johnson's Gunsmithing, Inc.
Oklahoma Ammunition Co.
Old Western Scrounger,Inc.
Paragon Sales & Services, Inc.
Petro-Explo Inc.
Precision Delta Corp.
R.E.T. Enterprises
Ramon B. Gonzalez Guns
RWS (See US Importer-Dynamit Nobel-RWS, Inc.)
Samco Global Arms, Inc.
Sentinel Arms
Southern Ammunition Co., Inc.
Stratco, Inc.
SwaroSports, Inc. (See JagerSport Ltd.)
T.F.C. S.P.A.
The BulletMakers Workshop
The Paul Co.
Victory Ammunition
Vihtavuori Oy/Kaltron-Pettibone
Vom Hoffe (See Old Western Scrounger, Inc., The)
Yukon Arms Classic Ammunition

ANTIQUE ARMS DEALER

Ackerman & Co.
Ad Hominem
Antique American Firearms
Antique Arms Co.
Aplan Antiques & Art, James O.
Arundel Arms & Ammunition, Inc., A.
Ballard Rifle & Cartridge Co., LLC
Bear Mountain Gun & Tool
Bill Johns Master Engraver
Bob's Tactical Indoor Shooting Range & Gun Shop
British Antiques
Buckskin Machine Works, A. Hunkeler
Buffalo Arms Co.
Bustani, Leo
Cape Outfitters
Carlson, Douglas R, Antique American Firearms
CBC-BRAZIL
Chadick's Ltd.
Chambers Flintlocks Ltd., Jim
Champlin Firearms, Inc.
Chuck's Gun Shop
Classic Guns, Inc., Frank S. Wood
Clements' Custom Leathercraft, Chas
Cole's Gun Works
Collectors Firearms Etc.
D&D Gunsmiths, Ltd.
David R. Chicoine
Dixie Gun Works, Inc.
Dixon Muzzleloading Shop, Inc.
Duffy, Charles E (See Guns Antique & Modern DBA)
Enguix Import-Export
Fagan & Co.Inc.
Fanzoj GmbH
Fish Mfg. Gunsmith Sptg. Co., Marshall F
Flayderman & Co., Inc.
Forgett Jr., Valmore J.
Frielich Police Equipment
Fulmer's Antique Firearms, Chet
Getz Barrel Co.
Glass, Herb
Goergen's Gun Shop, Inc.
Golden Age Arms Co.
Goodwin, Fred
Gun Hunter Trading Co.
Guncraft Sports Inc.
Guns Antique & Modern DBA/Charles E. Duffy
Hallowell & Co.
Hamilton, Jim
HandCrafts Unltd (See Clements' Custom Leathercraft)
Handgun Press
Hansen & Co. (See Hansen Cartridge Co.)
Hunkeler, A (See Buckskin Machine Works)
Kelley's
Knight's Mfg. Co.
Ledbetter Airguns, Riley
LeFever Arms Co., Inc.
Lever Arms Service Ltd.
Lock's Philadelphia Gun Exchange
Log Cabin Sport Shop
Mandall Shooting Supplies Inc.
Martin's Gun Shop
Michael's Antiques
Montana Outfitters, Lewis E. Yearout
Museum of Historical Arms, Inc.
Muzzleloaders Etcetera, Inc.
New England Arms Co.
Pony Express Sport Shop

Powder Horn Antiques
Retting, Inc., Martin B.
Robert Valade Engraving
Samco Global Arms, Inc.
Sarco, Inc.
Scott Fine Guns Inc., Thad
Shootin' Shack, Inc.
Sportsmen's Exchange & Western Gun Traders, Inc.
Steves House of Guns
Stott's Creek Armory, Inc.
Strawbridge, Victor W.
The Armoury, Inc.
The Gun Room
The Gun Room Press
The Gun Works
Vic's Gun Refinishing
Vintage Arms, Inc.
Wallace, Terry
Westley Richards & Co.
Wiest, M. C.
William Fagan & Co.
Winchester Sutler, Inc., The
Wood, Frank (See Classic Guns, Inc.)
Yearout, Lewis E. (See Montana Outfitters)

APPRAISER - GUNS, ETC.

Ackerman & Co.
Antique Arms Co.
Arundel Arms & Ammunition, Inc., A.
Barta's Gunsmithing
Beitzinger, George
Blue Book Publications, Inc.
Bob Rogers Gunsmithing
Bob's Tactical Indoor Shooting Range & Gun Shop
British Antiques
Broad Creek Rifle Works, Ltd.
Bustani, Leo
Butterfield & Butterfield
Camilli, Lou
Cannon's
Cape Outfitters
Chadick's Ltd.
Champlin Firearms, Inc.
Christie's East
Clark Firearms Engraving
Classic Guns, Inc., Frank S. Wood
Clements' Custom Leathercraft, Chas
Cole's Gun Works
Collectors Firearms Etc.
Colonial Arms, Inc.
Colonial Repair
Corry, John
Creekside Gun Shop Inc.
Custom Tackle and Ammo
D&D Gunsmiths, Ltd.
David R. Chicoine
DGR Custom Rifles
Dilliott Gunsmithing, Inc.
Dixon Muzzleloading Shop, Inc.
Duane's Gun Repair (See DGR Custom Rifles)
Epps, Ellwood (See "Gramps" Antique Cartridges)
Eversull Co., Inc., K.
Fagan & Co.Inc.
Ferris Firearms
Fish Mfg. Gunsmith Sptg. Co., Marshall F
Flayderman & Co., Inc.
Forgett Jr., Valmore J.
Forty Five Ranch Enterprises
Francotte & Cie S.A. Auguste
Frontier Arms Co.,Inc.
Gene's Custom Guns
George E. Mathews & Son, Inc.

Gerald Pettinger Books, see
    Pettinger Books, G
Getz Barrel Co.
Gillmann, Edwin
Gilmore Sports Concepts
Goergen's Gun Shop, Inc.
Golden Age Arms Co.
Gonzalez Guns, Ramon B
Goodwin, Fred
Griffin & Howe, Inc.
Gun City
Gun Hunter Trading Co.
Guncraft Sports Inc.
Guns
Hallberg Gunsmith, Fritz
Hallowell & Co.
Hammans, Charles E.
HandCrafts Unltd (See Clements'
    Custom Leathercraft)
Handgun Press
Hank's Gun Shop
Hansen & Co. (See Hansen
    Cartridge Co.)
Hughes, Steven Dodd
Irwin, Campbell H.
Island Pond Gun Shop
Jackalope Gun Shop
Jensen's Custom Ammunition
Kelley's
L.L. Bean, Inc.
Lampert, Ron
LaRocca Gun Works
Ledbetter Airguns, Riley
LeFever Arms Co., Inc.
Lock's Philadelphia Gun
    Exchange
Log Cabin Sport Shop
Madis, George
Mandall Shooting Supplies Inc.
Martin's Gun Shop
Mathews & Son, Inc., George E.
McCann Industries
McCann's Machine & Gun Shop
McCann's Muzzle-Gun Works
Montana Outfitters, Lewis E.
    Yearout
Museum of Historical Arms, Inc.
Muzzleloaders Etcetera, Inc.
New England Arms Co.
Nitex, Inc.
Pasadena Gun Center
Pentheny de Pentheny
Perazzi USA, Inc.
Peterson Gun Shop, Inc., A.W.
Pettinger Books, Gerald
Pony Express Sport Shop
Powder Horn Antiques
R.A. Wells Custom Gunsmith
R.E.T. Enterprises
Ramon B. Gonzalez Guns
Retting, Inc., Martin B
River Road Sporting Clays
Robert Valade Engraving
Safari Outfitters Ltd.
Scott Fine Guns Inc., Thad
Shootin' Shack, Inc.
Spencer Reblue Service
Sportsmen's Exchange &
    Western Gun Traders, Inc.
Steger, James R.
Stott's Creek Armory, Inc.
Stratco, Inc.
Strawbridge, Victor W.
Ten-Ring Precision, Inc.
The Armoury, Inc.
The Gun Room Press
The Gun Shop
The Orvis Co.
The Swampfire Shop (See
    Peterson Gun Shop, Inc.)
Thurston Sports, Inc.
Valade Engraving, Robert
Vic's Gun Refinishing
Walker Arms Co., Inc.

Wasmundt, Jim
Wayne Firearms for Collectors
    and Investors, James
Werth, T. W.
Whildin & Sons Ltd, E.H.
Wichita Arms, Inc.
Wiest, M. C.
William Fagan & Co.
Williams Shootin' Iron Service,
    The Lynx-Line
Winchester Sutler, Inc., The
Wood, Frank (See Classic Guns,
    Inc.)
Yearout, Lewis E. (See Montana
    Outfitters)
Yee, Mike

AUCTIONEER - GUNS, ETC.

"Little John's" Antique Arms
Buck Stix--SOS Products Co.
Butterfield & Butterfield
Christie's East
Fagan & Co.Inc.
Kelley's
Sotheby's

BOOKS & MANUALS (PUBLISHERS & DEALERS)

"Su-Press-On",Inc.
Accurate Arms Co., Inc.
Alpha 1 Drop Zone
American Handgunner Magazine
Armory Publications
Arms & Armour Press
Ballistic Product, Inc.
Ballistic Product, Inc.
Barnes Bullets, Inc.
Beartooth Bullets
Beeman Precision Airguns
Blacksmith Corp.
Blacktail Mountain Books
Blue Book Publications, Inc.
Blue Ridge Machinery & Tools,
    Inc.
Boone's Custom Ivory Grips,
    Inc.
Brown Co, E. Arthur
Brownells, Inc.
Bullet'n Press
Calibre Press, Inc.
Cape Outfitters
Cheyenne Pioneer Products
Colonial Repair
Colorado Sutlers Arsenal (See
    Cumberland States Arsenal)
Corbin Mfg. & Supply, Inc.
Cumberland States Arsenal
DBI Books Division of Krause
    Publications (Edito
Dixie Gun Works, Inc.
Dixon Muzzleloading Shop, Inc.
Ed~ Brown Products, Inc.
Executive Protection Institute
Flores Publications Inc, J (See
    Action Direct Inc)
Forgett Jr., Valmore J.
Galati International
Gerald Pettinger Books, see
    Pettinger Books, Gerald
Golden Age Arms Co.
Gun City
Gun Hunter Books (See Gun
    Hunter Trading Co)
Gun Hunter Trading Co.
Gun List (See Krause
    Publications)
Guncraft Books (See Guncraft
    Sports Inc.)
Guncraft Sports Inc.
Gunnerman Books
GUNS Magazine

Gunsmithing, Inc.
H&P Publishing
Handgun Press
Harris Publications
Hawk Laboratories, Inc. (See
    Hawk, Inc.)
Hawk, Inc.
Heritage/VSP Gun Books
High North Products, Inc.
Hodgdon Powder Co.
Home Shop Machinist The
    Village Press Publications
Hornady Mfg. Co.
Hungry Horse Books
Huntington Die Specialties
I.D.S.A. Books
Info-Arm
Ironside International
    Publishers, Inc.
J Martin Inc.
Jantz Supply
Kelley's
Koval Knives
Krause Publications, Inc.
Lapua Ltd.
Lethal Force Institute (See Police
    Bookshelf)
Lyman Products Corp.
Madis Books
Magma Engineering Co.
MarMik, Inc.
Milberry House Publishing
Montana Armory, Inc (See C.
    Sharps Arms Co. Inc.)
Mountain South
Mountain State Muzzleloading
    Supplies, Inc.
New Win Publishing, Inc.
OK Weber,Inc.
Outdoor Sports
    Headquarters,Inc.
Paintball Games International
    Magazine (Aceville
    Publications)
Pejsa Ballistics
Petersen Publishing Co.
Pettinger Books, Gerald
Police Bookshelf
Precision Reloading, Inc.
Precision Shooting,Inc.
Ray Riling Arms Books Co.
Remington Double Shotguns
Riling Arms Books Co., Ray
Rocky Mountain Wildlife
    Products
Rutgers Book Center
S&S Firearms
Safari Press, Inc.
Saunders Gun & Machine Shop
Scharch Mfg., Inc.
Semmer, Charles (See
    Remington Double
    Shotguns)
Sharps Arms Co., Inc., C.
Shootin' Accessories, Ltd.
Sierra Bullets
SPG LLC
Stackpole Books
Stewart Game Calls, Inc., Johnny
Stoeger Industries
Stoeger Publishing Co. (See
    Stoeger Industries)
The Gun Parts Corp.
The Gun Room Press
The Gun Works
The NgraveR Co.
The Outdoorsman's Bookstore
Thomas, Charles C.
Track of the Wolf, Inc.
Trafalgar Square
Trotman, Ken
Tru-Balance Knife Co.
Vega Tool Co.
Vintage Industries, Inc.

VSP Publishers (See
    Heritage/VSP Gun Books)
W. Square Enterprises
W. Square Enterprises
W.E. Brownell Checkering Tools
WAMCO--New Mexico
Wells Creek Knife & Gun Works
Wilderness Sound Products Ltd.
Williams Gun Sight Co.
Winchester Press (See New Win
    Publishing, Inc.)
Wolf's Western Traders
Wolfe Publishing Co.

BULLET CASTING, ACCESSORIES

Ballisti-Cast, Inc.
Bullet Metals
CFVentures
Ferguson, Bill
Lee Precision, Inc.
Magma Engineering Co.
Ox-Yoke Originals, Inc.
Rapine Bullet Mould Mfg. Co.
The Hanned Line
Thompson Bullet Lube Co.
United States Products Co.

BULLET CASTING, FURNACES & POTS

Ballisti-Cast, Inc.
Bullet Metals
Ferguson, Bill
Lee Precision, Inc.
Magma Engineering Co.
Rapine Bullet Mould Mfg. Co.

BULLET CASTING, LEAD

Action Bullets & Alloy Inc.
Ames Metal Products
Beartooth Bullets
Belltown Ltd.
Buckskin Bullet Co.
Bullet Metals
Bullseye Bullets
Hunters Supply, Inc.
Jericho Tool & Die Co., Inc.
Lee Precision, Inc.
Magma Engineering Co.
Muzzleloading Technologies,
    Inc.
Ox-Yoke Originals, Inc.
Penn Bullets
Proofmark Corp.
SPG LLC

BULLET PULLERS

Royal Arms Gunstocks

BULLET TOOLS

Brynin, Milton
Bullet Swaging Supply Inc.
Camdex, Inc.
Corbin Mfg. & Supply, Inc.
Cumberland Arms
Eagan, Donald V.
Holland's Gunsmithing
Hollywood Engineering
Lee Precision, Inc.
Necromancer Industries, Inc.
Niemi Engineering, W. B.
North Devon Firearms Services
Rorschach Precision Products
Sport Flite Manufacturing Co.
The Hanned Line
WTA Manufacturing

BULLET, CASE & DIE LUBRICANTS

4-D Custom Die Co.
Bonanza (See Forster Products)

Brown Co, E. Arthur
Buckskin Bullet Co.
Camp-Cap Products
CH Tool & Die Co (See 4-D
    Custom Die Co)
Chem-Pak Inc.
Cooper-Woodward
CVA
E-Z-Way Systems
Elkhorn Bullets
Ferguson, Bill
Forster Products
Guardsman Products
HEBB Resources
Heidenstrom Bullets
Hollywood Engineering
Hornady Mfg. Co.
Imperial (See E-Z-Way Systems)
Knoell, Doug
Le Clear Industries (See E-Z-
    Way Systems)
Lee Precision, Inc.
Lithi Bee Bullet Lube
MI-TE Bullets
Paco's (See Small Custom
    Mould & Bullet Co)
RCBS Div. of Blount
Reardon Products
Rooster Laboratories
Shay's Gunsmithing
Small Custom Mould & Bullet
    Co.
Tamarack Products, Inc.
Uncle Mike's (See Michaels of
    Oregon Co)
Warren Muzzleloading Co., Inc.
Widener's Reloading & Shooting
    Supply, Inc.
Young Country Arms

CARTRIDGES FOR COLLECTORS

"Gramps" Antique Cartridges
Ackerman & Co.
Ad Hominem
British Antiques
Cameron's
Campbell, Dick
Cartridge Transfer Group, Pete
    de Coux
Cherry Creek State Park
    Shooting Center
Cole's Gun Works
Collectors Firearms Etc
Colonial Repair
de Coux, Pete (See Cartridge
    Transfer Group)
Duane's Gun Repair (See DGR
    Custom Rifles)
Enguix Import-Export
Epps, Ellwood (See "Gramps"
    Antique Cartridges)
First Inc, Jack
Fitz Pistol Grip Co.
Forty Five Ranch Enterprises
Goergen's Gun Shop, Inc.
Grayback Wildcats
Gun City
Liberty Shooting Supplies
Mandall Shooting Supplies Inc.
MAST Technology
Michael's Antiques
Montana Outfitters, Lewis E.
    Yearout
Pasadena Gun Center
San Francisco Gun Exchange
SOS Products Co. (See Buck
    Stix-SOS Products Co.)
Stone Enterprises Ltd.
The Country Armourer
The Gun Parts Corp.
Vom Hoffe (See Old Western
    Scrounger, Inc., The)
Ward & Van Valkenburg

PRODUCT & SERVICE DIRECTORY

Yearout, Lewis E. (See Montana Outfitters)

CASE & AMMUNITION PROCESSORS, INSPECTORS, BOXERS

Ammo Load, Inc.
Ben's Machines
Scharch Mfg., Inc.

CASE CLEANERS & POLISHING MEDIA

3-D Ammunition & Bullets
Belltown Ltd.
G96 Products Co., Inc.
Lee Precision, Inc.
Penn Bullets
VibraShine, Inc.

CASE PREPARATION TOOLS

Hoehn Sales, Inc.
K&M Services
Lee Precision, Inc.
Match Prep--Doyle Gracey
RCBS Div. of Blount
Stoney Point Products, Inc.

CASE TRIMMERS, TRIM DIES & ACCESSORIES

Fremont Tool Works
Hoehn Sales, Inc.
K&M Services
Match Prep--Doyle Gracey
Ozark Gun Works

CASE TUMBLERS, VIBRATORS, MEDIA & ACCESSORIES

Berry's Mfg., Inc.
OK Weber,Inc.
Penn Bullets
VibraShine, Inc.

CASES, CABINETS, RACKS & SAFES - GUN

Alco Carrying Cases
All Rite Products, Inc.
Allen Co., Bob
Allen Co., Inc.
Allen Sportswear, Bob (See Allen Co., Bob)
Alumna Sport by Dee Zee
American Display Co.
American Security Products Co.
Americase
Art Jewel Enterprises Ltd.
Ashby Turkey Calls
Bagmaster Mfg., Inc.
Barramundi Corp.
Berry's Mfg., Inc.
Big Sky Racks, Inc.
Big Spring Enterprises "Bore Stores"
Bill's Custom Cases
Bison Studios
Black Sheep Brand
Brauer Bros. Mfg. Co.
Brown, H. R. (See Silhouette Leathers)
Browning Arms Co.
Bushmaster Hunting & Fishing
Cannon Safe, Inc.
Chipmunk (See Oregon Arms, Inc.)
Cobalt Mfg., Inc.
CONKKO
Connecticut Shotgun Mfg. Co.

D&L Industries (See D.J. Marketing)
D.J. Marketing
Dara-Nes, Inc. (See Nesci Enterprises, Inc.)
Deepeeka Exports Pvt. Ltd.
Doskocil Mfg. Co., Inc.
DTM International, Inc.
Elk River, Inc.
English, Inc., A.G.
Enhanced Presentations, Inc.
Eversull Co., Inc., K.
Fort Knox Security Products
Frontier Safe Co.
Galati International
GALCO International Ltd.
Gun Locker Div. of Airmold W.R. Grace & Co.-Conn.
Gun-Ho Sports Cases
Hafner World Wide, Inc.
Hall Plastics, Inc., John
Hastings Barrels
Homak
Hoppe's Div. Penguin Industries, Inc.
Huey Gun Cases
Hugger Hooks Co.
Hunter Co., Inc.
Hydrosorbent Products
Impact Case Co.
Johanssons Vapentillbehor, Bert
Johnston Bros. (See C&T Corp. TA Johnson Brothers)
Jumbo Sports Products
Kalispel Case Line
Kane Products, Inc.
KK Air International (See Impact Case Co.)
Knock on Wood Antiques
Kolpin Mfg., Inc.
Lakewood Products LLC
Liberty Safe
Marsh, Mike
Maximum Security Corp.
McWelco Products
Morton Booth Co.
MPC
MTM Molded Products Co., Inc.
Nalpak
Necessary Concepts, Inc.
Nesci Enterprises Inc.
Oregon Arms, Inc. (See Rogue Rifle Co., Inc.)
Outa-Site Gun Carriers
Palmer Security Products
Perazzi USA, Inc.
Pflumm Mfg. Co.
Poburka, Philip (See Bison Studios)
Powell & Son (Gunmakers) Ltd., William
Prototech Industries, Inc.
Quality Arms, Inc.
Rogue Rifle Co., Inc.
Schulz Industries
Silhouette Leathers
Southern Security
Sportsman's Communicators
Sun Welding Safe Co.
Sweet Home, Inc.
The Eutaw Co., Inc.
The Outdoor Connection,Inc.
The Surecase Co.
Tinks & Ben Lee Hunting Products (See Wellington Outdoors)
Universal Sports
W. Waller & Son, Inc.
WAMCO, Inc.
Wilson Case, Inc.
Woodstream
Zanotti Armor, Inc.
Ziegel Engineering

CHOKE DEVICES, RECOIL ABSORBERS & RECOIL PADS

3-Ten Corp.
Accuright
Action Products, Inc.
Allen Co., Bob
Allen Sportswear, Bob (See Allen Co., Bob)
Answer Products Co.
Arms Ingenuity Co.
B-Square Company, Inc.
Baer Custom, Inc, Les
Baker, Stan
Bansner's Gunsmithing Specialties
Bartlett Engineering
Briley Mfg. Inc.
Brooks Tactical Systems
Brownells, Inc.
Buffer Technologies
Bull Mountain Rifle Co.
C&H Research
Cape Outfitters
Cation
Clearview Products
Colonial Arms, Inc.
Connecticut Shotgun Mfg. Co.
CRR, Inc./Marble's Inc.
Danuser Machine Co.
Dina Arms Corporation
Elsen Inc., Pete
Frank Custom Classic Arms, Ron
Graybill's Gun Shop
Gruning Precision Inc.
Guns
Hammans, Charles E.
Harry Lawson Co.
Hastings Barrels
Hogue Grips
Holland's Gunsmithing
I.N.C. Inc (See Kick Eez)
J.P. Enterprises Inc.
Jackalope Gun Shop
Jenkins Recoil Pads, Inc.
Kickeez Inc.
Lawson Co., Harry
London Guns Ltd.
Lyman Products Corp.
Mag-Na-Port International, Inc.
Marble Arms (See CRR, Inc./Marble's Inc.)
Meadow Industries
Menck, Gunsmith Inc., T.W.
Middlebrooks Custom Shop
Morrow, Bud
Nelson/Weather-Rite, Inc.
Nu-Line Guns,Inc.
One Of A Kind
Original Box, nc.
Palsa Outdoor Products
PAST Sporting Goods,Inc.
Precision Reloading, Inc.
Pro-Port Ltd.
Protektor Model
Que Industries, Inc.
R.M. Precision
Shotguns Unlimited
Simmons Gun Repair, Inc.
Spencer's Custom Guns
Stone Enterprises Ltd.
Truglo, Inc.
Trulock Tool
Uncle Mike's (See Michaels of Oregon Co)
Universal Sports
Virgin Valley Custom Guns
Vortek Products, Inc.
Wilson Gun Shop
Wise Guns, Dale

CHRONOGRAPHS & PRESSURE TOOLS

Air Rifle Specialists
Brown Co., E. Arthur
Canons Delcour
Clearview Products
Competition Electronics, Inc.
Custom Chronograph, Inc.
D&H Precision Tooling
Hege Jagd-u. Sporthandels GmbH
Hornady Mfg. Co.
Hutton Rifle Ranch
Kent Cartridge Mfg. Co. Ltd.
Mac-1 Airgun Distributors
Oehler Research,Inc.
P.A.C.T., Inc.
Romain's Custom Guns, Inc.
Savage Arms, Inc.
Shooting Chrony, Inc.
SKAN A.R.
Stratco, Inc.
Tepeco

CLEANERS & DEGREASERS

Belltown Ltd.
Camp-Cap Products
G96 Products Co., Inc.
Hafner World Wide, Inc.
Kleen-Bore,Inc.
Lestrom Laboratories, Inc.
Modern Muzzleloading, Inc.
Northern Precision Custom Swaged Bullets
Prolixr Lubricants
R&S Industries Corp.
Sheffield Knifemakers Supply, Inc.
United States Products Co.

CLEANING & REFINISHING SUPPLIES

AC Dyna-tite Corp.
Accupro Gun Care
Alpha 1 Drop Zone
American Gas & Chemical Co., Ltd
Answer Products Co.
Armite Laboratories
Armsport, Inc.
Atlantic Mills, Inc.
Atsko/Sno-Seal, Inc.
Barnes Bullets, Inc.
Beeman Precision Airguns
Belltown Ltd.
Bill's Gun Repair
Birchwood Casey
Blackhawk East
Blount, Inc., Sporting Equipment Div.
Blue and Gray Products Inc (See Ox-Yoke Originals, Inc.)
Break-Free, Inc.
Bridgers Best
Brown Co., E. Arthur
Brownells, Inc.
C.S. Van Gorden & Son, Inc.
Camp-Cap Products
Cape Outfitters
Chem-Pak Inc.
CONKKO
Connecticut Shotgun Mfg. Co.
Creedmoor Sports, Inc.
CRR, Inc./Marble's Inc.
Custom Products (See Jones Custom Products)
Cylinder & Slide, Inc., William R. Laughridge
D&H Prods. Co., Inc.
Dara-Nes, Inc. (See Nesci Enterprises, Inc.)

Decker Shooting Products
Deepeeka Exports Pvt. Ltd.
Desert Mountain Mfg.
Dever Co., Jack
Dewey Mfg. Co., Inc., J.
Du-Lite Corp.
Dykstra, Doug
E&L Mfg., Inc.
Eezox, Inc.
Ekol Leather Care
Faith Associates, Inc.
Flashette Co.
Flitz International Ltd.
Fluoramics, Inc.
Frontier Products Co.
G96 Products Co., Inc.
Golden Age Arms Co.
Gozon Corp. U.S.A.
Great Lakes Airguns
Guardsman Products
Gunsmithing, Inc.
Half Moon Rifle Shop
Heatbath Corp.
Heckler & Koch, Inc.
Hoppe's Div. Penguin Industries, Inc.
Hornady Mfg. Co.
Hydrosorbent Products
Iosso Products
Jantz Supply
Johnston Bros. (See C&T Corp. TA Johnson Brothers)
Jonad Corp.
K&M Industries, Inc.
Kellogg's Professional Products
Kent Cartridge Mfg. Co. Ltd.
Kesselring Gun Shop
Kleen-Bore,Inc.
Knight Rifles
Laurel Mountain Forge
Lee Supplies, Mark
LEM Gun Specialties Inc. The Lewis Lead Remover
List Precision Engineering
LPS Laboratories, Inc.
Mac-1 Airgun Distributors
Marble Arms (See CRR, Inc./Marble's Inc.)
Mark Lee Supplies
Micro Sight Co.
Minute Man High Tech Industries
Mountain State Muzzleloading Supplies, Inc.
Mountain View Sports, Inc.
MTM Molded Products Co., Inc.
Muscle Products Corp.
Muzzleloading Technologies, Inc.
Neal Johnson's Gunsmithing, Inc.
Nesci Enterprises Inc.
Northern Precision Custom Swaged Bullets
Now Products, Inc.
October Country Muzzleloading
OK Weber,Inc.
Old World Oil Products
Omark Industries,Div. of Blount,Inc.
Original Mink Oil,Inc.
Otis Technology, Inc.
Outers Laboratories Div. of Blount, Inc.Sporting E
Ox-Yoke Originals, Inc.
P&M Sales and Service
Parker & Sons Shooting Supply
Parker Gun Finishes
Pendleton Royal, c/o Swingler Buckland Ltd.
Pete Rickard, Inc.
Precision Airgun Sales, Inc.
Precision Reloading, Inc.
Pro-Shot Products, Inc.

Prolixrr Lubricants
R&S Industries Corp.
Radiator Specialty Co.
Rickard, Inc., Pete
Rooster Laboratories
Rusteprufe Laboratories
Rusty Duck Premium Gun Care Products
Saunders Gun & Machine Shop
Schumakers Gun Shop
Sheffield Knifemakers Supply, Inc.
Shiloh Creek
Shooter's Choice
Shootin' Accessories, Ltd.
Silencio/Safety Direct
Sinclair International, Inc.
Sno-Seal, Inc. (See Atsko/Sno-Seal)
Southern Bloomer Mfg. Co.
Spencer's Custom Guns
Starr Trading Co., Jedediah
Stoney Point Products, Inc.
Svon Corp.
T.F.C. S.P.A.
TDP Industries, Inc.
Tetra Gun Lubricants (See FTI, Inc.)
Texas Platers Supply Co.
The Dutchman's Firearms, Inc.
The Lewis Lead Remover (See LEM Gun Specialties, Inc.)
The Paul Co.
Thompson Bullet Lube Co.
Thompson/Center Arms
Track of the Wolf, Inc.
United States Products Co.
Venco Industries, Inc. (See Shooter's Choice)
VibraShine, Inc.
Volquartsen Custom Ltd.
Vom Hoffe (See Old Western Scrounger, Inc., The)
Warren Muzzleloading Co., Inc.
WD-40 Co.
Wick, David E.
Willow Bend
Wolf's Western Traders
Young Country Arms

COMPUTER SOFTWARE - BALLISTICS

Action Target, Inc.
AmBr Software Group Ltd.
Arms Software
Arms, Programming Solutions (See Arms Software)
Ballistic Engineering & Software, Inc.
Barnes Bullets, Inc.
Beartooth Bullets
Canons Delcour
Corbin Mfg. & Supply, Inc.
Data Tech Software Systems
Gun Hunter Trading Co.
Hodgdon Powder Co.
Huntington Die Specialties
J.I.T. Ltd.
Jensen Bullets
Kent Cartridge Mfg. Co. Ltd.
Maionchi-L.M.I.
Oehler Research,Inc.
Outdoor Sports Headquarters,Inc.
P.A.C.T., Inc.
Pejsa Ballistics
Powley Computer (See Hutton Rifle Ranch)
RCBS Div. of Blount
Sierra Bullets
The Ballistic Program Co., Inc.
The Country Armourer
Tioga Engineering Co., Inc.

Vancini, Carl (See Bestload, Inc.)
W. Square Enterprises
W. Square Enterprises

CUSTOM GUNSMITH

A&W Repair
A.A. Arms, Inc.
Acadian Ballistic Specialties
Accuracy Unlimited
Ace Custom 45's, Inc.
Acra-Bond Laminates
Actions by "T" Teddy Jacobson
Ad Hominem
Adair Custom Shop, Bill
Ahlman Guns
Aldis Gunsmithing & Shooting Supply
Alpha Gunsmith Division
Alpine Indoor Shooting Range
American Custom Gunmakers Guild
Amrine's Gun Shop
Answer Products Co.
Antique Arms Co.
Armament Gunsmithing Co., Inc.
Arms Craft Gunsmithing
Arms Ingenuity Co.
Arnold Arms Co., Inc.
Art's Gun & Sport Shop, Inc.
Arundel Arms & Ammunition, Inc., A.
Autauga Arms, Inc.
Baelder, Harry
Baer Custom, Inc, Les
Bain & Davis, Inc.
Ballard Rifle & Cartridge Co., LLC
Bansner's Gunsmithing Specialties
Barnes Bullets, Inc.
Barta's Gunsmithing
Bear Arms
Bear Mountain Gun & Tool
Beaver Lodge (See Fellowes, Ted)
Behlert Precision, Inc.
Beitzinger, George
Belding's Custom Gun Shop
Bellm Contenders
Ben William's Gun Shop
Benchmark Guns
Bengtson Arms Co., L.
Biesen, Al
Biesen, Roger
Bill Adair Custom Shop
Billeb, Stephen L.
Billings Gunsmiths Inc.
BlackStar AccuMax Barrels
BlackStar Barrel Accurizing (See BlackStar AccuMax Barrels)
Bob Rogers Gunsmithing
Boltin, John M.
Bond Custom Firearms
Borden Ridges Rimrock Stocks
Borden Rifles Inc.
Borovnik KG, Ludwig
Bowen Classic Arms Corp.
Brace, Larry D.
Briese Bullet Co., Inc.
Briganti, A.J.
Briley Mfg. Inc.
Broad Creek Rifle Works, Ltd.
Brockman's Custom Gunsmithing
Broken Gun Ranch
Brown Precision,Inc.
Buckhorn Gun Works
Buckskin Machine Works, A. Hunkeler
Budin, Dave
Bull Mountain Rifle Co.
Bullberry Barrel Works, Ltd.
Burkhart Gunsmithing, Don
Cache La Poudre Rifleworks

Cambos Outdoorsman
Camilli, Lou
Cannon's
Carolina Precision Rifles
Carter's Gun Shop
Caywood, Shane J.
CBC-BRAZIL
Chambers Flintlocks Ltd., Jim
Champlin Firearms, Inc.
Chicasaw Gun Works
Chuck's Gun Shop
Clark Custom Guns, Inc.
Clark Firearms Engraving
Classic Arms Company
Classic Guns, Inc., Frank S. Wood
Clearview Products
Cleland's Outdoor World, Inc.
Cloward's Gun Shop
Cogar's Gunsmithing
Cole's Gun Works
Coleman's Custom Repair
Colonial Arms, Inc.
Colonial Repair
Colorado Gunsmithing Academy
Colorado School of Trades
Colt's Mfg. Co., Inc.
Conrad, C. A.
Corkys Gun Clinic
Cox, Ed. C.
Craig Custom Ltd., Research & Development
Creekside Gun Shop Inc.
Cullity Restoration
Curtis Custom Shop
Custom Checkering Service, Kathy Forster
Custom Gun Products
Custom Gun Stocks
Cylinder & Slide, Inc., William R. Laughridge
D&D Gunsmiths, Ltd.
D&J Bullet Co. & Custom Gun Shop, Inc.
Dangler, Homer L.
Darlington Gun Works, Inc.
Dave's Gun Shop
David Miller Co.
David R. Chicoine
David W. Schwartz Custom Guns
Davis, Don
Del-Sports, Inc.
Delorge, Ed
Dever Co, Jack
DGR Custom Rifles
DGS, Inc., Dale A. Storey
Dietz Gun Shop & Range, Inc.
Dilliott Gunsmithing, Inc.
Donnelly, C. P.
Duane A. Hobbie Gunsmithing
Duane's Gun Repair (See DGR Custom Rifles)
Duffy, Charles E (See Guns Antique & Modern DBA)
Duncan's Gun Works, Inc.
E. Arthur Brown Co.
Echols & Co., D'Arcy
Eckelman Gunsmithing
Ed~ Brown Products, Inc.
Eggleston, Jere D.
EGW Evolution Gun Works
Entre'prise Arms, Inc.
Erhardt, Dennis
Eskridge Rifles
Eversull Co., Inc., K.
Eyster Heritage Gunsmiths, Inc., Ken
Fanzoj GmbH
Ferris Firearms
Fish Mfg. Gunsmith Sptg. Co., Marshall F
Fisher, Jerry A.
Fisher Custom Firearms
Fleming Firearms

Flynn's Custom Guns
Forkin, Ben (See Belt MTN Arms)
Forkin Arms
Forster, Kathy (See Custom Checkering Service, Kathy Forster)
Forster, Larry L.
Forthofer's Gunsmithing & Knifemaking
Francesca, Inc.
Francotte & Cie S.A. Auguste
Frank Custom Classic Arms, Ron
Fred F. Wells/Wells Sport Store
Frontier Arms Co.,Inc.
Fullmer, Geo. M.
G.G. & G.
Gary Reeder Custom Guns
Gator Guns & Repair
Genecco Gun Works, K
Gentry Custom Gunmaker, David
George E. Mathews & Son, Inc.
Gilkes, Anthony W.
Gillmann, Edwin
Gilman-Mayfield, Inc.
Gilmore Sports Concepts
Giron, Robert E.
Goens, Dale W.
Gonic Arms/North American Arm
Gonzalez Guns, Ramon B
Goodling's Gunsmithing
Goodwin, Fred
Gordie's Gun Shop
Grace, Charles E.
Grayback Wildcats
Graybill's Gun Shop
GrE-Tan Rifles
Green, Roger M.
Greg Gunsmithing Repair
Griffin & Howe, Inc.
Griffin & Howe, Inc.
Gruning Precision Inc.
Guncraft Sports Inc.
Guns
Guns Antique & Modern DBA/Charles E. Duffy
Gunsite Custom Shop
Gunsite Gunsmithy (See Gunsite Custom Shop)
Gunsite Training Center
Gunsmithing Inc.
Hagn Rifles & Actions, Martin
Hallberg Gunsmith, Fritz
Halstead, Rick
Hamilton, Jim
Hamilton, Alex B (See Ten-Ring Precision, Inc)
Hammans, Charles E.
Hammond Custom Guns Ltd.
Hank's Gun Shop
Hanson's Gun Center, Dick
Hanus Birdguns Bill
Harris Gunworks
Harry Lawson Co.
Hart & Son, Inc.
Hart Rifle Barrels,Inc.
Hartmann & Weiss GmbH
Harwood, Jack O.
Hawken Shop, The (See Dayton Traister)
Hecht, Hubert J, Waffen-Hecht
Heilmann, Stephen
Heinie Specialty Products
Hensley, Gunmaker, Darwin
Heppler's Machining
Heppler, Keith M, Keith's Custom Gunstocks
Heydenberk, Warren R.
High Bridge Arms, Inc.
High Performance International
Highline Machine Co.
Hill, Loring F.
Hiptmayer, Armurier
Hiptmayer, Klaus

Hoag, James W.
Hodgson, Richard
Hoehn Sales, Inc.
Hoelscher, Virgil
Hoenig & Rodman
Hofer Jagdwaffen, P.
Holland's Gunsmithing
Hollis Gun Shop
Huebner, Corey O.
Hughes, Steven Dodd
Hunkeler, A (See Buckskin Machine Works, A. Hunkeler)
Hyper-Single, Inc.
Imperial Magnum Corp.
Irwin, Campbell H.
Island Pond Gun Shop
Ivanoff, Thomas G (See Tom's Gun Repair)
J&S Heat Treat
J.J. Roberts/Engraver
Jackalope Gun Shop
Jamison's Forge Works
Jarrett Rifles, Inc.
Jarvis, Inc.
Jeffredo Gunsight
Jensen's Custom Ammunition
Jim Norman Custom Gunstocks
Jim's Gun Shop (See Spradlin's)
Jim's Precision, Jim Ketchum
John Norrell Arms
Johnston, James (See North Fork Custom Gunsmithing, James Johnston)
Jones, J.D./SSK Industries
Juenke, Vern
Jungkind, Reeves C.
Jurras, L. E.
K-D, Inc.
KDF, Inc.
Keith's Custom Gunstocks
Keith's Custom Gunstocks (See Heppler, Keith M)
Ken Eyster Heritage Gunsmiths, Inc.
Ken Starnes Gunmaker
Ken's Gun Specialties
Ketchum, Jim (See Jim's Precision)
Kilham & Co.
Kimball, Gary
King's Gun Works
KLA Enterprises
Klein Custom Guns, Don
Kleinendorst, K. W.
Kneiper, James
Knippel, Richard
KOGOT
Korzinek Riflesmith, J
LaFrance Specialties
Lair, Sam
Lampert, Ron
LaRocca Gun Works
Larry Lyons Gunworks
Lathrop's, Inc.
Laughridge, William R (See Cylinder & Slide Inc)
Lawson Co., Harry
Lazzeroni Arms Co.
Lee's Red Ramps
LeFever Arms Co., Inc.
Lind Custom Guns, Al
Linebaugh Custom Sixguns
List Precision Engineering
Lock's Philadelphia Gun Exchange
Lone Star Rifle Company
Long, George F.
Mag-Na-Port International, Inc.
Mahony, Philip Bruce
Mahovsky's Metalife
Makinson, Nicholas
Mandall Shooting Supplies Inc.
Martin's Gun Shop

PRODUCT & SERVICE DIRECTORY

Martz, John V.
Mathews & Son, Inc., George E.
Mazur Restoration, Pete
McCament, Jay
McCann's Muzzle-Gun Works
McCluskey Precision Rifles
McFarland, Stan
McGowen Rifle Barrels
McKinney, R.P. (See Schuetzen Gun Co.)
McMillan Rifle Barrels
MCS, Inc.
Mercer Custom Stocks, R. M.
Michael's Antiques
Mid-America Recreation, Inc.
Middlebrooks Custom Shop
Miller Arms, Inc.
Miller Custom
Mills Jr., Hugh B.
Mo's Competitor Supplies (See MCS Inc)
Moeller, Steve
Monell Custom Guns
Morrison Custom Rifles, J. W.
Morrow, Bud
Mowrey's Guns & Gunsmithing
Mullis Guncraft
Muzzleloading Technologies, Inc.
Nastoff's 45 Shop, Inc., Steve
NCP Products, Inc.
Nelson, Stephen
Nettestad Gun Works
New England Arms Co.
New England Custom Gun Service
Newman Gunshop
Nicholson Custom
Nickels, Paul R.
Nicklas, Ted
Nitex, Inc.
North American Shooting Systems
North Fork Custom Gunsmithing, James Johnston
Nu-Line Guns,Inc.
Oakland Custom Arms,Inc.
Old World Gunsmithing
Olson, Vic
Ottmar, Maurice
Ox-Yoke Originals, Inc.
Ozark Gun Works
P.S.M.G. Gun Co.
Pagel Gun Works, Inc.
Parker Gun Finishes
Pasadena Gun Center
Paterson Gunsmithing
PEM's Mfg. Co.
Pence Precision Barrels
Pennsylvania Gunsmith School
Penrod Precision
Pentheny de Pentheny
Perazone-Gunsmith, Brian
Performance Specialists
Pete Mazur Restoration
Peterson Gun Shop, Inc., A.W.
Powell & Son (Gunmakers) Ltd., William
Power Custom, Inc.
Professional Hunter Supplies (See Star Custom Bullets)
Quality Firearms of Idaho, Inc.
R&J Gun Shop
R.A. Wells Custom Gunsmith
Ramon B. Gonzalez Guns
Ray's Gunsmith Shop
Renfrew Guns & Supplies
Ridgetop Sporting Goods
Ries, Chuck
Rifles, Inc.
Rigby & Co., John
River Road Sporting Clays
RMS Custom Gunsmithing

Robert Valade Engraving
Robinson, Don
Rocky Mountain Arms, Inc.
Rocky Mountain Rifle Works Ltd.
Romain's Custom Guns, Inc.
RPM
Rupert's Gun Shop
Ryan, Chad L.
Sanders Custom Gun Service
Savage Arms, Inc.
Schiffman, Mike
Schumakers Gun Shop
Score High Gunsmithing
Scott, Dwight
Scott McDougall & Associates
Sharp Shooter Supply
Shaw, Inc., E. R. (See Small Arms Mfg. Co.)
Shay's Gunsmithing
Shockley, Harold H.
Shooters Supply
Shootin' Shack, Inc.
Shooting Specialties (See Titus, Daniel)
Shotguns Unlimited
Sile Distributors, Inc.
Silver Ridge Gun Shop (See Goodwin, Fred)
Simmons Gun Repair, Inc.
Singletary, Kent
Sipes Gun Shop
Siskiyou Gun Works (See Donnelly, C. P.)
Skeoch, Brian R.
Sklany's Machine Shop
Slezak, Jerome F.
Small Arms Mfg. Co.
Small Arms Specialists
Smith, Art
Smith, Sharmon
Snapp's Gunshop
Speiser, Fred D.
Spencer Reblue Service
Spencer's Custom Guns
Sportsmen's Exchange & Western Gun Traders, Inc.
Springfield, Inc.
SSK Industries
Star Custom Bullets
Steelman's Gun Shop
Steffens, Ron
Steger, James R.
Stiles Custom Guns
Storey, Dale A. (See DGS Inc.)
Stott's Creek Armory, Inc.
Strawbridge, Victor W.
Sturgeon Valley Sporters, K. Ide
Sullivan, David S .(See Westwind Rifles Inc.)
Swann, D. J.
Swenson's 45 Shop, A. D.
Swift River Gunworks
Szweda, Robert (See RMS Custom Gunsmithing)
Taconic Firearms Ltd., Perry Lane
Talmage, William G.
Tank's Rifle Shop
Tar-Hunt Custom Rifles, Inc.
Tarnhelm Supply Co., Inc.
Taylor & Robbins
Ten-Ring Precision, Inc.
Terry K. Kopp Professional Gunsmithing
The Competitive Pistol Shop
The Custom Shop
The Gun Shop
The Gun Works
The Orvis Co.
The Robar Co.'s, Inc.
The Swampfire Shop (See Peterson Gun Shop, Inc.)
Thompson, Randall (See Highline Machine Co.)

Thurston Sports, Inc.
Time Precision, Inc.
Tom's Gun Repair, Thomas G. Ivanoff
Tom's Gunshop
Tooley Custom Rifles
Trevallion Gunstocks
Trulock Tool
Tucker, James C.
Unmussig Bullets, D. L.
Upper Missouri Trading Co.
Valade Engraving, Robert
Van Horn, Gil
Van Patten, J. W.
Van's Gunsmith Service
Vest, John
Vic's Gun Refinishing
Vintage Arms, Inc.
Virgin Valley Custom Guns
Volquartsen Custom Ltd.
Walker Arms Co., Inc.
Wallace, Terry
Wasmundt, Jim
Wayne E. Schwartz Custom Guns
Weaver Arms Corp. Gun Shop
Weber & Markin Custom Gunsmiths
Weems, Cecil
Weigand Combat Handguns, Inc.
Welsh, Bud
Wenig Custom Gunstocks
Werth, T. W.
Wessinger Custom Guns & Engraving
Western Design (See Alpha Gunsmith Division)
Westley Richards & Co.
Westwind Rifles, Inc., David S. Sullivan
White Barn Wor
White Shooting Systems, Inc. (See White Muzzleloading)
Wichita Arms, Inc.
Wiebe, Duane
Wiest, M. C.
Wild West Guns
Williams Gun Sight Co.
Williams Shootin' Iron Service, The Lynx-Line
Williamson Precision Gunsmithing
Wilson Gun Shop
Winter, Robert M.
Wise Guns, Dale
Wiseman and Co., Bill
Wood, Frank (See Classic Guns, Inc.)
Working Guns
Wright's Hardwood Gunstock Blanks
Yankee Gunsmith
Yee, Mike
Zeeryp, Russ

CUSTOM METALSMITH

A&W Repair
Ackerman & Co.
Ahlman Guns
Aldis Gunsmithing & Shooting Supply
American Custom Gunmakers Guild
Amrine's Gun Shop
Answer Products Co.
Antique Arms Co.
Arnold Arms Co., Inc.
Baer Custom, Inc, Les
Bansner's Gunsmithing Specialties
Baron Technology
Bear Mountain Gun & Tool

Behlert Precision, Inc.
Beitzinger, George
Benchmark Guns
Bengtson Arms Co., L.
Biesen, Al
Bill Adair Custom Shop
Billings Gunsmiths Inc.
Billingsley & Brownell
Bob Rogers Gunsmithing
Bone Engraving, Ralph
Brace, Larry D.
Briganti, A.J.
Broad Creek Rifle Works, Ltd.
Brown Precision,Inc.
Buckhorn Gun Works
Bull Mountain Rifle Co.
Bullberry Barrel Works, Ltd.
Burkhart Gunsmithing, Don
Bustani, Leo
Campbell, Dick
Carter's Gun Shop
Caywood, Shane J.
Champlin Firearms, Inc.
Checkmate Refinishing
Chicasaw Gun Works
Classic Guns, Inc., Frank S. Wood
Cleland's Outdoor World, Inc.
Colonial Repair
Colorado Gunsmithing Academy
Craftguard
Crandall Tool & Machine Co.
Cullity Restoration
Custom Gun Products
D&D Gunsmiths, Ltd.
D&H Precision Tooling
Dave's Gun Shop
Delorge, Ed
DGR Custom Rifles
DGS, Inc., Dale A. Storey
Duane's Gun Repair (See DGR Custom Rifles)
Duncan's Gun Works, Inc.
Eversull Co., Inc., K.
Eyster Heritage Gunsmiths, Inc., Ken
Ferris Firearms
Forster, Larry L.
Forthofer's Gunsmithing & Knifemaking
Francesca, Inc.
Frank Custom Classic Arms, Ron
Fred F. Wells/Wells Sport Store
Fullmer, Geo. M.
Gary Reeder Custom Guns
Gene's Custom Guns
Genecco Gun Works, K.
Gentry Custom Gunmaker, David
Gilkes, Anthony W.
Gordie's Gun Shop
Grace, Charles E.
Graybill's Gun Shop
Green, Roger M.
Griffin & Howe, Inc.
Guns
Gunsmithing Ltd.
Hagn Rifles & Actions, Martin
Hallberg Gunsmith, Fritz
Hamilton, Alex B (See Ten-Ring Precision, Inc)
Harry Lawson Co.
Hartmann & Weiss GmbH
Harwood, Jack O.
Hecht, Hubert J, Waffen-Hecht
Heilmann, Stephen
Heppler's Machining
Heritage Wildlife Carvings
Highline Machine Co.
Hiptmayer, Armurier
Hiptmayer, Klaus
Hoag, James W.
Hoelscher, Virgil
Holland's Gunsmithing
Hollis Gun Shop

Hyper-Single, Inc.
Island Pond Gun Shop
Ivanoff, Thomas G (See Tom's Gun Repair)
J&S Heat Treat
Jamison's Forge Works
Jeffredo Gunsight
Johnston, James (See North Fork Custom Gunsmithing, James Johnston)
KDF, Inc.
Ken Eyster Heritage Gunsmiths, Inc.
Ken Starnes Gunmaker
Ken's Gun Specialties
Kilham & Co.
Klein Custom Guns, Don
Kleinendorst, K. W.
Knippel, Richard
Lampert, Ron
Larry Lyons Gunworks
Lawson Co., Harry
List Precision Engineering
Mahovsky's Metalife
Makinson, Nicholas
Mazur Restoration, Pete
McCament, Jay
McCann Industries
McCann's Machine & Gun Shop
McFarland, Stan
Mid-America Recreation, Inc.
Miller Arms, Inc.
Morrison Custom Rifles, J. W.
Morrow, Bud
Mullis Guncraft
Nelson, Stephen
Nettestad Gun Works
New England Custom Gun Service
Nicholson Custom
Nitex, Inc.
Noreen, Peter H.
North Fork Custom Gunsmithing, James Johnston
Nu-Line Guns,Inc.
Olson, Vic
Ozark Gun Works
Pagel Gun Works, Inc.
Parker Gun Finishes
Pasadena Gun Center
Penrod Precision
Pete Mazur Restoration
Precise Metalsmithing Enterprises
Precision Specialties
R.A. Wells Custom Gunsmith
Rice, Keith (See White Rock Tool & Die)
Rifles, Inc.
River Road Sporting Clays
Robert Valade Engraving
Rocky Mountain Arms, Inc.
Score High Gunsmithing
Simmons Gun Repair, Inc.
Sipes Gun Shop
Skeoch, Brian R.
Sklany's Machine Shop
Small Arms Specialists
Smith, Art
Smith, Sharmon
Snapp's Gunshop
Spencer Reblue Service
Spencer's Custom Guns
Sportsmen's Exchange & Western Gun Traders, Inc.
Steffens, Ron
Steger, James R.
Stiles Custom Guns
Storey, Dale A. (See DGS Inc.)
Strawbridge, Victor W.
Taylor & Robbins
Ten-Ring Precision, Inc.

Terry K. Kopp Professional
Gunsmithing
The Custom Shop
The Gun Shop
The Robar Co.'s, Inc.
Thompson, Randall (See
Highline Machine Co.)
Tom's Gun Repair, Thomas G.
Ivanoff
Tooley Custom Rifles
Valade Engraving, Robert
Van Horn, Gil
Van Patten, J. W.
Waldron, Herman
Wallace, Terry
Weber & Markin Custom
Gunsmiths
Werth, T. W.
Wessinger Custom Guns &
Engraving
Westrom, John (See Precision
Metal Finishing)
White Rock Tool & Die
Wiebe, Duane
Wild West Guns
Williams Gun Sight Co.
Williams Shootin' Iron Service,
The Lynx-Line
Williamson Precision
Gunsmithing
Winter, Robert M.
Wise Guns, Dale
Wood, Frank (See Classic Guns,
Inc.)
Wright's Hardwood Gunstock
Blanks
Zufall, Joseph F.

DECOYS

A&M Waterfowl,Inc.
Baekgaard Ltd.
Belding's Custom Gun Shop
Boyds' Gunstock Industries, Inc.
Carry-Lite, Inc.
Deer Me Products Co.
Fair Game International
Farm Form Decoys, Inc.
Feather, Flex Decoys
Flambeau Products Corp.
G&H Decoys,Inc.
Herter's Manufacturing, Inc.
Hiti-Schuch, Atelier Wilma
Klinger Woodcarving
L.L. Bean, Inc.
Molin Industries, Tru-Nord
Division
North Wind Decoy Co.
Penn's Woods Products, Inc.
Quack Decoy & Sporting Clays
Russ Trading Post
Sports Innovations Inc.
Tanglefree Industries
Waterfield Sports, Inc.
Woods Wise Products

DIE ACCESSORIES, METALLIC

MarMik, Inc.
Rapine Bullet Mould Mfg. Co.
Sport Flite Manufacturing Co.

DIES, METALLIC

Carbide Die & Mfg. Co., Inc.
Dakota Arms, Inc.
Fremont Tool Works
King & Co.
Ozark Gun Works
Rapine Bullet Mould Mfg. Co.
RCBS Div. of Blount
Redding Reloading Equipment
Sport Flite Manufacturing Co.
Vega Tool Co.

DIES, SHOTSHELL

MEC, Inc.

DIES, SWAGE

Bullet Swaging Supply Inc.
Sport Flite Manufacturing Co.

ENGRAVER, ENGRAVING TOOLS

Ackerman & Co.
Adair Custom Shop, Bill
Adams & Son Engravers, John J.
Adams Jr., John J.
Ahlman Guns
Alfano, Sam
Allard, Gary/Creek Side Metal &
Woodcrafters
Allen Firearm Engraving
Altamont Co.
American Custom Gunmakers
Guild
American Pioneer Video
Anthony and George Ltd.
Baron Technology
Barraclough, John K.
Bates Engraving, Billy
Bill Adair Custom Shop
Bill Johns Master Engraver
Blair Engraving, J. R.
Bleile, C. Roger
Boessler, Erich
Bone Engraving, Ralph
Bratcher, Dan
Brooker, Dennis
Burgess, Byron
Churchill, Winston
Clark Firearms Engraving
Collings, Ronald
Creek Side Metal &
Woodcrafters
Cullity Restoration
Cupp, Alana, Custom Engraver
Davidson, Jere
Dayton Traister
Delorge, Ed
Dolbare, Elizabeth
Drain, Mark
Dremel Mfg. Co.
Dubber, Michael W.
Engraving Artistry
Evans Engraving, Robert
Eversull Co., Inc., K.
Eyster Heritage Gunsmiths, Inc.,
Ken
Firearms Engraver's Guild of
America
Flannery Engraving Co., Jeff W.
Forty Five Ranch Enterprises
Fountain Products
Francotte & Cie S.A. Auguste
Frank E. Hendricks Master
Engravers, Inc.
Frank Knives
French, Artistic Engraving, J. R.
Gary Reeder Custom Guns
Gene's Custom Guns
George, Tim
Glimm, Jerome C.
Golden Age Arms Co.
Gournet, Geoffroy
Grant, Howard V.
Griffin & Howe, Inc.
Guns
Gurney, F. R.
Gwinnell, Bryson J.
Hale, Engraver, Peter
Half Moon Rifle Shop
Hamilton, Jim
Hands Engraving, Barry Lee
Harris Gunworks
Harris Hand Engraving, Paul A.
Harwood, Jack O.

Hawken Shop, The (See Dayton
Traister)
Hendricks, Frank E. Inc., Master
Engravers
Heritage Wildlife Carvings
Hiptmayer, Armurier
Hiptmayer, Heidemarie
Ingle, Ralph W.
J J Roberts Firearm Engraver
J.J. Roberts/Engraver
J.R. Blair Engraving
Jantz Supply
John J. Adams & Son Engravers
Kamyk Engraving Co., Steve
Kane, Edward
Kehr, Roger
Kelly, Lance
Ken Eyster Heritage Gunsmiths,
Inc.
Kenneth W. Warren Engraver
Klingler Woodcarving
Knippel, Richard
Koevenig's Engraving Service
Kudlas, John M.
Larry Lyons Gunworks
LeFever Arms Co., Inc.
Leibowitz, Leonard
Lindsay, Steve
Little Trees Ramble (See Scott
Pilkington, Little
Lutz Engraving, Ron E.
Master Engravers, Inc. (See
Hendricks, Frank E)
McCombs, Leo
McDonald, Dennis
McKenzie, Lynton
Mele, Frank
Metals Hand Engraver/European
Hand Engraving
Mid-America Recreation, Inc.
Mittermeier, Inc., Frank
Montgomery Community
College
Nelson, Gary K.
New England Custom Gun
Service
New Orleans Jewelers Supply
Co.
Oker's Engraving
Pedersen, C. R.
Pedersen, Rex C.
Pilgrim Pewter,Inc. (See Bell
Originals Inc. Sid)
Pilkington, Scott (See Little
Trees Ramble)
Piquette, Paul R.
Potts, Wayne E.
Rabeno, Martin
Ralph Bone Engraving
Reed, Dave
Reno, Wayne
Riggs, Jim
Robert Valade Engraving
Rohner, Hans
Rohner, John
Rosser, Bob
Rundell's Gun Shop
Runge, Robert P.
Sampson, Roger
Schiffman, Mike
Sheffield Knifemakers Supply,
Inc.
Sherwood, George
Singletary, Kent
Smith, Mark A.
Smith, Ron
Smokey Valley Rifles (See Lutz
Engraving, Ron E)
The Gun Room
The NgraveR Co.
Theis, Terry
Thiewes, George W.
Thirion Gun Engraving, Denise
Thompson/Center Arms

Valade Engraving, Robert
Vest, John
Viramontez, Ray
Vorhes, David
W.E. Brownell Checkering Tools
Wagoner, Vernon G.
Wallace, Terry
Warenski, Julie
Warren, Kenneth W. (See
Mountain States Engraving)
Weber & Markin Custom
Gunsmiths
Welch, Sam
Wells, Rachel
Wessinger Custom Guns &
Engraving
Wood, Mel
Yee, Mike
Ziegel Engineering

GAME CALLS

Adventure Game Calls
African Import Co.
Arkansas Mallard Duck Calls
Ashby Turkey Calls
Bostick Wildlife Calls, Inc.
Cedar Hill Game Calls Inc.
Creative Concepts USA, Inc.
Crit'R Call (See Rocky Mountain
Wildlife Products)
Custom Calls
D&H Prods. Co., Inc.
D-Boone Ent., Inc.
Deepeeka Exports Pvt. Ltd.
Dr. O's Products Ltd.
Duck Call Specialists
Eddie Salter Calls, Inc.
Faulhaber Wildlocker
Faulk's Game Call Co., Inc.
Fibron Products, Inc.
Glynn Scobey Duck & Goose
Calls
Green Head Game Call Co.
Hally Caller
Haydel's Game Calls, Inc.
Herter's Manufacturing, Inc.
Hunter's Specialties Inc.
Keowee Game Calls
Kingyon, Paul L. (See Custom
Calls)
Knight & Hale Game Calls
Lohman Mfg. Co., Inc.
Mallardtone Game Calls
Marsh, Johnny
Moss Double Tone, Inc.
Mountain Hollow Game Calls
Oakman Turkey Calls
Outdoor Sports
Headquarters,Inc.
Penn's Woods Products, Inc.
Pete Rickard, Inc.
Philip S. Olt Co.
Primos, Inc.
Quaker Boy, Inc.
Rickard, Inc., Pete
Rocky Mountain Wildlife
Products
Russ Trading Post
Sceery Game Calls
Sports Innovations Inc.
Stanley Scruggs' Game Calls
Stewart Game Calls, Inc., Johnny
Sure-Shot Game Calls, Inc.
Tanglefree Industries
Tink's Safariland Hunting Corp.
Tinks & Ben Lee Hunting
Products (See Wellington
Outdoors)
Wellington Outdoors
Wilderness Sound Products Ltd.
Woods Wise Products
Wyant's Outdoor Products, Inc.

GAUGES, CALIPERS & MICROMETERS

K&M Services
Plum City Ballistic Range
Starrett Co., L. S.
Stoney Point Products, Inc.

GUN PARTS, U.S. & FOREIGN

"Su-Press-On",Inc.
A.A. Arms, Inc.
Actions by "T" Teddy Jacobson
Ahlman Guns
Amherst Arms
Antique Arms Co.
Aro-Tek Ltd.
Auto-Ordnance Corp.
Badger Shooters Supply, Inc.
Bar-Sto Precision Machine
Bear Mountain Gun & Tool
Bill's Gun Repair
Billings Gunsmiths Inc.
Bob's Gun Shop
Bohemia Arms Co.
Briese Bullet Co., Inc.
British Antiques
Brown Products, Inc., Ed
Buffer Technologies
Bushmaster Firearms (See
Quality Parts Co/Bushmaster
Firearms)
Bustani, Leo
Cape Outfitters
Caspian Arms, Ltd.
CBC-BRAZIL
Ciener Inc., Jonathan Arthur
Cole's Gun Works
Colonial Arms, Inc.
Colonial Repair
Cryo-Accurizing
Cylinder & Slide, Inc., William R.
Laughridge
Delta Arms Ltd.
DGR Custom Rifles
Dibble, Derek A.
Duane's Gun Repair (See DGR
Custom Rifles)
Duffy, Charles E (See Guns
Antique & Modern DBA)
E.A.A. Corp.
EGW Evolution Gun Works
Elliott Inc., G. W.
EMF Co., Inc.
Enguix Import-Export
Entre'prise Arms, Inc.
European American Armory
Corp (See E.A.A. Corp)
Federal Arms Corp. of America
Fleming Firearms
Forrest Inc., Tom
Glimm, Jerome C.
Goodwin, Fred
Granite Mountain Arms, Inc.
Greider Precision
Groenewold, John
Guns Antique & Modern
DBA/Charles E. Duffy
Hastings Barrels
Hawken Shop, The (See Dayton
Traister)
High Performance International
Hines Co, S C
I.S.S.
Irwin, Campbell H.
Jamison's Forge Works
Johnson's Gunsmithing, Inc,
Neal
K.K. Arms Co.
Kimber of America, Inc.
Knight's Mfg. Co.
Krico Jagd-und Sportwaffen
GmbH

Lampert, Ron
Laughridge, William R (See Cylinder & Slide Inc)
Leapers, Inc.
List Precision Engineering
Lodewick, Walter H.
Long, George F.
Mandall Shooting Supplies Inc.
Markell,Inc.
Martin's Gun Shop
McCormick Corp., Chip
MCS, Inc.
Merkuria Ltd.
Mid-America Recreation, Inc.
Mo's Competitor Supplies (See MCS Inc)
Morrow, Bud
North Star West
Northwest Arms
Nu-Line Guns,Inc.
Nygord Precision Products
Olympic Arms Inc.
P.S.M.G. Gun Co.
Parts & Surplus
Pennsylvania Gun Parts Inc.
Perazone-Gunsmith, Brian
Perazzi USA, Inc.
Performance Specialists
Peterson Gun Shop, Inc., A.W.
Pre-Winchester 92-90-62 Parts Co.
Quality Firearms of Idaho, Inc.
Quality Parts Co./Bushmaster Firearms
Ranch Products
Randco UK
Raptor Arms Co., Inc.
Ravell Ltd.
Retting, Inc., Martin B
Romain's Custom Guns, Inc.
Ruger (See Sturm, Ruger & Co., Inc.)
S&S Firearms
Sabatti S.r.l.
Samco Global Arms, Inc.
Sarco, Inc.
Savage Arms (Canada), Inc.
Scherer
Shockley, Harold H.
Shootin' Shack, Inc.
Silver Ridge Gun Shop (See Goodwin, Fred)
Simmons Gun Repair, Inc.
Sipes Gun Shop
Smires, C. L.
Smith & Wesson
Southern Ammunition Co., Inc.
Sportsmen's Exchange & Western Gun Traders, Inc.
Springfield Sporters, Inc.
Springfield, Inc.
Steyr Mannlicher AG & CO KG
STI International
Strayer-Voigt, Inc.
Sturm Ruger & Co. Inc.
Sunny Hill Enterprises, Inc.
T&S Industries, Inc.
Tank's Rifle Shop
Tarnhelm Supply Co., Inc.
The Gun Parts Corp.
The Gun Shop
The Southern Armory
The Swampfire Shop (See Peterson Gun Shop, Inc.)
Triple-K Mfg. Co., Inc.
VAM Distribution Co LLC
Vektor USA
Vintage Arms, Inc.
W. Waller & Son, Inc.
W.C. Wolff Co.
Walker Arms Co., Inc.
Weaver Arms Corp. Gun Shop
Wescombe, Bill (See North Star West)

Whitestone Lumber Corp.
Williams Mfg. of Oregon
Winchester Sutler, Inc., The
Wise Guns, Dale
Wisners Inc/Twin Pine Armory

GUNS & GUN PARTS, REPLICA & ANTIQUE

Ackerman & Co.
Ahlman Guns
Armi San Paolo
Auto-Ordnance Corp.
Ballard Rifle & Cartridge Co., LLC
Bear Mountain Gun & Tool
Billings Gunsmiths Inc.
Bob's Gun Shop
British Antiques
Buckskin Machine Works, A. Hunkeler
Buffalo Arms Co.
Cache La Poudre Rifleworks
Cape Outfitters
Cash Mfg. Co., Inc.
CBC-BRAZIL
CCL Security Products
Chambers Flintlocks Ltd., Jim
Cogar's Gunsmithing
Cole's Gun Works
Collectors Firearms Etc.
Colonial Repair
Custom Riflestocks, Inc., Michael M. Kokolus
Dangler, Homer L.
David R. Chicoine
Delhi Gun House
Delta Arms Ltd.
Dilliott Gunsmithing, Inc.
Euroarms of America, Inc.
Flintlocks Etc.
Flintlocks, Etc.
Forgett Jr., Valmore J.
George E. Mathews & Son, Inc.
Getz Barrel Co.
Golden Age Arms Co.
Goodwin, Fred
Groenewold, John
Guns
Hastings Barrels
Hunkeler, A (See Buckskin Machine Works, A. Hunkeler)
IAR Inc.
Ken Starnes Gunmaker
Kokolus, Michael M. (See Custom Riflestocks, Inc., Michael M. Kokolus)
L&R Lock Co.
Leapers, Inc.
Leonard Day
List Precision Engineering
Lock's Philadelphia Gun Exchange
Lucas, Edward E.
Mandall Shooting Supplies Inc.
Martin's Gun Shop
Mathews & Son, Inc., George E.
McKinney, R.P. (See Schuetzen Gun Co.)
Mountain State Muzzleloading Supplies, Inc.
Mowrey Gun Works
Museum of Historical Arms, Inc.
Muzzleloaders Etcetera, Inc.
Navy Arms Co.
Neumann GmbH
North Star West
Nu-Line Guns,Inc.
Pasadena Gun Center
Pecatonica River Longrifle
PEM's Mfg. Co.
Pennsylvania Gun Parts Inc.
Pony Express Sport Shop

Precise Metalsmithing Enterprises
Quality Firearms of Idaho, Inc.
R.A. Wells Custom Gunsmith
Randco UK
Ravell Ltd.
Retting, Inc., Martin B.
S&S Firearms
Samco Global Arms, Inc.
Sarco, Inc.
Shootin' Shack, Inc.
Silver Ridge Gun Shop (See Goodwin, Fred)
Simmons Gun Repair, Inc.
Sklany's Machine Shop
Southern Ammunition Co., Inc.
Starr Trading Co., Jedediah
Stott's Creek Armory, Inc.
Taylor's & Co., Inc.
Tennessee Valley Mfg.
The Gun Parts Corp.
The Gun Works
Tiger-Hunt Gunstocks
Triple-K Mfg. Co., Inc.
Uberti USA, Inc.
Upper Missouri Trading Co.
Vintage Industries, Inc.
Vortek Products, Inc.
Weisz Parts
Wescombe, Bill (See North Star West)
Winchester Sutler, Inc., The

GUNS, AIR

Air Arms
Air Rifle Specialists
Air Venture Airguns
Airrow
Allred Bullet Co.
Anschutz GmbH
Arms Corporation of the Philippines
BEC, Inc.
Beeman Precision Airguns
Benjamin/Sheridan Co., Crossman
Bohemia Arms Co.
Brass Eagle, Inc.
Brocock Ltd.
Bryan & Assoc.
BSA Guns Ltd.
Compasseco, Ltd.
Component Concepts, Inc.
Conetrol Scope Mounts
Creedmoor Sports, Inc.
Crosman Airguns
Crosman Products of Canada Ltd.
Daisy Mfg. Co.
Daystate Ltd.
Diana (See U.S. Importer - Dynamit Nobel-RWS, Inc.)
Domino
Dynamit Nobel-RWS, Inc.
European American Armory Corp (See E.A.A. Corp)
Frankonia Jagd Hofmann & Co.
FWB
Gamo USA, Inc.
Gaucher Armes, S.A.
Great Lakes Airguns
Groenewold, John
Hebard Guns, Gil
Interarms/Howa
Israel Arms International, Inc.
Labanu, Inc.
Leapers, Inc.
List Precision Engineering
Loch Leven Industries
Mac-1 Airgun Distributors
Marksman Products
Maryland Paintball Supply
Merkuria Ltd.

Neal Johnson's Gunsmithing, Inc.
Nygord Precision Products
Pardini Armi Srl
Precision Airgun Sales, Inc.
Precision Sales International, Inc.
Ripley Rifles
Robinson, Don
RWS (See US Importer-Dynamit Nobel-RWS, Inc.)
S.G.S. Sporting Guns Srl.
Savage Arms, Inc.
SKAN A.R.
Smart Parts
Smith & Wesson
Steyr Mannlicher AG & CO KG
Stone Enterprises Ltd.
The Gun Room Press
The Park Rifle Co., Ltd.
Theoben Engineering
Tippman Pneumatics, Inc.
Tristar Sporting Arms, Ltd.
Trooper Walsh
UltraSport Arms, Inc.
Valor Corp.
Vortek Products, Inc.
Walther GmbH, Carl
Webley and Scott Ltd.
Weihrauch KG, Hermann
Whiscombe (See U.S. Importer-Pelaire Products)
World Class Airguns

GUNS, FOREIGN MANUFACTURER U.S. IMPORTER

Accuracy Int'l. North America, Inc.
Accuracy Internationl Precision Rifles (See U.S. Importer-Wm Larkin Moore)
Air Arms
Armas Kemen S. A. (See U.S. Importers)
Armi Perazzi S.P.A.
Armi San Marco (See U.S. Importers-Taylor's & Co., Inc.)
Armi Sport (See U.S. Importers-Cape Outfitters)
Arms Corporation of the Philippines
Armscorp USA, Inc.
Arrieta S.L.
Astra Sport, S.A.
Atamec-Bretton
AYA (See U.S. Importer-New England Custom Gun Service)
B.C. Outdoors
BEC, Inc.
Benelli Armi S.P.A.
Benelli USA Corp
Beretta S.P.A., Pietro
Beretta U.S.A. Corp.
Bernardelli S.P.A., Vincenzo
Bersa S.A.
Bertuzzi (See U.S. Importer-New England Arms Co)
Bill Hanus Birdguns LLC
Blaser Jagdwaffen GmbH
Bohemia Arms Co.
Borovnik KG, Ludwig
Bosis (See U.S. Importer-New England Arms Co.)
Brenneke KG, Wilhelm
BRNO (See U.S. Importers-Bohemia Arms Co.)
Brocock Ltd.
Browning Arms Co.
BSA Guns Ltd.

Cabanas (See U.S. Importer-Mandall Shooting Supplies Inc.)
CBC
Chapuis Armes
Churchill (See U.S. Importer-Ellett Bros)
Cosmi Americo & Figlio s.n.c.
Crucelegui, Hermanos (See U.S. Importer-Mandall Shooting Supplies Inc.)
Cryo-Accurizing
Daewoo Precision Industries Ltd.
Dakota (See U.S. Importer-EMF Co., Inc.)
Davide Pedersoli and Co.
Diana (See U.S. Importer - Dynamit Nobel-RWS, Inc.)
Domino
Dumoulin, Ernest
EAW (See U.S. Importer-New England Custom Gun Service)
Effebi SNC-Dr. Franco Beretta
Euro-Imports
F.A.I.R. Techni-Mec s.n.c. di Isidoro Rizzini & C.
Fabarm S.P.A.
Fanzoj GmbH
Fausti Cav. Stefano & Figlie snc
FEG
Felk, Inc.
FERLIB
Fiocchi Munizioni S.P.A. (See U.S. Importer-Fiocchi Shooting Supplies, Inc.)
Firearms Co Ltd/Alpine (See U.S. Importer-Mandall Shooting Supplies, Inc.)
Firearms International
Flintlocks, Etc.
FN Herstal
Franchi S.P.A.
FWB
Galaxy Imports Ltd.,Inc.
Gamba S.P.A. Societa Armi Bresciane Srl
Gamo (See U.S. Importers-Arms United Corp, Daisy Mfg. Co.)
Garbi, Armas Urki
Gaucher Armes, S.A.
Gibbs Rifle Co., Inc.
Glock GmbH
Grulla Armes
Hammans, Charles E.
Hammerli Ltd.
Hartford (See U.S. Importer-EMF Co. Inc.)
Hartmann & Weiss GmbH
Heckler & Koch, Inc.
Hege Jagd-u. Sporthandels GmbH
Helwan (See U.S. Importer-Interarms)
Holland & Holland Ltd.
Howa Machinery, Ltd.
I.A.B. (See U.S. Importer-Taylor's & Co. Inc.)
IGA (See U.S. Importer-Stoeger Industries)
IMI
Imperial Magnum Corp.
Inter Ordnance of America LP
Interarms/Howa
Intrac Arms International
JSL Ltd (See U.S. Importer-Specialty Shooters Supply Inc.)
Kimar (See U.S. Importer-IAR,Inc)
Korth
Krico Jagd-und Sportwaffen GmbH

Krieghoff Gun Co., H.
KSN Industries Ltd (See U.S. Importer-Israel Arms International Inc.)
Lakefield Arms Ltd (See Savage Arms Inc)
Lanber Armas, S.A.
Lapua Ltd.
Laurona Armas Eibar, S.A.L.
Lebeau-Courally
Lever Arms Service Ltd.
Llama Gabilondo Y Cia
London Guns Ltd.
M. Thys (See U.S. Importer-Champlin Firearms Inc)
Madis, George
Magtech Ammunition Co. Inc.
Mandall Shooting Supplies Inc.
Marocchi F.lli S.p.A
Mauser Werke Oberndorf Waffensysteme GmbH
McCann Industries
MEC-Gar S.r.l.
Merkel Freres
Miltex, Inc.
Miroku, B C/Daly, Charles (See U.S. Importer-Bell'
Morini (See U.S. Importers-Mandall Shooting Supplies Inc.)
Navy Arms Co.
New SKB Arms Co.
Norica, Avnda Otaola
Norinco
Norma Precision AB (See U.S. Importers-Dynamit Nobel-RWS., Inc.)
Northwest Arms
OK Weber,Inc.
Para-Ordnance Mfg., Inc.
Pardini Armi Srl
Pease International
Perazzi USA, Inc.
Perugini Visini & Co. S.r.l.
Peters Stahl GmbH
Pietta (See U.S. Importers-Navy Arms Co, Taylor's
Piotti (See U.S. Importer-Moore & Co, Wm. Larkin)
PMC/Eldorado Cartridge Corp.
Powell & Son (Gunmakers) Ltd., William
Prairie Gun Works
Rigby & Co., John
Rizzini F.lli (See U.S. Importers-Moore & C England)
Rizzini SNC
Rossi Firearms, Braztech
Rottweil Compe
Rutten (See U.S. Importer-Labanu Inc)
RWS (See US Importer-Dynamit Nobel-RWS, Inc.)
S.A.R.L. G. Granger
S.I.A.C.E. (See U.S. Importer-IAR Inc)
Sabatti S.r.l.
Sako Ltd (See U.S. Importer-Stoeger Industries)
San Marco (See U.S. Importers-Cape Outfitters-EMF
Sauer (See U.S. Importers-Paul Co., The, Sigarms Inc.)
SIG
SIG-Sauer (See U.S. Importer-Sigarms Inc.)
Small Arms Specialists
Societa Armi Bresciane Srl (See U.S. Importer-Cape Outfitters)
Sphinx Engineering SA
Springfield, Inc.
Star Bonifacio Echeverria S.A.
Starr Trading Co., Jedediah

Steyr Mannlicher AG & CO KG
T.F.C. S.P.A.
Tanfoglio Fratelli S.r.l.
Tanner (See U.S. Importer-Mandall Shooting Supplies, Inc.)
Taurus International Firearms (See U.S. Importer-Taurus International Firearms, Inc.)
Taurus S.A. Forjas
Techno Arms (See U.S. Importer- Auto-Ordnance Corp.)
Tikka (See U.S. Importer-Stoeger Industries)
TOZ (See U.S. Importer-Nygord Precision Products)
Turkish Firearms Corp.
Uberti, Aldo
Ugartechea S. A., Ignacio
Ultralux (See U.S. Importer-Keng's Firearms Specialty, Inc./US Tactical Systems)
Unique/M.A.P.F.
Valtro USA, Inc.
Voere-KGH m.b.H.
Walther GmbH, Carl
Weatherby, Inc.
Webley and Scott Ltd.
Weihrauch KG, Hermann
Westley Richards & Co.
Whiscombe (See U.S. Importer-Pelaire Products)
Wolf (See J.R. Distributing)
Zabala Hermanos S.A.
Zanoletti, Pietro
Zoli, Antonio

GUNS, FOREIGN-IMPORTER

Accuracy International
AcuSport Corporation
Air Rifle Specialists
American Arms Inc.
American Frontier Firearms Mfg., Inc.
Amtec 2000, Inc.
Armsport, Inc.
Auto-Ordnance Corp.
B-West Imports, Inc.
Bell's Legendary Country Wear
Benelli USA Corp
Big Bear Arms & Sporting Goods, Inc.
Bill Hanus Birdguns LLC
Bohemia Arms Co.
Bridgeman Products
British Sporting Arms
Browning Arms Co.
Cabela's
Cape Outfitters
Century International Arms, Inc.
Champion Shooters' Supply
Champion's Choice, Inc.
Champlin Firearms, Inc.
Chapuis USA
Cimarron F.A. Co.
CVA
CZ USA
Dynamit Nobel-RWS, Inc.
E&L Mfg., Inc.
E.A.A. Corp.
Eagle Imports, Inc.
Ellett Bros.
EMF Co., Inc.
Euroarms of America, Inc.
Eversull Co., Inc., K.
Fiocchi of America Inc.
Fisher, Jerry A.
Flintlocks, Etc.
Forgett Jr., Valmore J.
Franzen International,Inc (See U.S. Importer for Peters Stahl GmbH)

G.U. Inc (See U.S. Importer for New SKB Arms Co)
Galaxy Imports Ltd.,Inc.
Gamba, USA
Gamo USA, Inc.
Giacomo Sporting USA
Glock, Inc.
Gremmel Enterprises
Griffin & Howe, Inc.
GSI, Inc.
Gunsite Custom Shop
Gunsite Training Center
Hammerli USA
Hanus Birdguns Bill
Heckler & Koch, Inc.
I.S.S.
IAR Inc.
Imperial Magnum Corp.
Import Sports Inc.
Interarms/Howa
Intrac Arms International
Israel Arms International, Inc.
Ithaca Gun Co. LLC
Johnson's Gunsmithing, Inc, Neal
K-Sports Imports Inc.
K.B.I. Inc.
Kemen America
Keng's Firearms Specialty, Inc./US Tactical Systems
Krieghoff International,Inc.
Labanu, Inc.
Legacy Sports International
Lion Country Supply
London Guns Ltd.
Magnum Research, Inc.
Magtech Ammunition Co. Inc.
Mandall Shooting Supplies Inc.
Marx, Harry (See U.S. Importer for FERLIB)
MCS, Inc.
MEC-Gar U.S.A., Inc.
Neal Johnson's Gunsmithing, Inc.
New England Arms Co.
New England Custom Gun Service
Nygord Precision Products
OK Weber,Inc.
P.S.M.G. Gun Co.
Para-Ordnance, Inc.
Pelaire Products
Perazzi USA, Inc.
Powell Agency, William
Precision Sales International, Inc.
Quality Arms, Inc.
S.D. Meacham
Savage Arms, Inc.
Schuetzen Pistol Works
Scott Fine Guns Inc., Thad
Sigarms, Inc.
SKB Shotguns
Small Arms Specialists
Southern Ammunition Co., Inc.
Specialty Shooters Supply, Inc.
Springfield, Inc.
Stoeger Industries
Stone Enterprises Ltd.
Swarovski Optik North America Ltd.
Taurus Firearms, Inc.
Taylor's & Co., Inc.
The Gun Shop
The Orvis Co.
The Paul Co.
Track of the Wolf, Inc.
Tradewinds, Inc.
Traditions Performance Firearms
Tristar Sporting Arms, Ltd.
Trooper Walsh
Turkish Firearms Corp.

U.S. Importer-Wm. Larkin Moore
Uberti USA, Inc.
VAM Distribution Co LLC
Vektor USA
Vintage Arms, Inc.
Weatherby, Inc.
Westley Richards Agency USA (See U.S. Importer for Wesley Richards & Co.)
Whitestone Lumber Corp.
Wingshooting Adventures
World Class Airguns

GUNS, SURPLUS, PARTS & AMMUNITION

Ad Hominem
Ahlman Guns
Alpha 1 Drop Zone
Armscorp USA, Inc.
Arundel Arms & Ammunition, Inc., A.
Bondini Paolo
Cambos Outdoorsman
Century International Arms, Inc.
Cole's Gun Works
Conetrol Scope Mounts
Delta Arms Ltd.
First Inc, Jack
Fleming Firearms
Forgett Jr., Valmore J.
Forrest Inc., Tom
Frankonia Jagd Hofmann & Co.
Garcia National Gun Traders, Inc.
Gun City
Hallberg Gunsmith, Fritz
Hank's Gun Shop
Hege Jagd-u. Sporthandels GmbH
Interarms/Howa
Jackalope Gun Shop
Ken Starnes Gunmaker
LaRocca Gun Works
Lever Arms Service Ltd.
Log Cabin Sport Shop
Lomont Precision Bullets
Mandall Shooting Supplies Inc.
Martin's Gun Shop
Navy Arms Co.
Nevada Pistol Academy, Inc.
Northwest Arms
Oil Rod and Gun Shop
Paragon Sales & Services, Inc.
Parts & Surplus
Pasadena Gun Center
Perazone-Gunsmith, Brian
Power Plus Enterprises, Inc.
Quality Firearms of Idaho, Inc.
Ravell Ltd.
Retting, Inc., Martin B.
Samco Global Arms, Inc.
San Francisco Gun Exchange
Sarco, Inc.
Shootin' Shack, Inc.
Silver Ridge Gun Shop (See Goodwin, Fred)
Simmons Gun Repair, Inc.
Sportsmen's Exchange & Western Gun Traders, Inc.
Springfield Sporters, Inc.
T.F.C. S.P.A.
Tarnhelm Supply Co., Inc.
The Gun Parts Corp.
Thurston Sports, Inc.
Vom Hoffe (See Old Western Scrounger, Inc., The)
Whitestone Lumber Corp.
Williams Shootin' Iron Service, The Lynx-Line

GUNS, U.S. MADE

3-Ten Corp.

A-Square Co.,Inc.
A.A. Arms, Inc.
Accu-Tek
Ace Custom 45's, Inc.
Acra-Bond Laminates
Airrow
Allred Bullet Co.
American Arms Inc.
American Derringer Corp.
American Frontier Firearms Mfg., Inc.
Angel Arms, Inc.
AR-7 Industries, LLC
ArmaLite, Inc.
Armscorp USA, Inc.
Austin & Halleck
Autauga Arms, Inc.
Auto-Ordnance Corp.
Baer Custom, Inc, Les
Ballard Rifle & Cartridge Co., LLC
Bar-Sto Precision Machine
Barrett Firearms Manufacturer, Inc.
Beretta S.P.A., Pietro
Beretta U.S.A. Corp.
Big Bear Arms & Sporting Goods, Inc.
Bond Arms, Inc.
Borden Ridges Rimrock Stocks
Borden Rifles Inc.
Brockman's Custom Gunsmithing
Brown Co, E. Arthur
Brown Products, Inc., Ed
Browning Arms Co.
Bushmaster Firearms (See Quality Parts Co/Bushmaster Firearms)
Calico Light Weapon Systems
Cambos Outdoorsman
Cape Outfitters
Casull Arms Corp.
CCL Security Products
Century Gun Dist. Inc.
Champlin Firearms, Inc.
Charter 2000
Colt's Mfg. Co., Inc.
Competitor Corp. Inc.
Conetrol Scope Mounts
Connecticut Shotgun Mfg. Co.
Connecticut Valley Classics (See CVC)
Coonan Arms (JS Worldwide DBA)
Cooper Arms
Creekside Gun Shop Inc.
Crossfire, L.L.C.
Cryo-Accurizing
Cumberland Arms
Cumberland Mountain Arms
CVA
CVC
Daisy Mfg. Co.
Dakota Arms, Inc.
DAN WESSON FIREARMS
Dangler, Homer L.
Davis Industries
Dayton Traister
Downsizer Corp.
E&L Mfg., Inc.
E. Arthur Brown Co.
Eagle Arms, Inc. (See ArmaLite, Inc.)
Ed~ Brown Products, Inc.
Emerging Technologies, Inc. (See Laseraim Technologies, Inc.)
Entre'prise Arms, Inc.
Essex Arms
Excel Industries Inc.
FN Herstal
Forgett Jr., Valmore J.
Fort Worth Firearms

PRODUCT & SERVICE DIRECTORY

Frank Custom Classic Arms, Ron
Freedom Arms, Inc.
Fulton Armory
Galena Industries AMT
Garcia National Gun Traders, Inc.
Genecco Gun Works, K.
Gentry Custom Gunmaker, David
Gibbs Rifle Co., Inc.
Gil Hebard Guns
Gilbert Equipment Co., Inc.
Goergen's Gun Shop, Inc.
Granite Mountain Arms, Inc.
Griffin & Howe, Inc.
Gunsite Custom Shop
Gunsite Gunsmithy (See Gunsite Custom Shop)
H&R 1871, Inc.
H-S Precision, Inc.
Hammans, Charles E.
Harrington & Richardson (See H&R 1871, Inc.)
Harris Gunworks
Hart & Son, Inc.
Hatfield Gun
Hawken Shop, The (See Dayton Traister)
Heritage Firearms (See Heritage Mfg., Inc.)
Heritage Manufacturing, Inc.
Hesco-Meprolight
Hi-Point Firearms
HJS Arms,Inc.
Hutton Rifle Ranch
IAR Inc.
Imperial Miniature Armory
Intratec
Ithaca Classic Doubles
Ithaca Gun Co. LLC
J.P. Enterprises Inc.
J.P. Gunstocks, Inc.
James Calhoon Mfg.
Jones, J.D./SSK Industries
JS Worldwide DBA (See Coonan Arms)
K.K. Arms Co.
Kahr Arms
Kel-Tec CNC Industries, Inc.
Kelbly, Inc.
Kimber of America, Inc.
Knight Rifles
Knight's Mfg. Co.
Kolar
L.A.R. Mfg., Inc.
L.W. Seecamp Co., Inc.
LaFrance Specialties
Lakefield Arms Ltd (See Savage Arms Inc)
Laseraim Technologies, Inc.
Lever Arms Service Ltd.
Ljutic Industries, Inc.
Lock's Philadelphia Gun Exchange
Lone Star Rifle Company
M.O.A. Corp.
Madis, George
Mag-Na-Port International, Inc.
Magnum Research, Inc.
Mandall Shooting Supplies Inc.
Marlin Firearms Co.
Maverick Arms, Inc.
McBros Rifle Co.
McCann Industries
Miller Arms, Inc.
MKS Supply, Inc. (See Hi-Point Firearms)
Montana Armory, Inc (See C. Sharps Arms Co. Inc.)
Mountain Rifles, Inc.
MPI Stocks
NCP Products, Inc.
New England Firearms
Noreen, Peter H.
North American Arms, Inc.

North Star West
Northwest Arms
Nowlin Mfg. Co.
October Country Muzzleloading
Olympic Arms Inc.
Oregon Arms, Inc. (See Rogue Rifle Co., Inc.)
Parker & Sons Shooting Supply
Phillips & Rogers, Inc.
Phoenix Arms
Precision Small Arms Inc.
Professional Ordnance, Inc.
ProWare, Inc.
Quality Parts Co./Bushmaster Firearms
Rapine Bullet Mould Mfg. Co.
Raptor Arms Co., Inc.
Remington Arms Co., Inc.
Republic Arms, Inc.
Rock River Arms
Rocky Mountain Arms, Inc.
Rogue Rifle Co., Inc.
Rogue River Rifleworks
RPM
Ruger (See Sturm, Ruger & Co., Inc.)
Savage Arms (Canada), Inc.
Scattergun Technologies, Inc.
Searcy Enterprises
Sharps Arms Co., Inc., C.
Shiloh Rifle Mfg.
Sklany's Machine Shop
Small Arms Specialists
Smith & Wesson
Sporting Arms Mfg., Inc.
Springfield, Inc.
STI International
Stoeger Industries
Strayer-Voigt, Inc.
Sturm Ruger & Co. Inc.
Sunny Hill Enterprises, Inc.
T&S Industries, Inc.
Taconic Firearms Ltd., Perry Lane
Tar-Hunt Custom Rifles, Inc.
Taurus Firearms, Inc.
Texas Armory (See Bond Arms, Inc.)
The Gun Room Press
Thompson/Center Arms
Time Precision, Inc.
Tristar Sporting Arms, Ltd.
U.S. Repeating Arms Co., Inc.
UFA, Inc.
Ultra Light Arms, Inc.
Volquartsen Custom Ltd.
Wallace, Terry
Weatherby, Inc.
Wescombe, Bill (See North Star West)
Wessinger Custom Guns & Engraving
Whildin & Sons Ltd, E.H.
Wichita Arms, Inc.
Wildey, Inc.
Wilson Gun Shop
Z-M Weapons

GUNSMITH SCHOOL

American Gunsmithing Institute
Bull Mountain Rifle Co.
Colorado Gunsmithing Academy
Colorado School of Trades
Cylinder & Slide, Inc., William R. Laughridge
Lassen Community College, Gunsmithing Dept.
Laughridge, William R (See Cylinder & Slide Inc)
Log Cabin Sport Shop
Modern Gun Repair School
Montgomery Community College
Murray State College

North American Correspondence Schools The Gun Pro
Nowlin Mfg. Co.
NRI Gunsmith School
Pennsylvania Gunsmith School
Piedmont Community College
Pine Technical College
Professional Gunsmiths of America,Inc.
Smith & Wesson
Southeastern Community College
Spencer's Custom Guns
Trinidad St. Jr Col Gunsmith Dept.
Wright's Hardwood Gunstock Blanks
Yavapai College

GUNSMITH SUPPLIES, TOOLS & SERVICES

Ace Custom 45's, Inc.
Actions by "T" Teddy Jacobson
Aldis Gunsmithing & Shooting Supply
Alley Supply Co.
Allred Bullet Co.
Alpec Team, Inc.
American Frontier Firearms Mfg., Inc.
B-Square Company, Inc.
Baer Custom, Inc, Les
Bar-Sto Precision Machine
Bauska Barrels
Bear Mountain Gun & Tool
Bengtson Arms Co., L.
Biesen, Al
Biesen, Roger
Bill Johns Master Engraver
Bill's Gun Repair
Blue Ridge Machinery & Tools, Inc.
Bob Rogers Gunsmithing
Break-Free, Inc.
Briley Mfg. Inc.
Brockman's Custom Gunsmithing
Brown Products, Inc., Ed
Brownells, Inc.
Buffer Technologies
Bull Mountain Rifle Co.
Burkhart Gunsmithing, Don
C.S. Van Gorden & Son, Inc.
Carbide Checkering Tools (See J&R Engineering)
Caywood, Shane J.
CBC-BRAZIL
Chapman Manufacturing Co.
Chem-Pak Inc.
Chicasaw Gun Works
Choate Machine & Tool Co., Inc.
Chopie Mfg.,Inc.
Ciener Inc., Jonathan Arthur
Colonial Arms, Inc.
Colorado School of Trades
Conetrol Scope Mounts
Craig Custom Ltd., Research & Development
Creekside Gun Shop Inc.
CRR, Inc./Marble's Inc.
Cumberland Arms
Cumberland Mountain Arms
Custom Checkering Service, Kathy Forster
Custom Gun Products
D&J Bullet Co. & Custom Gun Shop, Inc.
Decker Shooting Products
Dem-Bart Checkering Tools, Inc.
Dewey Mfg. Co., Inc., J.
Dixie Gun Works, Inc.
Dremel Mfg. Co.
Du-Lite Corp.
Echols & Co., D'Arcy

EGW Evolution Gun Works
Entre'prise Arms, Inc.
Erhardt, Dennis
Faith Associates, Inc.
FERLIB
Fisher, Jerry A.
Forgreens Tool Mfg., Inc.
Forkin, Ben (See Belt MTN Arms)
Forkin Arms
Forster, Kathy (See Custom Checkering Service, Kathy Forster)
Fortune Products, Inc.
Fred F. Wells/Wells Sport Store
Gentry Custom Gunmaker, David
Gilkes, Anthony W.
Grace Metal Products
GrE-Tan Rifles
Greider Precision
Groenewold, John
Gruning Precision Inc.
Gun Hunter Trading Co.
Gunline Tools
Half Moon Rifle Shop
Halstead, Rick
Hammond Custom Guns Ltd.
Hastings Barrels
Henriksen Tool Co., Inc.
High Performance International
Hines Co, S C
Hoelscher, Virgil
Holland's Gunsmithing
Huey Gun Cases
Ironsighter Co.
Ivanoff, Thomas G (See Tom's Gun Repair)
J&R Engineering
J&S Heat Treat
Jantz Supply
Jenkins Recoil Pads, Inc.
JGS Precision Tool Mfg.
Kasenit Co., Inc.
Kimball, Gary
Kleinendorst, K. W.
Kmount
Korzinek Riflesmith, J.
Kwik Mount Corp.
LaBounty Precision Reboring, Inc.
Lea Mfg. Co.
Lee Supplies, Mark
Lee's Red Ramps
List Precision Engineering
London Guns Ltd.
Mahovsky's Metalife
Marble Arms (See CRR, Inc./Marble's Inc.)
Mark Lee Supplies
Marsh, Mike
Martin's Gun Shop
McKillen & Heyer, Inc.
Menck, Gunsmith Inc., T.W.
Metalife Industries (See Mahovsky's Metalife)
Metaloy, Inc.
Michael's Antiques
MMC
Mo's Competitor Supplies (See MCS Inc)
Morrow, Bud
Mowrey's Guns & Gunsmithing
N&J Sales
New England Custom Gun Service
Nowlin Mfg. Co.
Nu-Line Guns,Inc.
Ole Frontier Gunsmith Shop
P.M. Enterprises, Inc.
Parker Gun Finishes
PEM's Mfg. Co.
Perazone-Gunsmith, Brian
Power Custom, Inc.
Practical Tools, Inc.

Precision Specialties
Professional Gunsmiths of America,Inc.
Prolixrr Lubricants
Ranch Products
Ransom International Corp.
Reardon Products
Rice, Keith (See White Rock Tool & Die)
Rocky Mountain Arms, Inc.
Romain's Custom Guns, Inc.
Roto Carve
Royal Arms Gunstocks
Rusteprufe Laboratories
Scott McDougall & Associates
Sharp Shooter Supply
Shooter's Choice
Simmons Gun Repair, Inc.
Smith Abrasives, Inc.
Southern Bloomer Mfg. Co.
Spencer Reblue Service
Spradlin's
Starr Trading Co., Jedediah
Starrett Co., L. S.
Stiles Custom Guns
Stoney Point Products, Inc.
Sullivan, David S .(See Westwind Rifles Inc.)
Sunny Hill Enterprises, Inc.
T&S Industries, Inc.
Terry K. Kopp Professional Gunsmithing
Texas Platers Supply Co.
The Dutchman's Firearms, Inc.
The NgraveR Co.
The Robar Co.'s, Inc.
Theis, Terry
Tom's Gun Repair, Thomas G. Ivanoff
Track of the Wolf, Inc.
Trinidad St. Jr Col Gunsmith Dept.
Trulock Tool
Turnbull Restoration, Doug
United States Products Co.
Van Gorden & Son Inc., C. S.
Venco Industries, Inc. (See Shooter's Choice)
W.C. Wolff Co.
Warne Manufacturing Co.
Washita Mountain Whetstone Co.
Weaver Arms Corp. Gun Shop
Weigand Combat Handguns, Inc.
Welsh, Bud
Wessinger Custom Guns & Engraving
Westrom, John (See Precision Metal Finishing)
Westwind Rifles, Inc., David S. Sullivan
White Rock Tool & Die
Wilcox All-Pro Tools & Supply
Will-Burt Co.
Williams Gun Sight Co.
Williams Shootin' Iron Service, The Lynx-Line
Willow Bend
Windish, Jim
Winter, Robert M.
Wise Guns, Dale
Wright's Hardwood Gunstock Blanks
Yavapai College

HANDGUN ACCESSORIES

"Su-Press-On",Inc.
4-D Custom Die Co.
A.A. Arms, Inc.
Ace Custom 45's, Inc.
Action Direct, Inc.
ADCO Sales, Inc.

PRODUCT & SERVICE DIRECTORY

Adventurer's Outpost
Aimpoint c/o Springfield, Inc.
Aimtech Mount Systems
Ajax Custom Grips, Inc.
Alpha 1 Drop Zone
Alpha Gunsmith Division
American Derringer Corp.
American Frontier Firearms
   Mfg., Inc.
Arms Corporation of the
   Philippines
Aro-Tek Ltd.
Astra Sport, S.A.
Autauga Arms, Inc.
Baer Custom, Inc, Les
Bagmaster Mfg., Inc.
Bar-Sto Precision Machine
Behlert Precision, Inc.
Berry's Mfg., Inc.
Bill's Custom Cases
Blue and Gray Products Inc (See
   Ox-Yoke Originals, Inc.)
Bond Custom Firearms
Bridgeman Products
Broken Gun Ranch
Brooks Tactical Systems
Brown Products, Inc., Ed
Bucheimer, J. M. (See Jumbo
   Sports Products)
Bushmaster Firearms (See
   Quality Parts Co/Bushmaster
   Firearms)
Bushmaster Hunting & Fishing
Butler Creek Corp.
Cannon Safe, Inc.
Catco-Ambush, Inc.
Centaur Systems, Inc.
Central Specialties Ltd (See
   Trigger Lock
   Division/Central Specialties
   Ltd.)
Charter 2000
Cheyenne Pioneer Products
Ciener Inc., Jonathan Arthur
Clark Custom Guns, Inc.
Classic Arms Company
Conetrol Scope Mounts
Craig Custom Ltd., Research &
   Development
CRR, Inc./Marble's Inc.
Cylinder & Slide, Inc., William R.
   Laughridge
D&L Industries (See D.J.
   Marketing)
D.J. Marketing
Dade Screw Machine Products
Delhi Gun House
DeSantis Holster & Leather
   Goods, Inc.
Doskocil Mfg. Co., Inc.
E&L Mfg., Inc.
E. Arthur Brown Co.
E.A.A. Corp.
Ed~ Brown Products, Inc.
Essex Arms
Euroarms of America, Inc.
European American Armory
   Corp (See E.A.A. Corp)
Federal Arms Corp. of America
Feminine Protection, Inc.
Fisher Custom Firearms
Fleming Firearms
Flores Publications Inc, J (See
   Action Direct Inc)
Frielich Police Equipment
FWB
G.G. & G.
Galati International
GALCO International Ltd.
Garcia National Gun Traders,
   Inc.
Garthwaite Pistolsmith, Inc., Jim
Gary Reeder Custom Guns
Gil Hebard Guns

Gilmore Sports Concepts
Glock, Inc.
Gould & Goodrich
Greider Precision
Gremmel Enterprises
Gun-Alert
Gun-Ho Sports Cases
H-S Precision, Inc.
H.K.S. Products
Hebard Guns, Gil
Heckler & Koch, Inc.
Heinie Specialty Products
Henigson & Associates, Steve
Hi-Point Firearms
Hill Speed Leather, Ernie
Hines Co, S C
Hobson Precision Mfg. Co.
Hoppe's Div. Penguin Industries,
   Inc.
Hunter Co., Inc.
Impact Case Co.
Israel Arms International, Inc.
J.P. Enterprises Inc.
Jarvis, Inc.
JB Custom
Jeffredo Gunsight
Jim Noble Co.
Jones, J.D./SSK Industries
Jumbo Sports Products
K.K. Arms Co.
Kalispel Case Line
KeeCo Impressions, Inc.
King's Gun Works
KK Air International (See Impact
   Case Co.)
L&S Technologies Inc (See
   Aimtech Mount Systems)
LaserMax, Inc.
Lee's Red Ramps
Loch Leven Industries
Lohman Mfg. Co., Inc.
Mag-Na-Port International, Inc.
Magnolia Sports,Inc.
Marble Arms (See CRR,
   Inc./Marble's Inc.)
Markell,Inc.
Maxi-Mount
McCormick Corp., Chip
MEC-Gar S.r.l.
Menck, Gunsmith Inc., T.W.
Merkuria Ltd.
Mid-America Guns and Ammo
Middlebrooks Custom Shop
Millett Sights
MTM Molded Products Co., Inc.
No-Sho Mfg. Co.
Omega Sales
Outdoor Sports
   Headquarters,Inc.
Ox-Yoke Originals, Inc.
Pachmayr Div. Lyman Products
Pager Pal
PAST Sporting Goods,Inc.
Pearce Grip, Inc.
Phoenix Arms
Practical Tools, Inc.
Precision Small Arms
Quality Parts Co./Bushmaster
   Firearms
Ram-Line Blount, Inc.
Ranch Products
Ransom International Corp.
Redfield, Inc.
Ringler Custom Leather Co.
Round Edge, Inc.
RPM
Simmons Gun Repair, Inc.
Southern Bloomer Mfg. Co.
Southwind Sanctions
Springfield, Inc.
Sturm Ruger & Co. Inc.
T.F.C. S.P.A.
TacStar
TacTell, Inc.

Tactical Defense Institute
Tanfoglio Fratelli S.r.l.
The Gun Parts Corp.
The Keller Co.
The Protector Mfg. Co., Inc.
Thompson/Center Arms
Trigger Lock Division/Central
   Specialties Ltd.
Trijicon, Inc.
Triple-K Mfg. Co., Inc.
Truglo, Inc.
Tyler Manufacturing &
   Distributing
United States Products Co.
Universal Sports
Valor Corp.
Volquartsen Custom Ltd.
W. Waller & Son, Inc.
W.C. Wolff Co.
Weigand Combat Handguns,
   Inc.
Western Design (See Alpha
   Gunsmith Division)
Wilson Gun Shop

HANDGUN GRIPS

A.A. Arms, Inc.
African Import Co.
Ahrends, Kim (See Custom
   Firearms, Inc)
Ajax Custom Grips, Inc.
Altamont Co.
American Derringer Corp.
American Frontier Firearms
   Mfg., Inc.
American Gripcraft
Arms Corporation of the
   Philippines
Art Jewel Enterprises Ltd.
Baelder, Harry
Baer Custom, Inc, Les
Bear Hug Grip, Inc.
Big Bear Arms & Sporting
   Goods, Inc.
Bob's Gun Shop
Boone Trading Co., Inc.
Boone's Custom Ivory Grips,
   Inc.
Boyds' Gunstock Industries, Inc.
Brooks Tactical Systems
Brown Products, Inc., Ed
Clark Custom Guns, Inc.
Cole-Grip
Colonial Repair
Crimson Trace Lasers
Custom Firearms (See Ahrends,
   Kim)
E.A.A. Corp.
EMF Co., Inc.
Essex Arms
European American Armory
   Corp (See E.A.A. Corp)
Fibron Products, Inc.
Fisher Custom Firearms
Fitz Pistol Grip Co.
Forrest Inc., Tom
FWB
Garthwaite Pistolsmith, Inc., Jim
H-S Precision, Inc.
Herrett's Stocks, Inc.
Hines Co, S C
HIP-GRIP Barami Corp.
Hogue Grips
Huebner, Corey O.
Jim Norman Custom Gunstocks
John Masen Co. Inc.
KeeCo Impressions, Inc.
Kim Ahrends Custom Firearms,
   Inc.
Korth
Lee's Red Ramps
Lett Custom Grips
Linebaugh Custom Sixguns
Michaels Of Oregon

Mid-America Guns and Ammo
Millett Sights
N.C. Ordnance Co.
Newell, Robert H.
Northern Precision Custom
   Swaged Bullets
Pachmayr Div. Lyman Products
Pardini Armi Srl
Peacemaker Specialists
Pilgrim Pewter,Inc. (See Bell
   Originals Inc. Sid)
Precision Small Arms
Radical Concepts
Rosenberg & Son, Jack A
Roy's Custom Grips
Sile Distributors, Inc.
Spegel, Craig
Stoeger Industries
Sturm Ruger & Co. Inc.
Sunny Hill Enterprises, Inc.
Tactical Defense Institute
Taurus Firearms, Inc.
Tyler Manufacturing &
   Distributing
Uncle Mike's (See Michaels of
   Oregon Co)
Vintage Industries, Inc.
Volquartsen Custom Ltd.
Western Gunstock Mfg. Co.
Wright's Hardwood Gunstock
   Blanks

HEARING PROTECTORS

Aero Peltor
Ajax Custom Grips, Inc.
Brown Co, E. Arthur
Brown Products, Inc., Ed
Browning Arms Co.
David Clark Co., Inc.
Dick Marple & Associates
Dillon Precision Products, Inc.
E-A-R, Inc.
Electronic Shooters Protection,
   Inc.
Flents Products Co., Inc.
Gentex Corp.
Gunsmithing, Inc.
Hoppe's Div. Penguin Industries,
   Inc.
Huntington Die Specialties
Kesselring Gun Shop
North Specialty Products
Paterson Gunsmithing
Peltor, Inc. (See Aero Peltor)
R.E.T. Enterprises
Ridgeline, Inc.
Rucker Dist. Inc.
Silencio/Safety Direct
Tactical Defense Institute
The Gun Room Press
Willson Safety Prods. Div.

HOLSTERS & LEATHER GOODS

A&B Industries,Inc (See Top-
   Line USA Inc)
A.A. Arms, Inc.
Action Direct, Inc.
Action Products, Inc.
Alessi Holsters, Inc.
American Sales & Mfg. Co.
Arratoonian, Andy (See
   Horseshoe Leather
   Products)
Autauga Arms, Inc.
Bagmaster Mfg., Inc.
Baker's Leather Goods, Roy
Bandcor Industries, Div. of Man-
   Sew Corp.
Bang-Bang Boutique (See
   Holster Shop, The)
Bear Hug Grip, Inc.
Beretta S.P.A., Pietro

Bianchi International, Inc.
Brauer Bros. Mfg. Co.
Brooks Tactical Systems
Brown, H. R. (See Silhouette
   Leathers)
Browning Arms Co.
Bucheimer, J. M. (See Jumbo
   Sports Products)
Bull-X, Inc.
Bushwacker Backpack & Supply
   Co (See Counter Assault)
Cathey Enterprises, Inc.
Chace Leather Products
Churchill Glove Co., James
Cimarron F.A. Co.
Classic Old West Styles
Clements' Custom Leathercraft,
   Chas
Cobra Sport S.r.l.
Colonial Repair
Counter Assault
Creedmoor Sports, Inc.
Delhi Gun House
DeSantis Holster & Leather
   Goods, Inc.
Dillon Precision Products, Inc.
Ekol Leather Care
El Dorado Leather (c/o Dill)
El Paso Saddlery Co.
EMF Co., Inc.
F&A Inc. (See ShurKatch
   Corporation)
Faust Inc., T. G.
Feminine Protection, Inc.
Flores Publications Inc, J (See
   Action Direct Inc)
Fobus International Ltd.
Forgett Jr., Valmore J.
Frankonia Jagd Hofmann & Co.
Gage Manufacturing
GALCO International Ltd.
Garcia National Gun Traders,
   Inc.
Gil Hebard Guns
Gilmore Sports Concepts
GML Products, Inc.
Gould & Goodrich
Gun Leather Limited
Gunfitters
Hafner World Wide, Inc.
HandCrafts Unltd (See Clements'
   Custom Leathercraft, Chas)
Hank's Gun Shop
Hebard Guns, Gil
Heinie Specialty Products
Hellweg Ltd.
Henigson & Associates, Steve
Hill Speed Leather, Ernie
HIP-GRIP Barami Corp.
Hobson Precision Mfg. Co.
Hogue Grips
Horseshoe Leather Products
Hoyt Holster Co., Inc.
Hume, Don
Hunter Co., Inc.
Israel Arms International, Inc.
Jim Noble Co.
John's Custom Leather
Jumbo Sports Products
K.L. Null Holsters Ltd.
Kane Products, Inc.
Kirkpatrick Leather Co.
Kolpin Mfg., Inc.
Korth
Kramer Handgun Leather
L.A.R. Mfg., Inc.
Lawrence Leather Co.
Lock's Philadelphia Gun
   Exchange
Lone Star Gunleather
Magnolia Sports,Inc.
Markell,Inc.
Marksman Products
Michaels Of Oregon

PRODUCT & SERVICE DIRECTORY

Minute Man High Tech Industries
Nikolai leather
No-Sho Mfg. Co.
Null Holsters Ltd. K.L.
October Country Muzzleloading
Ojala Holsters, Arvo
Oklahoma Leather Products,Inc.
Old West Reproductions,Inc. R.M. Bachman
Pager Pal
Pathfinder Sports Leather
Peacemaker Specialists
PWL Gunleather
Renegade
Ringler Custom Leather Co.
Rogue Rifle Co., Inc.
Rumanya Inc.
Safariland Ltd., Inc.
Safety Speed Holster, Inc.
Scharch Mfg., Inc.
Schulz Industries
Second Chance Body Armor
Shoemaker & Sons Inc., Tex
ShurKatch Corporation
Sile Distributors, Inc.
Silhouette Leathers
Smith Saddlery, Jesse W.
Southwind Sanctions
Sparks, Milt
Stalker, Inc.
Starr Trading Co., Jedediah
Strong Holster Co.
Stuart, V. Pat
Tabler Marketing
Tactical Defense Institute
Ted Blocker Holsters, Inc.
Thad Rybka Custom Leather Equipment
The Eutaw Co., Inc.
The Gun Works
The Holster Shop
The Keller Co.
Top-Line USA, Inc.
Torel, Inc.
Triple-K Mfg. Co., Inc.
Tristar Sporting Arms, Ltd.
Tyler Manufacturing & Distributing
Uncle Mike's (See Michaels of Oregon Co)
Valor Corp.
Venus Industries
Walt's Custom Leather, Walt Whinnery
Westley Richards & Co.
Whinnery, Walt (See Walt's Custom Leather)
Wild Bill's Originals
Wilson Gun Shop

HUNTING & CAMP GEAR, CLOTHING, ETC.

A&M Waterfowl,Inc.
Ace Sportswear, Inc.
Action Direct, Inc.
Action Products, Inc.
Adventure 16, Inc.
Adventure Game Calls
Allen Co., Bob
Allen Sportswear, Bob (See Allen Co., Bob)
Alpha 1 Drop Zone
Armor (See Buck Stop Lure Co., Inc.)
Atlanta Cutlery Corp.
Atsko/Sno-Seal, Inc.
B.B. Walker Co.
Baekgaard Ltd.
Bagmaster Mfg., Inc.
Barbour, Inc.
Bauer, Eddie
Bear Archery

Beaver Park Product, Inc.
Beretta S.P.A., Pietro
Better Concepts Co.
Bill Johns Master Engraver
Boss Manufacturing Co.
Brown, H. R. (See Silhouette Leathers)
Brown Manufacturing
Browning Arms Co.
Buck Stop Lure Co., Inc.
Bushmaster Hunting & Fishing
C.W. Erickson's Mfg. Inc.
Camp-Cap Products
Carhartt,Inc.
Churchill Glove Co., James
Clarkfield Enterprises, Inc.
Classic Old West Styles
Coghlan's Ltd.
Cold Steel Inc.
Coleman Co., Inc.
Coulston Products, Inc.
Creative Concepts USA, Inc.
Creedmoor Sports, Inc.
D&H Prods. Co., Inc.
Dakota Corp.
Danner Shoe Mfg. Co.
Deer Me Products Co.
Dr. O's Products Ltd.
Dunham Boots
Duofold, Inc.
Dynalite Products, Inc.
E-A-R, Inc.
Ekol Leather Care
F&A Inc. (See ShurKatch Corporation)
Flores Publications Inc, J (See Action Direct Inc)
Forrest Tool Co.
Fortune Products, Inc.
Fox River Mills, Inc.
Frontier
G&H Decoys,Inc.
Gerber Legendary Blades
Glacier Glove
Gozon Corp. U.S.A.
Hafner World Wide, Inc.
Heritage Wildlife Carvings
Hinman Outfitters, Bob
Hodgman, Inc.
Houtz & Barwick
Hunter's Specialties Inc.
John's Custom Leather
K&M Industries, Inc.
Kamik Outdoor Footwear
Kolpin Mfg., Inc.
L.L. Bean, Inc.
LaCrosse Footwear, Inc.
Langenberg Hat Co.
Leapers, Inc.
Lectro Science, Inc.
Liberty Trouser Co.
MAG Instrument, Inc.
Mag-Na-Port International, Inc.
Marathon Rubber Prods. Co., Inc.
McCann Industries
McCann's Machine & Gun Shop
Melton Shirt Co., Inc.
Molin Industries, Tru-Nord Division
Mountain Hollow Game Calls
Nelson/Weather-Rite, Inc.
North Specialty Products
Northlake Outdoor Footwear
Original Mink Oil,Inc.
Palsa Outdoor Products
Partridge Sales Ltd., John
Pointing Dog Journal, Village Press Publications
Powell & Son (Gunmakers) Ltd., William
Pro-Mark Div. of Wells Lamont
Pyramid, Inc.
Randolph Engineering, Inc.

Ranging, Inc.
Ringler Custom Leather Co.
Rocky Shoes & Boots
Russ Trading Post
Scansport, Inc.
Sceery Game Calls
Schaefer Shooting Sports
Servus Footwear Co.
ShurKatch Corporation
Simmons Outdoor Corp.
Sno-Seal, Inc. (See Atsko/Sno-Seal)
Streamlight, Inc.
Swanndri New Zealand
T.H.U. Enterprises, Inc.
TEN-X Products Group
The Eutaw Co., Inc.
The Orvis Co.
The Outdoor Connection,Inc.
Thompson, Norm
Thompson/Center Arms
Tink's Safariland Hunting Corp.
Torel, Inc.
Triple-K Mfg. Co., Inc.
United Cutlery Corp.
Venus Industries
Wakina by Pic
Walls Industries, Inc.
Wideview Scope Mount Corp.
Wilderness Sound Products Ltd.
Willson Safety Prods. Div.
Winchester Sutler, Inc., The
Wolverine Footwear Group
Woolrich, Inc.
Wyoming Knife Corp.
Yellowstone Wilderness Supply

KNIVES & KNIFEMAKER'S SUPPLIES

A.G. Russell Knives,Inc.
Action Direct, Inc.
Adventure 16, Inc.
African Import Co.
Aitor-Cuchilleria Del Norte S.A.
All Rite Products, Inc.
American Target Knives
Art Jewel Enterprises Ltd.
Atlanta Cutlery Corp.
B&D Trading Co., Inc.
Barteaux Machete
Belltown Ltd.
Benchmark Knives (See Gerber Legendary Blades)
Beretta S.P.A., Pietro
Beretta U.S.A. Corp.
Big Bear Arms & Sporting Goods, Inc.
Bill Johns Master Engraver
Bill's Custom Cases
Bob Schrimsher's Custom Knifemaker's Supply
Boker USA, Inc.
Boone Trading Co., Inc.
Boone's Custom Ivory Grips, Inc.
Bowen Knife Co., Inc.
Brooks Tactical Systems
Brown, H. R. (See Silhouette Leathers)
Browning Arms Co.
Buck Knives, Inc.
Buster's Custom Knives
Camillus Cutlery Co.
Campbell, Dick
Case & Sons Cutlery Co., W R
Chicago Cutlery Co.
Clements' Custom Leathercraft, Chas
Cold Steel Inc.
Coleman Co., Inc.
Colonial Knife Co., Inc.
Compass Industries, Inc.

Crosman Blades (See Coleman Co., Inc.)
CRR, Inc./Marble's Inc.
Cutco Cutlery
DAMASCUS-U.S.A.
Dan's Whetstone Co., Inc.
Degen Inc. (See Aristocrat Knives)
Delhi Gun House
DeSantis Holster & Leather Goods, Inc.
Diamond Machining Technology, Inc. (See DMT)
EdgeCraft Corp., S. Weiner
Empire Cutlery Corp.
Eze-Lap Diamond Prods.
Flitz International Ltd.
Flores Publications Inc, J (See Action Direct Inc)
Forrest Tool Co.
Forthofer's Gunsmithing & Knifemaking
Fortune Products, Inc.
Frank Knives
Frost Cutlery Co.
George Ibberson (Sheffield) Ltd.
Gerber Legendary Blades
Gibbs Rifle Co., Inc.
Glock, Inc.
Golden Age Arms Co.
H&B Forge Co.
Hafner World Wide, Inc.
HandCrafts Unltd (See Clements' Custom Leathercraft Chas)
Harris Publications
High North Products, Inc.
Hoppe's Div. Penguin Industries, Inc.
Hubertus Schneidwarenfabrik
Hunter Co., Inc.
Hunting Classics Ltd.
Imperial Schrade Corp.
J.A. Blades, Inc. (See Christopher Firearms Co.,
J.A. Henckels Zwillingswerk Inc.
J.R. Blair Engraving
Jackalope Gun Shop
Jantz Supply
Jenco Sales, Inc.
Johnson Wood Products
KA-BAR Knives
Kasenit Co., Inc.
Kershaw Knives
Knife Importers, Inc.
Koval Knives
Lamson & Goodnow Mfg. Co.
Lansky Sharpeners
Leapers, Inc.
Leatherman Tool Group, Inc.
Linder Solingen Knives
Marble Arms (See CRR, Inc./Marble's Inc.)
Matthews Cutlery
McCann Industries
McCann's Machine & Gun Shop
Molin Industries, Tru-Nord Division
Mountain State Muzzleloading Supplies, Inc.
Normark Corp.
October Country Muzzleloading
Outdoor Edge Cutlery Corp.
Pilgrim Pewter,Inc. (See Bell Originals Inc. Sid)
Plaza Cutlery, Inc.
Queen Cutlery Co.
R&C Knives & Such
R. Murphy Co., Inc.
Randall-Made Knives
Robert Valade Engraving
Rodgers & Sons Ltd., Joseph (See George Ibberson (Sheffield) Ltd.)
Scansport, Inc.

Schiffman, Mike
Sheffield Knifemakers Supply, Inc.
Smith Saddlery, Jesse W.
Spyderco, Inc.
T.F.C. S.P.A.
The Creative Craftsman, Inc.
The Gun Room
Theis, Terry
Traditions Performance Firearms
Traditions Performance Firearms
Tru-Balance Knife Co.
United Cutlery Corp.
Utica Cutlery Co.
Valade Engraving, Robert
Venus Industries
Washita Mountain Whetstone Co.
Weber Jr., Rudolf
Wells Creek Knife & Gun Works
Wenger North America/Precise Int'l
Western Cutlery (See Camillus Cutlery Co.)
Whinnery, Walt (See Walt's Custom Leather)
Wideview Scope Mount Corp.
Wostenholm (See Ibberson [Sheffield] Ltd., George)
Wyoming Knife Corp.

LABELS, BOXES & CARTRIDGE HOLDERS

Ballistic Product, Inc.
Berry's Mfg., Inc.
Blackhawk East
Brown Co, E. Arthur
Cabinet Mtn. Outfitters Scents & Lures
Cheyenne Pioneer Products
Del Rey Products
DeSantis Holster & Leather Goods, Inc.
Fitz Pistol Grip Co.
Flambeau Products Corp.
J&J Products, Inc.
Kolpin Mfg., Inc.
Liberty Shooting Supplies
Midway Arms, Inc.
MTM Molded Products Co., Inc.
Pendleton Royal, c/o Swingler Buckland Ltd.
Precision Reloading, Inc.
Ziegel Engineering

LEAD WIRES & WIRE CUTTERS

3-D Ammunition & Bullets
Bullet Swaging Supply Inc.
Northern Precision Custom Swaged Bullets
Sport Flite Manufacturing Co.
Star Ammunition, Inc.
Unmussig Bullets, D. L.

LOAD TESTING & PRODUCT TESTING

Ballistic Research
Bitterroot Bullet Co.
Bridgeman Products
Briese Bullet Co., Inc.
Buckskin Bullet Co.
CFVentures
Clearview Products
D&H Precision Tooling
Dead Eye's Sport Center
Defense Training International, Inc.
Duane's Gun Repair (See DGR Custom Rifles)

PRODUCT & SERVICE DIRECTORY

H.P. White Laboratory, Inc.
Henigson & Associates, Steve
Hoelscher, Virgil
Hutton Rifle Ranch
Jackalope Gun Shop
Jensen Bullets
Jurras, L. E.
Liberty Shooting Supplies
Linebaugh Custom Sixguns
Lomont Precision Bullets
Maionchi-L.M.I.
MAST Technology
McMurdo, Lynn (See Specialty
    Gunsmithing)
Middlebrooks Custom Shop
Multiplex International
Northwest Arms
Oil Rod and Gun Shop
Precision Reloading, Inc.
R.A. Wells Custom Gunsmith
Rupert's Gun Shop
SOS Products Co. (See Buck
    Stix-SOS Products Co.)
Spencer's Custom Guns
Tar-Hunt Custom Rifles, Inc.
Tioga Engineering Co., Inc.
Vancini, Carl (See Bestload, Inc.)
Vulpes Ventures, Inc. Fox
    Cartridge Division
Wessinger Custom Guns &
    Engraving
X-Spand Target Systems

LOADING BLOCKS, METALLIC & SHOTSHELL

Jericho Tool & Die Co., Inc.

LUBRISIZERS, DIES & ACCESSORIES

Ballisti-Cast, Inc.
Ben's Machines
Hart & Son, Inc.
Magma Engineering Co.
SPG LLC
Thompson Bullet Lube Co.
United States Products Co.
WTA Manufacturing

MOULDS & MOULD ACCESSORIES

American Products, Inc.
Ballisti-Cast, Inc.
Buffalo Arms Co.
Gun Hunter Trading Co.
Lee Precision, Inc.
Magma Engineering Co.
Old West Bullet Moulds
Penn Bullets
Rapine Bullet Mould Mfg. Co.
Redding Reloading Equipment
S&S Firearms

MUZZLE-LOADING GUNS, BARRELS & EQUIPMENT

Accuracy Unlimited
Ackerman & Co.
Adkins, Luther
Allen Mfg.
Armi San Paolo
Austin & Halleck
Bauska Barrels
Beaver Lodge (See Fellowes,
    Ted)
Bentley, John
Birdsong & Assoc, W. E.
Black Powder Products
Blackhawk East
Blue and Gray Products Inc (See
    Ox-Yoke Originals, Inc.)
Bridgers Best
Buckskin Bullet Co.

Buckskin Machine Works, A.
    Hunkeler
Butler Creek Corp.
Cache La Poudre Rifleworks
California Sights (See Fautheree,
    Andy)
Cash Mfg. Co., Inc.
CBC-BRAZIL
Chambers Flintlocks Ltd., Jim
Chopie Mfg.,Inc.
Cimarron F.A. Co.
Cogar's Gunsmithing
Colonial Repair
Colt Blackpowder Arms Co.
Conetrol Scope Mounts
Cousin Bob's Mountain
    Products
Cumberland Arms
Cumberland Mountain Arms
Curly Maple Stock Blanks (See
    Tiger-Hunt)
CVA
Dangler, Homer L.
Davide Pedersoli and Co.
Dayton Traister
deHaas Barrels
Delhi Gun House
Dixie Gun Works, Inc.
Dixon Muzzleloading Shop, Inc.
EMF Co., Inc.
Euroarms of America, Inc.
Feken, Dennis
Fellowes, Ted
Flintlocks Etc.
Flintlocks, Etc.
Forgett Jr., Valmore J.
Fort Hill Gunstocks
Fowler, Bob (See Black Powder
    Products)
Frankonia Jagd Hofmann & Co.
Frontier
Getz Barrel Co.
Goergen's Gun Shop, Inc.
Golden Age Arms Co.
Gonic Arms/North American
    Arm
Green Mountain Rifle Barrel Co.,
    Inc.
Hastings Barrels
Hawken Shop, The (See Dayton
    Traister)
Hege Jagd-u. Sporthandels
    GmbH
Hodgdon Powder Co.
Hoppe's Div. Penguin Industries,
    Inc.
Hornady Mfg. Co.
Hunkeler, A (See Buckskin
    Machine Works, A.
    Hunkeler)
Impact Case Co.
J.P. Gunstocks, Inc.
Jamison's Forge Works
Jones Co., Dale
K&M Industries, Inc.
Kalispel Case Line
Kennedy Firearms
Knight Rifles
Knight Rifles (See Modern
    Muzzle Loading, Inc.)
Kolar
L&R Lock Co.
L&S Technologies Inc (See
    Aimtech Mount Systems)
Legend Products Corp.
Lestrom Laboratories, Inc.
Lothar Walther Precision Tool
    Inc.
Lutz Engraving, Ron E.
Lyman Products Corp.
Lyman Products Corporation
Markesbery Muzzle Loaders,
    Inc.
Marlin Firearms Co.

McCann's Muzzle-Gun Works
Michaels Of Oregon
Millennium Designed
    Muzzleloaders
MMP
Modern Muzzleloading, Inc.
Montana Precision Swaging
Mountain State Muzzleloading
    Supplies, Inc.
Mowrey Gun Works
MSC Industrial Supply Co.
Mt. Alto Outdoor Products
Mushroom Express Bullet Co.
Muzzleloading Technologies,
    Inc.
Naval Ordnance Works
Navy Arms Co.
Newman Gunshop
North Star West
October Country Muzzleloading
Oklahoma Leather Products,Inc.
Olson, Myron
Orion Rifle Barrel Co.
Ox-Yoke Originals, Inc.
Pacific Rifle Co.
Parker & Sons Shooting Supply
Parker Gun Finishes
Pecatonica River Longrifle
Pioneer Arms Co.
Prairie River Arms
Prolixr Lubricants
Rusty Duck Premium Gun Care
    Products
S&B Industries
S&S Firearms
Selsi Co., Inc.
Shiloh Creek
Shooter's Choice
Simmons Gun Repair, Inc.
Sklany's Machine Shop
Smokey Valley Rifles (See Lutz
    Engraving, Ron E)
South Bend Replicas, Inc.
Southern Bloomer Mfg. Co.
Starr Trading Co., Jedediah
Stone Mountain Arms
Sturm Ruger & Co. Inc.
Taylor's & Co., Inc.
Tennessee Valley Mfg.
The Armoury, Inc.
The Eutaw Co., Inc.
The Gun Works
The House of Muskets, Inc.
Thompson Bullet Lube Co.
Thompson/Center Arms
Thunder Mountain Arms
Tiger-Hunt Gunstocks
Track of the Wolf, Inc.
Traditions Performance
    Firearms
Treso, Inc.
Truglo, Inc.
Uberti, Aldo
UFA, Inc.
Uncle Mike's (See Michaels of
    Oregon Co)
Upper Missouri Trading Co.
Venco Industries, Inc. (See
    Shooter's Choice)
Virgin Valley Custom Guns
Voere-KGH m.b.H.
W.E. Birdsong & Assoc.
Walters, John
Warne Manufacturing Co.
Warren Muzzleloading Co., Inc.
Wescombe, Bill (See North Star
    West)
White Owl Enterprises
White Shooting Systems, Inc.
    (See White Muzzleloading)
Williams Gun Sight Co.
Woodworker's Supply
Wright's Hardwood Gunstock
    Blanks

Young Country Arms
Ziegel Engineering

PISTOLSMITH

Acadian Ballistic Specialties
Accuracy Unlimited
Ace Custom 45's, Inc.
Actions by "T" Teddy Jacobson
Adair Custom Shop, Bill
Ahlman Guns
Ahrends, Kim (See Custom
    Firearms, Inc)
Aldis Gunsmithing & Shooting
    Supply
Alpha Precision, Inc.
Alpine Indoor Shooting Range
Armament Gunsmithing Co., Inc.
Aro-Tek Ltd.
Arundel Arms & Ammunition,
    Inc., A.
Baer Custom, Inc, Les
Bain & Davis, Inc.
Banks, Ed
Bar-Sto Precision Machine
Behlert Precision, Inc.
Bellm Contenders
Ben William's Gun Shop
Bengtson Arms Co., L.
Bill Adair Custom Shop
Bob Rogers Gunsmithing
Bowen Classic Arms Corp.
Broken Gun Ranch
Burkhart Gunsmithing, Don
Cannon's
Caraville Manufacturing
Carter's Gun Shop
Chicasaw Gun Works
Clark Custom Guns, Inc.
Cleland's Outdoor World, Inc.
Colonial Repair
Colorado School of Trades
Coonan Arms (JS Worldwide
    DBA)
Corkys Gun Clinic
Craig Custom Ltd., Research &
    Development
Curtis Custom Shop
Custom Firearms (See Ahrends,
    Kim)
Cylinder & Slide, Inc., William R.
    Laughridge
D&D Gunsmiths, Ltd.
D&L Sports
David R. Chicoine
Dayton Traister
Ed~ Brown Products, Inc.
EGW Evolution Gun Works
Ellicott Arms, Inc./Woods
    Pistolsmithing
Ferris Firearms
Fisher Custom Firearms
Forkin, Ben (See Belt MTN Arms)
Forkin Arms
Francesca, Inc.
Frielich Police Equipment
G.G. & G.
Garthwaite Pistolsmith, Inc., Jim
Gary Reeder Custom Guns
Genecco Gun Works, K.
Gentry Custom Gunmaker, David
George E. Mathews & Son, Inc.
Greider Precision
Guncraft Sports Inc.
Gunsite Custom Shop
Gunsite Gunsmithy (See Gunsite
    Custom Shop)
Gunsite Training Center
Hallberg Gunsmith, Fritz
Hamilton, Alex B (See Ten-Ring
    Precision, Inc)
Hammond Custom Guns Ltd.
Hank's Gun Shop
Hanson's Gun Center, Dick
Harris Gunworks

Harwood, Jack O.
Hawken Shop, The (See Dayton
    Traister)
Hebard Guns, Gil
Heinie Specialty Products
High Bridge Arms, Inc.
Highline Machine Co.
Hoag, James W.
Irwin, Campbell H.
Island Pond Gun Shop
Ivanoff, Thomas G (See Tom's
    Gun Repair)
J&S Heat Treat
Jarvis, Inc.
Jeffredo Gunsight
Jensen's Custom Ammunition
Johnston, James (See North
    Fork Custom Gunsmithing,
    James Johnston)
Jones, J.D./SSK Industries
Jungkind, Reeves C.
K-D, Inc.
Kaswer Custom, Inc.
Ken Starnes Gunmaker
Ken's Gun Specialties
Kilham & Co.
Kim Ahrends Custom Firearms,
    Inc.
Kimball, Gary
King's Gun Works
La Clinique du .45
LaFrance Specialties
LaRocca Gun Works
Lathrop's, Inc.
Lawson, John G (See Sight
    Shop, The)
Leckie Professional
    Gunsmithing
Lee's Red Ramps
Linebaugh Custom Sixguns
List Precision Engineering
Long, George F.
Mag-Na-Port International, Inc.
Mahony, Philip Bruce
Mahovsky's Metalife
Mandall Shooting Supplies Inc.
Marent, Rudolf
Marvel, Alan
Mathews & Son, Inc., George E.
Maxi-Mount
McCann's Machine & Gun Shop
MCS, Inc.
Middlebrooks Custom Shop
Miller Custom
Mitchell's Accuracy Shop
MJK Gunsmithing, Inc.
Mo's Competitor Supplies (See
    MCS Inc)
Mowrey's Guns & Gunsmithing
Mullis Guncraft
Nastoff's 45 Shop, Inc., Steve
NCP Products, Inc.
North Fork Custom
    Gunsmithing, James
    Johnston
Novak's, Inc.
Nygord Precision Products
Pace Marketing, Inc.
Paris, Frank J.
Pasadena Gun Center
Peacemaker Specialists
PEM's Mfg. Co.
Performance Specialists
Pierce Pistols
Plaxco, J. Michael
Power Custom, Inc.
Precision Specialties
Randco UK
Ries, Chuck
Rim Pac Sports, Inc.
Rocky Mountain Arms, Inc.
RPM
Score High Gunsmithing
Scott McDougall & Associates

PRODUCT & SERVICE DIRECTORY

Seecamp Co. Inc., L. W.
Shooters Supply
Shootin' Shack, Inc.
Singletary, Kent
Sipes Gun Shop
Spokhandguns, Inc.
Springfield, Inc.
SSK Industries
Steger, James R.
Swenson's 45 Shop, A. D.
Swift River Gunworks
Ten-Ring Precision, Inc.
Terry K. Kopp Professional
   Gunsmithing
The Robar Co.'s, Inc.
The Sight Shop
Thompson, Randall (See
   Highline Machine Co.)
Thurston Sports, Inc.
Tom's Gun Repair, Thomas G.
   Ivanoff
Vic's Gun Refinishing
Volquartsen Custom Ltd.
Walker Arms Co., Inc.
Walters Industries
Wardell Precision Handguns Ltd.
Weigand Combat Handguns,
   Inc.
Wessinger Custom Guns &
   Engraving
White Barn Wor
Wichita Arms, Inc.
Wild West Guns
Williams Gun Sight Co.
Williamson Precision
   Gunsmithing
Wilson Gun Shop
Wright's Hardwood Gunstock
   Blanks

POWDER MEASURES, SCALES, FUNNELS & ACCESSORIES

Fremont Tool Works
Frontier
Modern Muzzleloading, Inc.
RCBS Div. of Blount
Redding Reloading Equipment
Vega Tool Co.
VibraShine, Inc.

PRESS ACCESSORIES, METALLIC

R.E.I.

PRESS ACCESSORIES, SHOTSHELL

MEC, Inc.
Precision Reloading, Inc.
R.E.I.

PRESSES, ARBOR

K&M Services

PRESSES, METALLIC

Fremont Tool Works
RCBS Div. of Blount
Redding Reloading Equipment

PRESSES, SHOTSHELL

Ballistic Product, Inc.
MEC, Inc.

PRESSES, SWAGE

Bullet Swaging Supply Inc.
MAST Technology

PRIMING TOOLS & ACCESSORIES

Hart & Son, Inc.
K&M Services
RCBS Div. of Blount
Simmons, Jerry

REBORING & RERIFLING

Ahlman Guns
Bauska Barrels
BlackStar AccuMax Barrels
BlackStar Barrel Accurizing (See
   BlackStar AccuMax Barrels)
Chicasaw Gun Works
Collectors Firearms Etc.
H&S Liner Service
Hastings Barrels
IAI (See A.M.T.)
Ivanoff, Thomas G (See Tom's
   Gun Repair)
Jackalope Gun Shop
K-D, Inc.
LaBounty Precision Reboring,
   Inc.
Matco, Inc.
NCP Products, Inc.
Pence Precision Barrels
Pro-Port Ltd.
Redman's Rifling & Reboring
Rice, Keith (See White Rock Tool
   & Die)
Ridgetop Sporting Goods
Savage Arms, Inc.
Shaw, Inc., E. R. (See Small
   Arms Mfg. Co.)
Siegrist Gun Shop
Simmons Gun Repair, Inc.
Stratco, Inc.
Terry K. Kopp Professional
   Gunsmithing
The Gun Works
Time Precision, Inc.
Tom's Gun Repair, Thomas G.
   Ivanoff
Van Patten, J. W.
White Rock Tool & Die
Zufall, Joseph F.

RELOADING TOOLS AND ACCESSORIES

"Gramps" Antique Cartridges
4-D Custom Die Co.
Accurate Arms Co., Inc.
Advance Car Mover Co., Rowell
   Div.
Alaska Bullet Works, Inc.
American Products, Inc.
Ames Metal Products
Ammo Load, Inc.
Armfield Custom Bullets
Armite Laboratories
Arms Corporation of the
   Philippines
Atlantic Rose, Inc.
Atsko/Sno-Seal, Inc.
B-Square Company, Inc.
Bald Eagle Precision Machine
   Co.
Ballistic Product, Inc.
Belltown Ltd.
Ben William's Gun Shop
Ben's Machines
Berger Bullets Ltd.
Berry's Mfg., Inc.
Blackhawk East
Blount, Inc., Sporting Equipment
   Div.
Blue Mountain Bullets
Blue Ridge Machinery & Tools,
   Inc.
Bonanza (See Forster Products)
Break-Free, Inc.

Brown Co, E. Arthur
BRP, Inc. High Performance
   Cast Bullets
Brynin, Milton
Buck Stix--SOS Products Co.
Bull Mountain Rifle Co.
Bullseye Bullets
C&D Special Products (See
   Claybuster Wads & Harves
Camdex, Inc.
Camp-Cap Products
Canyon Cartridge Corp.
Carbide Die & Mfg. Co., Inc.
Case Sorting System
CFVentures
CH Tool & Die Co (See 4-D
   Custom Die Co)
Chem-Pak Inc.
CheVron Bullets
Claybuster Wads & Harvester
   Bullets
Clymer Manufacturing Co. Inc.
CONKKO
Cook Engineering Service
Cooper-Woodward
Crouse's Country Cover
Cumberland Arms
Curtis Cast Bullets
Custom Products (See Jones
   Custom Products)
CVA
D.C.C. Enterprises
Davide Pedersoli and Co.
Davis, Don
Davis Products, Mike
Denver Instrument Co.
Dever Co, Jack
Dewey Mfg. Co., Inc., J.
Dillon Precision Products, Inc.
Dropkick
E&L Mfg., Inc.
E-Z-Way Systems
Eagan, Donald V.
Eezox, Inc.
Efficient Machinery Co.
Eichelberger Bullets, Wm.
Elkhorn Bullets
Enguix Import-Export
Euroarms of America, Inc.
F&A Inc. (See ShurKatch
   Corporation)
Federated-Fry (See Fry Metals)
Feken, Dennis
Ferguson, Bill
First Inc, Jack
Fisher Custom Firearms
Fitz Pistol Grip Co.
Flambeau Products Corp.
Flitz International Ltd.
Forgett Jr., Valmore J.
Forster Products
Fremont Tool Works
Fry Metals
Fusilier Bullets
GAR
Gehmann, Walter (See
   Huntington Die Specialties)
Gozon Corp. U.S.A.
Graf & Sons
Graphics Direct
Graves Co.
Green, Arthur S.
Greenwood Precision
GTB
Gun City
Hanned Precision (See Hanned
   Line, The)
Harrell's Precision
Harris Enterprises
Harrison Bullets
Haydon Shooters Supply, Russ
Heidenstrom Bullets
Hirtenberger Aktiengesellschaft

Hoch Custom Bullet Moulds
   (See Colorado Shooter's
Hodgdon Powder Co.
Hoehn Sales, Inc.
Hoelscher, Virgil
Holland's Gunsmithing
Hollywood Engineering
Hondo Ind.
Hornady Mfg. Co.
Howell Machine
Hunters Supply, Inc.
Huntington Die Specialties
Hutton Rifle Ranch
Image Ind. Inc.
IMI Services USA, Inc.
Imperial Magnum Corp.
INTEC International, Inc.
Iosso Products
J&L Superior Bullets (See
   Huntington Die Specialties)
Javelina Lube Products
JGS Precision Tool Mfg.
JLK Bullets
Jonad Corp.
Jones Custom Products, Neil A.
Jones Moulds, Paul
K&M Services
Kapro Mfg.Co. Inc. (See R.E.I.)
King & Co.
Knoell, Doug
Korzinek Riflesmith, J
L.A.R. Mfg., Inc.
L.E. Wilson, Inc.
Lapua Ltd.
LBT
Le Clear Industries (See E-Z-
   Way Systems)
Lee Precision, Inc.
Legend Products Corp.
Liberty Metals
Liberty Shooting Supplies
Lightning Performance
   Innovations, Inc.
Lithi Bee Bullet Lube
Littleton, J. F.
Lock's Philadelphia Gun
   Exchange
Lortone Inc.
Loweth, Richard H.R.
Lyman Instant Targets, Inc. (See
   Lyman Products, Corp.)
Lyman Products Corp.
MA Systems
Magma Engineering Co.
MarMik, Inc.
Marquart Precision Co.
MAST Technology
Match Prep--Doyle Gracey
Mayville Engineering Co. (See
   MEC, Inc.)
McKillen & Heyer, Inc.
MCRW Associates Shooting
   Supplies
MCS, Inc.
MEC, Inc.
MI-TE Bullets
Midway Arms, Inc.
MMP
Mo's Competitor Supplies (See
   MCS Inc)
Montana Armory, Inc (See C.
   Sharps Arms Co. Inc.)
Mountain South
Mountain State Muzzleloading
   Supplies, Inc.
Mt. Baldy Bullet Co.
MTM Molded Products Co., Inc.
Multi-Scale Charge Ltd.
MWG Co.
Necromancer Industries, Inc.
NEI Handtools, Inc.
Newman Gunshop
North Devon Firearms Services
October Country Muzzleloading

Old West Bullet Moulds
Omark Industries,Div. of
   Blount,Inc.
Original Box, nc.
Outdoor Sports
   Headquarters,Inc.
Paco's (See Small Custom
   Mould & Bullet Co)
Paragon Sales & Services, Inc.
Pease Accuracy
Peerless Alloy, Inc.
Pinetree Bullets
Plum City Ballistic Range
Pomeroy, Robert
Ponsness/Warren
Prairie River Arms
Precision Castings & Equipment
Precision Reloading, Inc.
Prime Reloading
Pro-Shot Products, Inc.
Professional Hunter Supplies
   (See Star Custom Bullets)
Prolixr Lubricants
R.A. Wells Custom Gunsmith
R.E.I.
R.I.S. Co., Inc.
Rapine Bullet Mould Mfg. Co.
Redding Reloading Equipment
Reloading Specialties, Inc.
Rice, Keith (See White Rock Tool
   & Die)
Roberts Products
Rochester Lead Works
Rooster Laboratories
Rorschach Precision Products
Rosenthal, Brad and Sallie
S.L.A.P. Industries
SAECO (See Redding Reloading
   Equipment)
Sandia Die & Cartridge Co.
Saunders Gun & Machine Shop
Saville Iron Co. (See Greenwood
   Precision)
Scharch Mfg., Inc.
Scot Powder Co. of Ohio, Inc.
Scott, Dwight
Seebeck Assoc., R.E.
Sharp Shooter Supply
Sharps Arms Co., Inc., C.
Shiloh Creek
Shiloh Rifle Mfg.
Shooter's Choice
ShurKatch Corporation
Sierra Specialty Prod. Co.
Silver Eagle Machining
Simmons, Jerry
Sinclair International, Inc.
Skip's Machine
Small Custom Mould & Bullet
   Co.
Sno-Seal, Inc. (See Atsko/Sno-
   Seal)
SOS Products Co. (See Buck
   Stix-SOS Products Co.)
Spencer's Custom Guns
SPG LLC
Sportsman Supply Co.
SSK Industries
Stalwart Corporation
Star Custom Bullets
Starr Trading Co., Jedediah
Stillwell, Robert
Stoney Point Products, Inc.
Stratco, Inc.
Tamarack Products, Inc.
Taracorp Industries, Inc.
TCCI
TCSR
TDP Industries, Inc.
Tetra Gun Lubricants (See FTI,
   Inc.)
The Gun Works
The Hanned Line
The Protector Mfg. Co., Inc.

Thompson Bullet Lube Co.
Thompson/Center Arms
Timber Heirloom Products
Time Precision, Inc.
TMI Products (See Haselbauer Products, Jerry)
Trammco
Tru-Square Metal Prods., Inc.
TTM
United States Products Co.
Vega Tool Co.
Venco Industries, Inc. (See Shooter's Choice)
Vibra-Tek Co.
VibraShine, Inc.
Vihtavuori Oy/Kaltron-Pettibone
Vitt/Boos
W.B. Niemi Engineering
W.J. Riebe Co.
Walters, John
WD-40 Co.
Webster Scale Mfg. Co.
Welsh, Bud
White Rock Tool & Die
Whitetail Design & Engineering Ltd.
Widener's Reloading & Shooting Supply, Inc.
Wise Custom Guns
Wolf's Western Traders
Woodleigh (See Huntington Die Specialties)
WTA Manufacturing
Yesteryear Armory & Supply
Young Country Arms

RESTS BENCH, PORTABLE AND ACCESSORIES

Accuright
Adventure 16, Inc.
Armor Metal Products
B-Square Company, Inc.
Bald Eagle Precision Machine Co.
Bartlett Engineering
Borden Rifles Inc.
Browning Arms Co.
Bull Mountain Rifle Co.
C.W. Erickson's Mfg. Inc.
Canons Delcour
Chem-Pak Inc.
Clift Mfg., L. R.
Clift Welding Supply & Cases
Decker Shooting Products
Desert Mountain Mfg.
F&A Inc. (See ShurKatch Corporation)
Greenwood Precision
Harris Engineering Inc.
Hidalgo, Tony
Hoehn Sales, Inc.
Hoelscher, Virgil
Hoppe's Div. Penguin Industries, Inc.
Keng's Firearms Specialty, Inc./US Tactical Systems
Kolpin Mfg., Inc.
Kramer Designs
Midway Arms, Inc.
Millett Sights
MJM Mfg.
PAST Sporting Goods,Inc.
Protektor Model
Ransom International Corp.
Saville Iron Co. (See Greenwood Precision)
ShurKatch Corporation
Sinclair International, Inc.
T.H.U. Enterprises, Inc.
The Outdoor Connection,Inc.
Thompson Target Technology
Tonoloway Tack Drives
Varmint Masters, LLC

Wichita Arms, Inc.
Zanotti Armor, Inc.

RIFLE BARREL MAKER

Airrow
American Safe Arms, Inc.
Bauska Barrels
BlackStar AccuMax Barrels
BlackStar Barrel Accurizing (See BlackStar AccuMax Barrels)
Border Barrels Ltd.
Broad Creek Rifle Works, Ltd.
Brown Co, E. Arthur
Bullberry Barrel Works, Ltd.
Canons Delcour
Carter's Gun Shop
Christensen Arms
Cincinnati Swaging
Cryo-Accurizing
D&J Bullet Co. & Custom Gun Shop, Inc.
deHaas Barrels
DKT, Inc.
Donnelly, C. P.
Douglas Barrels Inc.
Fanzoj GmbH
Fred F. Wells/Wells Sport Store
Gaillard Barrels
Gary Schneider Rifle Barrels Inc.
Getz Barrel Co.
Granite Mountain Arms, Inc.
Green Mountain Rifle Barrel Co., Inc.
Gruning Precision Inc.
H-S Precision, Inc.
Half Moon Rifle Shop
Harris Gunworks
Hart Rifle Barrels,Inc.
Hastings Barrels
Hoelscher, Virgil
IAI (See A.M.T.)
Jackalope Gun Shop
K-D, Inc.
Knippel, Richard
Krieger Barrels, Inc.
LaBounty Precision Reboring, Inc.
Lilja Precision Rifle Barrels
Lothar Walther Precision Tool Inc.
Matco, Inc.
McGowen Rifle Barrels
McMillan Rifle Barrels
Mid-America Recreation, Inc.
Morrison Precision
Nowlin Mfg. Co.
Obermeyer Rifled Barrels
Olympic Arms Inc.
Orion Rifle Barrel Co.
Pac-Nor Barreling
Pell, John T. (See KOGOT)
Pence Precision Barrels
Perazone-Gunsmith, Brian
Raptor Arms Co., Inc.
Rocky Mountain Rifle Works Ltd.
Rogue Rifle Co., Inc.
Rosenthal, Brad and Sallie
Sabatti S.r.l.
Sanders Custom Gun Service
Savage Arms, Inc.
Schneider Rifle Barrels, Inc, Gary
Shaw, Inc., E. R. (See Small Arms Mfg. Co.)
Shilen, Inc.
Siskiyou Gun Works (See Donnelly, C. P.)
Small Arms Mfg. Co.
Specialty Shooters Supply, Inc.
Spencer's Custom Guns
Strutz Rifle Barrels, Inc., W. C.
Swift River Gunworks

Terry K. Kopp Professional Gunsmithing
The Gun Works
The Wilson Arms Co.
Unmussig Bullets, D. L.
Verney-Carron
Virgin Valley Custom Guns
W.C. Strutz Rifle Barrels, Inc.
Wiseman and Co., Bill

SCOPES, MOUNTS, ACCESSORIES, OPTICAL EQUIPMENT

A.R.M.S., Inc.
ABO (USA) Inc.
Accu-Tek
Accuracy Innovations, Inc.
Ackerman, Bill (See Optical Services Co)
Action Direct, Inc.
ADCO Sales, Inc.
Adventurer's Outpost
Aimpoint c/o Springfield, Inc.
Aimtech Mount Systems
Air Rifle Specialists
Air Venture Airguns
Alley Supply Co.
Alpec Team, Inc.
Apel GmbH, Ernst
ArmaLite, Inc.
Arundel Arms & Ammunition, Inc., A.
B-Square Company, Inc.
Baer Custom, Inc, Les
Barrett Firearms Manufacturer, Inc.
Beaver Park Product, Inc.
BEC, Inc.
Beeman Precision Airguns
Ben William's Gun Shop
BKL Technologies
Blount, Inc., Sporting Equipment Div.
Bohemia Arms Co.
Boonie Packer Products
Borden Rifles Inc.
Brockman's Custom Gunsmithing
Brown Co, E. Arthur
Brownells, Inc.
Brunton U.S.A.
BSA Optics
Bull Mountain Rifle Co.
Burris Co., Inc.
Bushnell Sports Optics Worldwide
Butler Creek Corp.
Carl Zeiss Inc.
Catco-Ambush, Inc.
Celestron International
Center Lock Scope Rings
Chuck's Gun Shop
Clark Custom Guns, Inc.
Clearview Mfg. Co., Inc.
Compass Industries, Inc.
Concept Development Corp.
Conetrol Scope Mounts
Creedmoor Sports, Inc.
Crimson Trace Lasers
Custom Quality Products, Inc.
D&H Prods. Co., Inc.
D.C.C. Enterprises
Daisy Mfg. Co.
Del-Sports, Inc.
DHB Products
E. Arthur Brown Co.
Eclectic Technologies, Inc.
Edmund Scientific Co.
Ednar, Inc.
Eggleston, Jere D.
EGW Evolution Gun Works
Emerging Technologies, Inc. (See Laseraim Technologies, Inc.)

Entre'prise Arms, Inc.
Excalibur Electro Optics Inc.
Excel Industries Inc.
Farr Studio,Inc.
Federal Arms Corp. of America
Forgett Jr., Valmore J.
Frankonia Jagd Hofmann & Co.
Fujinon, Inc.
G.G. & G.
Galati International
Gentry Custom Gunmaker, David
Gil Hebard Guns
Gilmore Sports Concepts
Groenewold, John
GSI, Inc.
Gun South, Inc. (See GSI, Inc.)
Guns
Guns Div. of D.C. Engineering, Inc.
Gunsmithing, Inc.
Hakko Co. Ltd.
Hammerli USA
Harris Gunworks
Harvey, Frank
Heckler & Koch, Inc.
Hertel & Reuss
Hines Co, S C
Hiptmayer, Armurier
Hiptmayer, Klaus
HiTek International
Holland's Gunsmithing
Impact Case Co.
Ironsighter Co.
Jeffredo Gunsight
Jena Eur
Jerry Phillips Optics
Jewell Triggers, Inc.
John Masen Co. Inc.
John Unertl Optical Co., Inc.
Johnson's Gunsmithing, Inc, Neal
Kahles A Swarovski Company
Kalispel Case Line
KDF, Inc.
Keng's Firearms Specialty, Inc./US Tactical Systems
KenPatable Ent., Inc.
Kesselring Gun Shop
Kimber of America, Inc.
Kmount
Kowa Optimed, Inc.
Kris Mounts
KVH Industries, Inc.
Kwik Mount Corp.
Kwik-Site Co.
L&S Technologies Inc (See Aimtech Mount Systems)
L.A.R. Mfg., Inc.
Laser Devices, Inc.
Laseraim Technologies, Inc.
LaserMax, Inc.
Leapers, Inc.
Lectro Science, Inc.
Lee Co., T. K.
Leica USA, Inc.
Leupold & Stevens, Inc.
Lightforce U.S.A. Inc.
List Precision Engineering
Lohman Mfg. Co., Inc.
London Guns Ltd.
Lyte Optronics (See TracStar Industries Inc)
Mac-1 Airgun Distributors
Mag-Na-Port International, Inc.
Marksman Products
Maxi-Mount
McBros Rifle Co.
McCann's Machine & Gun Shop
McMillan Optical Gunsight Co.
MCS, Inc.
MDS
Merit Corp.
Military Armament Corp.
Millett Sights

Mirador Optical Corp.
Mitchell Optics, Inc.
Mo's Competitor Supplies (See MCS Inc)
Mountain Rifles, Inc.
Muzzleloading Technologies, Inc.
MWG Co.
Neal Johnson's Gunsmithing, Inc.
New England Custom Gun Service
Nightforce (See Lightforce USA Inc)
Nikon, Inc.
Norincoptics (See BEC, Inc.)
Nygord Precision Products
Olympic Optical Co.
Optical Services Co.
Orchard Park Enterprise
Oregon Arms, Inc. (See Rogue Rifle Co., Inc.)
Ozark Gun Works
P.M. Enterprises, Inc.
Parsons Optical Mfg. Co.
PECAR Herbert Schwarz GmbH
PEM's Mfg. Co.
Pentax Corp.
Perazone-Gunsmith, Brian
PMC/Eldorado Cartridge Corp.
Precise Metalsmithing Enterprises
Precision Sport Optics
Premier Reticles
Quarton USA, Ltd. Co.
R.A. Wells Custom Gunsmith
Ram-Line Blount, Inc.
Ramon B. Gonzalez Guns
Ranch Products
Randolph Engineering, Inc.
Ranging, Inc.
Redfield, Inc.
Redfield/Blount
Rice, Keith (See White Rock Tool & Die)
Rocky Mountain High Sports Glasses
Rogue Rifle Co., Inc.
Romain's Custom Guns, Inc.
S&K Mfg. Co.
Sanders Custom Gun Service
Sanders Gun and Machine Shop
Schmidt & Bender, Inc.
Schumakers Gun Shop
Scope Control, Inc.
ScopLevel
Score High Gunsmithing
Segway Industries
Selsi Co., Inc.
Sharp Shooter Supply
Shepherd Enterprises, Inc.
Sightron, Inc.
Simmons Outdoor Corp.
Sinclair International, Inc.
Six Enterprises
SKAN A.R.
Slug Group, Inc.
Southern Bloomer Mfg. Co.
Sportsmatch U.K. Ltd.
Springfield, Inc.
SSK Industries
Stiles Custom Guns
Stoeger Industries
Stoney Point Products, Inc.
Sturm Ruger & Co. Inc.
Sunny Hill Enterprises, Inc.
SwaroSports, Inc. (See JagerSport Ltd.)
Swarovski Optik North America Ltd.
Swift Instruments, Inc.
T.K. Lee Co.
TacStar
Talley, Dave

Tasco Sales, Inc.
Tele-Optics
The Outdoor Connection,Inc.
Thompson/Center Arms
Time Precision, Inc.
Traditions Performance
  Firearms
Trijicon, Inc.
Truglo, Inc.
Ultra Dot Distribution
Uncle Mike's (See Michaels of
  Oregon Co)
Unertl Optical Co. Inc., John
United Binocular Co.
United States Optics
  Technologies, Inc.
Valor Corp.
Virgin Valley Custom Guns
Voere-KGH m.b.H.
Warne Manufacturing Co.
Warren Muzzleloading Co., Inc.
WASP Shooting Systems
Weatherby, Inc.
Weaver Products
Weaver Scope Repair Service
Weigand Combat Handguns,
  Inc.
Westley Richards & Co.
White Rock Tool & Die
White Shooting Systems, Inc.
  (See White Muzzleloading)
Wideview Scope Mount Corp.
Wilcox Industries Corp
Wild West Guns
Williams Gun Sight Co.
York M-1 Conversions
Zanotti Armor, Inc.

SHELLHOLDERS

American Sales & Mfg. Co.
Fremont Tool Works
Hafner World Wide, Inc.
Hart & Son, Inc.
K&M Services
Redding Reloading Equipment
Vega Tool Co.

SHOOTING/TRAINING SCHOOL

Alpine Indoor Shooting Range
American Gunsmithing Institute
American Small Arms Academy
Auto Arms
Beretta U.S.A. Corp.
Bob's Tactical Indoor Shooting
  Range & Gun Shop
Bridgeman Products
Cannon's
Chapman Academy of Practical
  Shooting
Chelsea Gun Club of New York
  City Inc.
Cherry Creek State Park
  Shooting Center
CQB Training
Defense Training International,
  Inc.
Executive Protection Institute
Feminine Protection, Inc.
Ferris Firearms
Front Sight Firearms Training
  Institute
G.H. Enterprises Ltd.
Gene's Custom Guns
Griffin & Howe, Inc.
Guncraft Sports Inc.
Gunsite Training Center
Henigson & Associates, Steve
Israel Arms International, Inc.
Jensen's Custom Ammunition
Jensen's Firearms Academy
L.L. Bean, Inc.
Lethal Force Institute (See Police
  Bookshelf)

Ljutic Industries, Inc.
McMurdo, Lynn (See Specialty
  Gunsmithing)
Mendez, John A.
Montgomery Community
  College
NCP Products, Inc.
Nevada Pistol Academy, Inc.
North American Shooting
  Systems
North Mountain Pine Training
  Center (See Executive
Paxton Quigley's Personal
  Protection Strategies
Pentheny de Pentheny
Performance Specialists
River Road Sporting Clays
SAFE
Shoot Where You Look
Shooter's World
Smith & Wesson
Specialty Gunsmithing
Starlight Training Center, Inc.
Steger, James R.
Tactical Defense Institute
The Firearm Training Center
The Shooting Gallery
Thunden Ranch
Western Missouri Shooters
  Alliance
Yankee Gunsmith
Yavapai Firearms Academy Ltd.

SHOTSHELL MISCELLANY

American Products, Inc.
Bridgeman Products
MEC, Inc.
Precision Reloading, Inc.
R.E.I.
T&S Industries, Inc.
Vitt/Boos

SIGHTS, METALLIC

Accura-Site (See All's, The Jim
  Tembelis Co., Inc.)
All's, The Jim J. Tembelis Co.,
  Inc.
Alley Supply Co.
Alpec Team, Inc.
Andela Tool & Machine, Inc.
Anschutz GmbH
Armsport, Inc.
Aro-Tek Ltd.
Ashley Outdoors, Inc.
Aspen Outfitting Co.
Baer Custom, Inc, Les
BEC, Inc.
Bo-Mar Tool & Mfg. Co.
Bob's Gun Shop
Bond Custom Firearms
Bowen Classic Arms Corp.
Bradley Gunsight Co.
Brockman's Custom
  Gunsmithing
Brooks Tactical Systems
Brown Co, E. Arthur
Brown Products, Inc., Ed
Brownells, Inc.
C-More Systems
California Sights (See Fautheree,
  Andy)
Cape Outfitters
Cash Mfg. Co., Inc.
Center Lock Scope Rings
Champion's Choice, Inc.
Colonial Repair
CRR, Inc./Marble's Inc.
DHB Products
E. Arthur Brown Co.
Evans, Andrew
Evans Gunsmithing (See Evans,
  Andrew)
Farr Studio,Inc.

Flintlocks, Etc
Forgett Jr., Valmore J.
Forkin Arms
G.G. & G.
Garthwaite Pistolsmith, Inc., Jim
Goergen's Gun Shop, Inc.
Gunsmithing, Inc.
Hank's Gun Shop
Heidenstrom Bullets
Heinie Specialty Products
Hesco-Meprolight
Hines Co, S C
Hiptmayer, Armurier
Hiptmayer, Klaus
Innovative Weaponry Inc.
Innovision Enterprises
J.P. Enterprises Inc.
Johnson's Gunsmithing, Inc,
  Neal
Keng's Firearms Specialty,
  Inc./US Tactical Systems
Knight Rifles
Kris Mounts
L.P.A. Snc
Leapers, Inc.
Lee's Red Ramps
List Precision Engineering
London Guns Ltd.
Lyman Instant Targets, Inc. (See
  Lyman Products, Corp.)
Madis, George
Marble Arms (See CRR,
  Inc./Marble's Inc.)
MCS, Inc.
MEC-Gar S.r.l.
Meprolight (See Hesco-
  Meprolight)
Merit Corp.
Middlebrooks Custom Shop
Millett Sights
MMC
Mo's Competitor Supplies (See
  MCS Inc)
Modern Muzzleloading, Inc.
Montana Armory, Inc (See C.
  Sharps Arms Co. Inc.)
Montana Vintage Arms
New England Custom Gun
  Service
Newman Gunshop
North Pass
Novak's, Inc.
OK Weber,Inc.
P.M. Enterprises, Inc.
PEM's Mfg. Co.
Quarton USA, Ltd. Co.
Redfield, Inc.
RPM
Sharps Arms Co., Inc., C.
Slug Site
STI International
T.F.C. S.P.A.
Talley, Dave
The Gun Doctor
The Gun Works
Thompson/Center Arms
Trijicon, Inc.
Truglo, Inc.
United States Optics
  Technologies, Inc.
Warne Manufacturing Co.
WASP Shooting Systems
Wichita Arms, Inc.
Wild West Guns
Williams Gun Sight Co.
Wilson Gun Shop

STOCK MAKER

Acra-Bond Laminates
Amrine's Gun Shop
Antique Arms Co.
Aspen Outfitting Co.
Bain & Davis, Inc.
Belding's Custom Gun Shop

Billings Gunsmiths Inc.
Bob Rogers Gunsmithing
Boltin, John M.
Bone Engraving, Ralph
Borden Ridges Rimrock Stocks
Boyds' Gunstock Industries, Inc.
Broad Creek Rifle Works, Ltd.
Burkhart Gunsmithing, Don
Caywood, Shane J.
Chuck's Gun Shop
Claro Walnut Gunstock Co.
Clear Creek Outdoors
Coffin, Charles H.
Colorado Gunsmithing Academy
D.D. Custom Stocks, R.H. "Dick"
  Devereaux
Dever Co, Jack
DGR Custom Rifles
DGS, Inc., Dale A. Storey
Fieldsport Ltd.
Fisher, Jerry A.
Genecco Gun Works, K.
George E. Mathews & Son, Inc.
Gillmann, Edwin
Great American Gunstock Co.
Gunsmithing Ltd.
Harper's Custom Stocks
Harry Lawson Co.
Heilmann, Stephen
Hensley, Gunmaker, Darwin
Heydenberk, Warren R.
Island Pond Gun Shop
Jamison's Forge Works
Jim Norman Custom Gunstocks
Jurras, L. E.
Keith's Custom Gunstocks
Knippel, Richard
Larry Lyons Gunworks
Lind Custom Guns, Al
Mathews & Son, Inc., George E.
McCament, Jay
McGowen Rifle Barrels
Mercer Custom Stocks, R. M.
Mid-America Recreation, Inc.
Mitchell, Jack
Morrow, Bud
Nelson, Stephen
Nettestad Gun Works
Nickels, Paul R.
Paul D. Hillmer Custom
  Gunstocks
Pawling Mountain Club
Pecatonica River Longrifle
Pentheny de Pentheny
R&J Gun Shop
Royal Arms Gunstocks
Sanders Custom Gun Service
Six Enterprises
Smith, Art
Smith, Sharmon
Stott's Creek Armory, Inc.
Talmage, William G.
Taylor & Robbins
Tiger-Hunt Gunstocks
Walker Arms Co., Inc.
Wayne E. Schwartz Custom
  Guns
Wessinger Custom Guns &
  Engraving
Williamson Precision
  Gunsmithing
Winter, Robert M.
Working Guns
Yee, Mike

STOCKS (COMMERCIAL)

3-Ten Corp.
Accuracy Unlimited
Acra-Bond Laminates
Ahlman Guns
Amrine's Gun Shop
Arms Ingenuity Co.

Arundel Arms & Ammunition,
  Inc., A.
Aspen Outfitting Co.
Baelder, Harry
Bain & Davis, Inc.
Balickie, Joe
Bansner's Gunsmithing
  Specialties
Barnes Bullets, Inc.
Beitzinger, George
Belding's Custom Gun Shop
Bell & Carlson, Inc.
Benchmark Guns
Biesen, Al
Biesen, Roger
Billeb, Stephen L.
Billings Gunsmiths Inc.
Blount, Inc., Sporting Equipment
  Div.
Bob Rogers Gunsmithing
Bob's Gun Shop
Bohemia Arms Co.
Boltin, John M.
Borden Ridges Rimrock Stocks
Borden Rifles Inc.
Bowerly, Kent
Boyds' Gunstock Industries, Inc.
Brace, Larry D.
Briganti, A.J.
Broad Creek Rifle Works, Ltd.
Brockman's Custom
  Gunsmithing
Brown Co, E. Arthur
Brown Precision,Inc.
Buckhorn Gun Works
Bull Mountain Rifle Co.
Bullberry Barrel Works, Ltd.
Butler Creek Corp.
Cali'co Hardwoods, Inc.
Camilli, Lou
Campbell, Dick
Cape Outfitters
Carter's Gun Shop
Caywood, Shane J.
Chambers Flintlocks Ltd., Jim
Chicasaw Gun Works
Churchill, Winston
Claro Walnut Gunstock Co.
Clear Creek Outdoors
Cloward's Gun Shop
Coffin, Charles H.
Coffin, Jim (See Working Guns)
Colonial Repair
Colorado Gunsmithing Academy
Colorado School of Trades
Conrad, C. A.
Creedmoor Sports, Inc.
Curly Maple Stock Blanks (See
  Tiger-Hunt)
Custom Checkering Service,
  Kathy Forster
Custom Gun Products
Custom Riflestocks, Inc.,
  Michael M. Kokolus
D&D Gunsmiths, Ltd.
D&G Precision Duplicators (See
  Greene Precision Du
D&J Bullet Co. & Custom Gun
  Shop, Inc.
D.D. Custom Stocks, R.H. "Dick"
  Devereaux
Dakota Arms, Inc.
Dangler, Homer L.
David W. Schwartz Custom Guns
Dever Co, Jack
Devereaux, R.H. "Dick" (See D.D.
  Custom Stocks, R.H. "Dick
  Devereaux)
DGR Custom Rifles
Dick Marple & Associates
Dillon, Ed
Dressel Jr., Paul G.
Duane's Gun Repair (See DGR
  Custom Rifles)

DIRECTORY

PRODUCT & SERVICE DIRECTORY

Duncan's Gun Works, Inc.
Echols & Co., D'Arcy
Eggleston, Jere D.
Erhardt, Dennis
Eversull Co., Inc., K.
Farmer-Dressel, Sharon
Fibron Products, Inc.
Fieldsport Ltd.
Fisher, Jerry A.
Folks, Donald E.
Forster, Kathy (See Custom
    Checkering Service, Kathy
    Forster)
Forster, Larry L.
Forthofer's Gunsmithing &
    Knifemaking
Francotte & Cie S.A. Auguste
Frank Custom Classic Arms, Ron
Fred F. Wells/Wells Sport Store
Game Haven Gunstocks
Gary Goudy Classic Stocks
Gene's Custom Guns
Gervais, Mike
Gillmann, Edwin
Giron, Robert E.
Goens, Dale W.
Golden Age Arms Co.
Gordie's Gun Shop
Grace, Charles E.
Great American Gunstock Co.
Green, Roger M.
Greenwood Precision
Griffin & Howe, Inc.
Guns
Gunsmithing Ltd.
H-S Precision, Inc.
Hallberg Gunsmith, Fritz
Halstead, Rick
Hamilton, Jim
Hanson's Gun Center, Dick
Harper's Custom Stocks
Harris Gunworks
Harry Lawson Co.
Hart & Son, Inc.
Harwood, Jack O.
Hastings Barrels
Hecht, Hubert J, Waffen-Hecht
Heilmann, Stephen
Hensley, Gunmaker, Darwin
Heppler, Keith M, Keith's
    Custom Gunstocks
Heydenberk, Warren R.
High Tech Specialties, Inc.
Hines Co, S C
Hiptmayer, Armurier
Hiptmayer, Klaus
Hoelscher, Virgil
Hoenig & Rodman
Hogue Grips
Huebner, Corey O.
Hughes, Steven Dodd
Island Pond Gun Shop
Ivanoff, Thomas G (See Tom's
    Gun Repair)
J.P. Gunstocks, Inc.
Jackalope Gun Shop
Jamison's Forge Works
Jarrett Rifles, Inc.
Jim Norman Custom Gunstocks
John Masen Co. Inc.
Johnson Wood Products
KDF, Inc.
Keith's Custom Gunstocks (See
    Heppler, Keith M)
Kelbly, Inc.
Ken's Rifle Blanks
Kilham & Co.
Klein Custom Guns, Don
Klingler Woodcarving
Knippel, Richard
Kokolus, Michael M. (See
    Custom Riflestocks, In
Lawson Co., Harry
Lind Custom Guns, Al

Mazur Restoration, Pete
McBros Rifle Co.
McCament, Jay
McCann's Muzzle-Gun Works
McCullough, Ken (See Ken's
    Rifle Blanks)
McDonald, Dennis
McFarland, Stan
McGuire, Bill
McKinney, R.P. (See Schuetzen
    Gun Co.)
McMillan Fiberglass Stocks, Inc.
Michaels Of Oregon
Mid-America Recreation, Inc.
Miller Arms, Inc.
Mitchell, Jack
Morrison Custom Rifles, J. W.
MPI Stocks
MWG Co.
NCP Products, Inc.
Nelson, Stephen
Nettestad Gun Works
New England Arms Co.
New England Custom Gun
    Service
Newman Gunshop
Nickels, Paul R.
Oakland Custom Arms,Inc.
Oil Rod and Gun Shop
OK Weber,Inc.
Old World Gunsmithing
One Of A Kind
Ottmar, Maurice
Pacific Research Laboratories,
    Inc. (See Rimrock R
Pagel Gun Works, Inc.
Paragon Sales & Services, Inc.
Paul D. Hillmer Custom
    Gunstocks
Paulsen Gunstocks
Pawling Mountain Club
Pecatonica River Longrifle
PEM's Mfg. Co.
Perazone-Gunsmith, Brian
Perazzi USA, Inc.
Pohl, Henry A. (See Great
    American Gun Co.
Powell & Son (Gunmakers) Ltd.,
    William
Precision Gun Works
R&J Gun Shop
R.A. Wells Custom Gunsmith
Ram-Line Blount, Inc.
Rampart International
Reagent Chemical & Research,
    Inc. (See Calico Hardwoods,
    Inc.)
Reiswig, Wallace E. (See Claro
    Walnut Gunstock, Co.)
Richards Micro-Fit Stocks
RMS Custom Gunsmithing
Robinson, Don
Robinson Firearms Mfg. Ltd.
Romain's Custom Guns, Inc.
Roto Carve
Ryan, Chad L.
Saville Iron Co. (See Greenwood
    Precision)
Schiffman, Curt
Schiffman, Mike
Schiffman, Norman
Score High Gunsmithing
Sile Distributors, Inc.
Simmons Gun Repair, Inc.
Six Enterprises
Skeoch, Brian R.
Smith, Sharmon
Speiser, Fred D.
Stan De Treville & Co.
Stiles Custom Guns
Storey, Dale A. (See DGS Inc.)
Stott's Creek Armory, Inc.
Strawbridge, Victor W.
Sturgeon Valley Sporters, K. Ide

Swann, D. J.
Swift River Gunworks
Szweda, Robert (See RMS
    Custom Gunsmithing)
T.F.C. S.P.A.
Talmage, William G.
Taylor & Robbins
Tecnolegno S.P.A.
The Gun Shop
The Orvis Co.
The Walnut Factory
Thompson/Center Arms
Tiger-Hunt Gunstocks
Tirelli
Tom's Gun Repair, Thomas G.
    Ivanoff
Track of the Wolf, Inc.
Trevallion Gunstocks
Tucker, James C.
Turkish Firearms Corp.
Tuttle, Dale
Vest, John
Vic's Gun Refinishing
Vintage Industries, Inc.
Virgin Valley Custom Guns
Volquartsen Custom Ltd.
Walker Arms Co., Inc.
Weber & Markin Custom
    Gunsmiths
Weems, Cecil
Wenig Custom Gunstocks
Werth, T. W.
Wessinger Custom Guns &
    Engraving
Western Gunstock Mfg. Co.
Williams Gun Sight Co.
Windish, Jim
Winter, Robert M.
Working Guns
Wright's Hardwood Gunstock
    Blanks
Yee, Mike
York M-1 Conversions
Zeeryp, Russ

STUCK CASE REMOVERS
MarMik, Inc.

TARGETS, BULLET & CLAYBIRD TRAPS
A-Tech Corp.
Action Target, Inc.
American Target
American Whitetail Target
    Systems
Autauga Arms, Inc.
Beeman Precision Airguns
Beomat of America, Inc.
Birchwood Casey
Blount, Inc., Sporting Equipment
    Div.
Blue and Gray Products Inc (See
    Ox-Yoke Originals
Brown Manufacturing
Bull-X, Inc.
Caswell Detroit Armor
    Companies
Champion Target Co.
D.C.C. Enterprises
Datumtech Corp.
Detroit-Armor Corp.
Diamond Mfg. Co.
Federal Champion Target Co.
Freeman Animal Targets
G.H. Enterprises Ltd.
Gozon Corp. U.S.A.
Great Lakes Airguns
H-S Precision, Inc.
Hiti-Schuch, Atelier Wilma
Hunterjohn
Innovision Enterprises
J.G. Dapkus Co., Inc.
Kennebec Journal

Kleen-Bore,Inc.
Lakefield Arms Ltd (See Savage
    Arms Inc)
Leapers, Inc.
Littler Sales Co.
Lyman Instant Targets, Inc. (See
    Lyman Products, Corp.)
Lyman Products Corp.
Marksman Products
Mendez, John A.
MSR Targets
N.B.B., Inc.
National Target Co.
North American Shooting
    Systems
Outers Laboratories Div. of
    Blount, Inc.Sporting E
Ox-Yoke Originals, Inc.
Palsa Outdoor Products
Passive Bullet Traps, Inc. (See
    Savage Range Systems,
    Inc.)
PlumFire Press, Inc.
Precision Airgun Sales, Inc.
Quack Decoy & Sporting Clays
Redfield, Inc.
Remington Arms Co., Inc.
Rockwood Corp.
Rocky Mountain Target Co.
Savage Arms (Canada), Inc.
Savage Range Systems, Inc.
Schaefer Shooting Sports
Seligman Shooting Products
Shoot-N-C Targets (See
    Birchwood Casey)
Shooters Supply
Target Shooting, Inc.
Thompson Target Technology
Trius Traps, Inc.
Universal Sports
White Flyer Targets
World of Targets (See
    Birchwood Casey)
X-Spand Target Systems
Z's Metal Targets & Frames
Zriny's Metal Targets (See Z's
    Metal Targets & Frames)

TAXIDERMY
African Import Co.
Kulis Freeze Dry Taxidermy
Montgomery Community
    College
World Trek, Inc.

TRAP & SKEET SHOOTER'S EQUIPMENT
Accurate Arms Co., Inc.
Allen Co., Bob
Allen Sportswear, Bob (See Allen
    Co., Bob)
American Products, Inc.
Bagmaster Mfg., Inc.
Baker, Stan
Ballistic Product, Inc.
Beomat of America, Inc.
Beretta S.P.A., Pietro
Bridgeman Products
Cape Outfitters
Clymer Manufacturing Co. Inc.
Elsen Inc., Pete
F&A Inc. (See ShurKatch
    Corporation)
Fiocchi of America Inc.
G.H. Enterprises Ltd.
Game Winner, Inc.
Hastings Barrels
Hoppe's Div. Penguin Industries,
    Inc.
Hunter Co., Inc.
Jamison's Forge Works
Jenkins Recoil Pads, Inc.
Jim Noble Co.

Kalispel Case Line
Kolar
Lakewood Products LLC
Ljutic Industries, Inc.
Mag-Na-Port International, Inc.
Maionchi-L.M.I.
Meadow Industries
MEC, Inc.
Moneymaker Guncraft Corp.
MTM Molded Products Co., Inc.
NCP Products, Inc.
Pachmayr Div. Lyman Products
Palsa Outdoor Products
PAST Sporting Goods,Inc.
Perazzi USA, Inc.
Pro-Port Ltd.
Protektor Model
Quack Decoy & Sporting Clays
Remington Arms Co., Inc.
Rhodeside, Inc.
Shootin' Accessories, Ltd.
Shooting Specialties (See Titus,
    Daniel)
ShurKatch Corporation
T&S Industries, Inc.
TEN-X Products Group
Trius Traps, Inc.
Truglo, Inc.
Universal Sports
Warne Manufacturing Co.
X-Spand Target Systems
Ziegel Engineering

TRIGGERS, RELATED EQUIPMENT
Actions by "T" Teddy Jacobson
B&D Trading Co., Inc.
Baer Custom, Inc, Les
Behlert Precision, Inc.
Bond Custom Firearms
Boyds' Gunstock Industries, Inc.
Bull Mountain Rifle Co.
Dayton Traister
Electronic Trigger Systems, Inc.
Eversull Co., Inc., K.
FWB
Galati International
Gentry Custom Gunmaker, David
    Guns
Hart & Son, Inc.
Hawken Shop, The (See Dayton
    Traister)
Hoehn Sales, Inc.
Hoelscher, Virgil
Holland's Gunsmithing
IAI (See A.M.T.)
Impact Case Co.
J.P. Enterprises Inc.
Jewell Triggers, Inc.
John Masen Co. Inc.
KK Air International (See Impact
    Case Co.)
L&R Lock Co.
List Precision Engineering
London Guns Ltd.
M.H. Canjar Co.
Mahony, Philip Bruce
Master Lock Co.
Miller Single Trigger Mfg. Co.
NCP Products, Inc.
OK Weber,Inc.
PEM's Mfg. Co.
Penrod Precision
Perazone-Gunsmith, Brian
Perazzi USA, Inc.
S&B Industries
Schumakers Gun Shop
Sharp Shooter Supply
Shilen, Inc.
Simmons Gun Repair, Inc.
Slug Group, Inc.
Target Shooting, Inc.
Time Precision, Inc.

MANUFACTURER'S DIRECTORY

A

A Zone Bullets, 2039 Walter Rd., Billings, MT 59105 / 800-252-3111; FAX: 406-248-1961

A&B Industries,Inc (See Top-Line USA Inc)

A&M Waterfowl,Inc., P.O. Box 102, Ripley, TN 38063 / 901-635-4003; FAX: 901-635-2320

A&W Repair, 2930 Schneider Dr., Arnold, MO 63010 / 314-287-3725

A-Square Co.,Inc., One Industrial Park, Bedford, KY 40006-9667 / 502-255-7456; FAX: 502-255-7657

A-Tech Corp., P.O. Box 1281, Cottage Grove, OR 97424

A.A. Arms, Inc., 4811 Persimmont Ct., Monroe, NC 28110 / 704-289-5356 or 800-935-1119; FAX: 704-289-5859

A.B.S. III, 9238 St. Morritz Dr., Fern Creek, KY 40291

A.G. Russell Knives,Inc., 1705 Hwy. 71B North, Springdale, AR 72764 / 501-751-7341

A.R.M.S., Inc., 230 W. Center St., West Bridgewater, MA 02379-1620 / 508-584-7816; FAX: 508-588-8045

A.W. Peterson Gun Shop, Inc., 4255 W. Old U.S. 441, Mt. Dora, FL 32757-3299 / 352-383-4258; FAX: 352-735-1001

ABO (USA) Inc, 615 SW 2nd Avenue, Miami, FL 33130 / 305-859-2010 FAX: 305-859-2099

AC Dyna-tite Corp., 155 Kelly St., P.O. Box 0984, Elk Grove Village, IL 60007 / 847-593-5566; FAX: 847-593-1304

Acadian Ballistic Specialties, P.O. Box 787, folsom, LA 70437 / 504-796-0078 gunsmith@neasolft.com

Accu-Tek, 4510 Carter Ct, Chino, CA 91710

Accupro Gun Care, 15512-109 Ave., Surrey, BC U3R 7E8 CANADA / 604-583-7807

Accura-Site (See All's, The Jim Tembelis Co., Inc.)

Accuracy Innovations, Inc., P.O. Box 376, New Paris, PA 15554 / 814-839-4517; FAX: 814-839-2601

Accuracy Int'l. North America, Inc., PO Box 5267, Oak Ridge, TN 37831 / 423-482-0330; FAX: 423-482-0336

Accuracy International, 9115 Trooper Trail, P.O. Box 2019, Bozeman, MT 59715 / 406-587-7922; FAX: 406-585-9434

Accuracy Internationl Precision Rifles (See U.S. Importer-Gunsite Custom Shop; Gunsite Training Center)

Accuracy Unlimited, 16036 N. 49 Ave., Glendale, AZ 85306 / 602-978-9089; FAX: 602-978-9089

Accuracy Unlimited, 7479 S. DePew St., Littleton, CO 80123

Accurate Arms Co., Inc., 5891 Hwy. 230 West, McEwen, TN 37101 / 800-416-3006 FAX: 931-729-4211

Accuright, RR 2 Box 397, Sebeka, MN 56477 / 218-472-3383

Ace Custom 45's, Inc., 1880 1/2 Upper Turtle Creek Rd., Kerrville, TX 78028 / 830-257-4290; FAX: 830-257-5724

Ace Sportswear, Inc., 700 Quality Rd., Fayetteville, NC 28306 / 919-323-1223; FAX: 919-323-5392

Ackerman & Co., Box 133 US Highway Rt. 7, Pownal, VT 05261 / 802-823-9874 muskets@togsther.net

Ackerman, Bill (See Optical Services Co)

Acra-Bond Laminates, 134 Zimmerman Rd., Kalispell, MT 59901 / 406-257-9003; FAX: 406-257-9003

Action Bullets & Alloy Inc, RR 1, P.O. Box 189, Quinter, KS 67752 / 913-754-3609; FAX: 913-754-3629

Action Direct, Inc., P.O. Box 830760, Miami, FL 33283 / 305-559-4652; FAX: 305-559-4652 action-direct.com

Action Products, Inc., 22 N. Mulberry St., Hagerstown, MD 21740 / 301-797-1414; FAX: 301-733-2073

Action Target, Inc., P.O. Box 636, Provo, UT 84603 / 801-377-8033; FAX: 801-377-8096

Actions by "T" Teddy Jacobson, 16315 Redwood Forest Ct., Sugar Land, TX 77478 / 281-277-4008

AcuSport Corporation, 1 Hunter Place, Bellefontaine, OH 43311-3001 / 513-593-7010 FAX: 513-592-5625

Ad Hominem, 3130 Gun Club Lane, RR, Orillia, ON L3V 6H3 CANADA / 705-689-5303; FAX: 705-689-5303

Adair Custom Shop, Bill, 2886 Westridge, Carrollton, TX 75006

Adams & Son Engravers, John J, 87 Acorn Rd, Dennis, MA 02638 / 508-385-7971

Adams Jr., John J, 87 Acorn Rd., Dennis, MA 02638 / 508-385-7971

ADCO Sales, Inc., 4 Draper St. #A, Woburn, MA 01801 / 781-935-1799; FAX: 781-935-1011

Adkins, Luther, 1292 E. McKay Rd., Shelbyville, IN 46176-8706 / 317-392-3795

Advance Car Mover Co., Rowell Div., P.O. Box 1, 240 N. Depot St., Juneau, WI 53039 / 414-386-4464; FAX: 414-386-4416

Adventure 16, Inc., 4620 Alvarado Canyon Rd., San Diego, CA 92120 / 619-283-6314

Adventure Game Calls, R.D. 1, Leonard Rd., Spencer, NY 14883 / 607-589-4611

Adventurer's Outpost, P.O. Box 547, Cottonwood, AZ 86326-0547 / 800-762-7471; FAX: 602-634-8781

Aero Peltor, 90 Mechanic St, Southbridge, MA 01550 / 508-764-5500; FAX: 508-764-0188

African Import Co., 22 Goodwin Rd, Plymouth, MA 02360 / 508-746-8552 FAX: 508-746-0404

AFSCO Ammunition, 731 W. Third St., P.O. Box L, Owen, WI 54460 / 715-229-2516

Ahlman Guns, 9525 W. 230th St., Morristown, MN 55052 / 507-685-4243; FAX: 507-685-4280

Ahrends, Kim (See Custom Firearms, Inc), Box 203, Clarion, IA 50525 / 515-532-3449; FAX: 515-532-3926

Aimpoint c/o Springfield, Inc., 420 W. Main St, Geneseo, IL 61254 / 309-944-1702

Aimtech Mount Systems, P.O. Box 223, Thomasville, GA 31799-1638 / 912-226-4313; FAX: 912-227-0222 aimtech@surfsouth.com www.aimtech-mounts.com

Air Arms, Hailsham Industrial Park, Diplocks Way, Hailsham, E. Sussex, BN27 3JF ENGLAND / 011-0323-845853

Air Rifle Specialists, P.O. Box 138, 130 Holden Rd., Pine City, NY 14871-0138 / 607-734-7340; FAX: 607-733-3261

Air Venture Airguns, 9752 E. Flower St., Bellflower, CA 90706 / 310-867-6355

Airgun Repair Centre, 3227 Garden Meadows, Lawrenceburg, IN 47025 / 812-637-1463; FAX: 812-637-1463

Airrow, 11 Monitor Hill Rd, Newtown, CT 06470 / 203-270-6343

Aitor-Cuchilleria Del Norte S.A., Izelaieta, 17, 48260, Ermua, S SPAIN / 43-17-08-50

Ajax Custom Grips, Inc., 9130 Viscount Row, Dallas, TX 75247 / 214-630-8893; FAX: 214-630-4942

Aker International, Inc., 2248 Main St., Suite 6, Chula Vista, CA 91911 / 619-423-5182; FAX: 619-423-1363

Al Lind Custom Guns, 7821 76th Ave. SW, Tacoma, WA 98498 / 206-584-6361

Alana Cupp Custom Engraver, P.O. Box 207, Annabella, UT 84711 / 801-896-4834

Alaska Bullet Works, Inc., 9978 Crazy Horse Drive, Juneau, AK 99801 / 907-789-3834; FAX: 907-789-3433

Alco Carrying Cases, 601 W. 26th St., New York, NY 10001 / 212-675-5820; FAX: 212-691-5935

Aldis Gunsmithing & Shooting Supply, 502 S. Montezuma St., Prescott, AZ 86303 / 602-445-6723; FAX: 602-445-6763

Alessi Holsters, Inc., 2465 Niagara Falls Blvd., Amherst, NY 14228-3527 / 716-691-5615

Alex, Inc., Box 3034, Bozeman, MT 59772 / 406-282-7396; FAX: 406-282-7396

Alfano, Sam, 36180 Henry Gaines Rd., Pearl River, LA 70452 / 504-863-3364; FAX: 504-863-7715

All American Lead Shot Corp., P.O. Box 224566, Dallas, TX 75062

All Rite Products, Inc., 5752 N. Silverstone Circle, Mountain Green, UT 84050 / 801-876-3330; FAX: 801-876-2216

All's, The Jim J. Tembelis Co., Inc., 216 Loper Ct., Neenah, WI 54956 / 920-725-5251; FAX: 920-725-5251

Allard, Gary/Creek Side Metal & Woodcrafters, Fishers Hill, VA 22626 / 703-465-3903

Allen Co., Bob, 214 SW Jackson, P.O. Box 477, Des Moines, IA 50315 / 515-283-2191 or 800-685-7020; FAX: 515-283-0779

Allen Co., Inc., 525 Burbank St., Broomfield, CO 80020 / 303-469-1857 or 800-876-8600; FAX: 303-466-7437

Allen Firearm Engraving, 339 Grove Ave., Prescott, AZ 86301 / 520-778-1237

Allen Mfg., 6449 Hodgson Rd., Circle Pines, MN 55014 / 612-429-8231

Allen Sportswear, Bob (See Allen Co., Bob)

Alley Supply Co., P.O. Box 848, Gardnerville, NV 89410 / 702-782-3800

Alliant Techsystems Smokeless Powder Group, 200 Valley Rd., Suite 305, Mt. Arlington, NJ 07856 / 800-276-9337; FAX: 201-770-2528

Allred Bullet Co., 932 Evergreen Drive, Logan, UT 84321 / 435-752-6983; FAX: 435-752-6983

Alpec Team, Inc., 201 Ricken Backer Cir., Livermore, CA 94550 / 510-606-8245; FAX: 510-606-4279

Alpha 1 Drop Zone, 2121 N. Tyler, Wichita, KS 67212 / 316-729-0800

Alpha Gunsmith Division, 1629 Via Monserate, Fallbrook, CA 92028 / 619-723-9279 or 619-728-2663

Alpha LaFranck Enterprises, P.O. Box 81072, Lincoln, NE 68501 / 402-466-3193

Alpha Precision, Inc., 2765-B Preston Rd. NE, Good Hope, GA 30641 / 770-267-6163

Alpine Indoor Shooting Range, 2401 Government Way, Coeur d'Alene, ID 83814 / 208-676-8824 FAX: 208-676-8824

Altamont Co., 901 N. Church St., P.O. Box 309, Thomasboro, IL 61878 / 217-643-3125 or 800-626-5774; FAX: 217-643-7973

Alumna Sport by Dee Zee, 1572 NE 58th Ave., P.O. Box 3090, Des Moines, IA 50316 / 800-798-9899

Amadeo Rossi S.A., Rua: Amadeo Rossi, 143, Sao Leopoldo, RS 93030-220 BRAZIL / 051-592-5566

AmBr Software Group Ltd., P.O. Box 301, Reistertown, MD 21136-0301 / 800-888-1917; FAX: 410-526-7212

American Ammunition, 3545 NW 71st St., Miami, FL 33147 / 305-835-7400; FAX: 305-694-0037

American Arms Inc., 2604 NE Industrial Dr, N. Kansas City, MO 64116 / 816-474-3161; FAX: 816-474-1225

American Bullet, 1512 W Chester Pike #298, West Chester, PA 19382-7754 / 610-399-6584

American Custom Gunmakers Guild, PO Box 812, Burlington, IA 52601 / 318-752-6114; FAX: 319-752-6114 acgg@acgg.org acgg.org

American Derringer Corp., 127 N. Lacy Dr., Waco, TX 76705 / 800-642-7817 or 817-799-9111; FAX: 817-799-7935

American Display Co., 55 Cromwell St., Providence, RI 02907 / 401-331-2464; FAX: 401-421-1264

American Frontier Firearms Mfg., Inc, PO Box 744, Aguanga, CA 92536 / 909-763-0014; FAX: 909-763-0014

American Gas & Chemical Co., Ltd, 220 Pegasus Ave, Northvale, NJ 07647 / 201-767-7300

American Gripcraft, 3230 S Dodge 2, Tucson, AZ 85713 / 602-790-1222

American Gunsmithing Institute, 1325 Imola Ave #504, Napa, CA 94559 / 707-253-0462; FAX: 707-253-7149

American Handgunner Magazine, 591 Camino de la Reina, Ste 200, San Diego, CA 92108 / 619-297-5350; FAX: 619-297-5353

American Pioneer Video, PO Box 50049, Bowling Green, KY 42102-2649 / 800-743-4675

American Products, Inc., 14729 Spring Valley Road, Morrison, IL 61270 / 815-772-3336; FAX: 815-772-8046

American Safe Arms, Inc., 1240 Riverview Dr., Garland, UT 84312 / 801-257-7472; FAX: 801-785-8156

American Sales & Kirkpatrick Mfg. Co., P.O. Box 677, Laredo, TX 78042 / 210-723-6893; FAX: 210-725-0672

American Sales & Mfg. Co., PO Box 677, Laredo, TX 78042 / 956-723-6893; FAX: 956-725-0672 holsters@kirkpatrick-leather.com http://kirkpatrickleather.com

American Security Products Co., 11925 Pacific Ave., Fontana, CA 92337 / 909-685-9680 or 800-421-6142; FAX: 909-685-9685

American Small Arms Academy, P.O. Box 12111, Prescott, AZ 86304 / 602-778-5623

American Target, 1328 S. Jason St., Denver, CO 80223 / 303-733-0433; FAX: 303-777-0311

American Target Knives, 1030 Brownwood NW, Grand Rapids, MI 49504 / 616-453-1998

American Whitetail Target Systems, P.O. Box 41, 106 S. Church St., Tennyson, IN 47637 / 812-567-4527

Americase, P.O. Box 271, 1610 E. Main, Waxahachie, TX 75165 / 800-880-3629; FAX: 214-937-8373

Ames Metal Products, 4323 S. Western Blvd., Chicago, IL 60609 / 773-523-3230; or 800-255-6937 FAX: 773-523-3854

Amherst Arms, P.O. Box 1457, Englewood, FL 34295 / 941-475-2020; FAX: 941-473-1212

Ammo Load, Inc., 1560 E. Edinger, Suite G, Santa Ana, CA 92705 / 714-558-8858; FAX: 714-569-0319

Amrine's Gun Shop, 937 La Luna, Ojai, CA 93023 / 805-646-2376

Amsec, 11925 Pacific Ave., Fontana, CA 92337

Amtec 2000, Inc., 84 Industrial Rowe, Gardner, MA 01440 / 508-632-9608; FAX: 508-632-2300

Analog Devices, Box 9106, Norwood, MA 02062

Andela Tool & Machine, Inc., RD3, Box 246, Richfield Springs, NY 13439

Anderson Manufacturing Co., Inc., 22602 53rd Ave. SE, Bothell, WA 98021 / 206-481-1858; FAX: 206-481-7839

Andres & Dworsky, Bergstrasse 18, A-3822 Karlstein, Thaya, AUSTRIA / 0 28 44-285

Angel Arms, Inc., 1825 Addison Way, Haywood, CA 94545 / 510-783-7122

Angelo & Little Custom Gun Stock Blanks, P.O. Box 240046, Dell, MT 59724-0046

Anics Firm Inc3 Commerce Park Square, 23200 Chagrin Blvd., Suite 240, Beechwood, OH 44122 / 800-556-1582; FAX: 216-292-2588

Anschutz GmbH, Postfach 1128, D-89001 Ulm, Donau, GERMANY / 731-40120

Answer Products Co., 1519 Westbury Drive, Davison, MI 48423 / 810-653-2911

Anthony and George Ltd., Rt. 1, P.O. Box 45, Evington, VA 24550 / 804-821-8117

MANUFACTURER'S DIRECTORY

Antique American Firearms, P.O. Box 71035, Dept. GD, Des Moines, IA 50325 / 515-224-6552

Antique Arms Co., 1110 Cleveland Ave., Monett, MO 65708 / 417-235-6501

Apel GmbH, Ernst, Am Kirschberg 3, D-97218, Gerbrunn, GERMANY / 0 (931) 707192

Aplan Antiques & Art, James O., James O., HC 80, Box 793-25, Piedmont, SD 57769 / 605-347-5016

AR-7 Industries, LLC, 998 N. Colony Rd., Meriden, CT 06450 / 203-630-3536; FAX: 203-630-3637

Arco Powder, HC-Rt. 1 P.O. Box 102, County Rd. 357, Mayo, FL 32066 / 904-294-3882; FAX: 904-294-1498

Arizona Ammunition, Inc., 21421 No. 14th Ave., Suite E, Phoenix, AZ 85027 / 623-516-9004; FAX: 623-516-9012 azam-mo.com

Arkansas Mallard Duck Calls, Rt. Box 182, England, AR 72046 / 501-842-3597

ArmaLite, Inc., P.O. Box 299, Geneseo, IL 61254 / 309-944-6939; FAX: 309-944-6949

Armament Gunsmithing Co., Inc., 525 Rt. 22, Hillside, NJ 07205 / 908-686-0960 FAX: 718-738-5019

Armas Kemen S. A. (See U.S. Importers)

Armas Urki Garbi, 12-14 20.600, Eibar (Guipuzcoa), / 43-11 38 73

Armfield Custom Bullets, 4775 Caroline Drive, San Diego, CA 92115 / 619-582-7188; FAX: 619-287-3238

Armi Perazzi S.p.A., Via Fontanelle 1/3, 1-25080, Botticino Mattina, / 030-2692591; FAX: 030 2692594+

Armi San Marco (See U.S. Importers-Taylor's & Co I

Armi San Paolo, 172-A, I-25062, via Europa, ITALY / 030-2751725

Armi Sport (See U.S. Importers-Cape Outfitters)

Armite Laboratories, 1845 Randolph St., Los Angeles, CA 90001 / 213-587-7768; FAX: 213-587-5075

Armoloy Co. of Ft. Worth, 204 E. Daggett St., Fort Worth, TX 76104 / 817-332-5604; FAX: 817-335-6517

Armor (See Buck Stop Lure Co., Inc.)

Armor Metal Products, P.O. Box 4609, Helena, MT 59604 / 406-442-5560; FAX: 406-442-5650

Armory Publications, 17171 Bothall Way NE, #276, Seattle, WA 98155 / 208-664-5061; FAX: 208-664-9906 armory-pub@aol.com www.grocities.com/armorypub

Arms & Armour Press, Wellington House, 125 Strand, London, WC2R 0BB ENGLAND / 0171-420-5555; FAX: 0171-240-7265

Arms Corporation of the Philippines, Bo. Parang Marikina, Metro Manila, PHILIPPINES / 632-941-6243 or 632-941-6244; FAX: 632-942-0682

Arms Craft Gunsmithing, 1106 Linda Dr., Arroyo Grande, CA 93420 / 805-481-2830

Arms Ingenuity Co., P.O. Box 1, 51 Canal St., Weatogue, CT 06089 / 203-658-5624

Arms Software, P.O. Box 1526, Lake Oswego, OR 97035 / 800-366-5559 or 503-697-0533; FAX: 503-697-3337

Arms, Programming Solutions (See Arms Software)

Armscorp USA, Inc., 4424 John Ave., Baltimore, MD 21227 / 410-247-6200; FAX: 410-247-6205 armscorp_md@ya-hoo.com

Armsport, Inc., 3950 NW 49th St., Miami, FL 33142 / 305-635-7850; FAX: 305-633-2877

Arnold Arms Co., Inc., P.O. Box 1011, Arlington, WA 98223 / 800-371-1011 or 360-435-1011; FAX: 360-435-7304

Aro-Tek Ltd., 206 Frontage Rd. North, Suite C, Pacific, WA 98047 / 206-351-2984; FAX: 206-833-4483

Arratoonian, Andy (See Horseshoe Leather Products)

Arrieta S.L., Morkaiko 5, 20870, Elgoibar, SPAIN / 34-43-743150; FAX: 34-43-743154+

Art Jewel Enterprises Ltd., Eagle Business Ctr., 460 Randy Rd., Carol Stream, IL 60188 / 708-260-0400

Art's Gun & Sport Shop, Inc., 6008 Hwy. Y, Hillsboro, MO 63050

Artistry in Wood, 134 Zimmerman Rd., Kalispell, MT 59901 / 406-257-9003

Arundel Arms & Ammunition, Inc., A., 24A Defense St., Annapolis, MD 21401 / 410-224-8683

Arvo Ojala Holsters, P.O. Box 98, N. Hollywood, CA 91603 / 818-222-9700; FAX: 818-222-0401

Ashby Turkey Calls, P.O. Box 1466, Ava, MO 65608-1466 / 417-967-3787

Ashley Outdoors, Inc, 2401 Ludelle St, Fort Worth, TX 76105 / 888-744-4880; FAX: 800-734-7939

Aspen Outfitting Co, Jon Hollinger, 9 Dean St, Aspen, CO 81611 / 970-925-3406

Astra Sport, S.A., Apartado 3, 48300 Guernica, Espagne, SPAIN / 34-4-6250100; FAX: 34-4-6255186+

Atamec-Bretton, 19 rue Victor Grignard, F-42026, St.-Etienne (Cedex 1, / 77-93-54-69; FAX: 33-77-93-57-98+

Atlanta Cutlery Corp., 2143 Gees Mill Rd., Box 839 CIS, Conyers, GA 30207 / 800-883-0300; FAX: 404-388-0246

Atlantic Mills, Inc., 1295 Towbin Ave., Lakewood, NJ 08701-5934 / 800-242-7374

Atlantic Rose, Inc., P.O. Box 10717, Bradenton, FL 34282-0717

Atsko/Sno-Seal, Inc., 2664 Russell St., Orangeburg, SC 29115 / 803-531-1820; FAX: 803-531-2139

Auguste Francotte & Cie S.A., rue du Trois Juin 109, 4400 Herstal-Liege, BELGIUM / 32-4-248-13-18; FAX: 32-4-948-11-79

Austin & Halleck, 1099 Welt, Weston, MO 64098 / 816-386-2176; FAX: 816-386-2177

Austin Sheridan USA, Inc., P.O. Box 577, 36 Haddam Quarter Rd., Durham, CT 06422 / 860-349-1772; FAX: 860-349-1771 swalzer@palm.net

Autauga Arms, Inc., Pratt Plaza Mall No. 13, Prattville, AL 36067 / 800-262-9563; FAX: 334-361-2961

Auto Arms, 738 Clearview, San Antonio, TX 78228 / 512-434-5450

Auto-Ordnance Corp., PO Box 220, Blauvelt, NY 10913 / 914-353-7770

Automatic Equipment Sales, 627 E. Railroad Ave., Salesburg, MD 21801

Autumn Sales, Inc. (Blaser), 1320 Lake St., Fort Worth, TX 76102 / 817-335-1634; FAX: 817-338-0119

Avnda Otaola Norica, 16 Apartado 68, 20600, Eibar,

AWC Systems Technology, P.O. Box 41938, Phoenix, AZ 85080-1938 / 602-780-1050 FAX: 602-780-2967

AYA (See U.S. Importer-New England Custom Gun Service)

B

B & P America, 12321 Brittany Cir, Dallas, TX 75230 / 972-726-9069

B&D Trading Co., Inc., 3935 Fair Hill Rd., Fair Oaks, CA 95628 / 800-334-3790 or 916-967-9366; FAX: 916-967-4873

B-Square Company, Inc., ;, P.O. Box 11281, 2708 St. Louis Ave., Ft. Worth, TX 76110 / 817-923-0964 or 800-433-2909 FAX: 817-926-7012

B-West Imports, Inc., 2425 N. Huachuca Dr., Tucson, AZ 85745-1201 / 602-628-1990; FAX: 602-628-3602

B.B. Walker Co., PO Box 1167, 414 E Dixie Dr, Asheboro, NC 27203 / 910-625-1380; FAX: 910-625-8125

B.C. Outdoors, Larry McGhee, PO Box 61497, Boulder City, NV 89006 / 702-294-0025

B.M.F. Activator, Inc., 12145 Mill Creek Run, Plantersville, TX 77363 / 936-894-2397 or 800-527-2881 FAX: 936-894-2397

Badger Shooters Supply, Inc., P.O. Box 397, Owen, WI 54460 / 800-424-9069; FAX: 715-229-2332

Baekgaard Ltd., 1855 Janke Dr., Northbrook, IL 60062 / 708-498-3040; FAX: 708-493-3106

Baelder, Harry, Alte Goennebeker Strasse 5, 24635, Rickling, GERMANY / 04328-722732; FAX: 04328-722733

Baer Custom, Inc, Les, 29601 34th Ave, Hillsdale, IL 61257 / 309-658-2716; FAX: 309-658-2610

Baer's Hollows, P.O. Box 284, Eads, CO 81036 / 719-438-5718

Bagmaster Mfg., Inc., 2731 Sutton Ave., St. Louis, MO 63143 / 314-781-8002; FAX: 314-781-3363

Bain & Davis, Inc., 307 E. Valley Blvd., San Gabriel, CA 91776-3522 / 818-573-4241 or 213-283-7449 cain-davis@aol.com

Baker, Stan, 10000 Lake City Way, Seattle, WA 98125 / 206-522-4575

Baker's Leather Goods, Roy, PO Box 893, Magnolia, AR 71753 / 501-234-0344

Balance Co., 340-39 Ave., S.E., Box 505, Calgary, AB T2G 1X6 CANADA

Bald Eagle Precision Machine Co., 101-A Allison St., Lock Haven, PA 17745 / 570-748-6772; FAX: 570-748-4443

Balickie, Joe, 408 Trelawney Lane, Apex, NC 27502 / 919-362-5185

Ballard Industries, 10271 Lockwood Dr., Suite B, Cupertino, CA 95014 / 408-996-0957; FAX: 408-257-6828

Ballard Rifle & Cartridge Co., LLC, 113 W Yellowstone Ave, Cody, WY 82414 / 307-587-4914; FAX: 307-527-6097

Ballisti-Cast, Inc., 6347 49th St. NW, Plaza, ND 58771 / 701-497-3333; FAX: 701-497-3335

Ballistic Engineering & Software, Inc., 185 N. Park Blvd., Suite 330, Lake Orion, MI 48362 / 313-391-1074

Ballistic Product, Inc., 20015 75th Ave. North, Corcoran, MN 55340-9456 / 612-494-9237; FAX: 612-494-9236 info@bal-listicproducts.com www.ballisticproducts.com

Ballistic Research, 1108 W. May Ave., McHenry, IL 60050 / 815-385-0037

Bandcor Industries, Div. of Man-Sew Corp., 6108 Sherwin Dr., Port Richey, FL 34668 / 813-848-0432

Bang-Bang Boutique (See Holster Shop, The)

Banks, Ed, 2762 Hwy. 41 N., Ft. Valley, GA 31030 / 912-987-4665

Bansner's Gunsmithing Specialties, 261 East Main St. Box VH, Adamstown, PA 19501 / 800-368-2379; FAX: 717-484-0523

Bar-Sto Precision Machine, 73377 Sullivan Rd., P.O. Box 1838, Twentynine Palms, CA 92277 / 760-367-2747; FAX: 760-367-2407

Barbour, Inc., 55 Meadowbrook Dr., Milford, NH 03055 / 603-673-1313; FAX: 603-673-6510

Barnes, 110 Borner St S, Prescott, WI 54021-1149 / 608-897-8416

Barnes Bullets, Inc., P.O. Box 215, American Fork, UT 84003 / 801-756-4222 or 800-574-9200; FAX: 801-756-2465 email@barnesbullets.com barnesbullets.com

Baron Technology, 62 Spring Hill Rd., Trumbull, CT 06611 / 203-452-0515; FAX: 203-452-0663

Barraclough, John K., 55 Merit Park Dr., Gardena, CA 90247 / 310-324-2574

Barramundi Corp., P.O. Drawer 4259, Homosassa Springs, FL 32687 / 904-628-0200

Barrett Firearms Manufacturer, Inc., P.O. Box 1077, Murfreesboro, TN 37133 / 615-896-2938; FAX: 615-896-7313

Barry Lee Hands Engraving, 26192 E. Shore Route, Bigfork, MT 59911 / 406-837-0035

Barta's Gunsmithing, 10231 US Hwy. 10, Cato, WI 54206 / 920-732-4472

Barteaux Machete, 1916 SE 50th Ave., Portland, OR 97215-3238 / 503-233-5880

Bartlett Engineering, 40 South 200 East, Smithfield, UT 84335-1645 / 801-563-5910

Basics Information Systems, Inc., 1141 Georgia Ave., Suite 515, Wheaton, MD 20902 / 301-949-1070; FAX: 301-949-5326

Bates Engraving, Billy, 2302 Winthrop Dr, Decatur, AL 35603 / 256-355-3690

Bauer, Eddie, 15010 NE 36th St., Redmond, WA 98052

Baumgartner Bullets, 3011 S. Alane St., W. Valley City, UT 84120

Bauska Barrels, 105 9th Ave. W., Kalispell, MT 59901 / 406-752-7706

Bear Archery, RR 4, 4600 Southwest 41st Blvd., Gainesville, FL 32601 / 904-376-2327

Bear Arms, 121 Rhodes St., Jackson, SC 29831 / 803-471-9859

Bear Hug Grip, Inc., P.O. Box 16649, Colorado Springs, CO 80935-6649 / 800-232-7710

Bear Mountain Gun & Tool, 120 N. Plymouth, New Plymouth, ID 83655 / 208-278-5221; FAX: 208-278-5221

Beartooth Bullets, P.O. Box 491, Dept. HLD, Dover, ID 83825-0491 / 208-448-1865 beartooth@trasport.com

Beaver Lodge (See Fellowes, Ted)

Beaver Park Product, Inc., 840 J St., Penrose, CO 81240 / 719-372-6744

BEC, Inc., 1227 W. Valley Blvd., Suite 204, Alhambra, CA 91803 / 626-281-5751; FAX: 626-293-7073

Beeline Custom Bullets Limited, P.O. Box 85, Yarmouth, NS B5A 4B1 CANADA / 902-648-3494; FAX: 902-648-0253

Beeman Precision Airguns, 5454 Argosy Dr., Huntington Beach, CA 92649 / 714-890-4800; FAX: 714-890-4808

Behlert Precision, Inc., P.O. Box 288, 7067 Easton Rd., Pipersville, PA 18947 / 215-766-8681 or 215-766-7301; FAX: 215-766-8681

Beitzinger, George, 116-20 Atlantic Ave., Richmond Hill, NY 11419 / 718-847-7661

Belding's Custom Gun Shop, 10691 Sayers Rd., Munith, MI 49259 / 517-596-2388

Bell & Carlson, Inc., Dodge City Industrial Park, 101 Allen Rd., Dodge City, KS 67801 / 800-634-8586 or 316-225-6688; FAX: 316-225-9095

Bell Reloading, Inc., 1725 Harlin Lane Rd., Villa Rica, GA 30180

Bell's Gun & Sport Shop, 3309-19 Mannheim Rd, Franklin Park, IL 60131

Bell's Legendary Country Wear, 22 Circle Dr., Bellmore, NY 11710 / 516-679-1158

Bellm Contenders, P.O. Box 459, Cleveland, UT 84518 / 801-653-2530

Belltown Ltd., 11 Camps Rd., Kent, CT 06757 / 860-354-5750 FAX: 860-354-6764

Ben William's Gun Shop, 1151 S. Cedar Ridge, Duncanville, TX 75137 / 214-780-1807

Ben's Machines, 1151 S. Cedar Ridge, Duncanville, TX 75137 / 214-780-1807 FAX: 214-780-0316

Benchmark Guns, 12593 S Ave. 5 East, Yuma, AZ 85365

Benchmark Knives (See Gerber Legendary Blades)

Benelli Armi S.p.A., Via della Stazione, 61029, Urbino, ITALY / 39-722-307-1; FAX: 39-722-327427+

MANUFACTURER'S DIRECTORY

Benelli USA Corp, 17603 Indian Head Hwy, Accokeek, MD 20607 / 301-283-6981; FAX: 301-283-6988 benelliusa.com

Bengtson Arms Co., L., 6345-B E. Akron St., Mesa, AZ 85205 / 602-981-6375

Benjamin/Sheridan Co., Crossman, Rts. 5 and 20, E. Bloomfield, NY 14443 / 716-657-6161; FAX: 716-657-5405

Bentley, John, 128-D Watson Dr., Turtle Creek, PA 15145

Beomat of America, Inc., 300 Railway Ave., Campbell, CA 95008 / 408-379-4829

Beretta S.p.A., Pietro, Via Beretta, 18-25063, Gardone V.T., ITALY / 39-30-8341-1 FAX: 39-30-8341-421

Beretta U.S.A. Corp., 17601 Beretta Drive, Accokeek, MD 20607 / 301-283-2191; FAX: 301-283-0435

Berger Bullets Ltd., 5342 W. Camelback Rd., Suite 200, Glendale, AZ 85301 / 602-842-4001; FAX: 602-934-9083

Bernardelli S.p.A., Vincenzo, 125 Via Matteotti, PO Box 74, Brescia, ITALY / 39-30-8912851-2-3; FAX: 39-30-8910249

Berry's Mfg., Inc., 401 North 3050 East St., St. George, UT 84770 / 435-634-1682; FAX: 435-634-1683 sales@berrysmfg.com www.berrysmfg.com

Bersa S.A., Gonzales Castillo 312, 1704, Ramos Mejia, ARGENTINA / 541-656-2377; FAX: 541-656-2093+

Bert Johanssons Vapentillbehor, S-430 20 Veddige, SWEDEN,

Bertuzzi (See U.S. Importer-New England Arms Co)

Better Concepts Co., 663 New Castle Rd., Butler, PA 16001 / 412-285-9000

Beverly, Mary, 3201 Horseshoe Trail, Tallahassee, FL 32312

Bianchi International, Inc., 100 Calle Cortez, Temecula, CA 92590 / 909-676-5621; FAX: 909-676-6777

Biesen, Al, 5021 Rosewood, Spokane, WA 99208 / 509-328-9340

Biesen, Roger, 5021 W. Rosewood, Spokane, WA 99208 / 509-328-9340

Big Bear Arms & Sporting Goods, Inc., 1112 Milam Way, Carrollton, TX 75006 / 972-416-8051 or 800-400-BEAR; FAX: 972-416-0771

Big Bore Bullets of Alaska, P.O. Box 872785, Wasilla, AK 99687 / 907-373-2673; FAX: 907-373-2673 doug@mtaonline.net ww.awloo.com/bbb/index.

Big Bore Express, 7154 W. State St., Boise, ID 83703 / 800-376-4010; FAX: 208-376-4020

Big Sky Racks, Inc., P.O. Box 729, Bozeman, MT 59771-0729 / 406-586-9393; FAX: 406-585-7378

Big Spring Enterprises "Bore Stores", P.O. Box 1115, Big Spring Rd., Yellville, AR 72687 / 870-449-5297; FAX: 870-449-4446

Bilal, Mustafa, 908 NW 50th St., Seattle, WA 98107-3634 / 206-782-4164

Bilinski, Bryan. See: FIELDSPORT LTD

Bill Austin's Calls, Box 284, Kaycee, WY 82639 / 307-738-2552

Bill Adair Custom Shop, 2886 Westridge, Carrollton, TX 75006 / 972-418-0950

Bill Hanus Birdguns LLC, P.O. Box 533, Newport, OR 97365 / 541-265-7433; FAX: 541-265-7400

Bill Johns Master Engraver, 7927 Ranch Roach 965, Fredericksburg, TX 78624-9545 / 830-997-6795

Bill Wiseman and Co., P.O. Box 3427, Bryan, TX 77805 / 409-690-3456; FAX: 409-690-0156

Bill's Custom Cases, P.O. Box 2, Dunsmuir, CA 96025 / 530-235-0177; FAX: 530-235-4959

Bill's Gun Repair, 1007 Burlington St., Mendota, IL 61342 / 815-539-5786

Billeb, Stephen L., 1101 N. 7th St., Burlington, IA 52601 / 319-753-2110

Billings Gunsmiths Inc., 1841 Grand Ave., Billings, MT 59102 / 406-256-8390

Billingsley & Brownell, P.O. Box 25, Dayton, WY 82836 / 307-655-9344

Billy Bates Engraving, 2302 Winthrop Dr., Decatur, AL 35603 / 205-355-3690

Birchwood Casey, 7900 Fuller Rd., Eden Prairie, MN 55344 / 800-328-6156 or 612-937-7933; FAX: 612-937-7979

Birdsong & Assoc, W. E., 1435 Monterey Rd, Florence, MS 39073-9748 / 601-366-8270

Bismuth Cartridge Co., 3500 Maple Ave., Suite 1650, Dallas, TX 75219 / 214-521-5880; FAX: 214-521-9035

Bison Studios, 1409 South Commerce St., Las Vegas, NV 89102 / 702-388-2891; FAX: 702-383-9967

Bitterroot Bullet Co., PO Box 412, Lewiston, ID 83501-0412 / 208-743-5635 FAX: 208-743-5635

BKL Technologies, PO Box 5237, Brownsville, TX 78523

Black Belt Bullets (See Big Bore Express)

Black Hills Ammunition, Inc., P.O. Box 3090, Rapid City, SD 57709-3090 / 605-348-5150; FAX: 605-348-9827

Black Hills Shooters Supply, P.O. Box 4220, Rapid City, SD 57709 / 800-289-2506

Black Powder Products, 67 Township Rd. 1411, Chesapeake, OH 45619 / 614-867-8047

Black Sheep Brand, 3220 W. Gentry Parkway, Tyler, TX 75702 / 903-592-3853; FAX: 903-592-0527

Blackhawk East, Box 2274, Loves Park, IL 61131

Blacksmith Corp., PO Box 280, North Hampton, OH 45349 / 800-531-2665; FAX: 937-969-8399 bcbooks@glasscity.net

BlackStar AccuMax Barrels, 11501 Brittmoore Park Drive, Houston, TX 77041 / 281-721-6040; FAX: 281-721-6041

BlackStar Barrel Accurizing (See BlackStar AccuMax Barrels)

Blacktail Mountain Books, 42 First Ave. W., Kalispell, MT 59901 / 406-257-5573

Blair Engraving, J. R., PO Box 64, Glenrock, WY 82637 / 307-436-8115

Blammo Ammo, P.O. Box 1677, Seneca, SC 29679 / 803-882-1768

Blaser Jagdwaffen GmbH, D-88316, Isny Im Allgau, GERMANY

Bleile, C. Roger, 5040 Ralph Ave., Cincinnati, OH 45238 / 513-251-0249

Blount, Inc., Sporting Equipment Div., 2299 Snake River Ave., P.O. Box 856, Lewiston, ID 83501 / 800-627-3640 or 208-746-2351; FAX: 208-799-3904

Blue and Gray Products Inc (See Ox-Yoke Originals, Inc.,)

Blue Book Publications, Inc., One Appletree Square, 8009 34th Ave. S. Suite 175, Minneapolis, MN 55425 / 800-877-4867 or 612-854-5229; FAX: 612-853-1486

Blue Mountain Bullets, HCR 77, P.O. Box 231, John Day, OR 97845 / 541-820-4594

Blue Ridge Machinery & Tools, Inc., P.O. Box 536-GD, Hurricane, WV 25526 / 800-872-6500; FAX: 304-562-5311

BMC Supply, Inc., 26051 - 179th Ave. S.E., Kent, WA 98042

Bo-Mar Tool & Mfg. Co., Rt. 8, Box 405, Longview, TX 75604 / 903-759-4784; FAX: 903-759-9141

Bob Allen Co.214 SW Jackson, P.O. Box 477, Des Moines, IA 50315 / 800-685-7020 FAX: 515-283-0779

Bob Rogers Gunsmithing, P.O. Box 305, 344 S. Walnut St., Franklin Grove, IL 61031 / 815-456-2685; FAX: 815-288-7142

Bob Schrimsher's Custom Knifemaker's Supply, P.O. Box 308, Emory, TX 75440 / 903-473-3330; FAX: 903-473-2235

Bob's Gun Shop, P.O. Box 200, Royal, AR 71968 / 501-767-1970; FAX: 501-767-1970

Bob's Tactical Indoor Shooting Range & Gun Shop, 90 Lafayette Rd., Salisbury, MA 01952 / 508-465-5561

Boessler, Erich, Am Vogeltal 3, 97702, Munnerstadt, GERMANY

Bohemia Arms Co., 17101 Los Modelos St., Fountain Valley, CA 92708 / 619-442-7005; FAX: 619-442-7005

Boker USA, Inc., 1550 Balsam Street, Lakewood, CO 80215 / 303-462-0662; FAX: 303-462-0668 bokerusa@world-net.att.net bokerusa.com

Boltin, John M., P.O. Box 644, Estill, SC 29918 / 803-625-2185

Bonanza (See Forster Products), 310 E Lanark Ave, Lanark, IL 61046 / 815-493-6360; FAX: 815-493-2371

Bond Arms, Inc., P.O. Box 1296, Granbury, TX 76048 / 817-573-4445; FAX: 817-573-5636

Bond Custom Firearms, 8954 N. Lewis Ln., Bloomington, IN 47408 / 812-332-4519

Bondini Paolo, Via Sorrento 345, San Carlo di Cesena, ITALY / 0547-663-240; FAX: 0547-663-780

Bone Engraving, Ralph, 718 N Atlanta, Owasso, OK 74055 / 918-272-9745

Boone Trading Co., Inc., P.O. Box BB, Brinnan, WA 98320

Boone's Custom Ivory Grips, Inc., 562 Coyote Rd., Brinnon, WA 98320 / 206-796-4330

Boonie Packer Products, P.O. Box 12204, Salem, OR 97309 / 800-477-3244 or 503-581-3244; FAX: 503-581-3191

Borden Ridges Rimrock Stocks, RR 1 Box 250 BC, Springville, PA 18844 / 570-965-2505 FAX: 570-965-2328

Borden Rifles Inc, RD 1, Box 250BC, Springville, PA 18844 / 717-965-2505; FAX: 717-965-2328

Border Barrels Ltd., Riccarton Farm, Newcastleton, SCOTLAND UK

Borovnik KG, Ludwig, 9170 Ferlach, Bahnhofstrasse 7, AUSTRIA / 042 27 24 42; FAX: 042 26 43 49

Bosis (See U.S. Importer-New England Arms Co.)

Boss Manufacturing Co., 221 W. First St., Kewanee, IL 61443 / 309-852-2131 or 800-447-4581; FAX: 309-852-0848

Bostick Wildlife Calls, Inc., P.O. Box 728, Estill, SC 29918 / 803-625-2210 or 803-625-4512

Bowen Classic Arms Corp., P.O. Box 67, Louisville, TN 37777 / 865-984-3583 bowsarms.com

Bowen Knife Co., Inc., P.O. Box 590, Blackshear, GA 31516 / 912-449-4794

Bowerly, Kent, 710 Golden Pheasant Dr, Redmond, OR 97756 / 541-595-6028

Boyds' Gunstock Industries, Inc., 25376 403RD AVE, MITCHELL, SD 57301 / 605-996-5011; FAX: 605-996-9878

Brace, Larry D., 771 Blackfoot Ave., Eugene, OR 97404 / 541-688-1278; FAX: 541-607-5833

Bradley Gunsight Co., P.O. Box 340, Plymouth, VT 05056 / 860-589-0531; FAX: 860-582-6294

Brass Eagle, Inc., 7050A Bramalea Rd., Unit 19, Mississauga,, ON L4Z 1C7 CANADA / 416-848-4844

Bratcher, Dan, 311 Belle Air Pl., Carthage, MO 64836 / 417-358-1518

Brauer Bros. Mfg. Co., 2020 Delman Blvd., St. Louis, MO 63103 / 314-231-2864; FAX: 314-249-4952

Break-Free, Inc., P.O. Box 25020, Santa Ana, CA 92799 / 714-953-1900; FAX: 714-953-0402

Brenneke KG, Wilhelm, Ilmenauweg 2, 30851 Langenhagen, GERMANY / 0511-97262-0; FAX: 0511-97262-62

Brian Perazone-Gunsmith, Cold Spring Rd., Roxbury, NY 12474 / 607-326-4088; FAX: 607-326-3140

Bridgeman Products, Harry Jaffin, 153 B Cross Slope Court, Englishtown, NJ 07726 / 732-536-3604; FAX: 732-972-1004

Bridgers Best, P.O. Box 1410, Berthoud, CO 80513

Briese Bullet Co., Inc., RR1, Box 108, Tappen, ND 58487 / 701-327-4578; FAX: 701-327-4579

Brigade Quartermasters, 1025 Cobb International Blvd., Dept. VH, Kennesaw, GA 30144-4300 / 404-428-1248 or 800-241-3125; FAX: 404-426-7726

Briganti, A.J., 512 Rt. 32, Highland Mills, NY 10930 / 914-928-9573

Briley Mfg. Inc., 1230 Lumpkin, Houston, TX 77043 / 800-331-5718 or 713-932-6995; FAX: 713-932-1043

British Antiques, P.O. Box 35369, Tucson, AZ 85740 / 520-575-9063 britishantiques@hotmail.com

British Sporting Arms, RR1, Box 130, Millbrook, NY 12545 / 914-677-8303

BRNO (See U.S. Importers-Bohemia Arms Co.)

Broad Creek Rifle Works, Ltd., 120 Horsey Ave., Laurel, DE 19956 / 302-875-5446; FAX: 302-875-1449 bcqw4guns@aol.com

Brockman's Custom Gunsmithing, P.O. Box 357, Gooding, ID 83330 / 208-934-5050

Brocock Ltd., 43 River Street, Digbeth, Birmingham, B5 5SA ENGLAND / 011-021-773-1200

Broken Gun Ranch, 10739 126 Rd., Spearville, KS 67876 / 316-385-2587; FAX: 316-385-2597

Brolin Arms, 2755 Thompson Creek Rd., Pomona, CA 91767 / 909-392-7822; FAX: 909-392-7824

Brooker, Dennis, Rt. 1, Box 12A, Derby, IA 50068 / 515-533-2103

Brooks Tactical Systems, 279-C Shorewood Ct., Fox Island, WA 98333 / 253-549-2866 FAX: 253-549-2703 brooks@brooks-stactical.com www.brookstactical.com

Brown, H. R. (See Silhouette Leathers)

Brown Co, E. Arthur, 3404 Pawnee Dr, Alexandria, MN 56308 / 320-762-8847

Brown Dog Ent., 2200 Calle Camelia, 1000 Oaks, CA 91360 / 805-497-2318; FAX: 805-497-1618

Brown Manufacturing, P.O. Box 9219, Akron, OH 44305 / 800-837-GUNS

Brown Precision,Inc., 7786 Molinos Ave., Los Molinos, CA 96055 FAX: 916-384-1638

Brown Products, Inc., Ed, 43825 Muldrow Trail, Perry, MO 63462 / 573-565-3261; FAX: 573-565-2791

Brownells, Inc., 200 S. Front St., Montezuma, IA 50171 / 515-623-5401; FAX: 515-623-3896

Browning Arms Co., One Browning Place, Morgan, UT 84050 / 801-876-2711; FAX: 801-876-3331

Browning Arms Co. (Parts & Service), 3005 Arnold Tenbrook Rd., Arnold, MO 63010 / 314-287-6800; FAX: 314-287-9751

BRP, Inc. High Performance Cast Bullets, 1210 Alexander Rd., Colorado Springs, CO 80909 / 719-633-0658

Brunton U.S.A., 620 E. Monroe Ave., Riverton, WY 82501 / 307-856-6559; FAX: 307-856-1840

Bryan & Assoc, R D Sauls, PO Box 5772, Anderson, SC 29623-5772 / 864-261-6810

Brynin, Milton, P.O. Box 383, Yonkers, NY 10710 / 914-779-4333

BSA Guns Ltd., Armoury Rd. Small Heath, Birmingham, ENGLAND / 011-021-772-8543; FAX: 011-021-773-084

BSA Optics, 3911 SW 47th Ave #914, Ft Lauderdale, FL 33314 / 954-581-2144 FAX: 954-581-3165

Bucheimer, J. (See JUMBO SPORTS PRODUCTS)

Bucheimer, J. M. (See Jumbo Sports Products), 721 N 20th St, St Louis, MO 63103 / 314-241-1020

Buck Knives, Inc., 1900 Weld Blvd., P.O. Box 1267, El Cajon, CA 92020 / 619-449-1100 or 800-326-2825; FAX: 619-562-5774 8

Buck Stix--SOS Products Co., Box 3, Neenah, WI 54956

Buck Stop Lure Co., Inc., 3600 Grow Rd. NW, P.O. Box 636, Stanton, MI 48888 / 517-762-5091; FAX: 517-762-5124

Buckeye Custom Bullets, 6490 Stewart Rd., Elida, OH 45807 / 419-641-4463

Buckhorn Gun Works, 8109 Woodland Dr., Black Hawk, SD 57718 / 605-787-6472

Buckskin Bullet Co., P.O. Box 1893, Cedar City, UT 84721 / 435-586-3286

Buckskin Machine Works, A. Hunkeler, 3235 S. 358th St., Auburn, WA 98001 / 206-927-5412

Budin, Dave, Main St., Margaretville, NY 12455 / 914-568-4103; FAX: 914-586-4105

Buenger Enterprises/Goldenrod Dehumidifier, 3600 S. Harbor Blvd., Oxnard, CA 93035 / 800-451-6797 or 805-985-5828; FAX: 805-985-1534

Buffalo Arms Co., 99 Raven Ridge, Samuels, ID 83864 / 208-263-6953; FAX: 208-265-2096

Buffalo Bullet Co., Inc., 12637 Los Nietos Rd., Unit A., Santa Fe Springs, CA 90670 FAX: 562-944-5054

Buffalo Rock Shooters Supply, R.R. 1, Ottawa, IL 61350 / 815-433-2471

Buffer Technologies, P.O. Box 104930, Jefferson City, MO 65110 / 573-634-8529; FAX: 573-634-8522

Bull Mountain Rifle Co., 6327 Golden West Terrace, Billings, MT 59106 / 406-656-0778

Bull-X, Inc., 520 N. Main, Farmer City, IL 61842 / 309-928-2574 or 800-248-3845; FAX: 309-928-2130

Bullberry Barrel Works, Ltd., 2430 W. Bullberry Ln. 67-5, Hurricane, UT 84737 / 435-635-9866; FAX: 435-635-0348

Bullet Metals, P.O. Box 1238, Sierra Vista, AZ 85636 / 520-458-5321; FAX: 520-458-1421 alloymetal-smith@theriver.com

Bullet Swaging Supply Inc., P.O. Box 1056, 303 McMillan Rd, West Monroe, LA 71291 / 318-387-3266; FAX: 318-387-7779

Bullet'n Press, 19 Key St., Eastport, ME 04631 / 207-853-4116 www.nemaine.com/bnpress

Bullet, Inc., 3745 Hiram Alworth Rd., Dallas, GA 30132

Bullseye Bullets, 8100 E Broadway Ave #A, Tampa, FL 33619-2223 / 813-630-9186 bbullets8100@aol.com

Burgess, Byron, PO Box 6853, Los Osos, CA 93412 / 805-528-1005

Burkhart Gunsmithing, Don, P.O. Box 852, Rawlins, WY 82301 / 307-324-6007

Burnham Bros., P.O. Box 1148, Menard, TX 78659 / 915-396-4572; FAX: 915-396-4574

Burris Co., Inc., P.O. Box 1747, 331 E. 8th St., Greeley, CO 80631 / 970-356-1670; FAX: 970-356-8702

Bushmann Hunters & Safaris, P.O. Box 293088, Lewisville, TX 75029 / 214-317-0768

Bushmaster Firearms (See Quality Parts Co/Bushmaster Firearms)

Bushmaster Hunting & Fishing, 451 Alliance Ave., Toronto, ON M6N 2J1 Canada / 416-763-4040; FAX: 416-763-0623

Bushnell Sports Optics Worldwide, 9200 Cody, Overland Park, KS 66214 / 913-752-3400 or 800-423-3537; FAX: 913-752-3550

Bushwacker Backpack & Supply Co (See Counter Assault)

Bustani, Leo, P.O. Box 8125, W. Palm Beach, FL 33410 / 305-622-2710

Buster's Custom Knives, P.O. Box 214, Richfield, UT 84701 / 801-896-5319

Butler Creek Corp., 290 Arden Dr., Belgrade, MT 59714 / 800-423-8327 or 406-388-1356; FAX: 406-388-7204

Butler Enterprises, 834 Oberting Rd., Lawrenceburg, IN 47025 / 812-537-3584

Butterfield & Butterfield, 220 San Bruno Ave., San Francisco, CA 94103 / 415-861-7500

Buzztail Brass (See Grayback Wildcats)

Byron Burgess, P.O. Box 6853, Los Osos, CA 93412 / 805-528-1005

C

C&D Special Products (See Claybuster Wads & Harvester Bullets)

C&H Research, 115 Sunnyside Dr., Box 351, Lewis, KS 67552 / 316-324-5445 www.09.net(chr)

C-More Systems, P.O. Box 1750, 7553 Gary Rd., Manassas, VA 20108 / 703-361-2663; FAX: 703-361-5881

C. Palmer Manufacturing Co., Inc., P.O. Box 220, West Newton, PA 15089 / 412-872-8200; FAX: 412-872-8302

C. Sharps Arms Co. Inc., 100 Centennial, Box 885, Big Timber, MT 59011 / 406-932-4353; FAX: 406-932-4443

C.S. Van Gorden & Son, Inc., 1815 Main St., Bloomer, WI 54724 / 715-568-2612

C.W. Erickson's Mfg. Inc., 530 Garrison Ave NE, PO Box 522, Buffalo, MN 55313 / 612-682-3665; FAX: 612-682-4328

Cabanas (See U.S. Importer-Mandall Shooting Supplies, Inc.)

Cabela's, 812-13th Ave., Sidney, NE 69160 / 308-254-6644 or 800-237-4444; FAX: 308-254-6745

Cabinet Mtn. Outfitters Scents & Lures, P.O. Box 766, Plains, MT 59859 / 406-826-3970

Cache La Poudre Rifleworks, 140 N. College, Ft. Collins, CO 80524 / 303-482-6913

Cali'co Hardwoods, Inc., 3580 Westwind Blvd., Santa Rosa, CA 95403 / 707-546-4045; FAX: 707-546-4027 calicohard-woods@msn.com

Calibre Press, Inc., 666 Dundee Rd., Suite 1607, Northbrook, IL 60062 / 800-323-0037; FAX: 708-498-6869

Calico Light Weapon Systems, 1489 Greg St., Sparks, NV 89431

California Sights (See Fautheree, Andy)

Cambos Outdoorsman, 532 E. Idaho Ave., Ontario, OR 97914 / 541-889-3138 FAX: 541-889-2633

Camdex, Inc., 2330 Alger, Troy, ML 48083 / 810-528-2300; FAX: 810-528-0989

Cameron's, 16690 W. 11th Ave., Golden, CO 80401 / 303-279-7365; FAX: 303-628-5413

Camilli, Lou, 600 Sandtree Dr., Suite 212, Lake Park, FL 33403

Camillus Cutlery Co., 54 Main St., Camillus, NY 13031 / 315-672-8111; FAX: 315-672-8832

Camp-Cap Products, P.O. Box 3805, Chesterfield, MO 63006 / 314-532-4340; FAX: 314-532-4340

Campbell, Dick, 20000 Silver Ranch Rd., Conifer, CO 80433 / 303-697-0150; FAX: 303-697-0150

Cannon, Andy. (See CANNON'S)

Cannon Safe, Inc., 9358 Stephens St., Pico Rivera, CA 90660 / 310-692-0636 or 800-242-1055; FAX: 310-692-7252

Cannon's, Andy Cannon, Box 1026, 320 Main St., Polson, MT 59860 / 406-887-2048

Canons Delcour, Rue J.B. Cools, B-4040, Herstal, BELGIUM / +32.(0)42.40.61.40; FAX: +32(0)42.40.22.88

Canyon Cartridge Corp., P.O. Box 152, Albertson, NY 11507 FAX: 516-294-8946

Cape Outfitters, 599 County Rd. 206, Cape Girardeau, MO 63701 / 573-335-4103; FAX: 573-335-1555

Caraville Manufacturing, P.O. Box 4545, Thousand Oaks, CA 91359 / 805-499-1234

Carbide Checkering Tools (See J&R Engineering)

Carbide Die & Mfg. Co., Inc., 15615 E. Arrow Hwy., Irwindale, CA 91706 / 626-337-2518

Carhartt,Inc., P.O. Box 600, 3 Parklane Blvd., Dearborn, MI 48121 / 800-358-3825 or 313-271-8460; FAX: 313-271-3455

Carl Walther GmbH, B.P. 4325, D-89033, Ulm, GERMANY

Carl Walther USA, PO Box 208, Ten Prince St, Alexandria, VA 22313 / 703-548-1400; FAX: 703-549-7826

Carl Zeiss Inc, 13017 N Kingston Ave, Chester, VA 23836-2743 / 804-861-0033 or 800-388-2984; FAX: 804-733-4024

Carlson, Douglas R, Antique American Firearms, PO Box 71035, Dept GD, Des Moines, IA 50325 / 515-224-6552

Carnahan Bullets, 17645 110th Ave. SE, Renton, WA 98055

Carolina Precision Rifles, 1200 Old Jackson Hwy., Jackson, SC 29831 / 803-827-2069

Carrell's Precision Firearms, 643 Clark Ave., Billings, MT 59101-1614 / 406-962-3593

Carry-Lite, Inc., 5203 W. Clinton Ave., Milwaukee, WI 53223 / 414-355-3520; FAX: 414-355-4775

Carter's Gun Shop, 225 G St., Penrose, CO 81240 / 719-372-6240

Cartridge Transfer Group, Pete de Coux, 235 Oak St., Butler, PA 16001 / 412-282-3426

Cascade Bullet Co., Inc., 2355 South 6th St., Klamath Falls, OR 97601 / 503-884-9316

Cascade Shooters, 2155 N.W. 12th St., Redwood, OR 97756

Case & Sons Cutlery Co., W R, Owens Way, Bradford, PA 16701 / 814-368-4123 or 800-523-6350; FAX: 814-768-5369

Case Sorting System, 12695 Cobblestone Creek Rd., Poway, CA 92064 / 619-486-9340

Cash Mfg. Co., Inc., P.O. Box 130, 201 S. Klein Dr., Waunakee, WI 53597-0130 / 608-849-5664; FAX: 608-849-5664

Caspian Arms, Ltd., 14 North Main St., Hardwick, VT 05843 / 802-472-6454; FAX: 802-472-6709

Cast Performance Bullet Company, 113 Riggs Rd, Shoshoni, WY 82649 / 307-856-4347

Casull Arms Corp., P.O. Box 1629, Afton, WY 83110 / 307-886-0200

Caswell Detroit Armor Companies, 1221 Marshall St. NE, Minneapolis, MN 55413-1055 / 612-379-2000; FAX: 612-379-2367

Catco-Ambush, Inc., P.O.Box 300, Corte Madera, CA 94926

Cathey Enterprises, Inc., P.O. Box 2202, Brownwood, TX 76804 / 915-643-2553; FAX: 915-643-3653

Cation, 2341 Alger St., Troy, MI 48083 / 810-689-0658; FAX: 810-689-7558

Caywood, Shane J., P.O. Box 321, Minocqua, WI 54548 / 715-277-3866

CBC, Avenida Humberto de Campos 3220, 09400-000, Ribeirao Pires, SP, BRAZIL / 55-11-742-7500; FAX: 55-11-459-7385

CBC-BRAZIL, 3 Cuckoo Lane, Honley, Yorkshire HD7 2BR, ENGLAND / 44-1484-661062; FAX: 44-1484-663709

CCG Enterprises, 5217 E. Belknap St., Halton City, TX 76117 / 800-819-7464

CCI Div. of Blount, Inc., Sporting Equipment Div.2299 Sn, P.O. Box 856, Lewiston, ID 83501 / 800-627-3640 or 208-746-2351; FAX: 208-746-2915

CCL Security Products, 199 Whiting St, New Britain, CT 06051 / 800-733-8588

Cedar Hill Game Calls Inc., 238 Vic Allen Rd, Downsville, LA 71234 / 318-982-5632; FAX: 318-368-2245

Celestron International, P.O. Box 3578, 2835 Columbia St., Torrance, CA 90503 / 310-328-9560; FAX: 310-212-5835

Centaur Systems, Inc., 1602 Foothill Rd., Kalispell, MT 59901 / 406-755-8609; FAX: 406-755-8609

Center Lock Scope Rings, 9901 France Ct., Lakeville, MN 55044 / 612-461-2114

Central Specialties Ltd (See Trigger Lock Division/Central Specialties Ltd.,)

Century Gun Dist. Inc., 1467 Jason Rd., Greenfield, IN 46140 / 317-462-4524

Century International Arms, Inc., 1161 Holland Dr, Boca Raton, FL 33487

CFVentures, 509 Harvey Dr., Bloomington, IN 47403-1715

CH Tool & Die Co (See 4-D Custom Die Co), 711 N Sandusky St, PO Box 889, Mt Vernon, OH 43050-0889 / 740-397-7214; FAX: 740-397-6600

Chace Leather Products, 507 Alden St., Fall River, MA 02722 / 508-678-7556; FAX: 508-675-9666

Chadick's Ltd., P.O. Box 100, Terrell, TX 75160 / 214-563-7577

Chambers Flintlocks Ltd., Jim, 116 Sams Branch Rd, Candler, NC 28715 / 828-667-8361 FAX: 828-665-0852

Champion Shooters' Supply, P.O. Box 303, New Albany, OH 43054 / 614-855-1603; FAX: 614-855-1209

Champion Target Co., 232 Industrial Parkway, Richmond, IN 47374 / 800-441-4971

Champion's Choice, Inc., 201 International Blvd., LaVergne, TN 37086 / 615-793-4066; FAX: 615-793-4070

Champlin Firearms, Inc., P.O. Box 3191, Woodring Airport, Enid, OK 73701 / 580-237-7388; FAX: 580-242-6922

Chapman Academy of Practical Shooting, 4350 Academy Rd., Hallsville, MO 65255 / 573-696-5544 or 573-696-2266

Chapman, J Ken. (See OLD WEST BULLET MOULDS J ken Chapman)

Chapman Manufacturing Co., 471 New Haven Rd., P.O. Box 250, Durham, CT 06422 / 860-349-9228; FAX: 860-349-0084

Chapuis Armes, 21 La Gravoux, BP15, 42380, St. Bon-net-le-Chatea, FRANCE / (33)77.50.06.96+

Chapuis USA, 416 Business Park, Bedford, KY 40006

Charter 2000, 273 Canal St, Shelton, CT 06484 / 203-922-1652

Checkmate Refinishing, 370 Champion Dr., Brooksville, FL 34601 / 352-799-5774 FAX: 352-799-2986

Cheddite France S.A., 99 Route de Lyon, F-26501, Bourg-les-Valence, FRANCE / 33-75-56-4545; FAX: 33-75-56-3587

Chelsea Gun Club of New York City Inc., 237 Ovington Ave., Apt. D53, Brooklyn, NY 11209 / 718-836-9422 or 718-833-2704

Chem-Pak Inc., PO Box 2058, Winchester, VA 22604-1258 / 800-336-9828 or 703-667-1341 FAX: 703-722-3993

Cherry Creek State Park Shooting Center, 12500 E. Belleview Ave., Englewood, CO 80111 / 303-693-1765

Chet Fulmer's Antique Firearms, P.O. Box 792, Rt. 2 Buffalo Lake, Detroit Lakes, MN 56501 / 218-847-7712

CheVron Bullets, RR1, Ottawa, IL 61350 / 815-433-2471

Cheyenne Pioneer Products, PO Box 28425, Kansas City, MO 64188 / 816-413-9196 FAX: 816-455-2859 cheyen-nepp@aol.com www.cartridgeboxes.com

Chicago Cutlery Co., 1536 Beech St., Terre Haute, IN 47804 / 800-457-2665

Chicasaw Gun Works, 4 Mi. Mkr., Pluto Rd. Box 868, Shady Spring, WV 25918-0868 / 304-763-2848 FAX: 304-763-3725

Chipmunk (See Oregon Arms, Inc.)

Choate Machine & Tool Co., Inc., P.O. Box 218, 116 Lovers Ln., Bald Knob, AR 72010 / 501-724-6193 or 800-972-6390; FAX: 501-724-5873

Chopie Mfg.,Inc., 700 Copeland Ave., LaCrosse, WI 54603 / 608-784-0926

Christensen Arms, 385 N. 3050 E., St. George, UT 84790 / 435-624-9535; FAX: 435-674-9293

Christie's East, 219 E. 67th St., New York, NY 10021 / 212-606-0400

Chu Tani Ind., Inc., P.O. Box 2064, Cody, WY 82414-2064

Chuck's Gun Shop, P.O. Box 597, Waldo, FL 32694 / 904-468-2264

Churchill (See U.S. Importer-Ellett Bros)

Churchill, Winston, Twenty Mile Stream Rd., RFD P.O. Box 29B, Proctorsville, VT 05153 / 802-226-7772

Churchill Glove Co., James, PO Box 298, Centralia, WA 98531 / 360-736-2816 FAX: 360-330-0151

CIDCO, 21480 Pacific Blvd., Sterling, VA 22170 / 703-444-5353

Ciener Inc., Jonathan Arthur, 8700 Commerce St., Cape Canaveral, FL 32920 / 407-868-2200; FAX: 407-868-2201

Cimarron F.A. Co., P.O. Box 906, Fredericksburg, TX 78624-0906 / 210-997-9090; FAX: 210-997-0802

Cincinnati Swaging, 2605 Marlington Ave., Cincinnati, OH 45208

Clark Custom Guns, Inc., 336 Shootout Lane, Princeton, LA 71067 / 318-949-9884; FAX: 318-949-9829

Clark Firearms Engraving, P.O. Box 80746, San Marino, CA 91118 / 818-287-1652

Clarkfield Enterprises, Inc., 1032 10th Ave., Clarkfield, MN 56223 / 612-669-7140

Claro Walnut Gunstock Co., 1235 Stanley Ave., Chico, CA 95928 / 530-342-5188; FAX: 530-342-5199

Classic Arms Company, Rt 1 Box 120F, Burnet, TX 78611 / 512-756-4001

Classic Arms Corp., P.O. Box 106, Dunsmuir, CA 96025-0106 / 530-235-2000

Classic Guns, Inc., Frank S. Wood, 3230 Medlock Bridge Rd., Suite 110, Norcross, GA 30092 / 404-242-7944

Classic Old West Styles, 1060 Doniphan Park Circle C, El Paso, TX 79936 / 915-587-0684

Claybuster Wads & Harvester Bullets, 309 Sequoya Dr., Hopkinsville, KY 42240 / 800-922-6287 or 800-284-1746; FAX: 502-885-8088 50

Clean Shot Technologies, 21218 St. Andrews Blvd. Ste 504, Boca Raton, FL 33433 / 888-866-2532

Clear Creek Outdoors, Pat LaBoone, 2550 Hwy 23, Wrenshall, MN 55797 / 218-384-3670

Clearview Mfg. Co., Inc., 413 S. Oakley St., Fordyce, AR 71742 / 501-352-8557; FAX: 501-352-7120

Clearview Products, 3021 N. Portland, Oklahoma City, OK 73107

Cleland's Outdoor World, Inc, 10306 Airport Hwy, Swanton, OH 43558 / 419-865-4713; FAX: 419-865-5865

Clements' Custom Leathercraft, Chas, 1741 Dallas St., Aurora, CO 80010-2018 / 303-364-0403; FAX: 303-739-9824

Clenzoil Corp., P.O. Box 80226, Sta. C, Canton, OH 44708-0226 / 330-833-9758; FAX: 330-833-4724

Clift Mfg., L. R., 3821 hammonton Rd, Marysville, CA 95901 / 916-755-3390; FAX: 916-755-3393

Clift Welding Supply & Cases, 1332-A Colusa Hwy., Yuba City, CA 95993 / 916-755-3390 FAX: 916-755-3393

Cloward's Gun Shop, 4023 Aurora Ave. N, Seattle, WA 98103 / 206-632-2072

Clymer Manufacturing Co. Inc., 1645 W. Hamlin Rd., Rochester Hills, MI 48309-3312 / 248-853-5555; FAX: 248-853-1530

Cobalt Mfg., Inc., 4020 Mcewen Rd Ste 180, Dallas, TX 75244-5090 / 817-382-8986 FAX: 817-383-4281

Cobra Sport S.r.l., Via Caduti Nei Lager No. 1, 56020 San Romano, Montopoli v/Arno (Pi, ITALY / 0039-571-450490; FAX: 0039-571-450492

Coffin, Charles H., 3719 Scarlet Ave., Odessa, TX 79762 / 915-366-4729 FAX: 915-366-4729

Coffin, Jim (See Working Guns)

Coffin, Jim. See: WORKING GUNS

Cogar's Gunsmithing, P.O. Box 755, Houghton Lake, MI 48629 / 517-422-4591

Coghlan's Ltd., 121 Irene St., Winnipeg, MB R3T 4C7 CANADA / 204-284-9550; FAX: 204-475-4127

Cold Steel Inc., 2128-D Knoll Dr., Ventura, CA 93003 / 800-255-4716 or 800-624-2363 FAX: 805-642-9727

Cole's Gun Works, Old Bank Building, Rt. 4 Box 250, Moyock, NC 27958 / 919-435-2345

Cole-Grip, 16135 Cohasset St., Van Nuys, CA 91406 / 818-782-4424

Coleman Co., Inc., 250 N. St. Francis, Wichita, KS 67201

Coleman's Custom Repair, 4035 N. 20th Rd., Arlington, VA 22207 / 703-528-4486

Collectors Firearms Etc, P.O. Box 62, Minnesota City, MN 55959 / 507-689-2925

Collings, Ronald, 1006 Cielta Linda, Vista, CA 92083

Colonial Arms, Inc., P.O. Box 636, Selma, AL 36702-0636 / 334-872-9455; FAX: 334-872-9540 colonialarms@mind-spring.com www.colonialarms.com

Colonial Knife Co., Inc., P.O. Box 3327, Providence, RI 02909 / 401-421-1600; FAX: 401-421-2047

Colonial Repair, 47 NAVARRE ST, ROSLINDALE, MA 02131-4725 / 617-469-4951

Colorado Gunsmithing Academy, 27533 Highway 287 South, Lamar, CO 81052 / 719-336-4099 or 800-754-2046; FAX: 719-336-9642

Colorado School of Trades, 1575 Hoyt St., Lakewood, CO 80215 / 800-234-4594; FAX: 303-233-4723

Colorado Sutlers Arsenal (See Cumberland States Arsenal)

Colt Blackpowder Arms Co., 110 8th Street, Brooklyn, NY 11215 / 212-925-2159; FAX: 212-966-4986

Colt's Mfg. Co., Inc., P.O. Box 1868, Hartford, CT 06144-1868 / 800-962-COLT or 860-236-6311; FAX: 860-244-1449

Compass Industries, Inc., 104 East 25th St., New York, NY 10010 / 212-473-2614 or 800-221-9904; FAX: 212-353-0826

Compasseco, Ltd., 151 Atkinson Hill Ave., Bardtown, KY 40004 / 502-349-0910

Competition Electronics, Inc., 3469 Precision Dr., Rockford, IL 61109 / 815-874-8001; FAX: 815-874-8181

Competitor Corp. Inc., Appleton Business Center, 30 Tricnit Road Unit 16, New Ipswich, NH 03071 / 603-878-3891; FAX: 603-878-3950

Component Concepts, Inc., 530 S Springbrook Dr, Newberg, OR 97132-7056 / 503-554-8095 FAX: 503-554-9370

Concept Development Corp., 14715 N. 78th Way, Suite 300, Scottsdale, AZ 85260 / 800-472-4405; FAX: 602-948-7560

Conetrol Scope Mounts, 10225 Hwy. 123 S., Seguin, TX 78155 / 210-379-3030 or 800-CONETROL; FAX: 210-379-3030

CONKKO, P.O. Box 40, Broomall, PA 19008 / 215-356-0711

Connecticut Shotgun Mfg. Co., P.O. Box 1692, 35 Woodland St., New Britain, CT 06051 / 860-225-6581; FAX: 860-832-8707

Connecticut Valley Classics (See CVC)

Conrad, C. A., 3964 Ebert St., Winston-Salem, NC 27127 / 919-788-5469

Cook Engineering Service, 891 Highbury Rd., Vict, 3133 AUSTRALIA

Coonan Arms (JS Worldwide DBA), 1745 Hwy. 36 E., Maplewood, MN 55109 / 612-777-3156; FAX: 612-777-3683

Cooper Arms, P.O. Box 114, Stevensville, MT 59870 / 406-777-5534; FAX: 406-777-5228

Cooper-Woodward, 3800 Pelican Rd., Helena, MT 59602 / 406-458-3800

Cor-Bon Bullet & Ammo Co., 1311 Industry Rd., Sturgis, SD 57785 / 800-626-7266; FAX: 800-923-2666

Corbin Mfg. & Supply, Inc., 600 Industrial Circle, P.O. Box 2659, White City, OR 97503 / 541-826-5211; FAX: 541-826-8669

Corkys Gun Clinic, 4401 Hot Springs Dr., Greeley, CO 80634-9226 / 970-330-0516

Corry, John, 861 Princeton Ct., Neshanic Station, NJ 08853 / 908-369-8019

Cosmi Americo & Figlio s.n.c., Via Flaminia 307, Ancona, ITALY / 071-888208; FAX: 39-071-887008+

Coulston Products, Inc., P.O. Box 30, 201 Ferry St. Suite 212, Easton, PA 18044-0030 / 215-253-0167 or 800-445-9927; FAX: 215-252-1511

Counter Assault, Box 4721, Missoula, MT 59806 / 406-728-6241 FAX: 406-728-8800

Cousin Bob's Mountain Products, 7119 Ohio River Blvd., Ben Avon, PA 15202 / 412-766-5114 FAX: 412-766-5114

Cox, Ed. C., RD 2, Box 192, Prosperity, PA 15329 / 412-228-4984

CP Bullets, 1310 Industrial Hwy #5-6, South Hampton, PA 18966 / 215-953-7264; FAX: 215-953-7275

CQB Training, P.O. Box 1739, Manchester, MO 63011

Craftguard, 3624 Logan Ave., Waterloo, IA 50703 / 319-232-2959 FAX: 319-234-0804

Craig, Spegel, P.O. Box 3108, Bay City, OR 97107 / 503-377-2697

Craig Custom Ltd., Research & Development, 629 E. 10th, Hutchinson, KS 67501 / 316-669-0601

Crandall Tool & Machine Co., 19163 21 Mile Rd., Tustin, MI 49688 / 616-829-4430

Creative Concepts USA, Inc., P.O. Box 1705, Dickson, TN 37056 / 615-446-8346 or 800-874-6965 FAX: 615-446-0646

Creedmoor Sports, Inc., P.O. Box 1040, Oceanside, CA 92051 / 619-757-5529

Creek Side Metal & Woodcrafters, Fishers Hill, VA 22626 / 703-465-3903

Creekside Gun Shop Inc., Main St., Holcomb, NY 14469 / 716-657-6338 FAX: 716-657-7900

Creighton Audette, 19 Highland Circle, Springfield, VT 05156 / 802-885-2331

Crimson Trace Lasers, 1433 N.W. Quimby, Portland, OR 97209 / 503-295-2406; FAX: 503-295-2225

Crit'R Call (See Rocky Mountain Wildlife Products)

Crosman Airguns, Rts. 5 and 20, E. Bloomfield, NY 14443 / 716-657-6161 FAX: 716-657-5405

Crosman Blades (See Coleman Co., Inc.)

Crosman Products of Canada Ltd., 1173 N. Service Rd. West, Oakville, ON L6M 2V9 CANADA / 905-827-1822

Crossfire, L.L.C., 2169 Greenville Rd., La Grange, GA 30241 / 706-882-8070 FAX: 706-882-9050

Crouse's Country Cover, P.O. Box 160, Storrs, CT 06268 / 860-423-8736

CRR, Inc./Marble's Inc., 420 Industrial Park, P.O. Box 111, Gladstone, MI 49837 / 906-428-3710; FAX: 906-428-3711

Crucelegui, Hermanos (See U.S. Importer-Mandall Shooting Supplies Inc.,)

Cryo-Accurizing, 2101 East Olive, Decatur, IL 62526 / 217-423-3070 FAX: 217-423-3075

Cubic Shot Shell Co., Inc., 98 Fatima Dr., Campbell, OH 44405 / 330-755-0349

Cullity Restoration, 209 Old Country Rd., East Sandwich, MA 02537 / 508-888-1147

Cumberland Arms, 514 Shafer Road, Manchester, TN 37355 / 800-797-8414

Cumberland Mountain Arms, P.O. Box 710, Winchester, TN 37398 / 615-967-8414; FAX: 615-967-9199

Cumberland States Arsenal, 1124 Palmyra Road, Clarksville, TN 37040

Cummings Bullets, 1417 Esperanza Way, Escondido, CA 92027

Cupp, Alana, Custom Engraver, PO Box 207, Annabella, UT 84711 / 801-896-4834

Curly Maple Stock Blanks (See Tiger-Hunt)

Curtis Cast Bullets, 527 W. Babcock St., Bozeman, MT 59715 / 406-587-8117; FAX: 406-587-8117

Curtis Custom Shop, RR1, Box 193A, Wallingford, KY 41093 / 703-659-4265

Curtis Gun Shop (See Curtis Cast Bullets)

Custom Bullets by Hoffman, 2604 Peconic Ave., Seaford, NY 11783

Custom Calls, 607 N. 5th St., Burlington, IA 52601 / 319-752-4465

Custom Checkering Service, Kathy Forster, 2124 SE Yamhill St., Portland, OR 97214 / 503-236-5874

Custom Chronograph, Inc., 5305 Reese Hill Rd., Sumas, WA 98295 / 360-988-7801

Custom Firearms (See Ahrends, Kim)

Custom Gun Products, 5021 W. Rosewood, Spokane, WA 99208 / 509-328-9340

Custom Gun Stocks, 3062 Turners Bend Rd, McMinnville, TN 37110 / 615-668-3912

Custom Products (See Jones Custom Products)

Custom Quality Products, Inc., 345 W. Girard Ave., P.O. Box 71129, Madison Heights, MI 48071 / 810-585-1616; FAX: 810-585-0644

Custom Riflestocks, Inc., Michael M. Kokolus, 7005 Herber Rd., New Tripoli, PA 18066 / 610-298-3013

Custom Tackle and Ammo, P.O. Box 1886, Farmington, NM 87499 / 505-632-3539

Cutco Cutlery, P.O. Box 810, Olean, NY 14760 / 716-372-3111

CVA, 5988 Peachtree Corners East, Norcross, GA 30071 / 800-251-9412; FAX: 404-242-8546

CVC, 5988 Peachtree Crns East, Norcross, GA 30071

Cylinder & Slide, Inc., William R. Laughridge, 245 E. 4th St., Fremont, NE 68025 / 402-721-4277; FAX: 402-721-0263

CZ USA, PO Box 171073, Kansas City, KS 66117 / 913-321-1811; FAX: 913-321-4901

D

D&D Gunsmiths, Ltd., 363 E. Elmwood, Troy, MI 48083 / 810-583-1512; FAX: 810-583-1524

D&G Precision Duplicators (See Greene Precision Du

D&H Precision Tooling, 7522 Barnard Mill Rd., Ringwood, IL 60072 / 815-653-4011

D&H Prods. Co., Inc., 465 Denny Rd., Valencia, PA 16059 / 412-898-2840 or 800-776-0281; FAX: 412-898-2013

D&J Bullet Co. & Custom Gun Shop, Inc., 426 Ferry St., Russell, KY 41169 / 606-836-2663; FAX: 606-836-2663

D&L Industries (See D.J. Marketing)

D&L Sports, P.O. Box 651, Gillette, WY 82717 / 307-686-4008

D&R Distributing, 308 S.E. Valley St., Myrtle Creek, OR 97457 / 503-863-6850

D-Boone Ent., Inc., 5900 Colwyn Dr., Harrisburg, PA 17109

D.C.C. Enterprises, 259 Wynburn Ave., Athens, GA 30601

D.D. Custom Stocks, R.H. "Dick" Devereaux, 5240 Mule Deer Dr., Colorado Springs, CO 80919 / 719-548-8468

D.J. Marketing, 10602 Horton Ave., Downey, CA 90241 / 310-806-0891; FAX: 310-806-6231

Da-Mar Gunsmith's Inc., 102 1st St., Solvay, NY 13209

Dade Screw Machine Products, 2319 NW 7th Ave., Miami, FL 33127 / 305-573-5050

Daewoo Precision Industries Ltd., 34-3 Yeoeuido-Dong, Yeong-deungoo-GU 15th Fl., Seoul, KOREA

Daisy Mfg. Co., PO Box 220, Rogers, AR 72757 / 501-621-4210; FAX: 501-636-0573

Dakota (See U.S. Importer-EMF Co., Inc.)

Dakota Arms, Inc., HC 55, Box 326, Sturgis, SD 57785 / 605-347-4686; FAX: 605-347-4459

Dakota Corp., 77 Wales St., P.O. Box 543, Rutland, VT 05701 / 802-775-6062 or 800-451-4167; FAX: 802-773-3919

DAMASCUS-U.S.A., 149 Deans Farm Rd., Tyner, NC 27980 / 252-221-2010; FAX: 252-221-2009

DAN WESSON FIREARMS, 119 Kemper Lane, Norwich, NY 13815 / 607-336-1174; FAX: FAX:607-336-2730

Dan's Whetstone Co., Inc., 130 Timbs Place, Hot Springs, AR 71913 / 501-767-1616; FAX: 501-767-9598

Danforth, Mikael. (See VEKTOR USA, Mikael Danforth)

Dangler, Homer L., Box 254, Addison, MI 49220 / 517-547-6745

Danner Shoe Mfg. Co., 12722 NE Airport Way, Portland, OR 97230 / 503-251-1100 or 800-345-0430; FAX: 503-251-1119

Danuser Machine Co., 550 E. Third St., P.O. Box 368, Fulton, MO 65251 / 573-642-2246; FAX: 573-642-2240

Dara-Nes, Inc. (See Nesci Enterprises, Inc.)

Darlington Gun Works, Inc., P.O. Box 698, 516 S. 52 Bypass, Darlington, SC 29532 / 803-393-3931

Darwin Hensley Gunmaker, P.O. Box 329, Brightwood, OR 97011 / 503-622-5411

Data Tech Software Systems, 19312 East Eldorado Drive, Aurora, CO 80013

Datumtech Corp., 2275 Wehrle Dr., Buffalo, NY 14221

Dave Norin Schrank's Smoke & Gun, 2010 Washington St., Waukegan, IL 60085 / 708-662-4034

Dave's Gun Shop, 555 Wood Street, Powell, WY 82435 / 307-754-9724

David Clark Co., Inc., PO Box 15054, Worcester, MA 01615-0054 / 508-756-6216; FAX: 508-753-5827

David Condon, Inc., 109 E. Washington St., Middleburg, VA 22117 / 703-687-5642

David Miller Co., 3131 E Greenlee Rd, Tucson, AZ 85716 / 520-326-3117

David R. Chicoine, 19 Key St., Eastport, ME 04631 / 207-853-4116 gnpress@nemaine.com

David W. Schwartz Custom Guns, 2505 Waller St, Eau Claire, WI 54703 / 715-832-1735

Davide Pedersoli and Co., Via Artigiani 57, Gardone VT, Brescia 25063, ITALY / 030-8912402; FAX: 030-8911019

Davidson, Jere, Rt. 1, Box 132, Rustburg, VA 24588 / 804-821-3637

Davis, Don, 1619 Heights, Katy, TX 77493 / 713-391-3090

Davis Industries, 15150 Sierra Bonita Ln., Chino, CA 91710 / 909-597-4726; FAX: 909-393-9771

Davis Products, Mike, 643 Loop Dr., Moses Lake, WA 98837 / 509-765-6178 or 509-766-7281

Daystate Ltd., Birch House Lanee, Cotes Heath Staffs, ST15.022, ENGLAND / 01782-791755; FAX: 01782-791617

Dayton Traister, 4778 N. Monkey Hill Rd., P.O. Box 593, Oak Harbor, WA 98277 / 360-679-4657; FAX: 360-675-1114

DBI Books Division of Krause Publications 700 E State St, Iola, WI 54990-0001 / 630-759-1229

de Coux, Pete (See Cartridge Transfer Group)

Dead Eye's Sport Center, RD 1, 76 Baer Rd, Shickshinny, PA 18655 / 570-256-7432

Decker Shooting Products, 1729 Laguna Ave., Schofield, WI 54476 / 715-359-5873

Deepeeka Exports Pvt. Ltd., D-78, Saket, Meerut-250-006, INDIA / 011-91-121-512889 or 011-91-121-545363; FAX: 011-91-121-542988

Deer Me Products Co., Box 34, 1208 Park St., Anoka, MN 55303 / 612-421-8971; FAX: 612-422-0526

Defense Training International, Inc., 749 S. Lemay, Ste. A3-337, Ft. Collins, CO 80524 / 303-482-2520; FAX: 303-482-0548

Degen Inc. (See Aristocrat Knives)

deHaas Barrels, RR 3, Box 77, Ridgeway, MO 64481 / 816-872-6308

Del Rey Products, P.O. Box 5134, Playa Del Rey, CA 90296-5134 / 213-823-0494

Del-Sports, Inc., Box 685, Main St., Margaretville, NY 12455 / 914-586-4103; FAX: 914-586-4105

Delhi Gun House, 1374 Kashmere Gate, Delhi, 0110 006 INDIA FAX: 91-11-2917344

Delorge, Ed, 6734 W. Main, Houma, LA 70360 / 504-223-0206

Delta Arms Ltd., P.O. Box 1000, Delta, VT 84624-1000

Delta Enterprises, 284 Hagemann Drive, Livermore, CA 94550

Delta Frangible Ammunition LLC, P.O. Box 2350, Stafford, VA 22555-2350 / 540-720-5778 or 800-339-1933; FAX: 540-720-5667

Dem-Bart Checkering Tools, Inc., 6807 Bickford Ave., Old Hwy. 2, Snohomish, WA 98290 / 360-568-7356; FAX: 360-568-1798

Denver Instrument Co., 6542 Fig St., Arvada, CO 80004 / 800-321-1135 or 303-431-7255; FAX: 303-423-4831

DeSantis Holster & Leather Goods, Inc., P.O. Box 2039, 149 Denton Ave., New Hyde Park, NY 11040-0701 / 516-354-8000; FAX: 516-354-7501

Desert Mountain Mfg., P.O. Box 130184, Coram, MT 59913 / 800-477-0762 or 406-387-5361; FAX: 406-387-5361

Detroit-Armor Corp., 720 Industrial Dr. No. 112, Cary, IL 60013 / 708-639-7666; FAX: 708-639-7694

Dever Co., Jack, 8590 NW 90, Oklahoma City, OK 73132 / 405-721-6393

Devereaux, R.H. "Dick" (See D.D. Custom Stocks, R.H. "Dick Devereaux)

Dewey Mfg. Co., Inc., J., P.O. Box 2014, Southbury, CT 06488 / 203-264-3064; FAX: 203-262-6907 deweyrods@world-net.att.net www.deweyrods.com

DGR Custom Rifles, 4191 37th Ave SE, Tappen, ND 58487 / 701-327-8135

DGS, Inc., Dale A. Storey, 1117 E. 12th, Casper, WY 82601 / 307-237-2414 FAX: 307-237-2414 dalest@trib.com www.dgsrifle.com

DHB Products, P.O. Box 3092, Alexandria, VA 22302 / 703-836-2648

Diamond Machining Technology, Inc. (See DMT)

Diamond Mfg. Co., P.O. Box 174, Wyoming, PA 18644 / 800-233-9601

Diana (See U.S. Importer - Dynamit Nobel-RWS, Inc., 81 Ruckman Rd., Closter, NJ 07624 / 201-767-7971; (FAX: 201-767-1589)

Dibble, Derek A., 555 John Downey Dr., New Britain, CT 06051 / 203-224-2630

Dick Marple & Associates, 21 Dartmouth St, Hooksett, NH 03106 / 603-627-1837; FAX: 603-627-1837

Dietz Gun Shop & Range, Inc., 421 Range Rd., New Braunfels, TX 78132 / 210-885-4662

Dilliott Gunsmithing, Inc., 657 Scarlett Rd., Dandridge, TN 37725 / 865-397-9204 gunsmithd@aol.com dilliottgunsmithing.com

Dillon, Ed, 1035 War Eagle Dr. N., Colorado Springs, CO 80919 / 719-598-4929; FAX: 719-598-4929

Dillon Precision Products, Inc., 8009 East Dillon's Way, Scottsdale, AZ 85260 / 602-948-8009 or 800-762-3845; FAX: 602-998-2786

Dina Arms Corporation, P.O. Box 46, Royersford, PA 19468 / 610-287-0266; FAX: 610-287-0266

Division Lead Co., 7742 W. 61st Pl., Summit, IL 60502

Dixie Gun Works, Inc., Hwy. 51 South, Union City, TN 38261 / order 800-238-6785;

Dixon Muzzleloading Shop, Inc., 9952 Kunkels Mill Rd., Kempton, PA 19529 / 610-756-6271

DKT, Inc., 14623 Vera Drive, Union, MI 49130-9744 / 800-741-7083 orders; FAX: 616-641-2015

DLO Mfg., 10807 SE Foster Ave., Arcadia, FL 33821-7304

DMT--Diamond Machining Technology Inc., 85 Hayes Memorial Dr., Marlborough, MA 01752 FAX: 508-485-3924

Doctor Optic Technologies, Inc., 4685 Boulder Highway, Suite A, Las Vegas, NV 89121 / 800-290-3634 or 702-898-7161; FAX: 702-898-3737

Dohring Bullets, 100 W. 8 Mile Rd., Ferndale, MI 48220

Dolbare, Elizabeth, P.O. Box 222, Sunburst, MT 59482-0222

Domino, PO Box 108, 20019 Settimo Milanese, Milano, ITALY / 1-39-2-33512040; FAX: 1-39-2-33511587

Donnelly, C. P., 405 Kubli Rd., Grants Pass, OR 97527 / 541-846-6604

Doskocil Mfg. Co., Inc., P.O. Box 1246, 4209 Barnett, Arlington, TX 76017 / 817-467-5116; FAX: 817-472-9810

Double A Ltd., P.O. Box 11306, Minneapolis, MN 55411 / 612-522-0306

Douglas Barrels Inc., 5504 Big Tyler Rd., Charleston, WV 25313-1398 / 304-776-1341; FAX: 304-776-8560

Downsizer Corp., P.O. Box 710316, Santee, CA 92072-0316 / 619-448-5510; FAX: 619-448-5780 www.downsizer.com

Dr. O's Products Ltd., P.O. Box 111, Niverville, NY 12130 / 518-784-3333; FAX: 518-784-2800

Drain, Mark, SE 3211 Kamilche Point Rd., Shelton, WA 98584 / 206-426-5452

Dremel Mfg. Co., 4915-21st St., Racine, WI 53406

Dressel Jr., Paul G., 209 N. 92nd Ave., Yakima, WA 98908 / 509-966-9233; FAX: 509-966-3365

Dri-Slide, Inc., 411 N. Darling, Fremont, MI 49412 / 616-924-3950

Dropkick, 1460 Washington Blvd., Williamsport, PA 17701 / 717-326-6561; FAX: 717-326-4950

DTM International, Inc., 40 Joslyn Rd., P.O. Box 5, Lake Orion, MI 48362 / 313-693-6670

Du-Lite Corp., 171 River Rd., Middletown, CT 06457 / 203-347-2505; FAX: 203-347-9404

Duane A. Hobbie Gunsmithing, 2412 Pattie Ave, Wichita, KS 67216 / 316-264-8266

Duane's Gun Repair (See DGR Custom Rifles)

Dubber, Michael W., P.O. Box 312, Evansville, IN 47702 / 812-424-9000; FAX: 812-424-6551

Duck Call Specialists, P.O. Box 124, Jerseyville, IL 62052 / 618-498-9855

Duffy, Charles E (See Guns Antique & Modern DBA), Williams Lane, PO Box 2, West Hurley, NY 12491 / 914-679-2997

Dumoulin, Ernest, Rue Florent Boclinville 8-10, 13-4041, Votten, BELGIUM / 41 27 78 92

Duncan's Gun Works, Inc., 1619 Grand Ave., San Marcos, CA 92069 / 619-727-0515

Dunham Boots, 1 Keuka business Park #300, Penn Yan, NY 14527-8995 / 802-254-2316

Duofold, Inc., RD 3 Rt. 309, Valley Square Mall, Tamaqua, PA 18252 / 717-386-2666; FAX: 717-386-3652

Dybala Gun Shop, P.O. Box 1024, FM 3156, Bay City, TX 77414 / 409-245-0866

Dykstra, Doug, 411 N. Darling, Fremont, MI 49412 / 616-924-3950

Dynalite Products, Inc., 215 S. Washington St., Greenfield, OH 45123 / 513-981-2124

Dynamit Nobel-RWS, Inc., 81 Ruckman Rd., Closter, NJ 07624 / 201-767-1971; FAX: 201-767-1589

E

E&L Mfg., Inc., 4177 Riddle By Pass Rd., Riddle, OR 97469 / 541-874-2137; FAX: 541-874-3107

E-A-R, Inc., Div. of Cabot Safety Corp., 5457 W. 79th St., Indianapolis, IN 46268 / 800-327-3431; FAX: 800-488-8007

E-Z-Way Systems, P.O. Box 4310, Newark, OH 43058-4310 / 614-345-6645 or 800-848-2072; FAX: 614-345-6600

E. Arthur Brown Co., 3404 Pawnee Dr., Alexandria, MN 56308 / 320-762-8847

E.A.A. Corp., P.O. Box 1299, Sharpes, FL 32959 / 407-639-4842 or 800-536-4442; FAX: 407-639-7006

Eagan, Donald V., P.O. Box 196, Benton, PA 17814 / 717-925-6134

Eagle Arms, Inc. (See ArmaLite, Inc.)

Eagle Grips, Eagle Business Center, 460 Randy Rd., Carol Stream, IL 60188 / 800-323-6144 or 708-260-0400; FAX: 708-260-0486

Eagle Imports, Inc., 1750 Brielle Ave., Unit B1, Wanamassa, NJ 07712 / 908-493-0333

EAW (See U.S. Importer-New England Custom Gun Service)

Echols & Co., D'Arcy, 164 W. 580 S., Providence, UT 84332 / 801-753-2367

Eckelman Gunsmithing, 3125 133rd St. SW, Fort Ripley, MN 56449 / 218-829-3176

Eclectic Technologies, Inc., 45 Grandview Dr., Suite A, Farmington, CT 06034

Ed~ Brown Products, Inc., 43825 Muldrow Trail, Perry, MO 63462 / 573-565-3261; FAX: 573-565-2791

Eddie Salter Calls, Inc., Hwy. 31 South-Brewton Industrial, Park, Brewton, AL 36426 / 205-867-2584; FAX: 206-867-9005

Edenpine, Inc. c/o Six Enterprises, Inc., 320 D Turtle Creek Ct., San Jose, CA 95125 / 408-999-0201; FAX: 408-999-0216

EdgeCraft Corp., S. Weiner, 825 Southwood Road, Avondale, PA 19311 / 610-268-0500 or 800-342-3255; FAX: 610-268-3545 www.chefschoice.com

Edmisten Co., P.O. Box 1293, Boone, NC 28607

Edmund Scientific Co., 101 E. Gloucester Pike, Barrington, NJ 08033 / 609-543-6250

Ednar, Inc., 2-4-8 Kayabacho, Nihonbashi Chuo-ku, Tokyo, JAPAN / 81(Japan)-3-3667-1651; FAX: 81-3-3661-8113

Eezox, Inc., P.O. Box 772, Waterford, CT 06385-0772 / 800-462-3331; FAX: 860-447-3484

Effebi SNC-Dr. Franco Beretta, via Rossa, 4, 25062, ITALY / 030-2751955; FAX: 030-2180414

Efficient Machinery Co, 12878 NE 15th Pl, Bellevue, WA 98005

Eggleston, Jere D., 400 Saluda Ave., Columbia, SC 29205 / 803-799-3402

EGW Evolution Gun Works, 4050 B-8 Skyron Dr., Doylestown, PA 18901 / 215-348-9892; FAX: 215-348-1056

Eichelberger Bullets, Wm, 158 Crossfield Rd., King Of Prussia, PA 19406

MANUFACTURER'S DIRECTORY

Ekol Leather Care, P.O. Box 2652, West Lafayette, IN 47906 / 317-463-2250; FAX: 317-463-7004

El Dorado Leather (c/o Dill), P.O. Box 566, Benson, AZ 85602 / 520-586-4791; FAX: 520-586-4791

El Paso Saddlery Co., P.O. Box 27194, El Paso, TX 79926 / 915-544-2233; FAX: 915-544-2535

Eldorado Cartridge Corp (See PMC/Eldorado Cartridge Corp.)

Electro Prismatic Collimators, Inc., 1441 Manatt St., Lincoln, NE 68521

Electronic Shooters Protection, Inc., 11997 West 85th Place, Arvada, CO 80005 / 800-797-7791; FAX: 303-456-7179

Electronic Trigger Systems, Inc., P.O. Box 13, 230 Main St. S., Hector, MN 55342 / 320-848-2760; FAX: 320-848-2760

Eley Ltd., P.O. Box 705, Witton, Birmingham, B6 7UT ENGLAND / 021-356-8899; FAX: 021-331-4173

Elite Ammunition, P.O. Box 3251, Oakbrook, IL 60522 / 708-366-9006

Elk River, Inc., 1225 Paonia St., Colorado Springs, CO 80915 / 719-574-4407

Elkhorn Bullets, P.O. Box 5293, Central Point, OR 97502 / 541-826-7440

Ellett Bros., 267 Columbia Ave., P.O. Box 128, Chapin, SC 29036 / 803-345-3751 or 800-845-3711; FAX: 803-345-1820

Ellicott Arms, Inc./Woods Pistolsmithing, 3840 Dahlgren Ct., Ellicott City, MD 21042 / 410-465-7979

Elliott Inc., G. W., 514 Burnside Ave, East Hartford, CT 06108 / 203-289-5741; FAX: 203-289-3137

Elsen Inc., Pete, 1523 S 113th St, West Allis, WI 53214

Emerging Technologies, Inc. (See Laseraim Technologies, Inc.)

Emap USA, 6420 Wilshire Blvd., Los Angeles, CA 90048 / 213-782-2000; FAX: 213-782-2867

EMF Co., Inc., 1900 E. Warner Ave., Suite 1-D, Santa Ana, CA 92705 / 714-261-6611; FAX: 714-756-0133

Empire Cutlery Corp., 12 Kruger Ct., Clifton, NJ 07013 / 201-472-5155; FAX: 201-779-0759

English, Inc., A.G., 708 S. 12th St., Broken Arrow, OK 74012 / 918-251-3399

Engraving Artistry, 36 Alto Rd., RFD 2, Burlington, CT 06013 / 203-673-6837

Enguix Import-Export, Alpujarras 58, Alzira, Valencia, SPAIN / (96) 241 43 95; FAX: (96) (241 43 95

Enhanced Presentations, Inc., 5929 Market St., Wilmington, NC 28405 / 910-799-1622; FAX: 910-799-5004

Enlow, Charles, 895 Box, Beaver, OK 73932 / 405-625-4487

Entre'prise Arms, Inc., 15861 Business Center Dr., Irwindale, CA 91706

EPC, 1441 Manatt St., Lincoln, NE 68521 / 402-476-3946

Epps, Ellwood (See "Gramps" Antique, Box 341, Washago, ON L0K 2B0 CANADA / 705-689-5348

Erhardt, Dennis, 3280 Green Meadow Dr., Helena, MT 59601 / 406-442-4533

Erma Werke GmbH, Johan Ziegler St., 13/15/FeldiglSt., D-8060 Dachau, GERMANY

Eskridge Rifles, Steven Eskridge, 218 N. Emerson, Mart, TX 76664 / 817-876-3544

Eskridge, Steven. (See ESKRIDGE RIFLES)

Essex Arms, P.O. Box 363, Island Pond, VT 05846 / 802-723-6203 FAX: 802-723-6203

Essex Metals, 1000 Brighton St., Union, NJ 07083 / 800-282-8369

Estate Cartridge, Inc., 12161 FM 830, Willis, TX 77378 / 409-856-7277; FAX: 409-856-5486

Euber Bullets, No. Orwell Rd., Orwell, VT 05760 / 802-948-2621

Euro-Imports, 905 West Main St Ste E, El Cajon, CA 92020 / 619-442-7005; FAX: 619-442-7005

Euroarms of America, Inc., P.O. Box 3277, Winchester, VA 22604 / 540-662-1863; FAX: 540-662-4464

European American Armory Corp (See E.A.A. Corp)

Evans, Andrew, 2325 NW Squire St., Albany, OR 97321 / 541-928-3190; FAX: 541-928-4128

Evans Engraving, Robert, 332 Vine St, Oregon City, OR 97045 / 503-656-5693

Evans Gunsmithing (See Evans, Andrew)

Eversull Co., Inc., K., 1 Tracemont, Boyce, LA 71409 / 318-793-8728; FAX: 318-793-5483

Excalibur Electro Optics Inc, P.O. Box 400, Fogelsville, PA 18051-0400 / 610-391-9105; FAX: 610-391-9220

Excel Industries Inc., 4510 Carter Ct., Chino, CA 91710 / 909-627-2404; FAX: 909-627-7817

Executive Protection Institute, PO Box 802, Berryville, VA 22611 / 540-955-1128

Eyster Heritage Gunsmiths, Inc., Ken, 6441 Bishop Rd., Centerburg, OH 43011 / 614-625-6131

Eze-Lap Diamond Prods., P.O. Box 2229, 15164 West State St., Westminster, CA 92683 / 714-847-1555; FAX: 714-897-0280

F

F&A Inc. (See ShurKatch Corporation)

F.A.I.R. Techni-Mec s.n.c. di Isidoro Rizzini & C., Via Gitti, 41 Zona Industrial, 25060 Marcheno (Bres, ITALY / 030/861162-8610344; FAX: 030/8610179

Fabarm S.p.A., Via Averolda 31, 25039 Travagliato, Brescia, ITALY / 030-6863629; FAX: 030-6863684

Fagan & Co.Inc, 22952 15 Mile Rd, Clinton Township, MI 48035 / 810-465-4637; FAX: 810-792-6996

Fair Game International, P.O. Box 77234-34053, Houston, TX 77234 / 713-941-6269

Faith Associates, Inc., PO Box 549, Flat Rock, NC 28731-0549 / 828-692-1916; FAX: 828-697-6827

Fanzoj GmbH, Griesgasse 1, 9170 Ferlach, 9170 AUSTRIA / (43) 04227-2283; FAX: (43) 04227-2867

Far North Outfitters, Box 1252, Bethel, AK 99559

Farm Form Decoys, Inc., 1602 Biovu, P.O. Box 748, Galveston, TX 77553 / 409-744-0762 or 409-765-6361; FAX: 409-765-8513

Farmer-Dressel, Sharon, 209 N. 92nd Ave., Yakima, WA 98908 / 509-966-9233; FAX: 509-966-3365

Farr Studio,Inc., 1231 Robinhood Rd., Greeneville, TN 37743 / 615-638-8825

Farrar Tool Co., Inc., 12150 Bloomfield Ave., Suite E, Santa Fe Springs, CA 90670 / 310-863-4367; FAX: 310-863-5123

Faulhaber Wildlocker, Dipl.-Ing. Norbert Wittasek, Seilergasse 2, A-1010 Wien, AUSTRIA / OM-43-1-5137001; FAX: OM-43-1-5137001

Faulk's Game Call Co., Inc., 616 18th St., Lake Charles, LA 70601 / 318-436-9726 FAX: 318-494-7205

Faust Inc., T. G., 544 minor St, Reading, PA 19602 / 610-375-8549; FAX: 610-375-4488

Fausti Cav. Stefano & Figlie snc, Via Martiri Dell Indipendenza, 70, Marcheno, ITALY

Fautheree, Andy, P.O. Box 4607, Pagosa Springs, CO 81157 / 970-731-5003; FAX: 970-731-5009

Feather, Flex Decoys, 1655 Swan Lake Rd., Bossier City, LA 71111 / 318-746-8596; FAX: 318-742-4815

Federal Arms Corp. of America, 7928 University Ave, Fridley, MN 55432 / 612-780-8780; FAX: 612-780-8780

Federal Cartridge Co., 900 Ehlen Dr., Anoka, MN 55303 / 612-323-2300; FAX: 612-323-2506

Federal Champion Target Co., 232 Industrial Parkway, Richmond, IN 47374 / 800-441-4971; FAX: 317-966-7747

Federated-Fry (See Fry Metals)

FEG, Budapest, Soroksariut 158, H-1095, HUNGARY

Feken, Dennis, Rt. 2, Box 124, Perry, OK 73077 / 405-336-5611

Felk, Inc., 2121 Castlebridge Rd., Midlothian, VA 23113 / 804-794-3744

Fellowes, Ted, Beaver Lodge, 9245 16th Ave. SW, Seattle, WA 98106 / 206-763-1698

Feminine Protection, Inc., 949 W. Kearney Ste. 100, Mesquite, TX 75149 / 972-289-8997 FAX: 972-289-4410

Ferguson, Bill, P.O. Box 1238, Sierra Vista, AZ 85636 / 520-458-5321; FAX: 520-458-9125

FERLIB, Via Costa 46, 25063, Gardone V.T., ITALY / 30-89-12-586; FAX: 30-89-12-586

Ferris Firearms, 7110 F.M. 1863, Bulverde, TX 78163 / 210-980-4424

Fibron Products, Inc., P.O. Box 430, Buffalo, NY 14209-0430 / 716-886-2378; FAX: 716-886-2394

Fieldsport Ltd, Bryan Bilinski, 3313 W South Airport Rd, Traverse Vity, MI 49684 / 616-933-0767

Fiocchi Munizioni S.p.A. (See U.S. Importer-Fiocchi of America, Inc.)

Fiocchi of America Inc., 5030 Fremont Rd., Ozark, MO 65721 / 417-725-4118 or 800-721-2666 FAX: 417-725-1039

Firearms Co Ltd/Alpine (See U.S. Importer-Mandall Shooting Supplies, Inc.)

Firearms Engraver's Guild of America, 332 Vine St., Oregon City, OR 97045 / 503-656-5693

Firearms International, 5709 Hartsdale, Houston, TX 77036 / 713-460-2447

First Inc, Jack, 1201 Turbine Dr., Rapid City, SD 57701 / 605-343-9544; FAX: 605-343-9420

Fish Mfg. Gunsmith Sptg. Co., Marshall F, Rd. Box 2439, Rt. 22 N, Westport, NY 12993 / 518-962-4897 FAX: 518-962-4897

Fisher, Jerry A., 553 Crane Mt. Rd., Big Fork, MT 59911 / 406-837-2722

Fisher Custom Firearms, 2199 S. Kittredge Way, Aurora, CO 80013 / 303-755-3710

Fisher Enterprises, Inc., 1071 4th Ave. S., Suite 303, Edmonds, WA 98020-4143 / 206-771-5382

Fisher, R. Kermit (See Fisher Enterprises, Inc), 1071 4th Ave S Ste 303, Edmonds, WA 98020-4143 / 206-771-5382

Fitz Pistol Grip Co., P.O. Box 744, LEWISTON, CA 96052-0744 / 916-778-0240

Flambeau Products Corp., 15981 Valplast Rd., Middlefield, OH 44062 / 216-632-1631; FAX: 216-632-1581

Flannery Engraving Co., Jeff W, 11034 Riddles Run Rd, Union, KY 41091 / 606-384-3127

Flashette Co., 4725 S. Kolin Ave., Chicago, IL 60632 FAX: 773-927-3083

Flayderman & Co., Inc., PO Box 2446, Ft Lauderdale, FL 33303 / 954-761-8855

Fleming Firearms, 7720 E 126th St. N, Collinsville, OK 74021-7016 / 918-665-3624

Flents Products Co., Inc., P.O. Box 2109, Norwalk, CT 06852 / 203-866-2581; FAX: 203-854-9322

Flintlocks Etc., 160 Rositter Rd, Richmond, MA 01254 / 413-698-3822

Flintlocks, Etc, 160 Rossiter Rd., P.O. Box 181, Richmond, MA 01254 / 413-698-3822; FAX: 413-698-3866 flintetc@vger-net.net pedersoli

Flitz International Ltd., 821 Mohr Ave., Waterford, WI 53185 / 414-534-5898; FAX: 414-534-2991

Flores Publications Inc, J (See Action Direct Inc), PO Box 830760, Miami, FL 33283 / 305-559-4652; FAX: 305-559-4652

Fluoramics, Inc., 18 Industrial Ave., Mahwah, NJ 07430 / 800-922-0075; FAX: 201-825-7035

Flynn's Custom Guns, P.O. Box 7461, Alexandria, LA 71306 / 318-455-7130

FN Herstal, Voie de Liege 33, Herstal, 4040 Belgium / (32)41.40.82.83; FAX: (32)41.40.86.79

Fobus International Ltd., P.O. Box 64, Kfar Hess, 40692 ISRAEL / 972-9-7964170; FAX: 972-9-7964169

Folks, Donald E., 205 W. Lincoln St., Pontiac, IL 61764 / 815-844-7901

Foothills Video Productions, Inc., P.O. Box 651, Spartanburg, SC 29304 / 803-573-7023 or 800-782-5358

Foredom Electric Co., Rt. 6, 16 Stony Hill Rd., Bethel, CT 06801 / 203-792-8622

Forgett Jr., Valmore J., 689 Bergen Blvd., Ridgefield, NJ 07657 / 201-945-2500; FAX: 201-945-6859

Forgreens Tool Mfg., Inc., P.O. Box 990, 723 Austin St., Robert Lee, TX 76945 / 915-453-2800; FAX: 915-453-2460

Forkin, Ben (See Belt MTN Arms)

Forkin Arms, 205 10th Ave SW, White Sulphur Spring, MT 59645 / 406-547-2344; FAX: 406-547-2456

Forrest Inc., Tom, PO Box 326, Lakeside, CA 92040 / 619-561-5800; FAX: 619-561-0227

Forrest Tool Co., P.O. Box 768, 44380 Gordon Lane, Mendocino, CA 95460 / 707-937-2141; FAX: 717-937-1817

Forster, Kathy (See Custom Checkering Service, Kathy Forster)

Forster, Larry L., P.O. Box 212, 220 First St. NE, Gwinner, ND 58040-0212 / 701-678-2475

Forster Products, 310 E Lanark Ave, Lanark, IL 61046 / 815-493-6360; FAX: 815-493-2371

Fort Hill Gunstocks, 12807 Fort Hill Rd., Hillsboro, OH 45133 / 513-466-2763

Fort Knox Security Products, 1051 N. Industrial Park Rd., Orem, UT 84057 / 801-224-7233 or 800-821-5216; FAX: 801-226-5493

Fort Worth Firearms, 2006-B, Martin Luther King Fwy., Ft. Worth, TX 76104-6303 / 817-536-0718; FAX: 817-535-0290

Forthofer's Gunsmithing & Knifemaking, 5535 U.S. Hwy 93S, Whitefish, MT 59937-8411 / 406-862-2674

Fortune Products, Inc., HC04, Box 303, Marble Falls, TX 78654 / 210-693-6111; FAX: 210-693-6394

Forty Five Ranch Enterprises, Box 1080, Miami, OK 74355-1080 / 918-542-5875

Fountain Products, 492 Prospect Ave., West Springfield, MA 01089 / 413-781-4651; FAX: 413-733-8217

4-D Custom Die Co., 711 N. Sandusky St., P.O. Box 889, Mt. Vernon, OH 43050-0889 / 740-397-7214; FAX: 740-397-6600

Fowler Bullets, 806 Dogwood Dr., Gastonia, NC 28054 / 704-867-3259

Fowler, Bob (See Black Powder Products)

Fox River Mills, Inc., P.O. Box 298, 227 Poplar St., Osage, IA 50461 / 515-732-3798; FAX: 515-732-5128

Foy Custom Bullets, 104 Wells Ave., Daleville, AL 36322

Francesca, Inc., 3115 Old Ranch Rd., San Antonio, TX 78217 / 512-826-2584; FAX: 512-826-8211

Franchi S.p.A., Via del Serpente 12, 25131, Brescia, ITALY / 030-3581833; FAX: 030-3581554

Francotte & Cie S.A. Auguste, rue de Trois Juin 109, 4400 Herstal-Liege, BELGIUM / 32-4-248-13-18; FAX: 32-4-948-11-79

Frank Custom Classic Arms, Ron, 7131 Richland Rd, Ft Worth, TX 76118 / 817-284-9300; FAX: 817-284-9300

Frank E. Hendricks Master Engravers, Inc., HC03, Box 434, Dripping Springs, TX 78620 / 512-858-7828

Frank Knives, 13868 NW Keleka Pl., Seal Rock, OR 97376 / 541-563-3041; FAX: 541-563-3041

Frank Mittermeier, Inc., P.O. Box 2G, 3577 E. Tremont Ave., Bronx, NY 10465 / 718-828-3843

Frankonia Jagd Hofmann & Co., D-97064 Wurzburg, Wurzburg, GERMANY / 09302-200; FAX: 09302-20200

Franzen International,Inc (U.S. Importer for Peters Stahl GmbH)

Fred F. Wells/Wells Sport Store, 110 N Summit St, Prescott, AZ 86301 / 520-445-3655

Freedom Arms, Inc., P.O. Box 150, Freedom, WY 83120 / 307-883-2468 or 800-833-4432; FAX: 307-883-2005

Freeman Animal Targets, 5519 East County Road, 100 South, Plainsfield, IN 46168 / 317-272-2663; FAX: 317-272-2674

Fremont Tool Works, 1214 Prairie, Ford, KS 67842 / 316-369-2327

French, Artistic Engraving, J. R., 1712 Creek Ridge Ct, Irving, TX 75060 / 214-254-2654

Frielich Police Equipment, 211 East 21st St., New York, NY 10010 / 212-254-3045

Front Sight Firearms Training Institute, P.O. Box 2619, Aptos, CA 95001 / 800-987-7719; FAX: 408-684-2137

Frontier, 2910 San Bernardo, Laredo, TX 78040 / 956-723-5409; FAX: 956-723-1774

Frontier Arms Co.,Inc., 401 W. Rio Santa Cruz, Green Valley, AZ 85614-3932

Frontier Products Co., 2401 Walker Rd, Roswell, NM 88201-8950 / 614-262-9357

Frontier Safe Co., 3201 S. Clinton St., Fort Wayne, IN 46806 / 219-744-7233; FAX: 219-744-6678

Frost Cutlery Co., P.O. Box 22636, Chattanooga, TN 37422 / 615-894-6079; FAX: 615-894-9576

Fry Metals, 4100 6th Ave., Altoona, PA 16602 / 814-946-1611

Fujinon, Inc., 10 High Point Dr., Wayne, NJ 07470 / 201-633-5600; FAX: 201-633-5216

Fullmer, Geo. M., 2499 Mavis St., Oakland, CA 94601 / 510-533-4193

Fulmer's Antique Firearms, Chet, PO Box 792, Rt 2 Buffalo Lake, Detroit Lakes, MN 56501 / 218-847-7712

Fulton Armory, 8725 Bollman Place No. 1, Savage, MD 20763 / 301-490-9485; FAX: 301-490-9547

Furr Arms, 91 N. 970 W., Orem, UT 84057 / 801-226-3877; FAX: 801-226-3877

Fusilier Bullets, 10010 N. 6000 W., Highland, UT 84003 / 801-756-6813

FWB, Neckarstrasse 43, 78727, Oberndorf a. N., GERMANY / 07423-814-0; FAX: 07423-814-89

G

G&H Decoys,Inc., P.O. Box 1208, Hwy. 75 North, Henryetta, OK 74437 / 918-652-3314; FAX: 918-652-3400

G.C.C.T., 4455 Torrance Blvd., Ste. 453, Torrance, CA 90503-4398

G.G. & G., 3602 E. 42nd Stravenue, Tucson, AZ 85713 / 520-748-7167; FAX: 520-748-7583

G.H. Enterprises Ltd., Bag 10, Okotoks, AB T0L 1T0 CANADA / 403-938-6070

G.U. Inc (See U.S. Importer for New SKB Arms Co)

G.W. Elliott, Inc., 514 Burnside Ave., East Hartford, CT 06108 / 203-289-5741; FAX: 203-289-3137

G96 Products Co., Inc., 85 5th Ave, Bldg #6, Paterson, NJ 07544 / 973-684-4050 FAX: 973-684-4050

Gage Manufacturing, 663 W. 7th St., A, San Pedro, CA 90731 / 310-832-3546

Gaillard Barrels, P.O. Box 21, Pathlow, SK S0K 3B0 CANADA / 306-752-3769; FAX: 306-752-5969

Gain Twist Barrel Co. Rifle Works and Armory, 707 12th Street, Cody, WY 82414 / 307-587-4919; FAX: 307-527-6097

Galati International, PO Box 10, Wesco, MO 65586 / 314-257-4837; FAX: 314-257-2268

Galaxy Imports Ltd.,Inc., P.O. Box 3361, Victoria, TX 77903 / 361-573-4867; FAX: 361-576-9622 galaxy@tisd.net

GALCO International Ltd., 2019 W. Quail Ave., Phoenix, AZ 85027 / 602-258-8295 or 800-874-2526; FAX: 602-582-6854

Galena Industries AMT, 5463 Diaz St, Irwindale, CA 91706 / 626-856-8883; FAX: 626-856-8878

Gamba S.p.A Societa Armi Bresciane Srl, Renato, Via Artigiani 93, ITALY / 30-8911640; FAX: 30-8911648

Gamba, USA, P.O. Box 60452, Colorado Springs, CO 80960 / 719-578-1145; FAX: 719-444-0731

Game Haven Gunstocks, 13750 Shire Rd., Wolverine, MI 49799 / 616-525-8257

Game Winner, Inc., 2625 Cumberland Parkway, Suite 220, Atlanta, GA 30339 / 770-434-9210; FAX: 770-434-9215

Gamebore Division, Polywad Inc, PO Box 7916, Macon, GA 31209 / 912-477-0669

Gamo (See U.S. Importers-Arms United Corp, Daisy Mfg. Co.,)

Gamo USA, Inc., 3911 SW 47th Ave., Suite 914, Ft. Lauderdale, FL 33314 / 954-581-5822; FAX: 954-581-3165

Gander Mountain, Inc., 12400 Fox River Rd., Wilmont, WI 53192 / 414-862-6848

GAR, 590 McBride Avenue, West Paterson, NJ 07424 / 973-754-1114; FAX: 973-754-1114

Garbi, Armas Urki, 12-14 20.600 Eibar, Guipuzcoa, SPAIN

Garcia National Gun Traders, Inc., 225 SW 22nd Ave., Miami, FL 33135 / 305-642-2355

Garrett Cartridges Inc., P.O. Box 178, Chehalis, WA 98532 / 360-736-0702

Garthwaite Pistolsmith, Inc., Jim, Rt 2 Box 310, Watsontown, PA 17777 / 570-538-1566; FAX: 570-538-2965

Gary Goudy Classic Stocks, 263 Hedge Rd., Menlo Park, CA 94025-1711 / 415-322-1338

Gary Reeder Custom Guns, 2710 N Steves Blvd. #22, Flagstaff, AZ 86004 / 520-526-3313; FAX: 520-527-0840 gary@reedercustomguns.com www.reedercustomguns.com

Gary Schneider Rifle Barrels Inc., 12202 N. 62nd Pl., Scottsdale, AZ 85254 / 602-948-2525

Gator Guns & Repair, 6255 Spur Hwy., Kenai, AK 99611 / 907-283-7947

Gaucher Armes, S.A., 46 rue Desjoyaux, 42000, Saint-Etienne, FRANCE / 04-77-33-38-92; FAX: 04-77-61-95-72

GDL Enterprises, 409 Le Gardeur, Slidell, LA 70460 / 504-649-0693

Gehmann, Walter (See Huntington Die Specialties)

Genco, P.O. Box 5704, Asheville, NC 28803

Gene's Custom Guns, P.O. Box 10534, White Bear Lake, MN 55110 / 612-429-5105

Genecco Gun Works, K, 10512 Lower Sacramento Rd., Stockton, CA 95210 / 209-951-0706 FAX: 209-931-3872

Gentex Corp., 5 Tinkham Ave., Derry, NH 03038 / 603-434-0311; FAX: 603-434-3002 sales@derry.gentexcorp.com www.derry.gentexcorp.com

Gentner Bullets, 109 Woodlawn Ave., Upper Darby, PA 19082 / 610-352-9396

Gentry Custom Gunmaker, David, 314 N Hoffman, Belgrade, MT 59714 / 406-388-GUNS

George & Roy's, PO Box 2125, Sisters, OR 97759-2125 / 503-228-5424 or 800-553-3022; FAX: 503-225-9409

George, Tim, Rt. 1, P.O. Box 45, Evington, VA 24550 / 804-821-8117

George E. Mathews & Son, Inc., 10224 S. Paramount Blvd., Downey, CA 90241 / 562-862-6719; FAX: 562-862-6719

George Ibberson (Sheffield) Ltd., 25-31 Allen St., Sheffield, S3 7AW ENGLAND / 0114-2766123; FAX: 0114-2738465

Gerald Pettinger Books, see Pettinger Books, G, Rt. 2, Box 125, Russell, IA 50238 / 515-535-2239

Gerber Legendary Blades, 14200 SW 72nd Ave., Portland, OR 97223 / 503-639-6161 or 800-950-6161; FAX: 503-684-7008

Gervais, Mike, 3804 S. Cruise Dr., Salt Lake City, UT 84109 / 801-277-7729

Getz Barrel Co., P.O. Box 88, Beavertown, PA 17813 / 717-658-7263

Giacomo Sporting USA, 6234 Stokes Lee Center Rd., Lee Center, NY 13363

Gibbs Rifle Co., Inc., 211 Lawn St, Martinsburg, WV 25401 / 304-262-1651; FAX: 304-262-1658

Gil Hebard Guns, 125-129 Public Square, Knoxville, IL 61448 / 309-289-2700 FAX: 309-289-2233

Gilbert Equipment Co., Inc., 960 Downtowner Rd., Mobile, AL 36609 / 205-344-3322

Gilkes, Anthony W., 26574 HILLMAN HWY, MEADOWVIEW, VA 24361-3142 / 303-657-1873; FAX: 303-657-1885

Gillmann, Edwin, 33 Valley View Dr., Hanover, PA 17331 / 717-632-1662

Gilman-Mayfield, Inc., 3279 E. Shields, Fresno, CA 93703 / 209-221-9415; FAX: 209-221-9419

Gilmore Sports Concepts, 5949 S. Garnett, Tulsa, OK 74146 / 918-250-3810; FAX: 918-250-3845 gilmore@webzone.net www.gilmoresports.com

Giron, Robert E., 1328 Pocono St., Pittsburgh, PA 15218 / 412-731-6041

Glacier Glove, 4890 Aircenter Circle, Suite 210, Reno, NV 89502 / 702-825-8225; FAX: 702-825-6544

Glaser Safety Slug, Inc., P.O. Box 8223, Foster City, CA 94404 / 800-221-3489; FAX: 510-785-6685 safetyslug.com

Glass, Herb, P.O. Box 25, Bullville, NY 10915 / 914-361-3021

Glimm, Jerome C., 19 S. Maryland, Conrad, MT 59425 / 406-278-3574

Glock GmbH, P.O. Box 50, A-2232, Deutsch Wagram, AUSTRIA

Glock, Inc., PO Box 369, Smyrna, GA 30081 / 770-432-1202; FAX: 770-433-8719

Glynn Scobey Duck & Goose Calls, Rt. 3, Box 37, Newbern, TN 38059 / 901-643-6241

GML Products, Inc., 394 Laredo Dr., Birmingham, AL 35226 / 205-979-4867

Gner's Hard Cast Bullets, 1107 11th St., LaGrande, OR 97850 / 503-963-8796

Goens, Dale W., P.O. Box 224, Cedar Crest, NM 87008 / 505-281-5419

Goergen's Gun Shop, Inc., 17985 538th Ave, Austin, MN 55912 / 507-433-9280 FAX: 507-433-9280

GOEX Inc., PO Box 659, Doyline, LA 71023-0659 / 318-382-9300; FAX: 318-382-9303

Golden Age Arms Co., 115 E. High St., Ashley, OH 43003 / 614-747-2488

Golden Bear Bullets, 3065 Fairfax Ave., San Jose, CA 95148 / 408-238-9515

Gonic Arms/North American Arm, 134 Flagg Rd., Gonic, NH 03839 / 603-332-8456 or 603-332-8457

Gonzalez Guns, Ramon B, PO Box 370, 93 St. Joseph's Hill Rd, Monticello, NY 12701 / 914-794-4515

Goodling's Gunsmithing, R.D. 1, Box 1097, Spring Grove, PA 17362 / 717-225-3350

Goodwin, Fred, Silver Ridge Gun Shop, Sherman Mills, ME 04776 / 207-365-4451

Gordie's Gun Shop, 1401 Fulton St., Streator, IL 61364 / 815-672-7202

Gordon Wm. Davis Leather Co., P.O. Box 2270, Walnut, CA 91788 / 909-598-5620

Gotz Bullets, 7313 Rogers St., Rockford, IL 61111

Gould & Goodrich, 709 E. McNeil, Lillington, NC 27546 / 910-893-2071; FAX: 910-893-4742

Gournet, Geoffroy, 820 Paxinosa Ave., Easton, PA 18042 / 610-559-0710

Gozon Corp. U.S.A., P.O. Box 6278, Folson, CA 95763 / 916-983-2026; FAX: 916-983-9500

Grace, Charles E., 1305 Arizona Ave., Trinidad, CO 81082 / 719-846-9435

Grace Metal Products, P.O. Box 67, Elk Rapids, MI 49629 / 616-264-8133

Graf & Sons, 4050 S Clark St, Mexico, MO 65265 / 573-581-2266 FAX: 573-581-2875

"Gramps" Antique Cartridges, Box 341, Washago, ON L0K 2B0 CANADA / 705-689-5348

Granite Mountain Arms, Inc, 3145 W Hidden Acres Trail, Prescott, AZ 86305 / 520-541-9758; FAX: 520-445-6826

Grant, Howard V., Hiawatha 15, Woodruff, WI 54568 / 715-356-7146

Graphics Direct, P.O. Box 372421, Reseda, CA 91337-2421 / 818-344-9002

Graves Co., 1800 Andrews Ave., Pompano Beach, FL 33069 / 800-327-9103; FAX: 305-960-0301

Grayback Wildcats, 5306 Bryant Ave., Klamath Falls, OR 97603 / 541-884-1072

Graybill's Gun Shop, 1035 Ironville Pike, Columbia, PA 17512 / 717-684-2739

GrE-Tan Rifles, 29742 W.C.R. 50, Kersey, CO 80644 / 970-353-6176; FAX: 970-356-9133

Great American Gunstock Co., 3420 Industrial Drive, Yuba City, CA 95993 / 530-671-4570; FAX: 530-671-3906

Great Lakes Airguns, 6175 S. Park Ave, New York, NY 14075 / 716-648-6666; FAX: 716-648-5279

Green, Arthur S., 485 S. Robertson Blvd., Beverly Hills, CA 90211 / 310-274-1283

Green, Roger M., P.O. Box 984, 435 E. Birch, Glenrock, WY 82637 / 307-436-9804

Green Genie, Box 114, Cusseta, GA 31805

Green Head Game Call Co., RR 1, Box 33, Lacon, IL 61540 / 309-246-2155

Green Mountain Rifle Barrel Co., Inc., P.O. Box 2670, 153 West Main St., Conway, NH 03818 / 603-447-1095; FAX: 603-447-1099

Greenwood Precision, P.O. Box 468, Nixa, MO 65714-0468 / 417-725-2330

Greg Gunsmithing Repair, 3732 26th Ave. North, Robbinsdale, MN 55422 / 612-529-8103

Greg's Superior Products, P.O. Box 46219, Seattle, WA 98146

Greider Precision, 431 Santa Marina Ct., Escondido, CA 92029 / 619-480-8892; FAX: 619-480-9800

Gremmel Enterprises, 2111 Carriage Drive, Eugene, OR 97408-7537 / 541-302-3000

MANUFACTURER'S DIRECTORY

Grier's Hard Cast Bullets, 1107 11th St., LaGrande, OR 97850 / 503-963-8796

Griffin & Howe, Inc., 36 W. 44th St., Suite 1011, New York, NY 10036 / 212-921-0980

Griffin & Howe, Inc., 33 Claremont Rd., Bernardsville, NJ 07924 / 908-766-2287

Grifon, Inc., 58 Guinam St., Waltham, MS 02154

Groenewold, John, P.O. Box 830, Mundelein, IL 60060 / 847-566-2365

GRS Corp., Glendo, P.O. Box 1153, 900 Overlander St., Emporia, KS 66801 / 316-343-1084 or 800-835-3519

Grulla Armes, Apartado 453, Avda Otaloa 12, Eiber, SPAIN

Gruning Precision Inc, 7101 Jurupa Ave., No. 12, Riverside, CA 92504 / 909-689-6692 FAX: 909-689-7791

GSI, Inc., 7661 Commerce Ln., Trussville, AL 35173 / 205-655-8299

GTB, 482 Comerwood Court, San Francisco, CA 94080 / 650-583-1550

Guarasi, Robert. (See WILCOX INDUSTRIES CORP)

Guardsman Products, 411 N. Darling, Fremont, MI 49412 / 616-924-3950

Gun Accessories (See Glaser Safety Slug, Inc.), PO Box 8223, Foster City, CA 94404 / 800-221-3489; FAX: 510-785-6685

Gun City, 212 W. Main Ave., Bismarck, ND 58501 / 701-223-2304

Gun Hunter Books (See Gun Hunter Trading Co), 5075 Heisig St, Beaumont, TX 77705 / 409-835-3006

Gun Hunter Trading Co., 5075 Heisig St., Beaumont, TX 77705 / 409-835-3006

Gun Leather Limited, 116 Lipscomb, Ft. Worth, TX 76104 / 817-334-0225; FAX: 800-247-0609

Gun List (See Krause Publications), 700 E State St, Iola, WI 54945 / 715-445-2214; FAX: 715-445-4087

Gun Locker Div. of Airmold W.R. Grace & Co.-Conn., Becker Farms Ind. Park, P.O. Box 610, Roanoke Rapids, NC 27870 / 800-344-5716; FAX: 919-536-2201

Gun South, Inc. (See GSI, Inc.)

Gun Vault, 7339 E Acoma Dr., Ste. 7, Scottsdale, AZ 85260 / 602-951-6855

Gun-Alert, 1010 N. Maclay Ave., San Fernando, CA 91340 / 818-365-0864; FAX: 818-365-1308

Gun-Ho Sports Cases, 110 E. 10th St., St. Paul, MN 55101 / 612-224-9491

Guncraft Books (See Guncraft Sports Inc), 10737 Dutchtown Rd, Knoxville, TN 37932 / 423-966-4545; FAX: 423-966-4500

Guncraft Sports Inc., 10737 Dutchtown Rd., Knoxville, TN 37932 / 423-966-4545; FAX: 423-966-4500

Gunfitters, P.O. 426, Cambridge, WI 53523-0426 / 608-764-8128 gunfitters@aol.com www.gunfitters.com

Gunline Tools, 2950 Saturn St., "O", Brea, CA 92821 / 714-993-5100; FAX: 714-572-4128

Gunnerman Books, P.O. Box 217, Owosso, MI 48867 / 517-729-7018; FAX: 517-725-9391

Guns, 81 E. Streetsboro St., Hudson, OH 44236 / 330-650-4563

Guns Antique & Modern DBA/Charles E. Duffy, Williams Lane, West Hurley, NY 12491 / 914-679-2997

Guns Div. of D.C. Engineering, Inc., 8633 Southfield Fwy., Detroit, MI 48228 / 313-271-7111 or 800-886-7623; FAX: 313-271-7112

GUNS Magazine, 591 Camino de la Reina, Suite 200, San Diego, CA 92108 / 619-297-5350 FAX: 619-297-5353

Gunsite Custom Shop, P.O. Box 451, Paulden, AZ 86334 / 520-636-4104; FAX: 520-636-1236

Gunsite Gunsmithy (See Gunsite Custom Shop)

Gunsite Training Center, P.O. Box 700, Paulden, AZ 86334 / 520-636-4565; FAX: 520-636-1236

Gunsmithing Ltd., 57 Unquowa Rd., Fairfield, CT 06430 / 203-254-0436; FAX: 203-254-1535

Gunsmithing, Inc., 208 West Buchanan St., Colorado Springs, CO 80907 / 719-632-3795; FAX: 719-632-3493

Gurney, F. R., Box 13, Sooke, BC V0S 1N0 CANADA / 604-642-5282; FAX: 604-642-7859

Gwinnell, Bryson J., P.O. Box 248C, Maple Hill Rd., Rochester, VT 05767 / 802-767-3664

H

H&B Forge Co., Rt. 2, Geisinger Rd., Shiloh, OH 44878 / 419-895-1856

H&P Publishing, 7174 Hoffman Rd., San Angelo, TX 76905 / 915-655-5953

H&R 1871, Inc., 60 Industrial Rowe, Gardner, MA 01440 / 978-632-9393; FAX: 978-632-2300

H&S Liner Service, 515 E. 8th, Odessa, TX 79761 / 915-332-1021

H-S Precision, Inc., 1301 Turbine Dr., Rapid City, SD 57701 / 605-341-3006; FAX: 605-342-8964

H. Krieghoff Gun Co., Boschstrasse 22, D-89079, Ulm, GERMANY / 731-401820; FAX: 731-4018270

H.K.S. Products, 7841 Founion Dr., Florence, KY 41042 / 606-342-7841 or 800-354-9814; FAX: 606-342-5865

H.P. White Laboratory, Inc., 3114 Scarboro Rd., Street, MD 21154 / 410-838-6550; FAX: 410-838-2802

Hafner World Wide, Inc., P.O. Box 1987, Lake City, FL 32055 / 904-755-6481; FAX: 904-755-6595

Hagn Rifles & Actions, Martin, PO Box 444, Cranbrook, BC V1C 4H9 CANADA / 604-489-4861

Hakko Co. Ltd., 1-13-12, Narimasu, Itabashiku Tokyo, JAPAN / 03-5997-7870/2; FAX: 81-3-5997-7840

Hale, Engraver, Peter, 800 E Canyon Rd., Spanish Fork, UT 84660 / 801-798-8215

Half Moon Rifle Shop, 490 Halfmoon Rd., Columbia Falls, MT 59912 / 406-892-4409

Hall Manufacturing, 142 CR 406, Clanton, AL 35045 / 205-755-4094

Hall Plastics, Inc., John, P.O. Box 1526, Alvin, TX 77512 / 713-489-8709

Hallberg Gunsmith, Fritz, 532 E. Idaho Ave, Ontario, OR 97914 / 541-889-3135; FAX: 541-889-2633

Hallowell & Co., PO Box 1445, Livingston, MT 59047 / 406-222-4770 FAX: 406-222-4792 morris@hallowellco.com hallowellco.com

Hally Caller, 443 Wells Rd., Doylestown, PA 18901 / 215-345-6354

Halstead, Rick, 313 TURF ST, CARL JUNCTION, MO 64834-9658 / 918-540-0933

Hamilton, Jim, Rte. 5, Box 278, Guthrie, OK 73044 / 405-282-3634

Hamilton, Alex B (See Ten-Ring Precision, Inc)

Hammans, Charles E., P.O. Box 788, 2022 McCracken, Stuttgart, AR 72106 / 870-673-1388

Hammerli Ltd., Seonerstrasse 37, CH-5600, SWITZERLAND / 064-50 11 44; FAX: 064-51 38 27

Hammerli USA, 19296 Oak Grove Circle, Groveland, CA 95321 FAX: 209-962-5311

Hammets VLD Bullets, P.O. Box 479, Rayville, LA 71269 / 318-728-2019

Hammond Custom Guns Ltd., 619 S. Pandora, Gilbert, AZ 85234 / 602-892-3437

Hammonds Rifles, RD 4, Box 504, Red Lion, PA 17356 / 717-244-7879

HandCrafts Unltd (See Clements' Custom Leathercraft, Chas,), 1741 Dallas St, Aurora, CO 80010-2018 / 303-364-0403; FAX: 303-739-9824

Handgun Press, P.O. Box 406, Glenview, IL 60025 / 847-657-6500; FAX: 847-724-8831 jschroed@inter-access.com

Hands Engraving, Barry Lee, 26192 E Shore Route, Bigfork, MT 59911 / 406-837-0035

Hanned Precision (See Hanned Line, The)

Hansen & Co. (See Hansen Cartridge Co.), 244-246 Old Post Rd, Southport, CT 06490 / 203-259-6222; FAX: 203-254-3832

Hanson's Gun Center, Dick, 233 Everett Dr, Colorado Springs, CO 80911

Hanus Birdguns Bill, PO Box 533, Newport, OR 97365 / 541-265-7433; FAX: 541-265-7400

Hanusin, John, 3306 Commercial, Northbrook, IL 60062 / 708-564-2706

Hardin Specialty Dist., P.O. Box 338, Radcliff, KY 40159-0338 / 502-351-6649

Harford (See U.S. Importer-EMF Co. Inc.)

Harper's Custom Stocks, 928 Lombrano St., San Antonio, TX 78207 / 210-732-5780

Harrell's Precision, 5756 Hickory Dr., Salem, VA 24133 / 703-380-2683

Harrington & Richardson (See H&R 1871, Inc.)

Harris Engineering Inc., Dept GD54, Barlow, KY 42024 / 502-334-3633 FAX: 502-334-3000

Harris Enterprises, P.O. Box 105, Bly, OR 97622 / 503-353-2625

Harris Gunworks, 20813 N. 19th Ave., PO Box 9249, Phoenix, AZ 85027 / 602-582-9627; FAX: 602-582-5178

Harris Hand Engraving, Paul A., 113 Rusty Ln, Boerne, TX 78006-5746 / 512-391-5121

Harris Publications, 1115 Broadway, New York, NY 10010 / 212-807-7100 FAX: 212-627-4678

Harrison Bullets, 6437 E. Hobart St., Mesa, AZ 85205

Harry Lawson Co., 3328 N. Richey Blvd., Tucson, AZ 85716 / 520-326-1117

Hart & Son, Inc., Robert W., 401 Montgomery St, Nescopeck, PA 18635 / 717-752-3655; FAX: 717-752-1088

Hart Rifle Barrels,Inc., P.O. Box 182, 1690 Apulia Rd., Lafayette, NY 13084 / 315-677-9841; FAX: 315-677-9610 hartrb@aol.com www.hartbarrels.com

Hartford (See U.S. Importer-EMF Co. Inc.)

Hartmann & Weiss GmbH, Rahlstedter Bahnhofstr. 47, 22143, Hamburg, GERMANY / (40) 677 55 85; FAX: (40) 677 55 92

Harvey, Frank, 218 Nightfall, Terrace, NV 89015 / 702-558-6998

Harwood, Jack O., 1191 S. Pendlebury Lane, Blackfoot, ID 83221 / 208-785-5368

Hastings Barrels, 320 Court St., Clay Center, KS 67432 / 913-632-3169; FAX: 913-632-6554

Hatfield Gun, 224 N. 4th St., St. Joseph, MO 64501

Hawk Laboratories, Inc. (See Hawk, Inc.), 849 Hawks Bridge Rd, Salem, NJ 08079 / 609-299-2700; FAX: 609-299-2800

Hawk, Inc., 849 Hawks Bridge Rd., Salem, NJ 08079 / 609-299-2700; FAX: 609-299-2800

Hawken Shop, The (See Dayton Traister)

Haydel's Game Calls, Inc., 5018 Hazel Jones Rd., Bossier City, LA 71111 / 800-HAYDELS; FAX: 318-746-3711

Haydon Shooters Supply, Russ, 15018 Goodrich Dr NW, Gig Harbor, WA 98329-9738 / 253-857-7557; FAX: 253-857-7884

Heatbath Corp., P.O. Box 2978, Springfield, MA 01101 / 413-543-3381

Hebard Guns, Gil, 125-129 Public Square, Knoxville, IL 61448

HEBB Resources, P.O. Box 999, Mead, WA 99021-0999 / 509-466-1292

Hecht, Hubert J, Waffen-Hecht, PO Box 2635, Fair Oaks, CA 95628 / 916-966-1020

Heckler & Koch GmbH, P.O. Box 1329, 78722 Oberndorf, Neckar, GERMANY / 49-7423179-0; FAX: 49-7423179-2406

Heckler & Koch, Inc., 21480 Pacific Blvd., Sterling, VA 20166-8900 / 703-450-1900; FAX: 703-450-8160

Hege Jagd-u. Sporthandels GmbH, P.O. Box 101461, W-7770, Ueberlingen a. Boden, GERMANY

Heidenstrom Bullets, Urdngt 1, 3937 Heroya, NORWAY,

Heilmann, Stephen, P.O. Box 657, Grass Valley, CA 95945 / 530-272-8758

Heinie Specialty Products, 301 Oak St., Quincy, IL 62301-2500 / 217-228-9500; FAX: 217-228-9502 rheinie@heinie.com www.heinie.com

Hellweg Ltd., 40356 Oak Park Way, Suite W, Oakhurst, CA 93644 / 209-683-3030; FAX: 209-683-3422

Helwan (See U.S. Importer-Interarms)

Hendricks, Frank E. Inc., Master Engravers, HC 03, Box 434, Dripping Springs, TX 78620 / 512-858-7828

Henigson & Associates, Steve, P.O. Box 2726, Culver City, CA 90231 / 310-305-8288; FAX: 310-305-1905

Henriksen Tool Co., Inc., 8515 Wagner Creek Rd., Talent, OR 97540 / 541-535-2309 FAX: 541-535-2309

Henry Repeating Arms Co., 110 8th St., Brooklyn, NY 11215 / 718-499-5600

Hensley, Gunmaker, Darwin, PO Box 329, Brightwood, OR 97011 / 503-622-5411

Heppler, Keith. (See KEITH'S CUSTOM GUNSTOCKS)

Heppler's Machining, 2240 Calle Del Mundo, Santa Clara, CA 95054 / 408-748-9166; FAX: 408-988-7711

Heppler, Keith M, Keith's Custom Gunstocks, 540 Banyan Cir, Walnut Creek, CA 94598 / 510-934-3509; FAX: 510-934-3143

Hercules, Inc. (See Alliant Techsystems, Smokeless Powder Group)

Heritage Firearms (See Heritage Mfg., Inc.)

Heritage Manufacturing, Inc., 4600 NW 135th St., Opa Locka, FL 33054 or 305-685-5966; FAX: 305-687-6721

Heritage Wildlife Carvings, 2145 Wagner Hollow Rd., Fort Plain, NY 13339 / 518-993-3983

Heritage/VSP Gun Books, P.O. Box 887, McCall, ID 83638 / 208-634-4104; FAX: 208-634-3101

Herrett's Stocks, Inc., P.O. Box 741, Twin Falls, ID 83303 / 208-733-1498

Hertel & Reuss, Werk fr Optik und Feinmechanik GmbH, Quellhofstrasse 67, 34 127, GERMANY / 0561-83006; FAX: 0561-893308

Herter's Manufacturing, Inc., 111 E. Burnett St., P.O. Box 518, Beaver Dam, WI 53916 / 414-887-1765; FAX: 414-887-8444

Hesco-Meprolight, 2139 Greenville Rd., LaGrange, GA 30241 / 706-884-7967; FAX: 706-882-4683

Heydenberk, Warren R., 1059 W. Sawmill Rd., Quakertown, PA 18951 / 215-538-2682

Hi-Grade Imports, 8655 Monterey Rd., Gilroy, CA 95021 / 408-842-9301; FAX: 408-842-2374

Hi-Performance Ammunition Company, 484 State Route 366, Apollo, PA 15613 / 412-327-8100

DIRECTORY

Hi-Point Firearms, 5990 Philadelphia Dr., Dayton, OH 45415 / 513-275-4991; FAX: 513-522-8330

Hickman, Jaclyn, Box 1900, Glenrock, WY 82637

Hidalgo, Tony, 12701 SW 9th Pl., Davie, FL 33325 / 954-476-7645

High Bridge Arms, Inc, 3185 Mission St., San Francisco, CA 94110 / 415-282-8358

High North Products, Inc., P.O. Box 2, Antigo, WI 54409 / 715-627-2331 FAX: 715-623-5451

High Performance International, 5734 W. Florist Ave., Milwaukee, WI 53218 / 414-466-9040

High Standard Mfg. Co., Inc., 10606 Hempstead Hwy., Suite 116, Houston, TX 77092 / 713-462-4200, 800-467-2228

High Tech Specialties, Inc., P.O. Box 387R, Adamstown, PA 19501 / 215-484-0405 or 800-231-9385

Highline Machine Co., Randall Thompson, 654 Lela Place, Grand Junction, CO 81504 / 970-434-4971

Hill, Loring F., 304 Cedar Rd., Elkins Park, PA 19027

Hill Speed Leather, Ernie, 4507 N 195th Ave, Litchfield Park, AZ 85340 / 602-853-9222; FAX: 602-853-9235

Hines Co, S C, PO Box 423, Tijeras, NM 87059 / 505-281-3783

Hinman Outfitters, Bob, 107 N Sanderson Ave, Bartonville, IL 61607-1839 / 309-691-8132

HIP-GRIP Barami Corp., 6689 Orchard Lake Rd. No. 148, West Bloomfield, MI 48322 / 248-738-0462; FAX: 248-738-2542

Hiptmayer, Armurier, RR 112 750, P.O. Box 136, Eastman, PQ JOE 1P0 CANADA / 514-297-2492

Hiptmayer, Heidemarie, RR 112 750, P.O. Box 136, Eastman, PQ JOE 1P0 CANADA / 514-297-2492

Hiptmayer, Klaus, RR 112 750, P.O. Box 136, Eastman, PQ JOE 1P0 CANADA / 514-297-2492

Hirtenberger Aktiengesellschaft, Leobersdorferstrasse 31, A-2552, Hirtenberg, / 43(0)2256 81184; FAX: 43(0)2256 81807

HiTek International, 484 El Camino Real, Redwood City, CA 94063 / 415-363-1404 or 800-54-NIGHT FAX: 415-363-1408

Hiti-Schuch, Atelier Wilma, A-8863 Predlitz, Pirming, Y1 AUSTRIA / 0353418278

HJS Arms,Inc., P.O. Box 3711, Brownsville, TX 78523-3711 / 800-453-2767; FAX: 210-542-2767

Hoag, James W., 8523 Canoga Ave., Suite C, Canoga Park, CA 91304 / 818-998-1510

Hobson Precision Mfg. Co., 210 Big Oak Ln, Brent, AL 35034 / 205-926-4662 FAX: 205-926-3193 cahobbob@dbtech.net

Hoch Custom Bullet Moulds (See Colorado Shooter's

Hodgdon Powder Co., 6231 Robinson, Shawnee Mission, KS 66202 / 913-362-9455; FAX: 913-362-1307

Hodgman, Inc., 1750 Orchard Rd., Montgomery, IL 60538 / 708-897-7555; FAX: 708-897-7558

Hodgson, Richard, 9081 Tahoe Lane, Boulder, CO 80301

Hoehn Sales, Inc., 2045 Kohn Road, Wright City, MO 63390 / 636-745-8144; FAX: 636-745-7868 hoehnsal@usmo.com benchrestcentral.com

Hoelscher, Virgil, 8230 Hillrose St, Sunland, CA 91040-2404 / 310-631-8545

Hoenig & Rodman, 6521 Morton Dr., Boise, ID 83704 / 208-375-1116

Hofer Jagdwaffen, P., Buchsenmachermeister, Kirchgasse 24, A-9170 Ferlach, AUSTRIA

Hoffman New Ideas, 821 Northmoor Rd., Lake Forest, IL 60045 / 312-234-4075

Hogue Grips, P.O. Box 1138, Paso Robles, CA 93447 / 800-438-4747 or 805-239-1440; FAX: 805-239-2553

Holland & Holland Ltd., 33 Bruton St., London, ENGLAND / 44-171-499-4411; FAX: 44-171-408-7962

Holland's Gunsmithing, P.O. Box 69, Powers, OR 97466 / 541-439-5155; FAX: 541-439-5155

Hollinger, Jon. (See ASPEN OUTFITTING CO)

Hollis Gun Shop, 917 Rex St., Carlsbad, NM 88220 / 505-885-3782

Hollywood Engineering, 10642 Arminta St., Sun Valley, CA 91352 / 818-842-8376

Homak, 5151 W. 73rd St., Chicago, IL 60638-6613 / 312-523-3100; FAX: 312-523-9455

Home Shop Machinist The Village Press Publications, P.O. Box 1810, Traverse City, MI 49685 / 800-447-7367; FAX: 616-946-3289

Hondo Ind., 510 S. 52nd St., I04, Tempe, AZ 85281

Hoover, Harvey, 5750 Pearl Dr., Paradise, CA 95969-4829

Hoppe's Div. Penguin Industries, Inc., Airport Industrial Mall, Coatesville, PA 19320 / 610-384-6000

Horizons Unlimited, PO Box 426, Warm Springs, GA 31830 / 706-655-3603; FAX: 706-655-3603

Hornady Mfg. Co., P.O. Box 1848, Grand Island, NE 68802 / 800-338-3220 or 308-382-1390; FAX: 308-382-5761

Horseshoe Leather Products, Andy Arratoonian, The Cottage Sharow, Ripon, ENGLAND / 44-1765-605858

Houtz & Barwick, P.O. Box 435, W. Church St., Elizabeth City, NC 27909 / 800-775-0337 or 919-335-4191; FAX: 919-335-1152

Howa Machinery, Ltd., Sukaguchi, Shinkawa-cho Nishikasug-ai-gun, Aichi 452, JAPAN

Howell Machine, 815 1/2 D St., Lewiston, ID 83501 / 208-743-7418

Hoyt Holster Co., Inc., P.O. Box 69, Coupeville, WA 98239-0069 / 360-678-6640; FAX: 360-678-6549

HT Bullets, 244 Belleville Rd., New Bedford, MA 02745 / 508-999-3338

Hubert J. Hecht Waffen-Hecht, P.O. Box 2635, Fair Oaks, CA 95628 / 916-966-1020

Hubertus Schneidwarenfabrik, P.O. Box 180 106, D-42626, Solingen, GERMANY / 01149-212-59-19-94; FAX: 01149-212-59-19-92

Huebner, Corey O., P.O. Box 2074, Missoula, MT 59806-2074 / 406-721-7168

Huey Gun Cases, P.O. Box 22456, Kansas City, MO 64113 / 816-444-1637; FAX: 816-444-1637

Hugger Hooks Co., 3900 Easley Way, Golden, CO 80403 / 303-279-0600

Hughes, Steven Dodd, P.O. Box 545, Livingston, MT 59047 / 406-222-9377; FAX: 406-222-9377

Hume, Don, P.O. Box 351, Miami, OK 74355 / 800-331-2686 FAX: 918-542-4340

Hungry Horse Books, 4605 Hwy. 93 South, Whitefish, MT 59937 / 406-862-7997

Hunkeler, A (See Buckskin Machine Works, A. Hunkeler) 3235 S 358th St., Auburn, WA 98001 / 206-927-5412

Hunter Co., Inc., 3300 W. 71st Ave., Westminster, CO 80030 / 303-427-4626; FAX: 303-428-3980

Hunter's Specialties Inc., 6000 Huntington Ct. NE, Cedar Rapids, IA 52402-1268 / 319-395-0321; FAX: 319-395-0326

Hunterjohn, P.O. Box 771457, St. Louis, MO 63177 / 314-531-7250

Hunters Supply, Inc., PO Box 313, Tioga, TX 76271 / 940-437-2458; FAX: 940-437-2228 hunterssupply@hotmail.com hunterssupply.net

Hunting Classics Ltd., P.O. Box 2089, Gastonia, NC 28053 / 704-867-1307; FAX: 704-867-0491

Huntington Die Specialties, 601 Oro Dam Blvd., Oroville, CA 95965 / 530-534-1210; FAX: 530-534-1212

Hutton Rifle Ranch, P.O. Box 45236, Boise, ID 83711 / 208-345-8781

Hydrosorbent Products, P.O. Box 437, Ashley Falls, MA 01222 / 413-229-2967; or 800-229-8743 FAX: 413-229-8743 orders@dehumidify.com www.dehumidify.com

Hyper-Single, Inc., 520 E. Beaver, Jenks, OK 74037 / 918-299-2391

I

I.A.B. (See U.S. Importer-Taylor's & Co. Inc.)

I.D.S.A. Books, 1324 Stratford Drive, Piqua, OH 45356 / 937-773-4203; FAX: 937-778-1922

I.N.C. Inc (See Kick Eez)

I.S.S., P.O. Box 185234, Ft. Worth, TX 76181 / 817-595-2090

I.S.W., 106 E. Cairo Dr., Tempe, AZ 85282

IAR Inc., 33171 Camino Capistrano, San Juan Capistrano, CA 92675 / 949-443-3642; FAX: 949-443-3647

IGA (See U.S. Importer-Stoeger Industries)

Ignacio Ugartechea S.A., Chonta 26, Eibar, 20600 SPAIN / 43-121257; FAX: 43-121669

Illinois Lead Shop, 7742 W. 61st Place, Summit, IL 60501

Image Ind. Inc., 382 Balm Court, Wood Dale, IL 60191 / 630-766-2402; FAX: 630-766-7373

IMI, P.O. Box 1044, Ramat Hasharon, 47100 ISRAEL / 972-3-5485617; FAX: 972-3-5406908

IMI Services USA, Inc., 2 Wisconsin Circle, Suite 420, Chevy Chase, MD 20815 / 301-215-4800; FAX: 301-657-1446

Impact Case Co., P.O. Box 9912, Spokane, WA 99209-0912 / 800-262-3322 or 509-467-3303; FAX: 509-326-5436 kkair.com

Imperial (See E-Z-Way Systems), PO Box 4310, Newark, OH 43058-4310 / 614-345-6645; FAX: 614-345-6600

Imperial Magnum Corp., P.O. Box 249, Oroville, WA 98844 / 604-495-3131; FAX: 604-495-2816

Imperial Miniature Armory, 10547 S. Post Oak, Houston, TX 77035 / 713-729-8428 FAX: 713-729-2274

Imperial Schrade Corp., 7 Schrade Ct., Box 7000, Ellenville, NY 12428 / 914-647-7601; FAX: 914-647-8701

Import Sports Inc., 1750 Brielle Ave., Unit B1, Wanamassa, NJ 07712 / 908-493-0302; FAX: 908-493-0301

IMR Powder Co., 1080 Military Turnpike, Suite 2, Plattsburgh, NY 12901 / 518-563-2253; FAX: 518-563-6916

Info-Arm, P.O. Box 1262, Champlain, NY 12919 / 514-955-0355; FAX: 514-955-0357

Ingle, Ralph W., Engraver, 112 Manchester Ct., Centerville, GA 31028 / 912-953-5824

Innovative Weaponry Inc., 2513 E. Loop 820 N., Fort Worth, TX 76118 / 817-284-0099; or 800-334-3573

Innovision Enterprises, 728 Skinner Dr., Kalamazoo, MI 49001 / 616-382-1681 FAX: 616-382-1830

INTEC International, Inc., P.O. Box 5708, Scottsdale, AZ 85261 / 602-483-1708

Inter Ordnance of America LP, 3305 Westwood Industrial Dr, Monroe, NC 28110-5204 / 704-821-8337; FAX: 704-821-8523

Interarms/Howa, PO Box 208, Ten Prince St, Alexandria, VA 22313 / 703-548-1400; FAX: 703-549-7826

Intercontinental Distributors, Ltd., PO Box 815, Beulah, ND 58523

Intrac Arms International, 5005 Chapman Hwy., Knoxville, TN 37920

Intratec, 12405 SW 130th St., Miami, FL 33186-6224 / 305-232-1821; FAX: 305-253-7207

Ion Industries, Inc, 3508 E Allerton Ave, Cudahy, WI 53110 / 414-486-2007; FAX: 414-486-2017

Iosso Products, 1485 Lively Blvd., Elk Grove Village, IL 60007 / 847-437-8400; FAX: 847-437-8478

Iron Bench, 12619 Bailey Rd., Redding, CA 96003 / 916-241-4623

Ironside International Publishers, Inc., P.O. Box 55, 800 Slaters Lane, Alexandria, VA 22313 / 703-684-6111; FAX: 703-683-5486

Ironsighter Co., P.O. Box 85070, Westland, MI 48185 / 734-326-8731; FAX: 734-326-3378

Irwin, Campbell H., 140 Hartland Blvd., East Hartland, CT 06027 / 203-653-3901

Island Pond Gun Shop, Cross St., Island Pond, VT 05846 / 802-723-4546

Israel Arms International, Inc., 5709 Hartsdale, Houston, TX 77036 / 713-789-0745; FAX: 713-789-7513

Israel Military Industries Ltd. (See IMI), PO Box 1044, Ramat Hasharon, ISRAEL / 972-3-5485617; FAX: 972-3-5406908

Ithaca Classic Doubles, Stephen Lamboy, PO Box 665, Mendon, NY 14506 / 706-569-6760; FAX: 706-561-9248

Ithaca Gun Co. LLC, 891 Route 34-B, King Ferry, NY 13081 / 888-9ITHACA; FAX: 315-364-5134

Ivanoff, Thomas G (See Tom's Gun Repair)

J

J J Roberts Firearm Engraver, 7808 Lake Dr, Manassas, VA 20111 / 703-330-0448 FAX: 703-264-8600

J Martin Inc, PO Drawer AP, Beckley, WV 25802 / 304-255-4073; FAX: 304-255-4077

J&D Components, 75 East 350 North, Orem, UT 84057-4719 / 801-225-7007

J&J Products, Inc., 9240 Whitmore, El Monte, CA 91731 / 818-571-5228; FAX: 800-927-8361

J&J Sales, 1501 21st Ave. S., Great Falls, MT 59405 / 406-453-7549

J&L Superior Bullets (See Huntington Die Specialties)

J&R Engineering, P.O. Box 77, 200 Lyons Hill Rd., Athol, MA 01331 / 508-249-9241

J&R Enterprises, 4550 Scotts Valley Rd., Lakeport, CA 95453

J&S Heat Treat, 803 S. 16th St., Blue Springs, MO 64015 / 816-229-2149; FAX: 816-228-1135

J-4 Inc., 1700 Via Burton, Anaheim, CA 92806 / 714-254-8315; FAX: 714-956-4421

J-Gar Co., 183 Turnpike Rd., Dept. 3, Petersham, MA 01366-9604

J. Dewey Mfg. Co., Inc., P.O. Box 2014, Southbury, CT 06488 / 203-264-3064; FAX: 203-262-6907

J. Korzinek Riflesmith, RD 2, Box 73D, Canton, PA 17724 / 717-673-8512

J.A. Blades, Inc. (See Christopher Firearms Co.,)

J.A. Henckels Zwillingswerk Inc., 9 Skyline Dr., Hawthorne, NY 10532 / 914-592-7370

J.G. Dapkus Co., Inc., Commerce Circle, P.O. Box 293, Durham, CT 06422

J.I.T. Ltd., P.O. Box 230, Freedom, WY 83120 / 708-494-0937

J.J. Roberts/Engraver, 7808 Lake Dr., Manassas, VA 22111 / 703-330-0448

J.M. Bucheimer Jumbo Sports Products, 721 N. 20th St., St. Louis, MO 63103 / 314-241-1020

J.P. Enterprises Inc., P.O. Box 26324, Shoreview, MN 55126 / 612-486-9064; FAX: 612-482-0970

J.P. Gunstocks, Inc., 4508 San Miguel Ave., North Las Vegas, NV 89030 / 702-645-0718

J.R. Blair Engraving, P.O. Box 64, Glenrock, WY 82637 / 307-436-8115

J.R. Williams Bullet Co., 2008 Tucker Rd., Perry, GA 31069 / 912-987-0274

J.W. Morrison Custom Rifles, 4015 W. Sharon, Phoenix, AZ 85029 / 602-978-3754

J/B Adventures & Safaris Inc., 2275 E. Arapahoe Rd., Ste. 109, Littleton, CO 80122-1521 / 303-771-0977

Jack Dever Co., 8590 NW 90, Oklahoma City, OK 73132 / 405-721-6393

Jack A. Rosenberg & Sons, 12229 Cox Ln., Dallas, TX 75234 / 214-241-6302

Jack First, Inc., 1201 Turbine Dr., Rapid City, SD 57701 / 605-343-9544; FAX: 605-343-9420

Jackalope Gun Shop, 1048 S. 5th St., Douglas, WY 82633 / 307-358-3441

Jaffin, Harry. (See BRIDGEMAN PRODUCTS)

Jagdwaffen, P. Hofer, Buchsenmachermeister, Kirchgasse 24 A-9170, Ferlach, AUSTRIA / 04227-3683

James Calhoon Varmint Bullets, Shambo Rt., 304, Havre, MT 59501 / 406-395-4079

James Churchill Glove Co., P.O. Box 298, Centralia, WA 98531

James Calhoon Mfg., Rt. 304, Havre, MT 59501 / 406-395-4079

James Wayne Firearms for Collectors and Investors, 2608 N. Laurent, Victoria, TX 77901 / 512-578-1258; FAX: 512-578-3559

Jamison's Forge Works, 4527 Rd. 6.5 NE, Moses Lake, WA 98837 / 509-762-2659

Jantz Supply, P.O. Box 584-GD, Davis, OK 73030-0584 / 580-369-2316; FAX: 580-369-3082

Jarrett Rifles, Inc., 383 Brown Rd., Jackson, SC 29831 / 803-471-3616

Jarvis, Inc., 1123 Cherry Orchard Lane, Hamilton, MT 59840 / 406-961-4392

JAS, Inc., P.O. Box 0, Rosemount, MN 55068 / 612-890-7631

Javelina Lube Products, P.O. Box 337, San Bernardino, CA 92402 / 714-882-5847; FAX: 714-434-6937

JB Custom, P.O. Box 6912, Leawood, KS 66206 / 913-381-2329

Jeff W. Flannery Engraving Co., 11034 Riddles Run Rd., Union, KY 41091 / 606-384-3127

Jeffredo Gunsight, P.O. Box 669, San Marcos, CA 92079 / 619-728-2695

Jena Eur, PO Box 319, Dunmore, PA 18512

Jenco Sales, Inc., P.O. Box 1000, Manchaca, TX 78652 / 800-531-5301 FAX: 800-266-2373

Jenkins Recoil Pads, Inc., 5438 E. Frontage Ln., Olney, IL 62450 / 618-395-3416

Jensen Bullets, 86 North, 400 West, Blackfoot, ID 83221 / 208-785-5590

Jensen's Custom Ammunition, 5146 E. Pima, Tucson, AZ 85712 / 602-325-3346 FAX: 602-322-5704

Jensen's Firearms Academy, 1280 W. Prince, Tucson, AZ 85705 / 602-293-8516

Jericho Tool & Die Co., Inc., RD 3 Box 70, Route 7, Bainbridge, NY 13733-9496 / 607-563-8222; FAX: 607-563-8560

Jerry Phillips Optics, P.O. Box L632, Langhorne, PA 19047 / 215-757-5037 FAX: 215-757-7097

Jesse W. Smith Saddlery, 16909 E. Jackson Road, Elk, WA 99009-9600 / 509-325-0622

Jester Bullets, Rt. 1 Box 27, Orienta, OK 73737

Jewell Triggers, Inc., 3620 Hwy. 123, San Marcos, TX 78666 / 512-353-2999

JGS Precision Tool Mfg., 100 Main Sumner, Coos Bay, OR 97420 / 541-267-4331 FAX: 541-267-5996

Jim Chambers Flintlocks Ltd., Rt. 1, Box 513-A, Candler, NC 28715 / 704-667-8361

Jim Garthwaite Pistolsmith, Inc., Rt. 2 Box 310, Watsontown, PA 17777 / 717-538-1566

Jim Noble Co., 1305 Columbia St, Vancouver, WA 98660 / 360-695-1309; FAX: 360-695-6835 jnobleco@aol.com

Jim Norman Custom Gunstocks, 14281 Cane Rd., Valley Center, CA 92082 / 619-749-6252

Jim's Gun Shop (See Spradlin's)

Jim's Precision, Jim Ketchum, 1725 Moclips Dr., Petaluma, CA 94952 / 707-762-3014

JLK Bullets, 414 Turner Rd., Dover, AR 72837 / 501-331-4194

Johanssons Vapentillbehor, Bert, S-430 20, Veddige, SWEDEN

John Hall Plastics, Inc., P.O. Box 1526, Alvin, TX 77512 / 713-489-8709

John J. Adams & Son Engravers, PO Box 66, Vershire, VT 05079 / 802-685-0019

John Masen Co. Inc., 1305 Jelmak, Grand Prairie, TX 75050 / 817-430-8732; FAX: 817-430-1715

John Norrell Arms, 2608 Grist Mill Rd, Little Rock, AR 72207 / 501-225-7864

John Partridge Sales Ltd., Trent Meadows Rugeley, Staffordshire, WS15 2HS ENGLAND

John Rigby & Co., 66 Great Suffolk St., London, SE1 0BU ENGLAND / 0171-620-0690; FAX: 0171-928-9205

John Unertl Optical Co., Inc., 308-310 Clay Ave., Mars, PA 16046-0818 / 724-625-3810

John's Custom Leather, 523 S. Liberty St., Blairsville, PA 15717 / 412-459-6802

Johnny Stewart Game Calls, Inc., P.O. Box 7954, 5100 Fort Ave., Waco, TX 76714 / 817-772-3261; FAX: 817-772-3670

Johnson Wood Products, 34968 Crystal Road, Strawberry Point, IA 52076 / 319-933-4930

Johnson's Gunsmithing, Inc, Neal, 208 W Buchanan St, Ste B, Colorado Springs, CO 80907 / 800-284-8671; FAX: 719-632-3493

Johnston Bros. (See C&T Corp. TA Johnson Brothers)

Johnston, James (See North Fork Custom Gunsmithing, James Johnston)

Jonad Corp., 2091 Lakeland Ave., Lakewood, OH 44107 / 216-226-3161

Jonathan Arthur Ciener, Inc., 8700 Commerce St., Cape Canaveral, FL 32920 / 407-868-2200; FAX: 407-868-2201

Jones Co., Dale, 680 Hoffman Draw, Kila, MT 59920 / 406-755-4684

Jones Custom Products, Neil A., 17217 Brookhouser Rd., Saegertown, PA 16433 / 814-763-2769; FAX: 814-763-4228

Jones Moulds, Paul, 4901 Telegraph Rd, Los Angeles, CA 90022 / 213-262-1510

Jones, J.D./SSK Industries, 590 Woodvue Ln., Wintersville, OH 43953 / 740-264-0176; FAX: 740-264-2257

JP Sales, Box 307, Anderson, TX 77830

JRP Custom Bullets, RR2 2233 Carlton Rd., Whitehall, NY 12887 / 518-282-0084 or 802-438-5548

JS Worldwide DBA (See Coonan Arms)

JSL Ltd (See U.S. Importer-Specialty Shooters Supply, Inc.)

Juenke, Vern, 25 Bitterbush Rd., Reno, NV 89523 / 702-345-0225

Jumbo Sports Products, J. M. Bucheimer, 721 N. 20th St., St. Louis, MO 63103 / 314-241-1020

Jungkind, Reeves C., 5001 Buckskin Pass, Austin, TX 78745-2841 / 512-442-1094

Jurras, L. E., P.O. Box 680, Washington, IN 47501 / 812-254-7698

Justin Phillippi Custom Bullets, P.O. Box 773, Ligonier, PA 15658 / 412-238-9671

K

K&M Industries, Inc., Box 66, 510 S. Main, Troy, ID 83871 / 208-835-2281; FAX: 208-835-5211

K&M Services, 5430 Salmon Run Rd., Dover, PA 17315 / 717-292-3175; FAX: 717-292-3175

K-D, Inc., Box 459, 585 N. Hwy. 155, Cleveland, UT 84518 / 801-653-2530

K-Sports Imports Inc., 2755 Thompson Creek Rd., Pomona, CA 91767 / 909-392-2345 FAX: 909-392-2354

K. Eversull Co., Inc., 1 Tracemont, Boyce, LA 71409 / 318-793-8728

K.B.I. Inc, PO Box 6625, Harrisburg, PA 17112 / 717-540-8518; FAX: 717-540-8567

K.K. Arms Co., Star Route Box 671, Kerrville, TX 78028 / 210-257-4718 FAX: 210-257-4891

K.L. Null Holsters Ltd., 161 School St. NW, Hill City Station, Resaca, GA 30735 / 706-625-5643; FAX: 706-625-9392

Ka Pu Kapili, P.O. Box 745, Honokaa, HI 96727 / 808-776-1644; FAX: 808-776-1731

KA-BAR Knives, 1116 E. State St., Olean, NY 14760 / 800-282-0130; FAX: 716-373-6245

Kahles A Swarovski Company, 1 Wholesale Way, Cranston, RI 02920-5540 / 401-946-2220; FAX: 401-946-2587

Kahr Arms, P.O. Box 220, 630 Route 303, Blauvelt, NY 10913 / 914-353-5996; FAX: 914-353-7833

Kalispel Case Line, P.O. Box 267, Cusick, WA 99119 / 509-445-1121

Kamik Outdoor Footwear, 554 Montee de Liesse, Montreal, PQ H4T 1P1 CANADA / 514-341-3950; FAX: 514-341-1861

Kamyk Engraving Co., Steve, 9 Grandview Dr, Westfield, MA 01085-1810 / 413-568-0457

Kane, Edward, P.O. Box 385, Ukiah, CA 95482 / 707-462-2937

Kane Products, Inc., 5572 Brecksville Rd., Cleveland, OH 44131 / 216-524-9962

Kapro Mfg.Co. Inc. (See R.E.I.)

Kasenit Co., Inc., 13 Park Ave., Highland Mills, NY 10930 / 914-928-9595; FAX: 914-928-7292

Kasmarsik Bullets, 4016 7th Ave. SW, Puyallup, WA 98373

Kaswer Custom, Inc., 13 Surrey Drive, Brookfield, CT 06804 / 203-775-0564; FAX: 203-775-6872

KDF, Inc., 2485 Hwy. 46 N., Seguin, TX 78155 / 210-379-8141; FAX: 210-379-5420

KeeCo Impressions, Inc., 346 Wood Ave., North Brunswick, NJ 08902 / 800-468-0546

Keeler, R. H., 817 "N" St., Port Angeles, WA 98362 / 206-457-4702

Kehr, Roger, 2131 Agate Ct. SE, Lacy, WA 98503 / 360-456-0831

Keith's Bullets, 942 Twisted Oak, Algonquin, IL 60102 / 708-658-3520

Keith's Custom Gunstocks (See Heppler, Keith M)

Keith's Custom Gunstocks, Keith M Heppler, 540 Banyan Circle, Walnut Creek, CA 94598 / 925-934-3509; FAX: 925-934-3143

Kel-Tec CNC Industries, Inc., P.O. Box 3427, Cocoa, FL 32924 / 407-631-0068; FAX: 407-631-1169

Kelbly, Inc., 7222 Dalton Fox Lake Rd., North Lawrence, OH 44666 / 216-683-4674; FAX: 216-683-7349

Kelley's, P.O. Box 125, Woburn, MA 01801 / 617-935-3389

Kellogg's Professional Products, 325 Pearl St., Sandusky, OH 44870 / 419-625-6551; FAX: 419-625-6167

Kelly, Lance, 1723 Willow Oak Dr., Edgewater, FL 32132 / 904-423-4933

Kemen America, 2550 Hwy. 23, Wrenshall, MN 55797

Ken Eyster Heritage Gunsmiths, Inc., 6441 Bishop Rd., Centerburg, OH 43011 / 614-625-6131

Ken Starnes Gunmaker, 15940 SW Holly Hill Rd, Hillsboro, OR 97123-9033 / 503-628-0705; FAX: 503-628-6005

Ken's Gun Specialties, Rt. 1, Box 147, Lakeview, AR 72642 / 501-431-5606

Ken's Kustom Kartridges, 331 Jacobs Rd., Hubbard, OH 44425 / 216-534-4595

Ken's Rifle Blanks, Ken McCullough, Rt. 2, P.O. Box 85B, Weston, OR 97886 / 503-566-3879

Keng's Firearms Specialty, Inc./US Tactical Systems, 875 Wharton Dr., P.O. Box 44405, Atlanta, GA 30336-1405 / 404-691-7611; FAX: 404-505-8445

Kennebec Journal, 274 Western Ave., Augusta, ME 04330 / 207-622-6288

Kennedy Firearms, 10 N. Market St., Muncy, PA 17756 / 717-546-6695

Kenneth W. Warren Engraver, P.O. Box 2842, Wenatchee, WA 98807 / 509-663-6123 FAX: 509-665-6123

KenPatable Ent., Inc., P.O. Box 19422, Louisville, KY 40259 / 502-239-5447

Kent Cartridge America, Inc, PO Box 849, 1000 Zigor Rd, Kearneysville, WV 25430

Kent Cartridge Mfg. Co. Ltd., Unit 16 Branbridges Industrial Esta, Tonbridge, Kent, ENGLAND / 622-872255; FAX: 622-872645

Keowee Game Calls, 608 Hwy. 25 North, Travelers Rest, SC 29690 / 864-834-7204; FAX: 864-834-7831

Kershaw Knives, 25300 SW Parkway Ave., Wilsonville, OR 97070 / 503-682-1966 or 800-325-2891; FAX: 503-682-7168

Kesselring Gun Shop, 400 Hwy. 99 North, Burlington, WA 98233 / 206-724-3113; FAX: 206-724-7003

Ketchum, Jim (See Jim's Precision)

Kickeez Inc, 301 Industrial Dr, Carl Junction, MO 64834-8806 / 419-649-2100; FAX: 417-649-2200 kickey@ipa.net

Kilham & Co., Main St., P.O. Box 37, Lyme, NH 03768 / 603-795-4112

Kim Ahrends Custom Firearms, Inc., Box 203, Clarion, IA 50525 / 515-532-3449; FAX: 515-532-3926

Kimar (See U.S. Importer-IAR,Inc)

Kimball, Gary, 1526 N. Circle Dr., Colorado Springs, CO 80909 / 719-634-1274

Kimber of America, Inc., 1 Lawton St., Yonkers, NY 10705 / 800-880-2418; FAX: 914-964-9340

King & Co., P.O. Box 1242, Bloomington, IL 61702 / 309-473-2161

King's Gun Works, 1837 W. Glenoaks Blvd., Glendale, CA 91201 / 818-956-6010; FAX: 818-548-8606

Kingyon, Paul L. (See Custom Calls)

Kirkpatrick Leather Co., PO Box 677, Laredo, TX 78040 / 956-723-6631; FAX: 956-725-0672

KK Air International (See Impact Case Co.)

KLA Enterprises, P.O. Box 2028, Eaton Park, FL 33840 / 941-682-2829 FAX: 941-682-2829

Kleen-Bore, Inc., 16 Industrial Pkwy., Easthampton, MA 01027 / 413-527-0300; FAX: 413-527-2522 info@kleen-bore.com www.kleen-bore.com

Klein Custom Guns, Don, 433 Murray Park Dr., Ripon, WI 54971 / 920-748-2931

DIRECTORY

Kleinendorst, K. W., RR 1, Box 1500, Hop Bottom, PA 18824 / 717-289-4687

Klingler Woodcarving, P.O. Box 141, Thistle Hill, Cabot, VT 05647 / 802-426-3811

Kmount, P.O. Box 19422, Louisville, KY 40259 / 502-239-5447

Kneiper, James, P.O. Box 1516, Basalt, CO 81621-1516 / 303-963-9880

Knife Importers, Inc., P.O. Box 1000, Manchaca, TX 78652 / 512-282-6860

Knight & Hale Game Calls, Box 468, Industrial Park, Cadiz, KY 42211 / 502-924-1755; FAX: 502-924-1763

Knight Rifles, 21852 hwy j46, P.O. Box 130, Centerville, IA 52544 / 515-856-2626; FAX: 515-856-2628

Knight Rifles (See Modern Muzzle Loading, Inc.)

Knight's Mfg. Co., 7750 9th St. SW, Vero Beach, FL 32968 / 561-562-5697; FAX: 561-569-2955

Knippel, Richard, 500 Gayle Ave Apt 213, Modesto, CA 95350-4241 / 209-869-1469

Knock on Wood Antiques, 355 Post Rd., Darien, CT 06820 / 203-655-9031

Knoell, Doug, 9737 McCardle Way, Santee, CA 92071

Koevenig's Engraving Service, Box 55 Rabbit Gulch, Hill City, SD 57745 / 605-574-2239

KOGOT, 410 College, Trinidad, CO 81082 / 719-846-9406 FAX: 719-846-9406

Kokolus, Michael M. (See Custom Riflestocks, Inc., Michael M. Kokolus)

Kolar, 1925 Roosevelt Ave, Racine, WI 53406 / 414-554-0800; FAX: 414-554-9093

Kolpin Mfg., Inc., P.O. Box 107, 205 Depot St., Fox Lake, WI 53933 / 414-928-3118; FAX: 414-928-3687

Korth, Robert-Bosch-Str. 4, P.O. Box 1320, 23909 Ratzeburg, GERMANY / 451-4991497; FAX: 451-4993230

Korzinek Riflesmith, J, RD 2 Box 73D, Canton, PA 17724 / 717-673-8512

Koval Knives, 5819 Zarley St., Suite A, New Albany, OH 43054 / 614-855-0777; FAX: 614-855-0945

Kowa Optimed, Inc., 20001 S. Vermont Ave., Torrance, CA 90502 / 310-327-1913; FAX: 310-327-4177

Kramer Designs, P.O. Box 129, Clancy, MT 59634 / 406-933-8658; FAX: 406-933-8658

Kramer Handgun Leather, P.O. Box 112154, Tacoma, WA 98411 / 206-564-6652; FAX: 206-564-1214

Krause Publications, Inc., 700 E. State St., Iola, WI 54990 / 715-445-2214; FAX: 715-445-4087

Krico Jagd-und Sportwaffen GmbH, Nurnbergerstrasse 6, D-90602, Pyrbaum, GERMANY / 09180-2780; FAX: 09180-2661

Krieger Barrels, Inc., N114 W18697 Clinton Dr., Germantown, WI 53022 / 414-255-9593; FAX: 414-255-9586

Krieghoff Gun Co., H., Boschstrasse 22, D-89079 Elm, GERMA-NY or 731-4018270

Krieghoff International,Inc., 7528 Easton Rd., Ottsville, PA 18942 / 610-847-5173; FAX: 610-847-8691

Kris Mounts, 108 Lehigh St., Johnstown, PA 15905 / 814-539-9751

KSN Industries Ltd (See U.S. Importer-Israel Arms International, Inc.,)

Kudlas, John M., 622 14th St. SE, Rochester, MN 55904 / 507-288-5579

Kulis Freeze Dry Taxidermy, 725 Broadway Ave., Bedford, OH 44146 / 216-232-8352; FAX: 216-232-7305 jkulis@kast-away.com

KVH Industries, Inc., 110 Enterprise Center, Middletown, RI 02842 / 401-847-3327; FAX: 401-849-0045

Kwik Mount Corp., P.O. Box 19422, Louisville, KY 40259 / 502-239-5447

Kwik-Site Co., 5555 Treadwell, Wayne, MI 48184 / 734-326-1500; FAX: 734-326-4120

L

L&R Lock Co., 1137 Pocalla Rd., Sumter, SC 29150 / 803-775-6127 FAX: 803-775-5171

L&S Technologies Inc (See Aimtech Mount Systems)

L. Bengtson Arms Co., 6345-B E. Akron St., Mesa, AZ 85205 / 602-981-6375

L.A.R. Mfg., Inc., 4133 W. Farm Rd., West Jordan, UT 84088 / 801-280-3505; FAX: 801-280-1972

L.E. Wilson, Inc., Box 324, 404 Pioneer Ave., Cashmere, WA 98815 / 509-782-1328; FAX: 509-782-7200

L.L. Bean, Inc., Freeport, ME 04032 / 207-865-4761; FAX: 207-552-2802

L.P.A. Snc, Via Alfieri 26, Gardone V.T., Brescia, ITALY / 30-891-14-81; FAX: 30-891-09-51

L.R. Clift Mfg., 3821 Hammonton Rd., Marysville, CA 95901 / 916-755-3390; FAX: 916-755-3393

L.S. Starrett Co., 121 Crescent St., Athol, MA 01331 / 617-249-3551

L.W. Seecamp Co., Inc., P.O. Box 255, New Haven, CT 06502 / 203-877-3429

La Clinique du .45, 1432 Rougemont, Chambly,, PQ J3L 2L8 CANADA / 514-658-1144

Labanu, Inc., 2201-F Fifth Ave., Ronkonkoma, NY 11779 / 516-467-6197; FAX: 516-981-4112

LaBoone, Pat. (See CLEAR CREEK OUTDOORS)

LaBounty Precision Reboring, Inc, 7968 Silver Lake Rd., PO Box 186, Maple Falls, WA 98266 / 360-599-2047 FAX: 360-599-3018

LaCrosse Footwear, Inc., P.O. Box 1328, La Crosse, WI 54602 / 608-782-3020 or 800-323-2668; FAX: 800-658-9444

LaFrance Specialties, P.O. Box 87933, San Diego, CA 92138-7933 / 619-293-3373; FAX: 619-293-7087

Lage Uniwad, P.O. Box 2302, Davenport, IA 52809 / 319-388-LAGE; FAX: 319-388-LAGE

Lair, Sam, 520 E. Beaver, Jenks, OK 74037 / 918-299-2391

Lake Center, P.O. Box 38, St. Charles, MO 63302 / 314-946-7500

Lakefield Arms Ltd (See Savage Arms Inc)

Lakewood Products LLC, 275 June St., Berlin, WI 54923 / 920-361-7719

Lamboy, Stephen. (See ITHACA CLASSIC DOUBLES)

Lampert, Ron, Rt. 1, Box 177, Guthrie, MN 56461 / 218-854-7345

Lamson & Goodnow Mfg. Co., 45 Conway St., Shelburne Falls, MA 03170 / 413-625-6564; or 800-872-6564 FAX: 413-625-9816 www.lamsonsharp.com

Lanber Armas, S.A., Zubiaurre 5, Zaldibar, 48250 SPAIN / 34-4-6827702; FAX: 34-4-6827999

Langenberg Hat Co., P.O. Box 1860, Washington, MO 63090 / 800-428-1860; FAX: 314-239-3151

Lanphert, Paul, P.O. Box 1985, Wenatchee, WA 98807

Lansky Levine, Arthur. (See LANSKY SHARPENERS)

Lansky Sharpeners, Arthur Lansky Levine, PO Box 50830, Las Vegas, NV 89016 / 702-361-7511; FAX: 702-896-9511

Lapua Ltd., P.O. Box 5, Lapua, FINLAND / 6-310111; FAX: 6-4388991

LaRocca Gun Works, 51 Union Place, Worcester, MA 01608 / 508-754-2887; FAX: 508-754-2887

Larry Lyons Gunworks, 110 Hamilton St., Dowagiac, MI 49047 / 616-782-9478

Laser Devices, Inc., 2 Harris Ct. A-4, Monterey, CA 93940 / 408-373-0701; FAX: 408-373-0903

Laseraim Technologies, Inc., P.O. Box 3548, Little Rock, AR 72203 / 501-375-2227

LaserMax, Inc., 3495 Winton Place, Bldg. B, Rochester, NY 14623-2807 / 800-527-3703 FAX: 716-272-5427

Lassen Community College, Gunsmithing Dept., P.O. Box 3000, Hwy. 139, Susanville, CA 96130 / 916-251-8800; FAX: 916-251-8838

Lathrop's, Inc., Inc., 5146 E. Pima, Tucson, AZ 85712 / 520-881-0266 or 800-875-4867; FAX: 520-322-5704

Laughridge, William R (See Cylinder & Slide Inc)

Laurel Mountain Forge, P.O. Box 52, Crown Point, IN 46065 / 219-548-2950; FAX: 219-548-2950

Laurona Armas Eibar, S.A.L., Avenida de Otaola 25, P.O. Box 260, Eibar 20600, SPAIN / 34-43-700600; FAX: 34-43-700616

Lawrence Brand Shot (See Precision Reloading, Inc.)

Lawrence Leather Co., P.O. Box 1479, Lillington, NC 27546 / 910-893-2071; FAX: 910-893-4742

Lawson Co., Harry, 3328 N Richey Blvd., Tucson, AZ 85716 / 520-326-1117 FAX: 520-326-1117

Lawson, John. (See THE SIGHT SHOP)

Lawson, John G (See Sight Shop, The)

Lazzeroni Arms Co., PO Box 26696, Tucson, AZ 85726 / 888-492-7247; FAX: 520-624-4250

LBT, HCR 62, Box 145, Moyie Springs, ID 83845 / 208-267-3588

Le Clear Industries (See E-Z-Way Systems), PO Box 4310, Newark, OH 43058-4310 / 614-345-6645; FAX: 614-345-6600

Lea Mfg. Co., 237 E. Aurora St., Waterbury, CT 06720 / 203-753-5116

Leapers, Inc., 7675 Five Mile Rd., Northville, MI 48167 / 248-486-1231; FAX: 248-486-1430

Leatherman Tool Group, Inc., 12106 NE Ainsworth Cir., P.O. Box 20595, Portland, OR 97294 / 503-253-7826; FAX: 503-253-7830

Lebeau-Courally, Rue St. Gilles, 386 4000, Liege, BELGIUM / 042-52-48-43; FAX: 32-042-52-20-08

Leckie Professional Gunsmithing, 546 Quarry Rd., Ottsville, PA 18942 / 215-847-8594

Lectro Science, Inc., 6410 W. Ridge Rd., Erie, PA 16506 / 814-833-6487; FAX: 814-833-0447

Ledbetter Airguns, Riley, 1804 E Sprague St, Winston Salem, NC 27107-3521 / 919-784-0676

Lee Co., T. K., 1282 Branchwater Ln, Birmingham, AL 35216 / 205-913-5222

Lee Precision, Inc., 4275 Hwy. U, Hartford, WI 53027 / 414-673-3075; FAX: 414-673-9273 leeprecision.com

Lee Supplies, Mark, 9901 France Ct., Lakeville, MN 55044 / 612-461-2114

Lee's Red Ramps, 4 Kristine Ln., Silver City, NM 88061 / 505-538-8529

LeFever Arms Co., Inc., 6234 Stokes, Lee Center Rd., Lee Center, NY 13363 / 315-337-6722; FAX: 315-337-1543

Legacy Sports International, 10 Prince St., Alexandria, VA 22314

Legend Products Corp., 21218 Saint Andrews Blvd., Boca Raton, FL 33433-2435

Leibowitz, Leonard, 1205 Murrayhill Ave., Pittsburgh, PA 15217 / 412-361-5455

Leica USA, Inc., 156 Ludlow Ave., Northvale, NJ 07647 / 201-767-7500; FAX: 201-767-8666

LEM Gun Specialties Inc. The Lewis Lead Remover, P.O. Box 2855, Peachtree City, GA 30269-2024

Leonard Day, 6 Linseed Rd Box 1, West Hatfield, MA 01088-7505 / 413-337-8369

Les Baer Custom,Inc., 29601 34th Ave., Hillsdale, IL 61257 / 309-658-2716; FAX: 309-658-2610

Lestrom Laboratories, Inc., P.O. Box 628, Mexico, NY 13114-0628 / 315-343-3076; FAX: 315-592-3370

Lethal Force Institute (See Police Bookshelf), PO Box 122, Concord, NH 03301 / 603-224-6814; FAX: 603-226-3554

Lett Custom Grips, 672 Currier Rd., Hopkinton, NH 03229-2652 / 800-421-5388 FAX: 603-226-4580

Leupold & Stevens, Inc., 14400 NW Greenbrier Pky., Beaverton, OR 97006 / 503-646-9171; FAX: 503-526-1455

Lever Arms Service Ltd., 2131 Burrard St., Vancouver, BC V6J 3H7 CANADA / 604-736-2711; FAX: 604-738-3503

Lew Horton Dist. Co., Inc., 15 Walkup Dr., Westboro, MA 01581 / 508-366-7400; FAX: 508-366-5332

Liberty Metals, 2233 East 16th St., Los Angeles, CA 90021 / 213-581-9171; FAX: 213-581-9351

Liberty Safe, 1060 N. Spring Creek Pl., Springville, UT 84663 / 800-247-5625; FAX: 801-489-6409

Liberty Shooting Supplies, P.O. Box 357, Hillsboro, OR 97123 / 503-640-5518; FAX: 503-640-5518

Liberty Trouser Co., 3500 6 Ave S., Birmingham, AL 35222-2406 / 205-251-9143

Lightfield Ammunition Corp. (See Slug Group, Inc.), PO Box 376, New Paris, PA 15554 / 814-839-4517; FAX: 814-839-2601

Lightforce U.S.A. Inc., 19226 66th Ave. So., L-103, Kent, WA 98032 / 206-656-1577; FAX: 206-656-1578

Lightning Performance Innovations, Inc., RD1 Box 555, Mohawk, NY 13407 / 800-242-5873; FAX: 315-866-1578

Lilja Precision Rifle Barrels, P.O. Box 372, Plains, MT 59859 / 406-826-3084; FAX: 406-826-3083 lilja@riflebarrels.com www.riflebarrel.com

Lincoln, Dean, Box 1886, Farmington, NM 87401

Lind Custom Guns, Al, 7821 76th Ave SW, Tacoma, WA 98498 / 253-584-6361 lindcustguns@worldnet.att.net

Linder Solingen Knives, 4401 Sentry Dr., Tucker, GA 30084 / 770-939-6915; FAX: 770-939-6738

Lindsay, Steve, RR 2 Cedar Hills, Kearney, NE 68847 / 308-236-7885

Lindsley Arms Cartridge Co., P.O. Box 757, 20 College Hill Rd., Henniker, NH 03242 / 603-428-3127

Linebaugh Custom Sixguns, Route 2, Box 100, Maryville, MO 64468 / 660-562-3031 sitgunner.com

Lion Country Supply, P.O. Box 480, Port Matilda, PA 16870

List Precision Engineering, Unit 1 Ingley Works, 13 River Road, Barking, ENGLAND / 011-081-594-1686

Lithi Bee Bullet Lube, 1728 Carr Rd., Muskegon, MI 49442 / 616-788-4479

"Little John's" Antique Arms, 1740 W. Laveta, Orange, CA 92668

Little Trees Ramble (See Scott Pilkington, Little

Littler Sales Co., 20815 W. Chicago, Detroit, MI 48228 / 313-273-6888; FAX: 313-273-1099

Littleton, J. F., 275 Pinedale Ave., Oroville, CA 95966 / 916-533-6084

Ljutic Industries, Inc., 732 N. 16th Ave., Suite 22, Yakima, WA 98907 / 509-248-0476; FAX: 509-576-8233

Llama Gabilondo Y Cia, Apartado 290, E-01080, Victoria, spain, SPAIN

Loch Leven Industries, P.O. Box 2751, Santa Rosa, CA 95405 / 707-573-8735; FAX: 707-573-0369

Lock's Philadelphia Gun Exchange, 6700 Rowland Ave., Philadelphia, PA 19149 / 215-332-6225; FAX: 215-332-4800

Lodewick, Walter H., 2816 NE Halsey St., Portland, OR 97232 / 503-284-2554

Log Cabin Sport Shop, 8010 Lafayette Rd., Lodi, OH 44254 / 330-948-1082; FAX: 330-948-4307

Logan, Harry M., Box 745, Honokaa, HI 96727 / 808-776-1644

Lohman Mfg. Co., Inc., 4500 Doniphan Dr., P.O. Box 220, Neosho, MO 64850 / 417-451-4438; FAX: 417-451-2576

Lomont Precision Bullets, RR 1, Box 34, Salmon, ID 83467 / 208-756-6819; FAX: 208-756-6824

London Guns Ltd., Box 3750, Santa Barbara, CA 93130 / 805-683-4141; FAX: 805-683-1712

Lone Star Gunleather, 1301 Brushy Bend Dr., Round Rock, TX 78681 / 512-255-1805

Lone Star Rifle Company, 11231 Rose Road, Conroe, TX 77303 / 409-856-3363

Long, George F., 1500 Rogue River Hwy., Ste. F, Grants Pass, OR 97527 / 541-476-7552

Lortone Inc., 2856 NW Market St., Seattle, WA 98107

Lothar Walther Precision Tool Inc., 3425 Hutchinson Rd., Cumming, GA 30040 / 770-889-9998; FAX: 770-889-4918 lotharwalther@mindspring.com www.lothar-walther.com

Loweth, Richard H.R., 29 Hedgegrow Lane, Kirby Muxloe, Leics, LE9 2BN ENGLAND / (0) 116 238 6295

LPS Laboratories, Inc., 4647 Hugh Howell Rd., P.O. Box 3050, Tucker, GA 30084 / 404-934-7800

Lucas, Edward E, 32 Garfield Ave., East Brunswick, NJ 08816 / 201-251-5526

Lucas, Mike, 1631 Jessamine Rd., Lexington, SC 29073

Lupton, Keith. (See PAWLING MOUNTAIN CLUB)

Lutz Engraving, Ron E., E1998 Smokey Valley Rd, Scandinavia, WI 54977 / 715-467-2674

Lyman Instant Targets, Inc. (See Lyman Products, Corp.)

Lyman Products Corp., 475 Smith Street, Middletown, CT 06457-1541 / 860-632-2020 or 800-22-LYMAN FAX: 860-632-1699

Lyman Products Corporation, 475 Smith Street, Middletown, CT 06457-1529 / 800-22-LYMAN or 860-632-2020; FAX: 860-632-1699

Lyte Optronics (See TracStar Industries Inc)

M

M. Thys (See U.S. Importer-Champlin Firearms Inc)

M.H. Canjar Co., 500 E. 45th Ave., Denver, CO 80216 / 303-295-2638; FAX: 303-295-2638

M.O.A. Corp., 2451 Old Camden Pike, Eaton, OH 45320 / 937-456-3669

MA Systems, P.O. Box 1143, Chouteau, OK 74337 / 918-479-6378

Mac-1 Airgun Distributors, 13974 Van Ness Ave., Gardena, CA 90249 / 310-327-3581; FAX: 310-327-0238 mac1@concentric.net mac1airgun.com

Macbean, Stan, 754 North 1200 West, Orem, UT 84057 / 801-224-6446

Madis, George, P.O. Box 545, Brownsboro, TX 75756 / 903-852-6480

Madis Books, 2453 West Five Mile Pkwy., Dallas, TX 75233 / 214-330-7168

MAG Instrument, Inc., 1635 S. Sacramento Ave., Ontario, CA 91761 / 909-947-1006; FAX: 909-947-3116

Mag-Na-Port International, Inc., 41302 Executive Dr., Harrison Twp., MI 48045-1306 / 810-469-6727; FAX: 810-469-0425

Mag-Pack Corp., P.O. Box 846, Chesterland, OH 44026

Magma Engineering Co., P.O. Box 161, 20955 E. Ocotillo Rd., Queen Creek, AZ 85242 / 602-987-9008 FAX: 602-987-0148

Magnolia Sports,Inc., 211 W. Main, Magnolia, AR 71753 / 501-234-8410 or 800-530-7816; FAX: 501-234-8117

Magnum Power Products, Inc., P.O. Box 17768, Fountain Hills, AZ 85268

Magnum Research, Inc., 7110 University Ave. NE, Minneapolis, MN 55432 / 800-772-6168 or 612-574-1868; FAX: 612-574-0109 magnumresearch.com

Magnus Bullets, P.O. Box 239, Toney, AL 35773 / 256-420-8359; FAX: 256-420-8360

MagSafe Ammo Co., 4700 S US Highway 17/92, Casselberry, FL 32707-3814 / 407-834-9966; FAX: 407-834-8185

Magtech Ammunition Co. Inc., 837 Boston Rd #12, Madison, CT 06443 / 203-245-8983; FAX: 203-245-2883 rfinemtek@aol.com

Mahony, Philip Bruce, 67 White Hollow Rd., Lime Rock, CT 06039-2418 / 203-435-9341

Mahovsky's Metalife, R.D. 1, Box 149a Eureka Road, Grand Valley, PA 16420 / 814-436-7747

Maine Custom Bullets, RFD 1, Box 1755, Brooks, ME 04921

Maionchi-L.M.I., Via Di Coselli-Zona, Industriale Di Guamo 55060, Lucca, ITALY / 011 39-583 94291

Makinson, Nicholas, RR 3, Komoka, ON N0L 1R0 CANADA / 519-471-5462

Malcolm Enterprises, 1023 E. Prien Lake Rd., Lake Charles, LA 70601

Mallardtone Game Calls, 2901 16th St., Moline, IL 61265 / 309-762-8089

Mandall Shooting Supplies Inc., 3616 N. Scottsdale Rd., Scottsdale, AZ 85252 / 480-945-2553; FAX: 480-949-0734

Marathon Rubber Prods. Co., Inc., 1009 3rd St, Wausau, WI 54403-4765 / 715-845-6255

Marble Arms (See CRR, Inc./Marble's Inc.)

Marchmon Bullets, 8191 Woodland Shore Dr., Brighton, MI 48116

Marent, Rudolf, 9711 Tiltree St., Houston, TX 77075 / 713-946-7028

Mark Lee Supplies, 9901 France Ct., Lakeville, MN 55044 / 612-461-2114

Markell, Inc., 422 Larkfield Center 235, Santa Rosa, CA 95403 / 707-573-0792; FAX: 707-573-9867

Markesbery Muzzle Loaders, Inc., 7785 Foundation Dr., Ste. 6, Florence, KY 41042 / 606-342-5553; or 606-342-2380

Marksman Products, 5482 Argosy Dr., Huntington Beach, CA 92649 / 714-898-7535 or 800-822-8005; FAX: 714-891-0782

Marlin Firearms Co., 100 Kenna Dr., North Haven, CT 06473 / 203-239-5621; FAX: 203-234-7991

MarMik, Inc., 2116 S. Woodland Ave., Michigan City, IN 46360 / 219-872-7231; FAX: 219-872-7231

Marocchi F.lli S.p.A, Via Galileo Galilei 8, I-25068 Zanano, ITALY

Marquart Precision Co., (See Morrison Precision)

Marsh, Johnny, 1007 Drummond Dr., Nashville, TN 37211 / 615-833-3259

Marsh, Mike, Croft Cottage, Main St., Derbyshire, DE4 2BY ENGLAND / 01629 650 669

Marshall Enterprises, 792 Canyon Rd., Redwood City, CA 94062

Marshall F. Fish Mfg. Gunsmith Sptg. Co., Rd. Box 2439, Rt. 22 North, Westport, NY 12993 / 518-962-4897 FAX: 518-962-4897

Martin B. Retting Inc., 11029 Washington, Culver City, CA 90232 / 213-837-2412

Martin Hagn Rifles & Actions, P.O. Box 444, Cranbrook, BC V1C 4H9 CANADA / 604-489-4861

Martin's Gun Shop, 937 S. Sheridan Blvd., Lakewood, CO 80226 / 303-922-2184

Martz, John V., 8060 Lakeview Lane, Lincoln, CA 95648 FAX: 916-645-3815

Marvel, Alan, 3922 Madonna Rd., Jarrestville, MD 21084 / 301-557-6645

Marx, Harry (See U.S. Importer for FERLIB)

Maryland Paintball Supply, 8507 Harford Rd., Parkville, MD 21234 / 410-882-5607

MAST Technology, 4350 S. Arville, Suite 3, Las Vegas, NV 89103 / 702-362-5043; FAX: 702-362-9554

Master Engravers, Inc. (See Hendricks, Frank E)

Master Lock Co., 2600 N. 32nd St., Milwaukee, WI 53245 / 414-444-2800

Match Prep--Doyle Gracey, P.O. Box 155, Tehachapi, CA 93581 / 661-822-5383; FAX: 661-823-8680

Matco, Inc., 1003-2nd St., N. Manchester, IN 46962 / 219-982-8282

Mathews & Son, Inc., George E., 10224 S Paramount Blvd, Downey, CA 90241 / 562-862-6719; FAX: 562-862-6719

Matthews Cutlery, 4401 Sentry Dr., Tucker, GA 30084 / 770-939-6915

Mauser Werke Oberndorf Waffensysteme GmbH, Postfach 1349, 78722, Oberndorf/N., GERMANY

Maverick Arms, Inc., 7 Grasso Ave., P.O. Box 497, North Haven, CT 06473 / 203-230-5300; FAX: 203-230-5420

Maxi-Mount, P.O. Box 291, Willoughby Hills, OH 44094-0291 / 216-944-9456; FAX: 216-944-9456

Maximum Security Corp., 32841 Calle Perfecto, San Juan Capistrano, CA 92675 / 714-493-3684; FAX: 714-496-7733

Mayville Engineering Co. (See MEC, Inc.)

Mazur Restoration, Pete, 13083 Drummer Way, Grass Valley, CA 95949 / 530-268-2412

McBros Rifle Co., P.O. Box 86549, Phoenix, AZ 85080 / 602-582-3713; FAX: 602-581-3825

McCament, Jay, 1730-134th St. Ct. S., Tacoma, WA 98444 / 253-531-8832

McCann Industries, P.O. Box 641, Spanaway, WA 98387 / 253-537-6919; FAX: 253-537-6919 mccann.machine@worldnet.att.net www.mccannindustries.com

McCann's Machine & Gun Shop, P.O. Box 641, Spanaway, WA 98387 / 253-537-6919; FAX: 253-537-6993 mccann.machine@worldnet.att.net www.mccannindustries.com

McCann's Muzzle-Gun Works, 14 Walton Dr., New Hope, PA 18938 / 215-862-2728

McCluskey Precision Rifles, 10502 14th Ave. NW, Seattle, WA 98177 / 206-781-2776

McCombs, Leo, 1862 White Cemetery Rd., Patriot, OH 45658 / 614-256-1714

McCormick Corp., Chip, 1825 Fortview Rd Ste 115, Austin, TX 78704 / 800-328-CHIP; FAX: 512-462-0009

McCullough, Ken. (See KEN'S RIFLE BLANKS)

McDonald, Dennis, 8359 Brady St., Peosta, IA 52068 / 319-556-7940

McFarland, Stan, 2221 Idella Ct., Grand Junction, CO 81505 / 970-243-4704

McGhee, Larry. (See B.C. OUTDOORS)

McGowen Rifle Barrels, 5961 Spruce Lane, St. Anne, IL 60964 / 815-937-9816; FAX: 815-937-4024

McGuire, Bill, 1600 N. Eastmont Ave., East Wenatchee, WA 98802 / 509-884-6021

Mchalik, Gary. (See ROSSI FIREARMS, BRAZTECH)

McKenzie, Lynton, 6940 N. Alvernon Way, Tucson, AZ 85718 / 520-299-5090

McKillen & Heyer, Inc., 35535 Euclid Ave., Suite 11, Willoughby, OH 44094 / 216-942-2044

McKinney, R.P. (See Schuetzen Gun Co.)

McMillan Fiberglass Stocks, Inc., 21421 N. 14th Ave., Suite B, Phoenix, AZ 85027 / 602-582-9635; FAX: 602-581-3825

McMillan Optical Gunsight Co., 28638 N. 42nd St., Cave Creek, AZ 85331 / 602-585-7868; FAX: 602-585-7872

McMillan Rifle Barrels, P.O. Box 3427, Bryan, TX 77805 / 409-690-3456; FAX: 409-690-0156

McMurdo, Lynn (See Specialty Gunsmithing), PO Box 404, Afton, WY 83110 / 307-886-5535

MCRW Associates Shooting Supplies, R.R. 1, Box 1425, Sweet Valley, PA 18656 / 717-864-3967; FAX: 717-864-2669

MCS, Inc., 34 Delmar Dr., Brookfield, CT 06804 / 203-775-1013; FAX: 203-775-9462

McWelco Products, 6730 Santa Fe Ave., Hesperia, CA 92345 / 619-244-8876; FAX: 619-244-9398

MDS, P.O. Box 1441, Brandon, FL 33509-1441 / 813-653-1180; FAX: 813-684-5953

Meadow Industries, 24 Club Lane, Palmyra, VA 22963 / 804-589-7672; FAX: 804-589-7672

Measurement Group Inc., Box 27777, Raleigh, NC 27611

Measures, Leon. (See SHOOT WHERE YOU LOOK)

MEC, Inc., 715 South St., Mayville, WI 53050 / 414-387-4500; FAX: 414-387-5802 reloaders@mayvl.com www.mayvl.com

MEC-Gar S.r.l., Via Madonnina 64, Gardone V.T. Brescia, ITALY / 39-30-8912687; FAX: 39-30-8910065

MEC-Gar U.S.A., Inc., Box 112, 500B Monroe Turnpike, Monroe, CT 06468 / 203-635-8662; FAX: 203-635-8662

Mech-Tech Systems, Inc., 1602 Foothill Rd., Kalispell, MT 59901 / 406-755-8055

Meister Bullets (See Gander Mountain)

Mele, Frank, 201 S. Wellow Ave., Cookeville, TN 38501 / 615-526-4860

Melton Shirt Co., Inc., 56 Harvester Ave., Batavia, NY 14020 / 716-343-8750; FAX: 716-343-6887

Men-Metallwerk Elisenhuette GmbH, P.O. Box 1263, Nassau/Lahn, D-56372 GERMANY / 2604-7819

Menck, Gunsmith Inc., T.W., 5703 S 77th St, Ralston, NE 68127

Mendez, John A., P.O. Box 620984, Orlando, FL 32862 / 407-344-2791

Meprolight (See Hesco-Meprolight)

Mercer Custom Stocks, R. M., 216 S Whitewater Ave, Jefferson, WI 53549 / 920-674-3839

Merit Corp., Box 9044, Schenectady, NY 12309 / 518-346-1420

Merkel Freres, Strasse 7 October, 10, Suhl, GERMANY

Merkuria Ltd., Argentinska 38, 17005, Praha 7 CZECH, REPUBLIC / 422-875117; FAX: 422-809152

Metal Merchants, PO Box 186, Walled Lake, MI 48390-0186

Metalife Industries (See Mahovsky's Metalife)

Metaloy, Inc., Rt. 5, Box 595, Berryville, AR 72616 / 501-545-3611

Metals Hand Engraver/European Hand Engraving, Ste. 216, 12 South First St., San Jose, CA 95113 / 408-293-6559

MI-TE Bullets, 1396 Ave. K, Ellsworth, KS 67439 / 785-472-4575; FAX: 785-472-5579

Michael's Antiques, Box 591, Waldoboro, ME 04572

Michaels Of Oregon, 1710 Red Soils Ct., Oregon City, OR 97045

Micro Sight Co., 242 Harbor Blvd., Belmont, CA 94002 / 415-591-0769; FAX: 415-591-7531

Microfusion Alfa S.A., Paseo San Andres N8, P.O. Box 271, Eibar, 20600 SPAIN / 34-43-11-89-16; FAX: 34-43-11-40-38

Mid-America Guns and Ammo, 1205 W. Jefferson, Suite E, Effingham, IL 62401 / 800-820-5177

Mid-America Recreation, Inc., 1328 5th Ave., Moline, IL 61265 / 309-764-5089; FAX: 309-764-2722

Middlebrooks Custom Shop, 7366 Colonial Trail East, Surry, VA 23883 / 757-357-0881; FAX: 757-365-0442

Midway Arms, Inc., 5875 W. Van Horn Tavern Rd., Columbia, MO 65203 / 800-243-3220 or 573-445-6363; FAX: 573-446-1018

Midwest Gun Sport, 1108 Herbert Dr., Zebulon, NC 27597 / 919-269-5570

Midwest Sport Distributors, Box 129, Fayette, MO 65248

Mike Davis Products, 643 Loop Dr., Moses Lake, WA 98837 / 509-765-6178 or 509-766-7281

Milberry House Publishing, PO Box 575, Corydon, IN 47112 / 888-738-1567; FAX: 888-738-1567

Military Armament Corp., P.O. Box 120, Mt. Zion Rd., Lingleville, TX 76461 / 817-965-3253

Millennium Designed Muzzleloaders, PO Box 536, Routes 11 & 25, Limington, ME 04049 / 207-637-2316

Miller Arms, Inc., P.O. Box 260 Purl St., St. Onge, SD 57779 / 605-642-5160; FAX: 605-642-5160

Miller Custom, 210 E. Julia, Clinton, IL 61727 / 217-935-9362

Miller Single Trigger Mfg. Co., Rt. 209, Box 1275, Millersburg, PA 17061 / 717-692-3704

Millett Sights, 7275 Murdy Circle, Adm. Office, Huntington Beach, CA 92647 / 714-842-5575 or 800-645-5388; FAX: 714-843-5707

Mills Jr., Hugh B., 3615 Canterbury Rd., New Bern, NC 28560 / 919-637-4631

Milstor Corp., 80-975 Indio Blvd., Indio, CA 92201 / 760-775-9998; FAX: 760-775-5229 milstor@webtv.net

Miltex, Inc, 700 S Lee St, Alexandria, VA 22314-4332 / 888-642-9123; FAX: 301-645-1430

Minute Man High Tech Industries, 10611 Canyon Rd. E., Suite 151, Puyallup, WA 98373 / 800-233-2734

Mirador Optical Corp., P.O. Box 11614, Marina Del Rey, CA 90295-7614 / 310-821-5587; FAX: 310-305-0386

Miroku, B C/Daly, Charles (See U.S. Importer-Bell's)

Mitchell, Jack, c/o Geoff Gaebe, Addieville East Farm, 200 Pheasant Dr, Mapleville, RI 02839 / 401-568-3185

Mitchell Bullets, R.F., 430 Walnut St, Westernport, MD 21562

Mitchell Optics, Inc., 2072 CR 1100 N, Sidney, IL 61877 / 217-688-2219 or 217-621-3018; FAX: 217-688-2505

Mitchell's Accuracy Shop, 68 Greenridge Dr., Stafford, VA 22554 / 703-659-0165

Mittermeier, Inc., Frank, PO Box 2G, 3577 E Tremont Ave, Bronx, NY 10465 / 718-828-3843

Mixson Corp., 7635 W. 28th Ave., Hialeah, FL 33016 / 305-821-5190 or 800-327-0078; FAX: 305-558-9318

MJK Gunsmithing, Inc., 417 N. Huber Ct., E. Wenatchee, WA 98802 / 509-884-7683

MJM Mfg., 3283 Rocky Water Ln., Suite B, San Jose, CA 95148 / 408-270-4207

MKS Supply, Inc. (See Hi-Point Firearms)

MMC, 2513 East Loop 820 North, Ft. Worth, TX 76118 / 817-595-0404; FAX: 817-595-3074

MMP, Rt. 6, Box 384, Harrison, AR 72601 / 501-741-5019; FAX: 501-741-3104

Mo's Competitor Supplies (See MCS Inc)

Modern Gun Repair School, P.O. Box 92577, Southlake, TX 76092 / 800-493-4114; FAX: 800-556-5112

Modern Muzzleloading, Inc, PO Box 130, Centerville, IA 52544 / 515-856-2626

Moeller, Steve, 1213 4th St., Fulton, IL 61252 / 815-589-2300

Molin Industries, Tru-Nord Division, P.O. Box 365, 204 North 9th St., Brainerd, MN 56401 / 218-829-2870

Monell Custom Guns, 228 Red Mills Rd., Pine Bush, NY 12566 / 914-744-3021

Moneymaker Guncraft Corp., 1420 Military Ave., Omaha, NE 68131 / 402-556-0226

Montana Armory, Inc (See C. Sharps Arms Co. Inc.), 100 Centennial, Box 885, Big Timber, MT 59011 / 406-932-4353

Montana Outfitters, Lewis E. Yearout, 308 Riverview Dr. E., Great Falls, MT 59404 / 406-761-0859

Montana Precision Swaging, P.O. Box 4746, Butte, MT 59702 / 406-782-7502

Montana Vintage Arms, 2354 Bear Canyon Rd., Bozeman, MT 59715

Montgomery Community College, P.O. Box 787-GD, Troy, NC 27371 / 910-576-6222 or 800-839-6222; FAX: 910-576-2176

Morini (See U.S. Importers-Mandall Shooting Supplies, Inc.,)

Morrison Custom Rifles, J. W., 4015 W Sharon, Phoenix, AZ 85029 / 602-978-3754

Morrison Precision, 6719 Calle Mango, Hereford, AZ 85615 / 520-378-6207 / morprec@c2i2.com (e-mail)

Morrow, Bud, 11 Hillside Lane, Sheridan, WY 82801-9729 / 307-674-8360

Morton Booth Co., P.O. Box 123, Joplin, MO 64802 / 417-673-1962; FAX: 417-673-3642

Moss Double Tone, Inc., P.O. Box 1112, 2101 S. Kentucky, Sedalia, MO 65301 / 816-827-0827

Mountain Hollow Game Calls, Box 121, Cascade, MD 21719 / 301-241-3282

Mountain Plains, Inc., 244 Glass Hollow Rd., Alton, VA 22920 / 800-687-3000

Mountain Rifles, Inc., P.O. Box 2789, Palmer, AK 99645 / 907-373-4194; FAX: 907-373-4195

Mountain South, P.O. Box 381, Barnwell, SC 29812 / FAX: 803-259-3227

Mountain State Muzzleloading Supplies, Inc., Box 154-1, Rt. 2, Williamstown, WV 26187 / 304-375-7842; FAX: 304-375-3737

Mountain View Sports, Inc., Box 188, Troy, NH 03465 / 603-357-9690; FAX: 603-357-9691

Mowrey Gun Works, P.O. Box 246, Waldron, IN 46182 / 317-525-6181; FAX: 317-525-9595

Mowrey's Guns & Gunsmithing, 119 Fredericks St., Canajoharie, NY 13317 / 518-673-3483

MPC, P.O. Box 450, McMinnville, TN 37110-0450 / 615-473-5513; FAX: 615-473-5516

MPI Stocks, PO Box 83266, Portland, OR 97283 / 503-226-1215; FAX: 503-226-2661

MSC Industrial Supply Co., 151 Sunnyside Blvd., Plainview, NY 11803-9915 / 516-349-0330

MSR Targets, P.O. Box 1042, West Covina, CA 91793 / 818-331-7840

Mt. Alto Outdoor Products, Rt. 735, Howardsville, VA 24562

Mt. Baldy Bullet Co., 12981 Old Hill City Rd., Keystone, SD 57751-6623 / 605-666-4725

MTM Molded Products Co., Inc., 3370 Obco Ct., Dayton, OH 45414 / 937-890-7461; FAX: 937-890-1747

Mulhern, Rick, Rt. 5, Box 152, Rayville, LA 71269 / 318-728-2688

Mullins Ammunition, Rt. 2, Box 304K, Clintwood, VA 24228 / 540-926-6772; FAX: 540-926-6092

Mullis Guncraft, 3523 Lawyers Road E., Monroe, NC 28110 / 704-283-6683

Multi-Scale Charge Ltd., 3269 Niagara Falls Blvd., N. Tonawanda, NY 14120 / 905-566-1255; FAX: 905-276-6295

Multiplex International, 26 S. Main St., Concord, NH 03301 / FAX: 603-796-2223

Multipropulseurs, La Bertrandiere, 42580, FRANCE / 77 74 01 30; FAX: 77 93 19 34

Mundy, Thomas A., 69 Robbins Road, Somerville, NJ 08876 / 201-722-2199

Murmur Corp., 2823 N. Westmoreland Ave., Dallas, TX 75222 / 214-630-5400

Murray State College, 1 Murray Campus St., Tishomingo, OK 73460 / 508-371-2371

Muscle Products Corp., 112 Fennell Dr., Butler, PA 16001 / 800-227-7049 or 412-283-0567; FAX: 412-283-8310

Museum of Historical Arms, Inc., 2750 Coral Way, Suite 204, Miami, FL 33145 / 305-444-9199

Mushroom Express Bullet Co., 601 W. 6th St., Greenfield, IN 46140-1728 / 317-462-6332

Muzzleloaders Etcetera, Inc., 9901 Lyndale Ave. S., Bloomington, MN 55420 / 612-884-1161 muzzleloaders-etcetera.com

Muzzleloading Technologies, Inc, 25 E. Hwy. 40, Suite 330-12, Roosevelt, UT 84066 / 801-722-5996; FAX: 801-722-5909

MWG Co., P.O. Box 971202, Miami, FL 33197 / 800-428-9394 or 305-253-8393; FAX: 305-232-1247

N

N&J Sales, Lime Kiln Rd., Northford, CT 06472 / 203-484-0247

N.B.B., Inc., 24 Elliot Rd., Sterling, MA 01564 / 508-422-7538 or 800-942-9444

N.C. Ordnance Co., P.O. Box 3254, Wilson, NC 27895 / 919-237-2440; FAX: 919-243-9845

Nagel's Custom Bullets, 100 Scott St., Baytown, TX 77520-2849

Nalpak, 1937-C Friendship Drive, El Cajon, CA 92020 / 619-258-1200

Nastoff's 45 Shop, Inc., Steve, 12288 Mahoning Ave, PO Box 446, North Jackson, OH 44451 / 330-538-2977

National Bullet Co., 1585 E. 361 St., Eastlake, OH 44095 / 216-951-1854; FAX: 216-951-7761

National Target Co., 4690 Wyaconda Rd., Rockville, MD 20852 / 800-827-7060 or 301-770-7060; FAX: 301-770-7892

Naval Ordnance Works, Rt. 2, Box 919, Sheperdstown, WV 25443 / 304-876-0998

Navy Arms Co., 689 Bergen Blvd., Ridgefield, NJ 07657 / 201-945-2500; FAX: 201-945-6859

NCP Products, Inc., 3500 12th St. N.W., Canton, OH 44708 / 330-456-5130; FAX: 330-456-5234

Neal Johnson's Gunsmithing, Inc., 208 W. Buchanan St., Suite B, Colorado Springs, CO 80907 / 800-284-8671; FAX: 719-632-3493

Necessary Concepts, Inc., P.O. Box 571, Deer Park, NY 11729 / 516-667-8509; FAX: 516-667-8588

Necromancer Industries, Inc., 14 Communications Way, West Newton, PA 15089 / 412-872-8722

NEI Handtools, Inc., 51583 Columbia River Hwy., Scappoose, OR 97056 / 503-543-6776; FAX: 503-543-6799

Neil A. Jones Custom Products, 17217 Brookhouser Road, Saegertown, PA 16433 / 814-763-2769; FAX: 814-763-4228

Nelson, Gary K., 975 Terrace Dr., Oakdale, CA 95361 / 209-847-4590

Nelson, Stephen, 7365 NW Spring Creek Dr., Corvallis, OR 97330 / 541-745-5232

Nelson/Weather-Rite, Inc., 14760 Santa Fe Trail Dr., Lenexa, KS 66215 / 913-492-3200; FAX: 913-492-8749

Nesci Enterprises Inc., P.O. Box 119, Summit St., East Hampton, CT 06424 / 203-267-2588

Nesika Bay Precision, 22239 Big Valley Rd., Poulsbo, WA 98370 / 206-697-3830

Nettestad Gun Works, RR 1, Box 160, Pelican Rapids, MN 56572 / 218-863-4301

Neumann GmbH, Am Galgenberg 6, 90575, GERMANY / 09101/8258; FAX: 09101/6356

Nevada Pistol Academy, Inc., 4610 Blue Diamond Rd., Las Vegas, NV 89139 / 702-897-1100

New England Ammunition Co., 1771 Post Rd. East, Suite 223, Westport, CT 06880 / 203-254-8048

New England Arms Co., Box 278, Lawrence Lane, Kittery Point, ME 03905 / 207-439-0593; FAX: 207-439-0525 info@new-englandarms.com www.newenglandarms.com

New England Custom Gun Service, 438 Willow Brook Rd., Plainfield, NH 03781 / 603-469-3450; FAX: 603-469-3471

New England Firearms, 60 Industrial Rowe, Gardner, MA 01440 / 508-632-9393; FAX: 508-632-2300

New Orleans Jewelers Supply Co., 206 Charters St., New Orleans, LA 70130 / 504-523-3839; FAX: 504-523-3836

New SKB Arms Co., C.P.O. Box 1401, Tokyo, JAPAN / 81-3-3943-9550; FAX: 81-3-3943-0695

New Win Publishing, Inc., 186 Center St., Clinton, NJ 08809 / 908-735-9701; FAX: 908-735-9703

Newark Electronics, 4801 N. Ravenswood Ave., Chicago, IL 60640

Newell, Robert H., 55 Coyote, Los Alamos, NM 87544 / 505-662-7135

Newman Gunshop, 119 Miller Rd., Agency, IA 52530 / 515-937-5775

Nicholson Custom, 17285 Thornlay Road, Hughesville, MO 65334 / 816-826-8746

Nickels, Paul R., 4789 Summerhill Rd., Las Vegas, NV 89121 / 702-435-5318

Nicklas, Ted, 5504 Hegel Rd., Goodrich, MI 48438 / 810-797-4493

Niemi Engineering, W. B., Box 126 Center Rd, Greensboro, VT 05841 / 802-533-7180; FAX: 802-533-7141

Nightforce (See Lightforce USA Inc)

Nikolai leather, 15451 Electronic ln, Huntington Beach, CA 92649 / 714-373-2721 FAX: 714-373-2723

Nikon, Inc., 1300 Walt Whitman Rd., Melville, NY 11747 / 516-547-8623; FAX: 516-547-0309

Nitex, Inc., P.O. Box 1706, Uvalde, TX 78801 / 888-543-8843

No-Sho Mfg. Co., 10727 Glenfield Ct., Houston, TX 77096 / 713-723-5332

Noreen, Peter J., 5075 Buena Vista Dr., Belgrade, MT 59714 / 406-586-7383

Norica, Avnda Otaola, 16 Apartado 68, Eibar, SPAIN

Norinco, 7A Yun Tan N, Beijing, CHINA

Norincoptics (See BEC, Inc.)

Norma Precision AB (See U.S. Importers-Dynamit Nobel-RWS, Inc.,)

Normark Corp., 10395 Yellow Circle Dr., Minnetonka, MN 55343-9101 / 612-933-7060 FAX: 612-933-0046

North American Arms, Inc., 2150 South 950 East, Provo, UT 84606-6285 / 800-821-5783 or 801-374-9990; FAX: 801-374-9998

North American Correspondence Schools The Gun Pro, Oak & Pawney St., Scranton, PA 18515 / 717-342-7701

North American Shooting Systems, P.O. Box 306, Osoyoos, BC V0H 1V0 CANADA / 604-495-3131; FAX: 604-495-2816

North Devon Firearms Services, 3 North St., Braunton, EX33 1AJ ENGLAND / 01271 813624; FAX: 01271 813642

North Fork Custom Gunsmithing, James Johnston, 428 Del Rio Rd., Roseburg, OR 97470 / 503-673-4467

North Mountain Pine Training Center (See Executive Protection Institute)

North Pass, 425 South Bowen St., Ste. 6, Longmount, CO 80501 / 303-682-4315; FAX: 303-678-7109

North Specialty Products, 2664-B Saturn St., Brea, CA 92621 / 714-524-1665

North Star West, P.O. Box 488, Glencoe, CA 95232 / 209-293-7010

North Wind Decoy Co., 1005 N. Tower Rd., Fergus Falls, MN 56537 / 218-736-4378; FAX: 218-736-7060

Northern Precision Custom Swaged Bullets, 329 S. James St., Carthage, NY 13619 / 315-493-1711

Northlake Outdoor Footwear, P.O. Box 10, Franklin, TN 37065-0010 / 615-794-1556; FAX: 615-790-8005

Northside Gun Shop, 2725 NW 109th, Oklahoma City, OK 73120 / 405-840-2353

Northwest Arms, 26884 Pearl Rd., Parma, ID 83660 / 208-722-6771; FAX: 208-722-1062

Nosler, Inc., P.O. Box 671, Bend, OR 97709 / 800-285-3701 or 541-382-3921; FAX: 541-388-4667

Novak's, Inc., 1206 1/2 30th St., P.O. Box 4045, Parkersburg, WV 26101 / 304-485-9295; FAX: 304-428-6722

Now Products, Inc., PO Box 27608, Tempe, AZ 85285 / 800-662-6063; FAX: 480-966-0890

Nowlin Mfg. Co., 20622 S 4092 Rd, Claremore, OK 74017 / 918-342-0689; FAX: 918-342-0624

NRI Gunsmith School, 4401 Connecticut Ave. NW, Washington, DC 20008

Nu-Line Guns,Inc., 1053 Caulks Hill Rd., Harvester, MO 63304 / 314-441-4500 or 314-447-4501; FAX: 314-447-5018

Null Holsters Ltd. K.L., 161 School St NW, Resaca, GA 30735 / 706-625-5643; FAX: 706-625-9392

Numrich Arms Corp., 203 Broadway, W. Hurley, NY 12491

NW Sinker and Tackle, 380 Valley Dr., Myrtle Creek, OR 97457-9717

Nygord Precision Products, P.O. Box 12578, Prescott, AZ 86304 / 520-717-2315; FAX: 520-717-2198

O

O.F. Mossberg & Sons,Inc., 7 Grasso Ave., North Haven, CT 06473 / 203-230-5300; FAX: 203-230-5420

Oakland Custom Arms,Inc., 4690 W. Walton Blvd., Waterford, MI 48329 / 810-674-8261

Oakman Turkey Calls, RD 1, Box 825, Harrisonville, PA 17228 / 717-485-4620

Obermeyer Rifled Barrels, 23122 60th St., Bristol, WI 53104 / 262-843-3537; FAX: 262-843-2129

October Country Muzzleloading, P.O. Box 969, Dept. GD, Hayden, ID 83835 / 208-772-2068; FAX: 208-772-9230 october-country.com

Oehler Research,Inc., P.O. Box 9135, Austin, TX 78766 / 512-327-6900 or 800-531-5125; FAX: 512-327-6903

Oil Rod and Gun Shop, 69 Oak St., East Douglas, MA 01516 / 508-476-3687

Ojala Holsters, Arvo, PO Box 98, N Hollywood, CA 91603 / 503-669-1404

OK Weber,Inc., P.O. Box 7485, Eugene, OR 97401 / 541-747-0458; FAX: 541-747-5927

Oker's Engraving, 365 Bell Rd., P.O. Box 126, Shawnee, CO 80475 / 303-838-6042

Oklahoma Ammunition Co., 3701A S. Harvard Ave., No. 367, Tulsa, OK 74135-2265 / 918-396-3187; FAX: 918-396-4270

Oklahoma Leather Products,Inc., 500 26th NW, Miami, OK 74354 / 918-542-6651; FAX: 918-542-6653

Old Wagon Bullets, 32 Old Wagon Rd., Wilton, CT 06897

Old West Bullet Moulds, J Ken Chapman, P.O. Box 519, Flora Vista, NM 87415 / 505-334-6970

Old West Reproductions,Inc. R.M. Bachman, 446 Florence S. Loop, Florence, MT 59833 / 406-273-2615; FAX: 406-273-2615

Old Western Scrounger,Inc., 12924 Hwy. A-I2, Montague, CA 96064 / 916-459-5445; FAX: 916-459-3944

Old World Gunsmithing, 2901 SE 122nd St., Portland, OR 97236 / 503-760-7681

Old World Oil Products, 3827 Queen Ave. N., Minneapolis, MN 55412 / 612-522-5037

Ole Frontier Gunsmith Shop, 2617 Hwy. 29 S., Cantonment, FL 32533 / 904-477-8074

Olson, Myron, 989 W. Kemp, Watertown, SD 57201 / 605-886-9787

Olson, Vic, 5002 Countryside Dr., Imperial, MO 63052 / 314-296-8086

Olympic Arms Inc., 620-626 Old Pacific Hwy. SE, Olympia, WA 98513 / 360-491-3447; FAX: 360-491-3447

Olympic Optical Co., P.O. Box 752377, Memphis, TN 38175-2377 / 901-794-3890 or 800-238-7120; FAX: 901-794-0676 80

Omark Industries,Div. of Blount,Inc., 2299 Snake River Ave., P.O. Box 856, Lewiston, ID 83501 / 800-627-3640 or 208-746-2351

Omega Sales, P.O. Box 1066, Mt. Clemens, MI 48043 / 810-469-7323; FAX: 810-469-0425

One Of A Kind, 15610 Purple Sage, San Antonio, TX 78255 / 512-695-3364

Op-Tec, P.O. Box L632, Langhorn, PA 19047 / 215-757-5037

Optical Services Co., P.O. Box 1174, Santa Teresa, NM 88008-1174 / 505-589-3833

Orchard Park Enterprise, P.O. Box 563, Orchard Park, NY 14227 / 616-656-0356

Oregon Arms, Inc. (See Rogue Rifle Co., Inc.)

Oregon Trail Bullet Company, P.O. Box 529, Dept. P, Baker City, OR 97814 / 800-811-0548; FAX: 514-523-1803

Original Box, nc., 700 Linden Ave., York, PA 17404 / 717-854-2897; FAX: 717-845-4276

Original Mink Oil,Inc., 10652 NE Holman, Portland, OR 97220 / 503-255-2814 or 800-547-5895; FAX: 503-255-2487

Orion Rifle Barrel Co., RR2, 137 Cobler Village, Kalispell, MT 59901 / 406-257-5649

Otis Technology, Inc, RR 1 Box 84, Boonville, NY 13309 / 315-942-3320

Ottmar, Maurice, Box 657, 113 E. Fir, Coulee City, WA 99115 / 509-632-5717

Outa-Site Gun Carriers, 219 Market St., Laredo, TX 78040 / 210-722-4678 or 800-880-9715; FAX: 210-726-4858

Outdoor Edge Cutlery Corp., 2888 Bluff St., Suite 130, Boulder, CO 80301 / 303-652-8212; FAX: 303-652-8238

Outdoor Enthusiast, 3784 W. Woodland, Springfield, MO 65807 / 417-883-9841

Outdoor Sports Headquarters,Inc., 967 Watertower Ln., West Carrollton, OH 45449 / 513-865-5855; FAX: 513-865-5962

Outers Laboratories Div. of Blount, Inc.Sporting E, Route 2, P.O. Box 39, Onalaska, WI 54650 / 608-781-5800; FAX: 608-781-0368

Ox-Yoke Originals, Inc., 34 Main St., Milo, ME 04463 / 800-231-8313 or 207-943-7351; FAX: 207-943-2416

Ozark Gun Works, 11830 Cemetery Rd., Rogers, AR 72756 / 501-631-6944; FAX: 501-631-6944 ogw@hotmail.com http://members.tripod.com~ozarkw1

P

P&M Sales and Service, 5724 Gainsborough Pl., Oak Forest, IL 60452 / 708-687-7149

P.A.C.T., Inc., P.O. Box 531525, Grand Prairie, TX 75053 / 214-641-0049

P.M. Enterprises, Inc., 146 Curtis Hill Rd., Chehalis, WA 98532 / 360-748-3743; FAX: 360-748-1802

P.S.M.G. Gun Co., 10 Park Ave., Arlington, MA 02174 / 617-646-8845; FAX: 617-646-2133

Pac-Nor Barreling, 99299 Overlook Rd., P.O. Box 6188, Brookings, OR 97415 / 503-469-7330; FAX: 503-469-7331

Pace Marketing, Inc., P.O. Box 2039, Stuart, FL 34995 / 561-871-9682; FAX: 561-871-6552

Pachmayr Div. Lyman Products, 1875 S. Mountain Ave., Monrovia, CA 91016 / 626-357-7771

Pacific Cartridge, Inc., 2425 Salashan Loop Road, Ferndale, WA 98248 / 360-366-4444; FAX: 360-366-4445

Pacific Research Laboratories, Inc. (See Rimrock R

Pacific Rifle Co., PO Box 1473, Lake Oswego, OR 97035 / 503-538-7437

Paco's (See Small Custom Mould & Bullet Co)

Page Custom Bullets, P.O. Box 25, Port Moresby, NEW GUINEA

Pagel Gun Works, Inc., 1407 4th St. NW, Grand Rapids, MN 55744 / 218-326-3003

Pager Pal, 200 W Pleasantview, Hurst, TX 76054 / 800-561-1603 FAX: 817-285-8769 www.pagerpal.com

Paintball Games International Magazine (Aceville Publications, Castle House) 97 High St., Essex, ENGLAND / 011-44-206-564840

Palmer Security Products, 2930 N. Campbell Ave., Chicago, IL 60618 / 800-788-7725; FAX: 773-267-8080

Palsa Outdoor Products, P.O. Box 81336, Lincoln, NE 68501 / 402-488-5288; FAX: 402-488-2321

Para-Ordnance Mfg., Inc., 980 Tapscott Rd., Scarborough, ON M1X 1E7 CANADA / 416-297-7855; FAX: 416-297-1289

Para-Ordnance, Inc., 1919 NE 45th St., Ste 215, Ft. Lauderdale, FL 33308

Paragon Sales & Services, Inc., 2501 Theodore St, Crest Hill, IL 60435-1613 / 815-725-9212; FAX: 815-725-8974

Pardini Armi Srl, Via Italica 154, 55043, Lido Di Camaiore Lu, ITALY / 584-90121; FAX: 584-90122

Paris, Frank J., 17417 Pershing St., Livonia, MI 48152-3822

Parker & Sons Shooting Supply, 9337 Smoky Row Rd, Straw Plains, TN 97871-1257

Parker Gun Finishes, 9337 Smokey Row Rd., Strawberry Plains, TN 37871 / 423-933-3286

Parker Reproductions, 124 River Rd., Middlesex, NJ 08846 / 908-469-0100 FAX: 908-469-9692

Parsons Optical Mfg. Co., P.O. Box 192, Ross, OH 45061 / 513-867-0820; FAX: 513-867-8380

Partridge Sales Ltd., John, Trent Meadows, Rugeley, ENGLAND

Parts & Surplus, P.O. Box 22074, Memphis, TN 38122 / 901-683-4007

Pasadena Gun Center, 206 E. Shaw, Pasadena, TX 77506 / 713-472-0417; FAX: 713-472-1322

Passive Bullet Traps, Inc. (See Savage Range Systems, Inc.,)

PAST Sporting Goods,Inc., P.O. Box 1035, Columbia, MO 65205 / 314-445-9200; FAX: 314-446-6606

Paterson Gunsmithing, 438 Main St., Paterson, NJ 07502 / 201-345-4100

Pathfinder Sports Leather, 2920 E. Chambers St., Phoenix, AZ 85040 / 602-276-0016

Patrick Bullets, P.O. Box 172, Warwick, QSLD, 4370 AUSTRALIA

Patrick W. Price Bullets, 16520 Worthley Drive, San Lorenzo, CA 94580 / 510-278-1547

Pattern Control, 114 N. Third St., P.O. Box 462105, Garland, TX 75046 / 214-494-3551; FAX: 214-272-8447

Paul A. Harris Hand Engraving, 113 Rusty Lane, Boerne, TX 78006-5746 / 512-391-5121

Paul D. Hillmer Custom Gunstocks, 7251 Hudson Heights, Hudson, IA 50643 / 319-988-3941

Paul Jones Moulds, 4901 Telegraph Rd., Los Angeles, CA 90022 / 213-262-1510

Paulsen Gunstocks, Rt. 71, Box 11, Chinook, MT 59523 / 406-357-3403

Pawling Mountain Club, Keith Lupton, PO Box 573, Pawling, NY 12564 / 914-855-3825

Paxton Quigley's Personal Protection Strategies, 9903 Santa Monica Blvd., 300, Beverly Hills, CA 90212 / 310-281-1762 www.defend-net.com/paxton

Payne Photography, Robert, Robert, P.O. Box 141471, Austin, TX 78714 / 512-272-4554

PC Co., 5942 Secor Rd., Toledo, OH 43623 / 419-472-6222

Peacemaker Specialists, P.O. Box 157, Whitmore, CA 96096 / 916-472-3438

Pearce Grip, Inc., P.O. Box 187, Bothell, WA 98041-0187 / 206-485-5488; FAX: 206-488-9497

Pease Accuracy, Bob, P.O. Box 310787, New Braunfels, TX 78131 / 210-625-1342

Pease International, 53 Durham St, Portsmouth, NH 03801 / 603-431-1331; FAX: 603-431-1221

PECAR Herbert Schwarz GmbH, Kreuzbergstrasse 6, 10965, Berlin, GERMANY / 004930-785-7383; FAX: 004930-785-1934

Pecatonica River Longrifle, 5205 Nottingham Dr., Rockford, IL 61111 / 815-968-1995 FAX: 815-968-1996

Pedersen, C. R., 2717 S. Pere Marquette Hwy., Ludington, MI 49431 / 616-843-2061

Pedersen, Rex C., 2717 S. Pere Marquette Hwy., Ludington, MI 49431 / 616-843-2061

Peerless Alloy, Inc., 1445 Osage St., Denver, CO 80204-2439 / 303-825-6394 or 800-253-1278

Peet Shoe Dryer, Inc., 130 S. 5th St., P.O. Box 618, St. Maries, ID 83861 / 208-245-2095 or 800-222-PEET; FAX: 208-245-5441

Peifer Rifle Co., P.O. Box 192, Nokomis, IL 62075-0192 / 217-563-7050; FAX: 217-563-7060

Pejsa Ballistics, 2120 Kenwood Pkwy., Minneapolis, MN 55405 / 612-374-3337; FAX: 612-374-5383

Pelaire Products, 5346 Bonky Ct., W. Palm Beach, FL 33415 / 561-439-0691; FAX: 561-967-0052

Pell, John T. (See KOGOT)

Peltor, Inc. (See Aero Peltor)

PEM's Mfg. Co., 5063 Waterloo Rd., Atwater, OH 44201 / 216-947-3721

Pence Precision Barrels, 7567 E. 900 S., S. Whitley, IN 46787 / 219-839-4745

Pendleton Royal, c/o Swingler Buckland Ltd., 4/7 Highgate St., Birmingham, ENGLAND / 44 121 440 3060 or 44 121 446 5898; FAX: 44 121 446 4165

Pendleton Woolen Mills, P.O. Box 3030, 220 N.W. Broadway, Portland, OR 97208 / 503-226-4801

Penn Bullets, P.O. Box 756, Indianola, PA 15051

Penn's Woods Products, Inc., 19 W. Pittsburgh St., Delmont, PA 15626 / 412-468-8311; FAX: 412-468-8975

Pennsylvania Gun Parts Inc, PO Box 665, 300 Third St, East Berlin, PA 17316-0665 / 717-259-8010; FAX: 717-259-0057

Pennsylvania Gunsmith School, 812 Ohio River Blvd., Avalon, Pittsburgh, PA 15202 / 412-766-1812 FAX: 412-766-0855 pgs@pagunsmith.com www.pagunsmith.com

Penrod Precision, 312 College Ave., P.O. Box 307, N. Manchester, IN 46962 / 219-982-8385

Pentax Corp., 35 Inverness Dr. E., Englewood, CO 80112 / 303-799-8000; FAX: 303-790-1131

Pentheny de Pentheny, 108 Petaluma Ave #202, Sebastopol, CA 95472-4220 / 707-573-1390; FAX: 707-573-1390

Perazone-Gunsmith, Brian, Cold Spring Rd, Roxbury, NY 12474 / 607-326-4088; FAX: 607-326-3140

Perazzi USA, Inc., 1207 S. Shamrock Ave., Monrovia, CA 91016 / 626-303-0068; FAX: 626-303-2081

Performance Specialists, 308 Eanes School Rd., Austin, TX 78746 / 512-327-0119

Perugini Visini & Co. S.r.l., Via Camprelle, 126, 25080 Nuvolera, ITALY / 30-6897535; FAX: 30-6897821

Pete Elsen, Inc., 1529 S. 113th St., West Allis, WI 53214

Pete Mazur Restoration, 13083 Drummer Way, Grass Valley, CA 95949 / 916-268-2412

Pete Rickard, Inc., 115 Roy Walsh Rd, Cobleskill, NY 12043 / 518-234-2731: FAX: 518-234-2454 rickard@telenet.net peterickard.com

Peter Dyson & Son Ltd., 3 Cuckoo Lane, Honley Huddersfield, Yorkshire, HD7 2BR ENGLAND / 44-1484-661062; FAX: 44-1484-663709

Peter Hale/Engraver, 800 E. Canyon Rd., Spanish Fork, UT 84660 / 801-798-8215

Peters Stahl GmbH, Stettiner Strasse 42, D-33106, Paderborn, / 05251-750025; FAX: 05251-75611

Petersen Publishing Co., (See Emap USA)

Peterson Gun Shop, Inc., A.W., 4255 W. Old U.S. 441, Mt. Dora, FL 32757-3299 / 352-383-4258; FAX: 352-735-1001

Petro-Explo Inc., 7650 U.S. Hwy. 287, Suite 100, Arlington, TX 76017 / 817-478-8888

Pettinger Books, Gerald, Rt. 2, Box 125, Russell, IA 50238 / 515-535-2239

Pflumm Mfg. Co., 10662 Widmer Rd., Lenexa, KS 66215 / 800-888-4867; FAX: 913-451-7857

PFRB Co., P.O. Box 1242, Bloomington, IL 61702 / 309-473-3964; FAX: 309-473-2161

Philip S. Olt Co., P.O. Box 550, 12662 Fifth St., Pekin, IL 61554 / 309-348-3633; FAX: 309-348-3300

Phillippi Custom Bullets, Justin, P.O. Box 773, Ligonier, PA 15658 / 724-238-2962; FAX: 724-238-9671 jrp@wpa.net http://www.wpa.net~jrphil

Phillips & Rogers, Inc., 100 Hilbig #C, Conroe, TX 77301 / 409-435-0011

Phoenix Arms, 1420 S. Archibald Ave., Ontario, CA 91761 / 909-947-4843; FAX: 909-947-6798

Photronic Systems Engineering Company, 6731 Via De La Reina, Bonsall, CA 92003 / 619-758-8000

Piedmont Community College, P.O. Box 1197, Roxboro, NC 27573 / 336-599-1181 FAX: 336-597-3817 www.piedmont.cc.nc.us

Pierce Pistols, 55 Sorrellwood Lane, Sharpsburg, GA 30277-9523 / 404-253-8192

Pietta (See U.S. Importers-Navy Arms Co, Taylor's & Co.,)

Pilgrim Pewter,Inc. (See Bell Originals Inc. Sid)

Pilkington, Scott (See Little Trees Ramble)

Pine Technical College, 1100 4th St., Pine City, MN 55063 / 800-521-7463; FAX: 612-629-6766

Pinetree Bullets, 133 Skeena St., Kitimat, BC V8C 1Z1 CANADA / 604-632-3768; FAX: 604-632-3768

Pioneer Arms Co., 355 Lawrence Rd., Broomall, PA 19008 / 215-356-5203

Piotti (See U.S. Importer-Moore & Co, Wm. Larkin)

Piquette, Paul R., 80 Bradford Dr., Feeding Hills, MA 01030 / 413-786-8118; or 413-789-4582

Plaxco, J. Michael, Rt. 1, P.O. Box 203, Roland, AR 72135 / 501-868-9787

Plaza Cutlery, Inc., 3333 Bristol, 161 South Coast Plaza, Costa Mesa, CA 92626 / 714-549-3932

Plum City Ballistic Range, N2162 80th St., Plum City, WI 54761 / 715-647-2539

PlumFire Press, Inc., 30-A Grove Ave., Patchogue, NY 11772-4112 / 800-695-7246; FAX: 516-758-4071

PMC/Eldorado Cartridge Corp., P.O. Box 62508, 12801 U.S. Hwy. 95 S., Boulder City, NV 89005 / 702-294-0025; FAX: 702-294-0121

Poburka, Philip (See Bison Studios)

Pohl, Henry A. (See Great American Gun Co.

Pointing Dog Journal, Village Press Publications, P.O. Box 968, Dept. PGD, Traverse City, MI 49685 / 800-272-3246; FAX: 616-946-3289

Police Bookshelf, P.O. Box 122, Concord, NH 03301 / 603-224-6814; FAX: 603-226-3554

Polywad, Inc., P.O. Box 7916, Macon, GA 31209 / 912-477-0669 polywadmpb@aol.com www.polywad.com

Pomeroy, Robert, RR1, Box 50, E. Corinth, ME 04427 / 207-285-7721

Ponsness/Warren, P.O. Box 8, Rathdrum, ID 83858 / 208-687-2231; FAX: 208-687-2233

Pony Express Reloaders, 608 E. Co. Rd. D, Suite 3, St. Paul, MN 55117 / 612-483-9406; FAX: 612-483-9884

Pony Express Sport Shop, 16606 Schoenborn St., North Hills, CA 91343 / 818-895-1231

Potts, Wayne E., 912 Poplar St., Denver, CO 80220 / 303-355-5462

Powder Horn Antiques, P.O. Box 4196, Ft. Lauderdale, FL 33338 / 305-565-6060

Powell & Son (Gunmakers) Ltd., William, 35-37 Carrs Lane, Birmingham, B4 7SX ENGLAND / 121-643-0689; FAX: 121-631-3504

Powell Agency, William, 22 Circle Dr., Bellmore, NY 11710 / 516-679-1158

Power Custom, Inc., 29739 Hwy. J, Gravois Mills, MO 65037 / 513-372-5684; FAX: 573-372-5799 pwpowers@laurie.net www.powercustom.com

Power Plus Enterprises, Inc., PO Box 38, Warm Springs, GA 31830 / 706-655-2132

Powley Computer (See Hutton Rifle Ranch)

Practical Tools, Inc., 7067 Easton Rd., P.O. Box 133, Pipersville, PA 18947 / 215-766-7301; FAX: 215-766-8681

Prairie Gun Works, 1-761 Marion St., Winnipeg, MB R2J 0K6 Canada / 204-231-2976; FAX: 204-231-8566

Prairie River Arms, 1220 N. Sixth St., Princeton, IL 61356 / 815-875-1616 or 800-445-1541; FAX: 815-875-1402

Pranger, Ed G., 1414 7th St., Anacortes, WA 98221 / 206-293-3488

Pre-Winchester 92-90-62 Parts Co., P.O. Box 8125, W. Palm Beach, FL 33407

Precise Metalsmithing Enterprises, 146 Curtis Hill Rd., Chehalis, WA 98532 / 206-748-3743; FAX: 206-748-8102

Precision Airgun Sales, Inc., 5247 Warrensville Ctr Rd, Maple Hts., OH 44137 / 216-587-5005 FAX: 216-587-5005

Precision Cartridge, 176 Eastside Rd., Deer Lodge, MT 59722 / 800-397-3901 or 406-846-3900

Precision Cast Bullets, 101 Mud Creek Lane, Ronan, MT 59864 / 406-676-5135

Precision Castings & Equipment, P.O. Box 326, Jasper, IN 47547-0135 / 812-634-9167

Precision Components, 3177 Sunrise Lake, Milford, PA 18337 / 570-686-4414

Precision Components and Guns, Rt. 55, P.O. Box 337, Pawling, NY 12564 / 914-855-3040

Precision Delta Corp., P.O. Box 128, Ruleville, MS 38771 / 601-756-2810; FAX: 601-756-2590

Precision Gun Works, 104 Sierra Rd Dept. GD, Kerrville, TX 78028 / 830-367-4587

Precision Munitions, Inc., P.O. Box 326, Jasper, IN 47547

Precision Reloading, Inc., P.O. Box 122, Stafford Springs, CT 06076 / 860-684-5680 FAX: 860-684-6788

Precision Sales International, Inc., P.O. Box 1776, Westfield, MA 01086 / 413-562-5055; FAX: 413-562-5056

Precision Shooting,Inc., 222 McKee St., Manchester, CT 06040 / 860-645-8776; FAX: 860-643-8215

Precision Small Arms, 9777 Wilshire Blvd., Suite 1005, Beverly Hills, CA 90212 / 310-859-4867; FAX: 310-859-2868

Precision Small Arms Inc, 9272 Jeronimo Rd, Ste 121, Irvine, CA 92618 / 800-554-5515; FAX: 949-768-4808 www.tcbebe.com

Precision Specialties, 131 Hendom Dr., Feeding Hills, MA 01030 / 413-786-3365; FAX: 413-786-3365

Precision Sport Optics, 15571 Producer Lane, Unit G, Huntington Beach, CA 92649 / 714-891-1309; FAX: 714-892-6920

Premier Reticles, 920 Breckinridge Lane, Winchester, VA 22601-6707 / 540-722-0601; FAX: 540-722-3522

Prescott Projectile Co., 1808 Meadowbrook Road, Prescott, AZ 86303

Preslik's Gunstocks, 4245 Keith Ln., Chico, CA 95926 / 916-891-8236

Price Bullets, Patrick W., 16520 Worthley Dr., San Lorenzo, CA 94580 / 510-278-1547

Prime Reloading, 30 Chiswick End, Meldreth, ROYSTON UK / 0763-260636

Primos, Inc., P.O. Box 12785, Jackson, MS 39236-2785 / 601-366-1288; FAX: 601-362-3274

PRL Bullets, c/o Blackburn Enterprises, 114 Stuart Rd., Ste. 110, Cleveland, TN 37312 / 423-559-0340

Pro Load Ammunition, Inc., 5180 E. Seltice Way, Post Falls, ID 83854 / 208-773-9444; FAX: 208-773-9441

Pro-Mark Div. of Wells Lamont, 6640 W. Touhy, Chicago, IL 60648 / 312-647-8200

Pro-Port Ltd., 41302 Executive Dr., Harrison Twp., MI 48045-1306 / 810-469-6727 FAX: 810-469-0425

Pro-Shot Products, Inc., P.O. Box 763, Taylorville, IL 62568 / 217-824-9133; FAX: 217-824-8861

Professional Gunsmiths of America, Inc., Route 1, Box 224F, Lexington, MO 64067 / 816-259-2636

Professional Hunter Supplies (See Star Custom Bullets,) PO Box 608, 468 Main St, Ferndale, CA 95536 / 707-786-9140; FAX: 707-786-9117

Professional Ordnance, Inc., 1215 E. Airport Dr., Box 182, Ontario, CA 91761 / 909-923-5559; FAX: 909-923-0899

Prolixr Lubricants, P.O. Box 1348, Victorville, CA 92393 / 800-248-5823 or 760-243-3129; FAX: 760-241-0148

Proofmark Corp., P.O. Box 610, Burgess, VA 22432 / 804-453-4337; FAX: 804-453-4337 proofmark@rivnet.net

Protektor Model, 1-11 Bridge St., Galeton, PA 16922 / 814-435-2442

Prototech Industries, Inc., Rt. 1, Box 81, Delia, KS 66418 / 913-771-3571; FAX: 913-771-2531

ProWare, Inc., 15847 NE Hancock St., Portland, OR 97230 / 503-239-0159

PWL Gunleather, P.O. Box 450432, Atlanta, GA 31145 / 770-822-1640; FAX: 770-822-1704 covert@pwlusa.com www.pwlusa.com

Pyromid, Inc., 3292 S. Highway 97, Redmond, OR 97756 / 503-548-1041; FAX: 503-923-1004

Q

Quack Decoy & Sporting Clays, 4 Ann & Hope Way, P.O. Box 98, Cumberland, RI 02864 / 401-723-8202; FAX: 401-722-5910

Quaker Boy, Inc., 5455 Webster Rd., Orchard Parks, NY 14127 / 716-662-3979; FAX: 716-662-9426

Quality Arms, Inc., Box 19477, Dept. GD, Houston, TX 77224 / 281-870-8377; FAX: 281-870-8524 arrieta2@excite.com www.gunshop.com

Quality Firearms of Idaho, Inc., 659 Harmon Way, Middleton, ID 83644-3065 / 208-466-1631

Quality Parts Co./Bushmaster Firearms, 999 Roosevelt Trail Bldg. 3, Windham, ME 04062 / 207-892-2005; FAX: 207-892-8068

Quarton USA, Ltd. Co., 7042 Alamo Downs Pkwy., Suite 370, San Antonio, TX 78238-4518 / 800-520-8435 or 210-520-8430; FAX: 210-520-8433

Que Industries, Inc., P.O. Box 2471, Everett, WA 98203 / 800-769-6930 or 206-347-9843; FAX: 206-514-3266

Queen Cutlery Co., P.O. Box 500, Franklinville, NY 14737 / 800-222-5233; FAX: 800-299-2618

R

R&C Knives & Such, 2136 CANDY CANE WALK, Manteca, CA 95336-9501 / 209-239-3722; FAX: 209-825-6947

R&D Gun Repair, Kenny Howell, RR1 Box 283, Beloit, WI 53511

R&J Gun Shop, 337 S Humbolt St, Canyon City, OR 97820 / 541-575-2130 rjgunshop@highdestertnet.com

R&S Industries Corp., 8255 Brentwood Industrial Dr., St. Louis, MO 63144 / 314-781-5400 polishingcloth.com

R. Murphy Co., Inc., 13 Groton-Harvard Rd., P.O. Box 376, Ayer, MA 01432 / 617-772-3481

R.A. Wells Custom Gunsmith, 3452 1st Ave., Racine, WI 53402 / 414-639-5223

R.E. Seebeck Assoc., P.O. Box 59752, Dallas, TX 75229

R.E.I., P.O. Box 88, Tallevast, FL 34270 / 813-755-0085

R.E.T. Enterprises, 2608 S. Chestnut, Broken Arrow, OK 74012 / 918-251-GUNS; FAX: 918-251-0587

R.F. Mitchell Bullets, 430 Walnut St., Westernport, MD 21562

R.I.S. Co., Inc., 718 Timberlake Circle, Richardson, TX 75080 / 214-235-0933

R.M. Precision, P.O. Box 210, LaVerkin, UT 84745 / 801-635-4656; FAX: 801-635-4430

R.T. Eastman Products, P.O. Box 1531, Jackson, WY 83001 / 307-733-3217 or 800-624-4311

Rabeno, Martin, 92 Spook Hole Rd., Ellenville, NY 12428 / 914-647-4567; FAX: 914-647-2129

Radack Photography, Lauren, 21140 Jib Court L-12, Aventura, FL 33180 / 305-931-3110

Radiator Specialty Co., 1900 Wilkinson Blvd., P.O. Box 34689, Charlotte, NC 28234 / 800-438-6947; FAX: 800-421-9525

MANUFACTURER'S DIRECTORY

Radical Concepts, P.O. Box 1473, Lake Grove, OR 97035 / 503-538-7437

Rainier Ballistics Corp., 4500 15th St. East, Tacoma, WA 98424 / 800-638-8722 or 206-922-7589; FAX: 206-922-7854

Ralph Bone Engraving, 718 N. Atlanta, Owasso, OK 74055 / 918-272-9745

Ram-Line Blount, Inc., P.O. Box 39, Onalaska, WI 54650

Ramon B. Gonzalez Guns, P.O. Box 370, 93 St. Joseph's Hill Road, Monticello, NY 12701 / 914-794-4515

Rampart International, 2781 W. MacArthur Blvd., B-283, Santa Ana, CA 92704 / 800-976-7240 or 714-557-6405

Ranch Products, P.O. Box 145, Malinta, OH 43535 / 313-277-3118; FAX: 313-565-8536

Randall-Made Knives, P.O. Box 1988, Orlando, FL 32802 / 407-855-8075

Randco UK, 286 Gipsy Rd., Welling, DA16 1JJ ENGLAND / 44 81 303 4118

Randolph Engineering, Inc., 26 Thomas Patten Dr., Randolph, MA 02368 / 800-541-1405; FAX: 800-875-4200

Randy Duane Custom Stocks, 110 W. North Ave., Winchester, VA 22601 / 703-667-9461; FAX: 703-722-3993

Range Brass Products Company, P.O. Box 218, Rockport, TX 78381

Ranger Products, 2623 Grand Blvd., Suite 209, Holiday, FL 34609 / 813-942-4652 or 800-407-7007; FAX: 813-942-6221

Ranger Shooting Glasses, 26 Thomas Patten Dr., Randolph, MA 02368 / 800-541-1405; FAX: 617-986-0337

Ranging, Inc., Routes 5 & 20, East Bloomfield, NY 14443 / 716-657-6161; FAX: 716-657-5405

Ransom International Corp., 1027 Spire Dr, Prescott, AZ 86302 / 520-778-7899; FAX: 520-778-7993 ransom@primenet.com www.ransom-intl.com

Rapine Bullet Mould Mfg. Co., 9503 Landis Lane, East Greenville, PA 18041 / 215-679-5413; FAX: 215-679-9795

Raptor Arms Co., Inc., 273 Canal St, #179, Shelton, CT 06484 / 203-924-7618; FAX: 203-924-7624

Ravell Ltd., 289 Diputacion St., 08009, Barcelona, SPAIN / 34(3) 4874486; FAX: 34(3) 4881394

Ray Riling Arms Books Co., 6844 Gorsten St., P.O. Box 18925, Philadelphia, PA 19119 / 215-438-2456; FAX: 215-438-5395

Ray's Gunsmith Shop, 3199 Elm Ave., Grand Junction, CO 81504 / 970-434-6162; FAX: 970-434-6162

Raytech Div. of Lyman Products Corp., 475 Smith Street, Middletown, CT 06457-1541 / 860-632-2020; FAX: 860-632-1699

RCBS Div. of Blount, 605 Oro Dam Blvd., Oroville, CA 95965 / 800-533-5000 or 916-533-5191; FAX: 916-533-1647 www.rcbs.com

Reagent Chemical & Research, Inc. (See Calico Hardwoods, Inc.)

Reardon Products, P.O. Box 126, Morrison, IL 61270 / 815-772-3155

Red Diamond Dist. Co., 1304 Snowdon Dr., Knoxville, TN 37912

Redding Reloading Equipment, 1089 Starr Rd., Cortland, NY 13045 / 607-753-3331; FAX: 607-756-8445

Redfield Media Resource Center, 4607 N.E. Cedar Creek Rd., Woodland, WA 98674 / 360-225-5000 FAX: 360-225-7616

Redfield, Inc., 5800 E Jewell Ave, Denver, CO 80224 / 303-757-6411; FAX: 303-756-2338

Redfield/Blount, PO Box 39, Onalaska, WI 54650 / 800-635-7656

Redman's Rifling & Reboring, 189 Nichols Rd., Omak, WA 98841 / 509-826-5512

Redwood Bullet Works, 3559 Bay Rd., Redwood City, CA 94063 / 415-367-6741

Reed, Dave, Rt. 1, Box 374, Minnesota City, MN 55959 / 507-689-2944

Reiswig, Wallace E. (See Claro Walnut Gunstock Co.,)

Reloaders Equipment Co., 4680 High St., Ecorse, ML 48229

Reloading Specialties, Inc., Box 1130, Pine Island, MN 55463 / 507-356-8500; FAX: 507-356-8800

Remington Arms Co., Inc., 870 Remington Drive, P.O. Box 700, Madison, NC 27025-0700 / 800-243-9700; FAX: 910-548-8700

Remington Double Shotguns, 7885 Cyd Dr., Denver, CO 80221 / 303-429-6947

Renato Gamba S.p.A.-Societa Armi Bresciane Srl., Via Artigiani 93, 25063 Gardone, Val Trompia (BS), ITALY / 30-8911640; FAX: 30-8911648

Renegade, P.O. Box 31546, Phoenix, AZ 85046 / 602-482-6777; FAX: 602-482-1952

Renfrew Guns & Supplies, R.R. 4, Renfrew, ON K7V 3Z7 CANADA / 613-432-7080

Reno, Wayne, 2808 Stagestop Rd, Jefferson, CO 80456 / 719-836-3452

Republic Arms, Inc., 15167 Sierra Bonita Lane, Chino, CA 91710 / 909-597-3873; FAX: 909-597-2612

Retting, Inc., Martin B, 11029 Washington, Culver City, CA 90232 / 213-837-2412

RG-G, Inc., PO Box 935, Trinidad, CO 81082 / 719-845-1436

Rhino, P.O. Box 787, Locust, NC 28097 / 704-753-2198

Rhodeside, Inc., 1704 Commerce Dr., Piqua, OH 45356 / 513-773-5781

Rice, Keith (See White Rock Tool & Die)

Richard H.R. Loweth (Firearms), 29 Hedgegrow Lane, Kirby Muxloe, Leics. LE9 2BN, ENGLAND

Richards Micro-Fit Stocks, 8331 N. San Fernando Ave., Sun Valley, CA 91352 / 818-767-6097; FAX: 818-767-7121

Rickard, Inc., Pete, RD 1, Box 292, Cobleskill, NY 12043 / 800-282-5663; FAX: 518-234-2454

Ridgeline, Inc, Bruce Sheldon, PO Box 930, Dewey, AZ 86327-0930 / 800-632-5900; FAX: 520-632-5900

Ridgetop Sporting Goods, P.O. Box 306, 42907 Hilligoss Ln. East, Eatonville, WA 98328 / 360-832-6422; FAX: 360-832-6422

Ries, Chuck, 415 Ridgecrest Dr., Grants Pass, OR 97527 / 503-476-5623

Rifles, Inc., 873 W. 5400 N., Cedar City, UT 84720 / 801-586-5996; FAX: 801-586-5996

Rigby & Co., John, 66 Great Suffolk St, London, ENGLAND / 0171-620-0690; FAX: 0171-928-9205

Riggs, Jim, 206 Azalea, Boerne, TX 78006 / 210-249-8567

Riley Ledbetter Airguns, 1804 E. Sprague St., Winston Salem, NC 27107-3521 / 919-784-0676

Riling Arms Books Co., Ray, 6844 Gorsten St, PO Box 18925, Philadelphia, PA 19119 / 215-438-2456; FAX: 215-438-5395

Rim Pac Sports, Inc., 1034 N. Soldano Ave., Azusa, CA 91702-2135

Ringler Custom Leather Co., 31 Shining Mtn. Rd., Powell, WY 82435 / 307-645-3255

Ripley Rifles, 42 Fletcher Street, Ripley, Derbyshire, DE5 3LP ENGLAND / 011-0773-748353

River Road Sporting Clays, Bruce Barsotti, P.O. Box 3016, Gonzales, CA 93926 / 408-675-2473

Rizzini F.lli (See U.S. Importers-Moore & C England)

Rizzini SNC, Via 2 Giugno, 7/7Bis-25060, Marcheno (Brescia), ITALY

RLCM Enterprises, 110 Hill Crest Drive, Burleson, TX 76028

RMS Custom Gunsmithing, 4120 N. Bitterwell, Prescott Valley, AZ 86314 / 520-772-7626

Robert Evans Engraving, 332 Vine St., Oregon City, OR 97045 / 503-656-5693

Robert Valade Engraving, 931 3rd Ave., Seaside, OR 97138 / 503-738-7672

Roberts Products, 25328 SE Iss. Beaver Lk. Rd., Issaquah, WA 98029 / 206-392-8172

Robinett, R. G., P.O. Box 72, Madrid, IA 50156 / 515-795-2906

Robinson, Don, Pennsylvaia Hse, 36 Fairfax Crescent, W Yorkshire, ENGLAND / 0422-364458

Robinson Firearms Mfg. Ltd., 1699 Blondeaux Crescent, Kelowna, BC V1Y 4J8 CANADA / 604-868-9596

Robinson H.V. Bullets, 3145 Church St., Zachary, LA 70791 / 504-654-4029

Rochester Lead Works, 76 Anderson Ave., Rochester, NY 14607 / 716-442-8500; FAX: 716-442-4712

Rock River Arms, 101 Noble St., Cleveland, IL 61241

Rockwood Corp., Speedwell Division, 136 Lincoln Blvd., Middlesex, NJ 08846 / 800-243-8274; FAX: 980-560-7475

Rocky Mountain Arms, Inc., 1813 Sunset Pl, Unit D, Longmont, CO 80501 / 800-375-0846; FAX: 303-678-8766

Rocky Mountain High Sports Glasses, 8121 N. Central Park Ave., Skokie, IL 60076 / 847-679-1012 or 800-323-1418; FAX: 847-679-0184

Rocky Mountain Rifle Works Ltd., 1707 14th St., Boulder, CO 80302 / 303-443-9189

Rocky Mountain Target Co., 3 Aloe Way, Leesburg, FL 34788 / 352-365-9598

Rocky Mountain Wildlife Products, P.O. Box 999, La Porte, CO 80535 / 970-484-2768; FAX: 970-484-0807

Rocky Shoes & Boots, 294 Harper St., Nelsonville, OH 45764 / 800-848-9452 or 614-753-1951; FAX: 614-753-4024

Rodgers & Sons Ltd., Joseph (See George Ibberson (Sheffield) Ltd.,)

Rogue Rifle Co., Inc., P.O. Box 20, Prospect, OR 97536 / 541-560-4040; FAX: 541-560-4041

Rogue River Rifleworks, 1317 Spring St., Paso Robles, CA 93446 / 805-227-4706; FAX: FAX:805-227-4723

Rohner, Hans, 1148 Twin Sisters Ranch Rd., Nederland, CO 80466-9600

Rohner, John, 186 Virginia Ave., Asheville, NC 28806 / 303-444-3841

Romain's Custom Guns, Inc., RD 1, Whetstone Rd., Brockport, PA 15823 / 814-265-1948

Ron Frank Custom Classic Arms, 7131 Richland Rd., Ft. Worth, TX 76118 / 817-284-9300; FAX: 817-284-9300

Ron Lutz Engraving, E. 1998 Smokey Valley Rd., Scandinavia, WI 54977 / 715-467-2674

Rooster Laboratories, P.O. Box 412514, Kansas City, MO 64141 / 816-474-1622; FAX: 816-474-1307

Rorschach Precision Products, P.O. Box 151613, Irving, TX 75015 / 214-790-3487

Rosenberg & Son, Jack A, 12229 Cox Ln, Dallas, TX 75234 / 214-241-6302

Rosenthal, Brad and Sallie, 19303 Ossenfort Ct., St. Louis, MO 63038 / 314-273-5159; FAX: 314-273-5149

Ross, Don, 12813 West 83 Terrace, Lenexa, KS 66215 / 913-492-6982

Rosser, Bob, 1824 29th Ave., Suite 214, Birmingham, AL 35209 / 205-870-4422; FAX: 205-870-4421

Rossi Firearms, Braztech, Gary Mchalik, 16175 NW 49th Ave, Miami, FL 33014-6314 / 305-474-0401

Roto Carve, 2754 Garden Ave., Janesville, IA 50647

Rottweil Compe, 1330 Glassell, Orange, CA 92667

Round Edge, Inc., P.O. Box 723, Lansdale, PA 19446 / 215-361-0859

Roy Baker's Leather Goods, P.O. Box 893, Magnolia, AR 71753 / 501-234-0344

Roy's Custom Grips, Rt. 3, Box 174-E, Lynchburg, VA 24504 / 804-993-3470

Royal Arms Gunstocks, 919 8th Ave. NW, Great Falls, MT 59404 / 406-453-1149 FAX: 406-453-1194 royalarms@lmt.net lmt.net/~royalarms

RPM, 15481 N. Twin Lakes Dr., Tucson, AZ 85739 / 520-825-1233; FAX: 520-825-3333

Rubright Bullets, 1008 S. Quince Rd., Walnutport, PA 18088 / 215-767-1339

Rucker Dist. Inc., P.O. Box 479, Terrell, TX 75160 / 214-563-2094

Ruger (See Sturm, Ruger & Co., Inc.)

Rumanya Inc., 11513 Piney Lodge Rd, Gaithersburg, MD 20878-2443 / 281-345-2077; FAX: 281-345-2005

Rundell's Gun Shop, 6198 Frances Rd., Clio, MI 48420 / 313-687-0559

Runge, Robert P., 94 Grove St., Ilion, NY 13357 / 315-894-3036

Rupert's Gun Shop, 2202 Dick Rd., Suite B, Fenwick, MI 48834 / 517-248-3252

Russ Haydon Shooters' Supply, 15018 Goodrich Dr. NW, Gig Harbor, WA 98329 / 253-857-7557; FAX: 253-857-7884

Russ Trading Post, William A. Russ, 23 William St., Addison, NY 14801-1326 / 607-359-3896

Russ, William. (See RUSS TRADING POST)

Rusteprufe Laboratories, 1319 Jefferson Ave., Sparta, WI 54656 / 608-269-4144

Rusty Duck Premium Gun Care Products, 7785 Foundation Dr., Suite 6, Florence, KY 41042 / 606-342-5553; FAX: 606-342-5556

Rutgers Book Center, 127 Raritan Ave., Highland Park, NJ 08904 / 732-545-4344 FAX: 732-545-6686

Rutten (See U.S. Importer-Labanu Inc)

RWS (See US Importer-Dynamit Nobel-RWS, Inc.), 81 Ruckman Rd, Closter, NJ 07624 / 201-767-7971; FAX: 201-767-1589

Ryan, Chad L., RR 3, Box 72, Cresco, IA 52136 / 319-547-4384

S

S&B Industries, 11238 McKinley Rd., Montrose, MI 48457 / 810-639-5491

S&K Mfg. Co., P.O. Box 247, Pittsfield, PA 16340 / 814-563-7808; FAX: 814-563-4067

S&S Firearms, 74-11 Myrtle Ave., Glendale, NY 11385 / 718-497-1100; FAX: 718-497-1105

S.A.R.L. G. Granger, 66 cours Fauriel, 42100, Saint Etienne, FRANCE / 04 77 25 14 73; FAX: 04 77 38 66 99

S.C.R.C., P.O. Box 660, Katy, TX 77492-0660 FAX: 713-578-2124

S.D. Meacham, 1070 Angel Ridge, Peck, ID 83545

S.G.S. Sporting Guns Srl., Via Della Resistenza, 37 20090, Buccinasco, ITALY / 2-45702446; FAX: 2-45702464

S.I.A.C.E. (See U.S. Importer-IAR Inc)

S.L.A.P. Industries, P.O. Box 1121, Parklands, 02121 SOUTH AFRICA / 27-11-788-0030; FAX: 27-11-788-0030

Sabatti S.r.l., via Alessandro Volta 90, 25063 Gardone V.T., Brescia, ITALY / 030-8912207-831312; FAX: 030-8912059

SAECO (See Redding Reloading Equipment)

Saf-T-Lok, 5713 Corporate Way, Suite 100, W. Palm Beach, FL 33407

Safari Outfitters Ltd., 71 Ethan Allan Hwy., Ridgefield, CT 06877 / 203-544-9505

Safari Press, Inc., 15621 Chemical Lane B, Huntington Beach, CA 92649 / 714-894-9080; FAX: 714-894-4949

Safariland Ltd., Inc., 3120 E. Mission Blvd., P.O. Box 51478, Ontario, CA 91761 / 909-923-7300; FAX: 909-923-7400

SAFE, P.O. Box 864, Post Falls, ID 83854 / 208-773-3624 FAX: 208-773-6819 staysafe@safe-llc.com www.safe-llc.com

Safety Speed Holster, Inc., 910 S. Vail Ave., Montebello, CA 90640 / 323-723-4140; FAX: 323-726-6973

Sako Ltd (See U.S. Importer-Stoeger Industries)

Samco Global Arms, Inc., 6995 NW 43rd St., Miami, FL 33166 / 305-593-9782 FAX: 305-593-1014

Sampson, Roger, 2316 Mahogany St., Mora, MN 55051 / 612-679-4868

San Francisco Gun Exchange, 124 Second St., San Francisco, CA 94105 / 415-982-6097

San Marco (See U.S. Importers-Cape Outfitters-EMF)

Sanders Custom Gun Service, 2358 Tyler Lane, Louisville, KY 40205 / 502-454-3338; FAX: 502-451-8857

Sanders Gun and Machine Shop, 145 Delhi Road, Manchester, IA 52057

Sandia Die & Cartridge Co., 37 Atancacio Rd. NE, Auquerque, NM 87123 / 505-298-5729

Sarco, Inc., 323 Union St., Stirling, NJ 07980 / 908-647-3800; FAX: 908-647-9413

Sauer (See U.S. Importers-Paul Co., The, Sigarms Inc.,)

Sauls, R. (See BRYAN & ASSOC)

Saunders Gun & Machine Shop, R.R. 2, Delhi Road, Manchester, IA 52057

Savage Arms (Canada), Inc., 248 Water St., P.O. Box 1240, Lakefield, ON K0L 2H0 CANADA / 705-652-8000; FAX: 705-652-8431

Savage Arms, Inc., 100 Springdale Rd., Westfield, MA 01085 / 413-568-7001; FAX: 413-562-7764

Savage Range Systems, Inc., 100 Springdale RD., Westfield, MA 01085 / 413-568-7001; FAX: 413-562-1152

Saville Iron Co. (See Greenwood Precision)

Savino, Barbara J., P.O. Box 51, West Burke, VT 05871-0051

Scanco Environmental Systems, 5000 Highlands Parkway, Suite 180, Atlanta, GA 30082 / 770-431-0025; FAX: 770-431-0028

Scansport, Inc., P.O. Box 700, Enfield, NH 03748 / 603-632-7654

Scattergun Technologies, Inc., 620 8th Ave. South, Nashville, TN 37203 / 615-254-1441; FAX: 615-254-1449

Sceery Game Calls, P.O. Box 6520, Sante Fe, NM 87502 / 505-471-9110; FAX: 505-471-3476

Schaefer Shooting Sports, P.O. Box 1515, Melville, NY 11747-0515 / 516-643-5466 FAX: 516-643-2426 rschaefe@optonline.net www.schaefershooting.com

Scharch Mfg., Inc., 10325 CR 120, Salida, CO 81201 / 719-539-7242 or 800-836-4683; FAX: 719-539-3021

Scherer, Box 250, Ewing, VA 24240 / 615-733-2615; FAX: 615-733-2073

Schiffman, Curt, 3017 Kevin Cr., Idaho Falls, ID 83402 / 208-524-4684

Schiffman, Mike, 8233 S. Crystal Springs, McCammon, ID 83250 / 208-254-9114

Schiffman, Norman, 3017 Kevin Cr., Idaho Falls, ID 83402 / 208-524-4684

Schmidt & Bender, Inc., 438 Willow Brook Rd., Meriden, NH 03770 / 800-468-3450 or 800-468-3450; FAX: 603-469-3471

Schmidtke Group, 17050 W. Salentine Dr., New Berlin, WI 53151-7349

Schmidtman Custom Ammunition, 6 Gilbert Court, Cotati, CA 94931

Schneider Bullets, 3655 West 214th St., Fairview Park, OH 44126

Schneider Rifle Barrels, Inc, Gary, 12202 N 62nd Pl, Scottsdale, AZ 85254 / 602-948-2525

Schroeder Bullets, 1421 Thermal Ave., San Diego, CA 92154 / 619-423-3523; FAX: 619-423-8124

Schuetzen Pistol Works, 620-626 Old Pacific Hwy. SE, Olympia, WA 98513 / 360-459-3471; FAX: 360-491-3447

Schulz Industries, 16247 Minnesota Ave., Paramount, CA 90723 / 213-439-5903

Schumakers Gun Shop, 512 Prouty Corner Lp. A, Colville, WA 99114 / 509-684-4848

Scope Control, Inc., 5775 Co. Rd. 23 SE, Alexandria, MN 56308 / 612-762-7295

ScopLevel, 151 Lindbergh Ave., Suite C, Livermore, CA 94550 / 925-449-5052; FAX: 925-373-0861

Score High Gunsmithing, 9812-A, Cochiti SE, Albuquerque, NM 087123 / 800-326-5632 or 505-292-5532; FAX: 505-292-2592

Scot Powder, Rt.1 Box 167, McEwen, TN 37101 / 800-416-3006; FAX: 615-729-4211

Scot Powder Co. of Ohio, Inc., Box GD96, Only, TN 37140 / 615-729-4207 or 800-416-3006; FAX: 615-729-4217

Scott, Dwight, 23089 Englehardt St., Clair Shores, MI 48080 / 313-779-4735

Scott Fine Guns Inc., Thad, PO Box 412, Indianola, MS 38751 / 601-887-5929

Scott McDougall & Associates, 7950 Redwood Dr., Suite 13, Cotati, CA 94931 / 707-546-2264; FAX: 707-795-1911 www.colt380.com

Searcy Enterprises, PO Box 584, Boron, CA 93596 / 760-762-6771 FAX: 760-762-0191

Second Chance Body Armor, P.O. Box 578, Central Lake, MI 49622 / 616-544-5721; FAX: 616-544-9824

Seebeck Assoc., R.E., P. O. Box 59752, Dallas, TX 75229

Seecamp Co. Inc., L. W., PO Box 255, New Haven, CT 06502 / 203-877-3429

Segway Industries, P.O. Box 783, Suffern, NY 10901-0783 / 914-357-5510

Seligman Shooting Products, Box 133, Seligman, AZ 86337 / 602-422-3607

Sellier & Bellot, USA Inc, PO Box 27006, Shawnee Mission, KS 66225 / 913-685-0916; FAX: 913-685-0917

Selsi Co., Inc., P.O. Box 10, Midland Park, NJ 07432-0010 / 201-935-0388; FAX: 201-935-5851

Semmer, Charles (See Remington Double Shotguns), 7885 Cyd Dr., Denver, CO 80221 / 303-429-6947

Sentinel Arms, P.O. Box 57, Detroit, MI 48231 / 313-331-1951; FAX: 313-331-1456

Service Armament, 689 Bergen Blvd., Ridgefield, NJ 07657

Servus Footwear Co., 1136 2nd St., Rock Island, IL 61204 / 309-786-7741; FAX: 309-786-9808

Shappy Bullets, 76 Milldale Ave., Plantsville, CT 06479 / 203-621-3704

Sharp Shooter Supply, 4970 Lehman Road, Delphos, OH 45833 / 419-695-3179

Sharps Arms Co., Inc., C., 100 Centennial, Box 885, Big Timber, MT 59011 / 406-932-4353

Shaw, Inc., E. R. (See Small Arms Mfg. Co.)

Shay's Gunsmithing, 931 Marvin Ave., Lebanon, PA 17042

Sheffield Knifemakers Supply, Inc., P.O. Box 741107, Orange City, FL 32774-1107 / 904-775-6453; FAX: 904-774-5754

Sheldon, Bruce. (See RIDGELINE, INC)

Shepherd Enterprises, Inc., Box 189, Waterloo, NE 68069 / 402-779-2424; FAX: 402-779-4010 sshepherd@shepherd-scopes.com www.shepherdscopes.com

Sherwood, George, 46 N. River Dr., Roseburg, OR 97470 / 541-672-3159

Shilen, Inc., 205 Metro Park Blvd., Ennis, TX 75119 / 972-875-5318; FAX: 972-875-5402

Shiloh Creek, Box 357, Cottleville, MO 63338 / 314-925-1842; FAX: 314-925-1842

Shiloh Rifle Mfg., 201 Centennial Dr., Big Timber, MT 59011 / 406-932-4454; FAX: 406-932-5627

Shockley, Harold H., 204 E. Farmington Rd., Hanna City, IL 61536 / 309-565-4524

Shoemaker & Sons Inc., Tex, 714 W Cienega Ave, San Dimas, CA 91773 / 909-592-2071; FAX: 909-592-2378

Shoot Where You Look, Leon Measures, Dept GD, 408 Fair, Livingston, TX 77351

Shoot-N-C Targets (See Birchwood Casey)

Shooter's Choice, 16770 Hilltop Park Place, Chagrin Falls, OH 44023 / 216-543-8808; FAX: 216-543-8811

Shooter's Edge Inc., P.O.Box 769, Trinidad, CO 81082

Shooter's World, 3828 N. 28th Ave., Phoenix, AZ 85017 / 602-266-0170

Shooters Supply, 1120 Tieton Dr., Yakima, WA 98902 / 509-452-1181

Shootin' Accessories, Ltd., P.O. Box 6810, Auburn, CA 95604 / 916-889-2220

Shootin' Shack, Inc., 1065 Silver Beach Rd., Riviera Beach, FL 33403 / 561-842-0990

Shooting Chrony, Inc., 3269 Niagara Falls Blvd., N. Tonawanda, NY 14120 / 905-276-6292; FAX: 416-276-6295

Shooting Specialties (See Titus, Daniel)

Shooting Star, 1715 FM 1626 Ste 105, Manchaca, TX 78652 / 512-462-0009

Shotgun Sports, PO Box 6810, Auburn, CA 95604 / 530-889-2220; FAX: 530-889-9106

Shotguns Unlimited, 2307 Fon Du Lac Rd., Richmond, VA 23229 / 804-752-7115

ShurKatch Corporation, PO Box 850, Richfield Springs, NY 13439 / 315-858-1470; FAX: 315-858-2969

Siegrist Gun Shop, 8752 Turtle Road, Whittemore, MI 48770

Sierra Bullets, 1400 W. Henry St., Sedalia, MO 65301 / 816-827-6300; FAX: 816-827-6300

Sierra Specialty Prod. Co., 1344 Oakhurst Ave., Los Altos, CA 94024 FAX: 415-965-1536

SIG, CH-8212 Neuhausen, SWITZERLAND

SIG-Sauer (See U.S. Importer-Sigarms Inc.)

Sigarms, Inc., Corporate Park, Exeter, NH 03833 / 603-772-2302; FAX: 603-772-9082

Sightron, Inc., 1672B Hwy. 96, Franklinton, NC 27525 / 919-528-8783; FAX: 919-528-0995

Signet Metal Corp., 551 Stewart Ave., Brooklyn, NY 11222 / 718-384-5400; FAX: 718-388-7488

Sile Distributors, Inc., 7 Centre Market Pl., New York, NY 10013 / 212-925-4111; FAX: 212-925-3149

Silencio/Safety Direct, 56 Coney Island Dr., Sparks, NV 89431 / 800-648-1812 or 702-354-4451; FAX: 702-359-1074

Silent Hunter, 1100 Newton Ave., W. Collingswood, NJ 08107 / 609-854-3276

Silhouette Leathers, P.O. Box 1161, Gunnison, CO 81230 / 303-641-6639

Silver Eagle Machining, 18007 N. 69th Ave., Glendale, AZ 85308

Silver Ridge Gun Shop (See Goodwin, Fred)

Simmons, Jerry, 715 Middlebury St., Goshen, IN 46526 / 219-533-8546

Simmons Gun Repair, Inc., 700 S. Rogers Rd., Olathe, KS 66062 / 913-782-3131; FAX: 913-782-4189

Simmons Outdoor Corp., PO Box 217, Heflin, AL 36264

Sinclair International, Inc., 2330 Wayne Haven St., Fort Wayne, IN 46803 / 219-493-1858; FAX: 219-493-2530

Singletary, Kent, 2915 W. Ross, Phoenix, AZ 85027 / 602-582-4900

Sipes Gun Shop, 7415 Asher Ave., Little Rock, AR 72204 / 501-565-8480

Siskiyou Gun Works (See Donnelly, C. P.)

Six Enterprises, 320-D Turtle Creek Ct., San Jose, CA 95125 / 408-999-0201; FAX: 408-999-0216

SKAN A.R., 4 St. Catherines Road, Long Melford, Suffolk, O10 9JU ENGLAND / 011-0787-312942

SKB Shotguns, 4325 S. 120th St., Omaha, NE 68137 / 800-752-2767; FAX: 402-330-8029

Skeoch, Brian R., P.O. Box 279, Glenrock, WY 82637 / 307-436-9655 FAX: 307-436-9034

Skip's Machine, 364 29 Road, Grand Junction, CO 81501 / 303-245-5417

Sklany's Machine Shop, 566 Birch Grove Dr., Kalispell, MT 59901 / 406-755-4257

Slezak, Jerome F., 1290 Marlowe, Lakewood (Cleveland), OH 44107 / 216-221-1668

Slug Group, Inc., P.O. Box 376, New Paris, PA 15554 / 814-839-4517; FAX: 814-839-2601

Slug Site, Ozark Wilds, 21300 Hwy. 5, Versailles, MO 65084 / 573-378-6430 john.ebeling.com

Small Arms Mfg. Co., 5312 Thoms Run Rd., Bridgeville, PA 15017 / 412-221-4343; FAX: 412-221-4303

Small Arms Specialists, 443 Firchburg Rd, Mason, NH 03048 / 603-878-0427 FAX: 603-878-3905 miniguns@empire.net miniguns.com

Small Custom Mould & Bullet Co., Box 17211, Tucson, AZ 85731

Smart Parts, 1203 Spring St., Latrobe, PA 15650 / 412-539-2660; FAX: 412-539-2298

Smires, C. L., 5222 Windmill Lane, Columbia, MD 21044-1328

Smith & Wesson, 2100 Roosevelt Ave., Springfield, MA 01104 / 413-781-8300; FAX: 413-731-8980

Smith, Art, 230 Main St. S., Hector, MN 55342 / 320-848-2760; FAX: 320-848-2760

Smith, Mark A., P.O. Box 182, Sinclair, WY 82334 / 307-324-7929

Smith, Michael, 620 Nye Circle, Chattanooga, TN 37405 / 615-267-8341

Smith, Ron, 5869 Straley, Ft. Worth, TX 76114 / 817-732-6768

Smith, Sharmon, 4545 Speas Rd., Fruitland, ID 83619 / 208-452-6329

Smith Abrasives, Inc., 1700 Sleepy Valley Rd., P.O. Box 5095, Hot Springs, AR 71902-5095 / 501-321-2244; FAX: 501-321-9232

Smith Saddlery, Jesse W., 16909 E Jackson Rd, Elk, WA 99009-9600 / 509-325-0622

Smokey Valley Rifles (See Lutz Engraving, Ron E)

Snapp's Gunshop, 6911 E. Washington Rd., Clare, MI 48617 / 517-386-9226

Sno-Seal, Inc. (See Atsko/Sno-Seal)

Societa Armi Bresciane Srl (See U.S. Importer-Cape Outfitters)

SOS Products Co. (See Buck Stix-SOS Products Co.), Box 3, Neenah, WI 54956

Sotheby's, 1334 York Ave. at 72nd St., New York, NY 10021 / 212-606-7260

Sound Technology, Box 391, Pelham, AL 35124 / 205-664-5860 or 907-486-2825

South Bend Replicas, Inc., 61650 Oak Rd.., South Bend, IN 46614 / 219-289-4500

Southeastern Community College, 1015 S. Gear Ave., West Burlington, IA 52655 / 319-752-2731

Southern Ammunition Co., Inc., 4232 Meadow St., Loris, SC 29569-3124 / 803-756-3262; FAX: 803-756-3583

Southern Bloomer Mfg. Co., P.O. Box 1621, Bristol, TN 37620 / 615-878-6660; FAX: 615-878-8761

Southern Security, 1700 Oak Hills Dr., Kingston, TN 37763 / 423-376-6297; FAX: 800-251-9992

Southwind Sanctions, P.O. Box 445, Aledo, TX 76008 / 817-441-8917

Sparks, Milt, 605 E. 44th St. No. 2, Boise, ID 83714-4800

Spartan-Realtree Products, Inc., 1390 Box Circle, Columbus, GA 31907 / 706-569-9101; FAX: 706-569-0042

Specialty Gunsmithing, Lynn McMurdo, P.O. Box 404, Afton, WY 83110 / 307-886-5535

Specialty Shooters Supply, Inc., 3325 Griffin Rd., Suite 9mm, Fort Lauderdale, FL 33317

Speedfeed, Inc., PO Box 1146, Rocklin, CA 95677 / 916-630-7720; FAX: 916-630-7719

Speer Products Div. of Blount Inc. Sporting Equipm, P.O. Box 856, Lewiston, ID 83501 / 208-746-2351; FAX: 208-746-2915

Spegel, Craig, PO Box 387, Nehalem, OR 97131 / 503-368-5653

Speiser, Fred D., 2229 Dearborn, Missoula, MT 59801 / 406-549-8133

Spencer Reblue Service, 1820 Tupelo Trail, Holt, MI 48842 / 517-694-7474

Spencer's Custom Guns, 4107 Jacobs Creek Dr, Scottsville, VA 24590 / 804-293-6836 FAX: 804-293-6836

SPG LLC, P.O. Box 1625, Cody, WY 82414 / 307-587-7621; FAX: 307-587-7695

Sphinx Engineering SA, Ch. des Grandex-Vies 2, CH-2900, Porrentruy, SWITZERLAND FAX: 41 66 66 30 90

Spokhandguns, Inc., 1206 Fig St., Benton City, WA 99320 / 509-588-5255

Sport Flite Manufacturing Co., P.O. Box 1082, Bloomfield Hills, MI 48303 / 248-647-3747

Sporting Arms Mfg., Inc., 801 Hall Ave., Littlefield, TX 79339 / 806-385-5665; FAX: 806-385-3394

Sporting Clays Of America, 9257 Bluckeye Rd, Sugar Grove, OH 43155-9632 / 740-746-8334; FAX: 740-746-8605

Sports Innovations Inc., P.O. Box 5181, 8505 Jacksboro Hwy., Wichita Falls, TX 76307 / 817-723-6015

Sportsman Safe Mfg. Co., 6309-6311 Paramount Blvd., Long Beach, CA 90805 / 800-266-7150 or 310-984-5445

Sportsman Supply Co., 714 E. Eastwood, P.O. Box 650, Marshall, MO 65340 / 816-886-9393

Sportsman's Communicators, 588 Radcliffe Ave., Pacific Palisades, CA 90272 / 800-538-3752

Sportsmatch U.K. Ltd., 16 Summer St., Leighton Buzzard, Bedfordshire, LU7 8HT ENGLAND / 01525-381638; FAX: 01525-851236

Sportsmen's Exchange & Western Gun Traders, Inc., 560 S. C St., Oxnard, CA 93030 / 805-483-1917

Spradlin's, 457 Shannon Rd, Texos Creek, CO 81223 / 719-275-7105 FAX: 719-275-3852 spradlins@prodigt.net jimspradlin.com

Springfield Sporters, Inc., RD 1, Penn Run, PA 15765 / 412-254-2626; FAX: 412-254-9173

Springfield, Inc., 420 W. Main St., Geneseo, IL 61254 / 309-944-5631; FAX: 309-944-3676

Spyderco, Inc., 4565 N. Hwy. 93, P.O. Box 800, Golden, CO 80403 / 303-279-8383 or 800-525-7770; FAX: 303-278-2229

SSK Industries, 590 Woodvue Lane, Wintersville, OH 43953 / 740-264-0176; FAX: 740-264-2257

Stackpole Books, 5067 Ritter Rd., Mechanicsburg, PA 17055-6921 / 717-796-0411; FAX: 717-796-0412

Stalker, Inc., P.O. Box 21, Fishermans Wharf Rd., Malakoff, TX 75148 / 903-489-1010

Stalwart Corporation, 76 Imperial, Unit A, Evanston, WY 82930 / 307-789-7687; FAX: 307-789-7688

Stan De Treville & Co., 4129 Normal St., San Diego, CA 92103 / 619-298-3393

Stanley Bullets, 2085 Heatheridge Ln., Reno, NV 89509

Stanley Scruggs' Game Calls, Rt. 1, Hwy. 661, Cullen, VA 23934 / 804-542-4241 or 800-323-4828

Star Ammunition, Inc., 5520 Rock Hampton Ct., Indianapolis, IN 46268 / 800-221-5927; FAX: 317-872-5847

Star Bonifacio Echeverria S.A., Torrekva 3, Eibar, 20600 SPAIN / 43-107340; FAX: 43-101524

Star Custom Bullets, P.O. Box 608, 468 Main St., Ferndale, CA 95536 / 707-786-9140; FAX: 707-786-9117

Star Machine Works, PO Box 1872, Pioneer, CA 95666 / 209-295-5000

Stark's Bullet Mfg., 2580 Monroe St., Eugene, OR 97405

Starke Bullet Company, P.O. Box 400, 605 6th St. NW, Cooperstown, ND 58425 / 888-797-3431

Starkey Labs, 6700 Washington Ave. S., Eden Prairie, MN 55344

Starkey's Gun Shop, 9430 McCombs, El Paso, TX 79924 / 915-751-3030

Starlight Training Center, Inc., Rt. 1, P.O. Box 88, Bronaugh, MO 64728 / 417-843-3555

Starline, Inc., 1300 W. Henry St., Sedalia, MO 65301 / 660-827-6640 FAX: 660-827-6650 bjhayden@starline-bra.com http://www.starlinebrass.com

Starr Trading Co., Jedediah, P.O. Box 2007, Farmington Hills, MI 48333 / 810-683-4343; FAX: 810-683-3282

Starrett Co., L. S., 121 Crescent St, Athol, MA 01331 / 978-249-3551 FAX: 978-249-8495

State Arms Gun Co., 815 S. Division St., Waunakee, WI 53597 / 608-849-5800

Steelman's Gun Shop, 10465 Beers Rd., Swartz Creek, MI 48473 / 810-735-4884

Steffens, Ron, 18396 Mariposa Creek Rd., Willits, CA 95490 / 707-485-0873

Stegall, James B., 26 Forest Rd., Wallkill, NY 12589

Steger, James R., 1131 Dorsey Pl., Plainfield, NJ 07062

Steve Henigson & Associates, P.O. Box 2726, Culver City, CA 90231 / 310-305-8288; FAX: 310-305-1905

Steve Kamyk Engraver, 9 Grandview Dr., Westfield, MA 01085-1810 / 413-568-0457

Steve Nastoff's 45 Shop, Inc., 12288 Mahoning Ave., P.O. Box 446, North Jackson, OH 44451 / 330-538-2977

Steves House of Guns, Rt. 1, Minnesota City, MN 55959 / 507-689-2573

Stewart Game Calls, Inc., Johnny, PO Box 7954, 5100 Fort Ave, Waco, TX 76714 / 817-772-3261; FAX: 817-772-3670

Stewart's Gunsmithing, P.O. Box 5854, Pietersburg North 0750, Transvaal, SOUTH AFRICA / 01521-89401

Steyr Mannlicher AG & CO KG, Mannlicherstrasse 1, A-4400, Steyr, AUSTRIA / 0043-7252-78621; FAX: 0043-7252-68621

STI International, 114 Halmar Cove, Georgetown, TX 78628 / 800-959-8201; FAX: 512-819-0465

Stiles Custom Guns, 76 Cherry Run Rd, Box 1605, Homer City, PA 15748 / 712-479-9945

Stillwell, Robert, 421 Judith Ann Dr., Schertz, TX 78154

Stoeger Industries, 5 Mansard Ct., Wayne, NJ 07470 / 201-872-9500 or 800-631-0722; FAX: 201-872-2230

Stoeger Publishing Co. (See Stoeger Industries)

Stone Enterprises Ltd., Rt. 609, P.O. Box 335, Wicomico Church, VA 22579 / 804-580-5114; FAX: 804-580-8421

Stone Mountain Arms, 5988 Peachtree Corners E., Norcross, GA 30071 / 800-251-9412

Stoney Point Products, Inc., PO Box 234, 1822 N Minnesota St, New Ulm, MN 56073-0234 / 507-354-3360; FAX: 507-354-7236 stoney@newulmtel.net www.stoney-point.com

Storage Tech, 1254 Morris Ave., N. Huntingdon, PA 15642 / 800-437-9393

Storey, Dale A. (See DGS Inc.)

Storm, Gary, P.O. Box 5211, Richardson, TX 75083 / 214-385-0862

Stott's Creek Armory, Inc., 2526 S. 475W, Morgantown, IN 46160 / 317-878-5489; FAX: 317-878-9489 www.sccalendar.com

Stratco, Inc., P.O. Box 2270, Kalispell, MT 59901 / 406-755-1221; FAX: 406-755-1226

Strawbridge, Victor W., 6 Pineview Dr., Dover, NH 03820 / 603-742-0013

Strayer, Sandy. (See STRAYER-VOIGT, INC)

Strayer-Voigt, Inc, Sandy Strayer, 3435 Ray Orr Blvd, Grand Prairie, TX 75050 / 972-513-0575

Streamlight, Inc., 1030 W. Germantown Pike, Norristown, PA 19403 / 215-631-0600; FAX: 610-631-0712

Strong Holster Co., 39 Grove St., Gloucester, MA 01930 / 508-281-3300; FAX: 508-281-6321

Strutz Rifle Barrels, Inc., W. C., PO Box 611, Eagle River, WI 54521 / 715-479-4766

Stuart, V. Pat, Rt.1, Box 447-S, Greenville, VA 24440 / 804-556-3845

Sturgeon Valley Sporters, K. Ide, P.O. Box 283, Vanderbilt, MI 49795 / 517-983-4338

Sturm Ruger & Co. Inc., 200 Ruger Rd., Prescott, AZ 86301 / 520-541-8820; FAX: 520-541-8850

Sullivan, David S .(See Westwind Rifles Inc.)

Summit Specialties, Inc., P.O. Box 786, Decatur, AL 35602 / 205-353-0634; FAX: 205-353-9818

Sun Welding Safe Co., 290 Easy St. No.3, Simi Valley, CA 93065 / 805-584-6678 or 800-729-SAFE FAX: 805-584-6169

Sunny Hill Enterprises, Inc., W1790 Cty. HHH, Malone, WI 53049 / 920-795-4722 FAX: 920-795-4822

"Su-Press-On",Inc., P.O. Box 09161, Detroit, MI 48209 / 313-842-4222

Sure-Shot Game Calls, Inc., P.O. Box 816, 6835 Capitol, Groves, TX 77619 / 409-962-1636; FAX: 409-962-5465

Survival Arms, Inc., 273 Canal St., Shelton, CT 06484-3173 / 203-924-6533; FAX: 203-924-2581

Svon Corp., 280 Eliot St., Ashland, MA 01721 / 508-881-8852

Swann, D. J., 5 Orsova Close, Eltham North Vic., 3095 AUSTRALIA / 03-431-0323

Swanndri New Zealand, 152 Elm Ave., Burlingame, CA 94010 / 415-347-6158

SwaroSports, Inc. (See JagerSport Ltd, One Wholesale Way, Cranston, RI 02920 / 800-962-4867; FAX: 401-946-2587

Swarovski Optik North America Ltd., 2 Slater Rd., Cranston, RI 02920 / 401-946-2220 or 800-426-3089 FAX: 401-946-2587

Sweet Home, Inc., P.O. Box 900, Orrville, OH 44667-0900

Swenson's 45 Shop, A. D., 3839 Ladera Vista Rd, Fallbrook, CA 92028-9431

Swift Bullet Co., P.O. Box 27, 201 Main St., Quinter, KS 67752 / 913-754-3959; FAX: 913-754-2359

Swift Instruments, Inc., 952 Dorchester Ave., Boston, MA 02125 / 617-436-2960; FAX: 617-436-3232

Swift River Gunworks, 450 State St., Belchertown, MA 01007 / 413-323-4052

Szweda, Robert (See RMS Custom Gunsmithing)

T

T&S Industries, Inc., 1027 Skyview Dr., W. Carrollton, OH 45449 / 513-859-8414

T.F.C. S.p.A., Via G. Marconi 118, B, Villa Carcina 25069, ITALY / 030-881271; FAX: 030-881826

T.G. Faust, Inc., 544 Minor St., Reading, PA 19602 / 610-375-8549; FAX: 610-375-4488

T.H.U. Enterprises, Inc., P.O. Box 418, Lederach, PA 19450 / 215-256-1665; FAX: 215-256-9718

T.K. Lee Co., 1282 Branchwater Ln., Birmingham, AL 35216 / 205-913-5222

T.W. Menck Gunsmith Inc., 5703 S. 77th St., Ralston, NE 68127

Tabler Marketing, 2554 Lincoln Blvd., Suite 555, Marina Del Rey, CA 90291 / 818-755-4565; FAX: 818-755-0972

Taconic Firearms Ltd., Perry Lane, PO Box 553, Cambridge, NY 12816 / 518-677-2704; FAX: 518-677-5974

TacStar, PO Box 547, Cottonwood, AZ 86326-0547 / 602-639-0072; FAX: 602-634-8781

TacTell, Inc., P.O. Box 5654, Maryville, TN 37802 / 615-982-7855; FAX: 615-558-8294

Tactical Defense Institute, 574 Miami Bluff Ct., Loveland, OH 45140 / 513-677-8229 FAX: 513-677-0447

Talley, Dave, P.O. Box 821, Glenrock, WY 82637 / 307-436-8724 or 307-436-9315

Talmage, William G., 10208 N. County Rd. 425 W., Brazil, IN 47834 / 812-442-0804

Talon Mfg. Co., Inc., 621 W. King St., Martinsburg, WV 25401 / 304-264-9714; FAX: 304-264-9725

Tamarack Products, Inc., P.O. Box 625, Wauconda, IL 60084 / 708-526-9333; FAX: 708-526-9353

Tanfoglio Fratelli S.r.l., via Valtrompia 39, 41, Brescia, ITALY / 30-8910361; FAX: 30-8910183

Tanglefree Industries, 1261 Heavenly Dr., Martinez, CA 94553 / 800-982-4868; FAX: 510-825-3874

Tank's Rifle Shop, P.O. Box 474, Fremont, NE 68026-0474 / 402-727-1317; FAX: 402-721-2573

Tanner (See U.S. Importer-Mandall Shooting Supplies Inc.,)

Tar-Hunt Custom Rifles, Inc., RR3, P.O. Box 572, Bloomsburg, PA 17815-9351 / 717-784-6368; FAX: 717-784-6368

Taracorp Industries, Inc., 1200 Sixteenth St., Granite City, IL 62040 / 618-451-4400

Target Shooting, Inc., PO Box 773, Watertown, SD 57201 / 605-882-6955; FAX: 605-882-8840

Tarnhelm Supply Co., Inc., 431 High St., Boscawen, NH 03303 / 603-796-2551; FAX: 603-796-2918

Tasco Sales, Inc., 2889 Commerce Pkwy., Miramar, FL 33025

DIRECTORY

Taurus International Firearms, Inc., 16175 NW 49th Ave., Miami, FL 33014 / 305-624-1115; FAX: 305-623-7506

Taurus S.A. Forjas, Avenida Do Forte 511, Porto Alegre, RS BRAZIL 91360 / 55-51-347-4050; FAX: 55-51-347-3065

Taylor & Robbins, P.O. Box 164, Rixford, PA 16745 / 814-966-3233

Taylor's & Co., Inc., 304 Lenoir Dr., Winchester, VA 22603 / 540-722-2017; FAX: 540-722-2018

TCCI, P.O. Box 302, Phoenix, AZ 85001 / 602-237-3823; FAX: 602-237-3858

TCSR, 3998 Hoffman Rd., White Bear Lake, MN 55110-4626 / 800-328-5323; FAX: 612-429-0526

TDP Industries, Inc., 606 Airport Blvd., Doylestown, PA 18901 / 215-345-8687; FAX: 215-345-6057

Techno Arms (See U.S. Importer- Auto-Ordnance Corp.)

Tecnolegno S.p.A., Via A. Locatelli, 6 10, 24019 Zogno, I ITALY / 0345-55111; FAX: 0345-55155

Ted Blocker Holsters, Inc., Clackamas Business Park Bldg A, 14787 SE 82nd Dr, Clackamas, OR 97015 / 503-557-7757; FAX: 503-557-3771

Tele-Optics, 630 E. Rockland Rd., PO Box 6313, Libertyville, IL 60048 / 847-362-7757

Ten-Ring Precision, Inc., Alex B. Hamilton, 1449 Blue Crest Lane, San Antonio, TX 78232 / 210-494-3063; FAX: 210-494-3066

TEN-X Products Group, 1905 N Main St, Suite 133, Cleburne, TX 76031-1305 / 972-243-4016 or 800-433-2225; FAX: 972-243-4112

Tennessee Valley Mfg., P.O. Box 1175, Corinth, MS 38834 / 601-286-5014

Tepeco, P.O. Box 342, Friendswood, TX 77546 / 713-482-2702

Terry K. Kopp Professional Gunsmithing, Rt 1 Box 224F, Lexington, MO 64067 / 816-259-2636

Testing Systems, Inc., 220 Pegasus Ave., Northvale, NJ 07647

Teton Arms, Inc., P.O. Box 411, Wilson, WY 83014 / 307-733-3395

Tetra Gun Lubricants (See FTI, Inc.)

Tex Shoemaker & Sons, Inc., 714 W. Cienega Ave., San Dimas, CA 91773 / 909-592-2071; FAX: 909-592-2378

Texas Armory (See Bond Arms, Inc.)

Texas Platers Supply Co., 2453 W. Five Mile Parkway, Dallas, TX 75233 / 214-330-7168

Thad Rybka Custom Leather Equipment, 134 Havilah Hill, Odenville, AL 35120

Thad Scott Fine Guns, Inc., P.O. Box 412, Indianola, MS 38751 / 601-887-5929

The Accuracy Den, 25 Bitterbrush Rd., Reno, NV 89523 / 702-345-0225

The Armoury, Inc., Rt. 202, Box 2340, New Preston, CT 06777 / 860-868-0001; FAX: 860-868-2919

The Ballistic Program Co., Inc., 2417 N. Patterson St., Thomasville, GA 31792 / 912-228-5739 or 800-368-0835

The BulletMakers Workshop, RFD 1 Box 1755, Brooks, ME 04921

The Competitive Pistol Shop, 5233 Palmer Dr., Ft. Worth, TX 76117-2433 / 817-834-8479

The Country Armourer, P.O. Box 308, Ashby, MA 01431-0308 / 508-827-6797; FAX: 508-827-4845

The Creative Craftsman, Inc., 95 Highway 29 North, P.O. Box 331, Lawrenceville, GA 30246 / 404-963-2112; FAX: 404-513-9488

The Custom Shop, 890 Cochrane Crescent, Peterborough, ON K9H 5N3 CANADA / 705-742-6693

The Dutchman's Firearms, Inc., 4143 Taylor Blvd., Louisville, KY 40215 / 502-366-0555

The Ensign-Bickford Co., 660 Hopmeadow St., Simsbury, CT 06070

The Eutaw Co., Inc., P.O. Box 608, U.S. Hwy. 176 West, Holly Hill, SC 29059 / 803-496-3341

The Firearm Training Center, 9555 Blandville Rd., West Paducah, KY 42086 / 502-554-5886

The Fouling Shot, 6465 Parfet St., Arvada, CO 80004

The Gun Doctor, 435 East Maple, Roselle, IL 60172 / 708-894-0668

The Gun Doctor, P.O. Box 39242, Downey, CA 90242 / 310-862-3158

The Gun Parts Corp., 226 Williams Lane, West Hurley, NY 12491 / 914-679-2417; FAX: 914-679-5849

The Gun Room, 1121 Burlington, Muncie, IN 47302 / 765-282-9073; FAX: 765-282-5270 bshstleguns@aol.com

The Gun Room Press, 127 Raritan Ave., Highland Park, NJ 08904 / 732-545-4344; FAX: 732-545-4344

The Gun Shop, 62778 Spring Creek Rd., Montrose, CO 81401

The Gun Shop, 5550 S. 900 East, Salt Lake City, UT 84117 / 801-263-3633

The Gun Shop, 716-A South Rogers Road, Olathe, KS 66062

The Gun Works, 247 S. 2nd, Springfield, OR 97477 / 541-741-4118; FAX: 541-988-1097 gunworks@world-net.att.net www.thegunworks.com

The Gunsight, 1712 North Placentia Ave., Fullerton, CA 92631

The Gunsmith in Elk River, 14021 Victoria Lane, Elk River, MN 55330 / 612-441-7761

The Hanned Line, P.O. Box 2387, Cupertino, CA 95015-2387 smith@hanned.com www.hanned.com

The Holster Shop, 720 N. Flagler Dr., Ft. Lauderdale, FL 33304 / 305-463-7910; FAX: 305-761-1483

The House of Muskets, Inc., P.O. Box 4640, Pagosa Springs, CO 81157 / 970-731-2295

The Keller Co., 4215 McEwen Rd., Dallas, TX 75244 / 214-770-8585

The Lewis Lead Remover (See LEM Gun Specialties Inc.)

The NgraveR Co., 67 Wawecus Hill Rd., Bozrah, CT 06334 / 860-823-1533

The Ordnance Works, 2969 Pidgeon Point Road, Eureka, CA 95501 / 707-443-3252

The Orvis Co., Rt. 7, Manchester, VT 05254 / 802-362-3622; FAX: 802-362-3525

The Outdoor Connection,Inc., 201 Cotton Dr., P.O. Box 7751, Waco, TX 76714-7751 / 800-533-6076 or 817-772-5575; FAX: 817-776-3553

The Outdoorsman's Bookstore, Llangorse, Brecon, LD3 7UE U.K. / 44-1874-658-660; FAX: 44-1874-658-650

The Park Rifle Co., Ltd., Unit 6a Dartford Trade Park, Power Mill Lane, Dartford DA7 7NX, ENGLAND / 011-0322-222512

The Paul Co., 27385 Pressonville Rd., Wellsville, KS 66092 / 785-883-4444; FAX: 785-883-2525

The Powder Horn, Inc., P.O. Box 114 Patty Drive, Cusseta, GA 31805 / 404-989-3257

The Protector Mfg. Co., Inc., 443 Ashwood Place, Boca Raton, FL 33431 / 407-394-6011

The Robar Co.'s, Inc., 21438 N. 7th Ave., Suite B, Phoenix, AZ 85027 / 602-581-2648; FAX: 602-582-0059

The School of Gunsmithing, 6065 Roswell Rd., Atlanta, GA 30328 / 800-223-4542

The Shooting Gallery, 8070 Southern Blvd., Boardman, OH 44512 / 216-726-7788

The Sight Shop, John G. Lawson, 1802 E. Columbia Ave., Tacoma, WA 98404 / 206-474-5465

The Southern Armory, 25 Millstone Road, Woodlawn, VA 24381 / 703-238-1343; FAX: 703-238-1453

The Surecase Co., 233 Wilshire Blvd., Ste. 900, Santa Monica, CA 90401 / 800-92ARMLOC

The Swampfire Shop (See Peterson Gun Shop, Inc.)

The Walnut Factory, 235 West Rd. No. 1, Portsmouth, NH 03801 / 603-436-2225; FAX: 603-433-7003

The Wilson Arms Co., 63 Leetes Island Rd., Branford, CT 06405 / 203-488-7297; FAX: 203-488-0135

Theis, Terry, HC 63 Box 213, Harper, TX 78631 / 830-864-4438

Theoben Engineering, Stephenson Road, St. Ives Huntingdon, Cambs., PE17 4WJ ENGLAND / 011-0480-461718

Thiewes, George W., 14329 W. Parada Dr., Sun City West, AZ 85375

Things Unlimited, 235 N. Kimbau, Casper, WY 82601 / 307-234-5277

Thirion Gun Engraving, Denise, PO Box 408, Graton, CA 95444 / 707-829-1876

Thomas, Charles C., 2600 S. First St., Springfield, IL 62794 / 217-789-8980; FAX: 217-789-9130

Thompson, Norm, 18905 NW Thurman St., Portland, OR 97209

Thompson Bullet Lube Co., P.O. Box 472343, Garland, TX 75047-2343 / 972-271-8063; FAX: 972-840-6743 thomlube@flash.net www.thompsonbulletlube.com

Thompson Precision, 110 Mary St., P.O. Box 251, Warren, IL 61087 / 815-745-3625

Thompson, Randall. (See HIGHLINE MACHINE CO.)

Thompson Target Technology, 618 Roslyn Ave., SW, Canton, OH 44710 / 216-453-7707; FAX: 216-478-4723

Thompson, Randall (See Highline Machine Co.)

Thompson/Center Arms, P.O. Box 5002, Rochester, NH 03867 / 603-332-2394; FAX: 603-332-5133

3-D Ammunition & Bullets, PO Box 433, Doniphan, NE 68832 / 402-845-2285 or 800-255-6712; FAX: 402-845-6546

3-Ten Corp., P.O. Box 269, Feeding Hills, MA 01030 / 413-789-2086; FAX: 413-789-1549

300 Below Services (See Cryo-Accurizing)

Thunden Ranch, HCR 1, Box 53, Mt. Home, TX 78058 / 830-640-3138

Thunder Mountain Arms, P.O. Box 593, Oak Harbor, WA 98277 / 206-679-4657; FAX: 206-675-1114

Thurston Sports, Inc., RD 3 Donovan Rd., Auburn, NY 13021 / 315-253-0966

Tiger-Hunt Gunstocks, Box 379, Beaverdale, PA 15921 / 814-472-5161 tigerhunt4@aol.com www.gunstock-wood.com

Tikka (See U.S. Importer-Stoeger Industries)

Timber Heirloom Products, 618 Roslyn Ave. SW, Canton, OH 44710 / 216-453-7707; FAX: 216-478-4723

Time Precision, Inc., 640 Federal Rd., Brookfield, CT 06804 / 203-775-8343

Tink's Safariland Hunting Corp., P.O. Box 244, 1140 Monticello Rd., Madison, GA 30650 / 706-342-4915; FAX: 706-342-7568

Tinks & Ben Lee Hunting Products (See Wellington Outdoors)

Tioga Engineering Co., Inc., P.O. Box 913, 13 Cone St., Wellsboro, PA 16901 / 717-724-3533; FAX: 717-662-3347

Tippman Pneumatics, Inc., 3518 Adams Center Rd., Fort Wayne, IN 46806 / 219-749-6022; FAX: 219-749-6619

Tirelli, Snc Di Tirelli Primo E.C., Via Matteotti No. 359, Gardone V.T. Brescia, I ITALY / 030-8912819; FAX: 030-832240

TM Stockworks, 6355 Maplecrest Rd., Fort Wayne, IN 46835 / 219-485-5389

TMI Products (See Haselbauer Products, Jerry)

Tom Forrest, Inc., P.O. Box 326, Lakeside, CA 92040 / 619-561-5800; FAX: 619-561-0227

Tom's Gun Repair, Thomas G. Ivanoff, 76-6 Rt. Southfork Rd., Cody, WY 82414 / 307-587-6949

Tom's Gunshop, 3601 Central Ave., Hot Springs, AR 71913 / 501-624-3856

Tombstone Smoke'n' Deals, 3218 East Bell Road, Phoenix, AZ 85032 / 602-905-7013; FAX: 602-443-1998

Tonoloway Tack Drives, HCR 81, Box 100, Needmore, PA 17238

Tooley Custom Rifles, 516 Creek Meadow Dr., Gastonia, NC 28054 / 704-864-7525

Top-Line USA, Inc., 7920-28 Hamilton Ave., Cincinnati, OH 45231 / 513-522-2992 or 800-346-6699; FAX: 513-522-0916

Torel, Inc., 1708 N. South St., P.O. Box 592, Yoakum, TX 77995 / 512-293-2341; FAX: 512-293-3413

TOZ (See U.S. Importer-Nygord Precision Products)

Track of the Wolf, Inc., P.O. Box 6, Osseo, MN 55369-0006 / 612-424-2500; FAX: 612-424-9860

TracStar Industries, Inc., 218 Justin Dr., Cottonwood, AZ 86326 / 520-639-0072; FAX: 520-634-8781

Tradewinds, Inc., P.O. Box 1191, 2339-41 Tacoma Ave. S., Tacoma, WA 98401 / 206-272-4887

Traditions Performance Firearms, P.O. Box 776, 1375 Boston Post Rd., Old Saybrook, CT 06475 / 860-388-4656; FAX: 860-388-4657 trad@ctz.nai.net www.traditionsmuzzle.com

Trafalgar Square, P.O. Box 257, N. Pomfret, VT 05053 / 802-457-1911

Traft Gunshop, P.O. Box 1078, Buena Vista, CO 81211

Trail Visions, 5800 N. Ames Terrace, Glendale, WI 53209 / 414-228-1328

Trammco, 839 Gold Run Rd., Boulder, CO 80302

Trax America, Inc., P.O. Box 898, 1150 Eldridge, Forrest City, AR 72335 / 870-633-0410 or 800-232-2327; FAX: 870-633-4788

Treadlok Gun Safe, Inc., 1764 Granby St. NE, Roanoke, VA 24012 / 800-729-8732 or 703-982-6881; FAX: 703-982-1059

Treemaster, P.O. Box 247, Guntersville, AL 35976 / 205-878-3597

Treso, Inc., P.O. Box 4640, Pagosa Springs, CO 81157 / 303-731-2295

Trevallion Gunstocks, 9 Old Mountain Rd., Cape Neddick, ME 03902 / 207-361-1130

Trico Plastics, 590 S. Vincent Ave., Azusa, CA 91702

Trigger Lock Division/Central Specialties Ltd., 1122 Silver Lake Road, Cary, IL 60013 / 847-639-3900; FAX: 847-639-3972

Trijicon, Inc., 49385 Shafer Ave., P.O. Box 930059, Wixom, MI 48393-0059 / 810-960-7700; FAX: 810-960-7725

Trilux, Inc., P.O. Box 24608, Winston-Salem, NC 27114 / 910-659-9438; FAX: 910-768-7720

Trinidad St. Jr Col Gunsmith Dept, 600 Prospect St., Trinidad, CO 81082 / 719-846-5631; FAX: 719-846-5667

Triple-K Mfg. Co., Inc., 2222 Commercial St., San Diego, CA 92113 / 619-232-2066; FAX: 619-232-7675

Tristar Sporting Arms, Ltd., 1814-16 Linn St., P.O. Box 7496, N. Kansas City, MO 64116 / 816-421-1400; FAX: 816-421-4182

Trius Traps, Inc., P.O. Box 471, 221 S. Miami Ave., Cleves, OH 45002 / 513-941-5682; FAX: 513-941-7970

Trooper Walsh, 2393 N Edgewood St, Arlington, VA 22207

Trophy Bonded Bullets, Inc., 900 S. Loop W., Suite 190, Houston, TX 77054 / 713-645-4499 or 888-308-3006; FAX: 713-741-6393

Trotman, Ken, 135 Ditton Walk, Unit 11, Cambridge, CB5 8PY ENGLAND / 01223-211030; FAX: 01223-212317

Tru-Balance Knife Co., P.O. Box 140555, Grand Rapids, MI 49514 / 616-453-3679

Tru-Square Metal Prods., Inc., 640 First St. SW, P.O. Box 585, Auburn, WA 98071 / 206-833-2310; FAX: 206-833-2349

True Flight Bullet Co., 5581 Roosevelt St., Whitehall, PA 18052 / 610-262-7630; FAX: 610-262-7806

Truglo, Inc, PO Box 1612, McKinna, TX 75070 / 972-774-0300 FAX: 972-774-0323 www.truglosights.com

Trulock Tool, Broad St., Whigham, GA 31797 / 912-762-4678

TTM, 1550 Solomon Rd., Santa Maria, CA 93455 / 805-934-1281

Tucker, James C., P.O. Box 1212, Paso Robles, CA 93447-1212

Tucson Mold, Inc., 930 S. Plumer Ave., Tucson, AZ 85719 / 520-792-1075; FAX: 520-792-1075

Turkish Firearms Corp., 522 W. Maple St., Allentown, PA 18101 / 610-821-8660; FAX: 610-821-9049

Turnbull Restoration, Doug, 6680 Rt 58 & 20 Dept. SM 2000, PO Box 471, Bloomfield, NY 14469 / 716-657-6338

Tuttle, Dale, 4046 Russell Rd., Muskegon, MI 49445 / 616-766-2250

Tyler Manufacturing & Distributing, 3804 S. Eastern, Oklahoma City, OK 73129 / 405-677-1487 or 800-654-8415

U

U.S. Importer-Wm. Larkin Moore, 8430 E. Raintree Ste. B-7, Scottsdale, AZ 85260

U.S. Patent Fire Arms, No. 25-55 Van Dyke Ave., Hartford, CT 06106 / 800-877-2832; FAX: 800-644-7265

U.S. Repeating Arms Co., Inc., 275 Winchester Ave., Morgan, UT 84050-9333 / 801-876-3440; FAX: 801-876-3737

U.S. Tactical Systems (See Keng's Firearms Specialty)

U.S.A. Magazines, Inc., P.O. Box 39115, Downey, CA 90241 / 800-872-2577

Uberti, Aldo, Casella Postale 43, I-25063 Gardone V.T., ITALY

Uberti USA, Inc., P.O. Box 469, Lakeville, CT 06039 / 860-435-8068; FAX: 860-435-8146

UFA, Inc., 6927 E. Grandview Dr., Scottsdale, AZ 85254 / 800-616-2776

Ugartechea S. A., Ignacio, Chonta 26, Eibar, SPAIN / 43-121257; FAX: 43-121669

Ultimate Accuracy, 121 John Shelton Rd., Jacksonville, AR 72076 / 501-985-2530

Ultra Dot Distribution, 2316 N.E. 8th Rd., Ocala, FL 34470

Ultra Light Arms, Inc., P.O. Box 1270, 214 Price St., Granville, WV 26505 / 304-599-5687; FAX: 304-599-5687

Ultralux (See U.S. Importer-Keng's Firearms Specia

UltraSport Arms, Inc., 1955 Norwood Ct., Racine, WI 53403 / 414-554-3237; FAX: 414-554-9731

Uncle Bud's, HCR 81, Box 100, Needmore, PA 17238 / 717-294-6000; FAX: 717-294-6005

Uncle Mike's (See Michaels of Oregon Co)

Unertl Optical Co. Inc., John, 308 Clay Ave, PO Box 818, Mars, PA 16046-0818 / 412-625-3810

Unique/M.A.P.F., 10 Les Allees, 64700, Hendaye, FRANCE / 33-59 20 71 93

UniTec, 1250 Bedford SW, Canton, OH 44710 / 216-452-4017

United Binocular Co., 9043 S. Western Ave., Chicago, IL 60620

United Cutlery Corp., 1425 United Blvd., Sevierville, TN 37876 / 865-428-2532 or 800-548-0835 FAX: 865-428-2267

United States Optics Technologies, Inc., 5900 Dale St., Buena Park, CA 90621 / 714-994-4901; FAX: 714-994-4904

United States Products Co., 518 Melwood Ave., Pittsburgh, PA 15213 / 412-621-2130; FAX: 412-621-8740

Universal Sports, P.O. Box 532, Vincennes, IN 47591 / 812-882-8680; FAX: 812-882-8680

Unmussig Bullets, D. L., 7862 Brentford Dr., Richmond, VA 23225 / 804-320-1165

Upper Missouri Trading Co., 304 Harold St., Crofton, NE 68730 / 402-388-4844

USAC, 4500-15th St. East, Tacoma, WA 98424 / 206-922-7589

Utica Cutlery Co., 820 Noyes St., Utica, NY 13503 / 315-733-4663; FAX: 315-733-6602

V

V.H. Blackinton & Co., Inc., 221 John L. Dietsch, Attleboro Falls, MA 02763-0300 / 508-699-4436; FAX: 508-695-5349

Valade Engraving, Robert, 931 3rd Ave, Seaside, OR 97138 / 503-738-7672

Valor Corp., 5555 NW 36th Ave., Miami, FL 33142 / 305-633-0127; FAX: 305-634-4536

Valtro USA, Inc, 1281 Andersen Dr, San Rafael, CA 94901 / 415-256-2575; FAX: 415-256-2576

VAM Distribution Co LLC, 1141-B Mechanicsburg Rd, Wooster, OH 44691 www.rex10.com

Van Gorden & Son Inc., C. S., 1815 Main St., Bloomer, WI 54724 / 715-568-2612

Van Horn, Gil, P.O. Box 207, Llano, CA 93544

Van Patten, J. W., P.O. Box 145, Foster Hill, Milford, PA 18337 / 717-296-7069

Van's Gunsmith Service, 224 Route 69-A, Parish, NY 13131 / 315-625-7251

Vancini, Carl (See Bestload, Inc.)

Vann Custom Bullets, 330 Grandview Ave., Novato, CA 94947

Varmint Masters, LLC, Rick Vecqueray, PO Box 6724, Bend, OR 97708 / 541-318-7306; FAX: 541-318-7306 varmintmasters@bendnet.com

Vecqueray, Rick. (See VARMINT MASTERS, LLC)

Vega Tool Co., c/o T.R. Ross, 4865 Tanglewood Ct., Boulder, CO 80301 / 303-530-0174

Vektor USA, Mikael Danforth, 5139 Stanart St, Norfolk, VA 23502 / 888-740-0837; or 757-455-8895; FAX: 757-461-9155

Venco Industries, Inc. (See Shooter's Choice)

Venus Industries, P.O. Box 246, Sialkot-1, PAKISTAN FAX: 92 432 85579

Verney-Carron, B.P. 72, 54 Boulevard Thiers, 42002, FRANCE / 33-477791500; FAX: 33-477790702

Vest, John, P.O. Box 1552, Susanville, CA 96130 / 916-257-7228

Vibra-Tek Co., 1844 Arroya Rd., Colorado Springs, CO 80906 / 719-634-8611; FAX: 719-634-6886

VibraShine, Inc., P.O. Box 577, Taylorsville, MS 39168 / 601-785-9854; FAX: 601-785-9874

Vic's Gun Refinishing, 6 Pineview Dr., Dover, NH 03820-6422 / 603-742-0013

Victory Ammunition, PO Box 1022, Milford, PA 18337 / 717-296-5768; FAX: 717-296-9298

Victory USA, P.O. Box 1021, Pine Bush, NY 12566 / 914-744-2060; FAX: 914-744-5181

Vihtavuori Oy, FIN-41330 Vihtavuori, FINLAND, / 358-41-3779211; FAX: 358-41-3771643

Vihtavuori Oy/Kaltron-Pettibone, 1241 Ellis St., Bensenville, IL 60106 / 708-350-1116; FAX: 708-350-1606

Viking Video Productions, P.O. Box 251, Roseburg, OR 97470

Vincent's Shop, 210 Antoinette, Fairbanks, AK 99701

Vincenzo Bernardelli S.p.A., 125 Via Matteotti, P.O. Box 74, Gardone V.T., Bresci, 25063 ITALY / 39-30-8912851-2-3; FAX: 39-30-8910249+

Vintage Arms, Inc., 6003 Saddle Horse, Fairfax, VA 22030 / 703-968-0779; FAX: 703-968-0780

Vintage Industries, Inc., 781 Big Tree Dr., Longwood, FL 32750 / 407-831-8949; FAX: 407-831-5346

Viper Bullet and Brass Works, 11 Brock St., Box 582, Norwich, ON N0J 1P0 CANADA

Viramontez, Ray, 601 Springfield Dr., Albany, GA 31707 / 912-432-9683

Virgin Valley Custom Guns, 450 E 800 N #20, Hurricane, UT 84737 / 435-635-8941; FAX: 435-635-8943 vvcguns@infowest.com www.virginvalleyguns.com

Visible Impact Targets, Rts. 5 & 20, E. Bloomfield, NY 14443 / 716-657-6161; FAX: 716-657-5405

Vitt/Boos, 2178 Nichols Ave., Stratford, CT 06614 / 203-375-6859

Voere-KGH m.b.H., P.O. Box 416, A-6333 Kufstein, Tirol, AUSTRIA / 0043-5372-62547; FAX: 0043-5372-65752

Volquartsen Custom Ltd., 24276 240th Street, P.O. Box 397, Carroll, IA 51401 / 712-792-4238; FAX: 712-792-2542

Vom Hoffe (See Old Western Scrounger, Inc., The), 12924 Hwy A-12, Montague, CA 96064 / 916-459-5445; FAX: 916-459-3944

Vorhes, David, 3042 Beecham St., Napa, CA 94558 / 707-226-9116

Vortek Products, Inc., P.O. Box 871181, Canton, MI 48187-6181 / 313-397-5656; FAX: 313-397-5656

VSP Publishers (See Heritage/VSP Gun Books), PO Box 887, McCall, ID 83638 / 208-634-4104; FAX: 208-634-3101

Vulpes Ventures, Inc. Fox Cartridge Division, P.O. Box 1363, Bolingbrook, IL 60440-7363 / 630-759-1229; FAX: 815-439-3945

W

W. Square Enterprises, 9826 Sagedale, Houston, TX 77089 / 713-484-0935; FAX: 281-484-0935

W. Square Enterprises, Load From A Disk, 9826 Sagedale, Houston, TX 77089 / 713-484-0935; FAX: 281-484-0935

W. Waller & Son, Inc., 2221 Stoney Brook Rd., Grantham, NH 03753-7706 / 603-863-4177

W.B. Niemi Engineering, Box 126 Center Road, Greensboro, VT 05841 / 802-533-7180 or 802-533-7141

W.C. Strutz Rifle Barrels, Inc., P.O. Box 611, Eagle River, WI 54521 / 715-479-4766

W.C. Wolff Co., PO Box 458, Newtown Square, PA 19073 / 610-359-9600; FAX: 610-359-9496

W.E. Birdsong & Assoc., 1435 Monterey Rd., Florence, MS 39073-9748 / 601-366-8270

W.E. Brownell Checkering Tools, 9390 Twin Mountain Cir, San Diego, CA 92126 / 619-695-2479; FAX: 619-695-2479

W.J. Riebe Co., 3434 Tucker Rd., Boise, ID 83703

W.R. Case & Sons Cutlery Co., Owens Way, Bradford, PA 16701 / 814-368-4123 or 800-523-6350; FAX: 814-768-5369

Wagoner, Vernon G., 2325 E. Encanto, Mesa, AZ 85213 / 602-835-1307

Wakina by Pic, 24813 Alderbrook Dr., Santa Clarita, CA 91321 / 800-295-8194

Waldron, Herman, Box 475, 80 N. 17th St., Pomeroy, WA 99347 / 509-843-1404

Walker Arms Co., Inc., 499 County Rd. 820, Selma, AL 36701 / 334-872-6231; FAX: 334-872-6262

Walker Mfg., Inc., 8296 S. Channel, Harsen's Island, ML 48028

Wallace, Terry, 385 San Marino, Vallejo, CA 94589 / 707-642-7041

Walls Industries, Inc., P.O. Box 98, 1905 N. Main, Cleburne, TX 76031 / 817-645-4366; FAX: 817-645-7946

Walt's Custom Leather, Walt Whinnery, 1947 Meadow Creek Dr., Louisville, KY 40218 / 502-458-4361

Walters, John, 500 N. Avery Dr., Moore, OK 73160 / 405-799-0376

Walters Industries, 6226 Park Lane, Dallas, TX 75225 / 214-691-6973

Walther GmbH, Carl, B.P. 4325, D-89033 Ulm, GERMANY

WAMCO, Inc., Mingo Loop, P.O. Box 337, Oquossoc, ME 04964-0337 / 207-864-3344

WAMCO--New Mexico, P.O. Box 205, Peralta, NM 87042-0205 / 505-869-0826

Ward & Van Valkenburg, 114 32nd Ave. N., Fargo, ND 58102 / 701-232-2351

Ward Machine, 5620 Lexington Rd., Corpus Christi, TX 78412 / 512-992-1221

Wardell Precision Handguns Ltd., 48851 N. Fig Springs Rd., New River, AZ 85027-8513 / 602-465-7995

Warenski, Julie, 590 E. 500 N., Richfield, UT 84701 / 801-896-5319; FAX: 801-896-5319

Warne Manufacturing Co., 9039 SE Jannsen Rd., Clackamas, OR 97015 / 503-657-5590 or 800-683-5590; FAX: 503-657-5695

Warren & Sweat Mfg. Co., P.O. Box 350440, Grand Island, FL 32784 / 904-669-3166; FAX: 904-669-7272

Warren Muzzleloading Co., Inc., Hwy. 21 North, P.O. Box 100, Ozone, AR 72854 / 501-292-3268

Warren, Kenneth W. (See Mountain States Engraving)

Washita Mountain Whetstone Co., P.O. Box 378, Lake Hamilton, AR 71951 / 501-525-3914

Wasmundt, Jim, P.O. Box 511, Fossil, OR 97830

WASP Shooting Systems, Rt. 1, Box 147, Lakeview, AR 72642 / 501-431-5606

Waterfield Sports, Inc., 13611 Country Lane, Burnsville, MN 55337 / 612-435-8339

Watson Bros., 39 Redcross Way, London Bridge, LONDON U.K. FAX: 44-171-403-336

Watson Trophy Match Bullets, 2404 Wade Hampton Blvd., Greenville, SC 29615 / 864-244-7948 or 941-635-7948

Wayne E. Schwartz Custom Guns, 970 E. Britton Rd., Morrice, MI 48857 / 517-625-4079

Wayne Firearms for Collectors and Investors, James, 2608 N. Laurent, Victoria, TX 77901 / 512-578-1258; FAX: 512-578-3559

Wayne Reno, 2808 Stagestop Rd., Jefferson, CO 80456 / 719-836-3452

Wayne Specialty Services, 260 Waterford Drive, Florissant, MO 63033 / 413-831-7083

WD-40 Co., 1061 Cudahy Pl., San Diego, CA 92110 / 619-275-1400; FAX: 619-275-5823

Weatherby, Inc., 3100 El Camino Real, Atascadero, CA 93422 / 805-466-1767 or 800-227-2016; FAX: 805-466-2527

Weaver Arms Corp. Gun Shop, RR 3, P.O. Box 266, Bloomfield, MO 63825-9528

Weaver Products, P.O. Box 39, Onalaska, WI 54650 / 800-648-9624 or 608-781-5800; FAX: 608-781-0368

Weaver Scope Repair Service, 1121 Larry Mahan Dr., Suite B, El Paso, TX 79925 / 915-593-1005

Webb, Bill, 6504 North Bellefontaine, Kansas City, MO 64119 / 816-453-7431

Weber & Markin Custom Gunsmiths, 4-1691 Powick Rd., Kelowna, BC V1X 4L1 CANADA / 250-762-7575; FAX: 250-861-3655

Weber Jr., Rudolf, P.O. Box 160106, D-5650, GERMANY / 0212-592136

Webley and Scott Ltd., Frankley Industrial Park, Tay Rd., Birmingham, B45 0PA ENGLAND / 011-021-453-1864; FAX: 021-457-7846

Webster Scale Mfg. Co., P.O. Box 188, Sebring, FL 33870 / 813-385-6362

Weems, Cecil, 510 W Hubbard St, Mineral Wells, TX 76067-4847 / 817-325-1462

Weigand Combat Handguns, Inc., 685 South Main Rd., Mountain Top, PA 18707 / 570-868-8358; FAX: 570-868-5218 sales@jackweigand.com www.jackweigand.com

Weihrauch KG, Hermann, Industriestrasse 11, 8744 Mellrichstadt, Mellrichstadt, GERMANY

Weisz Parts, P.O. Box 20038, Columbus, OH 43220-0038 / 614-45-70-500; FAX: 614-846-8585

Welch, Sam, CVSR 2110, Moab, UT 84532 / 801-259-8131

Wellington Outdoors, P.O. Box 244, 1140 Monticello Rd., Madison, GA 30650 / 706-342-4915; FAX: 706-342-7568

Wells, Rachel, 110 N. Summit St., Prescott, AZ 86301 / 520-445-3655

Wells Creek Knife & Gun Works, 32956 State Hwy. 38, Scottsburg, OR 97473 / 541-587-4202; FAX: 541-587-4223

Welsh, Bud, 80 New Road, E. Amherst, NY 14051 / 716-688-6344

Wenger North America/Precise Int'l, 15 Corporate Dr., Orangeburg, NY 10962 / 800-431-2996 FAX: 914-425-4700

Wenig Custom Gunstocks, 103 N. Market St., P.O. Box 249, Lincoln, MO 65338 / 816-547-3334; FAX: 816-547-2881 gunstock@wenig.com www.wenig.com

Werth, T. W., 1203 Woodlawn Rd., Lincoln, IL 62656 / 217-732-1300

Wescombe, Bill (See North Star West)

Wessinger Custom Guns & Engraving, 268 Limestone Rd., Chapin, SC 29036 / 803-345-5677

West, Jack L., 1220 W. Fifth, P.O. Box 427, Arlington, OR 97812

Western Cutlery (See Camillus Cutlery Co.)

Western Design (See Alpha Gunsmith Division)

Western Gunstock Mfg. Co., 550 Valencia School Rd., Aptos, CA 95003 / 408-688-5884

Western Missouri Shooters Alliance, P.O. Box 11144, Kansas City, MO 64119 / 816-597-3950; FAX: 816-229-7350

Western Nevada West Coast Bullets, PO BOX 2270, DAYTON, NV 89403-2270 / 702-246-3941; FAX: 702-246-0836

Westley Richards & Co., 40 Grange Rd., Birmingham, ENGLAND / 010-214722953

Westley Richards Agency USA (See U.S. Importer for Westley Richards & Co.,)

Westrom, John (See Precision Metal Finishing)

Westwind Rifles, Inc., David S. Sullivan, P.O. Box 261, 640 Briggs St., Erie, CO 80516 / 303-828-3823

Weyer International, 2740 Nebraska Ave., Toledo, OH 43607 / 419-534-2020; FAX: 419-534-2697

Whildin & Sons Ltd, E.H., RR 2 Box 119, Tamaqua, PA 18252 / 717-668-6743; FAX: 717-668-6745

Whinnery, Walt (See Walt's Custom Leather)

Whiscombe (See U.S. Importer-Pelaire Products)

White Barn Wor, 431 County Road, Broadlands, IL 61816

White Flyer Targets, 124 River Road, Middlesex, NJ 08846 / 908-469-0100 or 602-972-7528 FAX: 908-469-9692

White Owl Enterprises, 2583 Flag Rd., Abilene, KS 67410 / 913-263-2613; FAX: 913-263-2613

White Pine Photographic Services, Hwy. 60, General Delivery, Wilno, ON K0J 2N0 CANADA / 613-756-3452

White Rock Tool & Die, 6400 N. Brighton Ave., Kansas City, MO 64119 / 816-454-0478

White Shooting Systems, Inc. (See White Muzzleloading)

Whitestone Lumber Corp., 148-02 14th Ave., Whitestone, NY 11357 / 718-746-4400; FAX: 718-767-1748

Whitetail Design & Engineering Ltd., 9421 E. Mannsiding Rd., Clare, MI 48617 / 517-386-3932

Wichita Arms, Inc., 923 E. Gilbert, P.O. Box 11371, Wichita, KS 67211 / 316-265-0661; FAX: 316-265-0760

Wick, David E., 1504 Michigan Ave., Columbus, IN 47201 / 812-376-6960

Widener's Reloading & Shooting Supply, Inc., P.O. Box 3009 CRS, Johnson City, TN 37602 / 615-282-6786; FAX: 615-282-6651

Wideview Scope Mount Corp., 13535 S. Hwy. 16, Rapid City, SD 57701 / 605-341-3220; FAX: 605-341-9142 wvdon@rapidnet.com

Wiebe, Duane, 846 Holly WYA, Placerville, CA 95667-3415

Wiest, M. C., 10737 Dutchtown Rd., Knoxville, TN 37932 / 423-966-4545

Wilcox All-Pro Tools & Supply, 4880 147th St., Montezuma, IA 50171 / 515-623-3138; FAX: 515-623-3104

Wilcox Industries Corp, Robert F Guarasi, 53 Durham St, Portsmouth, NH 03801 / 603-431-1331; FAX: 603-431-1221

Wild Bill's Originals, P.O. Box 13037, Burton, WA 98013 / 206-463-5738; FAX: 206-465-5925

Wild West Guns, 7521 Old Seward Hwy, Unit A, Anchorage, AK 99518 / 800-992-4570 or 907-344-4500; FAX: 907-344-4005

Wilderness Sound Products Ltd., 4015 Main St. A, Springfield, OR 97478 / 503-741-0263 or 800-437-0006; FAX: 503-741-7648

Wildey, Inc., 45 Angevine Rd, Warren, CT 06754-1818 / 203-355-9000; FAX: 203-354-7759

Wildlife Research Center, Inc., 1050 McKinley St., Anoka, MN 55303 / 612-427-3350 or 800-USE-LURE; FAX: 612-427-8354

Wilhelm Brenneke KG, Ilmenauweg 2, 30851, Langenhagen, GERMANY / 0511/97262-0; FAX: 0511/97262-62

Will-Burt Co., 169 S. Main, Orrville, OH 44667

William Fagan & Co., 22952 15 Mile Rd., Clinton Township, MI 48035 / 810-465-4637; FAX: 810-792-6996

William Powell & Son (Gunmakers) Ltd., 35-37 Carrs Lane, Birmingham, B4 7SX ENGLAND / 121-643-0689; FAX: 121-631-3504

William Powell Agency, 22 Circle Dr., Bellmore, NY 11710 / 516-679-1158

Williams Gun Sight Co., 7389 Lapeer Rd., Box 329, Davison, MI 48423 / 810-653-2131 or 800-530-9028; FAX: 810-658-2140 williamsgunsight.com

Williams Mfg. of Oregon, 110 East B St., Drain, OR 97435 / 503-836-7461; FAX: 503-836-7245

Williams Shootin' Iron Service, The Lynx-Line, Rt 2 Box 223A, Mountain Grove, MO 65711 / 417-948-0902 FAX: 417-948-0902

Williamson Precision Gunsmithing, 117 W. Pipeline, Hurst, TX 76053 / 817-285-0064; FAX: 817-280-0044

Willow Bend, P.O. Box 203, Chelmsford, MA 01824 / 978-256-8508; FAX: 978-256-8508

Willson Safety Prods. Div., PO Box 622, Reading, PA 19603-0622 / 610-376-6161; FAX: 610-371-7725

Wilson Case, Inc., P.O. Box 1106, Hastings, NE 68902-1106 / 800-322-5493; FAX: 402-463-5276 sales@wilsoncase.com www.wilsoncase.com

Wilson Gun Shop, 2234 County Road 719, Berryville, AR 72616 / 870-545-3618; FAX: 870-545-3310

Winchester Div. Olin Corp., 427 N. Shamrock, E. Alton, IL 62024 / 618-258-3566; FAX: 618-258-3599

Winchester Press (See New Win Publishing, Inc.), 186 Center St, Clinton, NJ 08809 / 908-735-9701; FAX: 908-735-9703

Winchester Sutler, Inc., The, 270 Shadow Brook Lane, Winchester, VA 22603 / 540-888-3595; FAX: 540-888-4632

Windish, Jim, 2510 Dawn Dr., Alexandria, VA 22306 / 703-765-1994

Windjammer Tournament Wads Inc., 750 W. Hampden Ave., Suite 170, Englewood, CO 80110 / 303-781-6329

Wingshooting Adventures, 0-1845 W. Leonard, Grand Rapids, MI 49544 / 616-677-1980; FAX: 616-677-1986

Winkle Bullets, R.R. 1, Box 316, Heyworth, IL 61745

Winter, Robert M., P.O. Box 484, 42975-287th St., Menno, SD 57045 / 605-387-5322

Wise Custom Guns, 1402 Blanco Rd, San Antonio, TX 78212-2716 / 210-828-3388

Wise Guns, Dale, 333 W Olmos Dr, San Antonio, TX 78212 / 210-828-3388

Wiseman and Co., Bill, PO Box 3427, Bryan, TX 77805 / 409-690-3456; FAX: 409-690-0156

Wisners Inc/Twin Pine Armory, P.O. Box 58, Hwy. 6, Adna, WA 98522 / 360-748-4590; FAX: 360-748-1802

Wolf (See J.R. Distributing)

Wolf's Western Traders, 40 E. Works, No. 3F, Sheridan, WY 82801 / 307-674-5352 patwolf@wavecom.net

Wolfe Publishing Co., 6471 Airpark Dr., Prescott, AZ 86301 / 520-445-7810 or 800-899-7810; FAX: 520-778-5124

Wolverine Footwear Group, 9341 Courtland Dr. NE, Rockford, MI 49351 / 616-866-5500; FAX: 616-866-5658

Wood, Mel, P.O. Box 1255, Sierra Vista, AZ 85636 / 602-455-5541

Wood, Frank (See Classic Guns, Inc.), 3230 Medlock Bridge Rd, Ste 110, Norcross, GA 30092 / 404-242-7944

Woodleigh (See Huntington Die Specialties)

Woods Wise Products, P.O. Box 681552, 2200 Bowman Rd., Franklin, TN 37068 / 800-735-8182; FAX: 615-726-2637

Woodstream, P.O. Box 327, Lititz, PA 17543 / 717-626-2125

Woodworker's Supply, 1108 North Glenn Rd., Casper, WY 82601 / 307-237-5354

Woolrich, Inc., Mill St., Woolrich, PA 17701 / 800-995-1299; FAX: 717-769-6234/6259

Working Guns, Jim Coffin, 1224 NW Fernwood Cir, Corvallis, OR 97330-2909 / 541-928-4391

World Class Airguns, 2736 Morningstar Dr., Indianapolis, IN 46229 / 317-897-5548

World of Targets (See Birchwood Casey)

World Trek, Inc., 7170 Turkey Creek Rd., Pueblo, CO 81007-1046 / 719-546-2121; FAX: 719-543-6886

Worthy Products, Inc., RR 1, P.O. Box 213, Martville, NY 13111 / 315-324-5298

Wosenitz VHP, Inc., Box 741, Dania, FL 33004 / 305-923-3748; FAX: 305-925-2217

Wostenholm (See Ibberson [Sheffield] Ltd., George)

Wright's Hardwood Gunstock Blanks, 8540 SE Kane Rd., Gresham, OR 97080 / 503-666-1705

WTA Manufacturing, P.O. Box 164, Kit Carson, CO 80825 / 800-700-3054; FAX: 719-962-3570

Wyant Bullets, Gen. Del., Swan Lake, MT 59911

Wyant's Outdoor Products, Inc., P.O. Box 9, Broadway, VA 22815

Wyoming Bonded Bullets, Box 91, Sheridan, WY 82801 / 307-674-8091

Wyoming Custom Bullets, 1626 21st St., Cody, WY 82414

Wyoming Knife Corp., 101 Commerce Dr., Ft. Collins, CO 80524 / 303-224-3454

X

X-Spand Target Systems, 26-10th St. SE, Medicine Hat, AB T1A 1P7 CANADA / 403-526-7997; FAX: 403-528-2362

Y

Yankee Gunsmith, 2901 Deer Flat Dr., Copperas Cove, TX 76522 / 817-547-8433

Yavapai College, 1100 E. Sheldon St., Prescott, AZ 86301 / 520-776-2353 FAX: 520-776-2355

Yavapai Firearms Academy Ltd., P.O. Box 27290, Prescott Valley, AZ 86312 / 520-772-8262

Yearout, Lewis E. (See Montana Outfitters), 308 Riverview Dr E, Great Falls, MT 59404 / 406-761-0859

Yee, Mike, 29927 56 Pl. S., Auburn, WA 98001 / 206-839-3991

Yellowstone Wilderness Supply, P.O. Box 129, W. Yellowstone, MT 59758 / 406-646-7613

Yesteryear Armory & Supply, P.O. Box 408, Carthage, TN 37030

York M-1 Conversions, 803 Mill Creek Run, Plantersville, TX 77363 / 800-527-2881 or 713-477-8442

Young Country Arms, William, 1409 Kuehner Dr #13, Simi Valley, CA 93063-4478

Yukon Arms Classic Ammunition, 1916 Brooks, P.O. Box 223, Missoula, MT 59801 / 406-543-9614

Z

Z's Metal Targets & Frames, P.O. Box 78, South Newbury, NH 03255 / 603-938-2826

Z-M Weapons, 203 South St., Bernardston, MA 01337 / 413-648-9501; FAX: 413-648-0219

Zabala Hermanos S.A., P.O. Box 97, Eibar, 20600 SPAIN / 43-768085 or 43-768076; FAX: 34-43-768201

Zander's Sporting Goods, 7525 Hwy 154 West, Baldwin, IL 62217-9706 / 800-851-4373 FAX: 618-785-2320

Zanoletti, Pietro, Via Monte Gugielpo, 4, I-25063 Gardone V.T., ITALY

Zanotti Armor, Inc., 123 W. Lone Tree Rd., Cedar Falls, IA 50613 / 319-232-9650

ZDF Import Export, Inc., 2975 South 300 West, Salt Lake City, UT 84115 / 801-485-1012; FAX: 801-484-4363

Zeeryp, Russ, 1601 Foard Dr., Lynn Ross Manor, Morristown, TN 37814 / 615-586-2357

Zero Ammunition Co., Inc., 1601 22nd St. SE, P.O. Box 1188, Cullman, AL 35056-1188 / 800-545-9376; FAX: 205-739-4683

Ziegel Engineering, 2108 Lomina Ave., Long Beach, CA 90815 / 562-596-9481; FAX: 562-598-4734 ziegel@aol.com www.ziegelerg.com

Zim's, Inc., 4370 S. 3rd West, Salt Lake City, UT 84107 / 801-268-2505

Zoli, Antonio, Via Zanardelli 39, Casier Postal 21, I-25063 Gardone V.T., ITALY

Zriny's Metal Targets (See Z's Metal Targets & Frames)

Zufall, Joseph F., P.O. Box 304, Golden, CO 80402-0304

THE LASTEST NEWS ABOUT FIREARMS

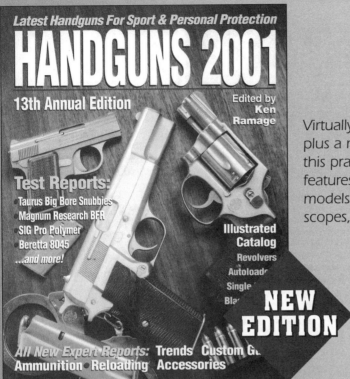

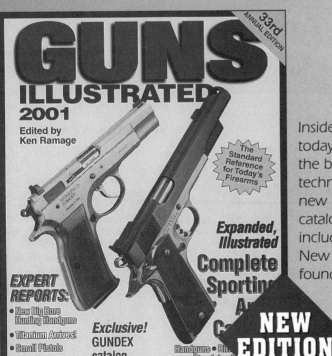

Handguns 2001
13th Annual Edition
Edited by Ken Ramage

Virtually every current production handgun sold in America - plus a new section on semi-custom handguns - is found in this practical volume. Pistol and revolver specifications, features and prices are included. Shooting tests of new models, an expanded, illustrated section of sights and scopes, plus a showcase of engraved guns are all on target!

Softcover ▪ 8-1/2 x 11 ▪ 352 pages
1,800 b&w photos
H2001 ▪ $22.95

Guns Illustrated 2001
33rd Annual Edition
Edited by Ken Ramage

Inside this new edition, you'll find the latest news about today's handguns, rifles and shotguns from the top writers in the business. Plus cutting-edge articles on breaking arms technology, like the detailed report on Remington's brand new electronic rifle and ammunition! The illustrated arms catalog lists more than 3,000 commercially available firearms, including muzzleloaders and airguns.
New to this edition - the catalog of Semi-Custom Firearms - found only in Guns Illustrated!

Softcover ▪ 8-1/2 x 11 ▪ 352 pages
2,000+ b&w photos
GI2001 ▪ $22.95

DBI BOOKS
a division of Krause Publications, Inc.

YOUR SEARCH FOR EXPERT FIREARMS INFORMATION ENDS HERE!

Cartridges of the World
9th Edition, Revised and Expanded
by Frank C. Barnes, Edited by M. L. McPherson
Whether you are searching for information on an obsolete cartridge or a new wildcat, a black powder round or a smokeless variety, you will find it here. Tables identify cartridges by measurement and offer ballistics and loading data. Learn the history of 1,500+ American and European cartridges in this single volume.
Softcover • 8-1/2 x 11 • 512 pages
450 b&w photos
COW9 • $27.95

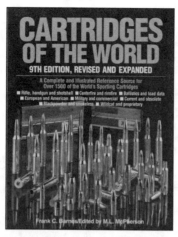

Knives 2001
21st Annual Edition
Edited by Joe Kertzman
You'll find "cutting edge" information inside this comprehensive volume of factory and custom knives. Track the latest designs, including tactical, sporting and the new semi-automatic knives. Admire the engraved, inlaid and scrimshawed works of the nation's keenest custom knifemakers. The industry's most comprehensive directory makes it easy to contact companies, custom makers and knifemaking supply firms.
Softcover • 8-1/2 x 11 • 304 pages
1,200 b&w photos
KN2001 • $22.95

Colt's Single Action Army Revolver
by "Doc" O'Meara
Learn more about the Colt Single Action Army Revolver as "Doc" O'Meara guides you through a historical look at the world's most famous revolver. With production figures and serial number ranges for early versions of the gun, this book is a must for any collector. O'Meara also mixes in stories about rare Colts and their owners that will both inform and entertain anyone interested in the gun that has come to symbolize the American cowboy.
Hardcover • 8-1/2 x 11 • 160 pages
250 b&w photos
16-page color section
CSAAR • $34.95

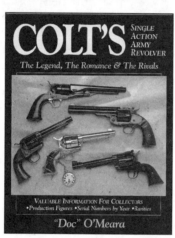

Action Shooting Cowboy Style
by John Taffin
Feel the rich gun leather and taste the smoke of America's fastest-growing shooting game. Every aspect is explained for shooters of all levels. Join the fun of cowboy-style shooting. Let John Taffin take you from the general store where he'll show you the latest in old western garb, to the firing line where some of the fastest guns around drop the hammer in search of a winning score.
Hardcover • 8-1/2 x 11 • 320 pages
300 b&w photos • 8-page color section
COWAS • $39.95

Gun Digest Book of Sporting Clays
2nd Edition
Edited by Harold A. Murtz
This book has something for shooters of all skill levels, including tips for new shooters, a discussion on the value of a coach/instructor and a guide to the best training for young shooters. Take a tour of clays courses around the country and learn what's new in guns, gear and ammunition.
Softcover • 8-1/2 x 11 • 256 pages
300 b&w photos
SC2 • $21.95

Custom Firearms Engraving
by Tom Turpin
Here is a broad and comprehensive look at the world of firearms engraving that covers exquisite examples of highly decorated handguns, rifles, shotguns and other firearms, as well as knives. More than 75 master engravers are represented with over 200 stunning photos in four-color presentation. Includes an up-to-date Engravers Directory so you can contact the craftsman of your choice.
Hardcover • 8-1/2 x 11 • 208 pages
200 color photos
CFE • $49.95

Shipping and Handling:
$3.25 1st book; $2 ea. add'l. Foreign orders $15 per shipment plus $5.95 per book.

Sales tax: CA, IA, IL, PA, TN, VA, WA, WI residents please add appropriate sales tax.

To place a credit card order or for a FREE all-product catalog

Call **800-258-0929**

Offer GNBR

M-F, 7 am - 8 pm • Sat, 8 am - 2 pm, CST
Krause Publications, Offer GNBR P.O. Box 5009, Iola, WI 54945-5009
www.krausebooks.com

Retailers call toll-free 888-457-2873 ext 880, M-F, 8 am - 5 pm

Satisfaction Guarantee:
If for any reason you are not completely satisfied with your purchase, simply return it within 14 days and receive a full refund, less shipping.

MUST-HAVE REFERENCES

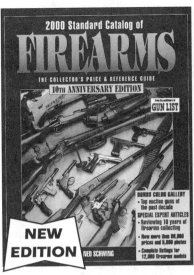

2000 Standard Catalog™ of Firearms
The Collector's Price & Reference Guide,
10th Anniversary Edition
by Ned Schwing
Packed with more than 80,000 real-world prices and over 5,000 photos, this is the must-have resource for every gun collector. This year's 10th Anniversary Edition boasts two first-time special features: A full-color gallery of some of the world's most rare and beautiful firearms; and an insightful look at the firearms industry over the last 10 years. In addition, several sections have been updated and expanded, offering comprehensive coverage on 12,000 different firearm models.
Softcover • 8-1/2 x 11
1,312 pages
5,000+ b&w photos • 40 color photos
Item # GG10 • $32.95

The Gun Digest Book of Assault Weapons
5th Edition
by Jack Lewis & David E. Steele
Here's the latest information (specifications, applications, etc.) on the world's assault weapons, reported in-depth by retired Marine Jack Lewis. Exclusive, detailed coverage of today's military and police weaponry from France, Germany, Russia, South Africa and the USA. Broad coverage of rifles, submachine guns, crew-served machine guns, combat shotguns - plus an educated look into the 21st century.
Softcover • 8-1/2 x 11
256 pages
500 b&w photos
Item # AW5 • $21.95

Military Small Arms of the 20th Century
7th Edition
by Ian V. Hogg and John S. Weeks
This is the complete and ultimate small arms reference by Ian Hogg, international military arms authority. Now expanded and updated to include every arm in service from 1900 to 2000; complete with specifications, history and insightful commentary on performance and effectiveness. There is no comparable book.
Softcover • 8-1/2 x 11
416 pages
800+ b&w photos
Item # MSA7 • $24.95

Mauser Military Rifles of the World
2nd Edition
by Robert W. D. Ball
Learn how to identify every Mauser model from 1871 to 1945 while looking over production figures and the relative rarity of each model. This updated edition of a collector's classic unveils 100 new photos of rare guns and the men who used them. Whether your interest is in collecting or military history, this book gives you all the details you won't find anywhere else.
Hardcover • 8-1/2 x 11
304 pages • 1,000 b&w photos
48-page color section
Item # FCM02 • $44.95

Standard Catalog™ of Winchester
Edited by David D. Kowalski
From 1886 to 1929 the Winchester Repeating Arms Company put its name on everything from garden tools to washing machines. Now there is a single price and identification guide covering the full gamut of the company's products. The Standard Catalog of Winchester identifies and values 2,500 collectibles, including firearms, cartridges, shotshells, fishing tackle, sporting goods, tools and pocket knives, plus provides unsurpassed coverage of the company's popular calendars, advertising materials and packaging. You will be amazed at the 2,500 photographs, including hundreds of rarely seen items and a gorgeous four-color gallery of the best Winchester offered.
Softcover • 8-1/2 x 11 • 704 pages
2,500 b&w photos
75 color photos
Item # SCW1 • $39.95

The Winchester Model 52
Perfection In Design
by Herbert G. Houze
Historical arms enthusiast Herbert Houze unravels the mysteries surrounding the development of what many consider the most perfect rifle ever made. The book covers the rifle's improvements through five modifications. Users, collectors and marksmen will appreciate each variation's history, serial number sequences and authentic photos.
Hardcover • 8-1/2 x 11
192 pages
190 b&w photos
Item # WIN • $34.95

FOR FIREARMS COLLECTORS

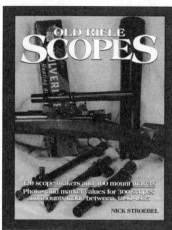

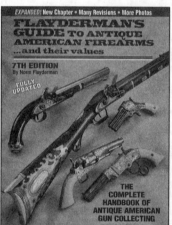
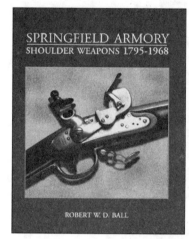
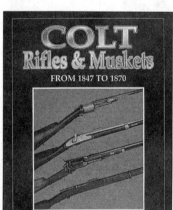